The Blackwell Encyclopedia of Sociology

Volume V

HE–LE

Edited by

George Ritzer

Blackwell
Publishing

© 2007 by Blackwell Publishing Ltd

BLACKWELL PUBLISHING
350 Main Street, Malden, MA 02148-5020, USA
9600 Garsington Road, Oxford OX4 2DQ, UK
550 Swanston Street, Carlton, Victoria 3053, Australia

The right of George Ritzer to be identified as the Author of the Editorial Material in this Work has been asserted in accordance with the UK Copyright, Designs, and Patents Act 1988.

First published 2007 by Blackwell Publishing Ltd

1   2007

Library of Congress Cataloging-in-Publication Data

Blackwell encyclopedia of sociology, the / edited by George Ritzer.
 p. cm.
Includes bibliographical references and index.
ISBN 1-4051-2433-4 (hardback : alk. paper) 1. Sociology—Encyclopedias. I. Ritzer, George.

HM425.B53 2007
301.03—dc22

                                             2006004167

ISBN-13: 978-1-4051-2433-1 (hardback : alk. paper)

A catalogue record for this title is available from the British Library.

Set in 9.5/11pt Ehrhardt
by Spi Publisher Services, Pondicherry, India
Printed in Singapore
by COS Printers Pte Ltd

The publisher's policy is to use permanent paper from mills that operate a sustainable forestry policy, and which has been manufactured from pulp processed using acid-free and elementary chlorine-free practices. Furthermore, the publisher ensures that the text paper and cover board used have met acceptable environmental accreditation standards.

For further information on
Blackwell Publishing, visit our website:
www.blackwellpublishing.com

Contents

health and medicine

Jeffrey Michael Clair and Jason Wasserman

Medical sociologists embrace a range of sociological concerns indigenous to the human condition – cultural, symbolic, personal, social, ecological, and biological. Medical sociology research can help us develop meaningful ways of thinking about the linkages between health and medicine, which involve a multitude of social factors. Health, medicine, and personhood dynamically interact through patient care. But despite this common insight, there is still much we do not know about the personal health and medicine relationship.

HISTORICAL RELATIONSHIP OF SOCIOLOGY TO HEALTH AND MEDICINE

The seed thoughts for a sociology applicable to health and medicine developed in Europe. The origins can be traced back to German physician Rudolf Virchow, who maintained that medicine was a social science and should be used to improve social conditions (Warbasse 1909, 1935; Walsh 1915; Rosen 1947, 1949, 1962, 1979; Ackerknecht 1953; Hyman 1967). Sixty years ago, medical historian Henry Sigerist (1946: 130) advocated the incorporation of a social science perspective into medical school curricula, arguing that "Social medicine is not so much a technique as rather an attitude and approach to the problems of medicine, one which I have no doubt will some day permeate the entire curriculum. This, however, will require a new type of clinical teacher and new textbooks." While sociologists have remained underrepresented in this new type of clinical role, sociological insights could increasingly benefit medical practice.

While there is a growing awareness that few, if any, patient care decisions are purely medical, the coming together of social and medical perspectives remains elusory (Kleinman et al. 1978; Eisenberg & Kleinman 1981). Often there seems to be little correspondence between the flow of new social knowledge and its application, despite the fact that social insights and

data clearly can inform the medical clinician's view of the problem. However, applicable findings tend to remain on the periphery of medical practice with much sociological evidence thought to be too abstract and uncertain to be helpful (Mechanic & Aiken 1986; Clair & Allman 1993).

Straus's (1957) dichotomy of sociological work "in" and "of" medicine characterizes two approaches to medical sociology. Some sociologists have tended to be critical toward applied sociology "in" medicine work. Research design and data collection structured more to serve medical interests have sometimes not been regarded as true sociological work. As a result, training has focused on sociology "of" medicine and health, where, while still focused on the medical/health arena as a source of data, the overall aim remained committed to contribute to the development of sociological theory.

HEALTH CARE UTILIZATION: HOW PATIENTS APPROACH MEDICINE

Although we know much about the volume and cost of medical care utilization, we still have difficulty explaining cause and variation in health care utilization rates. It is unclear whether service use is based on need or other factors (Cockerham 2005). The relationship between patients' health and their use of medical services is not necessarily direct, but related to class, race, and all sorts of social variables. Little is known about the decision-making process of patients across various social contexts and the ways in which they define a set of health symptoms as requiring medical treatment.

Previous work includes only "users" of health care services when testing health care-seeking patterns. This common approach can be seen as inherently problematic because it reduces relevant data and introduces severe sampling bias. It is a fair assumption that those studies focusing on only users of health services are really measuring *frequency of use* rather than the more generic issue of who is using and *not* using health services.

The vast majority of somaticized illnesses are managed almost exclusively outside institutionalized biomedical clinics (Kleinman et al. 1978). It is important to understand why large segments of the population are seeking alternative forms of health services. We now know that Americans are embracing complementary and alternative medicine (CAM) more than ever before. Sixty-eight percent of the adult population will use CAM at some point in their life (Eisenberg et al. 2001). Other studies consistently find that between 40 and 45 million American adults have used CAM within the previous 12 months (Astin 1998; Harris & Rees 2000). In 1997, Americans spent $27 billion out-of-pocket on CAM visits, a total dollar amount greater than that spent on conventional care that year (Eisenberg et al. 1998).

This is a phenomenon not limited to the United States. About half the citizens of other industrialized countries also use CAM (Bodeker & Kronenberg 2002). CAM visits are an estimated 49 percent for the French (Fisher & Ward 1994), 48 percent of the Australian population (MacLennan et al. 1996), and the World Health Organization (2003) estimates traditional herbal cures account for 30 to 50 percent of all medicinal consumption in China. If the term alternative medicine is expanded to include traditional (i.e., indigenous) medicine (T/CAM), the figure rises to almost 80 percent in Africa (Bodeker & Kronenberg 2002). Clearly, alternative medicine appears to be a sizable current in the medical stream.

We can see, then, that the decision to go to a doctor with an illness is the result of an interpretive process, taking place within the structural parameters of the distribution of available medical services. Factors other than need may be important in health care utilization. To routinely exclude non-users (or T/CAM users) from health services utilization analyses is severely problematic.

Explanations of individual determinants of health care utilization are classified into the three major factors of predisposing, enabling, and need (illness) characteristics (Andersen 1968; Andersen & Newman 1973). The model assumes that predisposing, enabling, and illness-need characteristics determine the use of health services. The predisposing variables represent individuals' inclinations to seek medical care. Predisposing characteristics exist prior to the incidence of an illness episode, and include subsets of demographic and social structural variables. An important assumption

of this model is that we should observe different patterns of health care utilization among individuals with different demographic and social structural characteristics.

The enabling characteristics reflect persons' access to social and institutional resources. The two levels of means are distinguished as family and community resources. When sufficient family and community resources exist, such as income and access to available medical care, then individuals needing health services are more likely to seek them out.

The illness-need characteristics of health care utilization are the third component in the behavioral model. Even when one is predisposed and able to access medical care services, there must be some perceived (individually assessed) or functional (physician assessed) condition serving as an impetus for health care utilization to occur.

Health care utilization is the outcome component of the behavioral model, and can be classified on a continuum between discretionary and non-discretionary use (Andersen 1968). At the discretionary end would be medical care use such as a dental visit. Although oral health care is vital to health and longevity, especially among older adults, dental services still tend to be an individual choice, even among those enabled to use them. The non-discretionary end of the continuum represents hospitalization, based on decisions made by physicians. In the middle of the continuum would be physician visits, ranging from initial perceived need-directed health care visits to more evaluative, physician-directed follow-up visits (see Andersen 1968; Andersen & Newman 1973; Wolinsky 1990).

Health and illness behaviors are ultimately influenced by how people think about their health. Individuals who place greater value on health potentially have different utilization patterns than those who attach less value. Indeed, individuals who have a greater confidence in their own ability to influence their health and those who are somewhat skeptical of the ability or trustworthiness of medical science are less likely to consult professionals.

There are over 40 million Americans with no health insurance. When we look at utilization research on this segment of the population, a variety of explanations are manifest. First, some research found a pattern of underusage by the uninsured, prior to the enactment of Medicare/Medicaid programs. Explanation for this pattern suggests that the poor are skeptical of the motives of professional practitioners, lack awareness and knowledge about their symptoms, do not practice preventive care, and tend to delay seeking medical care until symptoms are quite serious. These patterns place the poor at greater risk and result in higher health care costs. This traditional pattern finds the poor underutilizing medical services despite greater need, and attributes underutilization to financial problems, a culture of poverty, and/or systems barriers, both bureaucratic and interpersonal (Clair & Allman 1993).

The alternative pattern of health care-seeking behavior by uninsured patients finds that this population tends to utilize professional health services to a much greater extent than insured groups. Research by Cockerham (2005) and colleagues in a series of studies in Illinois, Germany, and the Netherlands shows that less-educated, low-income patients tend not to discriminate between symptoms on the basis of severity, are more likely to place responsibility for their health on physicians rather than themselves, and are relatively passive recipients of care. When ill, these poor tended to automatically visit physicians, while the more affluent were more likely to engage in self-treatment or to recognize minor ailments as self-limiting – likely to resolve without treatment. Earlier research in Illinois showed that blacks and the less educated had very positive attitudes about the health care system and believed that visiting doctors was the desirable course of action whenever any symptoms were present.

These two patterns of behavior are clearly influenced by the temporal context of the data. The traditional pattern of non-use has tended to be eroded among the poorest poor, those who qualify for Medicaid. Public policy has increased health care access for these groups and research suggests that they now tend to overuse medical care. But the working poor, who do not qualify for Medicaid, but also cannot afford private insurance, may still practice avoidance, thereby underusing medical care. Regardless, a planned intervention could substantially correct for the hypothesized extremes in the care-seeking behavior of the lower-income

population. The most efficacious provision of health care services must be based on communicating successfully with both those patients who delay too long before seeking help and those who arrive too early.

BIOMEDICAL CAREGIVING: HOW MEDICINE APPROACHES PATIENTS

Knowledge and practice of medicine, and the experience of illness, reveal key aspects of how social systems of meaning and identity are structured. The study of biomedical caregiving is important because a person's health is intimately related to social behavior and has pervasive effects on the performance of social roles and matrices of interpersonal relationships.

Evidence on the effect of social support in alleviating life stress is conceptualized largely in terms of informal support from family and friends. However, the effects of formal social support, such as effective physician communication and guidance, also are important. Examining social support at both informal and formal levels provides insight on how the formal social support network affects the ability of the patient and his or her informal care network to deal with the stressful physiological and psychosocial circumstances of an illness. From this perspective, physicians, representing the health care system, can be seen as providing formal support-counseling when caring for patients and their network of caregivers.

The life stress paradigm assumes that external stressors such as life events, role strains, and daily hassles, if unchecked, disrupt an individual's psychosocial equilibrium, induce physiological or psychological responses in the form of distress, and overall, challenge social resources. The premise is that psychosocial resources both alleviate existing distress and prevent or mitigate its occurrence. In addition to directly reducing distress, psychosocial resources play a primary role in mediating the detrimental effects of physiological and social stressors on the distress of both patients and caregivers (Lin et al. 1986; Clair et al. 1995). The concept of psychosocial resources should include not only personal coping and informal family and friendship support but also the *formal* support of professional health care providers.

Research on the mediation effect between life stressors, psychosocial resources, and distress is important. Such a focus can be expressed by the following propositions: (1) the frequency of undesirable life events and the daily pressures for individuals and caregivers are inversely related to social supports and psychological resources; (2) the extent and quality of an individual's informal and formal social supports and psychological resources are related inversely and directly to the extent of burden; and (3) the extent and quality of an individual's informal and formal social supports and psychological resources mediate the effects of undesirable life events and the daily pressures on burden.

Satisfaction with physician services, and the facilitation of services that extend beyond the medical mission of the clinic, are mutable conditions. Actions can be taken to improve physician–patient communication, and to expand a medical facility's domain so that a broader vision of illness and care can reduce burden on patients, family members, and/or primary caregivers.

CURRENT ISSUES AND FUTURE DIRECTIONS

Given a preponderance of health research based on self-reported health measures, it would seem advisable for researchers to gain close-up, first-hand knowledge of issues related to health service utilization by varied subcultural groupings in society, in an effort to determine the extent to which actual health behavior correlates with these self-reports. Such studies would then form the basis for generating research questions that are relevant and salient for the populations being studied.

As evidenced by informal health care behavior (e.g., T/CAM), those who utilize formal medical care are not necessarily sicker than those who do not. In fact, these two groups are indistinguishable when one compares the number and type of their symptoms. It would appear, then, that *symbolic* and *cultural* definitions of health are quite salient here. Those who manage their illnesses independent of traditional medicine may do so for a variety of reasons, one of which may entail negative experiences with, and reactions to, the idea of seeking traditional

medical care. Given the growing rate of both uninsured and underinsured persons, it is not hard to envision access to health care services becoming one of the major policy challenges of this century. Addressing issues of health care behavior and use as related to both access and differing symbolic and cultural meanings of health and illness is among the foremost future challenges for sociology.

How health information is being communicated to patients is another important social issue. Information must be presented in a way that takes into account patients' knowledge and values. Ignoring patients' broader social contexts may pose a barrier to adequate health care by creating misunderstandings about recommended treatment and prevention strategies. More importantly, patients may further aggravate their health by failing to adhere to such advice. A fuller understanding of uninsured patients' health values and beliefs, as well as health care-seeking behaviors, could yield appropriate intervention data.

Further, we may expect to see increasing use of home health care services as the "baby boomer" generation ages. Efforts should be made to integrate the care regimen across formal and informal structures. For example, home care should be carefully coordinated with clinic and hospital care through centralizing patient records, with a formal health care provider taking responsibility for closely documenting what treatments and services are provided at both loci. Formal–informal service coordination is especially important for caregivers of functionally impaired patients. Home-based formal support services may be the critical link to reducing burden, but such services should also enhance informal support services. Formal care providers may have to take responsibilities for what goes on outside the clinic by interjecting themselves into family support systems. For example, a care coordinator from the clinic could call a family meeting to institute a care-sharing system among family members. This would reduce burden on the patient, family, and primary caregivers. Current drives for universal health care are based on the premise that traditional biocentric medicine must expand its domain to include health promotion and prevention to be effective. Similarly, the scope of services can be broadened to include meaningful assistance to caregivers, because the patient's welfare and that of his or her caregivers go hand in hand.

Worldwide increases in the proportion of frail elderly raises a number of important questions regarding the motivations, satisfaction, and coping abilities of caregivers. Studying caregiver social networks and the appropriate responses to their needs is highly important and locating caregiving theoretically and empirically in a matrix of other roles and experiences adds substantially to our understanding of this critically important activity.

Caregivers are an especially important class of social actors in a society with an aging population, expanding health costs, and growing federal debt. Undoubtedly, individuals will be called on to do more caregiving, rather than less, in the near future. Under such circumstances, it is essential that we understand the caregiver distress process. To accomplish this difficult task, greater effort must be made to ground our knowledge of caregiving in more general psychosocial models of distress and to recognize the substantial impact of informal caregiving networks on patient care. Until this is accomplished, we cannot hope to design successful intervention programs for these critical health care providers. Instead we will remain puzzled as to why such programs have borne little fruit.

Proponents of alternative orientations toward the practice of medicine (and medical sociology) would like to see the emergence of new approaches and broadening conceptualizations of health and medicine, based on both traditional scientific methodology and new ways of knowing. To be sure, "any evaluation of sociology ought to focus not only on the way sociology is produced, but also on how it is consumed" (Merton & Wolfe 1995: 15). Sociology can be at the center of an integrative network of health and illness. However, by failing to make findings more accessible, sociologists enable health care providers to continue to view social factors as being outside their professional concern. Indeed, disciplinary jargons continue to be major obstacles (Freeman & Levine 1989). It will fall on sociologists to find ways of dealing with differences in our conceptual languages in order to infiltrate medicine and other physical and mental health settings, since invitations are not abundantly forthcoming.

SEE ALSO: Aging and Health Policy; Caregiving; Complementary and Alternative Medicine; Health Care Delivery Systems; Health and Culture; Health Locus of Control; Health and Race; Help-Seeking; Medical Sociology; Medicine, Sociology of; Social Support; Sociology in Medicine

REFERENCES AND SUGGESTED READINGS

Ackerknecht, E. H. (1953) *Rudolph Virchow: Doctor, Statesman, Anthropologist.* University of Wisconsin Press, Madison.

Andersen, R. (1968) *A Behavioral Model of Families' Use of Health Services.* Center for Health Administration Studies, Chicago.

Andersen, R. & Newman, J. (1973) Societal and Individual Determinants of Medical Care Utilization in the United States. *Memorial Fund Quarterly* 51: 95–124.

Astin, J. A. (1998) Why Patients Use Alternative Medicine: Results of a National Study. *Journal of the American Medical Association* 279: 1548–53.

Bodeker, G. & Kronenberg, F. (2002) A Public Health Agenda for Traditional, Complementary, and Alternative Medicine. *American Journal of Public Health* 92: 1582–91.

Clair, J. M. & Allman, R. M. (Eds.) (1993) *Sociomedical Perspectives on Patient Care.* University Press of Kentucky, Lexington.

Clair, J. M., Fitzpatrick, K., & LaGory, M. (1995) Caregiver Depression: Sociological Variations on a Gerontological Theme. *Sociological Perspectives* 38: 188–208.

Cockerham, W. (2005) *Medical Sociology.* Prentice-Hall, Upper Saddle River, NJ.

Eisenberg, D. M., Davis, R., Ettner, S. L., Appel, S., Wilkey, S., Van Rompay, M., & Kessler, R. C. (1993) Unconventional Medicine in the United States: Prevalence, Costs, and Patterns of Use. *New England Journal of Medicine* 328: 246–52.

Eisenberg, D. M., Davis, R., Ettner, S. L., Appel, S., Wilkey, S., Van Rompay, M., & Kessler, R. C. (1998) Trends in Alternative Medicine Use in the United States, 1990–1997. *Journal of the American Medical Association* 280: 1569–75.

Eisenberg, D. M., Kessler, R. C., Van Rompay, M. I., Kaptchuk, T. J., Wilkey, S., Appel, S., & Davis, R. B. (2001) Perceptions About Complementary Therapies Relative to Conventional Therapies Among Adults Who Use Both: Results from a National Survey. *Annals of Internal Medicine* 135: 344–51.

Eisenberg, L. & Kleinman, A. (1981) *The Relevance of Social Science for Medicine.* D. Reidel, Boston.

Fisher, P. & Ward, A. (1994) Medicine in Europe: Complementary Medicine in Europe. *British Medical Journal* 309: 107–11.

Freeman, H. & Levine, S. (1989) The Present Status of Medical Sociology. In: Freeman, H. & Levine, S. (Eds.), *Handbook of Medical Sociology*, 4th edn. Prentice-Hall, Englewood Cliffs, NJ, pp. 1–13.

Harris, P. & Rees, R. (2000) The Prevalence of Complementary and Alternative Medicine Use Among the General Population: A Systematic Review of the Literature. *Complemenatry Therapies in Medicine* 8: 88–96.

Hyman, M. (1967) Medicine. In: Lazarsfeld, P., Sewell, W., & Wilensky, H. (Eds.), *The Uses of Sociology*. Basic Books, New York.

Kleinman, A., Eisenberg, L., & Good, B. (1978) Culture, Illness, and Care. *Annals of Internal Medicine* 88: 251–8.

Lin, N., Dean, A., & Ensel, W. (Eds.) (1986) *Social Support, Life Events, and Depression*. Academic Press, New York.

MacLennan, A. H., Wilson, D. H., & Taylor, A. W. (1996) Prevalence and Cost of Alternative Medicine in Australia. *Lancet* 347: 569–73.

Mechanic, D. & Aiken, L. (1986) Social Science, Medicine, and Health Policy. In Aiken, L. & Mechanic, D. (Eds.), *Applications of Social Science to Clinical Medicine and Health Policy*. Rutgers University Press, New Brunswick, NJ, pp. 1–9.

Merton, R. & Wolfe, A. (1995) The Cultural and Social Incorporation of Sociological Knowledge. *American Sociologist* 26 (Fall): 15–39.

NCCAM (2001) *Horizons of Health Care: Five-Year Strategic Plan, 2001–2005*. National Center for Complementary and Alternative Medicine, Washington, DC. Online. altmed.od.nih.gov/about/plans/fiveyear/fiveyear.pdf. Retrieved April 10, 2004.

Rosen, G. (1947) What is Social Medicine? A Genetic Analysis of the Concept. *Bulletin of the History of Medicine* 21: 674–733.

Rosen, G. (1949) The Idea of Social Medicine in America. *Canadian Medical Association Journal* 61: 316–23.

Rosen, G. (1962) The Why and the How of Sociology in Medical Training. *Archives of Environmental Health* 4: 638–42.

Rosen, G. (1979) The Evolution of Social Medicine. In: Freeman, H., Levine, S., & Reeder, L. (Eds.), *Handbook of Medical Sociology*, 2nd edn. Prentice-Hall, Englewood Cliffs, NJ, pp. 23–50.

Sigerist, H. E. (1946) *The University at the Crossroads*. Henry Shuman, New York.

Straus, R. (1957) Nature and Status of Medical Sociology. *American Sociological Review* 22: 200–4.

Walsh, J. J. (1915) *Makers of Modern Medicine*. Fordham University Press, New York.

Warbasse, J. (1909) *Medical Sociology: A Series of Observations Touching Upon the Sociology of Health and the Relations of Medicine to Society*. Appleton, New York and London.

Warbasse, J. (1935) *The Doctor and the Public: A Study of the Sociology, Economics, Ethics, and Philosophy of Medicine, Based on Medical History*. P. B. Hoeber, New York.

Wolinsky, F. (1990) *Health and Health Behavior Among Elderly Americans: An Age-Stratification Perspective*. Wayne State University Press, Detroit.

World Health Organization (2003) *Fact Sheet # 134: Traditional Medicine*. WHO, Geneva.

health, neighborhood disadvantage

Christopher R. Browning and Kathleen A. Cagney

Although health is often seen as a product of individual or micro-level determinants, researchers are increasingly recognizing the role of neighborhood context in influencing a broad range of health outcomes. The concept of "neighborhood" typically refers to a geographically contained residential space the boundaries of which may be defined ecologically (e.g., major streets or railroad tracks), administratively (e.g., census tracts), socially (e.g., with respect to neighbor networks), or symbolically (e.g., shared identification with a local space). Extant research offers evidence of a link between economic disadvantage at the neighborhood level and outcomes such as mortality, morbidity, and functional status. A number of perspectives on the mechanisms linking neighborhood structural characteristics to health have emerged. These approaches emphasize social capital, subcultural orientations, stress, and access to care and other health-enhancing resources.

Neighborhood social capital and health. Social capital has been defined as aspects of social structure used by actors to facilitate the achievement of goals (Coleman 1990). We focus here on the role of social network ties and collective efficacy in promoting health at the community level. First, the increasingly vast literature on the role of informal social network supports in fostering health at the individual or egocentric network level has generated interest in the effects of community-level social network characteristics on health. Structurally disadvantaged neighborhoods may be less capable of sustaining viable social networks and may suffer from deficits in local social support and sociability. Berkman (2000) suggests, for example, that networks at the community level influence egocentric connectedness and health-enhancing processes such as social support, positive influence, and sociability. Evidence of the positive effects of social support on health is overwhelming and consistent, suggesting that the prevalence of social support activity and social engagement at the neighborhood level may also be relevant for health outcomes.

An additional social capital approach highlights the capacity for action on behalf of community goals as the critical intervening mechanism linking neighborhood structure with health. Robert Sampson and his colleagues (1997) have encapsulated this process in the concept of collective efficacy, which emphasizes mutual trust and solidarity (social cohesion) and shared expectations for prosocial action (informal social control). While acknowledging that local social ties may contribute to these dimensions of community social organization, the collective efficacy approach must be seen as distinct from the neighborhood social support and sociability perspective to the extent that it emphasizes the sense of attachment to community and the willingness of community residents to intervene on each other's behalf regardless of preexisting social ties.

The pathways through which neighborhood collective efficacy may influence health include the social control of health risk behavior, access to services and amenities, the management of neighborhood physical hazards, and psychosocial processes (Browning & Cagney 2003). First, Sampson et al. (1997) have demonstrated the powerful effects of collective efficacy on rates of violence, suggesting that health may be influenced by high levels of collective efficacy through limiting the health-damaging consequences of violent victimization. Other forms of problem behavior including illicit substance use, alcohol abuse, child and elder neglect/

abuse, and reckless behavior may also be held in check by high levels of collective social control. Second, collective efficacy may enhance the capacity of communities to attract and maintain high-quality health services and amenities such as community health clinics and safe recreational space. Third, collective efficacy may aid in correcting or avoiding the accumulation of neighborhood physical hazards such as decaying infrastructure and housing stock. Communities with the capacity to solicit and secure external resources to correct potentially risky conditions and monitor vulnerable residents (e.g., the elderly) are likely to enhance health. Finally, the effect of widespread trust and neighborhood attachment on factors such as fear and self-respect may improve the health and well-being of residents – even if they do not benefit from direct network support.

Subcultural transmission and health. Subcultural perspectives on health emphasize the health consequences of emergent alternative or oppositional cultural orientations primarily in economically disadvantaged communities. Fitzpatrick and LaGory (2000) suggest that disadvantaged communities with limited access to extra-local mainstream institutions may experience the emergence of "health-related subcultures." Two aspects of these subcultural orientations may have consequences for health: (1) tolerance for risky lifestyles and (2) anomie or detachment from conventional values. First, socially isolated communities are more likely to experience the cultural transmission of problematic behavioral strategies. Some of these behavioral orientations may be adaptive for survival (such as display of a "tough" or violent demeanor). However, modeling of violent and other risky behavior (such as smoking, drinking, risky sexual activity, and poor diet) in these contexts may have serious consequences for health.

Second, structural disadvantage, characterized by widespread poverty, lack of access to employment, and bleak economic prospects, may lead to anomic social conditions (Durkheim 1979 [1897]) in which neighborhood residents question basic normative orientations (e.g., the value of abiding by the law and of employing conventional means such as education and hard work to achieve success). Since the benefits of adherence to basic cultural values are perceived not to accrue to residents of some disadvantaged neighborhoods, the force of value-based pro-scriptions weakens in these contexts. Possible adaptations to these conditions include the emergence of largely short-term, instrumental orientations toward goals marked by little concern for the future. As applied to health, this hypoth-esis would suggest that anomie-induced, short-term, "here and now" orientations emphasizing satisfaction of immediate needs will tend to be associated with health-compromising behaviors.

Stress-based approaches. An additional per-spective focuses on the neighborhood context of exposure to stress-inducing conditions. Chronic high levels of exposure to stress may tax key systems within the body (e.g., the auto-nomic nervous system) resulting in diminished health (a condition known as "allostatic load"). Visible signs of community decay may contri-bute to stress through increased fear of victi-mization and social withdrawal. Abandoned and boarded-up buildings, vacant lots, graffiti, and other physical signs of deterioration com-bine with indicators of social decline such as public drinking, gang activity, and crime to convey the breakdown of social order and con-trol, particularly among the elderly. Thompson and Krause (2000), for instance, found that neighborhood deterioration, as measured by the condition of neighborhood buildings, roads, and the respondent's perceived level of safety from crime in the neighborhood, was positively associated with distrust and social isolation and negatively associated with physical health among older adults. Indeed, some elderly urban resi-dents may experience such intense fear of victi-mization that they live in a state of "self-imposed house arrest" (Dowd et al. 1981). Thus, in dis-advantaged contexts, the health consequences of fear-induced stress may be compounded by lim-ited social support and physical mobility.

Access to care and other health-enhancing resources. Finally, in addition to the informal aspects of neighborhood influence on health, the availability and quality of institutions that provide medical care and health-relevant resources are likely to vary across the commu-nity. Access to medical care depends upon who people are and where they live (Andersen et al. 2002). Research at the interface of sociology and health services has tapped these two dimen-sions, namely, via research on the behavioral determinants of access to care and variation in health outcomes across small areas. Variation at the community level may exist due to obvious differences in the number of physicians, clinics, or hospitals. It may also emerge from the com-munity's ability to attract and maintain health-enhancing resources or from factors associated with the organization and training of physicians. For instance, physicians disproportionately practice very near their initial training site, creating "clusters" of clinical norms and prac-tice patterns (Phelps 1992). Variation may also stem from the political level, given care for uninsured persons is driven largely by state and local policy (Cunningham & Kemper 1998). Access to care is critical for health and well-being, but may have benefits beyond those to the individual – good hospitals, for instance, may enrich the community apart from the deliv-ery of quality health care.

In summary, neighborhood structural charac-teristics, particularly economic advantage, may contribute to both formal and informal neigh-borhood-level mechanisms that are consequen-tial for health. To date, the research on the relative significance of these mechanisms – including networks, collective efficacy, social and physical disorder, and access to care – has been limited. However, data collection efforts designed to investigate these mechanisms are generating new insights into the potentially powerful role of neighborhood context in pro-moting, and diminishing, individual-level health status.

SEE ALSO: Aging and Social Support; Disease, Social Causation; Health and Culture; Health and Social Class; Hospitals; Social Capital and Health; Social Support; Stress and Health

REFERENCES AND SUGGESTED READINGS

Andersen, R. M., Yu, H., Wyn, R., Davidson, P. L., Brown, E. R., & Teleki, S. (2002) Access to Med-ical Care for Low-Income Persons: How Do Com-munities Make a Difference? *Medical Care Research and Review* 59: 384–411.

Berkman, L. F. (2000) Social Support, Social Net-works, Social Cohesion and Health. *Social Work and Health Care* 31: 3–14.

Browning, C. R. & Cagney, K. A. (2003) Moving Beyond Poverty: Neighborhood Structure, Social

Processes and Health. *Journal of Health and Social Behavior* 44(4): 552–71.

Coleman, J. S. (1990) *Foundations of Social Theory*. Harvard University Press, Cambridge, MA.

Cunningham, P. J. & Kemper, P. (1998) Ability to Obtain Medical Care for the Uninsured: How Much Does It Vary Across Communities? *JAMA* 280: 921–7.

Dowd, J., Sisson, R., & Kern, D. (1981) Socialization to Violence among the Aged. *Journal of Gerontology* 36: 350–61.

Durkheim, É. (1979 [1897]) *Suicide*. Free Press, New York.

Fitzpatrick, K. & LaGory, M. (2000) *Unhealthy Places: The Ecology of Risk in the Urban Landscape*. Routledge, New York.

Phelps, C. E. (1992) Diffusion of Information in Medical Care. *Journal of Economic Perspectives* 6: 23–42.

Sampson, R. J., Raudenbush, S. W., & Earls, F. (1997) Neighborhoods and Violent Crime: A Multilevel Study of Collective Efficacy. *Science* 227: 918–23.

Thompson, E. E. & Krause, N. (2000) Living Alone and Neighborhood Characteristics as Predictors of Social Support in Late Life. *Journal of Gerontology* 55: S245–S253.

health professions and occupations

Elianne Riska

A profession is a prestigious white-collar occupation that is based on theoretical and practical knowledge and training in a particular field, such as medicine. The specialized knowledge and the restricted practice is regulated by a central body of the profession to ensure the quality and the ethical conduct of its members. These characteristics separate the profession from an occupation which is a specific type of work done in the market. For example, caring is work done both outside and inside the labor market. In the latter case it is a collective activity organized as various health occupations. Sociologists differ in their views concerning the power of the professions, the character of health occupations, and on the division of labor in medicine.

The theoretical heritage of the sociology of health professions and occupations derives from a normative approach. Émile Durkheim saw professions as moral occupational communities in the new moral order and division of labor of the urban and industrial society. Based on this notion, Talcott Parsons (1951) defined professions in relation to a specific normative value system: the pattern variables. He viewed professions as occupational groups that had a special autonomy from the emerging bureaucracies of the modern society as depicted by Max Weber.

Special autonomy, knowledge and a service ideal towards clients were the three characteristics which defined the professions, not only as distinct from occupations, but also from the power of bureaucracies. Early research mapped the traits of occupational groups in order to identify to what extent they fitted the criteria of being a profession. This traits approach was considered too static, and a process and a power approach emerged in the 1970s.

Five major theoretical perspectives can be identified in the sociological debate about the character of health professions: the functionalist, the symbolic interactionist, the neo-Marxist, the neo-Weberian, and the social constructionist and poststructuralist perspectives. According to the functionalist perspective on professions, the physician's tasks are institutionalized as a social role, the function of which is the regulation of the kind of deviance interpreted as based on illness. The institutionalized roles of the physician and the sick person – the so-called sick role – contain certain expectations as well as obligations concerning the behavior related to the role. The role of the physician is acquired through a period of professional socialization where both the technical knowledge and the norms guiding professional behavior are taught. The views about the character of this socialization process were covered in a classic text, *The Student Physician* (Merton et al. 1957), which was based on a normative perspective.

The symbolic interactionist perspective on medical work has its earliest representative in a study on the professional socialization of medical students by a group of sociologists at the University of Chicago (Becker et al. 1961) and in Everett Hughes's (1958) collection of essays. For Hughes, the focus of a study of any kind of occupation is the "social drama of work." In his view, most occupations bring together people in definable roles and it is in their interaction that the content of work and occupational status are defined. An occupation is not *a priori* by means of its expertise and knowledge a profession, but a social status that is socially constructed and negotiated.

Everett Hughes's disciple Erving Goffman focused on the interaction between health professions and patients in a mental hospital and on the power and control function of the medical profession and the routine work of health care personnel. Like Hughes, Goffman (1961) perceived professions not as intrinsically distinct from occupations, but rather as a particular type of personal-service occupation based on expertise. Goffman emphasizes the social role of health professions as the basis of their power and he adheres to a Durkheimian approach to deviance. Goffman's complex and often conflicting views on social roles and structure have been pointed out in recent reviews.

A third representative working within the interactionist approach is Eliot Freidson, whose monopolization thesis set the field of sociology of professions on a new path. In contrast to the consensus perspective of the dominant functionalist approach to the study of the medical profession, Freidson (1970) reviewed the pattern variables and their validity for understanding the power of physicians in the division of labor in medicine. Rather than normative consensus, Freidson suggested that, like Hughes's (1958) thesis on the license and mandate of the medical profession, a monopoly of medical knowledge underlay the power of physicians as a profession. A decade later, Freidson (1984) witnessed a change in the character of the American medical profession, but argued that the profession had accommodated to the ongoing corporatization and rationalization of medicine by means of a new internal division of labor. This is Freidson's "restratification" thesis, which states that the medical profession is divided into three groups – the academic elite, administrators, and practicing physicians – in order to maintain its order in the hierarchy of medical work. In more recent work, Freidson (2001) has returned to the issue of professionalism as a special form of occupational control and the character of the market, professions, and bureaucratic and organizational control of work.

Both Parsons's and Freidson's work were focused on the medical profession and had little to say about other health occupations and the larger division of labor in medicine. Other theoretical perspectives not only challenged the narrow focus on the medical profession, but also pointed to the need to look at the broader division of labor within medicine and its basis in the class and gender structure of the larger society.

The neo-Marxist perspective relates the power of the profession to the larger underlying economic and political organization of society. According to the neo-Marxist perspective on health professions and occupations, the capitalist society determines the superstructure, of which the social organization of health care, the professions, and medicine as a science are but parts (Navarro 1975). The argument here is that the same hierarchy is found in the health sector as in the rest of the capitalist economy.

All the perspectives above perceive the medical profession as united and powerful. The prophecy of a gradual loss of power of the medical profession is attributed to two other sociologists, Marie Haug and John McKinlay, who advanced the deprofessionalization and proletarianization thesis, respectively (see Freidson 1984). For Haug, the knowledge monopoly of the medical profession is challenged both by various female health professionals and clients who have increasing access to medical knowledge through the information industry. Haug's prophecy was that the prerogatives of the medical profession will wither away because professions are rapidly losing their control over their knowledge domain. McKinlay and his colleagues adopted a neo-Marxist perspective: medicine is viewed as being taken over by capital-intensive and large corporations, a development that will result in physicians working increasingly as salaried employees of such organizations. The "proletarianization" of physicians denotes a process that will gradually result in the loss of the traditional power of the profession. The assumption is that all physicians will lose professional power and autonomy, since the corporatization of medicine is perceived as an ongoing universal process.

According to the neo-Weberian perspective, professions are occupational groups that operate in the marketplace and have been successful in demarcating the domain of their work as their exclusionary right (Larson 1977). The neo-Weberian approach to the professions emerged as a reaction to the functionalist and traits perspectives. In focus are the characteristics of medical work and the actions of the occupational group striving for a professional status and defending it through the strategy of closure. Witz (1992) has added a feminist perspective in her analysis of the power of the medical profession, nurses, and midwives in the UK and suggests that professions have always been gendered projects (i.e., the agents are either men or women).

The most recent theoretical perspective that combines the Freidsonian and the neo-Weberian views on the power of professions is Andrew Abbott's (1988) systems approach to professions. Here the term "professional jurisdiction" serves as the analytical tool to explain the power of both occupations and professions in the division of labor in knowledge-based work in the service sector.

The Foucauldian theory of the power of medicine (Foucault 1975) attracted in the 1990s those who wanted to understand changes taking place in the governance of health care. The conflict perspective on the medical profession presents the profession as a group exerting social control. While the social constructionist tradition viewed the medical profession as a self-interested group and patients as passive, the poststructuralist position in the structure-agency debate is more complex. The medicalization thesis suggests that the medical profession has crucial power in turning social phenomena into medical problems. The crude version harbors a victimization view of the patient, while the Foucauldian perspective contends that the medical discourse of the medical profession is merely one of many alternative discourses on health and medicine.

In more recent work on health professions, Foucault's notion of governmentality underlies the special role that scientific knowledge and professions have in regulating behavior. For example, a disciplinary regime of self-management serves as a "technology of the self" and represents a new kind of professionalism. Self-management is an internal normative mechanism whereby not only traditional professions but also new service occupations control their members.

The major theoretical perspectives on health professions have mainly focused on the medical profession. Two aspects have thereby been neglected. First, there is still little research on other health professions, such as nurses and midwives. The rise and struggle of these health professions to achieve professional status and a jurisdiction of their own have been the focus of recent studies (e.g., Witz 1992; De Vries et al. 2001). The theoretical frameworks used in these studies have been neo-Weberian or Abbott's systems approach. Second, early works on health professions viewed professions as either gender-neutral issues or male-dominated groups. In recent research, the gender perspective has been emphasized as a way to reach a broader understanding of the character of nursing and the status of women physicians within the medical profession.

The methodological approaches in the sociology of professions have varied, but can be classified as largely qualitative methods. Aside from statistics on the number of members and their distribution within specialties and sectors in the labor market, mapping of the historical trends and the professionalization process have been based on documents (e.g., organizational records, professional journals, legislation) and interviews with informants recruited from the profession. Recent studies on the job satisfaction or workload of physicians and nurses have used survey research, although a large part of this research has been done within the disciplines of health psychology or public health rather than sociology.

SEE ALSO: Functionalism/Neofunctionalism; Hospitals; Medical Sociology; Merton, Robert K.; Occupations; Parsons, Talcott; Professional Dominance in Medicine; Professions; Professions, Organized; Work, Sociology of

REFERENCES AND SUGGESTED READINGS

Abbott, A. (1988) *The System of Professions: An Essay on the Division of Expert Labor.* University of Chicago Press, Chicago.

Becker, H. S., Geer, B., Hughes, E. C., & Strauss, A. L. (1961) *Boys in White: Student Culture in Medical School.* University of Chicago Press, Chicago.

De Vries, R., Benoit, C., van Teijlingen, E. R., & Wrede, S. (2001) *Birth By Design: Pregnancy, Maternity Care, and Midwifery in North America and Europe*. Routledge, London.

Foucault, M. (1975) *The Birth of the Clinic*. Vintage Books, New York.

Fournier, V. (1999) The Appeal to "Professionalism" as a Disciplinary Mechanism. *Sociological Review* 47: 280–307.

Freidson, E. (1970) *Profession of Medicine*. Mead, New York.

Freidson, E. (1984) The Changing Nature of Professional Control. *Annual Review of Sociology* 10: 1–20.

Freidson, E. (2001) *Professionalism: The Third Logic*. Polity Press, Cambridge.

Goffman, E. (1961) *Asylums*. Doubleday, Anchor, Garden City, NY.

Hughes, E. C. (1958) *Men and Their Work*. Free Press, Glencoe, IL.

Larson, M. S. (1977) *The Rise of Professionalism*. University of California Press, Berkeley.

Merton, R. K., Reader, G., & Kendall, P. (1957) *The Student Physician*. Harvard University Press, Cambridge, MA.

Navarro, V. (1975) The Political Economy of Medical Care. *International Journal of Health Services* 5: 65–94.

Parsons, T. (1951) *The Social System*. Free Press, New York.

Witz, A. (1992) *Professions and Patriarchy*. Routledge, London.

health and race

Leigh A. Willis

Race interacts with health just as it does with other life-determining, sociodemographic factors like class, gender, and age. Race is best understood as a shared set of cultural and social experiences common to people of the same skin color. Research has shown that the notion of distinct biological races is misleading because often more genetic variation exists within a defined "race" than between them. Therefore, we all belong to the human race and thus race is a social construction rather than a "true" biological distinction. Even though race is socially constructed (American Sociological Association 2002), the manner in which it influences social relationships suggests that race is a valid construct with "real" repercussions.

Race, for example, is often associated with health, which the World Health Organization defines as a state of physical, mental, and social well-being. The relationship is important. By knowing an individual's race, that person's health lifestyle and illness behavior can frequently be predicted. Race and health interact on several levels, as seen in the health effects of racism and discrimination, class differences in health status, access to health care, doctor–patient interaction, health culture, representation in medical professions, and the racial health disparities in the United States and abroad.

There are substantial differences in health status among people of color in America and worldwide. For example, the rate of Hepatitis B is higher among Asians. Hispanics have a higher incidence of certain cancers, such as cancer of the cervix and stomach. Native Americans have high rates of alcoholism and diabetes. African Americans have an average life expectancy that is 7 years less than that of whites. So clearly there are differences in the health status of whites and non-whites.

One of the ways race influences health today is through racism and discrimination. All types of racism and discrimination contribute to this problem overtly, institutionally, and covertly. There are many overt ways in which racism affects health, such as through environmental racism, which is racial discrimination in environmental policy making, enforcement of laws, and regulations (Chavis 1993). This causes a disproportionately large number of health and environmental risks for people of color in the communities in which they live. These risks come in the form of housing placed near waste dumps, living in housing with lead-based paint, exposure to pesticides, and neighborhoods located in areas with contaminated land, air, and water. Environmental racism has existed for generations like other forms of racism, and is maintained by redlining, zoning, and political decision-making. Increased environmental exposure to pollutants in communities of color considerably elevates the risk of its inhabitants for a variety of diseases. Covert discrimination and racism in the medical system also influences health. Even when people of color have equal access and provision for health care services, they are less likely to be treated as aggressively as whites with procedures like chemotherapy and surgery (Jones 2000). Such treatment decisions ultimately exacerbate the health status of people of color by causing excess and premature mortality.

In order to understand the effects of racism and discrimination on health and how they influence health today, we must take into account its historical antecedents, using the concept of total discrimination. Historically, the institution of medicine was used as a basis of legitimization and justification for the oppression and disenfranchisement that non-white "races" have experienced. For instance, medicine was used to justify the enslavement and subjugation of many people of color. Nonwhites were viewed as subhuman animals, less intelligent, and biologically inferior to whites. More specifically, medical knowledge like virology has been applied to instances of genocide of native peoples. Native Americans receiving smallpox-infected blankets from Europeans is an example of these practices. In the same way, enslaved African Americans were used as human guinea pigs for medical procedures and treatments like abortion, hysterectomies, and amputation. Similarly, governments have sanctioned medical experiments on its minority citizens such as the Tuskegee Experiment (African Americans) and the South Dakota Hepatitis A-Vaccine Study (Native Americans). Both of these experiments ended relatively recently, in the 1970s and 1991, respectively.

The policies of the past have translated into a pervasive distrust of the medical establishment. This distrust has influenced three outcomes: (1) an underutilization of formal medicine, (2) the utilization of formal medicine in concert with traditional cultural-specific alternative means of healing, or (3) lack of participation in clinical trials. Every racial and ethnic group has its own culture-specific version of folk and faith healers; among Latinos, it is the Cuarandersmo/Cuarandersma; for African Americans, its root workers; for Asians, its acupuncturists and herbalists; for Native Americans, bonesetters. These healers use rudimentary health practices combined with aspects of religion and mysticism. Folk and faith healers are more effective in improving the patient's mental and spiritual sense of well-being than in improving physical health. Still, their contribution is not to be taken lightly given that mental well-being is directly related to immune-response. Furthermore, these healers offer a holistic (treating the body and mind as integrated units) approach to healing that most formal healers lack.

In the same way, the use of faith and folk healers is also due in part to the under-representation of people of color in health professions. The paucity of people of color among health care professions is partly due to non-whites formerly being prohibited and later discouraged from entering the health professions. This is important because when patients and professionals are of different backgrounds (races) there is a greater potential for racial stereotypes, prejudice, and lack of cultural sensitivity, as well as language barriers affecting the quality of medical encounters. Therefore, some people may decide if they cannot visit a health care professional with a similar racial background, they may avoid contact with formal medicine all together. Simply, many people of color feel more comfortable with health care providers and researchers of similar backgrounds who have an understanding or appreciation of their culture.

The unwitting participation of minorities in medical experiments in which people died or were disabled severely hinders efforts to recruit and enroll people of color in present-day clinical trials. Participation in clinical trials is critical to the development of cures, because clinical trials help determine if drugs are effective. Also, by participating in clinical trials participants receive new information about their disease. The under-representation in clinical trials also limits the potential for drugs to be designed specifically for people of color.

Access to care is another important factor that must be considered in looking at race and health. People of color are disproportionately poor, unemployed, or employed in jobs that do not provide health insurance. Therefore, they are more likely to be without or have limited access to health care. The costs of office visits, medicines, and therapy are an onerous burden for impoverished people. Also, the location of health care facilities influences access to care when there is closure of hospitals that formerly served non-white communities. Typically, non-white neighborhoods often do not have adequate medical facilities located within a suitable distance and thus make health care inconvenient for many. Also, many people of color obtain their health care through the public system of health care rather than the private system. The public system may feature long waiting periods, lack of adequate staff, and limited resources. Thus, it may not be able to provide the necessary treatment options that can impact the quality of care people of color receive. Due to the distrust of medicine, being on the receiving end of poor doctor–patient interaction, and the high cost associated with seeing a health professional, many people of color probably do not seek preventive care, such as routine physicals and screenings. Consequently, they may delay seeing a professional until their disease is in a critical or life-threatening stage.

Racism also affects health on a more personal level. A term for experiencing racism is "personally mediated racism." Personally mediated racism is defined as "prejudice and discrimination, where prejudice means differential assumptions about the abilities, motives, and intentions of others according to their race" (Jones 2000: 1214). Personally mediated racism manifests itself in day-to-day interactions through devaluation, suspicion, and dehumanization of people of color. Despite a greater utilization of a social support network, racism is a powerful stressor which takes a psychological and physiological toll over time. Psychologically, racism may lead to feelings of helplessness, anxiety, frustration, and nihilism (Clark et al. 1999). Physiologically, stressors like racism negatively impact cardiovascular, immune, and endocrine systems, thus leaving people of color particularly susceptible to a variety of ailments.

Besides racism, racial differences in health also result from patterns of health care utilization, genetics, and health culture. First, differences in health among races may be due to a greater reluctance of non-whites to use formal medicine for the reasons specified earlier. Genetics apparently plays some role, in that certain racial groups are predisposed to certain conditions, such as sickle cell anemia among African Americans and significantly higher rates of diabetes among Native Americans.

Health culture among different "races" may also explain differences. As mentioned earlier, people of color are more likely to utilize folk and faith healers from their own culture in concert with traditional medicine. Also, they

are more likely to use a lay-referral network, which is the process by which an individual consults lay people such as friends and family members to guide them in interpreting symptoms, deciding whether care is needed, and the type of care they should seek. This process may delay the seeking of professional help. In the same way, different racial groups have innate cultural means of promoting health. Some of these are the stress-buffering properties of the extended family network (social support); diet (nutrition); alternative healing practices (e.g., acupuncture); and subcultural emphasis on physical and mental health (e.g., yoga). In contrast, there are aspects of culture that are detrimental to health, such as lack of oral hygiene, internalization of stressors, and lack of disclosure of health status of family, friends, and sometimes the patients themselves.

Recently, racial health disparities between races have begun to receive greater attention in the US and worldwide. In the US efforts are being made to better understand the causes of health disparities. Some areas being examined are access to care and the effects of racism, genetics, diet, and health culture. Internationally, the WHO has been examining many of these issues, such as diseases that disproportionately affect people of color, such as HIV, TB, cholera, substance abuse, and a host of chronic diseases like cardiovascular disease, cancer, and mental illness.

There are methodological issues to be considered when examining the relationship between race and health. First, since race is a social construct, it is not measured consistently across societies. For example, racial categories in health data in America are not standardized. Second, in some situations, "race is not an attribute, but a dynamic characteristic dependent on other social circumstances" (Zuberi 2000: 172). So race is a construct that is defined differently and varies by country. For instance, in Brazil "races" are organized not only by skin color, but by hair type and language. Third, there is the problem of categorizing races. For instance, in some parts of the US, health data are only divided into white and non-white categories. This practice is problematic because researchers are unable to uncover key differences and report on the health of Hispanics, Asians, Native Americans, and African Americans. A standardization of racial categories across the world is needed, though creating a racial taxonomy would be difficult and perhaps cause misunderstanding.

As citizens of the world immigrate and migrate we will see greater diversity in societies as non-white populations increase. Thus, all developing and developed nations will have to grapple sooner or later with the issues raised here.

SEE ALSO: Ethnicity; Health and Culture; Health Lifestyles; Health Locus of Control; Health and Medicine; Health, Neighborhood Disadvantage; Health and Social Class; Mortality: Transitions and Measures; Race (Racism); Race/Ethnicity, Health, and Mortality; Stress and Health

REFERENCES AND SUGGESTED READINGS

American Sociological Association (2002) *Statement of the American Sociological Association on the Importance of Collecting Data and Doing Social Scientific Research on Race.* Online. www.asanet. org/media/racestmt02.pdf.

Chavis, B. F., Jr. (1993) *Confronting Environmental Racism: Voices from the Grassroots.* South End Press, Boston.

Clark, R., Anderson, N., Clark, V., & Williams, D. (1999) Racism as a Stressor for African-Americans: A Biopsychosocial Model. *American Psychologist* 54: 805–16.

Jones, C. (2000) Levels of Racism: A Theoretical Framework and a Gardener's Tale. *American Journal of Public Health* 90: 1212–25.

Simmons, B. (1995) *Environmental Liberty and Social Justice for All: How Advocacy Planning Can Help Combat Environmental Racism.* Online. www.igc. apc.org/envjustice/ejplan.html.

Zuberi, T. (2000) Deracializing Social Statistics: Problems in the Quantification Of Race. *Annals of the American Academy* 568: 172–85.

health and religion

Jeffrey Michael Clair

Concepts of health and illness in human society originated from traditional religious views about life and death. One of the first sociologists to study religion was Émile Durkheim, who found that distinctions between ideas about the sacred and profane were connected to notions of health and illness. Religious views of the sacred body, for example, were equated with health. When someone became ill, it was not because of hygiene, but because of a breach of social norms separating the sacred from the profane. Within this type of belief system, notions of sickness and misfortune generated attempts to justify and explain morally why a particular person was suffering from disease: "Why me?" (Turner 2004).

Fundamental notions of religion and health are apparent in modern everyday life, but as scientific concepts of disease develop, traditional notions of the religious character of illness and disease continue to be challenged. Over time, the social status of biomedicine has increased and the status of traditional healers diminished. During this transformation, we see the introduction of the mind-body dualism. This dualistic focus is responsible for the emergence of mental as well as physical health concerns (Turner 2004).

Contemporary studies show that religion is positively associated with physical and mental health, as well as longevity and mortality (Hummer et al. 1999; Sherkat & Ellison 1999). Religious involvement, measured by attendance at services and feelings of religiosity, is positively associated with physical health, general happiness, and satisfaction, as well as being inversely related to undesirable social psychological states, such as depression. Ellison and Sherkat (1995: 1256) suggest that religious involvement promotes physical and mental health in four ways: (1) shaping health behaviors and lifestyles in ways that reduce unhealthy and risky behavior; (2) by contributing to the individual's social psychological resource support network; (3) by enhancing self-esteem; and (4) by helping produce cognitive coping mechanisms.

Religious institutions and beliefs have long been recognized as control agents that can regulate individual behavior. We see this influence when we talk of religious groups promoting the body as a temple and discouraging negative practices like smoking, alcohol and drug use, and unhealthy diets (Cockerham 2004). Being involved in religious communities also tends to reduce deviant behavior, making an individual accountable for his or her health lifestyles. Some religious values encourage strong marital relationships, discouraging sexual experimentation. And religious beliefs often promote intergenerational relationships that promote shared meanings about life events and biographical histories (Ellison & Sherkat 1995).

Being involved in religious groups can also be seen as helping integrate individuals into caring social circles (Idler 1995) and therefore add to a person's psychosocial resources that mediate and/or moderate the health consequences associated with social stressors. Here, religious involvement can be seen as not only increasing the size of a person's support network, but also providing regular opportunities to cultivate support (Sherkat & Ellison 1999). Many congregations also provide formal programs for those in need, which enhances opportunities to receive needed information and social support. One result of such opportunities is that they increase an individual's confidence that friends and associates can be counted on to help in time of illness or injury. In general, being involved in such a community can promote aspects of self-esteem and efficacy (Ellison & Sherkat 1995). Religion provides not only support, but also structure, stability, and intimacy in dealing with health concerns.

Religious understandings have become "common and effective coping strategies for many individuals dealing with an array of chronic and acute stressors, particularly bereavement and health problems, including physical disability" (Sherkat & Ellison 1999: 374). This is in contrast to the "muscular Christianity" that links good health with the vitality of a nation (Cockerham 2004). Those with disabilities can find religious participation helps them to refocus on aspects of the self "to which a painful, or nonfunctioning, or unattractive physical body is irrelevant" (Idler 1995: 700). Such a refocus allows the individual to find a healthy inner-self and emphasize positive emotions such as contentment, love, hope, and optimism as they develop, integrate, and perpetuate their faith into everyday life. In this regard, even private religious activities (e.g., prayer, Bible reading and study) can produce an effect on health by providing meaning, which in turn reduces helplessness and increases optimism (Musick 1996). If religion is viewed as a source of comfort, the increase in individual hope provides a sense of control in a disadvantaged world, whether that disadvantage is physical health, social, or economic (Ellison et al. 2001).

Many people from a broad spectrum of religious backgrounds hold health and well-being as central spiritual concerns. Although there is evidence that spiritual, social psychological, and physical aspects of health are fundamentally interconnected, more research is needed. Postmodern developments will continue to challenge the synthesis of health and spirituality. Not only has human action become functionally separated into specialized institutions, but also biomedicine has displayed a predisposition toward differentiation from other institutional spheres, such as religion and the family. And while the general population does not generally disregard the power of medicine's explanations of disease causation, many consider medical explanations to be insufficient, and find themselves embracing complementary and alternative medicine and spiritual healing movements (McGuire 1993).

Future research will need to emphasize religious factors. We know that there is at least some evidence of the physical and mental health benefits of religion among men and women, different age groups, various racial and ethnic groups, and different socioeconomic classes, as well as geographical locations (Ellison et al. 2001). However, there often exist crude measures of religious identification, involvement, and participation. Not only do we find too many single-item indicators, but also mostly cross-sectional data. For instance, difficult measurement issues include being able to decipher when religious value is collectively produced versus it being a private good with intrinsic value (Ellison et al. 2001). Other suggestions for future work include an analysis of "insider documents" (Ellison & Sherkat 1995: 1265) in order to determine how institutions produce, distribute, and prepare material for religious communities. Because of its multidimensionality, religious involvement displays multiple causal pathways for its effects on physical and mental health. Attention to multidimensional measurement and a commitment to longitudinal data collection are needed. Epidemiological studies of large populations with extensive baseline health assessments and longitudinal follow-ups with measures of religious involvement are also required.

SEE ALSO: Health Behavior; Health and Culture; Health Lifestyles; Health Locus of Control; Religion; Social Support

REFERENCES AND SUGGESTED READINGS

Becker, M. (1993) A Medical Sociologist Looks at Health Promotion. *Journal of Health and Social Behavior* 34: 1–6.

Cockerham, W. (2004) *Medical Sociology*, 9th edn. Prentice-Hall, Upper Saddle River, NJ.

Coe, R. (1997) The Magic of Science and the Science of Magic: An Essay on the Process of Healing. *Journal of Health and Social Behavior* 38: 1–8.

Crosnoe, R. & Elders, G. (2002) Successful Adaptation in the Later Years: A Life Course Approach to Aging. *Social Psychology Quarterly* 65: 309–28.

Ellison, C. & Sherkat, D. (1995) Is Sociology the Core Discipline for the Scientific Study of Religion? *Social Forces* 73: 1255–66.

Ellison, C., Boardman, J., Williams, D., & Jackson, J. (2001) Religious Involvement, Stress, and Mental Health: Findings from the Detroit Area Study. *Social Forces* 80: 215–49.

Hummer, R., Rogers, R., Nam, C., & Ellison, C. (1999) Religious Involvement and US Adult Mortality. *Demography* 36: 273–85.

Idler, E. (1995) Religion, Health, and Nonphysical Senses of Self. *Social Forces* 74: 683–704.

Krause, N., Ingersoll-Dayton, B., Liang, J., & Sugisawa, H. (1999) Religion, Social Support, and Health Among the Japanese Elderly. *Journal of Health and Social Behavior* 40: 405–21.

McGuire, M. (1993) Health and Spirituality as Contemporary Concerns. *Annals of the American Academy of Political and Social Science* 527: 144–54.

Musick, M. (1996) Religion and Subjective Health Among Black and White Elders. *Journal of Health and Social Behavior* 37: 221–37.

Sherkat, D. & Ellison, C. (1999) Recent Developments and Current Controversies in the Sociology of Religion. *Annual Review of Sociology* 25: 363–94.

Turner, B. (2004) *The New Medical Sociology: Social Forms of Health and Illness*. Norton, New York.

health risk behavior

Deborah Lupton

Health risk behavior involves actions and related attitudes and perceptions that contribute to people's propensity to engage in, or avoid, activities that have been deemed by experts to be hazardous or dangerous to their health. Considerable research in public health and medicine has been devoted to identifying health risks and the behaviors associated with these risks in the attempt to assist people to avoid them.

The juxtaposition of the words "risk" and "behavior" often implies a psychological approach to understanding the processes by which people think about and react to risk. Cognitive science is a major approach within psychology that focuses on risk behaviors, including those related to states of health. From this perspective, people's behaviors are considered very much on an individual level. Research questions revolve around how people process information about risk and what they then do with this information. The "objective facts" of risk, as identified by scientists, medical researchers, and other experts, are considered the standard by which lay understandings are compared, and often found wanting. An individual's propensity to make inaccurate judgments about health risks is seen as based, for the most part, on ignorance, deficiency in self-efficacy, or biases.

One example of this perspective is the influential health belief model. People are seen as undergoing a series of cognitive steps when processing the possible threat posed by a health risk, presenting a linear relationship between knowledge, attitudes, and eventual practice. According to this model, risk-taking is an irrational and deviant act. Little attention is paid to the symbolic and emotional meanings that are associated with risk perception and risk-taking. People are represented as atomized and autonomous, largely removed from the influences of society and culture.

Sociological researchers often take a rather different perspective on health risk behaviors and beliefs. They are interested in exploring the ways in which people recognize phenomena as "health risks," how people identify the relationship between risk and behavior, which kind of risks they consider most threatening, who they see as posing the risks (e.g., are the risks viewed as imposed by outsiders or are they regarded as a product of personal lifestyle choices?), how social and cultural factors such as age, gender, ethnicity, and socioeconomic status influence health beliefs and behaviors, and what kinds of broader social and cultural meanings and beliefs are associated with health risk beliefs and understandings.

Various theoretical and methodological approaches have been taken by sociologists when researching health risk behavior and beliefs. Sociologists drawing on a critical approach based on Marxist or feminist writings focus their attention on the ways in which health risks are closely associated with social disadvantage and inequality. Rather than draw attention to an individual's personal responsibility for risks, therefore, such researchers emphasize that a person's social location is a major influence on their exposure to health risks and the opportunities they have to avoid them. People in disadvantaged areas both live in environments which are more conducive to health risk exposure, such as a subculture that supports cigarette smoking and a physical environment that is more polluted, and have less access to sources of knowledge and assistance in avoiding health risks than do those from more privileged backgrounds.

One influential sociologist, Ulrich Beck (1992), has written extensively on what he sees as the move to "risk society" in contemporary western societies. Risk society is characterized by a sensibility which is highly aware of, and concerned about, risks, including health risks. Beck is interested in the reasons why certain phenomena are singled out as "risks" and the political uses this serves. Many health risks, he argues, are seen as the result of human action, of modernizing processes that have gone too far: examples include pollution, chemical contamination of food, and epidemics of bacterial infections caused by the inappropriate use of antibiotics. Anthony Giddens's (1991) sociological writings on risk also emphasize these political aspects of risk. He particularly draws attention to lay people's growing loss of trust in experts, and the subsequent confusion they experience in knowing how best to deal with risks.

Researchers working from a social constructionist perspective are interested in the discourses, or organized ways of representing phenomena in language and practice, that surround health risks and give meaning to them. This perspective challenges the "objective facts" of risk themselves. Expert risk knowledge is viewed as equally subject to the influence of social and cultural processes as lay knowledge. Taking this perspective is not necessarily to challenge the accuracy of expert knowledge, but rather to emphasize that it is constructed in a social and cultural environment that shapes the knowledge in various ways. What phenomena are identified as "health risks," and therefore as hazardous and important for people to avoid, is partly a function of particular social and cultural environments and associated "ways of seeing," for both lay people and experts. Thus, for example, it may be argued that the current emphasis on the risks associated with overweight and obesity in western countries is influenced by a growing anxiety in the last decades of the twentieth century and into the first years of the twenty-first century about the shape and size of the body, not only in relation to health but also to physical attractiveness.

Sociologists are also interested in the ways that discourses about health risks serve to encourage people to view themselves and their bodies in certain ways. Thus, for example, the dominant popular and medical discourses surrounding health risks and cigarette smoking represent the smoker's body as vulnerable and open to serious illness, cigarette smoke itself as a contaminating substance, and smokers as ignorant or weak-willed, not interested enough in their health to give up the practice. Discourses are mutable, subject to change over time. Compare the positive discourses around cigarette smoking that were evident in the mid-twentieth century, which emphasized the glamor and health-giving effects of cigarettes, with those described above.

For sociologists, therefore, health risk behavior is not simply an individual's autonomous response to expert advice. Health risk behavior and the beliefs that accompany it are complex products of socialization and acculturation into certain expectations, assumptions, and norms. Behavior and beliefs are intimately associated with people's place in society, and are both political and surrounded by cultural meaning.

SEE ALSO: Health Behavior; Health and Culture; Health Lifestyles; Health Locus of Control; Health, Neighborhood Disadvantage; Health and Social Class; Risk, Risk Society, Risk Behavior, and Social Problems; Smoking

REFERENCES AND SUGGESTED
READINGS

Beck, U. (1992) *Risk Society: Towards a New Modernity*. Sage, London.
Giddens, A. (1991) *Modernity and Self-Identity*. Polity Press, Cambridge.
Lupton, D. (1999) *Risk*. Routledge, London.

health, self-rated

M. Christine Snead

Self-rated health, or self-reported health (SRH), is a measure of a respondent's subjective sense of health. The SRH is commonly used to capture a general sense of health from the perspective of the respondent, which is assessed by one simple global question about their overall health. There are many phrasings of this question, including "In general, would you say your health is ...," "How would you rate your overall health ...," and "How is your health, compared with others your age?" Response items for these questions are Likert-type scales with responses typically scored from 1–5 (excellent, good, fair, poor, very bad) or 1–3 (better, same, worse). Methodologically, the SRH has been found to be both a reliable and valid measure of a respondent's health status (Krause & Jay 1994; Lundberg & Manderbacka 1996; Miilunpalo et al. 1997).

The SRH question is purposely and ambiguously constructed to not specify what is meant by health. While most people tend to think of "health" as physical health, some respondents may use a frame of reference that includes emotional or mental well-being. Some researchers place the SRH question at the beginning of a questionnaire so that respondents will not be influenced by later questions. Other investigators, who favor a broad definition of health, deliberately place the SRH at the end of their questionnaire so that responses can be informed by earlier questions. The thinking behind the later placement of the SRH is that if earlier questionnaire items were related to physical, emotional, or social well-being, the respondent would utilize this perspective.

The SRH has for decades been used in numerous studies from around the world from many different disciplines. The popularity and wide use of the SRH are based on it being one of the most powerful predictors of health, clinical outcomes, morbidity, and mortality (Idler & Yael 1997; Fayers & Sprangers 2002; Goldman et al. 2004). Most people have an accurate idea of what their health status is and the SRH provides this measure. Therefore, the SRH question is commonly employed in health surveys. It is a common measure, for example, in large-scale studies like the Canadian National Population Health Survey, the Danish National Cohort Study (DANCOS), and the US Bureau of the Census's National Health Interview Survey. It has been employed successfully in smaller studies as well (Cockerham et al. 2002; Williams & Umberson 2004).

While the SRH is a powerful and useful measurement, it is not without limitations. It is a "subjective" measure and because of this "subjectivity" there will be differences in interpretations by respondents. The extent and ramifications of differing interpretations of what is meant by health and how respondents answer the SRH are not fully understood. Different social groups may interpret health in different ways. Researchers are currently investigating such issues and there appears to be a growing body of related literature. Gender differences, for example, have been noted in several studies examining SRH as a predictor of mortality. Women tend to rate their health poorer than men, even though they have longer life expectancies (Idler 2003).

Researchers have also noted relationships between other socio-demographic characteristics, SRH, and outcomes like mortality trends (Franks et al. 2003), including educational differences (Martinez-Sanchez & Regidor 2002) and socio-economic or income differences. Class differences in particular seem to have strong associations with SRH, but this finding has not been consistent in cross-national comparisons (Knesebeck et al. 2003). A variety of explanations have been used to describe such discrepancies, but there is no consensus as to why these discrepancies occur. There is, however, consensus that health is a multidimensional phenomenon that can be measured in a variety of ways, and that the SRH is a popular and widely used measure.

SEE ALSO: Aging, Mental Health, and Well-Being; Health Behavior; Health Lifestyles; Health Locus of Control; Health Risk Behavior; Sociometry

REFERENCES AND SUGGESTED READINGS

Cockerham, W. C., Snead, M. C., & De Waal, D. F. (2002) Health Lifestyles in Russia and the Socialist Heritage. *Journal of Health and Social Behavior* 43: 42–55.
Fayers, P. M. & Sprangers, M. (2002) Understanding Self-Rated Health. *Lancet* 359: 187–9.
Franks, P., Gold, M., & Fiscella, K. (2003) Sociodemographics, Self-Rated Health, and Mortality in the US. *Social Science and Medicine* 56: 2505–14.
Goldman, N., Glei, D., & Chang, M. (2004) The Role of Clinical Risk Factors in Understanding Self-Rated Health. *Annals of Epidemiology* 14: 49–57.
Idler, E. (2003) Discussion: Gender Differences in Self-Rated Health, in Mortality, and in the Relationship Between the Two. *Gerontologist* 43: 372–5.
Idler, E. & Yael, B. (1997) Self-Rated Health and Mortality: A Review of Twenty-Seven Community Studies. *Journal of Health and Social Behavior* 38: 21–37.
Knesebeck, O., Lüschen, G., Cockerham, W. C., & Siegrist, J. (2003) Socioeconomic Status and Health Among the Aged in the United States and Germany: A Comparative Cross-Sectional Study. *Social Science and Medicine* 57: 1643–53.
Krause, N. M. & Jay, G. M. (1994) What Do Global Self-Rated Health Items Measure? *Medical Care* 32: 930–42.
Lundberg, O. & Manderbacka, K. (1996) Assessing Reliability of a Measure of Self-Rated Health. *Scandinavian Journal of Social Medicine* 24: 218–24.
Martinez-Sanchez, E. & Regidor, E. (2002) Self-Rated Health by Educational Level in Persons With and Without Health Problems. *Journal of Health Psychology* 7: 459–69.
Miilunpalo, S., Vuori, I., Oja, P., Pasanen, M., & Urponen, H. (1997) Self-Rated Health Status as a Health Measure: The Predictive Value of Self-Reported Health Status on the Use of Physician Services and on Mortality in the Working Age Population". *Journal of Clinical Epidemiology* 50: 517–28.
Williams, K. & Umberson, D. (2004) Marital Status, Marital Transitions, and Health: A Gendered Life Course Perspective. *Journal of Health and Social Behavior* 45: 81–98.

health and social class

Eero Lahelma

The Black Report on Inequalities in Health (Townsend & Davidson 1982) refers to social class as "segments of populations sharing broadly similar types and levels of resources, with broadly similar styles of living and (for some sociologists) some shared perception of their collective condition." Two main sociological traditions of social class attach people to social structures, emphasizing either their relationships to production, ownership, and material resources (Marx) or their relationships to markets, status, power, and lifestyle (Weber). While in the Marxist tradition class positions between the bourgeoisie and the proletariat tend to be opposite, in the Weberian tradition social classes rather follow a hierarchical stratification. However, these sociological traditions of social class share the idea of unequal distribution of resources and assets in society. Both traditions have influenced the basic medical sociological assumptions that social divisions shape morbidity and mortality, and that poor health is likely to emerge from poor living conditions (Blaxter 1997).

Sociological studies often measure classes by occupations, but education, income, and wealth equally play a part in determining people's social class, or in broader terms, socioeconomic status. Thus, the topic of social class and health encompasses hierarchical inequalities in morbidity and mortality between upper and lower socioeconomic statuses as indicated by occupations and other socioeconomic indicators.

When examining social class differences in morbidity and mortality, it has become habitual to speak about "health inequalities" (Townsend & Davidson 1982). The term inequalities indicates not only neutral health differences between segments of people, but also suggests that most social class inequalities in health are artificial, undesirable, and (in principle) avoidable. Thus, a moral and political dimension of social class and health emerges, suggesting that a large part of health inequalities in modern societies can be regarded as unjust.

INTELLECTUAL AND SOCIAL CONTEXT

The examination of health inequalities dates back to the work of British scholars from the mid-seventeenth century, including John Graunt and William Petty, and later Edwin Chadwick and the German scholar Rudolf Virchow (Whitehead 1997). Within this tradition, hygienic as well as social and economic determinants of mortality and morbidity were emphasized. It is by now well known that social class inequalities in health are a universal issue, cutting across all western countries and probably equally developing countries. Health inequalities constitute a major scientific challenge for the sociological study of morbidity and mortality as well as a political challenge for public health.

The Black Report on Inequalities in Health, published in 1982, signaled a new wave of interest in social class inequalities in morbidity and mortality. In this report health inequalities were "re-found," since it had been believed that, with social and economic development, "in modern western countries the relationship between social class and the prevalence of illness is certainly decreasing and most probably no longer exits" (Kadushin 1964). Since the publication of the Black Report a large number of studies worldwide have reported on persistent health inequalities.

It is recognized within medical sociology that social class inequalities in health provide keys for understanding major social causes for morbidity and mortality. In addition, the study of health inequalities provides evidence for general sociology on the significance of class and other social structural divisions for people's life chances and their well-being. This is challenging evidence, since some sociologists have predicted the "death of class," implying that class divisions would give way to new divisions in society, such as those based on consumption and identity (Lee & Turner 1996). Nevertheless, the study of health inequalities shows that social class divisions continue to shape morbidity and mortality among populations.

Large hierarchical differences in morbidity and mortality between social classes persist in all countries from which evidence is available. This means that the public health challenge posed by health inequalities equally persists.

However, only slowly and in few countries have inequalities in morbidity and mortality been included in the agenda of health and welfare policies (Mackenbach & Bakker 2002). Political and moral reasons for tackling health inequalities have been raised, but successful reduction of health inequalities would not only contribute to equality and justice in society, but also to the overall level of health and life expectancy. For example, in Finland in the early 2000s the difference in life expectancy between upper non-manual employees and manual workers is 7 years for men and 3.5 years for women (Valkonen et al. 2000). There are very few equally large health divides as those for social class, and lengthening the life in lower classes provides a large potential to improve the overall public health in society.

MAJOR DIMENSIONS

Social class inequalities in morbidity and mortality exist for occupational class as well as other key socioeconomic indicators, such as educational attainment, individual and household income, and wealth (Lahelma et al. 2004). These inequalities typically follow a hierarchical pattern, called the health inequalities invariance: the lower the social class, the poorer the health. Although occupational class is a key socioeconomic indicator, each socioeconomic indicator reflects partly general and partly particular aspects of the comprehensive concept of social class. Accordingly, there is no a priori paramount social class indicator, and judging from the existing body of research we are unable to say whether social class inequalities in health by one indicator are universally larger than by another. In fact, people's social class is crystallized over the life course: education being achieved first, that contributing to occupational class, and these two together contributing to income. Thus, multiple socioeconomic circumstances jointly shape the overall social class inequalities in health that people will experience.

Inequalities are also found for a broad range of health indicators, and the patterns and magnitude of inequalities may depend on the health indicator employed. Social class inequalities exist for all main causes of death, but deviations are found, for example, for female and male cancers of the reproductive organs. For violent causes of death, inequalities among men tend to be particularly large (Valkonen et al. 2000). Social class inequalities equally exist for most domains of ill-health, including subjective health and functional as well as medically confirmed conditions. For example, large and consistent inequalities are found for self-rated health and physical functioning as well as many diseases. Only inequalities in mental health tend to be mixed and even reversed (i.e., mental health being somewhat poorer among upper social classes than lower classes).

A number of factors, such as age, gender, and ethnicity, are likely to modify social class inequalities in health. Inequalities in morbidity and mortality persist over the adult life and relative inequalities tend to be largest among middle aged people. However, for morbidity, there is a period of relative equalization in youth. Whether this is an artifact, or whether a true pattern exists, is not fully clear. Inequalities in morbidity and total mortality tend to be greater among men than women, since men more often die from causes in which inequalities are particularly great, such as accidents and violence, as well as cardiovascular diseases. Gender differences in inequalities in morbidity vary by domains of health, and there is a need for more accurate measurement of women's socioeconomic position. Ethnic background, furthermore, shapes health inequalities and being in a minority position tends to aggravate these inequalities (Krieger et al. 1997).

The patterns and magnitude of social class inequalities in morbidity and mortality vary between countries. According to European comparative evidence, inequalities in morbidity and mortality exist in all countries. For mortality, relative inequalities in the Scandinavian welfare states have appeared among the largest in Western Europe (Mackenbach et al. 2003). This geographic pattern for inequalities in mortality can partly be attributed to the leading cause of death (cardiovascular diseases), for which the decline has been particularly fast in the uppermost social classes. In addition to western countries, very large inequalities in mortality and morbidity among men have been found in the post-communist countries, including Russia and a number of Eastern European countries (Cockerham 1997).

Widening inequalities over time are observed for both morbidity (Kunst et al. 2005) and mortality (Mackenbach et al. 2003), and several Western European countries show widening health inequalities, with no single country showing narrowing inequalities. For morbidity, there was some stabilization in the Nordic welfare states during the 1990s.

CAUSES

So far, much descriptive evidence on social class inequalities in morbidity and mortality has been produced. However, the main intellectual challenge is a better understanding of the causes of health inequalities. Although the Black Report introduced a framework for main types of explanation in the early 1980s, only a small number of subsequent studies have examined causes for inequalities in morbidity and mortality. The explanations have repeatedly been revisited in the aftermath of the Black Report, and the main types include selection and social mobility, early and adult living conditions, health behaviors, and health care (Bartley 2004).

Selection and Social Mobility

Through intergenerational or intragenerational social mobility health directly or indirectly can contribute to social class positions. The natural selection explanation predicts that people are recruited to social classes on the basis of their (inherited) health, and therefore inequalities in morbidity and mortality may not be preventable. The social selection explanation predicts that some social factors, such as parental social class, may contribute both to people's health and their own social class. Social selection may play a role in the production of health inequalities (e.g., as people with disabilities are discriminated against in the labor market and run the risk of drifting down the social ladder). However, explanations other than those related to selection and mobility are causal in nature and predict unequal distributions of the determinants producing health inequalities between social classes.

Early Life Conditions

Unequally distributed circumstances in childhood and early life may have long-lasting consequences for later life inequalities in health, either directly or through adult circumstances. For example, material living conditions (e.g., poverty) and psychosocial living conditions (e.g., parental divorce in the childhood family) may contribute to adult health inequalities.

Adult Living Conditions

Equally, in adulthood, unequal distributions of life circumstances and resources are found. Material living conditions, including poor housing and working conditions, provide causes for health inequalities between social classes. Further potential causes include psychosocial living conditions, such as stress and lack of social contacts and support, comprehensively referred to as "social capital" (Szreter & Woolcock 2004).

Health Behaviors

Smoking, excessive drinking, sedentary behavior, and an unhealthy diet all tend to enhance excess health risks among the lower social classes, and thus cause health inequalities. Smoking, in particular, is worldwide a key health-compromising behavior which is likely to account for large part of inequalities in morbidity and mortality.

Health Care

Many sociologists tend to hold that health care plays a negligible role in the production of health inequalities. Although little is known about the impacts of health care on health inequalities, there are examples of specific treatments that are unequally distributed among patients, and may thus contribute to health inequalities.

While descriptive mapping of inequalities in morbidity and mortality continues where evidence is still lacking, analytic approaches are increasingly pursued to clarify the causes for health inequalities. Summarizing the existing evidence suggests that the most important groups of factors causing social class inequalities in health include past and present material and psychosocial living conditions, as well as unhealthy behaviors. Selection and social mobility are likely to provide only limited explanations for health inequalities. Although arguments have been presented for one or another group of factors constituting the key explanation, it is by now clear that the explanations are not mutually exclusive and there is no single "hard" explanation for health inequalities. It has been debated, for example, whether childhood or adulthood, health behaviors or living conditions, material or psychosocial factors, people's own income or income inequality in society, macro-level structural and political processes or individual characteristics, will provide the key explanation. However, inequalities in morbidity and mortality are complex phenomena, and "soft" explanations should be pursued, taking simultaneously into account key groups of explanatory factors. Thus, some studies have sought to find interrelationships and pathways between the key explanatory factors; for example, whether material disadvantage enhances unequal distributions of unhealthy behaviors and these together produce health inequalities, or whether material disadvantage and health behaviors independently produce health inequalities (Laaksonen et al. 2005).

CHANGES OVER TIME

There are a number of further challenges for a better understanding of social class inequalities in morbidity and mortality which future analyses of health inequalities need to take into account.

First, changes over time should be examined more often. While it is known that health inequalities tend to widen over time, the causes for such widening need to be searched for. Second, there is international variation in the magnitude of health inequalities and the factors producing such variation between countries should be examined. Third, there are variations in health inequalities by gender and stage of life course, but the causes for these remain largely unknown. Fourth, a broad range of health outcomes shows inequalities varying in magnitude and in some cases no inequalities are found. It is poorly understood why the magnitude of health inequalities varies from large to negligible and even to reverse inequalities. Fifth, health inequalities vary by socioeconomic indicator, such as occupational social class, education, income, and wealth. The causes for such variation, too, remain largely unknown. Even more importantly, we know very little about the interrelationships between the various dimensions of socioeconomic status in the production of health inequalities.

The last-mentioned complex of issues is a particular challenge for sociologists, since social class is a key structural concept in sociology. The challenges range from postmodernist tendencies to abandon social class, to methodological and measurement issues related to health inequalities. In any case, sociological theory and empirical research on health inequalities need closer links. On the one hand, within the sociology of social class, the medical sociological evidence on persisting social class inequalities in health has played a negligible role only. On the other hand, within medical sociology, the study of social class inequalities in health has been pursued with relatively little theoretical work. Nevertheless, there are examples of Marxist, Weberian, and combined strategies, which have made efforts to apply theoretically based social class schemes in medical sociological studies (Cockerham 1997).

Although a strong current trend within medical sociology, social class inequalities in health are by no means sociologists' property only. In fact, a number of neighboring disciplines are involved, such as psychology, economics, and social epidemiology. The importance of multidisciplinary examination is evident from the broad range of explanatory factors for inequalities in morbidity and mortality, covering economic, social structural, cultural, psychological, and biological factors. The study of health inequalities can be taken as an example of the advantages of multidisciplinary social research.

METHODOLOGICAL ISSUES

A key methodological issue includes the distinction between absolute and relative inequalities in health. Most studies on health inequalities rely on relative inequalities, indicating the proportion of people with ill-health among, for example, manual workers as compared to their non-manual counterparts. Absolute inequalities, in turn, express the difference in the number of people with ill-health between the manual class and the non-manual class.

In the examination of causes for health inequalities, relative inequalities are preferred, while for efficient egalitarian health policies absolute inequalities are the prime target. It is important to pay more attention to this distinction in order to obtain a better understanding of the unequal patterning of morbidity and mortality. To take an example, among Swedish men, relative social class inequalities in mortality in the 1990s were at a similar level with their Irish counterparts. However, absolute inequalities in mortality between the manual class and non-manual class are much smaller in Sweden, because the level of mortality among Swedish manual men is lower that that among Irish non-manual men (Lundberg & Lahelma 2001).

TACKLING INEQUALITIES

Inequalities in morbidity and mortality constitute a major public health problem worldwide, and the health inequalities invariance – the lower the social class, the poorer the health – holds true even in the most advanced societies. Health has proven an area where there are no signs of universal social class hierarchies giving way to some other social divisions, and health provides a case showing continuity in social class inequalities. Therefore, health inequalities should have a high priority in the agenda of future medical sociological research, as well as national health and welfare policies.

Reducing social class inequalities in morbidity and mortality still remains largely an open question. As health inequalities are deep-rooted, their prevention should start in early life. Promoting equality in society, such as equal opportunities for education, is likely to provide resources also for egalitarian health development. Specific egalitarian health and welfare policies, as well as interventions against health inequalities, have so far been scarce. Nevertheless, in the 1990s such policies and programs have been developed in several countries with the explicit aim of reducing future health inequalities (Mackenbach & Bakker 2002). While we lack compelling evidence showing which measures would be the most efficient ones, research on the causes for health inequalities suggests a number of potential measures. These include promoting (particularly among the lower classes) better living and working conditions, as well as healthier behaviors, and avoiding discrimination against people with poor health and disabilities.

SEE ALSO: Class, Status, and Power; Disease, Social Causation; Health Behavior; Health Lifestyles; Health Locus of Control; Health, Neighborhood Disadvantage; Health and Race; Health Risk Behavior; Inequality, Wealth; Life Chances and Resources; Medical Sociology; Race/Ethnicity, Health, and Mortality; Social Epidemiology; Stratification and Inequality, Theories of; Women's Health

REFERENCES AND SUGGESTED READINGS

Bartley, M. (2004) *Health Inequality: An Introduction to Theories, Concepts and Methods*. Polity Press, Cambridge.

Blaxter, M. (1997) Whose Fault Is It? People's Own Conceptions of the Reasons for Health Inequalities. *Social Science and Medicine* 44: 747–56.

Cockerham, W. C. (1997) The Social Determinants of the Decline of Life Expectancy in Russia and Eastern Europe: A Lifestyle Explanation. *Journal of Health and Social Behavior* 38: 117–30.

Kadushin, C. (1964) Social Class and the Experience of Ill Health. *Sociological Inquiry* 534: 67–80.

Krieger, N., Williams, D. R., & Moss, N. E. (1997) Measuring Social Class in US Public Health Research: Concepts, Methodologies, and Guidelines. *Annual Review of Public Health* 18: 341–78.

Kunst, A. et al. (2005) Trends in Socioeconomic Inequalities in Self-Assessed Health in 10 European Countries. *International Journal of Epidemiology* 34: 295–305.

Laaksonen, M., Roos, E., Rahkonen, O., Martikainen, P., & Lahelma, E. (2005) The Influence of Material and Behavioural Factors on Occupational Class Differences in Health. *Journal of Epidemiology and Community Health* 59: 163–9.

Lahelma, E. (2001) Health and Social Stratification. In: Cockerham, W. (Ed.), *Blackwell Companion to Medical Sociology*. Blackwell, Oxford, pp. 64–93.

Lahelma, E., Martikainen, P., Laaksonen, M., & Aittomäki, A. (2004) Pathways between Socioeconomic Determinants of Health. *Journal of Epidemiology and Community Health* 58: 327–32.

Lee, D. J. & Turner, B. S. (1996) Introduction: Myths of Classlessness and the "Death" of Class Analysis. In: Lee, D. J. & Turner, B. S. (Eds.), *Conflicts about Class: Debating Inequality in Late Industrialism*. Longman, London, pp. 1–25.

Lundberg, O. & Lahelma, E. (2001) Nordic Health Inequalities in the European Context. In: Kautto, M., Fritzell, J., Hvinden, B., Kvist, J., & Uusitalo, H. (Eds.), *Nordic Welfare States in the European Context*. Routledge, London, pp. 42–65.

Mackenbach, J. & Bakker, M. (Eds.) (2002) *Reducing Inequalities in Health: A European Perspective*. Routledge, London.

Mackenbach, J. et al. (2003) Widening Socioeconomic Inequalities in Mortality in Six Western European Countries. *International Journal of Epidemiology* 32: 830–7.

Marmot, M. & Wilkinson, R. (Eds.) (1999) *The Social Determinants of Health*. Oxford University Press, Oxford.

Szreter, S. & Woolcock, M. (2004) Health by Association? Social Capital, Social Theory, and the Political Economy of Public Health. *International Journal of Epidemiology* 33: 650–67.

Townsend, P. & Davidson, N. (1982) *Inequalities in Health: The Black Report*. Penguin, London.

Valkonen, T., Martikainen, P., Jalovaara, M., Koskinen, S., Martelin, T., & Mäkelä, P. (2000) Changes in Socioeconomic Inequalities in Mortality During an Economic Boom and Recession Among Middle-Aged Men and Women in Finland. *European Journal of Public Health* 10: 274–80.

Whitehead, M. (1997) Life and Death Over the Millennium. In: Drever, F. & Whitehead, M. (Eds.), *Health Inequalities: Decennial Supplement*. Office for National Statistics Series DS, no. 15. HMSO, London, pp. 7–28.

health and sport

Ivan Waddington

There is widespread acceptance of the idea that "sport is good for health." The ideology linking sport and health has a long history and the promotion and maintenance of the health of schoolchildren has long been an area of concern to physical educators in Europe and America.

The links between physical activity and good health have been endorsed in many official health publications in Britain and North America. In Britain, the Health Education Authority

(1997: 2) suggested "the health benefits of an active lifestyle for adults are well established." In the US, the Surgeon General's report, *Physical Activity and Health* (US Department of Health and Human Services 1996: 10), argued "significant health benefits can be obtained by including a moderate amount of physical activity on most, if not all, days of the week." In Canada, a discussion paper prepared for Health Canada and Active Living Canada (Donnelly & Harvey 1996) noted that a comprehensive examination of Canadian data had similarly identified several significant health benefits of physical activity. Can we conclude, then, that sport is good for one's health? Let us begin by examining the health benefits associated with physical activity.

EXERCISE, SPORT, AND HEALTH

Numerous studies indicate that moderate, rhythmic, and regular exercise has a beneficial impact on health. In the United States, the 1996 report of the US Surgeon General brought together what had been learned about physical activity and health from decades of American research. It concluded that regular physical activity is associated with lower levels of overall mortality for younger and older adults; decreased risk of cardiovascular, and especially coronary, disease; prevention or delay of onset of high blood pressure; reduction of blood pressure in people with hypertension; decreased risk of colon cancer; reduced risk of developing certain forms of diabetes; maintenance of normal muscle strength and joint structure; reduced risk of falling in older adults; lower levels of obesity; and improved mental health.

Five years after the Surgeon General's report, Britain's Department of Health (2001:1) stated there was "compelling evidence that physical activity is important for health" and listed health benefits similar to those identified in the American report. Most recently, the National Center for Chronic Disease Prevention and Health Promotion (2004) pointed out that regular physical activity substantially reduces the risk of dying of coronary heart disease (the leading cause of death in the USA) and has reiterated all the health benefits identified in the earlier reports in the US and Britain.

At first glance, studies like these might seem to indicate that the health-based arguments in favor of sport and exercise are overwhelming. Donnelly and Harvey (1996: 5) have noted, tongue-in-cheek, that the "numerous, almost miraculous claims for the benefits of physical activity lead one to wonder why it has not been patented by an innovative company"; more seriously, they go on to point out that the widespread nature of these claims should serve as a warning against a too-easy and uncritical acceptance, and that the context of the claims needs to be carefully examined. There are indeed some important provisos to be borne in mind when considering studies on the relationship between sport, exercise, and health. In particular, it is important to note that almost all the studies cited to support the idea that sport is good for health refer not to sport, but to physical activity or exercise. Physical activity and sport are not the same thing. Physical activity or exercise might involve lifestyle activities such as walking or cycling to work, dancing, gardening, or walking upstairs instead of taking the elevator. None of these are sport. There are important differences between physical activity and exercise, on the one hand, and sport on the other. Perhaps most importantly, whereas the competitive element is not central to most forms of physical activity, sport, in contrast, is inherently competitive and is becoming increasingly so (Waddington 2000). The increased competitiveness of modern sport, together with the increased emphasis which has come to be placed on winning, mean that, unlike most people who take part in non-competitive physical activities, those who play sport are, particularly at the higher levels, frequently subject to strong constraints to "play hurt," that is to continue playing while injured, "for the good of the team," with the associated health risks this behavior entails (Young et al. 1994; Roderick et al. 2000).

It is also important to remember that many sports (not just combat sports) are mock battles in which aggression and the use of physical violence are, to a greater or lesser degree, central characteristics (Dunning 1986: 270). In this context, many sports have, in present-day societies, become enclaves for the expression of physical violence, not in the form of unlicensed or uncontrolled violence, but in the form of socially sanctioned violence as expressed in violently aggressive "body contact"; indeed, in the relatively highly pacified societies of the modern West, sport is probably the main – for many people, the only – activity in which they are regularly involved in aggressive physical contact with others. As Messner (1990: 203) has noted, in the more violent contact sports, "the human body is routinely turned into a weapon to be used against other bodies, resulting in pain, serious injury, and even death."

The link between sport, aggression, and violence provides a key to understanding why sport is a major context for the inculcation and expression of gender identities and, in particular, for the expression of traditional forms of aggressive masculinity. As Young et al. (1994) have noted, these traditional concepts of masculinity involve the idea that "real" men play sport in an intensely confrontational manner; players are expected to give and to take hard knocks, to hurt and to be hurt and, when injured, to "take it like a man"; injury thus becomes a symbol of virility and courage and, for many players and fans alike, relatively violent sports, precisely because of their violent character, are arenas *par excellence* for young men to demonstrate their masculinity.

Young (1993: 373) has noted that professional sport is a violent and hazardous workplace which has its own unique forms of "industrial disease." He adds: "No other single milieu, including the risky and labor-intensive settings of miners, oil drillers, or construction site workers, can compare with the routine injuries of team sports such as football, ice-hockey, soccer, rugby and the like." In this context, one study of injuries in English soccer found that the overall risk of injury to professional footballers is 1,000 times greater than the risk of injury in other occupations normally considered high risk, such as construction and mining (Hawkins & Fuller 1999).

But risks are not confined to elite-level sport. There are health costs associated with sports participation even at the mass level.

THE EPIDEMIOLOGY OF SPORTS INJURIES

A leading British research team has commented that there "is a reluctance to recognize that increased participation in sports and exercise will also result in an increase in exercise related injuries" (Nichol et al. 1995: 232), while Hardman and Stensel (2003: 250) have noted that "the relationship between the benefits and risks associated with physical activity is not well described."

Research indicates that sports injuries are extremely common and have to be taken into account in any attempt to assess the "health costs" and "benefits" of sport and exercise. Community studies in Europe suggest that every sixth unintentional injury is associated with leisure-time physical activity, mainly sports, and that around 50 percent of people participating in team sports sustain one or more injuries over a season (Hardman & Stensel 2003: 226). At one university hospital in the Netherlands, sports injuries comprised about one fifth of all injuries treated over a 7-year period, making these the second highest cause of accidental injuries (Dekker et al. 2000). In the US, a prospective study of a physical activity intervention program (Hootman et al. 2002) found that a quarter of all participants reported at least one musculoskeletal injury, and such injuries were more likely to be reported by those participating in sports than those participating in other forms of physical activities.

Large scale, national studies of sports injuries are relatively rare, but a team from Sheffield University Medical School (Nichol et al. 1993, 1995) estimated that in England and Wales there are 19.3 million new injuries and a further 10.4 million recurrent injuries each year. The direct treatment costs of injuries were estimated at £422 million, with costs of lost production (11.5 million working days a year are lost due to sports injuries) estimated at £575 million (Nichol et al. 1993: 25, 31).

The Sheffield University researchers also sought to ascertain the direct economic costs and benefits of sports and exercise-related injuries to the health-care system. The health benefits of sport and exercise (e.g., avoidance of costs associated with the management of chronic illnesses) were weighed against the costs of treatment of exercise-related injuries. It was found that, while there were economic benefits associated with exercise for adults aged 45 and over, for younger adults (15–44 years old), the costs avoided by the disease-prevention effects of exercise (less than £5 per person per year) were more than offset by the medical costs resulting from participation in sport and exercise (approximately £30 per person per year). Thus, for every 15–44-year-old adult who regularly participates in sport, there is a net cost to the British taxpayer of £25 per year. The authors conclude "there are strong economic arguments in favour of exercise in adults aged 45 and over, but *not* in younger adults" (Nichol et al. 1993: 109; emphasis added). A Dutch study that produced similar findings to those of Nicholl et al. noted that this result "contrasts heavily with statements of people who use the supposed health effect of sport as an economic argument to promote sport" (cited in Nichol et al. 1993).

Although the data in these studies relate to injuries from both sport and exercise, the authors did note that injury risks vary markedly from one kind of physical activity to another; unsurprisingly, the highest risks are associated with contact sports and, in line with the analysis presented earlier, the Sheffield study found that the activities with the lowest risks of injury were the non-contact, rhythmic (and largely non-competitive) activities involved in "keep fit," swimming, and diving.

CONCLUSION

The relationship between sport and health is by no means simple. Moderate and regular physical activity has a beneficial impact on health. However, as we move from non-competitive activity to competitive sport, and from non-contact to contact sports, the health costs, in the form of injuries, increase. Similarly, as we move from mass sport to elite sport, the constraints to train more intensively and to continue competing while injured also increase, with a concomitant increase in the health risks. The health-related arguments in favor of regular and moderate physical activity are clear, but they are considerably less persuasive in relation to competitive, and especially contact, sport and very much less persuasive in relation to elite or professional sport.

The injury risks associated with competitive sport are increasingly being recognized by public health specialists. Significantly, almost all the examples of physical activity recommended in the 1996 Surgeon General's report are either lifestyle activities such as washing a car, gardening, or dancing, or non-contact, rhythmic exercises such as water aerobics, jumping rope, or walking. The only competitive sports which figure in the list of recommended examples of moderate activity are playing basketball for 15–20 minutes and playing volleyball for 45 minutes; all the other major competitive sports in the US, with their associated injury risks, are conspicuous by their absence from this list of recommended healthy activities.

SEE ALSO: Disability Sport; Exercise and Fitness; Health Behavior; Health Lifestyles; Leisure; Sport and the Body; Sport as Work; Violence Among Athletes; Youth Sport

REFERENCES AND SUGGESTED READINGS

Department of Health (2001) *Exercise Referral Systems: A National Quality Assurance Framework.* Department of Health, London.

Donnelly, P. & Harvey, J. (1996) *Overcoming Systematic Barriers to Active Living.* Discussion paper prepared for Fitness Branch, Health Canada and Active Living Canada.

Dekker, R., Kingma, J., Groothoff, J. W., Eisma, W. H., & Ten Duis, H. J. (2000) Measurement of Severity of Sports Injuries: An Epidemiological Study. *Clinical Rehabilitation* 14: 651–6.

Dunning, E. (1986) Sport as a Male Preserve: Notes on the Social Sources of Masculine Identity and its Transformation. In: Elias, N. & Dunning, E., *Quest for Excitement.* Blackwell, Oxford, pp. 267–83.

Hardman, A. E. & Stensel, D. J. (2003) *Physical Activity and Health.* Routledge, London.

Hawkins, R. D. & Fuller, C. W. (1999) A Prospective Epidemiological Study of Injuries in Four English Professional Football Clubs. *British Journal of Sports Medicine* 33: 196–203.

Health Education Authority (1997) *Young People and Physical Activity: Promoting Better Practice.* Health Education Authority, London.

Hootman, J. K., Macera, C. A., Ainsworth, B. E., Addy, C. L., Martin, M., & Blair, S. N. (2002) Epidemiology of Musculoskeletal Injuries among Sedentary and Physically Active Adults. *Medicine and Science in Sport and Exercise* 34: 838–44.

Messner, M. (1990) When Bodies are Weapons: Masculinity and Violence in Sport. *International Review for the Sociology of Sport* 25(3): 203–18.

National Centre for Chronic Disease Prevention and Health Promotion (2004) *The Importance of*

Physical Activity. Online. www.cdc.gov/nccdphp/dnpa/physical/importance/index.htm.

Nichol, J. P., Coleman, P., & Williams, B. T. (1993) *Injuries in Sport and Exercise: Main Report*. Sports Council, London.

Nichol, J. P., Coleman, P., & Williams, B. T. (1995) The Epidemiology of Sports and Exercise Related Injury in the United Kingdom. *British Journal of Sports Medicine* 29(4): 232–8.

Roderick, M., Waddington, I., & Parker, G. (2000) Playing Hurt: Managing Injuries in English Professional Football. *International Review for the Sociology of Sport* 35(2): 165–80.

US Department of Health and Human Services (1996) *Physical Activity and Health: A Report of the Surgeon General, Executive Summary*. US Department of Health and Human Services, Washington, DC.

Waddington, I. (2000) *Sport, Health and Drugs: A Critical Sociological Perspective*. E. & F. N. Spon, London.

Young, K. (1993) Violence, Risk and Liability in Male Sports Culture. *Sociology of Sport Journal* 10: 373–96.

Young, K., White, P., & McTeer, W. (1994) Body Talk: Male Athletes Reflect on Sport, Injury, and Pain. *Sociology of Sport Journal* 11(2): 175–94.

healthy life expectancy

Mark D. Hayward

Declining old-age mortality has motivated research on the interplay between mortality, chronic disease morbidity, and disability. Do declining mortality rates signal declining morbidity and disability rates? Are the substantial gains in *life expectancy* accompanied by an increase in the expected years in good health, i.e., healthy life expectancy? Investigations of healthy life expectancy are important for anticipating an aging population's demands on health care and evaluating the effects of interventions and policy changes on both the length and quality of life.

A CONCEPTUAL FRAMEWORK

Poor health is a complex concept denoting compromised well-being stemming from disability and disease, and mental, physical, and emotional problems. Health expectancy measures are typically based on the World Health Organization's (WHO) 1980 *International Classification of Impairments, Disabilities, and Handicaps* (ICIDH) and Lois Verbrugge's and Alan Jette's (1994) disablement framework. Disablement typically begins with the onset of a chronic disease that may have a cascading effect resulting in a loss of physical or mental function. Disability results if functional problems make it difficult to perform normal social activities. The pathway is neither unidirectional nor deterministic and death can occur at any point. Changes in the social and ecological environments can alter disablement.

Under the auspices of the WHO, a life-table model was developed to integrate and summarize the life cycle morbidity, disability, and mortality experiences of a population. The model allows survivorship to be decomposed into the probability of surviving without morbidity or disability, and the probability of death (see Fig. 1). The vertical axis denotes the probability of surviving to a given age without one of the health problems. The areas under the curves refer to the probability of being in a particular health state at a given age. For example, the area beneath the morbidity curve (A) represents the probability of being free of chronic disease at each age. By definition, the areas describe the person-years in a life-table cohort spent in each health state. Area C, for example, represents disabled person-years while areas of A and B represent disability-free person-years.

The life-table model provides the means to calculate healthy life expectancy, i.e., the expected length of time that an average individual can expect to be healthy (or unhealthy) according to some morbidity or disability criterion. The measure captures the *life cycle* burden of a health condition – i.e., the health-related quality of life in relation to the overall length of life. Healthy life expectancy has been used to assess whether declines in mortality lead to a compression of morbidity and/or disability during particular time periods and whether different groups have similar overall survival but differ in terms of life cycle morbidity and disability.

Demographers' use of the life-table model has produced a class of specific health expectancy

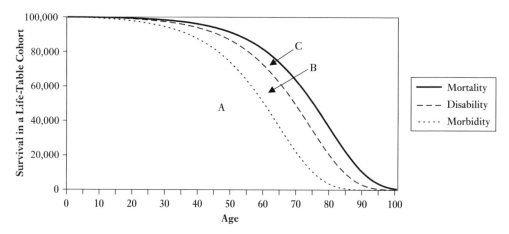

Figure 1 Hypothetical model of population health.

measures summarizing the life cycle health of a population:

- *Disease-free life expectancy*: The expected number of years the average person of a given age would expect to live free of disease (or a specific disease). Although this has not been a focus of demographers, researchers have calculated the number of years lived with heart disease, dementia, and lung cancer.
- *Disability-free life expectancy*: The expected number of years free of disability for persons who survived to a given age. Disability-free life expectancies have been calculated for a number of countries, for the United States over the past several decades, and for race/ethnic, educational, and gender groups. Socioeconomic differentials in healthy life expectancy typically exceed differentials in life expectancy.
- *Health-adjusted life expectancy*: This measure adjusts life expectancy according to weights assigned to health states. The measure is intended to identify the gap between life in perfect health and ill health. The measure has become a policy tool in evaluating the effects of interventions and international differences in disabled years. WHO estimates that disabled life is higher in poorer countries than in developed countries due to injury, blindness, paralysis, and the functional consequences of tropical diseases affecting the younger population.

MEASUREMENT AND METHODOLOGICAL ISSUES

An issue poorly addressed is the meaning of disability change. Disability is the combination of dysfunction (organ system or bodily function) *and* environmental demands on functioning. Changes in disability reports reflect differences in social and environmental support as well as changes in functioning – or adaptation. For example, marital status changes or the addition of technology can result in changes in individuals' reports of getting less help with tasks without improvements in functioning.

This problem points to the need to differentiate functional changes from environmental changes in longitudinal designs to understand how changes in healthy life expectancy occur. For example, a decline in disabled life could be a consequence of reductions in disabling diseases (e.g., cardiovascular disease), the reduction of environmental challenges, and new technology and medications. In the latter case, a reduction in disabled years is not a reflection of changes in functional problems but rather improvements in coping with functional problems.

Assessment of trends and differences in healthy life is also affected by studies' differences in life-table modeling approaches. Many studies rely on a prevalence-based approach called the Sullivan (1966) method, which weights the person-years in a hypothetical life-table cohort according to the observed proportion of persons in the population who have a health (morbidity or disability) problem at a point in time. Prevalence captures current health experience and experiences at younger ages that have stamped the surviving population. An advantage of the Sullivan method is its straightforward data requirements – observed prevalence rates of health conditions and mortality rates for the population. Mortality rates are typically obtained from a country's statistical agency. Prevalence rates are usually obtained from cross-sectional health surveys. These surveys are increasingly common internationally, inexpensive to field compared to longitudinal surveys, and yield reliable prevalence estimates.

A potential problem using the Sullivan method for examining trends in healthy life is its insensitivity to dramatic swings in disability and mortality. During periods of rapidly improving survival, the method underestimates improvements in healthy life relative to gains in survivorship.

With the availability of longitudinal data, multistate life tables are being used to model the interactions of morbidity, disability, and mortality. This approach relies on incidence rates rather than prevalence rates to model health changes with age. Incidence rates identify the probability of a change in health status. Unlike prevalence rates, incidence rates document both the onset and recovery from health conditions as well as mortality from each health state. Incidence rates used in multistate models are typically calculated for a relatively short time period (e.g., two years) for a cross-section of the population. Multistate models thus produce health expectancies that summarize the years of healthy and unhealthy life for a cohort if current incidence and mortality rates remained unchanged over time.

Health expectancies calculated by the Sullivan method and the multistate model are difficult to compare because of the models' assumptions and the fact that they use different sources of data (e.g., cross-sectional surveys versus panel studies). An advantage of the multistate model is that it can be used to assess the causes of changes in healthy life expectancy and the prevalence of health conditions. For example, Eileen Crimmins, Mark Hayward, and Yasuhiko Saito (1994) demonstrated how healthy life expectancy and prevalence respond to changes in the incidence rates governing declines and improvements in health, as well as changes in health-specific mortality.

Although the multistate model has desirable properties, the lack of longitudinal data for lengthy historical periods has limited its use in examining trends. Even if such data were available, the reliability of the incidence rates of health change – the usual inputs for the model – are potentially problematic because of the sparse numbers of health events at certain ages and for some groups. The implications of sample attrition for the incidence rates are also poorly understood.

SOME IMPORTANT LESSONS

Healthy life expectancy research has shown that mortality, morbidity, and disability are related but not isomorphic concepts. An individual may contract a fatal condition but not die from that cause. For some fatal conditions, individuals may live with the disease many years before death. Disability is not necessarily permanent nor does it inevitably precede death. Death is not always the evolutionary outcome of a process wherein individuals contract a fatal condition, the condition induces functional problems and disability, and, when advanced, results in death.

This complexity carries over to understanding group differences in healthy life. For example, sex affects mortality and disability in opposite directions such that women live longer than men, but they also have more disabled years. Men are more likely to die regardless of disability, but men are more likely to recover. Women are also more likely to become disabled. Other studies have documented educational differences in healthy life, showing that poorly educated persons have a higher incidence of disability, as well as higher death rates among persons without disability. Once disability occurs, educational differences in mortality are small. The end result is that education is associated with an increase of both total life and disability-free life, and a compression of disabled life.

Models of healthy life are thus important to identify health trajectories consisting of morbidity, disability, and mortality. These models also are important in evaluating group differences in healthy life and how these differences are tied to differences in morbidity, disability, and mortality. The models, in turn, help the development of theoretical models that articulate with the reasons for the interplay between morbidity, disability, and mortality.

CONCLUSIONS

Concerns about whether longer life signals better health has led to health monitoring systems and an ever expanding body of research. Health expectancy research has clarified that different components of health – disease, disability, and self-perceived health – need not move in the same direction at the same time. Some components may rise during periods of falling mortality, a natural part of the epidemiologic transition. Rising disability does not necessarily signal failure of public health policies.

Health expectancy research points to a shift in the United States toward less severe disability accompanying the decline in old-age mortality in recent decades. Research has begun to clarify the reasons for subgroup differences in healthy life, and life-table models' descriptions of how health problems unfold in groups are useful in refining theoretical arguments underlying health disparities. Within the scientific community, researchers are engaged in debates over health expectancy methods and measures, investigating how different facets of morbidity interact and change over time. These activities are frequently collaborative, involving teams of researchers from multiple disciplines and countries.

SEE ALSO: Aging, Demography of; Aging and Health Policy; Biodemography; Chronic Illness and Disability; Demographic Techniques: Life-Table Methods

REFERENCES AND SUGGESTED READINGS

Crimmins, E. M., Hayward, M. D. & Saito, Y. (1994). Changing Mortality and Morbidity Rates and the Health Status and Life Expectancy of the Older Population. *Demography* 31: 159–75.

Sullivan, D. F. (1966). Conceptual Problems in Developing an Index of Health. *Vital Health Statistics 1* 2(17): 1–18.

Verbrugge, L. M. & Jette, A. M. (1994). The Disablement Process. *Social Science and Medicine* 38(1): 1–14.

Hegel, G. W. F. (1770–1831)

Rob Beamish

Georg Wilhelm Friedrich Hegel rose from within the liberal milieu of Protestant refugees in Würtemberg to become Prussia's foremost post-Kantian, idealist philosopher in Berlin (1818–31). Hegel's major philosophical achievements were the *Phenomenology of Spirit* (1804), *Science of Logic* (1812–16), the *Encyclopedia of Philosophy* (1817), and his philosophy of history. Sociologists' interest in Hegel began with the posthumous 1930s publications of Karl Marx's 1840s manuscripts, Alexander Kojève's late 1930s lectures, and Herbert Marcuse's, Karl Löwith's, and Georg Lukács's analyses of Hegel's work.

Hegel's major sociological contributions stem first from the *Phenomenology*. Responding to the Cartesian and Kantian subject/object separation, Hegel argued that through a historical, dialectical subject/object mediation, the apparently unknowable "thing-in-and-of-itself" was revealed. Confronting the phenomenal world, consciousness became self-consciousness as mind (*Geist*) dialectically discovered self-reflexivity in the subject/object relation. An increasingly comprehensive intellectual Spirit (*Geist*) followed as a more all-inclusive Reason grasped the complex totality of reality, culminating in an Absolute form of knowledge. Phenomenological sociologists drew upon Hegel's conception of the subjective creation of meaning while Marx replaced "mental labor" with real, material labor as history's prime motive force, to reconceptualize Hegel's emphasis on historical development through conscious human action.

The *Logic*, Hegel's systematic account of dialectical method, was the methodological inspiration for Marx's critique of political economy and remains essential to genuinely understanding his method and overall critique.

Hegel's *Philosophy of Right* addressed the question of social order – now seen under changing historical conditions (placing Hegel among the first modernist, political theorists). Contrary to Rousseau, Hegel did not believe civil society could produce a fusion of individual wills – only the constitutional state, based on the principles of absolute rationality, could create a stable, historically evolving social order. Legislation could create the conditions that would allow freedom to flourish. Inspired by Greek philosophy, the *polis*, and Plato's rather than Aristotle's image of humankind as *zoon politikon* (political animal), Hegel argued that an impartial, philosophically educated civil service would act in the universal interest. Due to its largely eighteenth-century traditionalism, the *Philosophy of Right* contained many of the *Republic*'s shortcomings.

Hegel's political writings were never totalitarian in orientation although they were elitist; his view of the state guiding civil society was rooted in traditional conceptions of hierarchy, and although the universal grasped the complex totality of reality more comprehensively than the general, Hegel's experiences suggested universal, Absolute Knowledge was only within the grasp of a minority rather than a majority. Democratic outcomes would come from the policies of an educated, impartial, knowledgeable elite, leaving more than Marx's "inversion" of Hegel's idealism separating the two thinkers.

SEE ALSO: Dialectic; Labor/Labor Power; Marx, Karl; Phenomenology; Species-Being

REFERENCES AND SUGGESTED READINGS

Kojève, A. (1969 [1947]) *Introduction to the Reading of Hegel*. Trans. J. Nichols. Basic Books, New York.
Löwith, K. (1964 [1941]) *From Hegel to Nietzsche: The Revolution in Nineteenth-Century Thought*. Trans. D. Green. Holt, Rinehart, & Winston, New York.
Lukács, G. (1975 [1948]) *The Young Hegel*. Trans. R. Livingstone. Merlin Press, London.
Marcuse, H. (1941) *Reason and Revolution: Hegel and the Rise of Social Theory*. Oxford University Press, Oxford.

hegemonic masculinity

Don Levy

Developed in the 1980s (Carrigan et al. 1985) to provide a relational and socially constructed conception of men and masculinities, the term hegemonic masculinity describes the hierarchical interaction between multiple masculinities and explains how some men make it appear normal and necessary that they dominate most women and other men (Connell 1987).

Hegemonic masculinity describes a position in the system of gender relations, the system itself, and the current ideology that serves to reproduce masculine domination. In presenting the term, Connell demonstrates the essentialistic, ahistorical, and normative liabilities in previous men's studies scholarship. In the concept of hegemonic masculinity Connell joins the constructivist view of "doing gender" (West & Zimmerman 1987) with insights drawn from feminist scholars who described the ways in which gender relations shape social structures (Hartsock 1983).

Connell seeks to explain how some men succeed in making it appear normal, natural, and necessary for them to enjoy power over other men and most women; why it is that so many men and women participate willingly in their own oppression; and how resistance to hegemonic masculinity can promote gender justice. Connell posits four types of masculinities, more as positions in relation to one another than as personality types: hegemonic, complicit, subordinated, and marginalized. The hegemonic position is the currently accepted male ideal within a particular culture at a particular time. As such, the hegemonic male is an ideal-type (Weber 1946). Connell notes that this image changes over time and place, as well as being subject to contestation within a particular culture.

Most men fall within the second, category, complicit. These men accept and participate in the system of hegemonic masculinity so as to enjoy the material, physical, and symbolic benefits of the subordination of women and, through fantasy, experience the sense of hegemony and learn to take pleasure in it, and avoid subordination.

The relations among the four positions are hierarchical. A man in the subordinated position suffers that fate despite appearing to possess the physical attributes necessary to aspire to hegemony. Men run the risk of subordination when they do not practice gender consistent with the hegemonic system and ideology. The clearest examples are men who are openly gay. Gay men are defined in this system as not real men. They lack the legitimacy to aspire to hegemony. The many seemingly innocuous taunts of "Be a man" or "What are you, a fag?" are in reality active gender policing in which the fear of subordination, the loss of legitimacy, and the fall from complicity are actively enacted. Marginalized men are those who cannot even aspire to hegemony – most often, men of color and men with disabilities. Groups can contest marginalization when they seek authorization by making the claim: "I'm a man, too."

The second manner in which Connell uses hegemonic masculinity is to describe the current system of gender relations: current "configurations of practice" organize social relations and structures to the overall benefit of men in relation to women and of some men in relation to other men. Connell stresses that these configurations of practice take place across four dimensions: power, the division of labor, cathexis or emotional relations, and the symbolic. Connell's argument is that hegemonic masculinity as a system becomes built into social institutions so as to make it appear normal and natural for men's superordinate position to be maintained. For example, major societal institutions including government, the economy, and the family are structured so as to reinforce and reproduce male hegemony in ways ranging from structure, credentialing, and even cultural symbolic expressions. Additionally, the hierarchical relations of men with other men are expressed in both social structures as well as cultural expectations in examples such as resistance to gays in the military or the gendering of

occupations, including typically female jobs like librarian, elementary teacher, or nurse.

The third usage of hegemonic masculinity, as an ideology, provides the justification through which patriarchy is legitimated and maintained. As an ideology, hegemonic masculinity structures the manner in which all people experience and thereby know their world, although those experiences vary as both men and women are differentially situated by race, class, and sexuality. This ideology, referred to as hegemonic complicity, can be measured across four dimensions: ideal-type masculinity, hierarchical ranking of self and others, subordination of women, and the subordination of woman-like behavior (Levy 2005). The first dimension, ideal-type masculinity, is the belief that there is a single type of masculinity that is appropriate. Different men or groups of men and women can posit a different ideal-type, contesting the definition of that type, but the underlying belief in a single ideal-type typifies this dimension.

Hierarchical ranking of oneself and others is perhaps the least studied component of hegemonic masculinity as an ideology. Previous scholars (Lewis 1978) spoke of competition as a restrictive component of masculinity or as a barrier to meaningful interaction. This conceptualization fails to capture the ever present intrapsychic dimension of active hierarchic assessment. Hierarchical ranking is a process in which men compare themselves and others actively and incessantly to their general or contextual ideal-type.

Subordination of women and anyone or any trait perceived to be woman-like includes overt and covert sexism and homophobia. Although some would argue that both overt sexism and homophobia have been in decline, the lingering or residual effects, often in the form of beliefs about men, women, and sexuality, are quite active.

The three dimensions of hegemonic masculinity as a position, a system, and an ideology can be theoretically separated while their interaction and interconnections are still recognized. Those who criticize the concept of hegemonic masculinity for confusion, reification, or elitism (Lorber 1998; Martin 1998; Whitehead 1999; Demetriou 2001) need to recognize its multiple usages and see that those allegations have merit only if the critic refuses to consider simultaneously the three understandings of hegemonic masculinity – position, system, and ideology – or to appreciate Connell's continuing dedication to gender justice, a commitment he shares with some feminists often accused of essentialism. Connell calls for forming coalitions among those resisting the subtle but pervasive effects of hegemonic masculinity and feminists opposed to patriarchal and/or class and racial oppressions. Given the ubiquity of hegemonic masculinity as both a system of gender relations and as a justificatory ideology, resistance can be expressed politically or interactionally; that is, rather than contesting the hegemonic position, resistance seeks to alter the configuration of gender practice that reproduces the system of hegemonic masculinity.

SEE ALSO: Doing Gender; Femininities/ Masculinities; Gendered Organizations/Institutions; Homophobic; Patriarchy; Sex and Gender

REFERENCES AND SUGGESTED READINGS

Carrigan, T., Connell, R. W., & Lee, J. (1985) Toward a New Sociology of Masculinity. *Theory and Society* 14: 551–604.

Connell, R. W. (1987) *Gender and Power*. Stanford University Press, Stanford.

Demetriou, D. Z. (2001) Connell's Concept of Hegemonic Masculinity: A Critique. *Theory and Society* 30: 337–61.

Hartsock, N. (1983) *Sex and Power*. Longman, New York.

Levy, D. P. (2005) Hegemonic Complicity, Friendship and Comradeship: Validation and Causal Processes Among White, Middle-Class, Middle-Aged Men. *Journal of Men's Studies* 13(2): 199–224.

Lewis, R. A. (1978) Emotional Intimacy Among Men. *Journal of Social Issues* 34: 108–21.

Lorber, J. (1998) Symposium on R. W. Connell's *Masculinities. Gender and Society* 12: 469–72.

Martin, P. Y. (1998) Symposium on R. W. Connell's *Masculinities. Gender and Society* 12: 472–4.

Weber, M. (1946) *Essays in Sociology*. Ed. H. H. Oxford University Press, Oxford.

West, C. & Zimmerman, D. H. (1987) Doing Gender. *Gender and Society* 1: 125–51.

Whitehead, S. (1999) Hegemonic Masculinity Revisited. *Gender, Work and Organization* 6: 58–62.

hegemony and the media

Dave Harris

Before becoming applied to academic analysis of the media, the term "hegemony" referred more generally to indirect political control, which often replaced the need for constant and direct military or political domination, of the kind exercised by, for example, colonial states over rivals.

The concept takes on more specific implications from its use to explain forms of domination (e.g., by classes, ethnic groups, or genders) within a nation-state. Mass media can be seen as having an important role in justifying the rule of dominant groups by supporting their claims to superiority, and in trying to persuade the dominated to consent to this justification. People who specialize in formulating and disseminating ideas (such as journalists, priests, public relations companies, politicians, advisers, and academics) are constantly engaged in interpreting current events and debates so as to fit dominant conceptions and categories (not always conspiratorially). As examples, a violent incident in Iraq is interpreted as further evidence of worldwide terrorist conspiracy; economic crises are blamed on outsiders or seen as inevitable; national sporting successes vindicate political systems.

Scholars associated with the Birmingham Centre for Contemporary Cultural Studies (CCCS) in the UK, and later the Open University Popular Culture Group in the UK, were particularly significant in developing the concept of hegemony as a research tool, although there are also prominent North American writers in the field, such as Giroux, Grossberg, Jhally, and Radway (see their contributions in Grossberg et al. 1992). One aspect of the project was to elaborate the work of Antonio Gramsci, an Italian Marxist working in the 1930s and 1940s. Gramsci had used the term "hegemony" to draw attention to the cultural and political dimensions of class struggle in Italy. Struggle was not only focused on industrial and parliamentary matters, but extended to regional, religious, and local issues as well. One implication he drew from this was that the working class had to unite with other oppressed factions, such as the remaining peasantry, leading them in a cultural and political struggle with the dominant bourgeoisie, as well as using the usual tactics of industrial strikes and urban demonstrations. A successful socialist or communist revolution would impose the hegemony of the working classes on its rivals and subordinates so that the whole culture would become a socialist one.

Italian fascism combined direct force and cultural, political, and ideological argument and activity and gained mass support. It displayed an impressive flexibility and mobility, reacting quickly to emerging social, cultural, and political events and weaving them into its (underdeveloped) conceptual schemes. Gramsci's attempts to do the same for Marxist theory (but far more rigorously) led to a flexible and impressive set of concepts that departed quite significantly from previous Marxist positions and debates. In particular, the concept seemed to offer a helpful notion of "moving equilibrium" to describe how ideological dominance was continually achieved as part of a process.

A number of specific academic projects were pursued by British Gramscian writers, including analysis of political discourses such as Thatcherism, the local manifestation of the neoconservative turn in European and American politics in the 1980s. Briefly, Thatcherism had gained sufficient mass support at the ballot box thanks to its effective ideological work in knitting together various dissatisfactions, even when they were mutually exclusive – such as anxiety about social change and a promise to modernize British society (Hall & Jacques 1983). More specific analyses soon followed, in which the mass media were seen as a major player in the struggle for hegemony, doing the actual hegemonic work, and explaining emerging events and arguments in popular terms.

One such event was identified as emerging from spectacular youth subcultures in the 1970s and 1980s in Britain. British youth were wearing outlandish clothes, listening to aggressive music, choosing different sorts of recreational drugs, and developing their own distinctive set of tastes. Sometimes, this led them into open conflict, as when rival youth groups fought at seaside resorts. In general, the media (the analysis largely turned on newspapers in the early days) reacted to this challenge by attempting to demonize British youth, by

launching tirades against the "mindlessness" of the activity, or exaggerating its impact on law and order. Perhaps the most extensive analysis of this kind of activity occurs in Hall et al. (1978). Here, black youth are attacked by the press in the guise of a campaign of moral outrage about street crime: the black mugger came to symbolize all that seemed to threaten the stability of Britain in the 1970s – social change, urban unrest, youth unemployment, immigration, etc. Other writers had written about such "moral panics," but Hall et al. politicized their analysis. This particular moral panic took place at a time of a general shift towards an authoritarian solution to the unrest produced by industrial decline and social change: diverting attention towards a visible minority group would offer a popular way to justify the strengthening of the state.

Gramscian analyses of the media peaked with the publication of the Open University course on popular culture (Open University 1982), together with its series of influential textbooks and readers (see Harris 1992). They included attempts to show how current affairs programs on television were also offering a form of hegemonic discourse. Despite their apparent political neutrality, such programs were suggesting in effect that the only legitimate political conflicts took place between recognized political parties working within the dominant system of parliamentary politics. This discourse was often embodied in the physical layout of the studio discussion, with party spokespersons on either side of the set, and a neutral respected commentator in the middle, whose role it was to stress in a concluding summary the underlying virtues of democratic consensus.

Television coverage of the English FA Cup Final (soccer) sought to perform a resolution of national tensions. Particular football clubs symbolize important social divisions, typically those between northern and southern England, for example. They come together on a national occasion as sporting rivals. However, unifying national symbols are also on display in the television coverage: the entire crowd sings traditional hymns, while the commentary team does its best to remind its viewers that football as a whole is the winner, that the English are wonderfully sporting and generous towards losers, that at the end of the day fans of rival clubs can unite in support of the national team, and so on.

Some more abstract theoretical work supported these specific examples. Hall (1977) discussed how the media produce an "ideology effect" in general. Borrowing from Poulantzas, he argued that social problems can only be described in terms of ideological categories, such as differences of age, region, "race," and so on. Social class in the Marxist sense is never acknowledged, and is hidden by these apparently obvious alternatives. Ideological categories like these then permit the sort of magical resolution discussed above – conflicts can be forgotten as the nation celebrates Christmas, for example, or seen to be reformed away. The whole analysis clearly echoes Marx's own work in exposing the inadequacies and ideological effects of the categories of liberal political economy.

These studies were also criticized. The work on black youth in particular proved controversial: it was not clear whether this work was actually justifying criminal activity as "political," for example (Cohen 1979). Other criticisms turned on the precise relevance of high-powered theoretical digressions in the texts: Hall et al. (1978) engage as much in theoretical struggle with Althusserians as they do with the concrete issue of hegemonic moral panics about black crime. Frith (1984) suggests that the theoretical and political interest in spectacular confrontational youth subcultures led to a serious omission: the study of "normal youth."

Media professionals objected strongly to seeing their claims to neutrality questioned. They wanted to suggest that a good deal of creative work went into constructing a television program, and that it was not just a simple matter of using unconscious hegemonic categories. Some work undertaken from within the Open University Popular Culture Group itself expressed similar doubts. Bennett's initial analysis of the James Bond movie (Open University 1982) saw it as structured around some basic hegemonic codes stressing British claims to world importance, the need to subordinate challenging women, and the need to structure and manage desire (in Freudian terms). However, a later ethnographic study of the actual work involved in producing a Bond movie (Bennett & Woollacott 1987) found much more going on as well: attempts to adapt or parody

existing filmic conventions, to make references to other films, to include visual sequences for entertainment, to respond to a global audience, and so on. The role of the active audience was also acknowledged.

The focus on social class in early versions of the analysis led to serious challenge from feminists or black activists, on both political and theoretical grounds. Perhaps the privileged terms of Gramscian analysis were simply not adequate to grasp how sexual or ethnic minorities were depicted on modern television, implying that other concepts from different traditions were also required. Important feminist work critiqued CCCS Marxism (Coward 1977) and developed alternatives, some of them based on the rival Althusserian notion of how the media "positioned" individual subjects as gendered subjects.

The debate indicates a wider theoretical discussion going on about Marxism, and new thinking in poststructuralism and postmodernism. The privileged or "foundational" status of Marxist concepts was much debated following a series of close critical readings of Marx's key works. Perhaps the most devastating of these was delivered by Hindess and Hirst (see Crook 1991), who argued that Marxist concepts were incoherent, not consistently deployed, heavily contaminated with metaphorical reasoning, and usually applied dogmatically. In an allied attack, poststructuralists were tending to refer to Marxism as a discourse, one among many, and refusing to grant it any privileged status as offering unique access to some underlying social reality.

Gramscian notions and concepts, including the notion of hegemony, faced problems from this criticism. The notion of hegemony seemed especially vulnerable to the poststructuralist emphasis on discourse. In a nutshell, ideological conceptions were being analyzed as discourses already, but why was it necessary or desirable to add a particular Marxist political inflection to such analysis? Answers insisting on the necessary reality of underlying struggle seemed to deliver Gramscians back into facing charges of foundationalism. Gramscianism found itself in a very uncomfortable position, having to hold increasingly suspect Marxist conceptions to stave off the possibilities of rival politically undesirable theoretical systems.

Critics have identified a number of dubious maneuvers in the debates that followed. Gramscians sought salvation in incoherent terms such as "relative autonomy" (see the debate between Hirst and Hall in Hunt 1977) or oscillated tactically between the possibilities (Wood 1998). They failed to resolve perhaps the most fundamental problem of all: whether hegemonic struggle is a "real" one located in a concrete social formation, or a discursive one, located exclusively in discourses and their effects (Townshend 2004). The question remains: is the main effect of the media to construct discourses about reality (evidently true but rather trivial and obvious, since what else could they do?), or do they do so as a necessary part of a wider and real political struggle for social control (much more significant, but much less easy to establish)?

SEE ALSO: Audiences; Birmingham School; Cultural Studies; Encoding/Decoding; Gramsci, Antonio; Ideological Hegemony; Media; Media Monopoly

REFERENCES AND SUGGESTED READINGS

Bennett, T. & Woollacott, J. (1987) *Bond and Beyond: The Political Career of a Popular Hero*. Macmillan Education, London.
Cohen S. (1979) Guilt, Justice and Tolerance: Some Old Concepts for a New Criminology. In: Downes D. & Rock P. (Eds.), *Deviant Interpretations: Problems in Criminological Theory*. Oxford University Press, Oxford.
Coward, R. (1977) Class, Culture and the Social Formation. *Screen* 18(1).
Crook, S. (1991) *Modernist Radicalism and its Aftermath: Foundationalism and Anti-Foundationalism in Radical Social Theory*. Routledge, London.
Frith, S. (1984) *Sociology of Youth*. Causeway Books, London.
Grossberg, L., Nelson, C., & Treichler, P. (Eds.) (1992) *Cultural Studies*. Routledge, New York.
Hall, S. (1977) Culture, the Media and the "Ideology-Effect." In: Curran, J., Gurevitch, M., & Wollacott, J. (Eds.), *Mass Communication and Society*. Edward Arnold, in association with the Open University Press, London.
Hall, S. & Jacques, M. (Eds.) (1983) *The Politics of Thatcherism*. Lawrence & Wishart and Marxism Today, London.
Hall, S., Critcher, C., Jefferson, T., Clarke, J., & Roberts, B. (1978) *Policing the Crisis: Mugging, the State, and Law and Order*. Macmillan, London.
Harris, D. (1992) *From Class Struggle to the Politics of Pleasure: The Effects of Gramscianism on Cultural Studies*. Routledge, London.
Hunt, A. (Ed.) (1977) *Class and Class Structure*. Lawrence & Wishart, London.
Open University (1982) *Popular Culture (U203)*. Open University Press, Milton Keynes.
Thornham, S. (Ed.) (1999) *Feminist Film Theory: A Reader*. Edinburgh University Press, Edinburgh.
Townshend, J. (2004) Laclau and Mouffe's Hegemonic Project: The Story So Far. *Political Studies* 52: 269–88.
Wood, B. (1998) Stuart Hall, Cultural Studies and the Problem of Hegemony. *British Journal of Sociology* 49(3): 399–414.

help-seeking

Bernice A. Pescosolido

Help-seeking refers to efforts or actions designed to assist individuals with physical, mental, or emotional behaviors or manifestations somehow noticed as out of the ordinary. Often, this term is used interchangeably with service utilization, health care decision-making, or health/illness behavior. However, a number of factors differentiate the concept of help-seeking from the others.

First, help-seeking is broader than service utilization, which generally taps formal, scientific medical services. Individuals may seek out lay, scientific, or alternative sources of advice or assistance perceived as potentially useful. Further, help-seeking can mean going to a provider of a medical system but, just as readily, can be applied to using the Internet for information, talking to neighbors about their experience with similar conditions, buying over-the-counter medications, praying, or joining a self-help group.

Second, the term is narrower than health/illness behavior because, technically, it refers to an active search by the parties involved. Individuals may, indeed, seek out care; however, it is also likely that individuals will experience legal coercion into the formal medical care system. The issues of involuntary treatment for mental illness symptoms, contact by public health authorities regarding possible HIV exposure, or employees forced to use physicians for an insurance check-up before starting their job, all are likely to result in the use of formal services. Further, and perhaps most troubling to some existing theories attempting to explain illness behavior, individuals may "muddle through" an experience of illness, recounting a story of entry into the formal medical care system that can be described neither as a choice nor as resistance (Pescosolido, Gardner, & Lubell 1998).

Third, help-seeking is broader than decision-making for medical care, at least in its most usual usage. That is, decision-making tends to evoke an image of a single person weighing the costs and benefits of seeking out any of a variety of possible preventive or curative services. However, as Freidson (1970) points out, no small part of the significance of society's influence on the use of services is involved in motivating (encouraging or discouraging) an individual's movement toward assistance and giving them a sense of appropriate cultural solutions. In perceiving symptoms or the risk of a medical problem (for preventive services), or in pushing individuals toward or away from scientific or complementary, alternative services, others around the individual are crucial.

In Talcott Parsons's early, influential theory, help-seeking was a non-issue since modern societies required acceptance of the sick role (a community-based decision) and that an individual seek formal help as part of the obligations inherent in the status. In response, several theories were developed in the 1960s and 1970s that still dominate empirical evaluations at the present time (Pescosolido & Kronenfeld 1995). The only explicit theory of help-seeking was developed by David Mechanic (1968). Noting that both the process of definition of illness and the ability to cope with it are socially determined, Mechanic laid out ten determinants of the response to illness. These are: (1) the visibility, recognizability, or perceived salience of symptoms; (2) their frequency, persistence, or recurrence; (3) the perceived severity of symptoms; (4) the individual's or others' tolerance of the symptoms; (5) other belief systems or circumstances that may explain away the

symptoms as "expected" or "normal"; (6) the extent of medical or other cultural knowledge surrounding the individual; (7) other emotions (e.g., fear) that may trigger responses to the symptoms; (8) the extent to which "normal" individual or family routines are disturbed by the symptoms, as well as (9) other role obligations that may facilitate or impede the ability to go to or be taken to services; and (10) issues of access, whether geographical, financial, or logistical.

These factors are reflected in three other models that currently dominate the study of individual or population use of formal services. The Health Belief Model (HBM), targeting health behavior or prevention, was conceived originally by psychologist Irwin Rosenstock and developed further by sociologist Marshall Becker (1974). This model emphasizes perceptions, beliefs, and other social psychological characteristics that influence whether individuals feel at risk for problems and position themselves to change health behaviors and to utilize health care services. The Socio-Behavioral Model (SBM), targeting illness behavior and overall use of medical and health care, was developed by sociologist Ronald Andersen (1974) and emphasizes three types of contingencies: enabling characteristics (or access, whether perceived or actual, geographic or fiscal), need (hurt, bother, and worry associated with symptoms), and predisposing characteristics (social and other characteristics like age and gender consistently related to utilization). The Theory of Reasoned Action, developed in psychology by Martin Fishbein (1979), was designed to address behavior more generally, but has been applied to health, illness, and disability issues. Here, the focus is on the factors that influence behavioral intentions because individuals rationally assess information or beliefs about the planned behavior. It is a combination of the individual's own attitudes about the intended behavior as well as the individual's perceptions of social norms that shape the person's subjected probability of "performing" the "target" behavior (for a catalogue of these and another models, see Gochman 1997).

In opposition to these models, which tend to be static in nature, other sociologists and anthropologists have focused on tracing the process of help-seeking, calling this approach the "illness career" perspective. These sociologists, coming primarily from the qualitative tradition, offer a textured recounting of the events and emotions leading up to decisions to use formal services (for a review, see Pescosolido 1991). More recently, the Network-Episode Model has been offered as an attempt to bridge the differences between these two approaches, capturing their essential insights and reflecting new realities that face individuals in contemporary societies (e.g., decreasing reliance on tertiary care). The NEM is focused on the "illness or disability career" which marks all of an individual's attempts to cope with the onset of an episode of a health or physical impairment or associated acute illness. It requires charting what individuals do and when they do it through the concepts of patterns and pathways. Patterns of care describe the combination of advisers and/or practices used during the course of coping with a disability or illness episode. Pathways add the element of order; that is, the sequences of advisers and/or practices used to deal with a disability or confront an acute episode of health problems during the disability career.

In the NEM the underlying mechanism is interaction or social influence. The NEM starts with a basic idea: dealing with any health problem or physical disability is a social process that is managed through the contacts (or social networks) that individuals have in the community, the treatment system, and social service agencies (including support groups, churches, community recreation centers, etc.). The experience of illness is embedded in its social life and rhythms, constrained by social structure, and created in negotiation with others. While dominant models have not ignored networks, it is quite different to conceptualize social networks as yet another contingency of choice (e.g., part of normative influence in the HSM and TRA), or to conceptualize social networks as the engine of action in a dynamic model of utilization. Unlike the explicit or implicit rational-man assumptions underlying the other dominant models, in the NEM individuals are seen as pragmatic, having commonsense knowledge and cultural routines that they draw from past experience, from proactively talking to others, and from reactively responding to the comments of others when impairments, or other health problems associated with them, occur.

It questions whether every action in coping with a behavior outside the ordinary is the result of the complicated, cost-benefit calculus typical of many other models. This view allows for rational choice, forced choice, or even haplessness to explain how individuals try to deal with their problems. But, in general, people face disabilities in the course of their day-to-day lives by interacting with other people who may recognize (or deny) a problem; send them to (or provide) treatment; and support, cajole, or nag them about appointments, medications, or lifestyle.

Whatever the patterns or pathways, illness careers are not assumed to occur in a vacuum in the NEM. They are embedded in personal lives and changing communities. These community-based networks are referred to as "external" networks. Following Freidson (1970), the NEM sees the size of a network as calibrating the potential amount of influence that can be leveraged, and the beliefs and experiences of individuals in social networks guiding them in a particular direction (e.g., toward or away from scientific medical care services). Further, the NEM conceptualizes the medical system itself as a changing set of providers and organizations with which individuals may or may not have contact ("internal" or "inside" networks). Like the community and the disability career, formal treatment systems change over time in response to the problems people have, to the technology and medical knowledge, to health care policies, and to community preferences and demands. These structures determine resource and information flows across systems and organizations, and they influence the behavior of individuals who are connected to or operate within them. These two network systems meet at the interface of the treatment and community system and can work together and cooperate or work in opposition. By seeing interaction in social networks as the underlying mechanism at work, the NEM contextualizes the response to disabilities in everyday life.

Taking a dynamic approach, rooted in the community and its institutions of care, and incorporating ideas from other existing models, poses a number of challenges in understanding help-seeking. Such investigations of help-seeking require more theoretical, methodological, and analytic work. In addition to integrating more of the insights of dominant social science models, sociological approaches will have to incorporate new ideas about cognition, biology, psychiatry, and geography, for example, into its models. Moving to a more dynamic approach should bring other concepts from recent developments in the understanding of the life course. Social science methodologists have only begun to consider and develop suitable dynamic tools in the last decade. Further, moving to a more integrated approach will require serious theorizing about linking process and structures. Again, we are only beginning to consider how to integrate results from how one set of social and dynamic processes influences others. However, faced with current failures to explain critical aspects of help-seeking, the synthesizing approach of sociology has much to offer in addressing these challenges.

SEE ALSO: Health Behavior; Health Care Delivery Systems; Health and Culture; Health Lifestyles; Illness Behavior; Social Support

REFERENCES AND SUGGESTED READINGS

Andersen, R. (1974) *A Behavioral Model of Families' Use of Health Services.* University of Chicago, Chicago.

Becker, M. H. (Ed.) (1974) *The Health Belief Model and Personal Health Behavior.* Society for Public Health Education, San Francisco.

Fishbein, M. (1979) A Theory of Reasoned Action: Some Applications and Implications. *Nebraska Symposium on Motivation* 27: 65–116.

Fishbein, M. & Ajzen, I. (1975) *Belief, Attitude, Intention, and Behavior: An Introduction to Theory and Research.* Addison-Wesley, Reading, MA.

Freidson, E. (1970) *Profession of Medicine: A Study of the Sociology of Applied Knowledge.* Dodd, Mead, New York.

Gochman, D. S. (Ed.) (1997) Handbook of Health Behavior Research, Vol. 1: *Personal and Social Determinants.* Plenum Press, New York.

Mechanic, D. (1968) *Medical Sociology.* Free Press, New York.

Parsons, T. (1951) *The Social System.* Free Press, Glencoe, IL.

Pescosolido, B. A. (1991) Illness Careers and Network Ties: A Conceptual Model of Utilization and Compliance. *Advances in Medical Sociology* 2: 161–84.

Pescosolido, B. A. & Kronenfeld, J. C. (1995) Health, Illness, and Healing in an Uncertain Era: Challenges From and For Medical Sociology. *Journal of Health and Social Behavior* extra issue: 5–33.

Pescosolido, B. A., Gardner, C. B., & Lubell, K. M. (1998) How People Get Into Mental Health Services: Stories of Choice, Coercion and "Muddling Through" from "First-Timers." *Social Science and Medicine* 46(2): 275–86.

Rosenstock, I. (1966) Why People Use Health Services. *Millbank Memorial Fund Quarterly* 44: 94–127.

hermeneutics

Wendy Hilton-Morrow and Austin Harrington

Hermeneutics is a branch of sociology concerned with human understanding and interpretation. Originally applied solely to texts, sociologists have applied hermeneutics to social events by examining participants' understandings of the events from the standpoint of their specific historical and cultural context. Hermeneutics is opposed to the view that social phenomena can be grasped adequately by reference to invariant laws of cause and effect or statistical regularities, as with positivist and behaviorist approaches and some elements of functionalist theory. Hermeneutics is one among a range of approaches to meaning, symbolization, and representation in social life that includes semiotics, structuralism, deconstruction, and discourse analysis.

The term hermeneutics derives from the Greek verb *hermeneuein* ("to interpret"), thereby relating to the ancient Greek messenger of the gods, Hermes. His role was more complex than that of mere messenger because before Hermes could translate and communicate the words of the gods (which were unintelligible to humans), he first had to interpret and understand their meanings for himself. This complex process is key to theories of hermeneutics, in which texts are understood as intermediaries between writers and audiences. In particular, hermeneutics initially focused on interpreting the Bible in order to understand the word of God.

Among German Protestant writers of the seventeenth and eighteenth centuries, hermeneutics referred to the art of interpreting scripture in the light of philological evidence. Writing during the early nineteenth century within the Romantic movement, theologian and philosopher Friedrich Schleiermacher favored broadening the focus of hermeneutics, seeking a theory of interpretation that extended beyond religious texts. His writings influenced future work in that he understood the author as creator and the text as an expression of the creative self. Earlier traditions of hermeneutics theorized that a reader would understand intended meanings of a text until encountering incongruous or illogical passages. However, Schleiermacher proposed a radically different position in which understanding was taken as a process in which readers understand the text's context, including the author's creative individuality, the text's particular genre, and its historical circumstances.

Schleiermacher's most lasting contribution to hermeneutics was the concept of the hermeneutic circle, which he understood to operate at every level of interpretation. According to the theory of the hermeneutic circle, a reader can only understand a part within its relation to the larger whole; however, the larger whole can only be understood through its contributing parts. Therefore, readers find themselves oscillating between the part and the whole within this inescapable process of interpretation. For example, readers cannot know the meaning of a word without framing it within the context of the larger sentence. Likewise, they cannot understand the significance of a sentence without the context of the entire work. However, an understanding of the work is based upon its accumulated parts, as well as a context of the author's life and the culture as a whole in which it was created. Therefore, circularity exists across and between all levels of interpretation.

As subsequent theorists applied Schleiermacher's work to other areas of study, hermeneutics flourished in German academia. In modern social thought the first thinker to develop a distinctively hermeneutic program was philosopher and cultural historian Wilhelm Dilthey. Writing in the 1880s, Dilthey extended Schleiermacher's theory of interpretation to the human sciences, which studied all human expressions in disciplines ranging from archeology and history to sociology and anthropology. In an attempt to differentiate between the natural sciences and the "human sciences," or what he termed the *Geisteswissenschaften*, Dilthey claimed that whereas the natural sciences seek *erklären*, the explanation of phenomena according to laws of regular correspondence between cause and effect, the goal of the human sciences is *verstehen*, the understanding of human action based on intention and context. To interpret a historical event or social process in terms of meaningfully lived experience was itself to account adequately for its occurrence and did not require the support of law-like naturalistic generalizations to gain scientific validity. For Weber, Dilthey's ideas underlined the importance of "empathic understanding" and "subjectively intended meanings" and the fallacy of attempts to model social action exclusively on behavioral or psychological laws, such as in the writings of Auguste Comte, J. S. Mill, Herbert Spencer, and the classical political economists.

A second key source for hermeneutics is twentieth-century phenomenological and linguistic philosophy. In the 1920s and 1930s Edmund Husserl and Martin Heidegger argued that before human beings come to develop methodical scientific representations of the world, they possess a more primordial existential understanding of the world which they express in everyday life and ordinary communication. These ideas became important notably for Alfred Schütz, who restated Weber's interpretive sociology in the form of a phenomenology of the social world, based on the concepts of intersubjectivity and the lifeworld. Similarly, in the 1950s, drawing on Ludwig Wittgenstein's linguistic philosophy, Peter Winch (1958) argued that social science had the aim of studying social relations in terms of "forms of life" constructed in linguistic rules and "language-games" shared between speakers. Conceived of as an attempt to understand the most appropriate way to study human life, hermeneutics became focused largely on method.

German philosopher Hans-Georg Gadamer challenged the assumption that understanding was a methodological issue. Gadamer was greatly influenced by philosopher Martin Heidegger's ontological concerns, including his idea that readers bring presuppositions to their understandings of a text. Gadamer hoped to separate the human sciences from prior influences, like

Dilthey and Wittgenstein, that he believed failed to fully reject the scientific presuppositions of positivism. In his 1975 book *Truth and Knowledge* Gadamer proposed that knowledge could never be objective, and, therefore, social theorists were incapable of fully escaping their preexisting prejudices. They can however be brought to a state of reflective awareness by means of what Gadamer calls a "fusion of horizons" between the standpoint of the interpreter and the standpoint of the other culture.

In the 1960s and 1970s Gadamer's philosophy was criticised by Jürgen Habermas on grounds of failure to address issues of power, ideology, and material conflict in social life. Habermas (1988) argued that hermeneutics raises a false claim to universality when it overlooks the imbrication of linguistic communication with relations of domination. He argued that Gadamer's and other hermeneutic philosophies need to be emended to incorporate critical assessment of the rationality of social practices in a non-relativistic framework. Habermas compared hermeneutics to Marxian ideology-critique and Freudian psychoanalysis. He argued that as Marx showed how ideologies can disguise oppressive social-class relations, so Freud showed how all psychological interpretation is necessarily guided toward emancipation of the patient from irrational repressions.

Writers such as Ricoeur (1981) and Taylor (1985) have criticized Habermas's position for ignoring the sense in which both ideology-critique and Freudian psychoanalysis are themselves situated in specifically western post-Enlightenment contexts of thought and therefore reflect specific pre-judgments of their own. In general, however, Habermas's arguments point to some notable limits around the scope of hermeneutics in social theory. In a similar spirit, other critics such as Roy Bhaskar, Anthony Giddens, and Pierre Bourdieu have argued that hermeneutics is informative only when it does not collapse material, economic, and systemic factors in social life into purely "mental" or "subjective" elements. In this sense, hermeneutics does not obviate the requirements of realist epistemology in social science. It demonstrates that all ideas of social reality depend on interpretation, but it does not show that social reality is reducible to interpretation, or that all causal relations in social life

can be encompassed purely in terms of aspects of meaning or symbolization.

In addition to influencing current sociological thought, the hermeneutic tradition's attention to textuality and interpretation informs related scholarship in a range of academic disciplines, including philosophy and rhetoric.

SEE ALSO: Behaviorism; Deconstruction; Functionalism/Neofunctionalism; Phenomenology; Positivism; Semiotics; Structuralism; *Verstehen*

REFERENCES AND SUGGESTED READINGS

Bauman, Z. (1981) *Hermeneutics and Social Science*. Hutchinson, London.

Gadamer, H. G. (1975) *Truth and Method*. Continuum, New York.

Habermas, J. (1988) *On the Logic of the Social Sciences*. MIT Press, Cambridge, MA.

Harrington, A. (2001) *Hermeneutic Dialogue and Social Science*. Routledge, London.

Hekman, S. (1986) *Hermeneutics and the Sociology of Knowledge*. University of Notre Dame Press, Notre Dame, IN.

Mueller-Vollmer, K. (Ed.) (1994) *The Hermeneutics Reader*. Continuum, New York.

Ricoeur, P. (1981) *Hermeneutics and the Human Sciences*. Cambridge University Press, Cambridge.

Schleiermacher, F. D. E. (1977) *Hermeneutics: The Handwritten Manuscripts*. Scholars Press, Missoula.

Taylor, C. (1985) Interpretation and the Sciences of Man. In: *Philosophical Papers I*. Cambridge University Press, Cambridge.

Winch, P. (1958) *The Idea of a Social Science and its Relation to Philosophy*. Routledge, London.

heterosexual imaginary

Chrys Ingraham

Culture installs meaning in our lives from the very first moment we enter the social world. Our sexual orientation or sexual identity is defined by the symbolic order of that world through the use of verbal as well as nonverbal language. How we come to understand what it means to be heterosexual is a product of a culture's symbolic order and its organizing practices. Heterosexuality as a *social* category is much more than the fact of one's sexual or affectional attractions. What we think of when we talk about heterosexuality or refer to ourselves as heterosexual is a product of a society's meaning-making processes. In reality, heterosexuality operates as a highly organized social institution that varies across culture, history, region, religion, ethnicity, nationality, race, lifespan, social class, and ability.

The task of examining this highly pervasive and taken-for-granted social arrangement requires a conceptual framework capable of revealing how heterosexuality has become institutionalized, naturalized, and normalized. Any attempt to examine the institution of heterosexuality and its incumbent meanings requires a theory and methodology capable of inquiring into its naturalized operation and pervasive social practices (e.g., dating, proms, weddings, Valentine's Day, online dating services, etc.).

French psychoanalyst Jacques Lacan's concept of the imaginary is especially useful for this purpose. According to Lacan, the imaginary is the unmediated contact an infant has to its own image and its connection with its mother. Instead of facing a complicated, conflictual, and contradictory world, the infant experiences the illusion of tranquility, plenitude, and fullness. In other words, infants experience a sense of oneness with their primary caretaker. Louis Althusser, a French philosopher, borrowed Lacan's notion of the imaginary for his neo-Marxist theory of ideology, defining ideology as "the imaginary relationship of individuals to their real conditions of existence" (Althusser 1971: 52). The "imaginary" here does not mean "false" or "pretend" but, rather, an imagined or illusory relationship between an individual and their social world. Applied to a social theory of heterosexuality, the *heterosexual imaginary* is that way of thinking that relies on romantic and sacred notions of heterosexuality in order to create and maintain the illusion of well-being and oneness. This romantic view prevents us from seeing how institutionalized heterosexuality actually works to organize gender while preserving racial, class, and sexual hierarchies. The effect of this illusory depiction of reality is that heterosexuality is taken for granted and

unquestioned while gender is understood as something people are socialized into or learn. The heterosexual imaginary naturalizes male-to-female social relations, rituals, and organized practices and conceals the operation of heterosexuality in structuring gender across race, class, and sexuality. This way of seeing closes off any critical analysis of heterosexuality as an organizing institution and the ends it serves (Ingraham 1994, 1999). By leaving heterosexuality unexamined as an institution we do not explore how it is learned, what it keeps in place, and the interests it serves in the way it is currently practiced. Through the use of the heterosexual imaginary, we hold up the institution of heterosexuality as timeless, devoid of historical variation, and as "just the way it is" while creating social practices that reinforce the illusion that as long as one complies with this prevailing and naturalized structure, all will be right in the world. This illusion is commonly known as romance. Romancing heterosexuality is creating an illusory heterosexuality.

The lived reality of institutionalized heterosexuality is, however, not typically tranquil or safe. The consequences the heterosexual imaginary produces include, for example, marital rape, domestic violence, pay inequities, racism, gay bashing, femicide, and sexual harassment. Institutionalized heterosexuality and its organizing ideology – the heterosexual imaginary – establishes those behaviors we ascribe to men and women – gender – while keeping in place or producing a history of contradictory and unequal social relations. The production of a division of labor that results in unpaid domestic work, inequalities of pay and opportunity, or the privileging of married couples in the dissemination of insurance benefits are examples of this.

Above all, the heterosexual imaginary naturalizes the regulation of sexuality through the institution of marriage and state domestic relations laws. These laws, among others, set the terms for taxation, health care, and housing benefits on the basis of marital status. Rarely challenged – except by nineteenth-century marriage reformers and early second wave feminists – laws and public and private-sector policies use marriage as the primary requirement for social and economic benefits and access rather than distributing resources on some other basis, such as citizenship or ability to breathe, for example.

A related concept useful for the study of the heterosexual imaginary and of institutionalized heterosexuality is heteronormativity. This is the view that institutionalized heterosexuality constitutes the standard for legitimate and expected social and sexual relations. Heteronormativity represents one of the main premises underlying the heterosexual imaginary, again ensuring that the organization of heterosexuality in everything from gender to weddings to marital status is held up as both a model and as "normal." Consider, for instance, the ways many surveys or intake questionnaires ask respondents to check off their marital status as either married, divorced, separated, widowed, single, or, in some cases, never married. Not only are these categories presented as significant indices of social identity, they are offered as the only options, implying that the organization of identity in relation to marriage is universal and not in need of explanation.

The sociological importance of the theory of heterosexual imaginary is in its usefulness in researching issues related to gender and sexuality. Integrating this concept into sociological study holds enormous promise for placing a check and balance on a researcher's standpoint, thus ensuring a more objective outcome.

SEE ALSO: Compulsory Heterosexuality; Essentialism and Constructionism; Femininities/Masculinities; Heterosexuality; Homophobia and Heterosexism; Ideology

REFERENCES AND SUGGESTED READINGS

Althusser, L. (1971) *Lenin and Philosophy and Other Essays*. Trans. B. Brewster. Monthly Review Press, New York.

Ingraham, C. (1994) The Heterosexual Imaginary: Feminist Sociology and Theories of Gender. *Sociological Theory* 12(2): 203–19.

Ingraham, C. (1999) *White Weddings: Romancing Heterosexuality in Popular Culture*. Routledge, New York.

heterosexuality

Stevi Jackson

Before we can even discuss heterosexuality, we need some terminology clarification. The words "sex" and "sexual" can be used to refer to the erotic (e.g., "having sex," "sexual fantasies") or to denote differences between men and women (as in "the two sexes" or "the sexual division of labor"). This semantic confusion reflects some of the taken-for-granted assumptions underpinning everyday understandings of sexuality: that to be born with a particular set of genitals ("sex organs") defines one as a member of a particular "sex" (male or female) and as destined to be erotically ("sexually") attracted to and to "have sex" with the other "sex." The introduction of the concept of gender, which emphasized the social character of the division between women and men, and the emergence of social constructionist perspectives on sexuality have made it possible to demystify the relationship between genitals, gender, and heterosexuality. Some confusion, however, persists in that some theorists continue to use "sex" to denote what sociologists generally term "gender." In what follows, unless otherwise stated, gender refers to all aspects of the division and distinction between women and men, while the words sex, sexual, and sexuality are reserved for erotic aspects of life.

The term heterosexuality, as it is used in everyday language, denotes sexual attraction to and relationships between differently gendered individuals. In this sense it is a mode of erotic interaction between women and men. From a sociological perspective, however, heterosexuality entails more than merely a sexual practice or preference: it is deeply embedded in wider social relations and practices, institutionalized as the "normal" form of human sexual relationship and as the basis of marriage, family, and kinship relationships. It is recognized by the state through laws and practices governing welfare, taxation, inheritance, and other spheres of governance affecting families. Heterosexuality is inextricably interrelated with gender: it is defined by and helps perpetuate the division of society into two gender categories. Many aspects of gender division and inequality are associated with heterosexuality. For example, the domestic division of labor and the gap between wages earned by men and women are products of a social order where adults are expected to live in heterosexual couples in which men are the main breadwinners. One of the main foci of studies of heterosexuality, therefore, has been its relationship with gender. The other has been its normative and privileged status, which has marginalized those who do not conform and served to legitimate the stigmatization of gay men and lesbians – historically often with brutal effect.

Heterosexuality might seem to be a human universal, but it is also historically and culturally variable in form. Heterosexual unions can be polygamous or monogamous, based on personal choice or founded on arrangements between kin, and have coexisted at times with socially approved homoerotic and homosocial bonds. Heterosexuality cannot therefore be assumed to have the same meaning or the same place in all societies at all times. Moreover, heterosexuality itself has a history: the concept was coined in the nineteenth century, along with "homosexuality," in order to differentiate what was deemed "normal" from what was deemed "perverse."

The term heterosexuality is less often used in everyday language than "homosexuality," largely because it is simply the taken-for-granted norm. It is thus an "unmarked" term, one privileged through remaining unsaid. Heterosexual people are generally not expected to identify themselves as such, are rarely called upon to justify or explain their sexuality. Until the last few decades of the twentieth century sociologists largely shared this commonsense view. Thus, while many aspects of heterosexual relations, such as marriage, families, and kinship, had become objects of sociological enquiry, heterosexuality itself was assumed rather than analyzed, taken as given rather than being subjected to critical scrutiny.

During the late 1960s and early 1970s, with changes within sociology and in the wider social and political climate, heterosexual relations began to be questioned. Social constructionism gained ground within sociology, making more critical perspectives on heterosexuality possible. In their classic text, *Sexual Conduct* (1973), John Gagnon and William Simon argued that human sexuality, far from being ordained by nature, was the product of social scripts. Sociologists working on deviance redefined it as a product of the social rules that defined the boundaries of conventionality and the social processes whereby individuals were labeled deviant. The implications of these perspectives were that heterosexuality was no more natural than homosexuality, the boundary between them was a social construct rather than a natural given, and that heterosexuality was "normal" only by virtue of social definition. A new generation of sociologists, influenced by the rise of gay liberation and second wave feminism, began to draw on these and other radical perspectives to develop critiques of male-dominated heterosexual institutions and practices. Gay scholars such as Mike Brake (1976) began to name the heterosexual family as a source of exclusion and oppression, while feminists defined these same family structures as central to women's subordination. Feminists also began to question the assumption of "natural" differences between men and women and therefore the idea of a natural mutual attraction between "opposite sexes" destined to complement each other in conjugal unions.

From the early 1970s feminist scholars and researchers began documenting sources of women's discontent within heterosexual relationships, although they did not always identify heterosexuality as the object of critique. Where specifically sexual practices were concerned, feminists challenged the denial of sexual pleasure and agency to women on the one hand and, on the other, sexual coercion and violence. In arguing for women's sexual autonomy feminists not only attacked the double standard of morality, but also questioned the definition and ordering of "the sex act" itself. Following Anne Koedt's widely cited article "The Myth of the Vaginal Orgasm" (1972), feminists argued that equating sex with penetrative vaginal intercourse (prioritizing male orgasm while relegating acts producing female orgasm to the status of "foreplay") constituted a male-defined view of sex – though only a few noted that is was equally heterosexually defined. Feminists also paid considerable attention to sexual coercion and violence, making connections between being pressured into unwanted sex, everyday sexual harassment, and rape. Rape was seen as a reflection of everyday sexual mores, a product of the social construction of male sexuality as an unstoppable force expressed through pursuit and conquest of women. Moreover, fear of rape was identified as a form of social control, limiting women's freedom of movement and legitimating their appropriation by one man in order to protect them from others. Even here, though, heterosexuality per se remained unproblematized. For example, Brownmiller's (1975) classic and encyclopedic analysis of rape never wavered from the assumption of a universally heterosexual world.

At the same time, considerable attention was given to marriage, the linchpin of institutionalized heterosexuality. Through the 1970s and early 1980s a great deal of research accumulated on power and economic dependence within marriage and especially on housework and the domestic division of labor. From the mid-1970s some feminists began to make an explicit connection with heterosexuality. Charlotte Brunch, for example pointed out that "heterosexuality upholds the home, housework, the family as both a personal and economic unit." Most analyses of domestic labor in North America and the UK, however, were oriented to debates on its utility for capitalism, precluding a focus on the heterosexual contract within which this labor took place.

In France, however, a different approach was being elaborated by a group of radical materialist feminists organized around the journal *Questions féministes* who, in the first issue of their journal published in 1979, made explicit the connection between the social construction of the categories "men" and "women" and the divide between heterosexuality and homosexuality This group included Christine Delphy, who analyzed marriage as a relationship founded on men's appropriation of women's labor, and Colette Guillaumin, who analyzed male domination in terms of the individual and collective appropriation of women's bodies and labor. Drawing on these ideas, Monique Wittig published a series of articles between 1976 and 1981 in which she elaborates on an analysis of the category of sex (the socially constructed division between women and men) as "the product of a heterosexual society in which men appropriate for themselves the reproduction and production of women and their physical persons by means

of . . . the marriage contract" (Wittig 1992: 6). She argues that women and men are defined by virtue of their location within the heterosexual contract and likens lesbians, as fugitives from this contract, to runaway slaves and contends that since "woman" has no meaning outside heterosexual systems of thought, lesbians "are not women" (p. 32).

Another founding text of this time was Adrienne Rich's "Compulsory Heterosexuality and Lesbian Existence" (1980). Like Wittig, Rich contested heterosexuality's privileged status as an unquestioned norm. She argued that rather than being natural it was imposed upon women through the erasure of lesbian existence from history and by a range of social practices that constrained women into personal subjection to men. Compulsory heterosexuality thus kept women *in*, within its confines, and kept them *down*, subordinate. Whereas Wittig had argued that lesbians are not women, Rich suggested that all women were potentially lesbians. Rather than emphasizing the differences between lesbian and heterosexual women, Rich argued that all forms of sociality and solidarity among women were part of a lesbian continuum.

Wittig and Rich were both writing at a time when radical or political lesbianism was becoming an increasingly vocal political tendency within feminism on both sides of the Atlantic. Groups such as the New York Radicalesbians and later, in the UK, the Leeds Revolutionary feminists saw lesbianism as a form of resistance to patriarchy and heterosexual feminism as holding back the cause of women's liberation. While Wittig's work was more in tune with this perspective, Rich's was seen as insufficiently radical in allowing heterosexual feminists to consider themselves part of a lesbian continuum while they continued to consort with men (Jeffreys 1990). The concept of compulsory heterosexuality, however, has stood the test of time and continues, alongside some of Wittig's insights, to inform contemporary debates.

During the 1980s feminist discussions of heterosexuality became more muted, as debates shifted to new terrain. Competing perspectives on heterosexuality, however, remained an undercurrent in the heated exchanges between libertarian and anti-violence feminists. The former focused on the rigid morality of straight society and thus on heterosexuality's normative status. Rubin (1984), for example, analyzed the climate of "sex-negativity" that resulted in the penalization of all forms of sexuality that lay outside the "charmed circle" of heterosexual monogamy. The latter saw heterosexual relations as a locus of male domination. Thus, Catherine MacKinnon argued that gender was the product of men's appropriation of women's sexuality. Two quite separate lines of critique were emerging – of heteronormativity and of heterosexuality's interrelationship with gender hierarchy – which were to inform the debates of the 1990s.

At the same time, new perspectives on sexuality were emerging following the English publication of the first volume of Michel Foucault's *The History of Sexuality*. Foucault's (1979) approach to power as primarily productive rather than repressive and his analytical focus on the discursive constitution of objects of knowledge facilitated a rethinking of the heterosexual/homosexual distinction. From a Foucauldian perspective these concepts did not come into being in order to name preexisting categories; rather, they brought those categories into being. Whereas in previous eras it was particular sexual conduct that was policed, with particular acts condemned or outlawed, in the late nineteenth century categories of sexual persons were created – it became possible, as Foucault said, to *be* a homosexual. A corollary of this is that heterosexuality does not define a pregiven norm, but creates it – that far from being a natural state, heterosexuality is a historical construct, an invention (Katz 1995). Foucault's arguments were to inform a new perspective that emerged in the 1990s – queer theory – which was also influenced more generally by postmodern thinking and by such writers as Lacan and Derrida.

Queer theory is not easy to define and some contest the utility of the term, but it has become a convenient shorthand for approaches that seek in some way to trouble heterosexuality, to destabilize the boundaries between heterosexuality and homosexuality and to interrogate the binaries of gay/straight and man/woman. Queer theory's critique of heterosexuality tends to focus on its normative status, but also questions its stability, revealing the ways in which it depends upon its excluded "other" in order to secure its boundaries. Here sexuality is

seen as fluid and contingent and neither heterosexual nor homosexual identities are assumed to be fixed or unitary (Seidman 1997). While queer theory developed from rather different preoccupations from feminism, there was considerable overlap with feminist critique. Both questioned the inevitability and naturalness of heterosexuality and both, to some extent at least, linked the binary divide of gender with that between heterosexuality and homosexuality. This is probably most evident in the early work of Judith Butler, which is often identified as both feminist and queer. The object of her critique is the heterosexual matrix, the regulatory fictions that link sex, gender, and heterosexuality together as a seemingly natural, compulsory order, producing gender as an effect of compulsory heterosexuality. Butler's radical denaturalization of gender and of the heterosexual/homosexual binary owes much to Wittig's analysis, but reinterpreted through postmodern theory with the emphasis on bringing gender and sexual identities into question rather than on gender as a form of social inequality. As a result of this emphasis, even feminist variants of queer theory tend to focus on heteronormativity, saying rather little about what goes on *within* heterosexual relations.

Other feminists, however, continued to be concerned with relationships within heterosexuality. The rise of queer theory in the 1990s coincided with a revival of feminist work on heterosexuality, developing and reformulating earlier analyses of its intersection with gender. Rather than treating heterosexuality as a monolithic entity, feminists began to analyze its different facets, considering heterosexuality as institution and identity and in terms of everyday experience and practice (Richardson 1996; Jackson 1999). In so doing they recovered earlier feminist insights, pointing out that heterosexuality was not simply a form of sexual desire and conduct, but of the wider social relations between women and men. In the domestic arena, therefore, heterosexuality was as much about who washed and ironed the sheets as what went on between them (Jackson 1999). Hence, attention was refocused on the gendered character of heterosexuality while, at the same time, making evident the heterosexual character of gender relations. In a key article, "The Heterosexual Imaginary," Chrys Ingraham argued that since gender concerns relations between men and women, it is fundamentally ordered by heterosexuality.

These new feminist analyses facilitated a separation of the critique of heterosexuality as an institution from heterosexual identity, experience, and practice. It is now possible to discuss the potential pleasures of heterosexual sex as well as its constraints and to analyze the ways in which heterosexuality is implicated in the perpetuation of a male–dominated social order without being critical of individual women for *being* heterosexual. Heterosexual identity can then be analyzed as differing for women and men, but also as often being not an identity as such at all, but a means of validating other aspects of feminine and masculine identities – in asymmetrically gendered ways. For example, first heterosex is often seen as "making a boy a man," but not making a girl a woman (Holland et al. 1996). Focusing on actual everyday heterosexual experiences and practices enables sociologists to explore persistent inequalities in heterosexuality, while also taking account of its variability; to consider heterosexual sexuality, but to link it with wider aspects of gendered, heterosexual social relations. For example, recent empirical research has found that despite greater sexual freedom, aspirations towards gender equality, and women's greater social and economic autonomy, heterosexual sex remains male-dominated. Young women, in particular, find it difficult to achieve a sense of sexual agency (Tolman 2002). One group of researchers have suggested that heterosexual sex is not governed by the tensions between masculinity and femininity – it is *masculinity* that regulates the sexuality of both young men and young women (Holland et al. 1998). Such research suggests that, despite the late-modern rhetoric of female sexual autonomy and pleasure, women still discipline themselves to conform to an idea of sexuality that prioritizes men's desires. This parallels other aspects of heterosexual relationship where women continue to do the bulk of the emotional and physical work that maintains the heterosexual couple as a going concern.

The debates of the 1990s have given critical perspectives on heterosexuality a higher profile within social theory and social research. This is most evident in approaches to sexuality, where studies of heterosexuality can no longer masquerade as studies of sexuality in general. Heterosexuality is routinely named as such, treated as only one form of sexuality, its normative status subject to scrutiny rather than taken as given. In studies of gender, too, heterosexuality is less often merely assumed. Sociologists working on family life are now more likely to be aware of diversity of sexual relations as one of many aspects of family diversity and therefore less likely to take heterosexuality as given. In the wider social and political arena heterosexuality's privileged status is now more openly contested within debates on gay and lesbian rights, especially with respect to the issue of gay and lesbian marriage or civil partnerships. Yet, in everyday life, despite advances in the rights of lesbians and gays in many countries, heterosexuality's normative status is rarely questioned.

SEE ALSO: Family Diversity; Feminism; Feminism, First, Second, and Third Waves; Gay and Lesbian Movement; Heterosexual Imaginary; Homosexuality; Inequality/Stratification, Gender; Lesbian Feminism; Lesbianism; Queer Theory; Sex and Gender

REFERENCES AND SUGGESTED READINGS

Brake, M. (1976) I May Be A Queer But At Least I'm A Man. In: Leonard Barker, D. & Allen, S. (Eds.), *Sexual Divisions and Society: Process and Change*. Tavistock, London.

Brownmiller, S. (1975) *Against Our Will: Men, Women and Rape*. Secker & Warburg, London.

Butler, J. (1990) *Gender Trouble*. Routledge, New York.

Foucault, M. (1979) *The History of Sexuality*, Vol. 1. Allen Lane, London.

Holland, J., Ramazanoğlu, C., Sharpe, S., & Thomson, R. (1996) In the Same Boat? The Gendered (In)Experience of First Heterosex. In: Richardson, D. (Ed.), *Theorizing Heterosexuality*. Open University Press, Buckingham.

Holland, J., Ramazanoğlu, C., Sharpe, S., & Thomson, R. (1998) *The Male in the Head*. Tufnell Press, London.

Ingraham, C. (1999) *White Weddings: Romancing Heterosexuality in Popular Culture*. Routledge, New York.

Ingraham, C. (Ed.) (2004) *Thinking Straight: The Power, the Promise and the Paradox of Heterosexuality*. Routledge, New York.

Jackson, S. (1999) *Heterosexuality in Question*. Sage, London.

Jeffreys, S. (1990) *Anti-Climax: A Feminist Critique of the Sexual Revolution*. Women's Press, London.

Katz, J. N. (1995) *The Invention of Heterosexuality*. Dutton, New York.

Rich, A. (1980) Compulsory Heterosexuality and Lesbian Existence. *Signs* 5(4): 631–60.

Richardson, D. (Ed.) (1996) *Theorizing Heterosexuality*. Open University Press, Buckingham.

Rubin, G. (1984) Thinking Sex: Notes for a Radical Theory of the Politics of Sexuality. In: Vance, C. (Ed.), *Pleasure and Danger*. Routledge, London.

Segal, L. (1994) *Straight Sex: The Politics of Pleasure*. Virago, London.

Seidman, S. (Ed.) (1996) *Queer Theory/Sociology*. Blackwell, Oxford.

Seidman, S. (1997) *Difference Troubles: Queering Social Theory and Sexual Politics*. Cambridge University Press, Cambridge.

Tolman, D. L. (2002) *Dilemmas of Desire*. Harvard University Press, Cambridge, MA.

Wilkinson, S. & Kitzinger, C. (Eds.) (1993) *Heterosexuality: A "Feminism and Psychology" Reader*. Sage, London.

Wittig, M. (1992) *The Straight Mind and Other Essays*. Harvester Wheatsheaf, Hemel Hempstead.

hidden curriculum

Laura Hamilton and Brian Powell

The hidden curriculum refers to the unofficial rules, routines, and structures of schools through which students learn behaviors, values, beliefs, and attitudes. Elements of the hidden curriculum do not appear in schools' written goals, formal lesson plans, or learning objectives although they may reflect culturally dominant social values and ideas about what schools should teach. Of the three major approaches to the hidden curriculum, the functionalist orientation is most concerned with how hidden curricula reproduce unified societies, the conflict perspective focuses on the reproduction of stratified societies, and symbolic interactionism more fully incorporates interactional context to our understanding of the hidden curriculum.

Because of its focus on education as a tool in maintaining orderly societies and producing appropriately socialized individuals, functionalist works are often collected under the label of consensus theory. Consensus theory depicts schools as benign institutions that rationally sort and order individuals in order to fill high and low status positions, meeting society's need for both experts and low-skilled workers. As a concept, the hidden curriculum has its roots in Émile Durkheim's *Education and Sociology* (1922) and *Moral Education* (1925). Durkheim concluded that society could not function without a high degree of homogeneity and that education, as a highly regulated institution, could provide this level of similarity. Drawing upon Durkheim's work, Philip Jackson in *Life in Classrooms* (1968) coined the term "hidden curriculum." Along with other consensualist theorists of that period, he noted that British and American schools teach children to sacrifice autonomy, control, and attention to those with more power, repress their own personal identity and desires, and accept the legitimacy of being treated as a category along with others.

Although the concept of the hidden curriculum originated in the functionalist works of Durkheim, conflict theorists further developed theoretical concepts of the hidden curriculum. In general, conflict theorists argue that education serves to preserve the social class structure. Early challenges to the functionalist approach came from Neo-Marxist theorists who suggested that schooling serves the demands of more powerful social institutions and groups. In their influential work *Schooling in Capitalist America*, Samuel Bowles and Herbert Gintis (1976) contended that students are educated in ways that make them suitable for varying levels of ownership, autonomy, and control in the capitalist system. They learn skills, develop a consciousness, and internalize norms that suit their future work. This connection between the social relations of school life and the social relations of production was labeled the correspondence principle. Theories that rely on the correspondence principle are also known as reproduction theories, as they explain how education reproduces social inequalities.

Reproduction theories, however, faced criticism in the early 1980s as some conflict theorists pushed for a less deterministic view of education's role in maintaining the class system. In *Learning to Labor*, Paul Willis (1981) introduced the concept of resistance to reproduction theories. He found that the working-class English boys in his study resisted both the official and hidden curriculums of their secondary schools. Although resistance had the effect of channeling the boys into working-class futures, the idea of resistance loosened the rigid theoretical approach to the hidden curriculum. The concept of resistance allowed conflict theorists to see the hidden curriculum as contestable and perhaps malleable.

Similar to the conflict approach, symbolic interactionists who address the hidden curriculum see education as sorting students by their ascribed characteristics into stratified social positions. However, the symbolic interactionist approach shifts the focal point to a micro level, looking at how face-to-face interactions in the classroom contribute to the creation and maintenance of inequalities. Symbolic interactionists are most concerned with how classroom dynamics create patterned advantages and disadvantages and how academic interactions mold students' personalities, skills, and behaviors.

Early work in the symbolic interactionist tradition noted that certain students are labeled as "good learners" while others are seen as "troublemakers" and that these labels often corresponded to a student's race, class, or gender. Regardless of their previous ability level, negatively labeled students are more likely to perform poorly while positively labeled students are more likely to perform well. The labeling process therefore creates what Merton called the self-fulfilling prophecy; students internalize the labels assigned to them and learn to behave in ways that match their labels. More recent work in the symbolic interactionist tradition has extended the focus from labeling to examine other ways in which teachers mold students' bodies, behaviors, and attitudes. They also recognize the importance of peer interactions, the physical environment, and teachers' interactions with each other and the administration.

While the functionalist approach assumes a consensual relationship between schools and societies, both the conflict and symbolic interactionist approaches see educational processes as creating and perpetuating social inequalities. These two approaches illustrate how class, race, and gender identities are produced and how these markers are used to privilege some students over others. Nevertheless, scholars disagree over the extent to which class, race, and gender differences are intensified as a result of the hidden curriculum. This dissensus is due in part to the variability of hidden curricula over time, place, location, and interaction context and in part to the difficulty of studying and measuring a curriculum that is not explicitly stated.

Some scholars posit that the hidden curricula carry powerful class – based and race – based messages. Pierre Bourdieu and Basil Berstein, for example, suggest that schools also create social environments that better match with the class backgrounds of middle and upper class students. Through the hidden curriculum, students get the message that middle and upper class cultural values, norms, and attitudes are the standard by which all else is measured. Schools reward conformity to these cultural norms and certify certain methods of learning as the standard. These learning methods are likely to better match middle and upper class styles of interaction and penalize lower or working class students. Physical spaces can also be marked by class, making some students more at home than others. The marking of space is particularly salient at higher levels of schooling: the physical environments in institutions that produce elite members of society such as law or medical schools are often tailored to the cultural norms and tastes of the advantaged.

To the extent that the hidden, and formal, curriculum is geared to the white majority, it is possible that the hidden curriculum inadvertently encourages, in the words of John Ogbu, an "oppositional culture." He argued that racial minorities with a history of enslavement, conquest, or colonization come to see academic achievement and participation in the dominant culture as a threat to group identity and loyalty. Oppositional culture can be considered part of the hidden curriculum as involuntary minorities learn through school that academic success is "acting white." The theory of oppositional culture, however, has been challenged by Douglas Downey and James Ainsworth Darnell among others who find that minorities place just as much if not more value on academic success than do their white peers and that oppositional culture is a class- not race-based phenomenon.

Some scholars contend that the hidden curriculum – again in tandem with the formal curriculum – creates and supports gender differentiation. Some scholars have noted that starting in kindergarten, teachers use gender dichotomies that mark and make gender difference salient, using gender groupings to address students, separate them, and create adversarial groups in competitions. There is also some evidence that teachers respond differently to girls and boys. For example, some studies indicate that since boys are often more disruptive than girls in elementary classroom, they are given greater positive and negative attention while girls are left to their own devices. Teacher practices also may affect how girls and boys learn to move in their bodies, teaching girls to take up less space, react passively to threats, regulate movements and speech at higher levels, and place greater value on body adornment than boys. Other scholars have suggested that teachers' beliefs regarding sex differences in math, science, and verbal aptitude may influence their teaching practices and in turn students' performance and interest in different topics. In addition, the content of textbooks and lesson plans in which males are more represented than are females arguably may shape boys and girls' views regarding their own abilities as well as their ambitions.

Research on gender and the hidden curriculum has indicated that peer culture is one of the most influential ways in which gendered behaviors are encouraged and perpetuated. Early on, children also segregate by gender, maintaining cross-gender boundaries through romantic teasing. Studies indicate that boys achieve high status in middle and secondary schools on the basis of their athletic ability, coolness, toughness, social skills, and success in cross-gender relationships while girls gain popularity because of their parents' socioeconomic status, their own physical appearance, and social skills. These values also may be transmitted through extracurricular activities, most notably the greater financial support typically given to male sports.

Social markers such as class, race, and gender are not only salient within the hidden curricula of education systems. They also reflect forms of hierarchy and differentiation that exist in other societal institutions. In fact, what theorists now see as the hidden curriculum of social control in the United States was once part of the explicit mission of education. This curriculum only became "hidden" as discussion of education shifted to increasingly individualistic terms. Although scholarship of the past few decades has unearthed this hidden curriculum, we still know little about how hidden curricula enter, change, and move out of schools. Moreover, other institutions (e.g., family, medicine, religion, and economy) intersect and shape both the formal and informal curricula of schools. Studying how the hidden curriculum is embedded within these contexts could lead to more informative and potentially transforming scholarship.

SEE ALSO: Cultural Capital in Schools; Differential Treatment of Children by Sex; Educational Inequality; Extracurricular Activities; Gender, Education and; Race and Schools; Self-Fulfilling Prophecy; Stratification: Functional and Conflict Theories; Teaching and Gender

REFERENCES AND SUGGESTED READINGS

Bourdieu, P. & Passeron, J. (1977) *Reproduction in Education, Society, and Culture*. Sage, Beverly Hills.
Bowles, S. & Gintis, H. (1976) *Schooling in Capitalist America*. Carnegie Foundation, New York.
Giroux, H. & Purpel, D. (Eds.) *The Hidden Curriculum and Moral Education*. McCutchan, Berkeley.
Jackson, P. W. (1968) *Life in Classrooms*. Rinehart & Winston, New York.
Sadker, M. & Sadker, S. (1994) *Failing at Fairness: How American Schools Cheat Our Girls*. Charles Scribner's Sons, New York.

hierarchical linear models

J. Kyle Roberts

The history of hierarchical linear modeling (also called multilevel modeling) can be linked to the seminal work of Robinson (1950) in recognizing contextual effects. The theory that

Robinson illustrated is also sometimes referred to as the "frog/pond" theory and bears discussion here. Suppose that a biologist has two frogs lying on an examination table that both weigh 500 grams and are both 1 year old. Consider further that Frog A was drawn from Pond A where it was the largest 1-year-old frog in the pond, and Frog B was drawn from Pond B where it was the smallest 1-year-old frog in the pond. The possible disregard of the contextual effect of the frogs' habitat could lead to some erroneous conclusions about frog development if the two frogs were considered outside of the pond from which they were drawn.

Placing this same contextual argument in educational terms, let us suppose that a researcher is interested in monitoring reading proficiency among students within New Mexico's schools. In testing differences among the schools, the researcher might use an analysis of variance (or ANOVA) to test for differences between mean reading proficiency scores across schools. As was noted with the frog/pond illustration, doing so would neglect the fact that some of the schools closer to the border of Mexico might have a larger number of non-English-speaking students. Neglecting this structure might lead a researcher to assume that a school is doing poorly in reading education, when in fact that school might be doing a superb job given the make-up of students that attend that school.

The strength of the hierarchical linear model (HLM) is that it capitalizes on these contextual effects and models data analysis such that the effect of grouping structures can be included as an integral component of the analysis. Since hierarchical linear modeling may be regarded as an extension of the general linear model (GLM), it subsumes most statistical techniques like ANOVA (see above), analysis of covariance (ANCOVA; comparing group means on a dependent variable after controlling for a covariate), multivariate analysis of variance (MANOVA; comparing group means on multiple dependent variables), regression, and canonical correlation. The advantage of HLM over simple regression or ANOVA is that it allows the researcher to look at hierarchically structured data and interpret results without ignoring these structures.

The structure of data within an HLM design is relatively straightforward. Sometimes referred to as nesting, the structure of an HLM data set is defined when data at the lowest level of the hierarchy are organized inside higher levels that are considered to determine the context of the lower-level responses. Consider the following examples of hierarchical data sets: students nested within classrooms, students nested within schools, students nested within classrooms nested within schools (3 levels), people nested within districts nested within states, measurement occasions nested within subjects (repeated measures), students cross-classified by school and neighborhood, students having multiple membership within schools across time (longitudinal data), and children nested inside families. Each of these examples illustrates data that are considered hierarchical in structure. Data derived from such hierarchical designs may be correlated based on the context from which they are drawn, and any subsequent analysis must take this into account.

The structure of a hierarchical linear model looks surprisingly similar to a regression format. Let us suppose that we have a data set in which we are trying to predict the amount of delinquency in children based on student GPAs. If we were to consider this model in a normal regression setting, we would simply place all of our students in a single data set and then make generalities about the relative contribution of GPA in explaining child delinquency. As any good sociologist knows, this model could have surprisingly different outcomes based on the type of school in which the data are collected. Let us use the state of Texas as a test case. In rural west Texas, it would be surprising to find any relationship between GPA and delinquency. With graduating classes sometimes approaching the teens, generally all of the students of the same age in these small rural towns are involved in the same activities and would have similar levels of delinquency (if delinquency can even be measured in these areas). Contrast this school to an inner-city low-SES school in one of the four large metropolitan areas in Texas. In this school, it may well be that student GPA is a very good predictor of child delinquency. Although this is probably not the most robust of analyses, it does help prove a point: the ability of HLM to consider context could prove paramount in studies where social settings differ between samples.

So just how does HLM do this? Answering this question would take multiple volumes, and is not the point of this entry. However, a quick answer is merited. Conceptually, HLM honors the nesting structure of a data set by simultaneously performing multiple analyses based on the grouping variable. For example, suppose that the above example of GPA and delinquency was performed for 100 students housed in eight different schools. In the first step of HLM we would perform a regression for each school in which we used GPA to predict child delinquency. After this was done, we would have eight slopes and eight intercepts for each of the eight schools. Through maximum likelihood procedures we would then produce a weighted least-squares average of the eight intercepts to produce a fixed intercept value (also called the grand estimate for the intercept). Through the same procedures, we would produce a weighted average fixed slope. These estimates can be thought of as the "average" intercept and slope for the combination of the eight schools. We can then use these fixed estimates to go back and reestimate the corrected slopes and intercepts for individual schools based on empirical Bayesian procedures. These are called the random estimates. What we now have are grand estimates that give us information about what is going on in all schools simultaneously, and the random estimates for each school. This can be very helpful, as in the case of delinquency, for examining which schools are performing at different levels from other schools. Furthermore, we have moved beyond asking "Are the schools different?" to "Why are the schools different?"

SEE ALSO: ANOVA (Analysis of Variance); General Linear Model; Multivariate Analysis

REFERENCES AND SUGGESTED READINGS

Goldstein, H. (2003) *Multilevel Statistical Methods.* 3rd edn. Edward Arnold, London.

Hox, J. (2002) *Multilevel Analysis: Techniques and Applications.* Erlbaum, Mahwah, NJ.

Kreft, I. I. & de Leeuw, J. (1998) *Introducing Multilevel Modeling.* Sage, London.

Raudenbush, S. W. & Bryk, A. S. (2002) *Hierarchical Linear Models: Applications and Data Analysis Methods*, 2nd edn. Sage, Thousand Oaks, CA.

Robinson, W. S. (1950) Ecological Correlations and the Behavior of Individuals. *Sociological Review* 15: 351–7.

Snijders, T. & Bosker, R. (1999) *Multilevel Analysis: An Introduction to Basic and Advanced Multilevel Modeling.* Sage, Thousand Oaks, CA.

high school sports

C. Roger Rees

High school sports, arguably the most popular extracurricular activity in American schools, have been inextricably linked to the ideology of modernity. Conventional wisdom has it that participants in interscholastic athletics learn educational skills necessary for success in higher education and positive cultural values upon which they can draw as they develop into productive and well-balanced adults. In short, there is widespread public faith that participation in sports "builds character" in the broadest sense of the term. This faith has, for the most part, remained unshaken despite three decades of sociological research from diverse theoretical perspectives that has produced mixed findings about the effects of interscholastic athletic participation.

The belief that sport played a positive role in the character formation of students originated when organized sports were first developed in the private boarding schools of nineteenth-century Britain. In these schools a cult of athleticism formed the basis of the muscular Christian movement through which the sons (but not the daughters) of the upper-middle class learned "manly" characteristics of leadership, courage, fair play, and patriotism through competitive sports. This movement also developed in the elite boarding schools of New England, which adopted a similar athletic curriculum to their British counterparts, and the value of sports as a socializing agent became "democratized" by the Playground Movement, the Young Men's Christian Association, and the Public School Athletic League. By the second decade of the twentieth century the belief that school sport could be used to "socialize" students into positive academic and social values was institutionalized.

Contemporary proponents of school sports suggest that athletics is a positive influence on the formal education of students. They claim that participation in sports develops skills such as drive and determination, a positive self-concept, and self-confidence that are useful in the workplace. Sport increases high school athletes' positive attitudes towards the school, their academic aspirations and achievement, and provides them with opportunities to further their education at college. For less academically inclined students, sport provides the motivation to stay in school and therefore reduces the school dropout rate. Critics of school sport see it as part of a Faustian bargain between teachers and students, particularly students who are not academically motivated, by which sport provides the excitement to compensate for boring and irrelevant classes. Ethnically diverse students from different social strata can find unity in the drive for athletic victory against a common enemy symbolized by other schools. Because of their prominence in this struggle, athletes become the school leaders glorifying masculine values of achievement and aggression, and modeling a simplistic social Darwinist philosophy stressing survival of the fittest (although critics would say survival of the most belligerent) that legitimizes the status quo. Sport helps the school to reproduce the existing status hierarchy in society instead of providing students the skills and motivation to challenge it.

True to historically positivist traditions, research on school sports has examined the success of sport in providing athletes with skills necessary for future success. The relationship between athletics and academic success has been a popular research theme in this endeavor. Believers in the educational value of high school athletics argue that athletes have to practice efficient time-management skills because of the time constraints imposed by school athletics, and that the self-esteem supposedly gained from sports can transfer to academics. To support such claims they can point to research showing that athletes have similar or higher grade point averages than non-athletes, and to more recent results from longitudinal research showing that participation has a small positive effect on grades and on dropout rates. Skeptics suggest that this "athletic effect" is part of a larger selection

process, since athletes tend to come from socio-economically advanced backgrounds typical of students with higher grades. Also, they could be graded more leniently than non-athletes, could benefit from special tutoring, or take easy courses in order to remain academically eligible to play.

Disagreement over the positive and negative effects of sport has also characterized the research on the relationship between participation and "delinquent" behavior by high school athletes. Approaches based on functionalist theory depict involvement as having a deterrent or reform effect by providing a system of rules and a code of behavior that gives athletes a positive sense of direction and a legitimate means of achieving their goals. Critical perspectives highlight the power of "the sports ethic" to reinforcing "positive deviance" in which athletes attach so much importance to team victory that they will do whatever it takes to win, even if it means taking performance enhancing substances or injuring their opponents on purpose. Longitudinal research has also examined the relationship between participation and the recreational behavior of athletes outside sport, including "risky" behavior such as binge drinking and sexual activity. As before, the results have been mixed. For example, whereas female athletes reported lower rates of sexual experience and fewer partners than did non-athletes, the opposite was true for male athletes.

Clearly, the nature of the relationship between academics, delinquency, and school sports remains controversial. Although the longitudinal research has improved on the early cross-sectional research designs because it has been able to isolate athletic effects instead of just comparing athlete and non-athlete groups, it has not challenged the positivist assumptions that sport can help "fix" social problems such as lack of educational achievement or delinquency. The results of these studies need to be considered in conjunction with research that describes the relative importance of athletics and education in the social and cultural milieu of school life, and which examines sport as part of the "lived experience" of students. These studies tend to highlight the importance of high school sport to the social life of students and to place it at the center of the "hidden curriculum," the unofficial values system that students learn through informal interaction in extracurricular activities.

The issue of gender identity is a prominent theme here. Feminists have challenged the historically positivist assumptions behind the development of school sports through the assertion that sports have always been linked to the promotion of masculinity. The fear that males were becoming "feminized" led to the origination of school sports and to their contemporary popularity. Some sports are still seen as being suitable only for boys or for girls. For example, the defining characteristics of violence and aggression make football a "male" sport, whereas gymnastics with its emphasis on aesthetics is seen as a "feminine" sport. Such stereotyping supports an "oppositional" view of gender, and has negative repercussions for athletes who risk labels such as "fags" or "dikes" if they play sports that are not "appropriate" for their gender. The male "jock" identity is often constructed around dominant images of masculinity based on victory, physical power, and heterosexuality. The frequent location of male athletes at the top of the status hierarchy of the school and the characterization of them as "cool" by other groups means that boys from less "masculine" cliques sometimes include these macho characteristics in their own self-identities. Homophobia is also a common theme in the way male athletes treat females and in the content of hazing rituals by which entry to the team is unofficially "celebrated." It is not clear what effect if any the great increase in girls' participation in high school sport over the past 20 years is having on issues of masculinity and femininity. Critical feminists have argued that this increase has the potential for females to reduce the hypermasculine characteristics of high school athletics, but also that female sports run the risk of being coopted by the "male" model.

Race issues in high school sport are also controversial. Popular mythology sees sports as an ideal avenue for black youth to use their "natural" physical advantage over whites to gain athletic scholarships that allow them access to higher education and the long-term benefits of a college degree. However, most sociologists would reject the authenticity of a biological theory of race, and would consider this racial ideology to be a trap. Excelling at sport in high school is not a "way out of the ghetto" for the vast majority of African American males. Besides reinforcing the stereotype that all African American males live in ghettos in the first place, it marginalizes their academic credentials and encourages them to chase unrealistic "hoop dreams." The myth of genetic black athletic superiority also affects the sporting choices of white males who feel they are at a disadvantage when they compete in sports popular with African Americans. Negative racial ideology is also institutionalized in the naming of many high school mascots. Using caricatures of Native Americans trivializes their cultural heritage. Although the relationship between sports participation and ethnic identity in high school is understudied, current research calls into question the melting pot theory of high school sports. Sport can be used to reinforce ethnic identities, and can also be seen as a form of Anglo hegemony. For example, Doug Foley's (1990) study of Mexicanos in Texas high school football showed that involvement in sport was rejected by some working-class Mexicano males, and also that Mexicanos who did participate were generally marginalized. High school football perpetuated Anglo power and privilege in the community.

Given the powerful belief that "sport builds character," research will continue to address the question of whether or to what degree athletics experiences comprise a valuable investment for the future success of youth. However, there is no singular sports experience in American high schools, so research comparing the characteristics of "athletes" to non-athletes, or football players to swimmers, is likely to yield conflicting results. The power of sports to influence the life of students can be mediated by factors such as community and school traditions, past success, coaching philosophy, and the existence of an athlete identity. Accepting this reality means that future research should focus on in-depth studies of high school athletics interacting with the culture of the school and community and the identity dynamics associated with sport participation. This approach would provide insights into how students view their own racial and ethnic identity in relation to athletic participation and fill a gap in our knowledge, particularly with regard to female African American students. At the same time, the challenge for applied researchers interested in high school sports still remains how to help sport become more of a compassionate force in the social climate of the school and less of a haven for a jock culture that reinforces athletic elitism, hazing, bullying, and risky health practices such as binge drinking, steroid use, and extreme dieting. However, the excitement and controversy surrounding school sports is also "consumed" by the students and the public. Conceptualizing high school sport as a commodity stripped of functionalist assumptions about positive character development will increase among sociologists as the economics of big time sports (e.g., televising tournaments, naming rights for football fields and gymnasiums, expensive summer camps for elite players) become more prominent in high schools.

SEE ALSO: Gender, Sport and; Socialization and Sport; Sport; Sport, College; Sport and Race

REFERENCES AND SUGGESTED READINGS

Blackshaw, T. & Crabbe, T. (2004) *New Perspectives on Sport and 'Deviance': Consumption, Performativity and Social Control*. Routledge, London.

Foley, D. E. (1990) *Learning Capitalist Culture: Deep in the Heart of Tejas*. University of Philadelphia Press, Philadelphia.

Guest, A. & Schneider, B. (2003) Adolescents' Extracurricular Participation in Context: The Mediating Effects of Schools, Communities, and Identity. *Sociology of Education* 76(2): 89–109.

Joravsky, B. (1995) *Hoop Dreams: A True Story of Leadership and Triumph*. Harper Collins, New York.

Lesko, N. (2004) Act Your Age! A Cultural Construction of Adolescence. In: Ballentine, J. H. & Spade, J. Z. (Eds.), *Schools and Society*, 2nd edn. Thompson-Wadsworth, Belmont, CA, pp. 149–60.

Miller, K. E., Sabo, D. F., Farrell, M. P. et al. (1999) Sport, Sexual Behavior, Contraceptive Use, and Pregnancy Among Female and Male High School Students: Testing Cultural Resource Theory. *Sociology of Sport Journal* 16: 366–87.

Miracle, A. W. & Rees, C. R. (1994) *Lessons of the Locker Room: The Myth of School Sports*. Prometheus, Amherst, NY.

Pascoe, C. J. (2003) Multiple Masculinities? Teenage Boys Talk About Jocks and Gender. *American Behavioral Scientist* 46: 1423–38.

Rees, C. R. & Miracle, A. W. (2000) Education and Sports. In Coakley, J. & Dunning, E. (Eds.), *Handbook of Sports Studies*. Sage, London, pp. 277–90.

highbrow/lowbrow

David Halle

The distinction between "high culture" and "popular culture," or "highbrow" and "lowbrow," has underpinned most of the important debates about culture over the last 50 years in the US, Britain, and France especially, but also elsewhere. Theories of culture have tended either to presuppose this distinction or to debate various aspects of it. However, the nature of the debate has changed over time, and in particular the extent to which researchers and commentators are willing to stand by this distinction.

Partly this reflects the spread of higher education. Just after World War II there was a clear gap between an educated elite and the rest (only about 7 percent of the US population had a college degree) and it seemed plausible to talk about an elite of "highbrows" versus the rest. As a college degree became increasingly normal (held by over 25 percent of the US population these days) this education gap has faded, and so has the plausibility of maintaining that there are two radically different cultures, one pitched to an educated elite and the other pitched to the rest of the population. (The term "culture" itself is susceptible to many definitions, broad and narrow. Here I mostly use it in a fairly narrow sense to refer to the arts, namely literature, journalism, film, television, art, architecture, music, dance, and so on; but sometimes in the discussion below "culture" takes on a broader sense to include political beliefs, social attitudes, and religious beliefs.)

Four overall stages can be distinguished in the debates over "high/highbrow" and "popular/ mass culture." In the first stage, which flourished in the 1940s, 1950s, and 1960s, it was held that "highbrow" or "high culture" was unambiguously superior to "lowbrow" or "popular culture." From this perspective, "highbrow" culture was aesthetically rich and vital while "popular/lowbrow" culture was at best of little merit and at worst was harmful. "Popular/lowbrow" was often depicted as the standardized and homogenized products of large corporations who sold their wares to the unsophisticated "mass public." By contrast, "high/highbrow" culture was the product of the skilled artist or craftsman and was appreciated by an elite, cultured audience. For example, in 1939 Clement Greenberg stressed the superiority of avant-garde art over what he dismissed as "kitsch-infected" mass art. Theodore Adorno, in the tradition of the Frankfurt School of sociology, berated popular music such as jazz, writing that the culture industry rooted out all deviations and that jazz had achieved musical dictatorship "over the masses." In similar fashion, for about two decades after World War II the movies of Hollywood were typically denigrated by film critics (who were often based in New York City) as the epitome of commercial, mass culture and as the opposite of art, modernism, and New York City which, by contrast, was said to nurture serious, independent, and non-commercial filmmaking.

The second stage in the debates over "high" and "popular" culture began in the late 1950s and early 1960s when researchers, especially sociologists, undertook empirical studies of "popular/lowbrow" culture and of the associated audience. These studies often challenged, on empirical grounds, the earlier claims that the products of "popular/lowbrow" culture were of little or no aesthetic value and were experienced by the audience in an uncreative and unimaginative way. While not usually disputing the view that "high/highbrow" culture was aesthetically superior to "popular/lowbrow" culture, these studies typically argued that popular culture was not as bad as its critics had maintained. For example, Herbert Gans, in a classic 1967 account of Levittown, the large suburban housing development in New Jersey, chastised those who denigrated such new tract houses, and the suburban lifestyle of their working-class and middle-class inhabitants, as dull, homogenized, or lonely. Few of those who lived there experienced Levittown in that way, Gans insisted, although he added that he personally considered that urban life was aesthetically and culturally richer

than that of these suburbs. Seven years later in an influential comparative account of culture, Gans defended popular culture in general against its most dismissive critics.

The third stage of the debates overlapped in time with the research of stage two and took the debates in a more radical turn, upending earlier aesthetic evaluations and arguing that "popular/lowbrow" culture is, in some respects at least, aesthetically superior to "high/highbrow culture." For example, in *Learning from Las Vegas* in 1968, the architects Robert Venturi and Denise Scott Brown insisted that architects could learn much from studying the buildings on the Las Vegas strip, a place that many "highbrow" critics would have dismissed as the epitome of popular, vulgar culture. Venturi and Scott Brown argued that popular Las Vegas architecture was doing exactly what the classical medieval cathedral, a paragon of high culture, did, namely revealing from the shape of the building the function and activities that went on inside. The casinos of LasVegas were designed so that viewers could recognize, from a considerable distance, not only that the building was a casino but also the nature of the fantasy that customers could experience within. For example, the shimmering black glass pyramid of the Luxor showed that this was a casino decorated in a patina of classical Egypt. Venturi and Scott Brown argued that such architecture was engaging and refreshingly superior to the dreary glass and steel boxes that the "highbrow" School of International Architecture had been building for decades. These anonymous boxes, the design of which dominated the curriculum of elite architecture schools, gave the viewer no inkling of what went on within the building. A similarly radical claim about the merits of popular culture was made by the Pop Art movement of the 1960s and beyond, which celebrated the aesthetic qualities of mass-produced modern objects. The success of Pop Art legitimized the status of these objects as art, underlined by the installation of many of its works in the citadels of high culture. Thus, Claes Oldenburg's 10-foot high sculptural representations of a slice of blueberry pie on a scoop of ice cream (installed on the roof of the Museum of Modern Art) and his monumental lipstick sculpture (installed at Yale), and Andy Warhol's depictions of such products as Campbell's soup, forced those who would denigrate mass culture not only to take a closer look, but to consider the possibility that the products of "mass culture" might in some ways be more interesting than those associated with "high culture."

Also part of this third stage's radical challenge to the established aesthetic hierarchies is the work of the French sociologist Pierre Bourdieu, who argued in his book *Distinction* in 1979 that the driving force of culture had less to do with aesthetics and more to do with struggles for power between social classes. For Bourdieu, the "dominant class" (or classes) use high culture, which is often difficult to understand for those lacking higher education or upbringing in a dominant-class family, in order to exclude members of the dominated class(es) from positions of power and privilege. Individuals from the dominated classes, lacking a facility in high culture, which Bourdieu calls "cultural capital," are on that basis kept out of the dominant class-cultural rituals of social solidarity (the opera, ballet, etc.) and by that method are kept out of the dominant class even if they have managed to acquire significant economic assets. By arguing that high culture is at base about struggles for power between social classes, Bourdieu undermines its claims to intrinsic aesthetic superiority.

The fourth stage in the debate over "high culture" versus "mass culture" is more radical still, for it questions whether the basic distinction between one category of items that can be assigned as "high/highbrow culture" and another category than can be classified as "popular/lowbrow" is justifiable on any major grounds, not just aesthetic, at least as a basis for social theories that seek to lay out the main contours of modern society. This fourth stage, in short, seeks to dissolve the key terms in the "high culture/mass culture" debate and in so doing to dissolve the debate itself. Beginning in the late 1980s, researchers such as Paul DiMaggio and David Halle point out that surveys reveal that almost everyone, highly educated or not, is involved with at least some of the activities and products often designated as "popular culture." It remains true that some activities associated with "high culture" (e.g., attending the ballet, opera, or classical music concerts) are confined to a smaller group of people, who tend to be very well educated, but these same people for the most part engage in the popular activities too. Further, any exclusionary function that "high culture" performed in the past has been decreasing for some time, as the institutional world of culture is less and less willing to insist on sharp boundaries between social classes and cultural worlds. Thus, it is noteworthy that contemporary theorists such as George Ritzer, Sharon Zukin, and Terry Clark, who stress the importance of the "consumer/shopping society," the "commercialization of leisure," and the tendency of cities to become "entertainment machines," usually argue that almost everyone is caught up in these phenomena.

Although in the past the analysis of culture has thrived on some version of the distinction between "high/highbrow" and "popular/lowbrow" culture, it increasingly seems as though major cultural theorists will now have to look for their inspiration elsewhere than to this supposed divide. That is not to deny that aesthetic distinctions can be made (though they need to be justified with extreme care), that tastes vary somewhat with such factors as education, or that these distinctions may have more salience and staying power in some societies (e.g., France) than others (e.g., the US). But it is to question whether aesthetic distinctions and taste differences are sufficiently clear cut as to provide the basis on which can be constructed major sociopolitical theories of cultural difference and distinction.

SEE ALSO: Culture; Distinction; Elite Culture; Popular Culture; Taste, Sociology of

REFERENCES AND SUGGESTED READINGS

DiMaggio, P. (1987) Classification in Art. *American Sociological Review* 52: 440–55.
Gans, H. (1967) *The Levittowners*. Pantheon, New York.
Gans, H. (1999) *Popular Culture and High Culture: An Analysis and Evaluation of Taste*. Basic Books, New York.
Halle, D. (1993) *Inside Culture*. University of Chicago Press, Chicago.
Horkheimer, M. & Adorno, T. (1972) The Culture Industry: Enlightenment as Mass Deception. In: *Dialectic of Enlightenment*, trans. J. Cummings. Herder & Herder, New York.

Lamont, M. & Thévenot, L. (Eds.) (2000) *Rethinking Comparative Cultural Sociology*. Cambridge University Press, Chicago.

Ritzer, G. (1999) *Enchanting a Disenchanted World: Revolutionizing the New Means of Consumption*. Pine Forge Press, Thousand Oaks, CA.

Saverio, G. (2003) Hollywood is a State of Mind: New York Film Culture and the Lure of Los Angeles from 1930 to the Present. In: D. Halle (Ed.), *New York and Los Angeles: Politics, Society and Culture, a Comparative Approach*. University of Chicago Press, Chicago.

Venturi, R., Scott Brown, D., & Izenour, S. (1978) *Learning from Las Vegas: The Forgotten Symbolism of Architectural Form*. MIT Press, Cambridge, MA.

Zukin, S. (2003) *Point of Purchase: How Shopping Changed American Culture*. Routledge, New York.

high-speed transportation pollution

Koichi Hasegawa

High-speed transportation pollution refers to a type of environmental pollution consisting of high levels of noise, vibration, and air pollution brought about by high-speed transportation systems such as the airplane and airport, the "bullet" (super-express) train, or the traffic expressway. These disturbances cause damage to daily life such as sleep deprivation or the disturbance of conversation at home, as well as stress-related health issues like heart disease or gastrointestinal disease. Bullet trains, jet airplanes, and high-speed expressways are essential to highly industrialized modern urban life. They are basic conditions for developing efficient modern economies, greatly reducing the time and cost of moving goods and people over large distances. In most countries, high-speed transportation pollution is serious along the train line, the expressway, or the area surrounding the airport. It is especially serious in metropolitan areas and in high population density countries like Japan.

In many ways, high-speed transportation pollution is quite distinct from industrial pollution. At first glance, the impact on the environment for each flight, bullet train service, or individual automobile on the expressway looks inconsequential. It comes and goes away very quickly, at most within a few minutes. But an airplane takes off every several minutes at a major airport, and in the case of Japan's Tokaido line, a bullet train passes through every several minutes. They keep coming every day, including holidays, from early morning to the middle of the night (for the airport and bullet train) or all day and night (for the expressway). The cumulative effect is very great. In fact, as the number of flights and trains rapidly increased in response to growing demand, the pollution from bullet trains and jet planes became serious social problems.

For many years planners, engineers, suppliers, and administrators of the transportation system focused only on the "benefit sphere": the speed, safety, convenience for passengers or drivers, economy of the system, and economic effect for the surrounding area. They overlooked the "negative" environmental effects for local residents neighboring the transportation system. Effective regulation of the environmental effects only came about with the starting of protest movements and the coming of serious social issues.

In some cases of industrial pollution or daily life pollution, determining cause and effect is not always simple. But in most cases of high-speed transportation pollution, the cause is usually obvious: we feel the noise and vibration. Despite the obviousness, planners, suppliers, and passengers tend to miss the negative effects. The principles of remedy or countermeasure are very clear – making the polluter pay (the PPP or polluter-pays principle) and fixing the problem at the point where it occurs. These are basic and relatively cheap principles. But in Japan, the government administration and the railway companies tended to reject these principles.

In Japan, during the years of rapid economic growth in the early 1970s, high-speed transportation pollution, especially in the high-density areas of large metropolises, became a central issue for local residents' movements. This was because the national government tried to continue high economic growth by constructing many jet airports, bullet train lines, and expressways. This special social background at that time made high-speed transportation pollution into a major nationwide social problem.

Representative examples of these protest movements include movements to rectify the Osaka Airport pollution problem; oppose the construction of Narita Airport; rectify the Nagoya bullet train pollution problem; oppose the construction of the Tohoku and Joetsu bullet train lines in Saitama Prefecture and northern Tokyo; and oppose the construction of the Yokohama cargo line. In all of these cases, large groups of residents rapidly and successfully organized a powerful local residents' movement that remained active for a long time.

Each of these cases had a significant impact on subsequent local residents' movements, transportation policy, and the judicial system. The Nagoya bullet train Pollution Response Alliance organized 2,000 households residing within about 7km of the train line. The anti-bullet train movement in Urawa demanded that the line be built underground and at its peak could mobilize about 4,000 people to a mass rally (Funabashi et al. 1985, 1988). In other cases, groups of plaintiffs were organized from local residents' movements. For example, litigation over the pollution produced by Osaka Airport and the Nagoya bullet train line sought the suspension or prohibition of airplanes and trains to reduce the environmental damage.

Alongside the litigation over the four major industrial pollution cases, these cases helped to establish a kind of class-action lawsuit as an effective strategy for local residents' and citizens' movements, but also exposed the limited capacity of the judicial system to provide relief. Legal action by local residents' movements seeking redress against industrial pollution principally indicted the interest-seeking behavior of private firms, accrediting responsibility to them. In contrast, in the airport and railway cases mentioned above, the movements targeted the Ministry of Transportation and the public bodies in charge of designing and running the national railroads and airports, criticizing them for their refusal to accept responsibility for the harm they were causing or to implement effective policies to prevent noise pollution, and for their continuing defense of their destructive behavior in the name of "the public."

Here, the government actors/perpetrators responded to the residents/victims with attitudes and tactics that were chillingly similar to the corporations' responses to accusations of industrial pollution. The government and public agencies defined "the public good" according to the social benefit produced by public works and related projects. They used this benefit to justify the behavior of public authorities, to proceed with project construction, and to restrict private rights to reduce (or avoid) the resulting damage and harm.

Residents criticized the authoritarian and oppressive tone of this conceptualization of "the public." They argued that the public good ought to be defined through democratic processes, including a complete prohibition on any violation of fundamental human rights. They demanded, before any large projects proceeded, the informed consent of residents in surrounding areas through direct participation in the decision-making processes.

High-speed transportation pollution is just one example of the unintended but harmful pollution caused by transportation technology. As mass consumer society becomes increasingly technological, the environmental problems caused by the new technologies extend well beyond noise and vibration into new areas like destruction of the ozone layer by CFCs.

SEE ALSO: Daily Life Pollution; Local Residents' Movements; Pollution Zones, Linear and Planar

REFERENCES AND SUGGESTED READINGS

Funabashi, H., Hasegawa, K., Hatanaka, S., & Katsuta, H. (1985) *Shinkansen Kogai: Kosoku Bunmei no Shakai Mondai* (Bullet Train Pollution: Social Problems of a High Speed Civilization). Yuhikaku, Tokyo.

Funabashi, H., Hasegawa, K., Hatanaka, S., & Kajita, T. (1988) *Kosoku Bunmei no Chiiki Mondai: Tohoku Shinkansen no Kensetsu, Funso to Shakaiteki Eikyo* (Regional Problems of a High Speed Civilization: The Dispute over Construction of the Tohoku Bullet Train Line and Its Social Impacts). Yuhikaku, Tokyo.

Hasegawa, K. (2004) *Constructing Civil Society in Japan: Voices of Environmental Movements*. Pacific Press, Melbourne.

Hinduism

T. N. Madan

Use of the English term "Hinduism" (and its equivalents in various European languages) to designate certain aspects of the cultural traditions of Hindus anywhere is commonplace, but it is relatively recent and not wholly unproblematic. The idea that the Hindus must have a "religion" comparable to Christianity and worthy of study originated with British administrators and scholars in India in the last quarter of the eighteenth century. These scholars, known as the Orientalists, devoted themselves to the study and translation of textual materials, mainly in Sanskrit, some of which they identified as religious and others as secular texts. By the time the British parliament allowed proselytization among the "natives" of India in 1813, the word Hinduism had come into use. Christian missionaries also devoted themselves to the study of religious texts and the observation of religious practices, but unlike the admiring Orientalists their primary aim was to expose the "wickedness" of polytheistic and idolatrous religions and to highlight the "perfection" of Christianity.

The problematic aspect of these studies, often laudable for their reliability and detail, was the basic assumption that the Hindus had a religion which, however, was curiously deficient in significant ways given the absence of most notably, a founder, a single revealed text, and a church-like organization. But that the Hindus were a community of faith, united by a common religion, Hinduism, was considered unquestionable. The widespread use of the Hindu term *dharma* (*dharma* literally means "moral law," "that which sustains" the social order) in Indian languages, at least from medieval times onward, was deemed sufficient terminological evidence for the historical authenticity of Hinduism. When the first census of the peoples of India under British control was conducted in 1872, classification by religion was considered an obvious objective. The Hindus emerged as the numerically preponderant community. Towards the end of the nineteenth century, when a national movement for some measure of self-governance under the British imperium began to take shape,

the notion of India-wide religions, respectively claiming the allegiance of millions, was further strengthened, despite some initial skepticism among intellectuals well-versed in the Hindu tradition on the ground that the religious–secular dichotomization of areas of life was alien to their way of thinking. Simultaneously with the emergence of the notion of monolithic Hindu and Muslim religious communities, officially enumerated and described, came the idea of mutually exclusive identities and religious nationalisms, that eventually led to the partition of the subcontinent in 1947.

At this point, it may be recalled that the term "Hindu," like Hinduism, is a foreign coinage from around the middle of the first millennium before the Christian era. The Persians and the Greeks identified the peoples of the plains of northwestern India in the name of the river called Sindhu in Sanskrit. Sindhu became Hindu in Persian and Indos in Greek. The Arabs appeared as conquerors in this area in the eighth century CE and called it al-Hind and the peoples thereof, al-Hindi. In the course of time a distinction came to be made between the Hindi, an ethno-geographical category and the Hindu, a religious category. By further elaboration Hindus were those Indians (and even peoples further east) who remained outside the Islamic fold. By medieval times "Hindu" was established as a term of self-designation and Hindu *dharma* also came into use. And, as noted above, Hindu *dharma* became Hinduism in the early nineteenth century.

The roots of Hinduism as we know it now go back to the belief and ritual complex, marked by nature worship, of immigrant Aryan-speaking peoples, who were the composers of the body of hymns and instructions on ritual performances collectively known as the *Veda* ("knowledge"). The earliest of these collections of "texts," transmitted orally, are about 3,200 years old and have over the millennia acquired the status of revealed scriptures. Some elements of Hinduism have been traced further back in time to the Harrappan civilization of 5,000 years ago. As the carriers of the Vedic cults proceeded east and south, a widespread and longlasting process of give and take (called by anthropologists "parochialization" and "universalization") between them and local communities of faith ("folk religions") began, producing immense regional varieties of belief and ritual and generating a vast body of post-Vedic texts known as the *Purana* ("legends") from around 300–600 CE. New gods and goddesses and the cults, cosmogonies, and mythologies associated with them proliferated. Mutually hostile sectarian divisions crystallized around some of the new deities (notably Shiva, Vishnu, and the female Devi). These immense diversities rule out any notions of a linear development of Hinduism or of a subcontinentally homogeneous religious community. It must be noted, however, that efforts have also been made for a long time to overcome these diversities. A daring young intellectual and renouncer of South India, Shankara (ca. 788–820), instituted a non-sectarian form of domestic worship (*smarta puja*), combining devotion to Shiva, Vishnu, Devi, and other deities, and traveled to the far corners of India to stress the unity and sacredness of the land through pilgrimage and to propagate a monistic philosophy of the oneness of the divine or Absolute and the human in its true essence. This and other philosophies are known as *Vedanta*, the culmination of the Veda, or the ultimate true knowledge. The earliest of the Vedantic texts, concerned with metaphysical issues and known as the *Upanishad* (secret knowledge), are believed to have been composed about the same time as the birth of Buddhism and Jainism (around the middle of the first millennium BCE), which were the first major heresies, so judged by the Brahmans, the teachers and practitioners of the Vedic religion. These ritual specialists were the most privileged of the categories of people who constituted Vedic society.

SOCIAL ORGANIZATIONAL FRAMEWORK

One of the hymns in the *Rig Veda* mentions the birth of four major social categories of human beings, and indeed the whole cosmos, from the self-sacrificial dismemberment of the divine "primeval man." From his mouth came the Brahman, knower and teacher of sacred knowledge; the Rajanya (or Kshatriya), warriors, and protectors of the realm, were his arms; the Vaishya, working people, his thighs; and the Shudra, providers of services to the other categories, his feet. Besides the division of labor that they embodied, the four *varnas*, so-called, were ranked, the Brahman downward, in terms of ritual status and social privilege, but in a holistic framework. Over the long duration, the fourfold *varna* order became the caste (from the Dutch *casta*) order comprising numerous *jatis* through a variety of processes including inter-*varna* marriages, incorporation of outsiders, and fusion or fission of existing groups. In principle, however, the caste system is based on hereditary membership within a *jati*, endogamy, and the inheritance of occupation and ritual status. Consequently, the caste system is, at least in theory, the most rigid social order conceivable. It is a mirror image, as it were, of the looseness (liberalism) of the belief and ritual complexes that characterize Hinduism in its regional and sectarian diversities. In view of this, some sociologists have suggested that the unity of Hindu society rests not in Hinduism but in its social organization.

Indologists (specialists of classical texts) have long described Hinduism as *varna-ashrama dharma*, the morally grounded way of life appropriate to one's *varna* or *jati* and one's *ashrama*. The latter stands for stage of life, of which four are recognized: the preparatory stage of studentship, householdership, retirement, and finally renunciation of all worldly engagements. The renouncers (not all of them may have gone through all the earlier stages) turn their back on caste rules as well as family obligations. In textual Hinduism the three upper *varnas* (referred to as *dvija*, the twice-born, in view of the rites of initiation through which everyone must ideally pass) are guided by a grammar of value orientations (*purushartha*). Hierarchically ranked, these values are *dharma* (grounding in moral law), *artha* (rational pursuit of economic and political goals), and *kama* (aesthetic enjoyment and physical pleasure). The fourth value orientation, *moksha* (liberation), is the alternative to the first three taken together. It should be clarified that in a householder's life, being grounded in *dharma* acquires meaning through the pursuit of *artha* and *kama*; but *kama* must not violate the dictates of *artha* and *dharma*, and *artha*, of *dharma*. The renouncers who seek liberation from the web of kinship and other social obligations do not necessarily go out of society altogether: they may return awakened, as the Buddha did, and found new sects, some of which (most notably

Buddhism, Jainism, and Sikhism) blossom in the course of time into full religions. Social involvement and renunciation are not necessarily mutually exclusive: their relationship is dialectical and socially creative. The preoccupation of sociological literature with caste and renunciation, presumably because of their unique character, has led to the grievous neglect of the empirical presence and ideological vigor of the householder as a key bearer of the values and rituals of Hinduism.

The householder, man or woman, is ever engaged in *karma*. In its narrower connotation *karma* is ritual action, but broadly *karma* stands for the full range of legitimate purposive action. *Karma* is the enactment of the triple goals of *purushartha*. Every *karmic* act has consequences (*karma-phala*), whether intended or (because of interferences or inadequacies) unintended. A chain of cause and effect is thus constructed; its most significant implication is the belief in reincarnation. *Samsara*, the web of worldly entanglements, is considered a bondage, and *moksha* is the release from it. In practical terms these beliefs do not mean withdrawal from all activity, but rather its pursuit according to *dharma*, so that the secular and the religious make up (at least in principle) one seamless whole, and in a spirit of detachment.

From conception to death and thereafter a Hindu's life is involved in a succession of rites of passage, including the rituals of birth, initiation, marriage, death, and post mortem offerings. These periodic household ceremonies, daily rituals for the well-being of the family (steps in a process of moral maturation) and of adoration (*puja*) of one's chosen deities, are a major preoccupation of all households. Pilgrimages to holy places (for example in the high mountains, at the confluence of rivers, or on the seashore) carry Hindus away from home. The precise content of these ritual performances varies from region to region and caste to caste. But there is more commonality in this respect between the upper ("twice-born") castes than among the lower, owing to a greater adherence to textual Hinduism in the case of the former and to folk traditions in the case of the latter. Sociological studies of "popular" Hinduism bear witness to its richness and viability; they have also recorded the process named Sanskritization by which lower castes tend to move away from their

folk moorings and attempt to raise their ritual and social status by taking over the religious and secular practices of the upper castes. While such efforts at status enhancement are group based, it is noteworthy that Hinduism is a non-congregational religion: its principal agent is the individual and its primary locus is the home. Even in temples and places of pilgrimage, it is the individual or a family who offer worship.

Karma in its various expressions is, then, the way (*marga*) of religion among Hindus. But there are two other equally valid ways, those of *gyan* (knowledge) and *bhakti* (devotion to the chosen deity), and all three are recognized in the scriptural text *Bhagavad Gita* (first century CE), which has gradually emerged as the single most revered "revealed" book of Hinduism. Beginning with the ninth-century commentary of Shankara, there has been an unending tradition of commentaries on this text, including in the twentieth century those by the firebrand politician Bal Gangadhar Tilak, the mystic Aurobindo Ghosh, and the pacifist Mahatma Gandhi, each emphasizing a particular mode of interpretation. For Gandhi, the *Bhagavad Gita* is a moral treatise of selfless action (*anasakti*) in the service of humanity, which brings out the futility of violence and the imperative of divine grace in human affairs.

MEDIEVAL SYNTHESIS AND MODERN HINDUISM

Hinduism is not a static tradition. As we have seen, it has grown through dialogic processes involving different levels of articulation from the local (tribal, folk) to the regional and finally the subcontinental, in an increasing order of eclectic complexity. Rightly perhaps, Hinduism has been described as a family of religions. Moreover, internal heterodoxies, some of which have grown into fully-fledged independent religions, have also altered the character of the core tradition of Hinduism, one of the best-known examples being the value placed upon vegetarianism following the great emphasis on non-violence in Buddhism and Jainism.

The arrival of Islam as a proselytizing religion in the eighth century, accompanied by the establishment of pockets of Muslim rule, first of all in the northwest, that by the early seventeenth century had grown into the subcontinental Mughal empire, opened new possibilities of religious syncretism, particularly at the folk level, but also temporarily and unsuccessfully in the imperial court. Elements of Sufi religiosity blended well with Hindu theistic devotionalism (*bhakti*) that had originated in southern India, partly in reaction to the ritualism of Vedism and the atheism of Buddhism. New communities of faith with their distinctive cults, such as the medieval Kabir Panth, were born, providing a "home" to low-caste Hindus as well as Muslims, bound together by their ecstatic love of a formless (*nirguna*) divine, unblemished by idolatry and mechanical ritualism. It was in such an ambience that Sikhism took shape as an independent religion in the sixteenth and early seventeenth centuries.

After Islam it was Christianity that provided the new challenge, drawing from the Hindu intelligentsia a variety of creative responses. Bengal was the stage on which these dramas were enacted before they spread elsewhere. Christianity arrived in India early in the Christian era, but it was only in the sixteenth century that, under the aegis of Portuguese and other colonial powers, which gained footholds on Indian shores, that conversions began. Since it was the British who emerged as empire builders in the late eighteenth century, Christianity became a subcontinental presence, particularly after the British parliament lifted restrictions on evangelical activities in 1813. An early response to the new challenge was the search for the best in the Christian gospels – for instance, their ethical precepts – that could be welcomed into Hinduism. Thus the Brahmo Samaj (Society of God) sought to combine the best of Vedanta with the best of Unitarian Christianity, but fared no better than the great Mughal Emperor Akbar's *Din-i Ilahi* (Religion of God) in the late sixteenth century.

As the activities of missionaries (often excessively condemnatory of Hinduism) gathered force, a spirited Hindu response, combining reform and revivalism, virtually burst upon the Indian scene in the closing years of the eighteenth century. Its luminous torch bearer was the Bengali renouncer Vivekananda (1863–1902). Breaking with tradition, he traveled overseas to emerge at the World Parliament of Religions in Chicago in 1893 as one of its most charismatic participants. Taking his stand on Vedanta, which he claimed contained all the great truths of all religions, he proclaimed that the essence of Vedantic Hinduism was the acknowledgment of religious pluralism. All paths of religious seeking were true, but the tradition that acknowledged this principle, as Vedanta did, was the paradigm of perfection. Lecturing in the US, the UK, and India, he called upon the West to look beyond its materialist riches to the spiritualist treasures of India. To the Indian youth his message was social uplift of the down-trodden and the cultivation of rationalism at home and spiritual conquest abroad. Like Shankara, he died young at 39 years of age. Vivekananda was indisputably the founder of global Hinduism.

If Vivekananda's pluralism was under the umbrella of Vedanta as the essence of true religion, the pluralism of Mohandas Gandhi (1869–1948), known to the world as Mahatma (Great Soul), a name bestowed upon him by the great poet Rabindranath Tagore, was radical and his pluralism was open to the sky. All religions spring from divine inspiration, he said, but are imperfectly articulated because of the limitations of human reason. Things that are only implicit in some religions are explicit in others. Humanity, therefore, needs all religions. In judging each of them, moral sensibility, which he considered innate and universal, provides the yardstick. Whatever is in conflict with it, including ancient texts, must be discarded: the search for truth is unending. The strength of Hinduism, in Gandhi's view, lies in its inclusivism and willingness to listen and learn from other religious traditions. Indeed, he considered this the true Hindu perspective. That he should have died at the hands of Hindu bigots should therefore not cause any surprise.

Hinduism is today a global religion. By present estimates there are nearly 900 million Hindus spread over six continents. Asia is where most of them live: over 800 million in India, 18 million in Nepal, 14 million in Bangladesh, 3 million in Sri Lanka, and about a million in the US. Migrants and itinerant religious teachers are the principal agents of a globalized Hinduism. Some forms of Hinduism have grown in foreign settings in response to the internal crises of other cultural traditions. The best-known case, perhaps, is that of the International Society of Krishna Consciousness (ISKCON) in the US.

In India Hinduism remains a personal spiritual engagement for millions; but those who look upon it as a resource for political mobilization in the pursuit of power are also quite numerous. Their Hinduism is exclusive and often degenerates into communal hate and violence. Gandhi's assassination in 1948 did not bring the conflict between the two Hinduisms to a close.

CONCLUSION

The study of Hinduism in modern times has proceeded along two tracks. On the one hand, there have been the textualists whose studies have presented us with the ideals and norms of Hinduism as a way of life. On the other hand, the contributions of social scientists (particularly social anthropologists) have contributed richly to our understanding of "lived Hinduism" in its immense variety. Methodologically, the truth of Hinduism lies at the confluence of the textual and contextual perspectives. In recent years, both perspectives have become theoretically more sophisticated: structuralism, phenomenology, hermeneutics, cultural analysis, etc. have all been drawn upon with much benefit. As befits an expanding religious tradition, its study also seeks new points of departure and new frameworks of interpretation.

SEE ALSO: Asceticism; Buddhism; Folk Hinduism; Islam; Religion; Religion, Sociology of; Secularization

REFERENCES AND SUGGESTED READINGS

Biardeau, M. (1981) *Hinduism: The Anthropology of a Civilization*. Oxford University Press, Delhi.
Flood, G. (Ed.) (2003) *The Blackwell Companion to Hinduism*. Blackwell, Oxford.
Fuller, C. J. (1992) *The Camphor Flame: Popular Hinduism and Society*. Princeton University Press, Princeton.
Madan, T. N. (1987) *Non-renunciation: Themes and Interpretations of Hindu Culture*. Oxford University Press, Delhi.
Radhakrishnan, S. (Trans.) (1948) *The Bhagavadgita*. Allen & Unwin, London.
Srinivas, M. N. (1952) *Religion and Society among the Coorgs of South India*. Clarendon Press, Oxford.

Hirschfeld, Magnus (1868–1935)

Ken Plummer

One of a cluster of early sexologists – like Krafft-Ebing, Albert Moll, and Havelock Ellis – who came to prominence in the late nineteenth century, Magnus Hirschfeld was a German physician and sex researcher, as well as a homosexual and a pioneer of homosexual rights. In his early work, he endorsed the idea of Karl Ulrichs's "urning theory," whereby homosexuality was seen as less of a choice and more of a biological "developmental defect." In particular, he argued for a hormonal basis. Much of his work was concerned with "intermediate types." He believed that all human beings were intermediate between male and female – a varying mixture of both. He was also one of the first modern theorists of transgender/transsexualism. He invented the terminology in 1923 and came to be known as "the father of Modern Transsexualism." He produced the film *Anders als die Anden (Different from the Others)* (1919), probably the first documentary campaign film about the rights of the homosexual, banned in 1920. Amongst his key publications were *The Transvestites* (1910), *Homosexuality of Men and Women* (1914), *Sexual Pathology* (1917), and *Sexual Science* (the five-volume magnus opus published between 1926 and 1930).

Writing initially in the time of the Oscar Wilde trial, Hirschfeld was a reformist and activist until the end of his life. He developed ideas around sexual liberation in general, and on transgenderism and homosexuality in particular. He founded the Scientific Humanitarian Committee (which petitioned the German Parliament for law change in favor of homosexuals, especially the repeal of paragraph 175 of the Penal Code) and the Institute for Sexual Science (in 1919) – seen as a "Child of the Revolution" – which housed major archives, a marriage guidance bureau, and a petition that advocated social change. His work was also very influential on the development of sexual "science" in the UK, leading to the formation of the British Sexological Society in the 1920s.

But his work was also seen as a scandal. Moralists saw much of this work as dangerous to the public, and thought that it should not fall into the hands of ordinary people. Radical feminists were also very critical of his work, both at the time and later. These are not celebrants of sexual diversity, in the ways that many early and subsequent sex researchers have been. In contrast, they suggested that much of early sex research had prioritized men and their power, and had not adequately considered the lack of a woman's right to control her own body and its access. Many contemporary feminists have argued that the situation has become increasingly worse, with the ever and upward rise of so-called "sexual freedom" in the twenty-first century. In addition, Hirschfeld was the victim of much personal abuse, both as a Jew and as a homosexual. He was forced to leave Germany in 1930, his Institute was burned down by the Nazis in 1933, and he died in France in 1935. The archives, library, and all records, as well as a bust of Hirschfeld, were destroyed. Other homosexuals were subsequently interned in concentration camps and killed.

SEE ALSO: Ellis, Havelock; Gay and Homosexuality; Intersexuality; Krafft-Ebing, Richard von; Sexuality Research: History; Sexuality Research: Methods; Transgender, Transvestism and Transsexualism

REFERENCES AND SUGGESTED READINGS

Steakley, J. D. (1975) *The Homosexual Emancipation Movement in Germany*. Arno Press, New York.
Wolff, C. (1986) *Magnus Hirschfeld: A Portrait of a Pioneer in Sexology*. Quartet, London.

historical and comparative methods

Ian Varcoe

Among the classical figures, Max Weber stands out from the others in his devotion to comparative historical sociology. His lifelong quest was to find through the study of "rationalization processes" what sets the West off from the non-western civilizations. Concretely, the concern was with modern, rational, or bourgeois capitalism, its origins and development. This series of studies is "macro" and it deals with changes over long stretches of time.

Weber tackles systematic comparative study, whereby, rather than creating data experimentally, the investigator bases comparative analysis on real or natural events, trajectories, and cases. One class of "natural case" is historical sequences in large-scale comparative social contexts or units.

Weber is a leading inspiration of comparative historical sociology in the twentieth century. Chief exponents of this are Reinhard Bendix, S. N. Eisenstadt, Theda Skocpol, Charles Tilly, Barrington Moore, Michael Mann, and John A. Hall. Weber came closest among the classical writers to making major use of John Stuart Mill's method of (indirect) difference. Of Mill's two principal procedures, the method of difference is the one that usually features in explicitly comparative research; it is the most powerful of the "logics" he identified and studies usually try to approximate it as closely as possible.

Mill's method of agreement works as follows: (1) several cases are found to have the phenomenon to be explained (y); (2) they also share the hypothesized causal factors (x) (this is the crucial similarity); but (3) in other ways that might seem causally relevant according to alternative hypotheses, they vary (i.e., *overall* there are differences). Mill's method of difference, on the other hand, requires that the investigator take (positive) cases in which the phenomenon to be explained and the hypothesized causes are present ($x - y$); these are then to be contrasted to other (negative) cases in which the phenomenon and the causes are absent (not x – not y). These negative cases are as similar as possible to the positive cases in other respects. Comparative historical sociologists, in particular, can supplement the method of agreement by introducing into their analyses the method of difference; in short, a research design that combines elements of both is possible. Or the method of agreement can be applied twice over so as to approximate the method of difference.

Max Weber did this in his comparative studies of civilizations. Essentially, he conducted two sets of studies, of European societies that developed capitalism and non-western ones that did not. Weber thought he could see a number of factors linked to the former which the latter set of societies did not possess. But what if other factors he had not identified were operating? By comparing the two sets of societies, stressing as much as possible their likenesses, Weber was able to strengthen the presumption in favor of his selected factors as the cause of capitalism in the West, their absence as leading to its absence in China and India.

Weber's strategy was to extend an ideal type by developing a subtype effectively containing an implicit explanatory hypothesis concerning difference. Weber's approach to comparative studies was shaped in a fundamental way by his view of causation in the historical and cultural sphere; not general laws but unique constellations of multiple causal factors drew his attention.

In addition to being historical studies, most work by comparative historical sociologists studies one, two, or three cases. Why this tendency to a limited number? The argument for such a limitation is that the cases are intrinsically interesting (they may even exhaust the phenomenon in question) or that they are the most representative. Unraveling complex, compacted causes can only be attempted in a small number of cases treated as wholes. The nomothetic (or generalizing) type of inquiry was held in suspicion by Max Weber as more the province of the natural sciences: opponents of positivism and evolutionism in the social sciences have shared this preference for the idiographic. It is, however, a tendency only, shown in varying degrees by historical sociologists. Studies using a few cases can, and usually do, pose nomothetic or general questions. Both the idiographic and the nomothetic types of studies may seek to explain and the causal forces conceived theoretically may well be the same in both. The import of Weber's methodology for comparative studies is, however, open to interpretation. Being itself a synthesis of conflicting elements, it has proved open to being "read" in different ways – to support more causal analytic and more contrast-oriented positions. Comparative historical sociologists draw

methodological inspiration from approaches such as that of Durkheim (and latterly structuralist Marxism).

An interpretation of Weber that sees him as underwriting a highly tentative approach to causal statements is that of Bendix, who offers a sophisticated critique of the traditions of Marxism and structural functionalism. They are, he says, effectively single-factor, evolutionary theories confined to proposing a series of "stages." Bendix calls for the kind of comparative concepts that cover some but not all societies. They should allow significant comparison but be less than universal. He argues that these are to be found in the ideal type because such concepts (1) invite specification in historical or developmental terms and (2) provide benchmarks by which historical data can be ordered in a preliminary fashion. The aim of comparative research, for Bendix, is to isolate differences, or explore contrasts, so setting a limit on premature generalizations. Such generalizations are always vulnerable to hidden or unexamined third variables (which may have to be dealt with ad hoc) for which the overly ambitious investigator has not controlled. An ideal type's principal value is to rule out certain possible associations in history by placing limits on the field within which causal imputation is possible, although this does not rule out imputation at some later stage when knowledge is better than it is now, and to give access to complexity unsuspected by "grand" evolutionary theories.

Bendix's modest, self-denying strictures against overly generalized research designs are aimed at combatting what he sees as the organic assumptions of classical theory deriving from Marx and Durkheim where societies tend to be seen as bounded entities, the forces for change lying within them. However, if change is exogenous the comparative sociologist needs a way of separating and then relating endogenous and exogenous sources of change. To tackle this question theoretically, Bendix has drawn attention to non-bounded societies composed of "layers" of differing degrees of extension beyond permeable borders that predate the unified modern state, and to the phenomenon of what he calls "reference societies" through which influence flows from one society to another, e.g., with respect to models of industrialization. Concepts such as this sensitize comparative sociologists to the different degrees to which societies are less than self-contained units.

Mill's canons of inductive logic say nothing about where the data should come from. They do not stipulate, for example, that they should come from different times and places; nor from how many social systems or units, that is, from one or more than one. The logic of comparative analysis whereby an attempt is made to gain control over suspected causal factors is present in methods that do not necessarily involve a few large units (e.g., nation-states, societies, and civilizations). "Deviant cases" may be picked out for study; non-existent data randomized, i.e., rendered irrelevant for scientific purposes; and the "imaginary experiment" employed. The aspect of a situation suspected to be crucial in producing a given outcome is "thought away" in an effort to estimate the difference it would have made.

The dilemma of concept formation in comparative research generally is that concepts should be sufficiently abstract to cover the multiple cases such research requires, but not so abstract that it becomes difficult to devise rules for empirical specification of the concepts. Aside from this, the main methodological questions in research concern:

1 *Classification.* Placing in the same class means "rendering comparable," i.e., implicitly excluding as causal candidates the respects in which members of the class are alike. Once a definition has been created, a pattern of possible causal relations – of similarities and differences of characteristics – is engendered.

2 *Issues of measurement.* Every stage of comparative research – choice of variables, causal inference, the location of indicators and their choice, the selection of units (classification), these last three reflecting implicit causal theories – depends on theoretical ideas. Theory and methods form a seamless unity, although the components of this unity can be separated and analyzed.

In the 1970s a certain momentum was generated for a comparative historical sociology, to renew the classical tradition of macrosocial inquiry into major transformations of the human condition. Partly this was in reaction to trends like ethnomethodology, and partly the inspiration came from sociologists wishing to continue developing the legacy of Max Weber. But Marxists and neofunctionalists were also drawn in. Major figures were Eisenstadt (neofunctionalism), Bendix (Weber), Perry Anderson (neo-Marxism), and Barrington Moore (neo-Marxism). Forerunners of this type of sociology were seen to be the French Annales School of Fernand Braudel, who inspired Immanuel Wallerstein's world-systems theory, and the historian of the Middle Ages, Marc Bloch. Methodological analysis of the various studies of these scholars suggested that theory influenced research design in various ways. Only one of these was firmly in the camp of macrosocial explanation, using Mill's logical canons in combined ways. Perhaps the most outstanding example of such a study was Barrington Moore's *Social Origins of Dictatorship and Democracy: Lord and Peasant in the Making of the Modern World* (1966). It used eight cases to identify three "paths" to the modern world. It used many independent variables, but principally the nature of class relations – between lord and peasant – in the countryside, to explain the type of emergent polity following industrialization.

Moore was able to establish parallels between countries within his three pathways. But he also made comparisons and contrasts across them. As well as this, he introduced negative cases in his discussion of particular countries. By doing so he approximated the method of difference, shoring up the causal case that he was trying to make.

Comparative historical sociology as a candidate for a preeminent theoretical empirical orientation in sociology has receded since its heyday in the 1980s – it was arguably less a movement or school than a genre. Mainly this is because the agenda of key sociological issues has changed with the end of the Cold War. The coherence of nation-states has declined somewhat and issues like industrialization, urbanization, democracy, and revolution have ceded place to others that have flowed from US hegemony, globalization, the resurgence of militant

Islam, human rights, and so forth. None of these seems resolvable in terms of the development of societies as nation-states, or is fully understandable with reference to a distinction between a Western European pattern of development and the development of the rest of the world seen as taking place with reference to that pattern. The priority of the West still resonates. However, issues of development are now filtered through the global framework rather than through a direct confrontation with Western Europe and North America. There is no doubt, however, that social change over the very long term is still a vitally important topic. It is historical sociology, but perhaps not *comparative* historical sociology in the analytic sense, that will continue to be practiced and will continue to offer rewarding insights: for example, into "multiple modernities."

SEE ALSO: Annales School; Braudel, Fernand; Dependency and World-Systems Theories; Ideal Type; Methods; Mill, John Stuart; Multivariate Analysis; Social Change; Variables; Weber, Max

REFERENCES AND SUGGESTED READINGS

Bendix, R. (1963) Concepts and Generalizations in Comparative Sociological Studies. *American Sociological Review* 28: 535–39.

Collins, R. (1973) A Comparative Approach to Political Sociology. In: Bendix, R. (Ed.), *State and Society: A Reader in Comparative Political Sociology*. University of California Press, Berkeley, pp. 42–67.

Delanty, G. & Isin, E. (Eds.) (2003) *Handbook of Historical Sociology*. Sage, London.

Mahoney, J. & Rueschmeyer, D. (2003) *Comparative Historical Analysis in the Social Sciences*. Cambridge University Press, Cambridge.

Ragin, C. (1987) *The Comparative Method*. University of California Press, Berkeley.

Smelser, N. (1976) *Comparative Methods in the Social Sciences*. Prentice-Hall, Englewood Cliffs, NJ.

Vallier, I. (Ed.) (1971) *Comparative Methods in Sociology: Essays on Trends and Applications*. University of California Press, Berkeley and Los Angeles.

Weber, M. (1949) *The Methodology of the Social Sciences*. Trans. and Ed. E. Shils & H. Finch. Free Press, New York.

HIV/AIDS and population

Mark VanLandingham

The connections between human immunodeficiency virus (HIV) and population features are vast. While HIV has its largest impacts on population size and structure by increasing mortality among young adults, it also affects and interacts with the other key components of population makeup and change, namely, sexual behavior and fertility, and migration. Impacts on these key components in turn affect the well-being of populations in profound ways.

INTELLECTUAL AND SOCIAL CONTEXT

HIV is believed to have infected nearly 60 million persons worldwide, killing more than 20 million of them through the various complications associated with acquired immune deficiency syndrome (AIDS), the disease caused by HIV. The toll has been especially heavy in the developing world, where infection rates are highest and where effective medications are the least available.

The introduction and spread of HIV across the globe is a recent phenomenon and caught public health, population, and other social scientists by surprise. Although it is now thought that the virus probably existed in Africa for a number of years before it emerged within gay male populations in America and Europe, it was not until the early 1980s that this new deadly and infectious disease caught the attention of a scientific community heretofore convinced that the age of epidemics was nearing completion. It is not just the epidemiological transition paradigm that was uprooted by the spread of this new virus and the host of health problems it causes, but also the demographic transition paradigm, which predicted a steady decline of mortality and fertility in the developing world, and a gradual shift from a very young age structure – in which as much as half of the population may be under age 15 – to an older population with a much more evenly distributed age structure.

Instead, we find ourselves almost halfway through a third decade of an epidemic that has reversed decades of progress in increasing life expectancy in several Sub-Saharan countries, and has disrupted longstanding patterns of intergenerational relations and exchange, social institutions, and international relations in many others. In terms of numbers of deaths, the HIV/AIDS pandemic is certain to surpass all previously recorded epidemics, and in terms of the disruption it causes, will rival and perhaps even surpass the plagues that ravaged Europe up until the Industrial Revolution and the worldwide influenza epidemic of 90 years ago. Unlike earlier epidemics that spread their misfortune across the age distribution, AIDS affects primarily young adults, at the precise ages when child rearing and economic responsibilities are highest. Indeed, one of the most sinister aspects of AIDS is that in addition to killing those young adults it infects, it also harms in profound ways many in the age groups typically dependent upon those young adults who succumb to the disease.

But if the prevailing paradigms of demography and public health were ill-suited for the advent of AIDS, demographers' toolkits for estimating the potential consequences of the epidemic on population structure have proven well suited for the task. Well-honed techniques for conducting "what if" scenarios involving changes in age-specific mortality rates, even while employing far-from-ideal data, have facilitated major contributions from population scientists. Even so, there have been new and difficult obstacles to modeling HIV-impacts because of poor information regarding the rate of spread of infection (especially related to variability in rates of partner change and partner risk profiles; variability in degree of infectiousness during different stages of the illness; unanticipated changes in behavior, etc.) and variability in the period between infection and death. Changes in such assumptions have very large implications for the results of such models.

It has been much more challenging to investigate the substantive consequences of such impacts. The combination of such high rates of death and the concentration of deaths in the most productive age groups is unprecedented. Also, such deaths affect all other age groups traditionally dependent upon these working age adults for support, as is society more generally. Sensitivities regarding AIDS and especially its primary modes of transmission make data collection on such topics challenging; and long latency periods and potential delays in the manifestation of consequences after death also make the measurement of long-term psychological, social, and economic effects difficult.

DEMOGRAPHIC DIMENSIONS OF AIDS

Demographers have focused much of their attention on the effects of various levels and patterns of AIDS-related mortality on the age-sex structure and size of future populations. Botswana's population, for example, would most likely have doubled between 1990 and 2025 without AIDS; instead, with AIDS, its actual population will be substantially less than it was in 1990. Worse, the loss of working age adults relative to other age groups will strain traditional support mechanisms for the young and old.

Such projections have proven very useful for illustrating the implications of existing levels of infections for future populations, and also for showing how such dire consequences would be mitigated by lowering rates of new infections. Such efforts have played a major role in inspiring some governments and international organizations to action. Most of this modeling has focused on transmission and subsequent death rates among young adults, but in high-prevalence countries where AZT and other drugs that lower mother-to-child transmission have not yet become widespread, the infection of large numbers of children also implies non-trivial decreases in child survival and overall life expectancy.

Conversely, patterns and levels of AIDS-related mortality can affect the future spread of the virus. One feature of this relationship that can be readily modeled is the loss of the most susceptible members of a population through early infection, which will, ceteris paribus, lead to lower rates of infection and death among those remaining. More difficult to predict and model are changes in sexual practices that occur as a result of increasing AIDS-related mortality.

Prevalence of HIV also affects current and future levels of fertility, primarily by increasing mortality among adults of childbearing age. This results in fewer children than would have been born had these adults lived through these years. Other effects of HIV on fertility are mediated through one or more of the classic proximate determinants of fertility. First, widespread widowhood will leave many young adult survivors without child-producing and child-rearing partners. Second, HIV-induced morbidity reduces sexual activity among the infected – in proximate determinants parlance, these first and second mechanisms decrease exposure to intercourse. Third, HIV may lead to shifts from contraceptives more effective in preventing pregnancy, such as the pill, to methods less effective in preventing pregnancy but offering new protection against HIV, such as the condom; this third mechanism would affect exposure to conception. Fourth, HIV appears to increase fetal loss among infected women, affecting gestation.

These major mechanisms of HIV on fertility described above are fairly straightforward to incorporate into a projection. But a more difficult mechanism to model is that HIV may change the fertility desires of those infected and/or left behind by widowhood. This could result in either increased fertility among persons living with HIV and AIDS (PHAs) who wish to leave a child behind; or decreased fertility among those who do not want to risk having an infected child and/or a child without his biological parent to raise him.

On the other hand, an increase in fertility – if caused by changes in the frequency or onset of unprotected intercourse for reasons unrelated to HIV – could in principle stimulate subsequent increases in the spread of HIV. However, it is the underlying patterns of sexual practices affecting both fertility and HIV transmission that will have the most important impacts on both.

Migration patterns, too, can be a cause or consequence of HIV transmission. Most attention to this topic in the population sciences has focused on the former. Population scientists studying migration have long speculated that patterns of migration could facilitate the transmission of HIV among migrants, and facilitate the spread of HIV from urban centers to rural communities from which many migrants come. The past few years have seen increasing empirical investigations of this hypothesis. The focus is most frequently on rural-to-urban migration because it exposes young adults to new opportunities for sexual experimentation, provides them the discretionary income with which to do so, removes them from the oversight and control of extended kin, and may lead to extended periods of spousal separation among those who are married. Similarly, long-distance truckers experience extended periods of spousal separation, which increases the likelihood that they visit sex workers or engage in other types of high-risk sexual behavior. Hence, migrants and long-distance truckers tend to have above-average rates of HIV infection, and may transmit the virus to more permanent partners upon their return. Moreover, many migrants and truckers provide financial support for a large number of family members in their home communities. Consequently, AIDS-related morbidity and mortality among migrants and truckers can have a devastating economic impact on their home communities.

Less studied but also important are patterns of migration that result from AIDS. Migration of PHAs who had previously moved to urban areas for work back home to their villages for caretaking appears widespread. While the implications for population distribution of such return migrations may not be major, the implications of such widespread moves on intergenerational exchanges (both monetary and in-kind) and the welfare of their parental caregivers are likely to be significant.

In addition to interacting with the three traditional components of population growth and structure (mortality, fertility, and migration), HIV also affects other key features of population well-being. Mortality aside, the severe morbidity associated with HIV-infection severely diminishes the productivity of those infected, and draws away scarce labor and financial resources that would have otherwise been available for family investment or consumption. In high-prevalence societies, the loss of highly trained individuals such as teachers, nurses, and physicians to AIDS will affect critical social institutions such as education and health care. Clinics and hospitals may also become overwhelmed with AIDS patients seeking expensive and sophisticated treatments that the staff are ill-positioned to provide. And traditional patterns of care for children and the elderly, both of whom are dependent upon working age adults for their support, are also being disrupted. While the plight of children left behind has been well recognized, the many ways in which older parents have been affected have not. Increasing numbers of households headed by women may face special difficulties related to resource acquisition. Increasing numbers of households without adult women may face special difficulties related to truncated social networks and a shortage of household services that adult women normally provide.

CHANGES OVER TIME IN THE TOPIC AND ITS TREATMENT

Much of the attention given to AIDS by demographers has focused on modeling the impacts of HIV-related mortality on future population size and structure, as briefly described above. Impending expansion of antiretroviral drugs to prolong the lives of the infected will soon add a happy complication to modeling efforts aimed at predicting the number of infections and deaths, and their subsequent impacts on population size and structure. Demographers and statisticians have recently also turned their attention to forecasting other future consequences of the epidemic; for example, the number of older persons likely to experience the death of a child before their own deaths. Other models address how features and changes in sexual networks affect the spread of the virus. New sampling strategies, such as the PLACE method and Respondent Driven Sampling, have been developed to access difficult-to-reach populations, such as sex workers and intravenous drug users, that often play key roles in the spread of the virus throughout the more general populations. Other recent advances in computer assisted analysis of qualitative data have helped make more systematic the investigation of sensitive topics and subtle processes.

Substantive work by population scientists has broadened from a focus on sexual risk-taking to analyses of how non-infected relatives of PHAs, such as children and, more rarely, older parents, are affected by the epidemic; community reaction and stigma towards PHAs and their families; HIV-related domestic violence; and how communities respond to the epidemic.

Population scientists have also played an important role in programmatic research, including developing methodologies to conduct systematic assessments of the relative effectiveness of various types of HIV prevention interventions.

FUTURE DIRECTIONS

As the use of antiretrovirals becomes more widespread in the countries that need them over the next decade, there will be increasing demands for research on access to care, quality of care, and quality of life of PHAs. For example, interactions between nutrition and the progression of the disease are likely to command increasing attention. Although stigma and discrimination appear to diminish over time in most communities, given the sensitivities associated with AIDS and the primary modes of transmission, these are likely to remain central to the research agenda for the foreseeable future.

SEE ALSO: AIDS, Sociology of; Demographic Techniques: Life-Table Methods; Demographic Techniques: Population Projections and Estimates; Fertility: Transitions and Measures; Globalization, Sexuality and; Health Risk Behavior; Prostitution; Sex Tourism; Sexual Health; Sexuality Research: Methods; Stigma

REFERENCES AND RECOMMENDED READINGS

Dayton, J. & Ainsworth, M. (2002) The Elderly and AIDS: Coping Strategies and Health Consequences in Rural Tanzania. *Policy Research Division Working Paper* No. 160. Population Council, New York.

Knodel, J. & VanLandingham, M. (2003) Return Migration in the Context of Parental Assistance in the AIDS Epidemic: The Thai Experience. *Social Science and Medicine* 57(2): 327–42.

Knodel, J. & VanLandingham, M. (2002) The Impact of the AIDS Epidemic on Older Persons. *AIDS 2002* 16 (suppl. 4): S77–S83.

Morris, M. (Ed.) (2004) *Network Epidemiology: A Handbook for Survey and Design and Data Collection.* Oxford University Press, Oxford.

Project website: Impact of AIDS on Older Persons in Thailand. www.aidseld.psc.isr.umich.edu/index.html.

Ross, A., Van der Paal, L., Lubega, R., Mayanja, B. N., Shafer, L. A., & Whitworth, J. (2004) HIV-1 Disease Progression and Fertility: The Incidence of Recognized Pregnancy and Pregnancy Outcome in Uganda. *AIDS* 18(5): 799–804.

Stanecki, K. (2004) *The AIDS Pandemic in the 21st Century*. Census Bureau, Washington, DC.

United Nations AIDS (UNAIDS) website: www.unaids.org.

Yang, Y. (2004) Temporary Migration and HIV Risk Behaviors: A Case Study in Southwestern China. Paper presented at the Population Association of America meetings, Boston.

Zimmer, Z. & Dayton, J. (2003) The Living Arrangements of Older Adults in Sub-Saharan Africa in a Time of HIV/AIDS. *Policy Research Division Working Paper* No. 169. Population Council, New York.

Hobhouse, L. T. (1864–1929)

Stephen K. Sanderson

Leonard Trelawney Hobhouse was born in 1864 in Cornwall, England. His father was rector of the local parish church, and his grandfather had been a distinguished barrister and public servant (Owen 1974). Educated at Corpus Christi College, Oxford, he became a tutor there in 1887. In 1907 he became the first person to hold the Martin White Chair of Sociology at the University of London. In addition to his academic career, Hobhouse spent time as a journalist, working for the *Manchester Guardian* between 1897 and 1902. Later he spent time as a journalist in London (Owen 1974).

Hobhouse is generally regarded as the first British sociologist. He wrote numerous books, the most important of which dealt with long-term social evolution and its meaning for the present and the future. The most important of these books were *Mind in Evolution* (1901), *Morals in Evolution* (1951 [1906]), *The Material Culture and Social Institutions of the Simpler Peoples* (1965 [1915]), and *Development and Purpose* (1927 [1913]).

In *Morals in Evolution*, Hobhouse sketched out the evolution of systems of morality or ethics as part of a larger process of mental evolution. In this regard, he identified a process of mental evolution that began with the rudimentary and impulse-driven thought of early preliterate societies. The first real advance in mental evolution was the protoscience of ancient China, Babylonia, and Egypt. This was followed by a new stage of reflection between the eighth and fifth centuries BCE that was characterized by the rise of the earliest world religions of Judaism, Confucianism, Buddhism, and Hinduism. Then came the first truly critical and systematic secular philosophy of the Greeks, and then finally the rise of modern empirical modes of thinking in Europe beginning in the sixteenth century (Ginsberg 1951).

Hobhouse identified four stages in the evolution of morality. At the lowest stage, people feel obligations toward one another, but these are limited to human relations in very small groups, either the local community or the kin group. Life is regarded as important, but it is only protected through such mechanisms as blood feud, and there is no moral principle that life itself is something sacred. Right moral action means avenging a wrong done to a member of one's own group. A second stage of morality is reached when people conceptualize a duty not merely to avenge a wrong but to protect life and to guard property instead of just retaliating against thieves. Moral obligations have become broader, but they still apply only to the members of one's own group, and there are no general ethical principles. This second stage of morality roughly corresponds to the second stage of mental evolution, and thus makes its appearance for the first time in the earliest civilizations.

In the third stage of morality people formulate moral principles and ideals of character and conduct of a religious nature. Here we find morality and ethics as integral parts of the great world religions; this third moral stage corresponds roughly to the third mental stage. The fourth and highest moral stage is reached when an attempt is made to construct a rational ethical theory that prescribes rights and duties that apply universally. It was the ancient Greeks who first began to grope toward this sort of ethical universalism, which has been extended by philosophers and theologians in more modern times.

In *The Material Culture and Social Institutions of the Simpler Peoples*, written in collaboration with G. C. Wheeler and Morris Ginsberg, the authors classified societies according to their technological inventory. They produced a scheme of seven major "stages of economic culture": (1) Lower Hunters; (2) Higher Hunters; (3) Incipient Agriculturalists; (4) Middle Agriculturalists; (5) Highest Agriculturalists; (6) Lower Pastoralists; and (7) Higher Pastoralists. There is a rough evolutionary sequence here, except that agriculture and pastoralism stand to each other as subsistence alternatives rather than in an evolutionary relationship.

The authors related these economic stages to other dimensions of social life, especially morality, religion, law, and overall social organization by assembling data on over 400 ethnographically known societies. They found that the higher the economic stage, the more developed and formalized the system of government. In terms of the administration of justice, there was a pronounced trend from private redress of wrongs to public redress by chiefs or tribal councils. The authors also looked at the relationship between their economic stages and various dimensions of marriage and family life. Here the correlations were not always as dramatic or striking. But in the final analyses, which involved variables bearing on social stratification and property ownership, the results were again dramatic. There was a very marked trend from communal to private forms of property ownership and toward greater social and economic inequalities.

Given the emphasis on economic stages as the starting point for the whole book, and the correlations between these stages and other dimensions of social life, one might get the impression that Hobhouse, Wheeler, and Ginsberg were materialists. But this is not the case. Hobhouse was in fact a strong theoretical idealist. This is clear from his *Morals in Evolution*, but even more so from his capstone work, *Development and Purpose*, in which he presents an overall philosophy of evolution. Hobhouse was highly critical of Spencer and the social Darwinists, and claimed that it was the human mind, not the struggle for existence, that was the engine of social evolution. He contended that it was the "slowly wrought out dominance of mind [that] is the central fact of evolution" (Hobhouse 1951: 637). Even the stages of economic culture themselves are explained ideationally, as the results of the mind accumulating "stocks of knowledge" over the millennia.

Like many early evolutionists, Hobhouse was committed to a doctrine of social progress, even though he recognized that progress is not automatic and social evolution is by no means strictly unilinear. Human progress is erratic, with periods of retrogression interspersed with periods of progression. But on the whole, humankind has been improving itself, gradually moving toward a society based on harmony and a kind of ethical universalism in which all of humanity will eventually form a single social unit.

Hobhouse was a liberal humanitarian and social reformer who was a strong proponent of social harmony and internationalism. He spoke out against imperialism in all of its forms. His interest in practical affairs is clearly indicated by his journalistic activity and his work for many years on various trade boards, where he concerned himself with labor conditions. Several prominent British government officials came under Hobhouse's influence, either directly or indirectly. These included Harold Laski, Clement Atlee, Hugh Dalton, and Hugh Gaitskell (Owen 1974).

SEE ALSO: Civilizations; Evolution; Peace and Reconciliation Processes; Primitive Religion; Property, Private; Spencer, Herbert

REFERENCES AND SUGGESTED READINGS

Carter, H. (1927) *The Social Theories of L. T. Hobhouse*. University of North Carolina Press, Chapel Hill.

Ginsberg, M. (1951) Introduction to the Seventh Edition. In: Hobhouse, L. T., *Morals in Evolution: A Study in Comparative Ethics*, 7th edn. Chapman & Hall, London.

Hobhouse, L. T. (1901) *Mind in Evolution*. Macmillan, London.

Hobhouse, L. T. (1927 [1913]) *Development and Purpose: An Essay Towards a Philosophy of Evolution*, 2nd edn. Macmillan, London.

Hobhouse, L. T. (1951) *Morals in Evolution: A Study in Comparative Ethics*, 7th edn. Introduction by

M. Ginsberg. Chapman & Hall, London. (Originally published as two volumes, 1906; republished in one volume, 1915.)

Hobhouse, L. T., Wheeler, G. C., & Ginsberg, M. (1965 [1915]) *The Material Culture and Social Institutions of the Simpler Peoples.* Routledge & Kegan Paul, London.

Hobson, J. A. & Ginsberg, M. (1931) *L. T. Hobhouse: His Life and Work.* George Allen & Unwin, London.

Owen, J. (1974) *L. T. Hobhouse, Sociologist.* Ohio State University Press, Columbus.

Holocaust

Fred Emil Katz

The stark facts of the Holocaust can be summarized. When Adolf Hitler and his National Socialist Party came to power in Germany in 1933, they initiated measures against Germany's Jews. Before their rise to power the Nazis, under Hitler, had openly and vehemently blamed Jews for all of Germany's ills in the years following the country's loss of World War I (1914–18). After they gained power, the Nazi anti-Jewish measures included use of the existing legal machinery of the German state to devise and implement increasingly restrictive measures against Germany's Jewish population. These measures incrementally but inexorably deprived Jews of more and more rights of citizenship and capacity of living their daily lives. The legal measures were augmented by sporadic brutal attacks by organized thugs who molested and terrorized individuals and communities of Jews. The most extreme of these occurred on the night of November 9, 1938, the *Kristallnacht*, where a nationwide attack on Jews took place. Yet all of these eventually turned out to be preliminaries to an active and focused program to actually exterminate all Jews who came within Germany's reach during World War II – the war of 1939 to 1945. During the early years of that war Germany had overrun and conquered most of continental Europe, a land mass that included millions of Jews who had been living in the various countries now under German control. The actual extermination of Jews relied, at first, on the direct execution of individuals by individual German soldiers and paramilitary functionaries of the state – most notably the SS. Although this took place on a huge scale, the extermination plan was so grandiose that more elaborate systems of mass murder were devised, most notably a system of concentration camps that served as extermination factories, using lethal gas and the burning of bodies on a mass scale never before seen. The Auschwitz concentration camp, located in Poland, was the most notorious but not the only camp of this kind. Murdered at Auschwitz were some 2 million innocent persons, most of them Jews, but also others whom the Nazi ideologues regarded as unworthy of living in their utopian vision of the superstate dominated by pure Nordics. It is estimated that the Nazis managed to murder some 6 million Jews before their rampage was stopped by the victory of the Allies that ended the war. This genocide, this deliberate and systematic murder of 6 million humans beings, is doubtless the largest effort of its kind in all of human history.

Following a period of stunned silence, there has been a flood of responses. Within the academic community these have come from historians (e.g., Hilberg 1967; Bauer 1978), political scientists (e.g., Shirer 1960; Goldhagen 1996), and psychologists (e.g., Adorno et al. 1950; Milgram 1974) and social philosophers (e.g., Arendt 1964, 1968).

Apart from one conspicuous exception (Fein 1979), sociologists have been exceedingly silent in response to the Holocaust. In 1979, a Jewish sociologist said that "there is in essence no sociological literature on the Holocaust" (Dank), and in 1989 another sociologist said that the Holocaust work of sociologists "looks more like a collective exercise in forgetting and eye-closing" (Bauman). Bauman's assessment still seems to hold today.

Despite this silence, it seems that sociology can contribute insights about the Holocaust that no other discipline can. And that, in turn, the Holocaust can help us sharpen some of the most venerable sociological insights derived from Max Weber and Émile Durkheim (Katz 1993, 2003, 2004). The first begins from what is perhaps sociology's underlying premise: the need to explain ordinary people's ordinary social lives.

Applied to the Holocaust, a great many ordinary people – not crazy people, not marginal people, not zealous Nazis, but ordinary folks – became active participants in mass horrors. When it comes to monstrous behavior, it is not monsters we need to worry about, but ordinary people; they were active participants and contributors to the terrors we know as the ultimate genocide. It is ordinary people's ordinariness that must provide us with the clues of how genocide is practiced. The Nazis recruited many into becoming mass murderers who did not start out with murderous intentions.

Rudolf Hoess, the commandant of Auschwitz, was the ultimate bureaucrat. From Weber, we learned how the bureaucrat is the functionary who tries to bring rational processes to whatever tasks come his way. Hoess did just that, except that his task was mass murder. He also shows how the distinctive mindset of the bureaucrat enabled him to segregate an ongoing, fairly warm, nurturing home life from deep immersion in a grisly work setting. Weber was resurrected, but applied to a setting of which he could not have dreamed.

Émile Durkheim found an ally in Helen Fein (1979) in her study showing that the degree of Jews' integration into a country influenced the likelihood of becoming victims of the murderous assault. Durkheim's focus on social cohesion – based on what we would now call a group or society's shared culture – is also the focus of the "local moral universe" (Katz 2003, 2004). We humans get our sense of identity and purpose from a moral context, to which we try to contribute. Under such a moral umbrella, we may totally exclude those whom we regard as being on the outside. The result is that, as the Nazis displayed, these people can be treated not only with contempt but also with actual annihilation, and this can be done under the myth of operating on the basis of a high moral purpose and justification. This, Durkheim did not envisage. But his perspective applies and clarifies such a phenomenon.

The distinctive contribution of sociology to clarifying how a genocide operates – using the Nazi Holocaust as a source of insight – is that it can show how ordinary people can be recruited to do the most horrific acts, and do so using our existing social psychological proclivities and habits. It can show how bureaucratic administrative techniques, so central to modern life, can be hijacked in the service of evil. Furthermore, it can show how the moral umbrellas under which we are accustomed to living, and which serve as instruments for our most humane actions, can also become the instruments for our most inhumane actions. Sociologists can clarify just how these ordinary features of our social makeup actually work. From this knowledge we can not only demystify, but also actually find ways to counter, the evil we have come to call genocide.

SEE ALSO: Anti-Semitism (Religion); Anti-Semitism (Social Change); Ethnic Cleansing; Genocide; Ghetto; Pogroms; War

REFERENCES AND SUGGESTED READINGS

Adorno, T. et al. (1950) *The Authoritarian Personality*. Harper & Row, New York.

Arendt, H. (1964) *Eichmann in Jerusalem: A Report on the Banality of Evil*. Penguin, New York.

Arendt, H. (1968) *The Origins of Totalitarianism*. Harcourt, Brace, & World, New York.

Bauer, Y. (1978) *The Holocaust in Historical Perspective*. University of Washington Press, Seattle.

Bauman, Z. (1989) *Modernity and the Holocaust*. Cornell University Press, Ithaca, NY.

Dank, B. M. (1979) Review of "On the Edge of Destruction" by Celia S. Heller. *Contemporary Sociology* 8(1): 129–30.

Fein, H. (1979) *Accounting for Genocide: National Responses and Jewish Victimization During the Holocaust*. Free Press, New York.

Goldhagen, D. (1996) *Hitler's Willing Executioners: Ordinary Germans and the Holocaust*. Knopf, New York.

Hilberg, R. (1967) *The Destruction of European Jews*. Quadrangle Books, Chicago.

Katz, F. E. (1993) *Ordinary People and Extraordinary Evil: A Report on the Beguilings of Evil*. SUNY Press, Albany, NY.

Katz, F. E. (2003) *Immediacy: How Our World Confronts Us and How We Confront Our World*. Discern Books, Baltimore.

Katz, F. E. (2004) *Confronting Evil: Two Journeys*. SUNY Press, Albany, NY.

Milgram, S. (1974) *Obedience to Authority: An Experimental View*. Harper & Row, New York.

Shirer, W. L. (1960) *The Rise and Fall of the Third Reich*. Simon & Schuster, New York.

Homans, George (1910–89)

Thomas J. Fararo

George Caspar Homans was a major theoretical sociologist whose lucid writings helped to shape numerous developments in basic sociological research. His ideas about theoretical principles in sociology were much debated and often rejected.

Homans entered Harvard College in 1928 with an area of concentration in English and American literature. Among his electives was a course with the philosopher Alfred North Whitehead. Thereafter, in the period from 1934 to 1939, as a Junior Fellow of the newly formed Society of Fellows at Harvard, he interacted with Whitehead and other Harvard luminaries while undertaking independent studies in a variety of subjects, including sociology, mathematics, psychology, and anthropology. He attended a special faculty-student seminar on the newly translated general theoretical sociology of Vilfredo Pareto, which led in 1934 to his first published work in sociology, with Charles Curtis, *An Introduction to Pareto: His Sociology*. He also studied historical methods, and began doing original historical research that was published in 1941 as *English Villagers in the Thirteenth Century*. In 1939 he became a Harvard faculty member, a lifelong affiliation in which he taught both sociology and medieval history. By virtue of his later theoretical writings, by the 1960s he had become a major theorist and in 1964 was elected president of the American Sociological Association.

As a theorist, Homans's overall intellectual ambition was to create a more unified social science on a firm theoretical basis. He criticized his colleague Talcott Parsons, notable for a similar ambition, for creating only a conceptual scheme, but not a theory, defined as a deductively organized system of propositions that explain observable phenomena. His own approach to theory developed in two phases. In each phase, there is a presupposition concerning the nature of the subject matter and an associated mode of theorizing.

In his first phase, as presented in *The Human Group* (1950), there is an explicit process-philosophical presupposition about reality and a system model for its analysis, reflecting the intellectual influence of Whitehead and Pareto, respectively (Fararo 2001: ch. 3). Echoing Whitehead's stress on events and process, Homans proposes that social reality should be described at three levels: social events, customs, and analytical hypotheses that describe the processes by which customs arise and are maintained or changed. Social relations (e.g., kinship ties) are instances of such customs, defined as recurrent patterns amid the flux of social events.

The conceptual scheme in this first phase consists of three elements of social behavior called interaction, sentiment, and activity, together with emergent norms. Each of these is associated with variables such as frequency of interaction, similarity of activities, intensity of sentiment, and conformity to norms. These behaviors comprise the social system of the group. The system model, reflecting Pareto's influence, employs analogies drawn from physical science, especially thermodynamics. He argues that, like actual thermodynamic systems, social systems vary substantially in their "externals" (apparent differences) but that as in thermodynamics, they possess an underlying similarity described by the hypotheses that interrelate a small number of analytical elements. A year after it was published, Homans's social system theory was formalized by Herbert A. Simon as a system of differential equations, one of the earliest and most influential contributions to mathematical sociology. At the same time, Homans's book set out examples of emergent social structures of groups that have been of continuing interest to social network analysts. The subfield of sociology called "small groups" owes much of its inspiration to Homans.

In this first phase, Homans makes some use of the psychological principle of reinforcement and analyzes social exchange in one particular group. However, he was more attuned to the work of social anthropologists of his time. Chapters that treat theories of ritual, social control, and authority are brilliant forays into the subjects that draw upon and surpass the literature of the day. For instance, in a chapter on kinship, he anticipates the theory of structural balance in social psychology, as well as his later trenchant critique of functionalist theories of marriage in his 1955 book with David Schneider, *Marriage, Authority, and Final Causes.*

The second phase of Homans's theory program is based on the presupposition that satisfactory explanation in the social sciences must be based upon principles about individual behavior. His "Social Behavior as Exchange" (Homans 1958) proved to be seminal for what came to be known as exchange theory, an important paradigm in sociology. In this article he employed principles from behavioral psychology to explain and synthesize findings from experimental social psychology, and findings from earlier field studies. Social behavior as exchange means that a plurality of individuals form a system of interaction in which the activity of each provides part of the basis for an outcome that has sanction significance (reward or punishment) for each of them. Social approval is a fundamental reward actors can provide one another, functioning at an elementary level of interaction as money does in an advanced economy. He elaborated this approach in his treatise *Social Behavior: Its Elementary Forms*, which appeared first in 1961 and then in a revised edition in 1974, and set out his presuppositions about social science in his 1967 book, *The Nature of Social Science.*

One example of his more specific theoretical contributions concerns distributive justice. In the pioneering 1958 article, Homans had argued that distributive justice is one of the conditions required for "practical equilibrium" in a group. In the *Social Behavior* treatise, Homans elaborated on this theme and suggested the general principle that distributive justice holds in a group when, for any pair of members, the ratio of their rewards (e.g., wages) is equal to the ratio of their contributions or investments (e.g., job responsibilities). These ideas have stimulated a great deal of theoretical and empirical work on justice by social psychologists and sociologists.

In its mature form, Homans's general argument is that fundamental explanatory principles are to be true of individuals as members of the human species, not as members of particular groups or cultures. Furthermore, social psychological propositions (e.g., those pertaining to

interpersonal balance) should be derivable from these principles. Thus, a theory requires two sets of premises: principles of behavioral psychology, and statements applying them to a specific explanatory task. Disciplines differ as to their typical explanatory task. History tries to explain particular social events, economics tries to explain outcomes of one-time interactions of individuals, and sociology aims to explain emergent features of recurrent interactions among the same individuals. Hence, sociology is concerned with customs and social structure, but its theoretical aim is to explain these recurrent features in terms of patterns of rewards and punishments that individuals experience through interaction. For instance, status orders and authority relations are two such emergent features of social interaction. Each has a time-extended character rather than a transient character. The new presupposition, relative to the first stage, is the idea that a theory must have a deductive structure. Homans is a methodological individualist, but his focus is sociological in the sense that the aim is to explain how processes of interaction generate the generic types of social structural phenomena we observe: social structure as consequence rather than cause. Although structure and culture act back on individuals, they cannot alter the principles of behavior.

Homans's arguments apply to what he calls the subinstitutional level of social life: that which emerges spontaneously from interaction such as informal social ranking. The logical priority of this type of explanation is essential to Homans's research program. Institutions are like the macrolevel enduring objects of fundamental physics: their existence presupposes a level of interactions that accounts for them. In this sense, Homans adopts the reductionist stance inherent in the program of theoretical physics. In terms of the philosophy of social science, his approach is clearly in the tradition of methodological individualism, although in his case it might better be called methodological behaviorism.

Although others called his work exchange theory and treated it as one among a number of ever-growing theoretical paradigms in social science, Homans strongly rejected both the label and the multi-paradigmatic presupposition that came with it. For Homans, there is only one fundamental theory in social science. That theory is given by a system of deductive arguments based on the principles of behavioral psychology. The specific task of theoretical sociology is to explain how enduring social relational structures arise out of the interaction of human behavioral organisms (Fararo 2001: ch. 10). A somewhat more general perspective of this sort would apply it also to the explanation of culture, as in *A Theory of Religion* (1987) by Rodney Stark and William Sims Bainbridge, a theoretical work that adopts both the deductive and the behavioral elements of Homans's approach.

Other theories have reflected the influence of Homans's ideas, but in a more critical mode. Some take issue with the behavioral foundation and the scope restriction to elementary processes. For instance, Peter Blau (1964) attempted to create a general theory that starts with face-to-face interaction but also incorporates explicit macrosocial assumptions. For example, approval of leaders in the small group is paralleled by the legitimation of power at the macrolevel. Although emphasizing exchange processes, Blau adopted neither the deductive nor the behavioral aspects of Homans's approach. In turn, Blau's theory was criticized on the grounds that it lacked a deductive linkage between the micro and macrolevels – a criticism that embodies methodological individualism but not necessarily the behaviorist version favored by Homans. Thus the way was open for a more explicit formulation of a micro–macro deductive logic in social theory. Coleman (1990) set out such an approach. It departed from the behaviorist foundation in favor of an approach closer to that of neoclassical economics, grounded in a postulate of rational choice.

Richard Emerson's power-dependence theory was closer to Homans's approach. It has led to an experimental research program that, in some versions, retains the behaviorist principles employed by Homans. Power-dependence theory has been applied to patterns of exchange between actors in networks. In turn, this development led to a variety of competing research programs that differ in their theoretical assumptions, but that aim to predict outcomes in varying shapes and types of exchange networks defined under laboratory conditions.

Homans's work also remains relevant to various research efforts gaining momentum in the early twenty-first century. Through the use of computer simulation, a number of investigators are developing model-building approaches grounded in the idea that the basic task of social theory is to show how the interaction of a set of actors gives rise to emergent social phenomena. These simulations treat actors as knowledgeable agents whose behavior is generated by ever-changing knowledge shaped by perceptions of the behaviors of other agents and of the outcomes to which their joint efforts give rise. In this development, the strictly behavioral foundation favored by Homans has been replaced by a more cognitive approach. However, very much in the spirit of Homans, the general theoretical goal is the explanation of spontaneous social order.

SEE ALSO: Blau, Peter; Emerson, Richard M.; Power-Dependence Theory; Social Exchange Theory; System Theories; Theory Construction

REFERENCES AND SUGGESTED READINGS

Blau, P. M. (1964) *Exchange and Power in Social Life.* Wiley, New York.
Coleman, J. S. (1990) *Foundations of Social Theory.* Harvard University Press, Cambridge, MA.
Fararo, T. J. (2001) *Social Action Systems: Foundation and Synthesis in Sociological Theory.* Praeger, Westport, CT.
Homans, G. C. (1958) Social Behavior as Exchange. *American Journal of Sociology* 63: 597–606.
Homans, G. C. (1984) *Coming to My Senses: The Autobiography of a Sociologist.* Transaction Books, New Brunswick, NJ.

homelessness

David A. Snow, Jill Leufgen, and Matthew Cardinale

The sociological conceptualization of homelessness has pivoted on two dimensions: social disaffiliation and residential impermanence. The disaffiliation dimension, associated primarily with research on Skid Row alcoholics of the 1950s, emphasizes the interpersonal and institutional disconnection of the homeless. Although many homeless individuals lack the affiliative bonds that link most domiciled folks to various institutional structures, not all homeless are socially atomized. Many of them are connected interpersonally to other homeless, some maintain contact with relatives, and most are connected in various degrees to an array of street agencies and programs. Moreover, the majority of homeless individuals are not chronically homeless, as they cycle on and off the street and between street and mainstream agencies and institutions. Because there is considerable variation among the homeless along the atomization continuum, disaffiliation can be best regarded as a variable dimension of homelessness rather than the defining characteristic. Consequently, recent conceptualization emphasizes the residential dimension.

Defined in terms of residence, individuals or families without a permanent place of their own that meets the minimal standards of a residence in their respective cultures are generally thought of as homeless. This would include within the US and much of the developed world not only what Peter Rossi initially termed the "literal" homeless – that is, people living on the streets and/or in shelters – but also institutionalized individuals who have no place of residence upon their release, individuals and families who "double up" with others because they cannot afford a place of their own, and often even those who live in grossly substandard housing. Although this is a very broad conceptualization (referred to as "general" homelessness), it is thought to be too inclusive for research purposes because of the difficulty of reaching agreement, both nationally and cross-nationally, as to what constitutes an acceptable level of doubling-up and substandard housing. In many large cities throughout the world, for example, the residents of the numerous urban shantytowns, such as Brazil's favelas, are not typically considered homeless; in the US, by contrast, residents of similar makeshift shelter arrangements (e.g., encampments) are typically counted among the homeless. Because of such complicated issues, most research on homelessness at the end of the past century is based on the "literal" conceptualization, encompassing individuals sleeping in shelters, accommodations paid for by agency vouchers, or in places not intended as dwellings, such as the streets, abandoned buildings, automobiles, and parks.

HISTORICAL OVERVIEW

Whether viewing homelessness broadly (general homelessness) or more narrowly (literal homelessness), it has been a longstanding feature of the social landscape, particularly since the rise of cities. However, the size and character of homeless populations, and the extent to which they have been regarded as social problems, have varied over time. Homeless beggars and members of "floating populations" were characteristic features of the pre-industrial city, wherein the streets were teeming with people because of the blurring of the boundaries between home, work, and leisure. With the exception of a few vilifying pamphlets, such as Martin Luther's *The Book of Beggars*, the folk tradition of hospitality to beggars and itinerants, and the tendency to idealize poverty as a spiritual virtue, tended to mitigate the stigma of pre-industrial homelessness. This changed, however, with the social dislocation caused by industrialization and the breakdown of European agrarian economies, which led to dramatic increases in the numbers of homeless, then referred to derogatorily as vagrants, and to the development of laws and policies to control or eliminate those so labeled, particularly in England and its colonies.

One such law, the Vagrancy Act of 1597, led to the transportation of some number of England's homeless to its American colonies. These relocated folks, along with other transient poor who moved from community to community because they were denied settlement rights, constituted the first wave of homelessness in what eventually became the United States. A second wave occurred in the 1860s immediately following the Civil War, when large numbers of people were displaced but subsequently absorbed into the western frontier. The era of westward industrial expansion, from the late 1800s to the mid-1920s, called for a transient labor force that gave rise to a third wave of homelessness symbolized by "hoboes" – itinerant, seasonal workers – and the development of "hobohemias" in many large cities, both of which were immortalized in Nels

Anderson's classic sociological study, *The Hobo* (1923). The Great Depression resulted in a fourth surge in homelessness, which lasted until World War II, when many homeless were either absorbed into the expanding workforce or recruited into the armed forces.

The confluence of a number of factors in the wake of World War II – declining Skid Row populations in major US cities, post-World War II veterans' programs, the rise of optimistic urban planning programs, and a changing economy – prompted some observers to predict the end of homelessness in First World cities. But the early 1980s ushered in a new wave of homelessness that has persisted into the current century, not only in US cities but also in major, global cities throughout the world, such as Berlin, London, Paris, São Paulo, and Tokyo.

RESEARCH ON THE "NEW WAVE" OF HOMELESSNESS

From the mid-1980s to the turn of the century, homelessness was regarded as one of the most pressing social problems within the US, generating widespread public concern and debate manifested in intense media coverage, Congressional hearings, homeless protests and locality-based NIMBY movements seeking to control and contain the homeless, and literally volumes of social scientific research. Nearly all of this research can be classified into three basic genres. The first genre consists of either city-specific or national survey-based studies focusing on homeless individuals, and particularly on their numbers, demographics, disabilities, and transitions in and out of homelessness (Rossi 1989; Burt 1992; Burt et al. 2001); the second genre includes macrolevel, multivariate studies that assess the relationship among variation in rates of poverty, unemployment, housing affordability, and the like, and variation in rates of homelessness across cities (Ringheim 1990; Burt 1992; Shinn & Gillespie 1994); and the third genre consists of ethnographic field studies that focus primarily on the texture and dynamics of street life and on the adaptive, survival strategies of the homeless (Snow & Anderson 1993; Wright 1997; Duneier 1999).

Estimating the Number of Homeless

Due to the distinction between literal and general homelessness, and the difficulties in counting the "hidden" homeless (sleeping in abandoned buildings, parks, automobiles, etc.) and determining the ratio of street to shelter homeless, estimating the number of homeless city-wide or nationally has been a contested enterprise, with agency and advocacy estimates generally being considerably higher (2–3 million) than most research-based estimates. Research estimates are generally based on either "point prevalence "or "period prevalence" counts. The former encompasses counts of the number of people who are homeless at a single point in time, usually one day or night, and are typically based on shelter and street counts (Rossi 1989), shelter and soup kitchen counts (Burt 1992), or on counts of homeless in a range of assistance programs (Burt et al. 2001). Since there are no reliable national counts, those derived from a systematically selected sample of cities have been used as the basis for estimating the national homeless population. There have been two such widely cited estimates, both conducted by the Urban Institute and both contested, for the US: close to 700,000 in 1987 (Burt 1992) and around 850,000 for 1996 (Burt et al. 2001). Period prevalence estimates, in contrast, are based on counts of people who have been homeless for some period of time or indicate that they have been in response to a survey, and yield much larger estimates. For example, a 1990 nationwide survey of 1,507 domiciled US adults indicated 3.1 percent (5.7 million) experienced literal homelessness between 1985–90, and 4.6 percent (8.5 million) experienced general homelessness during the same period (Link et al. 1995).

Characteristics of the Homeless

Prior to the 1980s and the fifth wave of homelessness in the US, most homeless individuals were poor, unattached, alcoholic older men (Bahr & Caplow 1973). In the 1980s, as the homeless population grew, their characteristics began to change as well (Rossi 1989; Burt 1992; Burt et al. 2001). The majority of the "new" homeless were still unattached (single, divorced, separated, or widowed) males, but there were more homeless families and children than in the preceding decades. They were also considerably younger, with a mean age in the late 30s rather than the 50s; they were disproportionately minorities, with black Americans being conspicuously over-represented, particularly in large metropolitan areas; and a disproportionately large number were military veterans. As before, alcohol abuse was prevalent among the new homeless, but heavy drug use was more commonplace, spurred in part by the availability of cheap "crack" cocaine during the 1980s. In comparison to the general US population, a disproportionate number of the homeless also experienced a serious mental disability, with most research-based estimates ranging from one-quarter to one-third. A final defining characteristic of the homeless, both the old and the new, is that they are predominantly urbanites. Clearly, the new homeless can be found in all kinds of communities, both rural and urban, but they are most prominent in metropolitan areas, particularly in selected neighborhoods in central cities (Lee & Price-Spratlen 2004).

Causes of Homelessness

Historical fluctuations in the incidence of homelessness appear to be precipitated by the occurrence of two dislocating trends or events: large-scale structural changes, as in the case of industrialization, and systemic shocks, as associated with wars and depressions. Such changes, particularly of the structural variety, have been identified as the major precipitants of the end-of-the-century increase in homelessness as well. Especially noteworthy is a decline in affordable housing in the context of increasing economic hardship due to such factors as deindustrialization and declining wages. Indeed, the confluence of such trends suggests a general proposition regarding the structural roots of homelessness: it grows in the widening gap between subsistence needs, particularly housing, and the availability of economic resources to meet those needs among increasing numbers of individuals (Ringheim 1990; Shinn & Gillespie 1994; Koegel et al. 1996).

Structural factors alone, however, do not determine who becomes homeless. They designate which groups or classes of individuals are at risk of becoming homeless, but they do not specify which vulnerable individuals are most likely to fall onto the streets. In order to get a handle on this part of the causal equation, researchers have also examined the individual-level, biographic correlates of homelessness, such as demographic factors (e.g., race/ethnicity), human capital factors (e.g., educational level), social capital factors (e.g., family attachments), and disabilities (e.g., substance abuse and mental illness). In general, research concludes that the occurrence of homelessness among some individuals rather than others can be best understood by considering the intersection of structural and biographical factors (Snow & Anderson 1993; Koegel et al. 1996).

Survival Strategies

The homeless face specific challenges to survival and must negotiate ways to satisfy their basic human needs. Such challenges include finding food and shelter, establishing social relationships, and even making some subjective sense of their situation. The homeless adopt certain survival strategies that facilitate the satisfaction of these material, interpersonal, and psychological challenges. The strategies employed by the homeless are not uniform, but vary according to the individuals' personal characteristics and length of time on the streets. These survival routines are also embedded in specific organizational, political, and ecological contexts that encourage some strategies while making others less likely (Snow & Anderson 1993; Wright 1997; Duneier 1999).

To satisfy material needs, the homeless often engage in a number of different activities exclusively or in combination. Some homeless individuals receive institutional assistance, some perform wage labor, and some engage in "shadow work," which includes a variety of unconventional work pursued in the shadow of regular work, such as begging and panhandling and collecting and peddling discarded books, magazines, and cans.

The homeless, in general, are not inter-personally atomized and incompetent as often portrayed. However, their interpersonal relationships are often paradoxical in that they can provide security in the form of a non-stigmatizing reference group and a source for sharing resources, but they are often fleeting and fragile due to the transient nature of street life.

Like all individuals, the homeless must also make sense of their situation and negotiate meaning in their lives. Research suggests they tend to do so in two main ways: via existential-oriented meaning construction, which includes invoking causal accounts, such as "I'm down on my luck," to explain one's situation; and through various forms of identity talk, including distancing oneself from negative associations, embracing a positive association, or telling fictive stories to embellish one's status (Snow & Anderson 1993).

Responses to Homelessness

The turn-of-the-century wave of homelessness has elicited a variety of responses by different sets of actors across different geopolitical units, ranging from the local community to the states to the federal government. In terms of doing something about the "problem" of homelessness, the responses have generally been of four kinds. The most pervasive response can be described as "accommodative" in the sense of providing relief that aims to ameliorate the experience of homelessness by expanding, for example, the network of shelters and food providers. This has been the character of response by most governmental units, including the federal government's Stewart B. McKinney Homeless Act of 1987 and its subsequent amendments. Overlapping, yet distinctive, is the "restorative" response, which has sought primarily to repair or remedy chronically disabled homeless individuals through medical and/or religious intervention, as illustrated by the 43rd US president's chronic homeless initiative and faith-based charity programs. A third line of response is "preventive" in that the objective is to attack the structural causes of homelessness, such as unaffordable housing, rather than its individual-level symptoms. This response is illustrated by the July 2003 Bring America Home Act (HR 2897) and is championed by most homeless advocacy groups and protest movements. A final general response encompasses various "anti-homeless" efforts that seek to control and contain the homeless through sponsoring regulative ordinances and legislation that "criminalize" various subsistence strategies, such as panhandling and sleeping in public places.

Research on the various responses to homelessness has been relatively minuscule in comparison to the volume of research on the scope and causes of homelessness and on the characteristics of the homeless and their survival strategies. Nonetheless, there is increasing scholarly concern with relevant policy issues and with the efforts of advocacy groups and the homeless themselves to mobilize on behalf of homeless interests and rights (Wright 1997; Cress & Snow 2000).

SEE ALSO: Deindustrialization; Industrial Revolution; Inequality and the City; Metropolis; Poverty; Poverty and Disrepute; Social Exclusion; Urban Poverty; Urbanization

REFERENCES AND SUGGESTED READINGS

Bahr, H. M. & Caplow, T. (1973) *Old Men Drunk and Sober*. New York University Press, New York.
Burt, M. (1992) *Over the Edge: The Growth of Homelessness in the 1980s*. Russell Sage Foundation, New York.
Burt, M., Aron, L. Y., & Lee, E., with Valente, J. (2001) *Helping America's Homeless: Emergency Shelter or Affordable Housing?* Urban Institute Press, Washington, DC.
Cress, D. & Snow, D. A. (2000) The Outcomes of Homeless Mobilization: The Influence of Organization, Disruption, Political Mediation, and Framing. *American Journal of Sociology* 105: 1063–104.
Duneier, M. (1999) *Sidewalk*. Farrar, Strauss & Giroux, New York.
Koegel, P., Burnam, M. A., & Baumohl, J. (1996) The Causes of Homelessness. In: Baumohl, J. (Ed.), *Homelessness in America*. Oryx, Phoenix, pp. 22–4.
Lee, B. A. & Price-Spratlen, T. (2004) The Geography of Homelessness in American Communities: Concentration or Dispersion? *City and Community* 3: 3–27.

Link, B. G., Phelan, J., Bresnahan, M., Stueve, A., Moore, R., & Susser, E. (1995) Lifetime and Five-Year Prevalence of Homelessness in the United States: New Evidence on an Old Debate. *American Journal of Orthopsychiatry* 64: 247–354.

Ringheim, K. (1990) *At Risk of Homelessness: The Roles of Income and Rent.* Praeger Press, New York.

Rossi, P. (1989) *Down and Out in America: The Origins of Homelessness.* University of Chicago Press, Chicago.

Shinn, M. & Gillespie, C. (1994) The Roles of Housing and Poverty in the Origins of Homelessness. *American Behavioral Scientist* 37: 505–21.

Snow, D. A. & Anderson, L. (1993) *Down On Their Luck: A Study of Homeless Street People.* University of California Press, Berkeley.

Wright, J. D., Rubin, B. A., & Devine, J. A. (1998) *Beside the Golden Door: Policy, Politics, and the Homeless.* Aldine De Gruyter, New York.

Wright, T. (1997) *Out of Place: Homeless Mobilization, Subcities, and Contested Landscape.* State University of New York Press, Albany.

homicide

Leonard Beeghley

Unlike other western nations, thousands of people are murdered in the United States every year. Any large American city displays almost as many homicides as do many western nations (Beeghley 2003). A high rate of homicide – the intentional and illegal killing of another human being – makes the US anomalous.

Historically, homicide rates across Western Europe fell in a ragged but steady way from about 20–30 per 100,000 in the fourteenth century to around 1 per 100,000 in the nineteenth century. Although the data must be pieced together and the use of ranges (for example, 20–30) for past estimates suggests some uncertainty, the long-term process is clear (Gurr 1989). The average homicide rate in England and Wales was less than 1 per 100,000 throughout the twentieth century (Beeghley 2003). Other Western European nations exhibit similar rates.

By comparison, the US has always displayed much more violence (Adler 2005). In the twentieth century, the average US homicide rate was 7.6 per 100,000 (Beeghley 2003). Nationwide, about 16,000 persons were murdered in 2001 – a relatively low number, as homicide rates declined at the end of the century. The US rate in 2001, however, was 5.6 per 100,000, compared to only 1.6 in England and Wales. There were 648 murders in Chicago in 2002, 587 in New York, and 654 in Los Angeles – which were low compared to just a few years ago, and interpreted as showing that these cities are becoming safer places to live. By contrast, there were 858 homicides in all of England in 2002.

One way to understand homicide is to assess people's motives (Akers & Sellers 2004). One might posit, for example, that an individual's frustration and socialization to violence contributed to a homicide. Other factors could be involved as well, of course, but the point is to distinguish individual killers from non-killers, to explain one homicide. Although social psychological explanations like these are necessary and valuable, they reveal nothing about the structural factors leading to a high (or low) rate of homicide.

Dealing with that issue requires shifting the level of analysis (Messner & Rosenfeld 2001). Research shows that five structural characteristics make the US unique and combine to produce an anomalous homicide rate: (1) the availability of guns, (2) drug markets, (3) racial discrimination, especially in housing, (4) exposure to violence in the media, at home, in neighborhoods, and from government action, and (5) economic inequality (Beeghley 2003). With one exception, the relationship between each of these factors and the homicide rate is clear and unequivocal. The exception involves guns. This literature has become politicized in the US (but not in other nations, where observers take the relationship as established), which means conclusions must reflect an assessment of the preponderance of the evidence.

The combined impact of these factors is especially important. Scholars writing in each area, however, usually do not refer to works in other areas, which makes it hard to see the interconnections. For example, when studies find a correlation between gun availability and the homicide rate, the authors generally do not look at drug markets. Yet one reason drug markets are so violent in the US is the presence of so many guns. In addition, one reason economic inequality in the US is related to homicide is that so many people are exposed to so much violence. It is a sociological truism that the parts of society are not only connected, but also that their impact is often mutually reinforcing. No single cause exists in isolation.

We are not helpless. A half century ago, the fatality rate from automobile accidents in the US was much higher than today. Although some argued the problem was the "nut behind the wheel," design changes in roads and cars reduced auto fatalities – even though "nuts" still drive. In a modern society, that which can be explained can often be changed.

The structural factors identified in the literature suggest some possible directions for policy change. Thus, while people have a right to own guns (at least in the US), under what conditions should this right be exercised? Just as public safety dictates some restrictions on the use of cars, perhaps similar policies ought to be applied to guns. Perhaps the way guns are designed and sold should be modified. Similarly, since zero tolerance policies have not reduced demand for illegal substances in the US, perhaps this tactic should be reconsidered and jail reserved for those we fear, rather than those who anger us. This might mean providing users with treatment to undercut the illegal market and violence it engenders. It might also be useful to consider how to attack housing discrimination, reduce the level of inequality, and limit exposure to violence in the US. In evaluating these possibilities, the trick is to think radically but proceed cautiously, looking out for unintended results (Rosenfeld 2004).

But caution need not be stasis. The experiences of other nations suggest clearly that Americans are not fated to live with so much lethal violence. The US is anomalous for specific reasons that are reflected in public policy. The impact condemns thousands of people to death each year. These policies are not set in stone; they are choices. Choices made can be unmade.

SEE ALSO: Crime; Drugs, Drug Abuse, and Drug Policy; Index Crime; Violence; Violent Crime

REFERENCES AND SUGGESTED READINGS

Adler, J. (2005) *"First in Violence:" Homicide in Chicago, 1875–1920*. Harvard University Press, New Haven.

Akers, R. L. & Sellers, C. (2004) *Criminological Theories: Introduction, Evaluation, and Application*, 4th edn. Roxbury Press, Los Angeles.

Beeghley, L. (2003) *Homicide: A Sociological Explanation*. Rowman & Littlefield, Boulder.

Gurr, T. R. (1989) Historical Trends in Violent Crime: Europe and the United States. In: Gurr, T. R. (Ed.), *Violence in America*, Vol. 1. Sage, Newbury Park, CA.

Messner, S. & Rosenfeld, R. (2001) *Crime and the American Dream*, 3rd edn. Wadsworth Publishing, Belmont, CA.

Rosenfeld, R. (2004) The Case of the Unsolved Crime Decline. *Scientific American* 290 (February): 80–9.

homophobia

James J. Dean

Three important areas of research have emerged on homophobia over the last 30 years. Since Weinberg (1972) first popularized the term homophobia in his book *Society and the Healthy Homosexual*, where he defined it as "the dread of being in close quarters with homosexuals," we have seen the emergence of sophisticated psychological instruments, a vast array of surveys, qualitative ethnographies, and interview studies that explore the attitudes, feelings, and social practices that constitute homophobia.

While scholars such as Sears and Williams (1997) now define homophobia more broadly as "prejudice, discrimination, harassment, or acts of violence against sexual minorities, including lesbians, gay men, bisexuals and transgendered persons," psychological instruments have become more adept at detecting differences between homophobic attitudes and feelings. For example, MacDonald and Games's 30-item instrument Modified Attitudes Toward Homosexuality and Hudson and Rickett's Index of Homophobia, which uses a scale to measure reactions to homosexual individuals and situations, have become standard ways to assess homophobic attitudes and feelings in experimental studies. Although these instruments are able to differentiate between attitudes as cognitive beliefs about homosexuals and homosexuality and feelings as deeply seated emotional responses, they are still not able to capture how attitudes and beliefs affect social behavior and practices.

The second and largest area of research on homophobia is the development of a huge variety of surveys on homophobic attitudes among adults. The general findings of these surveys show that the demographic characteristics of those who hold negative attitudes about homosexuals are that they are more likely to live in the Midwest, the South, or small towns and rural areas (Herek 1984; Britton 1990; Bruce et al. 1990). Moreover, negative attitudes are more likely to be held by men who are older and less well educated (Roese et al. 1992; Herek & Glunt 1993). These surveys also show that men have stronger homophobic attitudes or feelings than women, and that men evidence a stronger dislike for gay male homosexuality than lesbianism (Herek 1988; Gallup 1995).

Other recent research on the relationship between homophobia and the formation of gender and sexual identities has emerged among scholars such as Sanday (1990), Mac An Ghaill (1994), Nayak and Kehily (1997), and Epstein and Johnson (1998). For example, Nayak and Kehily (1997) show through interviews and ethnographic observation how young men in secondary schools use homophobic practices to establish masculine heterosexual identities, emphasizing that masculinities are the basis upon which young men's homophobic practices and heterosexual identities are constructed.

Nayak and Kehily argue that identities are always constructed, and gain their meanings, through cultural oppositions. Hence, masculine identities are constructed through their opposition to feminine ones, gaining their meaning through excluding feminine identities but at the same depending upon them for definition. This understanding, they argue, explains why young men are not necessarily against homosexuality itself, but rather its associations with femininity and the lack of a masculine self-identity that it implies. They thus view homophobia as a practice that establishes boundaries of purity and pollution between pure heterosexual masculine men and polluted non-heterosexual feminine ones. They observed several patterns of homophobic practices among young men. For instance, they state that young men avoid intimate conversations with one another, fearing emotional homosocial bonding. That is, talking about feelings could elicit suspicions that an individual might possibly be homosexual. Further, boys avoid other boys who are suspected of being gay in order to maintain clear boundaries between a respected masculine heterosexual status and a denigrated gay one. Moreover, young males use homophobic practices to establish a heterosexual identity through a gendered sign system that categorizes feminine boys as polluted and potentially homosexual. For example, boys who are quiet, studious, well mannered, or do not participate in male bonding practices are often targets of derision, as well as boys who have high voices, a feminine walk, or a scrawny body. By making fun of other boys, deriding them as gay, or even using violence, young men establish a masculine heterosexual identity through excluding and sanctioning other boys.

An even more violent and aggressive heterosexual masculine identity, which depends on homophobia and homosexuality for its constitution, is analyzed by Sanday (1990) in her study of fraternity gang rape. Sanday shows that fraternity brothers promote compulsory heterosexuality in acts of gang rape by using homophobic social sanctions which deride those brothers who do not participate as homosexual or unmanly. At the same time, however, a sublimated homosexuality is expressed by the fact that the frat brothers are having sex with one another through the woman being gang raped. Homosexual desire is expunged out of the act of gang rape through homophobic and compulsory heterosexual discourses that construct masculine heterosexual brothers who "pull train," that is, gang rape a woman, as exclusively heterosexual.

In sum, homophobia has become an important topic in social science research. The growing sophistication of psychological instruments, the increasing number of surveys and qualitative studies analyzing homophobic attitudes, feelings, and practices have helped us to better understand the phenomenon and its continuing conceptualization as a form of deviance. However, future research on homophobic behavior by both quantitative and qualitative scholars would help to fill in important empirical gaps in the literature, especially on men who consciously and behaviorally identify as heterosexual and commit the largest number of hate crimes against gays and lesbians (Jenness & Broad 1997). Similarly, more research on the most effective strategies for reducing homophobia would be a valuable component in mitigating the pernicious effects of this social problem.

SEE ALSO: Compulsory Heterosexuality; Fear; Gay Bashing; Gay and Lesbian Movement; Homophobia and Heterosexism; Homosexuality; Sexual Deviance; Sexual Politics

REFERENCES AND SUGGESTED READINGS

Britton, D. (1990) Homophobia and Homosociality: An Analysis of Boundary Maintenance. *Sociological Quarterly* 31(3): 423–39.
Bruce, K., Shrumm, J., Trefethen, C., & Slovik, L. (1990) Students' Attitudes About AIDS, Homosexuality, and Condoms. *AIDS Education and Prevention* 2: 220–34.
Epstein, D. & Johnson, R. (1998) *Schooling Sexualities*. Open University Press, Buckingham.
Gallup, G. (1995) Have Attitudes Toward Homosexuals Been Shaped by Natural Selection? *Ethnology and Sociobiology* 16(1): 53–70.
Herek, G. (1984) Beyond Homophobia: A Social Psychological Perspective on Attitudes Toward Lesbians and Gay Men. *Journal of Homosexuality* 10(1/2): 1–18.
Herek, G. (1988) Heterosexuals' Attitudes Towards Lesbians and Gay Men: Correlations and Gender Difference. *Journal of Sex Research* 25(4): 451–77.
Herek, G. & Glunt, E. (1993) Interpersonal Contact and Heterosexuals' Attitudes Toward Gay Men. *Journal of Sex Research* 30(3): 239–44.
Jenness, V. & Broad, K. (1997) *Hate Crimes: New Social Movements and the Politics of Violence*. Aldine de Gruyter, New York.
Mac An Ghaill, M. (1994) *The Making of Men: Masculinities, Sexualities and Schooling*. Open University Press, Buckingham.
Nayak, A. & Kehily, M. (1997) Masculinities and Schooling: Why are Young Men So Homophobic? In: Steinberg, D., Epstein, D., & Johnson, R.

(Eds.), *Border Patrols: Policing the Boundaries of Heterosexuality*. Cassell, London.
Roese, N., Olson, J., Borenstein, M., Martin, A., & Shores, A. (1992) Same-Sex Touching Behavior: The Moderating Role of Homophobic Attitudes. *Journal of Nonverbal Behavior* 16(4): 249–59.
Sanday, P. (1990) *Fraternity Gang Rape: Sex, Brotherhood, and Privilege on Campus*. New York University Press, New York.
Sears, J. & Williams, W. (Eds.) (1997) *Overcoming Heterosexism and Homophobia: Strategies that Work*. Columbia University Press, New York.
Weinberg, G. (1972) *Society and the Healthy Homosexual*. St. Martin's Press, New York.

homophobia and heterosexism

Barry D. Adam

Homophobia is perhaps the most widely understood term to refer to anti-homosexual attitudes and practices, but comparison of such terms as homophobia, heterosexism, and heteronormativity reveals how these terms rely on different ideas of what homosexual means, and where opposition to same-sex relations originates. Homophobia typically denotes, like other phobias, an irrational fear or a set of mistaken ideas held by prejudiced individuals; its alleviation therefore likely comes through therapy or education. Popularized through George Weinberg's 1973 book, *Society and the Healthy Homosexual*, homophobia is a concept with strong roots in psychology. Its use tends to focus attention on individuals, to locate its origins in childhood socialization, and to conceive of it as a prejudice directed against homosexual persons. Heterosexism tends to be used less widely, but it offers a more sociological notion of practices that are embedded in social structures and reinforced by ideology. Use of a term like heterosexism shifts analysis to the ways in which the social institutions of government, workplace, religion, family, and media are organized to exclude or disadvantage same-sex relations. Resolving heterosexism implies reforming or reorganizing social institutions in ways that allow and support same-sex relationships. Finally, heteronormativity is a term used most often in literary studies, which see both homosexuality and anti-homosexuality as effects of binary distinctions made in language. Textual deconstruction typically seeks to find how and why such distinctions as heterosexual–homosexual arise and are reproduced. If distinctions of this kind were not made at all, or least were of little significance, then presumably anti-homosexuality could scarcely come about either. For queer theory, the issue is not one of appealing for tolerance or acceptance for a quasi-ethnic, twenty-first-century urban community of lesbians and gay men, but of shaking up or transgressing the entire heterosexual–homosexual binary that fuels the distinction in the first place.

There are several leading theories that lend credence to each of these conceptions. Gayle Rubin's influential essay on "The Traffic in Women" built on Claude Lévi-Strauss's work on kinship systems among hundreds of societies around the world that showed how kinship codes prescribe the exchange of women by male clans, thereby founding and organizing gender systems that order both same-sex and cross-sex relations. Heterosexuality is recreated each generation through a system of fraternal interest groups that exercise control over women's reproductive power in families. As a consequence, homosexuality among men and among women runs up against different but related difficulties. Homosexuality among men abstains from or transgresses the fundamental social "game plan" of the fraternal interest groups to acquire, control, and trade in the reproductive power of women. Homosexuality in men, according to this scenario, comes to be identified with the betrayal of masculinity and the inability to assert male domination over women. The sexuality of women in such a system is put at the disposal of men; their own sexual preferences are largely precluded. Lesbianism, as Monique Wittig argues in "The Straight Mind," violates the same social order by asserting will and subjectivity among the female gender, intended by patriarchal groups to be objects of exchange. Wittig calls female homosexuality a "revolt of the trade goods" in the "traffic in women." Adrienne Rich (1989) also characterizes lesbianism as an assertion of women's subjectivity and self-determination, and a direct challenge to patriarchy. Anti-lesbianism, then, for Rich is a variant of misogyny, a means of

enforcing "compulsory heterosexuality," and a system of keeping women subservient to male domination.

Still, it must be noted that anti-homosexuality is not the inevitable consequence of kinship organization. In many societies around the world, same-sex bonding is accepted and valued by becoming integrated into, and defined by, kinship codes. Same-sex connections may take "berdache," "two-spirited," or transgendered form in societies with weak fraternal interest groups where gender fluidity, gender mixing, or gender migration appear to be possible for some men and a few women. Where male sexual bonding appears in societies with strong fraternal interest groups, it typically takes the form of hierarchical, military, age-graded, and mentor/acolyte relationships, where adult men who exercise control over women's bodies also assume sexual rights over younger, subordinate males.

Gender panic theory focuses particularly on homophobia as an effect of gender. Masculinity, this theory contends, is an achieved and insecure status. Defensiveness against losing male status and privilege generates homophobia. Psychological research shows how homophobia appears to be particularly strong among gender conservatives intent on upholding gender differences, and among adolescent males who feel insecure in their access to masculine status. The queer theory of Judith Butler and Eve Sedgwick relies on, and extends, gender panic theory, contending that heterosexual masculinity builds itself on the simultaneous exploitation and denial of homosexuality. Since heterosexual masculinity can never constitute itself as secure and unassailable, and homosexuality is a default subject location against which heterosexuality defines itself, then homosexual possibilities can never be fully repressed and indeed remain necessary for the masculine self. Through extensive analyses of such cultural artifacts as novels, movies, advertising, and sport, queer theorists reveal how they covertly appeal to (sometimes thinly veiled) homoeroticism at the same time as they overtly deny it. This repetitive denial of homoeroticism in order to shore up the social construct of heterosexual masculinity reproduces heteronormativity. Again, it is noteworthy from a cross-cultural perspective that this cultural understanding of gender and masculinity is neither inherent in maleness nor universal.

While gender panic theory offers a strong explanation for homophobia in western and other patriarchal societies, it does not work for societies where same-sex bonding is itself regarded as masculine, and makes up a part of the socialization process to masculinize youths.

Sociohistorical theories are particularly interested in the social factors that fuel, or diminish, homophobia. These theories focus on the variability of homophobia by investigating why campaigns of persecution against homosexual relations break out in certain places and times, and among particular social constituencies, while at other times and among other social groups there is acceptance or support of lesbian, gay, bisexual, and transgendered (LGBT) people. Homophobia in western societies is associated with the roles non-heterosexual peoples have been assigned in history, meanings attributed to homosexuality by powerful social institutions, and the symbolic value of disenfranchised and "upstart" social groups to dominant forces. In nineteenth- and twentieth-century Europe and North America, the adherents of anti-homosexual worldviews have typically come from a range of social groups disturbed or threatened by modernity – usually traditional elites fearful of change and declining social classes resentful of groups on the rise. Status defense theories note that people with (or threatened with) declining living standards are especially susceptible to a politics of resentment, and have a tendency to strike out against those they see as "undeserving." Anti-gay persecution has often run parallel to campaigns of persecution directed against other disenfranchised groups. Perhaps the most egregious example is fascism, which swept up a range of people symbolizing modernity into the Holocaust. Thus gay men came to share the fate of Jews, communists, Roma, and disabled and racialized peoples when Nazism moved to reestablish the dominance of traditionally privileged social groups. Smaller-scale and less intense campaigns have mobilized similar constituencies in the United States, from McCarthyism in the 1950s to repeated referendum campaigns to repeal human rights legislation since the 1970s and subsequent electoral strategies on the part of the Republican Party. Sociohistorical theories, then, do not see homophobia as a "given" inherent in gender and social institutions, but focus on the forces that exacerbate or alleviate it over time.

Despite important gains in human rights legislation protecting the equality rights of LGBT people in many countries, homophobic attitudes and practices remain widespread. High schools appear to be a particular source of anti-gay harassment in the English-language world. Human Rights Watch found, in a recent investigation of US schools, that LGBT youth frequently find themselves the objects of verbal and physical attacks and that school officials provide them little or no protection or redress. Organizations such as the International Lesbian and Gay Organization, the International Gay and Lesbian Human Rights Commission, and, to a lesser extent, Amnesty International now monitor violence directed against LGBT people around the world. In some countries, state violence flows from laws that continue to criminalize homosexuality, particularly in postcolonial governments of South Asia, Africa, and the Caribbean – many still preserving British laws now abandoned by the United Kingdom itself – and Islamic governments of the Arab world, Southwest Asia, and Malaysia. Some jurisdictions have begun to take steps to curb homophobic violence in the form of hate crimes legislation, as in the United States, or prohibitions against incitement to hatred, as in Northern Europe, Spain, Canada, and Australia, but in many places anti-LGBT violence endures.

SEE ALSO: Compulsory Heterosexuality; Gay Bashing; Gay and Lesbian Movement; Hate Crimes; Homophobia; Queer Theory

REFERENCES AND SUGGESTED READINGS

Adam, B. D. (1998) Theorizing Homophobia. *Sexualities* 1(4): 387–404.

Butler, J. (1990) *Gender Trouble*. Routledge, New York.

Fone, B. (2000) *Homophobia*. Metropolitan, New York.

Herek, G. (2000) The Psychology of Sexual Prejudice. *Current Directions in Psychological Science* 9(1): 19–22.

Human Rights Watch (2001) *Hatred in the Hallways*. Human Rights Watch, New York.

Rich, A. (1989) Compulsory Heterosexuality and Lesbian Existence. In: Richardson, L. & Taylor, V. (Eds.), *Feminist Frontiers II*. Random House, New York.

Rubin, G. (1975) The Traffic in Women. In: Reiter, R. (Ed.), *Toward an Anthropology of Women*. Monthly Review Press, New York.

Stein, A. (2001) *The Stranger Next Door*. Beacon, Boston.

homosexuality

Gert Hekma

Homosexuality refers to sexual behaviors and desires between males or between females. *Gay* refers to self-identification with such practices and desires. Gay and homosexual are both terms mostly used only for men. Lesbian is its female counterpart. Such definitions have run into major problems, and nowadays the concept *queer* is used to indicate the fluency of sexual practices and gender performances.

SOCIAL CONTEXT

Since the 1970s, homosexuality has become the topic of an interdisciplinary specialization variously called gay and lesbian, queer or LGBT studies (Lesbian, Gay, Bisexual, and Transgender, to which sometimes are added QQI: Queer, Questioning, and Intersexual). The field is far removed from traditional sexology that has its base in psychology, medicine, and biology, and is closely linked to what once were called minority (black and women's) studies and now gender studies. Most of the disciplines involved belong to the humanities and social sciences: language and literature, history, cultural and communication studies, sociology, anthropology and political sciences, philosophy. Sociology had a late start, although some of the key figures in the field were sociologists (Mary McIntosh, Ken Plummer, Jeffrey Weeks), but their work was seen as primarily historical. Michel Foucault made a major imprint with the first volume of his *Histoire de la sexualité* (1976). Other major sociologists contributed to or supported the field, for example Pierre Bourdieu, Michel Maffesoli, and Steven Seidman (1997, 1998). Notwithstanding its important intellectual proponents, the field has a weak base in universities and departments of sociology, where few tenured staff have been nominated anywhere specifically for the field, not even for the sociology of sexuality. Most often, academics started to work on homosexual themes because of personal and social interests. Gay studies has kept a strong interdisciplinary quality, often with close cooperation between sociology, history, anthropology, and cultural studies.

HISTORY

The words homosexual and heterosexual were invented in 1868 and first used in print in 1869 by the Hungarian author Károly Mária Kertbeny (1824–82). In 1864 the German lawyer Karl Heinrich Ulrichs had come up with the words "uranism" and "uranian" to describe a similar social reality, while "philopedia" was created by the French psychiatrist C. F. Michéa in 1849. These words no longer referred to sexual acts that were sins and crimes and were called sodomy, unnatural intercourse, pederasty, and so forth, but to sexual identities and desires that were deeply embedded in persons. Ulrichs and Kertbeny were predecessors of the gay rights movement and wrote mainly against criminalization of sodomy. They spoke largely from personal experiences and historical examples. Most medical authors, who started to use the new terminologies, discussed mainly the causes of such identities and desires and the question whether they were pathological or normal. They set the standards for the search for a biological basis that continues to this day ("gay gene"). Most physicians started to believe that homosexuality is an innate condition (but not the Freudians) and took the position that it is a disease or abnormality that should be healed and prevented. The early research by psychiatrists was mainly based on case histories of what they called "perverts." They began to discuss not only homosexuality, but other perversions as well that got new names, such as masochism, sadism, fetishism, exhibitionism, necrophilia, zoophilia, and so forth. The centers of research were on the European continent: Berlin, Paris, Vienna.

The early medical research had several sociological angles. Ulrichs and Magnus Hirschfeld, the founder of the first homosexual rights movement in 1897, came up with the first statistics on the numbers of homosexuals that closely resemble the data of today. While Ulrichs thought his uranians were less than 1 percent of the population, an anonymous Dutch adept of his estimated the figure in 1870 at 2 percent, as Hirschfeld later did. The Dutch physician and homosexual rights activist Lucien von Römer worked with Hirschfeld on sexual statistics. In a survey of 308 Amsterdam students done in 1904, he counted not only the men who identified as homosexual (2 percent) and bisexual (4 percent), but also those who had gay sex during puberty (21 percent) or homosexual fantasies (6 percent). In the first Dutch gay novel that appeared this same year, the author Jacob Israël de Haan told how as a student he made fun of the questions as he answered them. He made clear how unreliable such data often are.

Hirschfeld also did the first urban geography, "Berlin's Third Gender" (1904), in which he described the city's gay subculture of bars and parks and the elaborate world of male prostitution. Mainly German books on the history of sexual morality (*Sittengeschichte*), which often included chapters on homosexuality, preceded and influenced the work of later sociologists and historians like Norbert Elias and Michel Foucault. The work of these psychiatrists who started to give names, definitions, and identities to disease, crime, and perversion made possible the work of sociologists creating stigma and labeling theory. In many ways, this early research paved the way for what would become the sociology of (homo)sexuality. The enormous body of work, available mainly thanks to early, prewar German sexology, was largely forgotten when the main location of sex research after World War II moved to another language, English, and to another country, the US.

Most of the scholarly work on homosexuality remained focused on psychiatry, both in Europe and the US. The major sociological breakthrough came from Alfred Kinsey (1894–1956).

He was a biologist specializing in wasps, but he is generally considered to be the founder of the sociology of (homo)sexuality by means of his two books *Sexual Behavior in the Human Male* (1948) and *Sexual Behavior in the Human Female* (1953). Although these studies have been criticized for methodological weaknesses and the reduction of sexuality to "outlets," this work has been pivotal in putting sexuality on the agenda of the social sciences. Kinsey was the first to come up with more or less reliable statistics on sexual behavior, and placed them in the larger contexts of biology and history. From his research stem ideas that 37 percent of US men have had homosexual experiences and 4 percent exclusively and lifelong. He was a man with a mission who did not hide his political agenda. He stressed time and again that the large majority of citizens would have to go to prison if US laws were applied rigorously, indicating that it was a better idea to change the laws. He did much to normalize taboo acts such as homosexuality, masturbation, premarital sex, adultery, and prostitution. His institute in Bloomington, Indiana, has become one of the world's most important archives and research centers on sexual behavior and culture.

Kinsey offered a sociological instead of a psychological perspective on the topic. In his footsteps and in the wake of the nascent homosexual rights movement in the US and the UK, Edward Sagarin and Michael Schofield began to write on homosexuality from a sociological perspective, using the pseudonyms Donald Webster Cory and Gordon Westwood. Cory's books gave an overview of what was known on the topic, while Westwood interviewed 127 homosexuals on their sexual life. Cory's work in particular had a wide readership among gay men. These works changed the focus from the aberrant homosexual who had gender identity problems or was abused as a boy, to the society that discriminated against homosexuals and largely contributed to their problems (for an overview of early sociological research in the US, see Minton 2001). The Dutch psychiatrist Tolsma, who earlier believed homosexuality was pathological and homosexuals recruited boys to their ranks, did research on its origins and discovered in 1957 that no gay man had become this way through seduction.

In the footsteps of Kinsey and Schofield, more surveys were done among gay men in the 1970s, in Germany by Martin Dannecker and Reimut Reiche, in France by Michel Bon and Antoine d'Arc, and in the US by Joseph Harry and William De Vall and by Alan Bell and Martin Weinberg of the Kinsey Institute. These surveys provided good pictures of local or national homosexual cultures, but as they could not use representative samples their results are difficult to compare. Frederick Whitam and Robin Mathy surveyed *Male Homosexuality in Four Societies* (1986) and found effeminacy in gay men in all four locations, which suggested, for them, innateness. The homosexual behavior of many non-homosexual men in these societies was explained as a secondary sexual outlet. Other de/constructivist perspectives would later change this line of thinking. Surveying quickly developed in the wake of AIDS.

Other centers of research and theorizing took over in the 1950s from the Kinsey Institute and independent gay researchers. The Chicago School of urban sociology started to include sexual variation in its agenda and to study urban gay subcultures. Maurice Leznoff and William A. Westley were the first to write on "The Homosexual Community" in 1956, discussing "a larger Canadian city." The topics range from cliques, their gossip and incest taboos, being secret or overt, and professions (many were hairdressers). The topics are still very close to those of psychiatry. Later work discusses the gay bar in more sophisticated ways. Manuel Castells wrote a landmark study on geographical distribution, community organizing, and political activity of San Francisco gays and lesbians. In 1979 the concept of "gay ghetto" was introduced in the article of the same title by Martin Levine. This was the first article on gay geography and included maps of several gay vicinities that had come into visible existence since the late 1960s. After the queer turn of the 1990s, several books on space and sexuality appeared that were more cultural studies, but still included sociological material, while the field of gay urban histories boomed with George Chauncey's landmark study *Gay New York* (1994) and David Higgs's collection *Queer Sites* (1999). In *Forging Gay Identities* (2002) Elizabeth Armstrong studied gay and lesbian movements in San Francisco that she divided into three stages: the more prudent

homophile movement before 1969, a short interlude of the radical gay movement that connected gay and left interests, and from the early 1970s the identity and one-issue gay (and lesbian) movement. The date of the Stonewall rebellion in 1969, when fairies, butch lesbians, and drag queens resisted a police raid in the bar of the same name in New York, is nowadays globally commemorated.

The major concept of the 1970s was stigma. Symbolic interactionism was added to urban sociology. It fit well with the change from psychology to sociology, from pathology to activism. What homosexual men suffered from was not their innate abnormality or viciousness, but social rejection. At the time that activists asked for removal of homosexuality from psychiatric classifications such as DSM, and came out of the closets into the streets, sociologists started to discuss sexual stigma. In a landmark study, Gagnon and Simon (1973) developed the concept of sexual script(ing). Their script was what others later named narrative or story (Plummer 1995). Gagnon and Simon wanted to turn away from biological and Freudian perspectives to a sociological one that combined the social and the individual. Persons become sexual beings in an interaction between both. With many examples, they indicate how the social influences the sexual and vice versa. Theories that focus on instincts and impulses proved to be less helpful to explain erotic experience and variation. Other work engaged with the homosexual "coming out," in which the various stages of this process – sensitivation, resistance, acceptance, integration – were studied and demarcated (Troiden 1988). A budding field was the theme of gay and lesbian youth and their organizations and sexual education. An early and most controversial contribution in the symbolic interactionist tradition was *Tearoom Trade* (1970) by Laud Humphreys, which was about casual homosexual encounters in a public toilet. The debate was both on the topic and on the ethics of the research method. Humphreys had used the vehicle registration plates of the men visiting tearooms to discover additional information without their knowledge. So he came to know that the men often were married and highly conservative.

The major line of research from the late 1970s became historical-sociological. In 1967 Mary

McIntosh wrote a promising article ("The Homosexual Role") in this direction, suggesting that such a role had only come into existence in the eighteenth century. The major studies were Michel Foucault's 3-volume *Histoire de la sexualité* (1976, 1984, 1984). The first volume – *La Volonté de savoir* – was the founding work of social constructionism, a term Foucault himself never used. In this work he remarks on the change from the legal concept of sodomy, an act, to the medical one of homosexuality, an identity, that will be insistently researched as part of the politics of the body. His work is a strong critique of the idea of sexual liberation, then prominent on the social agenda through the work of Wilhelm Reich and Herbert Marcuse. He showed how discourses of sexual liberation had been around since the eighteenth century and mainly contributed to normalization and stricter controls of sexuality. His theory of an omnipresent power that used such ideologies to get a firmer grip on sexual practices spurred a new generation to engage with sexual history, also because sexuality was reconceived as something that changed over time and may not in fact have existed as a special social reality before the rise of sexual sciences. Movements of resistance that were included in his theory of power played an ambivalent role, as they largely contributed to the innovation of body politics. Although the work of Foucault deals with sexual culture in general, his leading theme may well be said to have been homosexual pleasures. His studies extended the realm of Gagnon and Simon from the micro to the macro level and gave it a historical twist.

A sociologist who works in the same vein as Foucault is Jeffrey Weeks. He started in 1977 with a book on the development of the homosexual rights movement in England and continued with a general history of sexuality (Weeks 2000). His later work is about sexual ethics (Weeks 1995), while he recently took to researching "non-heterosexual" intimate relations (Weeks et al. 2001). The Foucauldian approach came at the same time as the establishment of gay and lesbian studies and inspired the first international conferences. Most new work was based on the idea of *The Making of the Modern Homosexual*, the title of a collection by Ken Plummer. Social constructionism was opposed to essentialism that sees sexual preferences as innate. Few people in gay and lesbian studies defend that position, while most of the biologists who research gay genes, brain parts, and hormonal systems are unaware of this critique. A main theme became the development of essentialist sexual sciences.

The rise of AIDS stimulated research on several aspects of gay life, especially on sexual and preventive practices. The main aim was to impede risky behaviors. The positive side was that it produced much information on gay sex and created greater openness. But too often the research neglected the social context, once more focusing strongly on sexual outlets of "men having sex with men" (MSM). Many countries saw major surveys on sexual behavior (for the US, see Laumann et al. 1994). The outcome of these surveys surprised the gay movement because the stated numbers of gay men were everywhere lower than those found by Kinsey in the 1940s. The higher numbers of gay men in cities cannot be explained fully by their migration to the more gay-friendly towns, as was expected, as cities themselves produce more men identifying as homosexuals.

SPECIAL TOPICS

With the development of gay and lesbian, and later queer studies, the research specialized. Apart from gay bars and urban cultures, particular groups started to receive attention. An early popular issue was male prostitution. These studies discussed the pay and the sexual identity of the hustlers who are often straight, their age and sexual techniques, the locations where they work, their drug use, ethnicity, and class. It is a circuit where the ganymedes, sexually unsure and unprofessional, rob and murder their clients. Later, bisexuals, drag queens, transsexuals, transgenders, intersexuals and s/m-ers emerged. A very controversial subject is pedophilia, which is often and unjustly seen as an exclusively gay issue. Anonymous sex on the streets and other places was studied. Other topics varied from gay men in ethnic groups, friendships, and suburban gay lives to violence, suicide, and aging. Masculinity became a topic, sometimes with a focus on the leather scene.

With the start of discussions on homosexuality and the army and same-sex marriage these issues arrived on the sociological agenda. The discussion on intimate relations was started by Weston (1991). Later studies showed opposite results. While Weeks et al. (2001) underlined the transgressiveness of same-sexual families that were more open to third parties and educated children in various social constellations, Carrington (1999) stated that the couples he researched largely imitated straight codes when it came to the gendered division of labor, household tasks, and financial arrangements. It is likely that these opposite results could be explained by different samples. Other scholars revived the culture of the 1970s, before the times of AIDS, when gay men developed a patchwork of sexual situations, passions, love relations, and friendships that bridged the gap between single and couple. They felt culpable for the epidemic, but with the knowledge of safe sex it is possible to recreate this culture "beyond shame."

With the breakdown of the difference between anthropology and sociology, themes of gay life in a non-western and globalized world start to draw more attention. Nowadays a growing number of books discuss same-sexual practices and cultures in a great variety of countries, as well as the interconnections between the various parts of the world through migration, tourism, media, the Internet, science, and politics. Globalization created "global gays" and multiethnic queer communities in the major capitals of the world, while global effects got local inflections, or were sometimes resisted by gay and anti-gay people (Altman 2001).

METHODOLOGICAL ISSUES

The main question in gay research is the definition of what is the object of study. Most research is dependent on self-identification of the interviewees, who may be unwilling to disclose their sexual interests. There are no objective criteria to define the homosexual. Kinsey therefore developed a homo–heterosexual scale from 0–6 in which he integrated sexual practices and sexual fantasies. Other authors created layered scales that included more facets or developments

in time as individuals move between sexual identifications during their lives. AIDS research focused on sexual practices, while some opposed this narrow perspective because behaviors are dependent on personal identifications and social contexts.

The confluence of homosexuality with effeminacy and passivity in practice and prejudice offers another challenge. Most biological research is based on the equation of effeminacy and sexual passivity in males with homosexuality, but most modern gay men stress their masculinity and exchange sexual roles with partners. All of these terms can have very different meanings. Transgenders may flaunt their femininity, but can be strong and masculine when they face violent confrontations. Straight men visit male-to-female transgender prostitutes and often prefer passive roles. Some females in Namibia call themselves "lesbian men" and were intransigent when the local gay and lesbian movement tried to teach them they were really butches – for them, there was a world of difference between the two. The advice to the researcher should be to learn and use the terminologies the respondents themselves use and clarify those instead of attributing names and qualities to them.

Another major stumbling block in research is the absence of representative groups. Most research uses the snowball method. Gay men are invisible, so researchers depend in surveys on self-disclosure. Several techniques have been developed to circumvent this problem, for example asking "how often did you have sex with men?" rather than "are you gay?" or embedding questions on sexual behavior in a series that deals with heterosexual experiences. The terminological changes pose another problem, every new generation creating a new word for its same-sexual experiences, moving from uranian, homosexual, homophile, and gay to LGTBQQI and queer, while these vocabularies always give different meanings to sometimes similar, sometimes quite dissimilar practices and desires. Translations into other languages pose specific problems. The use of any concept creates exclusions. The most inclusive word – queer – that is close to non-heterosexual is rejected by respectable gay men who consider the term insulting.

FUTURE DIRECTIONS

Some of the research is driven by social developments, so it can be expected that controversial issues such as same-sex marriage, homosexuals in the army, violence against LGBT people, or discrimination in various situations such as in offices or sports will remain high on the agenda. The same will apply to sexual education and queer initiation. Specific groups such as elderly, ethnic minority, and questioning young gays will receive more attention. The turn from biology to sociology in gay research means that attention will shift from genes and identities to space and time as context for the development of gay identifications and queer cultures. Urban queer geography will expand, while this will create an interest in suburban and non-urban environments of gay men.

The development of questioning sexual orientation to a next stage which might be queer has not been touched upon in most theories of coming out, which relied on people with stable homosexual identities, not on those who did not make such a transformation. Too little theorizing has taken place on changes in sexual identifications or object choices. Examples are those men who start with gay and move on to kinky interests, but the reverse rarely happens, from kinky to gay or queer. Many boys who start to have gay interests seek adult partners rather than those of their own age group, while others who begin with their own age group subsequently stay with it, go beyond it, or forget about gay sex. Such changes in identifications and sexual interests have rarely been explored in their social contexts and ramifications.

A major issue concerns the terrains in between homosexual and heterosexual and male and female identifications and their interconnections. Sociological research on self-identified bisexuals and transgenders is on the rise, but not on those who identify less along those lines, such as unmasculine men, or those persons who show a preference for intermediate cases. They even lack concepts of identification and can only be circumscribed in descriptive terminologies such as lovers of bisexuals, drag queens, or male-to-female transgenders.

In most cultures and the western world until about 1900, sexual desire was based on the idea of social distinction: between male and female,

younger and older, higher and lower class. Gay men were effeminate mollies who desired "normal" (straight) men, while others looked over class lines or desired boys or young men. In the literature a classification of homosexualities has been proposed based on gender, age and, less often, class difference (Greenberg 1988). The ideal of sexual connections has become over the last century an absence of social differences. Gay and lesbian relations fit this ideal better than heterosexual ones that still have to deal with a gender difference. But in most cultures connections between same-sexual partners continue to be based on gender and age difference. This is the case in most of Latin America, Africa, the Arab world, and Asia. Casual contacts between non-homosexual identified males that remain common in those cultures will often express a power difference, or be accompanied by a financial transaction. Many non-western urban centers may see the quick expansion of gay cultures where such differences are eliminated, but they are not standard, often even defined as "modern" or "western" in a negative sense. The actual situation with regard to gender and age is rarely researched, not even for the West, while this global and radical innovation from sexual desire based on equality instead of difference has attracted next-to-no attention. It parallels a similar change of a world that is divided along homosocial lines (separate worlds for men and women) to a heterosocial world in which men and women participate on a basis of equality. This major and remarkable change with its manifold consequences for homosexual desires and worlds has not been a topic of research.

Absent is research on sexual pleasure, both in its individual developments and social locations. Although gay and queer studies often have an implicit liberal or libertine agenda, the sociological aspects of pleasure and desire are rarely discussed or studied. Sex research in the context of AIDS prevention has been weak on this issue, while it has been otherwise largely neglected. Scripting theory would have been a good tool for such work, but has not been used. It could help to study relations between social context and the experience of pleasure or how sexual specialties develop. Important elements of gay culture such as the choreography of cruising and sexual practices have been regrettably neglected (Bech 1997), or studied from a literary perspective. Sexual subcultures attracted little attention, and their sexual organization remained in obscurity.

The concept of intimate or sexual citizenship (Bell & Binnie 2000; Plummer 2003) has been introduced to highlight the social and political aspects of sexuality. Such aspects were hidden by the traditional relegation of sexuality to the natural and private. This terminology draws attention to the intimate or sexual side of citizenship, next to its economic, religious, cultural, or gendered sides. It is about the body politics of societies that are ruled by straight norms and defined by heteronormativity. These codes pervade all societal institutions, from families and schools to armies and prisons.

SEE ALSO: Gay and Lesbian Movement; Heterosexuality; Homophobia; Homophobia and Heterosexism; Lesbianism; Postmodern Sexualities; Queer Theory; Sexualities, Cities and; Sexuality, Masculinity and

REFERENCES AND SUGGESTED READINGS

Altman, D. (2001) *Global Sex*. University of Chicago Press, Chicago.
Bech, H. (1997) *When Men Meet: Homosexuality and Modernity*. Polity Press, Cambridge.
Bell, D. & Binnie, J. (2000) *The Sexual Citizen: Queer Politics and Beyond*. Polity Press, Cambridge.
Carrington, C. (1999) *No Place Like Home: Relationships and Family Life among Lesbians and Gay Men*. University of Chicago Press, Chicago.
Dynes, W. R. & Donaldson, S. (Eds.) (1992) *Sociology of Homosexuality*. Garland, New York.
Gagnon, J. & Simon, W. (1973) *Sexual Conduct: The Social Sources of Sexual Meaning*. Aldine, Chicago.
Greenberg, D. (1988) *The Construction of Homosexuality*. University of Chicago Press, Chicago.
Laumann, E., Gagnon, J., Michael, R. T., & Michaels, S. (1994) *The Social Organization of Sexuality: Sexual Practices in the USA*. University of Chicago Press, Chicago.
Minton, H. (2001) *Departing from Deviance: A History of Homosexual Rights and Emancipatory Science in America*. University of Chicago Press, Chicago.
Nardi, P. & Schneider, B. E. (Eds.) (1998) *Social Perspectives in Lesbian and Gay Studies*. Routledge, New York.
Parker, R. G. & Gagnon, J. H. (Eds.) (1995) *Conceiving Sexuality. Approaches to Sex Research in a Postmodern World*. Routledge, London.
Plummer, K. (1995) *Telling Sexual Stories*. Routledge, London.
Plummer, K. (2000) Mapping the Sociological Gay. In: Sanfort, T. (Ed.), *Lesbian and Gay Studies*. Sage, London, pp. 46–60.
Plummer, K. (2003) *Intimate Citizenship: Private Decisions and Public Dialogues*. University of Washington Press, Seattle.
Seidman, S. (1997) *Difference Troubles: Queering Social Theory and Sexual Politics*. Cambridge University Press, New York.
Seidman, S. (Ed.) (1998) *Queer Theory/Sociology*. Blackwell, Oxford.
Troiden, R. R. (1988) *Gay and Lesbian Identity: A Sociological Analysis*. General Hall, Dix Hills, NJ.
Weeks, J. (1995) *Invented Moralities*. Polity Press, Cambridge.
Weeks, J. (2000) *Making Sexual History*. Polity Press, Cambridge.
Weeks, J., Heaphy, B., & Donovan, C. (2001) *Same Sex Intimacies: Families of Choice and Other Life Experiments*. Routledge, New York.
Weston, K. (1991) *Families We Choose: Lesbians, Gays, Kinship*. Columbia University Press, New York.

Horkheimer, Max (1895–1973)

Markus S. Schulz

Max Horkheimer is best known as the long-time director of the Frankfurt School and co-author of the *Dialectic of Enlightenment* (with Theodor W. Adorno). In the 1930s Horkheimer defined the Frankfurt School's agenda of interdisciplinary empirical research, guided the Institute through the years of exile, and succeeded in its reestablishment in Frankfurt after World War II.

There is a remarkable continuity in Horkheimer's thought, which some have characterized as a Schopenhauerian Marxism. Although Schopenhauer and Marx had a great impact on Horkheimer, he was also profoundly influenced by Kant, Hegel, Nietzsche, the French Enlightenment philosophers, and three of his contemporaries: lifelong friend and political economist Friedrich Pollock, his university mentor Hans Cornelius, a phenomenologist philosopher with left-Christian leanings, and Theodor W. Adorno, who became his close collaborator.

There were four major stages in Horkheimer's work: (1) formative years from World War I to the late 1920s, in which he sought the conceptual tools for understanding human suffering and exploitation; (2) a brief but ambitious period of setting the agenda for interdisciplinary research during the later years of the Weimar Republic; (3) the years in exile, initially in Switzerland, then in New York and California; and (4) the reestablishment of the Institute in Frankfurt after the Nazi defeat.

Max Horkheimer was born in Stuttgart-Zuffenhausen as the only son of a prosperous German-Jewish textile manufacturing family. He wrote his dissertation (1922) and *Habilitationsschrift* (1925) on Kant under the supervision of Hans Cornelius at the University of Frankfurt. In 1931, following the death of Carl Gruenberg, Horkheimer became the second director of the *Institut fuer Sozialforschung* (Institute for Social Research) – later known as the Frankfurt School – and professor at the University of Frankfurt. Horkheimer outlined his vision for the Institute's agenda in his inaugural lecture on "The Present Situation of Social Philosophy and the Tasks of an Institute for Social Research" (in Horkheimer 1993: 1–14). He rejected what he perceived as philosophy's engagement with irrelevant pseudo-problems and called for a close collaboration between economics, legal studies, psychology, philosophy, and sociology. The kind of social research and philosophy he envisioned was meant to change social conditions. As director, Horkheimer recruited Erich Fromm, Leo Loewenthal, Herbert Marcuse, Franz Neumann, and Adorno to the Institute. Horkheimer also founded the Institute's *Zeitschrift fuer Sozialforschung* (Journal for Social Research), which published a wide array of scholarly studies. Among the Institute's early empirical projects was a survey on the political attitudes of workers in the Weimar Republic. Although it was never concluded, its informal findings revealed to the Institute members the widespread absence of emancipatory values.

The Nazi rise to power forced the Institute into exile. Horkheimer was dismissed from his post at the university, and the Institute was closed and its belongings confiscated. Horkheimer had already opened Institute branches in London and Geneva, and so transferred the Institute's endowment to Switzerland. After a brief stay in Switzerland, he moved the Institute to New York, where Columbia University made a building available at Morningside Heights. Horkheimer continued to edit the *Zeitschrift* in German until 1939, when he established its English successor, *Social Studies in Philosophy and Social Science* (1940–2). Among other articles, Horkheimer contributed to the *Zeitschrift* his definitive essay "Traditional and Critical Theory" (in Horkheimer 1972), which set the Institute's stance vis-à-vis mainstream academic thought. Horkheimer's substantial focus shifted in this period from research on the failure of a liberating revolution to a theory of the misdevelopment of culture. He became chief research consultant for the American Jewish Committee and co-organizer of a large-scale research project on anti-Semitism, social prejudice, and authoritarianism, the results of which were published in several volumes (with Samuel H. Flowerman, 1949–50) under the series title *Studies in Prejudice*.

In 1940 Horkheimer moved to Pacific Palisades, California, where from 1941–4 he worked with Adorno on a manuscript first circulated in 1944, then published in 1947 as *Dialectics of Enlightenment*. It was a dark assessment of the history of western rationality, surely influenced by the experience of the Nazis' industrial-scale barbarism and by deep fears about the mass culture industries in the US. Although collaborative, the title essay and the chapter on de Sade were mainly Horkheimer's. He developed his position further in his major book *Eclipse of Reason*, published in 1947 and based on a series of lectures he had given at Columbia University. The book's later German title *Zur Kritik der instrumentellen Vernunft* (On the Critique of Instrumental Reason) probably reflected better his intent to critique a historically perverted type of reason without giving up reason as such.

In 1949 Horkheimer returned to Germany upon his reappointment as professor at Frankfurt, though he kept his American citizenship and frequently returned to the US as a visiting professor at the University of Chicago (1954–9). He succeeded in reestablishing the *Institut fuer Sozialforschung*, which undertook research on, among other issues, the political culture in post-war Germany. Horkheimer was elected rector of the University of Frankfurt from 1951 to 1953. In the late 1950s he moved to Switzerland and handed over the Institute's directorship to Adorno. Although Horkheimer retired in 1961, he remained active and served increasingly as a public intellectual via the press and radio. He received numerous civic honors. The student movement of the latter 1960s was inspired by Horkheimer's writings, although some distance developed when he later declined to condemn the US involvement in Vietnam. Horkheimer's accommodation with post-war Germany and his appreciation of the benefits of liberal-democratic institutions seem to have made him uneasy about the extremity of some of his previous positions. Only after years of hesitation did he agree to the German publication of *Eclipse of Reason* (1967). Yet, his posthumously published *Notizen* (Notes) and statements made shortly before his death expressed a profound "yearning for the totally Other" in a "totally administered world." Horkheimer died in Nuremberg and was buried at the Jewish cemetery in Bern-Wankdorf, Switzerland.

Horkheimer's relevance cannot be separated from the Frankfurt School. Although not as prolific in his academic publications as his close collaborator Adorno, his sensitivity and vision shaped the Institute's research agenda, and his organizational and leadership skills ensured its survival during the years of exile and beyond. Horkheimer's writings have recently attracted renewed attention not only in Germany but also in the US. Contemporary sociology's growing interests in culture and interdisplinary studies as well as in public sociology are likely to further fuel debate about Horkheimer's legacy.

SEE ALSO: Adorno, Theodor W.; Critical Theory/Frankfurt School; Culture Industries; Metatheory; Rational Choice Theories; Theory

REFERENCES AND SUGGESTED READINGS

Benhabib, S., Bonss, W., & McCole, J. (Eds.) (1993) *On Max Horkheimer: New Perspectives*. MIT Press, Cambridge, MA.

Horkheimer, M. (1947) *Eclipse of Reason*. Oxford University Press, New York; reprinted 1974, New Seabury Press, New York.

Horkheimer, M. (1972) *Critical Theory: Selected Essays*. Trans. M. J. O'Connell et al. Herder & Herder, New York.

Horkheimer, M. (1974) *Critique of Instrumental Reason: Lectures and Essays since the End of World War II*. Trans. M. J. O'Connell et al. New Seabury Press, New York.

Horkheimer, M. (1985–) *Gesammelte Schriften* [Collected Writings], 17 vols. Ed. A. Schmidt & G. Schmid Noerr. Fischer Verlag, Frankfurt.

Horkheimer, M. (1993) *Between Philosophy and Social Science: Selected Early Writings*. MIT Press, Cambridge, MA.

Horkheimer, M. & Adorno, T. W. (1947) *Dialektik der Aufklaerung: Philosophische Fragmente*. Querido, Amsterdam; trans. by E. Jephcott as *Dialectic of Enlightenment* (2002). Stanford University Press, Stanford.

hospitals

Sharyn J. Potter

Hospitals are institutions where people in need of medical care receive medical and surgical treatment from trained professionals. The discovery of antiseptics and medical technological advances transformed the American hospital from the death and poor houses of the eighteenth and nineteenth centuries to the cornerstone of today's medical care (Starr 1982). The twenty-first century American hospital provides the sick, injured, and healthy with a myriad of diagnostic, medical, and surgical treatment options. The federal government helped solidify the modern hospital as a local institution when the 1945 Hill Burton Act provided federal money for every community to build or expand their existing hospital (Stevens 1989). Hospitals ranging in size from 10–1,000 beds now dot the American landscape. In urban areas hospitals resemble small cities, complete with gourmet restaurants and banking services.

The twentieth-century hospital provided families with relief from the disruption of home care by providing medical care for the sick and injured in a manner that was less disruptive for society as a whole. In recent years hospitals have changed from places of treatment and recuperation to places constrained to treatment. The major payers of hospital care – government and private insurance companies – limit hospital stays by only reimbursing hospitals for the medical or surgical treatment. These payers no longer reimburse hospitals for convalescence care, thereby giving the responsibility of caring for the sick or injured to family or friends. This change in the provision of hospital care can be partially attributed to the passage of the Medicare Prospective Payment System (PPS) legislation in 1983.

With the implementation of the PPS legislation the hospital industry was faced with cost-containment legislation for the first time in its history. Previously, hospitals had used their own discretion in pricing hospital services. The PPS legislation eliminated such discretion by authorizing the government to establish uniform prices for all hospital services for Medicare patients. Therefore, hospitals were forced to incur costs lower than the reimbursement amount to make a profit. Many hospitals found that they were able to earn a profit or save money by discharging patients soon after their procedures were complete. "PPS was a fixed payment per case determined in advance . . . this approach offered hospitals the rewards of a profit or the penalty of a loss" (Altman & Young 1993: 12). Although this legislation was passed to regulate Medicare spending, the private insurance and managed care companies adopted similar methods of cost containment and initiated similar strategies for reimbursing hospitals in the US.

Three distinct types of hospitals (not-for-profit, for-profit, and public) play an integral role in the US health care industry. Not-for-profit hospitals comprise the largest hospital sector, accounting for approximately 60 percent of all short-term general hospitals. Many not-for-profit hospitals were opened and operated by various immigrants and fraternal and religious groups as a means to promote group cohesiveness and ensure care for their members. Since 1913 the federal government has formally exempted private and religious not-for-profit organizations from most revenue and property taxes in exchange for providing some free or below-cost medical services (Gray 1986; Roska 1989). This commitment was referred to as the "relief of poverty" requirement (Fox & Schaffer 1991; Stevens 1989). The tax exemption accorded to not-for-profit hospitals was viewed as an investment of public resources for charitable purposes. Care for millions of uninsured patients was exchanged for the forgiveness of billions of dollars in federal, state, and local taxes.

The "relief of poverty" requirement remained in effect until 1969, when the Internal Revenue Service (IRS) modified the language and replaced it with the more general requirement that such hospitals provide "community benefit" (Roska 1989; Fox & Schaffer 1991; Seay 1992). The language in the 1969 IRS ruling resulted in considerable confusion about the interpretation of community benefit and a transformation in how hospitals began to define it. Because the rhetoric in the ruling was ambiguous and community benefit was not explicitly defined, not-for-profit hospitals explored alternative ways to meet this newly named requirement (Fox & Schaffer 1991). While some not-for-profit hospitals continued to maintain their tax-exempt status in the traditional manner by providing medical care for underserved populations (Seay & Sigmond 1989; Seay 1992; Fox & Schaffer 1991; Gamm 1996), other NFP hospitals established their exemption status through more creative and non-traditional methods. Some NFP hospitals began to invest in high-tech equipment and new hospital and office buildings for the sake of the community (Fox & Schaffer 1991). Other hospitals developed a myriad of wellness and community education programs, that some suggest would more appropriately be called patient recruitment tools (Buchmueller & Feldstein 1996). As a result, it has been argued that the change in IRS requirements has enabled hospitals to provide "outreach activities focusing on the special health problems of the underserved" (Gamm 1996: 80; Seay & Sigmond 1989) and not necessarily on meeting the greatest needs in the community.

This conflict between charity care and community benefit continues (Kane & Wubbenhorst 2000: 186), and some believe the 1969 IRS ruling has blurred the distinction between services for the underserved and services that increase hospital visibility and revenues (Tuckman & Chang 1991; Buchmueller & Feldstein 1996). In an effort to ensure that NFP hospitals are earning their tax exemptions, some communities now require NFP hospitals to quantify and report the community benefit services they provide (Kane & Wubbenhorst 2000). Other communities are pursuing the revocation of their hospitals' tax-exempt status, believing that the increased tax revenue will give them needed funds for other projects.

Not-for-profit hospitals can earn profits; they are prohibited from distributing these profits. Instead, profits must be reinvested in the hospital. The major distinction between not-for-profit and for-profit hospitals involves the distribution of profits. For-profit hospitals can distribute their profits to their owners or shareholders. Therefore, stockholders demand that for-profit hospitals behave in a manner that results in healthy financial statements. Gray (1991) argues that profitability is the key indicator for evaluating the success of a for-profit hospital and poor financial performance can cost managers their position.

In the early 1900s many for-profit hospitals were operated by physicians in rural areas where other types of hospitals were non-existent. In urban areas, eminent surgeons opened for-profit hospitals for patients who preferred not to seek treatment at not-for-profit hospitals. In 1910, for-profit hospitals accounted for approximately 50 percent of all hospitals (Stevens 1989). Thereafter, the number of proprietary hospitals steadily decreased as "community hospitals opened their staffs to wider membership and doctors found that they were able to have the public provide the capital for hospitals and maximize their incomes through professional fees" (Starr 1982: 219). By 1928, according to Paul Starr, proprietary hospitals accounted for only 36 percent of all hospitals. The number of proprietary hospitals subsequently declined further to 27 percent and then 18 percent of all hospitals, in 1938 and 1946, respectively (Stevens 1989).

Today, for-profit hospitals account for 13 percent of all short-term general hospitals. For-profit hospitals choose to locate in affluent areas, purposely avoiding the provision of expensive charitable care that detracts from potential hospital profits. These well-defined profit goals are the most appropriate justification for policies that tend to exclude poor patients (Homer et al. 1984). Over the years some for-profit hospital

stocks have earned record returns for their investors. Critics indicate, however, that these record returns are not always gains for their communities. Potential stockholders do not base their purchasing decisions on how well the hospitals are meeting community needs (Rushing 1976).

The presence of public hospitals in a community influences the strategies of the other hospitals, both for-profit and private not-for-profit. Research indicates that public hospitals often care for patients that other hospitals consider undesirable. A disproportionate number of their patients are poor, uninsured, or Medicaid recipients (Brown 1983).

Since the 1700s, public hospitals have played a vivid role in the history of American hospitals. Many big-city public hospitals began as almshouses, including Bellevue in New York City, Charity in New Orleans, and Cook County in Chicago. In 1902 public hospitals were described as grim and barracks-like; they typically had wards for patients with syphilis, tuberculosis, and mental disorders, and for unmarried pregnant women (Stevens 1989). Policymakers predicted the closure of many government not-for-profit hospitals following passage of the 1965 Medicare and Medicaid legislation, which gave the poor the means to pay for hospital care (Fox & Schaffer 1991). In theory, all patients now were paying patients and were entitled to private care. This prediction did not come true, and a mass closing of government not-for-profit hospitals never occurred. Public hospitals currently account for 26 percent of all US acute-care hospitals.

Some researchers question whether the care at public hospitals is comparable to care at their private not-for-profit and for-profit counterparts. For example, researchers who recently compared the records of patients suffering from ischemic heart disease at the three types of hospitals found that patients at public hospitals received less extensive services than patients at for-profit and private not-for-profit hospitals. Likewise, other researchers find that patients at public hospitals received fewer diagnostic tests, fewer surgeries, and fewer follow-up visits.

Twenty-first century hospitals face a number of challenges. As cost pressures and medical technology facilitate the movement of many procedures away from the hospital to physician offices and less expensive free-standing facilities, hospitals will have to develop strategies to meet these challenges. Furthermore, many smaller communities struggle to support their hospitals and mergers occur on a regular basis, removing hospital access from local communities.

SEE ALSO: Health Care Delivery Systems; Health and Medicine; Health Professions and Occupations

REFERENCES AND SUGGESTED READINGS

Altman, S. H. & Young, D. A. (1993) A Decade of Medicare's Prospective Payment System: Success or Failure? *Journal of American Health Policy* March/April: 11–19.

Brown, E. (1983) Public Hospitals on the Brink: Their Problems and their Options. *Journal of Health Politics, Policy and Law* 7: 927–44.

Buchmueller, T. & Feldstein, P. (1996) Hospital Community Benefits other than Charity Care: Implications for Tax Exemption and Public Policy. *Hospital and Health Services Administration* 41: 461–71.

Fox, D. M. & Schaffer, D. C. (1991) Tax Administration as Health Policy: Hospitals, the Internal Revenue Service and the Courts. *Journal of Health Politics, Policy and Law* 16: 251–79.

Gamm, L. D. (1996) Dimensions of Accountability for Not-for-Profit Hospitals and Health Systems. *Health Care Management Review* 21: 74–86.

Gray, B. H. (1991) *The Profit Motive and Patient Care: The Changing Accountability of Doctors and Hospitals.* Harvard University Press, Cambridge, MA.

Gray, B. H. (1986) Committee on Implications of For-Profit Enterprise in Health Care: Access to Care. In: Gray, B. H. (Ed.), *For-Profit Enterprise in Health Care.* National Academy Press, Washington, DC, pp. 97–126.

Homer, C. G., Bradham, D. D., & Rushefsky, M. (1984) To the Editor, Investor-Owned and Not-for-Profit Hospitals: Beyond the Cost and Revenue Debate. *Health Affairs* 3: 133–6.

Kane, N. M. & Wubbenhorst, W. H. (2000) Alternative Funding Policies for the Uninsured: Exploring the Value of Hospital Tax Exemption. *Milbank Quarterly* 78: 185–212.

Roska, A. K. B. (1989) Non-profit Hospitals: The Relationship between Charitable Tax Exemptions and Medical Care for Indigents. *Southwestern Law Journal* 43: 759–83.

Rushing, W. A. (1976) Profit and Non-Profit Orientations and the Differentiations-Coordination Hypothesis for Organizations: A Study of Small General Hospitals. *American Sociological Review* 41: 676–91.

Seay, J. D. (1992) Community Benefit Prevails: Are Radical Changes in Hospital Tax-Exemption Laws Necessary? *Health Progress* 73: 42–7.

Seay, J. D. & Sigmond, R. M. (1989) Community Benefit Standards for Hospitals: Perceptions and Performance. *Frontiers in Health Service Management* 5: 3–39.

Starr, P. (1982) *The Social Transformation of American Medicine.* Basic Books, New York.

Stevens, R. (1989) *In Sickness and in Wealth: American Hospitals in the Twentieth Century.* Basic Books, New York.

Tuckman, H. P. & Chang, C. F. (1991) A Proposal to Redistribute the Cost of Hospital Charity Care. *Milbank Quarterly* 69.

households

Graham Allan

When people discuss family life there is often a confusion between family as kinship and family as household. The two ideas are so much part of commonsense understandings of "family" that they are elided together. Though less common in sociology, a similar lack of clarity over what aspect of "family" is being examined sometimes arises. In principle, the distinction is clear-cut. Family as kin are all those people who are linked to you genealogically or who you otherwise define as kin (Schneider 1968; Silva & Smart 1999). Typically, they remain kin whether or not they live with you, though the boundaries of inclusion and exclusion drawn around "my family" may alter across the life course. Households, on the other hand, are essentially those people who share a home with you. In this sense "my family" are those with whom I live and with whom I participate in a domestic economy. The membership of an individual's household will certainly change over time, and may for significant periods include people who are clearly not regarded as family.

Defining who belongs to a household appears relatively straightforward and for many people it is. There is a clear-cut group of individuals who normally eat together, share a common house-keeping, and sleep in the same dwelling. These are the essential criteria used for defining a household, criteria which in different combinations are utilized in official government practices, records, and statistics. However, both in the past and currently, these issues are not quite so simple for all. At times, for example, some people may eat many of their meals in one household but sleep in another. Thus, one or more children in large sibling sets may sleep at a grandparent's house where there is more room, but otherwise live with their parents. Or a daughter or son with an elderly, infirm parent may regularly sleep at the parent's house in order to provide care at night.

Contemporary demographic patterns are also making the boundaries of households more diffuse than they were. For example, increasing numbers of people are spending different times of the week in different houses, usually as a result of conflicts between employment and domestic demands. Thus, some people do weekly commutes to work, living in one household during the week – possibly a small apartment or shared house – while living in the "family home" at weekends. A growing number of couples are also now "living apart together," sometimes through choice rather than employment demands. Here each partner maintains their own home, but they also regularly spend time together in one or other of their homes. Whether the individuals involved in these arrangements are defined as living in one or two households, or as having a multiple household, is a moot point, as in some cases may be the question of whether they are "family" to one another. The central issue though is that the living arrangements people construct are flexible and variable and consequently cannot always be characterized as fitting neatly into a single household.

Other demographic changes have also had an impact on the composition of households. The rise in divorce, for instance, has clearly contributed to the higher numbers of lone-parent households there now are, as well as to the increased proportions of people living alone for periods in midlife. So too the rise in separation and divorce has resulted in an increasing number of children whose parents share care of them in separate households. In terms of

their own household experience, these children belong to more than one household, alternating between each parent's household for whatever periods of time have been agreed. Other demographic shifts that have affected household composition include changes in life expectancy resulting in longer periods spent without dependent children in the household and later marriage age. This latter has had consequences for both the number of single-person households and for the rise of non-familial shared households consisting of unrelated friends and others living together (Heath & Cleaver 2003).

Generally, these demographic shifts have contributed to a greater degree of household diversity and mobility. In the early phases of adulthood particularly, people's "household careers" are often less "ordered" than they were, with changes in living arrangements being quite common. As well as the growth of shared housing as a living arrangement, young people are also now more likely than previously to be involved in relatively temporary cohabiting relationships of different durations. Equally, at least in Britain and other European countries, there has been a marked tendency for the process of leaving the parental home to be less clear-cut than it was for previous generations (Holdsworth & Morgan 2005). That is, not only are adult children living for longer periods in the parental home, but there is also a noticeable trend for them to return to the parental home as circumstances in their lives – changing employment, relationship breakup, financial pressures – alter.

As a result of these different trends, overall patterns of household composition have been changing quite significantly in most western countries over the last 30 years. Taking Britain as an example, household size has continued to reduce, from nearly 3 people per household in 1970 to 2.3 in 2002 (National Statistics 2005). Currently, only a fifth (21 percent) of households consist of what used to be conceptualized as the "standard" family households of two adults and dependent children, compared to 31 percent at the end of the 1970s. And of course this number now includes increasing numbers of cohabiting unions and stepfamilies, as well as first-time marriages. Significantly, nearly a third of all households (31 percent) are single-person households (compared with

21 percent in 1978), though the routes into these single-person households and the length of time spent in them varies significantly. A further third of households (34 percent) now consists of couples living alone, either married or cohabiting; some have not had children and others have children who are no longer dependent. The remaining households generally comprise lone-parent households (8 percent) and those where people are living with friends/unrelated others (4 percent). Importantly, as discussed above, just as household composition has been altering, so too there is even greater flux over time in the personnel involved in each category as people's domestic circumstances and partnership status alter.

While these figures are about Britain, broadly similar trends are found in other western countries as a result of shifting family demography under the global processes of late modernity (Buzan et al. 2005). As noted, the growth of cohabitation, divorce, and separation and the lack of clarity over the processes of children leaving home are having an impact throughout the developed world. Clearly, though, the extent to which they occur and the impact they have depend in part on the social, fiscal, and urban policies impacting on family and household organization in the different societies. One significant element within this is the operation of the housing market. The availability of different forms of housing to different sections of the population, the costs and quality of such housing, and the alternatives which are considered acceptable all have an impact on the choices people make and the pattern of households they construct. To take one example, at a macro level, increased separation and divorce are likely to generate provision of more single-person housing, but in turn people's decisions about whether or not to remain in a particular partnership will be influenced to some degree by their perception of the housing that will be available to them. Similarly, decisions about leaving the parental home will be based on alternative housing options as well as ideas of appropriate independence.

SEE ALSO: Cohabitation; Couples Living Apart Together; Family Structure; Kinship; Second Demographic Transition

REFERENCES AND SUGGESTED READINGS

Buzan, S., Ogden, P., & Hall, R. (2005) Households Matter: The Quiet Demography of Urban Transformation. *Progress in Human Geography* 29: 413–36.

Heath, S. & Cleaver, E. (2003) *Young, Free and Single: Twenty-Somethings and Household Change.* Palgrave Macmillan, Basingstoke.

Holdsworth, C. & Morgan, D. (2005) *Transitions in Context: Leaving Home, Independence and Adulthood.* Open University Press, Maidenhead.

National Statistics (2005) *Living in Britain: The 2002 General Household Survey.* Online. www.statistics.gov.uk/cci/nugget.asp?id=818.

Schneider, D. (1968) *American Kinship: A Cultural Account.* Prentice-Hall, Englewood Cliffs, NJ.

Silva, E. & Smart, C. (1999) *The New Family?* Sage, London.

Howard, George Elliott (1849–1928)

Michael R. Hill

George Elliott Howard, a distinguished social scientist trained initially in history, rose to the presidency of the American Sociological Society in 1917. Howard earned the A.B. in 1876 at the University of Nebraska. Following two years of advanced study in Germany, Howard joined the Nebraska faculty in 1879. Howard's most prominent Nebraska student from this period, Amos Griswold Warner, later wrote *American Charities* (1894) – a standard classic in the field. Howard was named to the prestigious "First Faculty" of Stanford University in 1891.

At Stanford, when sociologist Edward Alsworth Ross was summarily fired in 1900 by university president David Star Jordan, Howard immediately defended Ross's right to free speech. Jordan demanded Howard's apology – or his resignation. Howard resigned, as did other Stanford faculty members in sequence. Instantly, Ross was hired by chancellor E. Benjamin Andrews to teach sociology at the University of Nebraska. The so-called "Ross affair" at Stanford resulted ultimately in the founding of the American Association of University Professors and the establishment of academic tenure in American universities.

After a series of brief appointments, including the University of Chicago (1903–4), Howard returned in 1904 to the University of Nebraska, where his colleagues included Edward A. Ross and Roscoe Pound. In 1906, with Ross's departure for the University of Wisconsin, Howard was named head of Nebraska's newly reorganized Department of Political Science and Sociology. Howard was an egalitarian, activist, and humane sociologist who championed women's suffrage, encouraged racial tolerance, and advocated prohibition. An exacting scholar, Howard's elaborate published syllabi on *General Sociology* (1907), *Social Psychology* (1910), *Present Political Questions* (1913), *Marriage and Family* (1914), and other topics remain extraordinary models of rigorous instructional guidance. Howard's later Nebraska protégée, Hattie Plum Williams, earned her PhD in 1915, and in 1923 – with Howard's encouragement and endorsement – became, at Nebraska, the first woman in the world to chair a co-educational doctoral degree-granting department of sociology. Howard retired in 1924.

The author of scholarly books and dozens of professional articles, Howard is best known today for his massive *History of Matrimonial Institutions Chiefly in England and the United States* (University of Chicago Press, 1904). A quintessential study in the sociology of institutions (Howard claimed for himself the invention of "institutional history" as a category of study), *Matrimonial Institutions* merited critical appraisal from Émile Durkheim and provided the intellectual foundations for the 1906 National Congress on Uniform Divorce Laws.

SEE ALSO: American Sociological Association; Divorce; Marriage; Pound, Roscoe

REFERENCES AND SUGGESTED READINGS

Ball, M. R. (1988) George Elliott Howard's Institutional Sociology of Marriage and Divorce. *Mid-American Review of Sociology* 13(2): 57–68.
Durkheim, É. (2000). A French Perspective on George Elliott Howard's *History of Matrimonial Institutions*. Trans. D. B. Mann. *Sociological Origins* 2(2): 81–6.
Hill, M. R. (2000) Epistemological Realities: Archival Data and Disciplinary Knowledge in the History of Sociology – *Or*, When *Did* George Elliott Howard Study in Paris? *Sociological Origins* 2, 1 (special supplement): 1–25.
Howard, G. E. (1988) Sociology in the University of Nebraska, 1898–1927. *Mid-American Review of Sociology* 13(2): 3–19.
Vincent, M. J. (1928–9a) George Elliott Howard: Social Scientist. *Sociology and Social Research* 13: 11–17.
Vincent, M. J. (1928–9b) George Elliott Howard: Social Psychologist. *Sociology and Social Research* 13: 110–18.
Williams, H. P. (1928–9) The Social Philosophy of George Elliott Howard. *Sociology and Social Research* 13: 229–33.

human genome and the science of life

Anne Kerr

Although the double helix structure of DNA was discovered in 1953 by James Watson, Francis Crick, Maurice Wilkins, and Rosalind Franklin, it was not until the 1980s that powerful sequencing and information technologies were developed that enabled scientists to identify particular genes associated with hereditary diseases and to begin to map all of the genes in human DNA: the so-called human genome. The human genome project was a massive international mapping exercise which began in the 1990s and culminated in the publication of a draft sequence by the International Human Genome Sequencing Consortium of the entire human genome in 2001, which is freely available on the Internet.

In the same period a broader range of biomedical knowledge was also developing, particularly in the fields of assisted conception. More recently, research into stem cells and tissue engineering, alongside the so-called "postgenomic sciences" of pharmacogenomics and proteomics, has also developed. This "science of life" involves detailed understanding of the basic cellular mechanisms involved in human development, as well as a focus upon copying and ultimately manipulating these processes in the laboratory. This is linked to a number of biomedical developments in the diagnosis and treatment of disease, particularly the move towards more targeted individualized treatments tailored to individuals' particular genetic makeup, and perhaps, in the future, utilizing cells and tissues taken from people's own bodies to develop treatments for them.

The use of embryos is a particularly contentious aspect of the science of life and human genomics. The dangers of surveillance and discrimination against a "genetic underclass" have also been raised, as have concerns about "designer babies." More generally, the optimism about these new developments has been criticized for being a form of hype which sustains the pharmaceutical, bioscience, and infertility industries, but will do little to tackle the major causes of ill health that the majority of the world's citizens face: poverty. In the UK the government has responded to these public and professional concerns by establishing a number of oversight bodies, notably the Human Fertilization and Embryology Authority, which enforced strict limits on the type of research that can be conducted upon human embryos. Across the world there are a range of similar bodies and more or less restrictive laws, but in some countries the science of life is largely unregulated, notably China and North Korea, where stem cell research is developing apace. In the US regulation is uneven. Although assisted conception is largely unregulated, there are stringent controls on federally funded biomedical research to prevent the use of human embryos.

Sociological work on these developments covers a wide remit. The early days of the human genome project saw sociologists, in common with their colleagues in the ethical and legal disciplines, exploring the implications of greater knowledge about individuals' genetic makeup, particularly the dangers of eugenics and genetic determinism. Others focused upon the political economy of the project, especially patenting (notably, indigenous people's DNA) and access to genetic information by the state (primarily with respect to large-scale genetic databases). As Waldby (2002) noted, this was part of a growing trend of "biovalue" in which bodily parts and processes were commodified. However, these

developments have not gone unchallenged. John Moore challenged the patenting of his own DNA by researchers at Johns Hopkins University. Although he lost his case, the ownership of DNA was politicized in the process. Indigenous peoples have also resisted so-called bioprospecting, where researchers take DNA samples from them to patent in the West, and this has resulted in a number of international treaties and legal claims which reassert the rights of ownership of individuals and communities over indigeneous natural resources.

The lay–expert divide is also being breached in other respects where genomics and the science of life are concerned. Many patients with hereditary diseases have considerable expertise about their condition, which can lead them to challenge costly treatments and research. A range of oppositional groups such as the disability rights movement have also challenged the biologization of illness and disability. An unlikely alliance of feminists and anti-abortion groups has attacked the commodification of women's bodies in assisted conception in particular, challenging, for example, reproductive tourism where rich western women travel to eastern countries to purchase eggs from local women for their assisted conception treatment. These criticisms are often focused upon the political and economic aspects of biomedical research and treatment within the context of late capitalism, and unpack widespread cultural assumptions about the nature of disability and infertility. Yet they can also perpetuate conservative notions of reproduction, where the sanctity of life is paramount. Nor is medical authority necessarily challenged in the process. Patient support groups often share with clinicians a discourse of objectivity and support for medical progress. And many of the people who become active in such organizations have a medical or scientific background. There are clearly a range of complex and sometimes contradictory views being expressed by particular groups and individuals in this area, which means that simple categories of "patient," "clinician," or indeed "activist" are largely unhelpful.

From an ethnographic perspective scholars have also spent considerable time exploring the practices of gene sequencing in the laboratory and tracking their utilization in the clinic. As Rapp (1999) and Sarah Franklin have shown, as the uncertainties of diagnosis are profound, clinicians' and clients' choices can be very difficult. Although foregrounded, the individual is not necessarily privileged as a result of these new insights into reproductive and genetic futures. Although some patients might welcome an insight into the human face of science which an ambivalent clinician might present, others struggle to find categorical meanings to match the categorical actions that they are ultimately obliged to take about reproduction, diagnosis, and treatment: you either act or you do not.

The complexity of molecular genetic and other new forms of biological information is often highlighted by Foucaldian scholars, particularly Nikolas Rose, who explicitly contrasts it with the crude genetics of the past, particularly in its eugenic guise. This fits with a wider theoretical emphasis upon complexity and messy systems in late modernity. Echoing the risk society thesis, the main argument here is that as biomedical science has evolved so too has its risks and uncertainties. The bureaucratic edifice of the twentieth century was unable to control and tame these risks by centralized rational means, and faith in expertise weakened to the extent that the authority of biomedicine itself came into question. At the same time, the individual became more important than the collective, and a cultural emphasis upon personal rights and choices emerged. Science has therefore evolved to develop more complex, decentred interpretations of life, where flexibility and contingency are key. Genomics and the science of life, alongside developments in information and computer technologies, are at the forefront of these complex sciences, particularly the trend towards individualization of treatment, and a move away from "one size fits all" drugs and procedures.

However, others argue that the transformative potential and complex underpinnings of contemporary biomedicine and genetics in particular have been overemphasized. As scholars such as Diane Paul (1998) have shown, the so-called "old eugenics" had myriad links to established scholars of genetics, and their understandings of human disease were far from monological or crude. Other studies, such as Kerr's work on cystic fibrosis, have shown that genetics has a history of multifunctional complex paradigms, which have often coexisted alongside other more determinist understandings of disease. This

suggests that complexity is not unique to the contemporary science of life, nor is it primarily a *response* to risk. Instead, it is an enduring feature of biological science.

The extent to which genetic tests and other diagnostic and screening services give patients informed choice about whether or not to participate have also been queried in a wide range of psychosocial, ethical, and sociological empirical studies. Theresa Marteau and colleagues have comprehensively demonstrated that the context in which pregnant women make decisions about antenatal screening is often one where information and interactions are subtly cued towards compliance. On the other hand, studies of familial testing for diseases such as Huntington's disease show how relationships with close relatives, wider family, and the community as a whole, as well as the very fact that these disorders are often untreatable, shape people's decisions about presymptomatic testing in such a way that it is often declined. Individuals who come from affected families also have complex responses to antenatal testing. For many, this is also fraught with difficulties and contradictions, as the potential to avert the birth of an affected child is weighted against the implicit denigration of affected individuals. The danger of too much information about one's future health being generated by these tests has also been discussed at length.

This work is often mobilized in debates about the extent and meaning of "geneticization," a term coined by Abby Lippman to stress the pernicious reach of genetic explanations for disease and behavior. Yet evidence about the uptake of genetic diagnosis and its effects upon attitudes to disabled people and social misfits is mixed. There is no comprehensive genetic paradigm being enforced by the biomedical establishment, yet it is not possible to say that the more widespread emphasis upon biological reasons for disease of which genetics is a part has no effects upon how people account for citizens' rights and responsibilities for health care in particular.

In any case, Lippman's term was always meant to be focused upon a broader trend towards reductionist notions of the genetic determinants of identity, disease, and antisocial behavior. Other critics such as Dorothy Nelkin have made similar arguments about the simplicity of much of the popular presentation of genetics, as well as the limited analysis of burgeoning fields such as evolutionary biology. Although some sociologists have called for a deeper engagement with these sciences and an end to the nature versus nurture debate, many remain committed to challenging the reductionism and circularity of this new form of biological determinism. Others, such as Peter Conrad and Alan Petersen, have focused their attention upon the popular presentation of genetic determinism in media accounts in particular, but policy documentation can also be subjected to similar analysis to show the prevailing emphasis upon "genes for …" stories alongside an underlying positive focus upon technological progress, individual choice, and personal responsibility. At the same time, new technologies of visualization have emerged to move our understanding of life from the now relatively humble ultrasound of the disembodied fetus to laser scanning of internal cellular dynamics, bringing with them discourses of mastery and control alongside those of complexity and uncertainty.

A considerable corpus of work has also been built up into the public understanding of genetics, exploring and unpacking people's understandings and ambivalent responses to genetic knowledge and its application. Media messages notwithstanding, this work shows that the public are far from ignorant about new developments. Although their technical proficiency is often wanting, their wider social intelligence about the institutional politics of science and their experiences of raising children and mixing with a range of social groups can generate sophisticated questioning of the hype around the science of life and profound concerns about commodification in particular. Just as with the analysis of the various interest groups involved in more public debates about these new technologies, the study of more general public discourse shows that it not possible to box people into particular categories of "right to life" or "patient advocate" when their arguments and experiences overlap in myriad ways. It is also clear from a range of studies of the ethics of genomics and the science of life that professionals share many of the so-called public's concerns, but that their ambivalence is often suppressed in more public spaces.

A further feature of sociological inquiry into genomics and the science of life concerns the emergence of new forms of ethics, primarily located in new institutional forms such as the HFEA. The perception of increasing public anxiety and newfound uncertainties of the science itself, particularly its application in the clinic and beyond, has meant that ethicists have moved out of academia into policy communities at a national and international level. This has been intensified by the globalization of biomedical research, signaled most clearly by the worldwide efforts of the HGP, but continued in the more routine arrangements of trade in information and bodily commodities which sustain the research networks in this field. Ethics has also been institutionalized in local research ethics committees which vet research applications from scientists and sociologists alike. A particular issue here is informed consent. This is a reflection of the rights-based culture in which we live, but also a response to a range of scandals about biomedical research where subjects' and/or their families' consent had not been obtained prior to the performance of dangerous and/or distressing procedures. This holds science to account in a more public way than ever before, but in a fairly limited and (some would argue) limiting way. In contrast, ethics writ large is often focused upon pushing the boundaries of appropriate practice in this area, and is dominated by a number of high-profile libertarians such as John Harris and Julian Savalescu, who make compelling arguments in favor of everything from genetic enhancement to reproductive cloning.

Once again, it is not possible to interpret the rise of bioethics as uniformly supportive or restrictive towards the science of life. It would also be wrong to see it as a response to particular aspects of the science or the technology itself, as it flows from a range of complex sociopolitical developments which have happened alongside the scientific discoveries and developments. Although a greater range of voices is now included in ethical reflection and debate than perhaps was the case in the past, ethical reflection in the public sphere is not unique to the contemporary period, and ethical restrictions on medical and scientific practice have long operated at various levels of formality and informality as a matter of course. And although the new institutional forms have developed a complex infrastructure of surveillance to control medical practice, it is still the case that in the clinical context where consent is sought for diagnosis, treatment, or donations to research, the complexities of consent forms and the interpersonal dynamics between provider and client can and often do engender consent, just like the paternalism of the past.

Other sociologists, such as Nik Brown, have tracked the evolution of the human genome into post-genomic and related areas of the life sciences, exploring the public presentation and interpretation of these developments, and the construction of expectations in particular. This involves innovators in packaging particular disorders and technical interventions in a way that emphasizes their relevancy and social usefulness while also generating and attempting to sustain an optimistic politics of hope in the face of profound uncertainty about medical and biological futures. The ethics of such hype has been questioned by scientists as well as sociologists, yet its place in the pharmacological armory seems fundamental. Profit drives innovation so the emphasis upon the future consumer of biomedical enhancement becomes necessary to the success of the industry, although the everyday practices of health services on the ground suggest that the ultimate operationalization of the "science of life" is more mirage than reality.

SEE ALSO: Eugenics; Gay Gene; Genetic Engineering as a Social Problem; New Reproductive Technologies; Science and Public Participation: The Democratization of Science

REFERENCES AND FURTHER READINGS

Brown, N. (2003) Hope Against Hype: Accountability in Biopasts, Presents, and Futures. *Science Studies* 16(2): 3–21.

Conrad, P. (1999) A Mirage of Genes. *Sociology of Health and Illness* 21(2): 228–39.

Gottweis, H. (2004) Human Embryonic Stem Cells, Cloning and Biopolitics. In: Ster, N. (Ed.), *Biotechnology: Between Commerce and Civil Society*. Transaction, New Brunswick, NJ, pp. 239–68.

Kerr, A. (2004) *Genetics and Society: A Sociology of Disease*. Routledge, London.

Kerr, A. & Franklin, S. (2006) Genetic Ambivalence: Expertise, Uncertainty, and Communication in the Context of New Genetic Technologies. In: Webster, A. & Wyatt, S. (Eds.), *Innovative Health Technologies: New Perspective Challenges and Change*. Palgrave Macmillan, London.

Kerr, A. & Shakespeare, T. (2002) *Genetic Politics: From Eugenics to Genome*. New Clarion Press, Cheltenham.

Lippman, A. (1992) Prenatal Genetic Testing and Genetic Screening: Constructing Needs and Reinforcing Inequalities. *American Journal of Law and Medicine* 17: 15–50.

Michie Susan, B. F., Bobrow, M., & Marteau, T. M. (1997) Nondirectiveness in Genetic Counseling: An Empirical Study. *Obstetrical and Gynecological Survey* 52(6): 344–6.

Nelkin, D. & Lindee, S. (1995) *The DNA Mystique: The Gene as Cultural Icon*. W. H. Freeman Press, New York.

Paul, D. (1998) *Controlling Human Heredity: 1865 to the Present*. Humanity Books, New York.

Petersen, A. (2001) Biofantasies: Genetic Medicine in the Print News Media. *Social Science and Medicine* 52(8): 1255–68.

Rapp, R. (1999) *Testing Women Testing the Fetus: The Social Impact of Amniocentesis in America*. Routledge, New York.

Rose, N. (2001) The Politics of Life Itself. *Theory, Culture and Society* 18(6): 1–30.

Waldby, C. (2002) Stem Cells, Tissue Culture and the Production of Biovalue. *Health* 6: 301–23.

human–non-human interaction

Clinton R. Sanders

Human interaction with non-human animals is a central feature of contemporary social life. The majority of households include at least one companion animal, more people visit zoos each year than attend professional sporting events, people are more likely to carry photographs of their pets than of their children, married women report that their pets are more important sources of affection than are their husbands or children, and more money is spent on pet food than on baby food (Arluke 2003). Despite the fact that human interactions with animals are so commonplace, they have, until fairly recently, been virtually ignored within sociology. This prosaic disregard of human–animal exchanges is based on a variety of core assumptions. Sociology is conventionally seen as the study of *human* social structures and relationships. Sociologists also hold to the Cartesian liguacentric assumption that because animals lack the ability to employ spoken language they are consequently mindless and selfless. And, as Arluke (2003) has observed, sociologists who specialize in the investigation of inequality and oppression tend to be suspicious of the study of non-human animals because it may be seen as trivializing their focal concerns.

Although anthropologists traditionally have attended to the cultural role of domestic animals in simple societies, sociologists have only fairly recently begun to systematically examine the relationships and interactions between people and the animals with whom they share their everyday lives. For example, sociologists working in such varied substantive areas as social movements, the sociology of the family, work and occupations, criminology and deviance, and sociological psychology have turned their attention to human–animal issues. In tandem with the growth of interest in human–animal relationships within sociology, a wide variety of social scientific disciplines (geography, history, feminist studies, political science, and consumer research, among others) have also begun examining the phenomenon. Evidence of the burgeoning interest in what is now commonly referred to as human–animal studies is seen in the publication of special issues of established journals and book series established by academic presses devoted to the topic. The disciplinary legitimacy of human–animal studies was affirmed in 2002 when the American Sociological Association officially recognized the Animals and Society section.

The few early discussions of people's interactions with animals were relatively unsystematic and unempirical. For example, in 1865 Harriet Martineau (a pioneer in observational methods) wrote about the problems presented by feral dogs, while in an 1872 issue of the *Quarterly Review* Frances Power Cobbe speculated about the impact of dogs' physical characteristics upon their consciousness. In a little-known but significant paper entitled "The Culture of Canines," Read Bain (1929) criticized the anthropocentrism of sociology and advocated the

development of "animal sociology." In his discussion of the "culture of canines" Bain stated: "Just as animal intelligent and emotional behavior, anatomical and physiological structure and function, and group life, have their correlates in human behavior, so the dividing line between animal and human culture is likewise vague and arbitrary."

Bain's contemporary, George Herbert Mead, frequently discussed non-human animals in his writing. He employed descriptions of the *behavior* of animals as the backdrop against which he juxtaposed his model of human *action*. Mead maintained that, while animals are social beings, their interactions involve only a primitive and instinctual "conversation of gestures" (the dog's growl or the cat's hiss, for example). From Mead's perspective, animals lack the ability to employ significant symbols and are therefore unable to negotiate meaning and take the role of cointeractants. Their behavior is directed toward achieving simple goals such as acquiring food or defending territory but, unable to use language, their behavior is devoid of meaning. They are mindless, selfless, and emotionless. Mead's perspective reflected the anthropocentric, rationalist views of Descartes; non-human animals could not think, therefore they were not worthy of serious analytic attention. This orientation laid the groundwork for the conventional discounting of animals and lack of attention to their interactions with humans that dominated interactionist social psychology (and sociology in general) until the last quarter of the twentieth century.

A significant turning point occurred in 1979 when *Social Forces* published an article by Clifton Bryant in which he advocated the importance of sociologists attending to the "zoological connection" evident in so many areas of social life. Soon, a few pioneering sociologists were beginning to investigate settings in which human–animal interaction was a central feature and to overtly call into question the Cartesian orthodoxy that held sway within sociology.

The major focus of this early work was on occupational settings in which workers routinely interacted with non-human animals. Some of the earliest sociological work on this topic was done by C. Eddie Palmer on animal control officers and game wardens, D. Lawrence Wieder (1980) on researchers working with chimpanzees, and William Thompson on slaughterhouse workers.

Arnold Arluke later emerged as the major figure in this topical area when his 1988 article based on the ethnographic research he conducted in biomedical laboratories was published in the interdisciplinary journal *Anthrozoös* (the sole academic journal devoted to human–animal studies at that time). Arluke's paper, and the various other related works he produced, laid the groundwork for a theme that became central to the substantive field: the dichotomy between defining animals as "pets" or functional objects and the impact of this determination on how animals are treated. Arluke expanded on this theme in his later writings, emphasizing the job-related ambivalence experienced by animal shelter workers, veterinary students, and researchers in primate labs (Arluke & Sanders 1996). The number of studies focused on animal-related occupations grew: Carole Case studied race track workers, Clinton Sanders (1999) wrote about veterinarians and guide dog trainers, and Mary Phillips discussed laboratory workers' perceptions of animal pain and emphasized the importance of whether or not laboratory animals were given names.

Arguably, the richest focus of systematic attention within sociological human–animal studies has been on the everyday interactions between people and their companion animals. This work has been done primarily by scholars working within the perspective of symbolic interactionism and centers on a direct critique of Mead's anthropocentric discounting of animal abilities. Key recent examples are Sanders' (1999) research with dog owners, Gene Myers' (1998) study of the interactions between children and animals in a preschool program, and Janet and Steven Alger's (2003) book on a cat shelter. These writers examine the intersubjectivity that emerges when people routinely interact with animals; the process by which people construct an understanding of the individuality, mindedness, emotionality, and identity of animal others and, in turn, how association with animals shapes the identities of human actors. Leslie Irvine's (2004) book, centering on her participation in an animal shelter, builds upon and extends this intersubjective focus by presenting a case for animals possessing a self. Basing her analysis on the work of William

James and studies of prelingual infants, Irvine makes the case for the animal self as being constituted by a sense of agency (being the author of one's action), a sense of coherence (understanding one's physical self as the locus of agency), a sense of affectivity (experiencing feelings associated with the self), and a sense of self-history (maintaining an understanding of continuity in the midst of change). Irvine concludes that the self is "a system of goals, which we pursue through relationships and experiences, which involves the ways in which we respond to and order the worlds around us … [A]nimals, like people, manifest evidence of selfhood … as they manifest agency, affectivity, history, and coherence, as well as the capacity for intersubjectivity" (pp. 172–3).

Three additional main foci in the extant sociological work on human–animal interactions deserve mention. Grounded primarily in the insights of Erving Goffman, some writers have explored the impact of how being with a companion animal in public facilitates and/or impedes human-to-human social interaction. Non-human animals have also emerged as the focus of criminological discussion, most notably in the works of Piers Beirne and Gertrude Cazaux, both of whom attend to situations in which animals are cast as violators of the criminal law and the relationship of animal abuse to people's violence toward other humans. This latter relationship has become a major focus of attention, since it incorporates broader issues of social inequality and is seen by some as offering insights into elements of a person's movement into and through a violent career. It should be noted that the predictive value of abusing animals with regard to eventual involvement in human-to-human violence is an issue of considerable controversy.

The third major focus is based within the traditional literature on social movements. While some writers do not see their work as overtly situated in human–animal studies (e.g., James Jasper and Dorothy Nelkin), investigations of the animal rights movement do speak directly to how social definitions of animals are constructed and are employed to establish principles governing "appropriate" and "inappropriate" interaction with, or treatment of, non-human animals. David Nibert (2002), a sociologist who overtly identifies with human–animal studies, combines an orientation based on principles of the animal rights movement, sociological perspectives on inequality, and critical theory to make the case for the oppression of non-human animals – like that of women, racial minorities, and other members of disvalued human groups – as being directly related to the political and economic structure of contemporary society.

Sociologists employ a variety of methods in their investigations of human–animal relationships and interactions. Some conduct surveys to ascertain people's perceptions of both domestic and wild animals. Others use photographs of people with animals in order to explore the impact of being in the company of animals on social and personal identity. Content analysis of advertisements, films, greetings cards, and other graphic depictions of animals have also been used to assess cultural definitions of animals. However, the most common approaches employed within sociological human–animal studies are ethnography and its variant autoethnography (the systematic recording of the researcher's personal experience). Ethnographic techniques have proven to be the source of the richest, most detailed, and theoretically sophisticated portrayals of human–animal interaction in both public and private social settings.

As a relatively new substantive area within sociology, the study of human–animal interaction offers a wide variety of alternatives for future research. Since most of the extant discussions are focused on people's everyday relationships with cats and dogs (the animals most commonly incorporated into households), studies of relationships with "exotic" animals such as ferrets, potbelly pigs, reptiles, insects, and rabbits would be new and instructive. There are also a number of unexplored animal-related occupations (e.g., the work of veterinary technicians, wildlife rehabilitators, zoo keepers, professional dog handlers, animal behavior consultants, circus personnel, and K-9 police) available for fruitful investigation. Finally, as Arluke (2003) has observed, sociologists have now amassed sufficient basic understanding of human–animal interaction to begin to apply this knowledge in an attempt to deal effectively with problems in urban human–animal relations, veterinary medicine, animal control activities, and other settings and exchanges that constitute the "dark side" of this key form of social interaction.

SEE ALSO: Animal Rights Movements; Anthrozoology; Friendship: Interpersonal Aspects; Popular Culture Forms (Zoos)

REFERENCES AND SUGGESTED READINGS

Alger, J. & Alger, S. (2003) *Cat Culture: The Social World of a Cat Shelter*. Temple University Press, Philadelphia.
Arluke, A. (2003) Ethnozoology and the Future of Sociology. *International Journal of Sociology and Social Policy* 23: 26–45.
Arluke, A. & Sanders, C. R. (1996) *Regarding Animals*. Temple University Press, Philadelphia.
Bain, R. (1929) The Culture of Canines. *Sociology and Social Research* 13(6): 545–56.
Bryant, C. (1979) The Zoological Connection: Animal Related Human Behavior. *Social Forces* 58(2): 399–421.
Irvine, L. (2004) *If You Tame Me: Understanding our Connection with Animals*. Temple University Press, Philadelphia.
Myers, G. (1998) *Children and Animals*. Westview Press, Boulder.
Nibert, D. (2002) *Animal Rights/Human Rights*. Rowman & Littlefield, Lanham, MD.
Sanders, C. (1999) *Understanding Dogs: Living and Working with Canine Companions*. Temple University Press, Philadelphia.
Wieder, D. L. (1980) Behavioristic Operationalism and the Life-World: Chimpanzees and Chimpanzee Researchers in Face-to-Face Interaction. *Sociological Inquiry* 50: 75–103.

human resource management

John Hogan and Miguel Martínez Lucio

Human resource management (HRM) has various definitions, but in the main there are two general approaches. The first descriptive approach states that HRM is the managing of employees and human assets at work and within the organization in an integrated and coherent manner. The second approach elaborates this further by stating that HRM is distinct to previous forms of personnel administration in being proactive and therefore strategic: it concerns itself with soliciting higher forms of employee commitment and motivation. It is therefore both a relationship with organizations and a dedicated field of academic enquiry that has developed under this heading since the early 1980s.

Intellectually, HRM draws from various academic disciplines and subdisciplines, which in turn vary according to its distinct national contexts. Firstly, HRM derives from both traditional personnel management and labor/industrial relations as an area concerned with the question of employee control, cooperation, and commitment. It has, however, managed to constitute itself as something distinct to these two dimensions, with key proponents arguing it is more individualistic, strategic, and performance driven in orientation and not "reactive" or collectively underpinned. Hence, the role of occupational psychology has dovetailed into discussions on HRM regarding leadership and motivation, for example, and even matters of occupational health. Secondly, there is an economics tradition within HRM studies which is very much drawn from labor economics and concerns itself with matters concerning the relation between HRM processes and outcomes, as well as the subject of changing (flexible) labor markets and their relation with the HRM strategies of firms. Thirdly, there is a sociological trajectory which concerns itself with employment matters and management–employee–trade union relations within the workplace, and the broader composition of the workforce.

HRM is therefore a multidisciplinary area of analysis in terms of its academic context. It is a highly "populated" subject in terms of academic researchers, in the main due to the prevalence of business schools within the academy during the past two decades. There has also been an increasing demand from a practitioner perspective for information and guidance. This demand has come from organizations seeking greater flexibility in their workplaces, greater employee commitment, and developments in the capabilities of employees (e.g., the move from technical skills to communication and social skills). These demands have been driven by a range of changes in product markets, competitive strategies, the structure of the firm, the competitive challenge through the globalization of economies, social changes and employee demands, and the changing context of regulation.

The topic is based on a growing belief that competitive success increasingly depends on securing more from employees in terms of commitment and resources rather than passive compliance to managerial instruction. The topics that have emerged were best described by Walton (1985), who agued that future competitive success required the eliciting of commitment rather than the imposing of control. There were five "pillars" to this:

1 High-commitment or high-involvement management: hence the increasing interest in forms of involvement and participation at work of a direct nature through team briefings and not just intermediaries such as trade unions.
2 Employee development: the emergence of the human resource development field with its interest in new forms of skills such as communication and interactive skills – seen as essential for service delivery in a service economy.
3 An emphasis on the individual employee: this dovetails with the manner in which reward and performance management systems begin to constitute the employee more as an individual and less as part of a collective.
4 An emphasis on leadership both at the senior and workplace levels: the changing nature of leadership through the proliferation of coaching and communication skills.
5 An adoption of a more "strategic approach" to HRM, which can take two forms in terms of (1) "internal fit" (i.e., that there is a consistent link and planned approach to the way elements outlined above are tied together around a "vision") and in terms of (2) "external fit" (which has this strategy linked to the needs and demands of the product market and external environment in a more responsive manner).

There emerged approaches that referenced such developments in terms such as "hard" and "soft" HRM. Normally, these were equated with the work of such American schools of HRM as Michigan ("hard") and Harvard ("soft"). The first approach is more drawn to questions of control and direction (e.g., the role of cultural imposition of values and surveillance) and the second to a more negotiated approach based on involving stakeholders in the elaboration of strategy. These approaches have been nourished by the development of total quality management, with its emphasis on performance management on the one hand and employee involvement in matters related to service quality on the other.

HRM has expanded as an area of study in part due to the manner in which it is seen as being less a department or management identity/profession, and more a feature of all managerial functions. It remains an integral feature of core management education at various levels, although it has not always been able to rival the strategic popularity of areas such "change management," and especially marketing, within the confines of the business school tradition.

There are two schools of thought and practice. One sees HRM as a series of techniques and practices which are transferable across time: the much-feted emergence of the Japanese model of HRM during the 1980s and early 1990s with its emphasis on teamworking, employee commitment, and performance management, has been integrated by an Anglo-Saxon model which prioritizes employment flexibility, financial control, and greater customer awareness. Both these models were seen as being transferable to other contexts in their attempts to develop competitive economies through labor management policies. The second school of thought is increasingly concerned with context – both regulatory and, to a greater extent, cultural. Hence the idea of prescribing models and strategies is increasingly being confronted with an emergent interest in environmental/regulatory constraint and mediation. Thus, questions of convergence are being discussed in relation to questions of divergence/contingency/context.

This is being mirrored in the debate on organizational culture and the emergent interest in the historical narratives of the firm. Not only are external national, economic, and cultural perspectives a focus of analysis; internal cultural and organizational specificities and identities have also emerged as a source of study and intrigue which mediate the nature and content of HRM.

There are traditions within the study of HRM in recent years that also draw attention to the way management strategies are constrained and even mediated by the question of employee rights. The issue of diversity has begun to impact on the HRM debate as the tradition of equal opportunities and legal intervention has been complemented by the organizational utilization of employees and their socially diverse characteristics in the form of the discourse of "managing diversity." HRM debates have placed great store on the fact that such issues as gender and ethnicity rights can be enhanced for social and economic gain, leading to the building of a business case for a diverse workforce. This business case is also apparent in the question of partnership, and a renewed interest in a form of cooperation between management and unions/employees based on the mutual gains both "sides" can achieve through a dialogue which removes traditional forms of adversarialism of a class nature and replaces it with a common alliance and strategy. Such developments, in the terms of representation and rights within HRM, are hotly disputed due to their slow progress, the concern with real gains for employees, and the nature of employer motives regarding social and representational issues (Kochan & Osterman 1994; Martínez Lucio 2004).

Current work is broad and research is expanding rapidly in the area due to the sheer scale of researchers within business schools and the dominance of consultancy practices. There are very broad sets of developments: the main ones are as follows. Firstly, there is growing interest in taking the question of "fit" discussed above and modeling it and studying it through quantitative research methods. This is known as the "bundles" approach, which aims to establish the ingredients that ensure effective HRM strategies and which allow for a match between product market pressures and HRM "recipes." This has its own political dynamics as a feature of HRM in that there are concerns about the extent to which employee involvement and trade unions are part of such recipes in leading-edge firms. There are various firm-specific approaches and national/geographical studies aimed at substantiating such links. Hence, a more qualitative approach to this subject in the form of the mutual gains approach (Kochan & Ostermann 1994) attempts to establish the role of labor – collectively and individually – as a key factor in ensuring greater quality and contentment at work and in terms of production.

Another departure is the question of meaning (i.e., the meaning of HRM in terms of its rhetoric, its contingent qualities, and its tendency to be more of a cultural and political veil than a measurable reality in terms of increasing levels of skill formation and involvement). In this respect there are studies and overviews aimed at revealing the rhetorical and political qualities of HRM (Legge 2004), its tendency to be driven by an imperative for control as suggested by the increasing levels of surveillance at work (which has drawn interest from Marxist and postmodernist accounts), and, with regards to postmodernism, the way HRM strategies have attempted to construct employees ideologically in a variety of manipulative ways. In turn, studies are showing that such strategies often lead to new forms of contestation and resistance – and even misbehavior (Ackroyd & Thompson 2000). Hence, there is a growing preoccupation with issues of employee dignity and work–life balance due to the pressure brought by HRM strategies.

There are fundamental tensions in the study of change and HRM, especially in relation to research methodology. The first is the tension between prescriptive studies of HRM which are common in the managerialist and guru/fad literature, with its recommendations as to what managers and organizations should do with regards to issues such as commitment, and the more descriptive and explanatory literature (Huczynski 1993). This tension is played out in terms of the practitioner dimension of the discipline and the academic end, with the former tending to reproduce itself in business schools, especially when there is no critical dimension or tradition present among HRM staff. The second tension revolves around quantitative and qualitative approaches. Increasingly, the dominance of North American academic paradigms means that organizational change and the evolution of HRM is understood through a quantitative prism and the concern with strategic and

organizational factors regarding issues of "fit" – both internal and external. Whereas qualitative research has focused on the more contradictory and contingent nature of change; it has also drawn attention, increasingly, to the distinct meanings of management processes and practices. Moreover, there are severe disputes between the sociological and economic perspectives on the one hand, with their interest in social relations and regulation, and psychological perspectives on the other, with their emphasis on distinct methodological concerns and research questions based on the individual.

The comparative agenda is the main challenge to the future research on HRM. Models of analysis still default to cultural perspectives or regulatory traditions of analysis. Mapping varieties of HRM at the macro and micro level is a major development, in part driven by the concern with efficient and "better" models of people management and by a cartographic desire to see if there are common features emerging in the way people are managed.

This is paralleled by a broad diffusion of interest in the changing nature of the firm as a space within which HRM strategies are elaborated. Firstly, with regards to spatial boundaries, there is the increasing internationalization of the firm. The development of transnational corporations brings the question of "fit" and employee management across boundaries up against the question of national regulatory and cultural context. Secondly, the firm's boundaries are changing in organizational terms: the impact of decentralization, subcontracting, and ICT means that the jurisdiction of management is mediated and influenced by a broader set of sub-actors. This has led to a growing interest in the role of social and corporate networks in the study of the firm, and inevitably to questions of social capital, transaction costs, and organizational coordination. There is also a third feature to this boundary issue in terms of the relation between HRM and other areas such as marketing, with its interest in communication/branding/ethics, and information management, for example, calling on academics to appreciate the interactive nature of management processes in an age of IT and image.

Finally, regardless of the initial talk of a break from traditional stakeholders and forms of organization there is an ongoing concern with (1) the sociological characteristics of management and employees (e.g., in terms of gender and ethnicity), (2) the challenge of cooperation and involvement, and (3) the ethical framework of the firm. The ethical dimension in terms of the role of corporate social responsibility within the firm is a major aspect of current concern.

SEE ALSO: Industrial Relations; Management; Management, Worker's Participation in; Unions

REFERENCES AND SUGGESTED READINGS

Ackroyd, S. & Thompson, P. (2000) *Organizational Misbehaviour*. Sage, London.
Huczynski, A. (1993) *Management Gurus*. Routledge, London.
Kochan, T. A. & Osterman, P. (1994) *The Mutual Gains Enterprise: Forging a Winning Partnership Among Labor, Management and Government*. Harvard University Press, Boston.
Legge, K. (2004) *Human Resource Management*. Palgrave, London.
Martínez Lucio, M. (2004) Swimming Against the Tide: Social Partnership, Mutual Gains and the Revival of "Tired" HRM. *International Journal of Human Resource Management* 15(2): 404–18.
Walton, R. (1985) From Control to Commitment in the Workplace. *Harvard Business Review* (March/April): 77–84.

human rights

Susanne Karstedt

"Human rights are those liberties, immunities, and benefits which, by accepted contemporary values, all human beings should be able to claim 'as of right' of the society in which they live" (*Encyclopedia of Public International Law* 1995: 886). Virtually all states embrace and support the idea of human rights, and they have indicated some general agreement as to their objectives and contents. This definition which casts human rights in legal terms barely mirrors the expectations that individuals, groups, and peoples have attached to them. When on December 10, 1948 the United Nations General Assembly adopted the Universal Declaration of Human Rights (UDHR), the Declaration was hailed as "an international Magna Carta of all mankind" that could set up a common standard of achievement (Risse & Sikkink 1999: 1). Five decades later, human rights are seen as "offering a framework for debate over basic values and conceptions of a good society" (Charlesworth & Chinkin 2000: 210), and as social claims made by individuals and groups against organized power for the purpose of enhancing human dignity. Human rights are a powerful discourse on the *moral nature* of society and individuals that is simultaneously a *legal discourse* on rights, obligations, and accountability.

Human rights discourse provides a normative legal basis that is obligatory, not optional for states. Human rights are entry points for individuals and collectivities into the sphere of international law and international relations. They require active and effective remedies in the international arena, and accountability in national and domestic arenas. Perhaps more than ever they are a constant source of hope for empowerment, identity, and self-determination for individuals, groups, and peoples who are invisible and suffer from exclusion, discrimination, and human rights abuses (Charlesworth & Chinkin 2000).

After a slow start, human rights discourse gained momentum in particular during the last decades of the twentieth century. Roughly between 1970 and 1990 the international social structure of human rights norms and institutions was built, including transnational human rights NGOs and advocacy networks. During this period major covenants came into effect, new international institutions emerged, bilateral and multilateral human rights policies were developed, and regional institutional structures were established in Europe, Latin America, and Africa. Since then and concomitantly with the third wave of democratization that took hold first in Latin America and then Eastern Europe, a process of genuine international "norms cascade" began as the influence of human rights norms and discourse spread rapidly around the globe. This norms cascade has promoted the "internationalization" of human rights norms in the international community and given them a taken-for-granted quality (Risse & Sikkink 1999). If its momentum can be sustained human rights will be increasingly accepted and embedded in national norms and justice systems. The extensive human rights discourse, however, also revealed basic controversies and paradoxes that are innate to the paradigm of human rights, to its institutions and history. Three of these are presently most widely debated: first, the paradox of "international accountability for the domestic practice of sovereign states" (An-Na'Im 2004); second and related to this, the controversy about the claim for universality of human rights against cultural relativism; and third, the claim for social and economic rights, in particular for the right to development.

Human rights have historical roots that reach far back into history. In particular those human rights that guarantee due process or security can be traced to ancient societies, Roman civil law, and the common law of Anglo-Saxon countries (Ishay 2004a). Tolerance was and is embedded in many religions throughout the world, and states entered into treaties which acknowledged tolerance for heterodox religious worship. Through many centuries communities existed where at least some of what are now considered fundamental human rights were well protected by bodies of law, institutions, and customary law. However, the modern paradigm of human rights emerged in and is part of the Enlightenment tradition in Europe and the US. It came out of the struggles against the modern state that was accumulating more power than ever before, the bitter religious wars that had haunted the continent for nearly two centuries, and the claim for independence made by a colonial people. The first of these were the Petition of Right in 1628 and the Bill of Rights in 1689 in Britain, followed by the more encompassing declarations of the American and French revolutionaries: the American Declaration of Independence (1776), the French Declaration of the Rights of Man and of the Citizen (1789), and the American Bill of Rights (1791).

They were designed to empower individuals as human beings and because of their moral identity, thus ensuring individuals as moral personalities. These early declarations of human rights also made the state responsible for guaranteeing these rights. The legacy of Enlightenment philosophy was twofold in this respect: it introduced the notion of individual autonomy and liberty, and simultaneously the notion – based on contract theories – that the state existed to secure the universal rights of all its inhabitants. This legacy entailed a lasting paradox for the role of the state in human rights regimes, "as both the guardian of basic rights and as the behemoth against which one's rights need to be defended" (Ishay 2004b), a paradox that has been meanwhile transported to the supranational level and international humanitarian intervention. In the course of the nineteenth and twentieth centuries bills of rights were adopted or otherwise incorporated into constitutions on the entire continent of Europe, and the movement spread to the Americas, Asia, and Africa. The declarations of human rights further inspired and entailed other bilateral and multilateral international agreements and treaties that later were incorporated into the present paradigm of human rights. A prohibition on slavery and slave trade became customary international law in the nineteenth century and was later codified in widely accepted treaties. Further, humanitarian international laws that prohibited particularly cruel weapons and protected prisoners of war and civilians during wars were developed before World War I.

It was only in the wake of World War II and the barbarous acts committed in its course that the members of the international community, the United Nations, finally pledged themselves in the UN Charter to "take joint and separate action" for the promotion "of universal respect for, and observance of, human rights and fundamental freedoms for all without distinction as to race, sex, language, or religion" (Article 55 of the UN Charter). This led to the successive development and adoption of what is today known as the International Bill of Rights, which comprises a declaration, covenants, and measures of implementation. The International Bill of Rights can be termed as a major achievement and breakthrough in international law as it established individuals and groups as subject and legitimate preoccupation of international law besides sovereign states. The four "instruments" of the International Bill of Rights are the Universal Declaration of Human Rights

(UDHR) of 1948, the International Covenant on Civil and Political Rights (ICCPR), the Optional Protocol to the International Covenant on Civil and Political Rights (ICCPR-OP), and the International Covenant on Economic, Social, and Cultural Rights (ICESCR), all adopted in 1966. The International Bill of Rights is enshrined in regional conventions that specify human rights obligations and norms for the member states of supranational regional organizations. The European Convention on Human Rights that entered into force in 1953, and in particular the establishment of the European Court of Human Rights, have been a model for other regions and the development of legal institutions to monitor the observance of human rights. In 1986 the African Charter on Human and Peoples' Rights was adopted, and in 1993 the Managua Declaration of the Organization of American States stated explicitly the obligation of its member states to promote and safeguard human rights. Other instruments mainly in the form of conventions cover specific violations of human rights (e.g., racial discrimination, forced labor, genocide, and torture) or address and protect the rights of specific groups like children, women, and migrant workers. The continuous development of these instruments over the decades in fact demonstrates the norms cascade of human rights.

The International Bill of Rights and its four instruments comprise 39 rights (or freedoms) (Condé 1999). It differs however in two important respects from the predecessors on which it is based. While these focused on individual autonomy, the UDHR and the ensuing Covenants are based on the notion of the "inherent dignity" of human beings, thus acknowledging the social and cultural embeddedness of human nature. While it was important for the Declarations of the Enlightenment era to establish the right to private property, thus promoting a free-market economy, the UDHR and both Covenants do not include this right and thus abstain from defining the economic order of member states. The rights are often, though controversially, described in terms of first, second, and third "generation" rights reflecting on their historical legacy. The UDHR invokes in its 30 articles all generations of universal rights, which are then detailed and supplemented in the Covenants. The first-generation rights consist of civil and political rights and liberties as they were conceptualized during the Enlightenment. They protect against arbitrary interference and deprivation of life, liberty, and security by the state, and make the state obey the principle of the rule of law. The first generation's major document is the ICCPR. The ICESCR details the second generation of human rights, such as those to health, housing, and education. In contrast to the first generation these require active intervention by the state to ensure their protection. Individuals and groups can claim from their governments to secure their subsistence which is necessary to lead a life in dignity. Both Covenants further include third-generation rights comprising peoples' or collective rights. Most prominent among these is the right to self-determination that was absent in UDHR. Third-generation rights further include the right to development and peace. Claims can be made against the international community and nation-states, and benefits will flow to individuals and the respective group. Third-generation rights are more often than not contained in the "soft" law instruments like UN General Assembly declarations and resolutions, with the African Charter of Human and Peoples' Rights a notable exception.

While there is agreement on the justiciability of first-generation human rights laws, the implementation and enforcement of second and third generation social, economic, and cultural human rights have raised debates about the general accountability of states for securing these rights for their citizens, and the actions necessary to achieve this. The Declaration on the Right of Development adopted by the UN General Assembly in 1986 epitomizes these controversies, as it links human rights language with international economic issues in a highly ambiguous way. Notwithstanding its symbolic significance in the UN system, it has also contributed to the sense that first-generation liberal values and rights have a permanence and solidity that second and third-generation rights do not possess (Charlesworth & Chinkin 2000: 207). However, these also have come under intense criticism. First, the right of states to international humanitarian intervention, and the legitimacy of such interventions, is debated (An-Na'Im 2004). Second, the claim of human rights to universality has recently emerged as a most contentious issue (Ishay 2004a, 2004b; An-Na'Im 2004). This concerns the popular, social, and cultural acceptability of human rights norms within specific social and cultural contexts. Since human rights are without doubt the product of a specific culture but nonetheless claim universality, a given set of human rights norms (in particular those based on individual autonomy and liberal values) can be perceived as alien and unacceptable in other cultures (e.g., rights for women). Further, human rights norms might not only be alien in some cultural and social contexts, but endanger those who they are supposed to benefit, by unraveling the social fabric which supported these groups. While western countries support the claims for universal rights, but are more reluctant in their endorsement of collective rights, Islamic and Asian cultures prioritize collectivistic over individual rights. It is important to address these issues in the effective and practical implementation of human rights.

Human rights law is constantly challenged, and though most states formally accept human rights regimes they undermine such commitment by use of extensive reservations, thus widening the gap between human rights promises and practices; further, many states are responsible for numerous human rights violations. The process of democratization and the development of full liberal democracy reduce the gap between promise and practice and generally the level of human rights violations. The implementation of human rights further requires processes of socialization that incorporate human rights regimes into the political identity of citizens and nations. Risse and Ropp (1999) identify three processes on the international and national level: adaptation and bargaining, moral consciousness raising, "shaming," and persuasion, and institutionalization and habitualization. The density and strength of international institutions and "advocacy coalitions" of NGOs on the international and national level both coalesce into the "world time" and norms cascade of human rights regimes. Their "spiral model" of five stages towards enduring change of human rights regimes reflects the importance of interaction between advocacy networks, national movements, and international support.

Notwithstanding the numerous problems of implementation and enforcement, human rights law has an expanding role in the international community as a statement "of the elements of humanity" (Galtung 1994). It is perhaps the most important development in international law during the last century, with its norms cascade reaching into and defining the twenty-first century. It has destroyed the myth that the way in which states treat their citizens is not the concern of anyone else. In the era of globalization human rights abuses are becoming the concern of everyone else.

SEE ALSO: Democracy; Global Justice as a Social Movement; Globalization and Global Justice; Law, Sociology of; NGO/INGO; Tolerance; Transnational and Global Feminisms; Transnational Movements; War

REFERENCES AND SUGGESTED READINGS

An-Na'Im, A. A. (2004) Human Rights. In: Blau, J. R. (Ed.), *The Blackwell Companion to Sociology*. Blackwell, Oxford.

Charlesworth, H. & Chinkin, C. (2000) *The Boundaries of International Law: A Feminist Analysis*. Manchester University Press, Manchester.

Condé, H. V. (1999) *A Handbook of International Human Rights Terminology*. University of Nebraska Press, Lincoln.

Encyclopedia of Public International Law (1995) Human Rights. Vol. 2. Elsevier, Amsterdam.

Galtung, J. (1994) *Human Rights in Another Key*. Polity Press, Cambridge.

Ishay, M. R. (2004a) *The History of Human Rights: From Ancient Times to the Globalization Era*. University of California Press, Berkeley.

Ishay, M. R. (2004b) What are Human Rights? Six Historical Controversies. *Journal of Human Rights* 3: 359–71.

Risse, T. & Ropp, S. C. (1999) International Human Rights Norms and Domestic Change: Conclusions. In: Risse, T., Ropp, S. C., & Sikkink, K. (Eds.), *The Power of Human Rights. International Norms and Domestic Change*. Cambridge University Press, Cambridge.

Risse, T. & Sikkink, K. (1999) The Socialization of International Human Rights Norms into Domestic Practices: Introduction. In: Risse, T., Ropp, S. C., & Sikkink, K. (Eds.), *The Power of Human Rights. International Norms and Domestic Change*. Cambridge University Press, Cambridge.

Humanism

Joseph Scimecca

Humanism, a philosophical movement that affirms the dignity of the human being, originated in Italy in the second half of the fourteenth century. While the twelfth and thirteenth centuries had been dominated by the philosophical school of Scholasticism (philosophy taught by the "schoolmen" of medieval universities who tried to reconcile the philosophy of the ancient classical philosophers with medieval Christian theology), by the fourteenth century, Scholasticism was more and more seen by thinkers outside the church and the universities as irrelevant to everyday life. This view of Scholasticism, along with the growth of cities and greater contact with the East and its differing views and customs, led thinkers such as Francesco Petrarch (1304–74) and Desiderius Erasmus (1466–1536) to view the world differently than had the Scholastics. Although, the early Humanists were still Christians who believed that God ruled the world, it was a world which they saw as in need of change, change that could be brought about by human reason. For the Humanists, human beings possessed free will and the ability to use their reasoning power to bring about a humane world.

Humanism spread throughout Europe over the next few centuries, finally culminating in the Enlightenment, and it was out of the Enlightenment that the fundamental underpinnings of the birth of social science and eventually sociology sprang forth. It was a group of Scottish and French Enlightenment philosophers (or *philosophes*, as they are collectively known) who laid the foundation of what Auguste Comte (1798–1857) would later call "sociology." The *philosophes* – John Locke (1632–1704), Baron de Montesquieu (1689–1755), Jean-Jacques Rousseau (1712–78), Adam Smith (1723–90) – called for a fusion of morals and science, for a social science that sought to liberate the human spirit and ensure the fullest development of the person. Whereas these traditions of moral philosophy and empiricism are now seen by modern sociologists as separate, they were for the Enlightenment *philosophes* intertwined. And it was this emphasis on both moral philosophy and empiricism, as modified by German Idealism and more recently by the American philosophical tradition of pragmatism, that constitutes the foundations of Humanism in sociology today.

THE *PHILOSOPHES* AND SOCIOLOGICAL HUMANISM

Although the Enlightenment *philosophes* initiated the discipline of sociology through their call for the application of scientific principles to the study of human behavior (Rossides 1998), it should not be forgotten that the *philosophes* were first and foremost moral philosophers. Science and morality were to be fused, not separated; the "is" and the "ought" were to be merged into a moral science, a science to be used for the betterment of humankind. Rousseau, with his arguments against inequality and for the dignity of the person, can be seen as an exemplar of this moral science tradition. Rousseau (1985) started with the fundamental assumption that all people are created equal but "everywhere they are in chains." Rousseau was wedded to the idea that individual liberty and freedom prospered only under conditions of minimal external constraint – that the "chains" had to be broken. For Rousseau and the *philosophes*, this could only be accomplished through a fusion of morals and science, by a social science that sought to liberate the human spirit and bring about the fullest development of the person.

This tradition of a "moral science" is overlooked by the majority of contemporary sociologists, who instead focus on the empiricism of the *philosophes*, which though it played a huge role in the rise of social science, is only one part of what the *philosophes* advocated (Goodwin & Scimecca 2005). By their dismissal of the "moral science" tradition and by almost unquestioningly embracing the positivism that Comte, Spencer, Durkheim, and the other early founders of sociology advocated, sociology as it began in France, England, and later in the US strayed from its humanist roots. Sociology, however, developed differently in Germany, and it is through German philosophy and social science that the tradition of Humanism in sociology was kept alive.

GERMAN IDEALISM

German social science (unlike its English, French, and later American counterparts) was much more influenced by idealism than by empiricism – an influence due to two giants of philosophy: Immanuel Kant (1724–1804) and Georg William Freidrich Hegel (1770–1831). Like the medieval Humanists, Kant (1965) was concerned with the basic question of how autonomy and free will were possible in a deterministic Newtonian universe. Kant's answer lay in moral philosophy and the basis of moral philosophy was to be found in the human mind; moral law was located a priori in the mind and could be deduced rationally.

Kant's explanation was that objects of scientific investigation were not simply discovered in the world, but were constituted and synthesized a priori in the human mind. The external world which human beings experience is not a copy of reality, but something that can only be experienced and understood in light of a priori forms and categories. According to Kant, these forms and categories determine the form but not the content of external reality. Morally right action, too, was located in the mind. Going back to Rousseau and before him to the medieval Humanists, Kant (1949) focused on the dignity of the human being, postulating the notion of the categorical imperative – that each person be treated as an end and never as a means. This solidified the importance of the person as the cornerstone of philosophical inquiry and of Humanism. Moral values come from human consciousness, but lacking a viable theory of consciousness Kant could only go so far. It would be Hegel who subsequently made further progress toward the development of a humanistic orientation in sociology.

Although Hegel (1967) held that Kant's epistemology was successful in explaining how scientific knowledge was possible, he differed with Kant by rejecting his belief that the categories were innate and therefore ahistorical. For Hegel, the human mind had to be understood in the context of human history. Human reason was the product of collective action and as such was constantly evolving toward an ultimate understanding of its own consciousness. Hegel is very close to modern sociology in numerous aspects of his thought and it is unfortunate that he is so often dismissed because of his ultimate reliance on the metaphysical assumption that total understanding would only come with the realization of the absolute spirit in human history, along with his conservative political views which some have seen as justifying a totalitarian system. Such interpretations overlook that Hegel was the first modern theorist to develop an anti-positivist, critical approach to society. Hegel rejected positivism because of its over-reliance on empiricism. As was Kant's philosophy, Hegel's philosophy was Humanist at its core.

Given the times in which they lived, neither Kant nor Hegel had a fully blown conception of self in society. It would be up to the American pragmatists to provide an active view of the self, laying the groundwork for contemporary Humanist sociology.

PRAGMATISM AND HUMANISM

Pragmatism assumes an active epistemology which undergirds an active theory of the mind, one which challenges the positivistic behaviorism of the time made popular by the likes of John B. Watson. For the pragmatists, how the mind comes to know cannot be separated from how the mind actually develops.

Mead (1974) exemplifies the pragmatists' view concerning the development of mind. Consciousness and will arise from problems. Human beings are capable of reflexive behavior, that is, they can turn back and think about their experiences. The individual is not a passive agent who merely reacts to external constraints as positivism holds, but someone who actively chooses among alternative courses of action. Individuals interpret data furnished to them in social situations. Choices of potential solutions are only limited by the given facts of the individual's presence in the larger network of society. This ability to choose among alternatives makes individuals both determined and determiners (Meltzer et al. 1977).

The individual is engaged in an active confrontation with the world; mind and self develop in a social process. Mead and the pragmatists provided an epistemological justification for freedom (*the* basic tenet of Humanism). The mind develops in a social context and comes to know as it comes into being. Any restriction on the freedom of the mind to inquire and know implies a restriction on the mind to fully develop.

Pragmatism, by joining epistemology and freedom via the social development of mind, also provided a solution for the seeming incompatibility between an instrumental and an intrinsic approach to values. The value of freedom is instrumental in that it is created in action (the action of the developing mind); but it is also intrinsic in that the mind cannot fully develop without the creation of an environment which ensures freedom (Scimecca 1995).

Pragmatism, however, did not go far enough in its assumption of freedom of choice. Choice among alternatives is always limited. It is in pointing out these limitations in the form of power relations and vested interests behind social structures that Humanist sociology built upon pragmatism and thereby confronted the basic sociological criticism of pragmatism – that it lacked a viable notion of social structure. Humanist sociology seeks to fashion a full-blown vision of the free individual within a society based on the principle of human freedom.

HUMANIST SOCIOLOGY TODAY

Humanist sociology has moved beyond pragmatism with its attempt to spell out the social structural conditions for the maximization of freedom. Humanist sociology is explicitly based on moral precepts – the foremost of which is that of freedom, "the maximization of alternatives" (Scimecca 1995: 1). This is assumed to be the most desirable state for human beings – and the goal of sociology is to work toward the realization of conditions that can guarantee this freedom. Given its Meadian theory of self (an active theory of self that chooses between alternatives), Humanist sociology is concerned with what type of society best ensures that the freedom of the individual is not thwarted by the institutions of the society. For the Humanist sociologist, there is one basic purpose: to develop a society where the dignity, interests, and values of human beings are always given the highest priority (Goodwin & Scimecca 2005).

SEE ALSO: Hegel, G. W. F.; Pragmatism

REFERENCES AND SUGGESTED READINGS

Goodwin, G. A. & Scimecca, J. A. (2005) *Classical Sociological Theory: Rediscovering the Promise of Sociology*. Wadsworth, Belmont, CA.

Hegel, G. W. F. (1967 [1821]) *The Philosophy of Right*. Clarendon Press, Oxford.

Kant, K. (1949 [1788]) *The Critique of Practical Reason*. University of Chicago Press, Chicago.

Kant, K. (1965 [1781]) *The Critique of Pure Reason*. St. Martin's Press, New York.

Mead, G. H. (1974 [1934]) *Mind, Self and Society*. University of Chicago Press, Chicago.

Meltzer, B. N., Petras, J. W., & Reynolds, L. T. (1977) *Symbolic Interactionism: Genesis, Varieties, and Criticisms*. Routledge & Kegan Paul, Boston.

Rossides, D. W. (1998) *Social Theory: Its Origins, History, and Contemporary Relevance*. General Hall, Dix Hills, NJ.

Rousseau, J. J. (1985 [1755]) *Discourse on Human Inequality*. Penguin, New York.

Scimecca, J. A. (1995) *Society and Freedom*, 2nd edn. Nelson-Hall, Chicago.

hybridity

Jan Nederveen Pieterse

Cut-'n'-mix experiences in consumer behavior, lifestyles, and identities are common and everyday, for example in food and menus. Hybridity refers to the mixture of phenomena that are held to be different, separate. Hybridization is defined as "the ways in which forms become separated from existing practices and recombine with new forms in new practices" (Rowe & Schelling 1991: 231).

The theme of hybridity matches a world of intensive intercultural communication, everyday multiculturalism, growing migration and diaspora lives, and the erosion of boundaries, at least in some spheres. Hence, hybridity has become a prominent theme in cultural studies. New hybrid forms are indicators of profound changes that are taking place as a consequence of mobility, migration, and multiculturalism. However, hybridity thinking also concerns existing or, so to speak, old hybridity, and thus involves different ways of looking at historical and existing cultural and institutional arrangements. This suggests not only that things are no longer the way they used to be, but were never really the way they used to be, or used to be viewed.

Anthropologists studying the travel of customs and foodstuffs show that our foundations are profoundly mixed, and it could not be otherwise. Mixing is intrinsic to the evolution of the species. History is a collage. We can think of hybridity as *layered* in history, including precolonial, colonial, and postcolonial layers, each with distinct sets of hybridity, as a function of the boundaries that were prominent at the time and their pathos of difference. Superimposed upon the deep strata of mixing in evolutionary time are historical episodes of long-distance cross-cultural trade, conquest, and empire and episodes such as transatlantic slavery and the triangular trade. Within and across these episodes we can distinguish further hybrid configurations. Taking a political-economy approach we can identify several general types of hybridity in history. Hybridity across modes of production gives rise to mixed social formations and combinations of hunting/gathering and cultivation or pastoralism, agriculture and industry, craft and industry, etc. Semi-feudalism and feudal capitalism are other instances of mixed political economies; modes of production did not simply succeed one another but coexisted in time. Hybrid modes of economic regulation include the social market in Europe and Scandinavia and market socialism in China, which organize economies by combining diverse principles. The mixed economy and the social economy of cooperative and nonprofit organizations are hybrid economic formations. Social capital, civic entrepreneurship, and corporate citizenship – prominent themes of our times – are also hybrid in character.

Hybridization as a process is as old as history, but the pace of mixing accelerates and its scope widens in the wake of major structural changes, such as new technologies that enable new forms of intercultural contact. Contemporary accelerated globalization is such a new phase. However, if practices of mixing are as old as the hills, the thematization of mixing as a perspective is fairly new and dates from the 1980s. In a wider sense it includes the idea of *bricolage* in culture and art. Dada made mixing objects and perspectives its hallmark and inspired the collage. Surrealism moved further

along these lines and so do conceptual and installation art. Psychoanalysis brought together widely diverse phenomena – dreams, jokes, Freudian slips and symbols – under new headings relevant to psychological diagnosis.

While hybridity may be unremarkable in itself, the critical contribution of hybridity as a theme is that it questions boundaries that are taken for granted. Thus, hybridity is noteworthy from the point of view of boundaries that are considered essential or insurmountable. Hybridity is an important theme also in that it represents one of three major approaches to globalization and culture. One is the idea that global culture is becoming increasingly standardized and uniform (as in McDonaldization); second is the idea that globalization involves a "clash of civilizations"; and third is globalization as hybridization or the notion that globalization produces new combinations and mixtures. The hybridity view holds that cultural experiences past and present have not been simply moving in the direction of cultural synchronization. Cultural synchronization does take place, for instance in relation to technological change, but counter-currents include the impact non-western cultures have on the West and the influence non-western cultures exercise on one another. The cultural convergence view ignores the local reception of western culture, the indigenization of western elements, and the significance of crossover culture and "third cultures" such as world music. It overrates the homogeneity of western culture and overlooks that many of the cultural traits exported by the West are themselves of culturally mixed character if we examine their lineages. Centuries of East–West cultural osmosis have resulted in intercontinental crossover culture, and European and western culture are part of this global mélange. For a long time Europe was on the receiving end of cultural influences from the Orient and the dominance of the West dates only from 1800 onward (Frank 1998).

The term hybridity originates in pastoralism, agriculture, and horticulture. Hybridization refers to developing new combinations by grafting one plant or fruit onto another. A further application is genetics. When belief in "race" played a dominant part, "race mixture" was a prominent notion. Now hybridity also refers to cyborgs (cybernetic organisms): combinations of humans or animals with new technology (e.g., pets carrying chips for identification, biogenetic engineering).

Hybridity first entered social science via anthropology of religion and the theme of syncretism. Bastide (1970) defined syncretism as "uniting pieces of the mythical history of two different traditions in one that continued to be ordered by a single system." Creole languages and creolization in linguistics was the next field to engage social science interest. Creolization came to describe the interplay of cultures and cultural forms (Hannerz 1992). In the Caribbean and North America creolization stands for the mixture of African and European elements (as in the Creole cuisine of New Orleans), while in Latin America *criollo* originally denotes those of European descent born in the continent. The appeal of creolization is that it goes against the grain of nineteenth-century racism and the accompanying abhorrence of *métissage* as miscegenation, as in the view that race mixture leads to decadence and decay, for in every mixture the lower element would be bound to predominate. The cult of racial purity involves the fear of and disdain for the half-caste. By foregrounding the *mestizo*, the mixed and in-between, creolization highlights what has been hidden and values boundary crossing. The Latin American term *mestizaje* also refers to boundary-crossing mixture. Since the early 1900s, however, this served as an élite ideology of "whitening" or Europeanization; through the gradual "whitening" of the population and culture Latin America was supposed to achieve modernity. In the US, crossover culture denotes the adoption of black cultural characteristics by European Americans and of white elements by African Americans. A limitation of these terms is that they are confined to the experience of the post-sixteenth century Americas and typically focus on "racial" mixing. A different perspective is the "orientalization of the world" and easternization, in contrast to westernization. This concerns the influence of Japan and the rise of East Asia, China, and India and the twenty-first century as an "Asian century." Each of these terms – creolization, *mestizaje*, crossover, and orientalization – opens a different window onto the global mélange and global intercultural osmosis.

Hybrid regions straddle geographic and cultural zones, such as the Sudanic belt in Africa. Southeast Asia combines Indo-Chinese and Malay features. The Malay world, Indo-China, Central and South Asia, Middle Eastern, North African, and Balkan societies are all ancient mélange cultures. Global cities and ethnic mélange neighborhoods within them (such as Jackson Heights in Queens, New York) are other hybrid spaces in the global landscape.

What hybridity means varies not only over time but also in different cultures. In Asia it carries a different ring than in Latin America. In Asia the general feeling has been upbeat, as in East–West fusion culture. Hybridity tends to be experienced as chosen, willed, although there are plenty of sites of conflict. In Latin America the feeling has long been one of fracture, and fragmentation and hybridity were experienced as a fateful condition that was inflicted rather than willed. The Latin American notion of mixed times (*tiempos mixtos*) refers to the coexistence and interspersion of premodernity, modernity, and postmodernity. In recent times Latin America's hybrid legacies have been revalued as part of its cultural creativity.

The domains in which hybridity plays a part have been proliferating over time, as in the hybrid car (combining gas and electricity), hybridity in organizations, and diverse cultural influences in management. Interdisciplinarity in science gives rise to new hybrids such as ecological economics.

The prominence of hybridity has given rise to a debate in which hybridity is being criticized as an élite perspective (Friedman 1999). A brief account of arguments against and in favor of hybridity is as follows (see Nederveen Pieterse 2004). Critics argue that asserting that all cultures and languages are mixed is trivial; a rejoinder is that claims of purity have long been dominant. Critics hold that hybridity is meaningful only as a critique of essentialism; which is true, but there is lots of essentialism to go around. Some question whether colonial times were really so essentialist; a rejoinder is that they were essentialist enough for hybrids to be widely despised. Critics object that hybridity is a dependent notion; but so are boundaries. Some critics argue that hybridity matters only to the extent that people identify themselves as mixed; but the existing classification categories hinder hybrid self-identification. Critics claim that cultural mixing is mainly for élites; but arguably cross-border knowledge is survival knowledge also or particularly for poor migrants. Critics hold that hybridity talk is for a new cultural class of cosmopolitans; but would this qualify an old cultural class policing boundaries? If critics ask what the point of hybridity is, a riposte is what is the significance of boundaries? Boundaries and borders can be matters of life or death and the failure to acknowledge hybridity is a political point whose ramifications can be measured in lives.

A next step is to unpack hybridity and to distinguish *patterns* of hybridity. The most conspicuous shortcoming of hybridity thinking is that it does not address questions of power and inequality: "hybridity is not parity" (Shohat & Stam 1994). This is undeniably true; but boundaries do not usually help either. In notions such as global mélange what is missing is acknowledgment of the actual unevenness, asymmetry, and inequality in global relations. What are not clarified are the *terms* under which cultural interplay and crossover take place. Relations of power and hegemony are reproduced *within* hybridity, for wherever we look closely enough we find the traces of asymmetry in culture, place, and descent. Hence, hybridity raises, rather than erases, the question of the terms and conditions of mixing. Meanwhile, it is also important to note the ways in which relations of power are not merely reproduced, but refigured in the process of hybridization.

Thus, according to the context and the relative power and status of elements in the mixture, hybridity can be asymmetric or symmetric. For instance, colonial society is asymmetric. We can think of types of hybridity along a continuum with, on one end, a hybridity that affirms the center of power, adopts the canon, and mimics hegemony and hegemonic styles, and, at the other end, mixtures that blur the lines of power, destabilize the canon, and subvert the center. The novels of V. S. Naipaul are an example of the former and Salman Rushdie's novels often match the latter. Menus that mix cuisines and health care practices that combine diverse methods may offer examples of the symmetric end of the hybridity continuum, but completely free-floating mixtures are rare, for even at a carnival the components carry different values.

SEE ALSO: Boundaries (Racial/Ethnic); Cultural Studies; Colonialism (Neocolonialism); Eurocentrism; Globalization; Globalization, Culture and; Glocalization; McDonaldization; Multiculturalism; Race

REFERENCES AND SUGGESTED READINGS

Bastide, R. (1970) Mémoire collective et sociologie du bricolage. *L'Année Sociologique* 21.

Canclini, N. G. (1995) *Hybrid Cultures.* University of Minnesota Press, Minneapolis.

Frank, A. G. (1998) *Re Orient: Global Economy in the Asian Age.* University of California Press, Berkeley.

Friedman, J. (1999) The Hybridization of Roots and the Abhorrence of the Bush. In: Featherstone, M. & Lash, S. (Eds.), *Spaces of Culture: City – Nation – World.* Sage, London, pp. 230–55.

Gruzinski, S. (2002) *The Mestizo Mind: The Intellectual Dynamics of Colonization and Globalization.,* Routledge, New York.

Hannerz, U. (1992) *Cultural Complexity.* Columbia University Press, New York.

Nederveen Pieterse, J. P. (2004) *Globalization and Culture: Global Mélange.* Rowman & Littlefield, Boulder.

Rowe, W. & Schelling, V. (1991) *Memory and Modernity: Popular Culture in Latin America.* Verso, London.

Shohat, E. & Stam, R. (1994) *Unthinking Eurocentrism: Multiculturalism and the Media.* Routledge, New York.

hyperconsumption/ overconsumption

Jeremy Schulz

Social critics and social scientists, on observing the transformations of American and Western European societies throughout the twentieth century, have relied on terms such as "overconsumption," "consumptionism," "new consumerism," and "hyperconsumption" to convey the increasingly central role played by the acquisition and consumption of goods and services in the lives of individuals, the shaping of cultural forms, and the dynamics of social organization.

This family of terms has a long history in the American context, where "consumptionism" entered the popular lexicon in a 1924 article by journalist Samuel Strauss. Like many other social critics of his time, Strauss sought to expose the ethical bankruptcy of a society in which a concern for the standard of living dominated all other aspects of national and individual welfare. Decades later, in *The Affluent Society* (1958), the economist John Kenneth Galbraith savaged the "overconsumption" fueled by the growth of mass markets and American merchandisers' insatiable appetites for huge sales volumes.

The term "overconsumption" also figured prominently in the critiques of the American lifestyle formulated by social critics and social scientists during the 1970s and early 1980s. Moving beyond earlier critiques, these treatments took aim not only at the ethical consequences of overconsumption, but at the effects of consumption-oriented lifestyles on physical health, psychological well-being, and social functioning. Scitovsky (1976) and Wachtel (1989), for example, argue that ever-increasing quantities of goods and services do not ensure gains in satisfaction at the individual or collective level. In such a society, individuals accustomed to more and more inevitably adapt their consumer expectations to their new circumstances. Consumers will constantly revise their consumption standards upwards, conceiving a whole new set of "must-haves" as general consumption standards rise. Other writers from this period address the theme of overconsumption from a less psychological standpoint. Hirsch (1976) considers the perverse social consequences of American society's extreme emphasis on private goods at the expense of public amenities. The profusion of private goods and services and the starvation of the public sector make it necessary for each consumer to meet their needs individually through market channels. In Hirsch's view, when all goods and services are supplied and consumed in this way, social and individual well-being suffers.

Combining the themes which preoccupied the critics of the 1970s with the concerns for status and emulation which inspired Veblen at the turn of the century, Frank (1999) focuses on the competition over status and social position in the consumerist America of the 1990s. Frank relates the "upscaling" of expectations about what constitutes a desirable wristwatch, suit, or car during the 1990s to the desire American consumers have for "positional goods" (Hirsch 1976) which assist people in creating the "invidious distinctions" Veblen mentioned in his writings on conspicuous consumption (Veblen 1967). Because they represent membership in certain reference groups to which they aspire, today's status-seeking consumers treat socially sanctioned "high-end" products, brand-name clothes, cars, and "trophy homes" as necessities. For the status-driven American consumer, a serviceable $50 wristwatch suddenly becomes inadequate when $1,000 wristwatches start appearing on the arms of well-off neighbors, successful co-workers, and even media celebrities. Frank's concern with adaptation and status-seeking surfaces in many journalistic accounts of overconsumption in the contemporary US. During the late 1990s, articles about expensive and oversized "trophy homes" and "McMansions" appeared frequently in the pages of the nation's newspapers.

Several recent works on overconsumption have shifted the focus somewhat away from the proliferation of luxury goods and the upscaling of consumer norms among the affluent. The predicament of the middle-class overconsumer who depends entirely on earned income and consumer credit to finance his acquisition of goods and services is now a central theme in writings about overconsumption. In her influential book *The Overspent American* (1998), the economist Juliet Schor examines the new wave of middle-class consumerism supported by earned income and consumer credit. In Schor's view, middle-class purchasing of status goods and services has exploded because of the visibility and transparency of the lifestyles associated with middle-class reference groups such as celebrities. The status insecurities of middle-class Americans who fear sliding down the social ladder add to this emulationist pressure and stimulates even more consumerist behavior.

For the status-conscious members of the middle class, the acquisition, ownership, and display of "socially visible" goods such as cars, houses, and clothing have become essential means of proving to themselves and others that they belong in the "really made it" and "doing very well" groups which have come to play the reference group role for more and more Americans. Today's middle-class overconsumers live in a social world where one cannot validate and affirm one's claims to membership in the "made it class" without owning and flaunting the cars, clothes, houses, and computers which are recognized as essential components of upper-middle class living. Indeed, George Ritzer (2001) remarks it is the very inconspicuousness of contemporary brand-name overconsumption which differentiates it from the kind of overconsumption characteristic of Veblen's elites. Consumerist individuals who want to be seen driving certain cars and wearing certain clothes are at once proclaiming their conformity to a particular generalized type and their distinctiveness as "individuals" (Baudrillard 1998).

A new interest in the institutional and infrastructural conditions of overconsumption has surfaced in the works of sociologists studying consumerist practices at the beginning of the twenty-first century. The American sociologist George Ritzer coined the term "hyperconsumption" (Ritzer 1999, 2001) to capture the vastly expanded scope and scale of mass consumption supported by the organizational and logistical innovations of the last quarter century. Ritzer has written extensively about the physical and virtual settings and contexts where the contemporary consumer interacts with producers and sellers of consumer goods. In his view, the emergent "cathedrals" and "landscapes" of hyperconsumption offer an irresistible combination of abundance, enchantment, and predictability. They lend ordinary acts of purchase a magical aura, while at the same time removing all obstacles and barriers to the pleasurable and efficient acquisition of goods and services.

Ritzer (1999) reminds us that American consumers encounter a more and more rationalized and "McDonaldized" set of organizations and practices on the supply side of today's consumer-oriented American economy, an economy where consumer spending now accounts, either directly or indirectly, for a constantly rising proportion of US GDP (now around 70 percent) and some 60 percent of all domestic employment (Toossi 2002). At the same time, the demand side of the American economy has been increasingly reorganized to support ever-growing levels of consumption. Equity-based credit cards and other innovations in the "means of consumption" (Ritzer 1999, 2001) give ordinary American consumers the capacity to spend far beyond their current means.

It is possible to distinguish three strands in recent empirical research into contemporary trends in overconsumption and consumerism. British and American ethnographers tend to concentrate on the experiential dimensions of shopping, whether at luxury stores or the large volume discount stores so prevalent in the US (Zukin 2004). More theoretically and structurally oriented researchers have dealt with the markets and organizations which supply the means – such as consumer credit (Calder 1999) – and the opportunities (Ritzer 1999) for overconsumption.

Emergent lines of research include, at the behavioral level, studies of individuals' use of and relationship with goods such as large homes and luxury cars and services, particularly leisure and entertainment services such as cruises, casinos, hotels, and restaurants. At the structural and institutional level, researchers are turning their attention to the orchestration of consumer credit services, the structuring of large-scale discount retailing/small-scale luxury retailing, and the diffusion of American models of retailing and credit provision in Europe, Asia, and other parts of the world. Finally, theoretically oriented researchers are rethinking the category of consumer. Zygmunt Bauman, for example, argues that in contemporary neoliberal societies the empowered consumer now wields a kind of agency inaccessible to the comparatively disempowered worker-employee who must cope with an ever-more rationalized workplace. For this reason, individuals and households who lack purchasing power because of their low incomes or status as unemployed members of society find themselves stripped of consumer sovereignty. The loss of consumer choice casts the poor and unemployed further into the social abyss and further into the ranks of the "repressed" (Bauman 1998).

SEE ALSO: Conspicuous Consumption; Consumption; Consumption, Cathedrals of; Consumption, Landscapes of; Consumption, Mass Consumption, and Consumer Culture; Lifestyle; McDonaldization; Shopping Malls

REFERENCES AND SUGGESTED READINGS

Baudrillard, J. (1998 [1970]) *The Consumer Society: Myths and Structures.* Sage, London.
Bauman, Z. (1998) *Work, Consumerism, and the New Poor.* Open University Press, Buckingham.
Calder, L. (1999) *Financing the American Dream: A Cultural History of Consumer Credit.* Princeton University Press, Princeton.
Cohen, L. (2002) *Consumer's Republic: The Politics of Mass Consumption in Postwar America.* Alfred Knopf, New York.
Frank, R. (1999) *Luxury Fever: Why Money Fails to Satisfy in an Era of Excess.* Free Press, New York.
Galbraith, J. K. (1984 [1958]) *The Affluent Society.* Houghton Mifflin, Boston.
Gottdiener, M (Ed.) (2000) *New Forms of Consumption: Consumers, Culture, and Commodification.* Rowman & Littlefield, Lanham, MD.
Hirsch, F. (1976) *Social Limits to Growth.* Harvard University Press, Cambridge, MA.
Humphery, K. (1998) *Shelf Life: Supermarkets and the Changing Cultures of Consumption.* Cambridge University Press, Cambridge.
Mason, R. (1981) *Conspicuous Consumption: A Study of Exceptional Consumer Behavior.* St. Martin's Press, New York.
Miles, S. (1998) *Consumerism as a Way of Life.* Sage, London.
Ritzer, G. (1999) *Enchanting a Disenchanted World: Revolutionizing the Means of Consumption.* Sage, Thousand Oaks, CA.
Ritzer, G. (2001) *Explorations in the Sociology of Consumption: Fast Food, Credit Cards and Casinos.* Sage, Thousand Oaks, CA.
Schor, J. (1998) *The Overspent American: Why We Want What We Don't Need.* Basic Books, New York.
Scitovsky, T. (1976) *The Joyless Economy.* Oxford University Press, New York.
Strasser, S. (1989) *Satisfaction Guaranteed: The Making of the American Mass Market.* Pantheon, New York.
Toossi, M. (2002) Consumer Spending: An Engine for US Job Growth. *Monthly Labor Review* (November).
Twitchell, J. B. (1999) *Lead us into Temptation: The Triumph of American Materialism.* Columbia University Press, New York.
Veblen, T. (1967 [1899]) *The Theory of the Leisure Class.* Penguin, New York.
Wachtel, P. (1989) *The Poverty of Affluence: A Psychological Portrait of the American Way of Life.* New Society Publishers, Philadelphia.
Warde, A. & Martens, L. (2000) *Eating Out: Social Differentiation, Consumption, and Pleasure.* Cambridge University Press, Cambridge.
Zukin, S. (2004) *Point of Purchase: How Shopping Changed American Culture.* Routledge, London.

hyperreality

Michael T. Ryan

The capitalist mode of production has gone through some significant changes in the twentieth century (according to Henri Lefebvre, a mutation). A number of French social theorists inspired by Marx have attempted to grasp this process with new concepts and theories, especially in relation to new cultural forms and processes (e.g., media technologies) that are no longer treated as epiphenomenal superstructures that are reducible to the economic substructure of capitalism as orthodox Marxists have traditionally conceptualized this relation. Cultural phenomena have become critical forces in the moments of distribution, exchange, and consumption of commodities in late capitalism. The heroic age of the revolutionary bourgeoisie ended around 1910 with the decline of all of the referentials of classic capitalism: clock time, the vanishing point in art, the work ethic and productive values, history, proletarian revolution, etc. Class strategy has shifted from the organization of production to the bureaucratic organization of consumption and everyday life. The age of simulation begins with the liquidation of referentials, according to Jean Baudrillard. Signs and signifiers have become detached from their referents, from reality, and now only refer to each other. For example, according to Mark Gottdiener, Las Vegas casinos have a variety of themes and constitute a structure of differences that have nothing to do with the gambling and profit-taking that goes on in them. What is the social and historical relation between a simulated pyramid and the gambling, entertainment, and profit-taking that takes place there? If fantasies connected to ancient Egypt do not do anything for the consumer, there are a number of other fantasies with which to play (e.g., tropical paradise, the Wild West, simulated urban environments, etc.). For Umberto Eco, in themed environments like wax museums "[absolute] unreality is offered as real presence . . . The sign aims to be the thing, to abolish the distinction of the reference." For Baudrillard, hyperreality "is the generation by models of a real without origin or reality." The production and reproduction of the real or the hyperreal is what material production is all about in our postmodern society. Simulations, signs, and codes now structure social relations and social practices rather than the capital/labor production relations of classical capitalism. Modern men and women have been set adrift in a sea of signifiers and simulations.

While commodification, industrialization, and market relations were seen as elements of an explosive process in early capitalism, Baudrillard, following Marshall McLuhan, sees an implosion of all binary distinctions and boundaries in late capitalism: high and low culture, past and present, good and evil, capital and labor, male and female, white and non-white, developed and underdeveloped nations, appearance and reality, urban and rural representation and reality, true and false, etc. The poles of every opposition have been absorbed into one another and have become undecidable. Although he is not explicit about this, one could trace this process of implosion as Lefebvre does to the failure of the working class to become an agent of revolutionary transformation, an agent that was supposed to explode all of the contradictions that had accumulated in the capitalist mode of production and to transcend all of the premodern and bourgeois institutions to create a new socialist mode of production and urban society. While Lefebvre sees the implosion of this over-organized society as a dystopic possibility, Baudrillard sees it as an accomplished fact and only offers us one alternative possibility: a return to symbolic exchange that structured tribal cultures and, along with the challenge (i.e., warfare as a mode of appropriating economic surpluses as well as martial sports, the

ancient Greek Olympics or medieval jousting matches that maintained warrior skills and discipline), structured agrarian societies as well. Simulation begins when the poles of all of these oppositions collapse. Indifference and neutralization of all of these formerly dialectical oppositions is the consequence. The media provide models for lived experience and interactions in everyday life (e.g., sex manuals, manuals for parenting, advice columns, radio and television call-in shows, etc.).

Hyperreality is seen by most of these social theorists as a constituent element and a structural tendency in the development of the consumer society and late capitalism. While most of these theorists connect this process to the political economy of the capitalist mode of production, Baudrillard sees postmodern society as a fundamental break from modern capitalism. We move from a society organized around production to a society organized by semiurgy. Capital is simply one sign among a multitude of signs that structure social experience and practices in everyday life. Many of Baudrillard's readers have recognized the importance of his early critical work, see it as an enrichment of Marxist theory, and incorporate it in their critical analyses of late capitalism. But as Douglas Kellner sees it, Baudrillard abandons a social scientific perspective for a metaphysical philosophical perspective in his later works after *The Mirror of Production.*

While hyperreality is a useful concept to grasp the effects of the media in late capitalism, there are a number of problems with Baudrillard's later works. First, unlike Lefebvre who situates linguistic phenomena and consumerism within the process of the reproduction of the capitalist relations of production, Baudrillard sees the hyperreal as taking on a life of its own disconnected from the capitalist mode of production. He has reduced our understanding of this society to a single form and process (i.e., formalism or technological reductionism). He has failed to lay out the mediations to political and economic forms and processes, and he has failed to situate this tendency in history and in the possibilities for social change.

Second, his analysis is abstracted from any notion of agency. Which agents have brought this situation into existence? Which agents can take up the task of transcending this closed system that apparently can only break down in a catastrophic manner? The only resistance is the passivity of the silent majority, which are the objects of his contempt. This often happens to radicals who live through a period of social movements that contest the powers that be and then fail, as happened in the 1960s/ 1970s. With social change unlikely in his lifetime, he abandoned these social movements to embrace some very reactionary political positions.

Third, his analysis is abstracted from the content of everyday life, the lived experience of consumers who are even more alienated than the workers of Marx's era. Does this postmodern society integrate all of its elements? Does this consumer society take care of all of our needs, especially social needs and services? Will the earth sustain a global consumer society? Are we not in the process of committing *terricide* as Lefebvre suggests?

Fourth, while Baudrillard is long on theory, he has failed to put together a research agenda, and in Kellner's judgment he has even failed to fully develop his theory. His concept of code is never satisfactorily defined. His work is often metaphorical; the logic of the metaphor displaces the logic of social processes (i.e., his use of DNA as a master code). For hyperreality to become a more useful concept, the students of Baudrillard will have to answer his critics.

SEE ALSO: Consumption; Culture; Implosion; Simulacra and Simulation; Social Change; Theory

REFERENCES AND SUGGESTED READINGS

Baudrillard, J. (1975) *The Mirror of Production*. Telos Press, St. Louis.
Baudrillard, J. (1976) *For a Critique of the Political Economy of the Sign*. Telos Press, St. Louis.
Baudrillard, J. (1994) *Simulacra and Simulation*. University of Michigan Press, Ann Arbor.
Eco, U. (1986) *Travels in Hyperreality*. Harcourt Brace Jovanovich, San Diego.
Gottdiener, M. (2001) *The Theming of America*, 2nd edn. Westview Press, Boulder.
Kellner, D. (1989) *Jean Baudrillard*. Stanford University Press, Stanford.
Kellner, D. (1994) *Baudrillard*. Blackwell, Oxford.

hypersegregation

Nancy A. Denton

Hypersegregation occurs when a race/ethnic group is highly segregated in multiple ways, no matter how segregation is conceptualized or measured. It is an explicit recognition of the fact that residential segregation by race is a complex phenomenon that is multidimensional in nature. First used in 1989 in an article by Massey and Denton about patterns of black–white segregation in large US metropolitan areas in 1980, the term now occurs in both the academic and popular literature to describe the extremely high residential segregation experienced by African Americans in the US. Though residential segregation has generally declined in recent decades for African Americans, hypersegregation was still documented for African Americans in both 1990 and 2000. For the first time in 2000, Hispanics are hypersegregated in two places as well. No other group experiences hypersegregation in US metropolitan areas.

The complex, multidimensional nature of segregation reflects the historical causes of racial residential segregation, which include prejudice, discrimination, the behavior of realtors and mortgage and insurance agents, as well as the FHA and the development of the suburbs. Associated with the Chicago School, segregation is used to gauge the spatial assimilation of diverse groups into US society, beginning with comparisons of the residential patterns of European immigrant groups to native-born whites and blacks. The theory was that as groups became more similar to native-born Americans in terms of language, education, income, and occupations, they would also reside in similar areas. The study of segregation is also linked to the development of long-term amortized mortgages for housing purchase. Though these enabled many people to own their own homes, the mortgages necessitated that the lender have some way of knowing that the home would still be valuable decades hence, and the future value was linked to characteristics of the neighborhoods where houses were located, including the race of the neighborhood residents. The tremendous post-World War II housing boom, combined with the baby boom and suburban development, resulted in urban landscapes that some described as "chocolate city, vanilla suburbs." In recent decades, residential segregation of blacks has been linked to the development of underclass areas where the spatial concentration of poverty also concentrates other social ills such as crime, joblessness, single parenthood, low levels of educational attainment, etc. Even for the non-poor, the linkage between housing appreciation and neighborhood and their exclusion from such neighborhoods, combined with denial of mortgages and higher rates of interest, has been estimated to have cost the current generation of blacks almost $95 billion in lost assets (Oliver & Shapiro 1995). This brief history of residential segregation serves to illustrate the complexity of it. Throughout all of these studies the segregation of African Americans always stood out because it was so consistently high across cities and over time. The concept of hypersegregation was developed as a way of measuring and describing this uniqueness.

Conceptually, hypersegregation occurs when a group has high segregation scores on four or five different dimensions of segregation. The first dimension is evenness: the extent to which all the neighborhoods in a metropolitan area show the same distribution of groups as the total area. Thus, if an area is 20 percent black and 80 percent white, there would be no segregation if each neighborhood had that racial distribution as well. Evenness is measured by the Index of Dissimilarity (D), the most commonly used measure of segregation. The next dimension is isolation: the extent to which a group shares its neighborhoods with only members of its own group. While evenness looks at distributions *across* all neighborhoods in a city or metropolitan area, isolation provides the view from *within* neighborhoods. A group may live in only a subset of the neighborhoods in a city, but if those neighborhoods are relatively integrated the group has contacts outside their group and their segregation is not as severe as when their neighborhoods are occupied only by their own group. The third dimension, concentration, refers to the relative proportion of the total land area a group occupies, relative to the group's size. This dimension addresses the issues of crowding, population density, and the advantages associated with housing on spacious suburban lots. Centralization, the fourth

dimension, measures how close to the central business district a group resides. In the past, the central business district was not a desirable place to live because of the presence of factories, and in more recent years it reflects the disadvantage associated with not living in the suburbs, where many jobs are now located. The last dimension of segregation, clustering, looks at whether the neighborhoods where a group lives are themselves clustered into one large area or are scattered throughout the metropolitan area. It addresses the aspect of whether a group member, regardless of the composition of their neighborhood of residence, interacts with non-group members if they leave their neighborhood. In hypersegregated metropolitan areas, black neighborhoods tend to form large contiguous ghettos.

The five dimensions used to measure hypersegregation were identified through a factor analysis of 20 different segregation indices, computed for blacks, Hispanics, and Asians in 60 metropolitan areas in 1980 (the 50 largest plus ten others with large Hispanic populations) (Massey & Denton 1988). After selecting a single index for each dimension, a group was defined as hypersegregated when their segregation was above a cutoff on four or five of the dimensions. The original criteria for defining hypersegregation were 0.6 for indices of evenness and clustering, 0.7 for isolation and concentration, and 0.8 for clustering (Massey & Denton 1988), though in later work (Massey & Denton 1993) the cutoff was simplified to 0.6 for all dimensions. The choice of a cutoff reflects the fact that in the literature segregation above 0.6 is usually considered high when indices range between 0 and 1. In a reanalysis of the dimensions of segregation for the same metropolitan areas using data from 1990, Massey, White, and Phua (1996) found that the clustering dimension was not as clearly defined in 1990. These researchers also analyzed all 318 metropolitan areas and found that the original five dimensions of segregation identified in 1980 were clearly observable in 1990, indicating that the structure of segregation had changed somewhat in the largest metropolitan areas, possibly because of the increased presence of Hispanics and Asians in these places, but that segregation could clearly be defined as comprising five dimensions in 1990 as in 1980. In terms of which index best represented each dimension, however, the choice was not as clear for clustering and concentration.

In summary, to define hypersegregation requires three decisions: first, which index will be used to measure each of the five dimensions; second, what value of each index will be considered "high"; and third, on how many of the five dimensions must a group be highly segregated to be called hypersegregated. Choices on each of these are made based on both the extant literature and the judgment of the researchers: in short, there is no absolutely correct choice, and changes will yield different lists of hypersegregated places and groups. While this may at first seem to imply that hypersegregation is an arbitrary idea, what it really reflects is that segregation is a continuous variable. Furthermore, as will be seen when specific hypersegregated places are discussed below, varying these choices does not dramatically change the overall pattern of results.

Where does hypersegregation occur and does its location change over time? Using data from the 1980 US Census, ten metropolitan areas were originally identified as hypersegregated: Baltimore, Chicago, Cleveland, Detroit, Milwaukee, and Philadelphia on all five dimensions, and Gary, Los Angeles, Newark, and St. Louis on four dimensions (Massey & Denton 1989). As noted above, these were selected by examining the 50 largest metropolitan areas in 1980, as well as ten others with large Hispanic populations. In 1993 an additional six areas were added to the list as a result of modifying the criteria for defining hypersegregation to be 0.6 for all indices: Atlanta, Buffalo, Dallas, Indianapolis, Kansas City, and New York. Thus, in 1980 hypersegregation was most often found in larger, formerly industrial cities of the Northeast and Midwest that had large African American populations. A decade later, looking at the same 60 metropolitan areas originally used, Denton (1994) found that African Americans in all of these metropolitan areas remained hypersegregated except those in Atlanta and Dallas. In addition, examination of black segregation in the remaining metropolitan areas revealed hypersegregation of African Americans in an additional 15 metropolitan areas. While eight are smaller metropolitan areas located in the South (Albany, GA, Baton Rouge, LA,

Beaumont-Port Arthur, TX, Monroe, LA, and Savannah GA) or Midwest (Benton Harbor, MI, Flint, MI, and Saginaw Bay City Midland, MI), the other seven are large metro areas, implying substantial black populations living in hypersegregated conditions: Birmingham, AL, Cincinnati, OH, Miami-Hialeah, FL, New Orleans, LA, Oakland, CA, Trenton, NJ, Washington, DC.

Research using data from the 2000 census reveals the continuance of hypersegregation for African Americans, as well as the emergence of hypersegregation for Hispanics. Wilkes and Iceland (2004) identify 29 metropolitan areas with black–white hypersegregation in 2000: Chicago, Cleveland, Detroit, Milwaukee, Newark, and Philadelphia on all five dimensions, and Albany, GA, Atlanta, Baltimore, Baton Rouge, Beaumont-Port Arthur, Birmingham, Buffalo-Niagara Falls, Dayton-Springfield, Flint, Gary, Houston, Jackson, Kankakee, IL, Los Angeles-Long Beach, Miami, Memphis, Mobile, Monroe, LA, New Orleans, New York, Saginaw-Bay City, MI, St. Louis, and Washington, DC on four dimensions. While most of these were also hypersegregated in 1990, Wilkes and Iceland used a different index to measure concentration than the one recommended by Massey and Denton. If a consistent set of indices is used across the three censuses, then nine metropolitan areas drop off the list of those hypersegregated in 2000 (Benton Harbor, Cincinnati, Indianapolis, Kansas City, Miami, New Orleans, Oakland, Savannah, and Trenton), though they remain highly segregated. However, three areas (Atlanta, Dayton, and Mobile) became hypersegregated in 2000. In addition, Hispanics in Los Angeles and New York are found to be hypersegregated in 2000.

Why is hypersegregation important? The multidimensional layers of segregation implied by hypersegregation mean that to the extent that blacks living in these places are denied access to the spatial resources in terms of schools, jobs, safety, and housing value appreciation that whites experience, then hypersegregation is a factor supporting the disadvantaged status of blacks in metropolitan America. It is of particular importance that Hispanics in New York and Los Angeles are now experiencing hypersegregation as well, for there is little reason to expect that it will not have similar effects for them as it has had for African Americans. Future research on hypersegregation will have to confront the fact that, currently, hypersegregation is defined relative to non-Hispanic whites. While this group is the most socioeconomically privileged, controls the opportunity structure in most metropolitan areas, and is usually the largest group numerically, metropolitan areas are increasingly diverse. Future studies of hypersegregation will have to include more groups and use multiple group indices such as the Theil Index, which is just beginning to be used in segregation studies (Fischer 2003; Fischer et al. 2004). In addition, increasing heterogeneity within groups, in both income and suburban location, implies that future work may show that some members of a group live in hypersegregated conditions while others do not (Alba et al. 2000; Fischer 2003).

SEE ALSO: Ethnicity; Inequality and the City; Race; Race (Racism); Residential Segregation; Segregation

REFERENCES AND SUGGESTED READINGS

Alba, R., Logan, J. L., & Stults. B. (2000) The Changing Neighborhood Contexts of the Immigrant Metropolis. *Social Forces* 79: 587–621.
Denton, N. A. (1994) Are African Americans Still Hypersegregated in 1990? In: Bullard, R., Lee, C., & Grigsby, J. E., III (Eds.), *Residential Apartheid: The American Legacy*. UCLA Center for Afro-American Studies, Los Angeles, pp. 49–81.
Fischer, C. S., Stockmayer, G., Stiles, J., & Hout, M. (2004) Distinguishing the Geographic Levels and Social Dimensions of US Metropolitan Segregation, 1960–2000. *Demography* 41: 37–59.
Fischer, M. J. (2003) The Relative Importance of Income and Race in Determining Residential Outcomes in US Urban Areas, 1970–2000. *Urban Affairs Review* 38(5): 669–96.
Massey, D. S. & Denton, N. A. (1988) The Dimensions of Segregation. *Social Forces* 67: 281–315.
Massey, D. S. & Denton, N. A. (1989) Hypersegregation in US Metropolitan Areas: Black and Hispanic Segregation Along Five Dimensions. *Demography* 26: 373–91.
Massey, D. S. & Denton, N. A. (1993) *American Apartheid: Segregation and the Making of the Underclass*. Harvard University Press, Cambridge, MA.
Massey, D. S., White, M. J., & Phua, V. (1996) The Dimensions of Segregation Revisited. *Sociological Methods and Research* 25: 172–206.
Oliver, M. L. & Shapiro, T. M. (1995) *Black Wealth/White Wealth: A New Perspective on Racial Inequality*. Routledge, New York.
Wilkes, R. & Iceland, J. (2004) Hypersegregation in the Twenty-First Century. *Demography* 41: 23–36.

hypotheses

Ivan Y. Sun

Hypotheses are predictions that specify the relationships among the variables. The role of hypotheses in scientific research is to provide explanations for certain phenomena and to guide the investigation of related others. The development of scientific knowledge hinges ultimately upon the results from hypothesis testing. Formalized hypotheses consist of two types of variables: the independent and dependent variables. The former is the cause and the latter is the outcome. A good and well-worded hypothesis should (1) indicate the specific relationship between the dependent and independent variables to be examined; (2) suggest the nature of the relationship; and (3) imply the nature of the research design (Cone & Foster 1993).

Hypotheses, which are derived directly from a theory or theories, have to be testable. The hypothesis-testing process generally involves three steps. The first step is to formulate two hypothesis statements: a null hypothesis (often symbolized as H_0) that predicts no relationship between the variables in the population (e.g., H_0: Social class is unrelated to deviant behavior) and an alternative hypothesis (H_1) that predicts a relationship between the variables (e.g., H_1: Social class is related to deviant behavior). The null hypothesis should be mutually exclusive of the alternative hypothesis, meaning that there is no overlap between the two hypotheses. They are also exhaustive, representing all possible outcomes in reality. If the null hypothesis is not correct or rejected, then the alternative hypothesis may be correct or accepted.

The second step is to select the level of significance. In order to decide whether to reject or fail to reject the null hypothesis, researchers must select a significance level (i.e., the α level) for the null hypothesis, which is typically at .05 or .01. If the alternative hypothesis specifies a direction of the relationship between the variables (e.g., H_1: Social class is negatively related to deviant behavior), then the test is called a one-tailed or directional hypothesis test of significance, which looks for either the increase or decrease of the dependent variable. If the alternative hypothesis does not specify a direction of the relationship (H_1: Social class is related to deviant behavior), then the test is called a two-tailed or non-directional hypothesis test of significance, which examines any change in the dependent variable.

A final step is to calculate the value of test statistic and compare the statistic to a critical value obtained from distribution tables (e.g., Distribution of t or Chi Square or F) based upon the α level. If the test statistic falls beyond the critical value, then the null hypothesis is rejected and the finding is significant (e.g., People with high and low social class differ significantly in their deviant behavior). If the test statistic does not exceed the critical value, then the null hypothesis cannot be rejected and the finding is not significant (e.g., People with high and low social class do not differ significantly in their deviant behavior), meaning that the difference in deviant behavior between people with high and low social class only occurs by random chance.

SEE ALSO: Evaluation; Fact, Theory, and Hypothesis: Including the History of the Scientific Fact; Statistical Significance Testing; Theory; Theory Construction; Variables, Dependent; Variables, Independent

REFERENCES AND SUGGESTED READINGS

Cone, J. & Foster, S. (1993) *Dissertations and Theses from Start to Finish: Psychology and Related Fields.* American Psychological Association, Washington, DC.

Gravetter, F. & Wallnau, L. (2004) *Statistics for the Behavioral Sciences.* Wadsworth, Belmont, CA.

Knoke, D., Bohrnstedt, G., & Mee, A. (2002) *Statistics for Social Data Analysis.* F. E. Peacock, Itasca, IL.

ideal type

Stewart Clegg

The notion of an ideal type is best known to sociologists through the work of Max Weber, although it was a term in common usage in nineteenth-century German historical social sciences. It was designed to solve the problem of comparison. A historical event cannot be described without reference to the persons involved and to the place and date of its occurrence. Thus, all historical events were unique and one could only tell specific local stories. Forcing these into some overall framework would usually prove, at worst, ideological and, at best, would do violence to the integrity of local detail.

What an ideal type captures is meaning: what counts for history is always the meaning of the people concerned in its production and interpretation. As Leopold von Mises (1976: 60) argued in his *Epistemological Problems of Economics*:

> An ideal type cannot be defined: it must be characterized by an enumeration of those features whose presence by and large decides whether in a concrete instance we are or are not faced with a specimen belonging to the ideal type in question. It is peculiar to the ideal type that not all its characteristics need to be present in any one example. Whether or not the absence of some characteristics prevents the inclusion of a concrete specimen in the ideal type in question, depends on a relevance judgment by understanding. The ideal type itself is an outcome of an understanding of the motives, ideas, and aims of the acting individuals and of the means they apply.

As Weber conceived them, ideal types were hypothetical and a reference not to something that is normatively ideal but to an ideational type, which serves as a mental model that can be widely shared and used because analysts agree that it captures some essential features of a phenomenon. The ideal type does not correspond to reality but seeks to condense essential features of it in the model so that one can better recognize its real characteristics when it is met. It is not an embodiment of one side or aspect but the synthetic ideational representation of complex phenomena from reality.

For instance, Weber's analysis took emergent terms and ideas that were current in actual bureaucracies at the time that he was writing and used them as the basis for theoretical construction of an ideal type of bureaucracy. They were a reconstruction of ordinary language in use into the ideal type. Now a certain normative slippage occurs in this process, because he is using ordinary language terms, as defined by members of organizations, to describe what it is that these members do. The members were those of the Prussian and German bureaucracies of the state and military. They were bounded by a ferociously strong sense of duty and conformance.

Schütz (1967) took issue with one aspect of Weber's approach to ideal types: were they a construct by the analysts, or were they the analysts' account of the constructs in use by the members of the research setting in question? For Schütz it was not clear whether Weber's ideal types, in their basis in social action, were a member's category or one that belonged to analysts. By this he meant that their construction out of the concepts of everyday life should ensure that they were grounded in the members' usage. However, once they were refined by an analyst, they become somewhat dissociated from everyday usage.

An example of how slippage could occur is evident in the history of the concept of bureaucracy. Weber's synthesis of its ideal type

2202 identity control theory

meaning became the basis for a narrow focus on "bureaucracy," which became, ultimately, much more compatible with an instrumental concern with "efficiency" overshadowing the cultural, historical, institutional, political, and economic analysis of the market which Weber (1978) pioneered. Bureaucracy had been identified with elite constructions of organization; these, in turn, were now taken to be the literal depiction of the phenomenon. Rationality in the empirical world became identified with top managerial prerogatives defining what the bureaucracy should be and irrationality became identified with deviations from it.

Some sociologists made a similar error: because the ideal type was a construct from a highly specific place and time, it would have been odd for later and different realities to correspond to it. When writers such as Gouldner (1954) investigated organizations, they compared the realities they found with the type that they had inherited. However, since the type was always an imaginary and synthetic construct from a specific place and time, this is not an immediately sensible activity. It ends up privileging the subjectivities of those members whose everyday usage first grounded the construct and neglects that in different circumstances other members might have constructed quite other usages, which should surely provide the material for constructions of other ideal types. What can happen, instead, is that the type becomes reified. It takes on a life of its own. The analysts' casting of the ideal type sets it in concrete and it is employed long past its use-by date. For example, once again this seems to be what happened with Weber's famous ideal type of bureaucracy. It was widely used in the 1950s and 1960s as the basis for both case studies, such as Gouldner (1954), and for the development of what were heralded as taxonomic approaches to organizations (Pugh & Hickson 1976). The latter saw the ideal type elements abstracted by Weber with respect to nineteenth-century German bureaucracy become the definitive features of a functionalist conception of organization structure as an essential form determined in its particular patterns by specific local contingencies, such as size or technology. Analysis then became caught in a historical cul-de-sac of ever-diminishing returns as scholars sought to defend the essential structure against all comers (Donaldson 1996).

Meanwhile, the members of actual organizations were, in practice, using quite different everyday concepts to construct their realities (supply chains, outsourcing, virtual organizations, etc.), which could not be captured adequately in the abstractions of the reified form. As Martindale (1960: 383) suggested, we should "compare different empirical configurations, not empirical configurations and types," as any specific type is always historically bounded and "destined to be scrapped."

SEE ALSO: Bureaucratic Personality; Charisma, Routinization of; Culture, Organizations and; Democracy and Organizations; Labor Process; Organization Theory; Organizational Careers; Schütz, Alfred; Weber, Max

REFERENCES AND SUGGESTED READINGS

Donaldson, L. (1996) The Normal Science of Structural Contingency Theory. In: Clegg, S. R., Hardy, C., & Nord, W. R. (Eds.), Handbook of Organization Studies. Sage, London, pp. 57–76.
Gouldner, A. W. (1954) Patterns of Industrial Bureaucracy. Free Press, New York.
Martindale, D. (1960) The Nature and Types of Sociological Theory. Routledge & Kegan Paul, London.
Mises, L. von (1976) Epistemological Problems of Economics. New York University Press, New York.
Pugh, D. S. & Hickson, D. J. (1976) Writers on Organizations. Penguin, Harmondsworth.
Schütz, A. (1967) The Phenomenology of the Social World. Heinemann, London.
Weber, M. (1978) Economy and Society: An Outline of Interpretative Sociology. University of California Press, Berkeley.

identity control theory

Peter J. Burke

Identity control theory (ICT) focuses on the nature of persons' identities (who they are) and the relationship between the persons' identities and their behavior within the context of the social structure within which the identities are embedded. ICT grows out of identity theory (Stryker 1994; Stryker & Burke 2000) and structural symbolic interaction theory more generally (Stryker 1980). Central to all of these theories, including the symbolic interaction perspective, is the idea that behavior is premised on a named and classified world and that people in society name each other and themselves in terms of the positions they occupy. Further, these positional labels or names and the expectations attached to them become internalized as the identities that make up the self. These self labels thus define persons in terms of positions in society and these positions carry the shared behavioral expectations. Further, these positions, conventionally labeled roles and groups, are relational in the sense that they tie individuals together. For example, with respect to roles, father is tied to son or daughter; with respect to groups, the in-group is related to the out-group and in-group members are related to other in-group members. This is reflective of William James's (1890) notion that people have as many selves as they have relationships to others. Thus, through their identities, people are intimately tied to the social structure.

The social structure, in this view, is not fixed or static. Fluidity of the structure of social relations is conceptually brought about by introducing Turner's (1962) concept of "role-making," which takes place situationally as persons interact and negotiate common meanings that may reshape, reinterpret, and otherwise change the situation. However, this is variable. Some structures (open) are more open to role-making, negotiation, and change than others (closed). In the more open structures, names and classes as well as possibilities for interaction may be modified through negotiation and interaction. In closed structures, such modifications are made only with difficulty.

MEANING

Central to ICT is the concept of meaning around which identities are formed. What does it *mean* to be "father," or "son"? What does it *mean* to be an "American"? An identity is a set of meanings applied to the self in a social role or as a member of a social group that define who one is (Burke & Tully 1977). Identity control theory takes the definition of meaning

from the work of Osgood et al. (1957), which in somewhat simplified terms is a response that a person has to a stimulus; meaning is a response. From Mead, a symbol is a stimulus to which people share a common response. Thinking about myself as a father (the stimulus) calls up in me a set of responses (set of meanings) similar to those called up in others. These responses define for a person what it means to be a father, e.g., being strong, being caring, or being the breadwinner. These common responses lead to common expectations and understandings about what a father is and what a father does, as well as shared understandings about the relation of father to son or daughter and the position of father in the family.

CONTROL OF PERCEPTIONS

Each identity is viewed as a control system with four components (Burke 1991). The set of meanings for a given identity is held in what identity control theory terms the *identity standard* – one of the components of an identity. In addition to the identity standard containing the self-defining meanings, an identity contains *perceptions* of meanings in the situation that are relevant to our identity (most of which come from the feedback from others about how we are coming across in the situation), a *comparator* that functions to compare the perceived meanings with the meanings in the identity standard, and an output function of the comparison, sometimes called an *error* or *discrepancy* that represents the difference between perceptions and the identity standard. Finally, as a function of the error or discrepancy, there is meaningful behavior enacted in the situation that conveys meanings about our identity.

If, in an interactive setting, people perceive their identity-relevant meanings to be congruent with the meanings in their identity standard, that is, the discrepancy is zero, people continue to do what they have been doing. If the discrepancy is not zero, people change their behavior in such a way as to counteract the disturbance and reduce the discrepancy back toward zero. By changing their behavior, people change meanings in the situation. These altered meanings are perceived and again compared to the meanings in the identity standard. Thus, each identity is a control system that acts to control perceptions (of meanings relevant to their identity) by bringing them into congruency with the meanings in their identity standards, thus reducing toward zero any discrepancy or error caused by a disturbance.

This process of controlling perceptions of identity-relevant meanings to make them congruent with the meanings in the identity standard is the process of identity verification. Thus, people act to verify or confirm their identities, and in so doing, they bring about a situation in which relevant (perceived) meanings are consistent with their identity standard. The meanings in the identity standard represent goals or the way the situation is "supposed to be." If the identity is a role identity, then the behavior that brings about the changes in the situational meanings to make them consistent with the identity standard is appropriate role behavior. If the identity is a group- or category-based identity, the behavior which verifies the identity is the behavior that maintains group boundaries and divisions in the social structure. Thus, by verifying identities, people create and maintain the social structure in which the identities are embedded.

Note that by controlling perceived situational meanings, role players and group members are bringing about and maintaining certain conditions or states of affairs by whatever behaviors accomplish that. They are not engaging in particular behaviors except insofar as those behaviors bring about the condition of meanings that are perceived to be the way things are "supposed to be." It is the outcome that is important; an outcome that is accomplished by various means in spite of various unpredictable disturbances. For this reason, the meanings in the identity standard may also be conceptualized as goals to be achieved or realized by having perceptions that match the outcomes indicated in the identity standard.

As discussed above, identities control perceived meanings to bring them into alignment with meanings held in the identity standard. Meanings, also discussed above, are responses to stimuli. Identity control theory distinguishes between two types of meanings: *symbolic* meanings and *sign* meanings (Lindesmith & Strauss 1956). Symbolic meanings are responses to stimuli that are shared with others. These stimuli

are symbols. The meaning of the symbol "pen" is understood and shared by persons in the same culture. When one person talks about a "pen," others understand. Signs, however, are stimuli whose meanings are not necessarily shared with others, but which help us manipulate resources in the situation (Freese & Burke 1994). Using a pen to take notes, a person feels how the pen fits into her hand, how it flows along the surface of a sheet of paper, and how it makes marks with ink that are controlled to form writing. The responses that she has to the pen in its use are sign meanings. Sign meanings allow us to control resources present in the situation.

RESOURCES

Resources within identity control theory are processes that sustain persons, groups, or interaction (Freese & Burke 1994). This is a functional definition in which resources are defined by what they do rather than what they are. Resources are of two types: *actual* and *potential* (Freese & Burke 1994). Actual resources are resources in the situation that are in use in the sense of currently sustaining persons, groups, and interaction (e.g., the pen that is writing, the chair that is supporting an individual, the idea that solves a problem). Potential resources are resources that are not being used, but have the potential for use at a future time (e.g., the pen or chair that is not in use, food in the pantry, oil in the pipeline). Sign meanings allow us to control actual resources. Symbolic meanings allow us to control potential resources through thinking, planning, and action. When an identity controls meanings relevant to the identity in the situation, it controls both sign and symbolic meanings, and through them it controls actual and potential resources.

As described at the beginning, identities are primarily defined in terms of the named categories and positions of the general social structure. Further, the identity's position in the social structure, i.e., in a group or network, governs its access to the actual and potential resources either directly or through network ties. In this way, the resources controlled by identities are those that sustain the social structure by sustaining the groups, the roles, the individuals, and the interaction that defines these. To understand identity functioning in an empirical sense then, one must understand the location of the identity in the social structure.

THE BASES OF IDENTITY

ICT distinguishes between three bases of identities. These are *role identities*, what it means to be in a role such as father, *social identities*, what it means to be in a group or category such as American, and *person identities*, or what it means to be the unique biological being that one is. Identities based on each of the different bases operate in the same way, wherein people seek to verify the identity or make the relevant situational meanings (both signs and symbols) match the meanings held in the identity standard by counteracting any disturbances. Analytically, each of these bases differs in the resources that are controlled through the control of meanings. For a role identity, control of meanings results in control of resources that sustain the role and the group within which it operates. For a social identity, control is of the resources that help sustain the group and maintain its boundaries. For a person identity, control is of the resources that sustain the individual as a unique biological being. Analytically, these differences are clear, although in practice and empirically, it is often difficult to know which resources go with which since we are often all of these at once: a biological being who is a group member in a role.

People have many identities, one for each of the many persons they claim to be, roles they have, and groups and categories to which they belong. This complexity of the self with its many identities reflects the complexity of society (Stryker 1980). In ICT, the multiple identities are arranged into a hierarchy of control systems in which some identities are higher than others in the sense that the outputs of those identities at the higher level are the standards of those identities at a lower level (Tsushima & Burke 1999). Higher-level identities have their own perceptions, standard, and comparator just as the lower-level identities.

While the output of the comparator of the lower-level identities leads to behavior that maintains (when there is no discrepancy) or alters (when there is a discrepancy) meanings in the situation, the output of the comparator of the higher-level identities acts to alter the standards (identity meanings) for lower-level identities. In this way, higher-level identities act as general principles that guide the programs of lower-level identities. Higher-level identities include such master statuses as one's gender, race, or class, and many person identities, the control systems of which are used across situations, roles, and groups. One may, for example, be not just a friend but a female friend; one may be not just an American but a black American; one may be not just a professor but a diligent professor. In each case, the master status of gender or race, or the person identity as diligent, acts to change the manner in which friend, American, or professor is played out.

IDENTITY CHANGE

The most obvious outcome of a discrepancy between the perceived identity-relevant meanings and the meanings held in the identity standard is behavior that counteracts any disturbance to the perceived meanings and quickly brings them back into alignment with the identity standard. At the same time, however, ICT recognizes the less obvious outcome that identities change: i.e., the identity standard slowly changes in the direction of the situational meanings. Both outcomes occur simultaneously, but at much different speeds. If the disturbed situational meanings are restored quickly, any change to the identity standard may not be noticed. If the discrepancy persists, however, because the person cannot change the situational meanings for one reason or another, the slowly changing identity standard will continue to move toward agreement with the situational meanings and the person will come to see herself as consistent with the situational meanings. The discrepancy has been removed not by changing the situational meanings to be in agreement with the identity standard, but by changing the identity standard to be in agreement with the situational meanings, although this generally takes a long time and most people would leave the situation rather than endure such changes to who they are.

Nevertheless, in persons who have been prisoners of war, in persons who are brought into cults, and in persons who are abducted and kept for a long period of time with their abductors, we see the changes in the identities that are brought about. In each case, these powerless persons are unable to verify their (former) identities by changing perceived meanings in the situation. These persons with their lack of power and status are unable to change their perceptions and their identity standards slowly change to match the perceptions. This result was shown in research that examined identity verification among status unequals (Cast et al. 1999). The identities of persons with less power or status came to be more in alignment with the perceptions of meanings provided by more powerful others. The reverse was not true. Of course, children have very little power and their identity standards are strongly set by their parents who have the power.

EMOTIONS

In ICT, the verification process of identities is tied to emotional outcomes that help guide the process (Burke 1991). When the discrepancy between identity-relevant perceptions and the identity standard is small or decreasing, people feel good. When the discrepancy is large or increasing, people feel bad or distressed. These consequences have been shown in research by Burke and Harrod (2005), who found that persons become distressed, angry, and depressed when their spouse's view of them is different (better or worse) than their self-view or identity standard. Current work in ICT examines the role of identity verification in the production of self-worth, self-efficacy, and feelings of authenticity (Cast & Burke 2002) and is developing predictions about the specific emotions that may be felt when identities are verified or not verified (Stets & Burke 2005).

FUTURE RESEARCH

Because ICT is part of a continuing research program, new developments and additions to the theory are always being made; the theory is not fixed. A few areas that new research is exploring include: (1) how identities change in response to external events and the other identities an individual holds; (2) how the multiple different identities an individual has relate to one another; (3) how the social context in

which identities are or are not verified influences the variety of emotions felt; (4) how identity verification is related to the health and well-being of individuals; (5) how the identities of persons in interacting groups influence interaction and group processes; and (6) how ICT relates to other developing theories in social psychology such as justice theory, exchange theory, expectation states theory, and status characteristics theory. It is clear that much work remains for the future development of this theory (Stryker & Burke 2000; Burke 2004).

SEE ALSO: Identity: The Management of Meaning; Identity: Social Psychological Aspects; Identity Theory; Role-Taking; Self; Social Psychology; Symbolic Interaction

REFERENCES AND SUGGESTED READINGS

Burke, P. J. (1991) Identity Processes and Social Stress. *American Sociological Review* 56(6): 836–49.
Burke, P. J. (2004) Identities and Social Structure: The 2003 Cooley-Mead Award Address. *Social Psychology Quarterly* 67: 5–15.
Burke, P. J. & Harrod, M. M. (2005) Too Much of a Good Thing? *Social Psychology Quarterly* 68.
Burke, P. J. & Tully, J. C. (1977) The Measurement of Role Identity. *Social Forces* 55(4): 881–97.
Cast, A. D. & Burke, P. J. (2002) A Theory of Self-Esteem. *Social Forces* 80(3): 1041–68.
Cast, A. D., Stets, J. E., & Burke, P. J. (1999) Does the Self Conform to the Views of Others? *Social Psychology Quarterly* 62(1): 68–82.
Freese, L. & Burke, P. J. (1994) Persons, Identities, and Social Interaction. *Advances in Group Processes* 11: 1–24.
James, W. (1890) *Principles of Psychology*. Holt Rinehart & Winston, New York.
Lindesmith, A. R. & Strauss, A. L. (1956) *Social Psychology*. Holt Rinehart & Winston, New York.
Osgood, C. E., Suci, G. J., & Tannenbaum, P. H. (1957) *The Measurement of Meaning*. University of Illinois Press, Urbana.
Stets, J. E. & Burke, P. J. (2005) New Directions in Identity Control Theory. *Advances in Group Processes* 22.
Stryker, S. (1980) *Symbolic Interactionism: A Social Structural Version*. Benjamin Cummings, Menlo Park, CA.
Stryker, S. (1994) Identity Theory: Its Development, Research Base, and Prospects. *Studies in Symbolic Interaction*.

Stryker, S. & Burke, P. J. (2000) The Past, Present, and Future of an Identity Theory. In: *The State of Sociological Social Psychology. Social Psychology Quarterly* 63, 4 (special issue): 284–97.

Tsushima, T. & Burke, P. J. (1999) Levels, Agency, and Control in the Parent Identity. *Social Psychology Quarterly* 62(2): 173–89.

Turner, R. H. (1962) Role-Taking: Process Versus Conformity. In: Rose, A. M. (Ed.), *Human Behavior and Social Processes*. Houghton Mifflin, Boston, pp. 20–40.

identity, deviant

Patricia A. Adler and Peter Adler

Identities refer to the way people think of themselves. This is important in the field of deviance because people's perceptions and interpretations of situations and themselves are likely to affect their behavior. If people conceive of themselves as deviant, they are more likely to engage in further deviant behavior than if they have a non-deviant identity. The study of deviant identities has focused on how people develop and manage non-normative self-conceptions. This processual approach has been fostered by the special interest in deviant identity taken by symbolic interactionists, with their rich heritage from labeling theory to dramaturgy. Central themes in the study of deviant identities include the ways that they develop, factors that foster their development, and consequences of having them.

Some structuralist scholars consider definitions of deviance rooted in absolutist elements intrinsic to people's attitudes, behavior, conditions, or social statuses. This approach sees unchanging, universal sources such as God or nature as responsible for differentiating between the deviant and the normative. Structuralists would likely view certain acts as so inherently abhorrent that these would be banned by all societies. Relativist scholars, such as Howard Becker, however, view deviance as the product of people's reactions to events, which are situationally variable by the era in which they occur, the relative social power of the perpetrator and victim, and the consequences that arise from them. Relativists believe that the likelihood of

an act becoming defined as deviant (and the punishment that accompanies it) depends on who commits it, who suffers from it, and who knows about it. This partly explains the higher likelihood that individuals of color who commit crimes against white people (or lower-class people who commit crimes against rich people) will be arrested, charged with a crime, and prosecuted, since such victims generally have high social power and the perpetrators' social power is relatively low. Relativists note that definitions of deviance have significantly evolved over time and continue to do so. Most conceptions of deviant identity follow this latter approach, recognizing that people are most likely to develop deviant identities when they experience situational factors where such self-conceptions are pressed upon them. In fact, Becker (1963) suggested that many people go through a range of experiences as "secret deviants," violating norms but doing so inconspicuously. As long as no others are aware of their transgressions, he suggests that people are unlikely to think of themselves as seriously outside of the norm.

The process of acquiring a deviant identity unfolds processually as a "deviant" (Becker 1963) or "moral" (Goffman 1963) career, with people passing through stages that move them out of their innocent identities towards one labeled as "different" by society. "Deviant identity careers" develop through seven stages. The point of departure, as Becker (1963) suggested, is getting caught and publicly identified. People commit deviant acts, such as theft; if they are apprehended, news of this spreads. Second, others begin to think of them differently. In light of this new information, others may engage in what Kitsuse (1962) called "retrospective reinterpretation," reflecting back onto individuals' pasts to see if their current and earlier behavior can be recast. For instance, people may wonder how someone now caught for college cheating got such good grades without studying much, and decide that he or she was probably cheating all along. Third, as this news spreads, either informally or through official agencies of social control, individuals develop "spoiled identities" (Goffman 1963), where their reputations become tarnished. Erikson (1966) noted that news about deviance is of high interest in a community, commanding intense focus from a wide audience. Deviant labeling is hard to reverse, he suggested, and once people's identities are spoiled they are hard to socially rehabilitate. He discussed "commitment ceremonies," such as trials or psychiatric hearings, where individuals are officially labeled as deviant. Few corresponding ceremonies exist, he remarked, to mark the cleansing of people's identities and welcome them back into the normative fold. Individuals may thus find it hard to recover from the lasting effect of such identity labeling, and despite their best efforts they often find that society expects them to commit further deviance. Merton (1968) referred to this as the "self-fulfilling prophecy," where people tend to enact the labels placed upon them, despite possible intentions otherwise.

Fourth, Lemert (1951) noted that the dynamics of exclusion then set in, where certain groups of people, organizations, employers, and others may not want to associate with the newly labeled deviants, who become ostracized from participation and membership with them. They may be cast out of honors societies, professional associations, relationships, or jobs. Fifth, Lemert highlighted the corollary to this point, discussing the dynamics of inclusion, which make people labeled as deviant more attractive to others. Their very acts may lead fellow deviants or would-be deviants interested or engaged in similar forms of deviance to seek them out. Thus, individuals may find that as they move down the pathway of their deviant careers that they shift friendship circles, being pushed away from the company of some, while being simultaneously welcomed into the company of others.

Sixth, others usually begin to treat those defined as deviant differently, indicating through their actions that their feelings and attitudes towards the newly deviant have shifted, often in a negative sense. They may not accord people the same level of credibility they previously had, and they may tighten the margin of social allowance they allot them. Seventh, and finally, people react to this treatment using what Charles Horton Cooley referred to as their "looking-glass selves." In the culminating stage of the identity career, they internalize the deviant label and come to think of themselves differently. This is likely to affect their future behavior. Although not all people who get caught in deviance progress completely through this full set of stages, Becker (1963) described this process as the effects of labeling.

Degher and Hughes (1991) have suggested that along the way to identity change people may be nudged out of their normative self-identities and into deviant ones by active and passive "status cues." Active status cues are communicated through interaction, such as when people make remarks that let their friends know that they appear different, or that they ought to reconsider something about themselves. Passive status cues derive from the environment, such as when people discover that they are no longer capable of doing something or appearing a certain way. While active status cues are direct, people may encounter passive status cues for a long time without recognizing them, and often require some sensitization to perceive and accept these as pointing towards themselves. These cues serve to press on individuals the realization that their conventional identity no longer fits, and to move them through the identity change process.

While we all juggle a range of identities and social selves, Hughes (1945) asserted that a known deviant identity often assumes the position of a "master status," taking precedence over all others. Many social statuses fade in and out of relevance as people move through various situations, but a master status accompanies people into all their contexts, forming the key identity through which others see them. Deviant attributes such as a minority race, heroin addiction, and homosexuality are prime examples of such master statuses. Others, then, may think of an actor, for example, as a Hispanic actor, a heroin-addicted actor, or as a gay actor, with the individual's occupation coming as secondary to his or her deviant attribute. Hughes noted that master statuses are linked in society to auxiliary traits, the common social preconceptions that people associate with these. Self-injurers, for example, may be widely assumed to be adolescent white women from either middle-class backgrounds or disadvantaged youth whose lives are unhappy. They may be thought of as lacking impulse control, seeking attention, possibly abuse survivors, mentally unstable, or as people who seek to inject control into their lives. The relationship between master statuses and their auxiliary traits in society is reciprocal. When people learn that others have a certain deviant master status, they may impute the associated auxiliary traits onto them. Inversely, when people begin to recognize a few traits that they can put together to form the pattern of auxiliary traits associated with a particular deviant master status, they are likely to attribute that master status to others. For example, if parents notice that their children are staying out late with their friends, wearing "alternative" clothing styles, growing dredlocks in their hair, dropping out of after-school activities, and hanging out with a "druggie" crowd of friends, they may suspect them of using drugs.

Lemert (1967) asserted another processual depiction of the deviant identity career with his concepts of primary and secondary deviance. Primary deviance refers to a stage when individuals commit deviant acts, but their deviance goes unrecognized. As a result, others do not cast the deviant label onto them, and they neither assume it nor perform a deviant role. Their self-conceptions are free of this image. Some people remain at the primary deviance stage throughout their commission of deviance, never advancing further. Yet a percentage of them do progress to secondary deviance. The seven stages of the identity career, described above, move people from primary to secondary deviance; their infractions become discovered, others identify them as deviant, and the labeling process ensues, with all of its identity consequences. Others come to regard them as deviant, and they do as well. As they move into secondary deviance, individuals initially deny the label, but eventually come to accept it reluctantly as it becomes increasingly pressed upon them. They recognize their own deviance as they are forced to interact through this stigma with others. Sometimes this internalization comes as a justification or social defense to the problems associated with their deviant label, as individuals use it to take the offensive. At any rate, it becomes an identity that significantly affects their role performance. Some people may compartmentalize their deviant identity, but others exhibit "role engulfment" (Schur 1971), becoming totally caught up in this master status.

Most individuals who progress to secondary deviance advance no further, but a subset of them moves on to what Kitsuse (1980) called tertiary deviance. In contrast to primary deviants who engage in deviance denial, and secondary deviants who engage in deviance acceptance, Kitsuse sees tertiary deviants as those who engage in role embracement. These are people who decide that their deviance is not a bad thing. They may adopt a relativist perspective and decide that their deviant label is socially constructed by society, not intrinsic to their behavior, such as individuals with learning differences who consider themselves more creative than "typical" people. Or they may hold to an essentialist perspective and embrace their deviant category as intrinsically real, such as gays who "discover" their underlying homosexuality and accept it as natural. They therefore strongly identify with their deviance and fight, usually with the organized help of like others, to combat the deviant label that is applied to them. They may engage in "identity politics" and speak publicly, protest, rally, pursue civil disobedience, educate, raise funds, lobby, and practice various other forms of political advocacy to change society's view of their deviance. Examples of this include people who fight to destigmatize labels such as obesity, prostitution, and race/ethnicity.

All of these identity career concepts encompass a progression through several stages. They begin with the commission of the deviance and lead to individuals' apprehension and public identification. They move through the changing expectations of others towards them, marked by shifting social acceptance or rejection by their friends and acquaintances. The breadth, seriousness, and longevity of the deviant identity label are significantly more profound when individuals undergo official labeling processes than when they are merely informally labeled. With their internalization of the deviant label, adoption of the self-identity, and public interaction through it, they ultimately move into groups of differential deviant associates and commit further acts of deviance.

Exiting a deviant identity is considerably more problematic than assuming one in the first place. Our society has many types of what Erikson (1966) has called "commitment ceremonies," where people are stripped of their respectable status and marked with a negative one. Such moral passages are more noteworthy than returns to the normative fold, and garner considerably more public attention. Institutions of social control thrive on processing deviants, and have vested interests in holding individuals within their domain. Members of society also tend to reinforce people's continued deviance by their social expectations that they will not become rehabilitated. Finally, avenues of opportunity often close for those negatively marked, making normative movement difficult from a practical standpoint. The route out of deviance, then, is often more gradual than precipitous, more solitary than social, more ascetic than pleasurable. Individuals seeking to exit deviant identity careers often have to hit bottom before they are willing to make the sacrifices necessary to reattain the mundane everyday status that they once disdained.

SEE ALSO: Accounts, Deviant; Attitudes and Behavior; Deviance; Deviance Processing Agencies; Deviant Careers; Friendship: Interpersonal Aspects; Gender, Deviance and; Identity: Social Psychological Aspects; Identity Theory; Looking-Glass Self; Master Status; Passing; Resocialization; Role-Taking; Self; Significant Others; Socialization, Primary; Symbolic Interaction

REFERENCES AND SUGGESTED READINGS

Becker, H. S. (1963) *Outsiders: Studies in the Sociology of Deviance*. Free Press, New York.

Degher, D. & Hughes, G. (1991) The Identity Change Process: A Field Study of Obesity. *Deviant Behavior* 12(4): 385–401.

Erikson, K. T. (1966) *Wayward Puritans*. Wiley, New York.

Goffman, E. (1963) *Stigma*. Prentice-Hall, Englewood Cliffs, NJ.

Hughes, E. (1945) Dilemmas and Contradictions of Status." *American Journal of Sociology* (March): 353–9.

Kitsuse, J. (1962) Societal Reactions to Deviant Behavior: Problems of Theory and Method. *Social Problems* 9: 247–56.

Kitsuse, J. (1980) Coming Out All Over: Deviants and the Politics of Social Problems. *Social Problems* 28: 1–13.

Lemert, E. (1951) *Social Pathology*. McGraw-Hill, New York.

Lemert, E. (1967) *Human Deviance, Social Problems, and Social Control*. Prentice-Hall, New York.

Merton, R. K. (1968) *Social Theory and Social Structure*. Free Press, New York.

Schur, E. M. (1971) *Labeling Deviant Behavior*. Harper & Row, New York.

identity: the management of meaning

Christine Coupland

This description is an attempt to provide an informed understanding of classical and contemporary approaches to identity. Studies of identities aim to understand the ways we socially constitute ourselves while considering the link between society and self-identity. The term "identity" was relatively unheard of in sociology and social psychology prior to 1940. Since then it has become the focus of vast amounts of research. Its theoretical, cultural, and empirical development has continued as academics apply, dispute, and discuss the concept. Precursors to the concept of identity developed in the disciplines of sociology, anthropology, and psychology. Importance was given within these early developments to self, character, and personality.

Identity is a broad term incorporating notions of the individual in interaction with other individuals and with social structures. There is a long tradition of research on identity from within many diverse areas (e.g., anthropology, organizational theory, philosophy, psychology, and sociology), each bringing particular frames of philosophical inquiries and methodologies. The resulting heterogeneity of the field has been further developed over time due to movements across the social sciences which affect how the individual is considered to be constituted in social relationships and the implications this has for the study of identities. These movements have challenged the assumptions that characterize modernity which underpin dominant understandings of the modern world. Criticisms have been raised on many fronts, political (Hall & Jacques 1989), from feminist perspectives (Luke & Gore 1992), through conceptions of reality (Baudrillard 1989) and claims to truth and knowledge (Lyotard 1984; Rorty 1989).

During these movements, identity has been theorized in three different ways. First, that of a knowing and conscious subject, second as a product or outcome of social relationships, and finally as both outcome and resource in interaction between the self and others. Definitions of identity thus vary according to different philosophical assumptions; from an essentialist, mainstream view there has been a tendency to represent the "self" as a unified construct, thus leading to definitions that suggest personal identity is defined as the distinct personality of an individual regarded as a persisting entity, or the individual characteristics by which a thing or person is recognized or known. From a social relationship perspective attention has tended to focus on societal or cultural influences on identities, and from a dialectic or discursive approach it is acknowledged that identity is a contentious concept, subject to ongoing dispute rather than one with ontological reality which can be easily seen and defined. This illustrates its socially constructed nature rather than an objectively defined one. Hence, more contemporary definitions of identity suggest that it is emergent, always in flux, and that it is a perception that each person develops about who he or she is in relation to others. This definition requires us to understand the concepts and resources on which social actors draw to structure their relationships and is concerned with issues surrounding power, conformity, deviance, and difference.

There may be many reasons for this shift in perspective on what identity is and how it may be examined, but one major reconceptualization of identity and views of the self surround a critique of a neutral representation of the person by instead highlighting identity claims and descriptions as doing important work in constructing and transforming individuals and the social world.

MAINSTREAM APPROACHES TO IDENTITY

The notion that an individual has an essential inner self, which is carried around and can behave appropriately, dominates the western concept of people in social situations. This view, as a historically bound notion, may be seen in the rise of individualism for which most would credit the Enlightenment as the birthplace of our contemporary beliefs about the self. Although social theorists from different standpoints have questioned the universality of the contemporary western concept of the person, this remains the dominant notion of the self. In support for this argument, studies of other cultures have shown their people as depersonalized from a western point of view, which implies its cultural specificity.

Underlying traditional or mainstream approaches to understanding identity is the assumption that identity is something an individual or society has. From this perspective, the questions asked in traditional studies of identity include: What criteria distinguish identities from one another? Or, what part do identities play in society? One aim of the studies is to use identity as a predictive variable. Working from the assumption that identities (e.g., middle class) correspond to an existing social structure, and are not just externally attributed but internalized through socialization, attempts have been made to link individuals with the social structure through this process. Two of the traditional or mainstream theories that attend to the individual/social structure/socialization process are role identity theory (e.g., Goffman 1959) and social identity theory (Tajfel 1978).

Role Theory

Role theorists propose that society is made up of roles which are internalized as identities that people take on. Goffman (1959) equated social interaction with dramaturgical performance. His work suggested that identity is a performance and that the actor's skills enable the management of impressions left on others, the audience. Although influential in terms of understanding work identities in particular, this theory has been criticized because it places the person in the position of "social dope" where the self comprises a "true" self and a "social" self. The view that individuals are actors performing roles provided by society has been further critiqued as a "calculating" and "intellectual" view of the self (Bruner 1990). Finally, other critics of role theory argue that the notion of a script from within this dramaturgical perspective implies that the words are already decided. This underestimates the creative potential of interaction for the construction of the self.

Social Identity Theory

Social identity theorists suggest that social identities have a reality in relation to social groups.

This approach developed from a concern within social psychology to include a relationship, theoretically and empirically, between individual psychological functioning and the wider social processes that both shape this functioning and are shaped by it (Tajfel 1978). Individuals become aware of group membership and their preference for particular groups. In this way, the structure of society is reflected in the structure of the self as category memberships are internalized.

Its close relation, self-categorization theory (Tajfel & Turner 1979), although concerned with people's categorizations of themselves, assumed them to be psychological, subjective, mental processes. They proposed that social identity is based on individual need to enhance self-esteem through social comparison processes and differentiation. These influential theories have been interpreted, modified, developed, challenged, and expanded in numerous studies since their inception, which is an indication of the author's contribution. However, one of the criticisms of the work was that language was simply not considered to be an issue. If discussed at all, it was in terms of a psychological process along with motivation. This reflected the orthodox view of the time embodied in psycholinguistics from within a structuralist framework.

These and other traditional or mainstream approaches to identity have theorized largely at the intra-individual level, regarding categorization as a cognitive process. With reference to understanding group identity, the question being asked from the mainstream approach has focused around how people identify with groups and what the consequences are of such identification. Finally, traditional or mainstream approaches share a view that language is a transparent medium or conduit onto some hidden, internal process and therefore they ignore the constitutive nature of the interaction.

CONTEMPORARY APPROACHES TO IDENTITY

Contemporary perspectives on understanding identity have been largely connected to a discursive approach. However, there were earlier writers in the field who considered how identity was a linguistic construction, for example Cooley (1902). More recent approaches focus on interindividual explanations where categories and groups are considered to be discursive resources. Perspectives from within this broad description share skepticism of many mainstream assumptions and explanations of the self and instead regard identity as a process, rather than a product, evolving subject to historical and cultural influences. Identity formation is both active and context-relevant. From within the contemporary approaches to identity two major schools of thought differ in terms of how identity may be constructed. For simplicity's sake these are labeled the poststructuralist and the interpretive schools. There are some distinct differences between the poststructuralist and interpretive approaches which are outlined briefly here, but this represents an oversimplification as there are also several similarities. For example, there is a shared proposal for a move from considering the self as an entity to considering the self as a construct (Gergen 1985), specifically in order to consider how the self is talked about.

Poststructuralist Approaches to Identity

The term "poststructuralist" is applied to those writers who presume that discourse operates as an organizing factor through which identities are produced. From this approach subjects are "interpellated," or called to identity-relevant positions. This version of positioning began with Althusser's (1971) argument that ideologies in institutions (e.g., church, school) mean that people are trained to recognize themselves in a particular way. The focus of the poststructuralist approaches' study of identity has largely been on the relationship between power and discourse in that we are all claiming and resisting identities from within prevailing discourses. Poststructuralist writers argue that living under prevailing ideologies creates the illusion that we have chosen our way of life. Poststructural theories emphasize the nature of discourses in terms of how they constrain and enable ways of being, identities, in the social world. One criticism, however, of the poststructuralist view of language is that it disregards language's constitution through argument, while focusing on how it operates to obliterate argument in the interests of domination (Billig 1996).

Interpretive Approaches to Identity

Writers who adopt an interpretive approach propose that identities are constructed "online," are situated in ongoing interactions, and are constructed to perform accounting or explanatory work in talk. Many share an ethnomethodological concern with people's own displays of understanding and pay attention to the micro detail of talk in order to explore the "online" construction of plausible, persuasive identities. Members of a work community, for example, draw on, deploy, and reconstruct resources, which are available in that context and the broader context in which the workplace is situated. In this way, identity is viewed as a situated self which is set within a wider system of possible identities. Interpretive scholars have been criticized for treating "discourses" as cultural or social resources, as if one could construct self at whim. This would also imply some leaning toward a "calculating" view of the self, if it were not for the "structures" of plausibility, authenticity, and reasonableness in the talk. To disregard these in interaction would be to risk being thought mad or at least being misunderstood. To attend to how these function in talk makes visible commonsense, hidden ideologies surrounding how we are able to talk about the self today. From this perspective, a salient identity is a local, occasioned matter where members construct categories and draw on their rights and obligations in talk.

FUTURE DIRECTIONS

It is clear that the widespread acceptance and use of the term identity does not suggest agreement upon or even a clear understanding of its many meanings. Furthermore, the emergent trends in theorizing about identity should not be regarded as enduring but rather as historically and culturally located concepts which are enmeshed with emergent trends in the social sciences more broadly. This is not to suggest that scholars are gradually refining their understanding of what identity is and how it should be examined; rather, the trends are indicative of, shaped by, and subsequently shape understandings and social practices surrounding identities. Theories abound regarding identity,

sharing a focus upon understanding the ways that we socially constitute ourselves while considering or exploring the link between society and self-identity. Future approaches will need to become aware of and analyze the transformations in nature and meanings of identity under conditions of modernity, late modernity, and beyond.

SEE ALSO: Cooley, Charles Horton; Discourse; Goffman, Erving; Identity Control Theory; Identity, Deviant; Identity: Social Psychological Aspects; Identity Theory; Role Theory; Self-Esteem, Theories of; Social Comparison Theory; Social Identity Theory; Socialization

REFERENCES AND SUGGESTED READINGS

Althusser, L. (1971) *Lenin and Philosophy and Other Essays.* New Left Books, London.

Baudrillard, J. (1989) *America.* Verso, London.

Billig, M. (1996) *Arguing and Thinking: A Rhetorical Approach to Social Psychology.* Cambridge University Press, Cambridge.

Bruner, J. (1990) *Acts of Meaning.* Harvard University Press, Cambridge, MA.

Cooley, C. H. (1902) *Human Nature and the Social Order.* Scribner, New York.

Gergen, K. J. (1985) The Social Constructionist Movement in Social Psychology. *American Psychologist* 40: 266–75.

Gergen, K. J. (1999) *An Invitation to Social Construction.* Sage, London.

Gergen, K. J. (2001) *Social Construction in Context.* Sage, London.

Goffman, E. (1959) *The Presentation of Self in Everyday Life.* Penguin, Harmondsworth.

Hall, S. & Jacques, M. (1989) *New Times: The Changing Face of Politics in the 1990s.* Lawrence & Wishart, London.

Luke, C. & Gore, J. (Eds.) (1992) *Feminism and Critical Pedagogy.* Routledge, New York.

Lyotard, J. F. (1984) *The Postmodern Condition: A Report on Knowledge.* University of Minnesota Press, Minneapolis.

Rorty, R. (1989) *Contingency, Irony, and Solidarity.* Cambridge University Press, Cambridge.

Shotter, J. (1993) *Conversational Realities: Constructing Life Through Language.* Sage, London.

Tajfel, H. (Ed.) (1978) *Differentiation Between Social Groups: Studies in the Social Psychology of Intergroup Relations.* Academic Press, London.

Tajfel, H. & Turner, J. C. (1979) An Integrative Theory of Intergroup Conflict. In: Tajfel, H. (Ed.), *Differentiation Between Social Groups: Studies in the Social Psychology of Intergroup Relations.* Academic Press, London, pp. 38–43.

identity politics/ relational politics

Leslie Wasson

Human society is no stranger to exercises of interpersonal power and identity politics. The annals of political history are replete with descriptions of these exercises. Power is the ability to get what you want with or without the consent or cooperation of others. Effects of deployed power are observable at the structural and institutional levels of society, and in face-to-face interactions. A discussion of identity politics (sometimes also called relational politics) may focus on either the class or group level or the level of personal interactions. The subject of interpersonal politics rests within a set of related concepts, such as the distribution of social power, social location and status, and a stratified system in which these interpersonal resources may be valued and utilized for purposes of individual or group advantage over other individuals or groups.

Groups in a stratified system, that is, a social system with a ranked structure of positions, may contend for advantage among themselves. Each group may seek to utilize group-level resources in addition to individual characteristics to secure a better or stronger position vis-à-vis the members of other groups in the social tapestry. This may not be a result of actual conspiracy: often, people acting in their own perceived self-interest serve the mutual desires of others in a similar social position.

In the struggle for relative advantage, winning groups succeed in marketing the notion that their group has characteristics that mark them collectively as the legitimate holders of a higher social position than members of other social groups. One example from recent American history was the successful claim by

men that group characteristics associated with maleness and masculinity were more valuable to society and thereby more deserving of monetary compensation for paid labor than the group attributes of females in equivalent positions. This is represented today in the tendency for women to earn between 65–70 percent on average of the amount men earn for similar work.

Members of different ethnic or cultural groups may also work collectively to deploy their ethnic and cultural capital to best advantage. Examples of research on this phenomenon include Bayard de Volo (2001), who examines gender politics in Nicaragua between 1979 and 1999; Finlay (2005) on the use of altercasting a group identity with negative connotations as a strategy in political conflict; House (2002), whose study of cultural continuity and language among the Navajo posits language shift as an indicator of identity politics; and Howard (2006), on the construction of Irish identity in the British 2001 census.

Kiely et al. (2005) suggest that perhaps new conceptual tools are needed to effectively analyze identity politics from a civil/territorial perspective rather than a more traditional ethnic or cultural approach, since their research indicates that some contemporary identities are more complex as a result of transience or competing political considerations.

While some identity politics plays out at the level of the political order and public discourse, individuals also engage in identity politics in face-to-face encounters. Goffman (1959) notes: "an individual may find himself [*sic*] making a claim or an assumption which he knows the audience may well reject ... when the unguarded request is refused to the individual's face, he suffers what is called humiliation." Later, Goffman (1963) calls the resulting damage to identity a "stigma" that is then managed well or poorly by the individual in succeeding interactions. Blumer (1986) describes how these patterned social interactions are real to their participants and result in mutual expectations for behavior in wider contexts.

Goffman (1970) also contributes the concept of strategic interaction. In strategic interaction, the individual manages self-presentation and social resources to maximize personal advantage in the situation vis-à-vis other participants. Using the Japanese concept of "face" or the social perception of the individual by others in the situation, Goffman is able to integrate ideas about impression management, saving and losing face, and the potential for emotional manipulation, which contribute to politics at the interpersonal level of interaction.

Scheff (1988) suggests an interactionist perspective rooted in emotion for the individual level of identity politics. For Scheff, individual self-concept is influenced by basic emotions of pride or shame. Individuals are therefore subject to manipulation on the basis of these emotions, which results in the acknowledgment of status hierarchy among them and deference to others as a result of that hierarchy.

One set of themes in the academic literature regarding identity politics involves the practices of identity claiming on the one hand, and altercasting, on the other. In identity claiming, an individual seeks to portray herself or himself as a certain kind of person, which portrayal may or may not be met with agreement from others. Altercasting occurs when another or others attempt to impute an identity to an individual, which the individual may or may not embrace. These processes may also operate with groups.

A second theme in research and theory about identity politics is the ongoing debate between essentialist models of identity and social constructionism, also referred to as anti-essentialist positions. This is particularly noticeable in the debates about gender and identity. Debating whether group-level characteristics are innate (essential) or socially constructed obscures a basic misunderstanding about the difference between diversity and inequality. Over time, identity politics has shifted somewhat from demands for equality of opportunity toward demands for recognition of and structural access for persons and groups of diverse views and practices.

A third theme that may be observed in the literature on identity and relational politics is the relationship between individual experience, personal status, or social roles and political stance. For example, one might examine the expectation that part of being gay is being political, or that only members of oppressed minorities can legitimately "belong" in their movements for equality, such as an African American rights group that only accepts European American members in "auxiliary" roles.

For recent summaries of these themes, one might consult Bernstein (2005) for an overview of the topic or Warnke (2005) for an examination of race, gender, and pluralistic or anti-integrationist identity politics.

SEE ALSO: Blumer, Herbert George; Deference; Facework; Goffman, Erving; Power, Theories of; Status

REFERENCES AND SUGGESTED READINGS

Bayard de Volo, L. (2001) *Mothers of Heroes and Martyrs: Gender Identity Politics in Nicaragua, 1979–1999*. Johns Hopkins University Press, Baltimore.

Bernstein, M. (2005) Identity Politics. *Annual Review of Sociology* 31(1): 47–74.

Blumer, H. (1986 [1969]) *Symbolic Interactionism: Perspective and Method*. University of California Press, Berkeley.

Finlay, W. M. L. (2005) Pathologizing Dissent: Identity Politics, Zionism, and the Self-Hating Jew. *British Journal of Social Psychology* 44(2): 201–22.

Goffman, E. (1959) *The Presentation of Self in Everyday Life*. Doubleday, New York.

Goffman, E. (1961) *Asylums*. Anchor/Doubleday, New York.

Goffman, E. (1963) *Stigma: Notes on the Management of Spoiled Identity*. Prentice-Hall, Englewood Cliffs, NJ.

Goffman, E. (1970) *Strategic Interaction*. University of Pennsylvania Press, Pittsburgh.

House, D. (2002) *Language Shift Among Navajos: Identity Politics and Cultural Conformity*. University of Arizona Press, Phoenix.

Howard, K. (2006) Constructing the Irish of Britain: Ethnic Recognition and the 2001 UK Census. *Ethnic and Racial Studies* 29(1): 104–23.

Kiely, R., Bechhofer, F., & McCrone, D. (2005) Birth, Blood, and Belonging: Identity Claims in Post-Devolution Scotland. *Sociological Review* 53(1): 150–71.

Scheff, T. (1988) Shame and Conformity: The Deference-Emotion System. *American Sociological Review* 53: 395–406.

Warnke, G. (2005) Race, Gender, and Antiessentialist Politics. *Signs: Journal of Women in Culture and Society* 31(1): 93–116.

identity: social psychological aspects

Kevin D. Vryan

Sociological social psychologists conceive of identities as social constructs – culturally and interactionally defined meanings and expectations – and as aspects of self-processes and structures that represent who or what a person or set of persons is believed to be. Identities define people in social terms; they depend upon shared meanings and situate their bearers within variously structured and enduring sets of social relations. If a person is believed to belong to particular categories of persons, the meanings and expectations attached to those categories are presumed to be relevant to the person. Identities affect self-conceptions and other intrapsychic structures and processes of the person believed to embody the identity as well as their actions, and affect how others will interpret, feel, and act in relation to the identified individual. The meanings of an identity draw upon sociocultural constructs attached to an identity type and may relate to relatively enduring positions within social structures, but they are actively and creatively presented, interpreted, and modified across different social contexts and over time. Identities are both reflections of socially structured sets of relations and are emergent and negotiable by social actors. As such, they can recreate and reinforce existing sets of social relations as well as alter them.

While the notion of identity is often used without further specification, it is useful to differentiate between several forms of identity (Vryan et al. 2003). The focus on *social identities*, *role identities*, constitutes much of sociologists' empirical study and theorizing on identity. A social identity defines a person or set of persons in terms of the meanings and expectations associated with a socially constructed group or category of people, and locates a person within socially structured sets of relations. Social identities define persons as members of particular groups or sets of people and hence not others (e.g., a Jew may define herself as Jewish and as therefore different than Christians and Muslims). They lead to expectations about how the identified person – whether self or other – is likely to think, feel, and act. At the same time, social identities represent how a person fits within various interactional, network-level, and sociocultural structures. Social identities commonly studied include those related to sex/gender, family, race and ethnicity, nationality, religion, occupation, sexuality, age, and voluntary subcultural memberships, but social identities may be based on any distinction socially constructed or interactionally defined as significant. An individual may possess many social identities, but those identities will vary in their importance, centrality, or salience within different contexts, in turn affecting behavior differentially.

A *situational identity* is defined in terms of the emergent structure of a localized, shared definition of a particular interactional situation. While social identities tend to be enduring as long as a person's relations within webs of social relations endure and are often considered to be essential aspects of their bearers, situational identities are facets of particular interactional episodes and are not usually considered to be enduring or essential to those who enact them. In any interaction, participants must define the situation and the other participants in order to determine their own courses of action and to know how to interpret others' talk and other behaviors. While various social identities may also be defined as relevant to a situation by interactants and affect behaviors and interpretive activities, situational identity enactments and negotiations are specific to a given type of social situation. For example, the situational identities of "student/audience member" and "teacher/lecturer" are defined as essential to the structure of a classroom lecture, while "salesperson" and "customer" are defined as essential to the structure of the situation of shopping in a retail store. Were someone to ask a lecturer if returns require a receipt, or to ask a salesperson if the price was going to be on the next exam, the lack of appropriate self- and other-attributions of situational identities would significantly problematize the interactions. While the particular situational identities that are deemed appropriate and the content of those identities may be indicated in sociocultural constructs (e.g., general social definitions of classroom and shopping situations, including the identities considered relevant and appropriate), they are actively interpreted, adapted, presented, and mutually negotiated during interaction. Much research on situational identities focuses on their emergence, creative presentation, and negotiation in interaction and how people manage potential and actual problematizations of them (e.g., Goffman 1963; Snow & Anderson 1987).

A *personal identity* is a set of meanings and expectations specific to a given individual. Personal identity is associated with a personal name, a body and appearance (e.g., a clothing style), a biography and personal history (e.g., within a particular family network), a unique constellation of social identities, and a set of personality characteristics and traits (Goffman 1963; Shibutani 1964). Of the three forms of identity discussed here, personal identity is considered the most enduring and essential representation of a person, although its content may be presented differently to different audiences and may be redefined over time. Whereas social and situational identities focus on people as members of categories of persons – as similar to other members – a personal identity identifies the individual as unique. No two people are likely to share the exact same set of social identities, much less the same personal history and personality. But as with other forms of identity, personal identity functions to situate individuals within socially structured worlds, such as by specifying the identified person's various social identities and embeddedness within a particular family. Personal identity has been much less studied and theorized than social and situational identity.

Sociological social psychological work on identity followed an early symbolic interactionist focus on the related concept of *self*. Early symbolic interactionists and those who influenced them (e.g., William James, George Herbert Mead, Charles Horton Cooley, W. I. Thomas, Herbert Blumer) did not explicitly theorize and study identity as much as the related notion of self, but their conceptualizations significantly shaped work that was to focus directly on identity. Identity emerged as a concept of growing interest to both psychological and sociological social psychologists in the wake of immigration and disrupted national and ethnic identities following World War II, developing alongside and influenced by subsequent social changes and identity movements of the 1950s (e.g., the Civil Rights Movement), 1960s (countercultural rejection of traditional role identities), and 1970s (Women's Movement) in the US. The relevance and importance of identity in academic work paralleled a growing modernization characterized by geographic and cultural mobility, rapid social changes in social roles and the meanings and expectations attached to identities, and personal and cultural "identity crises."

Sociologists applied the interactionist emphasis on the importance of meaning and its emergence in interaction to their conceptualizations of identities – or meanings applied to people – as key aspects of any self and interaction and as important in understanding human behavior. As people's actions and interpretive activities both constitute society and are shaped by it in an iterative process, identities are seen as constituted by and within particular cultures and social situations that specify certain meanings, expectations, rights, and constraints for those who are seen to possess them, and also as actively created and managed by people.

Among the first to argue for the importance of identity to sociology, Nelson Foote (1951) explained that identity was vital to understanding motivation and hence behavior. Humans know and act toward objects – including themselves and others – in relation to the symbols (meanings, especially as represented in language) that they attribute to those social objects. Our identities inform us as to how to act and not act, producing motivations and social action. More broadly, Foote and other interactionists argued that identity is an important way to conceive of how individuals relate to each other and to society at large. Anselm Strauss (1959) was also quite influential in shaping treatments of identity. As did other interactionists, he challenged psychological models and viewed identity formations and transformations as lifelong, socially determined (rather than determined by essential and universal human developmental trajectories), and actively negotiated processes. Strauss emphasized the significance of language and meaning (as socially constructed and negotiated) – an emphasis pervading sociological treatments of identity. In a line of thinking receiving increasing attention presently, Strauss linked identity with self-narratives; we construct and reconstruct our various selves and identities by naming them, thus assigning meanings to them. Linking social structure to identity transformations, Strauss discussed "turning points" as signals to institutionalized identity transformations, such as those experienced when getting married, graduating school, or becoming a parent. As socially structured realities change, so do the identities of the people embedded within them. And as identities change, so do social structures. While Strauss's primary focus was, at least initially, on identity processes in face-to-face interactions, he attended to the cultural, intergenerational, and historical realities that affect such situations (1995). Other recent work builds on these foci, infusing recent theoretical and methodological developments associated with a "cultural turn" in sociology (e.g., Holstein & Gubrium 2000).

Gregory P. Stone (1981) called attention to the significance of appearances in the process of identification. Initially, it is appearance (e.g., clothing, nonverbal behaviors such as gestures, location) that leads us to an identification of the other, which precedes taking the role of the other; we must identify a person before having the ability to conduct that fundamental social process. Our selves as well as our behaviors in interaction are shaped by our identifications of ourselves and others, whether those identifications confirm or challenge a given identity that is presented or attributed. When there is congruence between the presentation of an identity and attribution by others, then a socially meaningful identity emerges. Erving Goffman (1963) was the first to explicate the complexities and intricacies of how it is that people create and manage identities as they go about their everyday lives, calling attention to the many problems that can arise as people go about defining themselves, others, and their social worlds. He also explained how people work collectively and continuously to manage their own and others' identities, engaging in teamwork that seeks to protect or restore the identities of participants. Identities are understood as social accomplishments rather than properties of individuals, and ongoing behavior – even if it has other purposes and goals as well – is seen as a collective enterprise of identity management. In studying identities considered to be deviant in *Stigma*, Goffman (1963) showed how problematic identity management

can be, and how creative and resourceful people are in accomplishing their self-conceptions and social interactions.

In addition to the situationally focused work of those discussed above – sometimes referred to as Chicago School symbolic interactionism – some sociologists pursued approaches known as structural, Iowa School, and Indiana School interactionism. Their work focused less on the situational and interactional emergence of identity and its management, and more on its enduring and socially anchored qualities, infusing reference group and role theories into their versions of interactionism (Stryker 1980). They saw identity in terms of intrapsychic self-structures and in more clear relation to larger and more enduring social structures, developing models intended to enable the prediction of self and behavioral outcomes and to be testable via quantitative data analysis techniques consistent with traditional positivistic scientific practices. Key figures working along these lines include Manford H. Kuhn (Kuhn & McPartland 1954), Sheldon Stryker (1980), George J. McCall (McCall & Simmons 1978), and Peter Burke (Burke & Reitzes 1981).

Structural interactionists conceived of identities in terms of self-structures, with enduring social identities being most significant to individuals' self-conceptions. More important than situationally emerging and renegotiable identities, the social identities seen as key to self-concept and behavior tie people to particular reference groups and social structural arrangements. Complex societies characterized by multiplicity and complexity are seen as resulting in a multiplicity and complexity of selves and identities; when people hold many different social statuses they possess many different identities. Self-structures include multiple identities arranged according to their salience, or the likelihood of a given identity affecting behavior rather than another. Structural interactionists explain that social arrangements and statuses affect salience hierarchies and, in turn, salience affects behavior, such as is modeled in Stryker's version of identity theory. Others home in on intrapsychic identity processes and structures that operate to affect behavior, as in Burke's version of identity theory that applies a cybernetic control model (Stryker & Burke 2000).

Many lines of research and theoretical specifications have emerged from the theoretical approaches and methodological techniques sociologists have applied in their studies of identity. Those following the more situationalist approach explain with increasing depth how, and identify generic social processes according to which, identities are taken on as aspects of self and are presented and managed in interaction. They most often apply qualitative methods such as ethnography within localized, naturally occurring social contexts and in-depth interviewing among people sharing a particular identity in order to discover how people collectively accomplish "identity work" in their everyday lives and how identities are constructed via self- and group-narratives. Structural interactionist research models how it is that social arrangements writ large affect individuals via identification with the meanings associated with categories of people that are defined by their social locations within those structures, seeking to explain and predict self-structures as a function of social positions, and behavior as a function of identification in terms of those positions. They most often apply quantitative methods such as survey research and laboratory experimentation suited to their goals of theory testing, replicability, and prediction of intrapsychic self-structures and resulting behavior. Lines of research not explicitly or directly symbolic interactionist – such as expectation states theory and various psychological approaches – also inform our understandings of identity, although sociological treatments of the topic nearly universally share the interactionist emphases on identities as sets of meanings emerging and made meaningful only within social contexts.

Some scholarship theorizes identity generally, such as self-verification theories that posit that people will select interactions and relationships that confirm their self-identifications regardless of what the identity is. Other research and theories focus on particular identities or types of identities. Most often, these are social identities based upon socially constructed and structured distinctions such as sex/gender, race, ethnicity, and minority status (e.g., Porter & Washington 1993), occupation (or other statuses within occupational and educational systems), deviance/normativity, age, and national or other

collective identities. Lines of research also pursue particular behaviors as functions of identification, such as social movement participation (Stryker et al. 2000). In addition to these lines of research that more deeply flesh out social realities related to particular identities, identity types, or contexts that shape identity structures and processes, there is increasing attention being paid in recent years to the multiplicities of identity, with theory and empirical research attending to the ways that multiple identities are organized and managed within self-structures and interactional and sociocultural contexts, as well as how they intersect. This can be seen, for example, in recent emphases on multiracial identity and in a tendency to study the intersections of a greater number of distinct types of identities such as those based upon gender, class, race, and sexuality. Scholars are increasingly attending to the importance of emotions, the body, and embodiment in their work on identity, as well as mental and physical health (e.g., Charmaz 1995). In addition to continuing these recent emphases, future research on identity is likely to explore more thoroughly how identity is affected within mass- and computer-mediated contexts, as well as other new forms of social organization and interaction that relate to new ways of defining, presenting, and managing identities (e.g., Holstein & Gubrium 2000).

SEE ALSO: Affect Control Theory; Identity Control Theory; Identity, Deviant; Identity Theory; Identity: The Management of Meaning; Impression Formation; Role; Social Identity Theory; Stigma; Symbolic Interaction

REFERENCES AND SUGGESTED READINGS

Burke, P. J. & Reitzes, D. C. (1981) The Link Between Identity and Role Performance. *Social Psychology Quarterly* 44: 83–92.

Cerulo, K. A. (1997) Identity Construction: New Issues, New Directions. *Annual Review of Sociology* 23: 385–409.

Charmaz, K. (1995) The Body, Identity, and Self: Adapting to Impairment. *Sociological Quarterly* 36: 657–80.

Foote, N. N. (1951) Identification as the Basis for a Theory of Motivation. *American Sociological Review* 16: 14–21.

Gecas, V. & Burke, P. J. (1995) Self and Identity. In: Cook, K. S., Fine, G. A., & House, J. S. (Eds.), *Sociological Perspectives on Social Psychology*. Allyn & Bacon, Boston, pp. 41–67.

Goffman, E. (1963) *Stigma: Notes on the Management of Spoiled Identity*. Simon & Schuster, New York.

Holstein, J. A. & Gubrium, J. F. (2000) *The Self We Live By: Narrative Identity in a Postmodern World*. Oxford University Press, New York.

Kuhn, M. H. & McPartland, T. S. (1954) An Empirical Investigation of Self-Attitudes. *American Sociological Review* 19: 68–76.

McCall, G. J. & Simmons, J. L. (1978) *Identities and Interactions: An Examination of Human Associations in Everyday Life*, revd. edn. Free Press, New York.

Porter, J. R. & Washington, R. E. (1993) Minority Identity and Self-Esteem. *Annual Review of Sociology* 19: 139–61.

Shibutani, T. (1964) The Structure of Personal Identity. In: Sampson, E. E. (Ed.), *Approaches, Contexts, and Problems of Social Psychology*. Prentice-Hall, Englewood Cliffs, NJ, pp. 231–5.

Snow, D. A. & Anderson, L. (1987) Identity Work among the Homeless: The Verbal Construction and Avowal of Personal Identities. *American Journal of Sociology* 92: 1336–71.

Stone, G. P. (1981) Appearance and the Self: A Slightly Revised Version. In Stone, G. P. & Farberman, H. A. (Eds.), *Social Psychology through Symbolic Interaction*. John Wiley, New York, pp. 187–202.

Strauss, A. L. (1959) *Mirrors and Masks: The Search for Identity*. Free Press, Glencoe, IL.

Strauss, A. L. (1995) Identity, Biography, History, and Symbolic Representations. *Social Psychology Quarterly* 58: 4–12.

Stryker, S. (1980) *Symbolic Interactionism: A Social Structural Version*. Benjamin/Cummings, Menlo Park.

Stryker, S. & Burke, P. J. (2000) The Past, Present, and Future of an Identity Theory. *Social Psychology Quarterly* 63: 284–97.

Stryker, S, Owens, T. J., & White, R. (Eds.) (2000) *Self, Identity, and Social Movements*. University of Minnesota Press, Minneapolis.

Vryan, K. D., Adler, P. A., & Adler, P. (2003) Identity. In: Reynolds, L. T. & Herman-Kinney, N. J. (Eds.), *Handbook of Symbolic Interactionism*. Alta Mira, Walnut Creek, CA, pp. 367–90.

Weigert, A. J., Teitge, J. S., & Teitge, D. W. (1986) *Society and Identity: Toward a Sociological Psychology*. Cambridge University Press, Cambridge.

identity, sport and

Chris Stevenson

Identity is a rather loose concept which has various degrees of currency in a number of different disciplines. For example, Bosma et al. (1994) have argued that there is little consensus in the field of psychology about the phenomena to which the term identity might refer. They go on to suggest that, as a result, different definitions of identity not only have led to the development of different schools within psychology, each with its own theoretical and empirical traditions, but that scholars appear to know little about, or prefer to ignore, what is happening beyond the boundaries of their own school.

There is not quite the same situation within sociology, where considerable theoretical and methodological developments of the concept of identity have occurred primarily in the sociological tradition of symbolic interactionism, in both the Chicago and Iowa schools, and where, according to Weigert et al. (1986), the notion of identity has also had some limited currency in the sociological traditions of structural functionalism, critical theory, interpretive sociology, and the sociology of knowledge.

The sociological concept of identity is broadly understood to include notions of "social identity," "personal identity," and "ego identity." *Social identities* are those identities which tend to refer to the individual's position(s) in a social structure, understanding that various cultural and social factors influence the extent to which the individual is pressured into fitting into available identity "molds" (Côté & Levine 2002). They are identities which are either seen as providing some social value and are therefore claimed by the actor, or imputed or attributed to others in order to place or situate them as social objects. *Personal identities* are the self-designations and self-attributions which an individual brings into play or asserts during the course of interaction, and are essentially the meanings the individual attributes to the "self" (Snow & Anderson 1987). "Personal identity," then, is a concept which places the focus on the specific individualities that are peculiar to each of us, which arise as a result of the accommodations between the definitions of our social identities and the uniqueness and peculiarities of our actual lived experience (Côté & Levine 2002). The term "ego identity" refers to the sense of sameness or continuity in the "self" (or personality) which individuals experience over long periods of their life. Bosma et al. (1994) use the illustration of a tree, which, although it experiences great changes over the seasons, still remains the same tree. Similarly, although a person experiences tremendous changes between the times of her conception and death, she remains the same, unique individual.

Two major interests have been apparent in sociology's focus on identity: (1) the process(es) through which adult identity is formed and (2) the process(es) by which that identity is maintained once it is formed. Identity formation is a process through which, particularly in modern societies, individuals are able to choose from an array of potential self-definitions and personal meanings, and then may work to develop those identities in interaction with others (e.g., see Goffman's 1959 work on impression management). Modern societies, it is argued, provide many more models of social and personal identity and offer much more freedom to choose from among these models. The notion of identity maintenance picks up on the idea, associated with late modernity, of the increasingly transient and unstable nature of social identities, with the consequence that the sustained validation of such social identities by others constantly requires work (Côté & Levine 2002: 6). This approach to the management of identities suggests that, first, the individual is required to act in a manner that is appropriate to the identity/ies which he or she is claiming, and second, that the individual must gain a confirmation of the performed identity/ies from the responses and reactions of appropriate significant others.

These ideas about identity are clearly centered on such assumptions as: (1) individuals are able to choose their identities; that is, they have an array of potential identity options available to them; (2) they are active players in the interactions which lead to the creation, assumption or appropriation, and development of an individual identity; that is, individuals have agency; and (3) it is through the validations of others in social interaction with the individual that such identities are maintained; that is, one

must work at securing these validations and confirmations.

Various literatures within the field of sport sociology have focused on the role that "sport" (broadly understood to include the many forms of participation in a wide range of types of physical activity, considerations of the physical body in movement, and the many forms of secondary consumption of sporting activities) may play in the processes of identity formation generally, and of particular identities specifically, and in the processes through which individuals strive to sustain such identities. This work has examined the role of sport (1) in the formation of an identity as an "athlete"; (2) in the formation of identities specific to particular sports; and (3) in the formation of more generic identities, such as gender identity, racial/ethnic identity, or national identity. It has also examined the consequences of successfully claiming an athletic identity on the individual's future options for seeking alternative identities and career paths.

The generic identity of "athlete" has considerable saliency in many social settings and in many of the countries of the world – although the specific characteristics associated with this identity vary from sport context to sport context and from country to country. Nevertheless, such an identity is clearly valued and may provide many social benefits to the individuals who are able to successfully claim it – whether this occurs at an elementary school age, at high school or college, as a member of a professional or national team, or even as a masters athlete in his nineties. The success of such identity claims rests on, first, the individual's ability to satisfactorily or authentically present the main characteristics of this identity, and second, the validation of the identity claim provided by primarily non-athlete, significant others – one's peers, family, community, and so on.

There are also many, more specific, sporting identities that are available in a wide range of different sporting activities, and in these cases the sport sociology literature has focused on the processes of identity formation and maintenance of such identities. An excellent example of this focus is provided by the work of Donnelly and Young (1988), who show how identity claims are made in the context of existing sport groups, and that successfully claiming an identity as an athlete in a particular sport is an interactive process that occurs in social and cultural contexts in which social definitions and meanings serve as influencing factors.

Using their ethnographic work on the sporting subcultures of rugby and rock climbing, Donnelly and Young illustrate the various ways in which neophytes to these two sporting activities deliberately strive to take on and claim – in Donnelly and Young's words, "construct" – the social identity of "rugby player" or "rock climber." They describe how, upon entering the social context, these neophytes often have a limited or even erroneous understanding of the behaviors, values, and attitudes typically associated with the sporting identities they are attempting to claim. If they are to be successful in these identity claims, therefore, the "rookies" need to realign their public presentations of these identities to meet the expectations of the subcultural insiders, the "veterans." It is through an interactive process in which the rookies "try on" the potential identities and attempt to manage impressions that they become more "accurate" in and more comfortable with the presentations of these identities. More often than not, however, they make mistakes, misinterpreting the meanings and the significance of certain behaviors, expressions, and narratives from within the subculture. It is here that the role of subcultural insiders is critical in this interactive process, as Donnelly and Young demonstrate, as the insiders test the newcomers in order to validate the identity claims that they are making, particularly about the skills, abilities, and experiences they are claiming as part of the identity – such as having climbed certain routes which have an established level of difficulty, or about having played in certain positions in rugby or at certain levels of expertise in countries recognized as rugby powers. The result is that these insiders act to either support and confirm or refute the claimed identity.

The formation and maintenance of more societally generic identities through personal participation in sports as well as through watching sports has been another focus of the sport sociology literature. Sports are believed to be particularly efficacious in such identity processes because of their enormous popularity, the passion they can engender in both participant and spectator, and their potential to present

effective modeling of the different identities. For example, sociologists have explored the ways in which a wide variety of sports can be used to create and to reinforce gender identity, such as a "masculine" identity through participation in such sports as soccer, North American football, rugby, and ice hockey (e.g., see Burgess et al. 2003). Alternatively, scholars have also shown how participation in sport can be used to create and sustain gender identities which challenge traditional meanings and definitions – for example, gay athletes who challenge hegemonic definitions of masculinity (see Anderson 2002). Similarly, scholars have examined the role of sports in the construction of various racial and ethnic identities, such as baseball and the Latino identity, basketball, football, and athletics and the African American identity, and rugby and the Maori identity (e.g., see King 2004). And, of course, sociologists have investigated the role of soccer worldwide in the construction and reinforcement of various national identities, from Ireland and Scotland to Israel, Liberia, and Brazil (e.g., see Bairner 2003).

Finally, some literature in sport sociology has examined the consequences of successful claiming and maintaining sporting identities on an individual's future options for seeking alternative identities and career paths. This literature has looked at the ways in which such successfully claimed sporting identities, while on the one hand encouraging the deepening of the individual's commitment and "embeddedness" in sporting involvements, may, on the other hand, also act to constrain the individual's immediate and future life choices. For example, Stevenson's (1990) examination of the careers of elite athletes illustrates how many of these individuals were often recognized early (but not always) in their lives as potentially excellent "rugby players" or "field hockey players" by a number of significant others (including their peers and their community, their parents and siblings, and such significant adults as teachers and coaches). The initial consequences of being attributed such desirable identities were generally very positive, in that these individuals received considerable attention and praise, and were held in high esteem by their immediate social group. Such consequences served to heighten the commitment of these individuals to these identities and to their sporting activities, increasing the time, energy, and resources which they committed to them, while also simultaneously reducing the perceived value of pursuing alternative identities and other types of careers. So, as they enjoyed these benefits over their careers as athletes, they also found that their options to be "other-than-a-rugby-player" or "other-than-a-field-hockey-player" became constrained. As the costs of their identities as successful athletes began to mount – injuries, the intrusion on other aspects of their lives, including their relationships with others, the constraints on their ability to create other career and identity possibilities outside of the sporting context – the resultant difficulties in maintaining their identities as athletes became increasingly acute, until their athletic careers came to an inevitable end or became transformed into associated identities, such as coach, administrator, or media commentator.

SEE ALSO: Gender, Sport and; Goffman, Erving; Identity Theory; Impression Formation; Nationalism and Sport; Sport; Sport Culture and Subcultures; Sport and Race; Sports Heroes and Celebrities

REFERENCES AND SUGGESTED READINGS

Anderson, E. (2002) Openly Gay Athletes: Contesting Hegemonic Masculinity in a Homophobic Environment. *Gender and Society* 16(6): 860–77.
Bairner, A. (2003) Political Unionism and Sporting Nationalism: An Examination of the Relationship between Sport and National Identity within the Ulster Unionist Tradition. *Identities: Global Studies in Culture and Power* 10, 4 (October–December): 517–35.
Bosma, H. A., Graafsma, T. L. G., Grotevant, H., & de Levita, D. J. (1994) *Identity and Development: An Interdisciplinary Approach*. Sage, Thousand Oaks, CA.
Burgess, I., Edwards, A., & Skinner, J. (2003) Football Culture in an Australian School Setting: The Construction of Masculine Identity. *Sport, Education, and Society* 8, 2 (October): 199–212.
Côté, J. E. & Levine, C. G. (2002) *Identity Formation, Agency, and Culture*. Lawrence Erlbaum, Mahwah, NJ.
Donnelly, P. & Young, K. (1988) The Construction and Confirmation of Identity in Sport Subcultures. *Sociology of Sport Journal* 5(3): 223–40.
Goffman, E. (1959) *The Presentation of Self in Everyday Life*. Doubleday, Garden City, NY.
King, C. (2004) Race and Cultural Identity: Playing the Race Game Inside Football. *Leisure Studies*, 23, 1 (January): 19–30.
Snow, D. A. & Anderson, L. (1987) Identity Work Among the Homeless: The Verbal Construction and Avowal of Personal Identities. *American Journal of Sociology* 92(6): 1336–71.
Stevenson, C. L. (1990) The Early Careers of Elite Athletes. *Sociology of Sport Journal* 7(3): 238–53.
Weigert, A. J., Teitge, J. S., & Teitge, D. W. (1986) *Society and Identity: Toward a Sociological Psychology*. Cambridge University Press, Cambridge.

identity theory

Michael J. Carter

Identity theory is a social psychological theory based on the tenets of structural symbolic interactionism (Stryker 1980). Similar to other work that has emerged within this type of symbolic interactionism, identity theory treats society as stable rather than erratic – the result of repeated, patterned behaviors of individuals. The theory examines how the self is created and how actors attach meanings to the multiple roles which they play; research within this theoretical framework addresses how identities emerge within social structures. Macro-level structures are continually replicated through interactions between actors in a reflexive process; identity theory examines how micro-level processes serve to create and maintain the meanings actors have for themselves as well as others, and how these meanings perpetuate themselves over time. This perspective sees the self as emergent from social interaction and portrayed to others through identities that are appropriate in specific situations.

The term "identity" is used in various ways in sociological literature, and usually concerns one of the following contexts (Stryker & Burke 2000). First, identity is sometimes used in reference to *culture*, where distinctions between identity and ethnicity are often blurred or disregarded altogether. Second, identity is also used to refer to common identification within *collectivities* or *social categories*. Identity here focuses on how phenomena (such as social movements) serve to create a common unity among individuals. Third, and unique to those who work specifically within identity theory, identity is seen as a component of the self. Identities in this context provide meanings that actors apply to various roles which are played out through social interaction. This orientation is aligned with the work of G. H. Mead concerning the self and others, and the reflexive relationship between the two. As part of structural symbolic interactionism, identity theory examines the embeddedness of the actor in society and how the self is organized around identity structures and identity meanings.

Identity theory begins by addressing the ways in which the self is comprised of multiple identities. These identities determine how an actor behaves when alone, while engaged in a role, or when in a group. Thus, there are different types of identities for different social dynamics: *role identities*, *social identities*, and *person identities* (Burke 2004). Role identities (e.g., student, worker, father) are defined by the meanings an actor attributes to the self while performing roles. These meanings emerge from socialization and through culture, as well as by the unique, individual assessment of what the role means for the actor. Role identities are a combination of *shared* and *idiosyncratic* meanings which are negotiated by an actor during interactions (Stets 2006). Social identities describe how actors identify with groups or categories (e.g., Republican, Christian). Actors' social identities operate as an in-group/out-group dynamic, with others being categorized as either *similar* or *different*. Social identities allow actors to create a sense of unity with other in-group members and share common bonds, and provide mutual reinforcement to act in various ways. Person identities refer to the self-meanings that allow an actor to realize a sense of individuality. Person identities are self-meanings such as being competitive or passive, moral or immoral. These identities are frequently activated because they are not generally unique to any specific circumstance; they rather apply across many situations. All three types of identities can operate simultaneously, and in many situations an actor can have multiple identities activated – including role, social, and personal identities.

Contemporary work within identity theory generally has two emphases. One emphasis examines how social structures influence identity and behavior, and how actors' many role identities are organized in a *salience hierarchy* (Stryker 1980). The other addresses the ways in which internal dynamics within the self influence how individuals behave (Burke & Cast 1997; Burke & Stets 1999). An additional area within identity theory specifically emphasizes role identities (McCall & Simmons 1978). While all three emphases add to the general understanding of identity within structural symbolic interactionism, most current research is aligned with the first two areas, following the work of Stryker and Burke.

SALIENCE AND COMMITMENT

Stryker's hierarchical approach to identity seeks to explain how a social actor will behave in a situation based on how often and strongly identities are invoked. Behavior is a function of how salient and committed identities are for actors as they interact with others in the social structure (Owens 2003). Identity salience refers to the probability that an identity will be invoked by the self or others in social situations; identity commitment refers to the degree to which actors' relationships to others depend on specific roles and identities. A salient identity is an identity that is likely to be activated frequently in various contexts. The more salient an identity, the more likely a person will perform roles that are consistent with role expectations associated with the identity, perceive a situation as an opportunity to enact an identity, and seek out situations that provide an opportunity to enact the identity (Stets 2006).

One's commitment identifies the number of actors that one has connection to through an identity and how strongly one is attached to others based on the identity. When an actor is more committed to an identity, the identity is seen as high in the salience hierarchy. The structural aspect to identity is important here: identities that have strong commitment are the identities that are invoked most often across situations. Research that addresses these aspects of identity examines such themes as religion and how salient religious identities are for individuals. For example, studies have shown that actors committed to relationships based on religion have highly religious identities; these identities are a function of the amount of time people spend doing religious activities (Stryker & Serpe 1982). Stryker's work emphasizes how the salience hierarchy for identities is crucial in determining human behavior because one's identity level directly influences choice and action – the higher an identity in the hierarchy, the higher the probability the identity will be activated (Owens 2003).

INTERNAL DYNAMICS

Burke et al.'s work in identity theory addresses the internal dynamics within the self that influence behavior (Burke & Tully 1977; Burke & Reitzes 1991; Burke 2004). Early work within this emphasis focused on how identity and behavior are linked to common meanings – by identifying what meanings actors apply to identities, one can predict the meanings associated with individuals' actions. Recent research that examines how internal processes affect behavior reveals the connection between identity and behavior, showing that the internal process for invoked identities is a perpetual control system (Burke 1991). Here the internal dynamics of the self are highlighted and identities serve as standards that influence behavior; identities are sets of meanings attached to the self – these meanings provide references that guide behavior. The perpetual control system is a circular process and mechanism that explains how an actor's self-defined identity meanings are reflexively attached to experiences in the social environment. Basically, when an identity is activated in a situation, a feedback loop emerges. As the feedback loop operates across situations, actors act to verify their identities and identify both who they believe they are and who others believe them to be. Work within this emphasis of identity theory furthers the idea that behavior is guided by situations or internal meanings by revealing that behavior results from the relationship between situations and self-meanings.

ROLE IDENTITIES

The third emphasis examines role identities – an actor's subjective interpretation of him/herself as an occupant of a social position (McCall & Simmons 1978). Role identities have two dimensions: conventional and idiosyncratic. Conventional dimensions of role identities refer to expectations and self-meanings actors internalize concerning social positions within the greater social structure. Idiosyncratic dimensions regard the unique interpretations actors have for their specific roles. McCall and Simmons (1978) understand identity similarly with Stryker in terms of identities being arranged hierarchically, but give more emphasis to a prominence hierarchy of identities. A prominence hierarchy reflects how individuals see themselves according to what ideals and desires the individual has, as well as what is considered important to the individual. An identity's location in the prominence hierarchy depends on three things: the degree of support an individual obtains from others for an identity, the degree of investment or commitment an individual has for an identity, and the rewards one receives by invoking an identity. The prominence hierarchy basically represents how actors' sense of priority affects their behavior in situations; it represents one's *ideal self*. McCall and Simmons also identify a salience hierarchy, as do Stryker and his colleagues. A salience hierarchy here reflects more the situational self rather than the ideal self. An identity's location in the salience hierarchy is a function of the identity's prominence, need for support, and actor's need for the kinds and amounts of intrinsic and extrinsic rewards achieved by the identity, and the perceived degree of opportunity for its profitable enactment in the situation (Stryker 1980; Stets 2006). Actors negotiate their identities by considering who they encounter and the context in which the interaction occurs – identities are in relation to counteridentities that exist in interactions with others. For example, the role of "doctor" is dependent on another's role of "patient"; the role of "employee" is dependent on the role of "boss." Actors have expectations for their roles as well as the roles of others; when interchanges go smoothly (i.e., both actors act within one another's expectations for each role), relationships are maintained and prominence hierarchies are supported.

RESEARCH METHODOLOGIES

Research within identity theory incorporates multiple methodologies, both quantitative and qualitative. Past research has used surveys and interviews to examine self-definitions of identity, identity commitment and salience, and how identities provide meanings for actors in specific situations. For example, surveys created to measure identity salience and commitment have asked participants questions such as "how often do you see yourself as a student?" and "which people are you more likely to discuss a sensitive issue with?" Such methods allow researchers to measure how salient and committed identities are for participants by finding what importance a participant places on an identity and by identifying the amount and type of people a participant is connected to through an identity. Other methods have used survey instruments to examine what it means to *be* a specific identity by measuring how often a participant plays a particular role – for example, how often a person sees herself as a student or spouse. Recent methodologies within identity theory (specifically, identity control theory) have used a combination of surveys and laboratory experiments to measure identity processes and identity verification. Contemporary research designs also use surveys and laboratory experiments to measure undeveloped facets of identities, such as how individuals act in groups when they are not committed to a situational identity and how identities are invoked when actors are amidst unfamiliar others (Stets 2006).

Identity theory continues to be an influential subfield for the general study of self, identity, and symbolic interactionism. The theory continues to grow in terms of its theoretical development, methodological innovations, and research areas that address the dynamics of the self within greater society (Stets 2006). Scholars of identity theory attempt to reveal how individuals attach meanings to themselves and others, and continually strive to identify the mechanisms that explain how social structures affect and constrain individuals, as well as how individuals

create and maintain social structures. The prevalent emphases within identity theory differ in degree more than kind, and the corpus of work produced by scholars from all areas of the theory has furthered the understanding of both micro- and macro-level phenomena, within both sociological social psychology and sociology in general.

SEE ALSO: Identity Control Theory; Identity: The Management of Meaning; Identity: Social Psychological Aspects; Mead, George Herbert; Role-Taking; Self; Social Psychology; Symbolic Interaction

REFERENCES AND SUGGESTED READINGS

Burke, P. J. (1991) Identity Processes and Social Stress. *American Sociological Review* 56(6): 836–49.

Burke, P. J. (2004) Identities and Social Structure: The 2003 Cooley-Mead Award Address. *Social Psychology Quarterly* 67: 5–15.

Burke, P. J. & Cast, A. D. (1997) Stability and Change in the Gender Identities of Newly Married Couples. *Social Psychology Quarterly* 60: 277–90.

Burke, P. J. & Reitzes, D. C. (1991) An Identity Theory Approach to Commitment. *Social Psychology Quarterly* 54: 239–51.

Burke, P. J. & Stets, J. E. (1999) Trust and Commitment through Self-Verification. *Social Psychology Quarterly* 62: 347–66.

Burke, P. J. & Tully, J. C. (1977) The Measurement of Role Identity. *Social Forces* 55(4): 881–97.

McCall, G. & Simmons, J. S. (1978) *Identities and Interaction*, rev. edn. Free Press, New York.

Owens, T. J. (2003) Self and Identity. In: Delamater, J. (Ed.), *Handbook of Social Psychology*. Kluwer Academic/Plenum, New York, pp. 205–32.

Stets, J. E. (2006) Identity Theory. In: Burke, P. J. (Ed.), *Contemporary Social Psychological Theories*. Stanford University Press, Palo Alto, CA.

Stryker, S. (1980) *Symbolic Interactionism: A Social Structural Version*. Benjamin Cummings, Menlo Park, CA.

Stryker, S. & Burke, P. J. (2000) The Past, Present, and Future of an Identity Theory. In: *The State of Sociological Social Psychology*. *Social Psychology Quarterly* 63, 4 (special issue): 284–97.

Stryker, S. & Serpe, R. T. (1982) Commitment, Identity Salience, and Role Behavior: A Theory and Research Example. In: Ickes, W. & Knowles, E. S. (Eds.), *Personality, Roles, and Social Behavior*. Springer Verlag, New York, pp. 199–218.

ideological hegemony

Matthew C. Mahutga and Judith Stepan-Norris

Ideological hegemony theorizes the way in which relationships of domination and exploitation are embedded in the dominant ideas of society. To the extent that dominant ideas are internalized, they induce consent to these relationships on the part of the dominated and exploited. Consistent with the interconnected world in which we live, there are as many levels of ideological hegemony as there are levels of society.

The concept of ideological hegemony has deep historical and theoretical roots in the development of Marxist thought during the twentieth century. At the beginning of the twentieth century, Marxist theorists and parties were faced with the absence or failure of worldwide communist revolutions. The concept sought to explain why workers were not gaining control of their states.

One of the earliest theorists to develop these ideas and use the phraseology of bourgeois hegemony explicitly was Georg Lukács (1885–1971). Lukács was active in the Hungarian Communist Party after World War I. He remained loyal to the Communist Party throughout his lifetime, but became increasingly critical of it toward the end of his life. Lukács's most important contribution was arguably *History and Class Consciousness*, published in 1923. Though greatly influenced by the writing of V. I. Lenin, Lukács unequivocally claimed to have been producing an exposition of Marx's theory as "Marx understood it." In this work, Lukács drew a distinction between what he calls *objective* and *subjective* class consciousness. Objective class consciousness consists of the material interests facing the working class at any given historical moment. Subjective class consciousness, on the other hand, consists of the actual ideas and attitudes that the working class may have. Thus, "false consciousness" is the gap between the working class's objective class interests and their awareness of them.

Drawing the distinction between objective and subjective class consciousness moves away from the "pure economism" that dominated Marxist thought during this time, which suggested that communism was inevitable due to the inherent contradictions in capitalism. In addition to the notion of false consciousness, Lukács suggested that social classes that were not "purely" proletarian (i.e., the petty bourgeois, peasantry, or semi-wage earners) were unable to attain a revolutionary consciousness because their consciousness was limited by their objective interests within society, which were not driven toward the dissolution of capitalism. Thus, Lukács presents two mutually reinforcing explanations for why the working class failed to gain control of the state across Europe and the United States: either the working class's objective and subjective class consciousness failed to coincide, or the working class simply failed politically because they could not gain the allegiance of classes that were neither proletarian nor capitalist. Either way, the source of these failures was the "hegemony of the bourgeoisie," which not only dominated economically, politically, and militarily, but also naturalized capitalist social relations through the development of a theory of economics, politics, and society that dominated the intellectual milieu.

The most often cited author in connection with ideological hegemony is Antonio Gramsci (1891–1937). While in prison in Fascist Italy between 1927 and 1935, Antonio Gramsci developed the notion of ideological hegemony. His writings, in particular his conception of ideological hegemony in *The Prison Notebooks*, were directed at the Marxists of the Second International, who emphasized the primacy of science and materialist forces, and anticipated that working classes in advanced industrialized nations would vote out the representatives of the capitalist classes once they obtained the right to vote. Gramsci, in contrast, argued that perceptions and other mediations come between material forces and the meanings connected to them. The realm of ideas, or what Marx called the "superstructure" (religion, legal structures, the family, etc.), is affected by the interests of the ruling class such that they incorporate those interests without the appearance of doing so. Exploited people unwittingly adopt ideas and ways of life that are consistent with the continuation of their exploitation (Boggs 1978).

To get a grasp on how this process operates, Gramsci distinguished between different levels of the superstructure. "Civil society" represents all that we consider private, and "political society" refers to the state. In civil society, the dominant group exercises hegemony, whereas it utilizes the state for direct domination.

According to Gramsci, ideological hegemony is a project that the ruling class must accomplish. Therefore, the level of ideological hegemony varies between societies. Where it is strong, capitalists need not rule mainly by physical coercion, but instead rely on popular consensus. Here, power relations are mystified. Where it is weak, that is, where traditional social and authority relations have been undermined, where bourgeois culture and lifestyles have lost their appeal, physical coercion becomes more necessary. In the latter case, workers' revolutionary potential is higher. Still, workers need not only throw off the old, but must also develop counterhegemonies to successfully accomplish their revolutionary potential. The development of a counterhegemony is the main political task of the socialist movement (Boggs 1978).

Gramsci's development of the notion of hegemony and counterhegemony goes beyond theorizing to the realm of politics. Gramsci distinguished between a "war of position" and a "war of maneuver" as necessary parts of the socialist/communist movement's counterhegemonic project. The war of position entails a battle for the hearts and minds of individuals within civil society. The war of maneuver involves a violent "frontal attack" on the state with the purpose of total political victory. Gramsci brings the role of "organic intellectuals" to center stage, arguing that only this group of thinkers, who are intimately connected with the day-to-day lives of the working classes, can construct an alternative vision acceptable to civil society. According to Gramsci, the role of organic intellectuals flows from their position in civil society, which unifies their subjective and objective class consciousness through the philosophy of praxis. Through praxis – practical/critical activity – the working classes can win the allegiance of all workers as well as other classes. Finally, a victorious war of position makes a victorious war of maneuver possible.

Around the same period as both Lukács and Gramsci, the Institute of Social Research was founded at the University of Frankfurt. The Institute became known as the Frankfurt School and continued the development of Marxist ideas. One of the most influential members of the Frankfurt School was Herbert Marcuse. By the 1960s, Marcuse was one of the most influential scholars of the New Left. This same period witnessed the popularization and proliferation of the writings of Antonio Gramsci, as the New Left became disillusioned with the Soviet Union and sought an explanation for the brutality of Stalinism. Though Marcuse never used the word hegemony explicitly, his ideas can be viewed as an extension and explication of ideological hegemony to the highly developed nature of advanced capitalism.

In *One-Dimensional Man* (1964), Marcuse criticized both capitalist society and the Soviet Union. He moved his analysis of the failures of radical politics from the impediments of a revolutionary "class consciousness" to the impediments of an oppositional consciousness of any kind. To the modes of hegemony articulated by Gramsci, Marcuse added the advertising industry, industrial management, and the very act of consumption. The diffusion of mass consumption wedded the lower classes to an exploitative system through the act of consuming, which mitigates oppositional behavior and critical thinking. This analysis became the cornerstone of much of the New Left's critique of capitalist society for the implication that it creates false needs in human beings, which reproduces, unnecessarily, relationships of exploitation and domination.

The legacy of Gramsci, Lukács, and the ideas subsumed under the notion of ideological hegemony can be clearly seen in current writings of critical theorists. Perhaps the most influential of these is Jürgen Habermas, the last of the Frankfurt School writers. Though Habermas's range of subject matter is quite large, he is concerned with the very basic notion that a socialist society is possible, but that there are systemic impediments to its emergence. For Habermas, "advanced capitalism" has evolved past the pure wage labor/capital dichotomy outlined by Marx and has proved able to avert (at least temporarily) a terminal economic crisis. Advanced capitalism instead produces a series of distinct but connected crises leading ultimately to a legitimation crisis (Habermas 1973), in which the system might cease to produce the motivation for the masses to consent. Though space considerations preclude a further discussion of the evolution of the notion of hegemony, suffice it to say that the whole field of critical theory owes an undying legacy to the development of Marxist theory in general, and ideological hegemony in particular.

The notion that hegemony must be achieved by convincing people to accept its terms in civil society implies that capitalists dominate the cultural sphere. When not achieved, hegemonic groups must exercise control through state violence. Thus, the maintenance of hegemony hinges on the ruling class's monopolization of cultural transmission in civil society. Cultural institutions, broadly defined to include the media, educational system, religious institutions, and so on, become the media through which "legitimate" discourse is defined. As evidence for the notion that elites have disproportionate access to media of cultural dissemination, many empirical studies have shown that the highest levels of corporate, political, and cultural arenas are occupied by interlocking directorates (Domhoff 2002). The empirical findings of dense and exclusive elite networks that unite the highest echelons of political, economic, and cultural institutions provide evidence that a dominant class has the ability to both construct and disseminate an ideology that legitimates their interests.

Many scholars who do research on or use the concept of hegemony focus on the mechanisms through which consent is achieved on different levels. Special attention is given to demonstrating the reproduction of hegemony through interpersonal interaction. For example, on the level of production processes, scholars have shown how submission to relationships of domination and exploitation on the shop floor is embedded in the act of work itself. Michael Burawoy (1979) has shown that piece rates induce a proclivity toward competition and manipulation between workers, and thereby solidify workers' commitment to the status quo on the shop floor.

Research in the area of media studies has focused on the means by which popular culture, as expressed on television or through the film industry, projects consistent images of society that mitigate critical thinking. For example, the very format of television creates a reified view of reality impervious to radical change by proposing character themes that are fixed rather than developing in nature. Furthermore, the very act of consuming mainstream cultural transmission via television precludes public discourse and encourages passive absorption of dominant ideologies. Finally, critical media scholars also point to the profit logic driving media dissemination as creating a contradictory consciousness. Here the idea is that views toward profit create appetites for sensationalism in media, which at best distracts consumers from the redress of everyday problems.

The theory of ideological hegemony explicitly implies that there are real limits to hegemony. Because of the strong link between the economic/political structure of society and the ideology it produces, as well as the fact that the economic/political structure of society is constantly in a state of change, hegemonic ideology must always change in order to naturalize evolving social relations. Todd Gitlin has argued that television in the 1950s was able to exclude voices of dissent because of the relatively calm era of smooth economic expansion. By the 1970s, however, themes dealing with racism, sexism, and poverty were increasingly pushing their way into the mainstream. Thus, what emerged in mainstream television culture was an attempt to domesticate ideas of feminist and ethnic resistance by delegitimizing "radical" views in favor of those that were easily co-opted. One study of American labor during its height of effectiveness in the industrial heartland showed that the presence of a progressive union can not only mitigate hegemonic ideology in the workplace, but also initiate *counterhegemonic* orientations (Stepan-Norris & Zeitlin 2003).

Because of the historical legacy of Marxist theory on the development of the concept of ideological hegemony, it oftentimes assumes a Marxist epistemology. Even when ideological hegemony is used in explicitly non-Marxist ways, it still relies on the distinction developed by Lukács between objective interests and subjective consciousness to imply that there is an objective reality of domination/exploitation that people in power obfuscate. To the extent that whether or not social relationships are exploitative remains an empirical question, studies of hegemony run the risk of tautology. Consequently, sometimes studies of ideological hegemony lapse into a "reinterpretation" of a given phenomenon with the language of a critical perspective, rather than conducting empirical investigations into whether or not such a reality exists to be covered up. In the end, however, if relationships of exploitation/domination have been shown to exist, the concept of ideological hegemony always provides a language to decode them and explicate the mechanisms through which subordinate groups consent to both the relationships and their outcomes.

SEE ALSO: Civil Society; Class Consciousness; Conspicuous Consumption; Critical Theory/Frankfurt School; False Consciousness; Gramsci, Antonio; Hegemony and the Media; Ideology; Lukács, Georg; Marcuse, Herbert; Marx, Karl; Media Monopoly

REFERENCES AND SUGGESTED READINGS

Boggs, C. (1978) *Gramsci's Marxism*. Pluto Press, London.
Burawoy, M. (1979) *Manufacturing Consent: Changes in the Labor Process under Monopoly Capitalism*. University of Chicago Press, Chicago.
Domhoff, G. W. (1979) Prime Time Ideology: The Hegemonic Process in Television Entertainment. *Social Problems* 26(3): 251–66.
Domhoff, G. W. (2002) *Who Rules America?* McGraw-Hill, Boston.
Gottdiener, M. (1985) Hegemony and Mass Culture: A Semiotic Approach. *American Journal of Sociology* 90(5): 979–1001.
Gramsci, A. (1971) *Selections from the Prison Notebooks*. International Publishers, New York.
Habermas, J. (1973) *Legitimation Crisis*. Beacon Press, Boston.
Lukács, G. (1971) *History and Class Consciousness*. Merlin Press, London.
Marcuse, H. (1964) *One-Dimensional Man: Studies in the Ideology of Advanced Industrial Society*. Beacon Press, Boston.
Stepan-Norris, J. & Zeitlin, M. (2003) *Left Out*. Cambridge University Press, Cambridge. www.marxists.org/May 20, 2004.

ideology

Christoph Henning

An ideology is a system of shared beliefs that is relevant for social action, integration, and social stability, though it is not necessarily true. Ideologies are very important for sociology: if there was no ideology, we would not need sociology. Because people's opinions of how society works differ from how society actually works, a science of society is necessary in the first place. It is not necessary for society to function that people have true beliefs about society. Rather, every social group holds its own beliefs to be true. If one group of people believes another group of people's set of beliefs to be false, they will call this belief system an ideology. Implicit in this denunciation is the claim of the first group to possess a more accurate theory of society. But such claims have become rare nowadays – at least, the term ideology is hardly used any more. After the cultural turn, this term lost its former prominence, for a simple reason: today, the claim to possess the one and only "true" theory of society is highly discredited. It was replaced by postmodernist pluralism. Here you can only investigate different discourses, without claiming that they are false. All of them are part of a certain culture, whether we like them or not. Nevertheless, in current public discourse there are many sentiments that could very well be called ideological from a sociological point of view.

The term ideology in its modern sense was first used in 1796 by Destutt de Tracy in the context of the French Revolution. He intended a descriptive *science des idées* in the tradition of the Enlightenment, but with an almost positivistic approach. The "ideologues" became an influential school of thought in early nineteenth-century France. Yet the term was soon to be used much more polemically. Napoleon criticized the pure reason of the "ideologues" that abstracted from pragmatic political necessities and the "knowledge of the human heart," meaning the human need for pleasant illusion. This was the birth of ideological criticism, which mainly contains an accusation of a detachment of theory from reality (abstractification). It was later taken up by Marx and Engels's use of the term ideology, which they developed in their seminal, but long unpublished, book, *The German Ideology*.

The Marxian use of the term ideology has the following implications. First of all, like mythology, it refers to self-conceptions of a whole society. But the societies Marx has in mind are modern societies. This means two things: first, they employ a social division of labor, resulting in a class society or, as later sociology would call it, a "functional differentiation." Secondly, one of these classes dominates the others, mainly through control over the means of production. Resulting from the division of labor is a fundamental opacity of the way society functions (estrangement), which calls for easy explanations to reduce this complexity cognitively and symbolically. This leads to "false consciousness," to false ideas and pictures about the way society functions. Here, ideologies develop and spread without anybody intending it. Resulting from the dominance of the ruling classes, on the other hand, is an imposition of their worldview on all members of society. "The ruling ideas are the ideas of the ruling classes" (Marx). This later process can include consciously intended actions in order to obtain such hegemony – not necessarily, but possibly. Later Marxist writers (e.g., Gramsci, Lukács, and Adorno) investigated how capitalism, or specific parts of the bourgeoisie, managed to uphold an ideology of "just" capitalism in spite of its partly and seemingly catastrophic consequences. One of these ideologies, Marxists would claim, was nationalism and fascism, another one was Keynesianism and the welfare state, and the most recent one is neoliberalism with its meritocratic master narrative.

Large parts of leftist twentieth-century sociology were engaged in a criticism of ideology, most importantly Critical Theory. Yet even before the cultural turn there were two serious challenges. First, by the middle of the century Daniel Bell and others proclaimed an "end of ideology," resulting from the weakened class conflict and increased sociological knowledge that allowed for more planning (technocracy). This was a rather old claim: ideologies never declare themselves openly, they always try to sell themselves as "truths." And this was the case with Bell's narrative, as well. After some decades, it has become obvious that ideology is still alive, as

writers like Žižek, Hall, and Bourdieu have shown. The "end of ideology" thesis was nothing less than yet another ideology. It depends on the social standpoint of the spectator whether something appears as ideology or as "truth." This irony of Marx's was in many cases missed by his critics.

Exactly this insight was the starting point for another challenge to the criticism of ideology. Some important Marxists like Gramsci and Lenin had called Marxism an ideology. In consequence, Marxists no longer had a privileged standpoint, but could only maintain one among many other perspectives on society. Karl Mannheim spelled out this paradox: the "hermeneutics of suspicion" (Paul Ricoeur) needs to be "totalized." Every social theory is a potential ideology. Unfortunately, this totalization is self-defeating. In order to call something an ideology, you need to claim that your own standpoint is valid. If you call everything an ideology, by implication you cannot call anything an ideology, because that applies to your own theory, too. Thus, Mannheim transformed ideology criticism into a less polemical sociological approach. This approach was as much influenced by Nietzsche's perspectivism and Dilthey's hermeneutics as it was by Marx. For Mannheim, the way social classes perceive society is necessarily influenced by their position in society. In order to understand an ideology or worldview right – without claiming that it is "false," because there is nothing like the one, true picture of society – we need to relate it to this position in society. This is Mannheim's "relationism," which was very important for the modern sociology of knowledge, which moved ideology criticism from politics to science.

SEE ALSO: Adorno, Theodor W.; Critical Theory/Frankfurt School; Discourse; Division of Labor; Gramsci, Antonio; Ideological Hegemony; Ideology, Economy and; Ideology, Sport and; Knowledge, Sociology of; Lukács, Georg; Mannheim, Karl; Modernity; Myth

REFERENCES AND SUGGESTED READINGS

Bell, D. (1961) *The End of Ideology: On the Exhaustion of Political Ideas in the Fifties*. Collier Books, New York.

Eagleton, T. (1991) *Ideology: An Introduction.* Verso, New York.

Festenstein, M. & Kenny, M. (Eds.) (2005) *Political Ideologies: A Reader and Guide.* Oxford University Press, Oxford.

Mannheim, K. (1936) *Ideology and Utopia: An Introduction to the Sociolocy of Knowledge.* Harvest, New York.

Marx, K. & Engels, F. (1970 [1846]) *The German Ideology.* Lawrence & Wishart, London.

Thompson, J. B. (1984) *Studies in the Theory of Ideology.* Polity Press, Cambridge.

Žižek, S. (Ed.) (1994) *Mapping Ideology.* Verso, New York.

ideology, economy and

Edward G. Carmines and Michael W. Wagner

Two fundamental aspects of political life in advanced industrial democracies the world over are people's ideological preferences and their economic orientations. The interaction between these two factors helps organize citizens' value orientations and issue beliefs since there are several different ideological perspectives that people can have about the appropriate role for the involvement of government in managing a nation's economy. These distinctive ideological impulses range from extremely liberal (or "left") preferences favoring equality through more state control over the production, distribution, and pricing of a society's goods to extremely conservative (or "right") beliefs preferring individual freedom through allowing the market to control the production, distribution, and price decisions in a society.

The relationship between ideological preferences and economic orientations is important because they inform citizens' political choices and behavior. In order to understand how the dynamic and varying ways these concepts have been integrated in modern democracies, it is necessary to (1) define ideology and explain the general beliefs that make up important ideological perspectives; (2) define economy and describe various prominent economic systems; (3) illustrate the ways in which ideological preferences and economic orientations have commingled; (4) describe how issue preferences, other than economic, have further complicated

how citizens make political choices; and (5) compare the evolution of the interaction of ideology and economy in the United States to other advanced industrial democracies.

The sets of beliefs that people use to help organize their opinions on political issues are called ideologies. A great deal of research demonstrates that people often identify themselves as having some measure of either a liberal or conservative ideology. Generally speaking, liberals favor government intervention on political and economic problems, viewing change as progress, while conservatives often prefer the status quo over change and prefer a more limited government.

The differences between liberals and conservatives vary country by country. For example, in the United States, the public perceives only a modest difference between the Democratic Party and the Republican Party, with the Democrats generally representing American liberals and Republicans being the party of choice for most conservatives. On the other hand, French, British, and German people perceive sizable differences between the much larger numbers of political parties on each side of the ideological divide. Since the advanced industrial democracies of Europe have more political parties than the United States does, European parties vary widely on a liberal–conservative continuum, holding distinctly different, and sometimes more extreme, positions than the United States' two major parties.

Economics is the study of how a society produces and distributes its goods. There are various forms of economic systems, many of which are operating in contemporary political life. At the far right end of the economic spectrum is the pure capitalist system, where the market determines the pricing, production, and distribution of goods and services in a society while property is privately owned. This kind of capitalism is called "laissez-faire" for the French term that loosely means "let the people do as they see fit." The government does not play any role in the economy in this kind of system, allowing the market to dictate a society's economic actions. There are no pure capitalist societies in the world.

At the other end of the ideological spectrum is the socialist system. A socialist economic system is one in which the means of production, distribution, property ownership, and price controls are state run. Under a purely socialist system, it would be unjust for some people to own more property than others. Therefore, the government decides what a society needs, preventing individuals from having power over others.

In between these extremes lies the system of regulated capitalism that provides a capitalist economy generally protecting individuals from government encroachment and supporting private ownership while still allowing for government intervention designed to protect fair competition, individual rights, and other procedural guarantees. One prominent example of this economic middle ground began in the United States during the 1930s and was the inception of the New Deal.

The New Deal coalition is the classic case studied by scholars interested in how the interaction between ideological preferences and economic orientations influences political choices. What was remarkable about the American political landscape in the years following the first election of Franklin Delano Roosevelt to the presidency was that public opinion on nearly every issue that was salient to the American public revolved around people's answer to the question: "what is the proper role of government in providing for the general welfare of its citizenry?" At the New Deal's outset, the answer was largely class-based.

In general, those of lower status and incomes, unskilled workers, northern blacks, Catholics, Jewish people, union members, urban residents, and southern whites became Democrats, favoring government support of progressive tax rates, the creation of a limited welfare state, and economic intervention. At the same time, the Republicans' coalition was a near mirror-image of the Democrats' alliance. Upper- and middle-income earners, northern whites, non-union families, non-southerners, and rural residents preferred a more "laissez-faire" attitude to government economic intervention. As such, the terms *liberal* and *conservative* became synonymous with one's position on the proper role of government in the economy.

This ideological alignment, based on citizens' preferences about the government's role in the economy, produced Democratic victories at the ballot box when elections were contested over New Deal economic and social welfare issues.

Of course, the debate over social welfare issues extended beyond the issue of government involvement in the economy, ranging over questions of whether or not the particular social goals of the New Deal were desirable for the United States.

The first hundred days of FDR's presidency brought swift changes to the way that the US government became involved in the American economy. During that time, the Securities and Exchange Commission reformed the banking system, the Civilian Conservation Corps, the Federal Emergency Relief Administration, and the Civil Works Administration provided relief to many of the 15 million Americans who were unemployed as a result of the Great Depression, and the Tennessee Valley Authority was created to address issues of flood control and public electric power. Later in Roosevelt's presidency, the Social Security Act was passed, providing the elderly with government-financed income.

The political alignment of liberals favoring government intervention in the economy and conservatives favoring less government involvement dominated American politics for 30 years. However, as Edward G. Carmines and James A. Stimson (1989) argued in their book *Issue Evolution*, the introduction of racial issues transformed the American political system, adding a new dimension to the ideological divide. The 1964 presidential race between Democrat Lyndon Johnson and Republican Barry Goldwater introduced the idea of government involvement in issues of racial equality. While the major political parties had not taken consistent stands on racial issues during the New Deal's heyday, the 1964 election introduced Democrats as the party of racial liberalism and Republicans as the party of racial conservatism. While the conservative–liberal divide still existed, the coalitions that made them up began to change, complicating the clean economic ideological divide that existed before.

After becoming familiar with the parties' positions on racial issues, people began making political choices based on their ideological positions on race, in addition to the role of government in the economy. African Americans became, and continue to be, overwhelmingly Democratic, but southern whites gradually gravitated to the Republican Party. One long-term result of this shift is that the once powerful "Dixiecrat" wing of the Democratic Party has vanished from American politics. Racially liberal Republican members of Congress have similarly disappeared, even though many of them were central to passing civil rights legislation in the 1960s.

Further complicating matters in the United States, the introduction of the abortion issue to partisan politics in the 1970s and 1980s also began to influence ideological choices amongst elected officials and the electorate. Even though more Republicans than Democrats preferred abortion rights in the early 1970s, by the late 1980s Republicans had become the "pro-life" conservative party on abortion while Democrats offered the more liberal "pro-choice" position. The abortion issue is the most prominent of a new set of issues that are often referred to as "culture war" issues (such as women's rights, gay rights, gun control, prayer in public school, and the death penalty). One of the most crucial distinctions between liberals and conservatives on the abortion issue and other cultural questions is people's individual religiosity. The more evangelically religious an individual, the more likely he or she is to exhibit a conservative ideological perspective on cultural issues. Thus, the New Deal alignment of economic liberals and conservatives has been altered, but no similarly simple alignment has taken its place.

COMPARING EUROPEAN POSTMATERIALISM TO THE AMERICAN IDEOLOGICAL DIVIDE

The evolution in the United States from a purely economic divide to a more contemporary ideological landscape consisting of economic, racial, and cultural divisions seems unique when compared to the electorate's ideological preferences in Europe's advanced industrial democracies.

First, while the New Deal conflict provides a useful example regarding the impact of competing ideological orientations and economic preferences, many European nations have a much wider scope of conflict on the economic dimension of ideological conflict. For example, in his book *Citizen Politics*, Russell Dalton (2002) notes that in 1996, less than 40 percent of Americans believed that the government was

responsible for providing health care for the sick or a decent standard of living for the elderly, while more than 80 percent of the British and between 50 and 65 percent of Germans and the French supported such measures. Additionally, Europeans were much more likely to claim that the government should help reduce the income disparities between the rich and the poor. This more expansive scope of conflict is also treated differently in European nations than in the United States because of the significantly greater number of political parties European advanced industrial democracies have in comparison with the United States, which boasts only two major parties.

Second, and perhaps more importantly, Ronald Inglehart's theory of postmaterialism, the leading account of cultural conflict in European advanced industrial democracies, provides a much different understanding of the role that economic preferences play in ideological orientations. The increasing affluence of the post-war period, according to Inglehart, resulted in certain groups in the advanced industrial democracies of Europe focusing less of their attention on economic issues, or "material" goals, and more on non-economic, value-laden, or "postmaterial" matters. Thus, issues such as economic security and national defense, which tap into people's underlying needs for safety and security, represent material goals. On the other hand, if a society is able to successfully meet material needs for a significant portion of its population, its citizens can shift their attention to higher-order values such as personal freedom and participation; these represent postmaterial values.

Postmaterialism's rise changes the nature of political conflict because it results in some parts of the working class shifting their political support to the right, while portions of the middle class move their political support to political parties on the left. In the end, according to Inglehart, the most meaningful basis of political conflict in western democracies (other than the United States) has come to be between materialists and postmaterialists, rather than between liberals and conservatives divided over economic issues.

Overall, the influence of material–postmaterial value priorities in American politics does not seem to help explain the growth of conflicts over "culture war" issues during the past few decades. Still, the continuing passage of time and the occurrence of political change more generally require the further comparison of the evolution of the relationship between citizens' ideological orientations and economic preferences for Americans, Europeans, and members of developing democracies across the globe.

SEE ALSO: Conservatism; Culture, Economy and; Economy (Sociological Approach); Ideology; Liberalism; Political Parties; Post-Industrial Society; Public Opinion; Socialism

REFERENCES AND SUGGESTED READINGS

Adams, G. D. (1997) Abortion: Evidence of an Issue Evolution. *American Journal of Political Science* 41: 718–37.

Carmines, E. G. & Stimson, J. A. (1989) *Issue Evolution: Race and the Transformation of American Politics*. Princeton University Press, Princeton.

Dalton, R. J. (2002) *Citizen Politics: Public Opinion and Political Parties in Advanced Industrial Democracies*, 3rd edn. Chatham House, New York.

Inglehart, R. (1979) Value Priorities and Socioeconomic Change. In: Barnes, S. H. & Kasse, M. (Eds.), *Political Action: Mass Participation in Five Western Democracies*. Sage, Beverly Hills, CA.

Layman, G. (2001) *The Great Divide: Religious and Cultural Conflict in American Party Politics*. Columbia University Press, New York.

ideology, sport and

Peter Millward

Sport and ideology refers to the way in which the former, as a distinct form of leisure activity, impacts upon the body of ideas which reflect the beliefs of a social group or political system. Indeed, the ideological capacity of sport can be considered so great that it may now be apt to rework Marx's dictum, in that sport, rather than religion, might sensibly be considered to be the new opiate of the people. Unquestionably, explicit links between sport and ideology have their roots in the work of the Frankfurt School thinker Theodor Adorno. In sum, Adorno argued that sport, like many other forms of popular culture, was a frivolous activity which reinforced the inequalities of the capitalist system and prohibited critical thought. At the heart of Adorno's critique lay two defining principles: participant competition and the consumption of the sporting spectacle.

Addressing the first of these issues, Adorno argued that sport emitted dangerous social messages, which resonate with the sports-playing proletariat. A given example is that sport is ultimately tied to "instrumental reason," meaning that it serves a purpose of habituating those in subordinate social positions to the demands of material life. Therefore, Adorno's indictment was specifically aimed at the means-end rationality of bourgeois society, in that sport created the message that if the sports player worked/trained hard he or she would have more success. This was the ideological communication from the capitalist system. Building upon this, Adorno saw that the intrinsic value of sport was in permitting competition between members of the same social class, in that they risked physically damaging themselves and each other during participation. Adorno argued that this was a dystopian reality: members of the oppressed class should be galvanizing against the inherent power structures rather than indulging in masochism. Thus, in this sense, sport creates a false ideology in which instrumental reason is central, which carries a strong capitalist work ethic and hides the "real" bourgeois enemy.

However, the ideology which sport creates does not stop at sports competitors. Adorno saw that spectators offered remuneration for the privilege of watching competitive sport. Thus, Adorno and Horkheimer (1992) argued that sport, like much of popular culture, was part of the *culture industry*. They argued that sport, like the other institutions that create popular culture, was owned by members of the bourgeoisie but uncritically consumed by the proletariat masses. Taking the view that popular culture may numb the working-class's faculties of critical thought, Adorno and Horkheimer argued that the differences between the ideological propaganda of the Nazi party and key agents within popular culture (including sport, music, cinema, and newsprint) were minimal. Indeed, popular cultural forms and Nazi propaganda were alike in lulling cultural consumers into a false sense of security and in the process limiting their ability to think critically. Essentially, the ideological message was that as long as the preoccupied proletariat had access to popular culture, they would not challenge the existing power structures.

Furthermore, the cultural industries have bourgeois owners who, for entry into sports events or access to the mediatized spectacle, charge fees for a unit of their product. Inevitably, like any profit-making activity, this creates a surplus. Therefore, popular culture – including sport – pacifies the proletariat while producing a profit for the bourgeoisie. Indeed, Eco (1986) has voiced a similar opinion. Like Adorno and Horkheimer, he highlighted a belief that sport placates society by asking if it was "possible to have a revolution on a football Sunday?" With this, Eco suggested that sport – in this case football – negates the proletariat's ability to think and act critically. Therefore, for Adorno, Horkheimer, and Eco, the only real sporting results are the continued oppression of those in subordinate positions and eventually an accommodation to monopolistic capitalism. What is more, these concerns were voiced long before the expansion of the global media, which has allowed the most popular sports events – such as English Premiership football and US NBA Championship basketball matches – to be broadcast worldwide, aiding the spread of global capitalism. In this sense, Adorno and Horkheimer's condemnation was prophetic. Indeed, Adorno (1982) most succinctly summed up his concerns by arguing that "sport itself is not play but ritual in which the subjected celebrate their subjection," and therefore clearly demonstrating the role sport plays in developing an ideology which favors existing power structures.

Thus, Adorno demonstrates the linkage between sport and the ideology of the capitalist system. However, Bero Rigauer (1981) points out that sport has also been utilized as an ideological tool by "state socialists"/"communists." For instance, in the former USSR, the first socialist sports movement was organized by the state immediately after the revolution. Therefore, sport was used to create harmony

and practiced to promote the nation's fitness during the Civil War (1917–20). This use of sport was markedly different from its uses in western capitalist systems, in that competitive sport was not featured. However, the practices were designed by Russian communist intellectuals in order to cultivate a social consciousness which could eliminate a range of social problems (such as alcoholism and illness). In this case, the ideological capacity of sport was utilized to manipulate the actions of the public, beyond capitalistic measures. Thus, using this form of ideology, sport can undeniably have a cohesive (as well as destructive) dimension that can (re)unite disparate societies.

However, the illustrated links between ideology and sport have been broadly one dimensional, relating to the way the economic or state power base conditions a public culture. Taking this route, Rigauer, Adorno, and Horkheimer do not look at subordination and empowerment beyond the macro political structures. Eco, on the other hand, pinpoints an additional criticism within the domain of sport participation. Eco argues that sport gives rise to a needless inequity, which separates those who demonstrate sporting aptitude from those who do not, deepening cultural inequality. Although Eco drenches his point with irony, it is clear that other forms of ideology exist beyond the parameters set by the named thinkers. Indeed, the late twentieth and early twenty-first centuries have been characterized by the shift toward non-class based new social movements. An agenda for future research which considers sport-created ideology should be responsive to this, asking questions which relate to other forms of inequality in sport (and with links to the broader society). Such an agenda might, for example, specifically relate to issues of racism, xenophobia, gender, and sexuality, which pertain to both sporting and non-sporting dimensions of contemporary society. Therefore, future scholarly research may focus on the various ideologies of inclusion and exclusion, building upon the impressive work of Back et al. (2001), Hargreaves (1994), and King (2003), among others.

SEE ALSO: Adorno, Theodor W.; Ideology; Political Economy and Sport; Social Theory and Sport; Sport and Culture

REFERENCES AND SUGGESTED
READINGS

Adorno, T. W. (1982) *Prisms*. MIT Press, Cambridge, MA.
Adorno, T. W. & Horkheimer, M. (1992 [1944]) *Dialectic of Enlightenment*. Verso, London.
Back, L., Crabbe, T., & Solomos, J. (2001) *The Changing Face of Football: Racism, Identity and Multiculture in the English Game*. Berg, Oxford.
Eco, U. (1986) *Travels in Hyper Reality*. Pan Books, London.
Hargreaves, J. (1994) *Sporting Females: Critical Issues in the History and Sociology of Women's Sport*. Routledge, London.
King, A. C. (2003) *The European Ritual*. Ashgate, Aldershot.
Rigauer, B. (1981) *Sport and Work*. Columbia University Press, New York.

idioculture

Tim Hallett

Idioculture is defined as "a system of knowledge, beliefs, behaviors, and customs shared by members of an interacting group to which members can refer and employ as the basis of further interaction" (Fine 1979: 734). Termed by Gary Alan Fine, idioculture respecifies the content of culture by focusing on the level of small groups and the social interactions therein. Developed before the sociology of culture gained popularity in the discipline and at a time in which macro, structural, political, and economic approaches were dominant and culture was seen as a vague, amorphous, fractured, "indescribable mist" (Fine 1979: 733), idioculture makes the culture concept useful by focusing on empirically observable group interactions as the locus of cultural creation. To reground culture in group interactions, Fine draws from the symbolic interactionist tradition and research on group dynamics.

While the idioculture concept respecifies culture at the group level, it also identifies the process through which elements become a part of an idioculture. To become a part of an idioculture, an item must be Known, Useable, Functional, Appropriate, and Triggered (KUFAT). An item must be a part of a *known* pool of

background information. If the item is not known by at least two group members, it cannot become a stable basis of ongoing interaction. Though the focus of idioculture is local, the "known" criterion provides a link to broader social structural and cultural forces as they are experienced by group members. An item must also be *useable*, that is, it must be "mentionable in the context of group interaction," (Fine 1979: 739). If the item violates the morals of a group or has taboo implications, it will not survive as a part of the idioculture. To become a part of idioculture, an item must also be *functional*: it must help the group to fulfill some need. Items that have no purpose in terms of group tasks or group emotions are unlikely to become a basis of ongoing interaction. An item must also be *appropriate*. An item is appropriate when it supports the status relations within the group. Items that are hostile to high-status group members are censored, but items that are sponsored by high-status members are likely to be incorporated into the idioculture. An item must also be *triggered*, it must "spark" group interactions, and triggers which are notable or unusual are most likely to become a part of the idioculture. The creation of idioculture through this five-part process occurs via the interactions of group members.

The content of idioculture ranges from nicknames and jokes to stories and rules of conduct. The concept was generated inductively from Fine's (1979, 1987) ethnographic study of little league baseball teams, but features prominently in all of his works, from his study of fantasy gaming to his recent observations of weather forecasting. Among the many examples that Fine gives is an informal rule created by a little league team prohibiting the eating of ice cream in the dugout during a game (Fine 1979: 743–4). The rule was triggered by an unexpected loss, during which a younger, non-playing member ate an ice cream cone. The rule was drawn from a known background – the players knew that it was abnormal for a player in the "big leagues" to eat ice cream during a game. Likewise, the rule was useable because it did not deal with any childhood taboos. It was functional because it provided an emotional outlet while focusing the attention of the younger members and creating solidarity, and it was appropriate because it was enacted by high-status members against the actions of a low-status member. Though this feature of the idioculture was created through this interactive process, it sets the terms for ongoing actions: it effectively ended the eating of ice cream for the rest of the season.

This process of idiocultural creation emphasizes the non-random and therefore thoroughly sociological nature of culture. Different configurations of the five features explain how idioculture varies between different groups and how different forms appear and remain in different groups. That the "no ice cream" rule did not present itself in the idiocultures of other teams can be explained by the notable triggering (during a loss as opposed to a victory) and the status dynamics of the particular group.

The term idioculture is routinely referenced in the sociological literature as a synonym for small-group culture. However, it is rare for researchers to engage the full KUFAT apparatus, perhaps due to an implicit methodological implication. Because idioculture is local in nature, it must be studied at the group level, and though the process of idiocultural creation is empirically observable, it requires detailed microsociological data collection and analysis. Though fieldwork is increasingly viewed as a legitimate method, many sociologists do not have the interest or inclination to engage in this labor.

While the term is used more frequently than the full concept, a number of studies capture the "spirit" of idioculture by emphasizing the connection between groups and culture. In his research on "creative genius," Farrell (2001) debunks the image of solitary inspiration to show how groups such as the French Impressionists used friendship networks to form a "collaborative circle" that spawned creativity. Farrell presents a stage model of group creativity (formation, rebellion, quiet, creative work, collective action, separation, reunion) that is not unlike the KUFAT process. In their ethnographic studies of voluntary associations, Eliasoph and Lichterman (2003) propose a model of culture in which "group style" filters macro-level collective representations down to the micro-level of interaction. Eliasoph and Lichterman stress how the group style (composed of boundaries, bonds, and speech norms) mediates broader cultural categories, codes, and vocabularies, to make them useable in the context of everyday group life.

SEE ALSO: Culture; Ethnography; Groups; Social Psychology; Symbolic Interaction

REFERENCES AND SUGGESTED READINGS

Eliasoph, N. & Lichterman, P. (2003) Culture in Interaction. *American Journal of Sociology* 108: 735–94.

Farrell, M. P. (2001) *Collaborative Circles: Friendship Dynamics and Creative Work*. University of Chicago Press, Chicago.

Fine, G. A. (1979) Small Groups and Culture Creation: The Idioculture of Little League Baseball Teams. *American Sociological Review* 44 (5): 733–45.

Fine, G. A. (1987) *With the Boys: Little League Baseball and Preadolescent Culture*. University of Chicago Press, Chicago.

Hare, A. P., Borgatta, E., & Bales, R. F. (1965) *Small Groups*. Random House, New York.

Hollingshead, A. B. (1939) Behavior Systems as a Field for Research. *American Sociological Review* 4: 816–22.

McFeat, T. (1974) *Small Group Cultures*. Pergamon Press, New York.

Sherif, M. & Sherif, C. (1953) *Groups in Harmony and Tension*. Harper, New York.

ie

Takami Kuwayama

In Japanese, *ie* means "house," but it is often applied to a group of people residing in the same house to make a living together. This semantic shift is evident in the definitions given in the authoritative dictionary *Kōjien* (5th edition, 1998): (1) a structure for residence; (2) a collectivity of people living in the same house; and (3) a kinship group with common ancestors and property handed down from generation to generation. The sociological and anthropological discussion of the *ie* is inevitably concerned with the last two meanings. The *ie* is widely regarded as Japan's traditional family. There has been much controversy, however, about what it really is, particularly over the question of how the *ie* should be distinguished from the supposedly universal institution of family or *kazoku*. (*Kazoku* is written in two Chinese characters, the first of which is the same as the character for *ie*). Furthermore, the *ie* has been used as a structural principle of larger organizations, including the entire Japanese nation, and, as such, it is central to the debate on Japan's national identity.

Putting aside the enormous variation within Japan, it is safe to characterize the *ie* as a 4P institution: patrilineal (tracing descent on the father's side), patrilocal (the bride moving into the groom's house after marriage), primogenitural (house property being inherited by the eldest son), and patriarchal. There is general agreement that the structural core of the *ie* is the line of succession between the head and his successor. Succession has two different aspects: (1) accession to the headship and (2) inheritance of property. The *ie* headship is ordinarily passed on from father to eldest son, but many alternative strategies exist to maintain the group. For example, when there is no biological son to succeed within the *ie*, a son may be adopted from outside. The Japanese *ie* is distinguished from its Chinese or Korean or even Okinawan counterpart in that there is no strong feeling that the adopted son should be related to the head by blood. This fact correlates with the absence of a clear-cut distinction between kin and non-kin in traditional Japanese society. It is also related to the loose use of kinship terms in addressing non-kin. As for inheritance, *ie* property is passed on to one child, usually to the eldest son by the rule of primogeniture. In some regions, however, it is inherited by the eldest daughter if she is a first child. In this particular case, the headship is ordinarily assumed by her husband who has been adopted into the *ie*. Occasionally, ultimogeniture is practiced – a custom commonly related to the *inkyo* (retirement) system, in which the senior couple set up a separate residence after abandoning the headship. Generally speaking, non-inheriting children, including daughters, receive economic support from their parents when marrying out. In the case of a merchant *ie*, which incorporates unrelated employees as its members, branch shops are often set up for them, and they maintain fictive kinship relationships with the *ie* head. This custom supports the argument, to be explained later, that the *ie* is a corporate group, rather than a family, which functions as a managing body.

Many of the features mentioned above were found in the family system codified in the Civil Code of 1898, known as the "*ie seido*" (*ie* system). Because this Code was abolished after Japan's defeat in World War II, having been replaced in 1947 with a democratic civil code during the occupation period (1945–52), there is a widespread tendency to regard the *ie* as feudalistic and legally defunct. This tendency should be corrected in the light of two facts. First, as a social organization, the *ie* has developed over the long course of Japanese history, with its origin probably dating back to the twelfth century. It is not identical with that codified in 1898. Thus, the abolition of the Civil Code of 1898 does not automatically mean the demise of the *ie*. Second, legal changes do not bring about immediate changes in people's attitudes. The so-called "*ie ishiki*" (*ie* consciousness) is weakening, but it persists and unexpectedly reveals itself on ceremonial occasions, such as weddings and funerals, often to the surprise of the people involved.

Among the many controversies over the identity of *ie*, that between Kizaemon Aruga and Seiichi Kitano deserves the closest attention. Aruga (also called "Ariga"), best known for his study of the *dōzoku* (a federation of *ie* groups organized hierarchically with the *honke* [main *ie*] governing its *bunke* [branch *ie*]), maintained that the *ie* is a *seikatsu shūdan* (life group). According to him, the *ie* is not simply a family or a kinship group. Rather, it consists of people, both kin and non-kin, who live and work together to sustain themselves and, ultimately, to perpetuate the collectivity's *keifu* (genealogy). He further contended that the status of *ie* members is determined by their functional roles in maintaining the group and that positions within the *ie* may be filled by any competent person recruited from outside. Aruga thus considered the *ie* a task-oriented residential unit (Aruga 1954, 1972). Kitano (1976) took exception to Aruga's functional view. Drawing on the theory of *shōkazoku* (small family) formulated by Teizo Toda, founder of the Japanese sociology of family, he emphasized the emotional bond among family members. He argued that the family consists of only a small group of kinship members, centered on husband, wife, and children, who are affectively connected with each other. He therefore excluded people like servants, and severely criticized Aruga, saying that the *ie* or the Japanese family as conceptualized by Aruga is essentially a *jigyō dantai* (enterprise group).

Significantly, it is the analogy between *ie* and enterprise group that was later adopted in analyzing the Japanese company, especially its commitment to the welfare of employees as persons rather than workers contracted to provide labor in exchange for wages. Known as "corporate familism," this feature of the Japanese company has widely been regarded as a secret of Japan's post-war economic development.

The scholarly importance attached to the *ie* has eventually developed into what may be called the "*ie* model of Japanese society." It is a part of the well-known "group model," in which the Japanese emphasis on the group is contrasted with western individualism. The *ie* model contains two major approaches: sociological and psychological. In the sociological approach, the *ie* is defined as the basic unit in Japanese society, and other large groups, such as the *dōzoku*, the company, and even the entire nation, are considered structural extensions of the *ie*. Examples include concepts like "corporate familism," "*ie* society," and the "family state" (see below). In the psychological approach, the group orientation of the Japanese is highlighted. Attention is focused on the submission of the individual to the family will and the resultant suppression of personal needs and desires for the sake of the *ie*.

Chie Nakane, author of *Japanese Society* (1970), represents the sociological approach. In this influential book, Nakane argued that the idea of *ba*, "frame" or "field," is pivotal in organizing groups in Japan. In her mind, *ba* refers to "a locality, an institution or a particular relationship which binds a set of individuals into one group" (p. 1), and it takes precedence over a member's *shikaku* or attributes. Thus, being a member of a particular company is considered in Japan more important than being, for example, the president or a secretary of that company. In this idea is underscored the importance of group membership, as contrasted with individual achievement. Nakane maintained that the *ie* is the archetype of *ba*. The psychological approach, on the other hand, has extensively been used by American scholars. A classic example is found in Ruth Benedict's *The Chrysanthemum and the Sword* (1946), in which she wrote:

"The claims of the family come before the claims of the individual. ... Submission to the will of the family is demanded in the name of a supreme value in which, however onerous its requirements, all of them have a stake" (p. 55). In the United States, the argument that self-sacrifice is demanded of the Japanese for the common good has repeatedly been made to date (e.g., Kondo 1990).

Since the Restoration of Meiji in 1868, the *ie* has often been represented as Japan's national symbol. This representation is inseparable from that of the house or family, but it has transcended the original meaning to produce a broad discursive sphere in which different aspects of Japan are understood as manifestations of a single entity – the *ie*. A most dramatic example is that of the *kazoku kokka* (family state), a political ideology created by the authorities at the end of the nineteenth century, which worked as the country's spiritual foundation until the end of World War II. The family state likened the entire Japanese nation to a huge *ie*, in which the relationship between the emperor and his subjects was compared to that between father and children, on the one hand, and between main *ie* and branch *ie*, on the other. From the first comparison was derived the notion that *chū* (loyalty to the emperor) was identical with *kō* (filial piety). From the second comparison was derived the belief that the emperor's ancestors were genealogically related to those of his subjects. A sense of national unity, however fictitious, was thus fostered among the Japanese people. Through the moral training called *shūshin*, Japanese schoolchildren were taught to serve the emperor faithfully, if necessary through the ultimate sacrifice of their lives. In *shūshin*, self-sacrifice for the sake of the *ie*, on which the nation was believed to be based, was praised as a great virtue, which was then contrasted with the supposed "vice" of western individualism.

Japan's defeat in World War II put an end to the official ideology of family state. The notion persists, however, that the *ie* is a time-honored tradition of Japan and that it should be defended from foreign encroachments. The current debate on the Japanese government's proposal to install a *fūfu betsusei* (two-surname family) system, which would allow husband and wife to assume their own surnames, clearly attests to this point. Article 24 of the Constitution of 1946 stipulates that the individual should be respected in family life and that husband and wife hold equal rights. Article 750 of the Civil Code of 1947 allows a married couple to assume the surname of either husband or wife in accordance with the agreement made at the time of marriage. In reality, however, women are required to change their surnames to those of their husbands upon marriage. In order to cope with a widespread sense of inequality among the ever-growing number of working women, and also to comply with the international Convention on the Elimination of All Forms of Discrimination against Women, in the mid-1990s the Japanese government proposed to legalize the two-surname family. This proposal immediately met strong opposition from nationalists, who vehemently maintained that it would only enhance the already individualistic trend among the Japanese whose moral fiber has, in their judgment, been destroyed by western values. Surprised by this reaction, the Japanese government has withdrawn the proposal. The debate continues, however, and it is difficult to predict the final outcome. Whatever the outcome may be, these issues demonstrate the vulnerability of the *ie* to political manipulation.

SEE ALSO: *Ba*; Japanese-Style Management; *Nihonjinron*; Suzuki, Eitaro

REFERENCES AND SUGGESTED READINGS

Aruga, K. (1954) The Family in Japan. *Marriage and Family Living* 16(4): 362–8.
Aruga, K. (1972) *Ie* (*The Ie*). Shibundö, Tokyo.
Benedict, R. (1946) *The Chrysanthemum and the Sword*. Houghton Mifflin, Boston.
Kitano, S. (1976) *Ie to Dözoku no Kiso Riron* (*Basic Theories of the Ie and the Dözoku*). Miraisha, Tokyo.
Kondo, D. (1990) *Crafting Selves*. University of Chicago Press, Chicago.
Kuwayama, T. (1996) The Familial (*Ie*) Model of Japanese Society. In: Kreiner, J. & Olschleger, H. (Eds.), *Japanese Culture and Society*. Iudicium, Munich, pp. 143–88.
Kuwayama, T. (2001) The Discourse of *Ie* (Family) in Japan's Cultural Identity and Nationalism. *Japanese Review of Cultural Anthropology* 2: 3–37.
Nakane, C. (1970) *Japanese Society*. University of California Press, Berkeley.

illness behavior

Ronald Angel

While the phrase health behavior refers to behaviors that individuals engage in to maintain health, the phrase illness behavior has been used to refer to the responses that individuals engage in after they become ill, presumably in an effort to get well. Many classic theoretical attempts to understand this process focused on what was conceived of as the illness career or the sick role. These theories (and later approaches) attempted to understand how an individual's perceptions, experience, and expression of symptoms, as well as their decisions concerning the appropriate course of action, are influenced by and interact with professional models of illness, provided primarily by physicians, to determine how the illness career is structured. Indeed, one of the most intriguing and important aspect of illness behavior models has to do with understanding compliance and the identification of those individual, cultural, and social factors that lead individuals to ignore or to follow medical advice.

As the populations of the developed world age and as chronic diseases such as obesity and its complications become more common, effective control requires long-term compliance with regimens that include dietary changes, increased exercise, and proper medication use. In order to make profound changes in behavior and lifestyle, the individual must come to view him or herself as sick and accept the proposition that the lifestyle changes and medical interventions prescribed will substantially lower the risk of further illness and functional decline. Similarly for HIV/AIDS, cancer, mental illness, or any other malady: the patient's response to intervention is determined by their own assessment of the medical advice provided. Even in an age in which medical authority is high, individuals continue to consult chiropractors, massage therapists, the practitioners of oriental medicine, herbalists, and many other non-traditional healers. The uncertainty and ambiguity that surrounds so much of illness and its treatment leave a great deal of room for personal interpretation and evaluation.

The classic conceptions of illness behavior were largely functional and identified categories of variables or factors that potentially influence the illness career. In most of these models, the response to illness usually begins with the recognition of symptoms or with a medical diagnosis in the absence of symptoms. The theories of Talcott Parsons (1975), Edward Suchman (1965), David Mechanic (1972), and others focus on the factors associated with the symptomatic individual's recognition and assessment of the severity and meaning of symptoms, as well as on those factors that determine the actions an individual takes in order to get well. Certain of these theories also dealt with society's expectations of the sick individual and the structure of the social roles that the ill individual occupies.

Suchman, for example, developed a theoretical model of the relationship between social and medical factors and related those to demographic and social group structure, including cultural orientation, in their impact on medical care use. Suchman identified several stages in the process of recognition and response to illness. At each stage the symptomatic individual engages in a cognitive process that is influenced by demographic and social group factors that leads him or her to reject a medical definition of the problem and postpone the acceptance of treatment, or to accept a medical explanation and comply with the prescribed treatment regimen. If the patient seeks medical advice and accepts its legitimacy, he or she assumes the sick role, the ultimate objective of which is recovery of one's health and functioning. Suchman observed that the probability of acceptance of a medical explanation for what is wrong with one is influenced by one's level of education and sophistication. Parochial individuals who are scientifically uninformed and who hold a popular view of healing tend to procrastinate, deny symptoms, and delay seeking medical attention longer than more cosmopolitan individuals who more readily accept their need for medical treatment. Suchman saw this theory providing important insight into the degree of congruence between physicians' subculture and belief systems and those of groups that adhered to more or less scientific or popular conceptions of illness and its treatment.

In subsequent years other theorists and researchers extended this tradition to focus specifically on the cognitive structures and processes involved in the sick individual's response to illness and their relation to culture and the process of acculturation. Much of this research focused on the phenomenon of "somatization" – a clinical syndrome in which emotional and even social distress is expressed somatically – or on specific culturally defined syndromes such as "nervios" or "nerves" among Latinos (Kleinman 1986; Guarnaccia & Farias 1988). This theoretical tradition was motivated by the observation that in subjective experience individuals do not differentiate between their emotional and physical selves, but rather experience distress holistically. Modern scientific medicine and psychiatry differentiate between the physical and the mental for practical reasons, but most of humanity does not, and given the ambiguous nature of illness and treatment, emotional distress directly influences and accompanies physical illness. A large body of research has for years demonstrated that depression exacerbates the symptoms of physical diseases and increases suffering (Wells et al. 1989). A casual perusal of the Internet or journals such as *Psychosomatic Medicine* reveals many articles that demonstrate an association between depression and coronary artery disease, arthritis, chronic pain, and much more.

By now a rather large body of theoretically informed research has demonstrated that illness behavior relates to a process that is cognitively and socially quite complex. Leventhal (1986) and colleagues have elaborated such a cognitive model in relation to a number of specific conditions and to the degree and nature of compliance with prescribed treatments. Most of the research into illness behavior is based on surveys and more in-depth anthropological and clinical inquiry. Surveys such as the Health and Nutrition Examination Survey ask questions about mental and physical symptoms, medical care use, self-medications, etc., and they clearly demonstrate group differences in the level and structure of depressive affect and symptom reporting (Angel & Guarnaccia 1989). Although such data provide useful information on broad group differences it is beset by methodological problems related to self-reports. Surveys are highly structured and offer little opportunity for deep or extensive probing. Indeed, the problems of language and communication plague all illness behavior research, both because researcher and patient often do not speak the same language, and because of the fact that they have very different worldviews, as Suchman noted.

For the physician and for the social scientific or behavioral researcher, symptoms form much of the basis of assessment. Unlike signs, or the observable and objective evidence of disease, self-reported symptoms reflect privileged information. The individual who is suffering is the only one with access to his or her internal subjective realm. Those cognitive and social factors that influence the expression of symptoms and the language one uses to talk about the self must be better understood by epidemiologists and social policy researchers, as well as physicians (Angel & Williams 2000). In recent years much more concern about measurement issues related to health matters has appeared (Stone et al. 2000). By now it is clear that self-reported and subjective information is influenced by multiple factors, including those related to culture, education, and one's previous experience with illness (either one's own or someone else's), and much more (Angel & Thoits 1987).

Perhaps the complexity of the processes involved in illness behavior accounts for one of the practical weaknesses of this particular theoretical and research tradition. Although the theories posit useful associations between the mind and the body and the research demonstrates a clear association between depression and physical illness, neither the theories nor the research provide specific prescriptive insights into just who will engage in specific behaviors or who will comply with prescribed medical regimens. Certainly, it is of practical use to know that depression, anxiety disorder, and substance abuse are common in primary care and that the response to them is often inadequate. It is also useful to know that depressive affect is correlated with physical complaints, but it has been difficult to determine which patients are at highest risk.

Perhaps screening of primary care patients or better training of physicians and other health care professionals would increase the recognition of these problems, but just how they would be treated is not clear. The problem is seriously compounded when the patients are recent immigrants with low acculturation levels or when they do not speak English. We understand the general aspects of illness behavior, but those insights have not been translated into practical applications. Knowing, for example, that poorly educated individuals of Latin extraction are, as a group, more likely to somatize and to employ culture-bound expressions of distress does not allow us to identify which individuals of that group will do so. Individuals who share similar demographic and cultural characteristics can differ significantly in their personal response to illness. Indeed, the illness behavior tradition suffers from the shortcomings and offers the promises that Thoits (1995) identified in the area of the health outcomes of stress and coping. We know that some individuals cope better with specific stresses than others, but it is not often clear what gives them that capacity. It is clear that we need a better sense of the intervening factors that lead one individual to engage in one set of behaviors and another to deny. "Parochial" versus "cosmopolitan" orientations or the realization that individuals with a culturally traditional orientation are more likely to somatize and to delay seeking medical care are only general observations. They do not lend themselves to prescriptive statements, which is what practitioners often request of their more social scientific and anthropologically oriented colleagues.

Clearly, though, understanding the complex processes that fall into the very general category of illness behavior is important. Much of modern medicine and certainly the control of chronic disease involves changing the patient's conception of his or her personal vulnerabilities in order to bring about the appropriate behavioral changes. Understanding how and why individuals decide how to respond to symptoms or how they interpret medical advice requires that we go beyond the traditional models and employ the new insights of the cognitive sciences to understand how individuals frame illness vocabularies (Pelto & Pelto 1997). In order to move the understanding of illness behavior forward it will be necessary to employ the insights and techniques of the cognitive sciences in combination with more refined qualitative interviewing techniques. Brain imaging may even lead to the identification of specific structures or processes associated with specific behaviors. At the very least we need some better sense of how complex medical information, or fairly burdensome medical recommendations such as advising a middle-aged Mexican American man to alter his diet drastically, are interpreted. We also need a better understanding of the impact of family and local social structural factors on illness behavior. The dietary changes required to control a father's diabetes mean that the routines of the entire family may have to be altered and that one is required to reject local dietary traditions.

It would be impossible, of course, to end even a short entry on illness behavior without mention of the non-cognitive, non-psychological factors affecting individual behavior. Most of the traditional theories placed the symptom attention, evaluation, response process within a larger social and economic context. Rarely, though, was that context elaborated in detail. Yet we know that if one has few economic resources and no income, one is less likely to seek professional medical care or to comply with treatment and more likely to suffer adverse health consequences (Institute of Medicine 2002). One suspects that much of the impact of culture is really a reflection of social class. Of the over 40 million uninsured Americans a disproportionate number are African American and Hispanic. Mexican Americans who are concentrated in Texas (the state with the lowest rates of health care coverage for adults and children in the nation) are the most uninsured group in the nation (Angel et al. 2001). It is possible to attribute to culture or to low levels of acculturation effects that are, in fact, a result of the lack of social or economic resources. The cognitive processes that individuals engage in to decide whether or not to seek help or comply with prescribed regimens may well be quite rational and reflect reality. Clearly, illness behavior is a complex process with multiple explanatory layers. Since humans are not passive recipients of medical care though, and since the public's health generally depends on the collection of individual actions, understanding illness behavior in context remains a vitally important research initiative.

SEE ALSO: Health Behavior; Health Care Delivery Systems; Health Lifestyles; Health and Culture; Health and Race; Health and Social Class; Illness Experience; Illness Narrative; Medical Sociology

REFERENCES AND SUGGESTED READINGS

Angel, R. J. & Guarnaccia, P. J. (1989) Mind, Body, and Culture: Somatization among Hispanics. *Social Science and Medicine* 28: 1229–38.

Angel, R. J. & Thoits, P. (1987) The Impact of Culture on the Cognitive Structure of Illness. *Culture, Medicine, and Psychiatry* 11: 23–52.

Angel, R. J. & Williams, K. (2000) Cultural Models of Health and Illness. In: Cuéllar, I. & Paniagua, F. A. (Eds.), *Handbook of Multicultural Mental Health*. Academic Press, San Diego.

Angel, R. J., Lein, L., Henrici, J., & Leventhal, E. (2001) Health Insurance for Children and Their Caregivers in Low Income Neighborhoods. In: *Welfare, Children, and Families: A Three City Study*. Johns Hopkins University Press, Baltimore.

Guarnaccia, P. & Farias, P. (1988) The Social Meaning of *Nervios*: A Case Study of a Central American Woman. *Social Science and Medicine* 26: 1223–31.

Institute of Medicine (2002) *Care Without Coverage: Too Little, Too Late*. National Academy Press, Washington, DC.

Kleinman, A. (1986) *The Social Origins of Distress and Disease: Depression, Neurasthenia, and Pain in Modern China*. Yale University Press, New Haven.

Leventhal, H. (1986) Symptom Reporting: A Focus on Process. In: McHugh, S. & Vallis, T. M. (Eds.), *Illness Behavior: A Multidisciplinary Model*. Plenum, New York.

Mechanic, D. (1972) Social Psychological Factors Affecting the Presentation of Bodily Complaints. *New England Journal of Medicine* 286: 1132–9.

Parsons, T. (1975) The Sick Role and the Role of the Physician Reconsidered. *Milbank Memorial Fund Quarterly* 53: 257–78.

Pelto, P. J. & Pelto, G. H. (1997) Studying Knowledge, Culture, and Behavior in Applied Medical Anthropology. *Medical Anthropology Quarterly* 11: 1147–63.

Stone, A. A., Turkkan, J. S., Bachrach, C. A., Jobe, J. B., Kurtzman, H. S., & Cain, V. S. (Eds.) (2000) *The Science of Self-Report: Implications for Research and Practice*. Lawrence Erlbaum Associates, Mahwah, NJ.

Suchman, E. A. (1965) Social Patterns of Illness and Medical Care. *Journal of Health and Human Behavior* 6: 2–16.

Thoits, P. (1995) Stress, Coping, and Social Support Processes: Where Are We? What Next? *Journal of Health and Human Behavior* Extra Issue: 53–79.

Wells, K., Stewart, A., Hays, R. D., Burnam, A., Rogers, W., Daniels, M., Berry, S., Greenfield, S., & Ware, J. (1989) The Functioning and Well-Being of Depressed Patients: Results from the Medical Outcomes Study. *Journal of the American Medical Association* 262: 914–19.

illness experience

Graham Scambler

The term illness experience refers to the ways in which people define and adjust to perceived interruptions to their health. It is conventional in medical sociology to distinguish between illness and disease. Illness refers to people's "lay" or subjective definitions of health problems, while disease refers to "professional" or objective definitions of health problems based on signs and symptoms. The value of this distinction is that it allows us to acknowledge that people can be ill without having a disease, and can have a disease without being ill (Freidson 1970).

For all its utility, the illness/disease dichotomy can also be misleading. First, it is evident that lay understandings of illness are typically informed by direct (e.g., communicated by doctors) or indirect (e.g., mediated by the Internet) representations of professional conceptions of disease. Less obviously, professional notions of disease do not emerge out of a cultural vacuum. Rather, they have their genesis in, often reflect, and must, if they are to retain their authority and legitimacy, continue to be seen to have their basis in the broader culture inhabited by prospective patients. Second, the dichotomy erroneously equates healing with allopathic medicine. There is strong evidence in North America, Europe, and elsewhere that people are turning increasingly to complementary or alternative practitioners to treat their health problems, and many of these healers reject the philosophy, theory, and practice of professional biomedicine. Arthur Kleinman's (1985) anthropological notion of the "local health care system," comprising popular (self- or lay care), folk, and professional sectors, neatly captures the complexity and subtlety of contemporary healing.

The research literature on the myriad but patterned ways in which people cope with the illness experience within their local health care systems can be broken down by theme. The first concerns how they come to see themselves as ill and their subsequent decision-making regarding treatment and care. The second contextualizes these decisions in relation to the cultural norms that articulate morally appropriate and responsible behaviors around illness. The classical expression of these norms is Talcott Parsons's (1951) concept of the sick role, which establishes both rights and obligations attendant on illness in the US and kindred societies. The third theme focuses on the ongoing and negotiated relationships between ill people and their healers, typically, in the domain of research, doctors. The fourth concerns biomedical and other treatment regimes and, most conspicuously, those factors known to affect what has been variously called compliance, adherence, and, more recently, concordance. The fifth and final theme is the broadest: it covers how and with what results people accommodate to their illnesses. It is a theme usually identified as coping or adjustment/maladjustment, typically with chronic and disabling rather than acute conditions. The first two themes are dealt with in detail in other entries, so what follows concentrates on themes three, four, and five.

There is enormous variability in the manner in which illness intrudes on people. An illness with a dramatic impact may not indicate threatening disease. Similarly, life-threatening disease can begin with uneventful symptomatology. A dizzy spell, faint, or blackout or two can either be rationalized away, as the product of fatigue or stress, or precipitate a consultation leading to a medical diagnosis of epilepsy. Medical labeling of this sort changes people: it "makes them into epileptics" (Scambler & Hopkins 1986). A diagnosis of multiple sclerosis typically occurs long after the individuals affected define themselves as ill, and often long after specialist doctors initiate testing. People are notoriously intolerant of uncertainty, particularly in the face of illness for which "lay theories" seem inadequate. However, while people with epilepsy typically experience the biomedical termination of uncertainty as a set-back (i.e., an unwanted stigmatizing identity has been foisted on them), those with multiple sclerosis, if not their kin, typically experience it as a relief (i.e., at last they can begin to make sense of what is happening).

Diagnoses of this type can lead to "biographical disruption" (Bury 1982), sometimes encompassing a "loss of self" (Charmaz 1983). Chronic symptoms like epilepsy or diseases like multiple sclerosis, diabetes, or rheumatoid arthritis require a rethinking or reordering of selves, goals, and priorities. Gareth Williams (1984) refers to such processes as "narrative reconstruction." This may be self- or other-imposed. An individual with epilepsy, as it were incognito, may be affected more by "felt" than "enacted stigma": he or she may suffer more from a sense of shame or fear of being stigmatized than from actual stigmatization or other forms of discrimination on the part of others (Scambler & Hopkins 1986; Scambler 2004). Someone with motor neuron disease, AIDS, or multiple sclerosis is more likely to be confronted with a stark and other-imposed demand to reappraise his or her future.

The notion that people who are ill, acknowledge themselves as such, and seek professional help should recognize an obligation to comply with or adhere to appropriate medical counsel and regimens has been challenged, evidentially and in theory. It is known that compliance/adherence averages out at around 40 percent. The rationales people develop in relation to advice and medications bear testimony to the fact that they think for themselves and typically have multiple motivations and agendas. Freidson's discernment of a "clash of perspectives" between doctors treating disease in their clinics and patients coping with illness in their day-to-day lives remains salient: the two parties can talk past each other.

Future research is likely to build on a topical concern with medical accountability and patient choice around illness. The concept of the "expert patient" has had a mixed reception, some heralding it as a device for co-opting and limiting patient choice. In addition to continuing work on coping with illness, new challenges might be anticipated to the ubiquitous presumption that all phenomena to which the label disease has been or might yet be attached, from diabetes to smoking to wrong body image, make either victims or irresponsible citizens of their bearers.

SEE ALSO: Chronic Illness and Disability; Complementary and Alternative Medicine; Illness Behavior; Illness Narrative; Patient–Physician Relationship; Sick Role

REFERENCES AND SUGGESTED READINGS

Bury, M. (1982) Chronic Illness as Biographical Disruption. *Sociology of Health and Illness* 4: 167–82.

Charmaz, K. (1983) Loss of Self: A Fundamental Form of Suffering in the Chronically Ill. *Sociology of Health and Illness* 5: 168–95.

Freidson, E. (1970) *Profession of Medicine: A Study in the Sociology of Applied Knowledge.* Dodd, Mead, New York.

Kleinman, A. (1985) Indigenous Systems of Healing: Questions for Professional, Popular, and Folk Care. In: Salmon, J. (Ed.), *Alternative Medicines: Popular and Policy Perspectives.* Tavistock, London, pp. 138–64.

Parsons, T. (1951) *The Social System.* Routledge, London.

Scambler, G. (2004) Felt and Enacted Stigma Revisited: Challenges to the Sociologies of Chronic Illness and Disability. *Social Theory and Health* 2: 29–46.

Scambler, G. & Hopkins, A. (1986) "Being Epileptic": Coming to Terms with Stigma. *Sociology of Health and Illness* 8: 26–43.

Williams, G. (1984) The Genesis of Chronic Illness: Narrative Reconstruction. *Sociology of Health and Illness* 6: 175–200.

illness narrative

Lars-Christer Hydén

Illness narratives are mostly thought of as sick people's narratives about their illnesses and the effect on their lives. Illness narratives can also include the narratives of relatives about the effects the illnesses have had on their relationships with the sick people and on their own lives. They often occur as oral narratives in everyday conversations with family, friends, and colleagues. They can also appear as written and published biographical or autobiographical accounts of illnesses or pathographies (Hawkins 1993). Both oral and written illness narratives help to configure and articulate experiences and events that change one's life and its prerequisites as a result of illness.

Research on the forms and functions of illness narratives expanded rapidly during the last decades of the twentieth century (Bury 2001). The medical sociologist Arthur Frank (1995) suggests that this interest has to do with ill persons in late modernity wanting to have their own suffering recognized in its individual particularity. Patients' illness narratives capture the individual's suffering in an everyday context, in contrast to the medical narratives that reflect the needs of the medical professions and institutions.

The research on illness narratives is marked by diversity in the theoretical perspectives and methods that are brought to bear on a variety of problems. The field covers interview studies of patient narratives of illnesses, as well as studies of the way narratives are used in the interaction between medical staff and patients.

Medical sociologists and anthropologists (among others) have attempted to understand suffering and illness as they are experienced by ill persons and how their daily lives are affected by illness – this in opposition to describing the illness from the perspective of the medical profession and institution. This approach has been conceptualized by Mishler (1984) as a conflict and struggle between the "voice of the life world" and the "voice of medicine." Several researchers have tried to examine the "voice of the life world" in more detail and in that context used narrative both as an analytic and theoretical concept.

In what follows, three main areas of research will be discussed: illness narratives and identity, illness narrative and medical knowledge, and the functions of illness narratives. The first area is concerned with the ways individuals narratively reconstruct their identities in face of chronic illness. All types of illnesses affect the experience of continuity and inner coherence as it is called into question, perhaps becoming invalid altogether. Illness can be experienced as a more or less external event that has intruded upon an ongoing life process. At first, the illness may seem to lack all connection with earlier events, and thus it ruptures not only the sense of continuity but also identity (Bury 1982; Williams, 1984).

Narratives offer an opportunity to knit together the split ends of life, to construct a new context and plot that encompasses both the illness event and surrounding life events and recreates a state of interrelatedness. Depicting illness in the form of narratives is also a way of contextualizing illness events and illness symptoms by bringing them together within a biographical context. By weaving the threads of illness events into the fabric of our personal lives, physical symptoms are transformed into aspects of our lives, and diagnoses and prognoses attain meaning within the framework of personal biography. Narrativizing illness enables other people to comment on the narrative and to offer new interpretations and suggestions. Thus, narratives serve as arenas or forums for presenting, discussing, and negotiating illness and how we relate to illness.

In the second area of research, the narrative is primarily *about* the illness; that is, the narrative conveys knowledge and ideas about illness (Kleinman 1988; Hunter 1991; Charon 2001). Examples are situations in which doctors and other professional care staff talk *about* the patient's illness. Several researchers emphasize the importance of the illness narrative as a means by which doctors acquire a more detailed clinical picture of the patient. The medical practitioner must become versed in the patient's narratives, not only in order to make a correct diagnosis, but also in order to propose a treatment program that is acceptable to the patient. Becoming acquainted with the patient's illness narratives also plays an important role in determining how the communication between doctor and patient develops (Clark & Mishler 1992) and how the patient experiences the information conveyed by the doctor. Charon (2001) has argued for the development of a "narrative medicine." It is necessary for the doctor to learn the process of close, attentive listening to the patient in order to hear the patient's narrative questions, and to recognize that there are often no clear answers to these questions. Through emphatic listening a relationship is created that allows the physician to arrive at a diagnosis, interpret physical findings, and involve the patient in obtaining effective care.

A third area of research is concerned with the *functions* narratives have in various contexts. One example of this is how narratives can be used as means of transforming individual experience into collective experience. Traditionally, illness narratives concern the *individual's* experience of illness. Several chronic illnesses (e.g., HIV/AIDS) pose the question of whether the narrative is able to *collectivize* the illness experience and ask what the social implications of illness are. An analysis of men who have been diagnosed as HIV-positive, for example, shows how homosexual men reconstruct their identities and incorporate the cultural experiences of homosexuality into their life histories (Carricaburu & Pierret 1995). The illness experience is removed from the private sphere and becomes a part of an all-encompassing political and social narrative and context. Through the narrative, the illness experience becomes a collective experience.

The study of illness narratives is a research area that is still growing. Important new areas focus on the way illness narratives are represented in various media like photos and film, and also the bodily enactment and performance of illness narratives in contrast to verbally performed narratives.

SEE ALSO: Body and Society; Chronic Illness and Disability; Illness Experience; Medical Sociology; Medicine, Sociology of; Narrative

REFERENCES AND SUGGESTED READINGS

Bury, M. (1982) Chronic Illness as Biographical Disruption. *Sociology of Health and Illness* 4: 167–82.
Bury, M. (2001) Illness Narratives: Fact or Fiction. *Sociology of Health and Illness* 23: 263–85.
Carricaburu, D. & Pierret, J. (1995) From Biographical Disruption to Biographical Reinforcement: The Case of HIV-Positive Men. *Sociology of Health and Illness* 17: 65–88.
Charon, R. (2001) Narrative Medicine: A Model for Empathy, Reflection, Profession, and Trust. *Journal of American Medical Association* 286: 1897–902.
Clark, J. A. & Mishler, E. G. (1992) Attending Patient's Stories: Reframing the Clinical Task. *Sociology of Health and Illness* 14: 344–71.
Frank, A. W. (1995) *The Wounded Storyteller: Body, Illness, and Ethics*. Chicago University Press, Chicago.
Hawkins, A. H. (1993) *Reconstructing Illness: Studies in Pathography*. Purdue University Press, West Lafayette.
Hunter, M. K. (1991) *Doctor's Stories: The Narrative Structure of Medical Knowledge*. Princeton University Press, Princeton.
Kleinman, A. (1988) *The Illness Narratives: Suffering, Healing, and the Human Condition*. Basic Books, New York.
Mishler, E. G. (1984) *The Discourse of Medicine: Dialectics of Medical Interviews*. Ablex, Norwood, NJ.
Williams, G. (1984) The Genesis of Chronic Illness: Narrative Reconstruction. *Sociology of Health and Illness* 6: 175–200.

imagined communities

Paul R. Jones

Imagined communities is a term coined by Benedict Anderson (1983) in an influential book on the emergence and persistence of the nation. Anderson addresses a number of central sociological issues associated with belonging and cultural communities. A paradox of the modern age is that although many feel that the nation is our natural community, we do not know the vast majority of the other people who constitute this group. Indeed, Anderson famously defines the nation as *imagined* "because the members of even the smallest nation will never know most of their fellow-members, meet them, or even hear of them, yet in the minds of each lives the image of their communion" (p. 6). The nation is defined as a *community* because "regardless of the actual inequality and exploitation that may prevail in each, the nation is always conceived as a deep, horizontal comradeship" (p. 7). Therefore, the concept of imagined community assumes that nations, national identities, and nationalism are socially constructed; "imagined" in this context then does not mean false, but instead points to the socio-cognitive element in the construction of the nation.

Like many others working in this tradition, Anderson argues that culture is crucial to these constructions, placing major emphasis on the chance, yet highly dynamic, coincidence of the emergence of print culture and the development of industrial capitalism in the eighteenth and nineteenth centuries. Advances in printing technology, accompanied by increased literacy, allowed the concept of the nation to be disseminated through the media and through literature. The mass production of print also led to communication increasingly taking place within national-linguistic boundaries and markets, allowing the emergent bourgeoisie to "imagine" themselves and to form new solidarities not based on family structures or religion. Indeed, the nation performs many of the integrative functions carried out by premodern religious cultural associations.

For Anderson then, the promise of the nation as an "imagined community" is both as a mechanism for social integration among strangers – a key concern for modern states – and a coherent narrative of progress based upon a constructed remembering and, just as importantly, a forgetting. The impression, albeit an illusion, is of a united group moving together through history and into a common future. In questioning how such narratives are constructed and maintained through culture, the concept of imagined community has become central to much sociological research on nationalism, ethnicity, and identity.

SEE ALSO: Community; Culture; Modernity; Nationalism; State

REFERENCES AND SUGGESTED READINGS

Anderson, B. (1983) *Imagined Communities: Reflections on the Origin and Spread of Nationalism.* Verso, London.
Billig, M. (1995) *Banal Nationalism.* Sage, London.
Delanty, G. (2003) *Community.* Routledge, London.
Gellner, E. (1983) *Nations and Nationalism.* Cornell University Press, Ithaca, NY.
Greenfeld, L. (1992) *Nationalism: Five Roads to Modernity.* Harvard University Press, Cambridge, MA.
Wodak, R., de Cillia, R., Reisigl, M., Leibhart, K., Hofstätter, K., & Kargl, M. (1999) *The Discursive Construction of National Identity.* Edinburgh University Press, Edinburgh.

Imanishi, Kinji (1902–92)

Pamela J. Asquith

Kinji Imanishi was an ecologist, anthropologist, and founder of primatology in Japan. His basic view emphasized cooperation rather than competition in the natural world. This view held that "lifestyle partitioning" (*sumiwake*) among coexisting species explained the origin, or differentiation, of species. His concept of "species society" (*specia*) likewise focused on members of a species as a whole and their interactions with one another that maintain an equilibrium, rather than on the morphological differences and reproductive fitness of individual members of the species. He returned to these views many times in the course of his critiques of the predominance of natural selection theory to explain evolution.

Imanishi received a bachelor's degree in 1928 from Kyoto University, specializing in entomology. He then turned to the relatively new discipline of ecology for graduate research, excited by the prospect of studying living organisms interacting with their natural environment. He received a Doctor of Science degree in 1940 from Kyoto University based on nearly 10 years of research on the ecology and taxonomy of mayfly larvae of various genera living in Japanese river torrents. In the next year he published his first and perhaps best-known book, *Seibutsu no Sekai* (*The World of Living Things*). This was a philosophical statement of his views on the origins and interactions of organisms with their environment and development of the biosphere. It was a pivotal book that related the views that had supported his biological work thus far, and out of which he developed most of his future ideas and projects. The book enjoyed several reprintings and was widely read by laypersons as well as scholars in Japan. English and German translations of the book were published in 2002 (Asquith et al. 2002; Wuthenow & Kurahara 2002).

As an undergraduate and graduate student he witnessed the considerable debate among western ecologists about the efficacy of natural selection theory to explain evolutionary processes. He was to remain a lifelong "anti-selectionist," or critic of Darwinian and neo-Darwinian evolution, though not of evolution itself.

His personal study notes and papers (dating from 1919 to 1980) reveal a probing, restless scholar with a huge capacity for synthesis and for fieldwork in several fields (Asquith 2004). From his student days he considered individual action upon the environment and recognition of the species society to be of paramount importance in understanding the life of living things. The idea of animals as active in selecting their own environments, rather than as passive organisms acted upon by chance, stemmed in part from migration studies among British ecologists. Charles Elton's (1930) summary of factors likely to be important in evolution included, besides natural selection, sexual selection, "tradition" (or the transmission of learned behaviors between generations), the selection of the environment by individuals, and the spread of "indifferent" or non-adaptive variations (that might be adaptive in another situation). A further reflection of the importance attached to sociality in determining biological outcomes was that social ecology in the 1920s and 1930s was considered to be a school within American sociology (Alihan 1938). Similarly, the well-known *Animal Aggregations* (1931) by the University of Chicago's W. C. Allee was subtitled *A Study in General Sociology.*

Part of what impelled Imanishi's remarkably broad range of scientific interests was an accident of history. At every turn his research was cut off by world events, as he relates midway through his career (Imanishi 1966). He had planned a scientific expedition to Borneo to study orangutans during World War II, but conditions made that impossible. Instead, he went to Mongolia where he began field studies of the Mongol, a pastoral tribe. For this, he included study of the types of vegetation and its productivity on the Mongolian steppe as it formed the basis of the livelihood of the Mongol. In 1944 he became the first director of the Northwest Research Institute there. His studies in what would be called ecological anthropology found fruition many years later when one of his students founded the African Area Studies Research Institute at Kyoto University, which conducts studies both of primates and of human ecology in Africa.

Imanishi left Mongolia in 1946 when the Institute was closed in the aftermath of the war. Shortly after his return to Japan he initiated various studies of naturalistic animal behavior, which soon became focused on Japanese macaques. Japanese primatology was founded through Imanishi and his students' efforts in 1948. In 1950, at age 48, he became a lecturer in the Institute for Humanistic Studies at Kyoto University. In 1958 he traveled through Africa with his student Junichiro Itani to search for good field sites for studies of gorillas and chimpanzees. They also visited several pioneers of the developing primate studies centers in Europe and the United States. In 1959 he became Professor of Social Anthropology at Kyoto University. He also established the Laboratory of Physical Anthropology and in 1962 was appointed professor there too. After mandatory retirement from the Imperial University, he became Professor of Cultural Anthropology at Okayama University in 1965, and president of Gifu University in 1967, continuing actively to research and publish, particularly on evolution.

Imanishi's extraordinarily broad and pioneering scholarly career was matched only by his mountaineering career and exploration (on which he also wrote prolifically). The latter was very much the basis for his inspirational example and popularity among the general public in Japan. He helped to found the still active Academic Alpine Club of Kyoto in 1931 and scaled over 2,000 peaks in Japan. During the early 1950s Imanishi led mountaineering expeditions to the Himalayas and his Japanese team was the first to ascend some of the peaks in the Annapurna range. His personal qualities and contributions were recognized twice by the Japanese government. In 1962 he was designated a "Person of Cultural Merit" and in 1979 he was named to the "Second Order of the Sacred Treasure." Imanishi remained professionally active into his eighties. He died on June 15, 1992. Fifteen hundred people attended his funeral, including an envoy from the emperor.

Although Imanishi published comparatively few papers in English, the papers appear to mark turning points in the development of his ideas and application to his researches. Very often he had published from one to several volumes in Japanese on major concepts that appeared in his English publications. Among these were papers on nomadism, development of the family, the evolution of personality, social behavior of primates, human and animal ecology, and, at the age of 82, a paper on his proposal for *shizengaku* (nature study) as a culmination of his efforts to dissolve disciplinary boundaries and mechanistic approaches to nature that he saw in the ever increasing specializations in science. Imanishi also found inspiration and a way to express his views in the writings of philosopher Kitarô Nishida (1870–1945). Nishida's view that everything came from a single source and fit within a coherent whole was echoed in Imanishi's view of evolution and the current complexity of life. It is only up to us to find how the parts of the whole fit together. Imanishi set himself the task to try to understand the ecosystem shared by all organisms, living and non-living.

Imanishi's influence extended far in the Japanese academy, even if it is sometimes only remembered by the most senior generations of scholars now. Those who accompanied him on his field researches and whom he sent on projects became professors, directors of institutes, and researchers in a great array of disciplines including anthropology, folklore studies, primatology, philosophy, ecology, and psychology. Imanishi referred to his human and animal studies as comparative sociological studies, and to his idea of the species society as a sociological concept. Critics of Imanishi's anti-Darwinian views have suggested that these views were a reflection of his cultural and political viewpoint. However, his personal notes and papers reveal instead that he was in step with the debates surrounding natural selection theory – debates that only quieted after the modern evolutionary synthesis (bringing genetic bases to Darwin's theory) was formulated in the late 1930s. Imanishi was aware of all the advancements in genetic theory through the ensuing decades, but remained unconvinced by the priority of a single theory of evolution. The concept of species society is central to his views of the interconnectedness of things in nature. It is not just a conceptual construct, Imanishi noted, but it is an existent entity with an autonomous

nature, whose various individuals are continually contributing to the maintenance and perpetuation of the species society to which they belong. This shared life does not imply a conscious and active cooperation; rather, as the result of the interactive influences among individuals of the same species, a kind of continuous equilibrium results. The species society is a real entity in this world, or in other words, the world of species is a *social* phenomenon.

SEE ALSO: Ecological View of History; Evolution

REFERENCES AND SUGGESTED READINGS

Alihan, M. A. (1938) *Social Ecology: A Critical Analysis*. Columbia University Press, New York.

Asquith, P. J. (2004) *The Kinji Imanishi Digital Archive*. Online. imanishi.sunsite.ualberta.ca.

Asquith, P. J., Kawakatsu, H., Yagi, S., & Takasaki, H. (2002) *A Japanese View of Nature: The World of Living Things by Kinji Imanishi*. RoutledgeCurzon, London and New York.

Elton, C. (1930) *Animal Ecology and Evolution*. Clarendon Press, Oxford.

Ikeda, K. & Sibatani, A. (1995) Kinji Imanishi's Biological Thought. In: Lambert, D. & Spender, H. (Eds.), *Speciation and the Recognition Concept: Theory and Application*. Johns Hopkins University Press, Baltimore, pp. 71–89.

Imanishi, K. (1941) *Seibutsu no Sekai (The World of Living Things)*. Koudansha, Tokyo.

Imanishi, K. (1960) Social Organization of Subhuman Primates in their Natural Habitat. *Current Anthropology* 1(5–6): 393–407.

Imanishi, K. (1966) The Purpose and Method of Our Research in Africa. *Kyoto University African Studies* 1: 1–10.

Imanishi, K. (1984) A Proposal for *Shizengaku*: The Conclusion to My Study of Evolutionary Theory. *Journal of Social and Biological Structures* 7: 357–68.

Itô, Y. (1991) Development of Ecology in Japan, with Special Reference to the Role of Kinji Imanishi. *Ecological Research* 6: 139–55.

Kawade, Y. (1998) Imanishi Kinji's Biosociology as a Forerunner of the Semiosphere Concept. *Semiotica* 120(3/4): 273–97.

Kawade, Y. (2001) Subject-Umwelt-Society: The Triad of Living Beings. *Semiotica* 134(1/4): 815–28.

Nishida, K. (1990 [1921]) *An Inquiry into the Good.* Trans. M. Abe & C. Ives. Yale University Press, New Haven.

Sibatani, A. (1983) The Anti-Selectionism of Kinji Imanishi and Social Anti-Darwinism in Japan. *Journal of Social and Biological Structures* 6: 335–43.

Wuthenow, A. & Kurahara, S. (Trans.) (2002) *Imanishi Kinji: Die Welt der Lebewesen.* Iudicium, Munich.

immigrant families

Karin Wall

Overall, the sociology of immigrant families represents a significant lacuna in the research on international migration. Although migratory flows have been interpreted as complex negotiations involving a diversity of actors including the individual, the family, social and kin networks, the market, and the state, other topics have polarized the attention of the social sciences. The political, demographic, and economic conditions of sending and receiving countries, on the one hand, and the patterns and corresponding consequences of migration movements for societies, in particular the survival or the elimination of ethnicity, on the other hand, have been the major concerns of classical migration research.

The neglect of the *immigrant family* is related to various factors. In the first place, sociologists underline the fact that immigrants were for a long time mostly workers and men. Women immigrants and children were few and only attracted attention when the intensity of family reunification, the settlement of families, and the integration problems of second-generation migrants came to the forefront. Secondly, research shows that the feminization of migration and the diversification in women's patterns of migration have only recently become a noted trend. As Castles and Miller (1998) point out, women over the last decades became increasingly vital in all forms of migration in many regions and across the globe. Lastly, the linkages between sociology of the family and sociology of migration have been weak. The former has focused on family change and organization in general rather than seeking to understand family trajectories and dynamics in the context of immigration. In contrast, gender studies have taken up the issue of migrant women and of women left behind more systematically, thus approaching the impact of immigration on family life from the perspective of women.

The invisibility of the family is, of course, relative. Indirectly, the immigrant family underpins many of the well-known works on immigration, past and present. For example, Thomas and Znaniecki's *The Polish Peasant in Europe and America* (1918–20) analyzes the subjective experience and the integration of Polish immigrants – mostly young male workers but also married men who left families behind – by reference to the peasant family in Poland and to the maintenance of kinship ties, viewed as promoting adaptation, in the receiving country. The life stories also focus on the difficulties of the new nuclear families, labeled as *marriage groups* in order to distinguish them from traditional multigenerational families, in educating and controlling their children without the authority of the extended primary group. Changing family relationships and obligations, alongside the assertion of individualization in the host country, are thus a subtle but constant thread of interpretation woven into the analysis of the experiences of immigrant individuals.

In conceptual terms, immigrant families have been defined rather broadly as families that have one or more members who *moved from another country*: it may include only one member or both members of the couple (or a lone parent), and all, a few, or none of the children, as some may stay behind and others are born in the host country. A second approach is to define the immigrant family as one that relates to migration through a *variety of movements between countries*: some immigrate, some stay in the sending country, some come and go, others (children) go back temporarily. This type of *multilocal and multinational immigrant family* has become more frequent in a world of transnational mobility and communications. For labor immigrants, it is also stimulated by policies which are often restrictive in relation to family reunification and legalization. Members come or stay behind, remittances flow, and the family overarches two parts of the world, one rich, one poor. A third approach is to define an immigrant family as one where everyone in the family is an immigrant. This is the most restrictive definition and is probably less useful methodologically as fewer families meet this definition. Depending on the objectives of research, however, it is important to keep in mind the diversity in the criteria of definition as they are strongly related to the immigrant family's organization and identity.

The conceptual issue has not been high on the research agenda. Instead, research on migration and the family has traditionally worked along four main areas: the motivations of family migration; the forms of migration (how the family moves to another country); demographic trends; and the assimilation of immigrant families.

The decision to migrate is one of the oldest themes in migration research. Moving on from the simplistic idea of a push–pull model, research developed typologies which account for a variety of subjective and objective reasons, such as redundancy, poverty and hardship, aspirations based on the idea of searching for a better life, social rejection and political persecution, the wish to study or to specialize, starting a new life after divorce or single parenthood, the decision to marry or to obtain health care in another country, working for multinational firms or responding to offers for qualified labor in another country. All these reasons may apply to individuals or families, but immigrant families in mass migration have traditionally been linked to two motivational categories: hardship and the search for better life conditions.

Findings remind us, however, that family migration is a selective process and that the reasons leading up to the decision are frequently linked to other factors, such as close relatives who have already migrated – family networks stimulate and facilitate the migration process – or social contexts, such as the Caribbean or the Cape Verde islands, where, over the centuries, emigration has acquired the quality of an all-pervasive norm perceived as the only way of "making a life" (as L. Akesson describes it in her 2004 book of that title). Moreover, rather than searching for isolated motivations, research has emphasized that family immigration is linked to an ongoing *project* involving various aspects of family life: saving up, finding stable jobs in order to be able to build or buy a family house, having children and giving them a better education and opportunities, helping elderly relatives in the home country, returning to the sending country with better living conditions (which may involve setting up a family business, buying farmland, or building a house in view of future retirement). The concept of a migration *project* has the advantage of underlining not only initial motivations but also the meanings of family immigration over time. These change and develop, depending, among other factors, on living conditions in the host country and on marital and parent–child relationships. Women from rural settings usually hesitate in returning after experiencing more egalitarian marital relationships and holding down full-time jobs in the receiving society, whereas children often feel they belong to the host society where they were born or educated. As a result, parents may decide to return without adolescent or adult children, thus initiating a new coming and going between the countries. In summary, to understand family immigration as a *process* it is essential to analyze the migration project in time as well as the tensions and differing meanings of immigration within the family.

The forms of family migration have been roughly mapped out but inadequately analyzed concerning their impact on families. Family immigration is commonly associated either with *joint family* migration or a *man first* migration in which the male breadwinner arrives first and the family comes later (often referred to as *chain migration*). In the latter case, however, there may be various pathways into family immigration: the male worker, who may be married or single, arrives first, finds work and a home; if married, then the wife, with or without the children, comes later; if single, the worker either marries in the host country or returns home to find a wife. The impacts of the various *man first* forms of migration on the immigrant family may be quite diverse: for example, coping with marital separation entails a great deal of strain, but living with enforced separation from young children is highly stressful and leads to emotional and cultural tensions between parents and children. Other pathways may be mentioned: the male worker may form a new family in the receiving society while maintaining bonds with the family in the country of origin. On the other hand, single women, lone mothers, and wives now frequently immigrate alone. In highly skilled couples, it is frequent for the wife to find a job first and for the husband to come later. In poor countries, unskilled single and divorced mothers are among the first to emigrate alone, often illegally, to work as domestic employees and health workers in order to improve the living conditions of children left behind with a grandmother. Unskilled lone working mothers may become lone mothers again in the receiving country, a situation often linked to immigrant lone-parent poverty.

The demography of immigrant families has privileged the analysis of fertility, a research topic which has currently gained ground due to the policy issues surrounding aging populations in the receiving societies. Immigrant worker families have a high birth rate compared to the population of the countries they are living in. The migrants are young, and in the age group most likely to have children. They also come from countries where birth rates are high, although immigrant women tend to have lower fertility rates than comparable age groups in their home countries and that decrease over time. Analysis of immigrant family households has also shown that immigration stimulates the formation of extended horizontal families (young couples who lodge and support young relatives) rather than vertically extended families.

The permanence of ethnic minorities and the noted existence of female immigration and participation in the labor market led, in particular from the 1970s onwards, to more research on the assimilation and differing ethnicity of families and the children of immigrants (usually referred to as *second-generation* immigrants). Regarding the process of assimilation, most research thinks in terms of a partial blending of cultures, with significant differences, nevertheless, according to the stronger or weaker ethnic contrasts (social, cultural, familial, racial) of the immigrant families in relation to the majority population group. Other theories have sought to go beyond the theory of assimilation or mutual acculturation. For example, Portes's notion of *segmented assimilation* (Rumbaut & Portes 2001) suggests that the children of immigrants assimilate to particular sectors of American society, with some becoming integrated into the majority middle class and others remaining in the inner-city underclass. Rather than a mix of old and new, this research shows that second-generation migrants follow diverse trajectories into the receiving society.

Research related to immigrant families has thus centered essentially on the theoretical question of their integration or marginalization in the receiving societies, even if some work is also emerging on family dynamics. A recent study on the *reconciliation of work and family* in immigrant families in Europe showed that the first-generation ones lack kin networks to support childcare as well as information on childcare facilities. Class and ethnic status cut across reconciliation strategies: skilled immigrant families resort to paid informal or formal care whereas unskilled labor families with low resources may have to manage by leaving young children alone, with other children, or taking them to work (Wall & São José 2004). Research on the dynamics of *mixed couples* has also been a recent topic of interest. Differences in culture, religion, and attitudes to family and gender roles often exacerbate the internal difficulties of married life (Barbara 1993).

Future directions in research, theory, and methodology are linked to the above-mentioned development in the sociology of immigrant families. In methodological terms, systematic treatment of the typologies concerning motivations and forms of family immigration is needed if their impact is to be adequately understood. More emphasis on comparative work, across countries and different national origin groups, such as the research by Rumbaut and Portes (2001), is also to be expected in the context of continued and intense movements of families across the globe. On the other hand, diversification in research topics and theoretical approaches, considering the emphasis laid over the last decades on the paradigm of assimilation, represents an important challenge. Understanding patterns of marital, family, and intergenerational dynamics through the migration process may be one direction; stimulating linkages between gender studies, family studies, and migration research may be another pathway toward diversification.

SEE ALSO: Ethnicity; Family Migration; Feminization of Labor Migration; Immigration; Immigration Policy; Migration: International; Znaniecki, Florian

REFERENCES AND SUGGESTED READINGS

Barbara, A. (1993) *Les Couples Mixtes*. Bayard, Paris.

Booth, A., Crouter, A. C., & Landale, N. (Eds.) (1997) *Immigration and the Family: Research and Policy on US Immigrants*. Lawrence Erlbaum, Mahwah, NJ.

Castles, S. & Miller, M. (1998) *The Age of Migration*. Macmillan, London.

Fernández de la Hoz, P. (2001) *Families and Social Exclusion in the EU Member States*. European Observatory on the Social Situation, Demography, and Family, Austrian Institute of Family Studies, Vienna.

McAdoo, H. P. (Ed.) (1993) *Family Ethnicity: Strength in Diversity*. Sage, Newbury Park, CA.

Morokvasic, M. (Ed.) (1984) Women in Migration. Special issue. *International Migration Review* 18.

Pflegerl, J., Khoo, S.-E., Yeoh, B., & Koh, V. (Eds.) (2003) *Researching Migration and the Family*. Asian MetaCenter for Population and Sustainable Development Analysis, Singapore.

Rumbaut, R. & Portes, A. (2001) *Ethnicities: Children of Immigrants in America*. Russell Sage Foundation, University of California Press, Berkeley.

Suárez-Orozco, C. & Suárez-Orozco, M. M. (2001) *Children of Immigration*. Harvard University Press, Cambridge, MA.

Wall, K. & São José, J. (2004) Managing Work and Care: A Difficult Challenge for Immigrant Families. *Social Policy and Administration* 38: 591–621.

Zehraoui, A. (1999) *Familles d'origine algérienne en France: Étude sociologique des processus d'intégration*. L'Harmattan, Paris.

immigration

Hans van Amersfoort

People have always been on the move. Sometimes they migrated over great distances, sometimes only a few miles, sometimes in regular circular movements in rhythm with the seasons, sometimes never to return to their place of departure. The study of such a general phenomenon requires a perspective from which to select the characteristics that we want to analyze. In studies on the micro level, the focus is primarily on individuals: the migrant's decision whether to leave or to stay, his or her process of adaptation to the new environment, and so on. Sociologists, however, tend to concentrate on migration and its causes and consequences as a social phenomenon. The unit of analysis is not the individual migrant but the migration flow, not immigrants as individuals but immigrant populations and their characteristics. The volume of the migration flow, its demographic structure (e.g., only young males, whole families, etc.), and the homogeneity or heterogeneity of the immigrant population (the mix and levels of educational attainment) are all relevant variables for the description of immigration as a social phenomenon that cannot be studied at the individual level.

A second decision to be taken concerns the societal context of our field of study. Because migration is such a ubiquitous phenomenon, it has occurred and still occurs under very different circumstances. The world counts to date millions of people who have migrated of their own free will or who have been compelled to move by ethnic cleansing, civil wars, or natural disasters. The receiving societies differ fundamentally in nature and stability of state formation, to mention only one important characteristic. (Documentation of present–day world migration is available at www.migrationinformation.org/GlobalData/.) A most important historical development impinging on migration processes has been the rise of the modern state, at least in the western world. The American and French revolutions signaled the birth of a state wherein government was legitimized not by patrimonial rights but by the will of the people. Government by the people for the people implied a distinction, between citizens and non-citizens, between those who are part of the nation and those who are not. The amalgamation between government and people gave rise to the twin concept of the nation-state. This modern state eclipsed in the course of a few centuries other institutions (notably the church) and became by far the most important institution regulating societal life. Especially after World War I, there was an increasing influence of the state on the labor market, in the field of housing, and with regard to education and medical care. The modern state became a welfare state and although there are differences between the western welfare states, they belong clearly to one family. With the rise of the state as the dominant social institution, state borders became critical impediments for migration flows. The distinction between internal and external migration became accepted as a fundamental one for the analysis and assessment of migration processes. Neither geographical distance nor cultural differences between populations but state borders are at present the most relevant divides regulating human movements. Immigrants became defined as people settling in a country of which they are not citizens. Whereas in the nineteenth century the most important attribute of a citizen was the right to vote and to be eligible for public office, in the present-day situation the most important attribute is the undisputed right of abode.

All welfare states have developed a three-step system of migration regulation controlling entry, residence, and work. The states of the European Union, for instance, use the following categories in order to regulate migration: (1) nationals; (2) European nationals who have an agreed reciprocal right of residence and work; (3) foreigners, including (a) visitors: people who are supposed to stay only a limited period, sometimes subject to visa regulations but generally allowed to stay for a maximum of 3 months; (b) foreigners with a personal residence title, often tied to a job or function; (c) foreigners with a dependent residence title, such as children of legal residents; (4) (a) refugees: persons who are recognized as falling under the Geneva Refugee Convention; (b) asylum seekers: persons who claim to fall under the Geneva Convention, but whose claim is still under consideration.

Other welfare states use similar classifications to decide who is allowed to enter, reside, and work in the country. In all states migration control has become a political issue, often a very sensitive one, and studies about the regulation of migration and the links to other aspects of social traditions, definitions, and interests show a kaleidoscope of situations even within the category of welfare states, let alone in very different states such as the emirates around the Gulf (Cornelius et al. 1994; Brochmann & Hammar 1999). The definitions that look so clear on paper, for instance who is a refugee, in practice prove to be open to debate. The control of all visitors to prevent them overstaying their term and becoming illegal residents is virtually impossible, and many an employer is happy to work with undocumented workers.

There are two different principles that guide the practical application of migration rules, as is already visible in the categories mentioned above. All western states have signed the Geneva Convention (1951) on refugees, as amended in New York (1967) and, for the countries of the European Union, refined in Dublin (1990). Whatever the practical definitions, the basic idea is clear: the ground for the right to enter, reside, and work in the country of immigration is based on the human rights of the refugee. The needs of the refugee-immigrant supersede the interests of the immigration country. The consequence of this principle is that it is an open-ended regulation, leaving the receiving states without any control over the number of entrants. No government is in practice prepared to accept this outcome. Hence, governments continuously modify the definitions and rules in order to contain the flows of these kinds of immigrants, without directly rejecting the treaties.

Implementation of the migration control mechanisms with regard to general immigrants depends on an evaluation of the following four aspects: (1) numerical consequences (does the country need more people?); (2) economic consequences (do the immigrants contribute to the economy or at least to certain sections of it?); (3) social consequences (what are the implications for the educational system, the costs of health care, the social housing program?); (4) cultural consequences (are the immigrants potentially people with strange and objectionable customs, with regard to women, for instance?). Leaving aside the special cases of spies, criminals, or international terrorists, these points determine the political discussions and policy measures with regard to immigration control. A distinction is made between good immigrants, who are expected to contribute to society, and unwanted immigrants, who are expected to become a burden rather than a boon. The last three factors converge in the more general question of whether the immigrants will ultimately be integrated into society.

The relation between immigrants and the host society, considered under various dimensions – assimilation, integration, incorporation – has been the main theme in the sociology of migration, especially in the United States. The countries of the "New World" (US, Canada, Australia, New Zealand) had few doubts about the numerical aspects of migration, unlike European countries, with the notable exception of France. But the question of the role of immigrant populations in the society has always been on the agenda. Several ideologies and paradigms have played a role. It was soon clear that the massive immigration of the nineteenth century would change American society and that the immigrants would not all become white Anglo-Saxon Protestants. The idea that a homogeneous American culture would emerge from the mixture of cultures – American society as a gigantic melting pot – also proved to be too simple. Reality was more complex. Immigrants on the one hand became Americanized, but, on the other hand, they changed American society by introducing new religions, customs, and lifestyles. The great fears many Americans had about the immigration of Catholic Poles and Italians, not to mention East European Jews, proved unfounded. They did not become the average American, but they did become part of American life in the course of a few generations.

This last aspect, the temporal nature of immigrant assimilation, is emphasized in many studies by American scholars. Stanley Lieberson (1980) documented how, over a period of a hundred years, various immigrant populations found their way into American society, how separation and participation in central institutions (labor market, educational system) developed in a circular causation. Precisely because it is a complex process of several interlinked elements, immigrant integration is difficult to steer by policy measures. The first generation of an immigrant group, particularly if it is made up of a homogeneous, poorly educated population, is generally concentrated in neighborhoods where housing, schools, and public services are of inferior quality. This is clearly a consequence of their low incomes, which in turn result from restricted opportunities in the labor market. This lack of participation in society can also lead to low levels of achievement of the second generation in school. Factors that are positive in the short run (closeness to family or fellow countrymen, which reduces psychological tensions) may be negative when viewed from a longer time perspective. Still, however complicated the processes and whatever the variations in time

scale, regional factors, and other variables among various groups, the general conclusion has been that the immigrants adapted to American society and American society to them. It is precisely this overall conclusion that has been questioned by recent studies with regard to the present immigration situation.

The development of modern means of transportation and the globalization of the economy have resulted in unprecedented flows of people all around the world. Never before have there been so many travelers and migrants. This mobility raises the question of whether it is the numbers alone that have changed, or whether the new means of transportation and communication are contributing to the formation of new types of immigrant communities. Instead of the "classical immigrants" gradually shifting their orientation from the home to the host country, modern immigrants are supposed to remain oriented to the home culture. They are described as frequently traveling home, using television and websites to communicate among themselves, and adapting only partially, if at all, to the receiving society. They are not immigrants but transnationals. Such a general claim is difficult to prove or disprove, because first-generation immigrants often have remained oriented to their homelands in many ways; on the other hand, maintaining contacts over long distances has undoubtedly become much easier. The question whether modern immigration is indeed different in nature, and therefore must have different consequences for the countries of immigration, is the subject of a recent study by Alba and Nee (2003). They summarize the classical American studies and scrutinize the evidence with regard to the assimilation of modern immigrant communities. They point out that an important aspect of modern assimilation is to be found in the rapid change in the economy and labor market. The American mainstream now looks different from the mainstream in the industrial era, but this is not to say that there is no mainstream and that immigrants are not assimilating to it.

During the past decades, western European states have also become immigration countries. Their situation in that respect has become similar to that of the classical immigration societies. Only France had, since the nineteenth century, already welcomed immigration as contributing to the demographic strengthening of the nation. But France had, at the same time, always been confident that immigrants would become true French men and women in at most two generations. The centralized and strongly assimilative educational system would result in French citizens, whatever their surname or color. It is only during recent decades, when it became clear that the Muslim immigrants from North Africa were not assimilating in that way and remained recognizable communities, that immigration in France also became a sensitive issue. Were immigrants not threatening the integrity of the French Republic and becoming a source of cultural, if not political, separatism? As in other countries, the rise of international Islamic fundamentalist terror organizations has dominated the public discourse and greatly impeded an assessment of the role of immigrants in society. European countries other than France had no (recent) immigration tradition and had, on the contrary, regarded themselves as countries of emigration in the years after World War II. The UK and the Netherlands, as a legacy of their colonial past, had received postcolonial immigrants but regarded this as a historical accident, which would have no remaining consequences. It was only in the last quarter of the twentieth century that Western Europe realized that immigration was a permanent feature of its demographic and social development. In order to manage the immigration pressure that results from a fertility rate below replacement level in Europe and excessively youthful populations in other parts of the world, all European countries devised measures that aimed to keep the "good" immigrants in and the unwanted ones out. With the growth and further institutionalization of the European Union, the states of Western Europe try to arrive at a unified policy with regard to immigration. But a concept comparable to the American mainstream has as yet not emerged among these states, with historically different ideas of citizenship and different traditions with regard to the relation between public and private life.

SEE ALSO: Assimilation; Diaspora; Diversity; Immigrant Families; Immigration and Language; Immigration Policy; Migration: International; Refugee Movements; Refugees; Transnational Movements; Transnationalism; Transnationals

REFERENCES AND SUGGESTED READINGS

Alba, R. & Nee, V. (2003) *Remaking the American Mainstream: Assimilation and Contemporary Immigration.* Harvard University Press, Cambridge, MA.

Brochmann, G. & Hammar, T. (Eds.) (1999) *Mechanisms of Immigration Control: A Comparative Analysis of European Regulation Practices.* Berg, Oxford.

Cohen, R. (Series Ed.) (1996–) *The International Library of Studies on Migration: An Elgar Reference Collection.* Edward Elgar, Cheltenham.

Cornelius, W. A., Martin, P. A., & Hollifield, J. F. (Eds.) (1994) *Controlling Migration: A Global Perspective.* Stanford University Press, Stanford.

Lieberson, S. (1980) *A Piece of the Pie: Black and White Immigrants Since 1880.* University of California Press, Berkeley.

immigration and language

Gillian Stevens and Jennifer M. Ortman

Languages are a means of communication, and provide access to cultural and social resources. The use of specific languages can also signify speakers' national and racial heritages. Because all but the very youngest migrants learn to speak in their country of origin, their language skills at the time of migration may not overlap with the language skills demanded in their country of destination. Any disparity between migrants' language skills and those of the receiving society results in a complex and multifaceted response involving individuals, communities, and societies. Individual-level responses include language learning and language shift. Societal-level responses to immigrants' languages may be formalized in policies governing the use of languages in various social domains. In a few cases, the languages themselves change.

LINGUISTIC ADAPTATION AND INCORPORATION

The language repertoires of societies and of their residents can shift in several ways when immigrants enter a country. The languages introduced by immigrants can displace the languages spoken by the indigenous residents, as happened in the colonial US and in much of Latin America. More commonly, the immigrants are required to learn and use one or more new languages. The anticipatable difficulties associated with learning an additional language pressure prospective migrants to choose destinations in which their current language skills are useable. Migration streams thus form between countries that share a language, such as France and Morocco or the US and Canada. In spite of this selectivity, many migrants arrive in the receiving society without being conversant or literate in its major languages of communication.

Migrants who lack skills in a nation's dominant or official language(s) face formidable difficulties in adapting to their new society because the languages used by individuals in a society are laden with communicative, political, and cultural import. Migrants can encounter numerous communicative obstacles in major social arenas, and as a result often face diminished labor force prospects and other negative life outcomes. For example, poor oral and literacy skills in the destination country's dominant language(s) strongly depress occupational status and earnings among immigrant adults. In countries such as Germany and New Zealand, immigrants cannot become citizens without demonstrating proficiency in the country's official language. Moreover, the negative outcomes can persist into the next generation. For example, studies in a variety of countries, such as the US, Israel, and the Netherlands, show that children of migrants often encounter language-based difficulties in school.

These negative outcomes pressure migrants and their children to learn the appropriate language(s). The first stage in the linguistic adaptation of immigrants is thus learning the society's dominant or official language(s). However, the political and social considerations dictating which languages migrants and their children should learn can be very complex, especially in multilingual societies. In Barcelona, Spain, for example, children of immigrants are pressed to learn three languages: Spanish (the national language), Catalan (a regional language), and English (as an international language).

In spite of the pressures to learn the society's dominant language(s), not all immigrants are equally successful. Research has identified a wide variety of factors associated with successful language acquisition among immigrants, but the most important factors are time, age at immigration, and education. In general, immigrants who have been in the country longer, who migrated in childhood, and who are more educated are more likely to be successful in learning a second (or higher order) language.

Sociologists generally interpret the strong positive association between length of residence in the host country and second language acquisition as the result of length of exposure to the opportunities and incentives to learn the language. The relationship may also reflect selection processes associated with return migration because migrants who are less motivated or less adept at learning the receiving country's major language are more likely to return to their country of origin. Sociologists attribute the strong and negative association between age at migration and second language acquisition as reflecting the participation of children in school, usually an intensive language-learning environment. Many (but not all) sociolinguists interpret this association as reflecting the operation of maturational constraints (or critical periods), which result in children being able to learn a second language more successfully than adults.

The positive association between educational attainment and second language skills among immigrants also has several explanations. The costs associated with a continued reliance on a minority language, and thus the impetus for investment in second language proficiency, rise with educational attainment. Higher educational attainment among migrants may indicate exposure to, or formal instruction in, the language before arrival in the receiving country. Individuals with less education may have less practice exercising the cognitive skills required in learning a second language. Moreover, among very poorly educated adults, illiteracy in a first language impedes second language learning. Finally, it is possible that the causality is reversed and that migrants with better linguistic skills are better able to achieve more schooling.

Intergenerational language shift (or "mother-tongue shift"), the next stage in the linguistic adaptation of immigrants and their families, occurs when children learn only the society's dominant language(s) and do not learn their parent(s)' mother tongue. There are two ways to assess the extent of intergenerational mother-tongue shift. The first is to directly compare children's language repertoires with those of their parents – an analytic approach that limits investigations to children living in the same household as their parents at the time the data are collected. Studies using this approach often show high rates of mother-tongue shift between the first and later generations in countries such as the US or Australia. A second approach focuses on communal shift: the gradual substitution over an extended period of time of a minority or immigrant language with the society's dominant language.

The rapidity or extent of mother-tongue shift (or conversely minority language maintenance) depends on numerous factors. The attributes of individuals, especially the parents, within immigrant families are particularly important because mother-tongue shift presumes parents have learned and use the society's dominant language(s) with their children. Rates of mother-tongue shift thus tend to be higher, for example, if parents are highly educated and have lived longer in the receiving country. Other considerations include the community and societal contexts. Rates of mother-tongue shift tend to be lower (and levels of minority language maintenance higher) when the immigrant language communities are culturally cohesive, spatially concentrated, and larger in size. Societal considerations include the degree of tolerance of additional languages and the legal and social resources devoted to immigrant minority language populations and to minority language maintenance.

RECEPTION AND RESPONSE

The linguistic differences that historically mark immigrants as newcomers to a society include an inability to speak the society's dominant language(s) and fluency in some other language(s). Immigrants' language skills (or lack thereof) are easily observed by others and can therefore play an important role in the formation of attitudes and implementation of policies within the receiving society.

Immigrants' lack of proficiency in the society's dominant language(s) can be read as a reluctance to learn the language and thus a disinclination to participate in the society's cultural and political life. In extreme situations, lack of fluency in a dominant language is deemed a barrier to the integration of immigrants. In the 1910s, for example, when the "Americanization" movement held sway in the US, immigrants were herded into English-language classes because they purportedly could not understand the ideals of the nation if articulated in any language other than English.

Even if fluent in the dominant language, fluency in an immigrant language can signify an individual's race, national origins, and status as an immigrant. The links between language skills and race, national origins, and nativity can incite xenophobia or nativism among the society's citizens. The use of an immigrant language can be viewed as evidence of continued affiliation with a racial or national origin group and in extreme cases can be seen as portending potential treachery, as happened with the use of German in the US during World War I. On occasion, the links between language skills and race have been enshrined in immigration policy and used to deny entry to prospective immigrants of certain races. During the first part of the twentieth century, for example, Australian immigration officials had the power to exclude any person who failed to pass a 50-word dictation test in *any* European language.

These types of responses can encourage governments to enact policies supporting or favoring the use of specific languages within a society. The policies are sometimes a response to languages introduced by recent immigrant groups. However, they sometimes seek to counteract the dominance of colonial languages, which were introduced by immigrants a century or more ago, by reviving or solidifying indigenous languages. Ironically, in many countries, the population prefers the colonial language. Hong Kong residents, for example, have resisted the recent attempt of the Chinese government to implement the use of Chinese rather than English as the medium of instruction in schools. South Africans prefer the use of English and Afrikaans in their schools and therefore strongly oppose the attempt of their government to revitalize indigenous languages through a multicultural national language policy.

The government policies directed at contemporary migrants can concern the lack of skills in the country's dominant language(s) among prospective immigrants. Some countries, such as Canada and New Zealand, explicitly favor the entry of prospective migrants who demonstrate facility in the country's official language(s). Recent shifts in France's immigration policy require immigrants to sign an "integration contract" in which they agree to participate in language training and instruction on the values of French society in order to receive a ten-year (rather than a one-year) residence permit.

Government policies may also implicitly dictate the use of official or dominant languages in important social arenas such as schools, the judicial system, the health care system, the political system, or in the provision of social services. These policies often disproportionately affect immigrants and their children. But policies can also support immigrant or minority languages in important social arenas. These policies are often among the most complex and often contested. For example, there is an ongoing debate in the US on the relative merits of immersion, transitional bilingual, and immigrant language maintenance programs in schools.

LINGUISTIC SHIFT

When languages are "in contact" because two or more language groups share the same social space, sociologists generally concentrate on changes in what languages are spoken by migrants (or residents) and their descendants. However, the languages also can change, and new languages can emerge. For example, if the need (or opportunity) to communicate across language groups is very narrowly focused on trade or migrant labor, pidgin languages, which are restricted in vocabulary, can emerge. If learned by children, the pidgin becomes more complex because it is used within additional social domains, and is then often referred to as a Creole.

If a sizable number of migrants settle permanently in a receiving society, they can establish immigrant language communities. Because these communities are embedded in the larger society, the immigrants' language often "borrows" words, or more rarely, elements of other linguistic structures, from the socially dominant language. A dominant language can also change. American English, for example, borrowed *kindergarten* from its early German immigrants, *shtick* from its early Yiddish immigrants, and *rodeo* and *macho* from its Mexican immigrants. Bilingual immigrants may also mix elements from the two languages in conversations, a phenomenon known as code-switching.

Immigrants also often retain linguistic structures, especially phonological features, from their first language when speaking the society's dominant language. The result is often heard by linguistically naïve listeners as an accent. (Linguistic transference therefore aids the identification of immigrants as minority group members.) In some situations, a borrowed linguistic structure lingers into the linguistic repertoires of the immigrants' native-born descendants. The result can be distinctive ethnic or geographically bounded dialectical communities sharing features such as the treatment of low back vowels among the Boston Irish and the /o/-fronting found among Philadelphians in the US.

SEE ALSO: Bilingual, Multicultural Education; Bilingualism; Immigration; Immigration Policy; Language; Migration, Ethnic Conflicts, and Racism; Migration: International

REFERENCES AND SUGGESTED READINGS

Alba, R., Logan, J., Lutz, A., & Stults, B. (2002) Only English by the Third Generation? Loss and Preservation of the Mother Tongue Among the Grandchildren of Contemporary Immigrants. *Demography* 39: 467–84.

Chiswick, B. R. & Miller, P. W. (1992) Language in the Immigrant Labor Market. In: Chiswick, B. R. (Ed.), *Immigration, Language, and Ethnicity: Canada and the United States.* AEI Press, Washington, DC, pp. 229–96.

Hoffmann, C. (2000) Balancing Language Planning and Language Rights: Catalonia's Uneasy Juggling Act. *Journal of Multilingual and Multicultural Development* 21: 425–41.

McWhorter, J. H. (2003) Pidgins and Creoles as Models of Language Change: The State of the Art. *Annual Review of Applied Linguistics* 23: 202–12.

Portes, A. & Shauffler, R. (1994) Language and the Second Generation: Bilingualism Yesterday and Today. *International Migration Review* 28: 640–61.

Stevens, G. (1999) Age at Immigration and Second Language Proficiency Among Foreign-Born Adults. *Language in Society* 28: 555–78.

immigration policy

Susan K. Brown and Frank D. Bean

Immigration policy specifies the laws and practices that allow persons to move permanently to other countries and petition for citizenship or to enter and stay for delimited lengths of time without the right to apply for citizenship. In developed countries, such policies include not only voluntary work and occupation-based and family-based migration but also the admission of refugees and the acceptance of asylum seekers. In its most comprehensive form, immigration policy not only involves the admission of immigrants, but also endeavors to coordinate labor needs with the control of migrant flows, affect international policies that might alleviate the need for some migration, and integrate newcomers into the socioeconomic fabric of the destination society. Immigration policies also often cover non-immigrants, such as those who cross borders to travel, conduct business, work temporarily, visit, or study. Such policies also extend to the treatment of unauthorized immigrants, or those who enter a country without a visa or who overstay a visa, although the presence of such persons in the country does not directly result from admissions policies.

Immigration policies vary across countries, although relatively few countries receive many international migrants and have formal migration policies in place. Traditional migrant-receiving countries such as the United States or Canada have tended to try to control who enters their borders through visa systems. Continental countries, such as Germany, that had not considered themselves migrant destinations despite decades of in-migration, have tended over the years to control migration through residence and work permits, the parameters of which might become more favorable the longer

migrants stayed. While such distinctions of policy emphasis have blurred in recent years, policy conceptions between the traditional immigrant-receiving countries still perceive of policy differently from new immigrant destinations.

Until the late nineteenth century, none of the major immigrant-receiving countries sought to adopt laws and practices to regulate migration, nor did they mount substantial efforts to control the magnitude of immigrant flows. To a considerable extent, this owed to the relative absence of political forces compelling such restriction. Nativism was a relatively small cultural current in early nineteenth-century America; most Americans at the time – as well as Canadians and Australians – understood that they needed to populate and settle their countries. After decades of flows of settlers, however, anti-immigrant activity began to arise in the United States in the mid-nineteenth century, first against Catholics, particularly the Irish but also the Germans; then against Asians, starting with the Chinese and moving on to Japanese and Filipinos; and then against all immigrants, particularly as immigrant flows were increasing from southern and eastern Europe.

By the late nineteenth century, the major immigrant-receiving countries were beginning to restrict migration in response to anti-immigrant sentiment. In the United States, the Chinese Exclusion Act of 1882 initiated an escalating series of limitations that culminated in the national quotas set in the Immigration Act of 1924. In Canada, legislation in 1895 barred those whose incapacities rendered them likely to become public charges, those with moral flaws, and those considered "racially and culturally unassimilatable" (Lynch & Simon 2003). In 1923, Canada further prohibited most Chinese and other Asians. Meanwhile, Australia set up a dictation test in 1901, together with restrictions on public charges, the insane, prostitutes, and contract laborers. The dictation test – 50 words in any European language – effectively restricted immigration to Europeans.

THE GROWTH OF INTERNATIONAL MIGRATION

International migration (defined as legal movers from one country to another plus refugees and asylees) grew in the latter part of the twentieth century. Although according to the United Nations it was only about 3 percent of the world's population in the year 2000, international migration has been rapidly increasing, with the global number of such migrants more than doubling in the latter third of the twentieth century. For example, the United Nations Population Division estimates a rise from 75 million to 175 million international migrants between 1965 and 2000. And the increase occurring over the last 15 years of this period (1985 to 2000) represents a rate of growth of more than 4 percent per year, more than two and a half times the 1.5 percent annual rate in overall population growth. Most of this in-migration is concentrated in the developed countries, where international migrants make up almost 9 percent of the population overall. This proportion varies, from just over 1 percent in Japan to 21 percent in Australia to nearly 35 percent in Luxembourg as of 1997. Among the OECD countries, many of which have birth rates below replacement, immigrants account for about 65 percent of population growth.

Countries thus vary substantially in their concentrations of international migrants. Some nations, like the United States, have always been known as immigration countries (that is, as countries whose policies allow for substantial immigration). Others, like Japan and Spain, for example, have not. Still others, at least until recently, have not either seen themselves or been known as immigration countries even though they in fact have been or have become countries of immigration. Germany is a case in point. Like most developed countries in the world, Germany now receives migrants from elsewhere, either legally or "illegally." Most of the industrial countries of the world are now experiencing immigration, even though many have not yet come to view themselves as immigration countries. Certainly, the movement of peoples from country to country affects politics and economics both nationally and worldwide. Yet immigration policies often reflect these countries' ambivalence toward immigration. In 2004, Germany opted not to institute a point system to select immigrants with high levels of human capital but to maintain its recruitment ban (although with some limited exceptions for scientists, managers, and the self-employed).

RECENT IMMIGRATION POLICY IN THE UNITED STATES

Because the United States receives by far the most immigrants of any country, US immigration policy deserves special mention. The immigration quotas of 1924, which curtailed immigration from Europe, were the culmination of 75 years of rising nativism. Four decades later, in the civil rights era, the Hart-Celler Act lifted those quotas and established family reunification as the preeminent criterion for admission. By abolishing race and ethnic origin as grounds for exclusion, the act set good relations with recently independent Asian countries, but it also inaugurated an era of unforeseen expansion in immigration. While Canada and Europe contributed relatively few immigrants, more and more came from Asia and Latin America.

The end of the Bracero program for temporary workers from Mexico in 1964 also led to a major increase in unauthorized migration. The use of Mexicans as a source of labor was institutionalized throughout the Southwest, and demand for such labor was rising even as population growth in Mexico generated many more people than Mexico could employ. As the US economy slowed dramatically in the 1970s, even as the stream of immigrants picked up, debate grew on how to deal with the migration of low-skilled workers, particularly those who were unauthorized. In 1986, Congress passed the Immigration Reform and Control Act (IRCA), which made it illegal to hire workers lacking appropriate documents, though this provision of the act has not been heavily enforced (Fix & Hill 1990). IRCA further made longtime unauthorized aliens and agricultural workers eligible for legalized status. The act also authorized spending $4 billion for states' costs in providing public assistance, health care, and education for the newly legalized population; required states to verify that non-citizens were eligible for welfare benefits; and expanded enforcement of the border patrol and inspections. Though the act did not succeed in curbing unauthorized migration, through 1994 it helped about 2 million unauthorized migrants become legal.

In 1990, a new Immigrant Act capped overall immigration for the first time since 1924 at

700,000 until 1994, and 675,000 thereafter, with unlimited visas for immediate relatives of US citizens. But the term "cap" is misleading, in that the cap exceeded the existing levels of family admissions and could be pierced under certain circumstances. The law also increased the number of visas for workers and shifted the preference toward skilled and professional labor. Furthermore, the act set up "diversity" visas for citizens of countries less likely to send immigrants to the United States.

In the aftermath of a backlash against immigrants that began in California, the United States began to emphasize border control and tripled its spending on border enforcement between 1993 and 2004. The Illegal Immigrant Reform and Immigrant Responsibility Act of 1996 further tightened US borders, particularly in the Southwest, and stiffened the penalties for smuggling, visa fraud, and illegal entry. The act, together with the welfare reform act of the same year, restricted the rights of noncitizens to obtain federal means-tested benefits, such as food stamps or Supplemental Security Income.

Mexican Immigration and US Policy

Special mention should also be made of Mexican migration, because Mexico has sent more legal immigrants to the United States between 1964 and 2004 than any other country, as well as the largest number of unauthorized migrants. The high profile of Mexican migration for US policy is relatively new. Until recently, Mexican migration, compared to that from other nations, was not particularly large and, in practice if not always in law, relatively unrestricted, with exceptions such as the repatriation of large numbers of Mexican migrants in the 1930s and again in 1954. Compared to the massive immigrations from Europe in the last half of the nineteenth century and the first decades of the twentieth century, Mexican immigration contributed only a small part of US population growth until recently. Its pre-World War II peak occurred in the 1920s when the economic disruptions of the Mexican Revolution (1910–20) and the civil wars that followed led many Mexicans to migrate to the United States in search of jobs. In the 1920s,

459,000 Mexicans were registered as immigrating to the United States, equivalent to 3.2 percent of the total Mexican population in 1921. These numbers of Mexican immigrants were not to be surpassed until the 1970s, but they were not exceptional. Several European countries, Italy, Germany, and the United Kingdom, contributed similar numbers of immigrants, while twice that number of immigrants came from Canada in the 1920s. Even Ireland, long past the peak of its contribution to US population growth, sent a higher proportion of its population as immigrants to the United States than did Mexico in these years. Some 5.2 percent of the Irish population immigrated to the United States in the 1920s, despite the attainment of Irish independence that removed one of the major ostensible causes of Irish emigration.

Not only was Mexican migration not particularly voluminous, much of it was temporary in nature. Partly as a result, Mexican immigrants have had one of the lowest naturalization rates of any immigrant group. Census figures also suggest substantial emigration out of the United States by Mexican immigrants. While 728,000 Mexicans are recorded as immigrating to the United States between 1901 and 1930, the numbers of the Mexican-born population in the US in 1930 amounted to 641,000, and these would have included many who had not documented their immigration. By 1950, the Mexican-born in the census had dropped to 452,000, reflecting not only mortality and the low level of immigration after 1930, but also the forced repatriations of Mexicans in the 1930s. There are no satisfactory estimates of Mexican return migration to Mexico, but it is clear the amount of return migration has been quite high in virtually all years.

Unauthorized Mexican Migration

Mexican migrants to the United States until the 1960s were predominantly employed in types of work that were temporary and seasonal in nature. The rapid expansion of Californian agriculture depended on a seasonal labor force. So long as unauthorized Mexican migrants wished to return to Mexico, the arrangement suited both sides. Until the 1970s, most Mexican migrants did in fact wish to return;

but in the last three decades of the twentieth century, Mexican migration not only increased in volume, it also more and more involved longer-term migration. A major reason for this shift toward permanent immigration was and continues to be the gradual erosion of the economic viability of small-scale agriculture in Mexico, a change that has at once promoted migration to large metropolitan areas within Mexico and discouraged Mexican US migrants from returning to and investing in small-town and rural Mexican villages and enterprises.

Because so much of Mexican migration has been unauthorized (i.e., occurring outside the framework of legal immigrant visas), US immigration policy has often given special policy attention to this type of migration. This reflects in part the United States' longstanding ambivalence about unauthorized labor migrants, particularly unauthorized migrants from Mexico. A good example of this ambivalence can be found in the now eliminated policy contradictions embedded in the so-called "Texas proviso," a quirk of US immigration law for nearly 30 years which – until 1986 – made it legal to hire unauthorized workers (e.g., to employ them to take care of your lawn) but illegal to harbor them (e.g., to invite them into your home for a drink of water). Such anomalies have exemplified US policy approaches to unauthorized Mexican migration for several decades, practices that have repeatedly consisted of sporadic and highly public efforts to intercept unauthorized Mexican migrants as they cross the border into the United States (i.e., to "control the border") while "turning a blind eye" to migrants who enter via other means. Although messy and unseemly, this awkward mixture of de jure and de facto strategies served the interests of conflicting constituencies reasonably well. Agricultural and other employers of low-skilled workers who tend to favor the easy entry of unauthorized migrants continued to benefit from a rather steady flow of workers, whereas citizens who worry about the social, cultural, economic, and legal implications of such migration have been able to take solace in at least periodic efforts at border enforcement.

That such largely ad hoc arrangements have not been entirely satisfactory is evident in the numerous legislative efforts of one kind or another mounted during the post-war era to curb such migration, usually attempts taking place after periods of high unemployment. One of these occurred in 1986 when Congress adopted the Immigration Reform and Control Act introducing civil and criminal penalties for hiring unauthorized workers. Another occurred in 1994, when Congress ratified the North American Free Trade Agreement (NAFTA), a treaty whose negotiation expressly avoided dealing with migration matters but whose political marketing widely promised that it would generate effective migration control through enhanced Mexican economic development. And in 1996, also following the economic recession of the early 1990s, Congress sought to reduce the attractiveness of migration by limiting immigrant access to social services.

Despite these legislative efforts, however, illegal migration to the United States has apparently not diminished, even though it has sometimes been temporarily reduced either by slowdowns in the economy or short-term responses to legislative initiatives. This lack of abatement has caused many observers to argue that efforts at border control and enforcement are largely futile, that the pressures for entry into the countries of the world enjoying the strongest and most advanced economies are so great that border and migration control efforts inevitably fail (Cornelius et al. 2004). Others have argued that control policies, especially border enforcement emphases, are not merely ineffective but even counterproductive, at least in the case of Mexican unauthorized migration to the United States. Recent more strict enforcement policies have been argued to generate longer US stays on the part of circular migrants who might otherwise have remained in the country for shorter periods of time were it not for the fact that crossing the border had become more difficult. Whatever the case, the apparent persistence of migration under conditions of economic slowdowns and increased border enforcement raises new questions for future immigration policy research about the effectiveness of implicit and explicit policy efforts to control migration.

SEE ALSO: Immigrant Families; Immigration; Migration: International; Migration: Undocumented/Illegal; Refugee Movements; Transnationalism

REFERENCES AND SUGGESTED
READINGS

Andreas, P. (2000) *Border Games: Policing the US–Mexico Divide*. Cornell University Press, Ithaca, NY.

Bean, F. D. & Stevens, G. (2003) *America's Newcomers and the Dynamics of Diversity*. Russell Sage Foundation, New York.

Bean, F. D., Vernez, G., & Keely, C. B. (1989) *Opening and Closing the Doors: Evaluating Immigration Reform and Control*. Rand Corporation and Urban Institute Press, Santa Monica, CA, Washington, DC, and Lanham, MD.

Bean, F. D., Passel, J. S., & Edmonston, B. (1990) *Undocumented Migration to the United States: IRCA and the Experience of the 1980s*. Urban Institute Press, Washington, DC.

Bean, F. D., Chanove, R., Cushing, R. G., de la Garza, R. O., Freeman, G. P., Hayes, C. W., & Spener, D. (1994) *Illegal Mexican Migration and the United States/Mexico Border: The Effects of Operation Hold the Line on El Paso/Juarez*. US Commission on Immigration Reform, Washington, DC.

Binational Report of the Binational Study on Migration (1997) Mexican Ministry on Foreign Affairs and US Commission on Immigration Reform, Mexico City and Washington, DC.

Calavita, K. (1992) *Inside the State: The Bracero Program, Immigration, and the INS*. Routledge, New York.

Cornelius, W. et al. (Eds.) (2004) *Controlling Immigration: A Global Perspective*. Stanford University Press, Stanford.

Fix, M. & Hill, P. T. (1990) *Enforcing Employer Sanctions: Challenges and Strategies*. Rand Corporation and Urban Institute Press, Santa Monica, CA and Washington, DC.

Freeman, G. P. & Bean, F. D. (1997) Mexico and US Worldwide Immigration Policy. In: Bean, F. D., de la Garza, R. O., Roberts, B. R., & Weintraub, S., *At the Crossroads: Mexican Migration and US Policy*. Rowman & Littlefield, Lanham, MD.

Hailbronner, K., Martin, D. A., & Motomura, H. (Eds.) (1997) *Immigration Admissions: The Search for Workable Policies in Germany and the United States*. Berghahn Books, Providence.

Jasso, G. & Rosenzweig, M. (1990) *The New Chosen People: Immigrants to the United States*. Russell Sage Foundation, New York.

Lynch, J. P. & Simon, R. J. (2003) *Immigration the World Over: Statutes, Policies, and Practices*. Rowman & Littlefield, Lanham, MD.

Marcelli, E. & Cornelius, W. (2001) The Changing Profile of Mexican Migrants to the United States: New Evidence from California and Mexico. *Latin American Research Review* 36: 105–31.

Martin, P. & Widgren, J. (2002) International Migration: Facing the Challenge. *Population Bulletin* 57 (1): 1–40.

Massey, D., Durand, J., & Malone, N. J. (2002) *Beyond Smoke and Mirrors: Mexican Immigration in an Era of Economic Integration*. Russell Sage Foundation, New York.

Münz, R. (2004) New German Law Skirts Comprehensive Immigration Reform. Migration Policy Institute.

Reyes, B. I. et al. (2002) *Holding the Line? The Effect of the Recent Border Build-Up on Unauthorized Immigration*. Public Policy Institute of California, San Francisco.

Smith, J. P. & Edmonston, B. (1997) *The New Americans: Economic, Demographic, and Fiscal Effects of Immigration*. National Academy Press, Washington, DC.

United Nations (2002) *International Migration Report 2002*. United Nations Press, New York.

imperialism

Alberto Toscano

Imperialism designates the historical phenomenon whereby certain political entities have sought to exert control over and extract resources from others, whether through formal conquest, informal coercion, or a host of intermediate solutions (e.g., protectorates, alliances, occupations, and so on). It also denotes the multiple concepts or theories of imperialism, which continue to be the object of controversies that easily exceed the realm of academic debate, especially since "imperialist" still largely remains a term of reprobation. Initially coined to designate the existence and expansion of empires (from Ancient Rome to Napoleonic France), the notion of imperialism gained prominence in the late nineteenth century, when it came to identify the reality of European colonialism (from the British Raj to the "scramble for Africa"). The ensuing history of the concept registers a distinction between, on the one hand, purely political definitions of imperialism, which reduce it to an instance of power politics and foreground the issue of territorial gain, and, on the other, socioeconomic analyses, which, while not discounting the significance of physical expansion, emphasize the underlying and often invisible causes of imperialist policies, thereby accounting for the influence of material factors on geopolitical decisions. The penchant for a given concept or theory of imperialism invariably determines which processes and events count as cases of imperialism, so that analytical definitions are here inseparable from historical judgments.

The acceleration in colonizing ventures during what Eric Hobsbawm has termed the "age of empire" gave rise to the first great debates on imperialism. At first, imperialism served to designate a policy of nationalist expansion and international competition. It was also marked by the sense of a European civilizing mission, the so-called "white man's burden." The expansionist ideology was sustained by quasi-vitalist ideas of the need for certain nations to expand politically, economically, and culturally (as testified, for instance, by some of Weber's writings on Germany). Liberal opposition to imperialism attacked what it regarded as a jingoistic manipulation of mass sentiment for irrational ends or petty interests. In Schumpeter's analysis, this led to a focus on the use of irrational and "objectless" nationalist tendencies to condition the popular masses, and to promoting a democratic free-market polity that could sap the drives towards monopolization and hyper-exploitation both at home and abroad. Where Schumpeter defined the causes of imperialism as primarily sociopolitical in character, Hobson's *Imperialism* opened the way for its structural analysis as a necessary correlate of a particular socioeconomic order. While also highlighting the manufacture of expansionist consent against the very interests of the masses, Hobson contended that imperialism was driven by the needs of financial elites and monopolies which, failing to get sufficiently profitable returns on their investments in a saturated market constrained by the low purchasing power of workers, pushed for the forcible opening of overseas opportunities.

Hobson's ideas were of great import for what is certainly the most read and influential tract on the subject, Lenin's 1916 *Imperialism, the Highest Stage of Capitalism*. Compensating for the insufficient theorization of imperialism in

Marx's own works, Lenin followed Hobson in seeing finance and monopoly capital as the key factor (a position also held by Hilferding and later by Baran, Sweezy, and Magdoff). In the midst of World War I, Lenin tried to understand that conflagration as an effect of the conflict between great capitalist powers, now held captive by increasingly parasitic financial oligarchies (this theory of imperialist conflict is juxtaposed with Kautsky's theory of imperialist convergence, or "super-imperialism"). This was, of course, a contradictory phenomenon, which saw both a seeming decay in the capitalist system as a whole, as well as an increase in the "socialization of production." Importantly, Lenin also interpreted imperialism in a strategic political vein, and pushed for the formation of an anti-imperialist front and the reconsideration of nationalism as a weapon against capitalism. Rosa Luxemburg, in her 1913 *The Accumulation of Capital*, also attempted to integrate a political critique of the age of empire with an economic analysis – founded on the idea of underconsumption and capitalism's constant need to expand to non-capitalist zones to create markets and realize surplus-value. She also introduced the analysis of "militarism" both as an ideological tool and as a component (in the guise of the arms industry) of capital accumulation under conditions of imperialism, an analysis later expanded upon by Ernest Mandel in his *Late Capitalism*.

Marxist theories of imperialism – whose economic parameters have repeatedly come under attack by liberal economists and social theorists – grew in political significance and conceptual variety in the post-war period, as they came face to face with the Cold War (especially in Vietnam, but also in terms of the vexing question of "communist imperialism") and decolonization (which spawned neo-Marxist theories of dependency and "modernization" *qua* products of imperialism). The ebb of theories of imperialism in the 1980s seemed terminal, especially as the analysis of the political economy of the world market came under the aegis of globalization theories. Even from the Left, namely in the theory of "Empire" as a new form of virtual, decentered capitalist sovereignty, the notion of imperialism appeared to be relegated to another era, when capitalism was still, to use Marx's terms, in a phase of formal and not real subsumption. Reaction to the work of Hardt and Negri paradoxically laid the ground for a renaissance in the theorization of imperialism, a renaissance that became all the more timely in the wake of the invasion and occupation of Iraq by the US and the UK in 2003. The justification of the war in terms of security and democracy, together with Iraq's massive oil resources, have inevitably spurred new attempts to link the economic and political aspects of imperialism. "Empire" is no longer used so much to designate a placeless system of power, and is frequently qualified as "American," leading to a renewal of the debate – prominent in the 1970s – over whether America's form of primarily non-territorial economic power and influence should be defined as imperialism. David Harvey and Ellen M. Wood, two prominent Marxist theorists, have answered in the affirmative. The first, following Giovanni Arrighi, argues that the "new imperialism" must be understood in terms of two conjoined but irreducible logics: a territorial logic of political power and a molecular logic of capital accumulation. He thus regards the war as a means of securing American hegemony over energy resources and thus bolstering its increasingly labile standing in the world economy. Wood, in what is perhaps the boldest restatement yet of the theory of imperialism, defines capitalist imperialism – as opposed to previous empires of property (China, Rome) and empires of commerce (Arab Muslim, Venetian, Dutch) – in terms of the detachment of economic from political power. However, this economic power demands for its hegemony and expansion the presence of a system of multiple states, and the more globally integrated the system, the greater the tendency to the hegemony of one of these states (i.e., the American "empire") over the task of maintaining the capitalist system. Updating the methods of historical materialism, Wood thus returns to the key theme already broached by Luxemburg: the intimate correlation between capital accumulation, on the one hand, and expansionist or interventionist militarism, on the other. In historical terms, the study of imperialism has also been reinvigorated by an attention to its interaction with ecological factors, namely in Mike Davis's groundbreaking research on the murderous exacerbation of famines by imperial policies in his *Late Victorian Holocausts*.

SEE ALSO: Capitalism; Colonialism (Neocolonialism); Cultural Imperialism; Marxism and Sociology; Neo-Marxism; Postcolonialism and Sport

REFERENCES AND SUGGESTED READINGS

Arrighi, G. (2005) Hegemony Unravelling. *New Left Review* 32/33: 23–80, 83–116.

Biel, R. (2000) *The New Imperialism: Crisis and Contradictions in North/South Relations*. Zed Books, London.

Brewer, A. (1980) *Marxist Theories of Imperialism: A Critical Survey*. Routledge, London.

Hardt, M. & Negri, A. (2000) *Empire*. Harvard University Press, Cambridge, MA.

Harvey, D. (2005) *The New Imperialism*. Oxford University Press, Oxford.

Mommsen, W. J. (1980) *Theories of Imperialism*. University of Chicago Press, Chicago.

Wood, E. M. (2005) *Empire of Capital*. Verso, London.

implosion

Karen Bettez Halnon

French postmodernist critic Jean Baudrillard's theory of implosion is one of social entropy, wherein he asserts that a consumer age of information, media, and mass media has ushered in an accelerated and coercive hyperproduction of meaning and information to the "irrational" and "terroristic" extent that all meaning, knowledge, and subjectivity, and the "social" itself, are neutralized and ultimately collapse. All that is left, he says, is an imploding "mass," described dramatically as "an in vacuo aggregation of individual particles, refuse of the social and of media impulses; an opaque nebula whose growing density absorbs all the surrounding energy and light rays, to collapse finally under its own weight" (Baudrillard 1983: 3–4). In other words, amid ubiquitous and proliferating media-generated information in a consumer society of simulacra and simulation, information ceases to be productive, in the sense of transformation of it by human subjects. It is destructive energy, producing even more implosive density, more mass. Best and Kellner (1991: 121) further summarize Baudrillard's theory of implosion, a basic point of reference for postmodern theory: "The social thus disappears and with it distinctions implode between classes, political ideologies, cultural forms, and between media semiurgy and the real itself ... Baudrillard is not only describing a series of implosions (that is, between politics and entertainment, capital and labour, or high and low culture) but is claiming that the society in its entirety is implosive."

Baudrillard claims that the only "imaginary referent" remaining in a world of simulacra and semiurgy are the non-subject, non-object "silent majorities," or the purely "crystal ball" statistical morbid remains of status groupings. The "singular function" of the silent majorities is to absorb all meaning, but not refract it. Stated otherwise, having "become bored and resentful of their constant bombardment with messages and the constant attempts to solicit them to buy, consume, work, vote, register an opinion, or participate in social life," the "masses thus become a sullen silent majority in which all meaning, messages, and solicitations implode as if sucked into a black hole" (Best & Kellner 1991: 121).

Baudrillard claims there is a "fantastic irony" in the muteness of the masses and their "exasperating endless conformity" (Baudrillard 1983: 33). While "at no time are the masses politically or historically engaged in a conscious manner" (p. 38), they have only one practice: a "collective retaliation," a "refusal to participate" (p. 14). Baudrillard says, for the inert, indifferent, passive masses, the only non-conscious "strategic resistance" to the present phase of the system is that of a "refusal of meaning ... the hyperconformist simulation of the very mechanisms of the system, which is a form of refusal and non-reception" (p. 108). Forestalling any interpretation of the defiantly apolitical, he says, "the denial of meaning has no meaning" (pp. 40–1).

Explicitly challenging both critical theory and psychoanalytic interpretations that claim mystification or alienation, or that develop schemas aimed at liberating oppressed or repressed subjects, Baudrillard says that implosion "is inevitable, and every effort to save the principles of

reality, of accumulation, of universality, the principles of evolution which extol expanding systems, is archaic, regressive or nostalgic" (p. 60). In particular, with the death of human subjectivity and the "social," Baudrillard's theory of implosion declares the end of sociology and sociological inquiry. However, if it is any consolation, the continuity of an intellectual elite that thinks, acts, and interprets (aimlessly) outside or above "silent majorities" is implicit in Baudrillard's theory of implosion.

SEE ALSO: Consumption; Consumption, Mass Consumption, and Consumer Culture; Consumption, Spectacles of; Hyperreality; Mass Culture and Mass Society; Postmodern Consumption; Postmodern Culture; Simulation and Virtuality

REFERENCES AND SUGGESTED READINGS

Baudrillard, J. (1975) *The Mirror of Production*. Trans. M. Poster. Telos Press, St. Louis, MO.
Baudrillard, J. (1983) *In the Shadow of the Silent Majorities, Or, The End of the Social and Other Essays*. Semiotext(e), New York.
Best, S. & Kellner, D. (1991) *Postmodern Theory: Critical Interrogations*. Guilford Press, New York.
Gergen, K. J. (1991) *The Saturated Self: Dilemmas of Identity in Contemporary Life*. Basic Books, New York.
McLuhan, M. & Fiore, Q. (1967) *The Medium is the MASSAGE: An Inventory of Effects*. Random House, New York.

impression formation

Christopher D. Moore

Impression formation is the process by which individuals perceive, organize, and ultimately integrate information to form unified and coherent situated impressions of others. Internalized expectations for situated events condition what information individuals deem is important and worthy of their attention. Further, these expectations condition how individuals interpret this information. In face-to-face interaction, social cues including others' physical appearance, verbal and non-verbal behavior, and the social setting in which the exchange takes place combine with information in perceivers' memories to influence the ways in which they initially form impressions of others and themselves. These initial impressions serve as the basis for subsequent attributions.

Key findings regarding impression formation come from a variety of theoretical literatures. Most notable are social cognition theories, expectation states theory, and affect control theory. Specifically, research in social cognition provides explanations of general information gathering and processing, expectation states theory offers additional insights with regard to information integration, while affect control theory highlights the importance of affective meanings to the process of impression formation and provides a testable mathematical calculus designed to predict its outcomes.

PERCEIVING SOCIAL INFORMATION

Once raw information about a social object is gathered, it is organized and integrated to form a coherent conceptual impression of the social object. Cognitive limitations in our capacity to both perceive and process information affect the impressions we form about others. Specifically, we are limited in what we can pay attention to in a social situation, and we also rely on cognitive shortcuts to quickly and efficiently manage the information that we do gather. In addition to cognitive limitations, our social experiences serve to form preexisting expectations for events that affect the nature of information we notice and how we then interpret it.

Most people believe that first impressions are very important. Research in social cognition and related subfields extends this view by highlighting how the temporal ordering influences the processing of social information. For example, a concept related to the importance of first impressions is the *primacy effect*. The primacy effect is said to have occurred when individuals weight information acquired early in an interaction more than later information.

While the process of impression formation begins with perception, it is important to also consider that individuals' preexisting internalized expectations for how they expect events to

unfold serve to sensitize them to specific features of situations over others. The relative degree of attention given by an individual to a specific social object is a measure of that object's *salience* to that person. An object's salience also stems from the relationship between it and the social context. Specifically, any characteristic about a social object/person that provides an observer with a basis to differentiate it from other similar objects or others (however categorized) may make that characteristic more salient, and thus more likely to be usable as a cue for defining said object/person. For example, the relative height of another is less salient if the observer is of approximately the same height as the other who is being observed, or if said other is in a room populated by similarly statured individuals.

Once individuals form preliminary impressions about others, the evaluation of new information is often subject to the *confirmation bias*. This bias is in operation when individuals seek out or disproportionately favor new information that confirms their existing views. As interactions continue, new pieces of information that "fit" within the initially evoked schema are readily used to elaborate and bolster it, while potentially disconfirming information is treated with suspicion. The outcome of this process, through which individuals form general attitudes toward others by weighting the salience of new information more favorably if it matches what they already "know," is called the *halo effect*.

Alternatively, information that is "old" or sparse (e.g., not bolstered by subsequent readily available confirming information for extended periods of time) may be supplanted by new challenging information. Specifically, the "newness" of information may be such that it makes it more likely for it to earn the attention of observers simply because it is part of the immediate local situation. Thus, not only can early information be disproportionately weighted in terms of an individual's impression formations, but the most recent items of information – those that are freshest in one's mind – may also carry more than their "fair share" of weight with respect to impression formation. When this occurs, it is called the *recency effect*. These effects are difficult to self-monitor and consciously control and they may be related to a wide range of other biases such as ethnocentrism, groupthink, and self-serving bias.

An illustration of how individuals form impressions of others is found in a classic research study conducted by Solomon Asch (1946). In this study, a number of people were shown a series of seven adjectives describing an unidentified person's personality characteristics. All conditions contained the following six adjectives – intelligent, skillful, industrious, determined, practical, and cautious – but varied on whether the seventh characteristic was either warm, cold, polite, or blunt. These adjectives represented the first (and only) pieces of information that the participants were given about the unidentified other. The participants were then asked to describe the person to which the list pertained by selecting from a list of other descriptors: generous, wise, happy, good-natured, reliable, and important. The goal of this study was to see if individuals form organized impressions of others based on a combination of what they perceive and what they then assume to be likely given that information. Asch found that the participants who were shown lists containing the trait "warm" were more likely to rate the unidentified person as generous, happy, and good-natured; whereas the participants who were shown the list containing the trait "cold" most often rated the unidentified person as stingy, unpopular, and unhappy. Further, when participants were shown either lists containing the traits "polite" or "blunt," their assessments of the unidentified person did not significantly differ. Asch concluded that hot and cold acted as *central organizing traits* with respect to how these individuals formulated their impressions of the unidentified person. These traits were especially important because they colored the participants' interpretation of other traits they also were shown such that the impressions they formed about the person the lists purportedly described were very different.

Individual traits are more than mere additive pieces of information; they are components that operate in relation to one another to form a gestalt picture of an individual. We do not perceive individuals as a collection of itemized traits, but rather these traits invoke images in their perceivers' minds of a complex assortment of meanings and expectations that then subsequently serves as the basis for further social

attributions. Asch referred to individuals' beliefs about how personality traits are related as *implicit personality theories*. These beliefs may also be thought of as trait schemas or personality stereotypes in that both of these terms also highlight the dynamic and abstract nature of these beliefs, as opposed to equating them only to a collection of specific traits.

ORGANIZING AND INTEGRATING SOCIAL INFORMATION

Expectation states theory provides a particularly useful and well-supported explanation of how the social information is aggregated into organized subsets to form impressions of self and others (Berger et al. 1992). Specifically, to explain the effects of multiple and sometimes contradictory pieces of social information in situations, these researchers argue that all salient status information is combined for each actor to form an aggregated expectation state, with the difference between the focal actor's and others' aggregated expectation states representing the focal actor's expectation (dis)advantage. In other words, all salient information is organized into subsets analogous to person-schemas, which then serve as the basis for the emergent status and influence arrangement of the group. Further, these researchers also demonstrate that an attenuation function operates with respect to additional pieces of supporting information such that at some point, for example, there is a diminishing independent effect for each additional piece of information favorable to group leaders' expected competence on their overall status in the group. Also, new information is likely to have a greater independent effect on status outcomes when presented in opposition to a field of contrary information than if it were presented alone.

Inconsistent information affects impressions in other ways. For example, changes in observers' evaluations of others may occur if they observe others behaving in ways that challenge their initial expectations for them. For example, if a presumably good and nice person behaves cruelly toward an also good but weaker other, an observer's evaluations of the first person in this case might be reassessed in light of this action unless the observer can somehow otherwise justify the act. Such a justification may involve adjustments to the observer's definition of the action itself (e.g., it was not really that violent and hurtful after all), or perhaps to the observer's definition of the presumably "good but weaker other" (e.g., he actually deserved the treatment). Notice how each of these strategies involves the reassessment of some information, be it that which comes from the local situation or that which resides in the observer's memory. Also note that the schemas upon which the observer's expectations are based do not change; rather, adjustments are made with respect to "fit" between what she observes in the local situation and how she cognitively categorizes it.

Affect control theory (ACT) offers a mathematical formalization of the impression formation process that synthesizes elements of symbolic interactionism and role theory. Our understanding of the impression formation process owes much to ACT. According to ACT, individuals see themselves and the others around them as participating in situations by enacting social roles. Each person forms his or her definition of the situation by assigning an identity label to self and others after comparing the readily observable characteristics that each person possesses with internalized cultural expectations for what identities are appropriate given the setting they are in. ACT quantifies the affective definitions of these assigned labels on three dimensions: evaluation (goodness versus badness), potency (powerfulness versus powerlessness), and activity (liveliness versus passiveness). These dimensions have been shown to capture the culture-specific sentiments that individual actors (A) form about self, behaviors (B), other social object/persons (O), and settings (S). The core ACT argument is that individual actors will try to create behaviors that maintain their symbolic meanings of A-B-O-S situations. Once an individual has defined the setting and the actors/objects in it, cultural rules pertaining to these definitions provide the basis from which she can form expectations for the events (behaviors) that are likely to occur between herself and the others in the situation.

When the meanings of events interpreted from individuals' own localized experiences do not match those they anticipate, given their definition of the situation, ACT predicts they will act to restore them. In particular, ACT researchers argue that social events create predictable changes in individual actors' feelings and impressions about the situation. The localized (transient) impressions individuals form in the context of situations are compared to their preexisting (fundamental) sentiments about the identities, behaviors, and setting that they are in. If events unfold such that individuals' experiences become out of line with their initial expectations for a situation, ACT predicts they will act to restore this balance. Importantly, ACT shows both how cognitive definitions of situations lead to impression formation, and how impressions from events can operate to maintain or change the definition of situations. Research in ACT has shown that this process applies to the meanings of the entire A-B-O-S situation.

ACT researchers often utilize a computer program, INTERACT, that contains several culture-specific dictionaries of sentiments and impression formation equations. This program automates the lengthy calculations involved in processing A-B-O-S situations. Separate impression formation equations for the United States, Canada, and Japan are currently available. For investigations into other cultures for which sentiment dictionaries are available (such as Germany), the United States impression formation equations are generally used by default.

A number of assumptions are incorporated into the impression formation equations. One of these assumptions is that individuals' impressions tend to be stable. The *stability principle* states that once situational elements have been labeled and impressions about the evaluation, potency, and activity (EPA) of the A-B-O-S elements have formed, those impressions tend to remain relatively stable and carry over into subsequent interactions. For example, the negative shift in the evaluation (E) dimension of an actor who does an evil deed, such as raping another, will be remembered by observers and cause them to continue to see the actor as bad after the event. When this principle is applied to the evaluation of actors' behavior, such as in the above example, it is called the *morality effect* (e.g., "good" or "bad" behaviors reflect evaluative "credits" or "demerits" toward actors' identities).

The *consistency principle* states that individuals tend to expect that the feelings they have about actors and their behaviors, or behaviors and targeted object-persons, will be congruent. When events unfold that pair actors or object-persons with inconsistently evaluated behaviors, observers tend to form corresponding negative impressions. For example, good actors are expected to perform good behaviors and good object-persons are supposed to receive good treatment (and vice versa). Thus, if an actor behaves cruelly (bad) toward a nice (good) other, the actor violates the consistency principle and is then seen as less good (note that this negative evaluation is also reinforced by the morality effect). However, the consistency principle also yields some non-intuitive predictions. For example, if a "bad" actor behaves generously toward a good and weak other, the actor may experience a marginally increased evaluation according to the morality effect, but the consistency principle suggests that the act may be seen as so out of character by observers that their subsequent suspicion of the actor may mitigate the otherwise positive evaluation from the behavior. In addition, actors who are seen as having much greater power over others are faced with a disincentive to actively use their power. Specifically, powerful actors who behave very powerfully toward weaker others appear as "bullies" and subsequently lose (possibly transfer) some of their perceived power. In other words, in order to maintain power, the consistency principle suggests that powerful actors should be sparing in their utilization of power. Further, if the evaluation (good versus bad) of a behavior is matched to the targeted object-person, the consistency principle suggests that the actor, behavior, and object-person will benefit from a slight increase in evaluation. On the other hand, when actors treat object-persons in ways that are not consistent with their evaluation, the evaluation of the actor, behavior, and object-person suffers a decrease. This effect seems to provide a global incentive for situated actors to "play by the normative rules" for the collective good (assuming that achieving a more positive evaluation operates as an incentive for most actors). Finally, a range of *congruency effects* further explains how specific pairs of different EPA dimensions combine to form impressions. For example, behaving nicely toward weaker others will make actors seem merciful (more good), while behaving nicely toward more powerful others can make actors appear as flatterers (less good). Similarly, acting powerfully toward evil others will make actors seem righteous (more good), while acting "too" powerfully toward very nice others makes actors seem indecorous (less good).

The tendency of observers to accord more or less goodness to actors who behave in ways that result in an equilibrium state with respect to the evaluation and/or potency dimensions of all three core event elements (A-B-O) is called the *balance effect*. Using an equilibrium criterion consistent with cognitive balance theory, ACT posits that if the product of the combined valences (+/−) of an A-B-O structure is even (e.g., all three are + or any two are −), then the actor will be seen as more good. When applied to the evaluation (E) dimension of an A-B-O structure, this effect either reinforces or mitigates consistency effects based on evaluation (e.g., the effect enhances the consistency effect when object-person is good and mitigates it when object-person is bad). Also, when applied to the potency (P) dimension, the balance effect suggests that when powerful actors act potently toward powerful others, or when weak others act sheepishly toward similarly powerless others, they seem less nice. Interestingly, when powerful others direct potent acts toward weaker others, they and the targeted others seem more good (the latter reinforced by the consistency principle if the object-person was not viewed as highly good beforehand) – but in doing so, powerful actors take the risk of losing some of their power (if the act is "too powerful") according to the consistency principle.

SEE ALSO: Affect Control Theory; Attribution Theory; Cognitive Balance Theory (Heider); Cognitive Dissonance Theory (Festinger); Expectation States Theory; Facework; Identity: Social Psychological Aspects; Mead, George Herbert; Social Cognition

REFERENCES AND SUGGESTED READINGS

Asch, S. E. (1946) Forming Impressions of Personality. *Journal of Abnormal and Social Psychology* 41: 258–90.

Berger, J., Fisek, M. H., Norman, R. Z., & Zelditch, M., Jr. (1977) Status Characteristics and Expectation States: A Graph-Theoretic Formulation. In: Berger, J. et al., *Status Characteristics and Social Interaction*. Elsevier, New York, pp. 91–134.

Berger, J., Norman, R. Z., Balkwell, J. W., & Smith, R. F. (1992) Status Inconsistency in Task Situations: A Test of Four Status Processing Principles. *American Sociological Review* 57: 843–55.

Heise, D. R. (1979) *Understanding Events: Affect and the Construction of Social Action*. Cambridge University Press, New York.

MacKinnon, N. J. (1994) *Symbolic Interactionism as Affect Control*. SUNY Press, Albany.

Morgan, D. L. & Schwalbe, M. L. (1990) Mind and Self in Society: Social Structure and Social Cognition. *Social Psychology Quarterly* 53: 148–64.

Smith-Lovin, L. & Heise, D. R. (1988) *Analyzing Social Interaction: Advances in Affect Control Theory*. Gordon & Breach, New York. (Reprint of a special issue of the *Journal of Mathematical Sociology* 13.)

income inequality, global

Glenn Firebaugh

Income inequality refers to the unequal distribution of income across units (usually individuals). *Global* income inequality refers to the unequal distribution of income across the world's citizens.

Global income inequality consists of income inequality across nations and income inequality within nations. Income inequality across nations, or *between-nation income inequality*, refers to the unequal distribution of *average* income across nations. Income inequality within nations refers to the unequal distribution of income across individual units (individuals or households) within countries. Traditionally, sociologists have focused on within-nation inequality: on why inequality is higher in some nations, on the consequences of high (and low) inequality, and on why inequality changes, where "change in income inequality" refers to change in the *ratios* of individuals' incomes. If everyone's income doubles, so an income of $100 is boosted to $200 and an income of $1,000 is boosted to $2,000, inequality remains constant because the income ratio remains fixed at 10 to 1. Standard inequality measures, such as the Gini index, are based on the ratio concept of inequality (Allison 1978), and that is the concept of inequality used here.

Recently there has been a surge of interest in income inequality across nations, or between-nation inequality. This new attention to between-nation inequality reflects (1) a growing recognition that between-nation inequality is the larger component of global income inequality; (2) more reliable data on national incomes; and (3) debate over whether between-nation income inequality is now declining and, if so, whether the decline is steep enough to drive down global inequality as well.

First, with regard to between-nation inequality as a component of global inequality, suppose we eliminated all inequality within countries by moving all incomes to the income mean within each country. How much global inequality would remain? The surprising answer is, "most of it." Because of huge income disparities between the world's richest and poorest regions, most global income inequality lies across countries, not within them (Goesling 2001).

The prominence of between-nation inequality in today's world reflects profound spatial unevenness in income growth during the nineteenth century and first half of the twentieth century. During this period the world divided into three income camps as the industrializing West surged ahead economically and Asia and Africa lagged badly behind. Incomes in a middle group, consisting of most of Latin America and Eastern Europe (including the former Soviet Union), grew at roughly the world average. Because it was the richer regions that were growing faster, this unevenness in growth rates resulted in the massive inequality in income across regions and nations that we see today.

The legacy of the Industrial Revolution, then, is that of a world of much higher average income (Maddison 1995) much more unevenly distributed (Pritchett 1997). The growth in global inequality over this period was due entirely to growing inequality across countries since within-nation income inequality declined over most of the period (Bourguignon & Morrisson 2002).

In recent decades, however, income inequality has declined across nations and increased in the average nation, resulting in a "new geography" of global income inequality (Firebaugh 2003) where nationality is becoming less important in the determination of one's income. There is little consensus on why inequality has increased recently in many nations (but not all nations); the reasons are complex and likely vary from country to country. By contrast, the major source of declining inequality across nations is clear (Firebaugh & Goesling 2004): faster than world average income growth in many of the world's most populous poor nations in Asia. Although incomes continue to decline relatively (and in some instances absolutely) in many poor nations in Sub-Saharan Africa, many more poor *individuals* live in poor nations where incomes are growing faster than the world average than in poor nations where incomes are growing slower than average. The result is declining income inequality across countries.

There is less consensus over the direction of the global trend since the global trend represents the net effect of two trends going in opposite directions. While some studies conclude that global inequality is declining because the decline across nations more than offsets the increase within nations (Firebaugh 2003: Table 11.1), others conclude that the global trend is indeterminate because some income series yield different results. The recent downward trend in between-nation income inequality is steeper when one uses conventional national account (production) data than when one uses household survey data on consumption, and that can affect conclusions about the global trend. With regard to the within-nation trend, estimates suffer from the lack of systematic data collection on income inequality for many nations, including some large nations. Aside from the problem of missing data, extant data are often inconsistent with regard to whether they are based on pre-tax or post-tax income, on whether the units are individuals or households, and on whether a probability sample was used.

The major challenge for future research on global inequality is data reliability. The measurement issues are pretty well settled: there is general consensus on how to measure income, and on how to measure and decompose income inequality. But our measurements and decompositions are only as reliable as the data we input, and that is where much of the effort should be expended in future research on global income inequality.

SEE ALSO: Income Inequality and Income Mobility; Inequality, Wealth; Stratification and Inequality, Theories of

REFERENCES AND SUGGESTED READINGS

Allison, P. (1978) Measures of Inequality. *American Sociological Review* 43: 865–80.

Bourguignon, F. & Morrisson, C. (2002) Inequality Among World Citizens: 1820–1992. *American Economic Review* 92: 727–44.

Firebaugh, G. (2003) *The New Geography of Global Income Inequality*. Harvard University Press, Cambridge, MA.

Firebaugh, G. & Goesling, B. (2004) Accounting for the Recent Decline in Global Income Inequality. *American Journal of Sociology* 110: 283–312.

Goesling, B. (2001) Changing Income Inequalities Within and Between Nations: New Evidence. *American Sociological Review* 66: 745–61.

Maddison, A. (1995) *Monitoring the World Economy 1820–1992*. OECD, Paris.

Pritchett, L. (1997) Divergence, Big Time. *Journal of Economic Perspectives* 11: 3–17.

income inequality and income mobility

Wout Ultee

Research on income inequality within the social sciences took off as a byproduct of income taxation. Lists were published showing how many tax-paying units during a tax year had an income of a certain size. The distribution did not look like a bell-shaped curve, but was skewed at the upper end. The description of the distribution by one parameter started with Vilfredo Pareto, and his results led to the hypothesis that this statistic was more or less the same for all times and places. Later results, using better measures like the Gini-coefficient, found differences between countries, leading to a hunt for explanations. Due to the efforts of the World Bank and the Luxemburg Income Study, quite comparable income inequality data for various countries are now available, so that hypotheses-testing is possible.

Sociologists proposed basically two explanations for country-level differences in income inequality. The first invokes economic factors, the second political ones. It has been held that in more economically developed countries income inequalities are smaller. Similarly, it has also been proposed that countries with a more peripheral (as opposed to central) place in the world economy have larger income inequalities. As to political factors, it has been maintained that in highly industrialized societies a long democratic history as well as a social democratic government, by way of various policies, have diminished income inequalities. Among these policies are progressive taxation, free secondary and tertiary education for all, and collective insurance against such matters as unemployment, work-related disabilities, and old age.

By way of quite simple comparisons and more sophisticated statistical techniques, these hypotheses have generally proved their mettle. An important issue is exactly how income inequalities are measured and what hypotheses say about effects on this or that measure. According to some hypotheses, a democratic state is like Robin Hood: the state takes from the really rich and gives to the poorest of the poor. This hypothesis may be tested by using one measure of a country's income distribution, such as the Gini-coefficient. Other theories take a closer look as what democracy is all about. If the members of a governing coalition wish to enrich themselves, they exclude the richest persons in a society from governing. So a redistribution from the rich to the rest will occur. But to exactly whom? Not only to the poorest of the poor, since the coalition governing a democratic state comprises at least 51 percent of the population, and the richest members of the coalition want a piece of the pie, too. Upon opposition from the poorest of the poor, the richest members of the coalition may threaten to blow up the coalition, leaving the poorest of the poor nothing at all. This is the theory of the strategic middle proposed by Gordon Tullock. If it is to be tested, an overall measure for income inequality in a country (like the Gini-coefficient) will not do. Data on the income share of, say, the poorest and the richest 10 percent and 20 percent of the population are also necessary. The Robin Hood hypothesis in its strongest form predicts that upon the introduction of democracy the income share of the two richest decile groups will go down, and the income share of the poorest deciles will go up, with the decrease of the former as large as the increase of the latter. The hypothesis of the strategic middle predicts a decrease for the richest deciles and an increase for the poorest deciles only if parties representing the interests of the poor are part of the governing coalition.

If some measure for the inequalities in income for all the households of a country does not change in the course of time, this of course does not mean that the income of all these households remained the same. It is not difficult to imagine that higher income inequality within a country goes together with more income mobility. Until recently, data on income mobility calculated over a longer time span were rare, but with the implementation of panel surveys by statistical agencies more data are becoming available. They mainly have been analyzed by economists.

Sociologists have studied data on intergenerational mobility along a scale of occupational status. Blau and Duncan (1967) examined data from the US and found a correlation between father and son's occupational status of 0.4 (with zero indicating no correlation and unity full correlation and the strongest possible determination of son's by father's occupational status). When reviewing Blau and Duncan's results, an economist suggested that occupational status as measured by sociologists is a reasonably good indicator of permanent income: not a person's income during one particular year, but a person's income calculated over a longer period. The interesting question is to what extent occupational correlations agree with data from long-running income panels.

Earlier data from non-representative samples in the US take single-year earnings of fathers and sons, with father's earnings observed when the son was still in the parental home and son's earnings some decades after leaving it showing correlations below 0.2. Later studies used data from the Panel Study of Income

Dynamics, conducted annually since 1968 in the US. The data for father's earnings pertain to around 1970, with those for son's earnings around 1985. Age restrictions were applied so as to bypass the earnings of sons when they were under 30 years of age, when earnings supposedly are highly variable. This time the intergenerational correlation in single-year earnings of fathers and sons was 0.3. Taking father's earnings not as a single year measure, but as the average of 5 years, increased the correlation to 0.4. Averaging son's earnings over 5 years too, the correlation approached 0.5. These findings on income mobility indicate that correlations between father and son's occupational status are not far off the mark and definitely not too high.

Apart from depicting the US as a much less mobile society than earlier income mobility data indicated, comparisons of US intergenerational income mobility data with those of other countries do not seem to show particularly low correlations for the US. Research on Finland and Sweden using 3-year annual average earnings for fathers and sons found correlations closer to 0.1 than to 0.2. Strict comparisons of a large number of countries remain a promise for the future, but it does seem that, for highly industrialized countries, low inequality in yearly income goes together with high income mobility.

SEE ALSO: Educational Attainment; Income Inequality, Global; Inequality, Wealth; Intergenerational Mobility: Core Model of Social Fluidity; Intergenerational Mobility: Methods of Analysis; Mobility: Intergenerational and Intragenerational; Occupational Mobility

REFERENCES AND SUGGESTED READINGS

Blau, P. & Duncan, O. D. (1967) *The American Occupational Structure*. Wiley, New York.
Esping-Andersen, G. & van Kersbergen, K. (1992) Contemporary Research on Social Democracy. *Annual Review of Sociology* 18: 187–208.
Gagliani, G. (1987) Income Inequality and Economic Development. *Annual Review of Sociology* 13: 314–34.
Pen, J. (1971) *Income Distribution*. Penguin, London.
Solon, G. (1992) Intergenerational Income Mobility in the United States. *American Economic Review* 82: 393–408.
Solon, G. (2002) Cross-Country Differences in Intergenerational Earnings Mobility. *Journal of Economic Perspectives* 16(3): 59–66.
Tullock, G. (1986) *The Economics of Wealth and Poverty*. Harvester, Brighton.

index crime

Robert F. Meier

Index crimes are a series of eight crimes – murder and nonnegligent homicide, forcible rape, aggravated assault, robbery, burglary, larceny-theft, motor vehicle theft, and arson – about which police agencies report to the Federal Bureau of Investigation (FBI). They have been an important source of information about crime for more then three-quarters of a century. They are also an important part of a larger crime reporting program called the Uniform Crime Reports (UCR).

The UCR began in 1930 when police chiefs in various cities began to experience difficulties in keeping up with crime on a national basis. With greater use of the automobile in the 1920s, criminals were able to commit crimes over a larger geographic area. Offenders could commit a major crime in, say, Chicago in the morning, in Des Moines in the afternoon, and in Omaha that evening. Clearly, effective police efforts required more information about crime in other communities than had existed up to this time. In the late 1920s, the International Association of Chiefs of Police requested the FBI to serve as a collection agency for crime statistics. The plan was for police departments to send their information to the FBI which, in turn, would collate the information and publish the figures annually.

The UCR publishes its annual report, *Crime in the United States*, each year. The report contains information about crime for the preceding calendar year. Among the statistical information contained in the report is information about crimes known to the police, characteristics of persons who are arrested for those crimes, and data about police officers. The crime statistics are broken down into major geographic areas and specific jurisdictions (cities and counties) within states. The annual report is largely a compilation of tables containing this information.

The UCR crime statistics are the result of a voluntary reporting system. No police department is *required* to submit information, but the great majority of all departments – state police, sheriff's offices, municipal police departments, federal police agencies, and even university and college campus police departments – do report their information for publication in the UCR. Police agencies covering about 94 percent of the population submit statistics on a monthly basis for the reporting system.

The FBI recognized that not all crimes could be included in the UCR, so they distinguished between two categories of offenses. The original Part I crimes were a list of seven offenses, all felonies that were thought to represent an "index" of crime in the US. For this reason, they are often referred to as the Index Crimes. The original index crimes were homicide, aggravated assault, forcible rape, robbery, burglary, larceny, and auto theft. In 1979 arson was added as an eighth index offense, although information in the UCR is still sketchy about this newest index crime, more than 20 years after it was added. The Part II offenses are a collection of about 27 offenses about which some but not all information is recorded. In terms of detailed information, the emphasis in the UCR is on the Part I or index crimes.

Murder and nonnegligent manslaughter is defined as the willful (nonnegligent) murder of one human being by another. As with the other index crimes, the determination of this crime is made by police investigation only, not other means (e.g., coroner, medical examiner).

Forcible rape, as defined by the UCR, is the carnal knowledge of a female forcibly and against her will. Neither assaults of male victims nor statutory rape cases are included.

Robbery is defined as taking or attempting to take anything of value from the care of another person through force or threat of force.

Aggravated assault is an unlawful attack by one person on another with the purpose of inflicting severe or aggravating injuries. Usually, such assaults involve a weapon. Also included in this crime are threats of severe injury.

Burglary is defined in the UCR as the unlawful entry into a structure for the purpose of committing a theft or felony. Actual theft is not required and attempts are considered burglaries. Force is not required.

Larceny-theft is defined as stealing property of another. There are many different kinds of thefts, such as shoplifting, purse snatching, and bicycle thefts. Specifically excluded from this crime category are embezzlement, confidence games, forgery, and worthless checks. Motor vehicle theft is also excluded since it is another index crime.

Motor vehicle theft is defined as the stealing of a motor vehicle or its parts. Included are thefts of cars, trucks, motorcycles, and buses. Specifically excluded are thefts of vehicles which do not intend to deprive owners of their vehicles permanently, such as joy riding.

Arson is defined as the willful burning of property with the intent to defraud. Arson is defined as the result of an investigation and those fires that are considered only suspicious are not included.

Surely, if one is interested only in characteristics of persons who are arrested, the UCR is the best single source for this information. Criminologists, however, are often more interested in the amount of real crime in the community, and in this regard the UCR is inadequate.

SEE ALSO: Age and Crime; Homicide; Measuring Crime; Property Crime; Race and Crime; Rape/Sexual Assault as Crime; Robbery; Sex and Crime; Violent Crime

REFERENCES AND SUGGESTED READINGS

Federal Bureau of Investigation (2004) *Crime in the United States.* Government Printing Office, Washington, DC.
Mosher, C. J., Miethe, T. D., & Phillips, D. (2002) *The Mismeasure of Crime.* Sage, Thousand Oaks, CA.

indigenous movements

David Anthony Tyeeme Clark

From the homelands of aboriginal peoples in Canada's Northwest Territories to indigenous territories in four Andean countries – Peru,

Ecuador, Bolivia, and Colombia – indigenous peoples have demanded self-governing political institutions, asserted their rights to a greater measure of cultural self-determination, and reacquired legal control over their own territories and resources. While throughout the Americas certain indigenous peoples have reestablished land ownership, gained official recognition of indigenous forms of government and justice, got elected to public office, and, in some cases, established independent regions, at the same time, others are losing their fragile control over lands, waters, and other resources, as well as their access to sacred sites. Market-driven global processes, supported by state-sponsored efforts often led by the United States, are deepening environmental deterioration and increasing poverty among natives, seriously deterring the possibility of sustainable indigenous societies and nations well into the future.

In response, indigenous peoples are continuing old fights as well as mounting new forms of resistance and grassroots mobilization. Throughout the Americas, indigenous peoples are resisting state violence and subtle coercion. While often concerned with defending recently reacquired autonomy, the political and economic conjuncture brought on by market-oriented globalization has forced indigenous peoples to engage in new fights for survival.

The efforts of Indians in Latin America, for instance, have gained momentum in the last decade as government policies based on assimilation and paternalism are replaced with new approaches founded on participation and consensus building and a respect for the aspirations of indigenous peoples. In less than a decade, indigenous movements in Latin American countries have toppled two presidents and left their distinctive mark on parliaments, ministries, municipal governments, and even a vice presidency. There are nearly 50 million indigenous individuals among a total Latin American population of 400 million.

In some cases, governments have responded to indigenous movements with broad-based state-sponsored violence, such as in Ecuador in 1992 and 1994 where indigenous peoples constitute 3.5 million – 25 percent – of the total population. In Mexico, with 10 million indigenes, the Ejército Zapatista de Liberación Nacional took up arms against the Mexican government in 1994 to demand access to the institutions of democracy and justice. As a result of their armed resistance that, along with other factors, destabilized the political system dominated since 1929 by the Institutional Revolutionary Party (PRI), in 2000 Mexico for the first time in over 70 years swore in a non-PRI government.

In many cases, grassroots efforts have achieved success without bloodshed. For instance, the Aymara leader Víctor Hugo Cárdenas was Bolivian vice president from 1993 to 1997. Cárdenas has called on his allies to "go beyond legal and institutional changes and transform the entire culture surrounding policies on indigenous people, including the attitudes of national elites and bureaucracies." In Brazil, indigenous peoples have worked with government leaders to set aside lands not as reservations where the government attempts to "civilize" hunters and gatherers, but where the government serves to keep loggers, gold miners, and other intruders out of indigenous lands.

Contemporary indigenous movements, appearing in response to unevenly institutionalized reforms, pose a serious challenge to emerging democracies. These movements have sparked political debates and constitutional reforms over community rights, territorial autonomy, and multi-ethnic citizenry. Throughout the Americas – from Canada to Latin America – indigenous peoples remain as concerned as ever with safeguarding indigenous forms of government and governing, wresting control of resources away from states and state-protected corporations, protecting sacred sites, and revitalizing indigenous languages and cultures.

Indigenous governments and governing. In Bolivia, for instance, indigenous peoples who make up 55 percent of the total population control 35 percent of the country's municipalities – 311 in total. Local leaders set their own priorities and administer local financial resources. In the Mexican state of Oaxaca, residents of 412 of the state's 570 municipalities chose their leaders in open assemblies of elders, rather than by ballot. The communities also run their own criminal justice systems. In the northern border state of Sonora, 33,000 Yaquis are represented by their own governor and council of elders, enforce their own laws, and exercise jurisdictional rights over a 1,880 square mile territory in the southeast portion of the state.

Control of resources. In the United States, the Native American Rights Fund (NARF) is a non-profit organization that provides legal representation and technical assistance to tribes, organizations, and individuals nationwide. In recent years on the Pine Ridge Reservation in South Dakota, for instance, NARF has supported the Oglala struggle with unsafe drinking water, crumbling sewage systems operating without EPA permits, and widespread pollution of primary streams which are both unregulated and unmonitored. A 1994 survey of 149 tribes conducted by the National Tribal Environmental Council for NARF revealed that tribes face an array of environmental problems. More than 75 tribes reported polluted or insufficient drinking water.

Sacred sites. For decades, a growing number of American Indians have been alarmed by the desecration and destruction of sacred sites and have advocated for increased protection. Dozens of sacred sites, including Dzil Nchaa Si An in central Arizona and the home of the sacred deity Ma'l Oyattsik'i at Zuni Salt Lake in New Mexico, remain in 2005 the focus of ongoing struggles by indigenous activists and elders, as well as environmentalists and religious organizations concerned about protecting the spiritual welfare of indigenous peoples.

Indigenous languages and cultures. In the United States there is an "English-Only" political movement that questions the value of teaching languages other than English, including indigenous languages. Identifying language loss among their greatest challenges, indigenous peoples have responded in a variety of ways. In Hawai'i, for instance, the 'Aha Punana Leo grew in 1983 from a pioneer group of language nest immersion preschools into a non-profit Native Hawaiian family-based 501(c)(3) tax-exempt educational organization dedicated to reinstituting Hawaiian as a daily, living language.

Indigenous peoples of the Americas are not alone. Indigenous movements representing hope for the future are visible in Africa, Asia, and Europe, as well as among Pacific Island populations including those in Australia and New Zealand.

SEE ALSO: Colonialism (Neocolonialism); Culture, Social Movements and; Decolonization; Ethnic, Racial, and Nationalist Movements; Indigenous Peoples; Paternalism; Recognition

REFERENCES AND SUGGESTED READINGS

Dean, B. C. & Levi, J. M. (Eds.) (2003) *At the Risk of Being Heard: Identity, Indigenous Rights, and Post-colonial States.* University of Michigan Press, Ann Arbor.

LaDuke, W. (2005) *Recovering the Sacred: The Power of Naming and Claiming.* South End Press, Boston.

Mihesuah, D. A. (2003) *Indigenous American Women: Decolonization, Empowerment, Activism.* University of Nebraska Press, Lincoln.

Niezen, R. (2003) *The Origins of Indigenism: Human Rights and the Politics of Identity.* University of California Press, Berkeley.

Warren, K. B. & Jackson, J. E. (Eds.) (2003) *Indigenous Movements, Self-Representation, and the State in Latin America.* University of Texas Press, Austin.

indigenous peoples

Thomas D. Hall and Joane Nagel

Throughout most of the nineteenth and twentieth centuries, scholars and policymakers predicted the disappearance of Native Americans and indigenous peoples in general (see Dippie 1982 for many examples). Global patterns of urbanization, industrialization, and resource extraction indeed have led to a reduction in the number of indigenous people living traditional lifestyles on ancestral lands. However, those who predicted the demise of indigenousness did not anticipate the global resurgence of indigenous consciousness, political mobilization, and cultural renewal of the past several decades (Wilmer 1993; Nagel 1996; Bodley 1994, 2003; Hall & Fenelon 2004). Indigenous groups in North and South America, Australia and New Zealand, Central Europe and Central Asia, Asia and Africa are making land claims, petitioning for political rights, and demanding control of resources; many are doing so with remarkable success given their limited votes, money, or military capacity. To illustrate the resurgence in indigenous identities, communities, and cultures, after a brief discussion of terminology and the sociological significance of studying indigenous peoples, we focus here on contemporary demographic, economic, and political trends among Native Americans.

We use the term "indigenous" to refer to those peoples who either live or have lived within the past several centuries in nonstate societies, though virtually all indigenous communities are located within state societies. We note that the diversity of types of nonstate societies is far greater than the diversity of states. Attempts to organize this diversity have generated a plethora of terms: clans, bands, macrobands, tribelets, tribes, chiefdoms, segmentary lineages, etc. (see Chase-Dunn & Hall 1997).

The term "tribe" is one of the most common designations for indigenous peoples, but it is also one of the most controversial because of its connotation of primitiveness and savagery. Despite its baggage, the term "tribe" has political utility for those peoples who inhabited North America before Europeans arrived, since the tribe–nation distinction often has been used politically to support or to deny autonomy or sovereignty for indigenous groups and because some indigenous communities informally and officially refer to themselves as tribes, though many have replaced "tribe" with "nation." Even "Native American" can be problematic, since legally, anyone born in the United States is a "native" [born] American. We use "indigenous" peoples or communities throughout this discussion, and for peoples indigenous to North America, we alternate among Native Americans, American Indians, native, or Indian.

When referring to a specific indigenous community, we use the name of the group, but we note that official names are political and historical constructions that do not necessarily reflect some prior, pristine indigeneity. For instance, there are the historical accidents of naming and the vagaries of spelling that stemmed from colonial powers' lack of clear understanding of indigenous languages. Sometimes a name derived from a derogatory term, while other changes mark indigenous peoples' efforts to reclaim their name in their own language, such as Diné for Navajo, Ho-Chunk for Winnebago, or Tohono O'odham for Papago.

Changes and disputes over indigenous peoples' names stem also from historical changes in group boundaries in response to internal processes or encounters with outsiders. In early contact periods with Europeans, North American native peoples often shared a broad sense of identity but were not ruled by any single social or political organization (Cornell 1988). The need for unified resistance to European, then American, encroachments led to the formation of socio-political structures that encompassed new groupings of individuals and communities. Out of these alliances new names and identities emerged.

The modern organization of many historical indigenous cultures and communities has arisen, ironically, from efforts to destroy them, either by outright genocide, the devastations of disease, by assimilation into European societies, or by merger or amalgamation with other indigenous groups. At times these amalgamated communities were examples of "ethnogenesis," i.e., the creation of new ethnic groups whose contemporary names may or may not reflect their historical origins. In fact, a great deal of ethnographic and ethnohistorical research shows that the symbolic, demographic, and social boundaries of nonstate groups are extremely permeable (Brooks 2002). This suggests that the presumption of fixed, clear, rigid boundaries or borders is an artifact of contact with European states – the expectations of outsiders about the timeless nature of indigeneity and the needs of European and later postcolonial negotiators to identify "leaders" of native societies for purposes of treaty-making and land acquisition.

Indigenous peoples are of special interests to sociology and to sociologists for several reasons. First, in the United States, the Americas, and in many other countries, indigenous peoples comprised the earliest human settlements and interactions with indigenous peoples by immigrant or colonial populations were important in shaping contemporary legal, cultural, political, economic, and social organization. In many countries indigenous peoples are central to national images of past and present and components of ethnically diverse national populations. Thus, despite their relatively small numbers, they should be included in any general discussion of race or ethnicity, particularly since the historical treatment and contemporary status of native peoples are central to national questions of group rights, nation formation, justice, group formation, group transformation, and social change.

The study of indigenous peoples represents an invaluable opportunity for theory building and evaluation since indigenous peoples represent a wide variety of social structures that are not found among immigrant or settler groups. In the United States, the varieties of indigenous languages, kinship structures, political organization, or cultural formations present unique opportunities for understanding human pasts and presents. Further, since the founding of the United States, Native Americans have had a unique political and social relationship with the US government. They are the only ethnic community with legal rights connected directly to the federal government, rights that bypass county, city, and state governmental authority. This "government-to-government" tribal–federal relationship generates many politically and sociologically interesting interactions and exceptions that have led to controversies about gaming, Indian hunting and fishing rights, or the right to sell gasoline or tobacco on reservations without charging state taxes (see Bays & Fouberg 2002).

Finally, consideration of indigenous peoples is vital to understanding long-term social change and social evolution. On the one hand, omitting such groups biases the sample. On the other hand, it is erroneous to assume indigenous people, even those who live "traditionally," are models or "living artifacts" of earlier societies. Contemporary indigenous peoples have survived centuries, and in parts of Asia, millennia of contact and interaction with state societies. Their contemporary social structures have been shaped by their responses to those interactions. Ferguson and Whitehead (1992) caution against too much reliance on historical "first-contact" accounts for information about change in indigenous societies. This is because intergroup contacts change both societies so profoundly that even the earliest first-hand accounts must be approached with considerable skepticism. By the time a representative of a literate state society observes an indigenous group, typically

there already has been considerable prior contact and consequent social change. Thus, while first-hand accounts can be useful, they cannot be presumed to be unbiased snapshots of the pre-contact past. The rate of change resulting from intergroup contact in North America, for example, has led scholars to be cautious about assuming the accuracy of early nineteenth-century depictions of western US tribes by Meriwether Lewis and William Clark (see Fenelon & Defender-Wilson 2004).

CONTEMPORARY INDIGENOUS AMERICAN ISSUES AND TRENDS

The demography of indigenous peoples is another complex topic. First is the politics of numbers and their uses. Stiffarm and Lane (1992) argue that there is a tendency to underestimate the population of the Americas prior to European contact in order to minimize the decimation of the indigenous population. While estimates for the indigenous population of North American (US and Canada) range from 1 million to 30 million, Thornton (1987) argues for a figure in the neighborhood of 7 million, based on careful reconstruction of population densities, early population counts, and the effects of known epidemics. Native populations declined drastically, but not exclusively, from "old world" diseases. Native populations in the United States reached a nadir of about one-quarter million around the turn of the twentieth century. Since then the Native American population has grown so that, at the beginning of the twenty-first century, it is well over 2 million – between one-third and one-half of what it was in 1492. It is important to note that more than disease was involved in the depopulation of indigenous Americans; colonial and US land policies, population removals, and wars took on genocidal proportions and were major factors in the steep population decline.

Population recovery since World War II has been considerable: from 1960 to 1970 the number of Americans who reported their race to be "American Indian" in the US census grew 51 percent (from 523,591 to 792,730); from 1970 to 1980, the American Indian population grew faster, 72 percent (to 1,364,033); from 1980 to 1990, the American Indian population increased 37 percent (to 1,878,285); and from 1990 to 2000, the American Indian population increased 26 percent (to 2,366,639). The increase is due to improved enumeration techniques, a decrease in death rates, and an increasingly willingness of individuals to identify themselves as Native American. Native Americans intermarry with other groups more than any other ethnic group, giving rise to three different categories of "Indians": (1) "American Indians," persons who claim to be Indian racially and have a specific tribal identification; (2) "American Indians of multiple ancestry," persons who claim to be Indian racially, but who have significant non-Indian ancestry; and (3) "Americans of Indian descent," who do *not* claim to be Indian racially, but who report an Indian component in their background (Snipp 1986). This gives rise to questions about membership in Indian tribes and definitions of who is and is not "Indian" by tribal governments, federal officials, and Indian communities and individuals. The financial successes of some native communities (e.g., due to gaming or natural resources) makes identity an economic issue as well.

Urbanization, intermarriage, education, and increased participation in the paid labor force since World War II have spurred the most politically active period in American Indian history: formation of activist organizations such as the American Indian Movement and Women of All Red Nations, legal defense organizations such as Native American Rights Fund and Native Action, and lobbying groups such as National Congress of American Indians and National Tribal Chairmen's Association. These organizations comprised a backdrop and, in some cases, the infrastructure for Indian rights movements in cities and on reservations that took root and blossomed in the fertile political soil of the civil rights era in the US. Beginning in the 1960s, American Indians staged a variety of protest events: "fish-ins" in the Pacific Northwest in the mid-1960s, the 19-month occupation of Alcatraz Island beginning in 1969, the 71-day siege at Wounded Knee on the Pine Ridge Reservation in South Dakota in 1973, the occupation of Camp Yellow Thunder in the Black Hills in the 1980s, and protests against Indian athletic mascots since the 1980s. Out of such protests and the legal battles they gave rise to came a new "self-determination"

era in federal Indian policy. This opened the way to increased tribal control of budgets and decision-making, to the development of tribally owned natural resources, to the establishment of casinos and gaming on tribal land, and to opportunities for self-rule and economic development by Indian communities. These changes, in turn, have raised questions about how Native Americans fit into United States society.

In the twentieth century, access to wealth from mineral resources, gaming, and tourism has helped economic development on reservations and in American Indian communities. Although Snipp (1988) has shown that the differences between energy resource Indian nations and those without such resources tend to be minimal, gaming has brought profits and change to many native communities (Jorgensen 1998; Napoli 2002). A key problem facing Native American nations has been how to participate in economic development without undermining traditional Indian values (Cornell & Kalt 1992, 2005). The tension between development and tradition also are central to debates in many indigenous communities globally (Wilmer 1993; Gedicks 2001).

Economic development and the practice and preservation of traditional cultures are enmeshed in two important contemporary issues facing American Indians: the internal and external consequences of gaming as a strategy of economic development in Indian communities and non-native interest in American Indian spiritual practices. Because of their special relationship with the US federal government, reservation governments are able to sponsor gaming, to sell gasoline and cigarettes without paying local and state taxes, and to sell other typically locally or state-interdicted or regulated products such as fireworks. The growth of Indian casinos and the desire of non-Indian governments and businesses to compete with Indian enterprises, which they see as having unfair tax advantages, has spawned social movements that are nominally anti-gaming, but are often thinly disguised anti-Indian movements. In some cases they reflect conflicts of interest among local non-Indians, Indians, and local and state governments. Similar non-Indian opposition has resulted from renewed Indian land claims (such as by the Passamaquoddies in Maine in the 1980s and the Oneidas in New York in the 1990s).

These controversies have heightened identity politics both within Native groups and between Native groups and the general population.

While American Indian gaming might be viewed negatively by some non-Indians, American Indian religions and traditions (real or imagined) have attracted many non-Indians. Some religions welcome, and indeed, seek to convert others and expand their membership. This generally is not the case with Native American spiritual leaders and practitioners. Non-Indian appropriation of Indian spiritual traditions often is perceived by native people as theft – one in a long series of "Indian giving" by non-Indians. The presence of charlatans and hucksters (a few of whom are of native ancestry) involved in assorted "new age" appropriations of Indian cultural elements lifted from their indigenous context has heightened the controversy (Churchill 1996).

The spread of new age and "world music" that uses elements and occasionally performers from various indigenous populations has spawned analogous controversies at a global level (Feld 1991). Not the least of the subcontroversies is that it is non-Indian performers and producers who are making the large profits from the use of indigenous instruments, themes, music, and performances. Such controversies will not disappear quickly. They have, however, generated a new interest in relations with indigenous peoples and new attempts to reexamine the long, and often tawdry, history of Indian/non-Indian relations.

SEE ALSO: Decolonization; Ethnography; Indigenous Movements; Polyethnicity; Primitive Religion; Tribalism

REFERENCES AND SUGGESTED READINGS

Bays, B. A. & Fouberg, E. H. (Eds.) (2002) *The Tribes and the States: Geographies of Intergovernmental Interaction*. Rowman & Littlefield, Lanham, MD.

Bodley, J. H. (1994) *Cultural Anthropology: Tribes, States, and the Global System*. Mayfield, Mountain View, CA.

Bodley, J. H. (2003) *Power of Scale: A Global History Approach*. M. E. Sharpe, Armonk, NY.

Brooks, J. F. (2002) *Captives and Cousins: Slavery, Kinship, and Community in the Southwest Borderlands*. University of North Carolina Press, Chapel Hill.

Chase-Dunn, C. & Hall, T. D. (1997) *Rise and Demise: Comparing World-Systems*. Westview Press, Boulder, CO.

Churchill, W. (1996) Spiritual Hucksterism: The Rise of the Plastic Medicine Men. In: Churchill, W. (Ed.), *From A Native Son: Selected Essays on Indigenism, 1985–1995*. South End Press, Boston, pp. 355–65.

Cornell, S. (1988) *The Return of the Native: American Indian Political Resurgence*. Oxford University Press, New York.

Cornell, S. & Kalt, J. (1992) *What Can Tribes Do? Strategies and Institutions in American Indian Economic Development*. American Indian Studies Center, University of California, Los Angeles.

Cornell, S. & Kalt, J. (2005) *Constitutions, Culture, and the Wealth of Nations: Economic Development on American Indian Reservations*. Cambridge: Harvard University Press.

Dippie, B. W. (1982) *The Vanishing American: White Attitudes and US Indian Policy*. University Press of Kansas, Lawrence.

Feld, S. (1991) Voices of the Rainforest. *Public Culture* 4, 1 (Fall): 131–40.

Fenelon, J. V. & Defender-Wilson, M. L. (2004) Voyage of Domination, Purchase as Conaues, Skakawea for Savagery: Distorted Icons from Misrepresentation of the Lewis and Clark Expedition. *Wicazo sa Review* 19(1): 85–104.

Ferguson, R. B. & Whitehead, N. L. (Eds.) (1992) *War in the Tribal Zone: Expanding States and Indigenous Warfare*. School of American Research Press, Santa Fe, NM.

Gedicks, A. (2001) *Resource Rebels: Native Challenges to Mining and Oil Corporations*. South End Press, Cambridge, MA.

Hall, T. D. & Fenelon, J. V. (2004) The Futures of Indigenous Peoples: 9–11 and the Trajectory of Indigenous Survival and Resistance. *Journal of World-Systems Research* 10(1): 153–97.

Jorgensen, J. G. (1998) Gaming and Recent American Indian Economic Development. *American Indian Culture and Research Journal* 22(3): 157–72.

Meyer, M. L. (1994) *The White Earth Tragedy: Ethnicity and Dispossession at a Minnesota Anishinaabe Reservation, 1889–1920*. University Press of Nebraska, Lincoln.

Nagel, J. (1996) *American Indian Ethnic Renewal: Red Power and the Resurgence of Identity and Culture*. Oxford University Press, New York.

Napoli, M. (2002) Native Wellness for the New Millennium: The Impact of Gaming. *Journal of Sociology and Social Welfare* 29(1): 17–25.

Snipp, C. M. (1986) Who are American Indians? Some Observations About the Perils and Pitfalls of Data for Race and Ethnicity. *Population Research and Policy Review* 5: 237–52.

Snipp, C. M. (Ed.) (1988) *Public Policy Impacts on American Indian Economic Development*. Native American Studies, Development Series No. 4, Albuquerque.

Stiffarm, L. A. with Lane, P., Jr. (1992) The Demography of Native North America: A Question of American Indian Survival. In: Annette Jaimes, M. (Ed.), *The State of Native America: Genocide, Colonization, and Resistance*. South End Press, Boston, pp. 23–53.

Thornton, R. (1987) *American Indian Holocaust and Survival*. University of Oklahoma Press, Norman.

Wilmer, F. (1993) *The Indigenous Voice in World Politics: Since Time Immemorial*. Sage, Newbury Park, CA.

individualism

Jens Zinn

Individualism emphasizes the importance of the individual, for example the individual's freedom, interests, rights, needs, or beliefs against the predominance of other institutions in regulating the individual's behavior, such as the state or the church. A range of theories in different societal domains contributes to the dissemination of individualistic ideas in society. In particular, economic and political liberalism are vehicles of individualism.

The term individualism was introduced by de Tocqueville. Even though he distinguished individualism from egotism, his distinction is essentially one of degree, but individualism would in the long run lead to "downright egotism."

A strong impact on the development of individualistic thinking in Western Europe can be traced to religion. The Reformation and the development of Protestantism indicated a shift to more individualistic thinking. This can be linked to Luther's claim that a personal relationship with God cannot be mediated by the interpretation of the church.

Another important contribution to individualistic thinking was given in economics by Adam Smith's development of a system of economic liberalism. He assumed that a simple system of natural liberty and exchange of goods and services in free and competitive markets, with as few interventions by the state as possible, would best support societal development and welfare.

A growing political individualism became most influential with the French Revolution and the emphasis on individual rights, referring to the idea of natural justice in contrast to the absolutist state. Several of these developments came together in the bourgeois Enlightenment in the seventeenth and eighteenth centuries.

In Anglophone discourse there is a tendency to interpret individualism as egoistic and selfish behavior. For example, Bellah et al. (1985) prominently argued that the prevalence of individualistic behavior would destroy the moral integrity of American society, though this view was contested. More positively, individualism is interpreted in Beck's (1992) theorizing on the risk society. Here, *individualization* indicates liberation from traditional bonds. Thus, it opens up more options from which to choose, but at the same time forces people to choose.

Methodological individualism emphasizes that sociological phenomena can only be explained by the characteristics of individuals. It was developed in opposition to methodological collectivism or holism. For example, Durkheim justified a specific sociological contribution to the examination of the human being by claiming that social phenomena can only be explained socially, and thereby proposed a holistic approach.

Today, this fundamental contradiction is rather outdated. Sociologists are much more concerned with questions of how sociocultural and sociostructural factors on the one hand and individuals, their actions or characteristics, on the other hand, are mutually linked or constitute each other. Instead of stating extreme positions, today's research is more often engaged with how both aspects combine in social reality.

SEE ALSO: Collectivism; Durkheim, Émile; Liberalism; Tocqueville, Alexis de

REFERENCES AND SUGGESTED READINGS

Beck, U. (1992) *Risk Society: Towards a New Modernity*. Sage, Newbury Park, CA.

Bellah, R. N. et al. (1985) *Habits of the Heart: Middle America Observed*. Hutchinson Education, London.

Durkheim, E. (1950) The Rules of Sociological Method. Trans. S. A. Solovay & J. H. Mueller. Free Press Glencoe, IL.

Smith, A. (1970) *Inquiry Into the Nature and Causes of the Wealth of Nations*. Penguin: London.

induction and observation in science

Andrew Tudor

One of the most persistent commonsense accounts of science is that in which scientists are understood systematically to assemble observations and arrive at reliable generalizations based upon them. Sometimes, wrongly, this simple inductive-empiricist view is laid at the door of Francis Bacon (1561–1626) and dubbed "Baconian inductivism." In fact, Bacon's views were considerably more complex than this, but the hare that he set running – inductive inference as the heart of scientific method – has subsequently been pursued by all manner of hounds. The Scottish Enlightenment philosopher David Hume (1711–76) was preeminent among the early pursuers, and to this day "Hume's problem" continues to preoccupy philosophy of science. In the mid-twentieth century, there was a period when the seemingly more powerful hypothetico-deductive model of scientific inquiry appeared to have run inductivism and Hume's problem to exhaustion. However, it rapidly became apparent that the issues surrounding inductive inference had a peculiar capacity to reemerge from the coverts of deductive certainty, not least where the nature of observation itself was questioned. Into the space thus created have hastened newer, more relativistic epistemologies and, in full cry, the sociology of science.

Although Bacon was by no means a naïve inductivist, he did insist on the necessity of ridding the mind of certain kinds of preconceptions when examining the facts, so as to better discover the true workings of natural phenomena. In effect, then, the inferential process moved from neutral observation to generalization unencumbered by misleading beliefs likely to obstruct proper knowledge. In its period this was a bold formulation, and one crucial to the subsequent development of natural philosophy into modern science. But it immediately raised difficulties for those eager to underwrite the legitimacy of scientific method in inductive terms. For while deductive reasoning had a lengthy logical pedigree, inductive inference was to prove far more slippery.

It was David Hume who presented the central problem of inductivism in its most influential form. In essence, the argument is simple: that however many instances we may find of a specific phenomenon, this gives us no reason in logic to expect that observed pattern to continue in the future. In other words, we have no justification for making any reliable inference from past evidence. Nor, of course, can we lay claim to probabilistic justification in as much as at the heart of the problem is the very unpredictability of the future in relation to past experience. The future will hold surprises. And against those who suggest, more pragmatically, that our past successes with this kind of inductive inference should lead us to expect success in the future, Hume levels the charge of circularity: attempting to justify inductive inference by inductively inferring future success from past instances of inductive inference itself.

Unsurprisingly, then, the difficulties consequent upon accepting inductive inference as *the* distinguishing feature of scientific method gave way by the mid-twentieth century to more deductively inclined models of science. Rather than seeing science as founded on generalizations from data, these approaches afforded greater emphasis to the relative autonomy of theory. So, for example, variants of the hypothetico-deductive model were little concerned with the grounds on which we actually arrived at our theories and generalizations. Their interest lay, rather, with deducing predictive hypotheses from theory which could then be subjected to (experimental) test. In strict versions – for example, Popperian falsificationism – the test could only falsify and not confirm (Hume's problem again). But this, too, presented problems. Science clearly did not proceed on the basis of rigid, deductive tenets (let alone falsificationist ones), and at the heart of any process of testing lay "observation" – which apparently relied upon some form of inductive inference from experience to the observation statements describing that experience. Since this would re-raise a variation of Hume's problem, deductivism was forced to recognize the unavoidably theory-laden and conventional character of observation. The traditional logical positivist reliance on the distinction between theory-language and observation-language simply would not do. The language of observation was no less theoretical than the language of theory.

None of this, of course, dissolves the problem of inductive inference, if problem it is, for even if induction is not the defining element in so-called scientific method it remains an important feature of actual scientific practice. Scientists make inductive inferences, albeit within a context of inquiry which also involves deduction, intuition, competition, and even sheer bloody-mindedness. Accordingly, philosophers of science have continued to examine induction with a view to somehow resolving or bypassing the Humean difficulties. Within the pragmatist tradition, for example, Rescher (1980) has sought to reconceive inductive inference as essentially a kind of cognitive method, while others, such as Howson (2000), who retain more formal concerns, have leaned toward Bayesian probability theory as providing grounds for resolving at least some of Hume's problem(s). Such approaches are often illuminating about what kinds of presuppositions are involved in inductive practice, although their apparent goal of providing "justification" seems far less significant in a period which has come more fully to recognize the importance of sociological and psychological factors in scientific inquiry. Here, Collins's (1985: 145) "sociological resolution of the problem of induction" is interesting. By empirical examination of what he calls the "experimenters' regress," he seeks to show that the nature of experiments as "skillful practice" means that an attempted replication always leads to the necessity for yet further experimental tests to confirm the quality of each experiment in the chain. This regress can only be halted by contingent, collective decision. Observing, experimenting, and constituting "facts," then, are socially constructed achievements of human agents; they cannot, without loss, be rendered as logically justified processes under the grand rubric of Inductive Scientific Method.

SEE ALSO: Controversy Studies; Experiment; Fact, Theory, and Hypothesis: Including the History of the Scientific Fact; Falsification; Laboratory Studies and the World of the Scientific Lab; Positivism; Realism and Relativism: Truth and Objectivity

REFERENCES AND SUGGESTED READINGS

Black, M. (1967) *Induction*. In: Edwards, P. (Ed.), *The Encyclopedia of Philosophy*, Vol. 4. Macmillan, New York.

Collins, H. M. (1985) *Changing Order: Replication and Induction in Scientific Practice*. Sage, London.

Goodman, N. (1973) *The New Riddle of Induction*. In: Goodman, N., *Fact, Fiction, and Forecast*. Bobbs-Merrill, New York.

Howson, C. (2000) *Hume's Problem: Induction and the Justification of Belief*. Clarendon Press, Oxford.

Hume, D. (1999) *An Enquiry Concerning Human Understanding*. Oxford University Press, Oxford.

Latour, B. & Woolgar, S. (1986) *Laboratory Life: The Construction of Scientific Facts*. Princeton University Press, Princeton.

Medawar, P. B. (1969) *Induction and Intuition in Scientific Thought*. Methuen, London.

Rescher, N. (1980) *Induction: An Essay on the Justification of Inductive Reasoning*. Blackwell, Oxford.

industrial relations

John Hogan and Peter Nolan

The material origins of industrial relations, both in practice and in research, can be traced to the movement from early to advanced capitalism. The rise of capitalism, centering on the purchase and sale of labor power, ushered in a new structure of relations between the direct producers and their controllers. Workers were brought together in centralized work stations and subjected to an authority relationship and hierarchical division of labor. The bosses had the right to hire and fire their charges, set their wages, and dictate the hours and intensity of work. The detailed division of labor was entrenched and reinforced in the factories, thus rendering worker solidarity and collective organization difficult. But the unbridled authority of bosses eventually came to be challenged. Workers formed embryonic unions and relations between workers and their masters became increasingly fraught.

The study of industrial relations took its lead from these material developments in the workplace. It is no accident that the field of inquiry has been shaped by scholars operating from within the economies that have dominated the history of global capitalist development. The study of industrial relations is a predominantly Anglo-Saxon discourse. Initially, scholars focused on processes of rule-making and the elaboration of institutional arrangements to contain conflict. The formation, structure, and influence of unions dominated the early key texts, but researchers found that the character of workplace relations, employer practices, and the position of unions were strongly conditioned by the wider political economy and state interventions. Scholars in the United States took the lead.

In the 1920s and early 1930s, American unions suffered heavy membership losses and were marginalized by company-sponsored unions. Yet, they proved to be successful in expanding their membership in the runup to and beyond World War II. While much of the success followed on from bitterly fought battles to build organization, notably in Minneapolis for the Teamsters and in Michigan amongst car workers, the position of US unions was bolstered by legislation introduced under Roosevelt's New Deal, in particular the Wagner Act, which legalized workers' rights of association, and the Social Security Act, which underpinned the emerging welfare state. But the changing balance of forces between employers, employees, and the unions proved difficult to capture in theory. By the late 1950s the dominant framework was the "systems" model, which treated industrial relations as a relatively autonomous subset of relations influenced by politics, the state, technology, and the economy (see Dunlop 1958; Kerr et al. 1960). Viewed as independent exogenous forces, these wider systematic variables were set apart conceptually from the processes and outcomes of the politics of

production. The possibility, for example, that the pace and impacts of technological advances may be conditioned by the division of labor and power struggles in the workplace was never considered. The approach thus attracted a vast critical literature that, inter alia, highlighted its intrinsic determinism and failure to unravel the complex, non-linear connections and contradictions between the industrial relations "subsystem" and broader political, economic, and technological forces.

Though initially influential in the UK, the systems approach was modified and adapted to take account of the particular patterns of workplace bargaining and the limited role of the state in directly shaping the pattern of industrial relations. The politics of pluralism dominated the mainstream literature that was primarily focused on institution building at workplace level. Like their American counterparts, the mainstream largely failed to unravel the complex connections between production politics and the particular historical trajectory of the UK economy, which by the early 1960s exhibited an entrenched pattern of low wages and low productivity. Criticized for overreliance on description, and for assuming that historical continuities would prevail over the forces of change, the mainstream, according to one critic (Crossley 1968), inclined toward a historicist method that blinded it to the contradictions and fragility of Britain's workplace institutions, including collective bargaining.

The late 1970s recoded the high tide of industrial relations in the Anglo-Saxon countries. In the UK union membership peaked at over 13 million employees. But during the 1980s and 1990s successive Conservative governments promoted the view that industrial relations had become an irrelevant public policy area. Strikes were in decline, and major unions suffered heavy defeats in the face of a state-sponsored employers' offensive. For many commentators, the defeat of the National Union of Mineworkers after a year-long strike between 1984 and 1985 was the turning point in modern labor history. Rising levels of unemployment, which topped 3 million by the mid-1980s, and a series of draconian anti-union laws sapped the capacity of unions to fight back and resist the degradation of working conditions that was legion across UK firms and industries.

In the United States, a new discourse – human resource management – focusing on the individual rather than collective employment relations captured the research agenda and led practitioners in the field of personnel and industrial relations to reinvent themselves. The administration led by Ronald Reagan was deeply hostile to the labor movement that had already been weakened by broader economic forces. Taking an unusually high profile in breaking the 1981 air traffic controllers' strike, Reagan was determined to promote a sea change in management practices, emphasize the primacy of the individual in the workplace, and denigrate established collective bargaining relations. Union membership and influence plummeted and have yet to recover, a malaise that brought forth a highly significant split in the peak trade union federation AFL-CIO during 2005.

In continental Europe collective bargaining and the solidarity of trade unions across service and industrial sectors proved more enduring. Tensions were apparent, in the systems that evolved after 1945, but large employers accepted (sometimes reluctantly) their duties under the laws to negotiate and consult with the trade unions that represented their employees. Union membership levels remained high by comparison with the UK and the US, and the coverage of collective bargaining often approached levels in excess of 80 percent of the workforce. Despite the claims on behalf of the Anglo-Saxon deregulated labor markets, the evidence revealed that the more regulated economies of Germany, Scandinavia, and Italy continued to thrive at the expense of the UK and US economies (Nolan 1994, 2004).

Employment patterns in continental Europe, it should be stressed, are not homogeneous. The panoply of institutional arrangements, both voluntary and statutory, that regulate the employment relationship vary considerably. Yet until quite recently many scholars counterpoised the industrial relations systems of the Anglo-Saxon countries to a stylized model of highly regulated and highly unionized labor markets that embedded productivity-inhibiting working practices. To be sure, in line with the traditions of social democracy that became embedded in many (but by no means all) European countries, institutional structures did evolve to protect the rights of workers in ways

that far exceeded the rights of British and American employees.

Yet it is crucial to be aware of the nuances of the employment systems in different European countries. In France, for example, a relatively small and divided union movement has kept alive a tradition of militancy, one capable of mobilizing beyond its immediate ranks, that has brought discipline to the practices of management. The principle of management prerogative has never been successfully embedded. In Germany union density rates are high, and workers retain considerable leverage over their terms and conditions of employment. A highly regulated system, to be sure, but it has succeeded in economic terms in delivering high levels of productivity and economic efficiency. It remains unique among the advanced economies in retaining a strong manufacturing sector. Further contrasts are provided by Spain, where unionism only took root after the death of Franco, and where a substantial proportion of the workforce is engaged in part-time work, while in the former Soviet bloc, systems of industrial regulation and union formation are evidently in a state of flux.

The key conclusion is that countries within the European zone should be studied in their own terms and not be grouped under facile descriptions of a rigid and inefficient block of sclerotic economies burdened with high unemployment and low productivity growth rates.

The early evidence base for the study of industrial relations was forged in the last decades of the nineteenth century. Seminal contributions from the Webbs (1894, 1920) brought a new focus to the examination of the nature of employment, authority relations, and the position of wage labor that had not been attempted since Engels's study 50 years earlier, of the nature of employment in Halifax, Leeds, London, and Manchester (Engels 1993).

Writing in a period of growing tensions in major industries – railways, textiles, chemicals, and coal – and in the buildup to the General Strike of 1926, Sidney and Beatrice Webb laid the foundations for the modern study of industrial relations. Leading practitioners such as Montague Burton – who developed in Leeds the largest clothing factory in the world – commissioned independent research into the conditions of industrial peace. He funded three

Chairs at the Universities of Cambridge, Leeds, and Cardiff in the late 1920s to address the concerns of key businesses about achieving a degree of consensus on the shop floor. The incumbents of these Chairs brought pragmatic guidance to the key policymakers involved in employment relations, the practitioners in the expanding industries, and the growing trade union movement. The concept of partnership – a current public policy issue in the UK and continental Europe – had been anticipated by progressive employers and trade unions eager to establish negotiating rights in the factories in the third decade of the twentieth century. The situation in the US was far less hospitable and was not placed on a more constructive footing for at least two decades.

Industrial relations became an established source of public policy concern in the US and the UK in the 1960s. In the US the research led by economists (Lloyd Reynolds, Clark Kerr, and John Dunlop) took as a point of theoretical departure traditional neoclassical economics. But they invested their studies with an acute understanding of power relations in the workplace and the pluralism of interactions between trade unions, government, and employers. Their research engaged with the orthodox notion that the anonymous forces of supply and demand dictated employment levels, rates of pay, and the position of different segments of the workforce within organizational hierarchies. Detailed studies of firms' internal labor markets (e.g., Ozanne 1968) revealed how imprecise a guide to the world of work the traditional economic axioms were (and still are). A beacon of light at a time of growing policy and theoretical conservatism, their work provided much of the impetus for the development of the academic study of industrial relations in Britain.

The research that ensued in Britain was driven by immediate policy questions focusing on rising strike levels, productivity deficits, and complex wage systems that were allegedly bringing manufacturing companies to a standstill. The challenge for researchers was to get behind the political rhetoric of the day. The lead was taken by a group of historians and social scientists committed to interdisciplinary policy research, collectively known as the "Oxford School." Led by Hugh Clegg, the group included academic practitioners (notably Alan Flanders and Clegg) and historians of the labor movement (Alan Fox). Such was their political influence at this time, Clegg was asked by the then prime minister, Harold Wilson, to lead the 1965 Royal Commission on Industrial Relations. Notwithstanding the often inflated (sometimes inflammatory) claims of many writers who claimed to have detected a direct causal link between the UK's industrial relations and economic underperformance, no clear evidence was produced (see Nolan 1996 for an exposition of the debates).

Anecdotes were used by economists to support their accounts of the underlying institutional causes of productivity deficits with the ever more successful economies of continental Europe, but the economists rarely entered the factories and offices about which they had so much to say. Studies failed to demonstrate a clear causal link between the UK's economic underperformance and the pattern of industrial relations in firms and industries. Many commentators gave voice to the government's position that the established voluntary system of industrial relations in the UK had proved deleterious to economic performance, and that a regime change, involving restrictive legislation against the activities of trade unions, was required. As indicated below, there followed a sea change in the character of industrial relations.

The government was disturbed by the increasing incidence of strikes that were both unconstitutional (out of procedure) and unofficial (unauthorized by the leaders of the relevant unions). Sometimes referred to as "wildcat" strikes, because of their spontaneous character on the shop floor, these actions were particularly common in the ailing UK engineering industries. Coventry, Birmingham, and Liverpool were notable hotspots. In Leeds textiles and clothing featured prominently in the disputes stakes. Some commentators linked the strikes and the wage drift associated with the increasingly tight labor markets in the 1960s to loss of market share in international manufacturing markets.

Hugh Clegg commented thus:

Under employment of labour is one of the major scandals of the British economy. There may be few workers – outside the newspaper industry – who are paid to do nothing at all, but throughout British industry there must be hundreds of thousands of workers who are paid to do nothing for a considerable part of their time ... Then there are the machines and changes in technology – many of them in use in other countries – which would be introduced here but for the limits placed by workers on their output. (Clegg 1964)

On the face of it this statement by Clegg represented a severe attack on the disruptive powers of the organized trade union movement in the UK, but he was also careful to include in his prescriptions the failures of management to do their jobs properly and efficiently. The Oxford School were ambivalent. Always committed to mutual disputes resolution in the workplace and to the limited role of legislators, Clegg and his colleagues espoused a program of reform that would engage all key parties: employers, workers, and their representatives to collective bargaining and the elaboration of new workplace procedures to minimize the damage that ensued from unbridled conflict.

The underlying philosophy was pluralism, the central idea that there were multiple stakeholders in the workplace. The evidence that the Royal Commission assembled revealed that conflict was endemic in the workplace and that institution building was the best way of raising productivity and reducing strikes, absenteeism, and conflict. Their prognosis – most clearly registered in the Royal Commission Report – was that power should be shared through the elaboration of collective bargaining arrangements, that the emerging numbers of unpaid shop stewards in private and public sector organizations should be provided with facilities (office space, time off work for meetings) in order to resolve differences with management to avoid strikes and productivity-damaging acts by both employers and employees.

Throughout this period in which academics worked hand in glove with policymakers in the UK and US, there were powerful dissenting voices. The most prominent scholar in the UK was Professor Vic Allen, a self-proclaimed Marxist. The Oxford School ignored his contributions but failed to minimize their impact on successive generations of students of industrial relations that found in his work a refreshing challenge to the pluralist orthodoxy (Allen

1971). The argument, backed by careful empirical research, that workers and their employers had often differences that could not be reconciled by institution building as proposed by the 1968 Royal Commission was borne out by the severe conflicts of the 1970s.

The election of Mrs. Thatcher in the UK in 1979 signaled a major upheaval in the practice, perception, and study of industrial relations. The situation in the US was bleaker, with union membership plummeting and employers introducing tough measures to retard workers' "voice" (Freeman & Medoff 1984). The attack by the Thatcher government, through numerous legislative measures, effectively prevented unions from taking collective action at the workplace. Set-piece strikes in the steel, railway, and coal industries halted the threat of mass mobilization policies by workers as the government sought new legal powers to stem the tide of resistance to draconian closure and mass redundancy programs. No sector was protected.

The academic study of industrial relations suffered in line with the prevailing material conditions. The new advocates of human resource management seized upon the evidence of declining collective relations in the workplace and proclaimed a new regime change in which business would work with individuals to secure business success. Performance-related pay, regular performance appraisals, teamworking, empowerment, and skill development programs were the new watchwords in a managerial vocabulary deployed to win the commitment of employees. Industrial relations researchers remained skeptical, arguing, somewhat complacently, that this was a fashion that would not endure.

The declining status of academic industrial relations was also a result of the failure of the mainstream to engage with other social science disciplines, notably economics. It ceded the terrain of debate – arguably the most politically charged debate in Europe, the US, and the UK – to economists who made bold claims with their blunt tools about the complex causal relations between conduct in the workplace and the performance of companies, industries, and national economies. They claimed that the terrain that had been occupied by students of the labor market, collective bargaining, and dispute resolution could be scrutinized with new techniques and data that would yield more knowledge than the older tradition of micro-empirical inquiry and ethnographic research.

The orientation in the new business schools that mushroomed in the US and UK, and to a lesser degree in continental Europe, promoted new vocabularies centered on leadership, self-help, and unbridled individualism in pursuit of personal advancement in the organization. Collective solidarity among workers was consigned to history. Academics in the US developed a new institutional economics that broke with the public policy tradition of the "old" institutionalists (e.g., Kerr, Dunlop, and Reynolds) by elevating transaction costs, for example the costs of managing the employment relationship through an authority relationship as opposed to spot market hire and fire policies. Established research centers were closed or starved of resources. Indeed, in the UK, leading academics were accused of academic bias in favor of collective bargaining at a time when the government of the day was seeking to impose highly restrictive measures on the trade unions.

Did the state offensive against unionism produce new patterns of working and new management practices that redefined the landscape of industrial relations? The evidence for the UK suggests that the new hardline approach against collective bargaining and worker voice was counterproductive. It encouraged sloppy management systems and removed the incentive for employers to invest in new technologies and the up-skilling of their employees. UK businesses pursued a longstanding tradition of competing in international markets with a low-wage, poorly trained workforce. At the turn of the twentieth century, productivity levels in the UK remained significantly lower than in other European countries and the United States.

Industrial relations have become a major issue for public policy debate. The UK government has retreated from the draconian policies designed to marginalize collective relations in the workplace, in favor of a renewed attempt to generate the condition of industrial peace through institutional arrangements to generate partnership in the workplace. Current developments would have pleased Montague Burton. The attempt by policymakers and researchers to supplant the traditional issues that had for nearly 100 years formed the agenda for the practice and subject of industrial relations by

the rather vague and empirically ungrounded field of human resource management has failed (Nolan & O'Donnell 2003). Unions have begun to rebuild their activities in the UK with membership gains, and employers are increasingly keen to harness their influence in the workplace to bring forward much needed changes to secure productivity and innovation changes. Slowly and unevenly there is a creeping shift toward a more European model of employment relations and a retreat from the harsher climate of industrial relations that has characterized work experiences in the United States. There is an evolving agenda that will inevitably be shaped by the impacts of new information and communication technologies (ICT), global market shifts, and developments in the shape of organizations and production politics at workplace level.

The capacity of industrial relations researchers to engage with these unfolding transformations is demonstrated with explorations into the meaning and potential of the "information age." The analysis of the implications of ICTs, in particular the Internet, for the politics and processes of labor has generated a substantial literature. Debate has been driven by concern with finding ways of building more effective forms in the face of the widespread and global "crises" of trade unionism, while taking inspiration from the innovative countercoordination of workers who have already demonstrated the potentialities of new ICTs. In South Korea, for example, the Internet has been identified as central to the strategy of the Korean Confederation of Trade Unions to break free from clandestine status, while in the 1995–8 unofficial Liverpool dockers' dispute the Internet was used to generate the most widespread international simultaneous solidarity action the labor movement has ever witnessed (Carter et al. 2003).

Developments in union presence on the Internet, the routine use of electronic communications, and the sponsorship of practitioner and academic reflection upon the opportunities and "perils" provide clear indication of future possibilities (Hogan & Grieco 2000). There is now a widespread availability of communication technologies that can be utilized at relatively low and distributed cost and accessed in transit and from the home, with processing and storage capacities that are growing exponentially and which can be readily deployed for the receipt, storage, auditing, manipulation, and broadcast of information globally. Through intervention into these communicative spaces visibility is greatly enhanced, allowing for the auditing of the performance of individuals and institutions (Hogan & Greene 2002). The retention of memories and traditions that hitherto had so easily been broken or lost is also placed within grasp as never before. This drive to innovation can challenge established power relations within trade unions but can also be internalized within labor institutions by the adoption of servicing and organizing facilities which specifically address the need to operate outside of the disciplinary constraints of hostile workplaces and which recognize that the captured market of the occupationally concentrated community is no more (Hogan & Nolan 2005).

SEE ALSO: Democracy and Organizations; Human Resource Management; Institutional Theory, New; Internet; Labor/Labor Power; Labor Movement; Labor Process; Laborism; Unions

REFERENCES AND SUGGESTED READINGS

Allen, V. L. (1971) *The Sociology of Industrial Relations*. Longman, London.
Carter, C., Clegg, S., Hogan, J., & Kornberger, M. (2003) The Polyphonic Spree: The Case of the Liverpool Dockers. *Industrial Relations Journal* 34 (September): 290–304.
Clegg, H. A. (1964) *Restrictive Practices, Socialist Commentary*. Cited in: *Productivity Bargaining and Restrictive Labour Practices*. Research Paper 4. Royal Commission on Trade Unions and Employers' Associations. HMSO, London, 1968.
Crossley, J. R. (1968) The Donovan Report: A Case Study in the Poverty of Historicism. *British Journal of Industrial Relations* 6(3): 296–302.
Dunlop, J. (1958) *Industrial Relations Systems*. Southern Illinois University Press, Carbondale and Edwardsville.
Engels, F. (1993) *The Condition of the Working Class in England*. Oxford University Press, Oxford.
Freeman, R. B. & Medoff, J. L. (1984) *What Do Unions Do?* Basic Books, New York.
Hogan, J. & Greene, A. M. (2002) E-collectivism: On-Line Action and On-Line Mobilization. In: Holmes, L., Hosking, D. M., & Grieco, M. (Eds.), *Organizing in the Information Age: Distributed Technology, Distributed Leadership, Distributed Identity, Distributed Discourse*. Ashgate, Aldershot.
Hogan, J. & Grieco, M. (2000) Trade Unions On Line: Technology, Transparency, and Bargaining Power. In: Donnelly, M. & Roberts, S. (Eds.), *Futures: Proceedings of the Second Scottish Trade Union Research Network Conference*. Scottish Trades Union Congress, Paisley, Scotland.
Hogan, J. & Nolan, P. (2005) Foreword. In: Grieco, M., Hogan, J., & Martinez-Lucio, M. (Eds.), *The Globalization of Labour: Counter-Coordination and Unionism on the Internet. Critical Perspectives on International Business* 1(2/3).
Kerr, C., Dunlop, J., Harbison, F. H., & Myers, C. (1960) *Industrialism and Industrial Man*. Harvard University Press, Cambridge, MA.
Nolan, P. (1994) Labour Market Institutions, Industrial Restructuring, and Unemployment in Europe. In: Grieve-Smith, J. & Michie, J. (Eds.), *Unemployment in Europe: Policies for Growth*. Academic Press, London, pp. 61–71.
Nolan, P. (1996) Industrial Relations and Performance Since 1945. In: Beardwell, I (Ed.), *Contemporary Industrial Relations: Critical Essays*. Oxford University Press, Oxford.
Nolan, P. (2004) Shaping the Future: The Political Economy of Work and Employment. *Industrial Relations Journal* 35 (September): 378–87.
Nolan, P. & O'Donnell, K. A. (2003) Industrial Relations, Human Resource Management, and Performance. In: Edwards, P. K. (Ed.), *Industrial Relations: Theory and Practice*. Blackwell, Oxford, pp. 489–512.
Ozanne, R. (1968) *Wages in Theory and Practice*. University of Wisconsin Press, Madison.
Webb, S. & Webb, B. (1894) *A History of Trade Unionism*. Longman, London.
Webb, S. & Webb, B. (1920) *Industrial Democracy*. Longman, Green, London.

industrial revolution

François Nielsen

The Industrial Revolution (IR) is the rapid increase in the use of machines powered by inanimate forms of energy (such as waterfalls, steam engines powered by coal, or electricity) that began in England in the later part of the eighteenth century. There are two perspectives on the scope of the subject. The IR may be viewed both as (1) a well-defined historical episode, delimited in time and space, or (2) a much broader phase of sociocultural evolution that is continuing to this day. In the first approach there is much agreement about the place (England) and time (the late 1700s). The year 1750 can be taken as a reasonable nominal date for the beginning of the IR (Nolan & Lenski 2004), although it might be considered early by some historians. The second approach is more encompassing, as it views the economic and social transformations of the nineteenth and twentieth centuries as all part of the unfolding of the IR.

A broad approach to the causes of the IR is to say that it is the result of the accumulation of technological information in agrarian societies of western Europe in the centuries that preceded the revolution (Nolan & Lenski 2004). Among these were innovations in shipbuilding and navigation that made possible transoceanic travel and the discovery of the New World. This event would contribute to increase trade activity, especially in the North Atlantic area, and infuse the European economy with large quantities of gold and silver. The resulting inflation favored the ascent of commercial classes relative to the landed aristocracy, and motivated the latter to try improving productivity of their land, spurring great progress in agricultural production. Another specific technological innovation was the mid-fifteenth-century invention of the printing press, which favored the spread of literacy and information in general and perhaps the rise of the rationalism associated with the Enlightenment. The printing press also facilitated the success of the Protestant Reformation, which was premised on direct access to sacred texts by believers. Much has been made of Max Weber's argument in *The Protestant Ethic and the Spirit of Capitalism* that the Protestant ethic of frugality and hard work facilitated the IR, but a major role of religion in the IR is unlikely in view of the fact that the earliest industrialized areas on the continent tended to be Catholic rather than Protestant (Delacroix & Nielsen 2001).

SHORT-TERM CONSEQUENCES

Short-term consequences of the IR are taken to be those that were already in evidence by, say, 1850.

Successive technological innovations in the late 1700s, especially in the textile industry, led to the design of increasingly complex machines that became too heavy to be operated by muscle power alone. The factory system arose because of the need to organize work activities near machines connected to a central source of power, such as a water mill or later a steam engine. Factory-based production had the additional advantages of permitting a more elaborate division of labor and closer supervision of the workers. Eventually there would be a corresponding decline in home-based manufacturing production (the "putting out" or "cottage industry" system), although this consequence was not immediate.

Labor demand associated with the rise of factories exacerbated the influx of rural population to towns and cities. In the mid-1700s only 15 percent of the population of England lived in towns of 10,000 or more; this proportion increased to a quarter by 1800 and one half by 1840 (Weightman 2003: 77). Immediate consequences of rapid urbanization were crowding, pollution, disease, poverty, crime, and other social ills. Contributing to social disorganization was the uprooting of industrial workers and their families from kin-based and traditional support networks in the countryside. Local town officials were overwhelmed and unable to cope with social problems on such an unprecedented scale (Nolan & Lenski 2004).

Although the issue of the short-term impact of the IR on living standards is still controversial (Evans 2001), it is known that the first half of the nineteenth century was characterized by much economic instability and that many families were barely able to survive on low factory salaries, even with all members of the household employed (including children as young as 6) and despite long hours of work in often deplorable conditions. The obvious hardship of workers' lives made entirely reasonable Karl Marx's belief, shared by many contemporaries, that the development of capitalism would entail the progressive impoverishment of the proletariat, a prediction that turned out to be false in the long run.

LONG-TERM DEVELOPMENTS

The entire way of life characteristic of modern industrial societies has its roots in the IR, and thus can be viewed as a consequence of this historical episode. Some of the specific causal threads linking modern life to the IR can be distinguished.

Economy and Labor Force

Industrialization has transformed the predominant types of economic activity carried out by the population of industrial societies. The proportion of the labor force employed in the primary sector (extractive activities such as agriculture and mining) dwindled in most industrial societies from an overwhelming majority in 1750 to less than 5 percent by the close of the twentieth century. The secondary sector (manufacturing industries) rose to approximately a third of the labor force, reaching a maximum early in the second half of the twentieth century before declining in later decades. It is employment in the tertiary sector (services, or the production of intangible goods) that rose steadily throughout the course of industrialization, up to some three-quarters of the labor force in many industrial societies today. These trends in the nature of work activities have radically changed the daily life and worldviews of members of industrial societies.

Industrialization began changing the nature of firms around 1850 with the spread of corporations based on the bureaucratic mode of organization, with a parallel decline in individually or family-owned firms. One major advantage of the corporate form of organization, in which the firm is collectively owned by shareholders in the form of stock, was the principle of limited liability, a genuine legal innovation of the industrial era. Limited liability means that investors are risking only the amount invested in shares, rather than their entire assets, in the corporate venture. This allowed the spreading of risk and the consolidation of vast amounts of capital. Corporations were run on bureaucratic principles, including the assignment of positions on the basis of competence acquired through education and training. This development coincided with the increasingly systematic application of science to industrial production. The resulting demand for skills, from the elementary (literacy) to the most sophisticated (such as engineering or legal), must have contributed to the spread of education, although other factors such as national rivalries may have been at work. Most industrial societies had extensive systems of primary education by the late 1800s, often with compulsory attendance laws. Systems of mass secondary and tertiary (college-level) education involving large proportions of the corresponding age cohorts did not develop until the second half of the twentieth century, however.

An inherent feature of capitalism is the tendency to growth in the average size of firms and industrial concentration, resulting in the domination of an industrial sector by one firm (a situation of *monopoly*) or a few (*oligopoly*). The mechanism of industrial concentration is based on economies of scale, which imply that a firm producing more units can reduce production costs by further subdividing fixed costs (such as costs of machinery, product development, and advertising). An initial market share advantage thus permits reducing production costs, and capturing an even larger market share. This autocatalytic process ("snowball effect") inevitably leads to increase in the size of firms and industrial concentration, a trend that was already evident in the late 1800s. As corporations grew in size and complexity they became increasingly controlled by the appointed executives (who had the expertise needed to run the organization) as opposed to the stockholders.

Demography, Family, and the Role of Women

Industrializing societies (with some exceptions such as France) experienced the *demographic transition* which is marked by a decline in the death rate followed by a delayed decline in the birth rate. The decline in deaths was due to improved food distribution facilitated by better transportation networks in the form of canals and railroads, better sanitation such as sewers and water treatment systems, and other public health measures such as vaccination. The decline in birth rate was due to a decline in the desire for large families more than improvements in birth control technology; the phenomenon is still somewhat mysterious. During the demographic transition, as the decline in births lagged behind the decline in deaths, industrializing societies experienced a phase of rapid population growth.

Rising productivity of labor combined with tapering population growth at the conclusion of the demographic transition eventually produced a remarkable rise in living standards for a majority of the population of industrial societies, refuting the trend of impoverishment prophesied by Marx.

Declining birth rates entailed much smaller families. The trend was dramatic: of British couples married around 1860, 63 percent had five children or more; of those married around 1925, only 12 percent did (Nolan & Lenski 2004: 281). Smaller family size reduced demands on women in the household, facilitated employment of women outside the home, and contributed to make women (and individuals in general) increasingly independent from the family.

With the decline in family farms and home-based industry the household ceased to be the principal unit of production. In a parallel trend the family lost a number of its traditional functions, including caring for the sick and the elderly, part of the socialization of children, and even food preparation; these activities were taken over by specialized organizations such as hospitals, retirement homes, schools, and makers of frozen dinners. Raising children, their early socialization, and the provision of emotional support for members have remained important functions of the family in industrial societies. The development of labor-saving machines for household tasks during the twentieth century further freed women for outside employment.

Greater independence from the family due to employment opportunities for women and the economic safety net provided in some measure by most industrial societies cannot be unrelated to the secular increase in divorce rate (a trend also marked by major upward and downward swings) that affected most industrial societies.

Ideology and Politics

In the ideological realm industrialization witnessed the emergence of new secular ideologies, including free-market capitalism (Smith 1976 [1776]), and socialism in two principal flavors:

democratic and *revolutionary*. The polity was transformed by the remarkably steady progression of *democratic republicanism* or *mass democracy*, i.e., a system of government where political decisions are made by representatives elected by the entire citizenry. Using franchise or electoral turnout as an indicator, it appears that democracy has increased steadily from the early 1800s, only temporarily interrupted by the fascist takeovers of the 1920s and 1930s (Flora 1983; Nolan & Lenski 2004). The democratic trend can also be seen in the passage of successive legislative milestones such as universal male voting, women suffrage, or Jewish emancipation (Davies 1998).

Another political trend was growing support for democratic socialism in many industrial countries, often with the support of working-class organizations such as trade unions. Social democratic parties have achieved many of the goals of socialism, collectively referred to as the welfare state. These goals include social security, state pension systems, unemployment compensation, national health care, free education at all levels, family allowances, subsidized childcare, and so on. The extent to which the welfare state has been achieved varies considerably among modern industrial nations, being less developed in the US than in most European countries (Esping-Andersen 1990).

The development of the welfare state and other government activities has produced massive increases in the size of government in all industrial societies, whether size is measured as number of employees or as government share of gross domestic product. "Big government" is strongly correlated with the development of the welfare state (e.g., Nolan & Lenski 2004: 233).

Fewer people in industrial societies today attend religious services or believe in God. The decline in traditional religious beliefs has been less marked in the US, a particularity attributed variously to the historical salience of religion in the country's origins, the variety of denominations and resulting competition for members (resulting in a more "efficient" recruitment of believers), or the relative failure of socialist ideologies in the US (Lipset & Marks 2000). It is possible that the trend of religious skepticism is partly independent of industrialization per se, having deeper and independent roots in the Enlightenment.

The World System

In the international context the rapid increase in production beginning with the IR in industrializing areas of Europe (and later the US and Japan) initiated an unprecedented rise in overall world inequality, as the income gap kept widening between industrial and non-industrial nations for more than two centuries (Firebaugh 2003). The resulting development gap, and the associated imbalance in military technology and power, may well have provided the conditions for the phase of territorial expansion of industrial nations from about 1860 to the eve of World War I that has been called *imperialism* or *colonialism* (Chirot 1986). This historical episode set the stage for the current phase of globalization (increasing trade and interactions of all kinds) affecting societies within the world system.

INDUSTRIAL OR POST-INDUSTRIAL SOCIETY

Some authors argue that the transformations taking place at the turn of the twenty-first century are so profound that societies affected by them deserve the new name of *post-industrial* societies. The post-industrial type of society is deemed different from the industrial one in that it is based on the production of services rather than manufactured goods, the processing of information rather than material objects (Bell 1976). Others, such as Nolan and Lenski (2004), prefer to view these recent trends as part of a later phase of the IR. In that view, advanced industrial societies today are experiencing the continuation of the IR rather than moving toward a radically different post-industrial stage. Both views certainly have merits; analyzing today's social trajectories does not require choosing any particular terminology.

SEE ALSO: Capitalism; Demographic Transition Theory; Demography: Historical; Family, History of; Industrialization; Labor/Labor Power; Management History; Post-Industrial Society; Socialism; Urbanization

REFERENCES AND SUGGESTED READINGS

Bell, D. (1976) *The Coming of Postindustrial Society*. Basic Books, New York.

Chirot, D. (1986) *Social Change in the Modern Era*. Harcourt Brace Jovanovich, San Diego, CA.

Davies, N. (1998) *Europe: A History*. HarperPerennial, New York.

Delacroix, J. & Nielsen, F. (2001) The Beloved Myth: Protestantism and the Rise of Industrial Capitalism in Nineteenth-Century Europe. *Social Forces* 80: 509–53.

Esping-Andersen, G. (1990) *The Three Worlds of Welfare Capitalism*. Polity Press, Cambridge.

Evans, E. J. (2001) *The Forging of the Modern State: Early Industrial Britain, 1783–1870*, 3rd edn. Pearson Education, London.

Firebaugh, G. (2003) *The New Geography of Global Income Inequality*. Harvard University Press, Cambridge, MA.

Flora, P. (1983) *State, Economy, and Society in Western Europe, 1815–1975: A Data Handbook in Two Volumes*. Vol. 1: *The Growth of Mass Democracies and Welfare States*. St. James Press, Chicago.

Lipset, S. M. & Marks, G. (2000) *It Didn't Happen Here: Why Socialism Failed in the United States*. W. W. Norton, New York.

Nolan, P. & Lenski, G. (2004) *Human Societies: An Introduction to Macrosociology*, 9th edn. Paradigm, Boulder, CO.

Smith, A. (1976 [1776]) *An Inquiry into the Nature and Causes of the Wealth of Nations*. Clarendon Press, Oxford.

Weightman, G. (2003) *What the Industrial Revolution Did For Us*. BBC Books, London.

industrialization

Michael Indergaard

Industrialization is the process by which an economy shifts from an agricultural to a manufacturing base during a period of sustained change and growth, eventually creating a higher standard of living. Sociology's founders were keenly interested in the causes, correlates, and consequences of industrialization, which they considered a major development in the broader social transformation producing modern society.

For much of the twentieth century, however, broad analyses by classical sociologists such as Marx and Weber were overshadowed by narrow accounts featuring technology or efficiency. Sociologists often deferred to economic historians, accepting determinist narratives of a singular path of industrialization marked by a flurry of new gadgets, energy sources, and processes unleashed by *laissez-faire* policies. Sociologists drew on miscellaneous concepts and observations to compile profiles of industrial society featuring traits such as a division of labor, rationalization, the systematic application of science, urbanization, increased life expectancy, literacy, higher standards of living, and democracy. More recently, the humbling of western industry by newly industrialized countries (NICs) has led sociologists to examine how interactions of political, cultural, and economic factors in different contexts produce multiple paths of industrialization.

A key influence on discussion of industrialization was Adam Smith's notion that more specialization in the division of labor, though it had negative effects on workers, is more efficient and inevitably increases a nation's wealth if the state adopts a *laissez-faire* stance. Another was provided by French writers in the early 1800s who spoke of an Industrial Revolution, citing parallels between technological changes in manufacturing and the French Revolution. Engels drew on various romantic currents in exposing the conditions that the Industrial Revolution imposed on the English working class. In *Capital* (1867), Marx placed the Industrial Revolution in the historical development of the capitalist mode of production, arguing that the detailed division of labor abetted the introduction of machinery which subordinated and replaced workers. Social progress, he asserted, awaited an overthrow of capitalist class relations and the detailed division of labor. Victorian reformers, alarmed by the revolutionary critiques and growing urban poverty, embraced Toynbee's romantic denouncement of the Industrial Revolution which, ironically, echoed Engels: it established the idea among economic historians that industrialization occurred through rapid technological change causing social catastrophe (Coleman 1992).

Most sociologists rejected Marx's radicalism, preferring interpretations of industrialization compatible with reformist positions. They were attracted to Durkheim's argument that the division of labor had temporarily made social solidarity problematic and to Weber's early work on the Protestant ethic, touted as the culturalist answer to Marx's materialism. Discussions of industrialization largely ignored Marx's dialectical conception of history and the comprehensive analysis that Weber later developed of how cultural, political, and economic factors interacted to produce rational capitalism.

The reform inclination in the early twentieth century was particularly evident among American sociologists who, having agreed to stay out of turf claimed by economists, focused on social aspects of industrial society. The Chicago School organized around the study of social problems and forms of organization in industrial cities, while a broad subspecialty – industrial sociology – drew on institutional economics and human relations theories to explore relations and groups in industrial organizations and workplaces. Over time, industry sociology expanded to examine additional issues such as development, occupations, stratification, organizations, and labor markets before such topics were hived off by a host of emerging subspecialties in the discipline.

A new movement in economic history injected optimism into discussions of industrialization during the twentieth century, celebrating the Industrial Revolution's technological achievements (e.g., use of coal, the steam engine, the spinning jenny); it reinforced the idea that the British case defined a general path of industrialization. The Great Depression, fascism, and the Soviet Union's industrialization temporarily raised doubts about the one-path thesis. Free market accounts of industrialization also were challenged by Polanyi's argument that ideology and state interventions set the ground for industrialization and for unregulated markets themselves. However, the World War II triumph restored confidence in the US that industrializing countries would converge around a common path. Some economists advised that multiple paths were possible, but many sociologists embraced Rostow's modernization thesis that all developing societies would have to pass through five stages of development, with industrialization representing the takeoff stage. Similarly, industrial sociologists endorsed a convergence thesis proposing that functional imperatives of industrialization required societies to develop certain traits – e.g., an extended division of labor, separation of family and enterprise, and rational forms of calculation and investments. They added that industrialization would encourage secularization, social mobility, and democracy.

In the 1960s and 1970s, a new wave in economic history attacked the Industrial Revolution metaphor, using macroeconomic trends (e.g., growth in national income, growth and sectoral composition of the labor force) to argue that industrialization had been a gradual process. Achievement partisans, however, depicted the Industrial Revolution in ever more heroic terms, comparing it to the development of agriculture, monotheism, and even language. They bolstered their position, drawing on Schumpeter's claim that each long wave of growth was propelled by a distinctive set of innovations (Coleman 1992). Dominant accounts of industrialization also came under fire from the left. Neo-Marxians revisited western industrialization, arguing that its capitalist nature accounted for the calamities it inflicted on working people. Labor process studies showed how social control agendas drove efforts in factories to subdivide work and deskill workers. Dependency and world-systems theorists proposed that the development of poor nations was distorted or constrained by unequal relations with advanced nations.

In the 1970s and 1980s, the rise of state-guided industrial powers in East Asia, crisis in western industry, and promotion of free markets by Anglo-American neoliberals brought a sea change in studies of industrialization. Debates about flexible industrial systems and new global divisions of labor produced evidence that industrialization had taken multiple paths in the past as well as the present. Seeking an alternative to technology/efficiency explanations, a new economic sociology spearheaded a return to broad examinations of industrialization. Piore and Sabel's (1984) study of the triumph of mass production over craft production inspired a large body of work. They argued that political conflicts and competing visions influenced the path that industrialization takes in different nations and the respective capacities that result

(e.g., the flexibility of Japanese manufacturing). Institutionalists also cited political and cultural factors in challenging Alfred Chandler's argument that the industrial corporation gained the form that it did (modeled on railroad administration) because it was the most efficient way to coordinate a large number of geographically dispersed workers.

A second debate concerned the rise of Japan and the East Asian NICs (South Korea, Taiwan, Hong Kong, Singapore). Economists attributed their international competitiveness to free trade policies which gave them access to foreign capital and technology while exposing them to market discipline. In contrast, proponents of the developmental state model argued that a distinctive set of policies gave East Asian NICs an advantage in overcoming the internal obstacles that late industrializers face. As was the case with Japan earlier, an initial lack of capacity for innovation in products and processes forced late industrializers (e.g., Brazil, Turkey, India, Mexico, South Korea, Taiwan) to enter the global economy through emulation of foreign technology and reliance on cheap labor and tariffs. Developmental states allowed East Asian NICs to complete and develop beyond this initial stage much more quickly than other NICs. The developmental state devises national strategies, encourages the formation of business groups, and guides capital into targeted sectors. It also exercises discipline over business (e.g., performance standards) as a condition for subsidies, encouraging firms to excel in making incremental improvements and enabling entire segments to move into higher-value sectors (Amsden 1989). A second explanation (Gereffi 1994) for varying paths of industrialization among NICs stresses the different positions that their chief industries hold in new global divisions of labor. State strategies still matter, but are constrained by the dynamics of product cycles and by the structures of different kinds of international commodity chains dominated by multinational corporations. A third model stresses the hybrid nature of post-socialist development, a notion that is especially relevant for the case of China – an avowed practitioner of market socialism that is often considered an avatar of global market forces but also resembles a developmental state.

The post-industrial society thesis deems the recent decline in manufacturing in western nations to reflect a transition to a knowledge-based service economy. However, the credibility of the term post-industrial depends on how industrialization is defined. If one considers industrialization to be the rationalization of economic activities, as does Ritzer's McDonaldization thesis, then the standardization of work routines and the homogenization of products and consumption that one sees in a fast food restaurant imply that industrialization continues in the service sector. Other work suggests that the development of information technology represents the industrialization of information. Mokyr (2002) proposes that sustained growth in both the First and Second Industrial Revolutions was due to the broadening of the knowledge base. He raises the possibility that the increasing accessibility of scientific knowledge due to computers may have initiated a Third Industrial Revolution. Synthesizing the literature on industrialization in the past and present, Castells (2000) advises that we are undergoing an Information Technology Revolution based on the application of knowledge and information back to the very process of generating knowledge and information.

The term industrialization seems more the product of mythmaking and list-making than a coherent theoretical program. In the reductionist manner in which economics addresses the term, industrialization means so little; in sociology it has come to mean so much. After nearly two centuries of use, basic definitional and methodological issues remain unsettled. When can a nation be deemed to be industrialized? At what point does the process begin? Can industrialization be distinguished from a stage of capitalism or the process of rationalization? What social structures, institutions, and processes are as essential for industrialization as technology and how should we understand their interplay? Should the unit of study be the nation-state or some global segment?

Given industrialization's correlation with basic indicators of well-being, it is important to determine what can still be expected in cases where industrialization has stalled or never really started. That problem is becoming more complex and daunting as the industrialization of developing nations is increasingly structured by their links to global networks of production and information technology.

SEE ALSO: Capitalism; Division of Labor; Industrial Revolution; Information Technology; McDonaldization; Marx, Karl; Post-Industrial Society; Weber, Max

REFERENCES AND SUGGESTED READINGS

Amsden, A. H. (1989) *Asia's Next Giant: South Korea and Late Industrialization*. Oxford University Press, Oxford.

Carruthers, B. & Babb, S. (2000) *Economy/Society: Markets, Meanings, and Social Structure*. Pine Forge, Thousand Oaks, CA.

Castells, M. (2000) *The Rise of the Network Society*, 2nd edn. Blackwell, Oxford.

Coleman, D. C. (1992) *Myth, History, and the Industrial Revolution*. Hambledon Press, London.

Dobbin, F. (1994) *Forging Industrial Policy: The United States, Britain, and France in the Industrial Age*. Cambridge University Press, Cambridge.

Faunce, W. (1968) *Problems of an Industrial Society*. McGraw-Hill, New York.

Gereffi, G. (1994) The International Economy and Economic Development. In: Smelser, N. J. & Swedberg, R. (Eds.), *The Handbook of Economic Sociology*. Russell Sage Foundation, New York.

Gereffi, G. & Wyman, D. L. (Eds.) (1990) *Manufacturing Miracles: Paths of Industrialization in Latin America and East Asia*. Princeton University Press, Princeton.

Kerr, C., Dunlop, J. T., Harbison, F., & Meyers, C. A. (1973) *Industrialization and Industrial Man*. Penguin, London.

Mokyr, J. (2002) *The Gifts of Athena: Historical Origins of the Knowledge Economy*. Princeton University Press, Princeton.

Piore, M. J. & Sabel, C. F. (1984) *The Second Industrial Divide: Possibilities for Prosperity*. Basic Books, New York.

Rostow, W. (1960) *The Stages of Economic Growth*. Cambridge University Press, Cambridge.

Swedberg, R. (1998) *Max Weber and the Idea of Economic Sociology*. Princeton University Press, Princeton.

Toynbee, A. (1908) *Lectures on the Industrial Revolution of the 18th Century in England*, 2nd edn. Longman, London.

inequalities in marriage

Constance Shehan and Susan Cody

Women and men typically experience different rights and responsibilities in marriage, in spite of widespread beliefs in marital equality. These differences led sociologist Jesse Bernard (1972) to coin the phrase "his and her marriages." Gender-based patterns of marital inequality have existed historically in the US and other western nations, though they have declined somewhat in recent decades, and they persist in other parts of the globe, as well. For various reasons, which will be outlined below, there are systematic gender differences in the amount and type of domestic labor and family care performed by spouses, in power and authority in marital-decision making, in access to and control over household resources, and likelihood of experiencing severe injury as a result of spousal violence. Gender-based inequalities continue after divorce, characterizing property settlements and custody arrangements as well as the relative economic circumstances of former spouses.

INEQUALITIES IN THE DIVISION OF HOUSEHOLD LABOR

Studies of the division of household labor conducted over the past 40 years have shown that women allocate considerably more time each week than men to various household tasks and family care even when they are employed outside their homes. Today, women typically devote about 19 hours, and men about 10 hours, to housework each week (Bianchi et al. 2000). The types of household tasks performed by women and men also differ. Men tend to do those that are more flexibly scheduled and at least somewhat discretionary, whereas women perform routine and repetitive labor that must be performed on a regular basis (Hochschild 1989).

In terms of childcare, fathers are more likely to spend time with children in recreational activities while mothers allocate considerable time to basic "maintenance" chores. The gender-based patterns of family care are even more pronounced when it comes to elderly relatives. Nearly all the work that is done for ill or dependent elderly

people in private homes is done by women. British researchers estimate that the ratio of time women and men spend in elder care approaches 19 to 1 (Abel 1986). Even in households where time allocated to household tasks and family care by spouses is similar, wives perform an "executive" function, monitoring family needs and ensuring that they are met in a timely and effective fashion. This may mean hiring and supervising outside help, in which case wives are likely to use their own salaries to pay for the costs of the auxiliary help. As a result, women spend more of their time in various types of labor and have less time for leisure and sleep. Among married couples with infants, women work an extra day, or 24 hours more per week than their husbands (Rexroat & Shehan 1987).

INEQUALITIES IN POWER AND DECISION-MAKING

Marital power can be defined as one spouse's ability to impose his or her will on another, which can mean forcing the other spouse to act in certain ways or accept a specific "definition of reality" as one's own (Aulette 2002). Alternative explanations for the balance of marital power emphasize individual traits or abilities such as one partner's greater size or strength, greater knowledge or expertise, control over socioeconomic resources, or superior communication skills. Thus, the balance of power swings to the stronger spouse or the one who contributes more money and status. When decisions are contested, the partner with the greater interest in or knowledge about the issue may have greater say in the final outcome. Or, in some cases, the more persuasive partner may win out. These bases of marital power often favor husbands insofar as men, on average, are larger and stronger and earn higher wages than their wives. Gender differences in communication styles in which men tend to control the course of conversations by talking more, interrupting more, and vetoing topics, may also swing decision-making power to husbands. One of the most important bases of power in marriage is patriarchal authority: legitimate authority bestowed on men to act as the heads of their families and/or households. Patriarchy is institutionalized in religious customs and governmental policies.

In many cultures, women's secondary status is linked to social systems which connect kinship and patriarchy. In such societies, social relations, including those within families, are influenced by traditional views of women and men. Kin groups are built around male headship. Traditions of patrilinealism and patrilocality have restricted women's choices inside and outside the home (Lerner 1987). In recent years, however, extended families have become less common around the globe. While this change has been bemoaned by some as a loss of tradition and family ties, it is also linked to greater freedom for women.

Today, in most western societies, patriarchal authority in families and households does not have the same influence it once had, but it still exists and in certain segments of American society it continues to be strongly supported. Evangelical Christians, for instance, often adhere to patriarchal authority, as do other religious subcultures such as the Hasidic Jews, the Old Order Amish, and to a lesser extent, the Mormons. Some ethnic and nationality groups in the US also adhere fairly closely to a patriarchal ideology. These include people who have recently emigrated from the traditionally patriarchal cultures of the Middle East, Africa, Latin America, and Asia. African American and Latino populations have cultural elements that support patriarchy, although other aspects of their lives (such as the need for women to be employed) may counterbalance the traditional view of male dominance.

Patriarchy is also built into civil laws. In a very real sense, American state and federal governments create a hidden marriage contract through laws, administrative rulings, and court decisions. This contract defines the rights, responsibilities, and obligations of married persons and is based on traditional assumptions about the roles of husbands and wives which grew out of English common law. Any person who marries is agreeing to conform to any and all conditions of the hidden contract (Stetson 1991). Primary among these assumptions are the following: husbands are the heads of their households; husbands are responsible for the economic support of their wives and children; and wives are responsible for domestic services and childcare. Under the common law tradition, husbands had the right to decide where they and their families would live. They were also given control of the family's economic resources, including the wife's property and possessions at the time of their marriage. When a wife was employed under these conditions, her husband was entitled to her wages.

INEQUALITIES IN THE LIKELIHOOD OF INTIMATE PARTNER VIOLENCE

While men are more likely than women to be victims of reported violence in our society, they are considerably less likely to be victims of intimate partner violence. If women are violently assaulted, their assailant is most likely a husband or boyfriend. When women are assaulted, they are more likely to be injured if they have an intimate relationship with the perpetrator. Bureau of Justice statistics reveal the extent of the gender difference: roughly 7.5 women and 1.4 men in every 1,000 are victims of crimes with intimate perpetrators. Feminist scholars argue that gender inequality and the oppression of women are the central features of violence in families. Historically, there have been norms and laws that condone violence against women. In the nineteenth century, for example, many states had laws specifically approving of wife beating. Battering is a reflection of the inequality between women and men and is a conscious strategy used by men to control women and to maintain the system of gender inequality.

In 1993 the United Nations adopted the Declaration on the Elimination of Violence Against Women. UNIFEM, the branch of the United Nations which deals with women's issues, has focused its attention on the global epidemic of violence against women and girls, especially violence that occurs within families (Sev'er & Yurdakul 2006). Because of the strong preference for sons, girls face a high risk of violence beginning at or before birth. Parents may use practices such as sex-selective abortion or infanticide to increase their chances for a son (Ravindran 1986). Worldwide, millions of girls have been victimized by a practice known as female genital mutilation (FGM). This cultural practice involves some combination of procedures ranging from partial to total removal of the clitoris and/or sewing together the external genitalia, often under very harsh and unhygienic conditions. It is used to ensure the virginity of girls, thereby increasing their opportunities for marriage (World Health Organization 1995).

Cross-cultural studies indicate that wife-beating is the most common form of family violence (World Health Organization 1995). Estimates of the incidence of wife abuse are conservative, due to shame and guilt on the part of victims, lack of legal recourse, and fear of partner retaliation. In recent years, extreme forms of violence against wives have been exposed. In India, for example, wives are expected to express deep gratitude for selection into marriage and to show deference to husbands and other family members. Bride burnings may result from a wife's alleged infidelity or a family's inability to pay the dowry in full to the husband.

In recent years, honor killings have been publicized in such nations as Pakistan, Egypt, and Turkey (Sev'er and Yurdakul 2006). Such countries have a strong tradition of family-based patriarchy and may customarily mandate complete control over women's social, reproductive, and economic lives. In Turkey, for example, wives have virtually no rights to property, and their sexual behavior continues to be controlled even after a legal separation has been granted. Wives are not protected against marital rape unless they sustain a serious and obvious physical injury. Furthermore, law enforcement officials continue to hold very traditional ideas about sexual assault, believing that women provoke such crimes in most cases.

EQUALITARIAN MARRIAGES

Despite the prevalence of traditional or patriarchal marriages, it does appear that some couples today are attempting to create and maintain what has been described as egalitarian or "peer marriages." Greater awareness of gender inequalities, changing gender roles, as well as the need for two wage-earners, has prompted some couples to consider a more equitable type of intimate relating. Clearly, the inequalities associated with marriage have been a major source of marital dissatisfaction in the past. Couples who maintain or who perceive that they maintain equity in their relationships express higher levels of marital satisfaction. Sociologists have coined the term peer marriage to refer to relationships that are built on *equity* (i.e., each

partner gives to the relationship in the same proportion that she or he receives) and *equality* (i.e., each partner has equal status and is equally responsible for emotional, economic, and household duties). Peer marriages are difficult to achieve and maintain, however, due to the overwhelming acceptance and established traditions of patriarchal marriage. Couples who strive for egalitarianism are viewed with suspicion, disbelief, or hostility (Blumstein & Schwartz 1983). Not surprisingly, women are often the first to initiate or express a preference for peer marriage (Schwartz 1994), although feminist ideology is not often cited as the reason. More often, wives cite the desire for more shared parenting as their primary motivation. Peer marriages remain quite rare (Risman 1998).

Peer marriages have four important characteristics: a nearly equal division of household labor and childcare; equal influence over important decisions; equal control over the family money; and equal consideration given to both partners' work in family decision-making.

SEE ALSO: Child Custody and Child Support; Childcare; Divisions of Household Labor; Divorce; Domestic Violence; Feminization of Poverty; Gender, Work, and Family; Marital Power/Resource Theory; Marital Quality; Marriage; Patriarchy

REFERENCES AND SUGGESTED READINGS

Abel, E. (1986) Adult Daughters and Care for the Elderly. *Feminist Studies* 12(3): 479–93.

Aulette, J. (2002) *Changing American Families*. Allyn & Bacon, Boston.

Bernard, J. (1972) *The Future of Marriage*. Yale University Press, New Haven.

Bianchi, S., Milkie, M., Sawyer, L., & Robinson, J. (2000) Trends in the Gender Division of Labor. *Social Forces* 79(1).

Blood, R. & Wolfe, D. (1960) *Husbands and Wives: The Dynamics of Married Living*. Free Press, New York.

Blumstein, P. & Schwartz, P. (1983) *American Couples: Money, Work, and Sex*. William Morris, New York:.

Hochschild, A. (1989) *The Second Shift*. Viking Press, New York.

Lerner, G. (1987) *The Creation of Patriarchy*. Oxford University Press, Oxford.

2304 *inequality and the city*

Ravindran, S. (1986) *Health Implications of Sex Discrimination in Childhood*. World Health Organization, UNICEF, Geneva.

Rexroat, C. & Shehan, C. (1987) The Family Life Cycle and Spouses' Time in Housework. *Journal of Marriage and the Family* 49(3): 737–50.

Risman, B. (1998) *Gender Vertigo: American Families in Transition*. Yale University Press, New Haven.

Schwartz, P. (1994) *Peer Marriage*. Free Press, New York.

Sev'er, A. & Yurdakul, G. (2006) Culture of Honor, Culture of Change: A Feminist Analysis of Honor Killings in Rural Turkey. In: Rothenberg, P. S. (Ed.), *Beyond Borders: Thinking Critically About Global Issues*. Worth Publishers, New York.

Stetson, D. (1991) *Women's Rights in the USA: Policy Debates and Gender Roles*. Brooks/Cole, Pacific Grove, CA.

Straus, M., Gelles, R., & Steinmetz, S. (1980) *Behind Closed Doors: Violence in the American Family*. Doubleday, Garden City, NY.

World Health Organization (1995) *Female Genital Mutilation: Report of a WHO Technical Working Group*. World Health Organization, Geneva.

inequality and the city

James R. Elliott and Timothy J. Haney

Urban sociology emerged from the fertile ground of US cities during the early 1900s as a means of understanding social problems and the processes that produce them. Central to the field's conceptualization and analysis of these social problems was, and remains, the idea of inequality, defined loosely as the uneven distribution of social resources and actors relative to one another. As such, the term "inequality and the city" is best understood as a conceptual umbrella that spans a broad range of subtopics and research traditions within urban sociology, rather than as a single subfield in its own right. For heuristic purposes, we can organize this material into two subject matters: inequality *among* cities and inequality *within* cities.

INEQUALITY AMONG CITIES

Research on inequality among cities focuses on how cities emerge and develop through interaction with other places, that is, as connected nodes within a more expansive trade and settlement system. Early attempts to understand the nature of this system emphasized the hierarchical, or unequal, distribution of cities by size and economic function within national regions, attempting to explain why, for example, Chicago became a more dominant city than Dubuque.

This research tradition traces to the 1930s, when German geographer Walter Christaller (1966 [1933]) advanced two theoretical propositions: first, a positive correlation exists between the importance of a city's economic functions and its population size; second, cities tend to "space" themselves such that those of similar size and economic importance do not cut into each other's market area. From these two propositions, Christaller developed a theory of urban hierarchy in which a few "super" cities generate market control over a larger number of middle-order cities, which in turn generate market control over an even larger number of lower-order cities, which themselves generate market control over surrounding rural hinterlands. The result is an even, orderly, and unequal system of cities, with those at the top gaining demographically and economically from those beneath them.

Subsequent research has challenged the assumptions and deductive logic of Christaller's theory, but it has not displaced the idea of urban hierarchy. Most recently this idea has resurfaced prominently in the "global city" literature, which investigates how new processes of global trade are redefining the roles that major cities play in the world system. This line of investigation can be traced to the early 1900s, when Robert McKenzie (1927), an original member of the Chicago School of Sociology, advanced a global perspective on urban structure and change in which he argued that social development brings with it increasing specialization of parts and greater centralization of "coordination and control" functions over time. It follows, McKenzie reasoned, that similar processes would bring growing inequality among places around the world, with most settlements becoming increasingly specialized and subordinate to a few cities where these "coordination and control" functions would concentrate.

Today's literature on "global cities" advances a similar theme but also contends that today's world economy has changed radically over recent decades as multinational corporations have seized the reins of increasingly far-flung financial and production operations. These developments have reduced the systemic importance of cities that serve merely as political capitals and increased the systemic importance of cities that act as strategic command posts for global business. According to Saskia Sassen (1991), these developments have produced a new breed of global city, which functions in four ways that distinguish it from the past: (1) as a highly concentrated and influential node in the organization of the world economy; (2) as a strategic site for the location of sophisticated business services, which have replaced manufacturing as the leading engine of economic development; (3) as a production and innovation site for this new sector; and (4) as a place where corporations go to buy and sell these sophisticated business services – accounting, advertising, legal counsel, information management, and the like. Sassen's central point is that global control is not an inevitable byproduct of economic globalization; rather, it must be produced, and this production occurs in global cities.

According to many observers, these developments have changed not only the urban hierarchy but also the social structure of cities at its top (e.g., New York, Los Angeles, Tokyo, London). This line of research contends that the growth and development of today's "command and control" functions in global cities polarize job opportunities in the local labor market. The result is a large sector of highly skilled, well-paid, corporate professionals and a large sector of less skilled, poorly paid, non-professionals that serve the new elite as maids, janitors, dry-cleaners, nannies, private security, restaurant help, and the like. This polarization tends to push working-class natives out of global cities, attract low-skill immigrant labor, and reproduce, locally, forms of extreme inequality that these cities help to maintain on a global scale.

INEQUALITY WITHIN CITIES

These issues move us from viewing cities as nodes in a larger system to viewing the city as a system itself. This tradition traces to the early years of the Chicago School (1910s–1920s), when US cities were booming and flush with European immigrants from all regions. Prejudice and discrimination against Poles, Italians, and Irish were high and often bitter during this period, followed later by the great migration of Southern, rural African Americans to the same urban centers, generating new ethnic divisions. From this turbulent context emerged a rich tradition of research on ethnic, racial, and class inequalities in the city.

Anchoring this tradition is the ecological premise that social and spatial distance correlate positively in the city, such that groups with higher status will seek to remove themselves spatially, as well as socially, from those with lower status. This premise identifies segregation, especially residential segregation, as the chief mechanism behind durable inequality in the city. Early research within this tradition produced rich cultural studies of ethnic-urban neighborhoods created by this segregation, capped intellectually by Louis Wirth's (1928) classic study of Jews in *The Ghetto*. By mid-century, however, with immigration restrictions in place and European assimilation on course, scholars began steadily shifting their attention from the vibrant lives of ethnic villages to the dramatic segregation of whites and blacks across metropolitan space. This issue erupted onto the front pages in the late 1960s, when racial unrest from Watts to Detroit to Newark shook US cities and white consciousness.

Efforts to understand this unrest pointed squarely to racial segregation of whites and blacks in big cities and the disadvantages and frustrations that this segregation created for African Americans. Central to this literature was John Kain's (1968) "spatial mismatch" hypothesis, which continues to inspire research to this day. Stripped to the bone, the spatial mismatch hypothesis advances two claims: first, proximity to jobs increases odds of employment and reduces commuting costs; second, African Americans tend to live farther than whites from available jobs as a result of residential segregation and emergent patterns of suburbanization. As a result, African Americans as a group tend to have higher employment costs and lower job prospects than otherwise equal whites, leading to higher rates of joblessness and underemployment. In his study of data from the 1950s, Kain estimated that residential segregation cost African American workers as many as 9,000 jobs in Detroit and 24,000 jobs in Chicago.

A decade later William Julius Wilson (1978) tweaked this idea in his influential book, *The Declining Significance of Race*, when he argued that US society was entering a new era during the 1970s in which class, more than race, now determined the life chances of African Americans. Wilson rooted this claim in the growth of college-educated blacks in professional occupations beginning in the late 1960s. For them, and their white counterparts, Wilson claimed, class position, not race, would define their place in the stratification system. The fate of less-educated blacks, however, would differ radically. Wilson later argued in *The Truly Disadvantaged* (1987) that as the black middle class grew, it would exercise its new racial freedom and move from established inner-city neighborhoods, leaving behind an impoverished "urban underclass" that lacked the skills, job opportunities, and social resources needed to succeed in today's urban economy. The result, Wilson claimed, was not only poor people but also disorganized communities that suffered from their eroding class, not racial, status.

This line of argument generated a great deal of debate in urban studies, with perhaps the most prominent critique coming from Douglas Massey and Nancy Denton (1993) in their book *American Apartheid*. In this and subsequent work, the authors argue that recent shifts in the urban economy away from manufacturing toward professional services have been uniquely detrimental to African Americans because they have joined with racial segregation to produce extreme concentrations of poverty that expose poor blacks to remarkably harsh and disadvantaged neighborhood environments. At stake in the ensuing debate with Wilson was whether race and class could ever truly be viewed as separate causes of urban inequality and what the answer implied for policy efforts to redress this inequality. For Wilson, class-specific actions that avoided the stigma of racial politics were best – higher educational standards, better teacher development, more school funding, public childcare and parental leave, universal health care, school-to-work programs, job centers, public employment programs, and the like. For Massey, these laudable efforts would have to be accompanied by race-specific remedies to reduce discrimination and expand opportunities for African Americans specifically, who remain by far the most segregated group in US cities.

By the late 1990s, immigration began to push the intellectual pendulum back from concerns over black/white segregation to concerns over immigrant adjustment and its role in reshaping racial, ethnic, and class inequalities in cities. Central to this literature is the question of how millions of less-educated immigrants can enter the same urban environments that failed less-educated African Americans and succeed, growing in number. The current answer, while still evolving, seems to run roughly as follows. Less-educated immigrants are willing to take jobs that less-educated natives will not due to the stigma that these jobs carry in US society. Immigrants who accept these stigmatized jobs, in turn, help friends and relatives move to the area to take similar jobs. The result is an ethnically organized economy for less-educated workers, wherein racial and ethnic groups not only tend to live apart from one another but also work apart in labor markets regulated as much by ethnic networks as by market forces. Whether these developments constitute "success" for less-educated immigrants is open to question, but scholars have already begun to talk of a new "immigrant underclass" that, despite its steady employment and dense job networks, finds itself living and working in substandard conditions that appear difficult to escape.

A related concern in this area is whether immigration and its urban concentration have increased the difficulties facing less-educated African Americans. Sometimes referred to as the "immigrant competition" hypothesis, this question has generated much debate but mixed results. On the one hand, economists and social demographers, who generally expect immigration to harm the wages and employment opportunities of blacks due to open markets, have found little evidence to this effect. On the other hand, sociologists working from a "new economic sociology" framework, who generally assume that immigrant networks minimize competition with blacks, have found evidence of a negative effect of immigration on African Americans' job prospects. The argument here is that urban blacks have trouble finding decent jobs not because they lack the necessary education and experience but because immigration has divided urban labor markets along ethnic lines, reducing job opportunities for natives, especially less-skilled African Americans. Where these and related intellectual traditions on inequality and the city lead next remains for future researchers to decide.

SEE ALSO: City; Global/World Cities; Hypersegregation; Social Exclusion; Uneven Development; Urban Ecology; Urban Political Economy; Urban Poverty; Urban Renewal and Redevelopment

REFERENCES AND SUGGESTED READINGS

Christaller, W. (1966 [1933]) *Central Places of Southern Germany*. Prentice-Hall, Englewood Cliffs, NJ.

Kain, J. (1968) Housing Segregation, Negro Employment, and Metropolitan Desegregation. *Quarterly Journal of Economics* 82(2): 175–97.

McKenzie, R. (1927) The Concept of Dominance and World Organization. *American Journal of Sociology* 33: 28–42.

Massey, D. & Denton, N. (1993) *American Apartheid: Segregation and the Making of the Underclass*. Harvard University Press, Cambridge, MA.

Sassen, S. (1991) *The Global City: New York, London, Tokyo*. Princeton University Press, Princeton.

Wilson, W. J. (1978) *The Declining Significance of Race: Blacks and Changing American Institutions*. University of Chicago Press, Chicago.

Wilson, W. J. (1987) *The Truly Disadvantaged: The Inner City, the Underclass, and Public Policy*. University of Chicago Press, Chicago.

Wirth, L. (1928) *The Ghetto*. University of Chicago Press, Chicago.

inequality/stratification, gender

Michele Adams

Gender stratification refers to the level of inequality in society based on gender, the social characteristics associated with sex. Specifically, gender stratification refers to the differential ability of men and women to access society's resources and to receive its privileges. As gender stratification increases, so does the level of gender inequality, reflecting greater differences between men's and women's access to power. Because historically men have garnered greater social power, gender inequality has systematically disadvantaged women. Gender inequality is complicated, moreover, by the intersection of gender with race/ethnicity, social class, age, and sexuality. That is, every individual, categorized as either male or female, also falls somewhere within a matrix of domination that includes these other dimensions (Collins 1991).

Original applications of the terms sex and gender tended to confuse the two, which were often used interchangeably. More recently, most sociologists have begun to distinguish between them, agreeing that the terms should apply to different, but related, concepts. While sex is defined in terms of biology and the reproductive organs one is born with, gender is typically seen in more social terms, as society's idea of how people should be, based on their biological sex. Gender, that is, is socially constructed to reflect society's expectations about how men and women should act, dress, move, and comport themselves in the context of everyday social interaction.

Under what conditions did gender inequality originate and under what conditions has it been maintained? Early answers to this question drew on biological differences between men and women and their associated reproductive functions to posit a "natural" division of labor between the two. Accordingly, men were seen as having evolved from hunters to family breadwinners and providers, with women as childbearing, childrearing, and domestic experts. More sophisticated study of premodern societies, however, has discredited many of these assumptions, pointing to more diversity and fluidity in men's and women's roles than a natural division of labor could explain.

As more nuanced information emerged from research on early societies, perspectives on the origin of gender inequality became more complex. Two main explanatory approaches surfaced from these later analyses, one economic and the other political. One early economic perspective came from Friedrich Engels's book, *The Origins of the Family, Private Property and the State* (1884). Although some of his assumptions are now recognized as incorrect, he was accurate in suggesting that early societies were more gender egalitarian than later ones, based on the latter's accumulation of material surplus. Social theorists (Blumberg 1978; Huber & Spitze 1983; Chafetz 1990) have proposed varying economic perspectives on the origin of gender inequality, taking account of labor conditions, the kinship system, and larger social politics. Generally, economic perspectives on gender stratification suggest that a high demand for women's labor, combined with kinship systems that promote inheritance through the maternal line and residence with female kin, promotes women's economic power and reduces gender inequality. Increased gender equality is evidenced in women's greater control over their fertility, choice of marriage partners, sexuality, and greater authority in the home and local politics.

Political perspectives on the origins of gender stratification examine how military situations and the organization of the state affect the relative power of men and women. One political theory of gender stratification evaluates ways by which control of weaponry, overall military situation, and social stratification and economic surplus affect inequality (Collins 1975). This perspective suggests that gender stratification increases as fighting and weapons are increasingly monopolized by men, and economic surplus and class stratification are high. Under these conditions, women are controlled as sexual property.

The industrial revolution reduced the importance of sex differences in maintaining the gendered division of labor. Machines replaced muscle power, and men's brawn became less significant as a source of energy. By the beginning of the twentieth century, bottle sterilization techniques freed women from the necessity of breastfeeding with its associated time and schedule demands. Over the course of the twentieth century, the invention of the birth control pill and other reliable contraceptive methods allowed women greater control over their reproduction, giving them relative freedom to move into the paid workforce in increasing numbers. According to the *Statistical Abstract of the United States, 2004–2005*, by the end of the century, nearly 60 percent of women aged 25 or older, many mothers of young children, worked in the paid labor force. This is a trend, moreover, that

shows little sign of abating. The sheer volume of women now doing paid work has, to a significant degree, lowered the level of gender inequality in the workplace.

The women's movement has been instrumental in reducing gender inequality. In the US, the first wave of the movement emerged in the mid-nineteenth century as a reaction to women's lack of power in both the public and private spheres. Elizabeth Cady Stanton and Susan B. Anthony are well-known as initiators of the movement, which ultimately turned its sights toward women's suffrage. After gaining the vote in 1920, the women's movement in the US became relatively inactive for the next 50 years, only to reemerge in the 1970s. This second wave of feminism reinvigorated the quest for women's empowerment in marriage and family and sought to equalize women's involvement and opportunity in institutions such as the labor force, education, law, and politics. While the struggle for women's equality is far from over, second wave feminism was able to mobilize many women (and men) on behalf of women's rights, overturning a number of institutionalized inequities embedded in law and promoting women's involvement in professional occupations and politics at the highest levels.

Nevertheless, both in the US and globally, women continue to be negatively affected by gender stratification. Although inroads have been made, gender persists as a core organizing structure around which inequality is arranged. In the workplace, occupations remain gender segregated overall, with "women's work" providing lower pay, fewer benefits, and less security than "men's work," even if comparable in form or content. At home, women continue to shoulder the lion's share of household labor, childcare, and domestic responsibility, even when employed in the paid labor force. These trends, moreover, extend globally, such that while women now constitute over a third of the world's labor force, they also, according to the Population Crisis Committee (1988), constitute 70 percent of the world's poor.

In the US, education is one area in which women have made substantial gains. In 1970, women comprised roughly 42 percent of undergraduate college enrolment; by 2001, that figure had risen to approximately 56 percent, a trend that is projected to continue (Peter & Horn

2005). Similarly, women today are awarded the majority of bachelors degrees (57 percent). Less change has occurred in the areas in which men and women earn their degrees and the earnings realized from them. In 2001, men predominated in business and engineering programs, as they did in 1980, while women have continued to earn more degrees than men in education, the health professions, and psychology. Moreover, the gender wage gap for bachelors degree recipients employed full time one year after graduation actually increased between 1994 and 2001. In 1994, these women earned 84 percent of what these men earned; in 2001, women's earnings had dropped to 83 percent of men's earnings (Peter & Horn 2005).

Women have made less educational progress elsewhere in the world. A gender gap in education persists in much of the developing world, where women's enrolment lags behind men's enrolment at all educational levels. Nevertheless, research continues to demonstrate the importance of women's education, which is positively related to beneficial national outcomes such as economic growth, greater life expectancy, and improved functioning of political processes (Hill & King 1995).

Where women are denied education and other rights, their health tends to suffer. For instance, lack of access to information on preventing HIV/AIDS has contributed to women's increased susceptibility to this devastating disease. According to the UNAIDS report "Women, Girls, HIV and AIDS" (2004), of those infected with HIV worldwide, 47 percent are women; in Sub-Saharan Africa, that figure has risen to 57 percent. Besides lack of education, the spread of HIV/AIDS among women has been linked to their restricted access to employment, property ownership, and other rights, as well as their vulnerability to violence.

Violence against women continues to be a major problem, reflecting the extent of gender inequality worldwide. Domestic violence perpetrated against women by their intimate partners has become an issue of international concern, occurring in all countries and across all social, economic, religious, and cultural groups. Stranger rape has become a weapon of war, and women in war zones are habitually subject to sexual assault by their captors both during and after conflict. In some countries such as in Africa,

women ranging in age from infancy to maturity are subjected by custom to genital mutilation. This practice, condemned by international groups, reflects the second-class citizenship of women and related attempts to regulate their sexuality. By the same token, constraints on women's ability to control their own sexuality and reproduction have historically been a hallmark of societies with high levels of gender stratification. Lack of access to safe methods of birth control and information regarding family planning and other reproductive options continues to plague women in a number of developing countries (Pillai & Wang 1999).

The following theoretical perspectives are among those invoked to explain the persistence of gender inequality. Sociobiological explanations suggest that the gendered division of labor is based on biological differences between men and women. The greater physical power of men, these theories suggest, leads to economic and political power. Women's reproductive functions, on the other hand, leave them vulnerable, dependent on men for protection and support, and without social power. Sociobiological explanations have been criticized for ignoring relevant cultural and social factors that affect the balance of power between men and women.

Structural functionalism peaked in the US in the 1950s with the theorizing of Talcott Parsons. Reflecting the powerful pro-family sentiment that characterized this era, structural functionalists promoted the complementarity of gendered roles for men and women, particularly in the context of the family. Men were instrumental, rational, goal oriented, and unemotional, and their associated role involved acting as family breadwinner. Women were expressive, emotional, and nurturing, and, as a result, were expected to stay home, tend the hearth, and raise the children. Because of the economic aspect of the breadwinner role, men were valued more highly than women, whose family role involved no monetary benefit. Adherence to the structural functionalist notion of gender roles thus institutionalized gender stratification and inequality as a functional imperative of family life. Today, structural functionalism receives little academic support, as it, too, omits questions of power.

Conflict theory is another perspective that may be used to explain gender stratification.

In this account, issues of power do come into play, with gender inequality explained as resulting from the unequal distribution of resources and power between men and women. Men's institutionalized and superior access to resources keeps them in control, while women, who have less access to valued resources, are obliged to submit.

Feminist theory is a version of conflict theory, suggesting that the unequal distribution of resources, control, and power is intentionally (if subconsciously) exercised by men to dominate women. Women are at the center of feminist theory and patriarchy is represented as the social system that supports men's domination of women. The goal of feminist theory is to move beyond theory to actively reduce gender inequality in society and in women's everyday lives.

In some arenas, gender stratification appears to be declining; in others, it does not. Evidence of the former comes in the form of men's increasing participation in household labor and childcare, once thought to be exclusively women's work. Evidence of the latter can be seen in the intractability of the gender wage gap and the glass ceiling that women bump up against in the paid labor force. Moreover, while men are, in fact, sharing more labor in the home, most of the increase can be explained by women who do less rather than by men who do substantially more. Nevertheless, as women continue to press for equality and men recognize the benefits that shared parenting and involved partnering have for them, gender equality is more likely than not to become the norm rather than the exception.

SEE ALSO: Feminist Activism in Latin America; Gender, Development and; Gender Ideology and Gender Role Ideology; Inequalities in Marriage; International Gender Division of Labor; Matrix of Domination; Patriarchy; Stratification, Gender and; Women's Movements

REFERENCES AND SUGGESTED READINGS

Blumberg, R. L. (1978) *Stratification: Socioeconomic and Sexual Inequality*. William C. Brown, Dubuque, IA.

Chafetz, J. S. (1990) *Gender Equity: An Integrated Theory of Stability and Change*. Sage, Newbury Park, CA.

Collins, P. H. (1991) *Black Feminist Thought: Knowledge, Consciousness, and the Politics of Empowerment*. Routledge, New York.

Collins, R. (1975) *Conflict Sociology: Toward an Explanatory Science*. Academic Press, New York.

Coltrane, S. & Collins, R. (2001) *Sociology of Marriage and the Family: Gender, Love, and Property*. Wadsworth, Belmont, CA.

Hill, M. A. & King, E. M. (1995) Women's Education and Economic Well-Being. *Feminist Economics* 1: 21–46.

Huber, J. & Spitze, G. (1983) *Sex Stratification, Children, Housework, and Jobs*. Academic Press, New York.

Krug, E. G., Dahlberg, L. L., Mercy, J. A., Zwi, A. B., & Lozano, R. (Eds.) (2002) *World Report on Violence and Health*. World Health Organization, Geneva.

Leeder, E. (2004) *The Family in Global Perspective*. Sage, Thousand Oaks, CA.

Peter, K. & Horn, L. (2005) *Gender Differences in Participation and Completion of Undergraduate Education and How They Have Changed Over Time* (NCES-169). US Department of Education, National Center for Education Statistics. US Government Printing Office, Washington, DC.

Pillai, V. K. & Wang, G. (1999) Women's Reproductive Rights and Social Equality in Developing Countries. *Social Science Journal* 36: 459–68.

Population Crisis Committee (1988) *Poor, Powerless, and Pregnant: Country Rankings on the Status of Women*. Population Briefing Paper, No. 20. US Government Printing Office, Washington, DC.

inequality, wealth

Nico Wilterdink

In all human societies beyond a certain minimum size, material possessions (such as land, animals, houses, tools, and consumption goods) are distributed unequally among individuals and groups. Insofar as these possessions have a monetary or exchange value, this unequal distribution can be described as inequality of wealth. Besides, and related to, income inequality, wealth inequality is an aspect of economic inequality which in turn is a dimension of social inequality in the wide sense. *Wealth* can be defined as the monetary value of the sum total of assets or goods belonging to a certain unit. This unit may vary from a national society (national wealth) to an individual person (individual wealth). *Personal wealth* is the wealth owned by an individual person or a consumption unit consisting of more than one person (a household or family). *Wealth inequality* is usually understood as the unequal distribution of personal wealth in a society.

Wealth gives the owner certain advantages; in other words, it has functions for the owner. These functions vary with the relative amount of wealth, its composition (the specific goods that make up the wealth), and its institutional context (including laws of property). In general terms, three economic or material functions can be distinguished: wealth is a source of (1) income (profits, interest, rent, dividend as well as capital gains), (2) material comfort and consumption (the ownership of a house and various durable consumption goods), and (3) material security. This latter function is particularly important when collective arrangements that guarantee some minimum income (pension rights, life insurances, social insurance, welfare payments) are lacking. Personal wealth can also have wider functions for its owners: it is a basis of (4) relative freedom and autonomy, (5) status, and (6) power. It contributes to individual freedom to the extent that it widens the scope of alternatives in consumption and leisure, and gives the possibility to postpone work, or not to work at all. In most stratified societies in the past, the very wealthy were a leisure class that distinguished itself by its freedom from physical labor. Wealth is also a source of status. Large wealth-holders may impress others by showing their possessions (a big house, a large piece of land, expensive jewelry, etc.) or obliging others by their generosity and material help. This may also contribute to power. More directly, wealth is a basis of power when it enables the owner to make other people work for him (as employees, servants, or even slaves). And it may be helpful in acquiring wider political power, for example, as a basis for financing an election campaign. Finally, personal wealth is (7) an important vehicle for keeping privileges within the family as it is transferred to the next generation through inheritance. On all these accounts, wealth inequality is at the basis of, and connected to, various dimensions of social inequality.

In the course of human history, wealth inequality tended to increase with the growing size and complexity of societies. In larger agrarian societies, most arable land was typically owned by only a tiny fraction of the population. This landed aristocracy not only derived the bulk of its income from the land, but also had political rights and privileges with respect to those who tilled the land, the dependent peasantry. With commercialization and monetarization and the advance of capitalism, starting in Western Europe in the late Middle Ages, these "feudal" relations gradually disappeared, and property became more sharply differentiated from political power. It is only under these modern conditions that wealth inequality can be assessed with some degree of accuracy.

Several empirical studies have attempted to assess the degree of wealth inequality in a given society and trends over time on the basis of tax data. Most studies have been undertaken by economists and economic historians. Lindert (2000: 181) calculated on the basis of estate duty data that the wealthiest 1 percent of households in England and Wales in 1670 held 48.9 percent of total personal wealth; in 1700 this share had declined to 39.3 percent, but since then it rose to 43.6 percent in 1740, 54.9 percent in 1810, and 61.1 percent in 1870. These figures thus indicate a high and, for the period 1700–1875, rising inequality. A high concentration of wealth was also found in the city of Amsterdam, Holland, in the seventeenth century, where the richest 1 percent of families held 41 percent of total taxable wealth in 1631 and 45 percent in 1674 (Soltow & van Zanden 1998: 38). Less inequality has been found for the US in the nineteenth century, although here too wealth inequality tended to increase, the share of the top 1 percent of households rising, according to one estimate, from 21 percent in 1810 to 31 percent in 1900 (Schneider 2004: 29, Table 3.10).

For the twentieth century and beyond, more data and estimates are available. Table 1 summarizes findings on trends in three countries: the UK, the US, and Sweden.

Table 1   Share of top 1%/5% of wealth-holders in total personal wealth in the UK, the US, and Sweden, 1911–2000

Year	UK	US	Sweden
1911–13	69/87		
1920–2		37/–	50/77
1929–30	58/79	44/–	47/74
1935			42/70
1938–9	55/77	36/–	
1949–51	47/74	27/–	33/60
1960	34/60		
1969–70	30/54	31/–	23/46
1975			17/38
1979–80	20/43	21/–	
1983			21
1990–2	18/35	34/–	
2000	22/42		

Several conclusions can be drawn from the figures in this table as well as the outcomes of studies on other countries:

1   The degree of inequality in the distribution of personal wealth is much higher than that of income. The shares of the top 1 percent or 5 percent in total personal wealth are normally more than twice the shares of the top 1 percent or 5 percent in total disposable income.

2   During the first three-quarters of the twentieth century, wealth inequality in western countries tended to diminish, though this tendency was much less clear and outspoken for the US than for the UK and Sweden. The same trend has been observed for several other western countries as well, such as France, Belgium, (West) Germany, Canada, and the Netherlands.

3   Since the last 15–25 years of the twentieth century, this trend stopped or even reversed: wealth inequality increased in many western societies.

These developments more or less correspond, and are related, to trends in income inequality. In order to assess their sociological significance, one has to connect them to other social developments: the long-run growth of national wealth; the increasing significance of collective wealth, such as pension funds and government-owned assets; and the development of welfare

state arrangements that give a certain degree of material security and are, in this respect, a functional alternative to personal wealth. The tendency of decreasing personal wealth inequality, particularly in the period from about 1930 to 1975, went hand in hand with equalizing tendencies in other respects: decreasing income inequalities and the development and expansion of collective arrangements for material security, including pension rights and state-guaranteed social insurances. The inclusion of pension rights in the distribution of wealth among individuals or households results in a lower degree of wealth inequality. The ongoing expansion of pension funds alleviates to some extent the tendency of growing personal wealth inequality since the last few decades of the twentieth century. On the other hand, this tendency is reinforced by other trends in the direction of more inequality: growing income differences and declining levels of state-regulated transfer incomes.

Economic explanations of wealth distribution usually start with individuals. Basic determinants of individual wealth are: earned (non-property) income, the savings rate, age, returns on wealth (property income and capital gains), and inheritance. The larger the differences in these respects, the larger the resulting wealth inequality. Several factors explain why wealth inequality is much higher than income inequality. First, there is a strong positive correlation between income and savings rate. High-income groups save more not only in absolute terms, but also proportionally. Low-income groups often spend more than they get, and as a consequence their wealth amounts to zero or is even negative. Whereas households cannot survive for long with a zero or negative income (unless they are very wealthy!), they can do without wealth (apart from some basic consumption goods). Secondly, the accumulation of wealth on the basis of savings on current income takes time; therefore, older age groups are on average wealthier than younger ones, and the differences within the older age groups are larger. A third factor is the cumulative interaction between income and wealth which is particularly important in the creation of new fortunes. In a capitalist market, one or a few entrepreneurs get a competitive advantage in new expanding branches; high profits are made that can be reinvested and lead to a strong upward appreciation of the invested capital.

In the course of the twentieth century, labor incomes (wages and salaries) in western societies increased in absolute terms and relative to capital incomes: this explains, to some extent, why wealth inequality tended to diminish. Through savings on wages, small wealth was created that brought some redistribution in favor of formerly "propertyless" wage earners. A more specific factor, related to this, was the spread of home-ownership. The introduction of new or higher taxes on wealth and income from wealth and/or wealth transfers (particularly inheritances) may also have contributed to some leveling in the distribution of wealth. Short-term changes in wealth inequality are connected to differential capital gains, especially fluctuations on the stock market: since shares and bonds are highly concentrated among large wealth-holders, a booming stock market leads to increasing wealth inequality, a recession on the other hand to decreasing inequality. This partly explains why wealth inequality increased in many western countries from the 1980s when stock prices started to rise more strongly and steadily than in previous years. A more general explanation is that returns on capital increased relative to average wages and wage incomes became more unequal. Moreover, in several countries tax reforms were initiated that were particularly advantageous for the well-to-do.

These explanations can be given a more sociological twist by relating factors of production to social groups or classes and conceiving the relations between these groups in terms of power and interdependence. The growth of wage income relative to capital income resulting in decreasing wealth inequality can be regarded as the manifestation of a shift in the power relation between (large) capital owners and workers (manual and non-manual, on different levels) in favor of the latter, which was in turn connected to processes of industrialization, urbanization, and democratization. In the last decades of the twentieth century, on the other hand, processes of deindustrialization and globalization contributed to the weakening power position of organized labor in relation to corporations and their shareholders, which may help to explain the growth of income and wealth inequality.

SEE ALSO: Capital: Economic, Cultural, and Social; Class, Perceptions of; Class, Status, and Power; Income Inequality and Income Mobility; Poverty; Stratification and Inequality, Theories of

REFERENCES AND SUGGESTED READINGS

Lindert, P. H. (2000) Three Centuries of Inequality in Britain and America. In: Atkinson, A. B. & Bourguignon, F. (Eds.), *Handbook of Income Distribution*, Vol. 1. Elsevier, Amsterdam.
Schneider, M. (2004) *The Distribution of Wealth*. Edward Elgar, Cheltenham.
Soltow, L. & van Zanden, J. L. (1998) *Income and Wealth Inequality in the Netherlands, Sixteenth–Twentieth Centuries*. Het Spinhuis, Amsterdam.

infant, child, and maternal health and mortality

Michelle J. Hindin and Britta Mullany

According to the World Health Organization (WHO), health is a state of "complete physical, mental, and social well-being and not merely the absence of disease or infirmity." The health status of a population, including that of infants, children, and mothers, has traditionally been summarized via mortality. An infant death is defined as a death under the age of 1; the standard indicator used to measure infant death is the "infant mortality rate," equal to the number of infant deaths under the age of 1 per 1,000 live births in a given year. A child death is a death of a child under the age of 5; the "under-5 mortality rate" refers to the number of deaths of children under age 5 per 1,000 live births in a given year. Given the multiple periods of risk related to a pregnancy, the definition of maternal mortality is more complex. A maternal death is one which occurs while "pregnant or within 42 days of the termination of pregnancy, irrespective of the duration and the site of the pregnancy, from any cause related to or aggravated by the pregnancy or its management but not from accidental or incidental causes" (WHO 1948). The "maternal mortality ratio" is the most frequently used indicator to measure maternal deaths and is defined as the number of women who die as a result of complications of pregnancy or childbearing in a given year per 100,000 live births in that year.

INEQUALITIES IN INFANT, CHILD, AND MATERNAL HEALTH AND MORTALITY

The death of an infant or child is considerably more likely in a developing country as compared to more developed settings. According to data from 2003–4, almost 11 million child deaths occur annually – approximately 8 million of these deaths occur in the first year of life. The first 28 days of life (also known as the neonatal period) represent the period of greatest risk with approximately 4 million deaths worldwide occurring during this time. With average under-5 mortality rates of 89/1,000 live births for the developing world and 120/1,000 for the world's poorest countries, and 8/1,000 for high-income countries, a child's risk of dying before his or her fifth birthday is at least 11 times higher in developing countries than in developed countries. The majority of child deaths around the world occur in Sub-Saharan Africa and South Asia. High child mortality is strongly linked to high fertility rates, which in turn increases risks of maternal, infant, and child death; this cycle, known as the replacement effect, suggests that a decline in infant and child death rates is a necessary precursor for a decline in fertility.

In the scope of public health, maternal mortality is the health risk for which the largest divide exists between the developed and the developing world. Approximately 515,000 maternal deaths occur worldwide each year, 99 percent of which are in developing countries; consequently, a woman's risk of dying from pregnancy-related complications is 45 times higher in the developing versus the developed world. While the maternal mortality ratio (MMR) in the developed world is 12/100,000 live births, the MMR in the developing world is 440/100,000, with the highest risks being found in Sub-Saharan Africa and South Asia. For each

woman who dies due to complications of pregnancy or childbearing, an estimated 30 women are afflicted with chronic disease, disability, or physical injury resulting from pregnancy-related complications. The death of a mother can have dire ramifications on a family, particularly in the developing country context. In addition to the loss of the primary caregiver and of a productive worker, the risk of death for her children under the age of 5 is doubled (in some cases, even tripled).

THE CAUSES OF INFANT, CHILD, AND MATERNAL HEALTH AND MORTALITY

The causes of infant and child mortality vary substantially in developed versus developing countries. The major causes of infant and child death in the developing world include neonatal causes (including birth asphyxia and low birth weight), diarrhea, pneumonia, malaria, measles, and AIDS. As societies become more advanced, the leading causes of infant and child death shift toward congenital anomalies, preterm-related disorders, sudden infant death syndrome, and others.

The direct causes of maternal death are unpredictable and often occur within hours or days after delivery. Globally, hemorrhage, sepsis/infection, and pregnancy-induced hypertension are the leading causes of maternal mortality. Other prominent causes of maternal death, particularly in developing countries, include obstructed labor and complications of unsafe abortion. Ectopic pregnancies result in a small proportion of maternal deaths in more industrialized countries as well.

The vast inequities in risk between higher-income and lower-income countries are one of the most striking elements about infant, child, and maternal survival. Similar gaps in infant, child, and maternal mortality are increasingly being seen between wealthy and poor communities within most countries of the world. While the direct medical causes of maternal, child, or infant death can be roughly outlined as above, it is exceedingly difficult to divide the direct cause of a death from the individual, social, economic, and cultural factors that precede and impact that medical condition and its management.

As related to child survival, for example, recent research has indicated that the predominant underlying cause of the majority of global child deaths, including deaths attributed to diarrhea, pneumonia, malaria, and measles, is malnutrition, which itself is the consequence of numerous factors.

In an effort to simplify these complexities, Figure 1 presents a conceptual framework of infant, child, and maternal mortality. The framework depicts some of the pathways through which distal determinants, such as socioeconomic conditions and cultural factors, can influence more intermediate health determinants, such as hygiene and sanitation practices and in turn contamination of water or food, which subsequently impact infant, child, and maternal survival via proximate mechanisms (or actual causes of death), such as undernutrition or infectious disease.

The socioeconomic, cultural, and political context of a population is crucial in understanding patterns of health in that setting. These background factors set the stage for individual, household, and community-wide factors that ultimately influence health outcomes by acting through maternal and/or environmental pathways. Poverty, for example, is perhaps the most common underlying factor that both "increases exposure and reduces resistance to disease, a synergy that contributes to the wide inequities" in infant and child health, as well as maternal health (Victora et al. 2003). In addition, risks to health are frequently compounded by the reduced utilization of and access to health services often found in poorer communities. The WHO and UNICEF have, for example, described maternal mortality as "a litmus test of the status of women, their access to health care and the adequacy of the health care system in responding to their needs" (WHO/UNICEF 1996).

Individual, household/familial, and community factors can play an important role in influencing the utilization of health care, which can ultimately impact health outcomes. A woman who wishes to seek health care for a condition but who has no decision-making power in her household may, for instance, suffer the repercussions of being denied access to household finances to seek care by her husband or other family member. Other social factors acting at the household level, such as domestic violence

toward pregnant women, can also have serious repercussions both on a woman's health and on the health of her child(ren). Worldwide, as many as 25 percent of women are physically or sexually abused during pregnancy, usually by an intimate partner. Women who have experienced violence are more likely to delay seeking antenatal care; more likely to experience sexually transmitted infections, bleeding during pregnancy, and unwanted or mistimed pregnancies; less likely to gain sufficient weight; and more likely to experience a miscarriage, abortion, premature labor, fetal distress, and low birth weight infant.

Factors influenced by distal determinants but ultimately specific to the mother impact the survival of both her and her children. For instance, short intervals between pregnancies increase the risk of pregnancy complications, with children born three to five years after a previous birth having a greater chance of survival compared to children born less than two years after a previous birth.

Background factors, such as household sanitation, can also impact exposure risks to disease through contaminated air, water, or food, and increased insect and parasite vector transmission. As a result of distal determinants operating via these intermediate environmental factors, children in poor settings are more likely to experience malnourishment and have lower resistance to infectious diseases. Similarly, women in such settings are more likely to experience poor maternal nutrition and infections during pregnancy, which in turn increases their risk of giving birth to a low birth weight baby, who is susceptible to undernutrition and disease.

Each of these points along the pathways, as illustrated in Figure 1, represents potential points for health promotion interventions, in the form of both prevention activities (e.g., improved access to water and sanitation, immunizations for pregnant women and children) and curative activities (e.g., improved access to health facilities, oral rehydration treatment for diarrhea). The reduction of infant, child, and maternal mortality must thus be achieved through a multitiered approach that addresses underlying factors (e.g., poverty, education, sociocultural aspects), intermediate causes (e.g., environmental contamination, short birth intervals), proximate causes (e.g., malnutrition, disease), and the population-equitable introduction

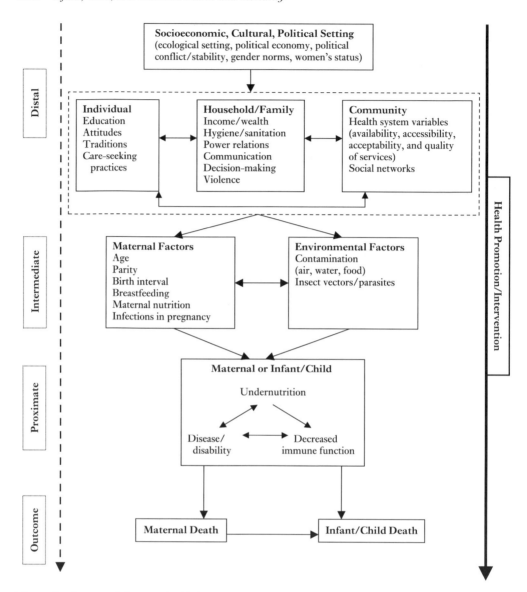

Figure 1   Conceptual framework of infant, child, and maternal health and mortality.

and monitoring of health promotion/disease prevention interventions (e.g., skilled attendance at birth, basic neonatal care, immunizations).

POLICY

The last two decades of the twentieth century witnessed an increased recognition of the important health needs and risks of women

and children globally. Figure 2 depicts an outline of the significant events impacting infant, child, and maternal health from the late 1970s to the present.

Numerous programs have been launched over recent years aimed at promoting infant and child health. In 1982, UNICEF, in collaboration with several other large international institutions, launched the Child Survival Revolution. In this initiative, reducing infant and child mortality

1976–1985	United Nations Decade for Women
1979	United Nations adopted the Convention on the Elimination of All Forms of Discrimination Against Women (CEDAW)
1982	UNICEF launched the Child Survival Revolution
1987	Safe Motherhood Initiative launched, Nairobi
1989	The convention on the rights of the child was adopted by the UN
1990	World Summit for Children and the Declaration on the Survival, Protection, and Development of Children
1992	Integrated Management of Childhood Illness (IMCI) Strategy by WHO and UNICEF began
1994	International Conference on Population and Development, Cairo
1995	The Fourth World Conference on Women: Action for Equality, Development, and Peace (including rights of girl-child), Beijing
1996	Generic guidelines for IMCI completed
2000	UN Millennium Goals launched through the United Nations Millennium Declaration
2000	Special Session of the UN General Assembly Women 2000: Gender Equality, Development, and Peace for the twenty-first century
2002	UN General Assembly Special Session on Children
2004	WHO strategy on Reproductive Health and Resolution on the Family

Source: www.un.org/esa/coordination/ecosoc/puc.htm (accessed August 5, 2004).

Figure 2   Timeline of recent significant events in maternal, child, and infant health.

was highlighted as an instrumental step along the journey of a country's development, and four low-cost interventions were singled out in an effort to reduce infant and child mortality. The acronym GOBI was used to summarize these four interventions (growth monitoring, oral rehydration therapy, breastfeeding, and immunization). Approximately a decade later, UNICEF and WHO introduced a new strategy named the Integrated Management of Childhood Illness (IMCI). Also aimed at reducing early childhood morbidity and death, the IMCI emphasized management of childhood illnesses with proper nutrition and immunization and improvement of service delivery at the household, community, and referral levels.

The launch of the Safe Motherhood Initiative (SMI) in 1987 represented an important commitment to maternal health, in the form of a partnership between WHO, the United Nations, the World Bank, and numerous governments and institutions. The primary aim of the SMI is to reduce maternal morbidity and mortality by encouraging the adoption of a number of maternal health promotion strategies (including family planning, post-abortion care, antenatal care, skilled assistance during childbirth, essential obstetric care, and adolescent reproductive health care).

An important perspective that has been gaining strength in maternal and child health movements has been an emphasis on human rights. The WHO estimates that 88–98 percent of maternal deaths are avoidable, and several international human rights committees consider the failure to address preventable causes of maternal death as being a violation of human rights. The Committee on the Elimination of Discrimination Against Women was one of the leading groups to clearly state this in its recommendations. Similar stances have been taken in relation to children; a shift toward viewing children as complete individuals has been crucial in framing their health rights as human rights, particularly in cases such as protection from sex trafficking of female children.

METHODOLOGICAL ISSUES

There are several methodological issues that arise for measuring infant, child, and maternal mortality. In the majority of settings where mortality risks run the highest, vital statistics registration systems are weak, and access to and utilization of health services are too low to provide accurate population estimates. Poor vital registration systems found in many settings lead to less than a full account of all births and deaths. Household surveys are often used; however, the relatively rare occurrence of death (particularly for maternal mortality) necessitates unusually large sample sizes, and consequently requires substantial financial and logistical inputs.

The calculation of infant, child, and maternal death rates can fall prey to seasonal effects; since many risk factors (e.g., malnutrition) and diseases (e.g., malaria) can change considerably throughout the seasons of a given year, caution must be exercised in surmising rates from data collected only in certain segments of a calendar year. Similarly, rapid shifts in fertility trends can result in misleading conclusions regarding maternal, infant, and child death rates.

There are specific issues that arise when measuring infant and child mortality, with data quality issues being the most prevalent. Members of a population most at risk for having a child death (e.g., individuals without a home or living in extreme poverty, migrant or conflict-affected communities) are also the most likely to be underrepresented in a vital events registration system; this problem is particularly problematic in developing country settings. Issues of underreporting and misclassification of mortality can be found for all ages of infant and child death, but are especially problematic for newborns. Beginning at the time of delivery, for instance, the correct identification of a live birth versus a stillbirth can be difficult. Though live births are used in the denominator for measuring rates of infant and child mortality, newborn infants who are born alive but die shortly (e.g., 1 minute) after birth may not be counted as live births, thereby underestimating the infant mortality rate. The timing of a death, or age at which a child dies, can be susceptible to both numerical rounding biases (i.e., respondents round up or down to the nearest age) and recall biases (i.e., respondents miscalculate the timing of the event). Retrospective recall difficulties can also result in misclassification of cause of infant or child death. In addition, child deaths are often the cause of sequential or concurrent illnesses, a factor that is important in ascertaining cause-specific risks to infant and child health. Greater efforts must therefore be made in correctly classifying a single cause of death, or multiple causes of death, allowing for the possibilities of co-occurrence of diseases or synergy in causes of death.

Assessing the levels of maternal mortality is also difficult since there are issues of measurement, misclassification, and underreporting. Despite being the most frequently cited indicator for measuring maternal mortality, the MMR has a number of weaknesses. The MMR uses live births in the denominator, although a sizable proportion of women each year experience (and survive) pregnancies that do not result in live births. Therefore, the MMR actually inflates the risk of maternal death. In addition, women die from pregnancy-related complications in the absence of a live birth, particularly women who experience unsafe abortions.

There are a number of alternatives to the MMR. Since most women become pregnant more than once in their lives, a more accurate measurement of maternal risk would take into account the lifetime risk of maternal death as a cumulative measure inclusive of fertility rates and the risk of dying from pregnancy-related causes. For instance, maternal mortality risk could be calculated per 100,000 pregnancies, rather than 100,000 live births; however, the near impossibility of counting the number of pregnancies makes this calculation unrealistic. The maternal mortality rate (number of maternal deaths in a given time period, usually one year, per 100,000 women of reproductive age) may better capture the risks introduced by exposure through fertility. The indirect sisterhood method of estimating maternal mortality relies on reports from the respondents of household surveys about pregnancy-related deaths among their sisters. This method, however, is costly since maternal mortality is relatively rare and therefore requires a very large sample size to obtain accurate population estimates. The WHO, UNICEF, and UNFPA have developed adjusted estimates of MMR that attempt to correct for underreporting and misclassification of maternal deaths.

Regardless of which estimation method is used to calculate maternal mortality, all methods are prone to misclassification bias and underreporting. Some examples of this include: the pregnancy status of a woman may be unknown at the time of her death; there may be fear or stigma preventing the report of an abortion-related, miscarriage-related, or other maternal death; or the medical cause of death may be unknown. Given these difficulties, proxy process indicators are used as monitoring tools. The "benchmark" proxy indicator promoted by UNICEF, WHO, and UNFPA is the percentage of all births attended by skilled health workers, including doctors, nurses, or midwives. These figures are often highly correlated with maternal mortality, are cost-effective, and easier to measure.

Data availability and quality are dependent on adequate funding. Several maternal health issues in particular are more sensitive to political shifts in resource allocation; data availability and quality are subsequently affected. Specifically, contraception, abortion, and comprehensive sex education, all of which influence women's reproductive health status, are particularly prone to political tides; the controversial aspects of these issues often manifest themselves in restrictions, terms, and/or conditions from funders of maternal health services. A paradoxical cycle of inadequate funding, followed by reduced availability of reliable data, is created; the less reliable data collected on these sensitive issues, the less funding that will be devoted to their improvement. There is a need for increased and improved event surveillance systems, as well as additional and stronger data concerning the identification of risk factors and the pathways between those risk factors and health outcomes, that will ultimately lead to more effective, affordable, and appropriate interventions for infant, child, and maternal health.

The sustained improvement of infant, child, and maternal health has faced major setbacks, and will inevitably continue to do so. Populations in crisis, such as those being persecuted, or those living or fleeing from war-torn or natural disaster-stricken areas, face greatly magnified health risks. The international community must learn to better address the health needs of these populations, including their amplified health risks as well as the often accompanying reduction or destruction of health infrastructure in such communities.

Perhaps the most prominent setback on the global stage has been the HIV/AIDS epidemic. Women account for almost half of the 40 million people living with HIV worldwide.

In the hardest-hit regions, most notably Sub-Saharan Africa, women make up the majority of people living with HIV, and maternal-to-child transmission of the virus is a major problem. Approximately 6 million children worldwide have been infected with HIV since the start of the pandemic, and access to the means of preventing vertical transmission from mother to child remains severely limited in many countries. In a 2004 call to action, several United Nations branches stated that in order to slow the spread of the epidemic and mitigate its consequences, the "triple threats" of gender inequality, poverty, and HIV/AIDS must be addressed.

FUTURE DIRECTIONS

A new set of benchmarks and policies may improve the global situation for infant, child, and maternal health. There is a growing focus on the significance of educating and empowering women, both for the sake of women themselves and for the overall health of their families. In 2000, the United Nations implemented a series of Millennium Development Goals, pledged to be met by all 191 United Nations member states. The third goal highlights the recognition of the importance of women's education by pledging to "eliminate gender disparity in primary and secondary education preferably by 2005, and at all levels by 2015." As more educated women enter the labor force, new infant, child, and maternal health issues will arise, creating the need for improved policies for women workers and workers with families. The International Labor Organization has played an active role in creating minimum standards for maternity leave, workers who are breastfeeding, and the needs of working families.

To improve infant, child, and maternal health, researchers, policymakers, and public health practitioners must go beyond the direct causes of death. The framework presented here attempts to capture social and contextual inputs that have traditionally been excluded or deemphasized in many health models and frameworks. Models need to consider a range of factors from the sociopolitical context to the power dynamics between couples to better understand the causes of infant, child, and maternal health and mortality. In addition, there is a critical need for research on improving strategies of health delivery systems and coverage of public health campaigns. Exploring multiple levels of influence on individual outcomes is required for increased understanding and prevention of mortality. In addition, a fundamental priority must be the improvement of surveillance and monitoring systems. The lack of high-quality population-representative data presents a major barrier to the development and implementation of more appropriate health promotion policies, particularly in developing country settings.

SEE ALSO: Family Demography; Family Planning, Abortion, and Reproductive Health; Gender, Health, and Mortality; Health Care Delivery Systems; Mortality: Transitions and Measures; Population and Development; Population and Gender; Socioeconomic Status, Health, and Mortality; Women's Empowerment; Women's Health

REFERENCES AND SUGGESTED READINGS

Black, R. E., Bryce, J., & Morris, S. S. (2003) Where and Why are 10 million Children Dying Every Year? *Lancet* 361(9376): 2226–34.

Cook, R. J. & Galli Bevilacqua, M. B. (2004) Invoking Human Rights to Reduce Maternal Deaths. *Lancet* 363(9402): 73.

Germain, A. (2004) Reproductive Health and Human Rights. *Lancet* 363(9402): 65–6.

Heise, L., Ellsberg, M., & Gottmoeller, M. (2002) A Global Overview of Gender-Based Violence. *International Journal of Gynecology and Obstetrics* 78 (Suppl. 1): S5–S14.

Setty-Venugopal, V. & Upadhyay, U. (2002) Birth Spacing: Three to Five Saves Lives. *Population Reports* L: 13.

United Nations (2003) *Indicators for Monitoring the Millennium Development Goals: Definitions, Rationale, Concepts, and Sources.* United Nations, New York.

Victora, C. G., Wagstaff, A., Schellenberg, J. A., Gwatkin, D., Claeson, M., & Habicht, J. P. (2003) Applying an Equity Lens to Child Health and Mortality: More of the Same is Not Enough. *Lancet* 362(9379): 233–41.

WHO (1948) Preamble to the Constitution of the World Health Organization. WHO, Geneva.

WHO/UNICEF (1996) Revised 1990 Estimates of Maternal Mortality: A New Approach by WHO and UNICEF. WHO, Geneva.

infertility

Arthur L. Greil

Infertility is a term used by medical professionals to refer to the physical inability to conceive a child or to successfully carry a child to term. Demographers typically employ the word "sub-fecundity" to describe this inability to have desired children. Some demographers use "infertility" to mean childlessness, regardless of childbearing intentions or contraception practices, but others utilize the term more narrowly and in conformity with popular and general sociological usage to refer to a woman's inability to give birth in the absence of contraception.

Although infertility must necessarily manifest itself in the female partner, the man or the woman or both may have the reproductive impairment. A specific male factor is identified in from 20 percent to 40 percent of those cases where a cause can be found. Since a major cause of infertility is female tubal factors related to reproductive tract infections (RTIs) spread through heterosexual intercourse, it is likely that men contribute to infertility in more than half of all infertile couples. It is thus ironic that, in many parts of the world, infertility is considered to be a "woman's problem."

Medical practitioners generally differentiate between "primary infertility," a situation in which an infertile woman has not had any pregnancies, and "secondary infertility," in which infertility has been preceded by at least one pregnancy. Demographers, epidemiologists, and other sociologists more often use these terms to refer to live births rather than pregnancies, using the term "primary infertility" to mean involuntary childlessness and the term "secondary infertility" to denote infertility experienced by couples who already have at least one biological child.

Most medical professionals consider a couple to be infertile if they have failed to conceive after 12 months of unprotected intercourse, reasoning that 90 percent of non-contracepting women will conceive within a year. This definition has been used by the National Survey of Family Growth (NSFG) in the United States and by researchers in the Netherlands, Norway, and other industrialized societies (Schmidt & Münster 1995). The World Health Organization (WHO) considers a couple to be infertile if they have experienced two years of unprotected intercourse (after which time 95 percent of non-contracepting women will have conceived), and some demographers have used longer intervals of either five or seven years (Larsen 2000). When self-reports are used to measure infertility, individuals are considered to be infertile if they state that it would be difficult or impossible for them to conceive a child. NSFG's definition of "impaired fecundity" combines medical considerations with self-reports (Chandra & Stephen 1998). Most studies of the social and psychological consequences of infertility utilize clinic samples, implicitly defining the infertile as those who are concerned enough about their fecundity to present themselves for treatment.

INCIDENCE

Various problems of methodology and data availability make it impossible to determine the incidence of infertility throughout the world with precision. The lack of consistent operational definitions of infertility makes it difficult to determine the numerator in an infertility rate with any confidence. But there is also uncertainty about the denominator, as no agreement exists with regard to who should be considered "at risk" for infertility. There are no agreed-upon upper and lower age limits for fertility; nor is there agreement about how to deal with women who have not "tested" their infertility by attempting to have children. Not all countries conduct population surveys based on random samples, and those that do employ various methodologies. Finally, many factors influence the accuracy of reporting, and there is no reason to assume that these factors will be consistent from one survey to another (Schmidt & Münster 1995).

Somewhere between 8 and 12 percent of couples or between 50 and 80 million people worldwide are affected by infertility (Inhorn 2002). Lifetime prevalence rates are probably considerably higher; it is likely that 20 to 40 percent of couples in any given society have been affected by infertility at some point in their lives (Schmidt & Münster 1995). There are wide

variations in the incidence of infertility from society to society and from region to region and ethnic group to ethnic group within societies. Infertility is particularly prevalent in Sub-Saharan Africa, to the extent that demographers often refer to a "Central African Infertility Belt." This higher rate is probably due to the higher incidence of RTIs. Secondary infertility appears to account for somewhat more than half of all cases of infertility in the industrialized world and is even more common in Sub-Saharan Africa.

SOCIAL AND CULTURAL CONTEXT

While infertility is clearly of interest to demographers, the study of infertility also has interest for sociologists interested in gender, help-seeking behavior, health care institutions, self-identity, and subjective well-being. Infertility is a health problem which can have far-reaching effects on life satisfaction, well-being, and psychological adjustment, especially for women. In societies throughout the world, parenthood is seen as an integral part of the transition to adult status. Because of the great importance attached to the childbearing and parenting roles, women often experience infertility as a catastrophic role failure, which can come to permeate every aspect of life (Sandelowski 1993).

Most research on the social and emotional impact of infertility has been marred by a reliance on clinic-based samples of treatment seekers. Because many infertile couples do not seek treatment, this makes it difficult to generalize findings to all infertile couples and confounds the consequences of fertility status, treatment seeking, and treatment itself. Descriptive and ethnographic studies have generally concluded infertility is a stressful experience that leads to psychological distress, feelings of social isolation, perceived stigma, and stressed relationships. The findings of quantitative studies using control groups have been more equivocal. In a review of the literature, Greil (1997) concludes that most well-designed studies find that the infertile are more distressed than the non-infertile, but not in a clinically significant way. McQuillan et al. (2003) conclude that infertility distress is found primarily among infertile women who remain childless. Most of the large body of research on the relationship between infertility and gender has found that women and men experience infertility differently, with women generally reporting greater distress.

Recently published ethnographic work (Inhorn & van Balen 2002) suggests that stigma and suffering of infertility may be more pronounced in developing societies, where parenting is culturally mandatory and where alternative roles for women may be less available. Infertility is both more common and more stigmatizing in many of the societies where fertility rates are highest and population pressures are greatest. Marcia Inhorn describes a "fertility–infertility dialectic," in which fear of infertility results in behaviors that lead both to high fertility rates and a high incidence of infertility. While infertility is seldom considered to be an important public health problem in societies where overpopulation is deemed to be the more serious problem, it may well be that controlling fertility rates will depend on dealing with women's concerns about *in*fertility.

TREATMENT

From 30 to 70 percent of infertile women in industrialized societies report that they have been to a physician or a clinic to seek treatment (Schmidt & Münster 1995). Treatment-seeking rates among industrialized countries appear to vary with access to health care, with treatment rates higher in societies with universal or near-universal health care coverage. Women with primary infertility are approximately twice as likely as those with secondary infertility to seek treatment. While reproductive impairments are actually more common among minority groups and those with lower incomes, whites and those with higher incomes are most likely to seek treatment. Many American women who are infertile according to the medical definition do not self-identify as infertile and therefore do not pursue treatment.

Increased media coverage in recent years has given the impression that the incidence of infertility has been rising dramatically in industrialized societies. In fact, this is not the case. It is, however, true that the number of *childless* infertile couples has been increasing in the

industrialized societies. Since female fertility declines with increasing age, the current trend in industrialized societies toward delayed childbearing means that a larger percentage of infertile couples than before are childless when they discover their infertility.

While the proportion of infertile women in industrialized societies has remained stable, the proportion of infertile women who have decided to seek medical treatment has increased dramatically in recent years in industrialized societies. Office visits for men have remained at virtually the same level as before. The trend toward delayed childbearing has meant that many women now discover their infertility at an older age when less time remains on the "biological clock." The advent of birth control technology may have given the infertile a stronger sense that conception is something that can be conquered via technology. Increased demand for medical services may also be related to the decreasing availability of non-medical solutions to the problem of involuntary childlessness, such as adoption.

Advances in medical treatment, including but not limited to such advanced reproductive technologies (ARTs) as *in vitro* fertilization (IVF) and intra-cytoplasmic sperm injection (ICSI), and the media attention that have surrounded them have contributed to a strengthening of the sense in developing societies that infertility is something that can be brought under control and that seeking medical treatment is the most appropriate response. A decline in the fertility rate has resulted in a drop in demand for obstetrical services in industrialized societies; when the supply of obstetricians exceeds the demand, gynecologists may be inclined to pay more attention to other kinds of services. Physicians may also have been encouraged to devote increased attention to infertility by the increased prestige that has come to infertility as a specialty as a result of publicity surrounding ARTs.

Treatment of infertility is often expensive, time-consuming, and invasive. The infertile often find that treatment regimens assume a central importance in their lives. The fact that reproductive technology has made the hope for a child more realistic can make infertility even harder to accept and can lead the infertile, especially infertile women, to become very treatment-oriented. A group of scholars influenced by feminist concerns has argued that overreliance on ARTs reinforces the notion of mandatory motherhood and reinforces traditional gender roles and patriarchal ideologies. Increasing reliance on ARTs has resulted in a dramatic rise in multiple births.

Demand for infertility treatment from both biomedical and traditional healers is quite strong in developing societies. For example, infertility is said to be the leading reason for gynecological visits in Nigeria. Clinics that offer IVF and other ARTs exist throughout the world, but access to them is typically limited to the wealthy. It is in the developing world, where demand for infertility services is greatest, that access to infertility treatment in general is most limited.

Areas where further research is needed include patterns of sociocultural variations in the experience of infertility; lay conceptions of infertility; help-seeking behavior; long-term consequences of infertility; and the socioeconomic context of infertility treatment.

SEE ALSO: Fertility: Low; Fertility: Transitions and Measures; Marriage; Medical Sociology; New Reproductive Technologies; Stigma

REFERENCES AND SUGGESTED READINGS

Chandra, A. & Stephen, E. H. (1998) Impaired Fecundity in the United States: 1982–1995. *Family Planning Perspectives* 30: 34–42.
Greil, A. L. (1997) Infertility and Psychological Distress: A Critical View of the Literature. *Social Science and Medicine* 45: 1679–1704.
Inhorn, M. C. (2002) Global Infertility and the Globalization of New Reproductive Technologies: Illustrations from Egypt. *Social Science and Medicine* 56: 1837–51.
Inhorn, M. C. & van Balen, F. (Eds.) (2002) *Infertility around the Globe: New Thinking on Childlessness, Gender, and Reproductive Technologies.* University of California Press, Berkeley.
King, R. B. (2003) Subfecundity and Anxiety in a Nationally Representative Sample. *Social Science and Medicine* 56: 739–51.
Larsen, U. (2000) Primary and Secondary Infertility in Sub-Saharan Africa. *International Journal of Epidemiology* 29: 285–91.
McQuillan, J., Greil, A. L., White, L., & Jacob, M. C. (2003) Frustrated Fertility: Infertility and Psychological Distress among Women. *Journal of Marriage and the Family* 65: 1007–18.
Sandelowski, M. (1993) *With Child in Mind: Studies of the Personal Encounter with Infertility.* University of Pennsylvania Press, Philadelphia.
Schmidt, L. & Münster, K. (1995) Infertility, Involuntary Fecundity, and the Seeking of Medical Advice in Industrialized Countries, 1970–1992: A Review of Concepts, Measurements, and Results. *Human Reproduction* 10, 1407–18.

infidelity and marital affairs

Kaeren Harrison

Infidelity is about being emotionally or sexually unfaithful. It is closely equated with non-monogamy, and as such is usually examined in the context of marriage. However, as constructions of marriage have changed since the middle of the twentieth century, the meanings attached to infidelity (or unfaithfulness, betrayal, or disloyalty) are no longer associated so exclusively with marriage. Awareness – and direct experience – of the fragility of marriage is high, ensuring that marriage is no longer uncritically perceived as a monogamous lifelong relationship. This is reflected in the popularity of prenuptial contracts, civil ceremonies, and the sharing of "relationship aspirations" rather than traditional marriage vows.

In his analysis of *The Transformation of Intimacy* (1992), Anthony Giddens provides a theoretical reappraisal of the nature of contemporary marital and partner commitment which is particularly interesting in the context of examining infidelity. In it, he describes the emergence of "confluent love," a form of intimacy based on mutual self-disclosure. The essence of confluent love lies in its contingency; couples construct a relationship of mutual trust and commitment alongside the knowledge that their relationship might not last for ever. The relationship will only last for as long as each member finds it emotionally and sexually fulfilling. Moreover, within confluent love, sexual exclusivity may or may not be significant, depending on the understandings negotiated by the couple.

Such views about transformations in the character of commitment in marriage and marriage-like relationships carry implications for understandings of infidelity. Of itself, a movement towards confluent love does not necessarily indicate that infidelity within partnerships is more acceptable than it once was. Indeed, it can be argued that monogamy (albeit serial rather than lifelong) remains a highly salient marker of commitment and stability in relationships because of the additional emphasis now placed on personal compatibility and long-term satisfaction (Allan & Harrison 2002). Nevertheless, the recognition that individuals have a right, and perhaps a responsibility, to seek fulfilment within their personal relationships, creates a cultural climate in which the exploration and development of new relationships is socially more acceptable than it once was.

Popular discourses around infidelity reflect these complexities. The terms "having an affair" or "becoming involved (or intimate) with someone else" carry different meanings and emotional overtones from "committing adultery" or "engaging in extramarital sex." The first two expressions convey greater tolerance and therefore a more ambiguous and muted moral message; the second two expressions retain a strong sense of social disapproval. In other words, responses to infidelity are shaped by the current understandings of marriage in the society and the social circle in question. Expressing this point slightly differently, the "rules" against infidelity are applied more readily to some people, and some groups, at some times, than others. An obvious example of this is the degree to which husbands' and wives' extramarital affairs have been understood very differently, with men's infidelity being condoned more readily than women's.

Attention must also be paid to the social or cultural variables that influence an individual's behavior. In agricultural societies, for example, marriage and kinship – with their associated land rights – represent the key structures around which social and economic organization is built. Under these conditions, it is likely that infidelity would be seen as a threat to the social

order as well as to the marital relationship, and would be condemned through a range of religious, moral, and social sanctions. Even today, there are some fundamentalist Muslim countries where infidelity may be punished by death. Cross-culturally, infidelity is the most frequently cited reason for divorce, and actual – or suspected – infidelity (usually on the part of the woman) is a primary cause of domestic violence and spousal homicide. These last two points, of course, indicate that for some women engaging in an affair carries very different risks and repercussions than it does for men, and therefore we should be cautious of an analysis of infidelity that is gender free.

However, recent research in Britain (Lawson 1988; Reibstein & Richards 1992; Wellings et al. 1994) has suggested that the incidence of affairs is increasing, and that behavior by men and women is converging. There is some evidence that many (or even most) men and women admit to having at least one affair in their first marriages (Lake & Hills 1979), indicating a move away from stereotypically gendered understandings of affairs based on "double standards," and suggesting a more complex understanding of sexuality, fidelity, and commitment where women's and men's needs are not highly differentiated. And yet both men and women in social attitude surveys in Britain and the US demonstrate continued disapproval of extramarital sexual relationships, with the percentage of people saying that such relationships were "always" or "mostly" wrong consistently being over 80 percent (Scott 1998). This would suggest that there is significant dissonance between what individuals feel their relationship practices should be like, and what they actually are like, making it increasingly difficult for people to make sense of affairs within the context of shifting normative frameworks.

Nevertheless, affairs – whether within heterosexual marriages or other forms of exclusive partnerships – are clearly important life events for those who have them. Unfortunately, despite the significance of affairs, there has been very little empirical research undertaken. This is a curious omission, given that sexual matters are now discussed far more openly and when there is greater ambiguity around the moral status of affairs. The recent resurgence of interest in family diversity and family practices has generated a lot of research on or about divorce, family dissolution and reordering, remarriage and, more recently, stepfamilies. However, little attention has been paid to the part that affairs might play in the process of marital breakdown and the character of new domestic arrangements. In other words, there would seem to be some disparity between the predominance of affairs on the one hand and the extent to which they have been studied academically on the other.

Among the reasons for the lack of sociological research into infidelity and marital affairs are the methodological issues and problems associated with the topic. Conducting research on issues of sex and secrecy raises serious ethical considerations, while the sheer variety of affairs makes any generalization difficult. This is a point that has been made by a number of authors who have investigated the broad nature of affairs and their consequences (Duncombe et al. 2004). Passion, transgression, secrecy and lies, betrayal, power, emotion work, identity construction, and gossip as a means of social control are common themes in Duncombe et al.'s edited collection, demonstrating the complex set of issues that face people who engage in affairs. There are few clues, however, as to why individuals might engage in affairs in the first place. Research is still in its early stages, but affairs tend to occur at different stages of marriage, possibly for different reasons. Early on, where partners have already engaged in premarital sex with others; after childbirth, when marital satisfaction dwindles; in early middle age, when individuals seek reassurance that they remain attractive; and in later years, when an affair may end an otherwise "empty" marriage. Men's affairs tend to cut across class, age, and marital status, whereas married women have markedly fewer relationships with young single men – a reflection, perhaps, of older men's greater resources and freedom, compared with women's "social depreciation" with age.

While the individuals involved (directly and indirectly) in affairs are important, it should also be remembered that these relationships develop, endure, and sometimes end within a wider complex of interacting forces. In other words, the patterns and pathways of affairs are framed within a societal context. The form affairs take, their importance in people's lives, the extent to which they are "allowed" to continue, and whether they are condemned or condoned, are all shaped by broader social and economic influences. The sociological study of how affairs are constructed at different historical points in time, among different social groups, would certainly contribute to an increased understanding of institutions and practices such as marriage, sexuality, morality, and gender relations.

SEE ALSO: Divorce; Intimacy; Marriage; Plastic Sexuality; Sexual Identities; Sexual Practices

REFERENCES AND SUGGESTED READINGS

Allan, G. & Harrison, K. (2002) Marital Affairs. In: Goodwin, R. & Cramer, D. (Eds.), *Inappropriate Relationships*. Lawrence Erlbaum, Mahwah, NJ, pp. 45–63.

Duncombe, J., Harrison, K., Allan, G., & Marsden, D. (Eds.) (2004) *The State of Affairs: Explorations in Infidelity and Commitment*. Lawrence Erlbaum, Mahwah, NJ.

Jamieson, L. (1998) *Intimacy*. Polity Press, Cambridge.

Lake, T. & Hills, A. (1979) *Affairs: The Anatomy of Extramarital Relationships*. Open Books, London.

Lawson, A. (1988) *Adultery*. Basic Books, New York.

Reibstein, J. & Richards, M. (1992) *Sexual Arrangements: Marriage and Affairs*. Heinemann, London.

Scott, J. (1998) Changing Attitudes to Sexual Morality: A Cross-National Comparison. *Sociology* 32: 815–45.

Wellings, K., Fields, J., Johnson, A., & Wadsworth, J. (1994) *Sexual Behaviour in Britain*. Penguin, London.

information and resource processing paradigm

Koichi Hasegawa

Tamito Yoshida's notion of the information and resource processing paradigm was influenced by information theory, particularly Norbert Wiener's *Cybernetics* (1948). At first,

Wiener was reluctant to relate his idea of cybernetic control to the social sciences, but he later came to apply the negative feedback process – the most basic principle of the cybernetic control mechanism – to organic bodies, human beings, and human society. The basic idea of Yoshida's (1990) general systems theory evolved from Wiener's work through the generalizing of his logic. His central hypothesis comprises the following.

The natural world is divided into "non-controlled nature," "inorganic nature" such as the universe, and "controlled nature." Controlled nature is composed of "organic nature" controlled by "genetic information" and "human nature" controlled by "cultural information." From Yoshida's "evolutionist" perspective, any natural system, including that of plants, animals, human beings, and any level of society, has the common basic structure of an "information and resource processing system." This means that any controlled system is "the system of resources and resource processing" controlled by "information and information processing." In this context, "information" and "resources" are defined in very broad and abstract terms. For instance, cherry blossoms only bloom when the temperature is higher than 20 degrees, hence they are controlled by temperature, by information. Similarly, human action involves a highly complicated process of information and resource processing. Human actions are controlled by a wide variety of cultural and social information such as language, signs, symbols, norms, and values. When we drive a car and come to a red signal, we press on the brake pedal. In this case, our behavior is controlled by the red signal, traffic rules, orders from cranial nerves and so on.

The structure of such systems is always configured by elements and patterns of information processing and resource processing. This structure is also controlled by information and information processing, such as norms and values. In family life, we can observe a pattern of action among family members (e.g., the sharing of housework, talking, the communal eating of meals, and so on). Social system is a "social information and resource processing system among two and more actors, including individuals and collectivities. Social resources are divided into material, informational, human,

and relational resources. Material resources include energy and energy resources. Money, influence, political power, love, and prestige are examples of relational resources.

Yoshida's ideas led to the development of his theory of the self-organizing system. An organic "information and resource processing system" is also a self-organizing system, with a built-in mechanism for structural change, so that when the performance of the system falls below a socially accepted level it has the potential to structurally change so as to increase its performance level. In cases where the system is performing adequately, it then remains stable and is able to maintain that performance level.

SEE ALSO: Social Change; System Theories

REFERENCES AND SUGGESTED READINGS

Wiener, N. (1948) *Cybernetics; or, Control and Communication in the Animal and the Machine.* MIT Press, New York.

Yoshida, T. (1990) *Jyoho to Jiko Soshiki-sei no Riron* (*Theory of Information and Self-Organizing Systems*). Tokyo, University of Tokyo Press.

information society

Hugh Mackay

The information society is a key way in which contemporary social transformation is conceived. Used commonly by policymakers, journalists, and futurists as well as sociologists, the notion encompasses a diversity of arguments which have in common that they see information, and information technology (IT), as at the heart of the burgeoning social order. Greater volumes of data are being communicated by a fast-growing range of technologies, with profound social consequences for nearly every aspect of social life. On the basis of the growth of information flows and technologies, information society theorists argue that the changes underway represent not just quantitative but qualitative social change – transforming almost every realm of social life, including households, communities, education, health, work, surveillance, democracy, and identities. Together, these changes are seen as constituting a new form of society, comparable to the shift from an agrarian to an industrial society. Rather than tightly defined, the scope of information society debates ranges widely and overlaps with other approaches to understanding contemporary social change. Other terms ("post-industrial society," "knowledge society," and "network society") carry similar and often overlapping meanings; while for some social theorists, different labels ("late modernity," "postmodernity," or "globalization") better characterize contemporary social transformations. Even those who focus on the "information society" use the term to refer to different social processes.

Information society theorists can be broadly categorized in terms of those who see technology as the driving force behind the change, versus those who see social factors as shaping technology and history. This debate, technological determinism versus "the social shaping of technology," lies at the heart of the sociology of technology. While sociologists have been concerned to refute technological determinism, countering the common, everyday way of conceiving of the relationship of technology to society, much work on the information society remains at least implicitly technologically determinist, while in the sociology of technology there is a growing interest in the constraining capacity of technology. Another key issue in the debate is whether and when quantitative changes (e.g., increasing flows of information, a larger information sector of the economy, or growing levels of ownership of IT devices) constitute qualitative change (the emergence of a new form of society, even an "IT revolution"). In other words, there is a debate about whether the situation is radically different from the past, or merely the continuation of long-running phenomena or tendencies. A further distinction is between optimists and pessimists, on which count the debate is remarkably polarized: for some (notably Daniel Bell), the information society is a progressive development, characterized by greater freedom and fulfillment, whereas others (Herbert Schiller, Jürgen Habermas, Nicholas Garnham, Frank Webster) point to the continuation or exacerbation of long-running

inequalities and patterns of control. Some contributors to the debate, and not just those in fiction and futurism, are normative in their writing, slipping into a mode of endorsing the changes that they identify as underway. Different theorists focus on different strands of the debate, notably the growth of technology, the transformation of the economy, the changing nature of work, new patterns of connection across time and space, and the coming to the fore of mediated culture. Contributors to the debate include economists (e.g., Fritz Machlup), geographers (e.g., David Harvey), planners (e.g., Manuel Castells), and cultural theorists (e.g., Mark Poster) as well as sociologists (e.g., Daniel Bell). The debate can be reviewed by considering the work of two key contributors to the field, Bell (who comes to the information society by identifying an information economy) and Castells (who provides a broad-ranging recent account of the information society).

The information society debate has its origins in the work of Daniel Bell, who has provided one of its most detailed accounts. Generally, he wrote about "post industrial society," but in some of his later work he refers to the "information society," and the distinction matters little to him. Bell argued that western economies had deindustrialized, by which he meant that they had a declining percentage of the workforce working in the manufacturing sector and growing employment in the service and information sectors. Figure 1 shows clearly the transformation which lies at the heart of his thesis.

Bell describes a "march through the sectors," from agrarian through industrial to post-industrial, or information, society. The shift of manufacturing to China and the growth of call-center employment are obvious contemporary manifestations of the changes to which he is referring. For Bell, pre-industrial society is characterized by muscle power, industrial society by machinery, and post-industrial society by information. The post-industrial society is about not only the transition to a service economy, but also the growth of scientific knowledge, which now drives history as never before.

Bell's thesis is rooted in, and draws heavily on, the empirical work of two economists, Fritz Machlup and Marc Porat. Machlup found that the knowledge industries between 1947 and

1958 expanded at a compound growth rate of 10.6 percent per annum, and thus established the high degree to which the US economy was dependent on its knowledge workforce. Machlup's definition of knowledge was his own subjective interpretation, Alistair Duff refers to this work as "riddled with errors," and Bell acknowledges that Machlup's data were "somewhat unsatisfactory." Nonetheless, there has been a dramatic growth in the use of codified knowledge which is transmitted systematically to others, and production and organization have become increasingly dependent on such knowledge. For Bell, knowledge has replaced labor as the source of added value, supplanting capital and labor as the central variable of society. Whether knowledge has *replaced* labor, or merely transformed it – perhaps increasing the skills required of the workforce – is debatable. Bell also used Porat's examination of the proportion of economic activity that can be attributed to information activities. Porat concluded that nearly 50 percent of the GNP and more than 50 percent of wages and salaries in the US in 1967 derived from the production, processing, and distribution of information goods and services.

Thus, Bell's analysis depends on definitions of "knowledge" and "service sector" and on the relationship between these and other sectors and occupations. There is considerable debate about such categorizations, and about how the processes are (or are not) related. Cleaning, transport, and accountancy, for example, might be classified as "services" if they are bought-in, but "manufacturing" if they are undertaken in-house. In other words, divisions into service and manufacturing can be unreliable or even meaningless. In his work there is some confusion about, and sometimes conflation of, knowledge and service work. Like futurists, but rather unusually for a sociologist, Bell is happy to play the role of social forecaster, presenting his vision of the future: his work moves readily from analysis to prognostication and even to prescription. He is remarkably optimistic, seeing the post-industrial society as one in which everyone will enjoy access to the world's traditions of art, music, and literature. Post-industrial society means the rise of professional work, professionals are oriented towards their clients, and society becomes transformed into a more caring, communal society. Education, care, public interest, and the environment, he wrote in the 1970s, become more important than restricted concerns to maximize the return on capital.

Finally, while Bell's analysis fuses data and argument about the economy, employment, and knowledge, underlying his work is a clear technological determinism. He epitomizes the information society literature by according to

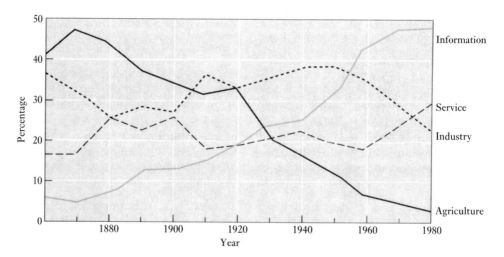

Figure 1 Four-sector aggregation of the US workforce, 1860–1980.
Source: Bureau of Labor Statistics, cited by Bell (1980: 521).

technology a central role in social change: technological innovation is seen as resulting in social change. By contrast, sociologists of technology reject the notion that technology is somehow outside society and that technological change causes social change. Rather, they have been concerned to explore how particular social formations *give rise to* (or shape) the development of specific technologies (MacKenzie & Wajcman 1999).

Castells's work on the "network society" provides a more recent account, again at a macro level, of contemporary, global, social transformation. His concern is to provide a cross-cultural theory of economy and society in the information age, specifically in relation to an emerging new social structure. While Castells uses a different term, his work resonates with the tenor of information society debates. Like Bell, Castells documents the demise of traditional, labor-intensive forms of industry and their replacement by flexible production. His account fuses the transformation of capitalism (notably, the growth of globalization) with changing patterns and forms of identity. He argues that, with the rise of the informational mode of development, we are witnessing the emergence of a new socioeconomic paradigm, one with information processing at its core. For Castells, the issue is not information as such, but the "informational society" – the "specific form of social organization in which information generation, processing, and transmission become the fundamental sources of productivity and power, because of the technological conditions" (Castells 1996: 21).

In other words, the issue is not simply that information is central to production, but that it permeates society. In the informational economy, networks are the new social morphology. Organizations are transforming from bureaucracies to network enterprises, responding to information flows, with economic activity organized by means of fluid project teams. Economic activity becomes spatially dispersed but globally integrated, reducing the strategic significance of place, but enhancing the strategic role of major cities. Networks are composed of interconnected nodes – places where information does not merely flow, but is collated, analyzed, and acted on. Thus, New York, Paris, Tokyo, and London are inhabited by a managerial class with a cosmopolitan lifestyle, extensive networks around the world, frequent air travel, and using exotic restaurants. In contrast with earlier time-space arrangements, there is in terms of flows no distance between nodes on the same network. In other words, geographical distance is irrelevant to connection and communication. So there are fundamental changes to the nature of time and space, with time compressed and almost annihilated; and space shifting to the space of flows: places continue to be the focus of everyday life, rooting culture and transmitting history, but they are overlaid by flows. The network of flows is crucial to domination and change in society: interconnected, global, capitalist networks organize economic activity using IT and are the main sources of power in society. The power of flows in the networks prevails over the flow of power – which might be read as some kind of "flow determinism." The Internet and computer-mediated communication are seen as transforming the fabric of society – though Castells explicitly rejects technological determinism.

The other main strands of Castells's argument are about identity and culture. The transformation of economies has been accompanied by the decline of traditional, class-based forms of association, particularly the labor movement. At the same time, state power has been eroded and new forms of collective resistance have emerged, notably feminism and environmentalism. The explosion of electronic media, specifically the development and growth of segmented audiences and interactivity, means the growth of "customized cottages" (as opposed to a global village) and a culture of "real virtuality." Although he acknowledges growing inequality, social exclusion, and polarization, Castells, rather like Bell, sees at least the possibility of a positive future, of new forms of communication and the network society offering democratizing possibilities.

While Bell focuses his analysis very much on the economy, and Castells provides a remarkably wide-ranging account, the work of these two key analysts of the information society addresses what can be seen as the four core themes of the information society, or of information society debates. First is the new patterning of work and inequality. This includes debates informed by Bell regarding the decline of manufacturing in western economies, and the growth of information and service sectors; the deskilling debate and the restructuring of work; and the growth of e-commerce. It also includes debates about the growing gulf between the rich and the poor, and social exclusion – the "digital divide." There is debate about the extent to which lack of access to information is a cause, rather than merely a reflection, of social exclusion.

Second is time-space reconfiguration, compression, or convergence – different authors use different terms. The shrinking of time and space, examined by Castells, is facilitated by instantaneous electronic communication. Globalization and digital information networks lie at the heart of information society debates. Some invoke McLuhan's notion of the global village and develop this in relation to the Internet, and a large and growing body of literature examines Internet communities, for example those of national diasporas. Multi-channel television and global television flows are key components of global cultural communication. The erosions of boundaries between home and work and public and private are other aspects of time-space reconfiguration.

Third is the huge growth of cultural activities, institutions, and practices. Culture has become increasingly significant in contemporary society, and with new ICTs the means to produce, circulate, and exchange culture has expanded enormously. The media and communications industries have a huge economic significance today, paralleling that of physical plant in the industrial era. Far from simply a matter of business and flow, culture connects closely with the constitution of subjectivity, with identity.

Fourth, there is a set of issues about the transformation of state power and democracy – with the growth of technologies of surveillance. Behavior in public space is routinely observed and recorded on video, while computer systems map personal movements, conversations, email traffic, consumption patterns, networks, and social activities. At the same time, democracy is facilitated by the capacity for many-to-many communication (as opposed to the broadcasting model of one-to-many) and the increasing accessibility of growing amounts of information, with the development of the Internet. New patterns of communication across time and space

enhance communication possibilities, and state control of the media is challenged by new technologies – satellite but especially the Internet – that easily cross national borders.

The notion of the information society has been highly influential in policy studies, notably in Japan, the EU, and the UN. From the end of the 1980s the EU identified the information society as a policy objective. It was seen that information and communication technology (ICT) could be harnessed to generate economic growth and to promote social cohesion. EU information society policies have their origins in economic policies to maintain competitive advantage, policies that followed the deregulation of state telecommunications in the 1980s. The Delors Report (1993) proposed a Task Force on European Information Infrastructures, which led to the Bangemann Report (1994) *Europe and the Global Information Infrastructure*. This referred to the spread of ICTs as a "new industrial revolution," and advocated financing the revolution through public-private partnerships. The Bangemann Report led to the Action Plan (1994), which has been revised subsequently but which remains the basis of the EU's information society policies. These have focused very much on IT infrastructure, encouraging businesses to get online and governments to deliver services electronically. At the same time as focusing on neoliberal economic development, there is a concern with social cohesion – in that policies focus, too, on the digital divide. The tenor of the EU information society discourse is both technologically determinist and highly positive, with reports routinely extolling the benefits of IT – at home and work, and in education and leisure.

There are important UN policies, which have focused on social exclusion and the digital divide. The World Summit on the Information Society, with its second phase in Tunis in 2005, was convened to set the global agenda, to build consensus between stakeholder groups (governments, civil society groups, NGOs, and corporations), and to develop an action plan (with target goals for 2015). The UN sees ICTs and access to information and knowledge as central to achieving development goals, and of value in resolving conflicts and attaining world peace.

The information society remains a term very much in vogue three decades after its formulation. In part because of its breadth, it is a malleable concept or debate. It continues to resonate because of the growing plethora of ICTs and their considerable significance in everyday social life. In turn, this has led to take-up by policymakers, making the information society an important area in which sociological debate connects with public policy. Research councils have responded to this connection with publicly funded research programs. In methodological terms, the field has been characterized by heterogeneity, with a prominent strand – that shows no sign of abating – that focuses on quantifying the information society.

SEE ALSO: Consumption and the Internet; Cyberculture; Globalization, Culture and; Information Technology; Internet; McLuhan, Marshall; Media and Diaspora; Technology, Science, and Culture

REFERENCES AND SUGGESTED READINGS

Bell, D. (1973) *The Coming Post-Industrial Society*. Basic Books, New York.

Bell, D. (1980) The Social Framework of the Information Society. In: Forester, T. (Ed.), *The Microelectronics Revolution*. Blackwell, Oxford.

Castells, M. (1996) *The Rise of the Network Society: The Information Age: Economy, Society and Culture*, Vol. 1. Blackwell, Oxford.

Castells, M. (1997) *The Power of Identity. The Information Age: Economy, Society and Culture*, Vol. 2. Blackwell, Oxford.

Castells, M. (1998) *End of Millennium. The Information Age: Economy, Society and Culture*, Vol. 3. Blackwell, Oxford.

Duff, A. (2000) *Information Society Studies*. Routledge, New York.

Garnham, N. (1990) *Capitalism and Communication: Global Culture and the Economics of Information*. Sage, London.

Habermas, J. (1989) The Structural Transformation of the Public Sphere. Trans. T. Burger & F. Lawrence. Polity Press, Cambridge.

Harvey, D. (1989) *The Condition of Postmodernity: An Enquiry into the Origins of Cultural Change*. Blackwell, Oxford.

Machlup, F. (1962) *The Production and Distribution of Knowledge in the United States*. Princeton University Press, Princeton.

MacKenzie, D. & Wajcman, J. (1999) *The Social Shaping of Technology*, 2nd edn. Open University Press, Buckingham.

Porat, M. U. (1977) *The Information Economy*, 9 vols. US Department of Commerce, Office of Telecommunications, Washington, DC.

Poster, M. (1990) *The Mode of Information: Poststructuralism and Social Context*. Polity Press, Cambridge.

Schiller, H. I. (1996) *Information Inequality: The Deepening Social Crisis in America*. Routledge, New York.

Webster, F. (2002) *Theories of the Information Society*, 2nd edn. Routledge, New York.

information technology

David Lyon

Information technology (IT) is generally taken to be a technical system for storing, transmitting, or processing information. As such it could refer to the paper documents and files of a bureaucratic organization, or even to hieroglyphs on rocks in the ancient world. While such broad meanings remind us of the larger context of human interaction with information, in the twenty-first century IT usually refers to electronically based systems that draw upon a combination of computing power and telecommunications. Indeed, IT is now central to many systems that are increasingly integrated, producing a fusion of what was once referred to separately as electronic media and information and communication technologies.

INTELLECTUAL AND SOCIAL CONTEXT

IT may be thought of by some computer scientists as a merely technical matter, but in fact a very good case can be made that such are relatively trivial. In the real world IT is the product of economic, political, social, and cultural contexts and choices, as well as technical knowledge, that shape its development and use. In these contexts the shaping and consequences of IT are far from trivial.

The changes that occurred in IT production and use between the start and the close of the twentieth century are nothing short of astonishing. While paper-based bureaucracies dominated the means of organizational practice at the start of the century, digital ones dominated them by the end, even though the "paperless office" never materialized as promised. But not only this – the ways in which production, education, administration, entertainment, travel, and other activities were done were transformed in large part through their interactions with and increasing dependence on IT. Today, for the vast majority in the global North, everyday life is unimaginable without a range of IT-based systems, tools, and gadgets, some of which – like call centers or smart refrigerators – were almost unheard of in the 1980s.

One crucial change was the convergence of telecommunications with computing power. Joining telecommunications with computing enabled many aspects of the taken-for-granted world that many in the global North now inhabit – of instant remote interactions with computers, credit and debit cards, computer-controlled machine tools, cell-phones, and iPods.

By the end of the twentieth century, IT was integrated with all aspects of modern life, such that many started to speak of an information age based on new forms of work and employment, a new global economy, a spatial division of labor, and a general sense of contracting space and accelerating time – as opposed to the industrial age ushered in by the Victorians a century before. And IT also ceased to be thought of as an "external" factor. It had become embedded in countless processes, practices, systems, and devices.

MAJOR SOCIAL DIMENSIONS

At the largest scale, IT must be seen as one dimension of modernity. IT is now a major contributor to the distinctive character of contemporary modernity and, in social science, to the debate over how modernity is transforming itself in the twenty-first century. If in early modern times a strong motif was reliance on science-and-technology as a vital determinant

of "progress," one could argue that the emphasis shifted decisively from "science" to "technology" during the twentieth century. While dependence on science is still demonstrably constitutive of today's modernity, it has in some ways been folded into technology, such that terms like technological society have far more popular resonance than scientific society. The term technoscience captures some of this folding.

More specifically, IT is implicated in a number of social, cultural, and political-economic changes that are referred to variously as late modernity or postmodernity, or are considered under the rubric of globalization. Alongside the shift towards consumption and consumer capitalism (Slater 1997), reliance on communication and IT has helped to reconfigure some of the central institutions of social life and to change the contours of modernity (Lyon 1999) in the global North and to a lesser extent and sometimes in different ways in parts of the global South. The very notion of global mobility of information, persons, goods, images, services, wastes, and entertainment – basic to any globalization thesis – is fundamentally enabled by IT. And equally the shift towards more fluid social relations (Bauman 2000) associated with the postmodern can only be understood in terms of remote connections and instant communication based on IT.

IT affects many aspects of social, political, economic, and cultural life, though not always in ways foreseen by the pundits and marketers. This is why serious sociological analysis is so vital for grasping the realities of change. Whether in military, workplace, domestic, or entertainment spheres, IT is increasingly a *sine qua non* (Webster 2004) of organization and practice, so it is worth exploring as a major theme of contemporary social analysis. This may involve examining ways that IT extends human capacities, but also looking at how IT may be implicated in actual alterations in social life (Gane 2004). And none of this may be adequately considered without seeing how IT is implicated in regimes of power, whether within labor processes, bureaucratic organization, or policing and state control. IT is intrinsically bound up with contemporary regimes of governance (Rose 1999).

SOCIAL RESEARCH ON IT

IT is an enabling technology that experienced – and is still experiencing – exponential growth just because it is basic to so many major processes of production and consumption. It started with a focus on microelectronics and now has to be considered in relation to the wholesale convergence and integration of many different media. The growth may be jerky at times, but the overall pattern is of steady expansion. IT is now a major economic player with huge ramifications in every area. IT is also a crucial enabler for globalization (whatever it means) and thus implicated in current developments.

The treatment of IT in the social sciences began as a fairly minor subfield, but it is now seen as one of the major areas for social science research. Four phases may be distinguished in its development. The first was what might be termed popular IT, and this first appeared under the rubric of the microelectronics revolution or the information technology revolution. These studies were very focused on the amazing capabilities and potential of these technologies to bring about "social transformations" of various kinds. While such studies rightly recognized the epochal character of IT, far too much stress was placed on what the technologies themselves would achieve and equally too much optimism was expressed about their benign character. However, such studies also stimulated serious critique (Webster & Robins 1986; Mosco 1996), which served to move the debate forward.

A second phase might be called IT studies in which workplace organization, government administration, and other areas such as "virtual communities" were examined in terms of the mediation of relationships by IT. This empirical contribution has produced a number of treatments of lasting value. A third phase, inspired largely by French theory, could be called poststructuralist IT studies, and these make much of the diverse contributions by Baudrillard and Lyotard. Later on, studies in the Foucauldian tradition and from authors such as Deleuze also became significant. Lastly, what might be called critical IT studies constitutes a fourth phase (and of course these "phases" overlap considerably with each other – they are neither historically nor conceptually independent). Such critical studies began by attacking the technological determinism of early popular accounts of "IT and society," but also made solid contributions of their own by stressing the political economy and the gendered and racialized developments of IT.

From the 1980s onward research councils in North America and Europe began to recognize the importance of IT and this was reflected in funding for studies of the social dimensions of electronically mediated relationships of all kinds. After the advent of the World Wide Web in the early 1990s, for example, the UK Economic and Social Research Council set up a multi-million pound initiative under the title "Virtual Society?" Similar work has been pursued in the US and Canada. Such developments tend to encourage empirical research and, with the late twentieth-century trend towards radical economic restructuring, they also tend to be tied more tightly to the competitiveness of the country in question (hence the Canadian Social Sciences and Research Council funding for work on "Knowledge-Based Economies" and then the "Initiative on the New Economy").

CURRENT EMPHASES

Classic work in social scientific treatments of IT was done by precursors in the field such as Canadians Harold Adams Innis and his student Marshall McLuhan, along with the philosopher George Grant (Kroker 1984). These and several others were also influenced by earlier and more general work on technology by Jacques Ellul and Martin Heidegger. One could say that Innis's work was the most doggedly empirical, even though he was to originate the important "bias of communication" perspective (Innis 1962). McLuhan's was less tied to political economy and attuned more to the cultural changes associated with new media in general, while Grant provided a deeper critique based in relational and ethical perspectives. These could be compared and contrasted with Ellul's searing attack on mere "technique" (that loses sight of what he argued are more significant goals of human activity, such as peace and justice) or Heidegger's argument that technology is not correctly understood as a "tool" or "means," but as a way of interacting with reality (and is not necessarily entirely under human control).

The most significant early sociological treatment of IT came from Daniel Bell, whose work still stands as a milestone in our comprehension of the social dimensions of what he called post-industrial society (Bell 1974). By examining carefully the occupational structure, Bell's "social forecast" proposed that "industrial society" – which it should be recalled was the standard sociological description of contemporary social relations for several decades in the twentieth century – was slowly but surely being replaced by something else. And among other things, a new kind of reliance upon organized technical knowledge was at the heart of this putative shift. In Bell's own work, and then in the work of others, the negative descriptor was soon exchanged for the more commonplace term "information society," a concept that retains its salience in the early twenty-first century.

More recently, however, the large-scale comparative studies of Manuel Castells (2000) under the general title of the *Information Age* have become the standard and the foil for analysis of the social aspects of IT. Castells's work is similar to Bell's in that he seeks some structural explanations for what he takes to be epochal shifts in economy, polity, and society, but different in several respects, too. Unlike Bell, Castells does not imagine that the US provides the model for "information society" or, as he calls it, "network society." Castells provides some comparative analyses of IT development in different societies, beginning with alterations in urban infrastructure – his interest was in "global cities" – but also examining new social and political movements whose existence and activities depend on the availability of IT, and new forms of criminality and social exclusion appearing in information societies (see also Stalder 2005).

During the last part of the twentieth century and into the present century IT studies proliferated into a number of constituent subfields. In addition to the macro-level studies of the information society, other distinct areas emerged. Internet studies became important in its own right (e.g., Jones 1999; Wellman & Haythornthwaite 2002), although this field is likely to change shape somewhat as other kinds of media (such as wireless cell-phones) are integrated with Internet access. Science, technology,

and society (STS) perspectives are also important in this field and combined with "information science" approaches have produced important studies such as Brown and Duguid's (2000) work on the "social life of information." This is turn relates to work done in organization studies and management information systems.

As noted above, IT is also studied in relation to globalization studies and in terms of divisions of access (digital divides) that may be socioeconomic but also associated with race and ethnicity and with gender (Wajcman 1991). IT studies are also implicated in surveillance studies and in the analysis of contemporary governance. Most strikingly, since the attacks of 9/11 and subsequent attacks in Madrid and London, IT companies have been competing for contracts with governments to upgrade security arrangements, especially at borders and within policing and intelligence services. The ideals of "convergence" and "integration" of systems and departments have never been as prominent as in the current quests for interoperability and for networked anti-terror techniques.

ANALYSIS AND CRITIQUE

The social analysis of IT does not of course take place in a philosophical or ethical vacuum. As with all social theory, explanations of processes, systems, and change inevitably refer to some kinds of valuing, to normative critique or at the most basic level, to views of the "good society" or its opposite. Rather than attempt the impossible, to purge theory of such features, it makes more sense to acknowledge the particular kinds of arguments being made and to debate the consequences of taking a specific stance. With regard to macro-level theories of the information society this is particularly evident, not least because some early studies seemed intent on optimistic forecasts of general human benefit in the wake of the new technologies. But it is also, though less obviously, true of STS, organization studies, and of studies of IT and social divisions.

A sociological understanding of IT cannot but notice the role of cultural factors in IT development. The ideas of information society or cyberspace are replete with mythical or even "sublime" characteristics (Mosco 2004). They relate to the supposedly beneficent effects of IT in their capacity to make life easier, more peaceful, or even to transcend the limitations of the body. Unfortunately, while there are of course labor-saving devices associated with IT, and while some quests for social justice are indeed facilitated by IT and some IT-based innovations (e.g., word processing) may be useful "prosthetic" extensions to the human body, IT in the real world is as caught up in the contradictions and struggles of social life as anything else.

But there is a further problem here. Those accounts of IT that gloss unavoidable aspects of the "real world" also distract attention from the questions of ethics and politics that responsible treatments of IT will always raise (even though these in themselves go beyond the purview of sociology; see Robins 1995, or, for another perspective, Lash 2001). Thus, while it is the case, for example, that globalization in all its manifestations is facilitated by IT, all the debates over globalization – who benefits, how distance "dies," where sweatshops and waste dumps are located, how superpower hegemony is maintained – thus also implicate IT. And as IT applications do not simply "appear" but are sought and developed for particular purposes, the argument that IT is a "neutral" technology and it is "how it is used" that matters is shown to be not only unsociological and hollow but also dangerous.

IT is today wrapped with the packaging of global consumerism, although it is also basic to the military systems that ultimately back up what appears to be a world of "free choices." That efficiency and productivity may be enhanced using IT is not questioned, but what might be worth questioning is whether these represent primary goals of social, economic, and political life. As Weber observed a century ago, the "demands of the day" make a significant call on sociology "as a vocation" (Gerth & Mills 1946). He argued strenuously against turning sociology into a vocation for "demagogues," but he also bemoaned the demise of seeing sociological work in the light of larger purposes and of politics and ethics. This is as true of the sociology of IT as the studies of bureaucracy or of comparative religion that Weber undertook.

FUTURE DIRECTIONS

The sociological analysis of IT is likely to continue for a long time to come, even though the discrete term IT may disappear as the technologies are increasingly embedded in systems and products. At a basic economic level, knowledge-based work, which accounts for a growing proportion of GDP in many countries around the world (including now, significantly, China and India), is highly dependent on IT. In every productive sector, IT makes an important difference and understanding this is in part a sociological issue. But IT is also involved in the ways that services, travel, education, and entertainment are organized, not to mention life in the domestic sphere. It is hard to think of an area of social life studies by sociologists in which IT has no impact.

IT is also implicated in several very significant current trends, especially those towards the safety state and the security economy. As concerns about terrorism have been added to the already-existing issues of the so-called risk society (Ericson & Haggerty 1997), security and surveillance will continue to play a prominent role in social, economic, and political life. The security economy is now a sector in its own right and commands massive markets, especially in the global North. These markets are frequently involved in dedicated surveillance technologies of various kinds and also in redeploying technologies developed in one area (consumer marketing in particular) for security purposes. Intelligence services, for example, in the quest for identifying potential terrorists, now use data mining tools invented for profiling consumers (Lyon 2003).

Social theories of IT are proliferating, but some key threads are likely to stand the test of time. Firstly, political economy perspectives that locate IT developments in the power relations of capitalist countries serve as a reminder that whatever the micro-level changes and however genuine improvements are made in human welfare, there is a constant tendency that IT will be developed in ways that benefit some groups at the expense of others. Secondly, technology studies look at the ways in which artifacts themselves are produced and how they interact with systems and users. This reminds us of the contingency of IT developments. Thirdly, the kinds of theory associated with particular aspects of IT development – in relation to race and ethnicity, gender, age, ability, access, and region – will continue to be important for the social understanding of IT. Fourthly, postmodern and poststructural theories (e.g., from Baudrillard, Foucault, and Deleuze) are likely to continue to stimulate new ways of thinking about IT as simulation, as discourse, or as assemblage.

Information technology has in some ways become as basic to social life as industrial organization was in the twentieth century. It thus warrants a commensurate degree of sociological attention that is clear, careful, and ethically critical.

SEE ALSO: Digital; Globalization; Globalization, Culture and; Information Society; Internet; Knowledge Societies; Surveillance; Technological Determinism; Technological Innovation; Technology, Science, and Culture; Women, Information Technology and (Asia)

REFERENCES AND SUGGESTED READINGS

Abbate, J. (1999) *Inventing the Internet*. MIT Press, Cambridge MA.
Bauman, Z. (2000) *Liquid Modernity*. Polity Press, Cambridge.
Bell, D. (1974) *The Coming of Postindustrial Society*. Penguin, London.
Beniger, J. (1986) *The Control Revolution: The Technological and Economic Origins of the Information Society*. Harvard University Press, Cambridge, MA.
Brown, J. S. & Duguid, P. (2000) *The Social Life of Information*. Harvard University Press, Cambridge, MA.
Castells, M. (2000) *The Information Age*, 3 Vols. Blackwell, Oxford.
Ericson, R. & Haggerty, K. (1997) *Policing the Risk Society*. University of Toronto Press, Toronto.
Gandy, O. (1993) *The Panoptic Sort: A Political Economy of Personal Information*. Westview Press, Boulder.
Gane, N. (2004) Back to the Future of Social Theory: An Interview with Nicholas Gane. *Sociological Research Online*. Online. www.socresonline.org.uk/9/4/beer.html.
Gerth, H. H. & Mills, C. Wright (Eds.) (1946) *From Max Weber: Essays in Sociology*. Oxford University Press, New York.
Innis, H. A. (1962) *The Bias of Communication*. University of Toronto Press, Toronto.
Jones, S. (1999) *Doing Internet Research*. Sage, Newbury Park, CA.
Kroker, A. (1984) *Technology and the Canadian Mind*. New World Perspectives, Montreal; St. Martin's Press, New York.
Lash, S. (2001) *Critique of Information*. Sage, London.
Lyon, D. (1988) *The Information Society: Issues and Illusions*. Polity Press, Cambridge.
Lyon, D. (1999) *Postmodernity*. Oxford University Press, Oxford.
Lyon, D. (2003) *Surveillance after September 11*. Polity Press, Cambridge.
Mosco, V. (1996) *The Political Economy of Communication*. Sage, London.
Mosco, V. (2004) *The Digital Sublime*. MIT Press, Cambridge MA.
Poster, M. (1995) *The Second Media Age*. Blackwell, Oxford.
Poster, M. (2001) *What's the Matter with the Internet*. University of Minnesota Press, Minneapolis.
Robins, K. (1995) Cyberspace and the World We Live In. *Body and Society* 1(3–4): 135–55.
Rose, N. (1999) *Powers of Freedom*. Cambridge University Press, Cambridge.
Slater, D. (1997) *Consumer Culture and Modernity*. Polity Press, Cambridge.
Stalder, F. (2005) *Manuel Castells*. Polity Press, Cambridge.
Wajcman, J. (1991) *Feminism Confronts Technology*. Polity Press, Cambridge.
Webster, F. (Ed.) (2004) *The Information Society Reader*. Routledge, New York.
Webster, F. & Robins, K. (1986) *Information Technology: A Luddite Analysis*. Ablex, Norwood, NJ.
Wellman, B. & Haythornthwaite, C. (2002) *The Internet in Everyday Life*. Blackwell, Oxford.

infotainment

Lauren Langman

The twentieth century, with its new forms of mass production and mass media, gave rise to what has been called consumer society, a world largely concerned with personal gratifications and desirable selfhood gained through consuming goods and experiences. An essential part of this new "amusement society" has been a focus on entertainment from watching television sit-coms to attending sport events, various rock concerts, or the symphony. As mass-mediated entertainment became a growing industry, there was a proliferation of cable programming and cable news outlets, greater fragmentation of audiences, and a growing concentration of ownership. Thus the gathering of "hard news," reports of breaking events of war and peace, prosperity and poverty, leadership, public affairs, or investigations of crimes became highly expensive, producing little revenue and ever less audience share. These various factors led to the erosion of barriers between reporting "hard news" and the production of "soft news" combining information and entertainment to produce "infotainment," pleasantries about peo-ple, places, or events which provide the viewer with an agreeable form of entertainment "that is unrelated to public affairs or policy, and is typically more sensational, more personality or celebrity oriented, less time-bound (meaning that the traditional journalistic norm of "time-liness" does not apply), and more incident-based than hard news" (Patterson 2001).

Thus we have seen that whether in print, radio, or television, almost half of the "news" now concerns such things as celebrity revela-tions – often conducted by celebrity journalists, in which the private thoughts of a Britney Spears on sex, diets, and clothes are far more entertaining than how changing tax codes more directly impact people. Various human interest stories, sensationalist tabloid journalism, life-style, personal finances, or the paranormal, what has been called "eye candy," pleasurable to view, have now become one of the main sources of information about the "world," or rather the world that many citizens inhabit, a world without war, hunger, poverty, or pollu-tion, but filled with information about the loves and marriage of celebrities, their affairs and divorces, and how they decorate their homes. Clinton's *affaire* Monica, from first revelation to published memoirs, garnered far more inter-est than his record on jobs, taxes, or the former Yugoslavia. While "infotainment" seems an aspect of television, it has also impacted much of print journalism, as for example *USA Today* reducing the vast complexities of events to a paragraph or so. To maintain or increase read-ership, many respectable newspapers have included more tabloid "infotainment" and have moved closer to *National Enquirer*-like reports on aliens in the government and monsters feed-ing on pollution.

It should also be noted that a great deal of talk radio and television that purports to be news and news commentary, generally presented by strong, charismatic "personalities," has become a channel for conservative viewpoints. While people like Rush Limbaugh, Don Imus, or Bill O'Reilly may very well be witty and entertain-ing, much of what they report is not just biased or distorted but blatantly wrong, and viewers/listeners are unlikely to have access to more accurate reportage. "Infotainment," whether celebrities' lives, UFOs, wonder diets, or most political talk shows, is however more than sim-ply amusing; it is part of a much larger set of processes that have encouraged personal gratifi-cations at the cost of public concerns and thus serves to erode democratic governance. This becomes most evident when celebrities become politicians and political news is entertainment, whether it involves Cicciolina the Italian porn star, Ronald Reagan, or Arnold Schwarzeneg-ger. As the Frankfurt scholars suggested, the "culture industries" serve an important conser-vative ideological function by reproducing the status quo and hiding its inequalities, injustices, and costs in human suffering.

SEE ALSO: Celebrity and Celetoid; Celebrity Culture; Culture Industries; Media and Con-sumer Culture; Popular Culture Forms; Popu-lar Culture Icons

REFERENCES AND SUGGESTED READINGS

McChesney, R. (1998) *Rich Media, Poor Democracy: Communication Politics in Dubious Times.* Univer-sity of Illinois Press, Urbana.
Patterson, T. (2001) *Doing Well and Doing Good: How Soft News and Critical Journalism Are Shrinking the News Audience and Weakening Democracy – And What News Outlets Can Do About It.* Joan Shorenstein Center for Press, Politics, and Pub-lic Policy at Harvard University, Cambridge, MA.

in-groups and out-groups

Michael J. McCallion

An in-group is a social unit an individual belongs to, interacts with, and shares a sense of "we-ness" with. An out-group, on the other hand, is a social unit or group of people that an individual neither belongs to nor identifies with. The construction and maintenance of boundaries (physical or symbolic) are the primary ways by which groups establish what it means to be "in" and, by contrast, what it means to be "out." The basis of in-group identity, then, is socially constructed through symbolic markers (boundaries) such as narratives, creeds, rituals, and social practices. Moreover, sociologists view such boundaries along a continuum of permeability (open) and impermeability (closed), which influences group member entrance and exit processes. In-group identity, in other words, is always an ongoing achievement in which group boundaries are collectively generated, affirmed, maintained, and employed to mark differences between insiders and outsiders (Hadden & Lester 1978).

In his classic study of folkways, William Graham Sumner (1906) articulated the enduring notions of in-groups and out-groups and the dialectical relation between them. Sumner stressed the negative reciprocity between in-groups and out-groups, especially in the context of conflict over scarce resources. In an environment of scarcity, Sumner argued, individuals need to band together to compete with other groups for survival. Without such conflict and scarcity, neither strong in-group attachment nor out-group hostility would occur, as Sherif and Sherif (1953) have confirmed in their work on intergroup behavior.

Indeed, Muzafer Sherif and his associates (1961) conducted various intergroup studies, in particular their classic field group study of 11- and 12-year-old boys. In stage one of their study, the researchers took a group of boys to summer camp and divided them into two groups, each group residing in its own cabin. Eventually two cohesive groups formed, with one group calling itself the Rattlers and the other the Eagles. In stage two, the groups engaged in competitive sporting activities, which soon gave way to name calling, accusations, fighting, and raiding of cabins, involving some structural damage. At this point the researchers discovered that negative stereotyping had developed toward the out-group, while in-group solidarity increased. Moreover, it was concluded that the social variable increasing each group's cohesiveness was threats toward the out-group. In stage three, the researchers attempted to unite the groups through various common social events, but the intergroup conflict continued. It was not until the two groups had to work together to accomplish common goals (all pushing their broken-down truck up a hill) that conflict decreased and cooperation ensued, leading to Sherif's hypothesis that conflict arose from mutually incompatible goals and cooperation from pursuing common goals.

In recent decades, much social research has confirmed Sumner's basic principle that conflict between groups often tends not to weaken, but rather to strengthen, groups internally. In other words, in-group favoritism and out-group negativity are strongly related, with some research (Tajfel 1982) finding that the mere categorization of people into groups can lead to increased attraction of in-group members and devaluation of out-group members. Ralph Dahrendorf (1964: 58) argues even more strongly that "it appears to be a general law that human groups react to external pressure by increased internal coherence." Even before Dahrendorf, however, Lewis Coser published a classic book, *The Functions of Social Conflict* (1956), which argued that intergroup conflict clarifies boundaries, strengthens in-group identity, increases unity and participation, and strengthens ideological solidarity within conflicted groups. Social scientists continue to observe these principles at work in a variety of settings, from ethnic relations (Gerard 1985) to military organizations (Elliot 1986). In particular, many studies in social psychology have confirmed the theory that out-group conflict builds in-group solidarity (e.g., Fisher 1993). Also, many studies in anthropology, psychology, and political science support these findings, with Stein (1976), in reviewing this literature, concluding: "In sum, then, there is a clear convergence in the literature in both the specific studies and in the various disciplines, that suggests that external conflict does increase internal cohesion."

Although research continues to confirm the findings that external conflict increases in-group solidarity, other research has found that mere categorization (Karp et al. 1993) or conflict (Allport 1954) are not key or absolutely necessary for the creation or maintenance of in-group solidarity and cohesion. Kollock (1998), reviewing this literature, writes that "it is the belief in future reciprocal exchanges between members . . . that moderates the temptation to defect and encourages cooperation. The expectation of in-group reciprocity seems to serve as a very deep heuristic that shapes our strategic decisions." Allport (1954) also found that attachment to one's in-group does not require conflict or hostility toward out-groups, which stands in contrast to the inherited wisdom of Sumner's work. Allport postulated, for instance, that in-groups are psychologically primary, in the sense that familiarity, attachment, and preference for one's in-group comes prior to development of attitudes toward specific out-groups. Moreover, he notes, in-group love can be compatible with a range of attitudes toward corresponding out-groups, including mild positivity and indifference or intense disdain and hatred. The bonds of in-group solidarity, in other words, are not necessarily based on conflict/hostility toward outsiders or born of altrusim via categorization of individuals into out-groups and in-groups, but rather, in many instances, in-group solidarity arises from the practices and beliefs in the interdependencies of group members and expectations of reciprocity among the members.

SEE ALSO: Groups; Idioculture; Networks; Social Worlds; Sumner, William Graham

REFERENCES AND SUGGESTED READINGS

Allport, G. W. (1954) *The Nature of Prejudice*. Addison-Wesley, Cambridge, MA.
Coser, L. (1956) *The Functions of Social Conflict*. Free Press, New York.
Dahrendorf, R. (1964) The New Germanies. *Encounter* 22: 50–8.
Durkheim, É. (1913) *The Elementary Forms of Religious Life*. Free Press, New York.
Elliot, W. A. (1986) *Us and Them: A Study of Group Consciousness*. Aberdeen University Press, Aberdeen.
Fisher, R. (1993) Toward a Social-Psychological Model of Intergroup Conflict. In: Larsen, K. (Ed.), *Conflict and Social Psychology*. Sage, Newbury Park, CA, pp. 109–22.
Gerard, H. (1985) When and How Minorities Prevail. In: Muscovici, S., Mugny, G., & Van Avermaet, E. (Eds.), *Perspectives on Minority Influence*. Cambridge University Press, Cambridge, pp. 171–251.
Hadden, S. & Lester, M. (1978) Talking Identity: The Production of Self in Interaction. *Human Studies* 1: 331–56.
Karp, D., Jin, N., Yamagishi, T., & Shinotsuka, H. (1993) Raising the Minimum in the Minimum Group Paradigm. *Japanese Journal of Experimental Social Psychology* 32: 231–40.
Kollock, P. (1998) Social Dilemmas: The Anatomy of Cooperation. *Annual Review of Sociology* 24: 183–214.
Sherif, M. & Sherif, C. W. (1953) *Group Relations at the Crossroads*. Harper & Row, New York.
Sherif, M., Harvey, O. J., White, B. J., Hood, W. R., & Sherif, C. W. (1961) *Intergroup Conflict and Cooperation: The Robbers Cave Experiment*. Institute of Group Relations, University of Oklahoma, Norman.
Stein, A. A. (1976) Conflict and Cohesion. *Journal of Conflict Resolution* 20: 143–72.
Sumner, W. G. (1906) *Folkways*. Ginn, Boston.
Tajfel, H. (1982) *Social Identity and Intergroup Relations*. Cambridge University Press, Cambridge.

insecurity and fear of crime

Philippe Robert

Insecurity and fear of crime are expressions designating the apprehension elicited by crime and, by extension, the field of research devoted to studying it.

In the United States, research on fear of crime took off following a study by a presidential commission on crime in the mid-1960s (President's Commission 1967), which tackled the problem of measuring crime from a new perspective. Growing doubts about the adequacy of police statistics at the time encouraged a search for non-institutional tools based on general population surveys. This led Joseph Bidermann, Philip Ennis, and Al Reiss, Jr. to invent the victimization survey. However, when people in a sample were questioned about their fear in addition to any victimizations they had suffered, the two measures turned out not to coincide that well: some victims were not very frightened, some non-victims were nonetheless fearful. Fear of crime thus gradually came to be singled out as an object of research. Even before this American tradition had taken hold in Europe, British sociologists had approached this research field from another angle: they had termed "moral panic" the excessive alarm elicited either by fights between youth gangs in holiday resorts (Cohen 1973) or by muggings (Hall et al. 1981). Elsewhere, sociologists or political scientists interested in local occurrences had studied rumors, such as reports that girls had been abducted by shopkeepers in one French city, or local signs of insecurity, the explanation for which was sought in the living conditions and social relations of insecure groups. The gradual reception of the American research tradition on fear of crime finally unified these different European strands to some extent.

Some subtle differences do exist, however, as evidenced in the terms used. North Americans tend to speak of fear of crime, whereas in Europe insecurity is increasingly becoming the accepted term, not only in German (*Unsicherheit*) and French (*insécurité* or *sentiment d'insécurité*), but also in European English. The two expressions are not exactly equivalent: recourse to one or the other may indicate, at least implicitly, differing conceptions.

Be that as it may, irrespective of whether we speak of fear of crime or insecurity, these expressions have become a part of the language of sociology because of the realization that apprehension is not a simple reflection of the risk incurred or of previous experience of victimization. Insecurity or fear of crime has become an object of research because it is felt to be *excessive*; attempts are made to dispel or to explain this apparent enigma. At the same time, these expressions continue to be used in public debate, and belong primarily to the language of the mass media and politics. Their conceptual coherence is faulty and sociologists may

consider whether research would not do better to replace them with more homogeneous objects of study.

The two main trends in research on insecurity and fear of crime may now be described. First, explaining why apprehension exceeds actual risk or experience has led to work exploring three themes. It may be claimed that insecurity is not so much caused by the intensity of the threat of crime to which one is exposed, or by one's experience as victim, but rather, that it results from media messages that unduly magnify crime. One may also wonder whether insecurity is not fed by disorder rather than by crime per se. Finally, the extent of apprehension may be adjusted by considering differences in exposure to risk or the greater vulnerability of some individuals.

Since apprehension of crime seems disproportionate in comparison with offenses actually committed, it seems common sense to accuse media coverage. The media everywhere devote a great deal of time and space to crime generally, as is readily observed, and most importantly, they mainly publicize the most spectacular and most frightening crimes, especially violent crime. The media, then, offer a dramatized image of criminality. Quite naturally, the media are deemed responsible for the gap between crime and the fear it elicits. Offending is good for filling up news columns, it is spectacular, in short, it helps to sell the media. Moreover, it is in the interests of certain other actors to feed the press, radio, and television with dramatic, fear-inducing information about crime: politicians play on fear as a vote-getting device or as a way of diverting public attention from more complex social problems such as unemployment; the police use it as an argument to support their demands for greater resources and to point up the importance of their work, sometimes even to silence criticism about their poor relationship with the public; lastly, some moral entrepreneurs find arguments to back their demands for greater repression, while pressure groups try to discredit some minorities by putting the blame for crime on them. As a sales gimmick, insecurity may serve a number of causes (Warr 2000).

However true all this may be, empirical research yields only lukewarm support for this commonsense argument. As usual, the message delivered by the mass media is easy to observe, but its impact is much more difficult to determine. It is very tempting to assume that what is delivered is received. On further reflection, however, this assumption is not very solid: it leads to the postulate that the target of media messages is like putty, passively molded by it. A handful of studies do come to the conclusion that media messages on crime are instrumental in producing insecurity. However, some have been subjected to serious methodological criticism that sheds doubt on their conclusions, whereas many other studies are unable to establish any definite causal relationship.

As a rule, the available research tends rather to reject the media's ability to create fear of crime out of nothing. It indicates that a media message suggesting a threat to security is only received as such if it corroborates some personal experience felt as security-threatening, or if it encounters a preexisting concern with security. If it falls on such fertile ground it may nourish insecurity, especially when people are subjected to constant media hype, particularly since people who are most sensitive to insecurity also tend to revel most in such alarmist messages. This may create a sort of vicious circle: people who are sensitive to insecurity problems welcome any corroboration provided by the authoritative media. Not only does the message then feed insecurity, it also legitimates it: this is not some personal whim, it is invested with the authority of the TV news program. But perhaps the influence of the media on insecurity stems mostly from the ability of mass communications to provide cognitive patterns, to give a definite shape to feelings of insecurity, its causes (*parental abdication* or *an overliberal justice system*), and the proper remedies (*zero tolerance*), thus furnishing ready-made frames of reference.

Whereas the mass media's responsibility in creating feelings of insecurity must be qualified, conversely, their enormous influence on political personnel should not be underestimated. It may be that political leaders' experience of their own sensitivity leads them to point an accusing finger at the media at regular intervals.

The discrepancy between the risk of crime and the fear it elicits has propelled research in a second direction, which ascribes feelings of insecurity to incivility rather than to crime, on the basis of Wilson and Kelling's (1982) article on broken windows. When signs of social disorder (e.g., drunkenness, youth gangs, harassment on the streets, drug dealing) and of physical disorder (e.g., vandalism, abandoned buildings, buildup of garbage and refuse) are allowed to accumulate in an area, the mechanisms of informal control are undermined, the housing market collapses, families who are able to leave move away to avoid being stigmatized by a neighborhood that is pulled into a downward spiral of disintegration, and feelings of insecurity prosper. The overview conducted by Skogan (1990) for the US conclusively marked the development of this type of research. The fact remains, however, that the underlying explanatory model may not be the same for those who think that incivility encourages crime, those for whom it primarily increases perception of crime (as is the case for LaGrange et al. 1992), and those who feel that it produces insecurity directly (e.g., Hale et al. 1994), the other possibility being that incivility affects both crime and fear simultaneously.

Another avenue of research has tried to correct the poor correlation between the extent of crime and the fear it elicits. In 1979, Balkin drew attention to the effect of exposure to risk: retirees and housewives who express great apprehension are less irrational than it would seem. Their risk of victimization should be correlated with their exposure, much less frequent than, for instance, a young man who goes out every evening; it is therefore greater than at first apparent. Stafford and Galle (1984) were the first to do empirical work in this direction. However, the Balkin effect can only work for street crime, not for housebreaking, burglary, or violence between intimates, which often have enormous repercussions. Many other factors operate in the same direction – differences in vulnerability, for instance. The prospect of being jostled is much more serious for an elderly man than for a youth of 20: any broken bone will heal rapidly in the latter's case, whereas the former risks permanent invalidity. The same is true of what Ferraro (1995) calls the *shadow effect* of fear of rape on women's fear of crime: behind any threatening situation lurks the far more terrifying risk of sexual violence.

However rich the three research currents outlined here, the fact remains that none has succeeded in completely dispelling the enigma of insecurity, and this legitimates the other broad area of research on insecurity and fear of crime. Are we dealing with a coherent social object, or do these labels, used in public debate, conceal more complex phenomena?

Many writers have attempted to break down the categories of fear of crime and insecurity in order to reach more consistent ones. Young Rifai, for example: as early as 1979 she made distinctions between general concern, at either a national or a local level, evaluation of actual risk in one's own neighborhood, and assessment of the probability of personally being a victim of a specific offense. The distinction between *fear* and *concern*, suggested by Furstenberg in 1971 (and adopted since in various forms – such as *concrete fear* and *formless fear* in the 1980 Figgie Report, and by a great many researchers) has finally prevailed. It is one thing to fear crime for oneself or one's loved ones, and quite another to view it as a serious societal problem. One may of course be both fearful and concerned, but the number of cases in which this is not true is sufficient to demonstrate the analytic cogency of this distinction. Although they may merge in some people, fear and concern are not driven by the same mechanism.

Fear for oneself and one's loved ones seems to be a kind of anticipation of a risk, hence its good correlation with local indicators of crime, be they police statistics or victimization rates, or with experience of victimization. To produce fear, however, the perception of danger combines with subjective feelings of vulnerability. The latter may depend either on physical causes, such as age or sex, or on living conditions. To take one example, some French studies show that people who are financially unable to leave their derelict urban area are particularly prone to fear crime, which they could only escape by moving out (Peretti-Watel 2000). Concern seems to be less concrete, less tied to a personal situation. It views insecurity as a social problem rather than a personal risk, and therefore seems to be relatively insensitive to variations in actual risk or personal victimization. It is apparently linked less to vulnerability with respect to crime than to apprehensiveness

about societal transformations, which makes people relatively intolerant of crime, viewed as a sign of disorder.

These distinctions help us to understand why the link between insecurity and the risk of crime or personal experience of victimization seems to vary with the form – concrete or abstract – of the question posed. Another point is that it is easier to apply a single indicator to the measurement of concern than to fear, which is both local and fragmented: in the same population, during the same investigation, scores and profiles may differ considerably depending on whether the question has to do with fear at night on the streets, at home, in different kinds of public transportation, or for one's children. Conversely, concern does not seem to be a black or white variable: there is a whole range of types, from people for whom security is an obsession to the relatively unconcerned, and including the strongly concerned.

Although the distinction was first made in the US, many observers have pointed out that North American research seems to deal increasingly with fear, whereas European research, although encompassing fewer studies, is directed at both facets of insecurity. The difference in vocabulary on either side of the Atlantic definitely reflects diverging scholarly orientations.

Be that as it may, scholarly interest in insecurity or fear of crime is part of a deep-seated change in ways of thinking about crime. Traditionally, interest focused on the extent of crime and its control, and even more specifically on offenders and what should be done with them. The main question then was: what should be done with that fringe of hardened repeat offenders who seem impervious to dissuasion by the law and the criminal justice system? Should they be rehabilitated when possible, and eliminated when not? The emphasis on insecurity places us within a conception in which crime is perceived as a mass risk, the harmful effects of which must be controlled while limiting the costs of public policies. The central variable is no longer the criminal as much as feelings about or experience of crime.

This change of emphasis seems to go along with the firm belief – carefully hidden but deeply rooted – among political leaders that public policies pertaining to security are mainly played out on the symbolic register, through statements of intention and the impact of calculated announcements. Perhaps this should be interpreted as reflecting a degree of powerlessness. Certainly, one of the bases of the nation-state is its claim to protect the security of people and their property. But concrete fears must be handled by local arrangements involving a number of protagonists, and these are difficult for national-level officials to comprehend. (Conversely, local governments are increasingly using security as an argument to attract people to their city or region.) As for concern with security, it may well turn out to be a bottomless pit: a government can prove its inclination for law and order, but have greater difficulty making the future less uncertain.

This juncture is stimulating for the development of research, for which the strong demand for knowledge is beneficial. But it also puts a tremendous onus on it, as is always the case when a subject of sociological research develops out of a controversial area of public debate, in which the very terms used are, in themselves, one element of the debate. Research on insecurity and fear of crime will continue to accumulate at a rapid pace; its fruitfulness, however, will depend on the ability of sociologists to call into question the obvious, immediate nature of the very formulations suggested by those who sponsor their work.

SEE ALSO: Crime, Broken Windows Theory of; Criminology; Dangerousness; Deviance, Criminalization of; Hate Crimes; Media and the Public Sphere; Social Disorganization Theory; Victimization; Violence

REFERENCES AND SUGGESTED READINGS

Balkin, S. (1979) Victimization Rates, Safety, and Fear of Crime. *Social Problems* 26(3): 343–57.

Cohen, S. (1973) *Folk Devils and Moral Panics: The Creation of the Mods and Rockers*. Paladin, London.

Crawford, A. (Ed.) (2002) *Crime and Insecurity: The Governance of Safety in Europe*. Willan, Cullampton and Portland, OR.

Ditton, J., Chadee, D., Farrall, S., Gilchrist, E., & Bannister, J. (2004) From Imitation to Intimidation:

A Note on the Curious and Changing Relationship between the Media, Crime, and Fear of Crime. *British Journal of Criminology* 44: 595–610.

Ferraro, K. F. (1995) *Fear of Crime: Interpreting Victimization Risk*. SUNY Press, Albany.

Figgie, H. E. (1980) *The Figgie Report on Fear of Crime: America Afraid*. Research and Forecasts, Inc., Willoughby, OH.

Furstenberg, F. F., Jr. (1971) Public Reaction to Crime in the Streets. *American Scholar* 40: 601–10.

Hale, C. (1996) Fear of Crime: A Review of the Literature. *International Review of Victimology* 4(1): 79–150.

Hale, C., Pack, P., & Salked, J. (1994) The Structural Determinants of Fear of Crime: An Analysis using Census and Crime Data Survey Data from England and Wales. *International Review of Victimology* 3(3): 211–33.

Hall, S., Critcher, C., Jefferson, T., & Roberts, B. (1981) *Policing the Crisis: Mugging. The State and Law and Order*. Macmillan, London.

LaGrange, R. L., Ferraro, K. F., & Supancic, M. (1992) Perceived Risk and Fear of Crime: Role of Social and Physical Incivilities. *Journal of Research in Crime and Delinquency* 29(3): 311–34.

Peretti-Watel, P. (2000) L'inscription du sentiment d'insécurité dans le tissu urbain (How Feelings of Insecurity are Inscribed in the Urban Fabric). *Les Cahiers de la sécurité intérieure* 39: 1–22.

President's Commission on Law Enforcement and Administration of Justice (1967) *The Challenge of Crime in a Free Society*. US Government Printing Office, Washington, DC.

Robert, P. (2002) *L'insécurité en France (Insecurity in France)*. La Découverte, Paris.

Robert, P. & Pottier, M. L. (1997) "On ne se sent plus en sécurité." Délinquance et insécurité: une enquête sur deux décennies ("We don't feel safe any more." Crime and Insecurity: A Survey Covering Two Decades). *Revue française de science politique* 47(6): 707–40.

Robert, P. & Pottier, M. L. (2004) Les préoccupations sécuritaires: une mutation? (Concern with Security: Have Things Changed?) *Revue française de sociologie* 45(2): 211–42.

Skogan, W. (1990) *Disorder and Decline: Crime and the Spiral of Decay in American Neighbourhoods*. Free Press, New York.

Stafford, M. & Galle, O. R. (1984) Victimization Rates, Exposure to Risk, and Fear of Crime. *Criminology* 22: 173–85.

Warr, M. (2000) Fear of Crime in the United States: Avenues for Research and Policy. In: Reno, J. et al., *Measurement and Analysis of Crime and Justice*. US Department of Justice, Washington, DC, vol. 4, pp. 452–89.

Wilson, J. Q. & Kelling, G. L. (1982) Broken Windows. *Atlantic Monthly* 249: 29–38.

Young Rifai, H. A. (1982) Methods of Measuring the Impact of Criminal Victimization through Victimization Surveys. In: Schneider, H. J. (Ed.), *The Victims in International Perspective*. De Gruyter, Berlin and New York, pp. 189–202.

institution

Christoph Henning

An institution is the fixing of stereotyped social interactions in the form of rules. In most cases these rules are made explicit and there are sanctioning mechanisms behind them. Yet sometimes these characteristics are absent, for example when people adhere to such rules simply because they feel urged to act in this way. An institution does not need to be a large organization. The largest institutions known are states or multinational organizations like the United Nations, yet there are also much smaller institutions, as for example marriage or monthly meetings of a group at a certain pub. Therefore, institutionalization is not a matter of size.

The term institution has become quite popular in the neo-institutional economics of Oliver Williamson and D. C. North. Their use of the term has recently spread back into sociology, in spite of the fact that it refers only to "constraints" on individual utility-maximizing behavior due to the fact that there are always others trying to do the same thing. It categorizes institutions in terms of the transaction costs people save if they agree to cooperate with others. In this individualistic perspective, the essentially social character of institutions is omitted from the start. That does not matter much for economics, but this conception is of little use for sociology. Sociological concepts of institutions, institutionalization, and institutional change have in fact influenced economics in the first place. An institution can determine what appears to the individual as a "utility" or an obligation. So if one starts from institutions, one can explain individual behavior, rather than the other way round. This is what the sociological concept of institution is aiming at.

The first sociologist to use the term was Herbert Spencer. He described society as an organism. Accordingly, for him institutions were society's "organs." He distinguished six different types of social institutions: those related to the family, politics, religion, the economy, ceremonies, and professions. Another naturalistic approach was developed by Bronislaw Malinowski, who started with the needs of the individual. The function of a social institution is to fulfill basic needs of a group. On this basis, higher- or second-order needs may develop which also call for satisfaction. This leads to a distinction between primary institutions, which can be legitimated with reference to nature, and secondary institutions, which must be legitimated with reference to culture. Here, institutions appear as the "concrete isolates of organized behavior" in which groups of people satisfy their needs together.

There is another tradition in social theory that starts not with nature but with ideas. Sometimes institutions enact power over the behavior of individuals even where it is against their interests. This cannot be explained by need alone, and there must be other sources of institutional credibility. For Émile Durkheim, who described sociology as the "science of institutions," these sources were the collective patterns of thought. They are as solid as physical objects for the socialized individual. But where does this normative and symbolic surplus come from? Following Maurice Hauriou (1865–1929), institutions are centered around a leading idea (*idée directrice*). This idea is shared by every member of a group and therefore constitutes institutions like law or the state. In order to provide continuity, this idea needs to be incorporated and personalized. Talcott Parsons further developed this approach: for him, too, society is based on norms and values. Yet in the Parsonian tradition, the term institution almost disappeared behind the more fundamental concept of the social "system."

A third way of dealing with institutions tries to combine the natural and the symbolic factors. For the German anthropologist Arnold Gehlen (1904–76), institutions are necessary in order to give directions to human beings. Compared to lower animals, human instincts are reduced. Yet social life without directions would lead to a Hobbesian war of all against all. Institutions therefore reduce complexity: they limit the possibilities to act. In so doing they not only fulfill the basic needs in a certain culturally fixed way, they also supply cultural meaning to all things, providing a "meaning of life." On the basis of this "background satisfaction," new possibilities appear which constitute the second-order freedom of cultivated man. This philosophical approach was taken up by the seminal work of Berger and Luckmann, *The Social Construction of Reality* (1966). Their work integrates different approaches into a general theory of institutionalization. Following them, social interaction becomes institutionalized when typified behavioral patterns crystallize into role models that are known to all or most members of society. Such models can last for generations. Therefore, their internalization (the counterpart of institutionalization) requires certain narratives in order to legitimize these institutions. Institutions do not necessarily need to become "total," as Goffman described in examples like prisons. The dimension of legitimation allows for an institutional adaptation to new challenges. For this reason, institutional analysis is not confined to finding formal organizational structures and necessities. It also needs to investigate the culture of an institution, which includes the legitimizing narratives as well as the informal narratives that allow for institutional continuity and institutional change.

Institutional economics has stressed the importance of institutional settings as restrictions on individual economic action. Economic sociology has reacted to this recent trend by showing that much more is at stake. Institutions matter even more than institutional economics admits. Economic action is always embedded in broader cultural and political settings. The market itself is an institution that needs regulation. This starts with a central bank that physically provides money, interest rates, loans, exchange rates, and so on; and it has cultural implications, as, for example, the issue of which "goods" should be allowed to be traded at all. Should there be markets for human organs and genetic codes? This is a question that is dealt with in ethical, political, and juridical institutions. The main object of economic analysis is the market. But there are

social institutions at work long before a market evolves. Therefore, the sociology of institutions is more relevant today than ever.

SEE ALSO: Culture, Nature and; Markets; Narrative; Organizations; Role; Social Change; Social Embeddedness of Economic Action; Socialization

REFERENCES AND SUGGESTED READINGS

Berger, P. L. & Luckmann, T. (1966) *The Social Construction of Reality: A Treatise in the Sociology of Knowledge*. Doubleday, New York.

DiMaggio, P. J. & Powell, W. W. (Eds.) (1991) *The New Institutionalism in Organizational Analysis*. University of Chicago Press, Chicago.

Gehlen, A. (1980) *Man in the Age of Technology*. Columbia University Press, New York.

Malinowski, B. (1944) *A Scientific Theory of Culture*. University of North Carolina Press, Chapel Hill.

North, D. C. (1990) *Institutions, Institutional Change, and Economic Performance*. Cambridge University Press, Cambridge.

Williamson, O. (1987) *The Economic Institutions of Capitalism: Firms, Markets, Relational Contracting*. Free Press, New York.

institutional review boards and sociological research

Zoë Blumberg Corwin and William G. Tierney

Institutional review boards (IRBs) are charged with ensuring the rights of volunteers who participate in research conducted through a university. Originally conceived after World War II to deter possible abuses in biomedical research, human subject review has expanded to research in the social sciences. The role of IRBs in research is not without controversy, especially as it pertains to sociological studies. Tension between IRBs and researchers centers on how the two parties interpret what constitutes research and the effects of IRB regulation on research in general.

ORIGINS AND HISTORY

During the Nuremberg War Crime Trials after World War II, news of abusive biomedical experiments conducted by the Nazis drew attention to the importance of establishing ethical parameters for conducting research. The Nuremberg Code (1947) expanded on earlier directives issued by the Prussian government to protect the welfare of research subjects, including obtaining consent from participants in medical experiments. The much-publicized Code outlined a broad protocol for judging the ethics and actions of scientists who performed biomedical research on human subjects, was intended for the international community, and served as the prototype for subsequent IRB regulations in the US.

The first major effort to establish IRBs at universities across the country and to articulate IRB guidelines occurred in 1974 when the US government created the National Commission for the Protection of Human Subjects of Biomedical and Behavioral Research. The commission was charged to determine the various distinctions between biomedical and behavioral research, establish a way to assess the risks and benefits of conducting research, outline the guidelines for subject selection, and define the boundaries of informed consent. The Commission's central policy document, the Belmont Report (1979), outlined guidelines for the Commission at the federal level and for individual IRBs at the institutional level. The report clarified distinctions between research and practice, identified three ethical principles intended to guide the protection of human subjects, and discussed the application of the three principles. The authors of the report intentionally utilized generalized language, thus leaving room for interpretations of details up to individual IRBs at each institution, a point with implications discussed below.

By 1991, oversight for human subjects policy in the US had been transferred to the Department of Health and Human Services which, in conjunction with 16 other federal departments, drafted what is commonly referred to as the Common Rule (45 CFR 46.111). The Common Rule expanded on earlier regulations and required that universities create IRBs if their researchers desire to access government funding for investigations. Many universities, however, have expanded IRB jurisdiction to cover all research activities with human subjects regardless of funding sources. The expanded IRB role is most likely due to increasing university concerns of being sued over improper research protocols and methods.

In 2001 the American Association of University Professors wrote a critical response to the Common Rule outlining concerns of social scientists over governmental regulations on research, questioning the constraints that IRBs potentially place on academic freedom, and studying the applications of governmental regulations on social science research. In particular, the document offered suggestions for improving how IRBs address qualitative research which comprises approximately 25 percent of all research reviewed by IRBs. The AAUP document underscored the challenge of interpreting IRB guidelines given the broad definitions articulated in the Belmont Report (AAUP 2001).

IRBs are not exclusive to the US. US IRBs provide protections for subjects participating in foreign research conducted by US researchers and many countries employ their own system of human subject protections within their universities. International IRBs are structured around similar issues to IRBS in the US, yet the details of implementation vary in nuanced ways. For example, in the Netherlands, social scientists are exempt from undergoing IRB review unless their research poses clear physical or psychological duress on subjects (Bosk & DeVries 2004), and Canadian IRBs differ slightly in how they define "minimal risk" and "human subjects" (Center for Advanced Study 2005). Debates entertained by IRBs and researchers in the international community are reflective of those that occur in the US.

JURISDICTION

IRBs are responsible for translating federal, state, and local regulations into institutional practice. As such, IRBs are mandated to approve, require modifications, or disprove of research activities related to human subjects and funded by federal resources. As noted, numerous universities now require all research, irrespective of funding source or researcher, to receive IRB approval. For example, any graduate student who writes a master's thesis or a dissertation must receive IRB approval. A recent study by the NIH found that few proposed studies were rejected by IRBs, but that approximately 80 percent required changes (AAUP 2001). The authority of IRBs is governed by principles outlined in the Belmont Report, but also is determined by the composition of IRBs, interpretation of exemptions and regulations, and treatment of informed consent. Most large institutions host separate medical and social behavioral IRBs. According to the Common Rule, IRBs must have at least five members, ideally from diverse backgrounds with respect to race, class, and gender, but also from various academic disciplines. Because the majority of IRB members come from biomedical fields, it is especially important for sociological researchers that IRBs are comprised of individuals who understand the nuances of social scientific work. If an IRB is faced with evaluating a proposal where no one is familiar with the research, experts are allowed to be consulted and participate in the review.

IRBs are guided by the three ethical principles outlined in the Belmont Report: (1) respect for persons, (2) beneficence, and (3) justice. Respect for persons emphasizes that individuals should be recognized as autonomous and treated with dignity and that persons with diminished autonomy (e.g., persons with certain types of mental illness, persons with restricted liberty such as prisoners) deserve special protections. The implications of this principle pertain to supplying participants with adequate information about the research project and ensuring voluntary participation. Beneficence requires researchers to do no harm and to maximize the possibility for benefits and minimize possible risks to subjects. The application of beneficence involves weighing the risks and benefits of each particular project. The third principle, justice, obliges researchers to distribute the benefits and burdens of research equitably. This principle relates to fair sample selection for the subject individually, but also

as a member of a social, racial, sexual, or ethnic group. The Tuskegee syphilis study of 1940, where rural African American men were used as research subjects and deprived of effective treatment, even though the disease affected a much wider population, is an example of how a specific population can be unfairly burdened through a selective sample.

Especially important to sociological researchers are the six concepts of exemption pertaining to social science research. They are (1) research in education settings on instructional techniques, curricula, or classroom-management methods; (2) research involving the use of educational tests, survey procedures, interview procedures, or observation of public behavior, unless the subject can be identified and disclosure of the subject's responses could put the individual at risk of criminal or civil liability or could damage the subject's financial standing, employability, or reputation; (3) research involving elected or appointed officials or candidates for public office; (4) studies using existing data, documents, or records, as long as these resources are publicly available or the human subject cannot be identified; (5) studies of public benefit or service programs; and (6) research focusing on consumer consumption of food and the taste and quality of food (AAUP 2001). These categories are exempt because they are believed to exhibit minimal risk. However, what qualifies as exempt is also open for interpretation by university-specific IRBs.

The majority of IRBs require written proof of informed consent to participate in research. Consent forms outline the study parameters, possible risks, and benefits of participating in the project, and require a signature from the research subject. Requiring written consent can pose problems for qualitative researchers in particular and at times must be negotiated with the institution's IRB. For example, the American Anthropological Association (2004) has argued that in some cases having research subjects sign a consent form can be alienating and even deter an individual from participating in a study. Examples of this include research with vulnerable populations such as individuals with stigmatizing illnesses (e.g., HIV/AIDS), or individuals who perform illegal activities (e.g., sex work, garment workers without immigration documents), or individuals who do not believe in signing government documents (e.g., *curanderos* – medicinal healers – from rural Mexico). Other issues arise, particularly in the field of education, if non-research activities, such as course evaluations, are conflated with exempt research. The Internet poses new challenges for obtaining informed consent, as researchers increasingly use email and chat rooms as sites for data collection. Still, researchers contend that obtaining consent should be a meaningful activity because it reflects the essence of individual autonomy (Brody 2001).

MAJOR DEBATES

Given the original purposes of IRBs, how well does institutional review fare with regard to sociological research? Despite the value they place on ethical conduct in research, sociological researchers are often at odds with the IRB process. On the one hand, IRBs have the potential to share resources and expertise with scholars, as well as highlight the importance of reflexivity in research. Yet researchers also complain that vague definitions and varying interpretations of research pose unique challenges to sociological work, that applying a biomedical model to social science research is ineffective, and that the implementation of IRB review inhibits academic freedom and restricts productivity. Further, many scholars perceive IRBs as increasingly more concerned with the protection of the university from lawsuits than with the protection of human subjects.

The amorphous character of definitions presented in the Belmont Report is particularly problematic for sociological researchers. For example, the report defines research as an activity designed to "test hypotheses, permit conclusions to be drawn, and thereby to develop or contribute to generalizable knowledge (expressed, for example, in theories, principles and statements of relationships)." This definition has perplexed social scientists who do not purport to test hypotheses or produce generalizable findings, but still are required to submit their proposed studies to their IRB for review. Also troubling for sociological researchers is the definition of the human subject as "a living individual about whom an investigator (whether professional or student) conducting research obtains (1) data

through intervention or interaction with the individual, or (2) identifiable private information." The terms "intervention," "interaction," and "private information" can be interpreted in different ways. Even measuring the costs and benefits of a research project is subject to interpretation. IRBs, for example, can determine that while the benefits of a research study are reasonable in relation to the risks imposed on subjects, the benefits with respect to new knowledge are not substantial and thereby deny approval or request modifications to the study. Here the interpretation of what constitutes knowledge is open for interpretation and strongly influenced by the composition of IRB members. As discussed below, how an IRB interprets the Belmont Report's definitions has significant ramifications for various types of sociological research.

In principle and in practicality, many researchers from the field of sociology voice concerns over the fact that IRB regulations derive from a biomedical model. Since the goals of sociological research as well as the methods often vary from biomedical research, this paradox poses problems for sociological researchers, especially for those who conduct qualitative studies. The examples of oral histories, ethnographies, and case studies illustrate the complexity of the inconsistency.

In 2003, after discussion with the American Historical Society, the federal government determined that oral histories do not constitute research and consequently are not subject to IRB review. Historians had voiced concern over how IRBs had been interpreting regulations intended for biomedical researchers which were "unsuited" to historical methods (Brainard 2003). The association argued that oral histories do not attempt to add to "generalizable knowledge" and that historians aim to describe a specific past and therefore do not need to undergo IRB review (Ritchie & Shopes 2003). At the core of this ruling was the interpretation of what it means to do research. While historians applauded the decision, they are now faced with the mixed message that what they do is not considered research. Consequently, a side effect of the loose interpretation of research is that it created a larger chasm between academic disciplines.

Unlike with oral histories, the American Anthropological Association (AAA) determined that ethnographies qualify as research, but should be evaluated on a case by case manner due to their often complex nature. In many cases, ethnographers are unable to articulate hypotheses and procedures formally prior to beginning data collection due to the dynamic nature of the method. In a 2004 statement on IRBs and ethnography, the AAA (2004) pointed out that, due to the fact that ethnographic research is based on cultivating trusting relationships over time, IRBs need to recognize that consent is a changing and ongoing process. The AAA stressed the need to evaluate the sociocultural environment of each research project in order to adequately assess risk. It is likely that most ethnographies will be classified as low risk since it is fairly simple to withdraw participation. A major area of contention for the AAA with regards to IRBs is the documentation of consent as discussed above, but also considering the intrusion that research paraphernalia (consent forms, tape recorders, writing pads, pencils, and pens) can have on securing trust with an interviewee.

The position of case studies is less clear. Some scholars argue that case studies aim to contribute to generalizable knowledge, can cause risk to participants, and thus are subject to IRB review; others argue that case studies do not rely on "systematic investigation" and generally invoke little risk and therefore should not be classified as research. How the IRB interprets research determines how case studies should be treated.

A practical result of this confusion is a logjam with regard to the approval process. The interpretation of IRB "rules" varies from campus to campus, and with different committees on the same campus. What was approved last year, or even last semester, may not gain approval this year. Graduate students, in particular, have faced delays in conducting research in large part because no one is certain how to proceed, so that everything needs to be reviewed by a committee. Even if the process were optimal, the result can be remarkably inefficient.

For many institutions, IRB review extends not just to research but into the classroom. Sociological scholars have emphasized the risk that increased surveillance, more rigid regulations, and emphasis on the institution over the individual place on academic freedom. Again, efforts to translate biomedical approaches to sociological research fuel the complexity of

ensuring academic freedom. Increased attention to human subjects as a result of biomedical failures, scrutiny of classroom teaching, and questions about what constitutes "evidence and scientific inquiry serve as fodder for limits on academic freedom" (Lincoln & Tierney 2004). It is suggested that this is partly because IRBs focus on research *plans* instead of potential publications, a method that works for biomedical research but has a complicated application to sociological work, since researchers often do not know what they will publish until the research is complete.

Debates in journal articles, conference papers, and online discussions suggest that IRBs have the potential to stifle innovations in research by discouraging research with populations who might appear to pose high risks to IRBs, slowing down the research process, and assuming a "one-size-fits-all" model for nuanced types of sociological studies (AAUP 2001). Delays in IRB approval adversely affect the actual production of scholarship, as well as the perceptions about how to design future research. Lincoln and Tierney (2004) point out that a growing reluctance to approve research with children as well as restrictions on reflexive research contribute to self-censorship on the part of researchers.

Concern has been expressed over burdening researchers with too much regulation and paperwork, a situation complicated by IRBs who are sometimes ignorant about sociological research methods (Pritchard 2002). At the same time, attention has turned to resisting "mission creep," or the inability of IRBs to cope with increased workloads caused by a misplaced focus on procedure over ethical issues (Center for Advanced Study 2005). Negative perceptions and experiences with IRBs have also been shown to demoralize faculty and students (Pritchard 2002). Graduate students witness the frustration experienced by their professors and opt to do research that they perceive will receive expedited or exempt review.

FUTURE

One solution to promoting understanding of sociological research is to ensure that members of sociology departments are represented on IRBs and that biomedical members are educated as to the nuances of sociological research. More in-depth understandings of the types of risks involved in sociological research can expand the potential for exempt review as well as lessen the number of required changes to research design. Other recommendations include sending research proposals to an IRB representative in home departments before submitting the document for review, thus decreasing the potential for an IRB member to misinterpret study goals or methods.

Kahn and Mastroianni (2002) pose an important question: How do we move from a culture of compliance to a culture of conscience? There are a host of innovative approaches to educating researchers about the IRB process. Universities now offer online certification for individuals conducting federal research, specialized journals highlight the continually changing issues facing IRBs, and online chat rooms provide a forum for discussing issues pertinent to IRB review (see www.irbforum.com). National conferences have also created venues for discussing the parameters of IRBs (American Sociological Association in 2005; Center for Advanced Study at the University of Illinois in 2003; Social and Behavioral Sciences Working Group in Human Research Protections in 2003). Graduate research seminars can incorporate sections on IRB review.

Given the public attention afforded to instances of university neglect of research volunteers and increasing concern of universities to protect themselves from lawsuits, it is unlikely that IRB regulations will relax in the future. In fact, trends in the last ten years indicate that IRBs have become more rigid. Consequently, it is critical that researchers continue to express vigilance over infringements on academic freedom and the adverse effects of IRB review on innovation in research. This can partially be facilitated through supporting sociological studies on how IRBs function (DeVries 2005). Continued dialogue and debate is productive not only at the institutional level, but in national forums as well.

SEE ALSO: Ethics, Fieldwork; Ethics, Research; Ethnography; Interviewing, Structured, Unstructured, and Postmodern; Methods, Case Study; Survey Research

REFERENCES AND SUGGESTED READINGS

Adler, P. A. & Adler, P. (2002) The Reluctant Respondent. In: Gubrium, J. & Holstein, J. (Eds.), *Handbook of Interview Research*. Sage, Thousand Oaks, CA, pp. 515–35.

American Anthropological Association (2004) Statement on Ethnography and Institutional Review Boards. Online. www.aaanet.org/stmts/irb.htm.

American Association of University Professors (2001) Protecting Human Beings: Institutional Review Boards and Social Science Research. *Academe* 87(3): 55–67.

Bosk, C. L. & DeVries, R. G. (2004) Bureaucracies of Mass Deception: Institutional Review Boards and the Ethics of Ethnographic Research. *Annals of the American Academy* 595: 249–63.

Brainard, J. (2003) Federal Agency Says Oral History Is Not Subject to Rules of Human Research Volunteers. *Chronicle of Higher Education*. Online. www.chronicle.com.

Brody, B. A. (2001) Making Informed Consent Meaningful. *IRB Ethics and Human Research* 23(5): 1–5.

Center for Advanced Study (2005) *Improving the System for Protecting Human Subjects: Counteracting IRB "Mission Creep."* University of Illinois, Urbana-Champaign.

Church, J. T., Shopes, L., & Blanchard, M. A. (2002) Should All Disciplines Be Subject to the Common Rule? Human Subjects of Social Science Research. *Academe* (May/June): 62–9.

DeVries, R. G. (2005) Deference and Scrutiny on a General IRB. Paper presented at the American Sociological Association Annual Meeting, Philadelphia, August.

Health and Human Services (n.d.) Institutional Review Board Guidebook. Online. www.hhs.gov/ohrp/irb.

Kahn, J. P. & Mastroianni, A. C. (2002) Point of View: Doing Research Well By Doing Right. *Chronicle of Higher Education*.www.chronicle.com.

Lincoln, Y. S. & Tierney, W. G. (2004) Qualitative Research and Institutional Review Boards. *Qualitative Inquiry* 10(2): 219–34.

National Commission for the Protection of Human Subjects of Biomedical and Behavioral Research (1979) *The Belmont Report: Ethical Principles and Guidelines for the Protection of Human Subjects of Research*. Department of Health, Education, and Welfare, Washington, DC. Online. www.ohsr.nih.gov/mpa/belmont.php3.

Pritchard, I. A. (2002) Travelers and Trolls: Practitioner Research and Institutional Review Boards. *Educational Researcher* 31(3): 3–13.

Ritchie, D. A. & Shopes, L. (2003) Oral history Excluded from IRB Review. Online. www.aaup. org/Issues/IBBs/Oralhistory.htm.

United States Department of Health and Human Services (1991) Title 45 Code of Federal Regulations, Part 46: Protection of Human Subjects. online. www.hhs.gov/ohrp/humansubjects/guidance/ 45cfr46.htm.

institutional theory, new

Chris Carter and Stewart Clegg

Emerging from the sociology of education in the 1970s, new institutional theory (NIT) has become one of the foremost positions within the mainstream of American management studies. It seeks to explain the ways in which institutions are created, sustained, and diffused. NIT's antecedents lay in the institutional theorizing of writers such as Philip Selznick a generation before. Adherents of NIT are keen to draw a distinction between "new" and "old" institutionalism. While old institutionalism emphasized politics and the role of conflict, NIT took legitimacy as its master concept. The old institutionalism focused on the existence of a negotiated order between different interest groups, while in its place NIT sought to understand the way in which the quest for legitimacy is a driving force behind the isomorphism of organizations. NIT is interested in understanding the means through which the socially constructed external environment enters the organization by "creating the lens through which actors view the world and the very categories of structure, action, and thought" (Powell & DiMaggio 1991).

Works by Meyer and Rowan (1977) and DiMaggio and Powell (1983) are generally held up as foundational or seminal statements of NIT. Constituting the two branches of NIT, they remain widely cited to this day. Meyer and Rowan examined why particular phenomena became institutionalized; that is, why certain forms were repeatedly enacted over time. Exploring the use of budgeting in the loosely institutionalized setting of a university, they argued that it came to play a more important

role because of the increasing need for university authorities to portray their actions to external agencies as following some form of "rationality," Their analysis highlights that such rationality is often a mere rhetorical veneer – an image existing only in a ceremonial and symbolic form – which might well be decoupled from what actually happens in the organization. Building on these insights, Suchman argues that this leaves three strategies open to organizational actors: (1) they ignore the actual performance of an initiative and choose to concentrate on celebrating the ceremonial aspects of the initiative; (2) they criticize and display cynicism towards the initiative, acknowledging that its results are problematic; (3) they champion reform of the initiative, thereby drawing a distinction between the troubled present and a more successful future.

The DiMaggio and Powell branch of NIT seeks to understand why it is that organizations are increasingly coming to resemble each other. They argue that this process of isomorphism is driven by the necessity of being seen to be legitimate in the eyes of important stakeholders, which, following Berger and Luckman, they see as an intersubjective process of social construction. DiMaggio and Powell identify coercive, normative, and mimetic dimensions of isomorphism. Coercive isomorphism, as the name suggests, occurs where an organization is compelled to institutionalize a particular policy, such as adopt an employment law or a tax standard. Coercive isomorphism is often found in global supply chains, where one powerful buyer coerces other parts of the supply chain to adopt a particular initiative or technology. Normative isomorphism refers to institutions adopting similar initiatives because they are regarded as constituting professional "best practice." The MBA qualification can be construed as a transmission mechanism for notions of best practice in management. The drive for legitimacy on these three dimensions increasingly leads organizations to resemble each other, at least superficially.

In management studies, contrary to their intentions, DiMaggio and Powell's concept of mimetic isomorphism has become by far the most widely used and tested of the three types of institutional isomorphism (Mizruchi & Fein 1999). It is this concept that underpins much of the burgeoning research in management fashion. According to this perspective, management fashions are ephemeral and are adopted by organizations seeking to demonstrate that they are in symphony with the spirit of the zeitgeist. In the adoption of an initiative, some organizations are regarded as being fashion leaders, on the catwalk at the leading shows, as it were, amidst a blaze of positive publicity, while others follow more slowly, less as *fashionistas* and more as diffusionists, as fashion gradually trickles and distills down to the high street (Mazza & Alvrarez 2000). After a few years, a fashion becomes *démodé*, leaving the organizational scene without an institutional trace. There is little empirical doubt that management fashion has become a feature of the organizational world. Some researchers (Mizruchi & Fein 1999) have suggested this is not the sole reason for the popularity of mimetic isomorphism. Its uncontroversial content – dealing with mimicry instead of power and conflict – make it perfect for making contributions to conservative American management journals. Thus, NIT has undergone a series of translations as it has entered the canon of management. These translations have taken it far from the initial work of DiMaggio and Powell and Meyer and Rowan.

NIT has been criticized for its weakness in being able to explain organizational change. As a social theory it has difficulty in explaining how change occurs. NIT's departure from old institutionalism marked a downplaying of power and politics, which means that, as a theory, it has little to say about conflict or hegemony. Similarly, NIT falls silent on agency. There have been recent calls to reintroduce agency into institutional analysis, a challenge that is being addressed by the emerging institutional entrepreneurship community.

Despite its limitations, NIT remains a popular position and it has the capacity to help understand aspects of the intersubjective relationship between an organization and its field (Powell & DiMaggio 1991). It can help us understand the adoption of innovations (Mazza & Alvarez 2000), long-term shifts in organization fields (Fligstein 1991), and variation among nation-states, an issue that is also addressed by the closely related societal effects school (Maurice et al. 1980). Indeed, with the latter we may say that a separate European New Institutional School, more attuned to the classical sociological concerns of power, has been established. However, lacking the citational impact of the leading US journals, because of its European provenance, its impact has been less influential. Indeed, in an ironical way, this serves as a final example of institutional theory at work: those theories that become most easily institutionalized are those that are seen to have been published in what are regarded, by a hegemonic system dominated by US scholarship, in the most legitimate journals. Needless to say, these are those sourced in the US rather than elsewhere.

SEE ALSO: Institution; Institutionalism; Management; Management Fashion

REFERENCES AND SUGGESTED READINGS

DiMaggio, P. J. & Powell, W. W. (1983) The Iron Cage Revisited: Institutional Isomorphism and Collective Rationality in Organizational Fields. *American Sociological Review* 48: 147–60.

Fligstein, N. (1991) The Structural Transformation of American Industry: An Institutional Account of the Causes of Diversification in the Largest Firms, 1919–1979. In: Powell, W. W. & DiMaggio, P. J. (Eds.), *The New Institutionalism in Organizational Analysis.* University of Chicago Press, Chicago, pp. 311–36.

Maurice, M., Sorge, A., & Warner, M. (1980) Societal Differences in Organizing Manufacturing Units: A Comparison of France, West Germany and Great Britain. *Organization Studies* 1(1): 59–86.

Mazza, C. & Alvarez, J. (2000) Haute Couture and Pret a Porter: The Popular Press and the Diffusion of Management Practices. *Organization Studies* 21: 567–88.

Meyer, J. W. & Rowan, B. (1977) Institutionalized Organizations: Formal Structure as Myth and Ceremony. *American Journal of Sociology* 83: 340–63.

Mizruchi, M. S. & Fein, L. C. (1999) The Social Construction of Organizational Knowledge: A Study of the Uses of Coercive, Mimetic, and Normative Isomorphism. *Administrative Science Quarterly* 44: 653–83.

Powell, W. W. & DiMaggio, P. J. (Eds.) (1991) *The New Institutionalism in Organizational Analysis.* University of Chicago Press, Chicago.

institutionalism

Paul Ingram

There are many definitions of institution in sociology. Most of them are subsumed in the following: institutions are persistent social facts that regulate social behavior. "Persistent" indicates the role of institutions in stabilizing social life. "Social facts" capture the idea that institutions are the product of interaction and association and that they exist externally to individuals. "Regulate social behavior" represents that institutions sanction certain forms of social behavior and discourage others.

According to this definition, most targets of sociological study qualify as institutions. At a minimum, organizations, the state, social norms, laws, cultural values, and socially constructed knowledge are, or are enlivened by, institutions, and each of these has been the focus of one or more variants of institutional argument. Indeed, Durkheim (1982: 59) defined sociology as "the science of institutions, their genesis and their functioning." There is really no question among sociologists that institutions matter for social life. Instead, sociological institutionalism is directed at questions of which institutions matter most, how they impact individual behavior, and how they emerge and change.

INSTITUTIONAL FORMS AND FORMS OF INSTITUTIONALISM

There are a number of variants of institutionalism based on different emphases on these three issues. One way to organize these is along two dimensions that identify the social structures with which the institutions are most closely associated. A public/private dimension identifies the subjects of the institution. Public institutions apply to all members of a nation, culture, or general sphere of interaction such as an industry, whereas private institutions apply to recognized members of an exclusive social structure, such as a group or an organization. A centralized/decentralized dimension refers to the source of institutional authority. Centralized institutions are those created and enforced by some designated agent, whereas decentralized institutions are emergent, and responsibility for their enforcement is diffuse. Archetypes of the four major forms of institutions identified by these two dimensions are laws (public–centralized), cultural values (public–decentralized), organizational rules (private–centralized), and social norms (private–decentralized). The social structures that house these institutional forms are, respectively, states, civil society, organizations, and networks.

Public–Decentralized: Culture, Values, and Civil Society

The public–decentralized quadrant is currently the most active in sociology, represented by the "new institutional" school that emerged in the late 1970s and closely associated with Stanford University (it is sometimes labeled the "Stanford School"). The seminal article was Meyer and Rowan (1977), which argued that many formal organizations implement structures that are consistent with widespread societal beliefs about legitimate approaches to organizing, and not necessarily a response to the task demands the organization faces. Organizing in this way can bring the organization resources, which are often dependent on legitimate action. However, it is not the conscious pursuit of the rewards of legitimacy that motivates action in this form of institutionalism. Rather, action here is more preconscious than calculative, based on the actor's socially constructed cognitions about their role and the expectations it entails (Berger & Luckmann 1967). This cognitive approach is a defining feature of this form of institutionalism.

The role of legitimacy as a mechanism for the new institutional school leads naturally to the question, "where does legitimacy come from?" The most common argument is that legitimacy is a function of frequency of occurrence, with a practice or structure becoming more cognitively familiar, and therefore more legitimate as it becomes more common, to the point where it may be sufficiently endemic as to be "taken for granted." The most compelling empirical evidence of this process comes from organizational ecology's theory of density dependence, which argues that an organizational form becomes more legitimate as a function of the number of organizations that employ it. The results of dozens of analyses of organizational founding and failure are seen as supporting that theory (e.g., Carroll & Hannan 1999).

Legitimacy-based institutionalism often examines the impact of institutional influence on organizations. The ultimate source of institutional influence from this perspective, however, is the concept of propriety inherent in civil society. Organizations are seen not generally as the source of institutional influence, but rather as a manifestation of it. Organizations stabilize the institutional environment by giving ideas a structural representation, which in turn reinforces them and facilitates their transition to taken-for-granted status. Although organizations are most often the target of institutional influence, an appealing element of this theory is that other social actors may be similarly affected. Some of the most exciting empirical applications of this form of institutionalism have examined states as the unit of analysis, identifying how they are subject to internationally embedded sentiments as to what types of activities are appropriate for a state (Meyer et al. 1997).

Within countries, pressure from institutions is not equal in all sectors of society. The relative importance of the legitimacy of organizational practices, as opposed to their direct implications for the organization's ability to achieve its goals, is greater in sectors that are more public. Consequently, studies on the structures of educational and health care organizations, and government offices, are among the most prominent in this literature. The literature is least compelling when it seeks to explain organizational features such as the marketing strategies of for-profit enterprises that cannot be clearly linked to ideas of propriety. This is not to say that this literature has nothing to say about the strategies and structures of for-profit organizations, however. There are a number of important studies on the processes by which organizational structures that represent societal values, particularly regarding labor relations and the role of women and minorities within organizations, become institutionalized among for-profit firms. A particularly interesting example in this line is Dobbin and Sutton (1998), which argues that the US federal government relied on its influence over the process of legitimation to affect a shift in employment rights that it did not have the administrative capacity to force on organizations.

Private–Decentralized: Interorganizational Ties and Group Norms

An influential paper by DiMaggio and Powell (1991) forges a bridge between public–decentralized and private–decentralized institutions, and between the legitimacy-based new institutionalism and its more realist ancestors. DiMaggio and Powell examine the tendency for organizations within a field of interaction to employ the same structures, practices, and procedures. Partly, they complement legitimacy-based institutional arguments by more precisely specifying the mechanisms by which ideals enter organizations, for example, through the influence of the professions. They also recognize more direct mechanisms of interorganizational influence, particularly the possibility that a powerful organization may coerce others that are dependent on it. Whereas the Stanford School sees institutions mainly as preconscious influences on cognition, the concept of coercive isomorphism is consistent with the idea that organizations may promote or adopt certain practices due to more conscious calculations regarding their costs and benefits to the organization's goals and to important interorganizational relationships. This idea connects firmly to what is called the "old institutionalism" in organizational sociology, represented famously by Selznick's (1949) classic study of the Tennessee Valley Authority (TVA). Selznick shows how, in its attempt to maintain control and sustain itself, the TVA became infused with the values of powerful constituents in its environment, coming to represent and pursue their values and interests at the cost of the TVA's original goals. As with the new institutionalism, the old institutionalism characterizes organizations as laden with external ideals, even when they are not needed or even helpful for achieving the organization's operational goals. The difference is the logic of action, which for the old institutionalists derives ultimately from utilitarian pursuits of organizations and their participants. Norms may be internalized in this view, but their origins are in the interests and values of the participants of a social system, and they are associated with regulatory rewards and punishments which are an important part of their influence (Parsons 1990).

Selznick and other old institutionalists are categorized as examining private institutions because organizations are not unavoidably subject to the influence of their interaction partners in the way that they are to the law or to public perceptions of legitimacy. At the same time, these institutions are decentralized because there is nothing official about the authority for influence among interdependent organizations. No bank is designated, for example, to encourage cooperative organizations to adopt capitalist organizing principles (a common empirical example of an ideal that leads to interorganizational coercion). Based on the behavioral constraints that emerge from voluntary association, the old institutionalism of organizational theory can be seen as comparable, at a higher level of social aggregation, to the norms of social groups. Indeed, the literature on social norms represents most of the sociology relevant to private–decentralized institutions.

Much of what sociologists know about normative control derives from social exchange theory. A fundamental work here is Homans (1950), which presents a number of insightful cases that show the micro-processes through which the benefits that members derive from groups become the basis for the group's control over them. More recently, researchers have used more formal models to show that norms can align individual and group interests by encouraging individuals to contribute to collective goods (e.g., Coleman 1990). Norms are of obvious sociological interest in their own right, but they are also important for understanding the operation of the most significant social structures. In particular, research on private–decentralized institutions is being used in economic sociology to better specify just how social networks that connect individuals, organizations, and states affect the behavior of those actors.

Private–Centralized: Bureaucracy and Organizational Rules

The third category of institutions, private–centralized, is based on the role played by organizations and organizational rules as the *source* (as opposed to the target) of institutional influence. The targets of private–centralized institutions are the participants in the organization, which may be individuals or other organizations in the case of a supra-organization such as a trade association. Attention to organizational policies and bureaucracy as determinants of individual behavior is the foundation of organizational theory. The foundational argument here is Weber's (1947) illustration of how authority may derive from the rules of bureaucracy. Merton (1957) contributed a potent essay on the micro-mechanisms by which bureaucratic rules grip participants, even to the point where they may sometimes inhibit the pursuit of the organization's goals. Subsequently, contingency theorists built theories that indicate which combinations of formal organizing principles are best to encourage particular behaviors from participants. Currently, the attention to private–centralized institutions from sociologists is low. Part of the reason is the success of new institutional arguments which have alerted analysts to the symbolic implications of formal organizational structures, rather than their direct influence on behavior. Private–centralized institutions are, however, the subject of a vibrant literature in organizational economics, one that borrows from and influences sociology. Williamson (1985) and others operating under the banner of "transaction cost economics" argue that formal organization and other institutional forms, notably the market, may be more or less effective for governance depending on characteristics of the transactions in question.

Public–Centralized: The State

The fourth category, public–centralized institutions, represents the state and the laws and policies it implements. Institutional arguments regarding the state's impact on the economy can be categorized into four broad types. First, the state is a fundamental source of the institutions that smooth exchange by helping citizens to make credible commitments (Campbell & Lindberg 1990; North 1990). This role of the state is particularly prominent in recent accounts of the transition from state socialism, where the costly absence of property rights, contract law, and the regulation of financial markets becomes starkly apparent. Second, the pattern of economic behavior within a state depends on whether the state can commit to not "bailing out" subjects when they struggle. If not, subjects may be diverted from productive activity toward efforts to "hold up" the state for subsidies. Third, subjects' willingness to invest in long-term projects will depend on whether the state has the checks and safeguards to resist appropriating subjects' wealth. Fourth, the state may affect the distribution of power and wealth, between rich and poor, between suppliers and consumers, or between rival organizational forms. Dobbin's (1994) comparison of the development of anti-trust institutions in France, the UK, and the US is an important example of the state's distributional influence. Beyond these direct effects of the state on the economy, institutionalists such as Skocpol (1985) have also theorized as to the source of the state's strength. Following Weber, they highlight bureaucracy as a key source of the state's capacity to implement policy, but they also consider the state's autonomy from other actors in society.

FUTURE DIRECTIONS FOR THEORY

The various institutionalisms all struggle with two questions: "how are different types of institutions interdependent?" and "how do institutions change?" The first question has become a pressing problem partly because of the pattern of development of institutionalism as a field of inquiry. Different schools of institutionalism have tended to focus on one kind of institution, typically arguing for its supremacy as an influence on behavior and slighting the relevance of other institutional forms. Nevertheless, some of the most exciting institutional arguments highlight the fact that the functioning of one institutional form, such as state regulation, depends on other institutions, such as norms derived from social cohesion. Indeed, Durkheim makes this claim in the preface to the second edition of *The Division of Labor in Society* (1984: liv), where he calls a modern state that governs unorganized individuals "a veritable sociological monstrosity" and claims "[a] nation cannot be maintained unless, between the state and individuals, a whole range of secondary

groups are interposed." The dependence of the state on other institutional forms makes for an even larger place for sociology among disciplinary approaches to institutionalism.

Kindred interdependencies exist between other institutional forms. As Homans's (1950) reanalysis of the bank-wiring room indicates, organizational rules may be frustrated by opposition norms among the participants. In part interdependence between institutional forms occurs because actors are almost always subject to various institutions – an individual in the US is subject to the law, the policies of an employing organization, the norms of friendship groups, and the values of culture. More than merely acting simultaneously on the same targets, however, different institutions may interact with and enable each other. For example, Fligstein (2001) presents an economic sociological account of markets that emphasizes that a range of different institutions, including property rights, rules of exchange, governance structures, and conceptions of control, are jointly necessary to make a market.

The second and most pressing challenge for all forms of institutionalism is to explain the origin and change of institutions. As institutions stabilize social structure and constrain behavior, it is perhaps unsurprising that theories say more about the persistence of institutions than their change. Furthermore, the arguments about institutional change that do exist emphasize incremental change processes in which the past weighs heavily. For the Stanford School, the key mechanism is diffusion, whereby a practice moves from actor to actor, gaining the momentum of legitimacy on the way (DiMaggio & Powell 1991). Other institutional schools highlight path dependence as a mechanism of institutional change (e.g., North 1990). Neither of these approaches accounts for the discontinuities in institutional trajectories which are perhaps the key moments of institutionalized life, or which institutions will be created in the first place. A promising development that targets such discontinuities is the combination of institutionalism with social movement theories. This approach sees institutional entrepreneurs playing a key role of motivating and organizing others to affect institutional change. To do so, they may broker between social sites and institutional ideas and frame potential institutions in ways that appeal to preexisting institutions. Furthermore, elements of the institutional framework may be reconstructed into new institutions in a form of bricolage. This approach therefore combines most extant institutional theories, recognizing that institutions affect individual interest but require collective consent, and that institutional change depends on preexisting institutions but may sometimes involve a turning point that shifts the institutional trajectory.

SEE ALSO: Capitalism, Social Institutions of; Durkheim, Émile; Economy (Sociological Approach); Institutional Theory, New; Institutionalism; Law, Economy and; Legitimacy; Organization Theory; Social Movements; State; Weber, Max

REFERENCES AND SUGGESTED READINGS

Berger, P. L & Luckmann, T. (1967) *The Social Construction of Reality*. Doubleday, New York.

Campbell, J. L. & Lindberg, L. N. (1990) Property Rights and the Organization of Economic Activity by the State. *American Sociological Review* 55: 634–47.

Carroll, G. R. & Hannan, M. T. (1999) *The Demography of Corporations and Industries*. Princeton University Press, Princeton.

Coleman, J. S. (1990) *Foundations of Social Theory*. Harvard University Press, Cambridge, MA.

DiMaggio, P. J. & Powell, W. W. (1991) The Iron Cage Revisited: Institutional Isomorphism and Collective Rationality in Organizational Fields. *American Sociological Review* 48: 147–60.

Dobbin, F. (1994) *Forging Industrial Policy*. Cambridge University Press, New York.

Dobbin, F. & Sutton, J. R. (1998) The Strength of a Weak State: The Rights Revolution and the Rise of Human Resource Management Divisions. *American Journal of Sociology* 104: 441–76.

Durkheim, E. (1982) *The Rules of Sociological Method*. Free Press, New York.

Durkheim, E. (1984) *The Division of Labor in Society*. Free Press, New York.

Fligstein, N. (2001) *The Architecture of Markets: An Economic Sociology of Twenty-First-Century Capitalist Societies*. Princeton University Press, Princeton.

Homans, G. C. (1950) *The Human Group*. Harcourt, Brace, & World, New York.

Merton, R. K. (1957) Bureaucratic Structure and Personality. In: Merton, R. K. (Ed.), *Social Theory and Social Structure*. Free Press, Glencoe, IL, pp. 195–206.

Meyer, J. W. & Rowan, B. (1977) Institutionalized Organizations: Formal Structure as Myth and Ceremony. *American Journal of Sociology* 83: 340–63.

Meyer, J. W., Boli, J., Thomas, G. M., et al. (1997) World Society and the Nation State. *American Journal of Sociology* 103: 144–81.

North, D. C. (1990) *Institutions, Institutional Change, and Economic Performance*. Cambridge University Press, New York.

Parsons, T. (1990) Prolegomena to a Theory of Social Institutions. *American Sociological Review* 55: 319–33.

Selznick, P. (1949) *TVA and the Grass Roots*. University of California Press, Berkeley.

Skocpol, T. (1985) Bringing the State Back In: Strategies of Analysis in Current Research. In: Evans, P. B., Rueschemeyer, D., & Skocpol, T. (Eds.), *Bringing the State Back In*. Cambridge University Press, Cambridge, pp. 1–43.

Weber, M. (1947) *The Theory of Social and Economic Organization*. Free Press, New York.

Williamson, O. E. (1985) *The Economic Institutions of Capitalism*. Free Press, New York.

intellectual property

Chris Rojek

Any form of literature, science, music, film, or computer program can be protected by copyright to prevent third parties from making copies without written permission. Copyright is the law of authorship and dates back to the Statute of Anne (1709) passed in England to protect the rights of authors and publishers from piracy. The law has been progressively elaborated in Europe and North America to grant copyright for a fixed term to the estate of deceased authors and protect authors from the violation of their rights through new technologies of reproduction and exchange. However, the balance between the rights of authors and freedom of information is a delicate one and is regularly subject to legal challenge. In the US the First Amendment, which guarantees free speech and a free press, has been used by litigants as the basis to contest the reach of copyright.

The issue has escalated in legal and popular culture as new electronic technologies of reproduction and file sharing, such as the photocopier, home audiotape, videotape machines, and computers, have become available. The First Amendment raises the issue of "fair use" through private educational and leisure practices, news reporting, comment, and criticism. The exchange of information and opinions in education and the press would be violated by an over-zealous application of copyright principles. In 1994 the US Supreme Court ruled that "transformative use," which alters the original to create a new work, through interpretation and parody, is acceptable. The ruling had widespread ramifications for hip hop, rap, and other forms of new music which employ sampling technology. The landmark case on this issue is *Acuff-Rose Music* v. *2 Live Crew* (1991). In 1965 Acuff-Rose Music acquired the rights to the song *Oh Pretty Woman* from its writers, the pop star Roy Orbison and William Dees. In 1990 the controversial rap group 2 Live Crew recorded its own version of the song without seeking copyright clearance. Acuff-Rose sued for infringement of its copyright. The Trial Court ruled that while 2 Live Crew had indeed infringed copyright, their version of the song constituted parody rather than imitation. It upheld the right of 2 Live Crew to engage in parody without legal constraint. However, the question of when "fair use" becomes "literary larceny" is extremely thorny and is obviously open to conflicting aesthetic judgments.

The Internet vastly increases the flow of data exchange and creates unprecedented challenges for policing and the application of copyright. Without a commercially viable system of monitoring file exchange, the integrity of copyright relies on the probity of Internet users. In the late 1990s the development of peer to peer (P2P) file exchange systems such as *Napster* seriously eroded the market share of record companies. This provoked a protracted and as yet unresolved series of legal disputes between P2P providers and copyright holders. The development of legal, fee-based download systems such as the *Apple Music Store* has been a partial solution to the problem. But it has not eliminated illegal file exchange. Broadband technology will exacerbate the problem by allowing more information to be downloaded at faster speeds, making the downloading of full-length feature films and computer programs as quick and easy as downloading a 3-minute pop single.

SEE ALSO: Consumption; Internet; Modernity; Popular Culture; Popular Culture Forms (P2P)

REFERENCES AND SUGGESTED READINGS

Goldstein, P. (2003) *Copyright's Highway*. Stanford University Press, Stanford.
Levine, S. (2004) *The Art of Downloading Music*. Sanctuary Press, London.
Pieterse, J. (2004) *Globalization and Culture*. Rowman & Littlefield, Boston.
US Department of Commerce (2000) *Falling Through The Net*. US Department of Commerce, Washington, DC.
Van Horebeek, B. (2003) Napster Clones Turn Their Attention to Academic E-Books. *New World Library* 104(1187/1188): 142–8.

intelligence tests

Aaron M. Pallas

Intelligence is a concept whose meaning has been fashioned by the discipline of psychology. Psychologists view intelligence as a set of mental abilities that are inferred from an individual's performance on an intelligence test. In defining intelligence as one or more abilities, psychologists seek to demarcate it from the accumulation of specific knowledge to which only some individuals are exposed. In this view, intelligence is a broad cognitive capacity that, though often correlated with the acquisition of specific knowledge, is conceptually distinct from it.

In emphasizing intelligence as a quality of individual cognition, psychologists differentiate it from other individual qualities, such as personality, character, social skills, and physical abilities. Such qualities may be highly valued by a society, and those who possess them may have different life chances than those who do not; but because they are not cognitive skills, they are not acknowledged by most scholars as forms of intelligence. The prevailing view of intelligence as an attribute of the individual also does not admit the more social view of cognition that sees human cognition as distributed across a group of individuals in a particular social setting, who use tools and artifacts to represent knowledge (Hutchins 1995).

Intelligence can be characterized as a hierarchical set of cognitive abilities, with Carroll's (1993) representation of three levels of mental abilities the most widely cited. At the lowest level are highly specific skills represented by performance on specific tests. One well-known intelligence test, the WAIS III (1997), has 14 specific tests, ranging from digit span (in which the examinee repeats an orally presented sequence of numbers either forwards or backwards) to picture completion (in which an examinee must identify what is missing from a color picture of a common object or setting). These specific tests are distinct in the sense that performance on one does not perfectly predict performance on another. But individuals may perform better on some clusters of these specific tests than on others, and the correlations among scores on such tests can be accounted for by a smaller number of factors than the original number of tests. Carroll (1993), in an exhaustive study of the correlations among mental test scores, concluded that there are eight factors that can adequately represent the clusters: broad visual perception, broad auditory perception, broad retrieval ability, broad cognitive speediness, processing speed, general memory and learning, crystallized intelligence, and fluid intelligence.

As was true for performance on specific tests, performance on one of these factors does not perfectly predict performance on another, indicating that the factors are distinct. But individuals who score highly on one factor are more likely to score highly on others, with the average intercorrelation among factors about .70 (Deary 2001). Carroll (1993) concluded that most of the variation among individuals on these eight factors could be accounted for by one general factor, which has historically been referred to as *g*, or general intelligence. Because *g* is abstracted from performance on a great many tests, it is often described as a context-free measure of general reasoning or problem-solving ability, and as the ability to comprehend and respond to complexity in one's environment.

Modern intelligence tests typically are constructed to have an overall mean of 100 and a standard deviation of about 15, and the distribution of scores within many populations assumes the shape of a bell curve, with about two-thirds of the scores clustered between 85 and 115, and fewer than 5 percent of the scores either below 70 or above 130. In the US, individuals identified as African American have historically scored on average about 15 points below those identified as white, an average group difference that parallels the gap observed on a variety of tests of educational achievement. The average black–white difference in IQ test scores cannot be explained by a simple form of cultural bias, as the differences are observed on tasks that appear to require little knowledge of white middle-class culture as well as those that are "culturally loaded" (Jencks 1998). Nor can the black–white test score difference be easily attributed to the lower socioeconomic status of blacks, as substantial differences are observed even when blacks and whites are matched on measurable social and economic characteristics (Phillips et al. 1998). Unmeasured social differences between blacks and whites may be important, but they are not yet an adequate explanation for the black–white difference in IQ test scores.

There is little question that performance on intelligence tests is a function of both genes and environment. Heritability, an attribute of a population of individuals at a particular historical moment, refers to the extent to which variation in individual intelligence scores is due to differences among individuals in their genes and environments. A heritability estimate of zero indicates that all of the variation among individual test scores is due to differences in those individuals' environments. A heritability estimate of one indicates that all of the variation among individual test scores is due to differences in those individuals' genes. Although scientists are not yet able to identify the specific genes associated with particular cognitive abilities, the shared genetic heritage of monozygotic ("identical") and dizygotic ("fraternal") twins provides some purchase on the relative influence of genes and environment. Within middle-class white populations in western societies, heritability estimates typically range from .50 to .70 (Cianciolo & Sternberg 2004).

Heritability estimates tell us little about the origins of a particular individual's cognitive abilities. In part this is because heritability is defined in relation to a population, not to an individual. But it would be difficult to summarize the mix of genetic and environmental influences in a single number, as individuals experience remarkably different social environments, due to both their social locations in society (Gottfredson 2000) and the unique experiences of individuals within the same general social location or the same family (Gottfredson 1997; Deary 2001). Moreover, individuals have the capacity both to select themselves into new environments and to modify the environments in which they are situated, and these adaptations may be more easily negotiated by individuals with greater cognitive ability.

Some scholars have succumbed to the temptation to link the average black–white difference in IQ scores to the high heritability of intelligence within the middle-class white population, suggesting that the origins of the black–white gap in intelligence scores are genetic (Herrnstein & Murray 1994). There is to date little empirical support for this view (Neisser et al. 1996). The existing evidence on black–white differences does not rely on a biological or genetic basis for racial classification, but rather a social basis, individuals' self-reports. Hence, the observed score difference represents a mixture of social and biological influences (Gottfredson 1997). Moreover, it is widely recognized that the magnitude of the heritability of a trait within a population, such as US blacks, does not imply a similar magnitude of its heritability between populations.

Individuals who score higher on intelligence tests have differing profiles of adult social and economic success than do those who score lower. Intelligence test scores are correlated with educational attainment, job performance, and income, and with the likelihood of delinquent behavior and incarceration. A functional interpretation of these associations is that they reflect the complexity of the modern world, in which only those with advanced cognitive skills can successfully navigate their environments over sustained periods of the life course. It is a logical fallacy, however, to conclude that the advantages enjoyed by people with high IQ test scores are a necessary, and hence natural, feature of modern society. The impact of individual differences in IQ test scores on adult success is expressed within a system of structured social inequality, in which social origins either open or close the doors to opportunity (Fischer et al. 1996). Differences among individuals are real, but their impact can be magnified or muted by the political choices a society makes. Under the current institutional arrangements, individual differences in measured cognitive ability do matter, and perhaps increasingly so.

SEE ALSO: *Bell Curve, The* (Herrnstein and Murray); Educational Inequality; Meritocracy; Scientific Racism; Standardized Educational Tests

REFERENCES AND SUGGESTED READINGS

Carroll, J. B. (1993) *Human Cognitive Abilities: A Survey of Factor Analytic Studies.* Cambridge University Press, Cambridge.

Cianciolo, A. T. & Sternberg, R. J. (2004) *Intelligence: A Brief History.* Blackwell, Malden, MA.

Deary, I. J. (2001) *Intelligence: A Very Short Introduction.* Oxford University Press, New York.

Fischer, C. S., Hout, M., Sanchez Jankowski, M., Lucas, S. R., Swidler, A., & Voss, K. (1996) *Inequality by Design: Cracking the Bell Curve Myth.* Princeton University Press, Princeton.

Gottfredson, L. S. (1997) Mainstream Science on Intelligence: An Editorial with 52 Signatories, History, and Bibliography. *Intelligence* 24: 13–23.

Gottfredson, L. S. (2000) Intelligence. In: Borgotta, E. F. & Montgomery, R. J. V. (Eds.), *Encyclopedia of Sociology*, 2nd edn. Macmillan, New York, pp. 1359–86.

Herrnstein, R. J. & Murray, C. (1994) *The Bell Curve: Intelligence and Class Structure in American Life.* Free Press, New York.

Hutchins, E. (1995) *Cognition in the Wild.* MIT Press, Cambridge, MA.

Jencks, C. (1998) Racial Bias in Testing. In: Jencks, C. & Phillips, M. (Eds.), *The Black–White Test Score Gap.* Brookings Institution Press, Washington, DC, pp. 55–85.

Neisser, U., Boodoo, G., Bouchard, T. J., Jr., Boykin, A. W., Brody, N., Ceci, S. J., Halpern, D. F., Loehlin, J. C., Perloff, R., Sternberg, R. J., & Urbina, S. (1996) Intelligence: Knowns and Unknowns. *American Psychologist* 51: 77–101.

Phillips, M., Brooks-Gunn, J., Duncan, G. J., Klebanov, P., & Crane, J. (1998) Family Background, Parenting Practices, and the Black–White Test Score Gap. In: Jencks, C. & Phillips, M. (Eds.), *The Black–White Test Score Gap*. Brookings Institution Press, Washington, DC, pp. 103–45.

interaction

Dirk vom Lehn

"Interaction" describes particular kinds of social relationship that are different from, but constitutive of, groups, organizations, and networks. Interaction occurs when two or more participants are in each other's perceptual range and orient to each other through their action and activity. It ends when the participants dissolve their mutual orientation and leave the social situation.

Sociological research only gradually recognized the significance of social interaction. It initially focused on groups and organized relationships before progressively finding that temporary bound social relationships are critical to understanding the emergence and organization of more persistent forms of relationship. Georg Simmel was one of the first sociologists to mark the difference between relatively persistent social relationships such as groups and fleeting social encounters such as the mutual exchange of glances. He differentiates various "forms of interaction" and demonstrates their significance for social life. Simmel's work has been of great importance for the development of sociological approaches to understanding interaction, in particular symbolic interactionism and conversation analysis.

George Herbert Mead argues that the emergence of interaction is grounded in the fact that people's actions function as social stimuli that affect a reaction of the other. He differentiates interaction mediated by gestures and symbolic interaction. The former, a "conversation of gestures," is relatively primitive and unreliable. Mead famously compares it to a "dog fight." Symbolic interaction uses "significant symbols" like language that stimulate the same reaction in the actor and the other. It provides the basis for

people's ability "to take the role of the other" and align each other's actions. Mead's work provides the intellectual basis for the emergence of symbolic interactionism (Mead 1934).

In light of these theories, early twentieth-century sociology began to take seriously interaction as a "social fact." *Functionalist approaches* investigate interaction as social system integrated by a common set of cultural symbols and norms that ensure people orient to situations in the same way (Parsons 1951). In recent years, Talcott Parsons's approach has been updated by Niklas Luhmann, who opposes social theories based on a consensus about meanings and values. He views social systems as *communication systems* that have developed specific mechanisms to organize their communication processes. Society's subsystems, such as politics or economy, organize their communication processes by virtue of generalized media such as power or money; they are autonomous from the co-presence of participants. Contrarily, the emergence of interaction systems relies on the co-presence of multiple participants who orient to each other's actions (Luhmann 1995). Systems theory remains relatively underdeveloped with regard to the social organization of interaction systems.

Exchange theory focuses on the individual and the "rationale" for his or her decision to engage in interaction. George Caspar Homans argues that interaction emerges because the actor who is a rational decision-maker anticipates to maximize his or her rewards by virtue of the exchange. He begins to develop psychological principles and rules that support the actor's decision to engage in exchanges (Homans 1961). Peter Blau has further developed exchange theory by linking it to contemporary theories concerned with social structure. He explores the relation between rational actions and the emergence of social structures (Blau 1964). In a related way, Richard Emerson investigates the origin of *exchange networks* by focusing on the exchange of valuable resources between parties (Emerson 1974).

Although there had been a growing sociological concern with interaction since the 1940s, relatively little research was undertaken to explore the process of interaction. Robert Bales's *Interaction Process Analysis* (1976) addresses this gap in research. IPA focuses on group activities that are undertaken to achieve a goal shared between group members. It provides quantitative methods through which people's actions are recorded and analyzed. The analysis reveals the phases of the activity a group is involved in and the different roles of the group members in the activity. In recent years, IPA has been further developed as a tool (Symlog) for people to enhance their effectiveness in group activities. IPA has been very influential in particular for small group research.

Symbolic interactionism was developed in opposition to functionalist approaches. In drawing on Mead's work, Herbert Blumer, who coined the term symbolic interactionism, considers "society as symbolic interaction" (Blumer 1969). He argues that society and its norms and values do not predefine how people act and interact. However, people act in situations according to the meaning these situations have for them. The "definition of the situation" is produced in interaction with others. Hence, symbolic interactionist research is particularly interested in the interpretive processes by virtue of which participants negotiate the definition of the situation.

Blumer's theoretical work has initiated the emergence of the Chicago School, which produced a large body of ethnographic studies tackling topics such as social problems, race relations, and industrial relations (Everett C. Hughes, Howard S. Becker). In recent years, sociologists like Mitchell Duneier have taken up the Chicago School's work and produced intriguing ethnographies of race relations (*Slim's Table*, 1992) or street vendors (*Sidewalk*, thnographies are not the only way in which symbolic interactionism developed. The Iowa School evolved a very different approach to further Mead and Blumer's concepts. Its work was initially interested in developing "scientific methods" to explore the structure of the self (Manford Kuhn). From the mid-1960s, Carl Couch and his colleagues introduced experimental methods to develop "a set of universal social principles" explaining how social units such as dyads and triads coordinate their activities (Couch & Hintz 1975). There also is a large body of research related to symbolic interactionism that explores how phenomena that are often viewed to be cognitive or material rather than social feature in interaction. For example,

investigations have been undertaken concerned with emotion and affect (Norman Denzin), the human body (Kathy Charmaz), or with the role of non-human objects in interaction (Joseph Cohen; Susan Leigh Star and Geoffrey Bowker).

Erving Goffman's famous work on *The Presentation of Self in Everyday Life* (1959) is often discussed in the context of debates in symbolic interactionism. Yet, it forms part of a research tradition that uses the "theater metaphor" for the inquiry of social life. His essay refers to Kenneth Burke's "dramatism," which explores the relationships between the act, the agent, the scene, agency, and the purpose of action ("dramatic pentad"). Goffman's "dramaturgical approach" explores how these relationships play out in social interaction and investigates the techniques participants employ to manage the impression others have of them. It has been very influential in sociological research and occasioned a wide range of ethnographic research concerned, for example, with the presentation of self of politicians and management gurus.

Goffman's investigations also draw on developments in human anthropology and cognate disciplines. Whilst sociology was still debating the significance of social interaction as a phenomenon, human anthropologists and ethologists (Heini Hediger; Irenaeus Eibl-Eibesfeldt) were long engaged in exploring the social production of culture. Gregory Bateson used film recordings to reveal the social organization of action and interaction. In light of Bateson's observations and related developments in other disciplines, a new communication theory emerged that conceived communication to be a "multichannel system." Researchers began to dissect the different communication channels to reveal the organization of their elements. Investigations have been undertaken that uncover the elements of language (Edward Sapir), the ways in which the meaning of utterances is influenced by the tone of voice, pitch, volume, and other paralinguistic cues, and bodily communication such as gestures and facial expressions (Michael Argyle, Paul Ekman, Adam Kendon; see Scherer et al. 1982).

These developments have initiated investigations that explore other aspects of human interaction and communication. Ray Birdwhistell (1970) uses film recordings to dissect the elements of body movement in concerted activities. Edward Hall (1966) investigates people's spatial behavior and experience of space. He conceives spatial behavior as a "language" by virtue of which people structure the social space in which they act and interact ("proxemics"). Hall's work provides the basis for inquiries into the spatial organization in conversations (Robert Sommer) or the use of personal space in public places. In the 1960s and early 1970s, Albert E. Scheflen (1972) explored how communicative systems such as psychotherapeutic encounters are structured and generate meaning by virtue of neatly organized verbal and bodily actions ("context analysis").

Goffman and later Adam Kendon (1990) drew on the observations made by the aforementioned investigations. They explored how through spatial and bodily behavior participants organize "relations in public" (Goffman 1971) and "focused" and "unfocused interaction" (Goffman 1963). These inquiries in the social organization of actions and activities reveal how participants bodily orient to each other and how they can shift the focus of an activity by virtue of changes in their bodily positions, postures, and gestures (Juergen Streeck). They reveal how people organize and structure their activities in social situations by virtue of body movements. Studies of people's spatial and bodily conduct in interaction have made important contributions to our understanding of interaction. However, they neglect how participants' talk is coordinated with their bodily conduct in interaction.

The development of *ethnomethodology* by Harold Garfinkel has been the beginning of a program of research that led to new developments in exploring how social interaction emerges from participants' actions and activities. Ethnomethodology aims to reveal the practices and reasoning that underlie people's action and interaction. Garfinkel investigates the in situ "indexical" character of interaction. The indexicality of people's practices and reasoning leads to the insight that the context of action is not predefined and stable, as symbolic interactionists may argue, but that action is "doubly contextual in being both context-shaped and context-renewing" (Heritage 1984).

In light of Garfinkel's *Studies in Ethnomethodology* (1967), Harvey Sacks and colleagues developed *conversation analysis* as a methodological framework to explore how language is used in practice. Conversation analysis employs audio recordings as principal data to investigate in detail the organization of brief fragments of talk. The original work by Harvey Sacks, Emanuel Schegloff, Gail Jefferson, and others has principally been concerned with talk as an institution in its own right. This work reveals how participants attend to each other's utterances moment by moment and begin to unpack the *sequential* organization of talk-in-interaction. They show how interactional encounters are opened and closed as well as how participants deal with interactional problems that arise in conversations. Key to the understanding of the organization of talk are "social mechanisms," such as adjacency pairs, repairs, and the like, that participants draw on in interaction. These mechanisms are independent from participants' cognitive disposition and motivation, institutional arrangements, and material constraints (Sacks 1974, 1992). In recent years, a body of research has emerged that expands the conversation analytic perspective. It explores how talk and its analysis are embedded in culture (Michael Moerman), how institutional arrangements influence the organization of "talk at work" (Paul Drew and John Heritage), and how participants orient to institutional settings and situations.

Various researchers have recently begun to augment the disembodied concept of interaction that pervades conversation analysis by exploring how the body and aspects of the material environment feature in interaction. They draw on Simmel and Goffman's work and use the analytic and methodological framework provided by ethnomethodology and conversation analysis to investigate how participants socially organize their talk and bodily conduct in social situations. The principal data of these investigations are audio/video recordings of naturally occurring social interaction. They employ the analytic and methodological framework of ethnomethodology and conversation analysis to explore the interactional and sequential production of talk and bodily conduct. They reveal how minute bodily movements such as a shift in gaze direction or the turn of a head can influence the way in which an interactional sequence develops. They demonstrate that speaking and hearing are closely intertwined activities. In speaking, the bodily actions of the hearer play a significant part in the way in which the talk is produced (Goodwin 1981). The observations and findings of these video-based studies of interaction provide the basis for a growing body of research concerned with the ways in which participants socially and sequentially organize their actions and activities in a variety of workplaces. The emerging field of *workplace studies* (Luff et al. 2000) reveals the social and sequential organization of work that involves the use of highly complex technologies in control rooms of urban transport systems, air traffic control, operating theaters, and news production. Workplace studies explore how participants orient to and embed objects and artifacts, such as paper documents, computer screens, or large displays, in the interactional production of work. They examine how participants produce a "reciprocity of perspectives" (Alfred Schutz) with regard to objects and artifacts, tools and technologies (Suchman 1987; Heath & Luff 2000). They also investigate the ways in which the human body becomes the focus of interaction. For example, in medical encounters, anesthesia, or surgical procedures, participants produce the status of the body as acting and feeling subject or inanimate object in and through social interaction. In recent years, related work has been undertaken in museums and galleries exploring how participants orient to and make sense of exhibits and exhibitions in interaction (Heath & vom Lehn 2004).

The development of video-based field studies that explore social interaction in material environments reflects a growing sociological interest in "materiality." Bruno Latour, Michel Callon, John Law, and others who have recently developed actor-network theory (ANT) have put the object and materiality firmly on the agenda of sociological debate. They argue for a fundamental rethink of the relationship between the social and the material. They ascribe objects the status of "actants" and explore how they participate in social situations. The body of research in ANT has been very influential in social studies of science (Latour 1987; Law 1991).

Recent technological developments challenge a fundamental principle of social interaction, namely, the physical co-presence of participants in social situations. Novel computer technologies seem to provide participants with sufficient resources to organize their action and activities "just like" in situations of co-presence. A large body of research has emerged in disciplines cognate to sociology, such as computer-supported cooperative work (CSCW), which explore interaction across distributed locations. They illuminate the difficulties of designers who try to create situations of "virtual presence" and of participants who attempt to organize their actions with others who are "in range" but not bodily present in a social situation. The exploration of distributed work has helped to reinvigorate the interest of sociologists in undertaking research on the social organization of interaction. However, it also has brought to the fore the tension between concepts of "interaction" used in the information and computer sciences and those developed in sociology, the former relying on a separation of "sender" and "receiver," the latter maintaining the particular social characteristics of interaction. The coming years will show whether sociology will be able to further develop its theories and methods to grasp the new forms of interaction emerging in light of the current technological revolution.

SEE ALSO: Actor-Network Theory; Bateson, Gregory; Blau, Peter; Blumer, Herbert George; Chicago School: Social Change; Conversation Analysis; Dyad/Triad; Emerson, Richard M.; Ethnomethodology; Friendship: Interpersonal Aspects; Goffman, Erving; Homans, George; Human–Non-Human Interaction; Interaction Order; Interpersonal Relationships; Language; Luhmann, Niklas; Mead, George Herbert; Mediated Interaction; Networks; Parsons, Talcott; Symbolic Interaction

REFERENCES AND SUGGESTED READINGS

Birdwhistell, R. L. (1970) *Kinesics and Context: Essays on Body Motion Communication.* University of Pennsylvania Press, Philadelphia.

Blau, P. M. (1964) *Exchange and Power in Social Life.* Wiley, New York.

Blumer, H. (1969) *Symbolic Interactionism: Perspective and Method.* University of California Press, Berkeley.

Couch, C. J. & Hintz, R. A. (Eds.) (1975) *Constructing Social Life: Readings in Behavioral Sociology from the Iowa School.* Stipes Publishing, Iowa.

Emerson, R. M. (1974) Social Exchange Theory. *Annual Review of Sociology* 2: 335–62.

Goffman, E. (1963) *Behavior in Public Places: Notes on the Social Organization of Gatherings.* Free Press, New York.

Goffman, E. (1971) *Relations in Public: Microstudies of the Social Order.* Basic Books, New York.

Goodwin, C. (1981) *Conversational Organization: Interaction Between Speakers and Hearers.* Academic Press, New York.

Hall, E. T. (1966) *The Hidden Dimension: Man's Use of Space in Public and Private.* Bodley Head, London, Sydney, and Toronto.

Heath, C. & Luff, P. (2000) *Technology in Action.* Cambridge University Press, Cambridge.

Heath, C. & vom Lehn, D. (2004) Configuring Reception: (Dis-)Regarding the "Spectator" in Museums and Galleries. *Theory, Culture, and Society* 21(6): 43–65.

Heritage, J. (1984) *Garfinkel and Ethnomethodology.* Polity Press, Cambridge.

Homans, G. C. (1961) *Social Behavior: Its Elementary Forms.* Harcourt Brace, New York.

Kendon, A. (1990) *Conducting Interaction: Patterns of Behavior in Focused Encounters.* Cambridge University Press, Cambridge.

Latour, B. (1987) *Science in Action.* Open University Press, Milton Keynes.

Law, J. (Ed.) (1991) *A Sociology of Monsters: Essays on Power, Technology, and Domination.* Routledge, London and New York.

Luff, P., Hindmarsh, J., & Heath, C. (Eds.) (2000) *Workplace Studies: Recovering Work Practice and Informing System Design.* Cambridge University Press, Cambridge.

Luhmann, N. (1995) *Social Systems.* Stanford University Press, Stanford.

Mead, G. H. (1934) *Mind, Self, and Society from the Perspective of a Social Behaviorist.* University of Chicago Press, Chicago.

Parsons, T. (1951) *The Social System.* Free Press, New York.

Sacks, H. (1974) A Simplest Systematics for the Organization of Turn-Taking for Conversation. *Language: Journal of the Linguistic Society of America* 50: 696–735.

Sacks, H. (1992) *Lectures on Conversation.* Blackwell, Oxford.

Scheflen, A. E. (1972) *Body Language and the Social Order.* Wiley, Hoboken.

Scherer, K. R., Ekman, P., Oatley, K., & Manstead, A. (Eds.) (1982) *Handbook of Methods in Nonverbal Behavior Research.* Cambridge University Press, Cambridge.

Suchman, L. (1987) *Plans and Situated Actions: The Problem of Human–Machine Communication.* Cambridge University Press, Cambridge.

interaction order

Mark D. Jacobs

The interaction order, as conceived by Erving Goffman, is constructed around systems of enabling conventions that – without recourse to social contract or social consensus, as often assumed – provide a basis of social order. The interaction order, Goffman insists, is a substantive domain in its own right, engendered by social situations, interactions in which at least two actors are co-bodily present. That is, against the claims of either micro- or macrosociological reductionism, Goffman insists on the analytical distinctness of the interaction order from both the underlying language games and conversational protocols of ethnomethodologists and the various overarching systems of macrostructuralists. For his part, Goffman dismisses the claim that macrostructural properties are epiphenomenal to the interaction order. The influence of Goffman's formulation extends even to theorists who reject the primacy of his analytic focus, as well as to those who embrace different characterizations of interactional dynamics.

As Goffman (1983) explains in his summative statement about the interaction order, enabling conventions arise as techniques of social management of the personal risks – both bodily and self-expressive – inherent in interpersonal interaction. These conventions "can be viewed . . . in the sense of the ground rules of a game" (p. 5); they are the shared base of cognitive and moral presuppositions that make interaction possible. Not merely tact but tact about tact (Goffman 1959) is one such convention; deference is another. By instructive contrast with the macrosociologist Edward Shils (under whose tutelage Goffman first studied deference), who declared: "Deference ... is a way of expressing an assessment of the self and others with respect to 'macrosocial' properties" (1975: 277), Goffman analyzes deference "as a means through which this self is established ... Deference and demeanor practices must be institutionalized so that the individual will be able to project a viable, sacred self and stay in the game on a proper ritual basis" (1967: 91).

As a theoretical construct, the interaction order is a Simmelian-Durkheimian hybrid. Goffman recapitulates Simmel's "The Problem of Sociology" (which famously declares: "Society exists where a number of individuals enter into interaction") (Simmel 1959a: 314), not only in its basic conception, but also in its methodological prescription: "The trick, of course, is to differently conceptualize these effects, great or small, so that what they share can be extracted and analyzed, and so that the forms of social life they derive from can be pieced out and cataloged sociologically, allowing what is intrinsic to interactional life to be exposed thereby" (Goffman 1983: 3).

He echoes Simmel's "How is Society Possible" (1959b) in declaring: "at the very center of interaction life is the cognitive relation we have with those present before us, without which relationship our activity, behavioral and verbal, could not be meaningfully organized" (Goffman 1983: 4). He explicitly draws on Durkheim in his assertion that enabling conventions are essentially symbolic and ritual. And he hearkens to Durkheim's analysis of the *corroboree* in *The Elementary Forms of the Religious Life* (1995) in his discussion of those intense ceremonials in the interaction order that have consequences for macrostructures.

In its relatively short career, the concept of the interaction order has already spawned a rich and variegated tradition. The concept animates such classic monographs as Schwartz's *Queuing and Waiting* (1975), which focuses on a paradigmatic form of the interaction order, and Fine's *With the Boys* (1987), which traces the emergence of "idiocultures" in primary groups involved in Little League Baseball. This tradition even encompasses theories that challenge the analytic distinctness of the interaction order: the macrosociological theories of Giddens (1984), for example, in which the interaction order cements the "duality of structure," as well

as the microsociological theories of Collins (2004), in which structural transformations derive their energies from interaction rituals.

SEE ALSO: Durkheim, Émile; Goffman, Erving; Idioculture; Interaction; Simmel, Georg

REFERENCES AND SUGGESTED READINGS

Collins, R. (2004) *Interaction Ritual Chains*. Princeton University Press, Princeton.

Durkheim, É. (1995 [1912]) *The Elementary Forms of the Religious Life*. Trans. B. Field. Free Press, New York.

Fine, G. (1987) *With the Boys*. University of Chicago Press, Chicago.

Giddens, A. (1984) *The Constitution of Society*. University of California Press, Berkeley.

Goffman, E. (1959) *The Presentation of Self in Everyday Life*. Doubleday Anchor, New York.

Goffman, E. (1967 [1956]) The Nature of Deference and Demeanor. In: *Interaction Ritual*. Doubleday Anchor, New York.

Goffman, E. (1983) The Interaction Order: American Sociological Association, 1982 Presidential Address. *American Sociological Review* 48: 1–17.

Rawls, A. (1987) The Interaction Order Sui Generis. *Sociological Theory* 5: 136–49.

Schwartz, B. (1975) *Queuing and Waiting*. University of Chicago Press, Chicago.

Shils, E. (1975 [1968]) Deference. In: *Center and Periphery*. Univeristy of Chicago Press, Chicago.

Simmel, G. (1959a [1908]) The Problem of Sociology. In: Wolff, K. (Ed.), *Essays on Sociology, Philosophy, and Aesthetics, by Georg Simmel et al.* Harper & Row, New York.

Simmel, G. (1959b [1908]) How is Society Possible? In: Wolff, K. (Ed.), *Essays on Sociology, Philosophy, and Aesthetics, by Georg Simmel et al.* Harper & Row, New York.

intergenerational conflict

Merril Silverstein

Intergenerational conflict refers to the collective tension, strain, and antagonism between older and younger generations over what constitutes the fair distribution of public resources across age groups. Intergenerational conflict is most often invoked in the context of the generational equity debate, an ongoing public dialogue about the cost and fairness of entitlement programs for the older population. One of the opening salvos in the debate over generational equity was the observation that the well-being of older and younger Americans diverged over the third quarter of the twentieth century as a result of public policies that favored older adults and lifted them out of poverty (Preston 1984). The popular press concluded from this that older adults had gained at the expense of younger adults, and it was not uncommon in the 1980s and 1990s for the elderly to be portrayed as a leisure class of affluent retirees unfairly benefiting from the taxes paid by a struggling working-age population.

Anxiety about the future viability of public programs for the aged has been on the rise, particularly among younger generations, driven by fears of population aging and consequent growth in the dependency ratio – a measure of the size of the working-age population relative to the retired population. Trends in population aging converged with national and international pressures to shrink government spending, raising fundamental questions about the nature of society's collective obligation to the elderly and the rights of older citizens to public benefits.

Economists, in particular, framed the issue of generational equity as a competition for limited resources in a zero-sum game between the young and the old. Using an approach known now as "generational accounting," they discussed how the financing of entitlement programs for the aged (Social Security, Medicare, and other government programs that use age to determine eligibility) was unfair to the younger generation that would ultimately pay the bill (Longman 1987). The public and scholarly debates that ensued opened the door to questioning the deservingness of older people as an entitled group, the inviolability of the contract between generations that began with the New Deal, and the wisdom of sustaining entitlement programs in their current form when the baby boom generation reaches old age. The "sacred cow" of the Social Security program was sacred no more, as conservative politicians began using the older population as a scapegoat to further their political agenda of shrinking the size of government (Binstock 1983).

The central tenet of generational accounting – that there are winners and losers in the competition between generations – was met with swift resistance by many social scientists. There was little evidence suggesting that generations were in conflict. Not only was public support for Social Security and Medicare programs very strong across all age groups, some research found that support for these programs was stronger among younger adults than it was among the elderly (Logan & Spitze 1995). In addition, when public opinion about various government programs was charted over time, entitlement programs serving older adults were the ones least likely to lose support. Thus, the slight declines observed in support for Social Security tended more to be the product of strengthening overall preferences for fiscal restraint and smaller government than of generational conflict. Scholars advocated for decoupling the fortunes of the young and the old, attributing them to unique historical processes. Where older people benefited from public programs initiated through the second half of the twentieth century, children were disadvantaged over this same period by family and economic change, such as the increase in single-parent families and the decline in real wages due to economic restructuring.

Social scientists discovered that the public's attitudes toward entitlement programs were more complex than could be measured on a single metric. Several orthogonal dimensions were identified: (1) perceptions about the legitimacy and social value of entitlement programs for the elderly; and (2) concerns over the cost of such programs. Thus, it is possible to support programs for the elderly while at the same time expressing concern over their costs. What explains the public's support for entitlement programs is the norm of reciprocity – the notion that older people previously contributed into the system and now deserve to be supported as an earned right. This argument has been extended to include the older population's earlier contribution to post-war economic expansion.

The principle of *generational justice* was brought into the scholarly debate to represent the moral dimension of public policy that emphasizes responsibility for older citizens as a collective duty. If reciprocity were relied upon as the sole underlying principle guiding intergenerational transfers, then older generations that presided over a particularly weak economy for most of their working lives would produce a moral hazard. This makes public programs all the more important, for they compel even the most reluctant contributors to make state-mediated transfers to the older generation.

One of the most compelling arguments against the existence of widespread intergenerational conflict is that younger and older adults are interdependent with each other within family lineages – what is known as the *interdependence of generations perspective*. Thus, individuals simultaneously occupy several types of generational positions: welfare generation as represented by age group or birth cohort at the macro level, and family generation as represented by position in the family lineage at the micro level (Attias-Donfut & Arber 1999). Resources that flow upward from later- to earlier-born cohorts through government transfer programs are then balanced against the sizable downward flow of resources from older parents to adult children in the form of inter-vivo transfers, bequests, and childcare. This circular flow of support builds solidarity across generations and suggests that obligations between welfare generations and family generations are not competing but complementary with each other. Whether intergenerational conflict continues to be minimal will hinge on how changes in public policies and family commitments alter the integrity of this implicit contract across generations.

SEE ALSO: Aging, Sociology of; Aging and Social Support; Intergenerational Relationships and Exchanges; Life Course; Life Course and Family

REFERENCES AND SUGGESTED READINGS

Attias-Donfut, C. & Arber, S. (Eds.) (1999) *The Myth of Generational Conflict: The Family and State in Aging Societies*. Routledge, London.
Bengtson, V. L. & Achenbaum, W. A. (Eds.) (1993) *Changing Contract Across Generations*. Aldine de Gruyter, New York.
Binstock, R. H. (1983) The Aged as Scapegoat. *Gerontologist* 23: 136–43.

Logan, J. R. & Spitze, G. (1995) Self-Interest and Altruism in Intergenerational Relations. *Demography* 32: 353–64.
Longman, P. (1987) *Born to Pay: The New Politics of Aging in America*. Houghton Mifflin, Boston.
Marmor, T. R. (Ed.) (1994) *Economic Security and Intergenerational Justice: A Look at North America*. Urban Institute Press, Washington, DC.
Preston, S. H. (1984) Children and the Elderly: Divergent Paths for America's Dependents. *Demography* 21: 435–57.
Ward, R. A. (2001) Linkages between Family and Societal-Level Intergenerational Attitudes. *Research on Aging* 23: 179–208.
Williamson, J. B., McNamara, T. K., & Howling, S. A. (2003) Generational Equity, Generational Interdependence, and the Framing of the Debate over Social Security Reform. *Journal of Sociology and Social Welfare* 30: 3–13.
Williamson, J. B., Watts-Roy, D. M., & Kingston, E. R. (Eds.) (1999) *The Generational Equity Debate*. Columbia University Press, New York.

intergenerational mobility: core model of social fluidity

Richard Breen

The analysis of intergenerational social mobility is usually carried out using log-linear or log-multiplicative statistical models applied to a contingency table which cross-classifies individuals' current class (usually called "class destination") with the class in which they were brought up ("class origin"). An important distinction is between absolute and relative mobility (sometimes called "social fluidity"). Absolute mobility refers to the distribution of cases in the mobility table. Social fluidity refers to the inequality between individuals from different classes in their chances of coming to occupy one rather than another destination class. It is captured by odds ratios which are measured as the proportion of cases that originate in class A and are found in destination class X rather than class Y, divided by the proportion of cases from origin class B which are found in destination X rather than Y. An odds ratio of one indicates that the chances of being in destination class X rather than in Y are the same for those originating in both A and B, while an odds ratio greater than one shows that those born in A are more likely than those born in B to be in X rather than Y, and conversely for an odds ratio less than one. An important feature of odds ratios is that they are unaffected by any scalar multiplication of one or more rows and/or columns of a table: thus, inequalities in access to particular class destinations can be compared across mobility tables, despite the fact that they differ in their distributions of origins and destinations.

One of the most widely reported findings of mobility research is that differences between mobility tables (when these tables represent, for example, sexes or ethnic groups in a given country, different time points within the same country, different countries, and so on) in the distribution of cases in the mobility table (i.e., absolute mobility) are overwhelmingly shaped by differences in the marginal distributions of origins and destinations rather than differences in social fluidity (Erikson & Goldthorpe 1992: 213–14). Despite this, by far the greater amount of research has been devoted to social fluidity – possibly because fluidity captures, in a very obvious way, inequality in the competition for more, rather than less, desirable destination class positions.

SOCIAL FLUIDITY IN LOG-LINEAR AND LOG-MULTIPLICATIVE MODELS

Assume that the mobility table has I rows (origin classes) and J columns (destination classes), indexed by I = 1,...,I and j = 1,...,J respectively. Because mobility tables are usually square, I = J. F_{ij} is the logarithm of the expected (under the model) frequency in the ij^{th} cell of the table and this is a function of a constant term, λ; an effect associated with being in the ith row (i.e., coming from the ith origin class), λ_i^O; an effect associated with being in the jth column (destination class), λ_j^D; and the effect, on the ij^{th} cell, of the association between origins and destinations, λ_{ij}^{OD}. That is:

$$F_{ij} = \lambda + \lambda_i^O + \lambda_j^D + \lambda_{ij}^{OD}, \text{ for all}$$

$$i = 1,...,I; \quad j = 1,...,J$$

The association between origins and destinations is captured in the λ_{ij}^{OD} terms which are functions of the logarithm of the odds ratios (the log odds ratios) in the table. A maximum of $(I - 1) \times (J - 1)$ such terms can be estimated (because this is the number of independent odds ratios in a table), and doing this would yield a model that exactly fitted the data. However, rather than fit all the association parameters we would like to reduce this to a few interpretable parameters which represent some underlying social processes that structure the pattern of fluidity. Such a set of parameters we will call a model of fluidity. How well a particular model reproduces the data (its "goodness of fit") is assessed by comparing the frequencies expected under the model with the observed data and several measures based on this comparison are widely used. A large number of models of social fluidity have been proposed: examples include Hout's (1984) "status, autonomy, and training" (SAT) model; Breen and Whelan's (1992) "agriculture, hierarchy, and property" (AHP) model; and the model developed by Jonsson and Mills in 1993. But Erikson and Goldthorpe's (1992) "core model" of social fluidity is the most widely used such model.

When we make comparisons of social fluidity between two or more mobility tables we are interested in whether the pattern of fluidity (or, equivalently, the odds ratios) differs significantly across the tables. In other words, is there more or less inequality in some tables compared with others? When comparing fluidity across tables, we must specify the manner in which the parameters of the chosen model of fluidity differ between them. In this way, we hope to gain insight into exactly where and how the fluidity regime varies.

CORE MODEL OF SOCIAL FLUIDITY

In 1975, Featherman, Jones, and Hauser put forward the FJH hypothesis: "the genotypical pattern of mobility (circulation mobility [i.e., social fluidity]) in industrial societies with a market economy and a nuclear family system is basically the same" (Featherman et al. 1975: 340). Since then many publications have been devoted to testing this hypothesis, the majority of which have found support for it (most notably, Erikson & Goldthorpe 1992), though with some influential exceptions (Ganzeboom et al. 1989; Breen 2004).

The FJH hypothesis refers to a "genotypical pattern" of fluidity, and Erikson and Goldthorpe (1987a, 1987b, 1992) developed the "core model of social fluidity" as an attempt to characterize this genotypical pattern. Having done this, they could test whether the purported pattern was indeed the same in industrial societies with a market economy and nuclear family system. The data that they used comprise mobility tables having seven classes of both origin and destination, defined according to the Goldthorpe or "EGP" (Erikson, Goldthorpe, and Portocarero) class schema (for details, see Erikson & Goldthorpe 1992: ch. 2). The seven classes are denoted by Roman numerals as follows:

1   Classes I+II: professionals, administrators and officials; managers
2   Class III: routine non-manual employees
3   Class IVab: small proprietors and artisans
4   Class IVc: farmers
5   Classes V+VI: technicians, supervisors, and skilled manual workers
6   Class VIIa: semi- and unskilled workers not in agriculture
7   Class VIIb: semi- and unskilled workers in agriculture

Erikson and Goldthorpe developed the core model as a theoretically informed account of the fluidity patterns of England and France (which were taken as the two nations whose fluidity patterns most closely corresponded to some putative common pattern). The model consists of eight components, usually expressed through a set of eight matrices, in each of which the cells of the table are assigned to one of two categories. These rows and columns of the matrices are ordered according to the ordering of origin and destination classes as they are listed above.

The first element of social fluidity in the core model concerns hierarchical movement; and in the first dimension of this (called HI1) the value 2 indicates movement between three ordered (from most to least desirable) groups of classes: (a) class I+II; (b) classes III, IVab and c, and V+VI; and (c) VIIa and b. (Erikson and Goldthorpe (1992: 46, 124) treat class IVc

(farmers) as lying at the lowest hierarchical level (c) in class origins, but at the second level (b) in destinations.) In other words, the value 2 is assigned to cells of the mobility table which indicate an origin in one group but a destination in another. The value 1 is applied to cells in the same group in both origins and destinations:

```
1 2 2 2 2 2 2
2 1 1 1 1 2 2
2 1 1 1 1 2 2
2 2 2 2 2 1 1
2 1 1 1 1 2 2
2 2 2 2 2 1 1
2 2 2 2 2 1 1
```

Another matrix, called HI2, is defined distinguishing movement across two levels:

```
1 1 1 1 1 2 2
1 1 1 1 1 1 1
1 1 1 1 1 1 1
2 1 1 1 1 1 1
1 1 1 1 1 1 1
2 1 1 1 1 1 1
2 1 1 1 1 1 1
```

Here the value 2 is applied to cells with an origin in a class in group (a) and a destination in a class in group (c), and vice versa. This element of the model thus distinguishes "long-range" mobility (as opposed to the short-range mobility captured by H1).

The second component concerns the inheritance of class position; that is, the tendency for men to enter the same class as their father – a tendency which is more marked in some classes than in others. The first inheritance matrix, IN1, distinguishes cells in which origin and destination are in the same class:

```
2 1 1 1 1 1 1
1 2 1 1 1 1 1
1 1 2 1 1 1 1
1 1 1 2 1 1 1
1 1 1 1 2 1 1
1 1 1 1 1 2 1
1 1 1 1 1 1 2
```

The second inheritance matrix, IN2, distinguishes three classes in which inheritance is more pronounced than elsewhere: these are classes I+II, IVab, and IVc:

```
2 1 1 1 1 1 1
1 1 1 1 1 1 1
1 1 2 1 1 1 1
1 1 1 2 1 1 1
1 1 1 1 1 1 1
1 1 1 1 1 1 1
1 1 1 1 1 1 1
```

The final inheritance matrix, IN3, reserves a single distinction for farmers (IVc), among whom class inheritance is particularly strong:

```
1 1 1 1 1 1 1
1 1 1 1 1 1 1
1 1 1 1 1 1 1
1 1 1 2 1 1 1
1 1 1 1 1 1 1
1 1 1 1 1 1 1
1 1 1 1 1 1 1
```

The third aspect of the core model is a single matrix, SE, that defines barriers to movement between the agricultural and non-agricultural sectors. Thus, all cells with agricultural origins (classes IVc and VIIb) and non-agricultural destinations, and vice versa, are assigned the value 2:

```
1 1 1 2 1 1 2
1 1 1 2 1 1 2
1 1 1 2 1 1 2
2 2 2 1 2 2 1
1 1 1 2 1 1 2
1 1 1 2 1 1 2
2 2 2 1 2 2 1
```

The final component of the model is two affinity matrices. The first, AF1, identifies movement between classes I+II and VIIb and assigns the value 2 to these cells:

```
1 1 1 1 1 1 2
1 1 1 1 1 1 1
1 1 1 1 1 1 1
1 1 1 1 1 1 1
1 1 1 1 1 1 1
1 1 1 1 1 1 1
2 1 1 1 1 1 1
```

while AF2 identifies reciprocal movement between I+II and III; between IVab and IVc; and between V+VI and VIIa; and non-reciprocal movement from IVc to VIIa and from VIIb to VIIa:

```
1 2 2 1 1 1 1
2 1 1 1 1 1 1
2 1 1 2 1 1 1
1 1 2 1 1 2 1
1 1 1 1 1 2 1
1 1 1 1 2 1 1
1 1 1 1 1 2 1
```

In the case of AF1, movement between I+II and VIIb is thought to be particularly unlikely (even over and above the hierarchy, inheritance, and sectoral effects already included), whereas the movements captured in AF2 are thought to be especially likely.

The model is derived from a number of propositions about the factors shaping inequality in mobility chances (for a full explanation, see Erikson & Goldthorpe 1987a). Because hierarchical movements are assumed to be more difficult than non-hierarchical ones, both HI1 and HI2 should have negative values. The inheritance effects, by contrast, should all be positive, while the sector effect, since it captures the difficulty of moving between the two sectors, should be negative. Of the affinity effects, AF1 should be negative (it captures a "disaffinity") and AF2 positive. Some of the parameters of the core model are to be interpreted incrementally. For instance, the relative likelihood of long-distance mobility is captured by the sum of the coefficients for HI1 and HI2, rather than by HI2 alone. HI2, in fact, tells us the degree to which long-range mobility is more difficult than short range. In the same way, the propensity to inheritance of class IVc is given by IN1 plus IN2 plus IN3. So IN3 itself measures the "extra" inheritance observed among farmers compared with classes I+II and IVab.

Erikson and Goldthorpe (1992: 173) argue that the FJH thesis requires, as the first criterion for its support, that a model of fluidity (in this case the "core model" of fluidity) should provide a reasonable fit to the data. But they find that the core model with the same parameter values for all countries in their sample does not provide an adequate fit to the data: in other words, there is statistically significant variation between countries in the parameters of the model. Allowing such variation, the model fits the data much better, and Erikson and Goldthorpe take the success of this as supporting the FJH hypothesis:

"We can at least maintain that . . . the . . . effects that our model comprises do tend to operate cross-nationally in the way anticipated, even if with differing strengths" (Erikson and Goldthorpe 1992: 174). Nevertheless, even allowing the parameters of the core model to differ between countries, they still find that everywhere except England and France, some adjustments have to be made to the core model itself in order successfully to capture national variations in fluidity. These are sometimes called the national variants of the core model. The adjustments are of two kinds. In some cases the existing matrices are redefined: so, for example, when applied to the West German data, IN2 assigns immobility in class I+II to level 1, rather than 2. That is, there is no tendency for class inheritance to be higher here than in any other class. In other cases, additional affinity matrices were included. So, in Hungary, an additional matrix, called AFX, captures the tendency for movement from the class of farmers, IVc, to the class of agricultural workers, VIIb.

CONCLUSIONS

The core model is nowadays very widely used (see, for example, the essays in Breen 2004) and its fit to empirical has often been adequate, and in some cases, good. The main reason for this is that it succeeds in capturing the features evident in most mobility tables, namely the tendency for clustering on some cells of the main diagonal of the table (inheritance effects), and the inequality that derives from a hierarchical ordering of the classes. But these features are common to almost all models of fluidity: indeed, given a number of mobility tables, it is usually quite difficult to decide which of a set of models is to be preferred because none provides an unequivocal best fit to all the tables. If there can be said to be any core features of fluidity it is the tendency for clustering on the diagonal and the hierarchical component. The latter can be modeled in various ways, and, indeed, Erikson and Goldthorpe's approach here is idiosyncratic, with most analysts preferring a simple scaling of the origins and destinations according to the mean prestige or mean income of the occupations that make up each class. Nevertheless, a model which only fits inheritance and hierarchical effects is unlikely

to fit any mobility table. The claims of the core model then rest on having found other processes (instantiated in the se and af terms) that are common to all fluidity regimes. Unfortunately, the need to introduce national variants of the model, which mainly modify the se and af terms, somewhat undermines that claim. As Sorenson (1992: 309) remarks: "*any* mobility regime can be represented as *some* core model with national variants."

The major weakness of the core model is that the effects hypothesized to shape fluidity are all operationalized as binary contrasts or "dummy variables" (on the other hand, this may also help to account for the model's popularity, since one requires no more than the mobility table itself in order to employ it). The alternative is to express log odds ratios as proportional to differences in scores on measured variables, and several other models of fluidity adopt this approach (e.g., Hout 1984; Breen & Whelan 1992; see also Breen & Whelan 1994). To illustrate: we might express the log odds ratios capturing hierarchical inequality as proportional to the difference in the mean earnings of the origin and destination classes involved in the comparison. Clearly, the choice of explanatory variables should follow from some hypothesized mechanisms rooted in individual action and interaction, and, in fact, the use of explanatory variables inevitably pushes mobility research away from a concentration on tabular data and towards analyses using data on individuals (Logan 1983; Breen 1994) which test hypotheses about the processes that shape individual mobility trajectories and account for the variation among them. A move in this direction would do much to advance the study of social fluidity both theoretically and empirically.

SEE ALSO: Class, Status, and Power; Intergenerational Mobility: Methods of Analysis; Log-Linear Models; Mobility, Horizontal and Vertical; Mobility, Intergenerational and Intragenerational

REFERENCES AND SUGGESTED READINGS

Breen, R. (1994) Individual Level Models for Mobility Tables and Other Cross-Classifications. *Sociological Methods and Research* 23: 147–73.

Breen, R. (Ed.) (2004) *Social Mobility in Europe*. Oxford University Press, Oxford.

Breen, R. & Whelan, C. T. (1992) Explaining the Irish Pattern of Social Fluidity: The Role of the Political. in: Goldthorpe, J. H. & Whelan, C. T. (Eds.), *The Development of Industrial Society in Ireland: Proceedings of the British Academy 79*. Oxford University Press, Oxford, pp. 129–52.

Breen, R. & Whelan, C. T. (1994) Modelling Trends in Social Fluidity: The Core Model and a Measured-Variable Approach Compared. *European Sociological Review* 10: 259–72.

Erikson, R. & Goldthorpe, J. H. (1987a) Commonality and Variation in Social Fluidity in Industrial Nations, Part I: A Model for Evaluating the FJH Hypothesis. *European Sociological Review* 3: 54–77.

Erikson, R. & Goldthorpe, J. H. (1987b) Commonality and Variation in Social Fluidity in Industrial Nations, Part II: The Model of Core Social Fluidity Applied. *European Sociological Review* 3: 145–66.

Erikson, R. & Goldthorpe, J. H. (1992) *The Constant Flux: A Study of Class Mobility in Industrial Societies*. Oxford University Press, Oxford.

Featherman, D. L., Jones, F. L., & Hauser, R. M. (1975) Assumptions of Mobility Research in the United States: The Case of Occupational Status. *Social Science Research* 4: 329–60.

Ganzeboom, H. B. G., Luijkx, R., & Treiman, D. J. (1989) Intergenerational Class Mobility in Comparative Perspective. *Research in Social Stratification and Mobility* 8: 3–84.

Hout, M. (1984) Status, Autonomy, and Training in Occupational Mobility. *American Journal of Sociology* 89: 1379–409.

Logan, J. A. (1983) A Multivariate Model for Mobility Tables. *American Journal of Sociology* 89: 324–49.

Sorenson, J. P. (1992) More Matter with Less Art: A Rejoinder to Erikson and Goldthorpe. *European Sociological Review* 8: 307–11.

intergenerational mobility: methods of analysis

Ruud Luijkx

This entry comprises an analysis of intergenerational mobility, and in particular mobility tables, in which parents' and children's positions are cross-classified. These positions can refer to the level of educational achievement, earnings, occupational position, religious denomination, social class, and so on. Intergenerational class mobility (social mobility) involves the class of the family in which respondents lived when young (the *origin* class), and their current class position (the *destination* class).

The analysis of social mobility has a long tradition within sociology and largely evolved within the context of the International Sociological Association's Research Committee 28 on Social Stratification and Mobility. Elaborate overviews of the results of the different "generations" of social mobility research have been published (Ganzeboom et al. 1991; Treiman & Ganzeboom 2000; Breen & Jonsson 2005).

DISTINGUISHING SOCIAL CLASSES

Usually, the origin class in an intergenerational mobility table is related to the occupational position fathers held when respondents were between 12 and 16 years of age, and the destination class is related to the *current* occupational position of respondents, although sometimes destination refers to the first occupation held. A typical age selection for respondents is between 25 and 64 years of age. How many categories do the origin and destination class have? Looking at the history of social mobility analysis, a whole range of social class variables has been used. Very crude classifications that only distinguished farm, manual, and non-manual occupations were used in early analyses (see, e.g., Lipset & Zetterberg 1959). Sometimes, for manual and non-manual occupations, a further distinction was made into an upper and a lower category. This five-category classification used to be standard in the United States and has been used as the basis for further refinements, leading to a seventeenfold categorization (Blau & Duncan 1967; Featherman & Hauser 1978). Another, now dominant, categorization is the Goldthorpe or EG(P) (Erikson, Goldthorpe, and Portocarero) class schema (Erikson & Goldthorpe 1992). To construct these more refined class schemes, detailed occupational information and information on the self-employment and supervising status of people holding the occupational positions is essential (Ganzeboom & Treiman 1996).

The criteria used to aggregate occupations into social classes are in many cases more pragmatic than theoretical, but classifications can be evaluated in terms of both homogeneity and structure. *Homogeneity* refers to the extent that, within an aggregate of occupations (social class), there are no barriers between any origin occupation and any destination occupation. *Structure* refers to pattern and strength of the barriers between origin and destination classes. These barriers should be similar for the occupations constituting the classes. When disaggregated information is available, the assumption that class boundaries (barriers) are in agreement with the requirements of homogeneity and structure is testable.

The following list makes use of the seven-class version of the Goldthorpe class schema:

1 Classes I + II: professionals, administrators and officials, managers.
2 Class III: routine non-manual employees.
3 Class IVab: small proprietors and artisans.
4 Class IVc: farmers.
5 Class V + VI: technicians, supervisors, and skilled manual workers.
6 Class VIIa: semi- and unskilled workers not in agriculture.
7 Class VIIb: semi- and unskilled workers in agriculture.

Table 1 presents an intergenerational mobility table based on data used by Breen and Luijkx (2004). The table is an "average" table based on 89 mobility tables for men from France, Germany, Great Britain, Hungary, Ireland, the Netherlands, Poland, and Sweden between 1970 and 2000. The number of cases in the table is rescaled for reasons of exposition from more than 250,000 to 1,000.

We distinguish origin O with subscript i and destination D with subscript j. Let $\{f_{ij}\}(i = 1, ..., I; j = 1, ..., J)$ be the observed frequencies for each cell (i, j) in the $I \times J$ mobility table of origin by destination (in this case $I = J = 7$); f_{ij} is the observed number of people with origin i and destination j. The observed row totals are designated by f_{i+}, the observed column totals by f_{+j}, and the grand total by f_{++} or N.

MEASURING ABSOLUTE MOBILITY

Using the data in Table 1, we can compute measures of absolute mobility. We observe that 340 out of 1,000 men are in the same class as their fathers. In other words, 34.0 percent of the men are immobile and thus the mobility rate in the table is 66.0 percent. The mobility rate (or gross change) depends on the number of classes being distinguished, as can be seen from Table 2. In Table 2, we combine the seven classes into three: (1) I + II, (2) III, IVab, IVc, and V + VI, and (3) VIIa and VIIb. Based on these data, we now conclude that 50.8 percent (9.5 + 33.3 + 8.0) of the people are immobile and that the mobility rate is 49.2 percent. Within the mobile, we can distinguish those who are upwardly mobile, going from (3) to (1) or (2) and from (2) to (1) – in total 31.2 percent; and those who are downwardly mobile, going from (1) to (2) or (3) and from

Table 1 A mobility table

O(rigin)	D(estination)							
	I + II	*III*	*IVab*	*IVc*	*V + VI*	*VIIa*	*VIIb*	*Total*
I + II	95	14	9	1	24	11	1	*155*
III	26	9	4	1	16	8	1	*65*
IVab	28	9	18	1	21	13	1	*91*
IVc	25	9	10	55	40	40	11	*190*
V + VI	67	21	16	1	102	44	2	*253*
VIIa	38	16	11	2	70	53	3	*193*
VIIb	5	3	2	2	17	16	8	*53*
Total	*284*	*81*	*70*	*63*	*290*	*185*	*27*	*1,000*

Table 2   A mobility table (percentages)

Origin	Destination			Total
	(1)	*(2)*	*(3)*	
(1)	9.5	4.8	1.2	*15.5*
(2)	14.6	33.3	12.0	*59.9*
(3)	4.3	12.3	8.0	*24.6*
Total	*28.4*	*50.4*	*21.2*	*100.0*

(2) to (3) – in total 18.0 percent. It is clear from these results that upward mobility is more typical for the last part of the twentieth century than downward mobility.

Outflow and Inflow Percentages

Using outflow and inflow percentages, one can answer the question of where people in a certain class are going and where they come from. Outflow percentages are defined as f_{ij}/f_{i+} and give the conditional distribution of destinations for each origin. They are used to answer the question of how likely it is that people from a certain origin will go to the different destinations. On the other hand, inflow percentages are defined as f_{ij}/f_{+j} and answer the question of which origins members are distributed from. Outflow and inflow percentages are presented in Tables 3a and 3b.

From the inflow percentages (Table 3b), we can conclude that origin matters. The origin distributions for the different classes differ, e.g., 87.3 percent of farmers are recruited from

Table 3a   Outflow percentages

Origin	Destination							Total
	I + II	*III*	*IVab*	*IVc*	*V + VI*	*VIIa*	*VIIb*	
I + II	61.3	9.0	5.8	0.7	15.5	7.1	0.7	*100.0*
III	40.0	13.9	6.2	1.5	24.6	12.3	1.5	*100.0*
IVab	30.8	9.9	19.8	1.1	23.1	14.3	1.1	*100.0*
IVc	13.2	4.7	5.3	29.0	21.1	21.1	5.8	*100.0*
V + VI	26.5	8.3	6.3	0.4	40.3	17.4	0.8	*100.0*
VIIa	19.7	8.3	5.7	1.0	36.3	27.5	1.6	*100.0*
VIIb	9.4	5.7	3.8	3.8	32.1	30.2	15.1	*100.0*
Total	*28.4*	*8.1*	*7.0*	*6.3*	*29.0*	*18.5*	*2.7*	*100.0*

Table 3b   Inflow percentages

Origin	Destination							Total
	I + II	*III*	*IVab*	*IVc*	*V + VI*	*VIIa*	*VIIb*	
I + II	33.5	17.3	12.9	1.6	8.3	6.0	3.7	*15.5*
III	9.2	11.1	5.7	1.6	5.5	4.3	3.7	*6.5*
IVab	9.9	11.1	25.7	1.6	7.2	7.0	3.7	*9.1*
IVc	8.8	11.1	14.3	87.3	13.8	21.6	40.7	*19.0*
V + VI	23.6	25.9	22.9	1.6	35.2	23.8	7.4	*25.3*
VIIa	13.4	19.8	15.7	3.2	24.1	28.7	11.1	*19.3*
VIIb	1.8	3.7	2.9	3.2	5.9	8.7	29.6	*5.3*
Total	*100.0*	*100.0*	*100.0*	*100.0*	*100.0*	*100.0*	*100.0*	*100.0*

a farmers' background, whereas only 33.5 percent of the people in class I + II are recruited from that class. However, when we look at Table 3a, we see that 29.0 percent of the people with a farmers' background become farmers themselves, but that 61.3 percent of the people with an origin in class I + II end up in that same class. An explanation for this can be derived from the column and row totals in Tables 3a and 3b, respectively: Class I + II expanded from 15.5 percent in the origin distribution to 28.4 percent in the destination distribution, while the relative size of the farmer class declined from 19.0 to 6.3 percent. This brings us to the dissimilarity index.

Dissimilarity Index

If we look upon the class distribution of destinations as an opportunity structure, we can say that economic and demographic changes in society contribute to the dissimilarity between the contemporary opportunity structure, i.e., the destinations, and the class origins of current workers. Looking at Table 1, it is evident that the decline in agricultural jobs is balanced by an increase in non-manual positions. A summary measure of these countervailing changes is the index of dissimilarity between the distribution of origins and the distribution of destinations:

$$\Delta = \sum_{i=1}^{I} \frac{|f_{i+} - f_{+i}|}{2N}$$

Δ is a measure of net change. It does not take into account the actual gross flows in the mobility table, only the net outcome of all flows. can be interpreted as the minimal proportion of people who have to be reclassified to make the origin and destination distributions identical (for Table 1 this is 0.182). Above we saw that the gross change (mobility rate) was 0.660. A high mobility rate results if the destination distribution differs substantially from the origin distribution or if origins and destinations are statistically independent, that is, if the conditional distributions of destinations are the same for all origins. A low mobility rate results if there is a similarity of origin and destination distribution *and* if the association between

origin and destination is strong. In the analysis of mobility, these two elements have to be separated: mobility due to dissimilar marginal distributions of origins and destinations (known as structural mobility) and mobility due to association between origins and destinations.

MEASURING RELATIVE MOBILITY

Mobility can also be described in terms of odds ratios. It is possible to compute many odds ratios from an $I \times J$ table, but the association in the complete table can be fully described by the odds ratios of a basic set of subtables: the 2×2 subtables formed from adjacent rows and adjacent columns. There are $(I - 1) \times (J - 1)$ basic subtables. The formula for the (adjacent) odds ratios is:

$$\theta_{ij} = \frac{f_{ij}/f_{i(j+1)}}{f_{(i+1)j}/f_{(i+1)(j+1)}}$$

In Table 4 this basic set is presented for the data from Table 1.

Goldthorpe (1980: 77) described odds ratios as indicating how unequal the outcomes are of competitions between persons of different origins to achieve or avoid certain jobs. For example, in Table 1, 95 men with origin I + II go to class I + II and 14 go to class III. The odds of going to class I + II instead of class III from origin I + II is 95/14 = 6.79. For people from class III background, this figure is 26/9 = 2.89. Although men from both origins are more likely to end up in class I + II instead of class III, the odds are 2.35 (6.79/2.89) times greater for men from origin I + II than for men from origin III. Were the odds for both origins equal, the odds ratio would have equaled one.

If all the odds ratios in the table are equal to one, we can speak of perfect mobility, i.e., destinations do not depend on origins. It is clear from the pattern in Table 4 that the odds ratios in the diagonal cells are much higher than the other ones, indicating that the propensity for men to stay in their own class is much higher than moving to another class.

An important feature of the odds ratio is that it is not dependent on the marginals: when all frequencies in a certain row or column are multiplied by a constant, the odds ratios remain the same. This property is useful in the case of stratified samples: the odds ratios are not sensitive to an over- or underrepresentation of a certain category. Even more important is the fact that it makes comparison of the origin–destination association possible between tables with different marginal distributions. This origin–destination association or relative mobility is also known as social fluidity.

Log-Linear Models to Constrain the Odds Ratio Patterns

The full set of contiguous odds ratios (Table 4) constitutes a complete account of the association pattern, the so-called saturated model or unconstrained association model. Log-linear models are used to constrain the odds ratios in the saturated model to a more parsimonious set in order to find a sociologically more meaningful and statistically more powerful account of the data. We define the following log-linear model:

$$\ln F_{ij} = \lambda + \lambda_i^O + \lambda_j^D + \lambda_{ij}^{OD}, \quad \text{for all}$$
$$i = 1, ..., I; \ j = 1, ..., J$$

where F_{ij} is the (under the model) expected frequency in the ijth cell of the table; λ is the grand mean; λ_i^O and λ_j^D are the one-variable effects pertaining to the origin and destination; and λ_{ij}^{OD} is the origin–destination association. Identifying restrictions on the parameters have to be defined. As fit measures, the conventional log-likelihood ratio χ^2 statistic (L^2), and the BIC statistic (Raftery 1986) are mostly used.

Which patterns of social fluidity can be modeled using log-linear analysis? The simplest

pattern would be the one with no origin–destination association, the already presented perfect mobility model (in that case all $\lambda_{ij}^{OD} = 0$). But such a model does not fit our data well ($L^2 = 336.9$; df $= 36$). A next model is that of quasi-perfect mobility. It assumes that people have a higher propensity to stay in their own class than moving to other classes (and that this propensity is different for each class), but that for people who are mobile, there is perfect mobility. We display this model as a matrix showing which association parameters of the model affect which cell of the table:

2	1	1	1	1	1	1
1	3	1	1	1	1	1
1	1	4	1	1	1	1
1	1	1	5	1	1	1
1	1	1	1	6	1	1
1	1	1	1	1	7	1
1	1	1	1	1	1	8

This model fits the data much better, but is still not statistically significant ($L^2 = 65.4$; df $= 29$). The highest immobility parameter belongs to class IVc (farmers), followed by VIIb (agricultural workers) and IVab (self-employed). Another pattern that improves the fit of the model further is the core model of social fluidity.

Scaled Association Models

Scaled association models have turned out to be very useful for summarizing relative mobility

Table 4 Odds ratios for the mobility table

Origin	Destination					
	(I + II):III	*III:IVab*	*IVab:IVc*	*IVc:(V + VI)*	*(V + VI):VIIa*	*VIIa:VIIb*
(I + II):III	2.35	0.69	2.25	0.67	1.09	1.38
III:IVab	0.93	4.50	0.22	1.31	1.24	0.62
IVab:IVc	1.12	0.56	99.00	0.03	1.62	3.58
IVc:(V + VI)	0.87	0.69	0.01	140.25	0.43	0.17
(V + VI):VIIa	1.34	0.90	2.91	0.34	1.76	1.25
VIIa:VIIb	1.43	0.97	5.50	0.24	1.24	8.83

(Goodman 1979). The "starting" point is the very restricted uniform association model that assumes all contiguous associations in a table to be identical: $\ln \theta_{ij} = \varphi$. This model uses one parameter to characterize all odds ratios in a table, which is parsimonious but also often too restrictive (in these data, $L^2 = 224.7$; df $= 35$). The stringent assumption can be meaningfully relaxed in three ways:

1 By including diagonal density parameters that represent within-class immobility over and above the association.
2 By scaling the distances between the row (μ_i) and column (ν_j) categories: $\ln \theta_{ij} = \varphi(\mu_{i+1} - \mu_i)(\nu_{j+1} - \nu_j)$; the category scalings μ_i and ν_j can be interpreted as measures of distance between or similarity among social categories with respect to the mobility chances. If categories are identically scaled ($\mu_1 = \mu_2$), this suggests that they can be regarded as a single social class. If the scalings are very different, this implies not only that mobility between the classes is extremely difficult, but also that they have very different mobility exchanges with other classes.
3 As a useful special restriction in this model we can introduce equal scalings for origins and destinations: $\mu_i = \nu_i$.

This model is known as the Goodman–Hauser model after its principal inventors (Goodman 1979; Hauser 1984). This model yields a very good fit to the data ($L^2 = 12.0$; df $= 23$). In Table 5 we present the scaling and immobility parameters.

Although not equidistant, we see from the scaling measures that the distance between the classes is ordered except for the farmers (IVc), who are better placed between unskilled manual workers (VIIa) and agricultural workers (VIIb). The immobility data show that inheritance is strong not only for farmers (IVc) and

the self-employed (IVab), but also for the service class (I + II).

In the Goodman–Hauser model the distance between the classes is estimated. An attractive alternative is the measured variable approach in which known characteristics are used as scalings for the classes. In Hout's (1984) SAT model, he scales origins and destinations using socioeconomic status (S), on-the-job autonomy (A), and specialized training (T). Breen and Whelan's (1994) AHP model scales origins and destinations with origin- and destination-specific measures for agriculture (A), hierarchy (H), and property (P).

COMPARATIVE ANALYSIS

The measures presented here for absolute mobility can also be used to compare the level of absolute mobility between countries and periods. An important prerequisite is that tables are comparable (of same dimension and using similar class categories). Dissimilarity indices can be computed to compare origin and destination distributions between tables, and in this way divergence or convergence between countries and periods can be assessed (see, e.g., Breen & Luijkx 2004).

For the comparative analysis of relative mobility, log-linear models are extremely well suited. To compare tables, we need to extend the log-linear model defined earlier:

$$\ln F_{ijk} = \lambda + \lambda_i^O + \lambda_j^D + \lambda_k^T + \lambda_{ik}^{OT} + \lambda_{jk}^{DT} + \lambda_{ij}^{OD} + \lambda_{ijk}^{ODT},$$

for all $i = 1, ..., I$; $j = 1, ..., J$; $k = 1, ..., K$

We now have an additional one-variable effect (λ_k^T) pertaining to the table totals, two additional two-variable effects ($\lambda_{ik}^{OT}, \lambda_{jk}^{DT}$) pertaining to the origin and destination distributions for the

Table 5 Parameters for the Goodman–Hauser model

Class	I + II	III	IVab	IVc	V + VI	VIIa	VIIb
Scaling	−0.48	−0.35	−0.23	0.38	−0.08	0.11	0.66
Immobility	0.69	0.21	1.13	2.82	0.41	0.21	0.20

distinct tables, and an additional three-variable effect (λ_{ijk}^{ODT}) pertaining to the variation in origin–destination association in the different tables.

Let us think of T as a number of tables from different periods within one country, although it could also be tables from different countries or a combination of periods and countries (the model can also be further extended to take period and country into account as distinct variables). A first model is the constant social fluidity (CnSF) model that assumes no variation in the odds ratios OD across the tables (all $\lambda_{ijk}^{ODT} = 0$). Erikson and Goldthorpe (1992) and Xie (1992) have proposed an elaboration of the CnSF model to test for trends, the UniDiff (uniform difference) or log-multiplicative layer effect model. UniDiff takes an intermediate position between CnSF (same pattern and strength of association in all tables) and the saturated model (different pattern and different strength of association for all tables) by using as a constraint that the set of odds ratios in one table differs from the set of odds ratios in the next table only by a log-multiplicative scaling factor: $\ln \theta_{ijk} = \beta_k * \ln \theta_{ij}$, where $\beta_1 = 1$ by convention. In this case $\ln \theta_{ij}$ refers to the set of log odds ratios in the first table.

The UniDiff model does not model the pattern of mobility in the tables, but simple extensions to do so can be made by elaborating on the scaled association model presented earlier: $\ln \theta_{ijk} = \varphi_k(\mu_{i+1} - \mu_i)(\nu_{j+1} - \nu_j)$. In this model, scalings μ_i and ν_j are assumed to be equal across tables and the association φ_k is allowed to differ (in a similar way as β_k in the UniDiff model). Both β_k and φ_k can be constrained linearly or curvilinearly.

General statistical programs like SPSS, SAS, and STATA can be used to estimate most of the models presented here. To estimate the log-multiplicative scaled association and UniDiff models, specialized programs such as LEM (Vermunt 1997) are more appropriate.

Although published more than 20 years ago, Hout's *Mobility Tables* (1983) is still one of the more comprehensive introductions to the log-linear analysis of mobility tables. A more recent work in which both substantive and methodological aspects of mobility analysis are presented is the collection of country papers in Breen (2004), which also includes a comparative analysis of eight nations over three decades.

SEE ALSO: Educational and Occupational Attainment; Income Inequality and Income Mobility; Intergenerational Mobility: Core Model of Social Fluidity; Mobility, Horizontal and Vertical; Mobility, Intergenerational and Intragenerational; Mobility, Measuring the Effects of; Occupational Mobility; Occupational Segregation; Transition from School to Work

REFERENCES AND SUGGESTED READINGS

Blau, P. M. & Duncan, O. D. (1967) *The American Occupational Structure*. Wiley, New York.

Breen, R. (2004) *Social Mobility in Europe*. Oxford University Press, Oxford.

Breen, R. & Jonsson, J. O. (2005) Inequality of Opportunity in Comparative Perspective: Recent Research in Educational Attainment and Social Mobility. *Annual Review of Sociology* 31: 223–43.

Breen, R. & Luijkx, R. (2004) Social Mobility in Europe between 1970 and 2000. In: Breen, R. (Ed.), *Social Mobility in Europe*. Oxford University Press, Oxford, pp. 37–75.

Breen, R. & Whelan, C. T. (1994) Modelling Trends in Social Fluidity: The Core Model and a Measured-Variable Approach Compared. *European Sociological Review* 10: 259–72.

Erikson, R. & Goldthorpe, J. H. (1992) *The Constant Flux: A Study of Class Mobility in Industrial Societies*. Oxford University Press, Oxford.

Featherman, D. L. & Hauser, R. M. (1978) *Opportunity and Change*. Academic Press, New York.

Ganzeboom, H. B. G. & Treiman, D. J. (1996) Internationally Comparable Measures of Occupational Status for the 1988 International Standard Classification of Occupations. *Social Science Research* 25: 201–39.

Ganzeboom, H. B. G., Treiman, D. J., & Ultee, W. C. (1991) Comparative Intergenerational Stratification Research: Three Generations and Beyond. *Annual Review of Sociology* 17: 277–302.

Goldthorpe, J. H. (1980) *Social Mobility and Class Structure in Modern Britain*. Clarendon Press, Oxford.

Goodman, L. A. (1979) Multiplicative Models for the Analysis of Occupational Mobility Tables and Other Kinds of Cross-Classification Tables. *American Journal of Sociology* 84: 804–19.

Hauser, R. M. (1984) Vertical Class Mobility in England, France, and Sweden. *Acta Sociologica* 27: 87–110.

Hout, M. (1983) *Mobility Tables*. Sage, Thousand Oaks, CA.

Hout, M. (1984) Status, Autonomy, and Training in Occupational Mobility. *American Journal of Sociology* 89: 1379–409.

Lipset, S. M. & Zetterberg, H. L. (1959) Social Mobility in Industrial Societies. In: Lipset, S. M. & Bendix, R. (Ed.), *Social Mobility in Industrial Society*. University of California Press, Berkeley, pp. 11–75.

Raftery, A. E. (1986) Choosing Models for Cross-Classifications. *American Sociological Review* 51: 145–6.

Treiman, D. J. & Ganzeboom, H. B. G. (2000) The Fourth Generation of Comparative Stratification Research. In: Quah, S. R. & Sales, A. (Eds.), *The International Handbook of Sociology*. Sage, Thousand Oaks, CA.

Vermunt, J. K. (1997) *LEM: A General Program for the Analysis of Categorical Data*. Tilburg University, Tilburg.

Xie, Y. (1992) The Log-Multiplicative Layer Effect Model for Comparing Mobility Tables. *American Sociological Review* 57: 380–95.

intergenerational relationships and exchanges

Timothy J. Biblarz, Vern L. Bengtson, and Merril Silverstein

The study of intergenerational relationships and exchange is about the structure and process of sharing that occurs in the linked lives of grandparents, parents, and children (and sometimes extended kin) as they move along the life course. Like the discipline of sociology, this subfield emerged in the wake of rapid industrialization, urbanization, and expansion of the state's role in families (e.g., the education of children and caring for the elderly), and is concerned with how these major social changes altered extended family ties, the role of grandparents, and parent–child relationships. Middletown researchers in the 1920s, for example, observed challenges to parental control as children's individualistic aspirations began to compete with family obligations. In the US, parents' relationships with children have since shifted from an emphasis on obedience and strict conformity to developing children's autonomy and independence. In Japan, South Korea, and other countries, the significance of filial piety seems to be diminishing, raising new questions about who should care for the old and young.

The study of intergenerational relationships and exchange has been guided by two questions. The first involves intergenerational transmission: what do families transmit from one generation to the next, how do processes of intergenerational transmission occur, and why? Sizable correlations have been found, for example, between the social class position of parents and that eventually held by children (the intergenerational reproduction of inequality), and between parents' and children's religious and political values, occupations, family behavior (e.g., propensity to divorce), health-related behavior (e.g., smoking), and other statuses, values, and behaviors. The family environment (as against genetic) component of intergenerational inheritance has been variously explained by patterns of parental investment in children (economic theory), children modeling their parents (learning theory), and levels of affect in the parent–child relationship (attachment theory). Research is just beginning to explore transmission across multiple generations, as in the case of grandparental influence on grandchildren, prompted in part by positive trends in the health, longevity, and socioeconomic status of older generations.

The second question involves how intergenerational relationships and exchange contribute to (or detract from) the well-being of individual family members. Under what circumstances do relationships and exchange provide members psychological and material well-being, a haven in a heartless world, or leave them in the cold? The concern most often has been with the well-being of society's two dependent populations, elders and children, although the well-being of the "sandwiched" generation has also received attention. A key feature is the study of caregiving, and of the timing and spacing of transfers up and down the intergenerational ladder over the life course. The core resources given altruistically or exchanged reciprocally that are most frequently studied include time and involvement, money, assets and goods, and love, affection, and intimacy, in part because these have proven essential to individual well-being.

Trends from the 1960s to the present – most notably, increases in divorce, maternal employment, nonmarital childbearing, and cohabitation – have stirred volumes of new research on consequences for parent–child relationships, child development and well-being, and intergenerational exchange. New research shows that the quality of early parent–child relationships is consequential years later, when aging parents may need help from adult children, or vice versa. Some studies show that fathers who divorce while their children are young, for example, get less from their children in old age. The role of grandparents in contributing to the well-being of grandchildren, particularly in the context of divorce and other stressors, is becoming an important focus of research.

While intergenerational relationships and exchange are studied in a variety of social science disciplines, the sociological approach has at least three key features. First, it pays attention to how patterns of intergenerational relationships and exchange are affected by the social contexts (neighborhoods, employment sites, economic conditions, and so on) in which families, and family members, are embedded. For example, a number of studies have shown that bad jobs make good parenting more difficult to achieve. The experiences and lessons learned in extra-family environments get brought into families, influencing family relationships and exchange.

Second, the life course perspective is often used as a framework for studying intergenerational relationships. It draws attention to the unique alignment of age or life stage (e.g., the nature of exchanges between parents and children will vary depending on whether children are in infancy, childhood, adolescence, or adulthood) and history (e.g., relationships will be colored both by the period under which family members came of age and the current climate), with an eye toward how individual development and primary relationships at the micro level

are affected by local, regional, national, and even global events. The life course approach is inherently longitudinal, viewing intergenerational relationships as beginning at birth and moving through old age, and sequential, where earlier intergenerational events and transitions along the life course will have essential implications for later ones.

Third, rooted in the expansion of the division of labor and population heterogeneity that accompanied modernization, sociology has become markedly attentive to the consequences of social inequalities – hierarchies based on the intersecting dimensions of education, occupation, economic status, age, race, ethnicity, nativity and immigration status, gender, sexual orientation, and family background. This "race, class, gender" approach has become an important component of studies of intergenerational relationships. Do class, race, and ethnicity, for example, shape the way parents raise children and adult children care for aging parents? Some evidence suggests that, controlling for resources, African American and Latino adults in the US are more likely to provide assistance to their parents, and that race, class, and gender shape the way parents raise their children.

Since its origin was in the disruptions of major social changes, this subfield traditionally has been concerned with family decline – the possibility that intergenerational relationships have weakened and exchanges have diminished. To date, the fear of intergenerational decline has been stronger than the empirical evidence. Even at the height of the apparent generation gap in the US – the 1960s – relatively high levels of shared values and bonds between family members were observed, and the vast majority of caregiving today continues to be provided by family members. Recent work has also shown that employment has not led to significant decline in the amount of time mothers spend with children. To be sure, at the beginning of the twenty-first century, intergenerational relationships and exchanges are more diverse and complicated than ever before, but remain crucially important to the well-being of individuals and society.

SEE ALSO: Aging, Sociology of; Family, Sociology of; Intergenerational Conflict; Life Course; Life Course and Family; Socialization

REFERENCES AND SUGGESTED
READINGS

Bengtson, V. L. (1975) Generation and Family
Effects in Value Socialization. *American Sociologi-
cal Review* 40: 358–71.
Bengtson, V. L. (2001) Beyond the Nuclear Family:
The Increasing Importance of Multigenerational
Bonds. *Journal of Marriage and the Family* 63: 1–16.
Bengtson, V. L., Biblarz, T. J., & Roberts, R. E. L.
(2002) *How Families Still Matter: A Longitudinal
Study of Youth in Two Generations.* Cambridge
University Press, New York.
Bianchi, S. M. (2000) Maternal Employment and
Time with Children: Dramatic Change or Surpris-
ing Continuity? *Demography* 37: 401–14.
Biblarz, T. J. & Raftery, A. E. (1999) Family Struc-
ture, Educational Attainment, and Socioeconomic
Success: Rethinking the "Pathology of Matriar-
chy." *American Journal of Sociology* 105(2): 321–65.
Caplow, T., Bahr, H. M., et al. (1982) *Middletown:
Fifty Years of Change and Continuity.* University of
Minnesota Press, Minneapolis.
Cherlin, A. J. & Furstenberg, F. F. (1986) *The New
American Grandparent: A Place in the Family, A
Life Apart.* Basic Books, New York.
Silverstein, M. & Schaie, K. W. (Eds.) (2005) *Annual
Review of Gerontology and Geriatrics*, Vol. 24:
Intergenerational Relations Across Time and Place.
Springer, New York.
Silverstein, M., Conroy, S., Wang, H., Giarrusso,
R., & Bengtson, V. L. (2002) Reciprocity in Par-
ent–Child Relations Over the Adult Life Course.
Journal of Gerontology: Social Sciences 57: S3–S13.
Treas, J. (1995) Older Americans in the 1990s and
Beyond. *Population Bulletin* 50(2). Population
Reference Bureau, Washington, DC.

international gender division of labor

Christine E. Bose

World systems theorists were among the first to
use the concept of an international division of
labor by illustrating how the production of
goods and services for "core" or more developed
countries relied on the material resources of
"peripheral" or developing nations (Wallerstein
1974). Their work describes the changing
political and economic relationships among
nations over the last six centuries, beginning
with the period of colonization when Western
European nations took possession of other countries in order to gain access to their raw materials
such as sugar, coffee, gold, silver, or labor sold
into slavery. By the middle of the twentieth
century most of those colonies had gained their
political freedom and titular control over their
own resources, but were never able to break
away from their economic dependence on highly
industrialized countries.

In the twentieth century a new process called
global or economic restructuring created a new
form of international division of labor between
the developed countries (now labeled the global
North, a term replacing the old Cold War label
"First World") and the developing nations
(now called the global South, which replaced
the concept of a "Third World"). Beginning in
the 1970s, in order to lessen production costs
and enabled by improvements in information
and production technologies, US, Japanese, and
Western European corporations began to "off-
shore" some of their production processes to the
global South, often moving to export-processing
zones (EPZs) within these countries, which are
defined as industrial zones that provide manufacturing infrastructure, tax reductions, low labor
costs, lax environmental regulations, and other
incentives. As a result of this worldwide economic restructuring, much basic manufacturing
and heavy industrial production were relocated
to developing nations, while corporate head-
quarters, service work, and final product finish-
ing stayed in developed nations. This process
was initially referred to as the growth of the
global assembly line or the global factory (Kamel
1990). Instead of taking raw material resources
from their former colonies, transnational corporations (TNCs) based in the global North rely
on residents of the global South to provide inexpensive labor for factories now located in developing countries.

In addition, international development or
funding agencies such as the International
Monetary Fund and the World Bank influence
global South economies when they loan money
to poor and developing nations, because loans
are tied to required austerity measures known
as structural adjustment programs (SAPs).
SAPs require the debtor countries to reduce

government expenditures on social services and increase production for export, rather than supporting independent local businesses that produce for local consumption, in order to earn more foreign currency to pay back these loans. An important byproduct of these two factors – TNCs relocating production overseas and structural adjustment programs – is that developing economies are indirectly controlled by transnational corporations and/or funding agencies located in developed nations, thus reinforcing a new international division of labor.

This international division of labor is profoundly gendered in many ways. Mies et al. (1988) observed there has been an international trend towards the "housewifization" of all labor – an interesting term that incorporates several aspects of the relationship between paid work and women's unpaid work at home. First, paid work is becoming increasingly feminized, with new jobs in the service sector drawing more on women's than men's labor. Indeed, some of women's traditional white and pink-collar jobs, such as data entry or telephone call-in work, are now being sent to workers in developing countries, especially to English-speaking, former British colony nations (Freeman 2000).

Second, paid work is increasingly organized like women's housework, with jobs that require flexible schedules and are occupationally segregated. Such "flexibilization" of the world economy refers to the growth of part-time, temporary, or seasonal employment. In developed countries, this process is most visible in the growth of the service sector. In developing economies flexibilization usually refers to the need for families to have multiple-income sources based on subsistence farming, vending, or other forms of self-employment, and perhaps some formal paid work.

Third, many of these jobs, like market trading, factory outwork, or off-the-books childcare, are found in the informal sector of the global economy that is rapidly expanding but, like housework, is not regulated by national labor laws. Therefore, increasing "informalization" of work often accompanies flexibilization.

Fifth, since women's traditional tasks are stereotyped as unskilled (although they are not), companies or individual employers can more easily pay less and provide less job security.

In other words, economic restructuring and the international division of paid labor created new jobs that have many of the characteristics of women's paid work and unpaid carework and housework, which is not surprising since women are the source of new labor in most countries worldwide.

Recent scholarship by Parreñas (2000), Hondagneu-Sotello and Avila (1997), and others illustrates that there also is an international division of reproductive or carework labor. This occurs when women from developing countries migrate internationally to more developed ones to perform paid carework for other women, then use their earnings to hire someone back home (often a rural-to-urban migrant or another family member) to take care of their own families. Parreñas (2000) argues that this labor chain, transferring white women's domestic and reproductive labor to women of color from developing nations, creates an international system of racial stratification in reproductive work and makes temporary overseas "contract workers" into a new export commodity for some developing countries.

While the international division of labor continues to change forms, one of the constant features is its gendered and raced nature.

SEE ALSO: Development: Political Economy; Division of Labor; Divisions of Household Labor; Feminization of Labor Migration; Global Economy; Women, Economy and

REFERENCES AND SUGGESTED READINGS

Freeman, C. (2000) *High Tech and High Heels in the Global Economy: Women, Work, and Pink-Color Identities in the Caribbean*. Duke University Press, Durham, NC.

Hondagneu-Sotello, P. & Avila, E. (1997) "I'm Here, But I'm There": The Meanings of Latina Transnational Motherhood. *Gender and Society* 11(5): 548–71.

Kamel, R. (1990) *The Global Factory: Analysis and Action for a New Economic Era*. Omega Press/American Friends Service Committee, Philadelphia.

Mies, M., Bennholdt-Thomson, V., & von Werlhof, C. (1988) *Women: The Last Colony*. Zed Books, London.

Parreñas, R. S. (2000) Migrant Filipina Domestic Workers and the International Division of Reproductive Labor. *Gender and Society* 14(4): 560–80.

Wallerstein, I. (1974) *The Modern World System I.* Academic Press, New York.

Internet

James Slevin

The Internet is a global network of interconnected computer hardware and software systems, making possible the storage, retrieval, circulation, and processing of information and communication across time and space. From a sociological perspective, the Internet is not synonymous with a global information machine as it is in some popular accounts. A sociological account encompasses the constituent Internet technologies and attends to these as social phenomena. It also includes the information and other content which is produced, transmitted, and received by individuals and organizations using the Internet. Finally, a sociological account of the Internet includes the socially and historically structured contexts and processes in which the production, transmission, and reception of information and communication are embedded.

Consider the simple act of writing and sending an email over the Internet. What can we say from a sociological perspective about communicating in this way? We could start by pointing out that communicating by email is not just an alternative way of producing and distributing information. It involves us in a complexity of new forms of action and interaction that stretch across the world. In order to send an email, we need to have access to technologies that allow us to store, process, and send information over the Internet. The resources we are able to muster in respect of communicating and in respect of accessing and distributing information over the Internet are not uniformly spread. Moreover, using these technologies is a skilled performance demanding particular capabilities, for example, knowing how to work a computer, knowing how to address an email, and knowing how to attach other items like photographs, if we so wish.

Sending an email is also embedded in various kinds of interlocking institutional arrangements. Sending email from a private Internet connection at home is different from sending an email from an office or from an Internet café. At home, we might need to negotiate time spent on the computer with others in our household who might also wish to use it. In an office, we might be restricted in sending private emails which are not strictly related to our work. In an Internet café, we might be paying for Internet access by the minute, feel uncomfortable because other people can read our screens, and leave as soon as we have finished our coffee. The circumstances of the recipient of our email may also be relevant to the process of sending it. It's no good sending an email and expecting a direct response if the recipient is away on holiday or is normally asleep at that time of day. The situated social contexts of both the sender and recipient also interlock with institutional arrangements that are instantiated in what happens online. Sending an email from an Internet café, for example, may involve us using the online services of a distant Internet provider. Such arrangements also enable and restrict communication and the accessing and distributing of information.

Finally, the content of an email also involves us in new forms of action and interaction and is constructed and organized differently from communication by letter, phone, or in face-to-face exchange. The content of email messages mostly does not display the same formalities that letters do. In such a situation where we want to communicate a complicated message which could easily be misunderstood, we might prefer to use a phone or meet face to face rather than communicate by email. Moreover, the choice to send a message by email rather than using a different means of communication is already an act that may be considered socially meaningful by a recipient. Sending highly consequential information via email, for example, may seem insensitive to a recipient's feelings and interests.

Email is only one of a baffling variety of available Internet applications. The World Wide Web, newsgroups, instant messenger systems, Virtual Learning Environments, to name but a few others, can all be approached from a similar sociological perspective.

The Internet deserves the attention of sociologists for three major reasons. First, the Internet facilitates a reorganization of information and social relationships across time and space. As such, its development and use have intended and unintended consequences for human social life, groups, and societies that need to be studied and understood. Second, in investigating and understanding the complex subject matter of sociology, the Internet is an important tool for collecting data and for accessing information relevant to such an endeavor. Third, the Internet deserves the attention of sociologists because it expands the opportunities for circulating research findings and for supporting critical reflection, learning, and debate. However, in staking out the relevance of the Internet for sociology, we need to be aware that as a social phenomenon, it is an expression of the radical interconnection of people, organizations, different sectors of society, and the problems that we take up for study. In this way, studying the Internet involves shifts and linkages to perspectives that might traditionally have been considered to lie beyond the disciplinary boundaries of sociology. A comprehensive understanding of the Internet can only be developed jointly, from a multidisciplinary approach.

Fundamental to a sociological account of the Internet is that its development and use are not accidental to a set of complex and contradictory changes that are taking place in our world today. As such, the Internet is in the midst of some of our most severe and exciting challenges. The world we live in is becoming increasingly globalized. As a global communication network, the Internet is transforming the complex relationships between local activities and interaction across distance. The world we live in confronts us with new opportunities and dilemmas as the certainties afforded by tradition, authority, and nature no longer direct our lives in the way that they once did. The Internet radicalizes this process by placing "horizontal" forms of communications center stage, by allowing the questioning and blurring over of authority, and by allowing the reordering and expansion of the built environment. The world we live in is increasingly reflexive and saturated with information. As a technology of communication, the Internet transforms our information environments by facilitating global attentiveness, visibility, and questioning. Moreover, as a technology of communication, the Internet does not simply impact on this set of complex and contradictory changes; it contributes to the construction, mediation, and disclosure of what these transformations are.

Globalization, detraditionalization, and the intensification of social reflexivity force themselves as major themes into all sorts of Internet topics addressed by sociological research. In connecting these themes to the topics they study, sociologists are concerned with a range of questions that follow from the challenges we face. First, to what extent is the Internet facilitating an advance in intelligent relationships between individuals, groups, and organizations arranged through dialogue rather than domination and violence? Second, how might the Internet empower individuals, groups, and organizations to make things happen rather than to have things happen to them in the context of overall goals and interests? Third, in what way does the Internet offer a new basis for solidarity and strategic alliances, bringing together in association individuals, groups, and organizations who were previously socially and geographically far apart? Fourth, in what way might the Internet open up new opportunities for limiting damage and conflict as new communication networks allow individuals, groups, and organizations to cross paths with others whose views differ from their own? In dealing with these questions, sociologists may opt to emphasize the communicational, political, economic, and normative aspects of the Internet and its use, or a combination of these.

In spite of all the excitement generated by the Internet over recent years, we would not be far off the mark if we were to conclude that it remains only poorly understood. Many debates about the social impact of the Internet have involved opposing sides taking almost completely contradictory views about its significance in modern life. On the one hand, we find the Internet radicals who claim that we are at the dawn of a new era of opportunity in which we can live our lives on the screen. On the other, we find the Internet skeptics, who warn of the onset of a terrible nightmare in which many people will find themselves disconnected and irrelevant to the important things that go on in their world. Sometimes optimistic and pessimistic views are raised by one and the same person.

While we might rejoice at the idea that people hold different opinions, this kind of understanding of an important communication medium is not at all satisfactory given the severity of the challenges that we face, both on the level of world society and institutions and on the level of our personal lives. Why is our understanding of the Internet so poor? More importantly, what can sociologists do about it?

Some commentators point to a lack of adequate research into the Internet and yet others to the sheer pace of social and technical change which they claim has overtaken us. The problem, however, also goes deeper than this. We urgently need to find concepts and frameworks that can be placed in the service of developing a more critical understanding of the Internet and we must continue to remain critical of what we may find.

A great deal of early knowledge of the Internet had an anecdotal and descriptive quality about it. As the sophistication of Internet studies advanced, research began to slot into an already growing interest in communication via the computer. Studies of computer-mediated communication and "cyberculture" developed from this and were taken up by researchers from diverse disciplinary backgrounds. This resulted in the research area becoming highly fragmented with different disciplines declaring different parts of it to be their own. While narrowly defined disciplinary approaches still exist today, Internet research has become increasingly multidisciplinary.

Another problem with early research is related to the use of the term "new media" to refer to technologies like the Internet. This was conveniently taken by some to mean that they could begin their understanding of the Internet with a fresh start without critically referring to existing theories and to existing media. Some commentators even claimed that media convergence would result in the new media swallowing up or replacing the old. Today, we are far more sensitized to the way in which the Internet reconfigures different media and the contrasting ways in which it reconfigures our information and communication environment.

The biggest shift in the treatment of the Internet, however, is that early research tended to focus on what was happening on the Net. Internet culture was understood to be an online phenomenon quite divorced from the social contexts within which, and by virtue of which, it was produced and received. There is now a growing realization that the Internet is not incidental to our lives but fundamental to the way we live now. This has resulted in far more comprehensive studies looking at the way in which the Internet enmeshes with the cultural transformations associated with the rise of modern societies and a far greater awareness of the situated and cultural contexts of its use.

With the Internet so centrally involved in the shakeup of our institutions, organizations, and our individual lives, the research topics addressed by sociologists are bounded only by the limits of their imagination. While the following list does not exhaust all possibilities, it contains some of the topics that sociological research has addressed.

1   The history of Internet-related technologies. The history of the Internet is only beginning to be written. Many early accounts hardly progress beyond the construction of timelines setting out important events without explaining why these came about or what they mean. More advanced approaches show the Internet not to be a sudden invention, governed solely by conditions internal to its own technological development. Instead, they argue that all Internet-related innovations are fundamentally social and their meaning, together with their meaningful use, is grounded in social contexts. The Internet is the result of tensionful, contradictory technical and social conditions and the consequences of its use are no less so.

2   Self-identity and everyday life. Globalization and detraditionalization mean that individuals face more opportunities in constructing their own lives than once was the case. Who we are, what we do, and how we do things together is increasingly mediated and fed by information and communication technologies. Sociological studies attempt to unravel the involvement of the Internet in transforming the nature of the self, experience, and communication in everyday life. Sociologists are sensitive to ways in which the Internet is furthering individual autonomy but also to ways in which the Internet might adversely affect individuals

by excluding them from its use or by involving them in problems of compulsion, addiction, and self-harm.

3 Networking and community. The turmoil of our modern world has resulted in the breakdown of traditional strategies for organizing solidarity. Critical awareness of this social disintegration is accompanied by a renewed interest in community. Online communication opens up vast opportunities for human interaction and association across time and space. Communities facilitated by the Internet often consist of individuals related to each other in terms of practice rather than proximity. There are worries, however, that new forms of human association using the Internet are undermining solidarity still further with individuals becoming increasingly disengaged from meaningful face-to-face relationships.

4 Organizations, business, and institutions. Modern organizations exist by virtue of the informed practices of their members. Internet technology has permeated all forms of organization in the form of intranets for their internal communication, extranets for their communication with other organizations, and the Internet for their external communication. Using these networks, some organizations have become more open and informed resulting from a decentralization of organizational authority, a shift toward supportive and facilitative leadership, a focus on knowledge sharing, horizontal communication, teamwork and empowerment, and a blurring of traditional organizational boundaries, for example, where individuals work from home and on the move. However, using these networks, organizations can also become highly centralized, hierarchical, inaccessible, exclusive, and fundamentalist rather than cosmopolitan in their outlook.

5 Publicness and democracy. The Internet is creating new opportunities and burdens as regards mediating visibility and making information available to others. Sociologists are interested in how the Internet is impacting on the public sphere, redefining freedom of expression and discussion. The new global information environment is a powerful democratizing force. Democratic institutions are being transformed under pressure of highly reflexive citizenries who are increasingly organizing themselves internationally.

6 Social movements and civil society. The rise of various social movements oriented toward challenges traditional democratic institutions have failed to cope with has snapped together with the new opportunities offered by the Internet. The civil rights movements, the feminist movements, the ecological and anti-nuclear movements, and the gay and lesbian movements, to name but a few, are all reinvigorating civil society, empowered by the Internet. For sociologists, their struggle for visibility, campaigns, and use of information technology have become important topics of study.

7 Globalization and the digital divide. Globalization is an inherent feature of our modern world and raises many questions and difficulties. We increasingly live in one world where globalized communication is relevant to all our lives. Yet the consequences of globalized communication are highly contradictory and most of the world's population is excluded from using it.

8 Regulation. New forms of policy and regulation are being researched, developed, and implemented affecting Internet access and content, stimulating economic development, promoting diversity, pluralism, and the deconcentration of power, and regulating the connections with other media.

9 Research and social theory. Sociologists have also attended to questions regarding Internet research and whether this demands new theoretical frameworks and research methodologies.

Sociological projects in these areas are set to continue and new projects will arise. Some will acquire new significance and urgency. None the more so than in the area of e-learning. Successful intervention in our world today is increasingly governed by decisions made on the basis of knowledge and competence which is revisable or can be rendered outdated in an instant. The Internet is set to play a key role in facilitating the building and rebuilding of knowledge and skills, at any time and in any place, and is already contributing to the refashioning of education, its institutions, and the way we learn.

As the radical interconnectedness afforded by the Internet propels its users into an increasingly challenging reality of cultural differences, people and organizations will increasingly cross paths with others whose views and interests may differ from their own. How people and organizations can best negotiate such a complexity of experiences will demand significant attention from sociologists.

There is also a growing awareness of the environmental impact of global communication systems. The Internet already consumes a vast amount of energy and produces a vast amount of waste. In this respect, as with other global technological systems of our times, the Internet only works because most of the world's population is excluded from using it. This poses tremendous challenges for finding ways of dealing with the digital divide.

New technological developments also call for new developments in sociological perspectives and imagination. Not only people but also technological systems, even ones we do not normally associate with communication and the Internet, will increasingly become interconnected. Our lives and the contexts in which we work and live will become ever more saturated with information which will create new demands for processing information and archiving it. Social problems and problems specifically related to the Internet will become more interconnected and complex. In meeting these challenges, sociologists will increasingly find themselves working with others across disciplines in a world acutely aware of the limitations of their expertise. In all of this, it is the sociologist's responsibility to contribute to understanding the ways in which technologies like the Internet are being used, to reflect critically on our complex world, to gain a better understanding of it, and to intervene in it the best we can.

SEE ALSO: Community and Media; Cybercrime; Cyberculture; Cybersexualities and Virtual Sexuality; Digital; Globalization, Education and; Information Society; Information Technology; Internet Medicine; Knowledge, Sociology of; Media and Globalization; Media Monopoly; Media, Network(s) and; Media and the Public Sphere; Mediated Interaction;

Multimedia; Politics and Media; Scientific Networks and Invisible Colleges; Social Movements, Participatory Democracy in; Surveillance; Technology, Science, and Culture

REFERENCES AND SUGGESTED READINGS

Castells, M. (2001) *The Internet Galaxy*. Oxford University Press, Oxford.

Donk, W. van de, Loader, B. D., & Nixon, P. (Eds.) (2003) *Cyberprotest: New Media, Citizens, and Social Movements*. Routledge, London.

Hafner, K. & Lyon, M. (1996) *Where Wizards Stay Up Late: The Origins of the Internet*. Simon & Schuster, New York.

Hamelink, C. J. (2000) *Ethics of Cyberspace*. Sage, London.

Jones, S. G. (Ed.) (1998) *Doing Internet Research: Critical Issues and Methods for Examining the Net*. Introduction by J. T. Costigan. Sage, London.

Miller, D. & Slater, D. (2000) *The Internet: An Ethnographic Approach*. Berg, Oxford and New York.

Slevin, J. (2000) *The Internet and Society*. Polity Press, Cambridge.

Tuomi, I. (2002) *Networks of Innovation: Change and Meaning in the Age of the Internet*. Oxford University Press, Oxford.

Webster, F. (2002) *Theories of the Information Society*. Routledge, London.

Wellman, B. & Haythornthwaite, C. (Eds.) (2002) *The Internet and Everyday Life*. Blackwell, Oxford.

Woolgar, S. (Ed.) (2002) *Virtual Society? Technology, Cyberbole, Reality*. Oxford University Press, Oxford.

Internet medicine

Michael Hardey

The engagement of medicine with information and communications technologies (ICTs) can be traced to the early part of the twentieth century when attempts were made to send X-ray images through the phone lines. By the 1970s, the desire to overcome the constraints distance imposed on contact between clinicians had produced a new specialist area of practice labeled "telemedicine." Since the emergence of the Internet, telemedicine has came to denote medical practices that use, for example, email, teleconferencing, and remote diagnosis. As Giddens (1991) notes, scientific disciplines in advanced modernity generate ever more subdisciplines. Consequently, specializations have emerged organized around telepsychiatry, teleneurology, teleorthopedics, medical informatics, and so forth. Despite this differentiation, a useful distinction can now be made between telemedicine and what is known as e-health. This recognizes the Internet as a key driver in the new "information age" where the "electronic" flows of information and capital form the "new economy" of the twenty-first century (Castells 2001). The prefix "e" has since become attached to activities that use the Internet to make interactive links between producers and consumers, so that together with e-commerce the category e-health has quickly become established. It can be defined sociologically as involving theoretically grounded and empirically informed attempts to understand the dynamic, emergent, and pluralistic nature of knowledge about health and illness that is mediated by the Internet. From this, four key themes that continue to frame research and debates within e-health are evident.

The first theme involves what might be termed the "quality debate," which has been significant since the initial use of the Internet to provide consumers with health information. It reflects the open, dynamic, global, and potentially anonymous nature of the media where the status of the providers of information and the veracity of material that is published may not be clear. To put it simply, the key issue in medical circles is whether information published on the Internet puts consumers at risk. Consequently, a range of organizations has emerged to provide "kite marks" which are awarded to Internet sites that only display reliable biomedical information. Such systems necessarily dismiss complementary and alternative (CAM) approaches to health that are not open to clear scientific verification.

The second theme is concerned with how individuals perceive and use information published on the Internet. Drawing on work by Anthony Giddens and others, it has been argued that people make sense of the choices that confront them in the information age through a reflexive engagement with diverse forms and sources of information. This involves the careful and rational discovery and assessment of information about health that offers to improve or shape aspects of individual lives. This highlights concerns about how medical treatments including drugs can be purchased or treatments entered into through the Internet in a way that escapes national regulations. For example, spam email advertising Viagra is widespread but there is no guarantee that the drugs purchased through ICTs will resemble those available through medical prescriptions. Similarly, how do consumers know that a doctor who offers email consultation is really what he or she purports to be? Trust is, as Parsons's (1991 [1951]) model of the sick role noted, central to the doctor–patient relationship. The third theme is therefore concerned with the way well-informed patients may transform this relationship (Hardey 1999). Reflecting broader aspects of the consumer society, the doctor–patient relationship is becoming democratized and one that is often better regarded as a partnership than an unequal encounter between expert and passive consumer.

Finally, the interactive nature of the Internet enables people to become producers as well as consumers of information. Research into newsgroups and similar peer-to-peer spaces have revealed how they are used to share information and experiences about illnesses. Whether the topic is "fatness," asthma, or any other health-related issue, it is possible to find newsgroups where individuals can post questions and offer advice to others. What has been called "wired self-help" has in effect opened up a global network of people with whom experiences can be shared that in the past was limited by sociability within geographically bound communities and families (Burrows & Nettleton 2002). There are also many web pages and blogs constructed by those who have experienced sometimes rare conditions and who want to share information in a global forum. Chronic illness may therefore not be such an isolating experience as it was in the past and people may come together to advocate new forms of treatment or call for more medical resources (Hardey 2004). Furthermore, those with "sick" bodies may leave them behind and interact on an equal basis with others in the disembodied digital domain of the Internet.

The Internet represents a challenge to established social research. Research has to capture the dynamic nature of the medium and often needs to embrace the local and global aspect of both users and the information that is published. This may involve the use of ICTs to generate data from, for example, email-based questionnaires or interactive interviews. Furthermore, the analysis of Internet resources may involve text, images, and languages other than English despite its domination of the Internet. Much work needs to be done on how CAM is represented and consumed through ICTs. The "digital divide" remains an important policy and research concern as unequal access to ICTs may further disadvantage the poor, who suffer disproportionately from chronic illness. Finally, we are only beginning to recognize how the Internet may be used to address the inequalities in health between people who live in the first and third worlds.

SEE ALSO: Complementary and Alternative Medicine; Cyberculture; Health and Culture; Health Lifestyles; Illness Behavior; Illness Experience; Illness Narrative; Internet; Medicine, Sociology of; Patient–Physician Relationship; Sick Role; Socialist Medicine

REFERENCES AND SUGGESTED READINGS

Burrows, R. & Nettleton, S. (2002) Reflexive Modernization and the Emergence of Wired Self-Help. In: Renninger, K. A. & Shumar, W. (Eds.), *Building Virtual Communities*. Cambridge University Press, New York.
Castells, M. (2001) *The Internet Galaxy*. Oxford University Press, Oxford.
Eysenbach, G., Powell, J., Kuss, O., & Sa, E. (2002) Empirical Studies Assessing the Quality of Health Information for Consumers on the World Wide Web: A Systematic Review. *JAMA* 287: 2691–2700.
Giddens, A. (1991) *Modernity and Self-Identity*. Polity Press, Cambridge.
Hardey, M. (1999) Doctor in the House: The Internet as a Source of Lay Health Knowledge and the Challenge to Expertise. *Sociology of Health and Illness* 6: 820–35.
Hardey, M. (2004) Internet et société: reconfigurations du patient et de la médecine? *Sciences sociales and santé* 22(1): 21–42.
Hardey, M. (2005) *iHealth: Health and Illness in the Information Age*. Routledge, London.
Parsons, T. (1991 [1951]) *The Social System*. London, Routledge.

interpersonal relationships

Terri L. Orbuch

In any relationship, two participants are interdependent, where the behavior of each affects the outcomes of the other. Additionally, the individuals interact with each other in a series of interactions that are interrelated and affect each other. Individuals form many different kinds of relationships with other people, some of which are intimate and close (e.g., parent–child, spouse–spouse, friendships) and others which are not intimate and close (e.g., neighbor, teacher–student). Most of the research on interpersonal relationships has focused on those relationships that are close, intimate, and have high interdependence. In an influential book, Kelley and colleagues (1983) define a close relationship as one that is strong, frequent, and with diverse interdependence that lasts over a considerable period of time. In sociology, although the classic distinction between primary and secondary relationships has been expanded in the public realm (fleeting, routinized, quasi-primary, and intimate-secondary relationships), these close relationships (as described above) also can be categorized as primary groups, which provide support and nurture and socialize individuals to the norms of society.

The concept of relationship historically has had a central and significant place in sociology. Some of the founding sociologists, such as Simmel and Marx, were concerned with attraction and interpersonal relationship issues. Even particular types of relationships and relationship processes – such as courtship, marriage, and parent–child relationships – have always been important to how and what sociologists study. For example, sociologists have been particularly interested in research on marriage and the family, specifically the structural and demographic correlates of these relations (e.g., Bernard 1972).

HISTORICAL CONTEXT

In the 1960s the initial focus of interpersonal relationship research was on the interpersonal attraction process, primarily between strangers meeting for the first time, rather than on the relationships themselves that might develop as a result of attraction. This research developed primarily out of mate-selection studies first begun by family sociologists in the 1930s and 1940s (Burgess & Cottrell 1939). Attraction typically is conceptualized as an attitude toward another consisting of feelings, cognitions, and behaviors and can be negative and/or positive in nature. Most of the early research on the interpersonal attraction process relied on self-report measures to assess the factors that lead a person (P) to be attracted to another person (O). For example, the bogus stranger paradigm (Byrne 1971) asked respondents (typically, young college students) to rate how much they were attracted to another person after being presented with minimal information about this other person. In these paradigms, respondents were actually participating in an experiment, where the information presented to respondents was manipulated, and the other persons were typically hypothetical others. Walster, Berscheid, and their colleages (e.g., Walster et al. 1966) also conducted numerous "get-acquainted interaction" studies in which real respondents were matched with each other and given the opportunity to interact, after which they self-reported their attraction to each other.

In the 1980s researchers turned their attention to the more intense sentiments and phenomena that occur within actual interpersonal relationships, and to the social context of various kinds of specific relationships. Although attraction was important, maybe even necessary for P (person) and O (other) to begin an interpersonal relationship, the majority of research started to focus on the "pulse" or quality of these interpersonal relationships and its link to processes inside (e.g., cognitions, depression, physical health) and outside (e.g., work satisfaction, financial strain, family cohesiveness) the individual. In addition, researchers began to examine the influence of factors in P (person)

(e.g., depression) and O (other) (e.g., physical attractiveness), along with the combination of those factors (P and O) (e.g., conflict, similarity) on the likelihood that P and O will stay in the relationship and are happy with it.

NEW DIRECTIONS IN RESEARCH

Even more recently, relationships have received considerable attention in sociology and the other social sciences. An examination of the research since 1980 illuminates several themes. First, an expanding and significant body of literature demonstrates that interpersonal relationships are vital and important to the physical and mental health of individuals. Studies show (House et al. 2003) that individuals are likely to suffer from depression, anxiety, ill health, and other physical problems if they lack interpersonal relationships of high quantity and quality. The interesting finding here is that quality and quantity of relationships are critical for individuals' overall health and well-being.

Second, the current research emphasizes specific relational processes that are relevant at various stages of the life course of a relationship. This literature tends to be organized according to relationship type and focuses on factors that are important to the development of a relationship (attraction, similarity, background factors), the maintenance of a relationship (communication, conflict, family interference and support), and the dissolution of a relationship (legal factors, effects on children, adjustment). There also is strong evidence to suggest that what factors predict divorce or dissolution of a relationship differ depending on the life course stage of the *relationship*. The age or life course stage of the *individual* also has been found to be relevant to what relational processes are important to individuals' evaluations of the relationship (relationship quality). Further, the recent emphasis on the life course of both relationship and individual has focused scholarly attention on the importance of making conceptual distinctions between (1) the intent to maintain a relationship (e.g., commitment) (see Johnson 1991), (2) personal evaluations within a relationship as perceived by individuals (relationship quality), and (3) the status of the relationship (relationship stability) (Veroff et al. 1997).

A third new direction in relationship research has been to concentrate on making the dyad the unit of analysis rather than the individual (Couch 1992). This change is both methodological and conceptual and has become an important contribution to the literature on relationships. Relationship scholars now find it important to collect information from both members of the dyad, rather than only one member, and assess how these reports may differentially affect the well-being and stability of the relationship (Duck 1990).

Fourth, given the prominence of symbolic interactionism in sociology (e.g., Mead 1934), another new direction of relationship research has been to apply symbolic interactionist concepts to the study of relationship well-being and stability (Burke & Cast 1997). The self is created out of the interactions and feedback from others, and the relational context is even more salient for how individuals view themselves. Further, to understand how adults define and describe themselves to others, relationship scholars turn directly to the context and status of their relationships.

The fifth new direction in relationship research has been to examine the construction of meaning within relationships for relationship quality and stability (Orbuch et al. 1993). In these studies, there is an acknowledgment that individuals may construct meanings of their relationship, based on the social context of that relationship and individual, which in turn has significant influence on individuals' evaluations and status of those relationships. Many relationship scholars now ask couples/dyads (separately or jointly) to use a narrative or account-as-stories technique to gain a better understanding of individuals' meanings of their relationship and relational processes over time (for a review, see Orbuch 1997). This technique allows individuals to have a "voice" in their reports about their relationships and permits variations in reports as a result of the "sociocultural ecology" within which the relationship is embedded. This approach also recognizes that these stories formulate, control, predict, and shape individuals' relational experiences over time.

Sixth, the larger environment and structural conditions that can be harmful or beneficial for a couple's well-being have been examined. Relationship scholars have begun to link these "sociocultural ecologies," or what sociologists term the norms, cultural meanings, settings, circumstances, or people outside the relationship, to relationship quality and stability. One specific contextual factor that has received a great deal of attention lately is social networks, or the link between the relationship and people outside the dyad. Specifically, relationship scholars have been interested in the influence of social networks of family and friends on the stability and quality of relationships (for a review, see Felmlee & Sprecher 2000). The majority of this research looks at how social networks can be a potential source of support or reduction of stress for couples, but this direct link has been challenged and revised by many (Kessler et al. 1995). The general notion that social networks are linked to the internal pulse of the relationship was first examined by Bott (1971).

Another important contextual factor that has received attention recently is the context of race/ethnicity for interpersonal relationships (McLoyd et al. 2000). Relationship scholars have begun to highlight the similarities and differences between and within various racial/ethnic groups. Recent studies find that both cultural and structural factors may affect relational processes differentially among various ethnic groups (Orbuch et al. 2002).

CONCLUSIONS AND FUTURE DIRECTIONS

The field of interpersonal relationships has a strong history and vibrant theoretical foundation in the discipline of sociology. Critical to sociological ideas and theories is the notion that individuals interact with others and that these interactions are interrelated and affect each other. Further, the topic of interpersonal relationships is the perfect arena to understand and illuminate many underlying sociological processes and concepts (e.g., development of self, culture, social networks, commitment, and emotions) that are critical to the discipline.

The study of interpersonal relationships is not yet the focus of an organized subspecialty in sociology, as it is in psychology and communication studies. Yet the research questions that have been asked about interpersonal relationships, whether in the past or present, are not inherently more psychological than sociological. It is imperative that sociologists continue to expand research on the topic of interpersonal relationships (Felmlee & Sprecher 2000). For sociologists, the list of questions is still very expansive and the research possibilities are endless.

SEE ALSO: Accounts; Divorce; Dyad/Triad; Family and Community; Friendship: Interpersonal Aspects; Interaction; Marriage

REFERENCES AND SUGGESTED READINGS

Bernard, J. (1972) *The Future of Marriage*. World, New York.

Bott, E. (1971 [1957]) *Family and Social Networks*. Tavistock, London.

Burgess, E. W. & Cottrell, L. S. (1939) *Predicting Success or Failure in Marriage*. Prentice-Hall, New York.

Burke, P. J. & Cast, A. D. (1997) Stability and Change in the Gender Identities of Newly Married Couples. *Social Psychology Quarterly* 60: 277–90.

Byrne, D. (1971) *The Attraction Paradigm*. Academic Press, New York.

Couch, C. (1992) Towards a Theory of Social Processes. *Symbolic Interactionism* 15: 117–34.

Duck, S. (1990) Out of the Frying Pan and Into the 1990s. *Journal of Social and Personal Relationships* 7(1): 5–28.

Felmlee, D. & Sprecher, S. (2000) Close Relationships and Social Psychology: Intersections and Future Paths. *Social Psychology Quarterly* 63(4): 365–76.

House, J. S., Landis, K. R., & Umberson, D. (2003) Social Psychology of Health. In: Salovey, P. & Rothman, A. J. (Eds.), *Social Relationships and Health*. Psychological Press, New York, pp. 218–26.

Johnson, M. P. (1991). Commitment to Personal Relationships. In: Jones, W. H. & Perlman, D. (Eds.), *Advances in Personal Relationships*, Vol. 3. Jessica Kingsley Publishers, London, pp. 117–43.

Kelley, H. H., Berscheid, E., Christensen, A. et al. (1983). *Close Relationships*. Freeman, New York.

Kessler, R. C., House, J. S., Anspach, R. R., & Williams, D. R. (1995) Social Psychology and Health. In: Cook, K. S., Fine, G. A., & House, J. S. (Eds.), *Sociological Perspectives on Social Psychology*. Allyn & Bacon, Boston, pp. 548–70.

Lofland, L. (1998) *The Public Realm*. Aldine de Gruyter, New York.

McLoyd, V. C., Cauce, A. M., Takeuchi, D., & Wilson, L. (2000) Marital Processes and Parental Socialization in Families of Color: A Decade in Review. *Journal of Marriage and the Family* 62: 1070–93.

Mead, G. H. (1934) *Mind, Self, and Society*. University of Chicago Press, Chicago.

Orbuch, T. L. (1997) People's Accounts Count: The Sociology of Accounts. *Annual Review of Sociology* 23: 455–78.

Orbuch, T. L., Veroff, J., Hassan, H., & Horrocks, J. (2002) Who Will Divorce: A 14-Year Longitudinal Study of Black Couples and White Couples. *Journal of Social and Personal Relationships* 19 (2): 179–202.

Orbuch, T. L., Veroff, J., & Holmberg, D. (1993) Becoming a Married Couple: The Emergence of Meaning in the First Years of Marriage. *Journal of Marriage and the Family* 55: 815–26.

Veroff, J., Young, A., & Coon, H. (1997) The Early Years of Marriage. In: Duck, S. (Ed.), *Handbook of Personal Relationships*. Wiley, New York, pp. 431–50.

Walster, E., Aronson, V., Abrahams, D., & Rottman, L. (1966) The Importance of Physical Attractiveness in Dating Behavior. *Journal of Personality and Social Psychology* 4: 508–16.

interracial unions

Alison Roberts

Interracial unions refer to romantic relationships between people of different racial categories. Generally, the term indicates married (and hence, heterosexual) status, as it is more feasible to identify and carry out social research on this population than non-married, non-cohabiting, and/or same-sex interracial couples. Sociological inquiry of racial intermarriage stems from the study of assimilation and understanding the social evolution of societies with significant immigration. Researchers employ both qualitative and quantitative methods to study interracial unions: a macro-level perspective involves examining demographic data to identify cultural patterns, and a micro-level approach focuses on the cultural meaning – derived from social interaction – of an interracial relationship to the couple and to their family, friends, and community. In recent years more attention has been devoted to the study of the identity of the offspring of interracial unions, but the study of interracial marriage remains sociologically relevant – the rate of interracial marriages can be an indicator of levels of proximity or distance across racial lines, tolerance or prejudice of different groups, and the malleability of the boundaries of racial categories. Interracial unions are studied by sociologists with an interest in racial and ethnic relations as well as those interested in the family.

Sociologists use the metaphor of the "marriage market" to analyze how people select their spouses: individuals will look for the most desirable partner they can attract given the resources available to them. This model explains why many married couples share similar characteristics such as educational background and socioeconomic status. However, individuals may compensate for any "mismatching" by providing each other with resources that the other does not possess. This status exchange hypothesis explains that members of higher-status groups could be inclined to marry members of lower-status groups if the individuals with the lower status could offer a resource to offset that lower status. In his 1941 article "Intermarriage and the Social Structure: Fact and Theory," Merton argued that racial minorities could compensate for their lower racial status with a higher socioeconomic position. Much of the research conducted on interracial marriages has focused on an exchange of racial status for socioeconomic status.

Sociologists who study racial and ethnic relations use assimilation theories to address immigrants' ability to adapt to the new environment and to integrate with other racial and ethnic groups. Milton Gordon established several stages of assimilation that explained what outcomes we can expect if immigrants adapt to and become part of their new culture. One such outcome would be marital assimilation, indicated by significant intermarriage between ethnic and racial groups. Over time, intermarriage among white, European American ethnic groups became quite commonplace, but that trend has not been replicated in the rate of interracial unions. Historical conditions such as colonialism and slavery are determinants of how interracial marriages are perceived within a society. Indeed, many states and nations legislated and enforced sanctions against interracial unions. In South Africa, interracial marriages were not entirely uncommon until the Prohibition of Mixed Marriages Act of 1949 and the Immorality Act of 1950 effectively outlawed interracial unions. Today interracial marriages remain rare occurrences even with the repeal of apartheid-induced racial laws in the late 1980s. In the United States, some states forbade interracial marriage up until 1967, when the Supreme Court overturned the last anti-miscegenation laws in the case of *Loving* v. *Virginia*.

A few trends characterize interracial marriages in the United States. Since 1967 the rate of interracial marriages has increased exponentially, and demographic trends and cultural patterns indicate that this rate will continue to increase in the same direction. However, the growing number of interracial unions does not bear out proportionately among racial groups. The amount of research on interracial marriages between blacks and whites belies the fact that these unions make up a very small percentage of interracial marriages overall. Interracial marriages among blacks remain relatively uncommon, especially when compared with the rates of interracial marriage among Asians, Latinos, and American Indians. Younger generations find interracial unions more acceptable: researchers find that interracial marriages are more common among newer immigrant groups from Asian and Latin American countries, particularly among the young, native-born population.

Qualitative analyses indicate that interracial couples face an array of challenges as a consequence of their decision to "cross the color line" in their selection of a spouse. Public opinion of interracial unions is much more favorable than it has ever been, but many people tend to be less accepting when an immediate family member chooses to date or marry interracially. Interracial couples may deal with strained relations with their families and perhaps even estrangement. They must also contend with a worldview that posits race as an essential quality, not a socially constructed element of a person's identity. They may find themselves defending their relationship in ways other couples are never called on to do. Finally, their own ideas about race may be tested – they may witness privilege and/or racism in new ways.

Research on interracial unions would be well served if the literature based on both demographic and qualitative approaches was synthesized. As new immigration patterns take shape, the world becomes more diverse, and racial boundaries continue to shift, it will be important for those studying interracial unions to employ innovative perspectives. In an increasingly global society, the field would benefit from a cross-cultural and cross-national examination of interracial unions.

SEE ALSO: Biracialism; Boundaries (Racial/Ethnic); Color Line; Endogamy; Marriage; One Drop Rule; Race

REFERENCES AND SUGGESTED READINGS

Dalmage, H. M. (2000) *Tripping on the Color Line: Black–White Multiracial Families in a Racially Diverse World.* Rutgers University Press, New Brunswick, NJ.

Fu, V. K. (2001) Racial Intermarriage Pairings. *Demography* 38(2): 147–59.

Kalmijn, M. (1993) Trends in Black/White Intermarriage. *Social Forces* 72(1): 119–46.

Kalmijn, M. (1998) Intermarriage and Homogamy: Causes, Patterns, Trends. *Annual Review of Sociology* 24: 395–412.

Lee, J. & Bean, F. D. (2004) America's Changing Color Lines: Immigration, Race/Ethnicity, and Multiracial Identification. *Annual Review of Sociology* 30: 221–42.

Moran, R. F. (2001) *Interracial Intimacy: The Regulation of Race and Romance.* University of Chicago Press, Chicago.

Qian, Z. (1997) Breaking the Racial Barriers: Variations in Interracial Marriage Between 1980 and 1990. *Demography* 34: 263–76.

Root, M. P. P. (2001) *Love's Revolution: Interracial Marriage.* Temple University Press, Philadelphia.

intersectionality

Cynthia Fabrizio Pelak

Most gender scholars agree that to understand historical and contemporary gender relations one must be attentive to how race, class, and other systems of power intersect with gender. The general consensus around intersectionality has emerged from an evolving interdisciplinary body of theory and practice that emphasizes the simultaneity of oppressions, the interlocking systems of inequalities, and the multiplicity of gendered social locations. Legal scholar Kimberlé Crenshaw (1989, 1991) was one of the first to use the term intersectionality to draw attention to the marginalization of black women's experiences within single-axis frameworks of anti-discrimination laws, feminist theories, and anti-racist politics. Sociologist Patricia Hill Collins (2000: 18) defines intersectionality as "particular forms of intersecting oppressions, for example, intersections of race and gender, or of sexuality and nation." She goes on to say: "intersectional paradigms remind us that oppression cannot be reduced to one fundamental type, and that oppressions work together in producing injustice." Intersectionality has its roots in numerous intellectual traditions, such as socialist feminism, race and ethnic studies, and postcolonial feminisms. The various identifiers of the projects in which intersectionality is central – black feminism, womanism, multiracial feminism, third world feminism, postcolonial feminism, indigenous feminism, and multicultural feminism – suggest divergent origins and analytical foci. In this entry, the term intersectionality is used to refer broadly to scholarship that uses theoretical approaches that foreground interlocking systems of inequality. Special attention is given to the contributions of scholars who were instrumental in developing the intersectionality perspective, namely black women intellectuals from North America and women of color scholars from the "third world."

An intersectionality framework is attentive to multiple levels of analyses: individual, interactional, institutional, cultural, and structural. Individuals are seen as occupying multiple and often-contradictory status positions as well as being embedded in institutional, cultural, or structural contexts that are multidimensional and fluid. By focusing on how systems of inequality are cross-cutting rather than operating in isolation from one another, intersectionality draws attention to differences among women (or among men) rather than simply differences between women and men. Beyond recognizing differences, this tradition understands systems of oppression as grounded in relational power differentials. Men's domination is thus related to (and dependent upon) women's subordination and the status of poor women of color is related to (and dependent upon) the status of affluent white women. Using a multi-lens approach or a race/gender/class approach allows researchers to understand consequential power differentials among women as well as those between women and men. Hence, this framework can help explain why women's common structural location as women is not sufficient for mobilization against gender inequalities.

Theorizing around intersectionality is directly rooted in the practical concerns of building diverse grassroots coalitions of women (and men) to fight against gender and other oppressions. Like feminist studies, the work on intersectionality did not develop in the rarefied atmosphere of academia, but among collectivities of people who sought to understand and change the systems of oppression called racism, patriarchy, and class exploitation (Collins 2000). To elucidate this framework, five basic assertions common to intersectionality approaches are identified (Baca Zinn & Thornton Dill 1996). They include the conceptualization of gender and race as structures and not simply individual traits, the rejection of an a priori assumption that women constitute a unified category, the existence of interlocking systems of inequality and oppression, the recognition of the interplay of social structure and human agency, and the necessity for historically specific, local analyses to understand interlocking inequalities.

CONCEPTUALIZATION OF GENDER AND RACE

Within intersectionality paradigms, gender and race are not simply conceptualized as a social characteristic of an individual, but are understood as structures, discourses, or sets of enduring relations that operate at multiple levels in connection with other structures, such as class, sexuality, and nationality. There is general agreement among social theorists that gender and race are social constructions rather than predetermined, transhistorical, biological or natural phenomena. The changing meanings of

gender and racial categories across time and place substantiate the fluid, social character of gender and race. Omi and Winant (1994) conceptualize race as an ever-changing complex of meanings that signifies and symbolizes sociopolitical conflicts and interests rather than a fixed, concrete, objective, or natural attribute. Likewise, scholars drawing on an intersectionality approach reject essentialist notions of gender and argue that sexed bodies do not exist outside of the social (Ferber 1998). Harding (1991: 79) explicates such a conceptualization within an intersectionality framework by claiming "there are no gender relations per se, but only gender relations as constructed by and between classes, races, and cultures."

ANALYTICAL CATEGORY OF WOMEN

Another basic assertion of gender scholars working within this framework is that the category of "women" is not assumed to be a homogeneous, unified group of individuals who experience a common oppression. The analytical category of "women" is not assumed prior to an investigation. As Mohanty et al. (1991: 58) argue, "sisterhood cannot be assumed on the basis of gender; it must be forged in concrete historical and political practice and analysis." Within an intersectionality framework, women's shared structural location as women is not sufficient for understanding their experiences of inequality.

INTERLOCKING SYSTEMS OF INEQUALITIES

A central component of intersectionality is the linkages of individual experiences with social structures. An intersectionality perspective assumes that individuals' lives are embedded within and affected by interlocking systems of inequalities, such as those based on race, gender, class, and sexuality. Individuals occupy multiple and often contradictory status positions that simultaneously advantage and disadvantage their lives. Collins (2000) identifies the interlocking systems of inequalities as a "matrix of domination," which is a model of interlocking rather than additive connections between inequalities and statuses. The notion of a matrix of domination is a criticism of the construction of binary oppositions of oppressed/oppressor or black/white; it rejects the "either/or" dichotomy while embracing a "both/and" position. Individuals can be simultaneously privileged and disadvantaged.

The notion of interlocking inequalities operates at two distinct analytical levels. At a macro level the concept refers to the connections between institutional and organizational structures of race, class, and gender. For example, the paid labor market is structured such that women of different racial and class backgrounds are differentially situated in the hierarchy of jobs. The labor market is thus simultaneously structured upon gender, race, and class hierarchies. The notion of interlocking oppressions at the micro level refers to how interactions between individuals and groups are shaped simultaneously by race, gender, and class structures. For example, the interactions between a female domestic worker and her employer are often shaped by unequal race and class statuses. At both levels of analysis, gender relations and inequalities cross-cut other systems of power rather than operating in isolation. A woman's gendered experiences are always framed in the context of her racial and class locations. Therefore, gender relations and gender inequalities are best examined simultaneously through lenses of race, class, and other systems of inequality. Using this multi-lens approach or the notion of the matrix of domination allows researchers to (1) ground scholarship on gender in the histories of racism, classism, imperialism, and nationalism; (2) highlight how status positions are relational such that positions of privilege and disadvantage are connected; and (3) understand consequential differences among women (or among men) rather than simply differences between women and men.

HUMAN AGENCY

Intersectionality also highlights the interplay between social structures and human agency. The importance of recognizing the interplay of social structures and human agency is that it allows for the possibility of social change. Scholars employing an intersectionality approach critique scholarship that overemphasizes the powerlessness of women and only represents women as victims, exploited, and dependent on men. Mohanty et al. (1991: 56), for example, criticize the research produced by western scholars that represent "third world" women as ignorant, poor, uneducated, tradition-bound, domestic, or family oriented, rather than agents of their own identity.

Intersectionality theorists tend to focus on the strategies of creative resistance that women employ to survive and thrive in oppressive situations. Social science scholarship typically focuses on overt, public political activity, while scholars drawing on intersectionality foreground the less visible politicized activities that are taken up by subordinated groups. For example, Berger's (2004) study of women of color with HIV/AIDS highlights how multiply stigmatized women develop a public voice and facilitate their political participation by drawing on resources rarely associated with political participation. Berger's work demonstrates that political resistance need not be formal or institutionalized. Collins (2000) recognizes two interdependent forms of black women's social activism: the subtle undermining of institutions through the creation of female spheres of influence within existing structures of oppression when direct confrontation is neither possible nor preferred, and the institutional transformation consisting of direct challenges in the form of trade unions, boycotts, sit-ins, marches, etc. By shifting our understanding of power relations based on a hierarchical, vertical model to a more fluid model of interrelatedness, intersectionality theorists argue that we can begin to analyze the dynamics of domination and resistance in new ways.

HISTORICALLY SPECIFIC AND LOCAL ANALYSES

The basic assumptions of intersectionality necessitate the need for historically specific, local analyses that allow for the specification of the complexities of particular modes of structured power relations. It is through such analyses that theoretical categories can be generated from within the context being analyzed. Intersectionality scholars reject universalizing and ahistorical approaches that try to explain, for example, patriarchal organization for all places at all times. The call for historically specific, local analyses also demands that researchers not impose a specific ideological or universal theoretical formula to interpret their findings. Postcolonial feminists, for example, offer a strong critique of the tendency of western feminists to interpret and judge "third world" women's activism through a western feminist or "first world" framework rather than indigenous understandings and definitions of feminist activism (Mama 1995). What is transgressive in one sociopolitical context may take on an entirely different meaning in another sociopolitical context.

Two early works that were influential in the development of an intersectionality approach are Angela Davis's book *Women, Race, and Class* *This Bridge Called My Back* (1983) edited by Moraga and Anzaldúa. Both of these texts center on the experiences of women of color to theorize differences among women and encourage alliances across racial, ethnic, class, sexual, and national boundaries. Davis (1981) addresses topics ranging from womanhood and the legacy of slavery, race and class dynamics of the early nineteenth-century women's movement in the US, rape and sexual assault, reproductive rights, and the politics of housework. Moraga and Anzaldúa (1983) grapple with the complexities of race, class, culture, homophobia, revolutionary politics, immigration, and motherhood through the voices of Chicana, black, Asian, Native, and third world women.

Another more recent exemplar of an intersectionality approach is Abby Ferber's book *White Man Falling* (1998). Ferber employs an intersectionality perspective to understand how the white supremacy movement articulates white male identity. Her analysis demonstrates that to fully appreciate the complexities of white supremacist identity one must explicate how race, gender, class, sexuality, family, religion, and nation intersect within the white supremacy movement.

The body of scholarship that builds upon insights of intersectionality is vast, diverse, and goes well beyond gender studies. Although there may be significant theoretical, methodological, and epistemological differences within this evolving interdisciplinary body of theory and practice, the thread that ties them together is the appreciation for the simultaneity of oppressions, the interlocking systems of inequalities, and the multiplicity of social locations. Even when intersectionality is not named or pioneering intersectionality scholars are not given credit for their ideas, the impact of this perspective has been deep and lasting.

SEE ALSO: Black Feminist Thought; Matrix of Domination; Multiracial Feminism; Racialized Gender; Third World and Postcolonial Feminisms/Subaltern; Womanism

REFERENCES AND SUGGESTED READINGS

Baca Zinn, M. & Thornton Dill, B. (1996) Theorizing Difference from Multiracial Feminism. *Feminist Studies* 22: 321–31.

Berger, M. T. (2004) *Workable Sisterhood: The Political Journey of Stigmatized Women with HIV/ AIDS*. Princeton University Press, Princeton.

Collins, P. H. (2000) *Black Feminist Thought: Knowledge, Consciousness, and the Politics of Empowerment*, 2nd edn. Routledge, New York.

Crenshaw, K. (1989) Demarginalizing the Intersection of Race and Sex: A Black Feminist Critique of Antidiscrimination Doctrine, Feminist Theory and Antiracist Politics. *University of Chicago Legal Forum*: 139–67.

Crenshaw, K. (1991) Mapping the Margins: Intersectionality, Identity Politics, and Violence against Women of Color. *Stanford Law Review* 43: 1241–99.

Davis, A. (1981) *Women, Race, and Class*. Random House, New York.

Ferber, A. L. (1998) *White Man Falling: Race, Gender and White Supremacy*. Rowman & Littlefield, Lanham, MD.

Harding, S. (1991) *Whose Science? Whose Knowledge? Thinking from Women's Lives*. Cornell University Press, Ithaca, NY.

Mama, A. (1995) *Beyond the Masks: Race, Gender and Subjectivity*. Routledge, London.

Mohanty, C. T., Russo, A., & Torres, L. (Eds.) (1991) *Third World Women and the Politics of Feminism*. Indiana University Press, Bloomington.

Moraga, C. & Anzaldúa, G. (Eds.) (1983) *This Bridge Called My Back: Writings by Radical Women of Color*. Kitchen Table: Women of Color Press, New York.

Omi, M. & Winant, H. (1994) *Racial Formation in the United States: From the 1960s to the 1990s*. Routledge, New York.

intersexuality

Laura M. Moore

Intersex refers to a variety of inborn conditions whereby an individual's sexual or reproductive anatomy varies from social expectations about "normal" male or female anatomy. Because the standards are arbitrary, "intersex" is not a discrete category – what counts as intersex depends upon who's counting. That said, about 1/2,000 babies is born with obvious enough differences to come to medical attention. This biological variation creates direct challenges to binary constructs of sex and gender and to the cultural institutional systems designed around assumptions that discrete sex categories naturally yield complementary gender roles and heterosexuality.

The medical treatment of intersexual infants in contemporary western cultures was first highlighted in Suzanne Kessler's (1990) publication, "The Medical Construction of Gender: Case Management of Intersexed Infants." This psychosocial theory presumes intersexuals must be normalized into one of two possible categories, male or female, so they can develop appropriate gender identities and meet society's gender role expectations. Hence, biological sex is forced to conform to socially constructed gender. Deconstruction analysis has revealed several sexist and heterosexist gender stereotypes embedded in the standard medical protocol, which prioritizes males' ability to penetrate and females' ability to procreate (Dreger 1998; Fausto-Sterling 1999). Among some gender theorists and scholars, intersexuality has become intertwined in nature versus nurture debates as well as identity politics arguments regarding the existence of an essential versus a socially constructed self (Turner 1999).

The most common surgeries performed on children with intersex conditions are removal of clitoral tissue and enlargement of the vagina. Though medical management of intersex drew the attention of media and the academy at the same time as African genital cutting, these parties have been largely unable to equate female genital cutting in Africa with clitoral surgeries in contemporary western culture (Chase 2002).

Individuals with intersex conditions entered the arena of gender and sexual identity politics with the formation of the Intersex Society of North America (ISNA) in 1993. Building on strategies employed by gender and sexual minority rights movements of the late twentieth century, ISNA members have demanded an end to cosmetic genital surgery on infants, noting the absence of empirical evidence supporting the practice and ethical, medical, and human rights concerns (Chase 2003; see also the ISNA website, www.isna.org). Sex assignment at birth has critical legal and social implications including marital rights, certain constitutional protections, military service, athletic program participation, and leadership opportunities in religious organizations. People with intersex argue the existing medical treatment protocol must be changed to reduce the shame and secrecy around their condition and to allow people with "ambiguous genitalia" the right to make their own decisions about plastic surgeries.

SEE ALSO: Gay and Lesbian Movement; Identity Politics/Relational Politics; Queer Theory; Transgender, Transvestism, and Transsexualism

REFERENCES AND SUGGESTED READINGS

Chase, C. (2002) "Cultural Practice" or "Reconstructive Surgery?": US Genital Cutting, the Intersex Movement, and Media Double Standards. In: Robertson, C. & James, S. M. (Eds.), *Genital Cutting and Transnational Sisterhood: Disputing US Polemics*. University of Illinois Press, Champaign.
Chase, C. (2003) What is the Agenda of the Intersex Patient Advocacy Movement? *Endocrinologist* 13: 240–2.
Dreger, A. D. (1998) "Ambiguous Sex" or Ambivalent Medicine? *Hastings Center Report* 28: 24–35.
Fausto-Sterling, A. (1997) How to Build a Man. In: Rosario, V. A. (Ed.), *Science and Homosexualities*. Routledge, New York.
Fausto-Sterling, A. (1999) *Sexing the Body: How Biologists Construct Sexuality*. Basic Books, New York.
Greenberg, J. (2003) Legal Aspects of Gender Assignment. *Endocrinologist* 13: 277–86.
Kessler, S. J. (1990) The Medical Construction of Gender: Case Management of Intersexed Infants.

Signs: Journal of Women in Culture and Society 16: 3–26.

Turner, S. S. (1999) Intersex Identities: Locating New Intersections of Sex and Gender. *Gender and Society* 13: 457–79.

intersubjectivity

Paul T. Munroe

Intersubjectivity refers to a shared perception of reality between or among two or more individuals. The term has been important in many aspects of sociology, from positivist and post-positivist research methods to studies of the lived experiences of individuals by ethnomethodologists and feminist scholars.

The term presupposes that we, as human beings, cannot know reality except through our own senses: sight, hearing, smell, taste, or tactile feeling. Accordingly, each individual's reality is necessarily subjective. We may extend and refine those senses through measuring devices such as telescopes, scales, cameras, and myriad other technologies, but ultimately each person's understanding of reality is individually subjective. One cannot see "blue" except through one's own senses. With social reality, we have even less certainty. It is easier to know that the sky is blue than it is to know that "James likes me."

However, most individuals also understand that we cannot change reality simply by thinking. Reality has an "obdurate" character (Turner & Boynes 2002). If one were to wake up and decide that "blue" is "yellow," it would be clear that one could not effect this change and make it real for many others. This is a duality of truths that presents a problem for people interested in studying how people live their lives; neither objectivity nor subjectivity is sufficient to explain the life experiences of the individual. Intersubjectivity is an intermediate position that sociologists use to solve this problem. We propose that the best people can, and often do, achieve is a common understanding of what is going on.

A related line of theorizing is work on the duality of agency and structure. As Giddens (1984) and Sewell (1992) argue convincingly, "actions," willed behaviors of free individuals, often follow and reproduce a given "structure," rules and patterns set in the external environment, even though actors have a choice to not do these acts. Part of what happens is that people perceive certain behaviors as normal, and if not compulsory, at least expected. Structure is thus enacted in everyday behavior. This enactment of structure could not happen without intersubjectivity.

INTERSUBJECTIVE TESTABILITY

Philosophers of science (Feigl 1953; Popper 1959) and social scientists (Cohen 1989) have used intersubjectivity, or often intersubjective testability, to discuss the day-to-day operations of a relatively successful science of human behavior. There is no way to know objectively the meaning of a particular behavior. Nor is there a way deterministically (with certainty) to predict that one process follows another every time, without fail. However, regularities do occur. Patterns of social behavior are often repeated; they can be observed to happen in similar ways in many instances, and these observations can be documented.

Since this is true, social science should be able to explain and predict, with better than chance results, the outcomes of certain situations based on some initial information and a theory of how things work. The concept of intersubjective testability is one answer to the question "how?" People in a particular field of study come to agree first on the rules of evidence. They obtain specialized training in order to be able to conduct tests of "knowledge claims" (Feigl 1953; Cohen 1989) about the regularities of patterns of behavior. Understanding is facilitated by clear definitions and precision in the theory, and by transparency in the research methods. Since the rules of evidence are agreed upon, different scientists looking at the same information can agree on its meaning. Social scientists obtain intersubjectivity on the results of a particular piece of research.

It is a value judgment on the part of people who share this view of social science that this intersubjectively tested knowledge, though short of perfectly certain or objective knowledge, is far better than many of its alternatives, such as intuition, tradition, "common sense," or guessing. Specialists trained in a certain field of science thus are and should be treated as authorities on how to evaluate knowledge claims in the field they dedicate their lives to studying. The knowledge that is generated through this rigorous process will be better and more reliable than knowledge produced through less systematic methods.

INTERSUBJECTIVITY IN EVERYDAY LIFE

In a quite different vein, phenomenologists (e.g., Schütz 1967) and ethnomethodologists (e.g., Garfinkel 1967) have used the term intersubjectivity to refer to the understandings people come to share in their everyday lives. Once again, the term presupposes that objectivity is not possible in human understanding. Here an emphasis is placed on the malleability of meaning, especially social meaning, and it is stressed that differences of subjective views are ubiquitous. Intersubjectivity in this context refers to the shared perspectives people sometimes actually achieve, and often assume they have achieved. People take for granted that reality is in fact obdurate. They may realize at times that there is no way objectively to know what is "real." But for day-to-day activity, this is treated as unimportant. People operate as if reality is knowable, as if people similar to themselves see things the same way, and that if reasonable people discuss matters, they will probably come to the same conclusions.

This assumption of intersubjectivity can become problematic when the reality of differences between people's expectations and interpretations becomes apparent. Garfinkel (1967) has pointed out that intersubjectivity is most visible, and its importance is highlighted, when it is violated. When taken-for-granted behaviors do not occur, or unexpected behaviors do occur, they call into question assumptions about reality. The resulting breakdown in intersubjectivity can be most unsettling. This line of work has led to an often repeated phrase among social constructionists that "reality is negotiated."

FEMINIST CONTRIBUTIONS TO INTERSUBJECTIVITY

Feminist scholars (see Lengermann & Niebrugge 1995) have pointed out that there are important aspects of power that are involved with intersubjectivity in interaction. Low-power actors are often required to share the perspectives of high-power actors, coming to an intersubjective agreement on "what you want, what you think, what you do." High-power actors are often afforded the right to concern themselves with "what I want, think, and need."

One kind of relation of power that qualitative researchers engage in is the interview setting. If researchers are more interested in what they want to know from their interviewees, they may miss the opportunity to learn what the interviewees want them to know. As a value statement, some qualitative researchers who wish to study human behavior from a feminist perspective claim that they should attempt to achieve an intersubjective view with their interviewees.

INTERSUBJECTIVITY IN THERAPEUTIC INTERACTIONS

Mitchell (2000) identifies four levels or modes of interaction which can be studied in a therapeutic situation: behavioral, in which relatively smooth interactions are facilitated by patterned, habitual repertoires of activities; primitive emotional, in which people's affect states transfer from one person to another – one person's anger invokes another's fear, one person's sadness makes another sad; self-oriented, in which the other person is thought of as a characteristic other in relation to the self (how does this person see me, what kind of person is this, and what is my role in this situation); and finally at the most useful and highest functioning level, intersubjectivity, in which two people are reacting in a genuine fashion to each other's conscious, willful, meaningful interactions. These modes of interaction hold much promise for the future study of interpersonal behavior in many other circumstances.

SEE ALSO: Ethnomethodology; Everyday Life; Interaction; Phenomenology; Schütz, Alfred; Structure and Agency

REFERENCES AND SUGGESTED READINGS

Cohen, B. P. (1989) *Developing Sociological Knowledge: Theory and Method*, 2nd edn. Nelson-Hall, Chicago.

Feigl, H. (1953) The Scientific Outlook: Naturalism and Humanism. In: Feigl, H. & Brodbeck, M. (Eds.), *Readings in the Philosophy of Science*. Appleton-Century-Crofts, New York.

Garfinkel, H. (1967) *Studies in Ethnomethodology*. Prentice-Hall, Englewood Cliffs, NJ.

Giddens, A. (1984) *The Constitution of Society: Outline of a Theory of Structuration*. University of California Press, Berkeley.

Lengermann, P. M. & Niebrugge, J. (1995) Intersubjectivity and Domination: A Feminist Investigation of the Sociology of Alfred Schutz. *Sociological Theory* 13(1): 25–36.

Mitchell, S. A. (2000) *Relationality: From Attachment to Intersubjectivity*. Analytic Press, Hillsdale, NJ.

Popper, K. (1959) *The Logic of Scientific Discovery*. Routledge, London.

Schegloff, E. A. (1992) Repair After the Next Turn: The Last Structurally Provided Defense of Intersubjectivity in Conversation. *American Journal of Sociology* 97(5): 1295–345.

Schütz, A. (1967) *The Phenomenology of the Social World*. Trans. G. Walsh & F. Lehnert. Northwestern University Press, Chicago.

Sewell, W. H. (1992) A Theory of Structure: Duality, Agency, and Transformation. *American Journal of Sociology* 98(1): 1–29.

Turner, J. & Boynes, D. (2002) Expectations, Need-States, and Emotional Arousal in Encounters. In: Szmatka, J., Lovaglia, M., & Wysienska, K. (Eds.), *The Growth of Social Knowledge: Theory, Simulation, and Empirical Research in Group Processes*. Praeger, Westport, pp. 97–101.

intertextuality

Matt Hills

The concept of intertextuality has been significant within a range of theoretical debates (Orr 2003). Though often assumed to be a matter of one text directly citing or quoting material from another, intertextuality has also been theorized as underpinning the general condition of textuality itself. As French structuralist Julia Kristeva (1969) argues: "Every text takes shape as a mosaic of citations." This has become a crucial concept in structuralist attacks on the authority of the author (Barthes 1977; Allen 2000). It is argued that language and textuality, as structuring systems, should form the proper objects of analysis, and not authorial agency.

Intertextuality's importance has not been restricted to structuralist debates, for it has also played a key role in definitions of the postmodern condition (Jameson 1985; Allen 2000). In Fredric Jameson's influential account, a specific type of intertextuality – thought of as a form of imitation – characterizes postmodernism: "Pastiche is . . . the imitation of a peculiar or unique style . . . but it is a neutral practice of such mimicry . . . Pastiche is blank parody" (Jameson 1985: 114). Here, intertextuality becomes an endemic social and cultural condition in postmodernism: signs, codes, and texts are subject to constant repetition, without any sense of "parody" as a critical or reflexive discourse. Instead, styles and texts are seemingly reiterated and re-represented, cut adrift from their original contexts and endlessly recombined as "pastiche."

However, this criticism lacks sociological context itself. Writers such as Collins (1989) and Lash (1990) have engaged more precisely with the sociology of "postmodern" intertextuality. Collins (1989) analyses how "intertextual arenas" operate in genre fiction, suggesting that authors and texts can position themselves in relation to their generic predecessors. Thus, texts such as detective fictions may bid for "literary" value by linking themselves to literary discourse, while others may seek deliberately to "mix" discourses, combining "High Art" and pop-cultural intertextualities so as to destabilize the cultural authority of the former, rather than simply deploying its cultural and social prestige. Moving this debate on, Lash (1990) argues that the wide-ranging intertextuality of postmodern culture may simply reflect the distinctive "cultural capital" of new middle-class groups of consumers – those who are able to spot many popular and elite cultural references. Indeed, we could go so far as to suggest that types of intertextuality carry "intertextual cultural capital" (Hills 2005): they specifically target educated, specialized, and highly media-literate audiences.

SEE ALSO: Barthes, Roland; Bourdieu, Pierre; Cultural Capital; Genre; Postmodern Culture; Postmodernism; Structuralism; Structure and Agency

REFERENCES AND SUGGESTED READINGS

Allen, G. (2000) *Intertextuality*. Routledge, London.
Barthes, R. (1977) *Image-Music-Text*. Fontana, London.
Collins, J. (1989) *Uncommon Cultures: Popular Culture and Post-Modernism*. Routledge, New York.
Hills, M. (2005) *The Pleasures of Horror*. Continuum, New York.
Jameson, F. (1985) Postmodernism and Consumer Society. In: Foster, H. (Ed.), *Postmodern Culture*. Pluto Press, London, pp. 111–25.
Kristeva, J. (1969) *Semeiotikè*. Points, Paris.
Lash, S. (1990) *Sociology of Postmodernism*. Routledge, New York.
Orr, M. (2003) *Intertextuality: Debates and Contexts*. Polity Press, Cambridge.

intervention studies

Robert F. Boruch

Intervention studies address one or more of the following five kinds of questions:

1   What is the nature and severity of problems to which an intervention is directed or may be directed, and what is the evidence of the problem?
2   How and how well is the intervention deployed, and what is the evidence for this?
3   Does the intervention work? Which intervention works better? And what is the evidence?
4   What are the cost-effect relationships among interventions, and what is the evidence?
5   What interventions work, or not, based on what cumulative evidence from repeated studies?

The phrase intervention studies is commonly used in epidemiology and medical research to refer to questions of the third kind (i.e., studies of the effects of health-related interventions). The phrase has also become common in prevention research, work on learning disabilities and behavioral disorders, and in other areas. Variations on the phrase are frequently in the context of studies of effects of interventions *other* than health-related ones. For instance, intervention studies "covers questions, posed in different academic disciplines and government agencies, that are also addressed under the rubrics of 'evaluation,' 'prevention research,' and 'randomized controlled trials'" (social experiments) (Rossi et al. 2004; see also Boruch 1997).

Questions of the third kind, on intervention effects, receive most attention then in what follows. The others are handled as precursors to or successors of this basic class of question. The interventions at issue vary with the problem's character and context. Across the social sciences, these can include *practices*, such as providing conventional welfare, police, or health services. They may include *programs* designed to provide better or more specialized services to individuals, organizations, or geopolitical jurisdictions. And at the broadest level, interventions may be construed as macro-level *policy* in welfare, environment, education, and other arenas.

In addressing the first question, on nature and severity of the problem, evidence may be generated by probability sample surveys of those people or organizations at risk, administrative records of service organizations, and ethnographic (street level) research. Each method, for instance, has been exploited to estimate the size of homeless populations in various cities, and the number and kinds of victims of crime. In health-oriented sociology and epidemiology, such studies include work to estimate incidence and prevalence of events such as injuries and survival rates. Good understanding of needs is usually a precursor to developing an intervention that could address the need, and is a precursor to testing the intervention's effects.

Theory drives the choice of what variables ought to be measured. In considering teenage pregnancy, for instance, one might focus on girls, or boys, or both, depending on one's theory about the problem or one's theoretical construal of the phenomenon in different cultures and countries.

At least for studies based on sample surveys, government statistical agencies and professional organizations have developed standards for judging the quality of the studies and their results. See, for instance, the standards enunciated by the US Census Bureau, as well as those for the UK, China, Sweden, Canada, and others.

The second question, on deployment of the intervention, falls under the rubrics of implementation studies, process research, and program monitoring, depending on the academic discipline and agency responsible for generating an evidential answer. Sociological theory might inform one's choices about what to measure and how (e.g., measuring social capital in the context of education interventions such as private versus public schools). Typically, the evidence to answer the question stems from performance indicators that permit one to judge progress of relevant agencies or the adequacy of the intervention services. Less often, the evidence may be generated through periodic surveys of clients' or customers' satisfaction with the intervention service, for instance. Anthropological studies may also be used to generate hypotheses and ideas about the character of service and delivery from the points of view of service recipients or other stakeholders in the process.

In health care, for example, studies that address the second question often aim to learn whether government or other professional guidelines for health care of the elderly (say) are operationalized in hospital or other care settings. Finding that fewer than half the guidelines are implemented well is important. Understanding whether, how, and how well particular interventions can be deployed in different settings is no easy matter. The need to understand has led to the production of systematic reviews of evidence on the topic, such as Fixsen et al. (2005), and to new peer reviewed journals such as www.implementaionsciences. com that cover new empirical work on how to deploy or not. For a new intervention, deeper questions hinge on whether it has been implemented with fidelity in a trial and how need for fidelity and need for flexibility in adaption can be balanced in larger-scale trials and in eventual deployment of the intervention beyond the trials.

The third question, on relative effects of interventions, invites attention to randomized controlled trials that produce the least equivocal evidence possible about whether one intervention is better than another or better than the ambient service or system (Boruch 1997). In these trials, individuals, organizations, or geopolitical jurisdictions are randomly assigned to each different intervention, including a control (ambient conditions). Well-run randomized trials generate a statistically unbiased effect of the interventions' relative effects and a legitimate statistical statement of one's confidence in the results. Put in other words, a trial's product is a fair comparison that takes into account chance variation in individual and institutional behavior.

In the US, for instance, randomized trials have been conducted to test the effect of programs that move poor people from high to low-poverty areas. These Moving to Opportunity trials (Gibson-Davis & Duncan 2005) include anthropological work on processes and people. Mexico's Progresa randomized trial was preceded by statistical work on severity of the school dropout problem in rural areas and informed by anthropological research on its nature and the intervention process. Villages were randomly assigned to an income support program or to control conditions to learn whether the program was effective in reducing a chronically high rate of school dropout (Parker & Teruel 2005).

Large-scale studies in which entire organizations or entities are randomly allocated to different interventions are often called cluster-randomized trials, or group randomized trials, or place-randomized trials, depending on the disciplinary context. Prevention researchers further distinguish between efficacy trials and effectiveness trials (Flay et al. 2005). Efficacy trials are well controlled and depend on experts and their collaborators to deploy an intervention in contexts that are well understood, with measures of outcome whose reliability is controlled, and so on. The effectiveness trials are mounted later, in environments that are real-world in the sense that the interventions may not be delivered as they ought to be, the measures of outcome are not as reliable, and so on. The interest in generating better evidence on effectiveness through such trials has led to the creation of specialized peer reviewed journals in which trial results and issues can be reported. These include the *Journal of Experimental Criminology* and www.trialsjournal.com.

When randomized trials are not ethical or feasible, evidence on what intervention works may be generated through quasi-experiments or through statistical model-based approaches. These are common in sociology and other social sciences. Quasi-experiments and observational studies produce more equivocal (i.e., potentially biased) estimates of effect than randomized trials.

Generally, these approaches try to approximate a randomized trial by using statistical methods to equate groups or to construct groups that are similar apart from the intervention. The methods and the independent variables used vary depending on the domain. The statistical approaches in the model-based approaches include propensity scores, selection models, structural models, instrumental variables, and other techniques that try to approximate the results of randomized trials.

Comparing the results of randomized controlled trials against quasi-experiments or observational studies on the same intervention is important for several reasons. Randomized trials ensure unbiased estimates of effect, but they are often more difficult to carry out than a quasi-experiment. The quasi-experiment may be easier to carry out, but does not provide the same level of assurance of unbiased estimates and instead relies on more assumptions. If the results of using each approach are similar, or lead to the same policy decisions, one might then opt for quasi-experiments. Empirical comparisons of the results of each suggest, however, that results often do differ and neither the magnitude nor the direction differences are predictable. The discrepancies have been explored through reviews of intervention studies in health (Deeks et al. 2003), employment and training (Glazerman et al. 2003), education and economic development (Rawlings 2005), and other areas. Identifying specific domains in which the nonrandomized intervention studies are dependable is crucial for science and for building better evidence-based policy.

Some professional societies and government organizations have developed standards for reporting based on studies of the effects of interventions. The standards have been constructed to ensure that the relevant evidence is presented completely and uniformly. In health care, for instance, the international CONSORT statement has been a model for reports on randomized controlled trials (Mohrer et al. 2001; Campbell et al. 2004). Analogous efforts have been made to ensure uniform reporting on quasi-experimental (nonrandomized) trials, notably TREND.

Standards for judging the trustworthiness of evidence from studies on the effects of interventions have also been developed. The international Society for Prevention Research, for instance, issued guidelines that distinguish between evidence on efficacy trials and effectiveness trials and also handles evidence on whether effective programs can be disseminated (Flay et al. 2005).

In education, substance abuse, and mental health, government agencies have developed systems for screening evidence from studies of the effects of the interventions. In the US, the Institute for Education Sciences put high priority on randomized trials, and put only certain quasi-experimental designs in second place. It eliminated many other study designs as a basis for dependable evidence. The Substance Abuse and Mental Health Administration (SAMSHA) sponsors the National Register of Exemplary Programs and Practices (NREPP) to assist people in identifying model programs that have been identified on the basis of quality of evidence, including randomized trials (www.modelprograms.samsha.gov). In crime and delinquency, Blueprints screens evidence and identifies model programs.

Addressing the fourth question, involving cost-effectiveness of different interventions, usually presumes evidence for answers to the first three questions. Few peer-reviewed journals that report on trustworthy studies of the effects of interventions also report on the intervention costs, however. Accountants, finance people, and economists can then add value beyond the first three questions addressed in intervention studies. Guidelines on the conduct of cost-effectiveness analyses of interventions have been developed for various substantive areas of study (National Institute of Drug Abuse 1999; on prevention and treatment, Levin & McEwan 2001; in education, Rossi et al. 2004).

The cumulation of results of studies of an intervention's effects and the analysis of this assembly of studies are important to science, of course. Systematic reviews of intervention studies of effect have developed remarkably since the 1990s. The scientific rubrics for development in this area include meta-analysis and systematic reviews, each of which emphasizes the quality of the evidence. The QUOROM Group in health research standards reports on meta-analyses of randomized trials (Moher et al. 1999). As yet, analogous guidelines have not yet been developed for the educational, social welfare, and criminological areas.

Beginning in 1993 the international Cochrane Collaboration (www.cochrane.org.) in health has led the way in generating uniform, systematic, high-quality reviews of assemblies of studies on effectiveness of interventions. The international Campbell Collaboration (www.campbellcollaboration.org.), Cochrane's younger sibling, focuses on social welfare, crime and justice, and education. The Cochrane Collaboration has produced over 1,500 systematic reviews since 1993. The topics range from effectiveness of psychosocial development interventions such as multi-systemic therapy, to summarizing efforts to manage colitis, heart disease, and other illness. Both the Cochrane Collaboration and the Campbell Collaboration have developed worldwide accessible registers of randomized trials. In this respect, the organizations compile information that addresses a variation on questions of the third kind in the context of intervention studies – What works? Or works better? – based on fair evidence.

SEE ALSO: Effect Sizes; Evaluation; Experiment; Experimental Methods; Prevention, Intervention; Structural Equation Modeling; Survey Research; Theory; Variables, Independent

REFERENCES AND SUGGESTED READINGS

Boruch, R. (1997) *Randomized Experiments*. Sage, Thousand Oaks, CA.

Campbell, M. K., Elbourne, D. E., & Altman, D. G. (2004) CONSORT Statement: Extension to Cluster Randomized Trials. *British Medical Journal* 328: 702–8.

Deeks, J. J., Dinnes, J., D'Amico, R., Sowden, A. J., Sakarovitch, C., Song, F., Petticrew, M., & Altman, D. G. (2003) Evaluating Nonrandomized Intervention Studies. *Health Technology Assessment* 7(27): 1–173.

Fixsen, D. L. et al. (2005) Implementation Research: A Synthesis of the Literature. University of South Florida, National Implementation Research Network. Online. www.nirn.fmhi.usf.edu.

Flay, B. R. et al. (2005) Standards of Evidence: Criteria for Efficacy, Effectiveness, and Dissemination. *Prevention Science* (May): 1–25.

Gibson-Davis, C. & Duncan, G. J. (2005) Qualitative/Quantitative Synergies in a Random Assignment Program Evaluation. In: Weisner, T. S. (Ed.), *Discovering Successful Pathways in Children's Development*. Sage, Thousand Oaks, CA, pp. 283–303.

Glazerman, D., Levy, D. M., & Myers, D. (2003) Nonexperimental versus Experimental Estimates of Earnings Impacts. *Annals of the American Academy of Political and Social Sciences* 589: 63–93.

Greenwood, P. W., Model, K. E., Rydell, C. P., & Chiesa, J. (1996) *Diverting Children from a Life of Crime: Measuring Costs and Benefits*. RAND Corporation, Santa Monica, CA.

Levin, H. M. & McEwan, P. J. (2001) *Cost-Effectiveness Analysis: Methods and Applications*, 2nd edn. Sage, Thousand Oaks, CA.

Mohrer, D., Schulz, K. F., & Altman, D. G. (2001) The CONSORT Statement. *Lancet* 357: 1191–204.

Mohrer, D., Cook, D., Eastwood, S., Olkin, I., Rennie, D., & Stroup, D. for the QUOROM Group (1999) Improving the Quality of Reports of Meta-Analysis of Randomized Controlled Trials: The QUORUM Statement. *Lancet* 354: 1896–900.

National Institute of Drug Abuse (1999) *Measuring and Improving Costs, Cost-Effectiveness, and Cost-Benefit for Substance Treatment Programs*. National Institutes of Health/NIDA, Washington, DC.

Parker, S. & Teruel, G. M. (2005) Randomization and Social Program Evaluation. *Annals of the American Academy of Political and Social Science* 599: 199–219.

Rawlings, L. (2005) Operational Reflections on Evaluating Development Programs. In: Pitman, G. K., Feinstein, O. N., & Ingram, G. N. (Eds.), *Evaluating Development Programs*. Transaction Books, London, pp. 193–204.

Rossi, P., Lipsey, M., & Freeman, H. (2004) *Evaluation: A Systematic Approach*, 7th edn. Sage, Thousand Oaks, CA.

interviewing, structured, unstructured, and postmodern

Andrea Fontana

Interviewing is a methodology based on asking questions in order to gain information from the respondent. The interview may be structured, unstructured, and postmodern. Structured interview seeks information with an emphasis on measurement, unstructured interview stresses understanding the world of the respondent, and postmodern interview focuses on the negotiated interaction between interviewer and respondent.

DEVELOPMENT

Interviewing first became popular in clinical diagnosing and in counseling; later, it was used in psychological testing. Charles Booth (1902–3) is credited with introducing interviewing to sociology, by embarking on a survey of social and economic conditions in London. Others followed, both in England and the US. Among the most notable early interview projects were Du Bois's (1899) study of Philadelphia and the Lynds' (1929, 1937) studies of Middletown.

During World War II the impetus of interviewing was magnified by large-scale interviews of American military personnel, some of which were directed by Samuel Stouffer and titled *The American Soldier*. In the 1950s, interviewing in the form of quantitative research moved into academia and dominated it for the next three decades. Some of the most notable proponents of this methodology were Paul Lazarsfeld and Robert K. Merton at the Bureau of Applied Social Research at Columbia University, Harry Field at the National Opinion Research Center in Denver and later in Chicago, and Rensis Likert with the Survey Research Center at the University of Michigan.

There were other developments in interviewing. Opinion polling was popularized by George Gallup; the documentary method focused on respondents' attitudes, and was initially used by W. I. Thomas and Florian Znaniecki; unstructured interviewing, often coupled with ethnographic research, was originally used by researchers at the Chicago School of sociology. Focus group interviewing moved from marketing to sociology and was employed both in quantitative and qualitative research. Oral history and creative interviewing were based on multiple, very lengthy interview sessions with the respondent. More recently, postmodern approaches have brought heightened attention to the negotiated collaboration in interviews between interviewer and respondents and the dynamics of gendered interviewing.

STRUCTURED INTERVIEWING

Telephone interviews, face-to-face interviews, and interviews associated with survey research are included in this category. Structured interviews make an effort to standardize both the instrument (the interview questions) and the interviewer. The questions posed are generally preestablished, provide a limited number of possible responses, and leave little room for variations. This approach makes it possible to numerically code each response a priori. The interviewer attempts to remain as neutral as possible and to treat each interview in exactly the same manner. The same questions are read in the same sequence to all respondents; explanations to be given to the respondents are prepared in advance by the supervisor and the interviewer should not deviate from them or try to interpret the meaning of any question. The interviewer must ensure that no one interrupts the interview or tries to answer for the respondent. The interviewer should not attempt to influence any answer or show agreement or disagreement in regard to any answers. The interviewer must never deviate from the preestablished questions and their exact wording. These efforts aim at minimizing errors and leaving little room for chance.

However, three types of problems arise in structured interviewing. Firstly, the task itself: the close-ended nature of the questions limits the breadth of the answers. Secondly, the interviewers: they do not in fact remain neutral but are influenced by the nature of the context and the variations among respondents. Additionally, the interviewers have been found to change the wording of questions. Thirdly, the respondents: there is an assumption that respondents will answer truthfully and rationally and will not let emotions or any personal agenda affect their answers.

FOCUS GROUP INTERVIEWING

Focus group interviews are basically a qualitative method; an interviewer/moderator assembles a small group of respondents in a conference room or similar setting in order to gather their collective opinions of the subject under study. The moderator directs the interaction among respondents and his or her approach can vary from very structured to completely unstructured, depending on the purpose of the interview.

Focus group interviewing originated in market research in order to collect consumers' opinions of various products. Sociologists use focus group interviewing for different purposes. Most common is to use the interview as an exploratory tool to fine-tune research topics or to pretest survey research structured questions. The interview can also be used for triangulation purposes to support and validate another method, either quantitative or qualitative. Finally, focus group interviews can be used as the sole basis of data gathering, often to elicit the respondents' recall of an event they all witnessed, such as a disaster or a celebration.

Focus group interviewers must possess skills similar to those of individual interviewers. Addressing a group, however, presents additional problems. The interviewer must ensure that all respondents are participating in the process and no one is dominating the interaction; also, the interviewer should be aware of the possibility of "group think." Focus groups are popular since they provide an alternative or addition to both qualitative and quantitative research methods and are relatively easy to assemble and fairly inexpensive.

UNSTRUCTURED INTERVIEWING

Unstructured interviewing, also called in-depth interviewing, is an open-ended methodological technique. The interviewer has a general idea about the topics of research but does not use any structured questions or formal approach to interviewing. There is no effort to ask the same questions of all respondents or to quantify the responses. The focus of this type of interviewing is to *understand* the way of life of the respondents and the meaning they themselves attribute to the events. We present three types of unstructured interviewing: traditional, oral history, and creative interviewing.

Traditional Interviewing

Traditional unstructured interviewing is often used in conjunction with ethnographic field-work and follows the same techniques. The interviewer has to *access the setting* of the group being studied, whether that be a welfare office or a massage parlor. Sometimes the study focuses on no group per se, as when studying homeless persons on the streets, and entrée must be negotiated anew with every individual. Next, the interviewer must make efforts to *understand the language and culture* of the respondents. Cultural anthropologists at times had to rely on interpreters, with perhaps disastrous misunderstanding of the cultural mores (Freeman 1983). Sociologists studying a subculture, such as physicians, also need to gain understanding of the language used. In addition, they must familiarize themselves with the cultural nuances of the group, such as not to ride a British bike while studying the Hell's Angels (Thompson 1985). *Locating an informant* is the next move. It is valuable to befriend a marginal member of the group under study with whom the interviewer can check the veracity of information being received by the others. *Gaining trust* and *establishing rapport* are next; the respondents must feel at ease and trust the interviewer or they will freeze them out, withhold information, or lie. Trust and rapport take time to achieve and are easy to lose, just by a wrong decision. Finally, the interviewer must find an inconspicuous way to collect information, ranging from debriefing oneself every night into a tape recorder to surreptitiously writing fieldnotes on toilet paper in a rest room.

This type of unstructured interviewing is still somewhat formal in its step-by-step approach and its attempt to find checks and balances in an effort to "scientize" the study. Interpreting the information received is also problematic. Since there is no close-ended questionnaire, the researcher finds there is a great deal of what often seems disconnected information and has to decide what to use and what not to use. There is also a tendency, as in structured interviewing, to view the interviewer as "invisible" while in fact who is doing the interviewing has a great influence on the interaction and results.

Oral History

Oral history is a very old approach to interviewing. It is based on lengthy, often multiple interviews with members of a specific group, such as a Native American tribe or elderly people in a chronic care facility. Its goal is to capture the daily forms of life of the group under study through the recollection of its members. Oral histories are not always published, but transcripts can be found in libraries – memories of a past waiting for someone to bring them back to life.

Creative Interviewing

Oral history straddles anthropology and sociology, while creative interviewing is more germane to sociology. Douglas (1985) coined this approach and it shares with oral history a technique based on multiple, lengthy, unstructured interviews with single respondents. Douglas's approach is more skeptical, raising doubts about the veracity of the respondents and suggesting techniques to help pry the "truth" from them. The interviewer should become close to the respondents and share with them facets of their own life in a sort of confidential quid pro quo.

POSTMODERN INTERVIEWING

Postmodern-informed researchers in both anthropology and sociology (Marcus & Fischer 1986) moved away from scientific claims about fieldwork and unstructured interviewing.

Instead, they are reflexive about the role and influence of the interviewer in their interaction with respondents. They suggest ways to minimize if not eliminate this influence, by increasing quotations from the actual, unretouched statements of the respondents. Also, postmodern interviewers use a *polyphonic* approach, using multiple voices of respondents with minimal intrusion by the interviewer. The interviewer became visible, actively drawn out in the reporting, to help inform the readers about the possible biases and gendered, social, and contextual distortions created by whomever, wherever, and whenever the interview occurred.

We present two types of postmodern informed interviewing: gendered interview and active interview.

Gendered Interviewing

There has been a pervasive tendency in traditional interviewing, whether structured or unstructured, to be paternalistic. It was not uncommon (in cultural anthropology) to give women researchers "temporary male status" to allow them to access settings and to talk to people with whom women would not otherwise be allowed to interact. The influence of gender in interviewing has been traditionally overlooked. Postmodern interviewers accuse traditional interviewers of ignoring gender differences in order to maintain the pretension of value-free and neutral research. Yet, as Denzin (1997) and other postmodern sociologists hold, interviews take place in a culturally paternalistic society where gender differences do matter.

In gendered interviews the interviewer must share herself with the respondent to gain her intimacy. Gendered interviewing is committed to maintaining the integrity of the phenomena studied and presenting the viewpoint of respondents. Yet this is not a ruse, as in creative interviewing, to get more information. Instead, the interviewer throws asunder pretenses of value neutrality and becomes an advocate for the women (or other oppressed individuals, such as African Americans or gay groups) being studied. It is reminiscent of C. W. Mills's ameliorative sociology.

Some have pointed out that there may be times when the researcher does not see things eye-to-eye with the group studied and advocacy becomes very problematic. Others have confessed that the "sharedness" between interviewer and respondent is artificial, since it is still the researcher who has the power of producing a text from the interview. Edwards and Mauthern (2002) feel that rather than pretend that differences between interviewer and respondents have been overcome, they should be pointed out, as they cannot be eliminated.

Active Interviewing

Holstein and Gubrium (1995) coined the term active interviewing to refer to the fact that interviews are actively negotiated accomplishments between the interviewer and the respondent. The two (or more) individuals actively collaborate in creating a text in a unique situation and a specific setting. According to Holstein and Gubrium, traditional interviews of all types stress too much the data gathered in the interview, regardless of how they were collected. The interviewer should also pay much closer attention to the latter, the ways in which data were collected – by whom, where, how, in what circumstances, and any other element that may have influenced the data. This approach is a very reflexive one, which rejects the notion that we merely gather data in interviews and use refined techniques to improve the quality of those data. Here the interview is a cooperative, negotiated text, created in the interaction and dependent upon it and the individuals involved.

Reporting Interviews

Postmodern interviewers are also experimenting with new modes of reporting their findings. Rather than mimicking the sparse language of science as do traditional sociologists, postmodern reports at times take the form of performances, plays, introspective recounting, and even poetry. The intent is to provide a more immediate and colorful picture for the readers, who can hopefully be more attracted to sociology and gain a better empathetic understanding

through the immediacy of the new reporting techniques.

Limits of Postmodern Interviewing

Postmodern interviewers have met with criticism from traditional interviewers. The question "but is it sociology?" has been repeatedly asked and not satisfactorily answered. Also, assuming that it is sociology, how does postmodern interviewing submit to the standard criteria of sociology, such as verifiability and replicability? Furthermore, how do sociologists judge the merits of the poetry or performance? Were these arbiters to judge them by literary standards they would fall very short; no other standards have thus far been suggested.

ELECTRONIC INTERVIEWING

A new development in interviewing is through electronic outlets, especially the Internet. Given the tremendous expansion of home computers this means of interviewing allows access to a huge population. The technique costs little and can have a very speedy response. Of course, there is no face-to-face or even voice-to-voice contact, so we are faced with a "virtual interviewing" with almost no checks and balances of who the respondent really is and the veracity of their statements. Currently, electronic interviewing tends to rely on questionnaires, but some are already exploring the world of chat rooms (Markham 1998) and delving into the fabricated realities and online lifestyles of virtual online selves.

ETHICAL ISSUES

Since the objects of inquiry in interviewing are human beings, there must be ethical considerations in their regards. All interviewers would agree to grant the respondents rights to informed consent, anonymity, and protection from harm. Much of structured and unstructured interviewing research has no stake per se in the world of the respondents, albeit at times social policy may arise from the findings of some studies. Postmodern interviewers aim for advocacy for oppressed and underserved individuals and groups whom they study, thus moving away from the traditional sociological goal of value neutrality and objectivity.

Another important ethical consideration is the relation and degree of involvement between researcher and respondents. Whyte (1943) has recently been accused (by Boelen 1992) of misrepresenting and exploiting his respondents, especially his closest informant, Doc. Having casual sexual relations with some of the respondents (as admitted by Goode 2002) certainly goes beyond the ethical involvement between interviewer and respondent.

Interviewing is a very varied methodology, but it ought to be, since human being are very complex and find themselves in a myriad of different vicissitudes. Each and every subtype of interviewing should be able to get to some kind of answer, to reach some life description from the respondents. This is the goal: not just asking questions, but being able to get answers – meaningful answers.

SEE ALSO: Ethics, Fieldwork; Ethnography; Key Informant; Methods; Postmodernism; Quantitative Methods

REFERENCES AND SUGGESTED READINGS

Boelen, W. A. M. (1992) Street Corner Society: Cornerville Revisited. *Journal of Contemporary Ethnography* 21: 11–51.

Booth, C. (1902–3) *Life and Labour of the People in London*. Macmillan, London.

Denzin, N. (1997) *Interpretive Ethnography: Ethnographic Practices for the 21st Century*. Sage, London.

Douglas, J. D. (1985) *Creative Interviewing*. Sage, Beverly Hills, CA.

Du Bois, W. E. B. (1899) *The Philadelphia Negro: A Social Study*. Ginn, Philadelphia.

Edwards, R. & Mauthern, M. (2002) Ethics and Feminist Research: Theory and Practice. In: Mauthern, M. Birch, M., Jessop, J., & Miller, T. (Eds.), *Ethics in Qualitative Research*. Sage, London, pp. 14–31.

Freeman, D. (1983) *Margaret Mead and Samoa: The Making and Unmaking of an Anthropological Myth*. Harvard University Press, Cambridge, MA.

Goode, E. (2002) Sexual Involvement and Social Research in a Fat Civil Rights Organization. *Qualitative Sociology* 25(4): 501–34.

Holstein, J. & Gubrium, J. (1995) *The Active Interview*. Sage, Thousand Oaks, CA.

Lynd, R. S. & Lynd, H. M. (1929) *Middletown: A Study in American Culture*. Harcourt, Brace, New York.

Lynd, R. S. & Lynd, H. M. (1937) *Middletown in Transition: A Study in Cultural Conflicts*. Harcourt, Brace, New York.

Marcus, G. E. & Fischer, M. M. J. (1986) *Anthropology as Cultural Critique: An Experimental Moment in the Human Sciences*. University of Chicago Press, Chicago.

Markham, A. N. (1998) *Life Online: Researching Real Experience in Virtual Space*. Alta Mira Press, Walnut Creek, CA.

Thompson, H. (1985) *Hell's Angels*. Ballantine, New York.

Whyte, W. F. (1943) *Street Corner Society: The Social Structure of an Italian Slum*. University of Chicago Press, Chicago.

intimacy

Lynn Jamieson

What is imagined by "intimacy" as a quality of relationships is often associated with particular ways of behaving (Davis 1973). Intimacy is sometimes defined narrowly to mean the familiarity resulting from close association. In this sense, domestic life across much of the life course in all societies is intimate. Living arrangements that involve sharing domestic space, a "hearth and home," the caring activities associated with bearing and raising children, and other forms of routinely giving or receiving physical care necessarily provide familiarity and privileged knowledge. Sometimes the term "intimacy" is also used even more narrowly to refer to sexual familiarity with another person. In everyday current usage, intimacy is often presumed to involve more than close association and familiarity, for example, also involving strong emotional attachments such as love. However, in both popular and academic commentaries, intimacy is increasingly understood as representing a very particular form of "closeness" and being "special" to another person founded on self-disclosure. This self-disclosing or self-expressing intimacy is characterized by knowledge and understanding of inner selves.

Privileged knowledge gained through close physical association is not a sufficient condition to ensure this type of intimacy. People living side by side can feel trapped together as strangers who know nothing of each other's inner worlds.

Studying how people generate and sustain intimacy leaves open the issue of what types of intimate relationships (sexual relationships, couple, kin, specific family relationships, friendship) are significant to people in different times and places. Popular and academic commentators of trends in affluent "western" societies make a range of claims and counterclaims about the nature of intimacy, its meaning and significance in everyday lives, and patterns of social change. These include claims that a focus on private intimacy has helped displace civic and community engagement, that individualized forms of intimacy have undermined conventional "family values," and counterclaims of heightened equality and democracy spreading from personal life to other domains.

"Self-disclosing intimacy" as an element of "good" couple, family, and, ultimately, friendship relationships has had widespread endorsement among the growing ranks of relationship experts, psychologists, psychiatrists, psychotherapists, and sexual counselors. This viewpoint was increasingly marketed and advertised in the late twentieth century through a range of cultural products advocating talking and listening, sharing your thoughts, showing your feelings to achieve and maintain a "good relationship," often privileging self-expression over more practical forms of "love and care." Advocates of "self-disclosing intimacy" claim participants in conversations of mutual self-revelation create a quality of relationship more intense than the knowing and understanding that can be gathered without such dialogue. Sexual intimacy may play a part, but for some advocates of this type of intimacy it is neither a necessary nor a sufficient condition, as an intimacy of inner selves is conceived as possible without an intimacy of bodies. However, if, as some theorists have argued, sexuality has come to be seen in western cultures as expressive of the very essence of the self, then sexual familiarity inevitably enhances the intimacy generated by verbal self-disclosures.

Academics across a range of disciplines have provided metacommentary on this cultural turn to "self-disclosing intimacy," generating both pessimistic and optimistic analysis of changes in intimate relationships. An influential optimistic analysis was produced by British sociologist Anthony Giddens in *The Transformation of Intimacy* (1992). Giddens argued that a qualitative shift in intimacy began to occur in the late twentieth century. In this period, the faster pace of social change and heightened awareness of risk and uncertainty meant that conventional ways of doing things, including "being a family" and constructing gender and sexual identities, were increasingly open to reworking, as people became more self-conscious of being makers of their own "narrative-of-the-self." In this climate, Giddens argued, people increasingly sought "self-disclosing intimacy" to anchor themselves in one or more particularly intense personal relationships. Relationships became more fragile, only lasting as long as they provided mutual satisfaction, but they were also potentially more satisfactory, equal, and democratic. Sex was no longer harnessed to set scripts; instead couples negotiated their own rules of sexual conduct on a "what-we-enjoy" basis. Although people continued to choose long-term intimate relationships, including marriage-like relationships and parenting relationships, diversity in styles of personal life inevitably also blossomed.

There has been continued discussion of whether and why women's relationships appear to involve more "self-disclosing intimacy" than men's (Duncombe & Marsden 1995). Some psychological and psychoanalytic accounts map this to the function of mothering and mother–child relationships. Historically produced gendered cultural discourses, together with inequalities in social constraints and opportunities, are also widely cited in the literature. Similarly, there are discussions of differences by social class, ethnicity, age, and life course stage in patterns of intimacy. Giddens suggested that women, and particularly lesbians and young women, were at the vanguard of his alleged transformation of intimacy: women because previous conventions and social conditions have made them more skilled at "doing intimacy"; women in same-sex relationships because they are less constrained by any prior script that suggests a particular division of labor; and young women because they have the most to gain in more equal and democratic relationships. The work of some feminist commentators has suggested that Giddens has underestimated the persistence of gender inequality (Jamieson 1999) and the ideological strength of a conventional heterosexual culture (Berlant 1997). Berlant argued in her analysis of US culture that the ideologies and institutions of heterosexual intimacy have provided support to a reactionary status quo by encouraging citizens to take refuge from the confusions of capitalism and politics. However, Giddens's argument also finds support among those who believe they are identifying a growing number of instances of people constructing intimate relationships outside of the "heteronorm" (Roseneil & Budgeon 2004).

Whereas Giddens's account suggested that cultural emphasis on "disclosing intimacy" is matched by positive social change in the everyday lives of men and women, there are many more pessimistic visions of what is happening to intimacy in this period of "postmodernity." According to a number of academic commentators, either intimacy has become attenuated (rather than more intense) or its intensity is of little social worth. Unrestrained market forces and mass consumer cultures are accused of promoting a self-obsessive, self-isolating, or competitive individualism which renders people incapable of sustaining meaningful intimate relationships. As one commentator puts it, concern to be sincere and responsible is replaced with worry about being true to one's self (Misztal 2000). Social scientists from a range of contexts have developed variations of this argument, sometimes in tandem with debate about "social capital" and concern that private intimacy supplants or undermines "community." Well-known examples include Bauman (2003) and Sennett (1998). This is also a longstanding subtheme in the work of Hochschild (2003; see also Bellah et al. 1985).

High rates of relationship breakdown, the associated disruption of wider social networks, and concerns, particularly in Europe and North America, about juggling family and work clearly do indicate strains in intimate life. However, detailed research on how people conduct specific intimate relationships commonly identifies strenuous efforts to create "good relationships" and to put children and "family" first, although generally it is women who continue to play the larger part in sustaining these intimate relationships. Much of the empirical research demonstrates neither self-obsession nor the primacy of "self-disclosing intimacy." In a review of research on couple relationships, sexual relationships, parent–child relationships, and friendship relationships, Jamieson (1998) concluded that the evidence demonstrated a wider repertoire of intimacy than "disclosing intimacy." The relationships people described as "good" relationships were often neither equal nor democratic. Moreover, equal relationships were sustained by more than "disclosing intimacy." For example, couples who had worked hard to have fair divisions of labor typically negotiated mutual practical care that did more to sustain their sense of intimacy than self-disclosure. As Vogler asserts, perhaps "not all intimacies are affairs of the self" (2000: 48; see also Holland et al. 2003). This is not, however, to deny the significance of "self-disclosing intimacy" in popular culture, or its discursive power to influence everyday perceptions of how to do intimacy.

SEE ALSO: Couples Living Apart Together; Heterosexuality; Inequalities in Marriage; Intimate Union Formation and Dissolution; Lesbian and Gay Families; Love and Commitment; Marriage

REFERENCES AND SUGGESTED READINGS

Bauman, Z. (2003) *Liquid Love: On the Frailty of Human Bonds*. Polity Press, Cambridge.

Bellah, R. N., Madsen, R., Sullivan, W. M., Swidler, A., & Tipton, S. M. (1985) *Habits of the Heart: Individualism and Commitment in American Life*. University of California Press, Berkeley.

Berlant, L. (1997) *The Queen of America Goes to Washington City: Essays on Sex and Citizenship*. Duke University Press, Durham, NC.

Davis, M. (1973) *Intimate Relations*. Free Press, New York.

Duncombe, J. & Marsden, D. (1995) "Workaholics" and "Whingeing Women": Theorizing Intimacy and Emotion Work – The Last Frontier of Gender Inequality? *Sociological Review* 43: 150–69.

Giddens, A. (1992) *The Transformation of Intimacy*. Polity Press, Cambridge.

Hochschild, A. (2003) *The Commercialization of Intimate Life: Notes from Home and Work*. University of California Press, Berkeley.

Holland, J., Weeks, J., & Gillies, V. (2003) Families, Intimacy, and Social Capital. *Social Policy and Society* 2: 339–48.

Jamieson, L. (1998) *Intimacy: Personal Relationships in Modern Societies*. Polity Press, Cambridge.

Jamieson, L. (1999) Intimacy Transformed: A Critical Look at the Pure Relationship. *Sociology* 33: 477–94.

Misztal, B. (2000) *Informality: Social Theory and Contemporary Practice*. Routledge, New York.

Roseneil, S. & Budgeon, S. (2004) Cultures of Intimacy and Care Beyond the Family: Personal Life and Social Change in the Early Twenty-First Century. *Current Sociology* 52: 135–59.

Sennett, R. (1998) *The Corrosion of Character: The Personal Consequences of Work in the New Capitalism*. London, Norton.

Vogler, C. (2000) Sex and Talk. In: Berlant, L. (Ed.), *Intimacy*. University of Chicago Press, Chicago, pp. 48–85.

intimate union formation and dissolution

Judith A. Seltzer

Ten years ago studies of couple relationships emphasized marriage formation and dissolution (both separation and divorce). Marriage is still the dominant heterosexual couple relationship, but increases in rates of nonmarital cohabitation, the growing recognition of couple relationships between individuals who do not live together, sometimes called LAT (Living Apart Together) couples, and same-sex unions have broadened the area of inquiry to include these other unions as well. A benefit of the broader perspective is that it allows for comparisons between marriage and less institutionalized relationships, such as cohabitation, to assess effects of social context and laws on couples' well-being.

Research on unions often distinguishes between unions as private, intimate relationships and unions as public phenomena that are a result of laws, policies, and social norms about the rights and obligations of members of the couple. Examples of the latter are tax policies and inheritance laws that treat married couples differently than unmarried couples who live together. The public nature of unions is also evident in attitude surveys that show general agreement about a gendered division of labor within marriage. The distinction between private and public unions is less useful than might appear at first. Private aspects of couples' relationships are, at least in part, a function of the laws, policies, norms, and economic organization of the public world. For instance, the relative wages of men and women may affect the timing of marriage and the kind of person someone marries. Social norms affect how husbands and wives divide household labor and childcare. Policies that change how difficult it is to divorce may also alter the quality of relationships within marriage. When divorce is less costly, spouses invest less in their relationship and pursue more of their own interests than when divorce is more difficult.

TRENDS

The US has seen an increase in the age at which couples marry. In 2003, half of US men were married by the time they reached age 27.1, an increase since 1970 of nearly 4 years. For women, the increase in median age at marriage to 25.3 was even greater, 4.4 years (US Bureau of the Census 2004). During this period, sex outside of marriage became more acceptable, rates of marital separation and divorce rose and then stabilized at high rates, and nonmarital cohabitation became much more common before and after marriage. By the late 1990s about half of first marriages ended in separation or divorce (some who end marriages do not formally divorce); and over half of first marriages were preceded by cohabitation. The probability of marital dissolution has been relatively stable for the past 20 years, although crude divorce rates have stabilized and even declined slightly for some subgroups. Late marriage and high divorce rates do not mean that individuals have stopped pairing off. Individuals still form couples and live together outside of marriage. Although rates of cohabitation have continued to rise, the increase in cohabitation has not compensated for the rise in age at marriage. That is, rates of union formation, where unions include marriage and nonmarital cohabitation, are still lower today despite the increase in cohabitation.

Within the US there are substantial class and race/ethnic differences in rates of union formation and dissolution. Men and women who have more secure economic prospects are more likely to marry than those who are economically disadvantaged. African Americans are much less likely to marry than are whites. This race difference cannot be explained fully by racial differences in economic characteristics. Marital dissolution is also more common among those with less education and among African Americans, as compared to whites. These disparities in separation and divorce appear to be widening over time.

Trends in union formation and dissolution in Western European countries are similar in several ways to those in the US. Age at marriage has risen and nonmarital unions, sometimes called consensual unions, have become increasingly common since the 1970s. Rates of divorce have also increased in most European countries. The combination of delayed or nonmarriage, increasing consensual unions, and high rates of marital instability support the claim that marriage has become less attractive compared to alternative arrangements.

ECONOMIC AND CULTURAL EXPLANATIONS

There are two broad categories of explanations for these trends and differentials: cultural change and changes in economic opportunities. Cultural explanations argue that changes in unions occurred because of a broad shift toward individualistic and egalitarian values. Some trace this ideological shift to the Protestant Reformation, while others identify a qualitative change toward the middle of the twentieth century, sometimes called the Second Demographic Transition. The rise in individualism fostered investment in personal goals which sometimes conflicted with marital goals, and resulted in delayed marriage and increases in marital dissolution. At the same time, a growing concern with equality between women and men fostered increases in women's education and labor force participation, contributing to declines in the number of children couples have. Without the

responsibility for children, individual spouses have less investment in their marriage and find divorce less costly. The driving force in these explanations, however, is changes in values.

Economic explanations for changes in marriage emphasize the rise in opportunities for wage labor, expansion of educational opportunities, and the relative wages of women and men. These theories argue that marriage and other unions are the result of cost-benefit calculations about whether the benefits of being married (or divorced) are greater than alternatives, such as being single or cohabiting. Delayed marriage and higher rates of marital dissolution occur because women have greater economic independence outside of marriage than they had earlier in the twentieth century. This interpretation derives from the "new home economics" theory advanced by Gary Becker and is consistent with Talcott Parsons's view of the family in which there are gains to specialization in marriage. In these theories, both husband and wife are better off when one (typically the husband), who has higher earning potential, specializes in market work and the other (typically the wife) specializes in housework and childcare. When women's earning potential increases, the gains to marriage are relatively smaller, and divorce rates rise.

Empirical evidence for the theories emphasizing women's economic opportunities is mixed. Several patterns suggest this explanation cannot on its own account for trends and differentials in union formation and dissolution. For example, US women with higher education and earnings are more likely to marry than women with lower earning potential. Education also reduces women's chances of divorce in the US. There is also some evidence that the education disparity in rates of marital dissolution has increased recently.

A second variant of economic interpretations focuses on men's economic prospects and security. According to this view, marriage in western societies has long been an economic arrangement, a prerequisite for which was that the couple must have sufficient economic resources to live independently from their parents. Even today, men's economic resources and potential earnings are an important predictor of marriage. In this view, marriage is delayed or foregone when men have difficulty establishing themselves in the labor market and earning a family wage, that is, among those who are less educated and minority group members. New research in this area, however, suggests that for recent cohorts both women's and men's earning potentials affect who marries and the kind of person they marry.

Although cultural and economic explanations for changes in unions are often posited as competing interpretations, efforts to compare them typically demonstrate that neither is sufficient on its own to explain either temporal or cross-sectional variation in union patterns. It is more likely that both ideological and economic factors contributed to changes in the formation and dissolution of marriage.

PRIVATE RELATIONSHIPS AND THE MARRIAGE MARKET

In the US the popular notion of finding a spouse is that two people fall in love and then marry. That marriage depends on more than love is evident from data on assortative mating, or the extent to which spouses resemble each other on social and demographic characteristics. Husbands and wives are very likely to have the same racial identification. They are also likely to be similar in the amount of schooling they have completed. In addition, spouses are likely to come from similar religious backgrounds, but religious intermarriage has been increasing in the US. Couples who are cohabiting are somewhat less homogamous or similar than married couples. This is probably in part because cohabitation is a period when individuals are evaluating whether or not they are a good match for each other, and in part because the social norms about what constitutes an appropriate marriage partner are different from those governing other unions. Members of cohabiting couples who are more similar have a greater likelihood of marrying. Marriages between more similar spouses are also more stable and less likely to end in divorce.

Similarities between spouses' or partners' characteristics are the result of a matching process in which each person seeks the best partner who will also have him or her. Social scientists sometimes describe the process of spouse selection as a marriage market. This analogy assumes that spouses find each other through an exchange process. The actors in marriage markets differ across cultures. Although in the US the potential spouses themselves are the primary actors, in some cultures matches are formed by kin groups seeking alliances with each other for political reasons or to protect property, and in other settings parents themselves or a third-party matchmaker bring a couple together.

Marriage markets also differ in the characteristics considered desirable in a potential spouse. For instance, in a secular society in which technical skills are highly valued, finding a highly educated spouse may be more important than marrying someone who is of the same religion. In the US, religious homogamy has declined at the same time educational homogamy has increased. There may also be gender differences in the characteristics desired in a spouse. If the roles of husband and wife differ, as in the Parsonian breadwinner–homemaker model of middle-class marriage, then the marital division of labor dictates that men with higher earning potential and women who are attractive and emotionally supportive would be highly sought after on the marriage market. Men's attractiveness and women's earning potential would be relatively less important compared to the characteristics that help fulfill the gendered role requirements of marriage.

Finally, marriage markets are also constrained by formal rules about who is an appropriate marriage partner (e.g., whether or not first cousins are allowed to marry; and whether racial intermarriage was permitted under previous US state laws governing marriage). Informal aspects of social organization also affect marriage market outcomes. Daily interaction between persons of the same race or education level in neighborhoods, schools, and work settings increases the likelihood of homogamous unions. By choosing where to live or where to send their children to school, families indirectly affect children's later decisions about whom to marry.

DELAY IN MARRIAGE AS AN EXTENDED SEARCH FOR A SPOUSE

Finding a spouse takes longer when it is unclear whether or not potential spouses have the desired characteristics. Physical appearance is easy to observe at a young age, but signs that someone will have a successful career or earn a lot of money are not apparent until individuals are older and have finished school and started working. That age is correlated with characteristics that matter on the marriage market is an insight that can be used to interpret the trend in age at marriage for US women and men. In the mid-twentieth century both women and men married at younger ages than they do today, in part because men completed schooling earlier and entered paid work at younger ages, thus revealing their potential as a breadwinner at younger ages. With the growth in demand for more highly educated workers, determining whether a potential husband would be a good economic provider takes longer as men (and women) stay in school longer and delay the age at which they marry. At the same time, the women's movement and improvements in women's economic opportunities increased the value to potential husbands of wives' earning potential. Uncertainty about women's economic potential when they are young also contributes to the rise in age at marriage, and probably accounts for the even greater rate of increase in women's age at marriage than men's. Much, but not all, of the delay in marriage in the US is compensated for by the increase in cohabitation before marriage. Living together before marriage is one way that couples learn more about whether a potential partner would be an appropriate spouse, even if couples do not consciously decide to cohabit as a step on the way to marriage.

Even with late marriage, there is still uncertainty about whether a potential spouse is a good match. Individuals change after marriage, sometimes in ways that make them more compatible and sometimes in ways that are unexpected. When individuals change in ways that are not anticipated (e.g., if a person is wrong about what kind of person their spouse will become or if one of the partners loses a job) these unexpected disruptions may increase the chance that the marriage will dissolve. The rise in US divorce rates in the 1960s and 1970s might be explained by unanticipated changes in spouses' expectations about each other's gender-role obligations in marriage associated with the women's movement and women's greater labor market opportunities and by decreasing costs of dissolving unsatisfactory matches.

FUTURE RESEARCH

Many theories about the formation and dissolution of intimate unions claim that unions depend on individuals' assessments of the relative benefits of being in the relationship as compared to an alternative. When cohabitation is rare, it is likely that the alternative to marriage is being single. When cohabitation is more widely accepted, there may be two alternatives to marriage: being single or cohabiting. New research should investigate the conditions that affect the alternatives individuals weigh in deciding whether, when, and with whom to form (or dissolve) a union.

Another productive area for new research is how individuals form expectations about potential partners' future characteristics (e.g., whether they will be good economic providers or good parents). It is especially important to learn more about the role of uncertainty in making decisions about unions and the degree to which individuals actually think of themselves as making a decision.

The challenge of designing studies that fully take into account the range of potential partners who might form a union, that is, the full marriage market, is a longstanding problem in studies of union formation and dissolution. Research that considers only unions or matches that have already been formed excludes important information about the alternatives or failed matches.

Finally, research on unions typically assumes that the partners or spouses co-reside, and that when the union dissolves, the partners no longer live together. Co-residence is important, but it is not the only dimension of intimacy and enduring ties that matters for couple relationships. Couples who are deeply committed to each other and their relationship may live apart (LAT relationships), and those who live together may not think of themselves as being in an enduring or satisfying relationship. Learning more about the continuum of relationships and the conditions under which they involve co-residence will shed new light on the meaning and effects of contemporary unions.

SEE ALSO: Cohabitation; Couples Living Apart Together; Divorce; Family Demography;

Marriage; Same-Sex Marriage/Civil Unions; Second Demographic Transition

REFERENCES AND SUGGESTED READINGS

Black, D., Gates, G., Sanders, S., & Taylor, L. (2000) Demographics of the Gay and Lesbian Population in the United States: Evidence from Available Systematic Data Sources. *Demography* 37: 139–54.

Bramlett, M. D. & Mosher, W. D. (2002) Cohabitation, Marriage, Divorce, and Remarriage in the United States. National Center for Health Statistics, *Vital Health Statistics* 23(22). Online. www.cdc.gov/nchs/data/series/sr_23/sr23_022.pdf.

Casper, L. M. & Bianchi, S. M. (2002) Continuity and Change in the American Family. Sage, Thousand Oaks, CA.

Kalmijn, M. (1998) Intermarriage and Homogamy: Causes, Patterns, Trends. *Annual Review of Sociology* 24: 395–421.

Oppenheimer, V. K. (1988) A Theory of Marriage Timing. *American Journal of Sociology* 94: 563–91.

Oppenheimer, V. K. (1997) Women's Employment and the Gain to Marriage: The Specialization and Trading Model. *Annual Review of Sociology* 23: 431–53.

Parsons, T. (1964 [1949, 1954]) The Kinship System of the Contemporary United States. In: *Essays in Sociological Theory*. Free Press, Glencoe, IL.

Raley, R. K. & Bumpass, L. (2003) The Topography of the Divorce Plateau: Levels and Trends in Union Stability in the United States after 1980. *Demographic Research* 8: 246–59.

Schoenmaeckers, R. C. & Lodewijckx, E. (1999) Demographic Behavior in Europe: Some Results from FFS Country Reports and Suggestions for Further Research. *European Journal of Population* 15: 207–40.

Seltzer, J. A. (2004) Cohabitation and Family Change. In: Coleman, M. & Ganong, L. H. (Eds.), *Handbook of Contemporary families: Considering the Past, Contemplating the Future*. Sage, Thousand Oaks, CA, pp. 57–78.

Sweeney, M. M. & Cancian, M. (2004) The Changing Importance of White Women's Economic Prospects for Assortative Mating. *Journal of Marriage and Family* 66: 1015–28.

Thornton, A. & Young-DeMarco, L. (2001) Four Decades of Trends in Attitudes Toward Family Issues in the United States: The 1960s through the 1990s. *Journal of Marriage and Family* 63: 1009–37.

US Bureau of the Census (2004) Estimated Median Age at First Marriage by Sex, 1890–Present. Online. www.census.gov/population/socdemo/hh-fam/tabMS-2.pdf.

Waite, L. J., Bachrach, C., Hindin, M., Thomson, E., & Thornton, A. (Eds.) (2000) The Ties That Bind: Perspectives on Marriage and Cohabitation. Aldine de Gruyter, Hawthorne, NY.

Weiss, Y. (1997) The Formation and Dissolution of Families: Why Marry? Who Marries Whom? And What Happens Upon Divorce. In: Rosenzweig, M. R. & Stark, O. (Eds.), *Handbook of Population and Family Economics*, Vol. 1a. Elsevier, Amsterdam, pp. 81–123.

invasion–succession

Barrett A. Lee

Invasion-succession (hereafter IS) has enjoyed considerable popularity among social scientists as a framework for understanding community change. In its simplest form, IS refers to the replacement of one population group or land use by another within a particular geographical environment. Due to mounting awareness of the complexities surrounding the process of change, however, the IS model no longer occupies the status of conventional wisdom that it did throughout much of the last century.

The historical roots of IS can be traced to the work of sociologists at the University of Chicago in the 1920s and 1930s. Borrowing ideas from plant and animal ecology, Park (1952), McKenzie (1968), and their colleagues stressed unfettered competition for valued resources (such as a desirable location or housing) as the driving force behind IS. Competition was believed to spur a natural, orderly, and irreversible transition from an equilibrium stage dominated by the incumbent group to a new equilibrium dominated by the "invading" group. According to the Chicago sociologists, the notion of passage through a sequence of stages could be helpful for depicting social change along multiple dimensions – demographic, cultural, economic – and across settings ranging from the local to the global.

Despite the Chicago School's broad view, the scope of IS has narrowed substantially over subsequent decades of empirical usage. Well before

World War II, IS research had already begun to focus on residential phenomena, including the settlement patterns of ethnic immigrants and shifts in community socioeconomic status. The meaning of IS became even more restricted after 1950. Studies by the Duncans (1957) and the Taeubers (1969) applied the term to a specific type of change in neighborhood racial composition: from white to African American occupancy. These studies defined additional stages (e.g., penetration, consolidation) in the IS process and spelled out the population dynamics that could produce an increase in the percentage of black residents. They also identified the conditions under which IS was likely to occur.

Many investigations conducted from the 1950s through the 1970s emphasized the pace and inevitability of white-to-black transition. Racial change was thought to proceed at a gradual rate until the representation of African Americans in an area reached some vague "tipping point." Once the area tipped, whites were deemed more likely to move out, leaving vacancies to be filled by black home-seekers eager for better housing and neighborhoods. The result of such "white flight" was accelerated change and, ultimately, resegregation. Put differently, this common version of the IS model precludes stable integration, black-to-white change, or other racial residential outcomes.

Recent scholarship has challenged the model on several fronts. One weakness is its overly descriptive character: IS predicts what should happen to a community over time but fails to explain why. In response to this weakness, students of racial change have devoted increased attention to decision-making – by both households and institutional actors – as an important explanatory mechanism (Hartmann 1993). Shifting racial composition can be seen as the cumulation of numerous household-level decisions to move out of, stay put in, or move into a given neighborhood. These decisions involve more than the ability to compete successfully for residential position, as implied by the IS model. Household members may take into account their own racial preferences, how they think residents from other racial groups will respond to them, perceived correlates of a neighborhood's racial mix (safety, school quality,

property values, etc.), and what kind of future they anticipate for the neighborhood.

Household decision-making is further influenced by a wide range of institutions ignored in IS research. Those institutional actors participating directly in the housing market tend to be key. Real estate agents, for example, have used "blockbusting" tactics to encourage panic selling on the part of white homeowners, speeding white-to-black change (Gotham 2002). Current evidence indicates that African Americans continue to receive less information and assistance from agents at all stages of the home-seeking process and are "steered" to certain types of areas (Yinger 1995). Lenders and insurers have also been shown to engage in discriminatory behavior. Similarly, local government policies and the efforts of residents' associations can constrain or facilitate household mobility decisions and thus modify the process of racial transition.

Beyond its explanatory deficiencies, the IS model seems out of step with certain kinds of community change. Gentrification, occasionally labeled "reverse" succession, offers a case in point. Since the 1970s, middle-class renovation of older housing in inner-city areas has typically been accompanied by an increasing (rather than decreasing) percentage of white residents and upward (rather than downward) socioeconomic movement. Another trend, the rise of multi-ethnic neighborhoods, defies the two-group logic of IS. With Latino and Asian populations growing rapidly across the metropolitan US, new trajectories of change are pushing more neighborhoods in the direction of greater diversity while reducing the number of all-white and all-black areas (Fasenfest et al. 2004). The IS prediction that African Americans will completely replace whites once they enter a neighborhood is less accurate now than in the past.

Multi-ethnic patterns of change highlight the significance of the larger context in which neighborhoods are embedded. Immigration policies and flows at the national level fuel these patterns, disproportionately affecting neighborhoods in "gateway" metropolises such as Los Angeles and New York. Variation across metropolitan settings in housing construction activity can have consequences for neighborhood change as well. When new housing units are occupied, the older vacated units become available, stimulating moves by members of different groups into and out of established residential areas in domino-like fashion.

The IS model appears to have worked best when a distinctive set of forces – notably, pervasive discrimination against an expanding African American population – made selected neighborhoods in Midwestern and Northeastern cities vulnerable to dramatic white-to-black transitions. In hindsight, the historical- and place-specific nature of the model is apparent. So are more fundamental shortcomings. To fully comprehend how communities evolve, one must be able to explain differences in the direction, pace, and magnitude of change on several dimensions, including but not limited to racial-ethnic composition. An adequate explanation must also incorporate causal factors operating at the social psychological, household, institutional, and contextual levels. In its most common form, IS fails to satisfy these criteria.

SEE ALSO: Blockbusting; Chicago School; Gentrification; Park, Robert E. and Burgess, Ernest W.; Redlining; Restrictive Covenants; Steering, Racial Real Estate; Urban Ecology

REFERENCES AND SUGGESTED READINGS

Duncan, O. D. & Duncan, B. (1957) *The Negro Population of Chicago: A Study of Residential Succession*. University of Chicago Press, Chicago.

Fasenfest, D., Booza, J., & Metzger, K. (2004) Living Together: A New Look at Racial and Ethnic Integration in Metropolitan Neighborhoods, 1990–2000. *Center on Urban and Metropolitan Policy, Living Cities Census Series*. Brookings Institution, Washington, DC.

Gotham, K. F. (2002) Beyond Invasion and Succession: School Segregation, Real Estate Blockbusting, and the Political Economy of Neighborhood Racial Transition. *City and Community* 1: 83–111.

Hartmann, D. J. (1993) Neighborhood Succession: Theory and Patterns. In: Hutchison, R. (Ed.), *Research in Urban Sociology*, Vol. 3. JAI Press, Greenwich, CT, pp. 59–81.

McKenzie, R. D. (1968) *On Human Ecology: Selected Writings*. University of Chicago Press, Chicago.

Park, R. E. (1952) *Human Communities: The City and Human Ecology*. Free Press, Glencoe, IL.

Taeuber, K. E. & Taeuber, A. F. (1969) *Negroes in Cities: Residential Segregation and Neighborhood Change*. Atheneum, New York.

Yinger, J. (1995) *Closed Doors, Opportunities Lost: The Continuing Costs of Housing Discrimination*. Russell Sage Foundation, New York.

investigative poetics

Stephen Hartnett

In his Beat-inflected manifesto, *Investigative Poetry*, Edward Sanders (1976) argued that "the essence of investigative poetry" is to create "lines of lyric beauty [that] descend from data clusters," hence both seducing and empowering readers with "a melodic blizzard of data-fragments." As illustrated in *America*, his epic collection of data-fragment-strewn poems, Sanders (2000) hoped to merge poetry with the pedagogical imperative to teach his readers their national history and the political goal of empowering them to re-enliven the great traditions of activism and artistry celebrated in his poems. By interweaving the emotional power of poetry with the pedagogical power of historical scholarship and the political power of fighting for social justice, Sanders's *America* embodies the theory explored in his *Investigative Poetry*, thus providing a model for writing layered, historically dense, yet beautiful, political poems (Bernstein 1990; Monroe 1996; Hartnett & Engels 2005).

While Sanders's version of investigative poetry is focused on US national history, other practitioners of the art have sought to write in a comparative, international mode. For example, Carolyn Forché's *The Country Between Us* (1981) shuttles between the US and El Salvador, where she was both witness to and participant in the nasty wars launched by presidents Reagan and Carter against supposed leftists. Peter Dale Scott's *Coming to Jakarta: A Poem about Terror* (1988) fulfills a similar role, oscillating back and forth between US political intrigue and the CIA-sponsored coup that brought Suharto to power in Indonesia and that led in 1965 and 1966 to the killing of half a million alleged communists (Blum 1995). For both Forché and Scott, witnesses propelled to chronicle terrible acts of violence while still honoring the aesthetic joys of poetry, investigative poetry can say what cannot otherwise be said, it can cut through stultifying genre expectations to interlace personal horror and historical fact, first-hand reports and philosophical flights of fancy.

Investigative poetry is more than just the expression of front-line reporting in poetic forms, however, for the works cited above by Sanders, Forché, and Scott also offer compelling meditations on the role of poetry as a survival mechanism in an age of mass-produced terror (Hartnett 1999; Kaplan 2006). As argued by Terrence Des Pres (1986) in a roundtable discussion on the possibilities of political poetry, "we turn where we can for sustenance, and some of us take poetry seriously in exactly this way," as a daily practice of making meaning. From this perspective, investigative poetry offers not only a creative vehicle for offering political criticism, but also a heuristic model of *how to live*, of how to take a critical stance against what Des Pres calls "empires in endless conflict" while not giving in to despair or quietude, all the while maintaining a daily commitment to producing art (see Hartnett 2003).

For example, after chronicling the horrors of the US-aided genocide in Indonesia, the closing section of Scott's *Coming to Jakarta* advises readers to cherish the small moments that make each day precious:

As for those of us
who are lucky enough
not to sit hypnotized
our hands on the steering wheel
which seems to have detached itself
from the speeding vehicle
it is our job to say
relax trust
spend more time with your children
things can only go
a little better
if you do not hang on so hard.

For Scott, investigative poetry includes ventures not only into international intrigue and bloody political crises, but also into the micrological mechanics of daily life. This inward turn is framed, of course, as part of a political response to empire, as an experiment in living an ethical life in the shadow of so much plenty earned largely through the mass-produced pain of so many others (Scott 1992, 2000; Hartnett 2006).

Whereas Sanders's work concerns US history, and whereas Forché's and Scott's contributions explore international political intrigue, a third major strand of investigative poetry includes work clumped loosely around a notion of ethnographic or anthropological poetry. Of the early practitioners of this genre, Jerome Rothenberg and Gary Snyder are perhaps the best known. The term *ethnopoetics* was coined in 1967 by Jerome Rothenberg and Dennis Tedlock and gained prominence via the work of *Alcheringa*, a magazine Rothenberg and Tedlock founded in 1970 (Statement of Intention 1970). Merging a fascination with premodern and developing cultures with a stinging rebuke of western modernity, ethnopoetics offered ecologically sensitive, culturally comparativist poems full of both wonder and anger (Rothenberg & Rothenberg 1983; Prattis 1985; Rothenberg 1990).

For example, Snyder's *Turtle Island* (1974) moves from a celebration of the Anasazi, a Native American tribe living in the sun-drenched Southwest, to "The Call of the Wild," a bitter poem attacking "All these Americans up in special cities in the sky / Dumping poisons and explosives." Published amid the war in Vietnam, this clear reference to the saturation bombings sanctioned by President Nixon invites readers to think about the deep historical connections among Indian genocide, environmental destruction, and the butchery under way in the name of defeating communism. By thinking in this multi-temporal manner, by holding the Anasazi and the Vietnamese in one's mind at the same time, Snyder gains historical and political leverage for his claim in "Tomorrow's Song" that "The USA slowly lost its mandate / in the middle and later twentieth century / it never gave the mountains and rivers, / trees and animals, / a vote. / all the people turned away from it." Reading these lines in light of another set of US-triggered wars in Afghanistan and Iraq, one is struck by the commonsensical argument that there is an intimate relation between the violence used to demolish nature and the violence used to murder our fellow humans. Indeed, in the face of the well-oiled machinery of death that slaughtered the Indians, that murdered millions of Vietnamese, that leveled Afghanistan and Iraq, and that has left a worldwide trail of ecological destruction in its path, one is struck by how relevant and powerful this poem feels 32 years after its first publication.

A fourth strain of investigative poetry builds upon the early work of ethnopoetics, yet infuses it with a stronger sense of anthropological depth. For example, consider Ivan Brady's masterful *The Time at Darwin's Reef* (2003). Whereas the ethnopoets mentioned above dabbled in studies of ancient and other non-western cultures – sometimes veering close to what could be called nostalgia or naïve Orientalism – Brady is an accomplished anthropologist who has studied Pacific Island cultures for over 25 years, meaning Brady's poems bristle with a lifetime of research and personal experience. As evidence of the book's remarkably broad sense of time and place, *Darwin's Reef* closes with an alphabetical "Place List" and a chronological "Date List," both of which include information relevant to the other. For example, the Place List begins with "Abaiang Island, February 14, 1840," closes with "USMCRD, San Diego, California, August 27, 1958," and includes 60 other place/time entries sandwiched in between. Readers recognize from glancing through the Place List and Date List that *Darwin's Reef* addresses the long history of naval conquest, beginning for the purposes of this book in the South Pacific during the 1840s, culminating in the world's largest floating arms depot, San Diego, during the late 1950s, and wreaking havoc on all the places in between. The Place List and Date List thus function as semiotic machines of imaginative yet historically grounded suggestions, producing juxtapositions, layerings, and clues meant to lead the reader on geographic and temporal journeys through the wreckage of colonialism (see Brady 2000).

As in Snyder's *Turtle Island*, "Time" at Darwin's Reef is less linear than in traditional historical writings and more like the twisting, reverberating, ecological, and even spiritual forms it often takes in folklore. For example, in the poem that names the book, "The Time at Darwin's Reef" – located with the place and date listings that preface each poem as "Playa de la Muerte, South Pacific, July 4, 1969" – Brady conveys time as "High Time, 1:05 p.m.,

Fiji time" (local clock time), as "Time to Get Down" (from the Cessna flying overhead), as "Island Time" (the deep ecological time of natural change), as "Copy Time in the coral" (the movements of coral reproduction as seen in "ejaculating rocks"), as "Magic Time," and so on, in a dizzying multiplication of possible times, most of them rooted not in western notions of clocks, but rather in the natural temporal forms of tides, seasons, and life cycles. Taken together, these layered "times" indicate a spiritual sense of completeness, of multiplicities woven into an organic whole, of ecological centeredness.

Lest readers assume that Brady's gorgeous experiments in temporal confusions lapse into political complacency, "Proem for the Queen of Spain" layers such temporal dislocations against spatial and political fragments, hence creating a sense of bitter poetic judgment. The bulk of the piece is a letter (fictional but true to its historical moment) from Fernando Junipero Dominguez, written in "New Spain" (Mexico) in 1539, in which the writer thanks the queen for bringing to his people "the Embrace of the Mission and the Love of God, Amen." The letter demonstrates how colonized peoples internalized oppression, in this case in the form of bowing to a foreign god brought to the New World by a foreign empire. The endmatter following the poem provides multiple historical references on the history of Dominguez, so the poem fulfills the pedagogical function of both seducing readers to think historically and then leading them to the necessary information to pursue their own further readings. Tucked within the letter, however, Brady offers expletive-laced commands from US troops who shout at Vietnamese peasants: "Nam fuckin' xuong dat! Lie the fuck down! Or y'all gonna fuckin' die!" Much like Snyder's juxtaposing of the Anasazi against Nixon's saturation bombing of Vietnamese peasants, Brady's insertion of dialogue from US soldiers within a 1539 letter to the queen of Spain illustrates a sense of continuity linking the Spanish invasion of Mexico to the US invasion of Vietnam. Against the deeply satisfying ecological times of "Time at Darwin's Reef," then, "Proem for the Queen of Spain" offers a chilling sense of *imperial time*, of the looping repetitive horrors of conquest.

Although attempts to define a genre are doomed to failure and inevitably invite a cascade of counter-arguments, refutations, and modifications, readings of Sanders, Forché, Scott, Rothenberg, Snyder, and Brady suggest that investigative poetry exhibits these characteristics:

- An attempt to supplement poetic imagery with evidence won through scholarly research, with the hope that merging art and archive makes our poetry more worldly and our politics more personal.

- An attempt to use reference matter not only to support political arguments but also as a tool to provide readers with additional information and empowerment.

- An attempt to problematize the self by studying the complex interactions among individuals and their political contexts, hence witnessing both the fracturing of the self and the deep implication of the author in the cultural and political systems that he or she examines.

- An attempt to problematize politics by witnessing the ways social structures are embodied as lived experience, hence adding to political criticism ethnographic, phenomenological, and existential components.

- An attempt to situate these questions about self and society within larger historical narratives, thereby offering poems that function as genealogical critiques of power.

- An attempt to produce poems that take a multi-perspectival approach, not by celebrating or criticizing one or two voices but by building a constellation of multiple voices in conversation.

- A deep faith in the power of commitment, meaning that to write an investigative poetry of witness the poet must put himself or herself in harm's way and function not only as an observer of political crises but also as a participant in them.

SEE ALSO: Anti-War and Peace Movements; Autoethnography; Buddhism; Capitalism; Class, Perceptions of; Class, Status, and Power; Collective Trauma; Colonialism (Neocolonialism); Crime, Corporate; Ethnography; Personal is Political; Poetics, Social Science; Time

REFERENCES AND SUGGESTED READINGS

Bernstein, C. (Ed.) (1990) *The Politics of Poetic Form: Poetry and Public Policy*. Roof, New York.

Blum, W. (1995) *Killing Hope: US Military and CIA Interventions since World War II*. Common Courage, Monroe, ME.

Brady, I. (2000) Anthropological Poetics. In: Denzin, N. & Lincoln, Y. (Eds.), *Handbook of Qualitative Research*, 2nd edn. Sage, Thousand Oaks, CA, pp. 949–79.

Brady, I. (2003) *The Time at Darwin's Reef: Poetic Explorations in Anthropology and History*. Alta Mira Press, Walnut Creek, CA.

Des Pres, T. (1986) Poetry and Politics. *Tri Quarterly* 65: 17–29.

Forché, C. (1981) *The Country Between Us*. Perennial, New York.

Hartnett, S. J. (1999) Four Meditations on the Search for Grace Amidst Terror. *Text and Performance Quarterly* 19: 196–216.

Hartnett, S. J. (2003) *Incarceration Nation: Investigative Prison Poems of Hope and Terror*. Alta Mira Press, Walnut Creek, CA.

Hartnett, S. J. (2006) "You Are Fit for Something Better": Communicating Hope in Anti-War Activism. In: Frey, L. (Ed.), *Communication Activism*. Erlbaum, Mahwah, NJ.

Hartnett, S. J. & Engels, J. (2005) "Aria in Time of War": Investigative Poetry and the Politics of Witnessing. In: Denzin, N. & Lincoln, Y. (Eds.), *The Handbook of Qualitative Enquiry*, 3rd edn. Sage, Thousand Oaks, CA, pp. 1043–67.

Jones, R. (Ed.) (1985) *Poetry and Politics: An Anthology of Essays*. Quill, New York.

Kaplan, B. A. (2006) *Unwanted Beauty: Aesthetic Pleasure in Holocaust Representation*. University of Illinois Press, Champaign.

Monroe, J. (Ed.) (1996) Poetry, Community, Movement. Special issue of *Diacritics* 26(3 & 4).

Prattis, J. I. (Ed.) (1985) *Reflections: The Anthropological Muse*. American Anthropological Association, Washington, DC.

Rothenberg, J. (1990) Ethnopoetics and Politics/The Politics of Ethnopoetics. In: Bernstein, C. (Ed.), *The Politics of Poetic Form: Poetry and Public Policy*. Roof, New York, pp. 1–22.

Rothenberg, J. & Rothenberg, D. (Eds.) (1983) *Symposium of the Whole: A Range of Discourse Toward an Ethnopoetics*. University of California Press, Berkeley.

Sanders, E. (1976) *Investigative Poetry*. City Lights, San Francisco.

Sanders, E. (2000) *America: A History in Verse*. Vol. 1: *1900–1939*. Black Sparrow, Santa Rosa, CA.

Scott, P. D. (1988) *Coming to Jakarta: A Poem About Terror*. New Directions, New York.

Scott, P. D. (1992) *Listening to the Candle: A Poem on Impulse*. New Directions, New York.

Scott, P. D. (2000) *Minding the Darkness: A Poem for the Year 2000*. New Directions, New York.

Snyder, G. (1974) *Turtle Island*. New Directions, New York.

Statement of Intention (1970) *Alcheringa/Ethnopoetics* 1(1): 1.

Islam

Khaled Fouad Allam

The birth of Islam coincided with radical change in the anthropological and sociocultural situation of Arab populations which, in about the seventh century CE, had already been affected by strong social tensions and by a number of important religious upheavals. If pre-Islamic societies are generally to be considered as polytheistic, the presence, since the beginnings of Islam, of important Christian and Hebrew communities must not be understated and from which elements of the Koran are taken. This "new" religion, Islam – whose etymology means "peace" but also "submission" in the sense of humankind's devotion to God's word – not only changed the extant religious language, but also deeply modified the social and anthropological structures of the peoples of the Arab peninsula. In analyzing the structures of Islamic societies it is clear how such an event resulted from the demand for change in a social universe – the tribal and clanic world – which claimed to be structured differently from the extant one, and which was crossed by deep tensions and crises.

According to Islamic tradition, God chose a man, Mohammad, who through the angel Gabriel's revelation (or *tanzil*, which means Word descent) would become God's messenger and prophet. The God of Abraham reveals definitively in the Word, the recitation of which corresponds to the term *Qur'an* in Arabic, the language that, according to the Koran, God chose because of its "clarity." This point represents an essential element in the definition of Islamic identity: the new religious conscience of Islam involves a linguistic and semantic specificity represented by the Arab language. In this way, signs and symbols define the whole religious universe of Islam and they are the foundations of Islamic dogma, the *I'gaz al-qur'an* (the inimitability of the Koran): "If all the humans and all the Jinns banded together in order to produce a Qur'an like this, they could never produce anything like it, no matter how much assistance they lent one another" (Koran, Surah XVII, verse 88).

The notion of inimitability refers to the notions of fascination and amazement: the divine language interrogates man, as the creator asks him to witness the eternity of his mystery (*gaib*) and the mystery of creation. An essential element of Islamic theology is the mystery behind the revelation of God, who does not allow man to attain such knowledge. Divine revelation in Islam is inseparable from "God's messenger" or *rasul*, Mohammad's path, which is divided into two phases, each corresponding to a collection of Surahs (chapters) of the Koran. The first phase, from the beginning of the revelation until 622, is called the Meccan period: it reflects the image of a solitary man, marginalized from Meccan society because of the revelation. The Meccan Surahs of this first period deal with a deeply spiritual, eschatological Islam – an Islam which could be referred to as being an interior Islam. In the second period, from 622 to 632, a change in the function of the Koran's message occurs: Islam appears and develops in Medina, where the first Muslim community is born and where individual religious identity becomes collective. The cycle of the revelation continues in Medina and the Prophet Mohammad dies in 632, leaving a society in the making.

The Koran's text, composed of 114 Surahs, is present in the memory of the Prophet's companions (the first four caliphs) and in the community's memory, but it is not yet structured, given that their culture is based on oral traditions and not the written word. This explains the reason for the great disagreements behind the authenticity of some verses and forms of transliteration. In fact, any passage which passes from oral to written form creates a filter that has consequences for an orally revealed religion.

The present text of the Koran, comprising 114 chapters, was codified during the age of caliph Utman (d. 656). His decision to arrive at a definitive version of the text intended to stop the violent polemics which the two different approaches to text created, due to the diverging views on Islam and its social structure. Sources for the contention were founded on issues of Arabic grammar. Two schools arose: the Bassora school and the Baghdad school. This implied two different ways to expound the revealed Word: one more closed, the other more open. Utman, to avoid disputes, opted for the more conservative system.

In the Koran, the order of chapters does not follow the chronological sequence of their revelation. Except for the first Surah, *Al Fatiha* ("the opening") that is Meccan, all the initial Surahs are from the Medina period, in that they essentially define the social organization of Islam and its ethical and juridical principles. Some scholars affirm that the historical sequence of the Surahs is inverted because they have been ordered beginning with the longer ones and ending with the shorter ones. Others affirm that this has to be interpreted as an accent on the Medina Surahs – those that refer to a specificity of Islam, the primacy of the community over the individual, a primacy that is historically defined in Medina and becomes the social archetype of the Muslim world.

In effect, Islamic identity is founded not only on the historically defined experience of the Medina community, but also, and essentially, on the prophetic function. The Prophet Muhammad embodies two roles in Islam. He is the messenger of God, whose Word he receives to transmit to the community, and he also represents the image of the perfect man (*insan kamil*), symbol of charismatic authority that is expressed through history, and therefore in a social construction consequent to the sacred experience of revelation. He is the archetype, the model which should inspire every Muslim community.

The first historical experience of Islam is that of Medina: it represents the collective memory for the entire Muslim world. In this way history becomes tradition (*Sunna*) and creates an individual and collective model for the whole community. From the outset, this passage in history involves a structural crux: if an initial historical experience is to be reproduced perpetually, Islam can no longer be empowered by history. Therefore, with the death of its

Prophet, profound disagreements arose regarding Islam's developments throughout history; the controversy between Sunnis and Shiites has its roots in the function of the Prophet. For the Sunnis, the cycle of prophecy concludes definitively with Muhammad's death. To subscribe to a historical perspective means to reproduce the founding elements of Islam, the categories and the interpretive patterns elaborated by the Prophet, since they are considered sufficient to preserve the social and religious elements of a community.

For the Shiites, on the contrary, the cycle of prophecy does not end, but continues throughout history. Islam has to be experienced permanently, in order to preserve a vital link between the sacred and the historical experience of its community. In the Shiite tradition, such continuity is made possible by prophetic descent, by the genealogical filiations which have their beginnings with Ali, cousin and son-in-law of the Prophet: in fact, the Shiite *faith-witness* mentions Muhammad alongside Ali.

These deep differences in the interpretive grid configure the Islamic universe into different dimensions and into contrasting anthropological and juridical patterns. In Islam, two perceptions of the connection between society and religious identity have developed. They correspond to different ways of interpreting the concept of authority. For the Shiites, the collective memory of Islam is kept alive, since the prophetic descent ensures the continuity of interpretation. The caliph is the principal figure of authority because it is he who maintains the interpretation of the Koran; the prophetic tradition does not conclude with the death of Muhammad, but it is continually enriched through the succession of the *imam*s, interpreters of Islam in its historical development. For the Sunnis, on the contrary, the historical cycle of interpretation concludes with the death of the Prophet in 632; Muslim society disposes of a definitively fixed pattern that can and must only repeat itself in following cycles of history.

Such deep disagreements produced a political and a theological divorce, since – according to the Shiite perspective – the caliphate had been usurped by the Sunnis. While Sunni Islamic theology is based upon a series of dogmas, Shiite Islamic theology is founded on the combination of the spiritual dimension and its achievement in history. While for the Shiites there is an uninterrupted investment in history with the sacred, for the Sunnis these two areas are distinct from one another and are always susceptible to conflict. For example, radical Islamism springs from the refusal of a historical investment in the interpretation of the Koran.

Sociologically, Sunni Islamism adapted to the cultural and cognitive contexts of the different peoples it encountered within its history, through the formulation of a legal system and not of a theology. Up to the present there are four schools of juridical interpretation: the Malikite, the Hanbalite, the Hanafite, and the Shafiite. Each of them extends over a wide area of the Muslim world. For example, the Malikite school is present in the Maghreb region and the Hanbalite school extends over the Middle West area (Mashreq), whereas the Hanbalite and Shafiite schools are in the areas of the so-called peripheral Islam (Central Asia, the Balkans, the Indian subcontinent, etc). Not only do these schools differ from each other in their juridical characteristics, but each of them also defines a specific approach to the Koran's exegetics, since each adopts a particular speculative methodology about the juridical corpus, varying from maximalist to minimalist interpretations.

There are four methods of reasoning in the formulation of the law in Sunni Islamism: *igma* (consent); *qiyas* (analogy); *ray* (personal opinion); and *igtihad* (interpretation), which provides an essentially closed praxis. The identity of a Sunni Muslim is not only founded upon the Koran and the prophetic tradition, but also upon his belonging to a certain juridical school which conditions his whole existence, from birth to death, through rites and religious praxis.

From the late Middle Ages, the European approach to Islam has been functional to the relation between religious identity and territory. The expansion of Islam in the Mediterranean basin has been interpreted in terms of competition between two patterns of medieval intelligibility, that is to say in terms of the different conceptions of truth, connected to revelation in the two sacred texts (the Koran and the Christian gospels). Intellectual and theological debates attempted to ascertain which of them held the truth.

Until the beginning of the twentieth century the interpreting grid of the Islamic phenomenon was based upon the more relevant historical events or changes. The birth of a wide Islamic empire in the heart of the Mediterranean has been the object of various interpretations, in particular the thesis of two prominent historians, the medievalist Henri Pirenne and the founder of the *Annales* school, Fernand Braudel. Pirenne affirmed that what distinguishes Islam from Christianity – and what corresponds to Islam's strategy of conquering new territories – is that Islam never integrates into other cultures, but always remains unchanged. Studying the texts of the Councils in Muslim Spain, Pirenne points out that the church had to translate its Latin texts into Arabic because Arabic was so widespread. His explanation is that the Muslim conquest implied an extension of its religious and sociocultural pattern. Pirenne places this specificity of Islam in opposition with the conquest of the Germans who, on the contrary, integrated and embraced the linguistic, cultural, and religious patterns of the people they conquered and who converted therefore to Christianity. Pirenne considers the fact that Islam never integrates a specificity of the religion, because he maintains that Muslim identity has a territorial character: Islam exists anywhere Muslims live.

The *Annales* school reflects a more complex position, in which religious matters are defined on the basis of material relations. From this point of view, the expansion of Middle Age empires has to be interpreted in relation to the exchange of goods and the control of maritime routes, which determines the logic of power and rule. If this logic is maintained until a certain date, then this is a consequence of the material, that is, economic characteristics of the period. In effect, the decline of the Muslim world historically coincides with the loss of control of the new trade routes. This happened in the sixteenth century, when trade moved from the Mediterranean to the Atlantic. In this case religious identity just seals the means of production and the consequent power relations of the period.

The nineteenth century and the first half of the twentieth saw the development of orientalism. This doctrine is considered as constitutive of a phenomenology of Islamic elements, such as the corpus of founding texts, the production of Muslim jurisprudence, the Arab language and its idioms, and the literature and the history of great dynasties. But orientalism certainly lacked the material history of the Muslim world, providing for it a series of interpreting grids, in the same way that the historical method did in the development of the western world. In fact, in Islam's historiography, the lack of a history of peoples is evident, since a history of dynasties and power has prevailed.

The conceptual frame of orientalism that provided a comprehensive and organic picture of Islam gradually crumbled in the face of the felt necessity to decodify those societies into a structural approach. A new approach to these societies was shaped in the field of social and cultural anthropology, where in fact more relevant methodological changes appeared. In the 1950s scholars like Jacques Berque, Jean-Paul Charnay, Germaine Tillon, and Clifford Geertz opened a new approach to Islam through structuralist research. They analyzed the kinship system and local economies; they conducted sociolinguistic studies of dialects; they began to analyze production in the Muslim world and its relations with territory. In this way they got over the issues that blocked these societies into rigid and decontextualized frames.

During the last few decades the consequences of decolonization together with the phenomenon of acculturation in Muslim countries have amplified the crisis and the re-Islamization of society, through the forming of religious parties and of a symbolic universe reintroducing religious order in socialization processes (veils for women, beards for men, etc.). Political science and sociology have analyzed all these changes. The phenomenon of Islamic terrorism, the geopolitical changes consequent to the Afghan crisis and the two Gulf wars, together with the question of the development of an Islamic Diaspora, both in the USA and in Europe, have raised the question of a public space for Islam in democratic western societies.

The role of sociologists and political analysts has therefore become relevant in providing a comprehensive frame for the great changes in Islam's progress. For example, scholars underline the deep fracture (*fitna*) afflicting contemporary Islam, dividing those who embrace a close relation between Islam and political order, and those who embrace a change of Islam in private life. The works of Gilles Kepel, Olivier Roy, and Jocelyne Cesari tend to demonstrate the complexity of the changes and conflicts in progress in Islam and in its relations with the West.

A multi-disciplinary approach to Islam in the social sciences gives an account of the present complexities and of the phenomena still in progress within Muslim societies. Such an approach is shared by many Muslim scholars, such as the anthropologist Abdellah Hamoudi, the philosopher Mohammed Arkoun, the political analyst Ghassan Salamé, the sociologist Leila Babès, and the historians Abdessalam Cheddadi and Abdellah Laroui. In all these studies the traits of contemporary Muslim societies are evident in the relationship between reality and change. Scholars have to face the difficulty of formulating appropriate interpreting grids to describe an ever changing reality. In studying and analyzing reality there is always a risk of using analytical frames which are surpassed by the constant transformation of reality, and of not having a conceptual frame that can account for reality and change.

The doctrine of orientalism has undergone a crisis because it fixed a method of study of those societies which did not take into consideration their transformation. Today, in the social sciences, the risk persists of fixing an immutable frame for Muslim societies by affirming that "Islam is . . ." The wording should probably be changed from Islam to Muslims, that is to say, those who live Islam.

The prospects for research on Islam and Muslim societies involve more than a shift towards field analyses, starting by singling out groups and segments of society, since collective identity tends today to shift toward individual identity. All this is related to the new forms of organization and structure of Muslim societies. What needs to be defined today is the Islamic Diaspora and Islamic nationalism, and what are the political procedures structuring Islam into political patterns like those of Morocco or Turkey. What should be analyzed is the crisis that is political Islam, as in Algeria. Finally, the crisis of contemporary Islam should be evaluated, in which the central questions troubling the Muslim world are the construction of a democratic space and the acknowledgment of human rights – the rights of the individual and religious freedom. Studying these questions society by society and country by country, the social sciences could provide a new framework that emphasizes the magnitude of the crisis, but also the significance of the changes that Islamic societies are already undergoing.

SEE ALSO: *'Asabiyya*; Fundamentalism; Islamic Sexual Culture; Khaldun, Ibn; Orientalism; Religion

REFERENCES AND SUGGESTED READINGS

Allam, K. F. (2002) *L'Islam globale*. RCS Libri, Milan.

Arkoun, M. (1970) *Comment lire le Coran?* Introduction to *Le Coran*. Garnier-Flammarion, Paris.

Arkoun, M. (1984) *Pour une critique de la raison islamique* (For a Criticism of Islamic Reason). Maisonneuve et Larose, Paris.

Association pour l'Avancement des Études Islamiques (1982) *Discours, écriture et société dans le monde islamique contemporain* (Speech, Writing and Society in Islamic Contemporary World). Actes du Colloque tenu au Collège de France à Paris le 4 et 5 février 1977. Paris.

Benkheira, M. H. (1997) *L'Amour de la Loi. Essai sur la normativité en islam* (Law's Sake: Essay on Normativeness in Islam). PUF, Paris.

Berque, J. (1991) *Relire le Coran* (To Reread the Koran). Albin Michel, Paris.

Charnay, J.-P. (1994) *Sociologie réligieuse de l'Islam* (Religious Sociology of Islam). Hachette, Paris.

Cheddadi, A. (2002) Introduction. In: Ibn Khaldun, *Le Livre des Exemples* (Book of Examples). Gallimard, Paris.

Chouémi, M. (1966) *Le Verbe dans le Coran* (The Verb in the Koran), n.VI – série 3: Études et Documents. *Études Arabes et Islamiques*. Librairie C. Klincksieck, Paris.

Filali-Ansary, A. (2001) La démocratie a-t-elle un avenir dans les pays du sud? (Has Democracy a Future in Southern Countries?). *Prologues – Revue maghrébine du livre*, 22–3 (Autumn).

Geertz, C. (1968) *Islam Observed*. Yale University Press, New Haven.

Gellner, E. (1981) *Muslim Society*. Cambridge University Press, Cambridge.

Hamès, C. (1987) La Filiation généalogique (nasab) dans la société d'Ibn Khaldun (The Genealogical Filiation (Nasab) in Ibn Khaldun Society).

L'Homme 102(27), École des Hautes Études en Sciences Sociales, Paris.

Hourani, A., Khoury, P. S., & Wilson, M. C. (Eds.) (2004) *The Modern Middle East*. I. B. Tauris, New York.

Kepel, G. & Richard, Y. (1990) *Intellectuels et militants de l'Islam contemporain* (Intellectuals and Militants of Modern Islam). Seuil, Paris.

Lapidus, I. M. (1988) *A History of Islamic Societies*. Cambridge University Press, Cambridge.

Laroui, A. (1999) *Islam et Histoire. Essai d'epistémologie* (Islam and History: Essay of Epistemology). Albin Michel, Paris.

Peters, R. (1979) *Islam and Colonialism: The Doctrine of Jihad in Modern History*. Mouton, The Hague.

Rodinson, M. (1980) *La Fascination de l'Islam* (Enchantment of Islam). Maspero, Paris.

Said, E. (1978) *Orientalism*. Routledge & Kegan Paul, London.

Islamic sexual culture

Hammed Shahidian

Delineating criteria for "Islamic sexuality" appears impossible because there exist no uniform codes for sexual behavior or relations. There are in fact many Islamic *sexualities*. Even so, one may deduce certain (relative) constants in sexual ideology. Islam considers sexual desire a natural aspect of human relationship and dissociates sexuality from guilt. In the Qur'an, just as plants and animals are created "in pairs, two and two" (13:3), humans are created with a mate. Several Qur'ânic verses (2:183–7; 4:1; 53:45) refer to mating as a divine design for making a harmonious family, a microcosm of the society wherein people can lead a peaceful life. Thus, sexuality in Islam is in nature heterosexual, with women being men's "tilth"; men are instructed to enter their "fields" as they please (2:223). Islamic sexuality reflects gender power hierarchy. Men are active and on top; women, boys, slaves, servants, and maids passive and at the bottom.

Having recognized the legitimacy of sexual desire, and having limited the legitimate outlet for sexual satisfaction to the marital bed, Islam promotes marriage (*nikâh*) at the earliest possible time. Yet in reality early marriage is not always possible. Marriage elevates intercourse from an act of lust to a sacred task and marks the boundaries of legitimate and illegitimate sexual liaisons. Marriage is an obligation of all believers. The restriction of sex to the marital bed – at least in theory – creates strict sexual and moral codes: *he* ought to display his manliness and *she*, her chastity. Any deviation is tantamount to anarchy and a revolt against God.

Islamic sexuality is ultimately procreational. The objective of lovemaking is not satisfying bodily desire but performing a divine mission (56:59). A quest for family "harmony" and raising healthy and virtuous children brings a couple together. Even when not resulting in procreation, marital intercourse performs its sacred mission by functioning as an antidote against the temptation of fornication.

Though these ideological "constants" are routinely negotiated and redefined in social practice, they are nonetheless significant in defining "normal" sexuality and how individuals must manage their sexual desires. Sexuality is intimately linked to religion, family law, and politics. The most blatant example is the Shari'ah-based notion of *tamkin*, according to which being financially provided for by her husband obligates a woman to live where he chooses and to serve him – including sexually – as he desires (unless his demands contradict the Shari'ah). States often regulate private erotic expressions to accord with the religiously defined "appropriate" sexuality and conservative moral standards. Deviation from sexual norms can be easily attributed to conspiracy with foreign powers to undermine religion and state.

Unequal power within the family severely compromises women's rights to consent and inextricably ties sexuality to violence. Passage to manhood involves rituals of violence (e.g., circumcision and conscription) that entail subordination of women. Circumcision or military training abuses inflict pain upon young men, yet this pain is celebrated and revered as a precondition to manhood. Crimes of honor, punishment for adultery (death by stoning), and female genital mutilation – neither of the latter prescribed by the Qur'an – are other manifestations of violence and sexuality.

Nationalist and modernization projects have drawn middle- and upper-class women into the public sphere, but they have also reemphasized women's maternal responsibility and have valorized them as symbols of nation and tradition, leading to new measures of control over female sexuality. In Turkey, for instance, women's chastity (*'iffet*) was a component of the Kemalist reconstruction of Turkish identity. In many Middle Eastern countries, a female student's chastity is a prerequisite for entitlement to formal education. Often, even married women cannot attend day classes in high school; they are required to enroll in evening classes with older students if they wish to continue their education.

According to Islamist ideologues, women stand at the vanguard of foreign intervention. Women are also the most significant bastion against external powers. Capitalizing on the perceived western threat to Islam and the Middle East, Islamist movements have promoted restrictive definitions of female gender roles and sexuality by assigning to women the task of preserving "authentic" culture. Traditions have been revived and invented. *Hejâb* (the Islamic dress code) has been referred to as the "flag" of Islam. Weakened customs such as *mut'a* (temporary marriage) have been reinforced (e.g., in Iran), and in some cases (e.g., Pakistan under President Zia) rape has been redefined as a form of *zinâ* (adultery).

Despite conservative tides, sexual ideologies and practices have undergone some changes. Emerging voices have addressed sexuality, especially restrictions on female sexuality, as a human rights issue. Feminists have attempted to move sexuality away from the sphere of metaphysical rules and place them in the context of social relationships. Progressive political movements are moving away from the belief that sexuality (and women's rights) concerns only the bourgeoisie. Evidence from a number of Islamic societies suggests that many youths are experiencing premarital sex. Though most women in Islamic countries marry, postponing marriage, even never marrying, is gaining gradual acceptance. Homosexuals are also slowly asserting their identities as gays and lesbians.

Studies of sexuality in Islamic cultures have been rather limited. There is a need for investigating the actual sexual behavior of the population, changes in attitude toward sex, and emerging sexualities. It is also pivotal to closely scrutinize classical and contemporary treatises on sexuality, paying attention not just to the text's overall message, but also to its underlying images, vocabularies, and assumptions.

SEE ALSO: Gender Ideology and Gender Role Ideology; Islam; Nationalism; Sexuality, Religion and

REFERENCES AND SUGGESTED READINGS

Bouhdiba, A. (1998) *Sexuality in Islam*. Saqi Books, London.

Ilkkaracan, P. (Ed.) (2000) *Women and Sexuality in Muslim Societies*. Women for Women's Human Rights, Istanbul.

Ilkkaracan, P. (Ed.) (2005) *Deconstructing Sexuality in the Middle East and North Africa: Contemporary Issues and Discourses*. Brill, Leiden.

Mernissi, F. (1987) *Beyond the Veil: Male–Female Dynamics in Modern Muslim Society*. Indiana University Press, Bloomington.

Sabbah, F. A. (1984) *Woman in the Muslim Unconscious*. Pergamon Press, New York.

James, William (1842–1910)

Frank J. Page

William James was the son of a theologian and brother of the novelist Henry James. He taught psychology and philosophy at Harvard University. His *Principles of Psychology* (1890) is the foundation of modern psychology. An annotated version, *On Psychology: Briefer Course*, was published in 1892. Other major works include *The Will to Believe* (1897), *Human Immortality* (1898), *The Varieties of Religious Experience* (1902), *Pragmatism* (1907), and *The Meaning of Truth* (1909). Along with Charles S. Peirce, Charles H. Cooley, and John Dewey, he was instrumental in establishing American pragmatism. This intellectual tradition has been an influential framework for symbolic interactionism, US educational practices, and many epistemological issues. James's conceptions of psychology, consciousness, cognition, self, self-esteem, stream of consciousness, and habit have a profound relevance for many sociological assumptions regarding the nature of society and its influence on human conduct.

As defined by James, psychology deals with consciousness, cognition, emotion, motivation, and conduct, all of which must be understood within the context of nature and evolution. His psychology rejects dualism, an ancient and prevalent assumption that asserts that mind (cognition and soul) and body are distinct and separate entities. James replaces dualism with parallelism, which posits that mind and body are linked through the central nervous system, and that there is a uniform correlation between thought and underlying physiological processes. In effect, cognition is made possible by the brain and central nervous system, an axiom central to modern psychology.

In harmony with his parallelism and modern evolutionary theory, James's psychology is predicated upon psychological functionalism, which asserts that the mind, consciousness, memory, and cognition are evolved traits that exist because they promote human survival. According to this paradigm, consciousness and the self-awareness it facilitates are made possible by the central nervous system and exist because of their adaptive value.

James describes the central nervous system as a biological machine that receives sense impressions and discharges reactions that promote survival of the organism. The biological principle that drives this process is homeostasis, the tendency of organisms to seek stability and respond in ways that will promote survival. In accord with this principle, humans are directed by sensations registered in the central nervous system. Accordingly, human behavior will tend toward those activities that are pleasurable and avoid those that are painful, because they promote survival. However, according to James, humans are not merely reactive organisms directed by biological instincts and drives. In humans, responses and interactions between the individual and the environment are mediated by consciousness.

According to James's concept of consciousness, early in childhood and forever after, many of the sense impressions that guide human conduct are mediated by and attached to signs and symbols that, as categories of thought, can be stored in memory and called to the forefront of consciousness. Through learning, people acquire these categories from society. In cognition, through the processes of association and disassociation, these categories facilitate discrimination, whereby people can categorize and differentiate between different objects and actions, and use this information to make decisions and choices. People think, perceive, and act on the basis of these categories, and it is not only the ability to discriminate that is made possible by categories, but also the sensations associated with categories that direct human thought and conduct.

In his analysis of consciousness, James describes the link between signs and sensations as "apperception." This physiological connection between signs and sensations is the mechanism by which signs and symbols direct human conduct. The sensory images that direct human conduct are "anticipatory images." These images and categories of thought enable people to anticipate the probable sensations associated with certain acts and objects, and thereby direct human conduct in ways that are generally beneficial to the individual and the species.

The concept of apperception is a core concept in James's model of consciousness. Several functions and implications are connected to this concept. First, apperception allows the cognitive processes of association and discrimination to be directed by sensations, however subtle, that occur when an individual thinks and interacts with the environment. Second, apperception is an incipient conception of sentiment, a key concept in Cooley's later conceptions of self and society. Third, apperception is intrinsic to James's principle of "ideo-motivation," which asserts that sensations associated with signs and symbols stored in the mind influence cognition in ways that direct and motivate conduct. Finally, apperception is a crucial component of James's concept of a "figured reality," which, like Peirce's concept of symbolic realism, posits that people can store signs and symbols that represent reality in their minds and use them for thinking, anticipating, and generally directing their conduct. This principle is central to later studies of cognition and symbolic interactionism.

James's principle of a figured reality is a central tenet in his functionalist model of consciousness. As such, it is also an important element in the American pragmatist conception of instrumental knowledge wherein knowledge is defined as information that guides human actions in a way that is useful and instrumental to well-being and survival. As conceptualized by James, all knowledge is composed of signs and symbols that are necessarily associated with sensations; this conception of knowledge also has implications for theories of meaning. Most importantly, if categories of thought are associated with sensation, meaning is not simply a matter of ascertaining what words refer to, but also a question regarding how acts and different ideas and things make people feel. Following this principle, acts and things that are meaningful are generally associated with certain pleasant and positive feelings, while those that are deemed meaningless are associated with bad and unpleasant feelings or no feelings at all. This principle, wherein knowledge is associated with a feeling state, underlies James's analysis of depression and the "sick soul."

A major tenet in James's conception of consciousness is the proposition that consciousness should always be conceptualized as something that is constantly changing, yet continuous, "a stream of consciousness." The validity of this concept is supported by the fact that, in accordance with James's principles, people do have the capacity for memory, cognition, learning, forgetting, habit, and the use of language to represent self and reality, all of which make consciousness and self-awareness a stable yet fluid experience. In *Principles of Psychology*, James carefully delineates these many capacities, their complex interrelationships, and the human qualities they facilitate. His analysis culminates with his depiction of the adaptive nature of habit which functions to simplify movements, conserve energy, limit fatigue, and allow people to multitask and become habituated to social norms. Accordingly, habit is not only personally empowering but also the "great flywheel of society," a notion that has considerable relevance for sociological conceptions of social control and order.

James's complex model of consciousness and human nature postulates that humans are evolved, sentient, cognitive, self-aware beings prone to habit and capable of learning, discrimination, and willful activity. However, the capstone of his psychology is his definition of self, and the related conceptions of the soul, will, motivation, and mental illness. As defined by James, self is composed of the "I and the Me." The I is the knower, thinker, and therefore the subject. The Me is that which empirically can be known by the knower about the knower as object. Basically, the knower is the consciousness and the changeable memory made possible by the central nervous system, whereas the Me is that which comes to be known about the knower through consciousness and awareness.

For analytical purposes, James divides the Me (that which can be known) into the Material Me, the Social Me, and the Spiritual Me. Each Me is important because, as known by the I, through the process of self-appreciation (evaluation), it may arouse instincts, feelings, and emotions that motivate and direct conduct. More specifically, if self-appraisal indicates that the self, be it the material, social, or spiritual aspect of self, is successful and secure, a person will experience self-complacency, and keep doing what he or she has been doing, or not doing. On the other hand, if self-appraisal leads to the conclusion that some aspect of the self is deficient or threatened, it will arouse instincts, emotions, and feelings that will generate self-seeking and self-preserving actions that attempt to remedy the problem by changing the self or the situation. Finally, if self-appraisal leads to a sense of hopelessness, the individual may experience lethargy, angst, depression, denial, and suicidal tendencies.

Because they are crucial aspects of the self that guide behavior, James carefully conceptualizes each aspect of the Me. The Material Me or self is not only the physical-bodily self, but also anything that a person can identify with. This may include family, friends, pets, lovers, houses, cars, a career, an art form, or a particular locality. However, in that the human body necessarily has the most direct connection with self, it is the innermost if not most important aspect of the material self. When threatened, as a matter of self-striving and self-preservation, strong instincts and emotions such as rage and anger will be automatically elicited.

In conceptualizing the Social Me, James delineates that part of the self that is aware of and responds to the expectations, influence, importance, and dependency on other people and groups. In many ways, his analysis of the Social Me adumbrates the conception of the "Me" that was developed by George Herbert Mead and later incorporated into symbolic interactionism. It also foreshadows what sociologists now describe as the social self, role-playing, situated identities, role conflict, and what Goffman later described as "impression management." That James saw the Social Me and social motivation as powerful is evident in his description of the American worship of success as a "Bitch Goddess" that creates workaholics.

James defines the Spiritual Me as that part of the self that, in being aware of itself as a thinking, feeling, acting creature, can ultimately deem life itself to be good, bad, meaningful, or meaningless. As a matter of self-striving, it is the spiritual self that directs conduct in terms of acquired intellectual, moral, religious, and philosophical beliefs and aspirations. However, while the spiritual self is an important and often dominant aspect of self, decisions are not always made by the spiritual self, but rather by that aspect of self that at a particular moment is the most engaged or threatened. When physical survival is at stake, the material self may predominate and overrule the social and spiritual self, a proposition that indirectly underscores the dangers of severe social disorganization and the moral importance of social order.

The Me(s) in James's model of self is an important organizing concept, because, in harmony with his functionalism and parallelism, as a matter of self-striving (self-protection), it responds when threatened. Consequently, when faced with a threat of injury or death, the Material Me, through instinct and emotion, strives for physical survival. When social rank is threatened, the Social Me, knowing of its dependence upon other people, strives for recognition as a means of security. When confronted with threats to cherished beliefs and values, the Spiritual Me attempts to direct conduct in terms of ideals and morals. Conceptually, each Me is an abstraction representing different aspects of the self as known by the I (the knower) that function as sources of motivation and direction.

James augments his analysis of the self and the motivation that springs from self-awareness with his mathematical formula for self-esteem (Self-esteem = Success/Pretenses to Success). According to this formula, a person's self-esteem level and the motivation that follows from it will be a function of the ratio of that person's actual success divided by his or her aspirations to success. When formulated in this ratio, self-esteem is low when a person has many aspirations to success and few actual successes, and high when a person has many successes and few aspirations. As a result, self-esteem can be heightened by success or by lowering aspirations for success. Charles Cooley and many modern theorists elaborated this concept.

A related and important, but often over-looked, principle regarding consciousness, motivation, and conduct developed by James that bespeaks his principle of ideo-motivation asserts that people will act on the basis of that image or idea that comes to the forefront of consciousness. According to this principle, whether or not a particular idea comes to the forefront of consciousness and thereby becomes a matter for thought and discrimination and a means of directing conduct will be a function of the intensity of the sensations associated with that particular idea or image. Due to apperception, all are accompanied by sensations, and James divides the ideas and images that compose consciousness into two types, those associated with instincts and drives, and those drawn from society. The values and beliefs drawn from society are "emotion-laden ideas." Paralleling Freud's discussion of the superego, James underscores how as part of the spiritual self these ideas direct conduct in prosocial ways. However, he notes that because instincts are associated with survival, they are also associated with strong sensations, and that when survival is at stake, an idea associated with an instinct, be it hunger, thirst, sex, or fear, may dominate consciousness and cognition and preempt the Social and Spiritual Me, and lead to conduct that is asocial and amoral.

According to James, consciousness is composed of ideas about the world and the self. Whether or not a particular idea or image will dominate consciousness and become the basis of cognition, perception, and motivation will be influenced by the strength of the sensations associated with it, the relative influence of instinct, society, the proper functioning of the central nervous system and the self, and the situation at hand. Consciousness, cognition, and the self are influenced by a variety of factors, but people think, make decisions, and act on the basis of intention and will. For

James, "will" or "will power," rather than being an amorphous metaphysical concept, is simply the individual's conscious attempt to keep certain ideas at the forefront of consciousness and thereby control her or his conduct. As to the issue of "free will," James's parallelism and functionalism, along with his conception of the self, implicitly imply that will is constrained by the functioning or dysfunctioning of the central nervous system and the nature, development, and health of the self.

While it does not often get the attention that the I, the Me, and self-esteem receive, James's concept of Soul is crucially important because it is the Soul that facilitates the interaction of the I and the Me. As defined by James, the Soul is that part of the I (the knower and thinker) that, as part of the stream of consciousness, functions as an ongoing, combining medium that allows for change and growth while maintaining continuity and a consistent sense of identity and self. While this concept is somewhat vague, it necessarily refers to the capacity of the individual to feel, know, learn, develop, and change. This ability to change yet maintain a continuous sense of identity is made possible by memory, learning, cognition, sensation, and, most importantly, the human use of language, all of which allow people to acquire new understandings of themselves and the world they live in, and selectively discard and forget older, inappropriate views. In terms of James's parallelism and functionalism, this is made possible by the central nervous system and the self-awareness that consciousness affords. However, as emphasized by James, the central nervous system, the Me(s), the Soul, and consciousness are subject to illness and aberrations that may lead to mental illness and human suffering.

In *Principles of Psychology*, James analyzes abnormal behavior in terms of mutations and multiplications of the self. These aberrations may be caused by alterations of memory brought about by changes, defects, or damage to the central nervous system or alterations in the material, social, and spiritual aspects of self. As conceptualized, a malady, be it a psychological problem that arises from a physiological deficit or a purely psychological problem associated with a damaged, threatened, or overreactive self, may lead to depression, insane delusions, alternating selves, mediumships or possessions, and false memories.

In *Varieties of Religious Experience*, James describes pathologies associated with the "sick soul" and the "divided self." These illnesses are driven by conditions where, in some individuals, the I's knowledge of the world gives rise to an awareness of inevitable suffering and the demise of self. This knowledge challenges and undermines the religious and philosophical ideas held by the spiritual self that give meaning and purpose to existence. As a result, the Soul, perceiving its own suffering and demise, is pained and sick. In addition, the self is divided and conflicted because the Spiritual Me is at a loss to provide direction to the Social Me and the Material Me which, without direction, may conflict with one another. In response, people may suffer neurosis, hopelessness, depression, and sadness, and some will search other religions and philosophies for more comforting beliefs that, in some cases, may relieve their anguish and give them a sense of being "reborn."

SEE ALSO: Cooley, Charles Horton; Goffman, Erving; Mead, George Herbert; Pragmatism; Self; Self-Esteem, Theories of; Social Psychology; Symbolic Interaction

REFERENCES AND SUGGESTED READINGS

James, W. (1890) *Principles of Psychology*. Henry Holt, New York.
James, W. (1892) *On Psychology: Briefer Course*. Henry Holt, New York.
James, W. (1897) *The Will to Believe, and Other Essays in Popular Philosophy*. Longmans, Green, London.
James, W. (1898) *Human Immortality*. Houghton Mifflin, Boston.
James, W. (1902) *The Varieties of Religious Experience*. Random House, New York.
James, W. (1907) *Pragmatism: A New Name for Some Old Ways of Thinking*. Longmans, Green, London.
James, W. (1909) *The Meaning of Truth*. Longmans, Green, London.
James, W. (1912) *Essays in Radical Empiricism*. Longmans, Green, London.

Japanese-style management

Ross Mouer

Japanese-style management (JSM) (*nihonteki kei-ei*) is a loosely defined term used to indicate the way employees are managed in firms and other organizations in Japan. Accordingly, its meaning changes as micro-economic realities change. At the same time, the term is used to distinguish from management practices in Japan more generally (*nihon no kei-ei* or *nihon ni okeru kei-ei*) to those employment practices that are alleged to be uniquely Japanese (*nihonteki*) and to have a peculiarly Japanese cultural imprint. Using the term to indicate the packaged set of practices which are described below, many acknowledge that what they refer to exists mainly in Japan's large firms. In this context, JSM was popularly used in the 1970s to delineate a number of interrelated practices demarcating the way work was organized in Japan (or at least in Japan's largest firms) from how it was conceived elsewhere.

The practices initially receiving attention were lifetime employment, seniority wages, and enterprise unionism. These came to be known as the three pillars, the three sacred treasures, or the three sacred emblems of industrial relations in Japan. Although the cultural uniqueness of each has been challenged, some have argued that it is the overall mix as an integrated system that has been unique. The belief that these practices were unique to Japan was bolstered by references to other phenomena alleged to be outcomes of the unique features: Japan's low levels of industrial disputes (reflecting a high value placed on social consensus), long hours worked in Japan (as part of a special culturally ordained work ethic), the provision of certain types of company welfare such as employee housing (emanating from familial and paternalistic orientations found in Japan's traditional agricultural communities), and lower labor turnover (reflecting an innate sense of loyalty to the company as a primary group; i.e., a surrogate family). In its second report on industrial relations in Japan in 1977, an OECD study team indicated that the three pillars were "kept in place" by a fourth: Japan's cultural values. Underpinning the three structures were a traditionally Japanese predilection for verticality in human relationships (e.g., seniority), for being part of a group (e.g., long-term employment), and for consensual relationships (e.g., enterprise unionism). By the 1970s these cultural features had come to be codified in academic accounts of nearly every aspect of Japanese society – a paradigmatic approach or viewpoint which came to be known as *nihonjinron*. This kind of cultural essentialism view came to dominate much of the Learn-from-Japan boom of the late 1970s and the 1980s.

The structures mentioned above were initially seen as part of an overall system of industrial relations that produced few strikes, wage restraint, and high levels of motivation as major factors facilitating Japan's rapid growth in the 1960s and 1970s. However, the literature about JSM shifted attention downward from the societal level and macroeconomic outcomes to the microeconomic concerns associated with employment relations in the firm. To some extent this shift reflected a general change in interest in the field internationally from the way tripartite frameworks for labor–management relations came to be institutionalized to a much more multi-dimensional mapping of employment relations and human resource management. Despite this shift, many in the field continued to assume that the industrial relations system in Japan was largely the sum of the HRM practices found in each Japanese firm. At this level the model was developed further to highlight "uniquely Japanese" approaches such as widespread bottom-up consultation (e.g., *nemawashi*, the memo system known as *ringi seido*), spontaneous and voluntary quality control circles, internal labor markets, joint labor–management consultations, the absence of a strong militant class orientation in ritualized conflicts such as the Spring Wage Offensive (the annual round of 6–8 weeks each spring when unions put forth their wage demands and settlements are negotiated between labor and management), and the highly integrated production systems which utilized large numbers of firms linked together to form enterprise groupings known as *keiretsukigyo*.

In the 1970s numerous scholars sought to codify the linkages between *nihonjinron* and *nihonteki kei-ei* (Ogishima 1984). In the late 1950s the anthropologist Abegglen coined the term "lifetime employment" to describe what he perceived to be a peculiar feature of management practices at the firms he studied in Japan. In the next decade Hazama (1963) began the codification by which he and others sought to link aspects of JSM to cultural underpinnings. However, it was in the 1970s that those foundations came to be seen as uniquely Japanese (and not just remnants from a tradition associated with all pre-industrial societies). As a kind of postmodern outcome, the Japanese firm was seen as being able to maintain a delicate balance between the push for greater social justice (as seen in the demands of left-wing unions) and the efforts of management (with the cooperation of business unions) to obtain greater efficiency. Nakayama (1974) wrote about a system generating true efficiency (*honrai no noritsu*) by combining an emphasis on economic rationality (*noritsu*) with an emphasis on fairness (*kosei*). For Tsuda (1977), the terms were cooperative community (*kyodo seikatsutai*), rationality (*gorisei*), and consensus (*goi*); for Hazama (1971), group-oriented labor–management relations (*shudanteki roshi kankei*), profit seeking (*eiri no tsuikyu*), and continuity of the company (*kaisha no eizoku*); for Iwata (1977), the formative principles of Japanese management (*nihonteki kei-ei no hensei genri*), organizational demands (*soshiki no yokyu*), and the demands of individual employees (*kojin no yokyu*). In hindsight an increased awareness of how the institutions associated with JSM were born out of the immediate post-war years, the shift in the balance of power first to unions and then back to management, and the ongoing ideological battle between Cold War camps has helped those interested in JSM to see how it was produced out of a peculiar historical milieu in which the tensions between capitalist and socialist views worked themselves out in the context of successful economic resurgence and the efforts to reestablish positive assertions of national identity.

In the 1980s debate revolved around the exportability of JSM, with many questions raised about the exportability of the cultural proclivities commonly associated with work organization in Japan. In the process the culturalist view was undermined by a growing acknowledgment that JSM practices were found primarily in Japan's large firms. Nevertheless, although firms with over 500 employees accounted for only 12 percent of the labor force in 1975 (and only 8.9 percent in 1999) (Mouer & Kawanishi 2004: 119), it was asserted by many that the model's significance was less in its prevalence as an actual reality and more in its role as an ideal to which many in the Japanese workforce aspired. Myth or not, the fact remains that notions of *nihonteki kei-ei* and the entire set of *emic* terms used to describe components of JSM have become important as a Japanese vocabulary for talking about work organization in Japan.

In the 1980s western managers, unionists, and academics made a concerted effort to find out more about JSM. Managers motivated by the desire to acquire a new kind of competitive advantage traveled to Japan to discover the secrets of JSM and to find "quick-fix" solutions. Unionists, however, came to feel the pressure of certain anti-union tactics which were seen as being characteristic of some Japanese investment in their own countries. Some of these views were captured in North America in the film *Gung-ho*. The efforts of these practitioners tended to shift attention back from the alleged essence of Japanese culture to the more easily observed concrete structures that could more easily be implemented in their own societies. By the early 1990s the literature had come to provide a more comprehensive view highlighting a number of structural features central to the functioning of JSM. Outside Japan a debate developed between those who saw JSM primarily in cultural terms as a post-Fordist phenomenon and those who saw it more in structural terms as an ultra-Fordist approach.

The structuralists paid attention to the very complex system of delayed wage payments and the importance of performance-linked criteria which markedly differentiated the age-wage (seniority) trajectories on which individual employees found themselves. Just-in-time systems (which had been contrasted with more costly just-in-case systems) were introduced without the full realization that the costs saved by the final assembling plants with reduced

stocks of parts had not been removed from the overall production process, but had rather been simply shifted further down through the production process, a situation reflected in continuing firm-size differentials in working conditions. Other ways in which internal and external labor markets were segmented – especially in terms of employment status and the distinction between regular employees and a huge range of non-regular employees – also came to be seen as integral to how the "Japanese system" of integrated production actually functioned. The use of excessive regulation and an opaque performance management system have also been mentioned as factors goading workers to work long hours and to accept assignments which physically removed them from being involved in their family on a day-to-day basis. These facets came to be documented by Kumazawa (1994, 1997) and by many others from the late 1980s onwards. Further to these correctives were studies showing that many Japanese firms governed by JSM were actually not very efficiently run; privatized public enterprises (from the Japan National Railways in the early 1980s to national universities at the end of the 1990s), retailers, and many financial institutions provide ready examples.

Mouer and Kawanishi (2004) argue that JSM needs to be understood in a broader social context in which choices at work have been fairly limited for many Japanese employees, including those in large firms. The absence of adequate safety nets for unemployment and the segmented approach to providing health insurance and pensions require all employees to think very carefully about choices which increase the risk that they might experience some form of downward intragenerational mobility as they are shifted out of Japan's more privileged labor markets and into its less attractive ones. Since the turn of the century a good deal has been written about widening income differentials and the difficulty of achieving intra- and intergenerational upward mobility (e.g., Sato 2000). Changes in the power relationship between peak organizations representing labor and management markedly affect the likelihood of progressive legislation being introduced to affect social welfare.

In recent years, however, Japan's affluence and a relatively high standard of living have altered the relationship between labor and management in the labor market. Fewer Japanese are willing to labor in jobs characterized by the 3 Ds (i.e., that are dirty, demanding, and dangerous) – or the 3 Ks in Japanese) (*kitanai*, *kitsui*, and *kiken*). Parasite singles (young persons in their late twenties and in their thirties who have not left home and continue to enjoy free accommodation at their parents' expense while working for good wages, as described in Yamada 1999) are less prone to seek "privileged employment" at all costs, and the number of *furitaa* (freelance casuals) has increased significantly over the 1990s. Widespread questioning of gender-derived segmentation has opened up the work place to greater competition. These changes only add to doubts about the uniqueness of JSM (*nihonteki kei-ei*), and in this sense JSM (*nihon ni okeru kei-ei*) will continue to be characterized by change and be difficult to capture in its entirety as managers use Japanese structural elements to respond to the spread of global standards. While the workers will continue to be guided by a strong sense of self-interest, the spread of multicultural thinking is likely to encourage variety in those responses. Over time new vocabularies for describing JSM are bound to emerge as perceptions and realities change, and as different conditions of possibility come to shape the environment in which work is performed in Japan.

SEE ALSO: Enterprise Unions; Labor–Management Relations; Management; *Nenko Chingin*; *Nihonjinron*; *Shushin Koyo*

REFERENCES AND SUGGESTED READINGS

Abegglen, J. C. (1958) *The Japanese Factory: Aspects of Its Social Organization*. Free Press, Glencoe, IL.

Hazama, H. (1963) *Nihonteki kei-ei no keifu* (The Evolution of Japanese-Style Management). Nihon Noritsu Kyokai, Tokyo.

Hazama, H. (1971) *Nihonteki kei-ei* (Japanese-Style Management). Nihon Keizai Shinbunsha, Tokyo.

Iwata, R. (1977) *Nihonteki kei-ei no hensei genri* (The Formative Principles of Japanese-Style Management). Bunchindo, Tokyo.

Kumazawa, M. (1994) *Shinhen Nihon no rodosha zo* (An Updated Portrait of the Japanese Worker). Chikuma Shobo, Tokyo.

Kumazawa, M. (1997) *Noryokushugi to kigyo shakai* (The Commitment to Ability and the Enterprise-Centered Society). Iwanami Shoten, Tokyo.

Mouer, R. & Kawanishi, H. (2004) *A Sociology of Work in Japan*. Cambridge University Press, Cambridge.

Nakayama, I. (1974) *Industrialization and Labor–Management Relations in Japan*. Trans. R. E. Mouer. Japan Institute of Labor, Tokyo.

Ogishima, K. (1984) *Japanese-Style Management: A Study of the Japanese-Language Literature*. School of Modern Asian Studies, Griffith University, Brisbane.

Organization of Economic Cooperation and Development (1977) *The Development of Industrial Relations Systems: Some Implications of the Japanese Experience*. OECD, Paris.

Sato, T. (2000) *Fubyodo shakai Nihon – Sayonara sochuryu* (The Unequal Society Japan: Farewell to the Mass Middle-Class Society). Chuo Koron Sha, Tokyo.

Tsuda, M. (1977) *Nihonteki kei-ei no ronri* (The Logic of Japanese-Style Mangement). Chuo Keizaisha, Tokyo.

Yamada, M. (1999) *Parasaito Shinguru no Jidai* (The Age of the Parasite Singles). Chikuma Shobo, Tokyo.

Jehovah's Witnesses

Massimo Introvigne

Rodney Stark and Laurence Iannaccone (1997) noted that, despite their millions of members, until recently Jehovah's Witnesses failed to attract the attention of most sociologists of religion (Beckford 1975 is one of the rare book-length studies). The difficult access to their international archives was a factor, together with a general underevaluation of non-mainline Christian groups by certain sociologists. In the 1990s and 2000s, however, the situation changed. Sociologists became interested in testing on such a large group hypotheses about the relative success of different religious movements, cognitive dissonance, routinization of charisma, and mainstreaming of once marginal religions, while a new Witnesses leadership was ready to cooperate.

The Jehovah's Witnesses are the largest among a group of several religious movements that claim the heritage of Pastor Charles Taze Russell (1852–1916). Born in Pittsburgh, Pennsylvania, Russell became involved in theological controversies within the American Adventist movement, which had predicted the end of the world for the year 1844 based on numerological speculations drawn from the Bible. After 1844, Adventists divided into several competing groups. Those who renounced any further date-setting eventually became the Seventh-Day Adventists, a large international denomination. Some of those who would still calculate prophetic dates focused their hopes on the year 1874, and constituted a loosely organized movement. After the new disappointment, the young Russell emerged as one of the leaders of those who had placed their hopes in 1874. Russell both predicted the end of the world as we know it for the year 1914 and shifted his focus on teachings other than prophetical date-setting.

In 1878, Russell separated himself from other factions of the movement and started editing a magazine, *Zion's Watch Tower and Herald of Christ's Presence*, which is still published today as *The Watchtower*. Russell's followers were known simply as Bible Students, but in 1884 the preacher formally established an organization known as the Zion's Watch Tower Society, later the Watch Tower Bible and Tract Society. Russell's ideas involved the denial of Trinity (Jesus Christ was regarded as God's first creature). He also preached conditionalism, a rejection of the traditional view of the immortality of the soul. These doctrines would later seem highly heterodox to mainline Christians. In the late nineteenth century, however, they were shared by quite a few preachers. Russell's notable success (almost all his books sold millions of copies) did not come so much from the alleged revolutionary character of his teachings as from the fact that they were perceived as being in continuity with, if not part of, mainline Christianity. This confirmed to later social science that new religious movements, in order to gain a large following, should exhibit only a moderate discontinuity with respect to mainline religion.

The prophetic failure of 1914 did not stop the movement's progress. The Bible Students, however, were radical Christian pacifists, who adamantly refused to be drafted and to fight in war. In several countries they were arrested in significant numbers. In this climate, the election as president of the Watch Tower Society of Joseph Franklin Rutherford (1869–1942) was not welcome by everybody, and several schismatic groups separated from the mainline movement, although all these splinter organizations remained quite small.

Not only did Rutherford promote speculations about a new date for the end of the world, 1925, he also transformed the loose network of Russell's times into a strongly centralized organization, changing its name in 1931 into the current one of Jehovah's Witnesses. With a peculiar and abrasive populist rhetoric, Rutherford consistently attacked organized religion, politics, and big business as "rackets" and corrupt monopolies up to no good. Although Rutherford would be later criticized for his early and, in retrospect, naïve attempt in 1933 to contact the Nazi regime and present a positive image of the German Jehovah's Witnesses, such contacts quickly failed and the Witnesses were severely persecuted in Nazi Germany, as in Fascist Italy and Communist Russia. Several hundred died in Nazi concentration camps.

Nathan Homer Knorr (1905–77) succeeded Rutherford in 1942. Again, the transition from one president to the next took place during a world war. The 115,000 active Witnesses, still committed to radical pacifism, were again experiencing difficult times in most countries of the world. Presiding over the Witnesses in an era that was now suspicious of charismatic leadership, Knorr struggled to depersonalize the movement's hierarchy and almost consciously organized a sustained routinization of charisma within the group. Articles in the Witnesses' magazines and books were now published anonymously, concluding a process initiated during the Rutherford era. Although still emphasizing the Witnesses as the only authorized organization representing the Lord's true church in the world, the style became less abrasive than it had been during the Rutherford administration. Missionary endeavors, now much more systematically organized, became the top priority.

At Knorr's death in 1977, the movement had grown to more than 2 million "publishers" (i.e., Witnesses engaged in the active "field service" of proselytization, mostly conducted by systematically visiting all homes in a given neighborhood) and more than 5 million participants to the memorial of the Lord's Supper, the only yearly "liturgy" of the movement. This difference emphasizes the problem in assessing the number of Jehovah's Witnesses statistically. While the Witnesses themselves would count only the "publishers" as members in full standing, adherents of other denominations are not counted by taking into account only those active in missionary enterprises. Participants in the yearly memorial offer a statistical assessment closer to how members of other religious organizations are normally counted, although it is true that the yearly memorial is occasionally attended also by friends and sympathizers. On the other hand, it is also true that the traditional Christian slogan "every member is a missionary" is taken much more literally by the Witnesses than by most other Christian denominations, and everybody is encouraged to devote a substantial amount of time to missionary endeavors. Although the effectiveness of the systematic door-to-door strategy has been called into question, sociologists have noted that the internal effects of the effort in reinforcing the members' identity and commitment are almost as important as its external success (see Beckford 1975).

A new prophetic enthusiasm seized the movement before 1975, a date regarded by many Witnesses as a likely end of this world. The disappointment many Witnesses experienced created several difficulties and energized an oppositional movement which received considerable media attention but in fact involved only a limited, if vocal, number of former members. The fact that the Witnesses survived prophetic failures in 1914, 1925, and 1975 has been regarded by some sociologists as a confirmation of the theory of cognitive dissonance as applied by Festinger et al. (1956) to instances "when prophecy fails." In order to avoid admitting their previous gullibility, members reinforce their missionary efforts and, by persuading others, re-persuade themselves. The theory would predict that, counterintuitively, movements can grow rather than enter into a crisis after a prophetic failure. More recently, however, others have argued that cognitive dissonance has very little to do with Witnesses' reactions to prophetic disconfirmation. First of all, in the immediate aftermath of failed date-setting, Witnesses *lost* members, and started growing again only after years of painful reorganization (Singelenberg 1989). On the other hand, prophecy in fact only fails for the

outsiders; from the point of view of the movement itself, prophecy does not fail but is regarded as having come true at other levels: perhaps *a* world, rather than *the* world, has ended, or the prophecy needs to be understood differently (Melton 1985).

In 1995 *The Watchtower* announced a "new point of view" on prophetic date-setting, still regarding the end of the world as we know it as quite near, but discouraging members from calculating precise dates. This evolution, as it did for Seventh-Day Adventists one century earlier, had the gradual effect of reducing the "other-worldliness" of the Witnesses, facilitating their further evolution toward the religious mainline. International expansion resumed (with more than 15 million participants at the yearly memorial in 2004), and the bureaucratization process continued. In 1976 the Witnesses started adopting a rotating presidency among the members of the governing body, the spiritual presiding body of the organization, thus further deemphasizing the presidency's charisma which had been so crucial in the Russell and Rutherford eras. In October 2000, after Milton Henschel (1920–2003) had succeeded Frederick Franz (1893–1992) as president of the Watch Tower Society, all members of the governing body voluntarily stepped aside from the board of directors of that Society, thus separating the spiritual from the administrative governance of the Witnesses.

In the late 1990s, renewed discrimination in countries such as Russia and France (where the Witnesses were involved in campaigns against so-called "cults" and "sects") led to what Pauline Côté and James Richardson (2001: 14) called a "deformation" or "reconfiguration" of the group's relationships with the external world. The two sociologists believe that external pressure, including persecution and legal harassment, may cause important changes in religious organizations. In other words, even when groups successfully resist pressure, how exactly they resisted may involve significant internal changes. In the cases of the Jehovah's Witnesses, Côté and Richardson report a first phase of "disciplined litigation" during and immediately after the Rutherford era. In the face of sustained legal discrimination, prominent Witnesses leader and lawyer Hayden Cooper Covington (1911–79) both reacted through any available legal means, and counseled the Witnesses to avoid the most abrasive slogans against "big business," politics, and other religions, which would not have fared well in courts of law. The introduction of "theocratic tact" showed how legal strategy contributed to mainstreaming the Witnesses after World War II (Zygmunt 1977).

However, after they had scored important victories before the US Supreme Court and other jurisdictions, the Witnesses did not continue with the "disciplined litigation" strategy and even appeared concerned not to lose their distinctiveness. Similar processes of backing off from what may be perceived as a too rapid integration into the religious mainstream have been described by Mauss (1994) with respect to the Mormons, and defined as "retrenchment." These retrenchment strategies may be very successful in terms of church growth because, as Stark and Iannaccone (1997: 152–3) have argued precisely with reference to Jehovah's Witnesses, keeping the "strict" features of the group may both reduce the number of free-riders and make a movement more attractive to the large conservative niche of the religious market.

In the case of the Witnesses, a certain retrenchment in the 1960s involved the closing in 1963 of the movement's in-house legal office, which had served as an important tool for contacts with religious liberty advocates and other religious groups, although limited to legal issues rather than involving ecumenical dialogue. However, renewed attacks led to the reopening of the legal office in 1981 and the emergence in the 1990s of a new strategy that Côté and Richardson (2001: 11) have defined as "vigilant litigation." Court cases are now used to prove to opponents, the media, and the members themselves that the Witnesses' lifestyle should no longer be regarded as marginal or controversial but is part of the mainline, although their theology remains unique. Law and the courts have thus been consciously used as a vehicle for moving toward the mainstream, although the results in countries like Russia or France remain quite uncertain.

SEE ALSO: Charisma; Charisma, Routinization of; Denomination; Fundamentalism; Globalization, Religion and; Millenarianism; New Religious Movements; Sect

REFERENCES AND SUGGESTED READINGS

Beckford, J. A. (1975) *The Trumpet of Prophecy: A Sociological Study of Jehovah's Witnesses*. Wiley, New York.

Côté, P. & Richardson, J. T. (2001) Disciplined Litigation, Vigilant Litigation, and Deformation: Dramatic Organization Change in Jehovah's Witnesses. *Journal for the Scientific Study of Religion* 40(1): 11–25.

Festinger, L., Riecken, H. W., & Schachter, S. (1956) *When Prophecy Fails*. University of Minnesota Press, Minneapolis.

Mauss, A. L. (1994) *The Angel and the Beehive: The Mormon Struggle with Assimilation*. University of Illinois Press, Urbana.

Melton, J. G. (1985) Spiritualization and Reaffirmation: What Really Happens When Prophecy Fails. *American Studies* 26(2): 17–29.

Singelenberg, R. (1989) "It Separated the Wheat from the Chaff:" The "1975" Prophecy and its Impact on Dutch Jehovah's Witnesses. *Sociological Analysis* 50: 23–40.

Stark, R. & Iannaccone, L. R. (1997) Why the Jehovah's Witnesses Grow So Rapidly: A Theoretical Application. *Journal of Contemporary Religion* 12: 133–57.

Zygmunt, J. R. (1977) Jehovah's Witnesses in the USA, 1942–1976. *Social Compass* 24(1): 45–57.

Jevons, William (1835–82)

Milan Zafirovski

William Stanley Jevons is best known as an early influential British neoclassical and utilitarian economist mostly influenced by and developing Benthamite utilitarianism (Schumpeter 1991). More precisely, he is renowned among economists as one of the founders (alongside Carl Menger and Leon Walras) of marginalism or marginal utility theory (during the 1870s) as what economist-sociologist Schumpeter (1954) describes as a Copernican Revolution in economics (for more on Jevons as an economist, see Mosselmans & White 2000). Overall, his sociologically minded disciple Philip Wicksteed (1905) describes Jevons as "one of the most powerful, bold, and original thinkers" in economics. While virtually unknown or neglected among sociologists, curiously enough, Jevons can probably be credited (Swedberg 2003) with inventing the term economic sociology (in the second 1879 edition of his main work, the *Theory of Political Economy*), though not the idea or concept. The idea of economic sociology is already contained or germane in Comte, especially his notion of social economy, as a branch of sociology distinguished from orthodox economics, and of the "economy of real society" subject to "sociological research."

Specifically, Jevons (1965) suggests "it is only by subdivision, by recognizing a branch of Economic Sociology, together possibly with two or three other branches of statistical, jural, or social science, that we can rescue our [economic] science from its confused state." He adds that economics (also called political economy) is in such a "chaotic state" owing to the need of subdividing a "too extensive sphere of knowledge," with economic sociology being one of the results of this subdivision. Hence, Jevons considers economic sociology not only a field of sociology, but also a branch of economics, alongside, for example, the mathematical theory of economics, systematic and descriptive economics, fiscal science, and others, as do similarly some later economists (e.g., Schumpeter 1954). In turn, he treats economics as a "branch of the social sciences," by implication of sociology understood as such a general science. Thus, Jevons (1965) states that the so-called new historical branch of social science, and implicitly economics, "is doubtless a portion of what Herbert Spencer calls Sociology." At this juncture, he adopts an apparent Spencerian or evolutionary definition of sociology as the "Science of the Evolution of Social Relations." Notably, Jevons defines economics by analogy to the Spencerian definition of sociology or in evolutionary terms, as "a science of the development of economic forms and relations." Further, he implies that economics as defined is "one branch of Mr. Spencer's Sociology," an implication also suggested by his followers Wicksteed and Edgeworth. Wicksteed (1933), noting that Jevons followed Comte "to erect a hierarchy of science," places economic science among the "branches of sociological study" and even urges

that "economics must be the handmaid of sociology." Similarly, Edgeworth (1967) describes Jevons's marginal utility economics as the "most sublime branch" of sociology in Comte's sense.

The Jevonian definitions of economics and sociology also yield an implicit Spencerian or evolutionary definition of Jevons's economic sociology as the study of the "development of economic forms and relations" in interrelation to and within the general "evolution of social relations." Thus understood, Jevons's economic sociology is a neoclassical economist's attempt at integration of economics and sociology, thus anticipating similar efforts by some sociologists (e.g., Parsons & Smelser 1956). Another implicit definition of economic sociology is found in Jevons's (1866) alternative, utilitarian–hedonistic specification of the "field of inquiry" of economics, deemed a "hedonic science," as consisting only of the "relations of ordinary pleasures and pains," or a "calculus of pleasure and pain" (Schumpeter 1991), and not of "all human motives." Viewing this field as "wide enough," he states "there are motives nearly always present with us, arising from conscience, compassion, or from some moral or religious source, which [economics] cannot and does not pretend to treat. These will remain to us as outstanding and disturbing forces; they must be treated, if at all, by other appropriate branches of knowledge" (Jevons 1866). By implication, one of these latter appropriate branches of knowledge is, as Jevons himself suggests in his later writings, economic sociology, thereby implicitly defined as the study of the relations of utilitarian–hedonistic motivation to other human motives as "disturbing forces" or, in Weber's words, material and ideal values/interests alike. Negatively, Jevons's statement, by denying that economics deals with "all human motives" and excluding non-economic factors from its field as "disturbing forces," does not suggest what has come to be known as the economic approach to "all human behavior" or rational choice theory. Positively, the statement in essence adopts and elaborates on Mill's earlier view that most "disturbing causes" do not belong to the domain of economics but to "some other science," specifically what he proposes as the "science of social economy" as an anticipation or equivalent of

Jevons's economic sociology (a proposal that also implies no rational choice theory).

The main part of Jevons's economic sociology is the sociology of the market, just as the (marginalist) theory of markets, value, and prices is the key element of his pure economics. One implied element of Jevons's sociology of the market is the observed impact of non-economic factors such as bargaining power and asymmetrical knowledge or information on market transactions. This is what he essentially suggests by observing that often market transactions "must be settled upon other than strictly economic grounds [supply and demand]" (Jevons 1965), specifically on bargaining and by implication power relations (an observation approvingly cited by his prominent marginalist disciple, Francis Edgeworth). In turn, Jevons predicts that the outcome of bargaining will "greatly depend on the comparative amount of knowledge of each other's position and needs which either bargainer may possess or manage to obtain in the course of the transaction" (i.e., simply, asymmetrical or private information as a particular ("soft") facet or source of differential power and domination). He therefore implies that the bargaining outcome such as the market price will be ultimately determined by what Weber calls power constellations, specifically economic domination "by virtue of a constellation of interests," and contemporary sociologists term differential positional power. Consequently, Jevons (1965) suggests "indeterminate bargains of this kind are best arranged by an arbitrator or third party," including political and other extraneous parties like government.

This indicates a second, related element of Jevons's sociology of the market: the role of political factors in markets. For illustration, he observes that the so-called political intelligence of the moment often affects "prospective" supply or demand (i.e., speculation) and its bearing on market equilibrium (Jevons 1965). A third element of Jevons's sociology of the market and economic sociology overall involves the influence of institutions on markets and the economy. For example, he notes the "hedonic bearing of our social institutions" (Jevons 1881), and thus suggests institutional influences

on market-economic behavior, including pursuit of pleasure or maximizing utility. Notably, he recognizes that non-economic institutions have such a hedonic-economic impact in virtue of their contribution to human wants or material (and other) well-being which he considers (like Adam Smith) the "sole object of all industry" (Jevons 1965).

In sum, while mostly unknown and overlooked among sociologists, Jevons is potentially interesting and intriguing for them on account of his proposal of economic sociology, thus formally contributing to the adoption and development, even within economics, of a classical sociological idea and field.

SEE ALSO: Comte, Auguste; Durkheim, Émile; Economic Sociology: Neoclassical Economic Perspective; Markets; Mill, John Stuart; Schumpeter, Joseph A.; Spencer, Herbert; Weber, Max

REFERENCES AND SUGGESTED READINGS

Edgeworth, F. (1967 [1881]) *Mathematical Psychics*. A. M. Kelley, New York.

Jevons, W. S. (1866) Brief Account of a General Mathematical Theory of Political Economy. *Journal of the Royal Statistical Society* 29: 282–7.

Jevons, W. S. (1881) A Review of Edgeworth's *Mathematical Psychics*. Mind 6: 581–3.

Jevons, W. S. (1965 [1879]) *The Theory of Political Economy*. A. M. Kelley, New York.

Mosselmans, B. & White, M. (2000) Introduction to W. S. Jevons, *Collected Economic Writings*. Palgrave Macmillan, New York, pp. v–xxv.

Parsons, T. & Smelser, N. (1956) *Economy and Society*. Free Press, New York.

Schumpeter, J. (1954) *History of Economic Analysis*. Oxford University Press, New York.

Schumpeter, J. (1991) *The Economics and Sociology of Capitalism*. Princeton University Press, Princeton.

Swedberg, R. (2003) *Principles of Economic Sociology*. Princeton University Press, Princeton.

Wicksteed, P. (1905) Jevons's Economic Work. *Economic Journal* 15 (59): 432–6.

Wicksteed, P. (1933) *The Common Sense of Political Economy*. Routledge & Kegan Paul, London.

Johnson, Charles Spurgeon (1893–1956)

Mary Jo Deegan

African American race relations authority and academic administrator Charles Spurgeon Johnson was born in Bristol, Virginia on July 24, 1893. The grandson of a slave and the son of a Baptist minister, Johnson was inspired by religious ideals and a commitment to end social inequality. He graduated from Wayland Academy and studied at Virginia Union University, both in Richmond, Virginia. He completed a BA in sociology from the University of Chicago in 1917. After America entered World War I, he enlisted in the army. He returned to the university in 1919 and begin his graduate studies with Robert Ezra Park.

In the summer of 1919 a major race riot occurred in Chicago, and the Chicago Commission on Race Relations, under the auspices of the Chicago Urban League, began to investigate the conditions leading up to it. Johnson directed this research from 1919 to 1921. In 1922 the commission published *The Negro in Chicago*, wherein Johnson made significant contributions.

In 1921 he moved to New York to direct research for the National Urban League. From 1923 to 1928 he edited their magazine, *Opportunity*, an important publishing outlet during the Harlem Renaissance. It influenced the careers of many artists including Langston Hughes, Zora Neale Hurston, and Arnaud Bontemps.

In 1929 Johnson moved to Nashville, Tennessee, where he chaired the social sciences department at Fisk University. He hired colleagues formerly associated with the Chicago School of Sociology, including Horace Cayton, E. Franklin Frazier, and Park after the latter's retirement from the University of Chicago.

Johnson's books *The Negro in American Civilization* (1930), *Shadow of the Plantation* (1934), and *The Negro College Graduate* (1936) emphasized the importance of scientific, objective goals to collect and interpret empirical data. Education was a major source for social change to obtain social equality. Johnson documented institutionalized discrimination in these books but rarely commented upon it or supported explicit reforms.

During World War II, Johnson shifted his conservative politics by openly attacking segregation. He published *The Monthly Summary*, which provided information on race relations throughout the country. In 1943 his work on segregation influenced Gunnar Myrdal's *An American Dilemma* (1944). In 1944, Johnson began annual Race Relations Institutes (RRI), attended by national leaders. Johnson became the first black president of Fisk University in 1946, a position he held until 1956.

National Association for the Advancement of Colored People (NAACP) attorney Thurgood Marshall often addressed the RRI in the 1950s and Johnson provided him with sociological data and interpretations that Marshall used in his legal briefs for *Brown* v. *Board of Education* (1954). This landmark decision eliminated the legal justification for "separate but equal" public facilities and set in motion many public protests in the later Civil Rights Movement.

By the late 1940s Johnson was appointed to several powerful positions: as a United States delegate to UNESCO (1946–7), a member of the Fulbright Board of Foreign Scholarships (1947–54), and a delegate to the Assembly of the World Council of Churches (1948). His balance between "objective" social science and a more critical, change-oriented stance helped Johnson obtain philanthropic funds, create a Southern center for studying racial injustice, and develop a global network supporting black artists.

On October 27, 1956, Johnson died suddenly in Louisville, Kentucky of a heart attack. He was mourned by educational, sociological, and political leaders who recognized his contributions to all these fields.

SEE ALSO: *American Dilemma, An* (Gunnar Myrdal); *Brown* v. *Board of Education*; Chicago School; Civil Rights Movement; Frazier, E. Franklin; Park, Robert E. and Burgess, Ernest W.

REFERENCES AND SUGGESTED READINGS

Gilpin, C. J. & Gasman, M. (2003) *Charles S. Johnson*. Foreword D. L. Lewis. SUNY Press, Albany, NY.
Robbins, R. (1996) *Sidelines Activist*. University of Mississippi Press, Jackson.

jōmin

Takami Kuwayama

Jōmin is a central concept in Kunio Yanagita's research into Japanese folklore. Yanagita (1875–1962), founder of Japanese folklore studies or folkloristics, invented this term by combining two characters – *jō* (also pronounced *tsune*), used either as a noun or a modifier, meaning "usual," "ordinary," "average," or "conventional," and *min*, a noun meaning "people." *Jōmin* thus means "common people" as distinguished from both elites in the ruling class and people placed at the bottom of society, including outcastes. No proper equivalent is found in European languages, but its meaning is close to that of the German *Volk* or the English "folk."

The importance attached to the study of *jōmin* in Yanagita's research may be explained in terms of his theory of history. Defining folkloristics as a historical science, Yanagita contended that orthodox historiography, using almost exclusively written documents as data, merely recorded the lives of great individuals and dramatic events. Commoners, who made up the majority of the population, were described as the anonymous masses without emotion and character, if described at all. Dissatisfied with this practice, Yanagita placed *jōmin* at the center of historical inquiry. He also proposed new methods for studying history. Instead of doing archival research, he conducted fieldwork. Yanagita reasoned that, since Japan modernized relatively late, premodern manners and customs were still practiced among the commoners. Even if they were no longer practiced, they could be reconstructed, Yanagita thought, from the memory of living people. Thus, he extensively used interviews, in addition to the observations of actual behavior, as a tool of investigation into the past. In Yanagita's mind, history did not refer to past events, but rather the past within the present. In today's terminology, he wrote the "social history" of the Japanese people at large, using the ethnographic methods that were developed in the early twentieth century.

There is agreement among Japanese folklorists that *jōmin* embody Japan's folk culture. Put another way, ordinary people are understood as active agents of historical development, not as passive subjects, who, with their own will, observe and pass on tradition from generation to generation. There is, however, some ambiguity as to the exact meaning of *jōmin* because Yanagita neither defined it precisely nor used it consistently, as was often the case with other concepts he proposed. Despite his admiration for science, Yanagita was essentially a man of letters, whose influence derived more from his literary talent than from his scientific achievement. Among later generations of scholars, therefore, there has been much debate about the meaning and the significance of *jōmin* for folklore research. Even today, it continues to be debated, with new interpretations presented from various fields.

One of the best interpretations has been presented by Ajio Fukuta, Japan's leading folklorist. Fukuta examined the frequencies of Yanagita's use of "*jōmin*," as well as its meanings, in his voluminous works. Having found that Yanagita's usages had changed over time, Fukuta classified them into three periods: (1) from the 1910s to the 1920s; (2) around the mid-1930s; and (3) after the 1940s. In the first period, when Yanagita first made his name as a governmental bureaucrat and later, after his resignation, as a pioneer in folkloristics, *jōmin* was used to mean peasants who had settled in a particular community located on flat land, as contrasted with non-peasants, such as hunters, wood-turners, and some sorts of religious practitioners, who moved from community to community in the mountains. In the second period, when Yanagita's scholarship fully developed, *jōmin* meant not simply peasants but "ordinary peasants," excluding the hereditary upper-class peasants who owned massive land and thus dominated local politics. Fukuta's interpretation is based on Yanagita's classic statement, made in his 1935 book *Kyōdo Seikatsu no Kenkyūhō* (*Methods in the Study of Local Community Life*), that *jōmin* were found in between the upper and the lower classes of people in a farming community, the former pointing to the hereditary ruling class, and the latter pointing to people engaged in specialized occupations, such as smiths, coopers, and itinerant priests. These people refused to settle in one community. In the last period, when Yanagita's research interest shifted from the study of local customs to that of Japan's national culture, *jōmin*'s meaning was extended to include the entire Japanese population, even the emperor. In Yanagita's observation, some aspects of ordinary people's life, rituals in particular, closely resembled those of the imperial family – hence the unity of the Japanese nation.

After Yanagita's death in 1962, much of the debate on *jōmin* focused on the extended usage just mentioned. Central to the debate was the question of whether *jōmin* constituted a specific category of people who really existed at a particular time and place or, by contrast, an abstract category comprising the entire Japanese people across time and space. Fukuta supported the former position, regarding *jōmin* mainly as *honbyakushō* (independent peasants), who, in the Tokugawa period, possessed their own land and house, as well as their descendants, who were believed to embody their ancestors' traditions in modern times. He thus objected to Yanagita's attempt to make *jōmin* an all-embracing category. Many folklorists supported Yanagita, however, and interpreted *jōmin* as meaning not only the Japanese people, but also the totality of their way of life. In their hands, *jōmin* became almost synonymous with Japanese culture – a view that later came to be called "*jōmin* as a cultural concept."

This identification of *jōmin* with Japanese culture aroused much controversy among historians. Historians directed their criticisms toward the folklorists' indifference to the time frame, which, according to the former, was derived from the latter's supposition of the "supertemporal nature" of *jōmin*. This concept was so named after the folklorists' assertion that *jōmin* was a transgenerational category. Indeed, the aforementioned "*jōmin* as a cultural concept" was divorced from a specific time frame, hence unable to indicate when particular customs were practiced – a criticism similar to that of "essentialism" in today's scholarship. Another criticism made by historians, especially those in the Marxist camp, was concerned with the folklorists' indifference to class, which derived from the supposed "superclass nature" of *jōmin*. Given Yanagita's view that *jōmin* included the emperor, this was only expected. All in all, the idea of *jōmin* has the same weaknesses as the anthropological notion of culture: both tend to be essentialist and gloss over internal differences and conflict.

Fukuta's approach, by contrast, is free from such ambiguities. It represents what has come to be called "*jōmin* as a substantial concept." This concept, however, has a different set of problems. For one thing, the proportion of the people Fukuta identified as *jōmin* (i.e., independent peasants in Tokugawa times and their descendants) has significantly diminished in post-war Japan as a result of urbanization and industrialization. Since *jōmin* is a pivotal concept in Japanese folkloristics, this demographic change implies the loss of the discipline's raison d'être. At least, the dramatic social change that has occurred since the end of World War II has made it necessary to reconsider the folklorists' customary emphasis on peasant culture. Some scholars, most notably Noboru Miyata, have tried to solve this problem by developing new fields, such as "urban folkloristics." For another, the attempt to restrict the meaning of *jōmin* to a narrowly defined group of people will eventually direct the researchers' attention away from the folk customs practiced outside that category. Accordingly, the scope of research will be considerably diminished, and folkloristics may lose its popularity among readers at large.

Despite his familiarity with western scholarship, Yanagita seldom mentioned the literature he had consulted in producing his voluminous works. This omission was probably intentional. Yanagita was convinced that folkloristics would only prosper in a country like Japan, where the old and the new coexisted, and that western scholars would sooner or later be forced to reexamine their findings in light of the Japanese research. Yanagita wanted to be the leader, if not the founder, of the world community of folklorists. Considering the passive role Japanese academics conventionally played in the international community, his ambition was exceptional. However, Yanagita's failure to properly acknowledge his intellectual debt has brought about unfortunate results among his followers – the difficulty of assessing his achievement in the global context and the subsequent isolation of Japanese folkloristics from western scholarship, which occupies a central place in the "academic world system" (Kuwayama 2004). Thus, it is unclear if Yanagita's concept of *jōmin*, around which his scholarship developed, has any connection with, for example, the Annales School of French social history, which developed at about the same time. The task of clarifying the "western roots" of Yanagita still remains to be done.

SEE ALSO: Annales School; *Minzoku*; *Nihonjinron*; Yanagita, Kunio

REFERENCES AND SUGGESTED READINGS

Amino, Y., Miyata, N., & Fukuta, A. (Eds.) (1992) *Nihon Rekishi Minzoku Ronshü*, 1 (*Selected Essays on Japanese History and Folklore*, Vol. 1). Yoshikawa Köbunkan, Tokyo.

Fukuta, A. (1984) *Nihon Minzokugaku Höhö Josetsu* (*An Introduction to the Methods in Japanese Folkloristics*). Köbundö, Tokyo.

Fukuta, A. (1992) *Yanagita Kunio no Minzokugaku* (*Kunio Yanagita's Folkloristics*). Yoshikawa Köbunkan, Tokyo.

Kuwayama, T. (2004) *Native Anthropology*. Trans Pacific Press, Melbourne.

Nakai, N. (1973) *Rekishigaku-teki Höhö no Kijun* (*Rules of Methods in Historiography*). Kö Shobö, Tokyo.

Yanagita, K. (1998) *Kyödo Seikatsu no Kenkyühö* (*Methods in the Study of Local Community Life*). In: Ito, M. et al. (Eds.), *Yanagita Kunio Zenshü*, 8 (*The Complete Works of Kunio Yanagita*, Vol. 8). Chikuma Shobö, Tokyo, pp. 195–368.

journaling, reflexive

Valerie J. Janesick

Journal writing as a reflexive research activity has been called reflexive journaling by many sociologists and researchers in training. It has been most used by qualitative researchers in the social sciences and other fields since these professionals are seeking to describe a given social setting or a person's life history in its entirety. Qualitative research has a long history of its own which includes discussion of the techniques of the qualitative researcher. Reflexive journaling has been one of the most described and often used techniques (Janesick 2004). It has proven to be an effective tool for understanding the processes of qualitative research more fully, as well as the experiences, mindsets, biases, and emotional states of the researcher.

Many researchers advocate the use of a reflexive journal at various points in the research project timeline. To begin with, a journal is a remarkable tool for any researcher to use to reflect upon the methods of a given work in progress, including how and when certain techniques are used in the study. Likewise, it is a good idea to track the thinking processes of the researcher and participants in a study. In fact, writing a reflexive journal on the role of the researcher in any given qualitative project is an effective means to describe and explain research thought processes. Often qualitative researchers are criticized for not explaining exactly how they conducted a study. The reflexive journal writing of a researcher is one device that assists in developing a record of how a study was designed, why certain techniques were selected, and subsequent ethical issues that evolved in the study. A researcher may track in a journal the daily workings of the study. For example, did the participants change an interview appointment? How did this subsequently affect the flow of the study? Did a serious ethical issue emerge from the conduct of the study? If so, how was this described, explained, and resolved? These and other such questions are a few examples of the types of prompts for the writer. In addition this emphasizes the importance of keeping a reflexive journal throughout the entire qualitative research project.

If one checks recent dissertations completed and catalogued on Dissertation Abstracts International, it is easy to see that many recent dissertations include the use of a reflexive journal. The inclusion of the use of the reflexive journal as part of the data collection procedure indicates, to some extent, the credibility of this technique. But, conversely, does it not also act as a source of credibility and validity for the overall project? As a research technique, the reflexive journal is user friendly and often instills a sense of confidence in beginning researchers and a sense of accomplishment in experienced researchers. Many researchers verify that the use of a reflexive journal makes the challenge of interviewing, observations, and taking fieldnotes much more fluid. Researchers who use the reflexive journal often become more reflective persons and better writers. Writing in a journal every day instills a habit of mind which can only help in the writing of the final research report.

In beginning the reflexive journal, regardless of the project, it is always useful to supply all the basic descriptive data in each entry. Information such as the date, time, place, participants, and any other descriptive information should be registered in order to provide accuracy in reporting later in the study. Especially in long-term qualitative projects, the specific evidence which locates members and activities of the project can become most useful in the final analysis and interpretation of the research findings. Now let us turn to the history of the reflexive journal and the creation of a reflexive journal, which are also critical aspects of the journaling process.

Journal writing began from a need to tell a story. Famous journal writers throughout history have provided us with eminent examples and various categories of journals (Progoff 1992). Some types of journal writing can be viewed from the perspective of chronicler, traveler, creator, apologist, confessor, or prisoner, as Mallon (1995) describes. No matter what orientation taken by the reflexive journal writer, it is generally agreed that reflexive journal writing is utilized for providing clarity, organizing one's thoughts and feelings, and for achieving understanding. Thus the social science researcher has a valuable tool in reflexive journal writing.

While journal writing has its seeds in psychology, sociology, and history, one can rely on understanding the use of the journal from social psychology and the symbolic interactionists. In addition, what Denzin (1989) calls "interpretive interactionism" is a useful tool for understanding the reflexive journal. Symbolic interactionists have historically argued that we all give meaning to the symbols we encounter in interacting with one another. Interpretive interactionists go a step further in that the act of interpretation is a communication act with one or more interactors. For the journal writer, one is interacting with one's self in a sense.

Basically, the art of journal writing and subsequent interpretations of journal writing produce meaning and understanding which are shaped by genre, the narrative form used, and personal cultural and paradigmatic conventions of the writer, who is either the researcher, participant, and/or co-researcher. As Progoff (1992) notes, journal writing is ultimately a way of getting feedback from ourselves. In so doing, it enables us to experience in a full and open-ended way the movement of our lives as a whole and the meaning that follows from reflecting on that movement.

One might ask, why should one invest the time in journal writing? Journal writing allows one to reflect, to dig deeper into the heart of the words, beliefs, and behaviors we describe in our journals. The act of writing down one's thoughts will allow for stepping into one's inner mind and reaching further for clarity and interpretations of the behaviors, beliefs, and words we write. Journal writing also allows for training the writer as a researcher in writing about a research project in progress. The journal becomes a tool for training the research instrument, the person. Since qualitative social science relies heavily on the researcher as research instrument, journal writing can only assist researchers in reaching their goals in any given project.

SEE ALSO: Biography; Culture; Education; Life History; Methods

REFERENCES AND SUGGESTED READINGS

Denzin, N. K. (1989) *Interpretive Biography*. Sage, Newbury Park, CA.

Janesick, V. (2004) *Stretching Exercises for Qualitative Researchers*, 2nd edn. Sage, Thousand Oaks, CA.

Mallon, T. (1995) *A Book of One's Own: People and their Diaries*. Hungry Mind Press, Saint Paul, MN.

Progoff, I. (1992) *At a Journal Workshop: Writing to Access the Power of the Unconscious and Evoke Creative Ability*. J. P. Tarcher, Los Angeles.

Judaism

Abraham D. Lavender

Judaism is one of the world's oldest religions, characterized by a belief in one God (monotheism), a belief that the Torah is the source of divine knowledge and law, and that the Jews, because the Torah was given to them after other peoples turned it down, have an obligation to be a light unto the world. The Torah is also referred to as the holy scriptures. It is the first five books (Genesis, Exodus, Leviticus, Numbers, and Deuteronomy) of what Christians refer to as the Old Testament. In Hebrew, the word *Torah* means "teaching." In a larger sense the Torah consists not only of the five books, but includes all of Jewish tradition. The belief in monotheism is affirmed in the Shema, the first line and essence of which comes from Deuteronomy 6:4, and is translated as "Hear, O Israel, the Lord our God, the Lord is One." Judaism does not claim to be the only true religion, but rather teaches that there are different ways of reaching God.

Some sources define Judaism as the religion of the Jews, but this then raises the question of how to define Jews. The definition has changed throughout history, and continues to change even until today. This situation exists largely because Jews also have been considered a race, an ethnic group, a culture, a civilization, or a nation. Today, a person born of a Jewish mother is considered Jewish even if he or she does not practice Judaism, unless there is a deliberate rejection of Judaism. Reform and Reconstructionist Judaism accept a child born of either a Jewish mother or father if the child is raised to accept Judaism. But until about 2,000 years ago the religion followed the father instead of the mother. In Israel today the issue of who is a Jew continues to be a hotly debated topic which changes according to the internal political situation and influences from the Diaspora.

Abraham (ca. 1600 BCE) is considered the first patriarch and the founder of Judaism. He was born and raised in Ur (present-day Iraq), and afer rejecting the idols of his culture and accepting the belief in monotheism, he migrated to Canaan. As with much of ancient history, researchers today question whether this is legend or fact, or a mixture of both, but Abraham is viewed as the founder of Judaism.

The initials used above, BCE, refer to Before the Common Era, and CE refers to the Common Era. They frequently are used by Jews instead of BC and AD, which are based on the birth and death of Jesus, and hence are viewed by some as Christian markers. However, the years are the same as in the Christian (Gregorian) calendar, so that one could, for example, say 2007 CE, which would be the same as AD 2007. However, within the Jewish community, and with Jewish calendars, the years differ, and one does not use any initials after the year. Because Judaism, like Islam, the Chinese culture, and others, uses a lunar calendar instead of a fixed calendar, the Jewish year does not begin on January 1, but on the Jewish holiday, Rosh Hashanah ("the head of the year"), which usually occurs in September or early October. The Jewish calendar adds 3,761 years to the Christian calendar, so that, for example, the Christian year of 2000–2001 was the Jewish year of 5760–5761. Judaism uses this system to date the beginning of the world with Adam and Eve. Abraham, and the beginning of Judaism, go back only about 3,600 or 3,700 years, but the Jewish calendar goes back 1,946 years before Abraham. The number of years is based on the 19 generations listed inclusively from Adam to Abraham (Abram) in Genesis 5:3–32 and Genesis 11:10–26. The Jewish day begins at sundown instead of at midnight.

While all of the Torah is very important to Judaism, the Ten Commandments (Exodus 20:1–17), revealed to Moses at Mount Sinai in the thirteenth century BCE, are viewed in Judaism as the basis of all legislation. About two centuries after Moses, King David (1010–970 BCE) made Jerusalem the center of the government and of Judaism. David's son Solomon built the first Temple, making Jerusalem the physical center of worship for Jews. But the strengthening of Jerusalem strained relations with the tribes outside of Jerusalem, leading to major effects on the future of Judaism.

Like most religions, Judaism has changed over time and has developed divisions with different definitions, degrees of traditionalism, and practices. The first major division was in 721 BCE when the ten northern tribes, known as Israel, were conquered by the Assyrians and sent into exile (becoming known as the Lost Tribes), while the two southern tribes, known as Judah and centered in Jerusalem, continued. In 2 Kings 17:7 it is said that Israel fell because "the people of Israel had sinned against the Lord their God." But in 586 BCE Judah also fell, victim of the large Babylonian Empire to the east. Solomon's Temple was destroyed and much of the population, especially much of the religious leadership, was deported to Babylonia.

Large numbers also went to Egypt. But only a few decades later, in 538 BCE, under new Babylonian leadership, Jews were allowed to return to Jerusalem. Some stayed in Babylonia and some returned. The exile was interpreted as punishment for sins, and the return was interpreted as God's forgiveness for the sins.

The Temple was rebuilt in Jerusalem (completed in 516 BCE) and referred to as the Second Temple. Rebuilding a Jewish life was not easy, but eventually Judah was reestablished with Judaism at its center and the Temple playing a major role. The Greek empire was the next threat to Judaism, partly by ruling over Judah, but also by presenting other perspectives and "hedonistic" philosophies. After 198 BCE the Seleucids ruled Jerusalem, banned the practice of Judaism, and raised an altar to Zeus in the Temple. In 165 BCE the Maccabees, a Jewish group, won independence for Judah and reestablished Judaism. Two groups arose during this period: the Pharisees, who maintained the Torah and the Oral Law and tried to adapt Judaism to new conditions, and the Sadducees, an aristocratic group who rejected the Oral Law and interpreted the Pentateuch (Genesis, Exodus, Leviticus, Numbers, and Deuteronomy) literally. Although they were frequently dominant in Temple worship, they disappeared as a group with the destruction of the Second Temple in 70 CE. Oral Law is the authoritative interpretation of the Written Law (the Pentateuch), and traditionally is considered as being given to Moses at Mount Sinai along with the Written Law.

The destruction of the Second Temple resulted from Roman rule. Religious conflict was dominant in Israel, partly leading to a weakened condition, and by 47 BCE Israel was ruled by the Roman Empire. This defeat brought great soul-searching, many individuals claimed to be the promised Messiah who would bring peace (Jesus, a rabbi, appeared in this context), and conflicts between religious groups were frequent. There were Jewish revolts against the Romans, and as a result in 70 CE the Second Temple was destroyed. In 135 CE a second revolt was crushed and most Jews were exiled from Israel.

Even by the end of the first century of the Common Era, shortly after the life of Jesus, the world Jewish population was about 7 million, with about 2.5 million in Israel and almost two-thirds in the Diaspora, especially in Egypt, Syria, Greece, Rome, and Babylonia. With a Temple no longer existing as the major center of Judaism, and with nearly all Jews expelled from Israel in 135 CE, the worship of Judaism would undergo major changes. Over a million Jews had been killed during the revolts in Israel, including rabbis and other scholars, and many yeshivot (Jewish academies) had been destroyed. A religious need existed. Rabbinic Judaism, which emphasized interpretations by rabbis, would become dominant. The synagogue increased in importance, becoming the focus of Jewish communal life. Because nearly all Jews were now in Diaspora, living in many countries, many interpretations of how to believe in and practice Judaism developed. The Babylonian Talmud was developed between the early third and late fifth centuries CE. It consists of Jewish history and customs, and interpretations of Jewish law. The less accepted Jerusalem Talmud was completed around the fifth century CE. Halakhah refers to the legal part of the Talmudic and later Jewish literature, including Oral Law, and is the traditionally accepted interpretation of the Written Law.

From a cultural perspective, Jews today are classified as Sephardic or Ashkenazic. Sepharad comes from the Hebrew word referring to Spain, and Sephardic Jews in a restricted sense are those Jews from Spain or Portugal. However, the term frequently is used also to refer to Jews from the Near East, the Middle East, North Africa, and a few other locations. A more correct terminology is to refer to Jews from the Eastern world as Mizrahim, *mizrahi* meaning "eastern" in Hebrew. Ashkenazi comes from the Hebrew word for Germany, but like Sephardi, has been extended to cover a much larger area. It includes all of Europe except a few areas such as Spain and Portugal, and in a larger sense, generally refers to those Jews who have lived in Christian lands. Jews lived in many of these areas long before the areas became Christian. By contrast, most Sephardim have lived in Islamic or Muslim lands since the advent of Islam in the seventh century, although most of these areas,, such as Iran,

Iraq, the Middle East, and North Africa, had sizable Sephardic populations long before the areas became Islamic.

Sephardim, living mostly in Islamic lands, were not treated as equals but generally were not treated as badly as the Ashkenazim (*im* is the masculine plural, and *ot* the feminine, in Hebrew). Sephardim were more likely to interact with the non-Jewish populations, whereas Ashkenazim, facing more oppression, were less likely to interact with non-Jews. Ashkenazim generally maintained Yiddish, that is, Hebrew mixed with German or other European languages, as their major language. Sephardim from Spain maintained Ladino, Hebrew mixed with Spanish, to a limited degree, and in some other areas maintained Hebrew mixed with the local language, such as Judeo-Persian. But Sephardim or Mizrahim largely spoke the language of the country. In all Arab countries Arabic remained the vernacular of the Jews to the present time, and a voluminous literature in Arabic was produced by Jews. Largely because of the interaction, or lack thereof, with non-Jewish neighbors, Sephardim and Ashkenazim developed different responses to discrimination and persecution. Ashkenazim have been more likely to approach persecution from a martyr perspective, whereas Sephardim have been more likely to temporarily adjust themselves to the demands of the oppressive society (sometimes converting to the dominant religion, with a secret maintenance of Judaism) with the expectation of being able to return to Judaism at a later date. Maimonides (1135–1204), a very famous rabbi, philosopher, and physician who was born in Spain, fled to Morocco to escape persecution, and spent most of his life in Egypt, taught this perspective. Some indications are that his family followed this perspective.

In 1170 there were 1,400,000 Sephardim in the world, and only 100,000 Ashenazim, Sephardim comprising 93.3 percent of world Jewry. World trade patterns shifted, some countries underwent difficult times, and by 1700 there were 2 million Jews in the world, evenly divided between Ashkenazim and Sephardim. In the next 200 years the Ashkenazim, largely in Eastern Europe, continued an explosive growth while the Sephardim declined. In 1900 there were 9,550,000 Ashkenazim and only 950,000 Sephardim, Ashkenazim comprising 90.5 percent of world Jewry.

Largely because of different experiences of Jews living in diverse areas, as well as the influences of modernization, Judaism historically has had religious divisions and movements. In the Common Era, the Karaites appeared in the Middle East in the early eighth century, and rejected the Talmudic and Rabbinic traditions. Kabbalah, emphasizing Jewish mysticism, became more important around the twelfth century. By the sixteenth century, Jerusalem, Safed, Tiberias, and Hebron were centers of Jewish mysticism in Israel. Shabbetai Zevi came out of Turkey in the seventeenth century, claimed to be the Messiah, and got a large following, but eventually converted to Islam under pressure. Hasidism arose in Eastern Europe in the eighteenth century as a pietist religious and social movement, emphasizing devotion of the masses rather than Talmudic learning for a few. The Haskalah, a modernization and Enlightenment approach to Judaism, arose in Germany, Italy, and Western Europe in general in the 1770s.

Today, there are several major branches of Judaism, which differ in their beliefs and practices. In most Ashkenazi areas the two main divisions are Orthodox, or Traditional, Judaism, and Liberal, or Progressive, Judaism. Orthodox Judaism accepts the totality of Judaism as based on the Torah, Oral Laws, and commentary, and requires a strong degree of traditional belief and daily observance. It is divided into Modern Orthodox and Traditional Orthodox. Liberal Judaism has made more adjustments with modern societies and is less demanding in both beliefs and practices.

The US, whose Jewish population is over 90 percent Ashkenazi, developed a threefold division of Orthodox, Conservative, and Reform Judaism, largely because of migration patterns which were not experienced in other countries. Although Sephardic Jews founded the US Jewish community in 1654 and remained the cultural elite until the 1700s, the first sizable Jewish population was established in the early and middle 1800s by German Jews. They usually had been influenced by Haskalah before migrating. Reform Judaism had begun in Germany and was brought to the US. In the 1880s large numbers of Jews began migrating to the US from Eastern Europe, which mostly had not yet experienced the Haskalah. Hence, they usually brought Orthodoxy with them. Many felt that Orthodoxy was too traditional for the US, which was much different from Eastern Europe, but many also felt that Reform Judaism had given up too much tradition. So a middle ground, Conservative Judaism, developed. Conservatism agrees with Orthodoxy in many beliefs, but is closer to Reform in practices. A fourth branch of Judaism in the US, Reconstructionism, views Judaism as an evolving religious civilization and follows some modern practices, such as ordination of women. Sephardic Jews did not follow this migration pattern to the US, and hence did not divide into either Reform or Conservative Judaism. Sephardic Judaism is Orthodox, but because it represents all Sephardim with various degrees of traditionalism and modernization, it tends to be more flexible than Ashkenazi Orthodoxy.

In contemporary Israel, because of political alignments within the Knesset (Israel's parliament), Orthodoxy (mostly of the Ashkenazi perspective) has been the arbiter of religious and cultural disagreements. This includes the question of who is a Jew, and has led to major conflicts between traditional and non-traditional Jews. A large number of Israeli Jews are secular rather than religious. Reform and Conservative Judaism have made some progress in Israel, but progress has been limited because of insufficient political power. The Masorti movement, founded in 1979, is the umbrella for Conservative Jews in Israel.

Judaism has several major holidays and a number of minor holidays. Most important are Rosh Hashanah, Jewish new year, and Yom Kippur, the Day of Atonement. Rosh Hashanah begins a 10-day period of repentance that ends with Yom Kippur, the holiest day of the Jewish year. As noted, both occur in September or October. Other major Jewish holidays are a reflection of Judaism's long religious and cultural history, including persecutions and victories. Purim (February–March) is a joyful holiday that celebrates the victory of the Jews over a plot to destroy them in ancient Persia. Pesach, or Passover (March–April) is a celebration of the Jewish escape from slavery in ancient Egypt in the thirteenth century BCE. Sukkot (September–October) is a joyful festival

symbolized by booths (sukkot) which represent the huts which Jews lived in during the years in the wilderness during their return from Egyptian slavery. Sukkot is celebrated for 7 days and nights and concludes with Simchat Torah, a joyful holiday which celebrates the completion of the annual reading of the Torah and the beginning of a new cycle. Hanukkah (usually December) lasts for 8 days and celebrates the victory of the Maccabees over the Seleucid oppression in 165 BCE. Historically, Hanukkah was a relatively minor holiday, but it has become more important in Christian countries partly to offset Christmas so that Jewish children do not feel left out.

Judaism has several life-cycle events beginning with circumcision (*brit milah*) for a male Jewish child on the eighth day after birth. This is to renew the covenant between Abraham and God (Genesis 17:9–13). When a child is 13 years of age, a rite of passage into adulthood is celebrated: bar mitzvah for the male and bat mitzvah for the female. In the US and some other places in recent decades, these ceremonies have become expensive celebrations for some youths. Bat mitzvahs, traditionally not celebrated as much as bar mitzvahs, have increased in importance in recent decades to lessen the gender gap. Marriage and death, as in most religions, also have special religious ceremonies.

Intermarriage of Jews with non-Jews has become very common in a number of places, including the US, in the last few decades. This reflects the extent to which Jews have been accepted in larger societies, but it also is a numerical threat to the Jewish community because of the tendency of children of intermarried couples to merge into the larger society. Assimilating often is easier than maintaining a separate identity. Some non-Jews who marry Jews convert to Judaism, but overall intermarriage is a numerical loss to the Jewish community.

At the same time that Judaism is losing people to intermarriage, there are two groups of people who are returning to Judaism. In the Americas, thousands of descendants of Jews who left Judaism during the Spanish Inquisition (especially 1391 to 1492) are returning to a Jewish identity. This is found especially in the Southwestern US, but is evident in most areas with large numbers of Hispanics, such as

California, Miami, Florida, and New York City. Some descendants of the Lost Tribes of Israel, exiled by the Assyrians in 721 BCE, also are returning to Judaism. Some, especially from India, have returned to Israel to live. Black Jews from Ethiopia also have returned to Israel in large numbers, undergoing conversion once in Israel. Among all these returnee groups, there is a desire, so far unfulfilled, for a return ceremony rather than a conversion ceremony.

The belief that Jews are a race has been held by most non-Jews and some Jews until recent decades, and historically has been used as an excuse for major anti-Semitic actions. The Crusades, the Inquisition in Spain and Portugal, the pogroms (mob attacks on Jews, often for fun) in Eastern Europe, and the Holocaust all have had various degrees of racial, religious, and social reasons for anti-Semitism. The racial dimension has often been the most severe, especially during the Holocaust. It was the pogroms in Russia which gave impetus to the First Aliyah in 1881–2 and began the large-scale return of Jews to Israel as part of the Zionist movement. In recent decades the concept of race has decreased in importance and more attention has been put on genetic (DNA) clusters. There is a Middle Eastern genetic base shared by about two-thirds of Jews in the world, and the closest genetic relatives of Jews as a group are other Middle Eastern groups such as Palestinians, Syrians, and Lebanese.

Recent studies conclude that there are about 13 million (12,950,000) Jews in the world today, with 60.7 percent (7,856,000) in the Diaspora and 39.3 percent (5,094,000) in Israel. The Americas account for 46.9 percent (6,071,100) of world Jewry, with the US alone accounting for 40.9 percent (5,300,000). This has decreased in the last few decades, largely because of intermarriage and loss of children to Judaism. In the Americas, other than the US, the largest populations are in Canada (370,500), Argentina (187,000), Brazil (97,000), and Mexico (40,000).

Hashoah (the Holocaust) killed about 6,000,000 Jews – 37 percent of all world Jewry – mostly in Europe. Until then, 60 percent of world Jewry lived in Europe. Now, Europe has only 12.0 percent (1,550,800) of world Jewry. The three largest populations are found in France (498,000), of whom many are post-1948 exiles from Morocco, Algeria, and other North African countries, the United Kingdom (300,000), and Germany (108,000), most of whom are immigrants from Eastern Europe. Next in size in Europe are Russia (252,000), Ukraine (95,000), Hungary (50,000), Belgium (31,400), the Netherlands (30,000), Italy (29,000), and Belarus (23,000). In the 1990s about 900,000 Jews left the former Soviet Union and moved to Israel. Iran, Iraq, and North African countries historically had large Jewish populations, but most of these Jews (about 870,000) left in the 15 years after 1948 because of hostility against them after Israel's independence in 1948 and the rise of Islamic-based nationalism in North Africa. About 600,000 moved to Israel, and today about half of the population of Israel is Sephardi or Mizrahi.

The above figures, given annually in the American Jewish Year Book, are estimates and include people who identify as Jewish, whether or not they are active followers of, or even believers in, Judaism. Once again, the definition of who is a Jew includes a mixture of religious and cultural identities, and, for countries where anti-Semitism persists, racial components.

SEE ALSO: Anthropology, Cultural and Social: Early History; Anti-Semitism (Religion); Anti-Semitism (Social Change); Assimilation; Ethnicity; Holocaust; Orthodoxy; Religion, Sociology of; Women, Religion and

REFERENCES AND SUGGESTED READINGS

Benbassa, E. & Attias, J. (2001) *The Jews and Their Future: A Conversation on Judaism and Jewish Identities*. Zed Books, London.

Kleiman, Y. (2004) *DNA and Tradition: The Genetic Link to the Ancient Hebrews*. Devora Publishing, Jerusalem.

Kriwaczek, P. (2005) *Yiddish Civilization: The Rise and Fall of a Forgotten Nation*. Alfred A. Knopf, New York.

Lavenda, R. & Schultz, E. (2003) *Core Concepts in Cultural Anthropology*. McGraw-Hill, Boston.

Lavender, A. (2005) Sephardi, Ashkenazi, and Kurdish Jewish DNA Patterns: Comparisons to Each Other and to Non-Jews. *HaLapid: Journal of Crypto-Judaic Studies* 12: 1–7.

Neusner, J. (1992) *A Short History of Judaism: Three Meals, Three Epochs*. Fortress Press, Minneapolis.

Patai, R. (1971) *Tents of Jacob: The Diaspora – Yesterday and Today*. Prentice-Hall, Englewood Cliffs, NJ.

Stillman, N. (1979) *The Jews of Arab Lands: A History and Source Book*. Jewish Publication Society of America, Philadelphia.

Viorst, M. (2002) *What Shall I Do With This People? Jews and the Fractious Politics of Judaism*. Free Press, New York.

Zohar, Z. (Ed.) (2005) *Sephardic and Mizrahi Jewry: From the Golden Age of Spain to Modern Times*. New York University Press, New York.

juvenile delinquency

Jeff Maahs

Juvenile delinquency refers to behaviors of children and adolescents that violate the legal code. Some jurisdictions further distinguish "delinquent offenses," those that violate criminal law, from "status offenses" (e.g., curfew violation, truancy) that apply only to minors. The legal status of "juvenile delinquent" is relatively new. The concept of delinquency is rooted, however, in an ancient debate over when children can form criminal intent and bear criminal responsibility for their actions, and whether/how they should be officially sanctioned. Some of the earliest written legal codes make distinctions in the punishments available for children and adult offenders. By the seventeenth century, English common law adopted a classification system where children under 8 years of age were immune from criminal prosecution. For youth aged 8 to 13 years, the state had the burden of proving that the youth possessed criminal intent (Butts & Mitchell 2000). In the United States, Progressive-era reformers went a step further and created an entirely new system to respond to juvenile offenders. The first juvenile court, created in Cook County, Illinois in 1899 and modeled thereafter by other states, was markedly different from criminal courts. The new court was quasi-civil and informal in nature, and under the doctrine of *parens patriae* (the state as parent), aspired to act in the best

interests of the child. The new philosophy and procedures required a new language. Thus, rather than finding juveniles guilty of a criminal offense and sentencing them to a sanction, youths were "adjudicated delinquent" and received a suitable "disposition."

The issues of criminal responsibility and age-appropriate responses to juvenile offending remain unresolved, as evidenced by wide variation in statutes defining juvenile delinquency across the United States. For example, the upper age limit for juvenile court jurisdictions ranges from 15 to 18 years. Additionally, many states have statutes that allow, for various reasons (e.g., seriousness of offense, prior juvenile offenses), youth to be waived to criminal court.

Aside from legal considerations and the formal response to juvenile misconduct, juvenile delinquency occupies a central position in the study of criminal behavior. This position is well justified for a number of reasons, chief among them the prevalence of juvenile offending. In the United States, juveniles aged 13–17 years make up only 6 percent of the population, yet account for roughly 30 percent of all arrests for Uniform Crime Reporting (UCR) index offenses. A plot of arrest rates versus age yields an "age–crime curve" that indicates offending rates peak during adolescence (around age 16 for property offenses, and age 18 for violent offenses) and diminish soon thereafter.

Unsurprisingly therefore, the major theoretical paradigms explaining crime, including social control theory (Hirschi 1969), social learning theory (Sutherland 1947), strain theory (Merton 1938), and labeling theory (Becker 1963), are derived from theories of juvenile delinquency. In the 1960s, several "subculture" theories evolved solely to explain the existence and nature of delinquent gangs (see, e.g., Cohen 1955). Although some of theses theories extend to account for adult offending, most focus explicitly on concepts (school experience, peer groups, parenting) that are germane to adolescence. More recently, juvenile delinquency interests criminologists for another reason – its ability to predict future criminal behavior.

Studies (using both self-report and official data) of cohorts of children indicate that a small minority of children (roughly 6 percent) account for a large portion (over 50 percent) of the delinquency in that cohort. Further, delinquency, and even non-delinquent behavior problems (e.g., severe, age-inappropriate temper tantrums, conduct disorder), are robust predictors of future criminal behavior. A major goal of developmental or life course criminology is to explain why antisocial behavior is stable over time. Some theorists argue that stability is due to a trait (impulsivity, low self-control) that is stable from early childhood onward. Others contend that delinquency itself has effects on the environment (school performance, peer and parent relationships) that mortgage the child's future prospects and narrow options for change. While this debate remains unsettled, there is some agreement with regards to other correlates of juvenile delinquency.

Gender is among the most agreed-upon correlate of crime. Regardless of how delinquency is measured (e.g., arrest data, self-report, victimization data), males are much more likely to engage in most forms of delinquency than females. The data are more ambiguous for social class and race. In the United States, official data (and some victimization data) indicate moderate to strong relationships between delinquency, class, and race, whereas self-report data often indicate weak or nonexistent associations. This may be due to police or court bias, or to differences in the nature of offenses measured by self-report and official data. Aside from gender, the most empirically supported individual-level correlates include socialization markers (parental supervision and discipline, parent–child bond), and the influence of delinquent peers. At the macro level, social disorganization theorists focus on neighborhood characteristics (high poverty, high residential mobility) conducive to delinquency. Sampson and Groves (1989), using data from the British Crime Survey, found that delinquency is more likely in neighborhoods where these ecological characteristics impede a neighborhood's ability to informally supervise and control youth.

SEE ALSO: Age and Crime; Crime, Life Course Theory of; Crime, Schools and; Crime, Social Control Theory of; Crime, Social Learning Theory of; Gangs, Delinquent; Index Crime; Measuring Crime; Race and Crime; Self-Control Theory; Social Disorganization Theory; Strain Theories

REFERENCES AND SUGGESTED READINGS

Becker, H. (1963) *Outsiders: Studies in the Sociology of Deviance*. Free Press, New York.
Butts, J. A. & Mitchell, O. (2000) Brick by Brick: Dismantling the Border between Juvenile and Adult Justice. In: *Criminal Justice 2000*, Vol. 2. National Institute of Justice, Washington, DC.
Cohen, A. (1955) *Delinquent Boys: The Culture of the Gang*. Macmillan, New York.
Hirschi, T. (1969) *Causes of Delinquency*. University of California Press, Berkeley.
Merton, R. (1938) Social Structure and Anomie. *American Sociological Review* 3: 672–82.
Sampson, R. & Groves, B. (1989) Community Structure and Crime: Testing Social-Disorganization Theory. *American Journal of Sociology* 94: 774–802.
Sutherland, E. H. (1947) *Principles of Criminology*, 4th edn. J. B. Lippincott, Philadelphia.

key informant

Jon H. Rieger

The term key informant is generally associated, though not exclusively, with qualitative research in which a researcher employs interviewing of knowledgeable participants as an important part of the method of investigation. During the often extended period of fieldwork that such research requires, a particular subject may become an especially useful source of information, be repeatedly interviewed, and thus earn designation as a key informant. It is not unusual in field research that at any particular time an investigator might have several informants who could be identified as performing in that role. Key informants can extend the investigator's reach in situations where he or she has not been, or cannot be a direct observer, and they can illuminate the meanings of behavior that the researcher does not understand. They can also serve as a check on the information obtained from other informants.

Varying circumstances may determine who actually ends up serving as a key informant. Sometimes a person becomes a key informant by merit of playing an important role in the social setting being studied. If the researcher is studying an organization, for example, a key informant might turn out to be that person who occupies a central structural position or who may be situated strategically in the communication network within the organization. An individual in such a position is likely to be unusually knowledgeable about the organization and its internal dynamics and may function as a gatekeeper. This circumstance can make his or her cooperation critically important to the success of the research. Properly cultivated, that person may serve not only as a key

informant, but may also function as a potential sponsor and guide.

Another kind of subject who might become a key informant would be an individual who has long experience with the phenomenon being studied: veteran participants are likely to be rich repositories of information. Long-term participants in a particular setting potentially provide not only a wealth of useful information but can also bring perspective to their accounts. Researchers tend to be acutely sensitive to those circumstances which may indicate that a particular subject has special or extensive knowledge and may therefore make special recruitment efforts to secure his or her service in that role. Classic studies by Whyte (1955) and Liebow (1967) demonstrate the successful utilization of key informants by social researchers in field settings.

Who will be a key informant is not always predictable, for as often as not, the person who fulfills that role emerges as the research is ongoing. While the researcher may have good reasons to surmise that certain individuals will become key informants, this is not always the way things turn out in field situations. A person who may be desirable as a potential informant may be, for various reasons, insufficiently accessible to the researcher. Issues of trust can interfere with development of the researcher–informant relationship, or there may arise simple conflicts of personality or temperament. Moreover, key informants may shift as the research is ongoing: different phases or aspects of the research may call forth different individuals who can serve as key informants.

The researcher must exercise some care in the choice and employment of informants and in reliance on any of them as key sources. For example, experienced field researchers are generally wary of subjects who present themselves early and enthusiastically to outsiders. Such individuals may actually be marginal or isolated within their own group. Uncritical use of these subjects may yield information of little value and interfere with gaining access to more reliable sources. The value of a key informant may also be adversely affected by his or her limitations as an observer, or lack of reportorial articulateness or sensitivity. To combat such problems some field researchers have even suggested that key informants be given training for their roles (Pelto & Pelto 1978).

Other perils accompany reliance on key informants. They may harbor unacknowledged biases or be driven by their own private agendas. Alternatively, key informants may distort, embellish, or exaggerate their accounts in an attempt to provide what they believe the researcher wants to hear. On the other hand, informants may willfully falsify or invent information. Chagnon (1977), for example, spent most of his initial field time being systematically lied to by supposed key informants among the Yanomamo Indians in South America, and it took 5 months of effort before he was able to connect with even a single source in the tribe that he could trust, and nearly a year to find a second informant to confirm the accounts of the first.

The value of informants in social research was well recognized at a fairly early stage in the evolution of contemporary research methodology and a substantial literature began to develop on the topic, especially in the 1950s. By the late 1960s virtually every aspect of the potentials and limitations of informant interviews had been pretty thoroughly explored. The basic insights into the use of informants generally, and key informants in particular, date to this classic literature. The value of this approach as a component of a robust social research methodology has thus been well established for several generations, and it has become a fairly standardized part of contemporary methods training (e.g., Warren & Karner 2005). In recent decades, the use of key informants has become a very common procedure in evaluation research, so much so that in some venues it has acquired more formal recognition as the "key informant method."

SEE ALSO: Ethics, Fieldwork; Ethnography; Evaluation; Grounded Theory; Interviewing, Structured, Unstructured, and Postmodern; Observation, Participant and Non-Participant; Rapport

REFERENCES AND SUGGESTED READINGS

Becker, H. S. & Geer, B. (1957) Participant Observation and Interviewing: A Comparison. *Human Organization* 16(3): 28–42.

Campbell, D. T. (1955) The Informant in Quantitative Research. *American Journal of Sociology* 60: 339–42.

Chagnon, N. A. (1977) *The Yanomamo: The Fierce People*, 2nd edn. Holt, Rinehart, & Winston, New York.

Dean, J. P. & Whyte, W. F. (1958) How Do You Know the Informant Is Telling the Truth? *Human Organization* 17(2): 34–8.

Liebow, E. (1967) *Tally's Corner: A Study of Negro Streetcorner Men*. Little, Brown, New York.

Pelto, P. J. & Pelto, G. H. (1978) *Anthropological Research: The Structure of Inquiry*. Cambridge University Press, Cambridge.

Warren, C. A. B. & Karner, T. X. (2005) *Discovering Qualitative Methods: Field Research, Interviews, and Analysis*. Roxbury Publishing, Los Angeles.

Whyte, W. F. (1955) *Street Corner Society*, 2nd edn. University of Chicago Press, Chicago.

Zelditch, M., Jr. (1962) Some Methodological Problems in Field Studies. *American Journal of Sociology* 67: 566–76.

Khaldun, Ibn (732–808 AH/1332–1406)

Syed Farid Alatas

Walī al-Dīn 'Abd al-Rahman ibn Muhammad ibn Khaldūn al-Tūnisī al-Hadhramī was born in Tunis on 1 Ramadhan of the Muslim year into an Arab family which originated from the Hadhramaut, Yemen and subsequently settled in Seville at the beginning of the Arab conquest of Spain. His ancestors left Spain for North Africa after the Reconquista and settled in Tunis in the seventh/thirteenth century. Ibn Khaldun was a scholar, teacher, and judge but is best known from the nineteenth century as the founder of historiography and sociology. Ibn Khaldun received a customary education in the traditional sciences, after which he held posts in various courts in North Africa and Spain. After a number of unsuccessful stints in office he withdrew into seclusion to write his *Muqaddimah*, a prolegomenon to the study of history that was completed in 1378 and which introduces what he believed to be a new science he called *'ilm al-'umrān al-basharī* (science of civilization) or *'ilm al-ijtimā'al-insānī* (science of human society). Ibn Khaldun's chief works are the *Kitab al-'Ibar wa Dīwān al-Mubtada' wa al-Khabar fī Ayyām al-'Arab wa al-'Ajam wa al-Barbar wa man Āsarahum min Dhawī al-Sultān al-Akbar* (*Book of Examples and the Collection of Origins of the History of the Arabs and Berbers*); *Muqaddimah* (*Prolegomenon*); *Lubāb al-Muhassal fī usūl al-dīn* (*The Resumé of the Compendium in the Fundamentals of Religion*), being his summary of Fakhr al-Dīn al-Rāzī's *Compendium of the Sciences of the Ancients and Moderns*; and his autobiography, *Al-Ta'rīf bi Ibn Khaldūn wa Rihlatuhu Gharban wa Sharqan* (*Biography of Ibn Khaldun and His Travels East and West*).

Ibn Khaldun lived during the period of the political fragmentation and cultural decline of the Arab Muslim world. The picture of chaos and disintegration that Ibn Khaldun grew up with must have influenced the development of his thought. His central concern was the explanation of the rise and decline of states and societies and he believed that he had discovered an original method for this purpose. In fact, his own classification of the major known fields of knowledge cultivated up to his time shows that his science of human society was unknown. The first category, that of the traditional sciences (*al-'ulūm al-naqliyya*), refers to sciences associated with revealed knowledge, while the second category, that of the rational sciences (*al-'ulūm al-'aqliyya*), refers to sciences which arise from the human capacity for reason, sense perception, and observation (ibn Khaldun 1981 [1378]: 435–7, 478). Neither ibn Khaldun's nor earlier classifications of the sciences include *'ilm al-'umrān al-basharī* or *'ilm al-ijtimā'al-insānī*.

Ibn Khaldun's *Muqaddimah* is a prolegomenon to his larger historical work on the Arabs and Berbers, the *Kitab al-'Ibar*. He begins the *Muqaddimah* by problematizing the study of history, suggesting that the only way to distinguish true from false reports and to ascertain the probability and possibility of events is the investigation of human society (ibn Khaldun 1981 [1378]: 38 [1967: I.77]). It is this investigation that he refers to as *'ilm al-'umrān al-basharī* (science of civilization) or *'ilm al-ijtimā'al-insānī* (science of human society), which may also be translated as sociology. Ibn Khaldun made the distinction between the outer forms (*zāhir*) and the inner meaning (*bātin*) of history (ibn Khaldun 1981 [1378]: 1 [1967: I.6]). The outer forms consist of facts and reports while the inner meaning refers to explanations of cause and effect. The new science, therefore, is presented by ibn Khaldun as a tool for the study of history and is directed to uncovering the inner meaning of history. The new field of inquiry consists of the following areas: (1) society (*'umrān*) in general and its divisions; (2) Bedouin society (*al-'umrān al-badawa*), tribal societies (*qabāil*), and primitive peoples (*al-wahshiyyah*); (3) the state (*al-dawlah*), royal (*mulk*) and caliphate (*khilāfah*) authority; (4) sedentary society (*al-'umrān al-hadharah*), cities; and (5) the crafts, ways of making a living, occupations. These areas roughly approximate, in the language of the modern social sciences, human or social ecology, rural sociology, political sociology, urban sociology, and the sociology of work. The brief introduction to Ibn Khaldun's sociology that follows looks at the empirical and theoretical aspects of his work.

Empirically, ibn Khaldun's interest was in the study of the rise and fall of the various North African states. This begins with theorizing the differences in social organization between nomadic (*al-'umrān al-badawa*) and sedentary societies (*'umrān hadharab*). Fundamental to his theory is the concept of *'asabiyyah* society with a strong *'asabiyyah* could establish domination over one with a weak *'asabiyyah* (ibn Khaldun 1981 [1378]: 139, 154 [1967: I.284, 313]). In this context, *'asabiyyah* refers to the feeling of solidarity among the members of a group that is derived from the knowledge that they share a common descent. Because of superior *'asabiyyah* among the Bedouin, they could defeat sedentary people in urban areas and establish their own dynasties. Having done so, they became set in the urban ways of life and experienced great diminution in their *'asabiyyah*. With this went their military strength and their ability to rule.

There are at least two general ways in which *'asabiyyah* declines. One is where the second generation of tribesmen who founded the dynasty experience a change "from the desert attitude to sedentary culture, from privation to luxury, from a state in which everybody shared in the glory to one in which one man claims all the glory for himself while the others are too lazy to strive for (glory), and from proud superiority to humble subservience. Thus, the vigour of group feeling is broken to some extent." By the third generation *'asabiyyah* disappears completely (ibn Khaldun 1981 [1378]: 171 [1967: I.352]). This left them vulnerable to attack by fresh supplies of pre-urban Bedouins with stronger *'asabiyyah* who replaced the weaker urbanized ones. And so the cycle repeats itself.

Another distinct way in which *'asabiyyah* declines is when the "ruler gains complete control over his people, claims royal authority all for himself, excluding them; and prevents them from trying to have a share in it" (ibn Khaldun 1981 [1378]: 175 [1967: I.353]). In other words, when a tribal group establishes a dynasty and its authority becomes legitimate, the ruler can dispense with *'asabiyyah*. The ascendant ruler then rules with the help not of his own people, but of those other tribal groups who have become his clients.

The social cohesion expressed by the concept of *'asabiyyah* is only partly derived from agnatic ties in tribal social organizations. While all tribal groups have stronger or weaker *'asabiyyah*s based on kinship, religion can also bring about such social cohesion, as was the case with the Arabs who needed Islam in order to subordinate themselves and unite as a social organization. But beyond this social psychological aspect of *'asabiyyah*, there are its material manifestations. *'Asabiyyah* refers to the authority that is wielded by the leader that derives, in addition, from his material standing as a result of profits from trade and appropriation from raiding activities. For ibn Khaldun, then, *'asabiyyah* referred to (1) kinship ties, (2) a socially cohesive religion such as Islam that provided a shared idiom legitimizing the leader's aspirations for power and authority, and

(3) the strength of the leader derived from trade, booty, pillage, and conquest.

Ibn Khaldun resigned himself to the eternal repetition of the cycle. He did not foresee developments that would lead to the elimination of the cycle. This happened with the Ottomans, the Qajar dynasty in Iran, and the state in the Yemen. The cycle ceased to be in operation when the basis of state power was no longer tribal. In Ibn Khaldun's world, ordinary folk were caught between the oppressive policies and conduct of a royal authority on one hand, and the other the prospects of conquest by bloodthirsty tribesmen led by a religious leader bent on destruction of the existing order.

Underlying the above substantive concerns is ibn Khaldun's interest in elaborating a new science of society. An understanding of the relationships among the state and society, group feeling or solidarity, and the question of the end of society requires an application of Aristotle's four types of causes, the formal, material, efficient, and final cause (Mahdi 1957: ch. 5). Understanding the inner meaning of history is to know the nature of society, which in turn requires the study of its causes. The causes are what gives society its constitution (material cause), its definition (formal cause), the motive forces of society (efficient cause), and society's end (final cause) (Mahdi 1957: 233–4, 253, 270). The material cause or the "substratum" of society is identified by ibn Khaldun as the constituent elements of society such as economic life and urban institutions (Mahdi 1957: 234). What gives definition to society, the formal cause, is the organizing ability of the state (Mahdi 1957: 235). But the material and formal causes are united by an efficient cause, solidarity or group feeling (*'asabiyyah*), which is the primary factor effecting societal change (Mahdi 1957: 253–4, 261). As society has a goal or end, the final cause also enters into the analysis. The end is the common good, for the sake of which the society, state, and solidarity (the material, formal, and efficient causes) exercise their causality (Mahdi 1957: 270). The above can be said to be the elements of ibn Khaldun's general sociology, applicable to all types of societies, nomadic or sedentary, feudal or prebendal, Muslim or non-Muslim.

There are numerous works on ibn Khaldun's life and thought, including an autobiography. There are not many modern biographies of ibn Khaldun, but a well-known one was authored by an early Egyptian sociologist, Muhammad Abdullah Enan, and is available in both the Arabic original and English translation (1941, 1953). Ibn Khaldun has been widely written on in the Arab and Muslim world as a precursor of modern sociology. Well-known examples are 'Abd al-'Aziz 'Izzat's thesis in 1932 entitled *Ibn Khaldun et sa science sociale* supervised by Fauconnier and Maunier in France (Roussillon 1992: 56 n48) and another work comparing ibn Khaldun and Émile Durkheim ('Izzat 1952). Ali Abd al-Wahid Wafi undertook a comparative study of ibn Khaldun and Auguste Comte (1951) and wrote a much-cited work on ibn Khaldun as the founder of sociology (1962).

Ibn Khaldun has been recognized as a founder of sociology by earlier generations of sociologists (Kremer 1879; Flint 1893: 158ff.; Gumplowicz 1928 [1899]: 90–114; Maunier 1913; Oppenheimer 1922–35: II.173ff., IV.251ff.; Ortega y Gasset 1976–8 [1934]). Becker and Barnes in their *Social Thought from Lore to Science*, first published in 1938, devote many pages to a discussion of the ideas of ibn Khaldun, recognizing that he was the first to apply modern-like ideas in historical sociology.

However, this degree of recognition has not been accorded to ibn Khaldun in contemporary teaching and the writing of the history of sociology. A neo-Khaldunian sociology has yet to be developed. There has always been little interest in developing his ideas, combining them with concepts derived from modern sociology, and applying theoretical frameworks derived from his thought to historical and empirical realities.

There have been few works which have gone beyond the mere comparison of some ideas and concepts in ibn Khaldun with those of modern western scholars toward the theoretical integration of his theory into a framework that employs some of the tools of modern social science (Gellner 1981; Lacoste 1984; Carre 1988; Alatas 1993).

SEE ALSO: *'Asabiyyah*; Gökalp, Ziya; Islam; Sociology; Theory

REFERENCES AND SUGGESTED READINGS

Alatas, S. F. (1993) A Khaldunian Perspective on the Dynamics of Asiatic Societies. *Comparative Civilizations Review* 29: 29–51.

Carre, O. (1988) A propos de vues Néo-Khalduniennes sur quelques systèmes politiques Arabes actuels. *Arabica* 35(3): 368–87.

Cheddadi, A. (1980) Le systeme du pouvoir en Islam d'après Ibn Khaldun. *Annales, Eco., So., Civ.* 3–4: 534–50.

Enan, M. A. (1941) *Ibn Khaldun: His Life and Work*. Muhammad Ashraf, Lahore.

Enan, M. A. (1953) *Ibn Khaldun: Hayātuhu wa turāthuhu al-fikrī*. Al-Maktabat al-Tijāriyat al-Kubra, Cairo.

Flint, R. (1893) *History of the Philosophy of History in France, Belgium, and Switzerland*. Edinburgh.

Gellner, E. (1981) *Muslim Society*. Cambridge University Press, Cambridge.

Gumplowicz, L. (1928 [1899]) *Soziologische Essays: Soziologie und Politik*. Universitats-Verlag Wagner, Innsbruck.

Ibn, Khaldun, 'Abd, al-Rahman (1981 [1378]) *Muqaddimat Ibn Khaldun*. Dār al-Qalam, Beirut. Page numbers in square brackets refer to Franz, Rosenthal's (1967) English translation, *Ibn Khaldun: The Muqadimmah – An Introduction to History*, 3 vols. Routledge & Kegan Paul, London.

'Izzat, 'Abd al-'Aziz (1952) *Étude comparée d'Ibn Khaldun et Durkheim*. Al-Maktabat Al-Anglo Al-Misriyyah, Cairo.

Kremer, A. von (1879) Ibn Chaldun und seine Kulturgeschichte der Islamischen Reiche. Sitzungsberichte der Kaiserlichen Akademie der Wissenschaften (Philosoph.-histor. Klasse) (Vienna), 93.

Lacoste, Y. (1984) *Ibn Khaldun: The Birth of History and the Past of the Third World*. Verso, London.

Mahdi, M. (1957) *Ibn Khaldun's Philosophy of History*. George Allen & Unwin, London.

Maunier, R. (1913) Les idées économiques d'un philosophe arabe au XIVe siècle. *Revue d'histoire économique et sociale* 6.

Michaud, G. (1981) Caste, confession et société en Syrie: Ibn Khaldoun au chevet du "Progessisme Arabe." *Peuples Mediterranéens* 16: 119–30.

Oppenheimer, F. (1922–35) *System der Soziologie*. Jena.

Ortega y Gasset, J. (1976–8 [1934]) Abenjaldún nos revela el secreto. *Revista del Instituto Egicio de Estudios Islámicos en Madrid* 19: 95–114.

Ritter, H. (1948) Irrational Solidarity Groups: A Socio-Psychological Study in Connection with Ibn Khaldun. *Oriens* 1: 1–44.

Roussillon, A. (1992) La représentation de l'identité par les discours fondateurs de la sociologie Turque et Egyptienne: Ziya Gökalp et 'Ali Abd Al-Wahid Wafi. In: *Modernisation et mobilization sociale II, Egypte–Turquie*. Dossier du CEDEJ, Cairo, pp. 31–65.

Wafi, Ali Abd al-Wahid (1951) *Al-falsafah al-ijtima'iyyah li Ibn Khaldun wa Aujust Kumt*. Cairo.

Wafi, Ali Abd al-Wahid (1962) Ibn Khaldun, awwal mu'assis li 'ilm al-ijtimā'. In: *A'māl Mahrajān Ibn Khaldun* (Proceedings of the Ibn Khaldun Symposium). National Center for Social and Criminological Research, Cairo, pp. 63–78.

kindergarten

Valerie E. Lee and David T. Burkam

The idea of a kindergarten originated in 1840, after the German educationalist Friedrich Froebel opened a Play and Activity Institute for children between the ages of 3 and 7 to develop their mental, social, and emotional faculties. The term is now used in many parts of the world for the initial stages of a child's classroom schooling. In some countries kindergarten is part of the formal school system, but in others it usually refers to preschool or day-care programs. In France and Germany such programs are separate from the schools and are often run by churches and local community groups. In India, Mexico, and the US kindergarten programs are available through both public and private schools.

Many aspects of children's education in kindergarten are important in a sociological context. However, the discussion here is restricted to a few important issues about kindergarten in the US: (1) differences in children's social and cognitive status as they begin their formal schooling in kindergarten; (2) how these social and cognitive differences map onto the quality of the schools where they experience kindergarten; and (3) how differences in children's cognitive growth in kindergarten are associated with whether their experiences are in full-day or half-day programs.

When US children should begin their formal schooling, and what the nature of that schooling should be, has been debated for almost two centuries (Ramey & Campbell 1991; Pianta & Cox 1999). Although the availability of publicly funded preschool education (including Head Start) is far from universal and is typically restricted to low-income children, virtually all US children now attend kindergarten. Despite its universality, the nature of the optimal kindergarten experience is widely debated among educators, early childhood specialists, parents, and researchers (Vecchiotti 2001). Since the 1960s, experts have called for more than "self-directed play." Among early childhood experts, "early intervention" typically refers to activities that include both play and academics.

Children neither begin nor end their education on an equal footing. Although kindergarten is where virtually all US children begin their formal schooling, many have early and informal schooling experiences in preschool, Head Start, or childcare (Olsen & Zigler 1989). Although all children enter kindergarten at close to the same age (typically, 5 years old), there is great variation in their cognitive and social skills as they start school (Alexander & Entwisle 1988; Ramey & Campbell 1991; Duncan et al. 1998; Pianta & Cox 1999). Moreover, cognitive and social status are typically associated with family background and race/ethnicity (Jencks & Phillips 1998). Using data from the current and nationally representative US Department of Education's Early Childhood Longitudinal Study, Kindergarten Cohort (ECLS-K), Lee and Burkam (2002) reported substantial differences in young children's test scores in literacy and mathematics by race, ethnicity, and socioeconomic status (SES) as they begin kindergarten.

Such substantial cognitive and social differences among children as they begin school present a serious conundrum. On the one hand, school is seen by the broader society as the location where social inequalities should be reduced. Advantages and disadvantages that children experience at home should not determine what happens to them in school. Rather, school is a place where children should have equal chances to make the most of their potential. On the other hand, schools often tailor children's educational activities to their perceived potential (or cognitive status), which would increase rather than equalize social differences. Kindergarten is where this conundrum about the proper role of schooling in either equalizing or magnifying cognitive and social differences begins.

Researchers and policymakers agree that social background factors are associated with school success. Moreover, research findings are consistent that social stratification in educational outcomes increases as children move through school. However, there is less agreement about the causes of increasingly stratified outcomes. One explanation for growing inequality is that children's educational experiences are differentiated as early as kindergarten – through reading groups, special education placement, and retention (Alexander & Entwisle 1988). Many educators see such differential experiences as appropriate responses to the cognitive and behavioral differences children bring to kindergarten. Such differentiation extends through elementary school through ability grouping, special education, and gifted and talented programs. They are well recognized by high school, through tracking, advanced placement, and the like.

Another explanation for increases in socially based cognitive differences relates to the schools children attend, although this link has typically been assumed rather than subjected to empirical scrutiny. The association between background and school quality means that disadvantages derived from the lack of home resources that might stimulate cognitive growth are frequently reinforced by a lack of school resources (both financial and human). The low resource base of such schools constrains their ability to compensate for poor children's weak preparation.

Lee and Burkam (2002) used ECLS-K to explore the link between young children's social background, defined by race/ethnicity and socioeconomic status (particularly poverty or economic need) and the quality of the schools where they attend kindergarten. School quality was broadly defined with a wide array of measures. Although background factors were not equally strongly associated with all measures of school quality, the patterns of association were strikingly consistent. Black, Hispanic, and lower-SES children begin school at kindergarten in systematically lower-quality elementary schools than their more advantaged and white counterparts. Whether defined by less favorable

social contexts, larger kindergarten classes, less outreach to smooth the transition to first grade, less well prepared and experienced teachers, less positive attitudes among teachers, fewer school resources, or poor neighborhood and school conditions, the least advantaged US children were shown to begin their formal schooling in consistently lower-quality schools.

The consistency of these findings across aspects of school quality very different from one another was both striking and troubling. The least advantaged children in the US, who also begin their formal schooling at a substantial cognitive disadvantage, are systematically mapped into the nation's worst schools. Moreover, there is a strong association between the type of communities where schools are located (large or medium city, suburbs, small town, or rural area) and the quality of their public schools. The lowest-quality schools are in large cities; the highest-quality schools are located in the suburbs, where the most affluent citizens reside. Those findings translate into a sobering conclusion: children who need the best schooling actually start their education in the nation's worst public schools.

As kindergarten attendance has moved toward universality, pressure has mounted among policymakers to increase the cognitive demands made on kindergarten students. One way to accomplish this is to keep children in school longer. Several demographic and sociocultural factors explain the growing implementation of full-day kindergarten. The proportion of working mothers with children under 6 is increasing; over 60 percent of these mothers are now in the workforce. Moreover, for growing numbers of children, rather than their first school experience, kindergarten fits into a continuum routinely beginning with childcare and/or a pre-kindergarten or preschool experience and moves through elementary school (Olsen & Zigler 1989). Since the mid-1970s more and more children under 5 have attended preschool programs: private or public preschools, Head Start, or childcare. Proponents of full-day kindergarten believe that, as a result of their childcare and preschool experiences, children are ready for more demanding and cognitively oriented educational programs. Recent scientific, technological, and economic developments have thrust the importance of academic success, especially in literacy and numeracy, into the forefront of social discourse. Public and political forces collectively impose enormous pressures on schools to focus on children's academic achievement, and this focus begins earlier and earlier.

Full-day kindergarten advocates suggest that a longer school day provides educational support that ensures a productive beginning school experience and increases the chances of future school success, particularly for poor children. The growing diversity among kindergarten children's racial, ethnic, cultural, social, economic, and linguistic backgrounds challenges educators to serve children well in increasingly complex classrooms. Full-day advocates suggest numerous advantages of a longer kindergarten day: (1) it allows teachers more opportunity to assess children's educational needs and individualize instruction; (2) it makes small-group learning experiences more feasible; (3) it engages children in a broader range of learning experiences; (4) it provides opportunities for in-depth exploration of a curriculum; (5) it provides opportunities for closer teacher–parent relationships; and (6) it benefits working parents.

Not all educators, researchers, and parents favor full-day kindergarten. Detractors argue that children in full-day programs risk stress and fatigue due to the long day. However, research reveals that children attending full-day kindergarten demonstrate less frustration than children in half-day programs and do not show evidence of fatigue (Elicker & Mathur 1997). Others argue that full-day kindergarten increases the chance that children will be expected to achieve and perform beyond their developmental capabilities (Olsen & Zigler 1989).

Full-day programs in public schools enroll less advantaged children (those whose families are lower SES and/or minority). Full-day programs are more common in public schools located in large US cities, which enroll less affluent and more minority children (Lee & Burkam 2002). A logical explanation for these trends focuses on public efforts to induce social equity. Despite the higher cost of operating full-day kindergarten programs, their implementation may have a compensatory purpose. Schools with disadvantaged populations are able to offer such programs because Title 1 funds (US federal money that assists schools with high numbers or percentages of poor children to ensure that all children meet academic achievement standards) could cover the added costs.

Although the relative impact of full-day and half-day kindergarten programs has been subjected to considerable empirical scrutiny, the quality of this research base is not strong. Many such studies are quite dated; many have weak research designs. Although some studies explore affective outcomes, most focus on cognitive performance. In general, research findings favor full-day (or extended-day) kindergarten over half-day programs for academic performance. Further, some studies suggest that full-day kindergarten is especially effective for socially and educationally disadvantaged children (Eliker & Mathur 1997). Whereas some studies document long-term benefits of full-day kindergarten, others report no long-term effects. No study demonstrates academic advantages for children in half-day kindergarten.

A recent study improved on the extant research based on this topic in several ways (Lee et al. 2001). First, it used current and representative samples from ECLS-K. Second, it made use of more appropriate multilevel analysis methods. Third, its conclusions were located within policies that consider costs and benefits of full-day programs. Although kindergarten is now close to universal in the US, only about half (55 percent) of schools offer kindergarten exclusively in a full-day format. Full-day programs are more common both in private schools and as compensatory programs (i.e., in inner-city schools enrolling high proportions of low-income and minority children).

Findings of the study strongly favored full-day programs, with between-school advantages of almost one standard deviation on gains over the kindergarten year in both literacy and mathematics achievement. This translated into over a month's learning advantage in both subjects. Although the time spent in school was twice as long in full-day than half-day kindergartens, the time spent on academic instruction was not double. Asking whether the benefits are worth the cost, the authors concluded that they are. Although costs for moving to full-day programs include doubling the numbers of kindergarten teachers and increasing classroom space, the benefits in academic terms are substantial, with potential long-term benefits of less remediation or retention. Evaluations of educational interventions, particularly at the national level, have seldom reported cognitive advantages this large.

Although offering kindergarten to all in the educational landscape of the US is no longer contested, there is considerably less agreement about the nature of the optimal kindergarten experience. Further research is needed to determine the ideal length of the kindergarten day, and how much of children's kindergarten experiences should focus on academics and how much should be devoted to play and socialization. In addition, numerous equity issues need to be addressed through careful investigations into whether children's academic experiences in kindergarten should be tailored to their cognitive status at entry, and whether full-day kindergarten should be an aspect of compensatory education, so that only low-income and/or low-performing children have access to such programs at public expense. As the first formal educational setting that virtually all US children experience, ongoing research needs to provide an understanding of how children's academic and social experiences in kindergarten lay the groundwork for their educational trajectories.

SEE ALSO: Childhood; Early Childhood; Educational Inequality; Ethnic Groups; Family Poverty; Poverty; Race and Schools; School Transitions; Urban Education; Urban Poverty

REFERENCES AND SUGGESTED READINGS

Alexander, K. & Entwisle, D. (1988) Achievement in the First Two Years of School: Patterns and Processes. *Monographs of the Society for Research in Child Development* 53(2), Serial No. 218.
Duncan, G., Yeung, J. Y., Brooks-Gunn, J., & Smith, J. (1998) How Much Does Childhood Poverty Affect the Life Chances of Children? *American Sociological Review* 63(3): 406–23.
Eliker, J. & Mathur, S. (1997) What Do They Do All Day? Comprehensive Evaluation of Full-Day Kindergarten. *Early Childhood Research Quarterly* 12: 459–80.
Jencks, C. & Phillips, M. (Eds.) (1998) *The Black/White Test Score Gap.* Brookings Institution, Washington, DC.
Lee, V. E. & Burkam, D. T. (2002) *Inequality at the Starting Gate: Social Background Differences in Achievement as Children Begin School.* Economic Policy Institute, Washington, DC.
Lee, V. E., Burkam, D. T., Honigman, J. J., & Meisels, S. J. (2001) Full-Day vs. Half-Day Kindergarten: Which Children Learn More in Which Program? Paper presented at the annual meeting of the American Sociological Association, Anaheim, August.
Olsen, D. & Zigler, E. (1989) An Assessment of the All Day Kindergarten Movement. *Early Childhood Research Quarterly* 4: 167–86.
Pianta., R. C. & Cox, M. J. (Eds.) (1999) *The Transition to Kindergarten.* Paul H. Brookes, Baltimore.
Ramey, C. T. & Campbell, F. A. (1991) Poverty, Early Childhood Education, and Academic Competence: The Abecedarian Experiment. In: Huston, A. C. (Ed.), *Children in Poverty.* Harvard University Press, Cambridge, MA, pp. 190–221.
Vecchiotti, S. (2001) *Kindergarten: The Overlooked School Year.* Foundation for Child Development, New York.

King, Martin Luther (1929–68)

John H. Stanfield

Dr. Martin Luther King, Jr., was not only an internationally renowned civil rights leader, but was also a public sociologist par excellence. King was born into a family and local community of socially involved ministers, deeply dedicated to issues of racial justice, in Atlanta, Georgia. His father was the pastor of Ebenezer Baptist Church, located in the now famous Auburn Avenue black community in Atlanta, who along with peers such as the Rev. William Borders, pastor of the Wheat Street Baptist Church, and John Dobbs, informally called the Mayor of Sweet Auburn, created a community culture that was highly critical of the racial status quo. It was in the Auburn Avenue community that King developed his lifelong commitment to social justice that would become refined as he was educated and went through the experiences of being a leader of a powerful social movement. This is important to keep in mind since often, while analyzing the contributions of King, it has been common to forget, or to undervalue, the influences of his community of origin. It was here that he was exposed, at an early age, to highly educated black men who took bold public stances against the racial oppression of their day.

His time at Morehouse College as an undergraduate (1944–8) coincided with the most influential years of Benjamin E. Mays, the institution's president, who was a practical theologian and public sociologist who published what was considered to be, for many years, the seminal text on the sociology of the black church. Mays, who was appointed as Morehouse president in the early 1940s, transformed this remarkable liberal arts college for black men into a sociological learning community teaching social justice and egalitarian values which permeated the culture of the campus and were reinforced by Mays's mandatory Tuesday Chapel talks to Morehouse men. Besides the leadership of Mays, the ideas and insights of Walter Chivers, the longtime chair of the Morehouse department of sociology in which he majored, had a profound influence on King. Chivers was the chief black community researcher for Arthur Raper's (1933) *The Tragedy of Lynching*, 1 of public sociological activist research in the South. From the 1940s until the late 1960s, when he retired, Chivers directed the Morehouse Family Institute, which sponsored annual conferences designed to translate academic knowledge about family issues for black community members who would be invited to these campus events. Chivers's approach would have a profound influence on how King subsequently valued the capacity of sociology as a discipline to bring about social transformation.

King would learn as well the importance of careful empirical sociological research from spending a summer working as a research assistant for the Afro-Caribbean Quaker sociologist Ira de A. Reid, who was on the Atlanta University Center faculty for a brief time. It should be mentioned that the reflective sociological reasoning typical of the culture of Morehouse College also involved the department of religion, which included professors such as S. M. Williams, who encouraged Morehouse students not only to study religious ideas, but also to be active in addressing questions of social inequality in a Jim Crow society. King's profound ethical and sociological critiques of race in American society, such as *The Letter from Birmingham Jail* and his "I Have a Dream" speech, were shaped by an older Morehouse professor, Howard Thurman, who was a theologian with a strong sociological imagination, as best seen in his book *Jesus and the Disinherited* (1949). (While Thurman was dean of Boston University's Marsh Chapel, he would introduce King, then a doctoral student, to the ideas of Gandhi.)

Thus, wherever King turned in the Morehouse curriculum there was the emphasis on thinking sociologically to promote the public good of racial justice. Surviving papers from King's Morehouse and Crozier Seminary days reveal a young man with a keen sociological approach to theology and community justice issues. This pattern would continue in his sermons, which also tended to have a deep reflective sociological focus. That King identified himself as a sociologist can be seen in his willingness to write prefaces to sociological texts such as Daniel Thompson's (1963) classical study of the black leadership class. He also wrote at least one essay on the use of the behavioral sciences in efforts to transform communities and societies. King's first book, *Stride Towards Freedom* (1958), was a personal ethnographic account of the origins and development of the 1955 Montgomery Bus Boycott, which is still a seminal handbook on how to organize a local social movement. It also includes one of the first sociological discussions about nonviolence as a means to achieve what would be eventually called restorative justice. Lastly, when King went to Stockholm in 1964, one of the people he most wanted to see was Gunnar Myrdal, the Swedish economist whose monumental *An American Dilemma* (1944) had greatly influenced his views on race as a social and moral problem in the US.

King's leadership of the Southern Christian Leadership Conference during the 1960s, like his command over the Montgomery Bus Boycott during the mid-1950s, demonstrated his skills as an applied public sociologist. His capacity to manage men and women with strong personalities and his extraordinary ability to delegate authority as a self-effacing leader were amazing. He was also a master of the media during an age in which television was beginning to become the dominant force in mass communications. If it were not for King's skill at dealing with the media, as well as his political acumen, his movement would not have been nearly as effective as it was. When King was assassinated in Memphis in 1968, he was being increasingly criticized, as his movement began to falter outside the South and due to his opposition to the Vietnam War. Also, as indicated in his 1964 Nobel Peace Prize lecture, he was beginning to turn, at least since the early 1960s, to economic questions, which made many traditional supporters of his movement, including those in the media, increasingly uncomfortable. That is to say, he began to inch closer to the perspectives of emerging Black Power leaders who were advocating black economic empowerment.

King's ability to take academically challenging theological and sociological ideas and translate them effectively for mass appeal made him a most unusual example of what a public sociologist does, and for whom. Nevertheless, the most distinctive dimension of King's sociology was his integration of spiritual and interfaith concerns into his social analysis of racial problems and other important issues during his time, such as poverty and war. His sermons, lectures, and books have fascinating illustrations of how his spiritual values are intertwined with his astute sociological analyses. In doing this, King's approach provides a model for those sociologists interested in the ethical and spiritual dimensions of human experiences, and an example for those theologians wishing to understand the sociological context for religious studies.

SEE ALSO: *American Dilemma, An* (Gunnar Myrdal); Civil Rights Movement; Leadership; Race and Ethnic Politics; Social Movements, Non-Violent

REFERENCES AND SUGGESTED READINGS

King, M. L., Jr. (1958) *Stride Toward Freedom: The Montgomery Story.* Harper, New York.
King, M. L., Jr. (1964) The Quest for Peace and Justice. Nobel Prize Lecture, December 11.
Mays, B. E. (1933) *The Negro's Church.* Arno Press, New York.
Myrdal, G. (1944) *An American Dilemma.* Harper, New York.
Raper, A. F. (1933) *The Tragedy of Lynching.* Arno Press, New York.
Thompson, D. C. (1963) *The Negro Leadership Class.* Prentice-Hall, Englewood Cliffs, NJ.
Thurman, H. (1949) *Jesus and the Disinherited.* Abingdon-Cokesbury Press, Nashville.

Kinsey, Alfred (1892–1956)

Ken Plummer

Alfred Kinsey was not by training a sociologist, but a biologist (specializing in the taxonomy of gall wasps) at Indiana University, Bloomington. Believing there was a need for a course about marriage and sexual behavior, in 1938 he was concerned to find little data on which to base such study. According to one small study at that time, some 96 percent of young Americans did not know the word masturbation and many thought it was a form of insanity. In general there was widespread ignorance, and he decided to conduct his own study of the sexual behavior of the American female and male during the 1930s to 1950s – most prominently as *The Sexual Behavior of the Human Male* (1948) and *The Sexual Behavior of the Human Female* (1953), and after his death, less well-known studies such as *Sex Offenders* (1965). Ultimately providing some 18,000 life stories of individuals (many of whom he interviewed himself), it was largely taxonomic – a "social book keeping" exercise showing who does what with whom, where, when, and how often. Using the interviews, he and his colleagues asked around 300 questions. When published, his work was a large statistical and scientific study, but curiously it became a national bestseller and played a prominent role in shaping US cultural life in the later part of the twentieth century (Reumann 2005).

His work was largely atheoretical, but his data showed dramatically how sexual behavior was related to social forces. (The theoretical implications were later drawn out by John Gagnon and William Simon, especially in their theory of social scripting.)

For Kinsey, matters such as social class, age, marriage, urban living, and religion seriously shaped social patterns of sexual behavior. His work documented significant differences between men and women, noting that "the range of variation in the female far exceeds the range of variation in the male" (Kinsey et al. 1953: 537–8: see tables in vol. 2), as well as across social classes. He also showed a wide range of variant sexual behavior; for example, finding very high rates of extramarital and premarital sex, high rates of masturbation, curiously high rates of zoophilia, and most famously of all very high rates of homosexual behavior. He found much higher rates of participation in homosexual acts than previously thought, and invented the heterosexual–homosexual continuum with a point scale ranging from "exclusively homosexual" (Kinsey 6) through to "exclusively heterosexual" (Kinsey 0) (Kinsey et al. 1953: 470).

Among his other major contributions was the refinement of interview research tools – a major appendix on research strategy is included in the first volume and it became required reading for many students of sociology during the 1950s and 1960s. His interviews required great sensitivity in eliciting material, and his sample depended upon volunteers. It remains one of the most detailed large sample studies to date, though it depended upon volunteers and did not use random sampling.

Kinsey's work has been much criticized. Apart from many moralists who condemned his work as obscene, there were others (such as Lionel Trilling) who argued that the focus on sexual behavior – of measuring who does what to whom, where, and when – managed to reduce sex to orgasm-counting while robbing it of meaningful humanity. The importance of love was minimized (but Kinsey argued that this was not measurable and this was his concern). Radical (or anti-libertarian) feminists came to criticize it for its tacit celebration of male power, for its emphasis on pleasure while ignoring the danger of sexuality, and for the violence often perpetrated upon women. (Although many also agued that it made women's hitherto neglected and denied sexuality much more active and visible.) Sociologists were later very critical of

its methodology: it did not employ a random probability sample but depended on volunteers, and hence, although large, the sample was seen as very biased. Further, the sample was not representative, and the interviews were not very accurate.

But others have seen it as a trailblazing study. For its time, the study was actually a remarkable methodological achievement, not least due to Kinsey's pioneering, single-minded efforts. In time, not only did it come to inspire many subsequent empirical works on human sexual behavior, but sociologists eventually became part of a team of researchers and helped the research take both a more theoretical (sexual scripting) and therapeutic turn. Robinson (1976) suggested that the key contribution of Kinsey's work was its impact on society: it rendered sexuality more democratic and generated an "ideology of tolerance" around sexuality that has now permeated culture. This, in turn, was built "on Kinsey's discovery of the remarkable variety of human experience." Kinsey also established the Kinsey Institute (formally known as the Kinsey Institute for Research in Sex, Gender, and Reproduction), which exists to this day in Bloomington, Indiana. Part of its work became therapeutic training for practitioners, and as such it played a prominent role in the development of sex therapy and sexology, though it has often been under continuing critiques.

Kinsey's own life has been the subject of both biography (Jones 1970; Gathorne-Hardy 1998) and film. He may have looked the picture of conservative America (complete with his bow tie): he was "happily married" and his work took on the mantle of objectivity and respectability. But as recent writing has shown, Kinsey and his colleagues were in fact "sexual enthusiasts," very accepting of a wide range of sexual diversities, and implicitly very critical of the moralism that dominated US sexual mores. He was ultimately attacked as a communist out to destroy the family and he became depressed – dying in ignominy of a heart attack at the age of 62. He was never to know his profound influence in making people aware of sexual issues, and in trailblazing the field of sexology and sex research. His work has played a major role in the development both of the study of sexuality as a serious area and in creating a very different sexual culture.

SEE ALSO: Homosexuality; Sexuality Research: Ethics; Sexuality Research: History; Scripting Theories; Sexuality; Sexuality Research: Methods

REFERENCES AND SUGGESTED READINGS

Gathorne-Hardy, J. (1998) *Alfred C. Kinsey: Sex, The Measure of All Things*. Chatto & Windus, London.
Gebhard, P., Gagnon, J., Pomeroy, W. B., & Christenson, C. V. (1965) *Sex Offenders: An Analysis of Types*. Heinemann, London.
Jones, J. H (1970) *Alfred C. Kinsey: A Public/Private Life*. Norton, New York.
Kinsey, A., Pomeroy, W. B., Martin, C., & Gebhard, P. (1948) *The Sexual Behavior of the Human Male*. W. B. Saunders, New York.
Kinsey, A., Pomeroy, W. B., Martin, C., & Gebhard, P. (1953) *The Sexual Behaviour of the Human Female*. W. B. Saunders, New York.
Reumann, M. G. (2005) *American Sexual Character: Sex, Gender and National Identity in the Kinsey Reports*. University of California Press, Berkeley.
Robinson, P. (1976) *The Modernization of Sex*. Elek, London.

kinship

Graham Allan

The study of kinship tends to be associated more closely with social anthropology than with sociology. In large part, this is a consequence of anthropologists frequently studying societies in which social and economic organization was premised to a great extent on the obligations and responsibilities that kin had towards one another. Consequently, understanding the kinship system operating in such a society provided the anthropologist with a means of revealing the society's dominant structural characteristics. In contrast, sociologists focused more on industrial societies in which family and kinship solidarities, while of consequence, were far less central to the overall organization of social and economic life. Indeed, often, family relationships were understood to be of declining significance within western societies. Like the collapse of community, the decline of kinship solidarities was understood as a necessary consequence of the economic specialization and bureaucratic rationalization associated with modernity and industrial development.

In focusing on kinship systems anthropologists are concerned with specifying the principles which underlie the dominant forms of kinship behavior, commitments, and solidarities occurring within the society they are studying. They examine such issues as who is recognized as kin; what the boundaries of kinship are; what the social and economic consequences of particular kinship positions are; whether some categories of kin (e.g., patrilineal or matrilineal kin) are privileged over others; how kinship groups operate to protect their economic interests; and the like. Such questions about the kinship system as a system can also be asked of western societies, even while recognizing that kinship is structurally of less importance in these societies. Indeed, in many ways, the long history of moral panics and polemical debates concerning the state of contemporary family life can be recognized as essentially debates about the character of the contemporary kinship system in the society in question.

Historically, the sociologist who has been most influential in analyses of western kinship systems is Talcott Parsons (1949, 1955). His argument, building on the work of earlier European social theorists, was that the family and kinship system emergent in developed industrial societies could best be characterized as a *nuclear family* system. This form of kinship system, according to Parsons, was best suited (i.e., functionally most compatible) to meet the economic requirements of industrial societies. The essence of the nuclear family system is that each individual's primary obligations are defined as being to his or her nuclear family of spouse/partner and dependent children. Parsons argues that the absence of extensive kinship obligations outside the nuclear family facilitates mobility among the labor force and limits the extent to which kinship obligations potentially undermine dominant organizational requirements for fair and equal treatment. Other sociologists, in particular W. J. Goode in his book *World Revolution and Family Patterns* (1964), developed Parsons's ideas further by attempting to demonstrate that a wide range of contemporary societies were merging towards a common nuclear family system.

In evaluating Parsons's views of kinship, it is important to recognize that his concept of structural isolation does not equate with either social isolation or an absence of all obligations. What it does assert is that responsibilities to nuclear family members are prioritized over obligations to other kin. In other words, the argument is that within the dominant kinship system a relatively strong boundary is drawn between nuclear family members and other kin. Other writers have queried how strong this boundary really is. Litwak and his associates in particular emphasized the important role that other family members outside the nuclear family household play in sustaining social life (see Harris 1983). Certainly, there is now ample evidence that in industrial societies primary kin – mothers, fathers, sons, daughters, siblings – generally remain significant throughout a person's life, and not just when they reside together as a nuclear family. Typically, though not invariably, these kin act as resources for one another, being part of an individual's personal support network for coping with different contingencies.

Thus, while a person's primary responsibilities are usually to their spouse/partner and dependent children, there remains a continuing solidarity with other kin. In particular, a parent's concern for children does not end when the child becomes adult, and few adult children have no sense of commitment to their parents. Yet importantly, this solidarity is *permissive* rather than *obligatory* (Allan 1979). That is, within most western societies, the "rules" of kinship are not tightly framed. Typically, neither the law nor custom specifies how relationships with non-nuclear kin should be ordered. Instead, there is a relative freedom for individuals to work out or "negotiate" how their kinship relationships should be patterned. Within this, of course, some groups or subcultures have stronger social regulation of kinship relations than others. For example, many migrant minority groups, especially those with a specific religious commitment, draw on kinship as a means of coping in a foreign and sometimes hostile environment, of advancing their economic interests, and of protecting and celebrating their culture.

The extent to which forms of negotiation occur between kin has been highlighted in Finch and Mason's (1993) research in Britain. They were concerned with the nature of kinship obligation in general, but more specifically with how families determine who provides support to elderly parents as they become more infirm. Their argument is that kinship obligations and responsibilities are not culturally specified – they do not follow "a preordained set of social rules." Rather, in any particular instance, a process of "negotiation" occurs through which decisions come to be made. Importantly, such negotiation does not occur in isolation, but is framed by the biographical development of the relationships in question. In other words, previous kinship behavior, as well as knowledge of the personalities and commitments of those involved, form part of the context in which the negotiation occurs. Moreover, Finch and Mason (1993) highlight three different modes of negotiation that can occur. These are: *open discussions*, *clear intentions*, and *non-decisions*. As the name implies, the first is where two or more kin openly discuss and negotiate potential responses to the issue in question. The second is where a particular individual decides on a course of action and conveys this to other kin involved without really allowing any wider discussion. The final category, non-decisions, arises where, because of the circumstances of those involved, a particular course of action emerges as "obvious" to all without any explicit decision-taking ever occurring.

The importance of Finch and Mason's analysis is that it highlights the role of agency as well as structure in kin behavior. While there are clear patterns in the ways kin behave toward one another (e.g., in the greater likelihood of daughters rather than sons providing parents with personal care in later old age) there is also a great deal of variation. As an illustration, there is solidarity between siblings, but the ways in which that solidarity is expressed vary depending on the circumstances of the siblings, their other commitments, and the history of their relationship. So too there can be diversity in who is regarded as kin, which kinship ties are honored, and what activities and topics of conversation are seen as relevant within different kin relationships. Furthermore, all these matters are liable to change over time as people's circumstances alter. Thus, within contemporary western society, kinship position does not of itself determine how people behave towards their kin or the responsibilities they feel.

The variation there is in people's attitudes and behavior towards kin has been compounded over the last 30 years by significant changes in patterns of family formation and dissolution. Most obviously, there has been the substantial growth in divorce and remarriage. Of themselves, these raise questions about the categorization and meaning of kinship. For example, are ex-spouses categorized as kin? Under what circumstances? When, if at all, are their kin categorized as kin? Similarly, to what degree and under what circumstances does a stepparent or a stepchild become kin? Are they likely to be so regarded without co-residence? Equally, what are the kinship consequences of cohabitation, a pattern of partnership which is becoming increasingly common? When do cohabitees come to be regarded as kin, either by their partner or by their partner's other kin? Such questions do not have clear-cut answers; there is a relative absence of kinship "rules" governing these matters. Instead, the nature of the relationships which develop and the extent to which they are understood as operating within a kinship frame are emergent, and in this sense "negotiated" in line with Finch and Mason's (1993) arguments.

One other important property of kinship is worth noting. As implied above, kinship is not just about individual relationships. The collective element of kinship is central to understanding kinship behavior. That is, kinship is a network of relationships in which each tie is influenced by, and in turn influences, the others. The effective boundaries of the network vary for different people, over time and for different contents. But typically news, information, and gossip flow readily through the network, with some individuals acting as "kinkeepers." For example, mothers often play a key role in passing news on to their children and facilitating contact at times of family ceremonial. In part it is because kinship operates as a network that a focus on negotiation is so useful for understanding kinship processes. Similarly, the issues raised above concerning when new partners come to be regarded as kin or whether stepparents are kin are not solely individual issues. In part, what matters is whether others in the kinship network regard them as "family," too. In many ways it is the network properties of kinship that distinguish it most clearly from other personal ties and which encourage the "diffuse, enduring solidarity" which Schneider (1968) defines as characteristic of American kinship – and by implication other western kinship.

SEE ALSO: Family Diversity; Family, Sociology of; Grandparenthood; Lesbian and Gay Families; Marriage; Parsons, Talcott; Sibling Ties; Stepfamilies

REFERENCES AND SUGGESTED READINGS

Allan, G. (1979) *A Sociology of Friendship and Kinship*. Allen & Unwin, London.
Allan, G. (1996) *Kinship and Friendship in Modern Britain*. Oxford University Press, Oxford.
Finch, J. & Mason, J. (1993) *Negotiating Family Relationships*. Routledge, London.
Harris, C. C. (1983) *The Family and Industrial Society*. Allen & Unwin, London.
Harris, C. C. (1990) *Kinship*. Open University Press, Buckingham.
Parsons, T. (1949) The Social Structure of the Family. In: Ashen, R. (Ed.), *The Family*. Haynor, New York, pp. 241–74.
Parsons, T. (1955) The American Family. In: Parsons, T. & Bales, R. (Eds.), *Family: Socialization and Interaction Process*. Free Press, Glencoe, IL, pp. 3–33.
Schneider, D. (1968) *American Kinship: A Cultural Account*. Prentice-Hall, Englewood Cliffs, NJ.
Simpson, B. (1998) *Changing Families*. Berg, Oxford.
Stack, C. & Burton, L. (1994) Kinscripts: Reflections on Family, Generation and Culture. In: Glen, E., Chang, G., & Forcey, L. (Eds.), *Mothering: Ideology, Experience and Agency*. Routledge, London.

Kitsuse, John I. (1923–2003)

Axel Groenemeyer

John I. Kitsuse was one of the premier and most influential contributors to the social constructionist movement from the 1960s, which changed the way sociologists approached the study of social problems, normality, deviance, and control. Born a second-generation Japanese American in California, Kitsuse was imprisoned in an internment camp for one year during World War II. He earned his bachelor's degree from Boston University and his master's and PhD from UCLA before he became professor of sociology at Northwestern University in 1958. From 1974 until 1991 he was professor of sociology at University of California San Diego. He served as president of the Society for the Study of Social Problems from 1978 to 1979. He died in California.

Kitsuse started his academic career with contributions on migration and social integration, especially of Japanese migrants in the US (Broom & Kitsuse 1955, 1956), and with research on education and the school system in the US (Chandler et al. 1962; Cicourel & Kitsuse 1963). However, he is primarily known as one of the founding fathers of the labeling approach to deviant behavior in the 1960s and for his contributions to the perspective of constructivism on social problems from the 1970s on.

The basic methodological and epistemological perspective of Kitsuse could best be described with a story, written at the beginning of his book *Constructing the Social* (Sarbin & Kitsuse 1994). Three referees are involved in a discussion. The first one, a self-confident realist, argued that he would punish every foul according to the rules of the game. The second one, more cautious and influenced by the perspective of symbolic interaction, answered: "I only punish the fouls as and how I see them." After that, the third one, a convinced constructivist, stated: "There will only be a foul when I punish it." There is no doubt that Kitsuse, at least after the early 1960s, followed the perspective of the third referee. Even if the basic ideas of the then so-called labeling approach had been developed long before by Tannenbaum (1938) and Lemert (1951), this radical subjectivism and relativism had not become convincing before the 1960s, with its political and intellectual climate of political mobilization for civil rights and other social movements, and the criminalizing reactions of the state. The reactions of agencies of social control and their consequences in the construction of deviant labels and careers, the scrutinizing of basic and commonly held categories of deviance and conformity, and the opening of sociology to the perspectives of "underdogs" became the main interests of a whole generation of sociologists and constituted the base for a fundamental criticism of the supremacy of structural functionalism in sociology and of positivist criminology, which had always been interested only in the individual pathologies of offenders.

Among the "fathers" of this new approach of the sociology of deviance – sometimes called the New Chicago School from California (David Matza, Sheldon L. Messinger, Howard B. Becker, Aaron V. Cicourel, Erving Goffman, Edwin M. Lemert, Harold Garfinkel) – Kitsuse was one of the first to formulate this research program in a radical way (Kitsuse 1962, 1964; Kitsuse & Cicourel 1963). Whereas this new perspective had been popularized by the work of Howard Becker (1963), who had been influenced more by Everett C. Hughes and Edwin H. Sutherland and the theory of learning, and by Erving Goffman's (1963) analysis of stigma and identity development, Kitsuse had already use a constructivist perspective (even if it had not been so named at this time).

Although the labeling approach very often has been linked to symbolic interaction, ethnomethodology, or phenomenology, it never developed a consistent theory. This has not only been a major criticism of the perspective from outside its ranks, but also by Kitsuse (1975) himself. However, against its critics (e.g., Gove 1975), he insisted on the methodological position that the process of labeling could not be reduced to another cause of deviance among others. In this, he followed the line of argumentation developed in the classic text of Kitsuse and Cicourel (1963). The objective of this analysis was not the dismantling of measurement problems of official statistics on crime, but to show that these statistics are basically *not* statistics of crime. Instead, they have to be seen as a representation of the activities of the agencies of social control. In this formulation there are no measurement problems of crime in official statistics because they do not measure criminal activities. Unlike Becker (1963) and Lemert (1951), Kitsuse insists there will only be a criminal offense if and when this label is successfully applied. From this perspective the idea of undetected crime does not make any sense. As a consequence the only interesting issue in the sociology of deviance and crime has to be the processes by which deviant labels are constructed and applied to certain categories of behavior and people. Deviant behavior cannot be explained by existing social norms, but must be analyzed as the activities of social control.

Even if the labeling perspective of Kitsuse had not been named constructivist, its central arguments certainly followed this idea and laid the groundwork for the more theoretical formulations that – since the publication of *Constructing Social Problems* (Spector & Kitsuse 1977) – dominated the sociology of social problems, at least in the US. This book, which was an elaboration of ideas published previously (Kitsuse & Spector 1973, 1975; Spector & Kitsuse 1973), defined the field of social problems from a new perspective. Social problems were no longer rooted in social structures and social change as in theories of social disorganization, anomie, and social pathology, but had to be analyzed as "activities of individuals or groups making assertions of grievances and claims with respect to some putative conditions" (Spector & Kitsuse 1977: 75). "Claims-making activities" now constitute the basic research question, and very often the perspective of reconstructing the establishment of specific issues as problematic in public discourses is seen as the only legitimate and characteristic research question in the sociology of social problems.

Criticisms about inconsistencies in his argumentation (for not having followed the methodological perspective of constructivism consistently) (Woolgar & Pawluch 1985) led Kitsuse to reformulate this perspective in a more linguistic form of discourse analysis (Ibarra & Kitsuse 1993). Whereas in *Constructing Social Problems* the main focus of analysis was on activities and collective actors that define issues as social problems on the public agenda, now social problems should be analyzed as cognitive structures – "vernacular constituents" – of texts and narratives. With this "linguistic turn" any reference to the real world of social conditions and actors was dismissed from the sociology of social problems: they are just a special game of rhetoric and counter-rhetoric. The role of sociological knowledge is reduced to that of developing convincing narratives that could offer some new perspectives. The central criterion for the validity of these narratives

is not a somehow-constructed correspondence with some social reality, but its coherence and dramatic structure (Sarbin and Kitsuse 1994). In principle, sociologists become storytellers like any other collective actor in society, perhaps with the difference that sociologists tell stories about the stories of other storytellers. As a consequence, one could ask whether this should still be called sociology, but in the perspective of his radical constructivism Kitsuse left this question open.

SEE ALSO: Constructionism; Crime; Deviance; Labeling; Social Problems, Concept and Perspectives

REFERENCES AND SUGGESTED READINGS

Becker, H. S. (1963) *Outsiders: Studies of the Sociology of Deviance*. Free Press, New York.

Broom, L. & Kitsuse, J. I. (1955) The Validation of Acculturation: A Condition to Ethnic Assimilation. *American Anthropologist* 57: 44–8.

Broom, L. & Kitsuse, J. I. (1956) *The Managed Casualty: The Japanese American Family in World War II*. University of California Press, Berkeley.

Chandler, B. J., Stiles, L. J., & Kitsuse, J. I. (Eds.) (1962) *Education in Urban Society*. Knopf, New York.

Cicourel, A. V. & Kitsuse, J. I. (1963) *Educational Decision Makers*. Bobbs-Merrill, Indianapolis.

Goffman, E. (1963) *Stigma: Notes on the Management of Spoiled Identity*. Prentice-Hall, Englewood Cliffs, NJ.

Gove, W. R. (Ed.) (1975) *The Labeling of Deviance: Evaluating a Perspective*. Wiley, New York.

Ibarra, P. R. & Kitsuse, J. I. (1993) Vernacular Constituents of Moral Discourse: An Interactionist Proposal for the Study of Social Problems. In: Miller, G. & Holstein, J. A. (Eds.), *Constructionist Controversies: Issues in Social Problem Theory*. Aldine de Gruyter, New York, pp. 21–54.

Kitsuse, J. I. (1962) Societal Reaction to Deviant Behavior: Problems of Theory and Method. *Social Problems* 9(3): 247–56.

Kitsuse, J. I. (1964) Notes on the Sociology of Deviance. In: Becker, H. S. (Ed.), *The Other Side: Perspectives on Deviance*. Free Press, New York, pp. 9–21.

Kitsuse, J. I. (1975) The "New Conception of Deviance" and its Critics. In: Gove, W. R. (Ed.), *The Labeling of Deviance: Evaluating a Perspective*. Wiley, New York, pp. 273–84.

Kitsuse, J. I. & Cicourel, A. V. (1963) A Note on the Uses of Official Statistics. *Social Problems* 11(2): 135–9.

Kitsuse, J. I. & Spector, M. (1973) Toward a Sociology of Social Problems: Social Conditions, Value-Judgments, and Social Problems. *Social Problems* 20(4): 407–19.

Kitsuse, J. I. & Spector, M. (1975) Social Problems and Deviance: Some Parallel Issues. *Social Problems* 22(5): 584–94.

Lemert, E. M. (1951) *Social Pathology: A Systematic Approach to the Theory of Sociopathic Behavior.* McGraw Hill, New York.

Sarbin, T. R. & Kitsuse, J. I. (Eds.) (1994) *Constructing the Social.* Sage, London.

Spector, M. & Kitsuse, J. I. (1973) Social Problems: A Re-Formulation. *Social Problems* 21: 145–59.

Spector, M. & Kitsuse, J. I. (1977) *Constructing Social Problems.* Cummings, Menlo Park, CA.

Tannenbaum, F. (1938) *Crime and the Community.* Columbia University Press, New York.

Woolgar, S. & Pawluch, D. (1985) Ontological Gerrymandering: The Anatomy of Social Problems Explanations. *Social Problems* 32(3): 214–27.

knowledge

Steve Fuller

Knowledge is relevant to sociology as the principle that social relations can be organized in terms of the differential access that members have to a common reality.

Until the late eighteenth century, Plato's *Republic* epitomized the role of knowledge as a static principle of social stratification. However, the Enlightenment introduced a more dynamic conception, whereby different forms of knowledge could be ordered according to the degree of freedom permitted to their possessors. An individual or a society might then pass through these stages in a process of development. Thus, thinkers as otherwise diverse as Hegel, Comte, and Mill came to associate progress with the extension of knowledge to more people.

However, this dynamic conception of knowledge produced a paradox: the distribution of knowledge and the production of power seem to trade off against each other. The more we know, the less it matters. Knowledge only

seems to beget power if relatively few people enjoy it. The distinctly sociological response to this paradox was to jettison Plato's original idea that a single vision of reality needs to be the basis for knowledge. This response, popularly associated with philosophical relativism, asserts simply that different forms of knowledge are appropriate to the needs and wants of their possessors.

The history of the sociology of knowledge is a tale of two traditions, French and German. Both came to fruition in the period 1890–1930. They are based on the proximity of knowers in space and time, respectively. Thus, the French tradition focused on how people of different origins who are concentrated in one space over time acquire a common mindset, whereas the German tradition focused on how people dispersed over a wide space retain a common mindset by virtue of having been born at roughly the same time.

The French tradition, exemplified by Lucien Lévy-Bruhl and Émile Durkheim, regarded sustained interpersonal contact as the means by which a "collective consciousness" is forged and maintained. Both took tribal rituals as the paradigmatic site for the formation of this sort of consciousness, whereby emotional energy is translated into such cognitively significant artifacts as sacred texts and canonical procedures.

In contrast, the German tradition, exemplified by Wilhelm Dilthey and Karl Mannheim, was influenced more by history – indeed, historicism – than anthropology. Instead of looking at how the physical environment, including artifacts, constrains cognitive development, the German tradition focused on the overall worldview exhibited by an array of texts produced by people who marched through time together, a "generational cohort."

Common to both the French and German traditions was the assumption that knowledge is constituted as acts of collective resistance to the environment. The exact nature of the resistance is explainable by the spatiotemporal arrangement of the people concerned. Thus, a Durkheimian might show how religious rituals enable the faithful to escape the limitations of their material conditions and stand up to potential oppressors, while a Mannheimian might show how a persistent ideology enables the experience of a particular generation to define the parameters of policy for the entire society. In both cases, the sociology of knowledge is meant to complement, not replace, the psychology of normal thought processes through which individuals adapt to a world that is largely not of their own making. Berger and Luckmann's *The Social Construction of Reality* (1967) eclectically mixes French and German traditions.

The addition of scientific knowledge as a potential object of inquiry complicated matters. Among the classical sociologists, Vilfredo Pareto was very clear about the "non-logical" status of the forms of knowledge eligible for sociological scrutiny. He declared that rationality is self-explanatory as the path of least resistance between ends and means, while sociology is needed to explain the friction of bias and error that usually gets in the way. The "rational choice" paradigm in the social sciences retains this perspective today. It was also how positivistic philosophers divided the intellectual labor between the epistemology and the sociology of knowledge. They presumed that science would always fall on the rational side of the divide, and hence not require special sociological treatment. Mannheim himself justified the presumption on reflexive grounds: sociology could not be trusted to study knowledge scientifically unless it was systematically immune to the kinds of frictions Pareto identified.

This general line of reasoning was overturned in the late 1970s by the self-styled sociology of scientific knowledge (Bloor 1976). It posed an empirical and a conceptual challenge to Mannheim's strictures. The empirical challenge lay in the irony that sociology seemed to have a mystified understanding of the form of knowledge it aspired to be. For example, Robert Merton's famous account of the normative structure of science had been based largely on the methodological pronouncements of distinguished scientists and philosophers. This was like constructing a sociology of religion solely out of the writings of theologians and priests. Consequently, the last quarter century has witnessed an efflorescence of studies applying some German but mainly French approaches to the sociology of knowledge to the understanding of science. As had been the case with religion, much of this work on science has been "demystifying" and hence a source of discomfort to professional scientists and philosophers of science.

The conceptual challenge pertained to the definition of science used to infer that it is necessarily a rational activity. Might not a religion or a political party also appear "rational," especially if evaluated in terms of its own goals? Conversely, were scientists judged in terms of all the consequences of their activities, both intended and unintended, might they not appear as "irrational" as priests and politicians? How, then, should the socially and ecologically transformative, sometimes even destructive, character of science be taken into any overall assessment of its "rationality." This challenge has been taken up most directly by "social epistemology" (Fuller 1988), which attempts to reconstruct a normative order for science in light of this socially expanded sense of consequences.

Perhaps the biggest challenge facing the sociology of knowledge today is science's tendency to become embedded in the technological structure of society as "technoscience" (Latour 1987). Under the circumstances, science's character as a form of knowledge is reduced to its sheer capacity to increase the possessor's sphere of action. Such a reduction characterizes the definition of "knowledge" used by sociologists who argue that we live in "knowledge societies" (Stehr 1994). For them, knowledge is a commodity traded in many markets by many producers. In this emerging political economy, institutions traditionally dedicated to the pursuit of knowledge (e.g., universities) no longer enjoy any special advantage.

SEE ALSO: Knowledge Management; Knowledge Societies; Knowledge, Sociology of; Mannheim, Karl; Merton, Robert K.; Scientific Knowledge, Sociology of

REFERENCES AND SUGGESTED READINGS

Berger, P. & Luckmann, T. (1967) *The Social Construction of Reality*. Doubleday, Garden City, NY.

Bloor, D. (1976) *Knowledge and Social Imagery*. University of Chicago Press, Chicago.

Fuller, S. (1988) *Social Epistemology*. Indiana University Press, Bloomington.

Latour, B. (1987) *Science in Action*. Open University Press, Milton Keynes.

Mannheim, K. (1936 [1929]) *Ideology and Utopia*. Harcourt Brace & World, New York.

Merton, R. (1977) *The Sociology of Science*. University of Chicago Press, Chicago.

Stehr, N. (1994) *Knowledge Societies*. Sage, London.

knowledge management

John Sillince

Knowledge management seeks to increase organizational capability to use knowledge as a source of competitive advantage. The field has risen to prominence along with the "knowledge worker," who is someone who does work which involves knowledge which is socially complex, causally ambiguous, and tacit. Relevant theories include social capital theory and the resource-based view of the firm. Practitioner approaches to knowledge management emphasize ways of creating, diffusing, using, and evaluating knowledge.

Strategy researchers attempt to create statements about the link between industry structure and firm performance in order to deliver guidance to leaders of firms. This guidance advocates either selection of an appropriate formula for changing industry structure, or diversification into more profitable industries. However, the value of such guidance is undermined by its key assumption of interfirm homogeneity – all firms can implement such strategies. An emerging theory of the resource-based view (RBV) of the firm and of sustainable competitive advantage implies that such strategies are not able to protect the firm against imitation or substitution. This has led to the rise in importance of theories of business strategy which privilege resources such as knowledge which are socially complex, tacit, and causally ambiguous.

Socially complex resources are routines and skills which, because of their relational nature, are difficult to imitate or substitute. Knowledge is a socially complex resource because its creation and use depend on networks of relationships and because it is collectively owned. Much

work in organizations is done in interaction with others, where the knowledge is created and used collaboratively rather than in isolation, and for this reason where it is difficult to disentangle what each person knows individually from the collectively generated knowledge. Other work is done in networks of friends and contacts who inform each other of opportunities, send warnings, and answer questions. The value of knowledge within social networks often depends on its surprise value. Such knowledge tends to come from "weak ties" – distant rather than near relationships. Networks also can act as passageways for accessing information. Through "weak ties" and "friends of friends" network members can gain privileged access to information and opportunities. In order to explicate such properties of networks and communities a theory of social capital has developed. Social capital theory argues that there are intangible goods such as knowledge, trust, goodwill, and reputation which animate social networks, constitute social structure, and facilitate the actions of individuals. It has been argued that organizations have advantages over markets for the development and use of social capital. This is because organizations are able to protect secrets and to create a trustful working environment better than markets. Such a view places knowledge as a central element within the organizational community, which concerns itself with the creation of new knowledge by means of combination and exchange of previous knowledge.

Causally ambiguous resources are ones which cannot be easily identified as inputs to performance improvements and so do not help competitors who wish to learn why a firm is so successful. However, the assumption is that organization members are sufficiently able to identify the value of those resources. Knowledge is a causally ambiguous resource because how firms do things is not just a question of procedures, policies, and routines. There are also experience, degree of care and heedfulness, cooperativeness and collective confidence which also facilitate the use to which knowledge is put and which help to improve business performance.

Tacit resources are implicit and therefore uncodifiable and so are again difficult to copy. Knowledge is a tacit resource because it is used and exchanged in language and interaction, where context cues and conversational sequence provide implicit information about the meaning of what is said. Even when written down, there is meaning to be gained by reading "between the lines."

Recent times have seen theoretical developments in how organization members are seen and how they see themselves in terms of a greater emphasis on knowledge. More educational qualifications and training, more reliance on an empowered, flexible workforce which is able to take the initiative, together with a shift from manufacturing into services, have all led to a greater emphasis on the intellectual content of work. These forces have all been behind the rise of the term "knowledge worker."

The simplest definition of knowledge worker is someone who does work which involves knowledge which is socially complex, causally ambiguous, and tacit. Many attempts have been made to measure "intellectual capital," which is defined as the knowledge dimension of social capital. Simple methods include a focus on observable and tangible assets such as patents and routines. However, this misses out many intangibles and any serious attempt to measure intellectual capital would need to take account of these. Intellectual capital is structurally embedded in the organization because the individual's knowledge is enriched and applied in a specific context created by the organization. That context includes routines, equipment, and people. Intellectual capital is relationally embedded in the organization because the individual's knowledge is enriched and applied in relationships with others. Knowledge is therefore partly a function of who one knows and what relationships one has with them. However, those relationships are only partly influenced by the organization – they may span across organizational boundaries. Intellectual capital is also influenced by cultural and cognitive factors such as inertia, cognitive bias, curiosity, and motivation.

Many employees now have responsibilities which are difficult to track and control and therefore employees are increasingly difficult to motivate. Employees with complex responsibilities are valuable because the tasks they perform would take some time to teach to a replacement, who may not be as good anyway. Employees are increasingly disloyal to their company, despite attempts by companies to develop "strong cultures." They are therefore free to leave and join other organizations. Old-fashioned, heavy-handed control methods may backfire in such cases, as the knowledge held by such workers "walks out the door."

The slimming down of workforces as a quick and simple method of economic stabilization in times of market difficulties has led to gaps in knowledge, or to gaps in organizational methods for handling knowledge. These gaps have added to the perceived importance of knowledge. If knowledge workers make up the organizational brain, removing whole levels of the hierarchy is analogous to small parts of the brain dying in a stroke, with its effect on dislocation of the organizational memory. Just as in the case of stroke in an individual, organizational memory may recover over time if there are suitable recovery practices.

The search for non-imitable organizational capabilities in line with resource-based theory of the firm has increased the importance of organizational identity. Organizational identity is "who we are as an organization." It increases one's sense of belonging, commitment, and identification. To conceive of knowledge as an individual competence misses the potential for linking individual knowledge to organizational identification. Instead, conceiving of organizational identity as the collective meaning of knowledge creation ensures that individual members feel part of a common activity, and discourages them from individualistic, alienated, and opportunistic means of gaining compensation. This is all to say that such management messages avoid drawing attention to individual competencies and instead draw attention to organization-level capabilities.

The view of knowledge in relation to organizational processes which has been most influential with practitioners has been the mechanistic view that there are different, separable processes. These are creation, diffusion, use, and evaluation of knowledge.

The realization that the creation of explicit knowledge can be measured whereas the creation of tacit knowledge cannot, and that the tacitness of knowledge prevents free transfer between a firm's workers, has led to at least two very different responses. One approach, of great appeal to practitioners, and influenced by a mechanistic view of knowledge, has been to suggest that tacit knowledge should be transformed into explicit knowledge rather like changing base metal into gold. This approach centers upon the transformations possible between tacit and explicit knowledge. These transformations are explicit to explicit (socialization), tacit to explicit (externalization), tacit to tacit (combination), and explicit to tacit (internalization). This classification has been linked to steps of learning. However, few empirical tests have been carried out of these ideas, perhaps because of the intractability of tacit knowledge.

The other approach to the creation of knowledge more favored by academic researchers has been to investigate tacit knowledge as a sociological phenomenon. For example, language is a rich field of investigation because much of the information contained in interactions is situated and context dependent. Another example is social networks in which knowledge is understood and evaluated as part of social relationships – the intellectual content of a piece of information may be less influential in its being believed compared to whether the source is liked or trusted. Another example is activity theory, which argues that knowledge is embedded in – and therefore inextricable from – tasks or, more precisely, interdependencies between tasks, "tools," and people.

The desire to measure and therefore control knowledge may be a misguided objective. The crucial question here is whether the control of knowledge leads to over-standardization. Individuals have their own "craft" ways of doing things, whereas organizational interest is furthered by standardization. Knowledge is continuously created by economic activity, and attempts to standardize too much may eradicate any novelties that eventually become sources of a firm's uniqueness. Over-standardization may also lead to the creation of routines which can be imitated by competitors.

The diffusion of knowledge has been investigated intensively for some years. Starting from the simple electricity analogy that knowledge starts from a source and eventually, despite resistance, reaches a destination or target, the field has changed considerably. The transfer of knowledge depends upon the target's ability to handle or understand it: its "absorptive capacity." Thus, a new industrial process will more

likely be taken up by another company if it has scientists and technologists who understand it, and if it has industrial processes which can turn it into valuable products. The barrier may not only be in terms of understanding the content of the knowledge to be transferred. It may also be a question of the cultural gulf which exists between the sending and receiving organization – a difficulty experienced by many multinationals. The idea of absorptive capacity has been generalized to say that the target must be treated carefully by the source in order to facilitate diffusion. For example, Edison bought up a gas company and designed electric lamps of similar dimness to gas lamps in order first to overcome the resistance of monopoly gas suppliers, and secondly to adapt to consumers' expectations of dimness. Only later did electric lights increase in brightness when the idea of the electric light had been accepted. This is an example of the value of institutional theory in understanding knowledge diffusion.

Institutional theory states that much organizational action is caused not by instrumental or rational objectives, but instead takes on the values or prescriptions contained in institutional rules. Organizations adopt many rational-seeming procedures and techniques not because they make members more knowledgeable about what they are doing, but just in order to be seen to be following methods accepted by other organizations. It may be that a lot of the value of knowledge, and of knowledge workers, may be of this institutional kind. That is, knowledge may often be valued because it provides the organization with legitimacy rather than because it makes things work better or faster.

When looked at in this way, knowledge becomes a political good, which adds to an organization's reputation and which is useful to specific professional groups in their attempts to increase their status and power. Historical studies have been undertaken of companies which have shown that the status and power of professional groups have changed markedly. In the early twentieth century, manufacturing and production engineering were the most powerful professionals. Since then there has been a rise in both the finance and the marketing functions, as companies have come to realize that scarce resources in their environment, first of finance and then of consumer demand, give precedence to people who have knowledge about such scarce resources.

One dimension of knowledge management of interest to practitioners is the extent to which the creation, diffusion, use, and evaluation of knowledge can be facilitated by information and communication technology, and how much it is facilitated by human resource management by creating a cultural environment which encourages information sharing and knowledge creation. Technology offers several tools, but requires cultural support to be fully effective. Intranets enable organizations to share background information such as procedures and policies and to make this information available on an as-needed basis. But intranets depend upon individuals adding information for others to read. Databases which contain organization members' area of specialization enable members to contact the most suitable person to help them solve their problem. But members may refuse to give the time requested to solve a problem, especially if the organization rewards individuals narrowly according to specific targets. Or members may refuse to share their knowledge because they do not wish to lose their indispensability and the power associated with it. Project diaries which chronicle surprises and problems surmounted are valuable sources of advice for the project teams that follow. But often project teams are too busy to fill in the diary, or members wish to hide mistakes. Multinationals spawn huge numbers of projects in each unit and subsidiary. These projects often duplicate each other in different regions or departments. Databases of projects and their main features enable members to avoid such duplication. But such databases also threaten team budgets and so often teams refuse to add their own project's details. Such databases also cross regional boundaries and so threaten the independence of regional units.

Where such methods have been systematized they therefore require a centralized system directing their use. An example is the use of Rapid Action for Process Improvement Deployment (RAPID) at all Ford's car factories as a method of publicizing new process improvements between plants. However, it is important that local subsidiaries have sufficient freedom to develop their own solutions to problems if they wish, because markets and regulations may vary

considerably between subsidiaries. Finding the right balance is partly judging the product as global (oil), nearly global (cars), or national (insurance). It is also a matter of giving regions the choice of getting the diffused and reused idea cheaply or the local solution at full cost.

These examples show the importance of the human factors involved in technology use with regard to knowledge management. Knowledge management is therefore as much an area of concern for human resource management as it is for information technology. The main aim of such policies is to encourage information sharing. One approach is to create a "strong culture," that is, a strong identification with the organization, a positive organizational identity. This is not just a job for a communications department, because what members consider their organization to be will affect, for example, how they train new recruits, how they deal with customers, and how they check quality. Another approach is to use rewards of both money and recognition. Most consultancy firms, in which knowledge sharing is vital, give their consultants high basic salaries so that doing "good citizen" activities such as sharing information with others does not lead to loss of the consultant's income. Consultancy firms which do not do this have problems motivating their staff to cooperate enough to share information. Directly rewarding specific actions such as how much an individual writes is difficult because it may be quality rather than quantity that counts. The best situation is when reputation as an expert is its own reward.

Behind all questions of effective knowledge management is the existence or nonexistence of trust in working relationships. After all, this is the advantage of organizations rather than markets as methods of creating economic value. Some organizations have trust and some do not. Inside most companies there exist departmental feuds, scapegoating, blame shifting, and ruthless competition for promotion. Trust takes time to build up. Trust exists between identifiable individuals. It is based on perceived goodwill to be likely to promise something and also on competence to do what the person promises to do. But there is also such a thing as institutional trust, where being from a certain company or department or region or nationality gives a person a guaranteed trustworthiness even when we do not know that person. Because of the growing importance of knowledge and therefore of information sharing, trust is also growing in importance. It is one of the fundamental qualitative features of organizational climate. Because it is impossible to acquire imitatively it is a potent source of competitive advantage.

Several routines have gained prominence as methods of facilitating knowledge sharing. One is the Peer Assist scheme at BP. When a difficult decision arises (e.g., when a new oil rig has to be started involving risky investment) the person who is responsible calls for experts to come to a meeting to give their views. This is resourced by the sending units on the argument that the visiting experts gain by picking up new experience and new credits on their CVs. Although conflicts between strangers might develop, it seems that the need of experts to get invited to such meetings leads them to control their level of criticism. Another routine is the Asset Consulting Team approach at Chevron, where if you have a problem, you go and visit a specialized internal consulting unit.

Most practitioners recognize knowledge management as talking about and spreading "best practice." One problem is that this year's best practice becomes last year's bad practice. Spreading best practice may also result in sharing ignorance. These problems occur when knowledge management becomes concerned merely with diffusion and not with creation of new knowledge.

SEE ALSO: Knowledge; Knowledge Societies; Knowledge, Sociology of; Management Theory; Scientific Knowledge, Sociology of

REFERENCES AND SUGGESTED READINGS

Alvesson, M. (2001) Knowledge Work: Ambiguity, Image and Identity. *Human Relations* 54(97): 863–86.

Carlile, P. R. (2004) Transferring, Translating and Transforming: An Integrative Framework for Managing Knowledge Across Boundaries. *Organization Science* 15(5): 555–69.

Cross, R. & Sproull, L. (2004) More Than an Answer: Information Relationships for Actionable Knowledge. *Organization Science* 15(4): 446–63.

Morris, T. (2001) Asserting Property Rights: Knowledge Codification in the Professional Service Firm. *Human Relations* 54(7): 818–38.

Nahapiet, J. & Ghoshal, S. (1998) Social Capital, Intellectual Capital and the Organizational Advantage. *Academy of Management Review* 23(2): 242–67.

Nickerson, J. A. & Zenger, T. R. (2004) A Knowledge-Based Theory of the Firm: The Problem-Solving Perspective. *Organization Science* 15(6): 617–33.

Shepherd, D. A. (2003) Learning from Business Failure: Propositions of Grief Recovery for the Self-Employed. *Academy of Management Review* 28(2): 318–28.

knowledge societies

Nico Stehr

The transformation of modern societies into knowledge societies continues to be based, as was the case for industrial society, on changes in the structure of the economies of advanced societies. Economic capital – or, more precisely, the source of economic growth and value-adding activities – increasingly relies on knowledge. The transformation of the structures of the modern economy by knowledge as a productive force constitutes the "material" basis and justification for designating advanced modern society as a knowledge society. The significance of knowledge grows in all spheres of life and in all social institutions of modern society. The historical emergence of knowledge societies represents not a revolutionary development, but rather a gradual process during which the defining characteristics of society change and new traits emerge. Until recently, modern society was conceived primarily in terms of property and labor. While the traditional attributes of labor and property certainly have not disappeared entirely, a new principle, "knowledge," has been added which, to an extent, challenges as well as transforms property and labor as the constitutive mechanisms of society.

Knowledge may be defined as a *capacity for action*. This definition indicates that implementation of knowledge is open, that it is dependent on or is embedded within the context of specific social, economic, and intellectual conditions. Knowledge is a peculiar entity with properties unlike those of commodities or of secrets, for example. Knowledge exists in objectified and embodied forms. If sold, it enters other domains – and yet it remains within the domain of its producer. Unlike money, property rights, and symbolic attributes such as titles, knowledge cannot be transmitted instantaneously. Its acquisition takes time and often is based on intermediary cognitive capacities and skills. Despite its reputation, knowledge is virtually never uncontested. Scientific and technical knowledge is uniquely important in modern social systems because it produces incremental capacities for social and economic action that may be "privately appropriated," at least temporarily. Knowledge has of course always had a major function in social life. Social groups, social situations, social interaction, and social roles all depend on, and are mediated by, knowledge. Power, too, has frequently been based on knowledge advantages, not merely on physical strength.

The emergence of knowledge societies signals first and foremost a radical transformation in the structure of the economy. What changes are the dynamics of the supply and demand for primary products or raw materials; the dependence of employment on production; the importance of the manufacturing sector that processes primary products; the role of manual labor and the social organization of work; the role of international trade in manufactured goods and services; the function of time and place in production and of the nature of the limits to economic growth. The common denominator of the changing economic structure is a shift away from an economy driven and governed by *material* inputs into the productive process and its organization, toward an economy in which the transformations of productive and distributive processes are increasingly determined by symbolic or knowledge-based inputs.

The transformation of modern societies into knowledge has profound consequences aside from those that pertain to its economic structure. One of the more remarkable consequences is the extent to which modern societies become fragile societies. Modern societies tend to be fragile from the viewpoint of those large and once-dominant social institutions that find it

increasingly difficult to impose their will on all of society. From the perspective of small groups and social movements more uncoupled from the influence of the traditional large-scale social institutions, however, modern societies are not more fragile, in the first instance. For such groups and social movements, the social transformations underway mean a distinct gain in their relative influence and participation, even if typically mainly in their ability to resist, delay, and alter the objectives of the larger institutions.

Knowledge societies (to adopt a phrase from Adam Ferguson) are the results of human action, but often not of deliberate human design. They emerge as adaptations to persistent but evolving needs and changing circumstances of human conduct.

Modern societies are also increasingly vulnerable entities. More specifically, the economy, the communication and traffic systems are vulnerable to malfunctions of self-imposed practices typically designed to avoid breakdowns. Modern infrastructures and technological regimes are subject to accidents, including large-scale disasters as the result of fortuitous, unanticipated human action, to non-marginal or extreme natural events that may dramatically undermine the taken-for-granted routines of everyday life in modern societies, and to deliberate sabotage.

Present-day social systems may be seen to be fragile and vulnerable entities in yet another sense. Such fragility results from the conduct as well as the deployment of artifacts designed to stabilize, routinize, and delimit social action (e.g., the so-called "computer trap" or, more generally, the unintended outcomes of intentional social action). In the process of evermore deeply embedding computers into the social fabric of society, that is, redesigning and reengineering large-scale social and socio-technical systems in order to manage the complexities of modern society, novel risks and vulnerabilities are created.

The fragility of modern societies is a unique condition. Societies are fragile because individuals are capable, within certain established rules, of asserting their own interests by opposing or resisting the (not too long ago) almost unassailable monopoly of truth of major societal institutions. That is to say, legitimate cultural practices based on the enlargement and diffusion of knowledge enable a much larger segment of society effectively to oppose power configurations that turned out or are apprehended to be tenuous and brittle.

Among the major but widely invisible social innovations in modern society is the immense growth of the "civil society" sector. This sector provides an organized basis through which citizens can exercise individual initiative in the private pursuit of public purposes. One is therefore able to interpret the considerable enlargement of the informal economy, but also corruption and the growth of wealth in modern society, as well as increasing but typically unsuccessful efforts to police these spheres, as evidence of the diverse as well as expanded capacity of individuals, households, and small groups to take advantage of and benefit from contexts in which the degree of social control exercised by larger (legitimate) social institutions has diminished considerably.

The future of modern society no longer mimics the past to the extent to which this has been the case. History will increasingly be full of unanticipated incertitudes, peculiar reversals, and proliferating surprises, and we will have to cope with the ever-greater speed of significantly compressed events. The changing agendas of social, political, and economic life as the result of our growing capacity to make history will also place inordinate demands on our mental capacities and social resources.

SEE ALSO: Economy, Networks and; Information Society; Knowledge; Knowledge Management; Knowledge, Sociology of; Network Society; Scientific Knowledge, Sociology of

REFERENCES AND SUGGESTED READINGS

Bell, D. (1973) *The Coming of Post-Industrial Society.* Basic Books, New York.

Stehr, N. (1994) *Knowledge Societies.* Sage, London.

Stehr, N. (2001) *The Fragility of Modern Societies: Knowledge and Risk in the Information Age.* Sage, London.

Webster, F. (2002) *Theories of the Information Society*, 2nd edn. Routledge, London.

knowledge, sociology of

E. Doyle McCarthy

The sociology of knowledge examines the social and group origin of ideas, arguing that the entire "ideational realm" ("knowledges," ideas, ideologies, mentalities) develops within the context of a society's groups and institutions. Its ideas address broad sociological questions about the extent and limits of social and group influence through an examination of the social and cultural foundations of cognition and perception. Despite significant changes over time, classical and contemporary studies in the sociology of knowledge share a common theme: the social foundations of thought. Ideas, concepts, and belief systems share an intrinsic sociality explained by the contexts in which they emerge.

From its origins in German sociology in the 1920s, sociology of knowledge has assumed that ideas (knowledge) emerge out of and are determined by the social contexts and positions (structural locations) of their proponents. Its major premise is that the entire ideational realm is functionally related to sociohistorical reality. According to its framers, *Wissenssoziologie* was developed as an empirical and historical method for resolving the conflicts of ideologies in Weimar Germany that followed the political and social revolutions of the late nineteenth and early twentieth centuries, conflicts grounded in competing worldviews and directed by intellectual and political elites. Outlined in early statements by Max Scheler and Karl Mannheim, the new discipline reflected the intellectual needs of an era, to bring both rationality and objectivity to bear on the problems of intellectual and ideological confusion. It was in this sense that the sociology of knowledge has been described as a discipline that reflected a new way of understanding "knowledge" within a modern and ideologically pluralistic setting. The approach defines a new "situation" (Mannheim 1936), summarily described as "modernity," a world where "knowledge" and "truth" have many faces. What we believe that we *know* varies with the cognitive operations of human minds and these vary by community, class, culture, nation, generation, and so forth.

Contemporary sociology of knowledge addresses a related but different set of concerns than those posed by its founders, and its subject matter extends beyond the problem of relativism and the social location of ideas and ideologies. Prominent among its current themes are the "local" features of knowledges and the study of their functions in everyday life. This redirection of the field from the study of conflicting ideologies to the study of the tacit and taken-for-granted understandings of everyday life can be characterized as a shift from concerns with the truth-status of ideas and ideologies to the concerns of a cultural "sociology of meaning." These changes also represent a movement away from a study of the ideological functions of elites and intellectuals to conceptions of knowledges as discursive (cultural) forms and as part of the entire range of symbolic and signifying systems operating in a society.

The term sociology of knowledge (*Wissenssoziologie*) was first used in 1924 and 1925 by Scheler (1980) and Mannheim (1952). From its inception, it described a field of inquiry closely linked to problems of European philosophy and historicism, particularly the nineteenth-century German philosophical interest in problems surrounding relativism that were linked to the legacies of Karl Marx, Friedrich Nietzsche, and the historicists, whose cultural philosophy of worldviews (*Weltanschauungsphilosophie*) was influential in German social science from the 1890s to the 1930s.

For Scheler (1980), who offered the first systematic outline of the discipline, the *forms* of mental acts, through which knowledge is gained, are always conditioned by the structure of society. For this reason, sociology of knowledge is foundational to all specialized studies of culture and to metaphysics. While Scheler's original essays provoked commentary and debate, it was Mannheim's formulation of the discipline in *Ideology and Utopia* that defined the subject matter of the field for years to come. Those who offered their own sociologies of knowledge, including Talcott Parsons (1961) and Robert K. Merton (1957), defined their positions relative to Mannheim's arguments concerning ideology, utopia, and relationism.

Mannheim's treatise begins with a review and critique of Marxism and proceeds toward a theory of ideology in the broader sense: the mental structure in its totality as it appears in different currents of thought and across different social groups. This "total conception of ideology" examines thought on the structural level, allowing the same object to take on different (group) aspects. This understanding of ideology refers to a person's, group's, or society's way of conceiving things situated within particular historical and social settings. Like ideologies, "utopias" arise out of particular social and political conditions, but are distinguished by their opposition to the prevailing order. Utopias are the embodiment of "wish images" in collective actions that shatter and transform social worlds. Both concepts form part of Mannheim's broad design for a critical but nonevaluative treatment of "ideology," one that supersedes the sociohistorical determinism and relativism of Marxism while moving toward a "relationist" notion of truth. From an analysis of the various and competing social positions of ideologists and utopians, a kind of "truth" emerges that is grounded in the conditions of intellectual objectivity and detachment from the social conditions that more directly determine ideas. *Ideology and Utopia* established the criteria for a valid knowledge, albeit a *relational* knowledge, of sociohistorical processes. More important, it raised the problems surrounding the historicity of thought and did this within the newly emerging academic discourse of sociology. In the process, it gave legitimacy to a new set of methodological issues involving the problems of objectivity and truth for the sciences and the humanities.

Despite the many criticisms of *Ideology and Utopia*, the work received wide attention and appreciation inside and outside the social sciences where the problems posed by relativism continued to attract the attention of those working in the sciences and the humanities. While reviews of the work focused on its failure to overcome relativism and Mannheim's excessive reliance on the Marxist conception of ideology, Mannheim's book provoked discussion and commentary in the decades after its publication.

Werner Stark's *The Sociology of Knowledge* (1991) prompted a major advancement and redirection of the field. It argued for the embedding of sociology of knowledge within the larger field of cultural sociology. Stark's book clarified the principal themes of earlier writers, especially sociologists, who had addressed the problem of the social element in thinking. He also intended it to serve as an introduction to the field that would prepare the way for a detailed and comprehensive history of the sociology of knowledge and its most significant ideas: theories of ideology of Marx and Mannheim; philosophical speculations of the neo-Kantians Heinrich Rickert and Max Weber; views of the German phenomenological school of the 1920s, especially Scheler. Stark's strongest affinity was with Scheler's struggle to reconcile the antithetical claims of idealism and materialism, and his view of the sociology of knowledge as the foundation for a knowledge of "eternal values." The sociology of knowledge is concerned with the "social determination of knowledge," not with the problem of ideology. This distinction is an indispensable precondition of the sociology of knowledge. It directs attention to the study of mental life as grounded in social and historical conditions, granting to "social determination" a depth that the theory of ideology does not accomplish. While the theory of ideology will always play a vital role in sociology and the history of ideas, it remains outside the principal concerns of the sociology of knowledge.

Berger and Luckmann's *The Social Construction of Reality* (1966) advanced a sociology of knowledge that was compatible with the view of sociology as a humanistic discipline and the notion that "human reality" is a "socially constructed reality." The work moved the field further away from theoretical knowledge or ideas and toward the (pre-theoretical) knowledge that social actors draw from in everyday life. Their treatise also redirected the traditional theory of social determination of ideas by social realities: social reality itself is a *construct*. It integrated the perspectives of classical European social thought (Marx, Durkheim, Weber) with the social psychology of the American pragmatist philosopher George Herbert Mead, thereby advancing Meadian social psychology as a theoretical complement to European sociology of knowledge (see Curtis & Petras 1970; Remmling 1973). What the authors proposed was that knowledge and social reality exist in a

reciprocal or dialectical relationship of mutual constitution. This work placed the sociology of knowledge on a new footing whose focus was the broad range of signifying systems that form and communicate the realm of social realities. Since its introduction, the idea of a "constructed reality" has summarized a number of concerns of writers in the sciences and humanities that may be described as the *problem of meaning* and the use of philosophical, literary, and historical approaches to study its social construction. Berger and Luckmann's treatise subsumed knowledges within a framework of interpretation, a *hermeneutics* that was decidedly cultural and semiotic, concerned with the symbolic and signifying operations of knowledges.

More recently, the "new sociology of knowledge" (Swidler & Arditi 1994; McCarthy 1996) can be seen as part of this larger movement in the social sciences, distinguished by a turn away from materialism and social structure toward semiotic theories that focus on the ways in which a society's meanings are communicated and reproduced. Swidler and Arditi (1994) focus on how social organizations (e.g., the media) order knowledges, rather than examining social locations and group interests. In light of new theories of social power and practice (Michel Foucault and Pierre Bourdieu), they also examine how knowledges maintain social hierarchies and how techniques of power are simultaneously and historically linked to knowledges. They join others in pointing out that newer theories of power, gender, and knowledge depart from the economic, class, and institutional focus of the classical sociology of knowledge.

Proponents of the new sociology of knowledge do not claim that the subfield has been entirely superseded by newer work in sociology and cultural studies. However, they note that the new sociology of knowledge is not a unified field, an argument also advanced by earlier writers who treated the sociology of knowledge as a "frame of reference" rather than a body of theory in its own right (Curtis & Petras 1970: 1; cf. Remmling 1973).

Two overriding factors can account for the persistence of a broad approach to knowledges. First, the propositions of Scheler, Mannheim, and other early writers in this field (e.g., in the US, works by Florian Znaniecki, C. Wright Mills, and Edward Shils) today serve as working propositions for a range of social scientists as well as for specialists in other disciplines, including the subfields of the history of ideas, social psychology, social studies of science, feminist theories, and cultural studies. For this reason, a sociology-of-knowledge perspective – concerning group life and mind – has been incorporated into the many subfields of sociology as well as sister disciplines from anthropology to history. Furthermore, as long as knowledges are understood as preeminently cultural phenomena, the more likely it is that the sociology of knowledge will be seen as a broadly inclusive set of theories and studies rather than a subfield with a distinct subject matter. Knowledges are no longer confined to the domain of "superstructure." They operate across the full extent of society, from the realm of everyday affairs to the institutions of law, politics, art, and religion, to the various sites and fields where knowledges are produced. The new sociology of knowledge examines the observable properties of knowledges in texts, modes of communication, and forms of speech within specific institutional settings.

SEE ALSO: Collective Memory; Constructionism; Ideology; Knowledge; Knowledge Management; Knowledge Societies; Mannheim, Karl; Scientific Knowledge, Sociology of

REFERENCES AND SUGGESTED READINGS

Berger, P. L. & Luckmann, T. (1966) *The Social Construction of Reality*. Doubleday, New York.

Curtis, J. E. & Petras, J. W. (1970) *The Sociology of Knowledge*. Praeger, New York.

McCarthy, E. D. (1996) *Knowledge as Culture: The New Sociology of Knowledge*. Routledge, New York.

Mannheim, K. (1936 [1929]) *Ideology and Utopia*. Harcourt, Brace, & World, New York.

Mannheim, K. (1952 [1925]) The Problem of a Sociology of Knowledge. In: Mannheim, K., *Essays on the Sociology of Knowledge*. Ed. P. Kecskemeti. Harcourt, Brace, & World, New York, pp. 134–90.

Merton, R. K. (1957) *Social Theory and Social Structure*. Free Press, Glencoe, IL.

Parsons, T. (1961) Culture and the Social System. In: Parsons, T., Shils, E., Naegele, K. P., & Pitts, J. R. (Eds.), *Theories of Society*, Vol. 2. Free Press, New York.

Remmling, G. (1973) *Towards A Sociology of Knowledge*. Routledge & Kegan Paul, London.

Scheler, M. (1980 [1924]) *Problems of a Sociology of Knowledge*. Trans. M. S. Frings. Routledge & Kegan Paul, London.

Stark, W. (1991 [1958]) *The Sociology of Knowledge*. Intro. E. D. McCarthy. Transaction, New Brunswick, NJ.

Swidler, A. & Arditi, J. (1994) The New Sociology of Knowledge. *Annual Review of Sociology* 20: 305–29.

Komarovsky, Mirra (1905–99)

Vicky M. MacLean

Mirra Komarovsky's research, teaching, and advocacy on behalf of women mark her as a pioneer in the sociology of gender and feminist scholarship. She was the second woman to serve as president of the American Sociological Association, thus furthering opportunities for women in the profession of sociology. Major contributions to sociology include her critique of the Parsonian functionalist perspective on gender roles, research on women's education and changing feminine identities, and the study of men and masculinity. Komarovsky's research focused on the nature of conflict and strains in gender roles during periods of uneven social change. Her 1953 book *Women in the Modern World: Their Education and Their Dilemma* anticipated Betty Freidan's *The Feminine Mystique* by more than a decade. Methodological contributions include refining the use of the qualitative case study method using in-depth interviewing and synthesizing sociological schedules and surveys with psychological tests of personality and gender.

Born to a Jewish family in Russia in 1905, Komarovsky migrated with her family from Baku to the United States in 1921, fleeing anti-Semitism and Bolshevik attempts to eradicate the middle class. Her childhood education in Russia was primarily from private tutors. In the United States Mirra's family initially settled in Wichita, Kansas where she graduated from Wichita High School. Then in 1922 her father moved the family to Brooklyn, New York to provide greater educational and career opportunities for Mirra. She took her bachelor's degree at Barnard College, majoring in economics and sociology. Komarovsky received the Caroline Durer Fellowship for graduate studies, taught as an instructor at Skidmore College, and then pursued her master's degree at Columbia University, writing her thesis under the direction of William Ogburn. Upon accepting a research associate position at the International Institute for Social Research, Komarovsky began graduate work for her doctorate under the direction of Paul Lazarsfeld, and returned to Barnard to teach (Reinharz 1989, 1991; Rieder 1999). Her dissertation, *The Unemployed Man and His Family* (1940), was a continuation of Max Horkheimer's *Studien uber Autoritat und Familie* (1936). Using the case study method, Komarovsky studied 59 skilled-worker families receiving government relief during the Depression. The study revealed that unemployment led to a deterioration of men's personalities, undermined their household authority, and affected marital satisfaction. A man's loss of status was experienced more in relation to his wife than his young children, but his status and authority over adolescent children suffered most.

Central to Komarovsky's scholarship were the objectives of identifying the functional significance of sex roles, their cultural contradictions, and prospects for social change. Whereas the dominant functionalist perspective emphasized the integrating functions of a sexual division of labor in maintaining a system's equilibrium, Komarovsky emphasized role strains and conflicts. Focusing on these dysfunctional aspects of sex roles, she emphasized the important relationship between men's changing roles (particularly in sharing domestic responsibilities) and women's emancipation. "Cultural Contradictions and Sex Roles," published in the *American Journal of Sociology* in 1946, launched four decades of research on the changing gender role attitudes of women entering an elite women's college and the dilemmas college women faced due to competing gender role expectations. This research culminated in *Women in College: Shaping New Feminine*

Identities (1985). Prominent influences on Komarovsky's work were Ogburn's cultural lag theory and Merton's role theory. She conceptualized role conflicts and strains as emerging from the discontinuities created by differential rates of change in norms, attitudes, and institutional arrangements. *Women in the Modern World* (1953) addressed post-World War II anti-feminist charges that colleges neglected the special functions of women in society. Critiquing biological and psychological theories of gender differences, Komarovsky offered a sociological explanation of the dilemmas faced by women. The foremost contradiction was in the competing expectations of the "traditional" feminine role and the "modern" role, the latter emphasizing women's intellectual and professional development. Whether a woman chose homemaking or to combine domestic and paid work, she was likely to experience internal conflicts and dissatisfactions. Komarovsky argued for social changes allowing men and women to reach their full potentials, advocating for women's employment in non-traditional fields, men's sharing in family responsibilities, and wider availability of quality childcare.

Women in the Modern World emphasized strategies employed by college-educated women in the 1940s to address gender role strains; for example, "think smart and act dumb" was an adaptive strategy used to protect male egos. In contrast, *Women in College* (1985) emphasized the growing complexities of shifting gender roles and competing expectations from family, institutional, and peer influences in the 1980s. Based on a longitudinal study of 240 Barnard freshman women, the study traced the school's influences on changes in gender role attitudes, career aspirations, and lifestyle preferences for marriage and motherhood. Over time, women were found to gain an increasing commitment to combining careers and family, became more certain in their career choices, and an increasing proportion were committed to sustaining uninterrupted full-time careers. In *Women in College* Komarovsky also examined outside factors that shaped women's career orientations, including the quality of their parents' marital relationships, mothers' satisfactions with the homemaker role, and mother–daughter relationships.

Blue-Collar Marriage (1962) is Komarovsky's study of stable working-class marriages based on in-depth interviews with 58 couples living in "Glenton," a mill town located in a major metropolitan area. Working-class, native-born white Protestant couples, under the age of 40, with no more than a high school education and at least one child, were interviewed. Marital satisfaction based on discrepancies between ideals and reality was examined. Certain discrepancies in marriage were found to be easily tolerated by couples while others led to dissatisfaction. High conformity between values and behaviors sometimes led to strains and stresses as opposed to greater satisfaction in marriage. The cultural lag between modern conceptions of companionate marriage and the means for achieving personal intimacy was the basis of dissatisfaction in marriage, particularly for high school-educated women who had high expectations for personal intimacy. Although working-class couples experienced a minimal level of work–family role conflicts, they lacked intimate communication and self-disclosure. Ironically, a consensus of values about sex roles among traditional couples led to frustrations in the form of social isolation and emotional disengagement, particularly for the men. Komarovsky concluded that traditional values were problematic for couples in a society that could no longer accommodate a rigid sexual division of labor. The absence of economic and social rewards generally increased social isolation, creating a drab and narrowly circumscribed life for blue-collar families.

Not only did Komarovsky study female gender roles, but a number of her studies addressed men and masculinity, paving the way for contemporary work on hegemonic, alternative, and intersecting masculinities. In *Dilemmas of Masculinity: A Study of College Youth* (1976), Komarovsky found that men are not unlike women in the dilemmas they face in meeting role expectations, and in balancing cultural contradictions and role ambiguities. Using a sample of 62 senior males from Columbia University, Komarovsky examined masculine role strains resulting primarily from incongruity between the ideals of egalitarian relationships on the one hand, and men's personal preferences for masculine privileges in relationships on the other. The cultural revolution of the 1960s resulted in changes in male attitudes; for example, men expected their

wives to work, but retained traditional views that work should not interfere with the primary roles of mother and wife. Role strains, defined as the perceived or latent difficulty in fulfilling role expectations, and/or the low rewards for role conformity, were analyzed in several spheres of men's lives. Stresses in the sexual sphere included anxieties surrounding virginal status, sexual performance, and guilt associated with sex outside of marriage (e.g., potential pregnancy, sexual exploitation, and infidelity). Strains and stresses related to future work roles were prominent, particularly those surrounding choosing and achieving career goals. Similarly, men's desires for emotional independence from parents created stresses in their family relationships due to their economic dependence. Unsatisfactory father–son relationships were more common than mother–son relationships and had consequences for men's abilities to handle role strains and to disclose their emotions in heterosexual relationships. In relations with women (apart from sex), power and emotional disclosure were the primary sources of role strain. Of particular importance were men's feelings of inadequacy in obtaining ideal masculine leadership or dominance, assertiveness, and, to a lesser degree, intellectual superiority. Komarovsky developed a theoretical typology of role strain: ambiguity in role expectations; incongruity between individual and society in role conformity; insufficiency of resources to fulfill role expectations; low rewards for role conformity; latent and manifest conflicts in role conformity; and overload of role obligations.

In her American Sociological Association "Presidential Address: Some Problems in Role Analysis" (1973), published in the *American Sociological Review*, Komarovsky addressed the most common criticisms of social structural role analysis by using illustrations from her own and other's research. To the criticism that role analysis obscures and neglects individuality, presenting as it were an "oversocialized" view of humans lacking in spontaneity or self-agency, Komarovsky highlighted the importance of integrating psychological variables into sociological research. In particular, she promoted understanding the social situational origins of psychological ambivalence as these become embedded in the structure of social statuses and roles. To the criticism that role analysis places too much emphasis on role conformity and stability, Komarovsky illustrated from her own analyses of *Blue-Collar Marriage Dilemmas of Masculinity* the ways in which role conformity can become problematic in times of social change, creating conflict and disorganization. In "The Concept of Social Role Revisited" (1992), Komarovsky specifically took up the criticisms of some feminists that the concept of social role is too limited in the sociological study of gender. Critics have argued, for instance, that the concept of sex role is too closely linked to biology and neglects the social construction of gender (p. 301). The use of the concept of "gender" or "gender roles," argued Komarovsky, is preferred to "sex roles" but this preferred language and clarification of definition does not undermine the utility of social role or gender role analyses. Others, such as Barrie Thorne, have stated that the language of roles is deeply embedded in functionalism with its emphases on "consensus, stability, and continuity" (p. 303). Komarovsky (1992) responded that although Parsonian sociology placed emphasis on the functional integration of differentiated instrumental (male) and expressive (female) roles in the family, for others interested in women's problems the concept of social role locates "dissensus, discontinuity, and change" (p. 303). Komarovsky concluded that while new conceptualizations of gender are important for illuminating selected aspects of gender, the new approaches are not all inclusive, and complement rather than undermine social role analysis.

"Some Reflections on the Feminist Scholarship in Sociology," published in the *Annual Review* in 1991, provides a retrospective look at the important contributions of feminist scholarship to sociology and is an indication of Komarovsky's continued involvement in the discipline. The article addresses how the women's movement of the 1960s influenced the feminist critique of sociology and the important contributions of feminist precursors (writing between the 1930s and 1960) to the "new feminist scholarship." The feminist critique, she argued, identified lacunae in knowledge, revealed distortions embedded in the traditional theoretical interpretations, and raised new questions for research. The new scholarship was particularly important in revealing the malleability of personality and its responsiveness to social structural opportunity, the strong sex-typing of occupations and resistance to women's work integration, and the importance of reconceptualizing work to include both paid and unpaid activities. While this early work took a "minimalist" approach to gender differences in personality traits that too often were used to legitimize women's subordination, later work attempted to revalue women's traditional activities and feminine traits, thus challenging the bias in the value system of the dominant group.

Komarovsky's affiliation with Barnard College spanned three-quarters of a century from her undergraduate years through her retirement. In personal interviews Komarovsky indicated that she experienced both personal and professional obstacles to fulfilling her potential as a sociologist, not receiving interpersonal or institutional support for her work until later in her career (Reinharz 1989, 1991). As a student she was discouraged from becoming a professional sociologist, instructed by her mentor, Ogburn, that her desire to teach was unrealistic for a woman, a foreigner, and a Jew. On the Barnard faculty, from 1935 to 1946, she did not advance beyond the level of assistant professor. An administrative change in the late 1940s, however, brought her promotions and the support needed to advance professionally. She served as chair of the Barnard Department of Sociology for 17 years and returned to teach and to serve as the director of Women's Studies after her retirement in 1970. For her years of service and accomplishments at Barnard, Komarovsky received the Emily Gregory Award for teaching excellence and the Distinguished Alumnae Award, Medal of Distinction. Her accomplishments in the profession included serving as: vice president (1949) and president (1955) of the Eastern Sociological Association, a member of the Council of the American Sociological Association (1966–9), associate editor of the *American Sociological Review*, and president of the American Sociological Association (1972–3) (Reinharz 1989, 1991; Rieder 1999).

SEE ALSO: Culture, Gender and; Family Conflict; Family, Men's Involvement in; Gender Ideology and Gender Role Ideology; Gender, Work, and Family; Hegemonic Masculinity; Inequality/Stratification, Gender;

Liberal Feminism; Marital Quality; Sex and Gender; Structural Functional Theory

REFERENCES AND SUGGESTED READINGS

Komarovsky, M. (1950) Functional Analysis of Sex Roles. *American Sociological Review* 15 (August): 508–16.
Komarovsky, M. (1962) *Blue-Collar Marriage*. Random House, New York.
Komarovsky, M. (1973) Presidential Address: Some Problems in Role Analysis. *American Sociological Review* 38 (December): 649–52.
Komarovsky, M. (1988) Women Then and Now: A Journey of Detachment and Engagement. *Barnard Alumnae* (Winter 9): 7–11.
Komarovsky, M. (1991) Some Reflections on the Feminist Scholarship in Sociology. *Annual Review of Sociology* 17: 1–25.
Komarovsky, M. (1992) The Concept of Social Role Revisited. *Gender and Society* 6(2): 301–13.
Reinharz, S. (1989) Finding a Sociological Voice: The Work of Mirra Komarovsky. *Sociological Inquiry* 59 (Fall): 374–95.
Reinharz, S. (1991) Mirra Komarovsky. In: Deegan, M. J. (Ed.), *Women in Sociology: A Biobibliographical Sourcebook*. Greenwood Press, New York.
Rieder, J. (1999) Mirra Komarovsky: Old World Grace and New World Ideas. *Footnotes* 27, 5 (May/June). American Sociological Association.

Kondratieff cycles

Immanuel Wallerstein

It is an elementary truism that no phenomena are absolutely stable. Whatever we measure in the real world shows fluctuations, whether we are speaking of basic economic phenomena (such as prices, production, employment, or investment), politico-military phenomena (such as wars, free trade policies, or geopolitical arrangements), or cultural phenomena (such as puritanical mores or family patterns). The question is always whether we can ascertain the existence of any kind of rules or systemic pressures that govern the ups and downs of phenomena, including the explanation of the fluctuations and their timing and frequency.

The most readily observed fluctuations are those that affect the income levels of a population. We refer popularly to such ups and downs as prosperity and bad times. It is therefore no surprise that social scientists have been trying to explain such cyclical happenings for at least two centuries. As long as a large proportion of the population was engaged in agricultural production, the distinction between good harvest years and bad ones was of great importance to almost everyone, since the fluctuations promptly affected the prices and distribution of the products and therefore the ability of ordinary people to survive.

When industrial production became a larger percentage of total production, it became clear that there were fluctuations in the rates of profit of entrepreneurs, and therefore of production and employment, and this had immediate implications for public policy. Some scholars were beginning to measure such fluctuations at the beginning of the nineteenth century. Cyclical phenomena of varying lengths began to be observed, recorded, and eventually predicted. It was towards the middle of the nineteenth century that analysts began to talk of waves (A + B phases) that were 50–60 years in length. It is waves of this length that we now refer to as Kondratieff cycles.

Kondratieff cycles are named after Nikolai Kondratieff, a Russian economist whose classic work on such cycles was published in 1925. Kondratieff was not the first person to write about such waves, but his name became attached to them. Kondratieff observed price cycles in some major industrial countries, beginning in the late eighteenth century. His choice of starting date was no accident since, by the time he was writing, the late eighteenth century was also commonly given as the date of *the* industrial revolution.

Economists speak of a number of other shorter economic cycles named after their original analysts: the Kitchin cycle (40 months), the Juglar cycle (8–10 years), and the Kuznets cycle (15–20 years). They are explained variously. More economists are willing to accept the existence of these shorter cycles than are willing to give credence to the existence of Kondratieff cycles. Nonetheless, Kondratieff cycles have a wide, distinguished, and intellectually very varied set of proponents. Among economists the most prominent was no doubt Joseph Schumpeter in his book *Business Cycles*, who is primarily responsible for labeling these cycles with Kondratieff's name. The concept found strong supporters among Marxist economists (Helphand, van Gelderen, de Wolff, Trotsky, Mandel) but just as strong opponents (probably a larger group). It also found strong support among non- and anti-Marxist economists (Dupriez, Hansen, Rostow, Forrester, Mensch) but just as strong opponents (probably again a larger group).

If one turns to economic historians, one finds a very large group (e.g., Simiand, Braudel) who describe Kondratieff waves without using that name for earlier periods – the sixteenth to eighteenth centuries, and for some beginning much earlier. And then there is a group of political scientists and sociologists who find such cycles in the political and cultural arenas (again, often without using that name). Some see these cycles as linked to wars, some as linked to the rise and fall of hegemonic powers. Some find even longer economic cycles, to which Cameron (1973) gave the name of "logistics" because of their S-shape.

The critics of Kondratieff cycles point to inconsistencies among proponents concerning the dating and argue that the statistical evidence is inadequate, and often conclude with name-calling ("science fiction," according to Paul Samuelson). The debates among the proponents are more substantive and have to do with the underlying explanation of the cyclical patterns and a secondary debate about how, once in the B-phase, the system ever renews an expansionary phase.

If one looks at Kondratieff's classic work one notices immediately that all the data are about a very few countries (England, France, the US, and Germany). Only one graph and chart are comparative; all the rest are about either England or France. The earliest data are for 1780. The data deal with prices, wages, foreign trade turnover, and production of raw materials. Kondratieff does note, however, that the rising phase seems to have more social upheavals (revolutions, wars). His basic explanation of the start of a cycle is the possibility of profitable investment in "new basic productive forces" (Kondratieff 1984: 104). It is Schumpeter who took what was no more than empirical data in Kondratieff and

turned it into a theory. Schumpeter made two basic additions to the description Kondratieff had made. First, he argued that the three described forms of waves – the Kitchin, the Juglar, and the Kondratieff – fitted within each other: "It is possible to count off, historically as well as statistically, six Juglars to a Kondratieff and three Kitchens to a Juglar – not as an average but in every individual case" (Schumpeter 1939 I: 174–5).

The second change was to shift from a two-stage model of a long wave (prosperity and recession, or A and B) to a four-stage model, which he named prosperity, recession, depression, and revival. The four stages were bracketed at each end by equilibrium. This allowed Schumpeter to locate temporally the process of innovation (something for him quite distinct from invention), which he defined as "the setting up of a new production function" (p. 87). He called it "the outstanding fact in the economic history of capitalist society" (p. 86). It is spurred by the third phase (depression) and bears fruit in the fourth phase (revival) and accounts for the return to equilibrium and prosperity.

The Schumpeterian emphasis on innovation as the explanation of the long waves and the reason why they are a fundamental feature of a capitalist world has given rise to one entire school of Kondratieff theorizing, which was revived when the world-system entered a Kondratieff B-phase in the 1970s. Whereas the innovation school tends to emphasize the self-regenerating capacities of capitalist entrepreneurs (they innovate when they can no longer make profits on the basis of previous products), the class–conflict school of Kondratieff theorists insists that regeneration is a political process. Renewal of capital accumulation requires capitalists to "increase the rate of surplus value and to foster deterioration of general working conditions for the working class" (Mandel 1980: 46). Their capacity to do this depends on the latter's "capacity to mount resistance and counterattack" (p. 47). Hence, the upswing depends on a dialectic between objective and subjective factors, "in which the subjective factors are characterized by relative autonomy" (p. 49).

In a sense, both the innovation school and the class–conflict school see a decline in the rate of profit inherent in the capitalist process as accounting for the downturns. For Schumpeter, it is the inevitable speculative overreach, when there is prosperity and profits are high, which leads to excessive credit to producers who are not sufficiently efficient. For Mandel, it is essentially the expansion of production beyond the possibilities of buyers in the market. For both the innovation and the class-conflict schools the downturns are inevitable, and the question really is what permits the upturns. Suter (1992) adds evidence that national debt cycles are linked to the downturn phase.

There are of course some analysts, such as Rostow (1978), who see the downturns as the result of the fact that "investment decisions tend to be determined by current indicators of profitability rather than by rational long-range assessments" (p. 307). There is here the implicit suggestion that these decisions are irrational "mistakes," mistakes that might be corrected by greater wisdom. And indeed, it is clear that, in the last 50 years, central banks and world financial institutions have frequently undertaken measures in order to dampen cyclical behavior, which has no doubt affected the process somewhat.

While the innovation school looks primarily at the economic arena (indeed, primarily at the level of entrepreneurial activity), the class-conflict school tries to effectuate a "dialectic" between the economic (objective) processes and the political or class-conflict (subjective) processes. However, there are analysts who wish to turn our attention primarily to the political arena, and indeed to the geopolitical arena of the relations between states and the existence of "hegemonic powers" or "leadership cycles." These analysts tend to speak of "long cycles" rather than of "Kondratieff cycles" and these cycles turn out in general to be longer than those of Kondratieff.

Wars – to be more exact, world wars – play a central role in these analyses of grand political long cycles. Modelski (1987) traced over five centuries of such cycles, seeing them as having four phases: global war (ending with a victor or leader), world power (or world peace led by the victor), delegitimation (or decline of the leader), and deconcentration (lack of order and presence of a strong challenger to the leader). He suggested that in these conflicts the "continental" powers lose out to the "oceanic" powers. He saw this as "the major rhythm of the modern world" (p. 34), in which the result of the global war is the key decision.

The political long-cycle group shares one characteristic with the economic historians who speak of A- and B-phases. They agree that the processes they are describing go back at least to the sixteenth century, and are not a product merely of the so-called industrial revolution, often dated as beginning in the last decades of the eighteenth century (and which was the temporal foundation of Kondratieff's original discussion). So, be it noted, does Schumpeter.

There have been attempts to blend the discussion about Kondratieff cycles and political long cycles, using the longer time frame. Goldstein (1988) sought to "integrate" virtually all the emphases into a complex theoretical model which includes six "basic two-way causality relationships ... portrayed as negative feedback loops with time delays [whose] primary relationship is between production and war" (p. 277). Wallerstein (1983) saw two separate cycles in the workings of the modern world-system. One is the cycle of hegemony, in which the achievement of temporary hegemony is rooted in the ability of one state to command simultaneous primacy in production, trade, and finance. The other is the Kondratieff cycle which relates to the achievement of temporary quasi-monopolies in leading industries (Wallerstein 2004: 30–2). In both cases, the maximal positions (hegemony, quasi-monopoly with its concomitant maximal capital accumulation) are self-liquidating, which takes the form of long cycles with four phases.

It has been remarked that the popularity of theorizing about Kondratieffs is correlated with whether the world-system is in an A- or a B-phase. People living in A-phases seem to dislike long-wave theorizing because it suggests that the A-phase is not eternal, whereas people living in B-phases seem to like such theorizing, since it suggests that the B-phase will come to an end.

The literature on Kondratieff cycles and on "long cycles" is extensive. It has always been controversial. Indeed, few hypotheses about the modern world or about capitalism as a system seem to arouse as much negative passion among its opponents. One has to ask the question why. There seem to be several major arguments against the existence of Kondratieff cycles. One is a debate about the quality of the data put forward in its favor. This is of course a perfectly legitimate debate. But it is doubtful that the quality of the data is significantly weaker than that for any other hypothesis that deals with macrophenomena over long historical time.

The second is that the hypothesis is mechanistic, in that it suggests exact time parameters for the presumed phases of the cycles. But this is simply unfair, since all proponents explicitly state that the timing is only approximate and has varied from cycle to cycle. Indeed, proponents of the Kondratieff cycles argue among themselves constantly about the dating one wishes to assign to various cycles.

The heart of the debate involves two issues. One is whether there are any general rules governing large-scale social phenomena. The school of social scientists whose emphases are exclusively idiographic of course reject this. But so do social scientists whose epistemology is reductionist, emphasizing microphenomena and rejecting the idea of emergent properties. The second issue is among those who are willing to accept the existence of large-scale generalizations, but are quite unhappy about the policy implications of Kondratieff cycles. For some, they suggest that a Whig interpretation of history is unsustainable since the structures of the modern world provide constantly for "downturns." For others, it is the opposite. They see Kondratieffs as minimizing the element of agency and the possibilities of basic transformation of the existing system.

It is clear that the debate about Kondratieffs hides other, more important debates about the understanding of large-scale social processes and the historical development of the modern world. These questions will never be resolved at the level of the existence or non-existence of Kondratieff cycles, but must be tackled directly. In the meantime, there is a significant group of historical social scientists who are trying to add evidence and clarify theoretically their observations about macro-fluctuations in the real world.

SEE ALSO: Braudel, Fernand; Dependency and World-Systems Theories; Schumpter, Joseph A.

REFERENCES AND SUGGESTED READINGS

Cameron, R. (1973) The Logistics of European Economic Growth: A Note on Historical Periodization. *Journal of European Economic History* 2(1): 145–8.

Goldstein, J. S. (1988) *Long Cycles: Prosperity and War in the Modern Age.* Yale University Press, New Haven.

Kondratieff, N. (1984 [1926]) *Long Wave Cycle.* Richardson & Snyder, New York.

Mandel, E. (1980) *Long Waves of Capitalist Development: The Marxist Interpretation.* Cambridge University Press, Cambridge.

Modelski, G. (1987) *Long Cycles in World Politics.* University of Washington Press, Seattle.

Rostow, W. W. (1978) *The World Economy: History and Prospect.* University of Texas Press, Austin.

Schumpeter, J. A. (1939) *Business Cycles: A Theoretical, Historical, and Statistical Analysis of the Capitalist Process,* 2 Vols. McGraw-Hill, New York.

Suter, C. (1992) *Debt Cycles in the World-Economy: Foreign Loans, Financial Crises, and Debt Settlements, 1820–1990.* Westview Press, Boulder.

Wallerstein, I. (1983) The Three Instances of Hegemony in the Capitalist World-Economy. *International Journal of Comparative Sociology* 24(1–2): 100–8.

Wallerstein, I. (2004) *World-Systems Analysis.* Duke University Press, Durham, NC.

Krafft-Ebing, Richard von (1840–1902)

Ken Plummer

Richard von Krafft-Ebing was an influential Viennese psychiatrist who invented a massive taxonomy of non-procreative sexual classifications in his influential text, *Psychopathia Sexualis with specific reference to the Antipathy Sexual Instinct: A Medico-Forensic Study* (1886). Never a sociologist, he gathered some 1,500 "clinical" case studies, developing a simplified version of life stories/autobiography as a tool for gathering unique subjective worlds of sexuality which could then be placed in the public domain (Plummer 1995). Many were introduced – in a fairly random way – as newly discovered medical perversions and disorders such as masochism, fetishism, necrophilia, sadism, inversion, and even heterosexuality – combining, for example, a wide range of case studies from men who were attracted to handkerchiefs with detailed case studies of necrophiliac murders. It was the first book of its kind and played a very significant social role in bringing to recognition an array of diverse sexualities. Much of this is discussed very critically in Foucault's key work, *The History of Sexuality* (1978), where Krafft-Ebing is implicitly seen as a key figure in creating the sexual confessional, the medical construction of sexual perversion, and the contemporary organization of sexual discourses. For Foucault's influential work, Krafft-Ebing was a theorist of the Victorian "repressive hypotheses."

Initially, Krafft-Ebing theorized homosexuality as a degenerate inherited trait (although it can be caused by masturbation or debauchery), and his work was very significant in establishing the ideas that homosexuals were specific kinds of people, that their state was a sickness, and that cure may well be possible. As such, it could seem that Krafft-Ebing was a conservative regulator of sexuality. In fact, he was a sympathetic liberal doctor who was concerned with the ways in which many sexual deviations had become criminalized, seeing them as unjust. He was influential on both Havelock Ellis and Sigmund Freud, even though they both rejected his theory. Putting his work in context, his study must be seen as one strand of late nineteenth-century thinking in which sexuality was becoming separated out from its procreative function. The sexual impulse was no longer seen as dominated by the reproductive instinct, and could indeed be linked to pleasure and personal fulfillment. Many of the so-called perversions were part of this wider pleasure and desire (Oosterhuis 2000).

Psychopathia Sexualis was first published in 1886 and went through 12 editions. It was published in English in 1892, although much of the sexual language was left in a medicalized scientific form – "written in Latin" – to prevent the titillation of non-medical readers, who were largely excluded from reading it. By the final edition he was much more critical of his own ideas

of morbidity and degeneracy, but he did not live to see his own critique published. In the end, his work offered a humanistic account of widespread human sexual differences.

SEE ALSO: Ellis, Havelock; Foucault, Michel; Hirschfeld, Magnus; Homosexuality; Repressive Hypothesis; Sexuality Research: History

REFERENCES AND SUGGESTED READINGS

Foucault, M. (1978) *The History of Sexuality*. Vol. 1: *An Introduction*. Trans. R. Hurley. Pantheon, New York.

Katz, J. N. (1995) *The Invention of Heterosexuality*. Plume, New York.

Krafft-Ebing, R. von (1924 [1886]) *Psychopathia Sexualis*, 17th edn. Enke, Stuttgart.

Oosterhuis, H. (2000) *Stepchildren of Nature: Krafft-Ebing, Psychiatry, and the Making of Sexual Identity*. University of Chicago Press, Chicago.

Plummer, K. (1995) *Telling Sexual Stories: Power, Change, and Social Worlds*. Routledge, London.

Kuhn, Thomas and scientific paradigms

Ron Stanfield and Mary Wrenn

Thomas S. Kuhn (1922–96) was born in Cincinnati, Ohio, and attended Harvard University. After graduating with a bachelor's degree in physics, Kuhn worked for the US government during World War II, then returned to Harvard for graduate study in physics. Having entertained an interest in philosophy since his undergraduate days, Kuhn agreed to teach a newly developed history of science class as part of his graduate work. As a result, in the last stages of his doctoral program, he decided to change his field to the history of science, a change which allowed him an entrée into the study of philosophy by focusing on the philosophical implications of change within a discipline. Kuhn continued down this intellectual pathway, dedicating much of his professional academic career to the study of the history of science, and was especially intrigued by the shifting of gestalts within a discipline through time.

Although Kuhn's work focused almost exclusively on change within the natural sciences, it is perhaps in the social sciences that Kuhn's work made the deepest impact and where it continues to resonate today. Kuhn's emphasis on the social construction of a body of scientific knowledge appealed to social scientists who had long suffered in comparison to formal precision and elegance of the natural sciences. By seeming to emphasize consensus over rigor, Kuhn supported the scientific claim of social studies. He also opened the door to the study of the sociology of science through his work on the influence of cognitive values upon what is considered acceptable science, what Kuhn refers to as *normal science*, within any particular discipline.

Kuhn's most recognized and enduring work is *The Structure of Scientific Revolutions*. In *Structure*, Kuhn describes a process of a discipline's articulation or extension of a given developmental path up to the point at which that path no longer is able to furnish or resolve interesting problems. This crisis of normal science provokes extraordinary science and the possibility of scientific revolution in which the basic paradigm of a discipline is changed. A paradigm is a worldview, a set of implicit and explicit guides or examples defining the world and the questions and methods for analyzing the world.

The basic stages of Kuhn's scientific revolution or history of science paradigm are the following: pre-paradigm; normal science; crisis and, possibly, extraordinary science; and normal science again after the crisis is resolved. The pre-paradigm stage is characterized by the existence of several competing schools of thought, each offering a potential paradigm, none of which is persuasive enough to gain the (near) universal acceptance associated with normal science. There is a lack of direction as to what research should be done and as to the appropriate methods for doing it. Each competing group tends to seize upon a set of problems, facts, and methods. Published works take the form of extensive treatises that define and justify the scope and method of the research.

When one or a synthesis of the competing schools begins to attract ever-larger shares of practitioners, the transition to normal or mature science begins. Paradigms gain this acceptance by being considered more capable of solving a set of problems that have come to be accepted as the most important. The transition to normal science is marked by a withering away of competing schools, caused by conversion of old adherents, lack of recruits from a new generation, or simply defining out of the science the diehards who refuse to convert.

The discipline also is given a narrower, more rigid definition. This more rigid definition changes the nature of scientific publications, as general books (except textbooks) are replaced by shorter articles or research reports that assume prior knowledge of the paradigm on the part of the reader. The textbook tradition also arises. Textbooks generally include only that past scientific work relevant to the current paradigm. This creates the accumulated-knowledge illusion of a science, since past scientists are seen as sharing the same worldview, that is, as studying the same puzzles, data, and phenomena as current scientists, albeit somewhat less adroitly. Students learn from texts, not by using original sources. The discipline grows more insular, with its own standards and communications system increasingly separated from the lay public. Indeed, scientific revolutions tend to become invisible because of the textbook tradition.

Normal science is achieved when the discipline more or less universally accepts the dominant paradigm, which then directs the practitioner as to the key questions and appropriate methods of normal research. Normal science encompasses a period of paradigm articulation involving the manipulation of fact and theory to expand the scope and precision and to resolve the ambiguities of the paradigm. Significantly, normal science is characterized by a lack of intent to uncover phenomenal or theoretical novelties. The accepted paradigm defines the appropriate problems to pursue and the procedures to be used for this pursuit, and it guarantees that solutions to the problems can be found by using these procedures. Normal science involves puzzle solving. When an experiment fails to produce the anticipated result, the puzzle solver, not the puzzle (paradigm), is considered inadequate. This point is important because scientific revolutions are rejections of paradigms that do not make good their guarantees. Normal science is thus characterized by a period of relative quiescence, but this should not be interpreted as an equilibrium or static period. Normal science features calm and orderly cumulative change; it is not an equilibrium situation to be disturbed only by exogenous happenstance. As an articulation or day-to-day working out of the directions given by a paradigmatic axial structure, normal science itself sows the seeds for a period of storm, crisis, and redirection.

A situation of crisis occurs with the interruption of the normal science pattern. The existence of one or several anomalies marks the first stage of such a crisis. An anomaly is a violation of expectation or failure of a set of paradigm puzzles to come out right. As such, an anomaly may be associated with conflicting experimental or empirical discoveries or with an insistent theoretical ambiguity that defies resolution by paradigm articulation. An anomaly may not lead to crisis; it may exist and be recognized but be considered peripheral. Or the paradigm may be adjusted to resolve the anomaly. To evoke a crisis, an anomaly must question explicit, fundamental generalizations of the paradigm; be important to the solution of a pressing practical problem; or involve a long history of persistently defying resolution within the paradigm. When, for these or other reasons, an anomaly becomes recognized as more than merely a difficult problem, the transition to crisis and extraordinary science has begun. More attention is afforded the anomaly, and it may come to be recognized as the subject matter of the discipline.

The period of extraordinary science is similar in many ways to the pre-paradigm state. There occurs a relaxation of the rules of normal science, which results in more speculative, random research. Increasingly divergent articulations occur, which may involve the formation of schools of thought. This pattern often leads to an increase in discoveries and a shift to philosophical analyses or explicit methodological debates on the rules of the paradigm. In essence, then, a state of flux exists in which the discipline searches for a new departure by reconsidering data, questioning structural institutions, evaluating received doctrine, and the like. The state of flux which occurs during extraordinary science is necessary but not sufficient to invoke a battle of paradigms. The period of

extraordinary science ends in one of three ways. The anomaly may be resolved finally by normal science; the anomaly may resist all offered approaches, in which case the discipline accepts it as insoluble given the state of the art; or a new paradigm may emerge and a battle for its acceptance ensues. In the last case, the ascension to dominance of a new paradigm is, of course, the consummation of a scientific revolution.

The paradigm battle occurs when dissenting opinion is molded into a synthetic paradigm that can be used to challenge the extant conventional wisdom. The challenge to conventional opinion is weakened by the existence of several dissenting schools, each insisting on its own doctrinal integrity and expending vital energy to do so. The true testing in a science occurs within the paradigm battle. Normal science does not involve testing the paradigm with fact. It is a process of matching fact and theory with the burden of failure resting upon the tool user, not the tool. Testing occurs in the paradigm battle when competing paradigms are tested for their ability to gain the allegiance of the discipline. This testing cannot be done precisely by proof either of the falsifiability criterion or of the probability of accurate prediction types, since competing paradigms are incommensurate. That is, holding different worldviews, standards, delineations of the science, and connotations of terminology, practitioners with different paradigms cannot agree on an objective operational test of the paradigms. The testing and conversion process is one of persuasion. Frequently members of the old generation remain unpersuaded and either are defined out of the discipline or manage to stave off conversion of the discipline until their deaths.

There are three principal persuasive arguments for a new paradigm: that it is capable of resolving the crisis-producing anomaly; that it permits the admission of new phenomena inadmissible under the old paradigm; and that it is aesthetically more pleasing, neater, more suitable, or simpler than the old paradigm. More generally, Kuhn notes that to gain acceptance the new paradigm must be seen as preserving most or all of the problem-solving capacity of the old paradigm while offering additional capacity of its own. Of course its chances for success increase with the amount of importance that can be attached to this additional capacity. Although the new paradigm retains the problem-solving capacity of the old, the new paradigm is not simply a cumulative process of attaching a new layer to the old foundation. Rather, it is the social construction of a new foundation involving new fundamental laws, generalizations, and behavioral functions; often new methods and applications; and a redefinition of the character and standards of the science. It is because of this marked deviation from the previously established paradigm that the new paradigm arises in the minds of one or a few individuals whose research is usually concentrated in the anomaly area, and who generally are young or new to the discipline and therefore have less invested in the propagation of the old paradigm. Indeed, the new paradigm is a change in worldview to such an extent that the world itself is changed. The perception and cognition of data and even the data to be collected are redefined.

Kuhn's work indicates the importance of social structure in any discussion of a scientific community. For example, a clear picture of socialization or acculturation emerges from the discussion of the intergenerational process of recruitment and accreditation. Paradigm discipline to sustain an integral core of fundamental problems and methods is a social process. The most visible aspect of this process is the structure and function of a penalty–reward and status system in the discipline's hierarchy of journals, departments, and associational offices of function and sinecure. There is also the tacit knowledge aspect in that the members of a science have internalized shared commitments, values, and research guides that remain tacit in a period of normality. Their existence, however, can be recognized consciously and their content deliberately scrutinized in periods of crisis and extraordinary science. The hierarchy of departments, journals, and associations may also be subject to critical scrutiny in such times.

In discussing normal science as a puzzle-solving activity, Kuhn notes that the paradigm, and not society, defines the scope and method of a science, but this is not to say that paradigm shifts within a science occur in complete autonomy and that the wider society or social structure bears no influence upon paradigmatic change. Given the subjective character of paradigm acceptance, any social forces that play upon an investigator's sense of self and

sense of collegiality may play a role. Kuhn cites nationality as an example of an external criterion that could influence the rate of change within a discipline. Darwinism, Kuhn notes, ascended to normal science before its adaptation in other countries. As well, an individual scientist's values and norms influence the disciplinary choices made. As such, both shared and personal criteria figure into the decision-making process and work to determine the openness with which paradigm changes might be greeted and the type and degree of change which the individual practitioner will tolerate. The degree of influence by these external values is directly correlated with the degree of upheaval generated by the paradigm battle internal to the discipline. Subjective values thus rise to guide the individual and fill the lacuna left by the conflation or absence of objective rule criteria. In the interest of maintaining "objective science," the part played by an individual's values and norms is generally unacknowledged in the evolution of a science. Moreover, Kuhn points out that in understanding the ascension to dominance of a new paradigm, reference must be made not only to the shared criteria of the scientists who chose the new paradigm, but also to those points on which they differ.

Kuhn's work has had enormous influence not only in the history and philosophy of science but also in the language of everyday life. His emphasis on the social construction of science is part of a general movement, dating at least to Marx, toward a sociology of knowing. If a unification of scientific knowledge is in the offing near term, it will likely build upon this growing concern with the process of human cognition.

SEE ALSO: Evolution; Fact, Theory, and Hypothesis: Including the History of the Scientific Fact; Falsification; Paradigms; Science, Social Construction of; Scientific Knowledge, Sociology of; Scientific Revolution

REFERENCES AND SUGGESTED READINGS

Bird, A. (2000) *Thomas Kuhn*. Princeton University Press, Princeton.
Hoyningen-Huene, P. (1992) The Interrelations between the Philosophy, History, and Sociology

of Science in Thomas Kuhn's Theory of Scientific Development. *British Journal for the Philosophy of Science* 43(4): 487–501.

Kuhn, T. (1970) *The Structure of Scientific Revolutions*, 2nd edn. University of Chicago Press, Chicago.

Kuhn, T. (1977) *The Essential Tension*. University of Chicago Press, Chicago.

Kuhn, T. (1992) *The Trouble With the Historical Philosophy of Science*. Harvard University Press, Cambridge, MA.

Nickles, T. (Ed.) (2003) *Thomas Kuhn*. Cambridge University Press, Cambridge.

Stanfield, J. R. (1979) *Economic Thought and Social Change*. Southern Illinois University Press, Carbondale.

Yonay, Y. (1998) *The Struggle Over the Soul of Economics*. Princeton University Press, Princeton.

Kurauchi, Kazuta (1896–1988)

Kenji Kosaka

Kazuta Kurauchi was born in Okayama Prefecture in Japan. His father was the head teacher of Chinese classics at Kojokan, which was a local private school specializing in Chinese literature studies. From his early days, Kurauchi was greatly influenced by both Keiken Sakata, the famous scholar who owned and managed the school he attended, and his father.

Kurauchi graduated from the Faculty of Letters at the then Tokyo Imperial University – now Tokyo University – where he studied sociology under Tongo Takebe, who was a follower and proponent of Comtean sociology. As sociology was not yet a well-developed academic discipline in Japan, Kurauchi also studied history, literature, and philosophy, all of which combined to give a much broader perspective to his sociological work. Thus, although a sociologist, he was also well versed in classical Chinese and western (particularly German and French, but also English and Italian) and Japanese literature studies, both classical and contemporary. This wide intellectual background informed his sociological studies, and distinguished him from other Japanese

sociologists, both those who were his contemporaries and those who came after him.

After graduation, Kurauchi was employed by the Ministry of Education to research educational matters in Japan, but continued his sociological studies with colleagues at the Tokyo Society of Sociological Study. He also taught at various universities as a part-time instructor at this time. Eventually he moved into teaching as full-time academic work, becoming a faculty member at Kyushu University (1933–46), Osaka University (1948–60), Kwansei Gakuin University (1960–7), and Otemon University (1967–74). He was granted a doctoral degree in sociology for his book *Bunka Shakaigaku* (*Sociology of Culture*), written in 1943.

Among his other major works are the books *Bunka to Kyoiku* (*Culture and Education*, 1948), *Shakaigakubu Gairon* (*Outline of Sociology*, 1953), and *Shakaigaku – Zohoban* (*Sociology, Enlarged Edition*, 1966), which, with his many academic papers, are all included in his *Collected Papers* (1976–84). Kurauchi served as president of the Kansai Sociological Association (1956–60), and was a member of the Science Council of Japan from 1960 to 1963. He died at his home in Osaka Municipal Prefecture on July 6, 1988, having actively written about and explored new sociological research areas of study until the very end of his life.

Kurauchi was a creative scholar who lived in the Meiji era and who attempted to integrate western and Japanese philosophy, having first studied and learned Comtean sociology from Takebe, but later becoming inclined toward the sociological thinking of Tarde and Georg Simmel. His graduation thesis was "Considerations on the Causes of the Decline of Societies." He was later also influenced by the strong currents in German sociology, particularly by phenomenology and the sociologies of culture and knowledge. The research interest which sustained his work was in the "social" dimension of society and sociology as an academic discipline.

In 1922, a new movement emerged at Tokyo Imperial University among the younger sociologists. This movement sought to absorb the new waves of European sociology that had developed while Japanese scholars had been isolated due to World War I. *Tokyo Shakaigaku Kenkyukai* (Tokyo Society of Sociological

Study) was formed in 1924 by Hisatoshi Tanabe (a committed French sociologist being a follower of both Durkheim and Tarde), Kurauchi, and Takashi Akiba (well known for his studies of ethnic groups in Korea and in China) in order to promote this new movement. Although Kurauchi was committed to phenomenological sociology, Japanese sociology as a whole became more diverse and more independent in the years following the formation of the Tokyo Society of Sociological Study.

Kurauchi's principal influences were Simmel, Kracauer, Husserl, Vierkandt, Tönnies, Scheler, Litt, Geiger, and Mannheim, all of whom are considered phenomenological sociologists. Following study and research methods developed by this prominent group of sociologists, Kurauchi attempted to have a clearer understanding of the essence of "society" in the lived experiences of the self as an individual. Theodor Litt was perhaps the most influential phenomenological sociologist on Kurauchi's sociology. It was Litt's insights into lived space and the conceptualization of the essence of society in terms of the reciprocity of perspectives that most affected Kurauchi's sociological thinking. Kurauchi applied Litt's insights to both the spatial and temporal perspectives. Other prominent sociologists greatly influenced Kurauchi, such as Durkheim, Tarde, Gurvitch, and other French sociologists. No multiplication of names of people who influenced Kurauchi's intellectual odyssey, however, would be sufficient.

Kurauchi is known as a pioneer in three areas of sociological study and research in Japan: the sociology of education, cultural sociology, and theoretical sociology. Among his major contributions was the development of unique and creative theories and concepts of sociological thought from a phenomenological perspective. His creativity and innovativeness can be seen in the sociological analytical framework and in the uniquely coined sociological concepts and terms he developed. He considered society to be a whole that contains many subjects. This whole is experienced by each individual subject, rather than by the whole subjectivity. The contemplation of society must be considered from three points: the wholeness of society, individuals, and the many varied relations that hold between and among individuals.

The experience of society is always defined in terms of time and place, where three group types can be distinguished according to the lived experience of individuals: preceding group (*Vorgruppe*), present group (*Jetztgruppe*), and subsequent or succeeding group (*Nachgruppe*). Preceding group is defined as a social group which exists prior to a given nation-state, and which is involved in the transformation process of that nation-state from within, with the collective energy of a social group being retained. An example is tribal groups, on whose allegiance a given nation-state is based, these groups existing prior to the creation or construction of the state system, and maintaining their group allegiances after the system is formed. Such groups are often agitating elements in the state system, and there is always the possibility that these groups may withdraw from that system.

Present groups are those necessary for the construction or creation of the nation-state system. Bureaucratic groups and military groups are prime examples of this group type in that they play important roles – as far as formal roles are concerned – in sustaining the state as such. However, as concerns their informal roles, these groups can easily deviate from normative standards set by the state. Since such groups are deeply connected to the state system, having been instrumental in the creation of the state system, they can also have great effects on social changes (e.g., in a coup d'état). Succeeding groups emerge after the creation or construction of the state system has been initiated, and are created or recreated by the system itself. These groups may become discontented with the state system, in which case they may also become agents of revolutionary change through their resistance to the system.

These notions of society were quite original to Kurauchi, although he got the idea from the work of early Chinese and Japanese historians such as Su Dongpo (1036–1101) and Rai Sanyo (1780–1832). Kurauchi combined the three group-type model with a fourfold schema to fully develop his own theory of societal change – which he called *ri-ho-say-may* – by integrating various sociological insights, both eastern and western. Society in its totality and societal change can be analyzed, he claimed, by reference to *ri* (law), *ho* (norm), *say* (current), and *may* (destiny), as shown in Figure 1.

	Universal	Particular
Ultra-societal	law (*ri*; *Gesetz*)	destiny (*may*; *Geschick*)
Societal	norm (*ho*; *Norm*)	current (*say*; *Strom*)

Figure 1 Societal change.

In the conceptual schema in Figure 1, *ri* refers to "external" general laws that serve to regulate societies and events and manage the thinking, actions, and behavior of humans. Our individual lives are also determined by *may* in that we cannot choose when, where, or with what socio-economic status we are born. *Ho* refers to societies' "internal" laws and institutions, whereas *say* represents more transient entities such as social currents, fads, mobs, and public opinion. In Kurauchi's theoretical thinking, *ri* and *ho* are much more stable than *may* and *say*. All these terms originated in eastern or Oriental literature, but are readily translatable into terms clearly understood in western philosophy.

Kurauchi uses this fourfold typological schema to explain various social phenomena; even the architecture of a house, seen from Kurauchi's sociological perspective, can be interpreted using the four concepts. A house in Kurauchi's conceptual schema is a representation of material culture, it being a creation and adaptation of humans in the midst of their natural surroundings (*ri*). The house embodies human values (*ho*), and is a reflection of a variety of manners that show social currents (*say*). The house, consisting of three major components – roof, wall, and floor – is also a place where someone happens to live (*may*). The natural environment coupled with the human need to protect oneself from possible violent assault by outsiders, for example, together determine different housing styles, which reflect different cultures and ways of thinking and behaving (e.g., eastern/Oriental and western/Occidental, modern and premodern, etc.).

Kurauchi uses this same explanatory schema to illustrate, for example, how elements of Confucianism have affected modernization and the development of democracy in Japanese society, how the history of a society is to be analyzed in general terms, and how religion is formed and transformed during historical processes. Thus, Kurauchi's fourfold schema provides a powerful interpretive framework in sociology. Kurauchi's culture and his original social analyses reminded him of early literature, both eastern and western. At the same time, the opposite occurred: he was provided with useful clues or hints to formulating sociological concepts and theories by recalling early literature. For Kurauchi, even the past can be classified into three types. First there is the "age of direct contemporaries," secondly "the age of direct transmission of tradition," and lastly "the age of indirect records and literature." This further utilization of Kurauchi's conceptual and theoretical framework was suggested to him by Chun Gin, a Chinese scholar of the Gong Yang school at the end of the Qing dynasty. This typology was also easily linked to the concepts of *Vorwelt* (world of predecessors), *Umwelt* (fellow-men in direct experiences), *Mitwelt* (world of contemporaries), and *Folgewelt* (world of successors), which were developed by Alfred Schütz.

Kurauchi applied his unique phenomenological perspective to the interpretation of numerous historical events as well as cultural and artistic works. The *I Ching*, for example, remained one of his longstanding academic interests. *Doroumi-koki*, which was an orally constructed legend in Japan of the creation of humans, describes the philosophy of Miki Nakayama (1798–1887), the founder of the Shinto sect named *Tenri-kyo*. Kurauchi reinterpreted *Doroumi-koki* as an elaborate philosophy for ordinary people based on both the *I Ching* and his own sociological perspectives.

The legend known as *Doroumi-koki* begins by describing how humans were created. Gods of (the) sun and (the) moon looked down upon *doroumi* (muddy sea), only to find loaches. The gods soon grew tired of looking at this monotonous scenery and decided to create humans. Kurauchi interprets this as an embodiment of *K'un* (ground), represented as loaches in *doroumi* and gods in *Ch'ien* (heaven), a combination of the two trigrams of *ying* and *yang* which, he says, imply the production or creation of something – in this case, humans.

Other phenomena can be interpreted in terms of a combination of two out of eight trigrams. A seemingly ridiculous legend, involving a variety of fish and reptiles, such as tortoises, eels, globefish, plaice, flatfish, black snakes, and killer whales, is now codified as representing three layers of humans, animals, and vegetables. Furthermore, in the process of that codification the legend acquires a deep sociological interpretation. This analysis thus recalls Aristotelian anthropology and Lévi-Straussian structuralism as well as Chinese and Japanese philosophy. No other sociologist, Japanese or otherwise, can compete with Kurauchi's analysis explaining the entire discourse of *Doroumi-koki*.

Kurauchi's sociology may very well be characterized as an attempt to integrate sociology with its western origins into the social thought and literature of the eastern/Oriental and Asian experiences. In 1974 Kurauchi stated,

> [I am] dissatisfied with the situation where Japanese sociologists view sociology as an imported science subservient to the authority of Western scholars, while lessons from Chinese and Japanese classical and contemporary works are ignored. It is unnaturally dogmatic that we do not investigate that literature and continue to treat it as irrelevant. This is a cultural tragedy. ("Sociology and I," in *Collected Papers*, V.456)

Kurauchi never once mentioned or spoke of "globalization" in the sense in which the term was used at about the end of the twentieth century. The three-group model discussed above may well reflect the world system in the 1960s as Kurauchi viewed it. However, Kurauchi's ideas and theories will never become outdated since they are concerned deeply with the fundamental structures and processes of the lived experiences of humans, and with society. Kurauchi's ideas, concepts, and theoretical explanations, analyses, and interpretations are readily applicable to any society at any level of discussion or analysis, and at any time. The many newly emerging difficult tasks, and the turmoil which gives rise to an urgency of confronting those tasks in the twenty-first century, can be readily addressed by carefully looking at and applying Kurauchi's general theoretical schema.

SEE ALSO: Confucianism; Culture; Durkheim, Émile; Knowledge, Sociology of; Phenomenology; Religion; Schütz, Alfred; Shintoism; Simmel, Georg; Takata, Yasuma; Theory

REFERENCES AND SUGGESTED READINGS

Kurauchi, K. (1976–84) *Kurauchi Kazuta Chosakushu (Collected Papers)*, 5 vols. Ed. Editorial Committee of the Publications of Kazuta Kurauchi. Kwansei Gakuin Daigaku Seikatsu Kyodo Kumiai Shuppankai, Nishinomiya, Japan.

L

labeling

Thomas Calhoun and Mark Konty

In the sociology of deviance the concept of labeling is used in two interrelated ways. One involves the labeling of people as *deviants*. When people are so labeled, they are judged to be deviant by some standard and the label has important sociological and psychological consequences. The other is the labeling of actions as *deviance*. When actions are labeled as such, there tends to be an actual or assumed non-normative behavior, and that reaction reflects the feeling and attitude of a person or group toward that behavior.

Although functionalism and conflict theory contributed to the labeling concept, it is most firmly rooted in symbolic interactionism. As suggested by symbolic interactionism, people and their behavior are labeled deviant via social interaction with others, and the feedback we receive from those interactions structures our view of ourselves. In effect, labeling behavior as deviant constitutes and defines its deviant status, and, as a result, the person so labeled experiences the consequences of being labeled deviant.

LABELING PEOPLE AS DEVIANTS

Deviant labels are *negative*. Frank Tannenbaum (1938) was the first sociologist to argue that society creates criminals by "dramatizing the evil" of the offender. The person is "defined," "identified," "segregated," and made "conscious and self-conscious" of his or her failings. The label identifies the negative character of the offender.

Deviant labeling produces negative *reactions*. Edwin Lemert (1951) made a conceptual distinction between primary and secondary deviance. Primary deviance is norm-violating behavior that goes undetected by others and consequently escapes being labeled deviant. This type of deviation does not affect the individual's social relationships or self-concept. Secondary deviance, however, is known to others and provokes negative "societal response." Lemert was not concerned with what prompted people to commit the deviant act in the first place, but was interested in how the negative responses to deviance shaped future behavior. A person may commit rule-breaking acts, but with no response from others the individual simply carries on as before. A person, then, is not a deviant unless others respond in a negative way to the person's behavior.

Deviant labeling depends upon *social relationships*. All labels emerge from social relationships. These negative reactions ascribe negative characteristics to the individual. These reactions, however, are not the same for all kinds of people. Instead, as Howard Becker (1963) observed, some individuals are more likely to be labeled deviant than others, even when the same rule is broken. The likelihood of being labeled deviant, however, depends on the relationship between one person and others. Generally, the greater the difference in power and status between the two parties, the more likely one is labeled deviant by the other. Also, the more distant the relationship, the more likely labeling is to occur. Thus, labeling is more likely to occur among strangers than among friends and family members.

Deviant labels are *noxious*, an "undesired differentness" (Goffman 1963: 5). They tend to threaten or destroy the labeled person's career, social position, and relationship with friends, acquaintances, and others. As a result, people generally try to avoid deviant labels and they use various strategies to manage the situation to avoid the label. Erving Goffman (1963) draws a distinction between people who are "discredited" (already stigmatized) and "discreditable" (may be stigmatized at any time) and suggests some of the ways that each manages the situation to avoid the noxious effects of the deviant label.

Deviant labels make *social interaction difficult*. Generally, people prefer to interact with others who are more like them. The deviant label lets us know that the deviant is not like us, seems to oppose our values, or has different tastes and preferences. We consequently feel uncomfortable interacting with the deviant person. Moreover, interacting with deviants carries the risk of guilt by association or what Goffman (1963) called "courtesy stigma," whereby conventional people are labeled deviant simply because they associate with a deviant. As a consequence, conventional people tend to steer clear of the deviant.

Another effect on social interaction occurs when the rule-breakers are shamed for their behavior. According to John Braithwaite (1989), shaming takes one of two forms, each with different consequences. In "disintegrative" shaming the rule-breaker is stigmatized and rejected by the group, resulting in the likelihood of further deviance. "Reintegrative" shaming, on the other hand, involves showing compassion and understanding for the rule-breaker while simultaneously making him feel shame for his behavior. The result is the likelihood that deviance will desist. The effect of labeling on social interaction thus depends upon the type of shaming practiced by the group.

Deviant labels tend to produce *deviant self-concepts*. In symbolic interactionism, the self is a product of social interaction. If the interaction involves a person being labeled as a deviant, that person is likely to develop a deviant self-concept. The altered self-concept in turn affects future outcomes. This can occur even if the individual has done nothing wrong.

William Chambliss (1973) demonstrated that not only does social status affect who gets labeled, but that this difference also affects the self-concepts accordingly. The "Roughnecks" came from the community's lower social strata. They engaged in some petty larceny and

occasionally fought with each other. The community labeled them as the town troublemakers. The "Saints" were members of the community's upper social strata. They were actually more deviant than the Roughnecks, not only because they committed more deviant acts but also because their deviant acts were more serious and harmful. These boys were nonetheless considered upstanding members of the community, and when they were caught breaking rules, the behavior was excused as "boys being boys." Following high school graduation the Saints did better than the Roughnecks. The Saints became the respectable citizens they were projected to be, while the Roughnecks continued a life of petty crime and low-paying jobs. The only exception was two Roughneck boys who went away to college on athletic scholarships. Free from the negative feedback of the deviant label, they developed positive, successful self-concepts. They returned to their home community and occupied the same positions as the Saints. This reveals a situation where two groups of youth, both engaged in delinquency, had very different outcomes because their social statuses determined how their behavior was reacted to, and those reactions shaped the boys' futures in different ways.

LABELING BEHAVIOR AS DEVIANCE

Becker (1963) observed, "deviant behavior is behavior that people so label." This seems to be stating the obvious, but this subjective, or reactive, definition of deviance opened the door for new analytical and theoretical insights in the study of deviance. Analytically, this definition of deviance allows researchers to set aside their own judgments of right and wrong and instead focus on the judgments and consequent reactions of the society being observed. Theoretically, this definition calls attention to the role of power in defining behavior as deviant.

How can we know what is regarded as deviant in a society? Becker analyzed several approaches and found each wanting. One approach is to calculate some statistical mean and use that as a standard of what is "normal," but this may or may not actually fit what the society considers desirable or deviant. Some typical behaviors (e.g., lying) are quite common but still considered deviant. Some atypical behaviors (e.g., eating pancakes for lunch) are not considered deviant at all. Another approach is to determine if a behavior is harmful to the individual or society, but there is often little consensus as to what is harmful or not. The approach with the most intuitive appeal is to simply ask what the rules are or look for some absolute moral code (e.g., the Bible) which the group references. In complex societies, however, people reference many different groups, each under different rules, and figuring out which rules apply at what time and in which setting makes analysis difficult, if at all possible. On top of all this is the fact that some formal rules are rarely enforced while other informal rules carry more weight. How could the observer know what is deviant and what is not? The answer, Becker contended, is that the observer can know deviance by how people react to an individual's behavior. If they react negatively, he reasoned, then the act must be deviant.

Some critics question the moral validity of this approach. They argue deviants are unusual, deviance is harmful, and the moral code is absolute rather than relative. Deviance is an objective phenomenon, they conclude, not a product of social construction. Unfortunately, this approach is analytically useless and doesn't reflect empirical reality. To the researcher, it doesn't matter what *should* be deviant, but rather what *is* regarded as deviant in a particular society. Simply observing the world around us tells us that definitions of deviance do vary across groups, time, and space.

The labeling, reactive definition provides a parsimonious solution to the problem of defining a phenomenon with so much variance. People don't react negatively if they believe a behavior is positive, so if there is a negative reaction, there must have been a negative behavior in the eye of the observer. Of course, this definition also includes people who may have actually done nothing wrong, but are still labeled deviant, what Becker called the "falsely accused." There is a problem, though, with this reactive definition. It may include the subjective view of deviance as *positive*, which runs counter to most sociologists' assumption that deviance is always negative (Heckert & Heckert 2002).

A key utility of the reactive definition of deviance is that it allows sociologists to examine the role of power in defining deviant and normative behavior. A normative definition of deviance, which regards deviance as a norm violation, says nothing about where the norms came from or why the norm violation does not have the same consequences for different categories of people. The more power and resources a social category commands, the greater is its capacity to resist being labeled as deviant and the more impact its definitions of deviance have. More powerful social sectors of the society are more likely than less powerful sectors to have their definitions of deviance valorized and institutionalized. Taken collectively, the more influence a social category has, the more likely its views on right and wrong will have influence on the educational curriculum, the content of the media, political discourse, and the actions and policies of the criminal justice system.

AN ASSESSMENT OF LABELING THEORY

The labeling *process* is distinct from labeling *theory*. The process of labeling, a process that takes place in all societies and all times, has manifestations and consequences that are distinct from any theoretical claims made by labeling theorists. Labeling theory can be critiqued independent of the phenomena observed during the labeling process. As a theory, labeling can be both dependent and independent variable. Labeling theorists have attempted to explain why certain people are more likely to be labeled than others, taking labels as result dependent upon other factors. Substantial evidence indicates that factors like power and status differences, resources, social distance, and visibility affect the likelihood that a label will be applied. Labeling theorists also posit that labels have their own independent effects on social interaction, self-concepts, and behavior.

Over the years a number of criticisms have been leveled at labeling as an independent variable. The most common is the charge that the labeling perspective does not explain initial acts of deviance, as it only explains deviance after the behavior has been detected and the label applied. But supporters of the labeling theory counter that the theory is not intended to explain initial deviance but instead secondary, continued, or repeated deviance as a result of the societal responses to initial deviance. However, research has yielded mixed results on the presumed validity of the theory. Labeling by friends, family, and other informal social agents has strong effects on self-concepts (Matsueda 1992), while labels from the criminal justice system and other formal social control agencies seem to have weak or no effects on individual's self-concepts (Akers & Sellers 2004).

SEE ALSO: Crime; Deviance; Deviance, Crime and; Deviance, Criminalization of; Deviance, Explanatory Theories of; Deviance, Theories of; Goffman, Erving; Identity, Deviant; Labeling Theory; Lemert, Edwin M.; Stigma; Symbolic Interaction

REFERENCES AND SUGGESTED READINGS

Akers, R. L. & Sellers, C. (2004) *Criminological Theories: Introduction, Evaluation, and Application*, 4th edn. Roxbury, Los Angeles.
Becker, H. S. (1963) *Outsiders*. Free Press, New York.
Braithwaite, J. (1989) *Crime, Shame, and Reintegration*. Cambridge University Press, Cambridge.
Chambliss, W. J. (1973) The Saints and the Roughnecks. *Society* 11: 24–31.
Goffman, E. (1963) *Stigma: Notes on the Management of Spoiled Identity*. Prentice-Hall, Englewood Cliffs, NJ.
Heckert, A. & Heckert, D. M. (2002) A New Typology of Deviance: Integrating Normative and Reactivist Definitions of Deviance. *Deviant Behavior* 23: 449–79.
Lemert, E. (1951) *Social Pathology*. McGraw-Hill, New York.
Matsueda, R. L. (1992) Reflected Appraisals, Parental Labeling, and Delinquency: Specifying and Symbolic Interactionist Theory. *American Journal of Sociology* 97: 1577–1611.
Scheff, T. (1966) *Being Mentally Ill: A Sociological Theory*. Aldine, Chicago.
Schur, E. (1971) *Labeling Deviant Behavior: Its Sociological Implications*. Harper & Row, New York.
Tannenbaum, F. (1938) *Crime and Community*. Ginn, Boston.
Thomas, W. I. (1931) *The Unadjusted Girl*. Little, Brown, Boston.

labeling theory

Ross Matsueda

Unlike most theories of crime and deviance, which emphasize the causes of deviant behavior, labeling theories focus on society's reaction to crime and deviance. Labeling theorists argue that society's reaction to deviance is fundamental for three reasons. First, individuals who are labeled as deviant by society often become stigmatized and isolated from society, leading them into a deviant lifestyle. Second, the very definition of deviance lies not in the objective behavior of "deviants," but in powerful groups' ability to define and label the behavior of the powerless as deviant or criminal. Thus, deviance is socially constructed. Third, society's reaction to deviance provides positive functions for society by defining the boundary between deviant and conventional behavior and by reaffirming social solidarity.

LABELING, STIGMA, AND DEVIANCE AMPLIFICATION

Labeling theory argues that initial acts of child misbehavior are harmless acts of primary deviance; if left alone, children would mature out of misbehavior. While the children define such acts as "play" or "mischief," the adult community defines them as "bad" or "evil." The community, which includes parents, teachers, and juvenile justice officials, labels the acts as "delinquent," and the child as "bad" or "evil," in need of treatment or reform. The label, in turn, affects the self-image of the child, who comes to internalize the label, which produces more deviance, and more labeling. This escalating process of labeling can eventuate in the youth caught up in the legal system, stigmatized by society, isolated from conventional groups, and left with a deviant self-image. The result can be a self-fulfilling prophecy, as an otherwise conforming child fulfills the prophecy of the initial labeling of harmless acts, through deviance amplification (Matsueda 1992).

Lemert (1951) used the term primary deviance to refer to harmless initial acts of deviance, and secondary deviance to refer to deviance resulting from the negative effects of labeling. Labeling theorists have identified many examples of secondary deviance. For example, because of the stigma of their arrest records, ex-prisoners have difficulty getting jobs, finding affordable housing in good neighborhoods, and finding non-criminal companions, all of which impedes reentry into conventional society. Mental patients institutionalized in mental hospitals are stripped of their identities and forced to adapt to a custodial environment, which can hamper their attempts to recover. The poor are sometimes labeled as lazy and slothful, which can undermine their self-esteem and attempts to secure and maintain jobs.

These propositions of labeling theory led to policy changes in the 1970s. In juvenile justice, non-intervention policies were introduced to remove youth from the tangle of juvenile corrections and community treatment. In mental health, deinstitutionalization and mainstreaming were adopted to move non-chronic mental patients into the community. Such policies resulted in some successes, but also unanticipated consequences, such as widening the net of community controls of juveniles and increasing the ranks of mentally ill in the homeless population. Thus, the policies were no panacea for the complex problems addressed.

SOCIAL CONSTRUCTION, POLITICAL POWER, AND THE DEFINITION OF DEVIANCE

Perhaps more than any other theory of deviance, labeling theory takes seriously a social constructionist view. Rather than assuming that deviance and crime are objective behaviors "out there" to be discovered, labeling theorists argue that deviance is socially constructed through an institutional process involving politics and the legal system, and an interactional process involving the powerful applying of labels to the powerless. As a social construction, then, deviance is relative to a given society and

historical period. Out of the nearly limitless variety of human acts, societies settle on a small range of acts to label as deviant; most entail harm to others, but some entail little harm. The relativity of deviance is underscored by labeling theorists' definition of deviance.

In contrast to the usual definitions of deviance (or crime) as behavior violating social norms (or criminal laws), most labeling theorists adopt a "labeling definition of deviance," in which deviance is a label or status conferred by a social audience. Deviance, then, is not a behavior but a label: "The deviant is one to whom that label has successfully been applied; deviant behavior is behavior that people so label" (Becker 1963). When introduced, this definition created confusion, as critics argued that, taken literally, the definition excludes the possibility of actual deviant behavior, independent of whether or not it is labeled. Becker (1973) responded by saying the entire process of creating rules, violating rules, and labeling violators constitutes labeling: "Social groups create deviance by making the rules whose infraction constitutes deviance, and by applying those rules to outsiders." Such a definition spawned studies of the entire process, beginning with rule creation.

A hallmark of labeling theory is the observation that labels are not distributed equally in society, but rather are disproportionately applied to the powerless, the disadvantaged, and the poor. This begins with the creation of rules that define deviance. Labeling theorists argued that generally the powerful succeed in creating rules and laws outlawing behavior that violates their self-interests. Thus, rule creation is a result of group conflict in society, in which the powerful have a distinct advantage. Becker (1963) showed how moral entrepreneurs, typically drawn from the ranks of the middle and upper classes, create moral crusades by mobilizing disparate interest groups to outlaw behaviors that violate their common interest. Classic examples include the Marihuana Tax Act, prohibition, sexual-psychopath laws, and the creation of the juvenile court.

Labeling theorists also maintain that once laws are passed they tend to be enforced by the justice system in unfair ways, again more likely to single out the less powerful for the same behavior.

At the extreme, some theorists claimed that everyone commits crimes, but only a select few – including minorities, the poor, and the powerless – are arrested and incarcerated. Finally, an offshoot of labeling theory, termed the medicalization of deviance perspective, showed how the powerful medical profession increasingly succeeds in defining deviance as a medical problem or illness requiring treatment by licensed medical professionals. Once the deviant act is medicalized, other approaches to explaining, treating, and policymaking are ignored.

POSITIVE FUNCTIONS OF DEVIANCE

Building on the works of Durkheim and Mead, Erikson (1962, 1966) examined the positive functions of labeling for society. Durkheim (1964) argued that punishment of criminals served two functions. First, by punishing criminals with outrage and passion, society reaffirms the moral order – including the values, beliefs, and morals that bind society together –threatened by criminals' transgressions. Second, by punishing criminals, society draws a line between moral and immoral conduct, which is necessary because what constitutes crime and deviance is relative to a given society. Durkheim argued that in a "society of saints," trivial deviations – which we would consider merely "bad taste" – would be punished to reaffirm the moral order. Mead (1918) maintained that punishment allows members of society to express impulses of hostility and outrage, which creates a strong emotional identification with conventional society and feelings of anger at the criminal.

Erikson notes that labeling, such as imprisonment or hospitalization, does not reform or cure the deviant (the manifest function), but instead stigmatizes and segregates the deviant, resulting in a self-fulfilling prophecy in which deviants return to their deviant ways. Erikson concludes that labeling serves the latent function of maintaining a pool of deviants for defining moral boundaries and reaffirming social solidarity. He studied the Salem witch trials and showed how Puritans expressed their emotional hysteria by condemning witches and labeling them sinners and agents of the devil, which reduced tensions and factions among Puritans, Quakers, and other sects.

CRITICISMS AND PROMISING NEW DIRECTIONS

In the 1970s labeling theory achieved prominence as a major theory of deviance; through the 1980s it was subjected to several major critiques; by the 1990s, new theoretical developments emerged. Critiques came from disparate sources. Conflict and Marxist criminologists argued that labeling theory's analysis of rule creation and enforcement was rudimentary and ignored the contradictions of capitalism, which are revealed by a Marxist critique of capitalist social relations. Positivist criminologists, who advocate using scientific principles to study crime, argued that actual deviance did exist, the concept of secondary deviance was bankrupt, and labels were not disproportionately applied in society, when controlling for actual behavior.

Three recent developments in labeling theory have addressed the positivist critique by responding to Becker's (1973) call for an interactionist theory of all aspects of deviance, including primary deviance, labeling, and secondary deviance. Link and his colleagues (1989) have developed a modified labeling theory of mental illness in which a community's tolerance of mental illness colors how mental patients cope with the stigma of official labeling by treatment agencies. Depending on whether the community discriminates and devalues mental patients, the patient either minimizes the stigma by enlightening others, hides the treatment history, or withdraws from prejudicial groups.

Braithwaite (1989) developed a theory of shame and reintegration, in which he argues that labeling can have both positive and negative effects on future behavior. When offenders are severely punished, they are stigmatized as an outcast, cut off from conventional groups, and are likely to turn to subcultures, which ensnarls them in a web of criminality. In contrast, when offenders are publicly shamed by the community expressing disapproval, but then reintegrated into society, the stigmatizing effects of labeling will not lead to secondary deviance. Reintegrative shaming is most effective in communitarian societies like Japan, in which members are intertwined in each other's lives, making shaming and reintegration likely and successful.

Matsueda (1992) and his colleagues (Heimer & Matsueda 1994) used Mead's theory of role-taking and social cognition to develop a theory of both primary and secondary deviance, termed differential social control. In problematic situations in which habitual behavior is blocked, individuals take the role of others, form a self as an object from the standpoint of others, and consider alternate solutions to problems from the standpoint of others. This cognitive process links the self and social groups to behavioral decisions: the self is a reflection of appraisals made by significant others, including reference groups. They find support for a causal chain, in which labeling by others influences future delinquency by altering reflected appraisals.

In sum, labeling theory has shaped how we view deviance and crime in society by underscoring the importance of society's reactions to deviance, analyzing political power and deviant labels, and showing how labeling can amplify deviance. Left for dead in the 1980s by some researchers, labeling theory is enjoying a revival by researchers responding to Becker's (1973) call for an interactionist theory of all aspects of deviance, including primary deviance, labeling, and secondary deviance.

SEE ALSO: Crime; Deviance; Deviance, Crime and; Deviance, Criminalization of; Deviance, Theories of; Interaction; Labeling; Lemert, Edwin M.; Social Problems, Concept and Perspectives; Social Psychology; Theory

REFERENCES AND SUGGESTED READINGS

Becker, H. S. (1963) *Outsiders: Studies in the Sociology of Deviance*. Macmillan, New York.
Becker, H. S. (1973) Labeling Theory Reconsidered. In: *Outsiders: Studies in the Sociology of Deviance*. Free Press, New York, pp. 177–212.
Braithwaite, J. (1989) *Crime, Shame, and Reintegration*. Cambridge University Press, Cambridge.
Durkheim, E. (1964) *The Division of Labor in Society*. Free Press, New York.
Erikson, K. T. (1962) Notes on the Sociology of Deviance. *Social Problems* 9: 307–14.
Erikson, K. T. (1966) *Wayward Puritans*. Wiley, New York.
Heimer, K. & Matsueda, R. L. (1994) Role-Taking, Role-Commitment, and Delinquency: A Theory of Differential Social Control. *American Sociological Review* 59: 365–90.
Lemert, E. M. (1951) *Social Pathology: A Systematic Approach to the Theory of Sociopathic Behavior*. McGraw-Hill, New York.
Link, B. G., Cullen, F. T., Struening, E., Shrout, P. E., & Dohrenwend, B. P. (1989) A Modified Labeling Theory Approach to Mental Disorders: An Empirical Assessment. *American Sociological Review* 54: 400–23.
Matsueda, R. L. (1992) Reflected Appraisals, Parental Labeling, and Delinquency: Specifying a Symbolic Interactionist Theory. *American Journal of Sociology* 97: 1577–611.
Mead, G. H. (1918) The Psychology of Punitive Justice. *American Journal of Sociology* 23: 577–602.

labor/labor power

Rob Beamish

While establishing their materialist position, Marx and Engels argued that one may distinguish humankind from other biological entities by consciousness, religion, or whatever else one chose, but humankind fundamentally distinguished itself from animals and other living organisms when it began to produce its means of life. Labor, they argued, is an eternal, naturally imposed condition of human life, common to all forms of society. Finally, Marx and Engels noted, while producing its means of life, humankind indirectly produces the material conditions for its ongoing existence.

Two decades later, Marx again stressed labor's ontological nature and importance. In *Capital*, Marx distinguished labor "in general" from labor involved in "the valorization process." The latter is a particular sociohistorical form of labor that produces commodities that are sold in the market and functions as the source of surplus value. Labor in general is the general form of labor through which materials from the natural world are appropriated and converted to products that directly or indirectly meet human needs and wants. Labor in general actualizes the fundamental interchange between humankind and nature through which humankind engages with nature, changes its understanding of nature, and influences its own character. More than 130 years of scholarship in the physical, biological, and social sciences have refined, but not fundamentally altered, Marx's position on labor's ontological character.

Humankind is directly part of the material order of nature and inescapably bound to its laws (e.g., gravity, mitosis and meiosis, aging). As living creatures, there are specific material needs which we must meet (e.g., we must metabolize oxygen, water, protein, and caloric energy to live), but they are not all met immediately and directly. Through time and the evolutionary processes of the material order, the human order became dirempted or alienated from the material order. Whereas the material order of nature is direct, concrete, and thingly, the human order is concurrently immediate and mediate, concrete and abstract, and objective and subjective. Labor in general is the activity through which humankind indirectly or mediately engages with the material order and draws upon the concrete and abstract aspects of its being to create and recreate its existence.

It was Marx's 1844 critique of Hegel's *Phenomenology* that led to his deepest and most perceptive analyses of labor as the material, ontological basis to human life. Read through Marx's emerging materialist position, Hegel's conception correctly emphasized the creative aspects of labor, but limited it to the self-conscious mind. For Marx, human self-development stemmed from labor that was simultaneously concrete and abstract. Through labor, a material object is created which is separate from the producer as he or she externalizes an idea in a material form. This object stands "opposite" and outside the producer, but it simultaneously remains a part of him or her insofar as it represents the culmination of his or her creative activity. Subject to the laws of the material order – including humankind's material being – labor is an activity that is simultaneously objective and subjective because in producing an object – in the creation and externalization of an idea – the producer also gains subjective knowledge that did not exist before production began. Ontologically, labor is a concrete process that is inescapably creative. The mediate relation of humankind to the material order interposes,

through the labor process, a grid of culture between humankind and the natural order.

If labor is the eternal, naturally imposed condition of human life, labor power is the eternal, active, mediating capacity and force between humankind and the material order. Living labor, Marx argued in *Capital*, is the fire that infuses energy into raw materials, tools, and machinery, and turns them from moribund objects into newly formed products that can meet human needs and wants through consumption.

The notion of labor power originates in Adam Smith's *Wealth of Nations*, where he attributed the "productive powers" of labor to the division of labor. Noting the conception of "productive faculties" in one of his 1844 study notebooks, Marx refocused the term when wrestling with the question of what a worker actually brings to the production process. Marx argued that labor was brought to the marketplace as a potential. The living worker represented and carried an ability (or abilities) and the capacity to engage in labor – the product that was of ultimate interest to the capitalist purchaser. While Marx used several terms in his early work, he tended to use labor power in his later works to describe the capacity or commodity that the worker brought to the valorization process, but labor power always represented a complex conception of potential, ability, power, and force which brought life to the material order in the concurrently concrete and abstract, objective and subjective, immediate and mediate process of labor.

In class societies, labor power is the sole source of value creation. Because labor power is a capacity, the purchaser pays only as much as is required for the worker – the bearer of this potential – to meet his or her socially determined needs to reproduce him or herself and return to work day after day. The expenditure of labor power produces more value than the replacement value of labor power, giving rise to surplus value. As a result, labor power is the unique source of surplus value. The identification of labor power as the source of surplus in societies of social labor, in general and capitalist society in particular, was among Marx's most significant discoveries.

SEE ALSO: Alienation; Engels, Friedrich; Hegel, G.W.F.; Marx, Karl; Smith, Adam; Value

REFERENCES AND SUGGESTED READINGS

Krader, L. (2003) *Labor and Value*. Peter Lang, New York.

Lukacs, G. (1978) *The Ontology of Social Being: Labour*. Trans. D. Fernbach. Merlin Press, London.

Marx, K. (1975) *Early Writings*. Trans. G. Benton. Pelican, London.

Marx, K. (1976) *Capital*, Vol. 1. Trans. B. Fowkes. Penguin, London.

Marx, K. & Engels, F. (1981) *Marx-Engels Gesamtausgabe* (Marx–Engels Complete Works), Pt. 4, Vol. 2. Dietz Verlag, Berlin.

Schmidt, A. (1971) *The Concept of Nature in Marx*. Trans. B. Fowkes. New Left Books, London.

labor–management relations

Casten von Otter

The study of labor–management relations (LMR) refers to the rules and policies which govern and organize employment, how these are established and implemented, and how they affect the needs and interests of employees and employers. LMR has implications for the organization of work as well as economic policy. Focus gradually has broadened from the formation and operation of national and local institutions and collective bargaining to strategic human resource policies. Most recently a multi-level agenda has formed, following new needs for regulation in world trade, in the extended European Union, and in former communist and newly industrialized countries.

The freedom of collective bargaining is an important instrument of citizenship in a democracy, as expressed by the UN Declaration of Human Rights and the International Labor Organization's statement of core labor standards. Based on a norm of accommodation of interests, LMR eases the burden placed on parliamentary institutions. Respect for the freedom of association for all workers is generally seen as a prerequisite for a sustainable system of free trade.

To sociology, LMR is a momentous arena in which a political order intersects with the market system, which affects social differentiation, the distribution of social and economic welfare, and numerous other social dimensions in which sociologists take great interest. The field is important, as well, to many other disciplines – economics (labor economics), management science, political science, labor law, and social history. Industrial (or labor) relations was established as an academic discipline in the US in the early twentieth century. LMR is unusually rich in interdisciplinary theories, as well as international comparative studies. Its academic history is marked by strong ideological and normative commitments and the evident inputs to theorizing from political ideologies as well as the social sciences.

Two analytical paradigms have dominated the field. The traditional industrial relations systems perspective as laid out by John Dunlop is focused on the governance of work. Conflicts of interest between employees and management are seen as legitimate and often structural in origin. The favored vehicle for conflict resolution is collective bargaining (ultimately backed by the right to strike and lock-out) and regulated procedures for arbitration. Legislation is a useful instrument to be applied, however, mostly when self-determination by the parties has failed. While this theoretical perspective does not preclude accommodation of interests at the individual level, it maintains the importance of a collective regulatory framework that establishes a countervailing force against unfettered market forces and unilateral decisions of the employer. The industrial relations perspective has been critized for being too top-down, for disregarding workplace practices, and (initially) lacking in agency theory.

The other perspective is personnel or human resource management (HRM) and is underpinned by application of behavioral science (human relations theory) to organizational design. Corporate culture is important in integrating the employees with the aims and long-term objectives of the firm. Thus, wage systems and benefit schemes should be molded, not only to fulfill a contractual obligation, but also as proactive instruments to promote skills and beneficial attitudes and actions. New human resource policies are related to the increased pressure to compete in terms of speed, innovation, customization, etc. Conflicts and power relations are played down, as both parties supposedly have a strong interest in maintaining a consentient culture. HRM schemes have been controversial for their alleged use to foster complacent attitudes and to shift focus from trade union relations to personnel policy. More recently, the two fields are becoming integrated, as policies associated with HRM are introduced into collective agreements in Europe and the US.

HISTORY

Labor relations as a theme evolved out of the social problems that became evident during the industrial revolution. In all countries a period of social struggle preceded the resolution of labor conflict in institutional forms, bearing witness to the strong adversarial potential of unregulated LMR. In the words of Marx, workers were treated like commodities and should organize to overthrow the capitalist system. Sidney and Beatrice Webb inspired the reformist labor movement, favoring the improvement of LMR through legislated labor standards and collective bargaining, which ultimately could lead to industrial democracy. The basic idea – then and to this day – is to take wages, benefits, safety, and security standards out of economic competition. Germany under Bismarck pioneered legislation in health and safety, unemployment and workers' compensation insurance, retirement benefits, etc. Social model institutions for LMR or utopian communities such as those established by Robert Owen or Henry Ford served to demonstrate the viability of more human policies, but failed for different reasons in the long run.

J. R. Commons laid the foundation of the academic theory of industrial relations and the vocational practice in the US. The New Deal took his ideas further and established a national industrial relations framework with the National Labor Relations Act and the Fair Labor Standards Act, etc., which set an example to many countries. Since then the formal structure has expanded in scope, detail, and complexity.

During the politically radical 1970s attention was drawn to industrial democracy and new less-alienating models of work. The thinking owed inspiration both to the Webbs and to Japanese management, and to experiments with work organization by the Tavistock Institute (sociotechnical theory), especially in Norway and Sweden, which tackled issues such as employee participation in cross-functional learning, innovation, and quality. After a century of progressive evolution of workers' rights through collective bargaining and legislation, the trajectory for these approaches to LMR seemed to decline in the 1980s.

INSTITUTIONS OF LMR

There are three main processes of employment regulation: legal enactment, collective bargaining, and unilateral regulation confirmed by the individual when accepting his or her employment contract. LMR regimes involve a mix of substantive and procedural matters, but beneath them all are two parties in asymmetric positions, trying to make the most of their relative positions. Notions of interests, fairness, and effectiveness are profoundly important, within the action frame of reference. There is across nations a wide variety of arrangements, a mix of public and private, firm-specific, state and tripartite forms, reflecting particular national experiences, attitudes, and key political relationships, etc.

National clusters of LMR regimes have been identified as the European model, which is the more encompassing, and the Anglo-American, which is more minimalist. Some argue that there is more than one path to competitive advantage, and speak of the former as "coordinated" and the latter as "liberal market economies." Defining characteristics of the coordinated model are a combination of multi-employer bargaining, legal enforceability, and the practice of extension (of collective agreements), as well as provisions for information and consultation.

Few dispute the need for some government legislation in defining rules for collective bargaining and labor conflicts and establishing core standards (e.g., prohibiting forced and child labor, and more recently discrimination, sexual harassment, etc.). Issues regulated variably by law or contract or in combination include minimum wages, working hours, holidays, sick leave, dismissals, and redundancy and supplementary benefit schemes. Health plans, severance pay, unemployment insurance, pension plans, etc. are in some countries general entitlements, in others mediated through collective agreements or not at all. Issues of worker participation can similarly be regulated to give the workers – either as employees or through a trade union – representation on corporate boards, in work councils, or similar entities. An active labor market policy, assisting in the relocation and training of workers, is in most countries an integral part of the industrial relations system, seen as instrumental in obtaining compliance with structural economic change from the unions.

Over the years the general tendency has been for bargaining to become less differentiated between the private and public sectors, salaried and wageworkers, etc. A prominent feature when comparing Europe, the US, and the leading Asian economies is the persistent high degree of interest in organization among workers and employers in Western Europe. In the US union membership is considerably lower than in most of Europe, and the peak-level organizations command little authority. Employers' organizations are strong in Europe, barely feature in the US, and are weak in Japan.

The effectiveness of a union as negotiator and political lobbyist depends on its ability to command the loyalty of its members in mobilizing for action and respect for collective agreements. This makes internal governance and strategic leadership of unions of basic interest. Unions hold different views on how far they should allow themselves to be involved with government and management. Positions taken vis-à-vis employee stock ownership plans, quality circles, and productivity programs reflect varying deliberations and political inclinations (e.g., communist, social democratic, or catholic).

Union membership as percent of the active labor force was at its peak in most western countries in the 1970s. Only in a few mainly Northern European countries is a majority of the workforce engaged in trade unions. In countries such as the US, the UK, Australia, France, and Italy membership has declined by two thirds or more. Countries with stable density have legislation that favors membership.

In the last few decades US managers have been actively anti-union, while in Europe the focus has been on new arrangements rather than derecognition of unions. Non-union representation does not exclude workers' consultation. Many multinational corporations which are non-union have developed systems for employee regulation and representation as part of their personnel policy. The rules are then determined unilaterally and can be altered at management's discretion.

ENCOMPASSING REGIMES

Fundamental to the role of collective bargaining as theorized by the economist Mancur Olson is the degree of coordination in encompassing units. Where there is peak-level bargaining and trade unions have a near-total coverage of the community, they need to take into account wage, price, and employment effects, which induce restraint and concern for inflation. While under disintegrated bargaining, where the beneficial results are concentrated in the members and the negative impact is dispersed, the union will disregard inflationary and other external effects.

This line of reasoning is the rationale for neocorporatist arrangements, such as a government-led incomes policy. Most such schemes were eliminated in the neoliberal ascendancy of the 1980s. However, there has been an unexpected revival of "social pacts" as instruments for preparing for global competitiveness and the EMU (the European currency). In these, reform of LMR and wage moderation, labor market flexibility, and revised welfare provisions hold a key role.

European integration has prompted a multi-level system of governance, introducing a supranational level and encouraging resort to decentralization within national systems. The effects of harmonizing social standards in the Euro-zone need to take into account the vast regional economic differences in the expanded community. Compared to the US, labor market mobility remains much lower in Europe, for obvious cultural and traditional reasons.

All of the Western European countries, except the UK, are characterized by an inclusive structure of multi-employer bargaining.

The impact of collective bargaining only vaguely reflects the density of union membership. Most countries hold statutory extension provisions by which the terms of the collective agreement are extended throughout a sector or country. A consequence is that there is little correlation in Europe between trade union membership (on average below 50 percent) and coverage by collective agreement (around 80 percent). In the UK and Ireland by contrast, collective agreements are voluntary and enforceable by law only if the parties are agreed. Collective bargaining in the US never covered more than about a third of the labor market, but collective agreements are intensively developed to cover a wide range of issues. Some agreements have ramifications outside their constituency as a benchmark for non-union firms. This might explain why many Americans (between 40–50 percent) think favorably of unions, although fewer than 10 percent are members.

A NEW PARADIGM?

Over the last few decades momentous events have transformed the field of LMR practice and research. Inflexible markets were blamed for the stalled growth of the old industrialized countries in the 1970s, in comparison to rapidly developing economies in Asia. New global product markets created strong competitive pressures. In response, employers and a new range of neoclassical economists called for the deconstruction of LMR to reassert management authority and enhance flexibility.

Deregulation of the economy has left both parties with less room for contingent accommodation. Workers' bargaining power has suffered threefold because of the new international mobility of capital, technology driven vertical disintegration into global production networks, and monetary policy upholding an equilibrium level of unemployment (two or three times the previous full employment level). International dispersion of work enables employers to evade existing labor regulation and makes a unified workers' front more difficult.

With the macroeconomic policy shift in the 1980s from demand to supply-side economics, industrial relations' effects took center stage in the economic policy discourse. The neoliberal transformation process began in the US and the UK, and was followed by many other countries, including New Zealand, Australia, and many of the East European countries. Most of the emerging market economies in Asia and Latin America have a liberal market model, when LMR is not coercively regulated by the state.

The Reagan and Thatcher governments set out fundamentally to reform the industrial relations system and curb militant unionism and a mounting number of strikes, irregularities inside unions, and fierce labor–management disputes, plus inflationary pressure from wages. The Anglo-American axis was formed around a shift in policy towards more pro-individualism, private ordering, and free markets, and against collectivism and regulation of markets. Union immunities were reduced, strikes restricted, etc. The protection of workers in the UK was replaced by a legislative approach (traditionally condemned by the unions) to discrimination, unfair dismissal, and the like. The procedure continued under the subsequent Labour government, which introduced the first ever minimum wage law.

The blow to the unions also affected industrial relations research to the degree that it was symbiotic with the bipartisan structure. The situation eventually led to invigorated interest in workplace practices and HRM. Several facets of the scheme, such as flattened organizational hierarchy, gain sharing, and extensive communication, could be incorporated into and controlled under the participative management doctrine. In Scandinavia, where new laws on codetermination had been enacted in the mid-1970s, the basic principles had entered collective agreements, with clauses that gave the local union a say in their implementation.

MANAGEMENT PRACTICES

Alternative ways of thinking about LMR have long existed along lines parallel to the collective bargaining framework. Japanese (and to a degree Northern European) unions have for more than a generation acted on the presumption that there is a close link between high productivity, employment, and wages. The human relations theory associated with Elton Mayo is part of the legacy in these countries, as well as in American business schools. The focus in the 1990s on competitive advantage and industrial reengineering was evoked by globalization and deregulation, and brought emphasis to a strategic approach to employment management. The classic works of sociologists and psychologists like Argyris, Herzberg, McGregor, and Whyte guided the link to integration of LMR with business strategy.

In the deregulated market firms typically pay lower or more differentiated wages and they utilize work systems and employment contracts that are more flexible. Some exploit nonstandard employment arrangements that shift economic risks onto the workforce. However, work and employment are not changing as fast as may have been expected, and are unlikely to do so. Work is not disappearing. Surveys indicate that labor-force participation and hours of work have remained stable in the OECD area. People are highly committed to work. The evidence on workforce changes (e.g., with regard to tenure, training, and wage inequality) is mainly within occupations, indicating that there is an increasing diversity in workforce and individualized remuneration. Organizations are using a variety of skills in cross-functional teams, and there has been a drastic reduction in management and supervisory jobs. Managers become coaches and workers are expected to act more on their own commitment. Voluntary quits have declined, so have perceptions of job security. Dual-career patterns make work and family decisions highly interdependent. Union membership continues its long-term decline, even though significant innovations are made in union–management relations. Taken together, the changes have exerted a profound effect on explicit and implicit employment contracts and conditions of employment.

The bulk of surveys indicate strong pressure in all countries for numerical and functional flexibility, but also that environmental factors impinge in systematic ways on how work structures evolve – though they are not deterministic. A study by the ILO (Auer & Cazes 2003) suggests that stable employment relationships are in fact quite resilient. Arguments in favor of unconditional flexibility miss the fact that with high turnover human and organizational capital may be eroded. In Japan, policies are still geared towards employment maintenance and

thus social protection is low, while in Denmark the opposite is the case. When social protection outside the firm is kept at a high standard even though job security is low, workers perceive a lower degree of insecurity compared to the opposite situation.

FUTURE DIRECTIONS

The study of LMR, although relevant to innumerable disciplines, is held together by the existence of a politically urgent real-life problematic. Where the field has lost its central policy relevance, so has the demand for a multidisciplinary research community, as analyzed by Kaufman (2004). The need for systematic theories of LMR, however, has not disappeared, resulting in claims to new interesting research combinations.

Labor–management relations are deeply embedded in sociopolitical traditions and narratives, pointing to their relevance for the discourses of cross-national institution building and "varieties of capitalism." Human resource management has emerged intellectually stronger by infusing some industrial relations thinking. Monitoring of welfare effects under deregulation has become increasingly rewarding for sociological analysis. Finally, globalizing trade and production defines a distinctly international and challenging research agenda, where the basic assumption upon which organized labor has acted for well over 150 years – "to take wages out competition" – has met with some challenging complications. The western bias, which has prevailed throughout history in this field, might be approaching the end.

SEE ALSO: Collective Action; Labor Markets; Labor Movement; Management, Workers' Participation in; Stratification, Gender and; Unions; Welfare Regimes

REFERENCES AND SUGGESTED READINGS

Auer, P. & Cazes, S. (Eds.) (2003) *Employment Stability in an Age of Flexibility*. International Labor Organization, Geneva.

Basu, K. et al. (Eds.) (2003) *International Labor Standards*. Blackwell, Oxford.

Crouch, C. (1982) *Trade Unions: The Logic of Collective Action*. Fontana, Glasgow.

Dunlop, J. (1958) *Industrial Relations Systems*. Holt, New York.

Elvander, N. (2002) *Industrial Relations: A Short History of Ideas and Learning*. National Institute for Working Life, Stockholm.

Ferner, A. & Hyman, R. (Eds.) (1998) *Changing Industrial Relations in Europe*. Blackwell, Oxford.

Freeman, R. B. & Medoff, J. L. (1984) *What Do Unions Do?* Basic Books, New York.

Kaufman, B. E. (2004) *The Global Evolution of Industrial Relations: Events, Ideas and the IIRA*. International Labor Organization, Geneva.

Kerr, C. et al. (1960) *Industrialism and Industrial Man*. Harvard University Press, Cambridge, MA.

Marginson, P. & Sisson, K. (Eds.) (2004) *European Integration and Industrial Relations: Multi-Level Governance in the Making*. Palgrave Macmillan, New York.

Webb, S. & Webb, B. (1902) *Industrial Democracy*. Longmans, London.

labor markets

Anne Fearfull

In principle a labor market is the primary method of allocating people to paid work, of whatever nature, within capitalist economies/societies. Within capitalism, the separation of the producer of a good or service from the means of its production has rendered a situation where labor power (that is, the capacity of a person to work) has become a commodity to be bought and sold. In theory both buyers and sellers of labor power are free to choose from or to whom they would like to buy or sell. Thus, the "market" can be represented as an efficient, voluntary mechanism of exchange wherein the economic rules of efficiency, perfect competition, and supply and demand apply, and equilibrium will be achieved. From such a perspective market imperfections (or disequilibria) when they occur do so because interest groups within a market are, for example, able to strengthen their position, restrict entry to their group, or force pay changes. Actions or events such as these are regarded essentially as "glitches" and, over time, theory suggests, equilibrium will be reachieved.

From a general picture of labor markets within the context provided, we can hone our examination by considering the notion of both external and internal labor markets. The model of the dual labor market developed by Doeringer and Piore (1971) introduced the idea of the primary and secondary sectors. The primary sector represents core skill areas for which employers were prepared to pay higher levels of wages and provide better employment terms and conditions as a means of ensuring as far as possible a secure, committed, and competitive labor force. By contrast, workers in the secondary sector would not expect to have so secure a position. Indeed, it is this sector which facilitates flexibility for employers, as workers within this context would tend to have contracts based on, for example, seasonal requirements or part-time availability of or for work. Within this sector would be subcontracted workers or even businesses, and significant levels of labor turnover would be both expected and tolerated. This pattern of duality has been further popularized through the model of the flexible firm proposed by Atkinson (1984). This model proposed a range of flexibilities for operationalization by employers, including numerical, functional, and financial. The basis of this proposal was the employment of distinct core and secondary workforces, the latter, in extreme cases, attracting so-called "zero-hour" contracts. The agreement for people working under such a contractual term would be that they had no fixed hours or times of work, but would be called upon as and when the employer required their services.

From a sociological perspective, focus is placed upon the relationship between those groups within the labor market and within individual workplaces and occupations. Broadly speaking there is a rejection of the economists' notion of market efficiency. The basis of this alternative position is the inequitable nature of the employment relationship. The root of such inequity is firmly planted in the nature of capitalism and the dispossession of workers from the means of production, of either goods or services, including their lack of ownership of raw materials, tools, and places of production.

Attempts have been made by labor to manage the ensuing competition within labor markets. Some of these attempts have driven wedges between the different sectors within the labor force. Trades unions and other employee associations engage in collective bargaining to influence pay and conditions for their constituencies. Social closure has been one method used by trades unions to limit competition by restricting access to particular jobs to their members alone. While this is no longer an option for trades unions following the outlawing of closed shops, it remains a means by which professional bodies establish and maintain their power within their sectors. This is achieved by their ability to devise and establish systems of practice and codes of ethics within their fields of work and to have these formally recognized through the gaining of chartered status. Similarly, buyers of labor power (i.e., employers) have effected their own methods of managing labor markets and some of these have been addressed above in the outline of the dual market and its associated models.

The points suggested so far suggest that, while we might be able to form a neat definition of the term labor markets, and indeed we frequently see variations on such definitions in dictionaries and textbooks, the practice of and experience within them are far from neat. There are a number of reasons for this, some of which have already been outlined. By expanding upon those outlines we can appreciate the complexity of labor markets and the extent to which competition within them is anything but "perfect." If we take Littler's (1985: 3) position that "differences in labor market status help to create (or reinforce) different orientations to work," then we begin to gain greater insight into the nature of variations and experiences of labor within the labor market in general, and within specific labor markets in particular. Although not an exhaustive list, status markers include, being:

- Professionally qualified
- Trade qualified
- Skilled
- Unskilled
- Male
- Female
- A full-time employee
- A part-time employee
- Experienced
- Relatively inexperienced
- A school leaver

- From an ethnic minority group
- Already employed
- Unemployed

To explore the sociology of labor markets further we can use examples from the above. Beginning with young people entering the labor market we can consider the notions of structure and agency and the important interplay between these factors in that context. The socialization of individuals plays an enormous role in mediating our perception of agency since it heightens our awareness of the choices which can or cannot be made, as the case might be or might be perceived. It is clear that agency is affected by structures in place which might limit choice, and also by the extent to which individuals (in this case young people) are aware of the opportunities available to them and the contexts in which they might exercise their agency. Giddens's (1984) theory of structuration recognizes the inextricable link between structure and agency. However, while critically we can appreciate the boundaries placed upon people and their choices as a result of structures at the levels of both society and organization, we might also appreciate how structures enable opportunities to be formed and a context in which choices can be made.

The issue of class and class consciousness is particularly relevant when considering structuration and labor markets. This is especially so within the context of young people newly entering the labor market. The extent to which they are conscious of their "place" or "level" within the structure of society, and the degree to which they see this as determining the occupational choices they are able to make, may lead to lack of development and/or realization of their aspirations. Family support is also central to the developing aspirations of young people entering or preparing to enter the labor market.

If we consider the unemployed and their relation to labor markets we can see other levels of complexity. Attempting to re-enter a labor market from a position of unemployment, the unemployed are often met with difficult and sometimes insurmountable barriers. To some extent this is due to our often implicit understanding of the latent functions of work (Jahoda 1982). These functions are the sociopsychological factors rendered as a result of being employed; for example, having an imposed time structure to one's day; having social relationships beyond those formed within the family unit; having a sense of purpose; and the development of identity. For those people becoming unemployed, these positive, essentially unintended consequences of work can fade quickly as one begins to doubt oneself and one's contribution to both society and family. Long-term unemployment, or a situation where one has never been employed, can have more extensive and significant implications, as such a situation can be regarded as rendering a person work-incapacitated. Such incapacitation is with regard to skill levels and changes in skill requirements due to technological advancements, but just as importantly, with regard to the sociopsychological implications of unemployment.

Gershuny (1994) demonstrated the severity of the sociological and psychological implications of unemployment. So severe are they, in fact, that they might render people's potential participation in any labor market extremely difficult; due to the traditionally tighter tie between men and work, this can be particularly debilitative for men, as their sense of identity diminishes. Thus, the notion of a reserve army of unemployed people ready, willing, and able to be called back into the labor market when required might be regarded as nonsensical. Amid severely high levels of unemployment in the UK in the 1980s, an alternative perspective emerged whereby the notion of the Protestant work ethic, central to the functioning of western labor markets, was questioned as appropriate and proposals made to replace or amend it with the "usefulness ethic." This view is typified by Robertson (1985), who proposed an "ownwork agenda," the basis of which would move us away from employment where our working time is controlled through labor markets, to a system in which people would take control of the use of their own time. As we know, this proposal did not come into being. And yet we have seen an increasing interest in alternative lifestyles as people seek to effect improved work–life balance.

Using another example from our labor market groups above, we can examine the dynamic between women and labor markets. The dual role of women within society as both economically active and having primary responsibility for social reproduction renders their role or potential role within labor markets as problematic, both for themselves and for potential employers. The ensuing gender stereotyping and female subordination in the sexual division of labor prevails even today and in spite of legislation designed and introduced to outlaw inequities in access, opportunity, and pay. Women's particular place within, or displacement from, labor markets was discussed by Lewis (1988) when outlining past law which "denied women access to property and political rights." From a radical feminist perspective, the dominance of men in both legal and political environments and the fact that education was withheld from women until the late nineteenth century provides insight into the roles taken up by women, or aspired to by them, within the labor market in general. In this regard, we can reiterate Littler's suggestion, cited above, about the creation or reinforcement of orientations to work in the light of the nature of the gender relationship within both labor markets and society in general.

Over the past two decades feminist writers have extended the debate about the opportunities available to women and the degree to which they have been seriously curtailed by the patriarchal nature of western society. Cockburn (1987), for example, considered the level of discrimination apparent in training opportunities. The gendered nature of both occupational and job segregation has been considered by a range of authors (Crompton & Sanderson 1990; Reskin & Roos 1990; Cockburn 1991; Boterro 1992). These writers argue that such segregation is a result of practices within both employing organizations and the nature of societal organization, each of which is considered as being patriarchal. Extending this type of argument, Reskin and Roos (1990) illustrated the advantaged position with regard to job and occupational opportunities, as well as pay, enjoyed by white men, in general, over men of color and all women. Using an American focus, they provided a historical context for the inequitable distribution of workplace participation for men and women on the basis of gendering, race, and ethnicity. Again, the importance of the domestic sphere is emphasized as a means of shaping job and pay equity through raising the issues of aspirations and orientations of people entering the labor market and even targeting particular labor markets.

Extending the notion of inequalities for people within labor markets, we can draw further on the questions of race and ethnicity. The issues faced by ethnic minority people in the labor market are more complex than for indigenous populations. As Jenkins (1986) has shown, ethnic minority people in general face discriminatory processes due to potential employers' sensitivity around the extent to which people from such groups would "fit in" within an existing workforce. This notion of "acceptability" therefore extends requirements beyond those of a person's technical "suitability" for a post, which is a determinant for most people's employment. Thus, in spite of legislation introduced both nationally and internationally over the past three decades or so, we can consider notions of institutional racism (Macpherson 1999) as being a considerable threat to multi-ethnic workforces within organizations and the equitable treatment of ethnic minority groups within more widely defined labor markets. For ethnic minority women, any such circumstances are exacerbated further. Facing multiple roles in excess of those faced by many women in general in both internal and external labor and primary and secondary markets, ethnic minority women find their career aspirations challenged by stereotyping in relation to their sociocultural and religious affiliations, as well as those in relation to perceptions of their roles within family and community life (Kamenou 2002).

Although we have not considered each one of the labor market status markers listed above, we have developed an ongoing theme which challenges the dominant economic perspective on labor markets, including the notion that buyers and sellers of labor power are free to choose to whom they would like to buy from or sell to. From the perspective taken here, we can see that the concept of the efficient market, perfect competition, and the achievement of equilibrium is highly questionable. A more realistic position recognizes market imperfections, or disequilibria, and that they emerge because of the varying strengths of the numerous interest groups.

SEE ALSO: Class Consciousness; Ethnic and Racial Division of Labor; Gender Ideology and Gender Role Ideology; Labor/Labor Power; Labor–Management Relations; Labor Movement; Labor Process; Structure and Agency; Unemployment; Work, Sociology of

REFERENCES AND SUGGESTED READINGS

Atkinson, J. (1984) Manpower Strategies for Flexible Organizations. *Personnel Management* (August).

Atkinson, J. (1985) Flexibility: Planning for an Uncertain Future. *Manpower Policy and Practice* 1: 25–30.

Boterro, W. (1992) The Changing Face of the Professions: Gender and Explanations of Women's Entry into Pharmacy. *Work, Employment and Society* 6(3): 329–46.

Cockburn, C. (1987) *Two-Track Training: Sex Inequalities in the YTS.* Macmillian, Basingstoke.

Cockburn, C. (1991) *In the Way of Women: Men's Resistance to Sex Equality in Organizations.* Macmillan, Basingstoke.

Crompton, R. & Sanderson, K. (1990) *Gendered Jobs and Social Change.* Unwin Hyman, London.

Doeringer, P. B. & Piore, M. J. (1971) *Internal Labour Markets and Manpower Analysis.* D. C. Heath, Lexington, MA.

Gershuny, J. (1994) The Psychological Consequences of Unemployment: An Assessment of the Jahoda Thesis. In: Gallie, D., Marsh, C., & Vogler, C. (Eds.), *Social Change and the Experience of Unemployment.* Oxford University Press, Oxford.

Giddens, A. (1984) *The Constitution of Society: Outline of the Theory of Structuration.* Polity Press, Cambridge.

Jahoda, M. (1982) *Employment and Unemployment: A Social-Psychological Analysis.* Cambridge University Press, Cambridge.

Jenkins, R. (1986) *Racism and Recruitment: Managers, Organizations and Equality in the Labour Market.* Cambridge University Press, Cambridge.

Kamenou, N. (2002) The Impact of Gender, Race and Ethnicity on Career Progression for Ethnic Minority Women in Northern England. Unpublished PhD thesis. Leeds University Business School.

Lewis, J. E. (1988) Women Clerical Workers in the Late Nineteenth and Early Twentieth Centuries. In: Anderson, G. (Ed.), *The White-Blouse Revolution: Female Office Workers since 1870.* Manchester University Press, Manchester.

Littler, C. R. (1985) The Texture of Work. In Littler, C. R. (Ed.), *The Experience of Work.* Gower, Aldershot.

Macpherson, Report (1999) *The Steven Lawrence Inquiry: Report of an Inquiry by Sir William Macpherson.* HMSO, London.

Reskin, B. & Roos, P. (1990) *Job Queues, Gender Queues.* Temple University Press, Philadelphia.

Robertson, J. (1985) *Future Work: Jobs, Self-Employment and Leisure After the Industrial Age.* Gower, Aldershot.

labor movement

Rick Fantasia and Kim Voss

The labor movement is a broad, multidimensional social formation that is generated from the social structures of work and industry in a society. It may comprise both legally recognized and formally sanctioned institutions (like trade unions, political parties, and works councils) as well as less formal groupings of workers and their allies (industrial actions, organizations of strike supporters, dissident movements within unions, cultural forms, etc.). Labor movements operate at the intersection of economic practice, civil society, and the state. They are more or less firmly institutionalized in any given society in any given historical period, and can be partly characterized by the extent to which extra-institutional practices are permitted and have been incorporated into the routine operations of industrial and labor relations. The social and organizational composition of a labor movement as well as the degree to which its practices have been institutionalized are thus two important analytical axes through which the social logic of a labor movement can be discerned.

Having been born in and by the industrial order, the labor movements of the most developed capitalist societies generally took on their characteristic appearance over the course of the nineteenth century, with political parties and trade unions being the most prevalent organizational forms. Contrary to conventional wisdom, in its formative decades the US labor movement was not a particularly exceptional case relative to other industrial societies, although the arc of its trajectory would become increasingly distinctive later on. Thus, just as in England and France, two countries whose socioeconomic development was roughly comparable to the

United States, for much of the nineteenth century the American labor movement was composed of skilled craft workers whose cultures and practices had been constructed to protect traditional skills and craft prerogatives in the face of machine technologies and standardized work practices that employers had specifically designed and implemented to erode. By the last quarter of the nineteenth century, however, the character of the American labor movement began to take an "exceptional" form, although not at all in the manner in which conventional wisdom has often held. The labor movement in the US was becoming militant and class conscious in ways similar to those Karl Marx had envisaged in his analyses of the development of capitalist society, most notably expressed in the explosive growth of the Knights of Labor. The Knights was a remarkably egalitarian organization of workers and artisans that, by its height in 1886, had mobilized almost 10 percent of the US working class across skill level, nationality, race, and gender into militant local assemblies spread out across the entire country.

In contrast to perspectives in sociology and historical studies that have viewed the US labor movement as intrinsically and exceptionally weak, or conservative, or lacking in collective solidarity (variously attributed to affluence, or the possibilities for upward social mobility, or the spatial expansiveness of the American frontier, or early universal male suffrage, among other factors), the existence of the Knights of Labor in the late nineteenth century suggests the need for an alternative interpretation. A consideration of the dynamics of both their rise and their fall provide us with the lessons for such a reinterpretation. Ironically, it was the rapid and widespread mobilization of workers into the Knights that provoked a powerful mobilization of employers to counter them, with the ferocity of the reaction leading to their equally rapid downfall, as well as to a general weakening of the US labor movement for at least another generation. Unlike in England and France where the state often intervened to encourage or demand employer concessions in labor disputes, the US government at the time did little to constrain the actions of employers, allowing them free reign to destroy the Knights of Labor. Considered altogether, this suggests that (1) the

US labor movement was not intrinsically weak and, if anything, at one time was perhaps *more* militant and class conscious than its counterparts; and (2) the reaction by employers to the militancy of the Knights reshaped the legal, political, and social terrain in ways that made militant worker organizations much more difficult to mobilize and sustain, thus demonstrating the "exceptional" power enjoyed by *employers* in the US context. One outgrowth of the defeat of the militant Knights was the ascendancy of a more pragmatic, conservative, craft-based unionism embodied by the American Federation of Labor (AFL), which became the overwhelmingly dominant institutional force within the US labor movement well into the twentieth century.

What this brief example illustrates is that labor movements can never be properly understood without considering them in their mutually constituting relationship to the corporate employers of labor (capital). Moreover, the nature of this relationship will strongly affect the role of the state in the society. In the case of the US, the state has not been as strong a force for regulation as it has been in other societies and this has meant that large corporations have been relatively free to operate. With such freedom, large corporations have become firmly ensconced as the dominant institutional player in US society, thus ensuring a relatively weak labor movement. In most other capitalist societies the state has tended to foster more balance in this relationship, by limiting (or regulating) the power of large corporations. It is important to recognize at the same time, however, that because the society is not a static one, the power and position of the labor movement in US society have not always been as weak as they have at other times.

Moreover, the labor movement has never been monolithic and has always combined various competing tendencies. For example, by the turn of the twentieth century, a massive increase in European immigration was underway, with millions of relatively unskilled workers pouring into the United States, attracted to the huge factory complexes where assembly lines and other mass production techniques were fast becoming the bases for most forms of manufacture. A craft-based capitalism was giving way to highly industrialized forms, thereby paving the way for a new form of unionism.

The AFL, which had openly rejected the militant social unionism of the Knights of Labor, was made up of organizations largely shaped by the prerogatives of their own members, native-born skilled craftsmen concerned with protecting their own relatively privileged status within the working class more than with opening their ranks to the unskilled immigrants whom they often looked upon with contempt.

Not until the 1930s was a widespread effort undertaken to organize the unskilled workers from the mass production industries into industry-wide unions. It meant bringing into the same organizations men and women of all races and ethnic backgrounds, regardless of skill level, and these industrial unions formed together under the overall banner of the Congress of Industrial Organizations (CIO). The attempts to form the CIO unions were met by ferocious resistance by the large corporations, often including organized violence and thereby necessitating a more militant stance and a more combative political framework on the part of the new unions. Openly encouraged in the early stages of the New Deal by laws such as the Wagner Act of 1935 and by the administration of President Franklin Delano Roosevelt, who saw unionism as a strategy for overcoming the effects of the Great Depression, the CIO unions were often organized by socialists, communists, and other left-wing radicals who set the terms for a more broadly based social vision than had been held by the AFL unions. It was an outlook that both reflected and corresponded to ideologies that were familiar to and respected in the European immigrant communities that tended to make up the membership of the new unions.

Through the first half of the twentieth century, the US labor movement showed two faces, partly reflected in the divisions between the AFL unions and their craft base, and the CIO unions with their industrial base. While the former was more pragmatic and politically moderate, the latter tended toward militancy and political radicalism, and was much closer in tone to the version of unionism represented in most other capitalist societies. By the close of World War II, however, after more than a decade of CIO mobilization, the large corporations quickly moved to reassert and consolidate their power within US society by seeking to curtail the militancy and radicalism of the CIO.

This was accomplished by the powerful pressures they brought to bear on Congress to pass the Taft-Hartley Act, a broad set of statutes drafted by corporate lawyers to essentially repeal the Wagner Act that had earlier encouraged industrial unionism. The Taft-Hartley Act achieved a number of longstanding goals of American corporate employers, including weakening union security in a variety of ways; forbidding the most effective forms of industrial action; imposing a stifling regime of bureaucratic governance over labor relations practice, as well as on the practices of union leaders; and purging communists and radicals from the ranks of the union leadership, thereby removing the clearest and strongest voices for social change from positions of authority in the unions.

Whereas the labor movement in the United States had once shown two distinctive faces, by the mid 1950s the AFL and the CIO had merged together, while largely adopting the political visage of the AFL. It was a period characterized by rapid post-war economic growth, rising American military intervention throughout the less developed world, and a profound ideological conformity imposed under the name of McCarthyism. The corporate-imposed domestication of the US labor movement that was noted above was often misinterpreted by social scientists as a kind of "natural" outgrowth of institutional maturation that was thought to characterize labor relations in all developed societies. A related version of the same theme saw the "end of ideology" as the inevitable accompaniment to modern socioeconomic development, whereby societies would simply discard any need for radical criticism or ideological debate with regard to the future. However, underneath such obvious signs of approval that were stamped on the social order by conservative social scientists or the bureaucratic practices that had been imposed on labor relations in the process of domesticating it, there were important countertendencies apparent to the few who took notice. These took the form of dissident movements of workers, often radicalized by their experiences in the largest unions, who fought against the sorts of things that the Taft-Hartley Act had imposed (i.e., they struggled to replace union leaders who were insufficiently militant, overly bureaucratic, or undemocratic, and to wield militant forms of

protest and collective action, such as wildcat strikes). In other words, the actions of employers to constrain the labor movement had generated new forms of organization and new forms of action from deep within the labor movement itself.

By the beginning of the 1970s, facing strong competitive pressures from European and Japanese firms, US manufacturing corporations began to squeeze more from their domestic operations by forcing down wages and by mounting a formidable and wide-ranging assault on union organization in the United States. Drawing upon a legal arsenal that had been earlier put in place by the Taft-Hartley Act, they were also assisted by a burgeoning industry of management consultants specializing in both union avoidance (slowing the creation of new unions in those sectors of the economy where unions had not had traditional roots, like health care and much of the services) and in breaking unions in the traditional sectors of labor strength (food processing, meat packing, newspapers, airlines, etc.). While the assault against unionism reached its peak during the decade of the 1980s, it continued through the 1990s and up to the present, with union density rates falling from a high point of 35 percent in the mid-1950s to approximately 13 percent and falling in 2005 (where in the private sector it is only 9 percent).

In the mid-1990s, faced with the demise of its institutions and its position in the society, the leadership of the US labor movement began to forge a process of internal change in an attempt to reverse its fortunes. The change began with a "palace coup" within the top ranks of the AFL-CIO, which replaced a conservative, bureaucratic leadership with a reform leadership group drawn from some of the more militant and dynamic unions. Once in place, the new leadership group began a campaign to encourage, cajole, and coerce the leadership of the approximately 60 unions in the Federation to turn more of their efforts and budgets toward organizing new members, rather than servicing the needs of existing union members. They have encouraged new, more militant union organizing tactics, including circumventing the bureaucratic system of union representation elections in favor of collective action and disruption; developing "corporate campaigns" to pressure institutional shareholders to protest corporate anti-unionism; and have sought to envelop labor struggles within a wider circle of community solidarity, narrowing the distinction between the labor movement and other social movements. With their own elections dependent upon the votes of existing members, there has been a considerable amount of resistance from many labor leaders, but the use of new tactics, in certain economic sectors and regions of the country, has also been able to show some positive results. The future of the labor movement in the US is still quite uncertain.

The labor movements in the most advanced economies of Western Europe have traditionally been stronger politically, and more firmly rooted institutionally, than US unions. Indeed, the practice of "social partnership" has, for decades, characterized the relationship between large corporations and the labor movement in much of Western Europe, and is still intact. What this has generally meant is a more consultative and less openly combative relationship than in the US, represented by the active existence of works councils in many of the largest enterprises and trade associations that afford labor a voice in corporate planning. However, the deregulation of global markets and the imposition of many neoliberal reforms across Europe (often pioneered in the US, where labor has not been able to offer firm resistance) have shown that societies are now faced with some very similar competitive pressures (to privatize public services, to deregulate markets, to treat short-term shareholder value as a guide in economic policy, etc.). The tendency to cheapen the cost of labor is therefore increasingly an international effort, so that there is a drive to eliminate the differences between national labor movements by weakening them all. Ironically, then, faced with the competitive pressures from US corporations in many world markets (ironic given the reverse impetus for wage cuts and union busing in the 1970s within the US), European societies have seen corporate intransigence increase and union power decline in recent years, expressed most explicitly in the erosion of a host of state social welfare policies across Europe in recent years. Across Europe a debate rages between the labor movement and allied social forces who would uphold a European model of social solidarity, and those who would subordinate social and labor policies to the exigencies of the market alone.

SEE ALSO: Capitalism; Class; Collective Action; Labor–Management Relations; Laborism; Neoliberalism; Political Economy; Social Movements; Socialism; Unions

REFERENCES AND SUGGESTED READINGS

Clawson, D. (2003) *The Next Upsurge: Labor and the New Social Movements*. Cornell University Press, Ithaca, NY.

Fantasia, R. (1988) *Cultures of Solidarity: Consciousness, Action, and Contemporary American Workers*. University of California Press, Berkeley and Los Angeles.

Fantasia, R. & Voss, K. (2004) *Hard Work: Remaking the American Labor Movement*. University of California Press, Berkeley and Los Angeles.

Freeman, R. B. (Ed.) (1994) *Working Under Different Rules*. Russell Sage Foundation, New York.

Kimeldorf, H. (1999) *Battling for American Labor: Wobblies, Craft Workers, and the Making of the Union Movement*. University of California Press, Berkeley and Los Angeles.

Lopez, S. (2004) *Reorganizing the Rust Belt*. University of California Press, Berkeley and Los Angeles.

Milkman, R. & Voss, K. (Eds.) (2004) *Rebuilding Labor: Organizing and Organizers in the New Union Movement*. Cornell University Press, Ithaca, NY.

Stepan-Norris, J. & Zeitlin, M. (2003) *Left Out: Reds and America's Industrial Unions*. Cambridge University Press, Cambridge.

Vanneman, R. & Cannon, L. W. (1987) *The American Perception of Class*. Temple University Press, Philadelphia.

Voss, K. (1993) *The Making of American Exceptionalism: The Knights of Labor and Class Formation in the Nineteenth Century*. Cornell University Press, Ithaca, NY.

Western, B. (1997) *Between Class and Market*. Princeton University Press, Princeton.

labor process

Alan McKinlay

Braverman's *Labor and Monopoly Capitalism* (1974) was a craftsman's roar of indignation against the relentless deskilling of modern work. His starting point was explicitly Marxist:

the distinction between labor power and labor. That is, all forms of management are not neutral forms of coordination and mobilization, but necessarily involve the transformation of the *potential* productivity latent in labor power into *actual* work and output. Exploitation is not an unfortunate lapse but inherent in the employment relationship in capitalist societies. From the industrial revolution onwards, management had skirted around the stubborn opposition of skilled labor by indirect means, such as the use of ramshackle incentive systems or craft supervisors to navigate between craft norms and managerial demands. Braverman argues that modern management, a management that did not accept craft methods as a given, was inaugurated by F. W. Taylor. Taylorism, for Braverman, consisted of three essential principles. First, that management must accumulate and then codify all the knowledge of tools, tasks, and techniques held by skilled labor. This both redressed the imbalance of working knowledge that was the historic weakness of management and allowed them to experiment systematically with alternative, more efficient production methods. Second, the separation of conception from execution, the first step in the rigorous fragmentation and recombination of *all* tasks. Refractory, wayward workers were to be orchestrated for maximum discipline, efficiency, and predictability. "Scientific management" offered not just efficiency and control, but also reduced labor to something entirely interchangeable, an activity with no purpose other than to complete the working day and which offered no intrinsic satisfaction. Such was the ideological appeal of this objective "science," Taylor argued, that the worker would willingly accept her or his complete subjugation at the factory gates, and surrender all agency and knowledge to become a "mere appendage to the machine." *This* was the hallmark of modern "scientific management." Third, once management had wrested the necessary knowledge from skilled labor, tasks would be defined in advance and labor would now work according to the tempo set by management planning rather than craft norms. In part, Taylorism represented the accumulation, codification, and reordering of the craftsman's traditional knowledge in order to raise overall productive efficiency. No less important,

however, Taylorism offered a powerful critique of early twentieth-century American management, which had allowed the productive potential of major technological changes to be blunted by craft resistance. For Taylor, management had tacitly accepted its relative ignorance and was complicit with craft labor in maintaining inefficient working practices. The modern manager was to derive his authority not from the maintaining of output using established practices, but from his mastery of the theory and practice of Taylor's new science of work.

Taylorism and deskilling had a political importance that stretched far beyond the workplace. Braverman offered a new philosopher's stone, a way of understanding the long-run dynamics of class and political change. This was the political promise of labor process theory: as deskilling and the degradation of work became more extensive and profound, so it would erode, if not obliterate, distinctions inside the working class. As automation spread ever further, not just particular skills but entire occupational categories would disappear. The result would be degraded work, under-employment and the creation of an ever-expanding reserve army of labor that placed ever greater downward pressure on wages and working conditions of an increasingly homogenized working class. This vicious cycle of automation, degradation, and immiseration held enormous promise for revolutionary political change.

BEYOND BRAVERMAN

"First wave" labor process theory offered important correctives to Braverman's deskilling thesis, but endorsed its underlying analytical and political principles (Thompson & McHugh 2002). Certain criticisms quickly became routine – above all, that Braverman neglected not just union bargaining power but also informal worker resistance to technical and organisational change. In social history Braverman's focus on skill echoed the "history from below" that sought to recapture the lived experience of working people. Although this shift towards the grassroots inevitably flirted with a romanticization of working-class life, studies of construction, cotton, engineering, printing, and shipbuilding all pointed to the tenacious survival or, more accurately, the resilience of skilled labor and its ability to blunt or absorb much of the deskilling potential of new technologies. Nor does compliance with routinized work regimes necessarily imply a complete loss of agency. Michael Burawoy's pathbreaking studies show how workers turn production targets into games in which they negotiate the rules, which means that they can retain and display agency in even the most hostile environments (Burawoy 1985). A second criticism was that Braverman – like Taylor – ignored the often hidden or unrecognized skills of routine "unskilled" workers. Such tacit skills ensure safety, efficiency, and equity in the workplace and are important parts of even the most unsophisticated types of job. Braverman (1974) offered little guidance on how to measure changing skill levels over time, between occupations, sectors, or national economies. A third criticism was that Braverman underestimated the range of strategies deployed by employers. Management would cede control to skilled labor when confronted with major technical or market uncertainties or decide not to impose Taylorist principles where groups of workers had erected substantial defenses.

But however significant the qualifications to Braverman's original thesis, the implicit position was that – ceteris paribus – management would pursue a deskilling strategy. Other things were, however, seldom equal. Even at the height of its popularity in 1920s America, very few employers deployed the full range of techniques defined by Taylor as essential characteristics of scientific management (Nelson 1975; Edwards 1979). Similarly, faced with smaller, more fragmented product markets, and the significant fixed costs of developing the organizational infrastructure necessary to sustain some form of Taylorism over the long run, British and European employers, for example, consistently shunned full-blown scientific management (Littler 1982). Maintaining productive flexibility was a vital strategic consideration, far more important than any long-run gains that might result from a protracted and hugely risky transition to mass production (Zeitlin & Sabel 1997). Until the 1970s, the decentralized organizational structures of British corporations together with the disdain for "professional" management proved major barriers to anything more systematic than ad hoc bursts of Taylorism. The range of caveats, qualifications, and special pleading whittled away the coherence of Braverman's original position until Taylorism had assumed an almost metaphysical quality: the search for control, much more than profitability, was something that was assumed to be implicit in *all* managerial maneuvers. Braverman's original deskilling thesis was being asked to bear an impossible analytical burden.

NEW THEORETICAL DIRECTIONS

The last two decades have witnessed a waning of Braverman's influence. There have been two broad reasons for this. On the one hand, the emergence of teamworking as the dominant organizational form in manufacturing and clerical and service work over the last two decades has placed a question mark over the continued relevance of scientific management as the key driver of labor process change. Indeed, depicting the shift to teamworking as a revolt against Taylorism and managerial bureaucracy has been a prime source of legitimacy for corporate change programs. Just as the rhetoric of Taylorism was more important than its practice, so the dominant ideology of radical managerialism belies its more restricted practice.

The dynamics of routine service work *can* be accommodated within the original labor process perspective, but only by an increasingly strained use of the assembly line as a metaphor rather than an organizational reality. Analytically, Braverman has been pushed aside as the cornerstone of radical interpretations of work in favor of eclectic borrowings from post-modernism. Above all, Foucault has moved to the fore as the theorist that offers insights into the power of electronic and peer surveillance in the contemporary workplace, the ambiguous play of discipline on individual identity (McKinlay & Starkey 1998; Sewell 1998). Too often, this "linguistic turn" has assumed the coherence and durability of corporate cultural projects and the malleability of workers bewildered by managerial ideology and with scant alternative sources of meaning. The result has been an

2524 *laboratory studies and the world of the scientific lab*

analytical readiness to read workers as cultural dopes, analogous to the deskilled automata of Taylor's fantasy and Braverman's nightmare. On the other hand, Taylorism has little appeal to managers of high-value-added "knowledge work" in which innovation and creativity are valued more highly than efficiency. For knowledge-intensive firms – in adverting, design, pharmaceuticals – competitive advantage derives from management's ability to assemble project teams to maximize their creativity far more than their ability to codify, simplify, and deskill work. That is not to say that there are not significant competitive and managerial pressures to accelerate knowledge labor processes or to introduce project management tools, but that is a far cry from Taylorized work. Understanding the dynamics of control, knowledge, and creativity is fast becoming the focus of much mainstream and radical research into the dynamics of contemporary competitiveness and organization.

For all the claims to greater theoretical sophistication, the gradual retreat of the labor process perspective has involved a real loss of any sense of connection between shifts in the nature of capitalist economies and work organization or how that intersects with trade unionism or popular politics. The labor process debate sparked by Braverman initiated an enormous range of historical and contemporary research into the interplay of skill and technology, the long-run recomposition of labor markets, and management ideologies and practices. The turn to the study of work as a form of discourse which is shaped almost exclusively by management has resulted in the neglect of material issues of wages and working conditions, tools and tasks, and of conflict as something more than a clash of signs and symbols. The rejection of the very *possibility* of grand narratives has dissolved work as a key moment in political economy, a term that has become deeply suspect. A return to the ambitious historical sweep of Braverman's original focus on the political and economic centrality of the workplace is now overdue.

SEE ALSO: Capitalism, Social Institutions of; Labor/Labor Power; Labor–Management Relations; Labor Markets; Laborism; Organizational Careers

REFERENCES AND SUGGESTED READINGS

Braverman, H. (1974) *Labor and Monopoly Capitalism: The Degradation of Work in the Twentieth Century*. Monthly Review Press, New York.

Burawoy, M. (1985) *The Politics of Production*. Verso, London.

Edwards, R. (1979) *Contested Terrain: The Transformation of the Workplace in the Twentieth Century*. Heinemann, London.

Littler, C. (1982) *The Development of the Labor Process in Capitalist Societies*. Heinemann, London.

McKinlay, A. & Starkey, K. (Eds.) (1998) *Foucault, Management and Organization Theory: From Panopticon to Technologies of the Self*. Sage, London.

Nelson, D. (1975) *Managers and Workers: Origins of the New Factory System in the United States 1880–1920*. University of Wisconsin Press, Madison.

Sewell, G. (1998) The Discipline of Teams: The Control of Team-Based Industrial Work through Electronic and Peer Surveillance. *Administrative Science Quarterly* 43: 397–428.

Thompson, P. & McHugh, D. (2002) *Work Organizations*. Palgrave, London.

Zeitlin, J. & Sabel, C. (Eds.) (1997) *Worlds of Possibilities: Flexibility and Mass Production in Western Industrialization*. Cambridge University Press, Cambridge.

laboratory studies and the world of the scientific lab

Daniel Lee Kleinman

The most prominent laboratory studies – produced in the late 1970s and early 1980s – continued a trend in the sociology of science and technology away from attention to the institutional character of science and toward a sociological understanding of the process of knowledge production itself and the "technical core" of science. To comprehend the process through which knowledge is *constructed*, these studies undertook ethnographic investigations of the work that goes on in scientific laboratories. Among the central findings of this body of scholarship are: (1) contrary to standard images of science, which suggest that the methods, practices, and outcomes of science are universal (or trans-contextual), knowledge production occurs at a local level and is subject to local variation; (2) instead of the characterization of science as fundamentally logical and rational, science is the product of contingent factors; (3) scientific work does not merely read its results from nature, but instead nature is transformed in the laboratory; (4) if the view of science as "reading off nature" amounts to an understanding of science as a descriptive practice, the early laboratory studies show, by contrast, that scientific results are the product of construction.

Initially published in 1979, Latour and Woolgar's *Laboratory Life* (1986) is probably the most prominent laboratory study. This book traces the struggle to define the structure of an important human hormone. The authors show that the scientists they study are centrally engaged in efforts to persuade colleagues of the validity of their findings. To do this, these researchers begin with "inscription devices" – pieces of equipment that transform a material substance into a figure or a diagram. Unlike standard images of science as linear processes that lead inevitably to "findings," the movement from experimental work to inscription, as witnessed by Latour, was instead messy and uneven. In the end, however, the process was forgotten or taken for granted and scientific discussion focused on figures and diagrams. As a result, scientists came to see their inscriptions as direct indicators of the substance being studied, rather than as contingent and constructed outcomes.

With an inscription, scientists work to persuade colleagues to drop qualifications in any statements they make about the inscription. The researchers aim to move their competitors from statements like "Smith's work appears to suggest that x plays a crucial role in the onset of lung cancer" to "x plays a crucial role in the onset of lung cancer." This is all part of the process of knowledge construction. A fact only exists when qualification is gone and it is taken for granted and is drawn on as part of an accepted body of knowledge.

Another canonical laboratory study is Knorr-Cetina's *The Manufacture of Knowledge* (1981),

which studied the work of plant protein researchers. Knorr-Cetina stresses the contingent and local character of knowledge production, showing that how an experiment proceeds depends as much on what equipment happens to be available, what money has been allocated for, and how resource use needs to be justified as on widely accepted procedures. In addition, Knorr-Cetina suggests that scientists are not linear reasoners, but reason analogically. Knorr-Cetina shows that the messy and contingent process of knowledge production is masked by scientific papers which suggest an orderly and linear movement from introduction, to methods, to data and analysis and conclusions.

Another especially prominent laboratory study is Lynch's *Art and Artifact in Laboratory Science* (1985). Coming from the ethnomethodological tradition and drawing on data collected in a university brain-sciences laboratory, this book, like Knorr-Cetina's work, points to the disjunction between scientific writing and what actually happens in the laboratory. Even more than Knorr-Cetina, Lynch stresses the local character of scientific work, suggesting that, for example, what counts as an artifact in experimental work is determined in the local laboratory context through discussion of the local situation and not measured against an external standard. Lynch focuses on talk among laboratory workers and shows that standards for matters like experimental competence are settled for practical purposes.

A final canonical text, Traweek's *Beamtimes and Lifetimes* (1988), offers a quite different perspective. Based on a comparative analysis of high energy physics research in the US and Japan, Traweek focuses more on the culture of laboratory practice than on the epistemological concerns that drive the other prominent laboratory studies. Looking especially at the large and expensive equipment at the center of high energy physics, Traweek shows how the different cultures of the two countries affect the construction and use of these crucial tools. Most prominently, Traweek describes how equipment is proposed by researchers in the Japanese case and then built outside the laboratory environment and not subject to subsequent modification. In the US, particle detectors, while initially developed based on scientific specifications, are also altered on the basis of everyday use. This difference in orientation to equipment construction affects the way in which research is undertaken and the outcomes produced.

Broadly speaking, the classic laboratory ethnographies treat the laboratories studied in isolation from a larger social world in which we might view them as embedded. Kleinman (2003) moves laboratory ethnography in a new direction. Situating the plant pathology laboratory he studies within a broader political economy, Kleinman shows the multiple subtle and indirect ways in which university laboratory practices can be affected by the world of commerce.

SEE ALSO: Actor-Network Theory; Knowledge Societies; Merton, Robert K.; Political Economy of Science; Scientific Knowledge, Sociology of

REFERENCES AND SUGGESTED READINGS

Hess, D. J. (1992) Introduction: The New Ethnography and the Anthropology of Science and Technology. *Knowledge and Society* 9: 1–26.

Hess, D. J. (1997) *Science Studies: An Advanced Introduction*. New York University Press, New York.

Kleinman, D. L. (2003) *Impure Cultures: University Biology and the Commercial World*. University of Wisconsin Press, Madison.

Knorr-Cetina, K. (1981) *The Manufacture of Knowledge: An Essay in the Constructivist and Contextual Nature of Science*. Pergamon, Oxford.

Knorr-Cetina, K. (1995) Laboratory Studies: The Cultural Approach to the Study of Science. In: Jasanoff, S., Markle, G. E., Petersen, J. C., & Pinch, T. (Eds.), *Handbook of Science and Technology Studies*. Sage, Thousand Oaks, CA, pp. 140–66.

Knorr-Cetina, K. (1999) *Epistemic Cultures: How the Sciences Make Knowledge*. Harvard University Press, Cambridge, MA.

Latour, B. & Woolgar, S. (1986) *Laboratory Life: The Construction of Scientific Facts*. Princeton University Press, Princeton.

Lynch, M. (1985) *Art and Artifact in Laboratory Science: A Study of Shop Work and Shop Talk in a Research Laboratory*. Routledge, London.

Traweek, S. (1988) *Beamtimes and Lifetimes: The World of High Energy Physics*. Harvard University Press, Cambridge, MA.

laborism

Peter Beilharz

Laborism refers to the theory and practice of the labor movement, articulated as its own kind of socialism or social protection. Laborism is best understood as the project which seeks to defend and extend the interests of workers and their families under capitalism. Laborism is peculiar to Anglo imperial cultures, such as Britain, Australia, and New Zealand. Its intellectual advocates are often associated with the ideological trend of reformism called Fabianism in these countries, or progressivism in the United States. The peculiarity of laborism as an Anglo phenomenon is that it results from the shift a hundred years ago of the labor movement into politics. Laborism, or labor socialism, as the defensive cliché indicates, is what labor parties do.

Laborism, then, indicates a distinct path of development in contrast to European socialism, or social democracy. Classical social democratic parties on the European continent were based on the German model, which was not only socialist but also explicitly Marxist. Laborism is less doctrinal than this, often seeking as a maximum program universal health care provision and free schooling or decent public housing. This is not to say that laborism is always meek in its reformism. Certainly the British, Australian, and New Zealand labor parties were home to various radicals and Marxists, though the rise of organized communism after 1917 took such activists elsewhere. If the labor parties often then argued for socialization after World War I, their greatest moment came with World War II, when the Savage government pioneered the welfare state "cradle to the grave" in New Zealand from 1935, the Attlee government introduced the National Health Service (NHS) in Britain over the period of its reign, 1945–51, and the Curtin and Chifley governments presided over the program of post-war reconstruction in Australia.

Laborism was then transformed into managerialism in the post-war boom, and then washed away by the new wave of globalization into the 1980s. As the greatest organized social movement of the twentieth century, the labor movement lost its national reforming impact in the face of the rise of neoliberalism. Having dropped their socialist claims in the managerial atmosphere of the 1950s, labor parties now spearheaded neoliberal innovation, first in the Antipodes, then most illustriously in the shape of Blair's New Labour in Britain. The transformation of the post-war world – Keynesian, based on high growth, full male employment, and the nuclear family as the unit of consumption – dissolved the basis of this kind of left labor politics. The theory and practice of laborism were transformed sociologically from below.

SEE ALSO: Labor Movement; Management, Workers' Participation in; Political Sociology; Social Movements; Socialism; Solidarity; Unions; Welfare State; Welfare State, Retrenchment of

REFERENCES AND SUGGESTED READINGS

Beilharz, P. (1994) *Transforming Labor: Labor Tradition and the Labor Decade in Australia*. Cambridge University Press, Melbourne.
Elery, G. (2002) *Forging Democracy: The History of the Left in Europe, 1850–2000*. Oxford, New York.
Miliband, R. (1971) *Parliamentary Socialism: A Study of the Politics of Labour*. Merlin, London.
Sassoon, D. (1996) *One Hundred Years of Socialism*. Tauris, London.

Lacan, Jacques (1901–81)

Christine A. Monnier

Jacques Marie Émile Lacan received his medical degree in psychiatry in 1932 based on a doctoral dissertation analyzing a famous case of paranoid psychosis. This work marked the beginning of a clinical and theoretical career in psychoanalysis that would span over 50 years and make him one of the major, and most controversial, figures of the post-World War II French intellectual milieu. Lacan defined his approach as a "return to Freud." By this,

he did not simply mean the establishment of a literal Freudian orthodoxy, but the rediscovery of Freud's most controversial and subversive insights. He also succeeded in underlining the importance of Freud, beyond the field of psychoanalysis, to other human and social sciences. It is therefore not surprising that his conceptual developments integrated insights from the arts (Surrealism), philosophy (Spinoza, Hegel, Heidegger, Merleau-Ponty), linguistics (Saussure, Jakobson), anthropology (especially in the structuralist anthropology initiated by Lévi-Strauss), and mathematics. Such a wide range points to two major difficulties in studying Lacan: first, he constantly redefined his concepts to integrate insights from other fields; second, this integration made Lacan notorious for his deliberately "unreadable" style.

One of the major controversial insights that Lacan retrieved from Freud is the radical deconstruction of the classical Cartesian view of the *subject*. Through his famous formulation *cogito ergo sum* Descartes posited a unified subject, able to know himself through conscious thinking. This conception of the status of the subject was a pillar of western thought. By introducing the concept of the unconscious, Freud and Lacan showed that complete knowledge and unity of the subject is impossible. In addition, Lacan demonstrated that human life (mental and sexual) is not governed by biological processes and instinct (as biologism sees it), but by linguistic processes that create meaning; in other words, the source of human behavior is to be found in social rather than biological reality. Although it is impossible to review all of Lacan's conceptual developments, it is important to examine those that are relevant for the social sciences.

The first of these is known as the *mirror stage*. Infants reach the mirror stage between the ages of 6 and 18 months. At this stage, they become able to identify themselves in a mirror, as complete individuals, in spite of their lack of motor and coordination skills. According to Lacan, the mirror stage involves a dialectic process: the child, as it recognizes itself in the mirror, also identifies the image as its *reflection*, something separate from itself, an *other*; this stage marks the emergence of the ability to distinguish between self and other. Where the child experiences itself as fragmented, uncoordinated, and disorganized, it experiences the image as complete, thus providing for what Lacan calls the ego-ideal, the perfect, complete image of the ego that the subject tries to achieve through identifications. If the mirror stage is essential to the development of the ego, it also involves a fundamental alienation – a split – as the subject will always rely on an *other*, a mirror, for his identity.

Coinciding with the mirror stage is the development of language, the child's entry into the Symbolic order according to the Lacanian version of the Oedipus complex. The acquisition of language corresponds to the child's separation from the world of the mother and movement into the social world (the Big Other, in Lacanian terms), the patriarchal world, the world of the father (a symbolic, rather than biological entity). Lacan calls the former the "real," marked by complete enjoyment or *jouissance*, and the latter the "symbolic," marked by the loss of this *jouissance*, which gives rise to sexual desire in the subject. For Lacan, the fear of castration involved in the Oedipus complex is a symbolic more than real notion; it reflects the anguish associated with the irremediable loss of the real, the world of the mother where the subject is complete, and the entry into the symbolic, the social world, governed by language, where the subject is split. The mirror stage and the symbolic domain are at the root of the subject's identity in society, albeit an incomplete one.

The *Symbolic* and the *Real* are two components in the tripartite order that defines the human subject. The other is the *Imaginary*, the domain of appearances and images. Lacan represented the relation between these three orders in the image of the Borromean knot (for an illustration, see Evans 1997).

For many feminists, Lacan merely reproduced Freud's misogyny. However, for others, the infamous statement that "the Woman does not exist" can be interpreted as a description, rather than endorsement, of the fact that there is no feminine essence or nature but that such nature is only the product of men's desires and cultural determinations in the symbolic domain, that is, patriarchal reality. Moreover, Lacan also uses the symbolic concept of phallus (as opposed to the biological penis) as a limitation on men's libido. Indeed, Lacan showed that if men are limited to phallic pleasure,

women have access to a surplus of *jouissance* or sexual enjoyment.

The result of the split of the subject is the never-ending search for complete identity through identifications in the sociopolitical reality. But since this split is the result of the loss of the real, a full identity can never be achieved – although different ethnically based political movements (identity politics) may promise such fullness. Much nationalistic and exclusionary thinking is based on the idea that "others" (immigrants, minorities, homosexuals, etc.) have access to *jouissance* at the expense of the subject's "natural right" to such. In addition, most political utopian projects (Nazism, communism, communitarianism) are based on the idea of creating such fullness at the social level. Such projects offer an imaginary vision of a harmonious society, as if the real had been recuperated (Stavrakis 1999). However, since social reality is riddled with conflicts and other problems, such utopian projects always need a scapegoat to blame for delays in achieving the imaginary society, and therefore to be exterminated. For Stavrakis, this explains the failure of such utopian projects as well as the double threat to democracy: the threat of totalitarianism (the utopia of completeness) and the threat of particularism (the utopia of irreconcilable difference as source of complete identity). Democracy is the only viable Lacanian political project because it is based on the acceptance and institutionalization of conflict. Democracy is the only system that does not try to fill the lack that is constitutive of human existence, but integrates this lack and turns it into sociopolitical institutions.

SEE ALSO: Freud, Sigmund; Postmodernism; Poststructuralism; Psychoanalysis

REFERENCES AND SUGGESTED READINGS

Evans, D. (1997) *An Introductory Dictionary of Lacanian Psychoanalysis*. Routledge, London.
Grosz, E. (1990) *Jacques Lacan – A Feminist Introduction*. Routledge, London.
Rabate, J. M. (2003) *The Cambridge Companion to Lacan*. Cambridge University Press, Cambridge.

Roudinesco, E. (1997) *Jacques Lacan*. Columbia University Press, New York.

Stavrakis, Y. (1999) *Lacan and the Political*. Routledge, London.

Žižek, S. (1991) *Looking Awry: An Introduction to Jacques Lacan through Popular Culture*. MIT Press, Boston.

laicism

Jean Baubérot

The French Constitution defines France as a "*République laïque*," a lay republic, and the French generally consider laicism to be a "French exception." This aspect of singularity was recently reinforced with the passing of a law in March 2004 banning ostentatious religious signs in public schools. But it is impossible to simplify laicism in terms of this particular law. Laicism is also a possible means for relationships between the state, religion, society, and every human being. Such relationships can function only if there is flexibility and adaptability to all situations present in society.

Classically, sociologists dealt with the notion of secularization as being the decline of the influence of religion on modern society. For example, according to Peter Berger, secularization is "the process by which the sectors of society and culture are freed from the authority of religious institutions and symbols." Nowadays, not only is it obvious that the decline is incomplete (for Berger, the turning point of the twentieth and twenty-first centuries was "furiously religious"), but also such a notion of secularization can be criticized as being too broad. For a better understanding, a distinction can be made between two long-term sociohistoric processes, a cultural process of secularization and a political process of laicization.

When the cultural process of secularization is predominant compared with the political process of laicization, the relative decline of a religion's influence takes place in the form of cultural mutations, with no major tensions between religious and political or other social forces. Certainly, religious changes, as well as economic and political changes, may produce

internal tensions. But triumphant forces participate in the same cultural and social dynamic. Therefore, there is no important clash between the changes within the religious sphere and other social changes. This is the reason that Scandinavian countries are seen as exemplary of a secular state. The switch to Lutheran Protestantism, particularly linked to the Bible's translation, has favored the development of a national culture. Theological arguments have prevented the autonomy of the nation-state toward religion from provoking important conflicts. Moreover, a joint and progressive democratization of state and church has taken place.

In Scandinavian countries, and in other countries like the United Kingdom, religion contributed in various ways to secularization and particularly to the development of democratic sociability. In certain cases, the development of secularization that occurred in the eighteenth and nineteenth centuries is described by the paradoxical term "religious secularization." It is feasible, then, that a national church can continue to be the symbol of the identity of nations that have been culturally secularized.

Laicization is a process in which there is a double movement at the end of a political "theocracy," a movement of institutional differentiation between the political and the religious sphere, a movement of emancipation of the nation-state and the institutions toward religion. When the political process of laicization is predominant compared with the cultural process of secularization, the tensions between various social forces generally take on the aspect of an open conflict where religion becomes a politico-cultural stake. For example, the symbolization of the national culture is controversial. Either the state imposes religion on society (clericalism) or refuses that religion should continue to be the symbol of national identity (laicization). The French case is the main example of such a process.

In 1789, religion pervaded French society. From the Revocation of the Edict of Nantes (1685), the monolithic Roman Catholic faith was made compulsory for the French. Communion at Easter and confession were imposed on the people. The clergy was the first of the three "orders" of the kingdom. The monarchy possessed religious justification, given the theory of the divine right of kings. The king possessed politico-religious power, and one of his basic duties was to defend Catholicism. Gradually, the monarchy also established widespread autonomous political and administrative power. A Gallican movement emerged, which developed the idea of a French Catholic Church that would be autonomous from the pope and protected, as well as partly controlled, by the monarchy. An anticlerical dimension appeared in the French philosophy of the Enlightenment that had permeated a part of the nobility and bourgeoisie. This spirit differed from the English Enlightenment or the German *Aufklärung*. The latter appeared as a confrontation within a diversified Protestantism wanting "enlightened religion," the former directly attacked the Roman Catholic Church.

The French Revolution removed the privileges of the clergy and confiscated the church's large property holdings. Revolutionaries worked to "emancipate" civil and political society from the influence of the church, particularly in social matters relating to marriage, divorce, and education. The Declaration of Human Rights of 1789 proclaimed the principle of religious freedom. In 1791, the Constitution divested the monarchy of its religious features, and it was implemented the following year. The republic was established, although rather conflictually. However, it was not clear that the founding of the republic was considered as the first day of the new era (as is the birth of Christ for the Gregorian calendar). In 1793, the institutions of revolutionary cults ("Eternal Reason," "Saint Liberty," or the more conciliatory "Cult of the Supreme Being") struggled violently against all revealed religions. The significance of the new forms of religion was represented by ritualized gatherings of the community around common values that were socially fundamental and regarded as sacred (cf. Émile Durkheim). It was a conflictual and, eventually, impossible laicization.

Napoleon Bonaparte inherited a chaotic situation. In 1801 he signed a concordat with the pope: the Roman Catholic Church was proclaimed the "religion of the great majority of the French," but without the status of a state religion. In 1802, the plurality of religions became official: Lutheran and Reformed churches and, later, Judaism were recognized.

In 1804, the Civil Code made no reference to religion.

It is possible to evaluate the situation using the abstract notion of the first threshold of laicization (constructed on the basis of Weber's ideal type). It is marked by three characteristics:

1 *Institutional fragmentation*: Roman Catholicism was no longer an inclusive institution. The clergy had to confine itself to its religious activities, which were clearly distinguished from profane activities. Educational and health needs assumed gradual autonomy, related to religious needs, and were provided for by specific institutions that underwent progressive development.

2 *Recognition of legitimacy*: The French Revolution did not destroy religious needs, which continued to exist objectively and within the general society. Religion was a public service and the state paid ministers of recognized religions. Religions were politically recognized as a foundation of social morality.

3 *Religious pluralism*: The state recognized several but not all religions; it protected and controlled them since they could satisfy the religious needs of their followers and develop moral values. Other religions were more or less tolerated. Relative freedom was even granted to those who decided to do without the "help of religion."

This profile delineates a logic that dominated for a century. But the situation was not static or rigid. This was due especially to the fact that, for a long period, a number of aspects of the first threshold of laicization were not entirely evident; other institutions were not sufficiently developed to become totally autonomous. Then there was growing conflict between those who regarded France mainly as a Roman Catholic nation and partisans of the liberal values of 1789. Similar conflicts also rose during the nineteenth century in other countries where Catholicism continues to predominate today, among them Belgium, Spain, Italy, and Mexico, whilst in the 1870s a few countries, such as Germany with the *Kulturkampf* movement, held firm against Catholicism. But, at present, there is not necessarily any conflict between church and state in predominantly Catholic countries. Catholicism can represent a national sentiment (as, for example, in Ireland under British rule, or in Poland).

Conflict grew in the nineteenth century between "clericalism," that is, a religion's political dominion over a country, and "anticlericalism," which actively fought this claim. Rooted in scientific ideology, radical forms of anticlericalism perceived religion as an outdated explanation of the world that offered only a backwards orientation, irrelevant to the context of modern democracies.

In France, the founding of laicism was rooted in the political victory of the anticlerical movement. The impression prevailed that the republic (established again in 1870) was threatened by clericalism. A 1901 law excluded religious congregations from the right to free association. A new law passed in 1904 (and in effect until 1914) prohibited members of religious orders from teaching. But, essentially, the combative anticlerical movement gave birth to a progressive pacifist form of laicism. It is as if a revolutionary socialist party, assuming power by democratic process, ultimately gave birth to a social democratic system.

During the 1880s, the republicans introduced a religiously neutral educational system, which included a "laic morality." This morality borrows elements from a number of origins: classical antiquity, Christianity, the Enlightenment (from Voltaire to Kant), and, occasionally, from Confucius. Different traditions are interpreted according to two notions: dignity of the human person (which creates rights and duties) and social solidarity. Further, the republicans hoped that the structure of the lay school would engender morality. As a place for learning tolerance, it enabled all French children, irrespective of social class or religion, to come to know and accept one another. Through school, the republic itself was the bearer of values. This moral was a compromise, and, because of the conflict, a significant anticlerical section asserted that religion was dangerous for the republic and its ideals.

In 1904–5, after the crisis that arose out of the Dreyfus affair, the separation of church and state became inevitable in a climate of confrontation.

Two models were possible. One was combative, as represented by the bill of Prime Minister Émile Combes. However, it was rejected, especially by the celebrated socialist leader Jean Jaurès, who hoped to achieve a law that would bring peace and make it possible to combat social inequalities. A liberal model prevailed ensuring freedom of conscience, guaranteeing the freedom to exercise religion, and respecting the self-organization of each religion (art. 1 and 4), even though it neither "recognized" nor subsidized any religion (art. 2).

Even in liberal dominance, this model of separation completed a religiously neutral educational system and found a new logic. This can be seen as the second threshold of laicization. As for the first, there are three characteristics:

1 *Institutional dissociation*: Religion was entirely optional because it was no longer considered an institutional structure of society but rather as a mode of free association.
2 *Social neutrality regarding religious legitimacy*: Religious needs became a private matter. The question as to the usefulness of religion for society was no longer publicly relevant. But, within the framework of freedom of expression and association, religions could participate in public debates on social questions and the meaning of life.
3 *Freedom of religion and conviction*: Various religious societies belonged to the public sphere. The state guaranteed each citizen freedom of conscience and allowed citizens to meet within religious societies or associations.

A twofold aspect marked a separation in 1905: the victory of the lay camp in the conflict of a divided France, and an implicit covenant with opponents whose ultimate aim was to attain peace rather than achieve victory in the short term. The conflict vanished progressively because religion ceased to be a political problem, except in the field of education. So, by 1945, the bishops held that there could be a positive meaning to the term laicism and the following year laicism was officially proclaimed and recognized by the Constitution.

Other countries also underwent a process of laicization. Belgium was not situated in a similar

logic to the second threshold of French laicization but integrated laicism in its system of
recognized religions: non-confessional morality
in school, lay advisers in hospitals or prisons,
and so on. The Spanish and Italian systems tend
to resemble a laicism that corresponds a little
more to the first threshold of laicization, with
more liberty and more pluralism.

The American situation is characterized by
the separation between church and state (the
1st Amendment of the Constitution, 1791) and
this is linked to the central function of religion.
Stephen Warner indicates the main differences:

- Religion is constitutive for some American
  subcultures.
- Religion in America has historically promoted the formation of associations among
  mobile people.
- Religion in America serves as a refuge of
  free association and autonomous identity –
  a "free social space."
- The second generation of immigrants often
  transmutes ethnicity into religion because it
  allows immigrants to assimilate and conserve their identity.

The American situation is heavily influenced
by civil religion. There is an ambivalence
between civil religion and laicization. Civil religion historically favors dissociation between
social links and the hegemony of a religion,
but civil religion renders the political values of
the collectivity sacred.

Is the French situation the most laic? The
answer is no, since, for example, the separation
between state and church in Mexico from 1917
to 1992 created a time of austerity for religion.
The 1917 Mexican Constitution forbade mon-
astic orders, ensuring that religious ceremonies
could only take place in churches, which were
permanently under the authorities' supervision,
and according to the Constitution religious ministers of all cults were denied the right to vote.
Since the 1990s, though, there has been more
flexibility and such rigidity is not as common.
Turkish laicism is also historically harsher than
French laicism. It expanded after World War I,
questioning the logic of Islam, which was considered to be the principal cause of social
decline. This position explains the reason for
the armed forces' important role in religion.

A moderate Islamic movement tried to make it
more liberal. The international situation does
not favor such a development because a new
form of conflict that might be characterized by
a new anticlericalism has arisen between fundamentalist religious groups and laicized and/or
secularized societies. Examples are evident in
several Islamic countries, in Israel (orthodox
Jews), and in the United States (fundamentalist
Christians). Whether or not headscarves may be
worn, a passionate issue for many French people, is a typical example of these new tensions.
Several problems are interwoven, concerning
not only how best to deal with fundamentalism,
but also the most appropriate strategy to prevent social exclusion, the various conceptions of
school, and the different notions of plurality
compatible with national identity.

However, the idea of the universal has changed within the last 50 years. Today, the universal is no longer considered as the imposition
of the nation-state's values upon the civil
society, no more than it is the imposition of
western values on the rest of the world. It is
the result of the building up of positive comparisons between values provided by different cultures, religions, philosophies, and civilizations.
We are in the age of globalization. This represents a considerable change for laicism, which is
linked with the development of the nation-state.

Another issue worthy of attention is that,
historically, laicization and secularization were
two different processes of modernization. Now,
changing from a process to a movement, modernization is a hegemonic but disillusioned reality. In the nineteenth century, morality was
based on science. Now, science and morality
tend to be dissociated in the context of many
problems. Science was increasingly seen as technoscience, the functional efficiency of which was
undeniable but which, far from helping to
resolve moral questions, created new ones that
were more difficult to resolve because of their
intrinsic power. Is all possible progress also
desirable? This is now an important topical
question, not just in the biomedical field but
in other areas as well: consider everything that
contributes to environmental degradation. This
new disillusionment changes the relationship
to temporality. Ephemeral effects thus are
becoming more important than investments in
long-term projects. Mass communication favors

sensationalism over analysis in the news, emphasizing its entertainment value. This entertainment broadcasts heroism, intrigue, sex, and wealth in large doses. It can lead to resentment because of the sizable gap between the imaginary notions conveyed and the nature of daily life, with all its banality, difficulty, and routine. In addition, it is necessary to be self-sufficient, each person has to assume responsibility. Such disillusionment leads to problems and various identity constructions are available that help individuals move toward the necessities of self-realization. Once again, the new cultural and religious demands have to be understood within this context. Indirect discrimination and reasonable accommodation are becoming new important problems.

SEE ALSO: Civil Religion; Globalization; Globalization, Religion and; Modernization; Religion; Secularization

REFERENCES AND SUGGESTED READINGS

Baubérot, J. (2003) *Histoire de la laïcité en France* (*History of Laicism in France*). PUF, Paris.
Baubérot, J. (2004) *Laïcité 1905–2005, entre passion et raison* (*Laicism 1905–2005, Between Passion and Reason*). Le Seuil, Paris.
Baubérot, J. (Ed.) (2004) *La laïcité à l'épreuve, religions et libertés dans le monde* (*Laicism on Trial, Religions and Liberties in the World*). Universalis, Paris.
Baubérot, J. & Mathieu, S. (2002) *Religion, modernité et culture au Royaume Uni et en France* (*Religion, Modernity and Culture in the United Kingdom and France*). Le Seuil, Paris.
Blancarte, R. (2000) *Laïcidad y valores en un Estado democratico* (*Laicism and Values in a Democratic State*). El Colegio de Mexico, Mexico.
Casanova, J. (1994) *Public Religions in a Modern World*. University of Chicago Press, Chicago.
Garber, M. (Ed.) (1999) *One Nation Under God? Religion and American Culture*. Routledge, New York.
Kaboglu, I. O. (2001) *Laiklik ve Democratie* (*Laicism and Democracy*). Imge Dagitim, Ankara.
Kurtz, L. R. (1995) *Gods in the Global Village*. Pine Forge Press, Thousand Oaks, CA.
Milot, M. (2002) *Laïcité dans le nouveau monde* (*Laicism in the New World*). Brepols, Turnhout.
Warner, R. S. (1992) Work in Progress Toward a New Paradigm for the Sociological Study of Religion in the United States. *American Journal of Sociology* 98(5): 1044–93.

language

J. I. (Hans) Bakker

Language is a very important topic in its own right (Crystal 1987) and in terms of philosophical debates in the social sciences (Rorty 1967; Calhoone 2003), yet, surprisingly, many sociologists pay scant attention to language and find communication entirely unproblematic. For some, for example, it is mainly a question of tracing the history and etymology of specific words (Stevenson 1983). Many classical sociologists did not pay specific attention to language as a phenomenon, but recently there has been a reexamination of the work of outstanding linguists and logicians. The important debates between those who identify with Enlightenment modernism (Chomsky 1998) and those who adhere to postmodernism (Jameson 1991) have forced many social scientists to reexamine long-held assumptions.

However, there were important precursors among the moderns, including Johann Gottlieb Fichte, a dialectical thinker who defined language in 1794 as the "expression of our thoughts by means of arbitrary signs" (Surber 1996: 32). Critical approaches to the study of gender, race, and class have often involved a rethinking of basic linguistic categories by scholars such as Foucault, Baudrillard, Derrida, Bauman, and many others. For example, Foucault (1985: 91) has a very ingenious way of defining "aphrodisia" as "acts intended by nature." Hence, in a sense, the study of language is a window to all of the social sciences, especially as cutting-edge theory is shaping up in the early twenty-first century. For many, there has been a philosophical shift from Cartesian "subject-centered reason" and rational action, to Fichtean "communicative social action" (Habermas 1989) and symbolic interaction. Nevertheless, many theorists resist that change in worldview. The battleground where many issues are fought out is the study of language and communication generally.

Both as a subject matter (i.e., an "object" of study) and as a key aspect of theorizing (e.g., in terms of epistemology), language is a highly contentious topic (Crystal 1987). The ways in which languages have been studied have changed. There is still interest in such topics as the emergence of alphabets and writing. Much in the way of traditional linguistics is still carried out. But there have been many changes over the last few decades. Comparative philology has given way, for the most part, to various forms of linguistics and semiotics. Many writers have discussed the "linguistic turn" in contemporary thought, a paradigm shift that may have started with "ordinary language philosophy" and other trends in the 1960s, or even earlier (Rorty 1967). Modernist, structuralist epistemologies stressing the Cartesian subject–object dichotomy have been confronted by postmodernist, poststructuralist epistemologies which stress the "habitus" (Bourdieu 1977) and the "lifeworld" (Habermas 1989). Often, the study of language is seen as part and parcel of all aspects of human (and even non-human) communication. Since no one can speak a language that is entirely idiosyncratic and still be understood, all languages tend to be social. A critique of the meaning and function of language in general (or perhaps a particular jargon) is often implicit in efforts to reform a disciplinary paradigm. Philosophers who emphasize linguistic questions (e.g., the later Wittgenstein) sometimes argue as if all that is necessary to dissolve certain intellectual problems is simply a reform of the language, thereby eliminating what are often called merely "semantic arguments." Yet it is not altogether clear that certain questions can be considered mere "pseudo-problems." It is also not clear that "ideal language philosophy" is a realizable possibility (Rorty 1967).

Languages come in an amazing variety of forms, including dialects and *lingua francas* (Wardhaugh 1986). We rely on "euphemism" and "jargon" (Goshgarian 1998). There are many distinctive national, vernacular languages in the world. Of the approximately 5,500 currently still-viable languages the most commonly spoken are Mandarin Chinese, English, Arabic, Spanish, and Hindi. Several ancient languages ("dead languages") are nevertheless still in use, including Medieval Latin and Sanskrit. Other languages have died out and either can or cannot be reconstructed. (The Ancient Greek used by those who wrote in Linear B in Minoan civilization has been reconstructed, but Linear A – as well as the writing on the Phaistos Disc, also found in Crete – is still undeciphered.)

There are many definitions of the term language. Commonsense views of language stress the grammar and vocabulary of a specific natural language, like Swahili, Russian, Frisian, Mandarin, or English. Many people think of English, for example, as one and only one language. Crystal (2004) has stressed, however, that the history of English involves not just one consistent narrative (centered on English as spoken by the upper classes in England), but many different "stories" (including many versions of English historically and regionally). It is not just a matter of a "standard language" with many different offshoots. Since there are many legitimate forms of English spoken around the world, there is not just "one English language" today. This leads Crystal to look at English as a "global language." His encyclopedic coverage of English as a language is matched by a similar range of coverage on languages in general (Crystal 1987).

Linguistics, the study of language and languages, can be viewed as sets of answers to a host of different intellectual questions or problems. For example, a group of linguists may be concerned with (1) *philosophical problems* (e.g., rationalist vs. empiricist aspects of philology as clues to deeper epistemological truths); (2) *social science questions* (e.g., the study of language acquisition by children, speech communities, and dialect patterns); and (3) *challenges in the humanities and arts* (e.g., the study of rhetoric and literatures). Some authors, of course, develop complex theoretical ideas concerning all three areas of inquiry. Thus, for example, Roman Jakobson, a member of the Prague Circle of the 1920s, wrote on questions of literary theory but also got involved in questions related to grammar. His "Quest for the Essence of Language" (Jakobson 1987: 413–27) is an aspect of his "semiotic" theory. Moreover, some authors argue strongly in favor of one viewpoint but later find that their theoretical ideas concerning language may have implications for a range of questions on which they themselves had not previously focused. A good example is the work of Edward Said on "Orientalism," a very broad critique that has many implications for textual criticism and cultural criticism (Said, 1983). Habermas (1989) has attempted to steer clear of certain excesses in postmodernism while nevertheless incorporating many of the discoveries which have attended the linguistic turn.

The simplest form of language study is taxonomic and descriptive. However, for some, the term taxonomic linguistics is pejorative, since such classification systems tend to rely on "finite states" versus phases or transformations. There are different branches of linguistics. Historical linguistics looks at language change (diachronic, comparative philology), while general linguistics examines the characteristics of human language as a structured phenomenon (synchronic, contrastive structural linguistics). Language families have been analyzed by comparative linguists working in both diachronic and synchronic modes of investigation. Language usage is sometimes viewed as the most important aspect of what it means to be human. That could make linguistics a kind of queen of the social sciences, with interdisciplinary contacts with many other disciplines outside of the social sciences.

For many, the study of psychological linguistics is a subset of linguistics. For others, like Chomsky, the study of language is merely an aspect of the general discipline of psychology. That is because the key to language usage is considered to be a "generative grammar" that is part of our cognitive makeup. Chomsky argues that little children do not get enough experience with linguistic examples for them to be able to speak a language simply through memorization of clearly demonstrated patterns. Instead, human beings are "hard wired" with neurolinguistic abilities. Since those are universal it is possible to have a scientific approach to language acquisition and hence to language structure. In early work Chomsky views "transformational grammars" as heuristic, but more recently the standard "transformational-generative" theory of the 1960s has been questioned and further refined.

An examination of the anthropological and sociological aspects of language includes the study of such topics as the creation of artificial languages with simplified grammars (e.g., Esperanto). Language affects social structures and social structures, in turn, affect language. In general, it is a truism to point out that human beings interact with one another through the use of languages. But while that is well known, what interests the social scientist are the complex patterns that emerge from the human use of language. This leads to ethnolinguistics and

anthropological linguistics. In sociology the focus is on sociolinguistics.

The sociological use of the philosophical term *Verstehen* evokes for many an image of language in which the isolated individual speaker or writer in his or her personal "singularity" is able to have a fairly clear inner knowledge of the motivations and intentions of other speakers or writers, living or dead. Thus, Dilthey (1996) sometimes tended to write as if it is a matter of the scholar personally "reliving" (*Nacherleben*, *Nachbildung*) the mindset of a previous thinker (e.g., Marx attempting to interpret Hegel). Weber utilizes Dilthey's concept of *Verstehen* but modifies it to make it more sociological rather than psychological. (Dilthey himself was heading toward a broader conceptualization of *Verstehen* at the end of his life.) But various poststructuralist scholars have indicated that such a Dilthey-Weber use of *Verstehen* – and "romantic hermeneutics" in general – may still be too individualistic and may neglect the importance of the sociolinguistic "field," the conscious and unconscious coordination of a group due to its shared language (Bourdieu 1977). Hence, we move from the individual scholar to the social actor and then to the "bundle of habits."

In the discipline of linguistics the field of "pragmatics" concerns the ways in which language usage is linked to contextual background features. This has a recognized overlap with sociological ethnomethodology. How do people "accomplish talk"? Knowledge of the sociocultural context and the social psychological situation can help us, for example, to distinguish between angry and joking behavior. We might want to examine the specific details of how a group of people are able to believe that their words are understood. Thus, for example, speech act theory concerns the ways in which linguistic utterances are meant to accomplish specific goals (e.g., to apologize, to threaten). Conversation analysis examines the structure of human dialogues.

The study of "symbolic interaction" by sociologists who call themselves symbolic interactionists is based in part on George Herbert Mead's insight that in order for two or more people to interact they need to have "significant symbols" in common. A significant symbol is a symbol that all participants to the interaction understand fairly clearly in terms of its practical consequences. For most Americans a Ugandan flag is not a significant symbol, but an American flag is. Similarly, when two specialists use their own jargon they use words that are significant symbols in that one specialized context (e.g., motorcycle mechanics discussing the "fork" on a "hog" or astrologers debating the "sidereal" versus the "tropical" star chart). All human interaction relies on the ability of members of a collectivity to share certain significant symbols. This is partially a matter of customary norms.

Bourdieu (1977) has made it clear that one's habituated ways of doing and saying things (one's *habitus*) involves indicators such as language usage that can be correlated with social class. Those from upper-class households will be accustomed to speaking in a more formal and literary version of the language. Their language usage is "distinctive." Moreover, public recognition of a change of linguistic usage can evoke a crisis because the new expressions involve "objective signs of recognition" that were previously only privately held. Bourdieu worked with poststructuralist thinkers like Derrida. Bourdieu's *habitus* can be regarded as a sociological version of the idea of a semiotic system of meanings. Just like the air we breath, the semiotic symbols we use are part and parcel of our very being. We are like fish swimming in a linguistic sea. Take away the language context upon which we rely and we are no longer cognitive beings.

Some authors, following clues found in Saussure and Peirce, have argued that there should be a shift from linguistics to a much more generalized approach that is sometimes called semiotics (Hall 2002). Semiotics can take the form of a separate discipline, albeit one with very general implications (like mathematics or philosophy). However, semiotics is also often associated with interdisciplinary approaches. For example, both the psychologist and the sociologist might be interested in studying advertising in terms of the process of signification ("semiosis").

Reflexivity about language usage has led not only to specific questions about language and languages, but also to broader philosophical questions about how we know anything with any certainty (epistemology) and whether or not we ever really know "obdurate reality"

(other than perhaps concrete material things) in any direct sense (ontology). The use of careful distinctions in philosophical discourse is often disparaged by labels like "casuistry" or "Scholasticism." Nevertheless, there is a need to be precise and to articulate subtle but important distinctions that may not be easily conveyed by the use of natural languages. An example is the distinction often made between something being "real versus not real" and the separate analytical question of whether or not something "exists versus not." It has been argued that "God exists but is not real."

In philosophy some stress that in principle natural languages cannot be precise (e.g., the later Wittgenstein), while others attempt to develop an artificial, logical symbolic language that is precise, like mathematics (e.g., the early Russell). Of course, not all vague languages are naturally occurring languages. In computer science there have been a number of artificial program languages which are based on mathematical logic, but that does not always make computer algorithms crystal clear. The field of symbolic logic in philosophy also uses artificial signs. This is much like mathematics and statistics in general. But Gödel's proof that it is impossible to be both consistent and complete in mathematics had a significant impact on linguistics. Ever since Gödel's ingenious theory it has been argued that an entirely non-circular, non-tautological verbal language is also not logically possible.

One philosophical approach, associated with Peirce, is that languages of all kinds can be broadly conceived of as systems of "signs" which constitute a "code" or semiotic system (Sebeok 2001; Hall 2002). Such codes can affect our ways of seeing other human beings and classifying them as "others" in terms of their sex-gender, race-ethnicity, and class status. Peirce (1923) argues that the aspect of reality that is being signified is something "represented" by an interpretive community and not by an isolated individual. The interpretive community always signifies "the representant" through the use of a system of signs. Hence, language is a semiotic system that allows for human *and* animal communication.

For some, it is not possible to study anthropological linguistics, ethnolinguistics, sociolinguistics, or psycholinguistics without evoking all aspects of human communication (anthropo-semiotics). The argument is also frequently extended to include communication among other animals. Thus, the study of "the language of bees" is a study in animal communication (zoo-semiotics). The underlying premise is that there is a high degree of continuity between other animals and the human animal in the way in which we communicate.

The linguist Ferdinand de Saussure also constructed a view of language that stresses the importance of how "the signifier" (the form) represents "the signified" (the concept). When we use language, he argues, we make differentiations. For example, we can differentiate between the signs "mother" and "father." When signs can be interpreted in a meaningful way we have a language that is meaningful. Hence, the sign system and its usage constitute a social construction of reality. Our cultural codes are linguistic systems which we use in various ways and constantly modify as we apply them. Hence, language is constantly changing and always somewhat imprecise. Saussure introduced the distinction between the structure of a language (*langue*) and the way in which that language is commonly spoken (*parole*). The formal patterns are reinvented and simultaneously subverted every time we speak. No language can remain "pure" for long. Most languages are amalgams of many components.

There are many kinds of signs that are important to human languages (Sebeok 2001), but perhaps the most important are "symbols" such as words and phrases (Jakobson 1987). A set of such symbols, perhaps supplemented by iconic or indexical signs, can constitute a "text" (Dilthey 1996). Any piece of recorded symbolic communication is a kind of text, but when we think of language we think primarily in terms of written language and the formal "ground" of such a language, what Saussure refers to as *la langue*.

It is often argued that language has an important impact on how we think. The stronger form of the Sapir-Whorf hypothesis is rejected today, but it is widely recognized that a weaker form of that theory is valid. Edward Sapir and his student Benjamin Lee Whorf were struck by how subtle distinctions found in one language might be difficult to convey into another language. Moreover, the structure

of a language largely determines commonsense notions of time, space, and causation. In standard European languages there is, for example, a notion of events as discrete and countable, while in Native American languages that may not be the case (Wardhaugh 1986).

The study of symbolic interaction involves ethnographic use of language through such research techniques as the interview. Ethnomethodologists and conversation analysts have paid special attention to nuances in the construction of semiotic systems. Garfinkel (2002) attempts to examine the "haecceity" (immediacy) of accomplishments and Sacks and colleagues (1974) examine topics like turn-taking in conversations and the comprehension of puns. Others study membership categorization. Goffman (1981) studies forms of talk. Various kinds of discourse have been examined in many ways.

Langer (1979) argues that "true language" is always discursive. Hence, she rejects such metaphorical constructs as a "language of musical tones" or a "language of colors." For Langer, a discursive language can be broken down into analytical units and those units can be conceptualized as having a syntax. Without a true syntax to create composite structures, she argues, it is difficult to conceive of a true language. In human languages the basic unit may be the "word" as an elementary aspect of meaning. At the same time, it is also possible to have logical categories that are derived from immediate bodily experience which are "presentational." That is, we are "presented" with feelings and emotions which cannot be expressed in any language. This is similar to Foucault's (1985) discussion of language and sexuality.

Complex hypothetical and deductive linguistic theories have been postulated by many thinkers, including those who have emphasized the importance of "semiotics" (Deely et al. 1986). Writers such as A. J. Greimas have utilized insights from thinkers like Saussure, Merleau-Ponty, Lévi-Strauss, Dumezil, Barthes, Lacan, Propp, and Jakobson (1987) to develop arguments concerning the relationship between language and communicative symbols in general. Such "structural" views tend to postulate the existence of a narrated universe of "deep semantic structures" that are reflected in the underlying grammar of all human languages. The surface "narrative" is viewed as "syntagmatic." That is, the syntactical rules, such as "linear succession," tend to determine the fundamental semantic structures. This can be seen as a further refinement of Saussure's distinction between *parole* (the spoken language) and *langue* (the underlying structure), which utilizes ideas from Propp and others to give a more complete account of the way in which such semantic structures exist in human emotions, dreams, and passions, as well as in the rigor of scientific reason and the precision of technological design. One's epistemology shapes one's view of language and vice versa (Bourdieu 1977). The study of language and communications is central to philosophical aspects of social science theory and methodology (Calhoone 2003).

SEE ALSO: Bilingualism; Cultural Studies; Epistemology; Habitus/Field; Hermeneutics; *Langue* and *Parole*; Media; Postmodernism; Representation; Saussure, Ferdinand de; Semiotics; Sociolinguistics; Structuralism; Symbolic Interaction

REFERENCES AND SUGGESTED READINGS

Bourdieu, P. (1977) *Outline of a Theory of Practice*. Cambridge University Press, Cambridge.

Calhoone, L. (Ed.) (2003) *From Modernism to Postmodernism: An Anthology*. Blackwell, Oxford.

Chomsky, N. (1998) *On Language: Chomsky's Classic Works in One Volume*. New Press, New York.

Crystal, D. (1987) *The Cambridge Encyclopedia of Language*. Cambridge University Press, Cambridge.

Crystal, D. (2004) *The Stories of English*. Overlook Press, Peter Mayer Publishers, Woodstock, NY.

Deely, J., Williams, B., & Kruse, F. E. (Eds.) (1986) *Frontiers in Semiotics*. Indiana University Press, Bloomington.

Dilthey, W. (1996 [1860–1903]) *Hermeneutics and the Study of History: Selected Works Volume 4*. Princeton University Press, Princeton.

Foucault, M. (1985) *The Use of Pleasure: Volume 2 of The History of Sexuality*. Pantheon, New York.

Garfinkel, H. (2002) *Ethnomethodology's Program: Working Out Durkheim's Aphorism*. Rowman & Littlefield, Lanham, MD.

Goffman, E. (1981) Footings. In: *Forms of Talk*. University of Pennsylvania Press, Philadelphia, pp. 124–59.

Goshgarian, G. (1998) *Exploring Language*. Addison Wesley Longman, New York.

Habermas, J. (1989) *The Theory of Communicative Action: Lifeworld and System: A Critique of Functionalist Reason*. Beacon Press, Boston.

Hall, S. (Ed.) (2002) *Representation: Cultural Representations and Signifying Practices*. Open University, London.

Jakobson, R. (1987) *Language in Literature*. Belknap Press of Harvard University Press, Cambridge, MA.

Jameson, F. (1991) *Postmodernism, or, The Cultural Logic of Late Capitalism*. Duke University Press, Durham, NC.

Langer, S. K. (1979) *Philosophy in a New Key*. Harvard University Press, Cambridge, MA.

Peirce, C. S. (1923) *Chance, Love and Logic: Philosophical Essays*. Harcourt Brace, New York.

Rorty, R. (Ed.) (1967) *The Linguistic Turn: Recent Essays in Philosophical Method*. University of Chicago Press, Chicago.

Sacks, H., Schegloff, E., & Jefferson, G. (1974) A Simplest Systematics for the Organization of Turn-Taking for Conversation. *Language* 50(4): 696–735.

Said, E. W. (1983) *The World, the Text and the Critic*. Harvard University Press, Cambridge, MA.

Sebeok, T. A. (2001) *Signs: An Introduction to Semiotics*. University of Toronto Press, Toronto.

Stevenson, V. (Ed.) (1983) *Words: The Evolution of Western Languages*. Van Nostrand Reinhold, Toronto.

Surber, J. P. (1996) *Language and German Idealism: Fichte's Linguistic Philosophy*. Humanities Press, Atlantic Highlands, NJ.

Wardhaugh, R. (1986) *An Introduction to Sociolinguistics*. Blackwell, Oxford.

langue and *parole*

J. I. (Hans) Bakker

Ferdinand de Saussure distinguishes between a "language" (*langue*) in its structural form and the spoken word (*parole*). Linguistics studies patterns of communication using an auditory mode, but vocalized sounds in one language are structurally related to sounds in other languages, particularly languages of the same language family. Chomsky makes a similar distinction between "competence" and "performance." When a native speaker speaks a language, he or she "performs" the *parole* but is not necessarily aware of the linguistic structure of that language as a generalized "competence" in the linguistics of that *langue*. It is possible to speak a *langue* in a grammatically correct manner without any knowledge of the discipline of linguistics in general, or even the application of linguistic rules to that specific language. The distinction is similar to the anthropological terms "etic" and "emic," which are taken by analogy from phonetics and phonemics. In anthropology an "etic" approach to ethnographic fieldwork data is the outsider's academic perspective concerning patterns and structures, while the "emic" aspect is the indigenous knowledge of the culture in practice in daily life. An anthropological fieldworker attempts to learn the implicit rules and must become as adept at the local dialect as a native speaker. But the researcher then takes the data and makes broader generalizations than most indigenous speakers are likely to be concerned with in their everyday use of subtle distinctions. In linguistics, phonemics studies the phonemes, which are a class of phonetically similar "phones" or speech sounds (from the Greek word for voice), while phonetics is also concerned with patterns of sound changes in a language or group of languages. Grimm's law is a law of phonetics. Something similar is meant by Saussure's distinction, but it is not entirely clear whether he thought of *langue* as an ontologically real structure or merely an epistemologically ideal device. Saussure's distinction is synchronic rather than diachronic; the actual utterance by a person is a product of that speaker's having been socialized into a language which is relatively fixed during his or her lifetime. There is some indication that Saussure may not have been entirely settled on the methodological importance of the distinction for general linguistics; however, many structuralist theorists have utilized it. Hence, the structuralist tradition in anthropology that is associated with Claude Lévi-Strauss uses Saussure's distinction, which may be part of the reason why it was eventually transformed into the etic/emic distinction. A structuralist approach to *langue* is compatible with "semiology," "signology," or – as it is usually called now, semiotics (Seung 1982). The implications of Saussure's distinction have been debated by philosophers influenced by the "linguistic turn." The linguistic turn is often associated with "ordinary language philosophy" and with Wittgenstein's later philosophy, which stresses the ordinary use of words in "natural language" (Rorty 1967). Walter Benjamin was opposed to Saussure's ontological assumptions concerning the arbitariness of the signifier.

SEE ALSO: Benjamin, Walter; Emic/Etic; Language; Saussure, Ferdinand de; Semiotics; Sociolinguistics

REFERENCES AND SUGGESTED READINGS

Chomsky, N. (1957) *Syntactic Structures*. Mouton, The Hague.
Rorty, R. (Ed.) (1967) *The Linguistic Turn: Recent Essays in Philosophical Method*. University of Chicago Press, Chicago.
Seung, T. K. (1982) *Structuralism and Hermeneutics*. Columbia University Press, New York.

late-life sexuality

Judith A. Levy

Considerable ambiguity surrounds both scientific and popular attempts to define the term "late-life sexuality." Agreement as to when "late life" begins increasingly has moved upward over the last century with the lengthening of the average life course in most industrial societies. Meanwhile, the term "sexuality" has come to connote a wide variety of human sociobiological responses that range from varying levels of social attraction or physiological arousal to intimate body contact that may or may not include physical penetration. The failure of research scientists to define what they mean by "sexuality," "sexual behavior," or "late life" when designing studies or publishing their results complicates attempts to compare research findings within older age groups and across societies and sociocultural environments. Still, at least five themes emerge as constant premises in the literature concerning sexual desire and activity in later life as defined by some form of mental and/or physical sexual response at age 50 or older.

First, scientific evidence widely documents that sexual norms and behaviors differ by societies and culture, historical time, generational influences, group characteristics, and individual beliefs and preferences. In this regard, the sexual attitudes and behaviors of today's oldest Americans are believed to have been shaped by their having come of sexual age during an era when intimate relations were less openly discussed and less acceptably variable. Thus older people now in their late sixties and older generally are perceived to be more sexually conservative, less comfortable discussing sexual topics, and more prone to hiding sexual behavior defined as deviant than their younger US counterparts. Such judgments also are applied frequently to anyone seen as advancing toward middle or older age.

Second, the "sexual revolution" of the 1960s that redefined sexual mores for youth and young adults in western societies appears largely to have bypassed popular beliefs and stereotypes about sexuality in later life. Today's older adults, many of whom as youth in the 1960s helped to push the boundaries of acceptable sexual behavior, now find themselves part of a generation commonly believed to be disinterested in and/or incapable of sex. This view is reinforced by popular culture that often portrays sexuality in old age as humorous, fraught with frustration, and aesthetically distasteful to others.

Third, despite stereotypes to the contrary, general agreement exists among researchers and clinicians that sex and sexuality are a normal and valued part of human existence among adults at any age and that many older persons remain sexually active until they die. Sometimes compared in the literature to riding a bicycle, sex is seen as something that once learned is never forgotten and always remains potentially enjoyable. Scientific findings support this view through statistics drawn from studies documenting a wide range of sexual interest and activity occurring in later life. As with many aspects of human behavior, sexuality appears to follow lifelong patterns, with those individuals who were the more active in youth being the most active in old age.

Fourth, although desire for sexual gratification appears to continue typically throughout life, opportunity may not. Lack of a sexual partner is the most commonly cited reason given for late-life celibacy. Because they outnumber men demographically at age 65 and older, heterosexual women are more likely than their male counterparts to be without a partner (Deacon et al. 1995). Meanwhile, age norms that define mature adults as becoming less attractive and sexually desirable as they age tend to produce an ever-shrinking pool of younger candidates as sex partners for older persons, irrespective of their sexual preference. Lack of a social and/or physical environment conducive for sex also affects both sexual partnering and self-pleasuring opportunities. For example, older persons who live with their offspring or others may lack the private space needed for intimate behavior. For those living in a nursing home, staff attitudes and organizational policies often reflect negative judgments that hinder the expression of sexuality among residents.

Fifth, despite its potential for offering continued enjoyment, considerable evidence indicates that sexual behavior of all types occurs less frequently and differs physiologically with age from that of adolescence and earlier adulthood (Zeiss & Kasl-Godley 2001). Among peri- and post-menopausal women, natural changes due to aging commonly include general atrophying and loss in elasticity of vaginal tissue, decreases in rate and amount of vaginal lubrication, lesser labial and clitoral engorgement during sexual arousal, decrease in estrogen levels with a corresponding shrinkage in the size of the cervix, uterus, and ovaries, and more dependence on androgens for sexual response. Common changes among aging men include a slower rate of sexual arousal, the need for greater genital stimulation to reach full erection, less firm tumescence, lengthening of the refractory period prior to a new erection, and less semen and urgency in ejaculation due to loss of prostate elasticity. None of these biological changes, however, necessarily reduces sexual enjoyment for either sex (Lauman et al. 2005). Challenges and barriers to sexual fulfillment in later life are far more likely to be linked to the person's earlier sexual history, general health, the possible effects of medication that reduce desire or inhibit sexual function, and psychosocial factors that support or discourage sexual thoughts and actions.

NEW OPPORTUNITIES AND PERILS FOR SEX IN LATER LIFE

The development and popularization within the last decade of the chemical compound known as "Viagra" (sildenafil) may well mark the start of a sexual revolution, rivaling that of the contraceptive "pill" of the 1960s, with enormous opportunities and consequences for late-life sex (Loe 2004). With public figures appearing in the mass media extolling the benefits of the drug in treating male erectile dysfunction, sex among older adults has become more publicly visible and possibly better accepted by Americans of all ages. Both older women and men have become the focus of scientific, marketing, and media attempts to gauge how they view, use, and physiologically respond to its effects. Such scrutiny clearly documents Viagra's pharmacological success in treating erectile dysfunction, allowing an unknown number of men who otherwise experience difficulties to attain and maintain a penile erection sufficient for satisfactory sexual performance.

This biological achievement is not without social consequences. To assure maximal effects, sexual performance achieved through pharmaceutics also requires advanced decision-making and precalculations in timing that militate against sexual spontaneity. The use of Viagra and similar compounds (verdenafil, tadalafil) also has generated a plethora of comic monologues and media humor featuring the sex lives of older persons as the butt of the joke. Also, not all sexual partners of men experiencing renewed sexual capacity report welcoming this change. An unknown number of women and possibly men who are the sexual partners of aging males appear satisfied with or prefer reduced sexual activity as they or their partners age. In addition, the use and abuse of sexually enhancing pharmaceutics has crossed generational borders as an increasing number of younger men avail themselves of their effects to facilitate or prolong sexual intercourse or to enhance orgasms. The promise of "better sex through chemistry," using pharmaceutical enhancements obtained through medical prescription, the Internet, or illicit sources, has called into question previous assumptions about what is sexually "normal" at any age.

While Viagra, Cialis, and other similar substances have enhanced or restored the sexual lives of many aging males, older women have had less pharmaceutical success in treating age-related female sexual dysfunction. Clinicians commonly use variations of the term "hypoactive sexual desire disorder" to define persistent reduction or loss of sexual fantasies, a condition often associated with lower hormonal levels of androgens and estrogen with age. In addition to affecting libido, estrogen decline can reduce vaginal lubrication during sexual arousal and result in painful intercourse when vaginal walls become excessively thin. Hormone replacement therapy (HRT), even when begun after age 60, can retard or reverse such vaginal changes to some extent, but not without health risk. While testosterone replacement can increase libido in aging women, little is known of proper dosage and potential adverse side effects include masculinization with acne and excess body hair, scalp hair loss, deepening of the voice, and enlargement of the clitoris. Meanwhile, the search for a female Viagra has proved elusive despite considerable efforts by pharmaceutical companies to develop and test a range of clitoral therapy devices, vasoactive agents, and steroids. Their quest has added fuel to feminist and others' concerns that the framing of women's sexuality has become medicalized to the exclusion of other key social and cognitive factors (Kaschak & Tiefer 2001).

The Internet has emerged over the last two decades as a second technological innovation with enormous potential for transforming the sex lives of many older adults. As with their younger counterparts, an increasing number of individuals over age 50 seek friendship, romance, and opportunities for sexual interaction through websites and personal advertisements posted on the Internet (Adams et al. 2003). A global network of users offers opportunities for courtship and sexual partnering that transcend local geographical boundaries and the limits of personal social networks. Unlike face-to-face introductions, older adults can initiate online relationships without age-related physical declines being immediately apparent. Meanwhile, the Internet also supplies older adults with ready access to erotica, pornography, and online purchases of sex toys and adult-rated books without having to risk potentially embarrassing live encounters with sales clerks and other customers.

Increase in dating opportunities among older adults is not without worries. Although considered clinically safe for older males when used under physician supervision, some men experience undesirable side effects with Viagra or Cialis that force a choice between safeguarding health or enjoying better sex. Similarly, while HRT can ease menopausal changes that can inhibit sexual drive and activity among older women, increasing evidence suggests that its use heightens women's risk for breast and endometrial cancer. Meanwhile, as is true of all adults, people over age 50 who engage in sexual behavior outside of a monogamous relationship increasingly confront the dangers of acquiring sexually transmitted diseases including HIV/AIDS. CDC statistics reported by Karin Mack and Marcia Ory in a special issue of *JAIDS* devoted to AIDS and aging reveal that adults over age 50 account for about 10 percent of newly diagnosed cases of AIDS annually in the US. Over the next decade, the number of older persons living with HIV/AIDS is expected to rise substantially as treatment success of highly active antiretroviral therapy (HAART) prolongs the lives of people of all ages living with HIV. Increased prevalence of the virus among people over age 50 undoubtedly in some way will affect how this population views the use of condoms, sexual partnering, and sexual behavior in general.

SEE ALSO: Aging, Sociology of; Body and Sexuality; Cybersexualities and Virtual Sexuality; Sexual Health; Sexuality; Viagra; Women, Sexuality and

REFERENCES AND SUGGESTED READINGS

Adams, M. S., Oye, J., & Parker, T. S. (2003) Sexuality of Older Adults and the Internet: From Sex Education to Cyberspace. *Social and Relationship Therapy* 18(3): 405–15.

Deacon, S., Minichiello, V., & Plummer, D. (1995) Sexuality and Older People: Revisiting the Assumptions. *Educational Gerontology* 21: 497–513.

Hartmann, U., Philippsohn, S., Heiser, K., & Rüffer-Hesse, C. (2004) Low Sexual Desire in Midlife and Older Women: Personality Factors, Psychosocial Development, Present Sexuality. *Menopause* 11, 6 (Suppl.): 726–40.

Kaschak, E. & Tiefer, L. (Eds.) (2001) *Looking Beyond Viagra for a New View of Women's Sexual Problems*. Hawthorne Press, New York.

Lauman, E., Nicolosi, A., Glasser, D. B., Paik, A., Gingell, C., Moreira, E., & Wang, T. (2005) Sexual Problems Among Women and Men Aged 40–80 Years: Prevalence and Correlates Identified in the Global Study of Sexual Attitudes and Behaviors. *International Journal of Impotence Research* 17(10): 39–57.

Loe, M. (2004) *The Rise of Viagra: How the Little Blue Pill Changed Sex in America*. University of New York Press, New York.

Walsh, K. E. & Berman, J. R. (2004) Sexual Dysfunction in the Older Woman: An Overview of the Current Understandings and Management. *Drugs Aging* 21(10): 655–75.

Zeiss, A. M. & Kasl-Godley, J. (2001) Sexuality in Older Adults' Relationships. *Generations* 25(2): 19–35.

latent growth curve models

Oliver Christ and Elmar Schlueter

Longitudinal methods permit the systematic study of stability and change over time and thus are a powerful tool for examining processes underlying social phenomena and the causal relation between different constructs. There are many different statistical methods to analyze longitudinal data (for an overview, see Crowder & Hand 1996; Menard 2002). Most of these techniques are related to applications of the general linear model to continuously distributed repeated measures (e.g., repeated *t* tests, ANOVA, multiple regressions, autoregressive models). A major shortcoming of these methods is that they are fixed-effects models assuming that there are no interindividual differences in change. One prominent and powerful method to overcome this shortcoming are latent growth curve models (LGMs; synonymous terms used in literature are "latent curve models" or "latent trajectory models") as one variant of structural equation modeling (Bollen & Curran 2006). With LGM it is possible to analyze individual trajectories and related processes of change over time. Meredith and Tisak (1990) first proposed LGM based on the seminal work of Tucker and Rao in 1958. LGMs are based on the assumption that a set of observed repeated measures taken on a given individual over time can be used to estimate an unobserved underlying trajectory. This assumption can be formally expressed as

$$y_{it} = \alpha_i + \lambda_{i2}\beta_i + \varepsilon_{it}.$$

y_{it} are the measured variables of time t which are explained by two latent factors (α_i and β_i) in the measurement model. α_i models the initial level in the measured variable (intercept factor), whereas β_i expresses the linear growth rate (slope factor). ε_{it} is the random error. The subscript i indicates that both the latent intercept and the latent slope factor are allowed to vary across individuals. These individual intercept and slope components of growth can be expressed by the following function specifying group and individual influences:

$$\alpha_i = \mu_\alpha + \zeta_{\alpha i}.$$

$$\beta_i = \mu_\beta + \zeta_{\beta i}.$$

Both latent factors, α_i and β_i, are defined by their means (μ_α and μ_β) and their residuals ($\zeta_{\alpha i}$ and $\zeta_{\beta i}$) in the structural equations. Since there are no exogenous variables specified, $\zeta_{\alpha i}$ and $\zeta_{\beta i}$ can be interpreted as the deviations from the group mean of the intercept and the slope

factor. A prerequisite of LGM is that the measurement model is constant over time, otherwise growth cannot be meaningfully modeled by LGM.

In Figure 1 a simple unconditional LGM is presented with three repeated measures assessed at equal intervals. "Unconditional" means that both latent factors are not affected by other variables (see below). Factor loadings on the intercept factor are set to 1 and the three factor loadings on the slope factor equal $\lambda_t = t - 1$, where t is 1, 2, 3. Thereby, the slope factor is constrained to a linear growth. In this example, the intercept reflects the model-implied value of the outcome measure at the initial period of measurement because factor loading on the slope factor for the first measure was set to zero and factor loadings on the intercept factor are constrained to one. It is also possible to use alternative codings of time to define other meanings of the intercept term. In the case of an unconditional LGM with three measures, eight parameters have to be estimated from the data. The model is just over-identified ($df = 1$), since the empirical covariance matrix has six and the mean vector has three elements.

In LGM, besides linear growth, nonlinear trajectories can also be modeled. In linear LGM, change over time is constant over all points in time. That means a one-unit change in time is associated with a μ_β-unit change in the outcome. This relation is constant for all equally spaced assessments, but can vary in the

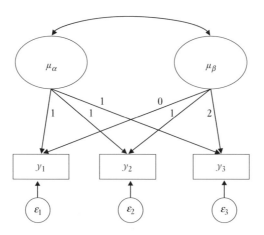

Figure 1   Unconditional linear latent growth curve model for three repeated measures.

nonlinear case. In some cases it is theoretically plausible to assume nonlinear growth instead of linear changes. One possibility to test such relations is to use a quadratic function. Whereas the linear LGM has only one intercept and one slope factor, the quadratic LGM includes a third latent factor to capture any curvature that might be present in the individual trajectories. The quadratic model implies differential change in the measured variable between equally spaced time assessments. For example, change in a construct can be large at the beginning, but constantly becomes smaller in the further course of time. Alternatives to quadratic trajectories are exponential trajectories which are not time bound and as such are often more plausible for describing change in constructs. Du Toit and Cudeck developed techniques to implement exponential functions into the LGM framework. All trajectories, presented so far define a specific growth function that relates the repeated measures to the passage of time. Sometimes such assumptions are too restrictive and do not cover the pattern of change in an optimal way. An alternative is the free estimation of a part of the factor loadings of the repeated measures on the slope factor (Meredith & Tisak 1990). For example, in the case of three repeated measures, the loading of the last measure on the slope factor can be freely estimated to get a better adjustment of the trajectory on the observed data.

Besides the question of the functional form of the trajectory, it is often of interest to identify variables which affect the development of constructs. The LGM can be easily extended by including exogenous predictor variables (Willett & Sayer 1994). In these models it is examined in such a way that the intercept and the slope of a repeated measure are affected by time-invariant predictors.

A further extension of the LGM is the inclusion of time-variant repeated measures. Such multivariate LGMs take into account the change of several repeated measures simultaneously. Besides the consideration of several time-variant repeated measures it is also of interest to consider time-specific relations of the repeated measures within or between constructs. The autoregressive latent trajectory model (ALT) developed by Bollen and Curran (2004) connects LGM with autoregressive

models and allows, in addition to the analysis of random trajectories, the examination of autoregressive relations within constructs, as well as cross-lagged relations between constructs.

Further possibilities to extend LGM include the examination of moderational and mediational hypotheses, as well as the use of multiple indicator latent factors. Mediation is indicated when the effect of a predictor on the intercept or slope of a time-variant repeated measure is explained by a further time-invariant predictor. In the case of two time-invariant predictors as described before, normal methods to test mediation can be used. If predictors and mediators are also time variant, mediational analysis is much more complex (see Bollen & Curran 2006). In many cases it is of interest to proof moderating effects of variables in the change of a construct. There are two general types of analysis techniques to examine such moderational effects. In one case, the interaction term of two exogenous predictors can be included in an LGM analysis. A moderational effect is indicated by a significant effect of the interaction term on the two latent growth factors. Alternatively, multigroup analysis can be used to test for moderation. Here, specific parameters can be compared between two or more subgroups of a sample. Significant differences in parameters of the LGM indicate moderational effects of the moderating variable which was chosen to divide the sample into subgroups (e.g., age, sex). By using multiple indicator latent factors it is possible to control for measurement error. In the case of LGMs with multiple indicator latent factors, the growth in the latent factors is estimated, not in the measured variables.

As with all applications of structural equation modeling, LGM allows us to analyze missing data using powerful methods to impute missing data like multiple imputation or full information maximum likelihood (FIML). In addition, it is also possible to calculate LGM even when the normal distribution assumption is violated, which is often the case in social science (Bollen & Curran 2006).

Figure 2 illustrates a conditional growth curve model for anomia – defined as a state of mind expressed by individuals living under societal conditions of anomie – over a three-year period ($N = 825$) based on data from an

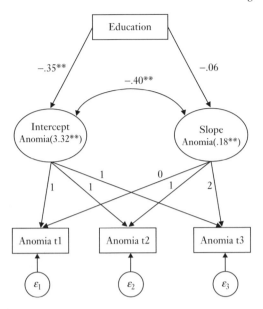

Figure 2 Conditional latent growth curve model for anomia over a three-year period with education as an exogenous predictor variable.
Notes: Anomia t1 = Anomia at wave 1; Anomia t2 = anomia at wave 2; Anomia t3 = Anomia at wave 3; ** p < .001.

ongoing panel survey of the German general population. In this example, education is used as a time-invariant predictor variable.

For the latent intercept indicating respondents' initial level of anomia, a significant mean value of 3.23 ($p < .001$) is estimated. The significant variance of the mean value equals .56 ($p < .001$), suggesting that there is substantial variability in respondents' average levels of anomia at time one.

For the latent slope, the data reveal a significant mean value of = .18 ($p < .001$). According to this finding, respondents' level of anomia increases on average .18 units for every measurement one year apart. Further, the data reveal a significant parameter estimate for the variance of the latent slope (.09, $p < .001$). Therefore, it can be concluded that there is considerable variability in the respondents' latent trajectories for anomia over the period under study.

The significant negative correlation of $r = -.40$ ($p < .001$) between the latent intercept and slope factors indicates that the higher respondents' initial level of anomia, the lower the change over time.

Next, we examine possible effects of education on the latent intercept and latent slope of anomia. For the latent intercept, the significant parameter estimate of education is $\beta = -.35$ ($p < .001$). Substantially, this suggests that individuals with higher education show significantly lower initial levels of anomia. However, according to the results, education exerts no significant effect on the latent slope of anomia ($\beta = -.06$, ns). That means change in anomia is independent from respondents' level of education.

LGM is a powerful method for longitudinal analyses. It allows social science researchers to examine many different theoretical questions of change. LGMs can easily be extended by using multiple indicator latent factors to model measurement error, integrating predictors of change as well as mediators and testing moderating influences of measures. But there are of course a number of limitations of latent growth curve modeling. A minimum of three repeated measures is needed. Still problematic is the handling of missing data and deviations from normal distributions, although there are powerful techniques to take these problems into account, such as FIML in the case of missing data and robust maximum likelihood in the case of deviances from normal distribution (for more details, see Bollen & Curran 2006). But the most critical factor for LGM and all other statistical methods is the underlying theory which guides the statistical analyses.

SEE ALSO: Aging, Longitudinal Studies; Correlation; Hierarchical Linear Models; Quantitative Methods; Structural Equation Modeling

REFERENCES AND SUGGESTED READINGS

Bollen, K. A. & Curran, P. J. (2004) Autoregressive Latent Trajectory (ALT) Models: A Synthesis of Two Traditions. *Sociological Methods and Research* 32: 336–83.

Bollen, K .A. & Curran, P. J. (2006) *Latent Curve Models: A Structural Equation Approach*. Wiley, New York.

Crowder, D. & Hand, M. (1996) *Practical Longitudinal Data Analysis*. Chapman & Hall, London.

Duncan, T. E., Duncan, S. C., Strycker, L. A., Li, F., & Alpert, A. (1999) *An Introduction to Latent Variable Growth Curve Modeling: Concepts, Issues, And Applications*. Erlbaum, Mahwah, NJ.

Menard, S. (2002) *Longitudinal Research*, 2nd edn. Sage, Newbury Park, CA.

Meredith, W. & Tisak, J. (1990) Latent Curve Analysis. *Psychometrika* 55: 107–22.

Willett, J. B. & Sayer, A. G. (1994) Using Covariance Structure Analysis to Detect Correlates and Predictors of Individual Change Over Time. *Psychological Bulletin* 116: 363–81.

later-life marriage

Liat Kulik

With the aging of the population and increased life expectancy in western societies, there has been growing research interest in the period of late adulthood, which can span several decades. That life stage is characterized by three major events that can affect the individual as well as the marital unit: decline in health, retirement

from work, and entry into the role of grandparent or sometimes even great-grandparent. The following main aspects of the dyadic unit are emphasized here in light of their relevance to late adulthood: caregiving, satisfaction with marriage and quality of marital life, power relations, and the division of household tasks.

CAREGIVING

In late adulthood, caregiving involves a considerable investment of time and energy by spouses, who are usually the main caregivers. Some couples report that the caregiving role increases their sense of commitment, closeness, and love. Husbands usually approach caregiving as a project and are comfortable delegating tasks, whereas caregiving wives usually give more direct assistance in the form of ADLs (activities of daily living) and IADLs (instrumental activities of daily living) (Miller 1990). Caregiving wives usually look for activities that will involve their spouses, and are concerned with providing for their spouses' needs, whereas caregiving husbands usually prefer to do things on their own. In addition, wives are more negatively affected than their husbands by caregiving. For example, Miller (1990) found that caregiving wives have less access to social support, although they do not differ from their husbands with regard to emotional strain. Other researchers indicate that caregiving wives feel burnout, because the responsibilities of providing care may cause them to feel trapped at a time when they should be free. By contrast, caregiving husbands may feel less burnout because they are more likely to supplement the care for their wives with formal services. It has also been argued that husbands are better able than wives to cope with problems in the marital relationship and maintain an emotional distance (for a review, see Walker 1999).

SATISFACTION WITH MARRIAGE AND QUALITY OF MARITAL LIFE

In general, researchers have found that most older people report happy marriages, and attribute this perception to the selective examination of couples whose marriage did not end in divorce (for a review, see Huyck 1995).

Cross-sectional studies of older people have revealed that, compared with younger populations, older couples report fewer marital problems, although there is a decline in positive interaction compared with earlier stages of marriage. As for gender differences, husbands typically report higher marital satisfaction than do wives (Walker 1999). In this connection, qualitative studies suggest that husbands tend to idealize the situation and deny existing tensions, whereas wives tend to recognize problems and initiate changes as the children start leaving home. Wives who have been married for 20 years indicate that resolving disagreements becomes more difficult (Vaillant & Vaillant 1993), and tend to report lower marital adjustment over time, whereas husbands tend to report a greater decline in sexual satisfaction. Among elderly couples, wives are more likely to consider separating than husbands. Elderly wives are also less likely than their husbands to name their spouse as their main confidant, although both elderly partners consider their spouse as a companion. Kulik (2001) found fluctuations in marital satisfaction at different stages of the retirement process. In the remote pre-retirement stage (about seven years before retirement), couples express more emotions (tension and marital enjoyment) than in the near pre-retirement and post-retirement stages. Kulik also found that levels of burnout, i.e., feeling tired of the marriage or feeling trapped in late adulthood, are much lower than in earlier stages of marriage, and that when marital relations are egalitarian, both spouses feel less burnout in marital life.

POWER RELATIONS

Few studies have focused on marital power relations, and even fewer have dealt with the topic in late adulthood. In their well-known study *Husbands and Wives* (1960), Blood and Wolfe found that a husband's power increases from the time the first child is born until the youngest child enters school. Afterwards there is a steady decline in the husband's power, which reaches a particularly low point when the oldest child leaves home. The husband's power continues to decline after retirement, when he loses some of the resources that he had while he was working.

Recently, Kulik found that throughout the retirement process (remote pre-retirement, near pre-retirement, and after retirement), men show a greater tendency than women to report an advantage in the areas of major decisions (e.g., budget). With respect to domestic power (decisions about household matters), women have reported an advantage, although no gender-based differences were found regarding decisions about such issues as time use. Moreover, attempts have been made to analyze power relations in late adulthood as a function of occupational status and timing of retirement among couples. For example, a comparative study of synchronous couples (both spouses retired or employed) and asynchronous couples (one spouse retired and the other employed) revealed that all types of couples tend to have relatively egalitarian power relations, as expressed in decision-making in all areas of life (Kulik 2001).

DIVISION OF HOUSEHOLD TASKS

According to family development perspectives, role differentiation declines in the late stage of family life, when work obligations and the demands of childrearing diminish. However, findings are inconclusive and inconsistent. Some studies have found that after retirement most couples continue the traditional patterns, which are characterized by a clear differentiation between gender roles. According to this perspective, men continue to perform typically masculine tasks such as household repairs and gardening, and even increase their involvement in those activities (Vinick & Ekerdt 1991), whereas women maintain traditional feminine roles such as cooking, cleaning, and laundry. In a similar vein, researchers have found that retired men with employed wives do not seek to increase their involvement in household tasks, and that certain women even increase their involvement in household tasks after retirement (Szinovacz & Harpster 1994). In contrast to these findings, which indicate that traditional gender roles persist after retirement, other studies have revealed that gender role differences diminish (for a review, see Atchley 1992). Additionally, some studies have found that the husband's participation in typically feminine household tasks increases after retirement. Kulik

(2001) found that the division of feminine tasks such as cooking, cleaning, and ironing, as well as general tasks such as paying bills and purchasing household commodities, is usually more egalitarian among synchronous retired couples than among synchronous pre-retired couples. The division of feminine tasks was relatively egalitarian among asynchronous couples (retired husbands/employed wives). However, no differences were found between different types of couples with respect to masculine tasks such as household repairs, which are almost always carried out by men.

As for future research, with the increase in life expectancy in western societies and the growing population of elderly couples over the age of 80, it would be worthwhile to focus studies on that age group. Additionally, because most studies on later-life marriage are cross-sectional, longitudinal studies that follow the development of marital relations in late adulthood among the same group of couples would be very useful.

SEE ALSO: Divisions of Household Labor; Emotion Work; Gender, Aging and; Inequalities in Marriage; Marital Power/Resource Theory; Marital Quality; Marriage; Retirement

REFERENCES AND SUGGESTED READINGS

Atchley, R. C. (1992) Retirement and Marital Satisfaction. In: Szinovacz, M., Ekerdt, D. J., & Vinick, B. H. (Eds.), *Families and Retirement.* Sage, Newbury Park, CA, pp. 145–58.

Huyck, M. H. (1995) Marriage and Close Relationships of the Marital Kind. In: Blieszner, R. & Hilkevitch, V. (Eds.), *Handbook of Aging and the Family.* Greenwood Press, Westport, CT, pp. 181–200.

Kolsberg, J. I., Cairl, R. E., & Keller, D. M. (1990) Components of Burden: Interventive Implications. *Gerontologist* 30: 236–42.

Kulik, L. (2001) Marital Relationships in Late Adulthood: Synchronous versus Asynchronous Couples. *International Journal of Aging and Human Development* 52: 323–9.

Miller, B. (1990) Gender Differences in Spouse Caregiving Strain: Socialization and Role Expectations. *Journal of Marriage and the Family* 52: 311–21.

Szinovacz, M. & Harpster, P. (1994) Couples: Employment/Retirement Status and the Division of Household Tasks. *Gerontology: Social Sciences* 49: S125–S136.

Vaillant, C. O. & Vaillant, G. E. (1993) Is the U-Curve of Marital Satisfaction an Illusion? A 40-year Study of Marriage. *Journal of Marriage and the Family* 55: 230–9.

Vinick, B. H. & Ekerdt, D. J. (1991) The Transition to Retirement: Responses of Husbands and Wives. In: Hess, B. B. & Markson, E. (Eds.), *Growing Old in America*, 4th edn. Transaction, New Brunswick, NJ, pp. 305–17.

Walker, A. J. (1999) Gender and Family Relationships. In: Sussman, M. B., Steinmetz, S. K., & Peterson, G. W. (Eds.), *Handbook of Marriage and the Family*, 2nd edn. Plenum, New York, pp. 439–74.

Latinidad and consumer culture

Lisa Peñaloza

Latinidad, most literally, is the identity of Latinos/as. More figuratively, it is a sensibility and way of being-in-the-world that expresses who one is and what one's culture is about. This quality emanates from a community of very diverse people and is used by them to relate to one another, drawing from their similarities, even as they contest it based on their differences. Born at the multiple intersections of Native American peoples, Europeans, and blacks, it connotes an amalgam of ritual traditions and values – *amor, familia, respeto, compromisos, pasion*; that is, love, family, respect, accomplishment, and a passion for living – at once very real, yet imagined, dynamic and organic. The geographical coordinates of its diaspora are no less complex, in pertaining to those of Latin American ancestry in the US and in Central and South American nations, the Caribbean, Spain, and, to a lesser degree, southern Italy and France. Like other social phenomena, it is individually and collectively engineered and reproduced; internally by Latinos/as, and externally, as attributed to us by non-Latinos/as. When linked to consumer culture, the body of work has sparse but long roots, and has gained in abundance and currency with the rapid growth of the people.

Terminology continues to be a challenge, for Latinos/as in identifying ourselves and distinguishing among our various subgroups, and for non-Latinos/as in referring to us. Issues of race, geography, nationality, social class, generation, politicization, language, and colloquial usage context complicate its meaning and use, as does variation in the strength of affiliation of members to the group as a whole and to the various subgroups, and dramatic sociodemographic shifts, particularly geographical mobility and the increased incidence of mixed ethnic background. A major distinction lies between those from the US, where Latinos/as are a minority, and those from the many other nations where Latinos/as constitute the mainstream. In the US, subgroups of different historical trajectories and sociocultural characteristics impact Latinidad. Here, traces of regional concentrations remain such that Mexicans and Mexican Americans live predominantly in the US Southwest; Cubans and Cuban Americans in Florida; and Puerto Ricans in New York. However, the cultural character of each of the regions has changed dramatically since the 1980s due to interstate migration and immigration from other Central and South American countries and the Caribbean.

As with other groups of people and fields of ideas examined within the sociology of science, studies of Latinidad and consumer culture have changed as each generation of scholars grapples with the issues of its time. Socially, gains made by Latinos/as in the US in the 1970s and 1980s in political representation, legislation for equal rights, census inclusion, and more accurate counting were followed by affirmative action programs in government and in business, academic studies programs in universities, and attention as a consumer market through the early 1990s to the present. Buoyed by increased numbers and buying power, Latinos/as in the US have come to enjoy a much heralded popularity in media representation, political canvassing, job recruitment, and market targeting. Yet while those comprising the middle class experienced dramatic gains in income in the 1990s, the majority continues to lag socioeconomically, with overall indicators remaining well below

those of their white counterparts. In contrast, the social context of Latinidad in Latin American and Caribbean nations is marked by the challenges of socioeconomic development, postcolonial relations, alliances with other Latin American and Caribbean nations and nations in Europe and Asia, internal political differences, and the struggles of indigenous peoples.

Academic studies in the US have come a long way since the early demands for Chicano and Puerto Rican studies programs in universities as part of El Movimiento, the Civil Rights Movements in the 1960s and 1970s. Early work such as Ernesto Galarza's *Merchants of Labor* (1964) and Rodolfo Acuña's *Occupied America* (1988) display a mix of academic and social activist research, as scholars worked to educate and remedy the violence, exclusions, and discrimination of postcolonization. The early, androcentric work of Latino scholars was soon joined by their Latina counterparts, as exemplified by Gloria Anzaldúa and Cherríe Moraga's classic edited volume, *This Bridge Called My Back: Writings by Radical Women of Color* (1981). This book, and many that would follow (e.g., Carla Trujillo's *Living Chicana Theory*, 1998; Richard Delgado and Jean Stefanic's *Critical White Studies*, 1997), are not pegged to Latinos/as alone, and have stimulated and challenged Latino/a and non-Latino/a scholars alike to incorporate and attempt to better understand the simultaneous social impacts of ethnicity, race, gender, sexuality, class, and the market on social phenomena, and the differential effects experienced by various subgroups.

A mix of activism, literature, and research characterizes the history of Latino/a consumer culture. Activists have operated on the terrain of consumer culture in the US for decades; an early example is their challenge to the racial stereotyping of the cartoon character, the Frito Bandito, in Frito Lay advertisements in the 1960s. They protested against the marketing of cigarettes and alcohol in Latino/a neighborhoods in the 1980s. Priests called for spending curbs on lavish *quinciañera* celebrations (young 15-year-old women's coming-of-age parties), and actors and community activists fought for more Latino/a roles and more Latinos/as playing Latino/a characters in film and on TV through the 1990s. More recently, Internet blogs were used successfully to stop offensive insinuations of Latina sexuality in Tecate Beer promotions in 2004. In Latin America, consumer culture peppers the literature, from indictments of US imperialism and multinational capitalism in the poems of José Marti and Pablo Neruda; the pedagogical essays of Ariel Dorfman articulating a critical approach to such pop cultural characters as Donald Duck and Babar the elephant; to the intricate literary and political analyses of Carlos Fuentes.

Academically, theoretical and empirical studies of Latino/a consumer culture have flourished since the 1980s on such topics as postcolonial identity and cultural adaptation, physical and mental health care, community development, media representations and ownership, and globalization. Critical literary studies are arguably the most prevalent, with early scholars such as Américo Paredes, Ana Castillo, and Rina Benmayor, joined more recently by Norma Alarcón and Ramon Saldívar in directing attention to the contributions of Latino/a authors, poets, and musicians, both historical and contemporary, and challenging theoretical conventions by which such work is evaluated.

Dimensions of Latinidad and consumer culture reflect the multiple disciplines comprising its study and the diversity of the people. Geographical considerations, national and subcultural background, language, socioeconomic class, political orientation, generation, disciplinary structure, and theoretical perspective are discernable across a wide array of topics. Areas of study include border studies, colonialization and postcolonialism, labor organization and exploitation, immigration patterns, family life and socialization, language acquisition, bilingual education, and political representation. The work has changed dramatically over time, even as it is marked by continuities. Initially oriented by the cultural background and disciplinary training of its major scholars, the body of work has expanded toward the full realm of the social sciences and humanities. Scholars such as David Montejano, Henry Triandis, Amado Padilla, Rodney Hero, José Limón, Fernando Peñalosa, Alfredo Mirandé, Vickie Ruiz, Enrique Trueba, Doug Foley, Elizabeth Fox, Anghy Valdivia, and Lisa Peñaloza, to name a few, have focused on replacing pejorative accounts of Latinos/as based on naïve comparisons with the Anglo mainstream,

in books and the journals of their disciplines – history, psychology, political science, anthropology, sociology, education, communication, and marketing. Economics is the most recent addition to the fold. Works by George Borges and Marta Tienda, Silvia Pedraza-Baily, and Bárbara Robles investigate cultural patterns affecting community economic development in the US, while Hernando De Soto examines such issues in Latin America.

Current emphases of this body of work stem from the many paradoxes and contradictions of consumer culture, together with unique qualities related to particular mainstream/margin cultural dynamics. First, agency in reproducing one's identity and one's culture is a key concern. It is important to consider the power dynamics in who is consuming whose culture, as signs and values drawn from the ritual holidays and everyday life of Latinos/as are packed into consumer objects and activities associated with Latino/a culture for consumption by Latinos/as and non-Latinos/as. The general availability and widespread use of the piñata for children's birthday parties is one example. Consumer culture is empowering, in that Latinos/as support a big part of their consumer culture in buying the accouterments, products, and services they employ in being Latino/a. However, in a key displacement of power, a formative influence stems from the ways Latino/a consumer culture is subject to the whims of non-Latino/a consumers in cultural crossovers and tourism.

Second is the paradox of market legitimization. That is, being a market brings a type of social legitimacy, yet it is not without its limitations. Simply put, it is easier to be Latino/a now than ever before. Yet this legitimacy comes at a price, for not all aspects and dimensions of this diverse identity and culture are recognized, reproduced, and thus valued in the market. This is a major concern among Latinos/as and community organizations, for it requires much work to redirect attention to qualities more vital to the community, but much less marketable. In a second key displacement of power, marketers play an important role in reproducing Latino/a culture in the marketplace, for consumption by Latinos/as and non-Latinos/as. What often follows is that the most different and threatening among Latino/a elements are elevated in cultural stereotypes, even as marketers emphasize the most assimilated and the less threatening qualities in their efforts to target Latinos/as.

Third, in addition to examining non-Latino/a–Latino/a dynamics, it is crucial to examine relations of power among Latinos/as. That is, an important part of the development of Latino/a consumer culture occurs as cultural members with knowledge of Latino/a culture educate Latino/a- and non-Latino/a-owned consumer products companies, as Dávila notes in *Latinos, Inc.* (2001). Of importance here is examining the ways Latinos/as work to reproduce Latino/a identity in such consumer cultural institutions as the media and advertising (Peñaloza, *Media Studies Journal*, 1995).

In short, basic to Latinidad and consumer culture is a conflation of region, nationality, class, and political leanings that are not easily sorted out, and from which stem important methodological implications. A key concern in this body of work is incorporating fundamental precepts of social justice into our disciplines, as Sandoval, San Juan, Jr., and Pérez encourage, in examining the ways such ideals as democratic representation, opportunity, and community development are compromised in capitalist socioeconomic systems in the US and Latin American nations. These works employ self-reflexivity and social engagement, while attending to a diversity of positions and perspectives. As such, additional challenges relate to the complexities of agency and subjectivity, for both researchers and those whom they study. Identity dynamics remain a challenge in attending to relations of power between many levels of mainstream and marginal subgroups, while retaining a critical perspective in attending to the full range of their intragroup impacts. Other methodological challenges relate to scope and scale, as important inroads are being made in attending to the dynamics of globalization, while not losing sight of the contours of localized struggles.

Regarding future directions in research and scholarship, while the work is likely to continue to examine persistent traditions and change in the competing pulls of family, culture, and society, it shows tendencies of moving beyond who we are as a people and how we are represented in the market, toward exploring fundamental contradictions between democracy and capitalism. Important inroads are to be made in linking across the various groups in the US and in other nations, and not getting derailed by the many differences, while acknowledging their substance and significance. Further advances are to be made by globalizing our studies, and comparing the experiences of Latinos/as in the US to those in Latin America and other nations of the Latino/a diaspora. Ultimately, much work is to be done to better understand dimensions of race, class, and gender as they impact cultural inclusion and exclusion, of identity and community development, and institutional and government treatment as played out in the terrain of consumer culture.

SEE ALSO: Capitalism; Community and Economy; Consumption, Mass Consumption, and Consumer Culture; Culture; Globalization, Consumption and

REFERENCES AND SUGGESTED READINGS

De Soto, H. (2000) *The Mystery of Capital: Why Capitalism Triumphs in the West and Fails Everywhere Else.* Basic Books, New York.

Dorfman, A. (1983) *The Empire's Old Clothes: What the Lone Ranger, Babar, and Other Innocent Heroes Do to Our Minds.* Pantheon, New York.

Hero, R. (1992) *Latinos and the US Political System: Two-Tiered Pluralism.* Temple University Press, Philadelphia.

Peñaloza, L. (1994) Atravesando Fronteras/Border Crossings: A Critical Ethnographic Exploration of the Consumer Acculturation of Mexican Immigrants. *Journal of Consumer Research* 21, 1 (June): 32–54.

Peñaloza, L. (1995) Immigrant Consumers: Marketing and Public Policy Implications. *Journal of Public Policy and Marketing* 14, 1 (Spring): 83–94.

Peñaloza, L. (2004) *Generaciones/Generations: Cultural Identity, Memory, and the Market.* Documentary film.

Peñaloza, L. & Gilly, M. (1999) Marketers' Acculturation: The Changer and the Changed. *Journal of Marketing* 63, 3 (July): 84–104.

Rodriguez, C. E. (Ed.) (1998) *Latin Looks: Images of Latinas and Latinos in the US Media.* Westview, Boulder, CO.

San Juan, Jr., E. (2002) *Racism and Cultural Studies: Critiques of Multiculturalist Ideology and the Politics of Difference.* Duke University Press, Durham, NC.

Sandoval, C. (2000) *Methodology of the Oppressed*. University of California Press, Berkeley.

Trueba, E. T. (1999) *Latinos Unidos: From Cultural Diversity to the Politics of Solidarity*. Rowman & Littlefield, Lanham, MD.

law, civil

Stephen E. Brown

Civil law entails two distinct categories of meaning. It is used to reference Romano-Germanic law, one of four broad forms of legal systems that presently are most practiced throughout the world. In this context, civil law is best understood in juxtaposition to common (Anglo-Saxon), religious (e.g., Islamic), and socialist law. Civil law systems are most widespread in the world. Their most central feature is the codification of law, an approach historically linked to the Justinian Code of ancient Rome, and that became characteristic of continental Europe.

The second fundamental connotation of civil law relates to the division of some legal systems into segments that address what are construed as distinct types or categories of legal problems. Such division is not universal, but reflects a larger philosophy of law, the authority underlying it, and the goals of social control. Islamic law, for example, does not distinguish civil matters from criminal. Instead, all behaviors are morally assessed from the framework of the Koran and the *Sharia*, identifying the word of God regarding how humans are to behave. Under this system the view is that law comes from God and cannot be compromised. Both Romano-Germanic and common law traditions, however, view the state as having a vested interest in and authority over public issues such as crimes (which are offenses against the state or community at large), but not in regard to private disputes. The latter fall in the realm of civil law. In this vein, then, civil law refers to the segment of legal systems that addresses grievances between individual citizens, as opposed to conflicts that are theoretically between the state and individual citizens.

All law serves as a form of social control in the sense that it manages social conflict. All forms of law are also shaped by social forces. These points probably are most widely appreciated in the context of criminal law, but apply equally to civil law. Moreover, the way that laws control and are shaped have greater bearing on the civil realm because these cases impact far more people. Civil law governs social obligations across a vast array of human activity. It governs the nature and parameters of family relations such as marriage, divorce, child custody, adoption, provision of medical treatment to family members, and innumerable other domestic issues. Civil law governs privileges such as licensure to operate vehicles, to engage in certain occupations, to participate in sporting activities, the pursuit of education, eligibility for many financial benefits, ownership of property, and all other realms of human endeavor. It also provides the framework for determining which individuals have been wronged and how the damages are to be rectified. In short, civil law provides the rules and procedures for resolving conflicts between individuals over any and all matters within a society.

Civil or private law, as opposed to public law, is structured differently because it is presumed that public law is pitting individuals against a more powerful state. Within civil law the defendant is not accorded nearly as much protection because it is presumed that there is not such a dramatic power imbalance between the two sides to the conflict. Moreover, the state is empowered to take life or liberty, sanctions unavailable in private disputes. A single event, however, may have the potential to be jointly addressed by civil law (a plaintiff sues for civil damages) and criminal law (the state pursues criminal charges). Nevertheless, because it is so far-reaching, civil law dramatically shapes the nature and quality of social life.

SEE ALSO: Crime, White-Collar; Law, Criminal; Law, Sociology of; Legal Profession

REFERENCES AND SUGGESTED READINGS

Black, D. (1998) *The Social Structure of Right and Wrong*. Academic Press, San Diego.

Calvi, J. V. & Coleman, S. (2000) *American Law and Legal Systems*. Prentice-Hall, Upper Saddle River, NJ.

Grana, S. J., Ollenburger, J. C., & Nicholas, M. (2002) *The Social Context of Law*. Prentice-Hall, Upper Saddle River, NJ.

law, criminal

Victoria Time

Criminal law is a body of law that defines and grades crimes, and indicates corresponding punishments. These definitions and punishments are found in statutes and in criminal codes within each state, and within each country. Due to the dual system of government that obtains in the US, the federal government has its own criminal code different from that of the various states.

Besides defining and stipulating sanctions, criminal law also explains constitutional limits on the power of government in enforcing criminal laws. It explains general principles of criminal liability and discusses parties to a crime, as well as defenses to criminal responsibility.

In the US, criminal law differs from civil law in that the latter (also referred to as private law) regulates private rights and remedies. Further, while a higher burden is required to prove guilt in criminal cases (beyond a reasonable doubt), liability in civil cases is proven based on a preponderance of the evidence. The penalties for criminal violations range from jail time and any intermediate sanction to death, while those in civil cases are limited to damages and injunctions. Some crimes, such as assault and battery, may be prosecuted in both a criminal court and a civil court. The prosecutor, on behalf of the state or the federal government, brings charges against defendants in criminal cases, while the victim or friends and family as plaintiffs file charges against defendants in civil cases.

OBJECTIVES AND CHARACTERISTICS OF CRIMINAL LAW

The primary purpose of criminal law is to regulate people's behavior in efforts to curb crime.

In this regard, delineating behavior which is criminal is necessary, and punishing wrongdoers is vital. In compliance with the rule of law, also known as the principle of legality, one can be punished only if there is a law that expressly defines conduct as criminal, and prescribes a fitting punishment for that conduct. Hence, if there is no crime, there can be no punishment. Criminal law attempts to achieve several goals, including deterrence, retribution, incapacitation, rehabilitation, and restitution. The following are characteristics of criminal law:

- It states behavior that people must comply with and those from which people must refrain.
- These stipulations are put into law by appropriate authorities.
- Violations of these stipulations result in punishments.
- Everyone in that jurisdiction is subject to the law.
- Not only the victim is affected by a crime; the community at large becomes a symbolic victim.
- Punishments against perpetrators signify a collective will of the people.

SOURCES OF CRIMINAL LAW

The following provide the various sources of law in the US.

US Constitution

Even though the US Constitution focuses on procedural law in the Bill of Rights, it touches on criminal law in that it defines the crime of treason in Article 3.III.

US Criminal Code

The US code embodies federal crimes defined by Congress. These crimes, which include illegal possession of drugs and weapons, as well as crimes perpetrated against the US, its employees, and property, are prosecuted in federal courts.

State Constitutions

As the most dominant source of law in a state, state constitutions embody laws that define the parameters of the powers of the various agents that work within the criminal justice system. Further, it incorporates precepts of criminal law.

State Criminal Codes

State-defined crimes are largely a heritage of common law. However, where necessary, each state has modified common law definitions of crimes as well as punishments in ways that reflect changing times, as well as the unique circumstances of the state.

Common Law of England

Initially, common law of England comprised unwritten customs and regulations which were interpreted and enforced differently throughout England. In efforts to create some uniformity in the interpretation and enforcement of the law, William the Conqueror requested that the various customs and regulations be codified, and applied in similar fashion throughout England. These written customs and regulations became known as common law. In order to maintain some semblance in the ways cases with similar facts were decided, judges felt compelled to follow precedent. The principle of *stare decisis* which mandated judges to follow precedent was developed.

When the founding fathers migrated to the US they brought many of these English laws and practices and incorporated them into the legal systems. Today, some common law definitions of crimes, as well as practices, still exist, while others have been modified or stricken out.

Judicial Decisions

Appellate court judges (the US Supreme Court Justices are the highest) make law through judicial rulings. Usually, they follow precedent when cases have similar facts. When there are substantive differences, judges distinguish the cases and provide a rationale for their new decision.

Local and Municipal Ordinances

It is not uncommon to find ordinances that are endemic to a particular municipality. Based on their unique economic and social factors, each jurisdiction defines crimes and infractions, and stipulates punishments for behavior that contravenes aspects of those factors.

Administrative Law

Although administrative laws mostly generate civil litigation, violation of some may sometimes give rise to criminal litigation. For example, the administrative agency for Alcohol, Tobacco and Firearms requires that firearms be registered. Possession of an unregistered firearm may lead to criminal prosecution.

CLASSIFICATION OF CRIMES

Offenses are classified in various ways in order to determine an appropriate punishment. Worthy of note is the fact that classifications based on the type of punishment are not uniform among the states, since each state legislature draws limits on sentences.

Classification Based on Severity of Offense

A more popular way of classifying offenses is based on the degree of seriousness of the offense. Crimes are divided into three categories: felonies, misdemeanors, and infractions. Felonies are the most serious crimes, for which the punishment ranges from one year in prison to death. Death sentences are usually reserved for capital offenses such as treason and aggravated murder. In non-death penalty states, a capital offense carries a punishment of life.

Misdemeanors are less serious offenses than felonies and their punishments are usually less than a year in jail. Some states differentiate gross misdemeanors from petty misdemeanors. Gross misdemeanors carry sanctions ranging from six months to one year. Infractions or violations such as traffic violations are the least serious offenses, whose punishments are usually fines.

Felonies are tried in courts of general jurisdiction, while misdemeanors and infractions are tried in courts of limited jurisdiction.

Classification Based on Moral Turpitude

Offenses that are egregious (such as murder) are deemed *mala in se* or inherently wrong. Others (such as polygamy) are *mala prohibita* or acts made illegal by laws of a state or country.

Crimes can also be classified based on the subject matter. For instance, battery may be classified as a crime against a person, while treason and sedition may be classified as crimes against the state.

ELEMENTS OF A CRIME

In order to convict a defendant, a prosecutor has to prove the elements of a crime. Sometimes, it may not be necessary to prove all the elements. The elements are (1) the guilty or evil act (*actus reus*), (2) the guilty mind (*mens rea*) or the evil intent, (3) concurrence of the guilty act and mind, (4) attendant circumstances, or "facts surrounding an event" (Black 1990: 127), (5) causation, which may relate to cause in fact, that is, the act that creates the harmful result. Courts look at two types of causation in determining who should be held responsible for cause of death: (1) "but for" or *sine qua non* causation, and (2) legal causation, which relates to the proximate cause of a result when some intervening factor affected the chain of events from when an initial act was perpetrated until when death occurred.

PARTIES TO CRIMES

Criminal liability may attach for those who commit crimes, as well as those who aid and abet, assist, entice, or encourage criminal acts. The doctrine of complicity explains circumstances under which accomplices assume criminal responsibility based on the extent of their participation in a criminal venture. Common law grouped parties to a crime in four categories: accessories before the fact, principals in the

first, principals in the second, and accessories after the fact. Changes have been made over time to this classification. Participants to crimes are classified in modern statutes as (1) principals (those who carry out the crime), (2) accomplices (those who act before and during the commission of the crime, as for instance those who act as look-outs) and (3) accessories after the fact (individuals who, knowing fully well that principals and accomplices have committed a crime, willingly provide them a safe haven, or provide them with any type of assistance in order to impede their arrest or prosecution). Accomplices and accessories can be punished even when the principal is still at large.

Culpability may also attach vicariously based on the relationship of the offender and a third party. For example, an employer may be held responsible for the crimes of an employee that fall within the scope of employment. A person may also be held liable under the doctrine of strict liability, even when the person did not have the requisite guilty mind, as long as some harm ensued from the person's act.

TYPES OF CRIME

Some offenses are classified as anticipatory/ inchoate or incomplete crimes. These offenses, in order of their seriousness, are attempt, conspiracy, and solicitation. Attempt is distinguished from mere preparation, in that attempt requires that "substantial steps" are taken towards the commission of a crime. Conspiracy requires an agreement between two or more persons to engage in illegal activities. Solicitation is a request or an inducement to someone to commit a crime.

With regard to other types of crimes, the list is lengthy. Some of the more common are (1) crimes against a person, which include murder, manslaughter, rape, assault, battery, and kidnaping; (2) property offenses, which include larceny, burglary, embezzlement, forgery, etc.; (3) crimes against public order and morality, which may include but are not limited to vagrancy, disorderly conduct, aggressive panhandling, and prostitution; (4) crimes against the administration of government, which include treason, perjury, obstruction of justice, etc.; and (5) crimes against a person as well as property, for example, robbery.

DEFENSES TO CRIMINAL LIABILITY

There are three broad categories of defenses to criminal liability: (1) alibi, which is raised by defendants who contend that they were somewhere else when the crime was committed; (2) defenses of justification, such as self-defense, defense of home and property, defense of others, consent, necessity/choice of evils, and execution of public duty, which may be raised by defendants who accept responsibility for the crime but argue that based on the circumstances, their actions were justified; and (3) defenses of excuse, such as insanity, entrapment, intoxication, age, mistake, syndromes, etc., which may be raised by those who shift blame to something that to them precipitated the commission of the crime. Some of the syndromes that defendants have raised are Vietnam/Gulf War syndrome, premenstrual syndrome, and spousal abuse syndrome. When a syndrome defense is raised, the defendant contends that some abnormality brought about by unpleasant experiences triggered anti-social behavior.

LIMITATIONS ON CRIMINAL LAW

Even though many legislative and judicial rulings affect criminal procedure, some of them set limitations on how criminal law can be enforced. Some limitations are (1) void for vagueness and overbreadth: laws that are not precise or those that are so broad as to encompass constitutionally protected rights cannot be enforced; (2) *ex post facto* laws: retroactive laws cannot be enforced if they punish acts which were committed before the laws were passed; neither can they increase the punishment nor the gravity of an offense; (3) cruel and unusual punishments such as those that are barbaric or those that are disproportionate to the crimes are forbidden; (4) free speech, which includes expressive conduct, may not be "abridged" except they constitute obscenity, profanity, fighting words, slander, libel, and expressions that may give rise to "clear and present danger"; and (5) due process and equal protection of the laws may not be denied anyone. Without a valid state interest that has to be articulated, courts will not enforce laws that are discriminatory.

SOME CHANGES IN CRIMINAL LAW OVER TIME

Changes over time are quite evident in the sanctions, definitions, and types of crimes. Most felonies at common law carried a death penalty sanction; today, the death penalty is mostly reserved for capital offenses and treason. The penalties for other felonies in recent times typically carry terms of incarceration, while punishments for misdemeanors range from fines to a year in jail in most states. Flogging, which is outlawed, and punishments which are disproportional to the crimes are considered cruel and unusual in contemporary times.

Besides changes in sanctions, definitions of offenses have also changed over time. Two examples are burglary and rape. The definition of burglary used to comprise the breaking and entering of a dwelling during the night with the intent to commit a felony. The current definition of burglary entails breaking, entering, and remaining in any structure at any time of day with the intent to commit a crime. Rape, which was considered to be an unwanted sexual offense by a man to a woman other than his wife, today in many states has a gender-neutral definition. The elements of the crime of rape, particularly that of force, have in modern times been revised to include both intrinsic force (normal force) and extrinsic force (more force than normal). While non-consent at common law required resistance by the victim, today, simply saying "no" suffices for non-consent.

SEE ALSO: Age and Crime; Alcohol and Crime; Capital Punishment; Corrections; Courts; Crime; Criminal Justice System; Death Penalty as a Social Problem; Deviance; Deviance, Crime and; Hate Crimes; Law, Civil; Law, Sociology of; Legal Profession; Prisons; Property Crime; Violent Crime

REFERENCES AND SUGGESTED READINGS

Black, H. C. (1990) *Black's Law Dictionary*, 6th edn. West Publishing, St. Paul, MN.

Dix, G. & Shralot, M. M. (1999) *Criminal Law*, 4th edn. West/Wadsworth Publishing, Belmont, CA.

Reid, S.T. (2001) *Criminal Law*, 5th edn. McGraw-Hill, Boston.

Samaha, J. (2004) *Criminal Law*, 8th edn. Thompson/Wadsworth Learning, Belmont, CA.

Time, V. (2002) Criminal Law. In: Kritzer, H. M. (Ed.), *Legal Systems of the World*, Vol. 1. ABC-CLIO, Santa Barbara, CA, pp. 375–81.

law, economy and

Robin Stryker

The law–economy relationship has been an important object of inquiry for sociologists. Classical theorists Durkheim and Weber promoted sociology as a discipline by offering theories of this relationship. Today, sociological research on law and the economy provides ideas and empirical evidence to help answer such key questions as: Where do firms and markets come from? How and why do they operate and evolve as they do? How do legislatures and courts shape inequalities of income and wealth? How do legislatures and courts affect the participation in paid labor markets, jobs, and earnings of people of different races, ethnic groups, religions, and genders?

Among classical theorists, Marx assumed "bourgeois" law would reflect and reinforce capitalist relations of production. At most law was an object of class conflict among factory owners and workers, but it was not a major causal force in its own right. Durkheim focused much attention on the law–economy relationship, making it central to his analyses of economic modernization. For Durkheim, shifts in law from punitive to restitutive legal principles and sanctions indicated changes in social bases of solidarity. Societies moved from solidarity rooted in similarity to that rooted in difference and complementarity, as a consequence of increased economic division of labor. In contrast to Durkheim and Marx, who viewed the nature of legal ideas, behavior, and institutions as consequence rather than cause of economic ideas, behavior, and institutions, Weber emphasized the conjoint, mutually reinforcing rise of a formal-rational legal system and of capitalism in Western Europe. Weber's ideas

have been especially influential in economic sociology and for contemporary perspectives on law and economy (Trevino 1996; Swedberg 2000; Stryker 2003; Edelman & Stryker 2004).

According to Weber, formal-rational law provided legal rights and guarantees to parties in exchange, enhancing predictability and certainty in contractual relations. This increased the probability that promises were kept, promoting market exchange, which in turn promoted further changes in business and contract law. Though full-blown capitalist economies were unlikely without legal enforcement of contracts, economic exchange and markets could exist without such enforcement. One among many sources of legal rationalization itself was separation of sacred and secular law going back to republican Rome's practice of refusing to let priests interfere in daily life (Trevino 1996).

Similarly, legal concepts and tools of negotiability, agency, and the juristic or legal person probably were necessary for developing economic action and institutions with very high degrees of systematization, calculability, and predictability. Banknotes, checks, and bills of exchange are signed legal documents including unconditional promises to pay. As Trevino (1996) points out, because such negotiable instruments were not promoted until the seventh century, markets but not full-blown capitalism could develop in ancient Rome. Finally, by making business organizations bearers of universal rights and duties, entitled to formal equal treatment under the law, the legal personhood concept provided a bridge between developing ideas of rule of law and rule-oriented legality in the polity, and development and reproduction of capitalist ideologies, firms, and markets.

Contemporary treatments follow Weber in presuming that law operates both as an independent and dependent variable with respect to the economy (Edelman & Stryker 2004). With respect to centrality of law in the social construction of firms and markets, for example, Roy (1990) showed that anti-trust policy contributed to a massive merger wage in the US at the turn of the twentieth century. Focusing on an 1897 Supreme Court decision that unexpectedly declared key provisions of the Interstate Commerce and Sherman Acts to be constitutional, Dobbin and Dowd (2000) showed how this decision triggered a chain of events leading the railroad industry away from cartel forms of business organization to oligopoly-enhancing friendly mergers. Not only did firm and market structures change, so too did business models of appropriate and efficient profit-oriented behavior.

Business activity shapes the nature of law, as well as vice versa. For example, Fligstein and Stone-Sweet (2002) showed that increased cross-border trade within the European Community promoted more litigation of EC law, that the two together promoted more EC legislation, and that all three of these together promoted the founding of new EC-oriented lobbying groups in Brussels. Here, firm economic behavior and concomitant legal and political behavior are transforming legal ideas, action, and institutions, creating a new EC-level regulatory system and transforming a treaty-based common market into a constitution-based transnational legal system.

With respect to economic inequality, research shows how economic and social regulations, including legislation governing collective bargaining, health and safety, pensions, and equal employment opportunity, have reshaped the nature of the American workplace, transforming workplace governance, business hiring, firing and promotion procedures, and impacting labor market outcomes for women and minorities (Stryker 2003). As well, redistributive tax and social welfare legislation at the core of the welfare state ideal led to measurable reductions in income inequality in advanced industrial democracies, though these reductions were not of the magnitude that many anticipated (Lempert & Sanders 1986).

Conversely, Edelman et al. (1999) showed that courts take into account managers' business concepts and routines, including their business-adapted interpretations of equal employment opportunity and affirmative action laws, when making formal adjudicative rulings on whether or not firms have violated equal employment laws. Thus, more "covert" day-to-day managerial interpretations diffusing across firms and economic sectors, as well as more "overt" business attempts to influence legal rules through litigation, often have dramatic effects on law enforcement, such that the impact of equality-promoting legislation is minimal or even the converse of that intended (Yeager 1990; Stryker

2003; Edelman & Stryker 2004). Law and society scholars highlight such differences by contrasting "law on the books" with "law in action" (Trevino 1996; Stryker 2003; Edelman & Stryker 2004). The legal profession itself – in addition to advancing members' interests in creating and monopolizing markets for their services – also shapes the content of legal rules and the structure of legal institutions (Lempert & Sanders 1986; Dezalay & Garth 1996).

Consistent with many recent studies and findings, current sociological ideas about the law–economy relationship emphasize co-evolution (Stryker 2003). Legal ideas, actions, and institutions reciprocally shape and are shaped by economic ideas, action, and institutions in intersecting institutional fields. An excellent example is provided by Dezaley and Garth (1996) in their study of the emergence of a transnational legal order of commercial business arbitration. This new legal field, which transforms international and national business disputing, emerges and itself becomes transformed through interconnected power struggles over business, markets, and the state within and among lawyers and businesspersons operating in and across local, national, and transnational organizations and institutions.

Social mechanisms through which law–economy co-evolution occurs are a topic of lively debate. Some scholars emphasize how law reshapes actors' cost-benefit calculations and interests. Others emphasize how legal and economic concepts and institutions are mutually constitutive, with law's power in and for economic life rooted in taken-for-granted meanings, norms, and values. Where scholars emphasizing rational calculation tend to conceptualize law as a set of state-promulgated formal rules, scholars emphasizing how law helps to construct cognitive frameworks for economic behavior tend to emphasize a broader concept of law as legality (Stryker 2003; Edelman & Stryker 2004). Legality encompasses codified rules as well as symbolic and ritual elements of law and social behaviors mobilizing and enacting both state-made formal laws and law-like principles and processes outside the formal legal system.

Stryker (2003) suggests that both formal legal rules and broader notions of legality affect the economy through multi-dimensional resource mobilization processes involving instrumental calculations by economic and legal actors, and also these actors' cognitive-interpretive frames and their normative evaluations (see also Dezalay & Garth 1996; Kelly 2003). Reviewing extant research, Edelman and Stryker (2004) suggest that political mechanisms involving resource mobilization and counter-mobilization and institutional mechanisms involving hegemony and diffusion of taken-for-granted meanings and practices combine to account for the mutual endogeneity of legal and economic ideas, actors, and institutions. They show how a "sociological" approach to law and the economy, emphasizing that ideas of economic efficiency and rationality are socially constructed, is different from a "law and economics" approach. The latter relies on a priori concepts of rationality and efficiency as assumptions for its theories about business behavior and as a normative standard to evaluate legal rules and institutions. Finally, law plays facilitative, constitutive, and/or regulatory roles with respect to economic ideas, actors, and institutions. Sometimes it plays all three at once. For example, corporation law constitutes corporations as bona-fide economic actors and legal persons while it also facilitates and regulates capital accumulation (Edelman & Stryker 2004).

Diverse quantitative and qualitative methods are used productively to study law and the economy. Both quantitative modeling and case-oriented comparative techniques have been used to investigate the impact of statutes, directives, executive orders, and court rulings on, for example, business behavior, unionization, strikes, economic growth, employment, unemployment, international trade, and transformation of market structures, as well as on the labor market participation, jobs, and wages of minorities, women, and members of diverse ethnic and religious groups (Donahue & Heckman 1991; Fligstein & Stone-Sweet 2002; Edelman & Stryker 2004). Quantitative methods likewise have proved useful for assessing diffusion of new business structures and practices in response to changing regulatory laws and for investigating distinct periods in law and economy dynamics. Case-oriented comparative historical methods have been especially helpful in examining key events or turning points in mutually constitutive legal and economic processes (Stryker 2003). Precisely because the

over-time role of law in constructing currently taken-for-granted economic concepts, actors, behaviors, and institutions tends to become invisible from contemporary vantage points, research investigating short and long-term law–economy dynamics is important for understanding current economic phenomena, as well as for appreciating the possibilities and probabilities of future economic transformations.

SEE ALSO: Capitalism; Culture, Economy and; Economic Development; Economic Sociology: Classical Political Economic Perspectives; Economy (Sociological Approach); Enterprise; Global Economy; Institutionalism; Law, Sociology of; Markets; Modernization; Occupations; State and Economy; Unions; Weber, Max; Women, Economy and

REFERENCES AND SUGGESTED READINGS

Cooter, R. & Ulen, T. (2000) *Law and Economics*. Addison-Wesley, Reading, MA.
Dezalay, Y. & Garth, B. G. (1996) *Dealing in Virtue: International Commercial Arbitration and the Construction of a Transnational Legal Order*. University of Chicago Press, Chicago.
Dobbin, F. & Dowd, T. (2000) The Market that Antitrust Built: Public Policy, Private Coercion and Railroad Acquisitions, 1825–1922. *American Sociological Review* 65: 635–57.
Dobbin, F., Sutton, J. R., Meyer, J. W., & Scott, W. R. (1993) Equal Employment Opportunity Law and the Construction of Internal Labor Markets. *American Journal of Sociology* 99: 396–427.
Donahue, J. J. & Heckman, J. (1991) Continuous vs. Episodic Change: The Impact of Civil Rights Policy on the Economic Status of Blacks. *Journal of Economic Literature* 29: 1603–43.
Ebbinghaus, B. & Visser, J. (1999) When Institutions Matter: Union Growth and Decline in Western Europe, 1950–1995. *European Sociological Review* 15: 135–58.
Edelman, L. B. & Stryker, R. (2004) A Sociological Approach to Law and the Economy. In: Smelser, N. & Swedberg, R. (Eds.), *Handbook of Economic Sociology*, 2nd edn. Princeton University Press, Princeton.
Edelman, L. B., Erlanger, H., & Uggen, C. (1999) The Endogeneity of Law: Grievance Procedures as Rational Myth. *American Journal of Sociology* 105: 406–54.

Fligstein, N. & Stone-Sweet, A. (2002) Constructing Politics and Markets: An Institutionalist Account of European Integration. *American Journal of Sociology* 107: 1206–43.

Kelly, E. (2003) The Strange History of Employer-Sponsored Childcare: Interested Actors, Ambiguity and the Transformation of Law in Organizational Fields. *American Journal of Sociology* 109: 506–49.

Lempert, R. & Sanders, J. (1986) *An Invitation to Law and Social Science: Desert, Disputes and Distribution.* Longman, New York.

Nelson, R. & Bridges, W. (1999) *Legalizing Gender Inequality: Courts, Markets and Unequal Pay for Women.* Cambridge University Press, Cambridge.

Roy, W. (1990) Functional and Historical Logics in Explaining the Rise of the American Industrial Corporation. *Comparative Social Research* 12: 19–44.

Stryker, R. (2003) Mind the Gap: Law, Institutional Analysis and Socio-Economics. *Socio-Economic Review* 1: 335–68.

Swedberg, R. (2000) *Max Weber and the Idea of Economic Sociology.* Princeton University Press, Princeton.

Trevino, A. J. (1996) *The Sociology of Law: Classical and Contemporary Perspectives.* St. Martins Press, New York.

Yeager, P. (1990) *The Limits of Law: The Public Regulation of Private Pollution.* Cambridge University Press, Cambridge.

law, sociology of

Robert Dingwall

The sociology of law is one of the oldest specialty fields in the discipline, reflecting the influence of nineteenth-century jurists like Sir Henry Maine (1861) on writers of the founding generation like Tönnies, Weber, and Durkheim. Although it has been a less significant area over the last half century, it is currently undergoing a revival, mainly through its contribution to interdisciplinary studies in law and society alongside law, history, political science, anthropology, and social psychology.

The sociology of law can be distinguished from criminology in two ways. First, it has a broader attention to the scope of law's impact on society. Where criminology focuses particularly on the coercive effect of law, the sociology of law is also interested in its regulatory and facilitative aspects in relation to civil society, commerce, and domestic life. Second, it has a less applied orientation. Although there are significant critical currents in criminology, which are often closely linked to the sociology of law, much criminological work is essentially a form of problem-solving for the criminal justice system, where prior definitions of crime and institutional solutions have been laid down by research sponsors. It is important not to overstate this because there are also empiricist elements in law and society studies that are equally sponsor driven (Campbell & Wiles 1976).

Early sociologists had a central interest in explaining the transition to modernity that they believed they were witnessing, in their own lifetime and that of their immediate predecessors. Changes in the nature of law were thought to be part of this transition, creating the conditions for the development of a capitalist economy. Maine described this as the movement from a society based on *status* to one based on *contract*, a distinction reformulated by Tönnies as *Gemeinschaft* to *Gesellschaft* and by Durkheim as *mechanical* to *organic* solidarity (Nisbet 1966). To the extent that law could be said to exist in traditional societies, it was an expression of sovereign or collective will, designed to impose order through repressive sanctions and sustain relations between individuals that reflected inherited or ascribed positions within the community. Modern law was a resource that individuals could use to structure episodic relationships between themselves, particularly within the economic sphere, by means of contracts that provided a basis for stability and predictability in their interactions by codifying promises and penalizing breaches. Contemporary anthropologists of law are highly critical of this representation of traditional societies, which their research has shown to be more strongly marked by informal sanctions and an emphasis on restitution and peace-making than on coercion. Nevertheless, the model was important in stimulating reflection and empirical work on the relationship between law and the rise of capitalism.

The division of analysts over the extent to which law is an integrative element in society, facilitating action in a broadly neutral fashion, or an expression of the coercive power of a dominant class persists to the present day. Durkheim (1984) saw law as one of the solutions to the problem of social and moral fragmentation that arose from the division of labor. The creation and articulation of enforceable contracts provided for the specification and definition of a wide range of social relationships – from the economic sphere of consumption, employment, or property to the domestic sphere of marriage and intimate relationships. However, in contrast to many of his contemporaries writing from more narrowly legal or economic backgrounds, Durkheim underlined the importance of the institutional embeddedness of law: contracts depended on a non-contractual basis of values, which could only be imperfectly sustained by legal means. For Durkheim, though, the division of labor was a spontaneous process: its unilateral imposition on workers by the owners of capital was a pathological form, the *forced* division of labor, that he sought to oppose. Marx, in contrast, saw this imposition, in pursuit of greater profit, as the essential driver of the process, so that law was primarily an ideological tool of the capitalist, supplying legitimacy to the power imbalance between owner and laborer (Cain & Hunt 1979). The apparent neutrality of law as an arbiter between interests cloaks the "hard power" of the capitalist state's monopoly of violence. In practice, laws are written by one class to serve their goals of expropriation from, and domination over, another. The courts are no more open to all than the Ritz Hotel.

Weber (1978) took over Marx's recognition of the role of law in legitimizing state power, although he argued that the control of the state and the nature of struggles between different groups of citizens were more complex phenomena than Marx had allowed. Law was not a simple servant of the interests of a capitalist class because such a single, homogeneous social grouping could not be identified as easily as Marx thought. Weber put more emphasis on the role of law in the spread of rationalization in modern societies. It was one of the impersonal metrics that both ordered social and economic relations and, ultimately, undermined their spontaneity and creativity. If the modern world was being experienced as an inhumane place, law was part of that inhumanity, while,

at the same time, being one of the conditions that made possible the advance of Enlightenment values and of material prosperity. This tradition remains important in, for instance, the work of Teubner (1993).

The straightforward model of Marx's original writing proved unsustainable under the conditions of the twentieth century's experiments with communism. Marx had seemed to suggest that the overthrow of the capitalist order would lead to the creation of a self-organizing society in which law would be redundant. In practice, communist societies found it hard to dispense with law. The Soviet Russian theorist Pashukanis, writing in the 1920s and 1930s, noted the continuing use of contracts to define relationships between state-owned or controlled enterprises, for example. He distinguished the repressive character of law under capitalism from the facilitative character of law under communism (Beirne & Sharlet 1980). Even the self-styled "workers' states" found it hard to dispense with a framework of law to regulate economic and social relationships or to supply legitimacy to coercive acts in defense of the revolutionary order.

The contemporary sociology of law focuses on a research agenda that can conveniently be summarized in the terms of one of its classic papers: naming, blaming, and claiming (Felstiner et al. 1980–1). Naming refers to the recognition by a social actor that a problem is potentially a legal problem, that is to say a grievance or a dispute to which the law may offer a useful response. This generates a set of questions about what kinds of problems people encounter in their daily lives, whether as family members, workers, consumers, tenants, borrowers, employers, landlords, lenders, or whatever. How do some of these come to be selected into the legal system? What happens to the others? These questions generate studies of legal consciousness, what the prospective users of law think that the law can offer them, and when it is appropriate to make use of it. Legal consciousness is in turn linked to studies of culture, of the images of law presented in different forms of mass media, and of the outreach activities of professional legal actors seeking to recruit problems for resolution by the system from which they derive their living. Blaming involves the identification of a second party who is responsible for the problem and against whom the law's resources may be mobilized. The law is a means to compel the wrongdoer to make some redress for the wrong. In this sense, at least, it is an alternative to the peer pressures of a community or the unregulated use of private violence. The law may ultimately rest on coercion to deliver redress, but this response is the measured employment of the modern state's monopoly of legitimate force, sanctioned by a judicial decision. Claiming describes the processes of mobilization, considering the social and economic influences on access to the law, the relative role of formal and informal legal institutions, the role of the legal professions and regulatory agencies in managing claims or grievances, and the role of court processes in constructing outcomes.

In general, scholars draw attention to the "iceberg" of potential legal business: potential causes for litigation are endemic in everyday life, but are rarely named as such and mobilized as claims (Greenhouse et al. 1994). While there is a widespread contemporary belief in the recent growth of a "compensation culture," where both citizens and corporations, stimulated by entrepreneurial lawyers, are making increasing use of formal legal means to make claims and resolve disputes, there is no substantial empirical evidence to support this (Daniels & Martin 1995). Even in an area like medical malpractice, where claim rates have attracted much discussion, the best evidence suggests that only a relatively small proportion of physician errors lead to claims, most of which are settled without trial. Compensation tends to reflect the real losses sustained by plaintiffs, even in countries like the US where, at least in the first instance, juries decide awards (Vidmar 1995). The perception of a compensation culture is in part the product of a popular imagery of law, derived from novels, TV, and film, that massively overstates the role of trials in modern legal systems. Whether in relation to criminal or civil issues, most legal outcomes are negotiated.

A good deal of recent scholarship, then, concentrates on the factors that tend to divert cases from the legal system. Is the diversion of problems structured in ways that exclude certain social groups and favor others? Some of the barriers are cultural. Ewick and Silbey (1998),

for example, identify three ways in which ordinary people understand the law: one is based on an idea of the law as magisterial and remote, not for "people like us"; a second views the law as a game with rules that can be manipulated, and where some people are always advantaged; a third sees the law as an arbitrary power to be resisted in favor of local and traditional ways of dealing with problems. However, even business actors tend to avoid referring their disputes to the legal system wherever practicable (Macaulay 1963). Individual litigants and small businesses are indeed structurally disadvantaged by their limited resources and unfamiliarity with the nature of the game. Galanter's (1974) analysis of the imbalances between "one-shotters" and repeat players has had a wide influence and continues to be sustained in current work (Kritzer & Silbey 2003). Research on court procedures has examined the extent to which legal language excludes or disadvantages certain social groups, although there is some disagreement about the degree to which these features either arise from the functional logic of a truth-seeking process or are more or less self-conscious devices for protecting the interests of the powerful (Dingwall 2000). The legal profession itself has become increasingly organized in larger units focused on serving the repeat players, with a growing distinction between those firms and lawyers serving corporate and individual interests (Heinz & Lauman 1982; Galanter 1994; Heinz et al. 2005). This has not necessarily compromised the profession's ethical standards: large firms may have greater economic and cultural resources for resisting pressure to engage in deviant behavior (Carlin 1962; Shapiro 2002). However, it is argued that the law contributes increasingly to the social and economic integration of an elite, supplying predictability in their corporate relationships and providing for the settlement of their disputes, mainly by negotiation between their lawyers and only occasionally by the maverick process of trial.

Those who are not well served by this closure have been offered two other institutional developments: the rise of alternative dispute resolution (ADR) and of regulation as an alternative to litigation. ADR is an uneasy coalition of two very different interests. One dimension is inherited from experimental social programs in the 1960s and 1970s intended to strengthen the capacity of poor neighborhoods to resolve their own disputes by supporting the mobilization of community resources. It is intended to overcome the perceptions of remoteness and arbitrariness attaching to the formal legal system. Problems will be solved by the intervention of a third party, who may either facilitate direct negotiation between disputants, seek to communicate between the parties to bring about a compromise, or, more rarely, to make a decision that will bind the parties. It should be noted that none of these are exclusive to the settlement of the grievances of the poor: the powerful also prefer to avoid courts and have long used similar means to resolve disputes among themselves. However, this community oriented concept has been increasingly transformed by the sponsorship of governmental actors seeking to reduce public expenditure on the legal system by diverting low-value cases from the courts, which have relatively high fixed costs. ADR reduces the resources offered by the state to poor people while telling them that it is morally better for them to solve their own disputes among themselves (Nader 2002).

The twentieth century saw the wholesale growth of regulation as an alternative to relying on victims to mobilize the law in search of redress. Regulation is based on the proactive screening of various areas of social and economic activity by a formal bureaucracy empowered to administer legal penalties or to refer cases to the courts for sanction. It has been particularly evident in areas where harms are diffuse (environment, obscenity), where there are great economic inequalities between parties (health and safety, discrimination), or where there are great informational inequalities (consumer protection, finance and investment, professional licensing). However, the results have been mixed. Sociologists have pointed to the way in which regulatory agencies tend to become "captured" by those who they seek to regulate, forming alliances inimical to the public interest that they are supposed to represent. As with so much of the law, compliance is negotiated rather than imposed. In part, this often reflects state ambivalence about their use of enforcement powers and willingness to resource

agencies accordingly. The revival of neoliberal social theories has produced calls to roll back the regulatory state in favor of action by robust individuals. As with ADR, private enforcement by individual litigants is held to be morally preferable to collective action on their behalf by a "nanny state."

The resurgence of the sociology of law is in part attributable to the resurgence in the role of law in society. The discipline's founders observed a world of "small states," with limited spheres of action, and sought to develop replacements for the ineffectiveness of traditional legal forms as a basis for the new forms of social and economic organization that were emerging. A modern world required a modern form of law, forming part of a much wider system of governmentality. The perceived crisis of that system has allowed its critics to roll back many of its state-based elements, returning individual acts of legal mobilization to a position that they have not occupied for some generations.

SEE ALSO: Criminology; Durkheim, Émile; Law, Civil; Law, Criminal; Law, Economy and; Legal Profession; Marx, Karl; Social Control; Tönnies, Ferdinand; Weber, Max

REFERENCES AND SUGGESTED READINGS

Anleu, S. L. R. (2000) *Law and Social Change.* Sage, London.
Beirne, P. & Sharlet, R. (Eds.) (1980) *Evgeny Pashukanis: Selected Writing on Marxism and Law.* Academic Press, London.
Braithwaite, J., Parker, C., Lacey, N., & Scott, C. (Eds.) (2004) *Regulating Law.* Oxford University Press, Oxford.
Cain, M. & Hunt, A. (Eds.) (1979) *Marx and Engels on Law.* Academic Press, London.
Campbell, C. M. & Wiles, P. (1976) The Study of Law in Society in Britain. *Law and Society Review* 10: 547–78.
Carlin, J. E. (1962) *Lawyers on Their Own: A Study of Individual Practitioners in Chicago.* Rutgers University Press, New Brunswick, NJ.
Cotterell, R. (1992) *The Sociology of Law: An Introduction.* Butterworths, London.
Daniels, S. & Martin, J. (1995) *Civil Juries and the Politics of Reform.* Northwestern University Press and American Bar Foundation, Evanston, IL.

Dingwall, R. (2000) Language, Law and Power: Eth-nomethodology, Conversation Analysis and the Politics of Law and Society Studies. *Law and Social Inquiry* 25: 885–911.

Durkheim, E. (1984 [1893]) *The Division of Labor in Society*. Free Press, New York.

Ewick, P. & Silbey, S. S. (1998) *The Common Place of Law: Stories from Everyday Life*. University of Chicago Press, Chicago.

Felstiner, W. L. F., Abel, R., & Sarat, A. (1980–1) The Emergence and Transformation of Disputes: Naming, Blaming, Claiming. *Law and Society Review* 15: 631–54.

Galanter, M. (1974) Why the Haves Come Out Ahead: Speculation on the Limits of Legal Change. *Law and Society Review* 9: 95–160.

Galanter, M. (1994) *Tournament of Lawyers*. University of Chicago Press, Chicago.

Greenhouse, C., Yngvesson, B., & Engel, D. (1994) *Law and Community in Three American Towns*. Cornell University Press, Ithaca, NY.

Heinz, J. P. & Lauman, E. O. (1982) *Chicago Lawyers: The Social Structure of the Bar*. Basic Books, New York.

Heinz, J. P., Nelson, R. L., Sandefur, R. L., & Lauman, E. O. (2005) *Urban Lawyers: The New Social Structure of the Bar*. University of Chicago Press, Chicago.

Kritzer, H. M. & Silbey, S. (Eds.) (2003) *In Litigation Do The "Haves" Still Come Out Ahead?* Stanford University Press, Stanford.

Macaulay, S. (1963) Non-Contractual Relations in Business: A Preliminary Study. *American Sociological Review* 28: 1–19.

Macaulay, S., Friedman, L. M., & Stookey, J. (Eds.) (1995) *Law and Society: Readings on the Social Study of Law*. W. W. Norton, New York.

Maine, H. (1861) *Ancient Law*. Murray, London.

Nader, L. (2002) *Life of the Law: Anthropological Projects*. University of California Press, Berkeley.

Nisbet, R. (1966) *The Sociological Tradition*. Basic Books, New York.

Ross, H. L. (1980) *Settled Out of Court: The Social Process of Insurance Claims Adjustment*. Aldine, New York.

Shapiro, S. P. (2002) *Tangled Loyalties: Conflict of Interest in Legal Practice*. University of Michigan Press, Ann Arbor.

Teubner, G. (1993) *Law as an Autopoietic System*. Blackwell, Oxford.

Vidmar, N. (1995) *Medical Malpractice and the American Jury: Confronting the Myths about Jury Incompetence, Deep Pockets, and Outrageous Damage Awards*. University of Michigan Press, Ann Arbor.

Weber, M (1978 [1914]) *Economy and Society*. University of California Press, Berkeley.

Lazarsfeld, Paul (1901–76)

Brian Starks

Paul Lazarsfeld, founder of the Bureau for Applied Social Research at Columbia University, was a pioneering empirical sociologist. Trained as a mathematician and initially self-identifying as a psychologist, he only later came to recognize himself as a sociologist.

Lazarsfeld was born to a Jewish family in Vienna and first came to the US as a Rockefeller Fellow in 1933. As an active socialist at the time, Lazarsfeld chose to remain in the US after his fellowship ended in 1935 rather than return home to persecution (a ban against social democrats had just been enacted in Austria, and Hitler had begun his rise to power in Germany). This experience of being a heavily accented foreigner and a Jew transplanted into the US left an enduring impact on Lazarsfeld's self-image. Throughout most of his life he saw himself as a marginalized individual despite his vast accomplishments and recognition among peers, which included being chosen as president of the American Association for Public Opinion Research (1949–50) and the American Sociological Association (1961–2).

While many of Lazarsfeld's concepts remain foundational in the field of mass communication, he may be best remembered for his sociological approach to voting (focusing on social location) and his theory of the two-step flow of communication, which highlights the importance of "opinion leaders" and personal influence in the process of decision-making, especially voting. Lazarsfeld's work is recognized as exceptional not just for the wealth of concepts he left behind but also for its methodological innovation. From his early work on unemployment (in the Marienthal project), to later work on mass communication and voting and finally in his research on higher education, Lazarsfeld developed ingenious ways of measuring and analyzing concepts. Cornerstones of modern social science such as survey analysis, focus groups, and panel studies, while not invented by him, were pioneered by him through his creative application of them to practical, empirical puzzles. Additionally, his development of "latent structure analysis" and use of contingency tables helped to build a secure foundation for the use of contingency tables and loglinear models in later research (e.g., in studies of class mobility).

Lazarsfeld was also dedicated to collaboration and institution building. He founded several research institutes over the course of his career. The first was the Research Center for Business Psychology in Vienna, but his most famous was the Bureau for Applied Social Research at Columbia. Finally, in a partnership with Robert Merton that lasted more than three decades, Lazarsfeld advised hundreds of graduate students at "the Bureau" and helped to shape a generation of empirically oriented sociologists.

SEE ALSO: American Sociological Association; Mathematical Sociology; Merton, Robert K.; Survey Research

REFERENCES AND SUGGESTED READINGS

Donsbach, W., Lipset, S. M., Noelle-Neumann, E., Worcester, R., & Robert M. (Eds.) (2001) *International Journal of Political Opinion Research* 13(3).
Merton, R. K., Coleman, J. S., & Rossi, P. H. (1979) *Qualitative and Quantitative Social Research: Papers in Honor of Paul F. Lazarsfeld*. Free Press, New York.
Sills, D. L. (1987) Paul Lazarsfeld 1901–1976: A Biographical Memoir. *Biographical Memoirs* 56: 251–82.

leadership

Tyrone S. Pitsis

There are several definitions of leadership available; however, it can be broadly defined as the process of inspiring, directing, coordinating, motivating, and mentoring individuals, groups of individuals, organizations, societies, and/or nations. While the origins of leadership can be traced back to ancient times in Africa, Asia, and Europe, it is only relatively recently that systematic attempts have been made to understand, operationalize, and conceptualize leadership. In sociology, Weber (1947) conceptualized leadership as legitimated by virtue of subordinates' understanding of bureaucratic authority, rules, and legitimacy. Weber identified three general typologies of leadership in bureaucracy: charismatic, traditional, and legal. Charismatic leaders were attributed powerful qualities by those who follow them; traditional leaders were powerful by virtue of hereditary wealth or peerage; legal leadership draws its power from professional knowledge and technical expertise, and formal authority was legitimized through roles or position in the bureaucratic hierarchy. As such, formal authority is legitimated by subordinates' understanding and respecting rules and authority (Clegg et al. 2005). In contrast to Weber's approach, more recent sociological approaches to leadership have been more concerned with notions of power rather than leadership per se. As such, the study of leadership is less about the individual and more about how power structures allow domination and control over others.

At a broader level, and in contrast to sociology, the origin of leadership research and theory is embedded in psychological trait theories of personality. Trait-based approaches to leadership distinguish leaders from non-leaders by attempting to identify specific biological and genetic personality traits, such as honesty, integrity, intelligence, strength of character, and confidence. Research results, however, have been quite mixed, and so critics sought to develop newer ways of understanding leadership. The issue for the trait approach was that leaders proved no more likely to possess special traits than did "non-leaders." As a result the behavioral school gained strength, especially in the US, because it argued that what distinguished leaders from non-leaders was not so much their traits but rather their observable behaviors. A leader, therefore, is what he or she does. Such notions of leadership dominated until the 1970s, when arguments emerged stating that effective leadership was contingent upon certain situational factors. If leadership was about how one acts, then one would have to act the same way all the time. Situational leadership theory moved away from individual difference psychology back to the social psychological and sociological notions of leadership. For some, there was a return to Weber's idea that leadership is a function of the willingness of subordinates to be led. For others, there was an attempt to define leadership as a function of a number of situational contingencies. Newer versions of contingency theories see leaders' ability to influence performance as a function of their cognitive capacity to deal with situational stressors and organizational environment (Fiedler 1995).

Over the last two decades the study of charismatic, transformational, and transactional leadership has dominated the leadership landscape and, to a certain extent, reflects Weber's three typologies of leadership. The charismatic leader, as the name suggests, exhibits character that followers are attracted to, and has the ability to inspire and build dreams and sell vision. The transactional leader attends to all the necessary functional aspects of management, such as coordination, control, and budgeting. The emphasis on the transformational leader emerged out of the sociological work of Burns (1978) on political leaders. The transformational leader sets examples through inspirational performance, inspired change and innovation, and deals in abstract concepts, such as vision and mission (Bass 1985; Avolio & Bass 1988). While there is a certain degree of overlap between transformational and charismatic leadership, charismatic leaders tend not to transform followers into future leaders. Adolf Hitler, for example, was a charismatic leader in that he inspired followership, but he also protected his rule and authority over all others. A transformational leader would also mentor his or her followers so that they might become future leaders.

Most recently a number of newer – or recycled older – approaches to leadership have emerged, most notably from a positive psychological perspective, but also from postmodernist conceptions. Positive psychology has its roots in William James and the humanist approaches of Gordon Allport, Carl Rogers, and Abraham Maslow. Interest in positive psychology has been reinvigorated more recently by Seligman (1999) and has recently entered organizational behavior and organization theory – not without its critics. The positive psychology of leadership draws upon Bass and Avolio's notions of transformational leadership, with some additions. Current work on positive leadership has a sociological dimension: it concentrates on a person's ability to create social as well as psychological capital (Luthans & Youssef 2004). Other approaches to leadership present leadership less as pious behavior and more as a problematic endeavor typified by tension, challenges, and mistakes. What characterizes a "good" leader, then, is the ability and commitment to build strong communities through principles of economic, social, and environmental sustainability (Dunphy & Pitsis 2005).

Another interesting area of leadership theory and research with sociological underpinnings is that of leadership substitutes and dispersed leadership theories. Leadership substitutes are those things that replace or make a leader obsolete. For example, the empowerment of teams and the use of self-managing work teams are believed to make the requirement for individual leaders obsolete. Dispersed leadership, however, returns to the analysis of leadership as power and addresses how leadership power is transferred to structure, rules, procedures, and technologies. Such notions may draw upon Foucault's (1979) analysis of Jeremy Bentham's Panopticon as a form of managerial surveillance and control. That is, while the leader may not be physically there, she or he is always watching you – say via time cards, surveillance cameras, email, etc. More interestingly, some go as far as to argue that even leadership substitutes such as empowerment are advanced and ingeniously designed forms of power. Sewell (1988), for example, argues that the use of teams produces stronger forms of control and surveillance than could any individual leader. What better way to control people than to have them monitored by their peers?

In a postmodern sense leaders do not exist to lead but to be servants – they are servants to the frontline people who are servants to customers. In other words, consumers and consumerism are king and we are all servants to consumption. In essence postmodern leaders provide running commentary on how the organization is doing, and how people fit within it; they construct the stories and rituals around life in organizations, where the organization will go and can go, and how one can become a better servant of the learned helplessness

consumer (Boje & Dennehey 1999; Greenleaf 2002). Of course, leadership might also be a social construction of our collective imagination. In this sense what makes a leader a leader is how observers construct their understanding around a person's specific behavior who is labeled a leader, and so the role and performance of leadership is overstated (Meindl 1995; Parry & Meindl 2002).

SEE ALSO: Political Leadership; Power, Theories of; Social Movements, Leadership in; Weber, Max

REFERENCES AND SUGGESTED READINGS

Avolio, B. J. & Bass, B. M. (1988) Transformational Leadership, Charisma, and Beyond. In: Hunt, J. G., Baliga, B. R., Dachler, H. P., & Schriesheim, C. A. (Eds.), *Emerging Leadership Vistas*. Lexington Books, Lexington, MA, pp. 29–49.

Bass, B. M. (1985) *Leadership and Performance Beyond Expectation*. Free Press, New York.

Boje, D. & Dennehey, R. (1999) Managing in a Postmodern World. Online. www.cbae.nmsu.edu/~dboje/mpw.html.

Burns, J. M. (1978) *Leadership*. Harper & Row, New York.

Clegg, S. R., Kornberger, M., & Pitsis, T. S. (2005) *Managing and Organizations: An Introduction to Theory and Practice*. Sage, Thousand Oaks, CA.

Dunphy, D. & Pitsis, T. S. (2005) Wisdom. In: Barker, C. & Coye, R. (Eds.), *The Seven Heavenly Virtues of Leadership*, 2nd edn. McGraw Hill, Brisbane.

Fiedler, F. E. (1995) Cognitive Resources and Leadership Performance. *Applied Psychology: An International Review* 44: 5–28.

Foucault, M. (1979) *Discipline and Punish*. Penguin, London.

Greenleaf, R. (2002) *Servant Leadership: A Journey into the Nature of Legitimate Power and Greatness*. Paulist Press, Mahwah, NJ.

Luthans, F. & Youssef, C. (2004) Human, Social, and Now Positive Psychological Capital Management: Investing in People for Competitive Advantage. *Organizational Dynamics* 33(2): 143–60.

Meindl, J. (1995) The Romance of Leadership as a Follower-Centric Theory: A Social Constructionist Approach. *Leadership Quarterly* 6(3): 329–41.

Parry, K. W. & Meindl, J. R. (Eds.) (2002) *Grounding Leadership Theory and Research: Issues, Perspectives and Methods*. Information Age Publishing, Greenwich, CT.

Seligman, M. E. P. (1999) The President's Address. *American Psychologist* 54: 559–62.

Sewell, G. (1988) The Discipline of Teams: The Control of Team-Based Industrial Work Through Electronic and Peer Surveillance. *Administrative Science Quarterly* 43: 397–428.

Weber, M. (1947) *The Theory of Social and Economic Organization*. Trans. T. Parsons & A. M. Henderson. Free Press, New York.

learned helplessness

Bridget Conlon and Christabel L. Rogalin

Learned helplessness is the group of motivational, cognitive, and emotional deficits that can result from repeated exposure to events if they are perceived to be uncontrollable. The phenomenon was discovered serendipitously in the laboratory of Richard Solomon by his students including Seligman, Maier, Leaf, and Overmier (Overmier & Seligman 1967; Seligman & Maier 1967). During experiments in which dogs in Pavlovian hammocks (harnesses used to restrict movement) were exposed to a tone (conditioned stimulus) paired with an electric shock (unconditioned stimulus), researchers realized that the dogs were unable to learn to escape shocks in a later controllable situation.

In order to examine the hypothesis that deficits were due to exposure to non-contingent (uncontrollable by the dogs) events, researchers designed "triadic design" experiments where animals were first exposed to one of three training phases: (1) no training; (2) training with outcomes that were not controllable by the animals; and (3) training with controllable outcomes. In the control condition, dogs were not exposed to any shock. In the second condition, experimenters shocked the dogs for 5 seconds 64 times. The dogs were able to cut the shocks short by pressing panels on either side of their heads. Dogs in the third condition were "yoked" to dogs in the second condition. Yoked means that the dogs were shocked simultaneously for identical lengths, yet the dogs in the second condition controlled the shocks while the dogs in the third condition were not able to control the frequency or length of shocks.

During the second (test) phase of the experiments, animals performed a task related to the task in the training phase and their performance was measured. The goal was to test whether performance during the test phase was affected by the condition in the training phase. Researchers found that the animals that were exposed to controllable shocks during the training phase were able to learn to escape shocks during the test phase. Animals exposed to uncontrollable shocks in the training phase were unable to learn to escape shocks during the test phase. In essence, the animals learned that they were unable to control outcomes and generalized that knowledge to a similar situation when they actually had control of outcomes. The *expectation* of uncontrollability is a key to learned helplessness.

LEARNED HELPLESSNESS IN HUMANS

Martin Seligman is considered a major contributor in extending the original observations to studies of learned helplessness in humans. Seligman suggested that the symptoms dogs exhibited were similar to symptoms of depression in humans. He proposed a learned helplessness model of human depression. Depressed people often exhibit similar motivational difficulties, believing that their behaviors are futile. They also often show cognitive deficiencies such as the inability to learn when their responses can affect outcomes. Finally, depressed people experience frequent sadness and anhedonia that may appear similar to the helpless whimpering of dogs exposed to non-contingent shocks. Anhedonia refers to the inability to experience pleasure from things that one would normally find pleasurable. The translation of the concept from animals to humans required some reworking of the original theory. Specifically, researchers studying humans found that when exposed to uncontrollable stimuli, such as inescapable noise or unsolvable puzzles, some individuals showed signs of learned helplessness while others exhibited increased activity that facilitated their performances.

The reworking of the learned helplessness model to fit humans included increased emphasis on attributions. Abramson et al. (1978) suggested that individual people have a stable (trait-like) explanatory style when they encounter unpleasant events. Explanatory style has three dimensions: internal–external, stable–unstable, and global–specific. In practice, these dimensions are measured using Likert scales from one to seven. The internal–external dimension refers to the extent to which an individual feels a specific event is caused entirely by one's self versus entirely by others. The stable–unstable dimension refers to the extent to which an individual believes that the cause of an event will never again be present versus always being present. The global–specific dimension refers to the extent to which an individual believes an event is caused by something that only influences the particular situation versus influencing all situations in one's life. The distinction between stability and globality is a fine one. Stability refers to causes repeating over time, while globality refers to causes that repeat across different types of situations. Many theorists argue that explanatory (or attribution) style is a trait-like characteristic that develops during childhood. The reformulated theory posits that when faced with negative events, people who tend to attribute the events to external, unstable, specific causes (referred to as pessimistic explanatory style) are less likely to experience depression than people who attribute the events to internal, stable, and global causes (referred to as optimistic explanatory style). Thus, in the reformulated theory, learned helplessness only occurs when an event is perceived to be beyond an individual's control and that individual has a more pessimistic rather than optimistic explanatory style.

MEASURING ATTRIBUTIONS

Because of the increased emphasis on attributions in the reformulated model of learned helplessness, researchers developed two standard procedures for measuring attributions: Attributional Style Questionnaire (ASQ; Peterson et al. 1982) and the Content Analysis of Verbatim Explanations (CAVE; Peterson et al. 1983). For the ASQ, respondents imagine that an event has happened to them. They are asked to give a cause for the event and then give ratings of internality, stability, and globality for each cause for each event. A more recent (and slightly more reliable) version of ASQ includes only negative events rather than both positive and negative (Peterson & Villanova 1988). There is also a children's version of the questionnaire (CASQ; Seligman et al. 1984).

Whereas the researcher gives respondents hypothetical situations to explain in the ASQ, researchers using the CAVE approach read documents such as autobiographies, interviews, or therapy transcripts to measure how respondents explain events in their lives. Events and attributions are extracted and scored by independent judges on the dimensions of internality, stability, and globality.

OTHER APPLICATIONS OF LEARNED HELPLESSNESS

Researchers have found that learned helplessness affects organisms' immune system function. In addition, learned helplessness has been used as an explanation for why some but not all people who experience traumatic events develop post-traumatic stress disorder (PTSD). After exposure to a traumatic event, the attribution an individual makes about the internality, stability, and globality of the cause of the event affects whether he or she develops PTSD.

Learned helplessness can also be applied in an educational setting. Students could perceive repeated failures to indicate that they lack control over their academic success and cause them to develop signs of learned helplessness. Sedek and Kofta (1990) focus on a specific aspect of learned helplessness. Specifically, they argue that cognitive exhaustion is the reason previous exposure to uncontrollable events results in reduced performance. They argue that poorer performance is not due to helpless feelings or believing one cannot control the situation. Rather, the uncontrollable event decreases the individual's ability to process information and develop conclusions. Note that these researchers, along with many others, suggest different mechanisms through which learned helplessness occurs than the original theory suggested.

A somewhat controversial application of learned helplessness is the battered woman syndrome. Walker (1984) suggested that repeated exposure to domestic violence causes women to develop learned helplessness so that they are unable to protect themselves or escape the relationship. Research evaluating this hypothesis has found at best mixed results. Many researchers see attributional style as a trait-like characteristic that is probably developed during childhood. A recent article suggests that pessimistic attribution style contributed to whether battered women developed symptoms of depression or PTSD. Yet the researchers found that battered women were no more likely to exhibit learned helplessness than women in a comparison group from the community. This suggests that experiencing domestic violence does not lead to learned helplessness, but that if a person tends to have a pessimistic attribution style, he or she is more likely to experience depression or PTSD due to the experience than if he or she had an optimistic attribution style (Palker-Corell & Marcus 2004).

CURRENT AND FUTURE DIRECTIONS IN LEARNED HELPLESSNESS RESEARCH

As mentioned above, researchers in this area often argue that explanatory style is a characteristic that develops during childhood. Few investigators have explored the conditions in which children develop this trait. Some argue that experiencing trauma at a young age leads to development of learned helplessness. Others believe that exposure to crowded or inadequate living conditions causes children to develop feelings of helplessness. Recent research also suggests that interpersonal relationships, particularly parent–child relationships, can affect the type of explanatory style individuals develop. Specifically, children can learn explanatory styles watching how their parents explain events in their own lives and their children's lives.

Maier's research has continued to focus on learned helplessness. His research evaluates the physiological and neurological aspects of learned helplessness. In particular, he explores the relationship between the brain and the immune system to understand cognitive difficulties, stress, and pain perception.

Seligman has turned his attention to positive psychology and learned optimism. He currently directs the Positive Psychology Center at the University of Pennsylvania. Positive psychology suggests that people have varying levels of 24 strengths such as leadership, humor, industriousness, and love of learning that they categorize into six cross-culturally valued virtues: wisdom and knowledge, courage, humanity, justice, temperance, and transcendence. Further happiness can be cultivated by focusing on one's strengths rather than one's weaknesses and frequently using one's strengths in day-to-day life.

SEE ALSO: Attribution Theory; Behaviorism; Experimental Methods; Self-Fulfilling Expectations

REFERENCES AND SUGGESTED READINGS

Abramson, L. Y., Seligman, M. E. P., & Teasdale, J. (1978) Learned Helplessness in Humans: Critique and Reformulation. *Journal of Abnormal Psychology* 87: 49–74.

Garber, J. & Seligman, M. E. P. (1980) *Human Helplessness: Theory and Applications*. Academic Press, New York.

Overmier, J. B. & Seligman, M. E. P. (1967) Effects of Inescapable Shock Upon Subsequent Escape and Avoidance Responding. *Journal of Comparative and Physiological Psychology* 63: 28–33.

Palker-Corell, A. & Marcus, D. K. (2004) Partner Abuse, Learned Helplessness, and Trauma Symptoms. *Journal of Social and Clinical Psychology* 23: 445–62.

Peterson, C. & Villanova, P. (1988) An Expanded Attributional Style Questionnaire. *Journal of Abnormal Psychology* 97: 87–9.

Peterson, C., Semmel, A., von Baeyer, C., Abramson, L. Y., Metalsky, G. I., & Seligman, M. E. P. (1982) The Attributional Style Questionnaire. *Cognitive Therapy and Research* 6: 287–99.

Peterson, C., Luborsky, L., & Seligman, M. E. P. (1983) Attributions and Depressive Mood Shifts: A Case-Study Using the Symptom-Context Method. *Journal of Abnormal Psychology* 92: 96–103.

Sedek, G. & Kofta, M. (1990) When Cognitive Exertion Does Not Yield Cognitive Gain: Toward an Informational Explanation of Learned Helplessness. *Journal of Personality and Social Psychology* 58(4): 729–43.

Seligman, M. E. P. & Maier, S. F. (1967) Failure to Escape Traumatic Shock. *Journal of Experimental Psychology* 74: 1–9.

Seligman, M. E. P., Kaslow, N. J., Alloy, L. B., et al. (1984) Attributional Style and Depressive Symptoms Among Children. *Journal of Abnormal Psychology* 93: 235–8.

Walker, L. E. (1984) *The Battered Woman Syndrome*. Springer, New York.

leaving home in the transition to adulthood

Frances Goldscheider and Berna Torr

Full adulthood normally involves attaining the stable adult roles of worker, partner, and parent. Childhood, in contrast, is normally associated with net dependency on one's own parents. The transition to adulthood, then, comprises two steps: (1) ending childhood dependency and (2) making progress on the central responsible roles of adulthood. In the study of the transition to adulthood, these processes are bound together in complex ways.

Given this complexity, it is not surprising that the transition to adulthood, which might be viewed as a near-uniform, biological progress to physical maturity, actually varies greatly across societies and over time. Dramatic changes in both work and family have increased this complexity. The time needed to attain stable adult work roles has lengthened. This reflects both the increased need for higher education and greater job turnover in early adulthood. Related in part to these changes in work roles, the establishment of stable family roles has also been delayed throughout the industrialized world, postponing full adulthood for most young adults. This has created an ambiguous life course stage between the ages of 18 and 25 marked by "semi-adulthood," when living arrangements such as (1) living in the parental home, (2) residing alone or with roommates (non-family living), or (3) entering into uncommitted partnerships (cohabitation) are common and become alternatives to the more traditional route of forming one's own family through marriage. Frank Furstenberg and colleagues (2004) have argued that we have a new stage in life in the US and many other developed economies, a stage of "early adulthood" that is no longer adolescence but is also not full adulthood either.

TIES TO THE PARENTAL HOME

Parents are the major source of the many transfers of resources needed by the next generation. In most industrialized countries, the generation of later-middle-aged adults is wealthier than any in history, and has relatively small families, so parents can afford to provide reasonable space for their children and financial support for an extended number of years. Parents use their income to retard very early departures (e.g., before high school is completed), which are linked with the most negative outcomes, but use their income to facilitate leaving home at older ages.

As a result of the rural–urban transformation that unfolded over the twentieth century, parents are now more likely to be living in areas where there are more economic opportunities for young adults and where young adults often do not have to leave home to attend school or find jobs. However, families once provided their children with jobs. Inheritance of the family farm or business was an important factor structuring many young people's economic opportunities and their relationships with their parents. Nepotism has not totally vanished from modern economies; many parents can "pick up the phone" and procure opportunities for their children in the businesses of friends and associates. Nevertheless, most parents who want to help their children must now find other ways to do so. Financing their children's college education, which often delays complete financial and residential independence of those children, is one way parents achieve this end.

An important resource is money. Not all parents are willing to provide monetary support to their children once they enter adulthood and financial help appears to be contingent on what young adults are doing. A 1980 study of mothers found that although most (88 percent) expect to provide at least some help with the expenses of college for their unmarried children, many fewer would help with college costs if the child were married, and fewer still would help out a child struggling with job or relationship difficulties. Further, there appeared to be substantial variation among mothers in their support priorities. Some would be more likely to help a married child while others would be more likely to help an unmarried one. Some would be more likely to provide support to a child living away from home while others would only help a child living at home.

LEAVING AND RETURNING TO THE PARENTAL HOME

Leaving the parental home, and particularly the routes young people take out of the home, play key roles in the transition to adulthood. In most industrialized countries, the cohort of the *parents* of today's young adults not only is relatively wealthy, but also left home younger than any cohort before or since. They appear to expect their children to follow in their footsteps, despite the much later ages at marriage and the more fragile economic situation confronting their children than they faced growing up. Parents often express dismay at the recent increase in the proportions of young adults remaining in or returning to the parental home, an increase that has accompanied the later age at marriage and greater instability in the job market. A frequently invoked norm of adulthood requires residential independence from an early age, in most cases long before marriage. This rhetoric suggests that young adults are refusing to grow up and may not deserve their parents' financial and residential support. However, pressures on young adults to leave home early can be problematic, given the negative effects of early, non-college nest-leaving on educational attainment.

The increase in marital disruption among parents also affects family support for the young adults and the timing of residential independence. Young people leave home faster from disrupted families than from two-biological-parent families. The differences are particularly large when leaving home to attend college is separated from other routes, as young adults from non-traditional families are significantly less likely than young adults from stable, two-parent families to leave home for college. In addition, young adults of divorced parents are more likely to report leaving home because of friction. Young adults from non-traditional families are also much less likely to return home, suggesting that the home and its resources are less available to them.

There are also longstanding gender and race/ethnic differentials in nest-leaving by young adults. Girls tend to leave home earlier than boys, in part because they are likely to marry or otherwise form families earlier. Non-Hispanic whites also tend to leave home earlier than African Americans, Asians, or Hispanics. Hispanics and Asians are more likely than non-Hispanic whites to leave home for marriage, while blacks are more likely to leave home single because of later ages at marriage. There was a crossover, however, in age at leaving home for blacks and whites in 1960. Prior to 1960, blacks left home earlier than whites, while in the post-1960 period blacks left home later, reflecting the differential impact many trends affecting leaving the parental home have on population subgroups.

The transition out of the parental home is not always a permanent one. Another form of support that parents provide is a home to return to. Those who leave home for marriage are less likely to return home than those who leave home for other reasons. Thus, the likelihood of returning home has increased as young adults have become more likely to leave home for reasons other than marriage. However, the older young adults are when they leave, the less likely they are to return. The availability of jobs and the cost of housing are also important: stable employment both facilitates residential independence and lowers the risk of returning home. Finally, state policies also affect when young adults leave the parental home and whether they return. When the state facilitates human capital growth, such as through access to affordable higher education, parental resources become less important; when it does not, the parental home and parental resources increase in importance for young adults' educational attainment and progress in taking on adult work and family roles.

NON-FAMILY LIVING

Non-family living is an increasingly important pathway out of the parental home. Although unmarried adolescents have often lived away from their parents, they normally lived with other families, in family-based lodgings, or in colleges considered to be *in loco parentis*. Extensive non-family living in separate households, however, is quite recent (mid-twentieth century), beginning among the elderly with the expansion of state support for pensioners. It spread to young adults as delayed marriage and parenthood, divorce, and cohabitation became more common. In the transition to adulthood, non-family living provides a "quasi-adult" alternative to committed family roles, in that living independently reduces the power of parental authority and increases individual autonomy for young people (and their parents). An increasingly common non-family living arrangement, cohabitation, shares with the other living arrangements (and jobs) in early adulthood the flexibility/impermanence that so often marks this life course segment. The majority of cohabitations are fairly short-lived. On the economic side, there is evidence that cohabitation may serve as an adaptive strategy for young couples facing uncertainty about their careers.

A HISTORICAL EXAMPLE FOR THE UNITED STATES

A full analysis of trends in young adults' living arrangements did not emerge until the 1990s. This reflected a lack of both data and interest in the subject in the early years of the development of family demography, but it also reflected the difficulty of conceptualizing it. When Paul Glick and his colleagues (1965) defined the family life cycle and outlined how its contours had been changing in the United States, they were forced by lack of data to assume that young people leave home when they marry. During the period in which Glick wrote – the baby boom – this was a more nearly tenable assumption than either before or after, since marriage ages then were so young that few young adults had the time to leave home in other ways.

Trends in young adult living arrangements in the United States are illustrated with an examination of the period from 1900 to 2000. The solid line in Figure 1 shows the proportions of all 18- to 24-year-olds who were living with their parents; that is, those who were

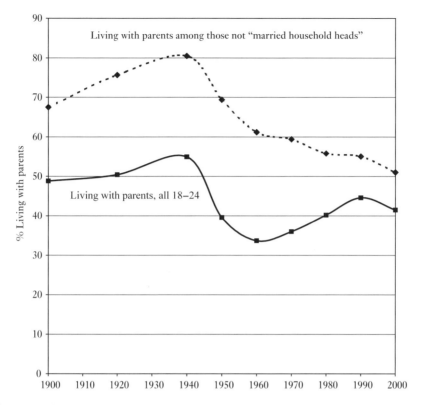

Figure 1 Percent living with parents and percent living with parents among those not "married household heads" (aged 18–24).
Source: Computed by the authors from the Integrated Public Use Sample (Ruggles & Sobek, University of Minnesota, 2003).

reported in the census as "child of head." In 1940, just over half of young adults were living at home at this age, a level that had changed only slightly in the previous 40 years, increasing from 49 percent to 55 percent. This slight increase likely reflected a combination of three factors. First, declining adult mortality increased the availability of parents for young adults to live with. Second, the ongoing rural–urban transformation meant that an increasing proportion of young adults were living in cities and therefore able to live at home while working. And third, the Great Depression of the 1930s delayed young adults' achievement of stable jobs and family formation, and kept home many of those who were employed in order to help their impoverished parents.

Between 1940 and 1960 there was a substantial decline in the proportion of all 18- to 24-year-olds living with their parents, decreasing more than 20 percentage points to 34 percent. Much of this decline was the result of the rapid decline in age at marriage, with the growth in early marriage that accompanied the post-World War II baby boom in the United States. However, some of this decline in the proportion of young adults living in the parental home during this 20-year period resulted from the increase in non-family living.

This increase in non-family living is illustrated by the dotted line in Figure 1, which shows a substantial decrease in the proportion of *unmarried* young adults living with their parents. This measure removes all married young adults from the ratio, and represents the proportion of *unmarried* young adults who are living in the parental home (and thus not living in a non-family situation). The proportion of unmarried young adults living in the parental home increased during the 1900 to 1940 period to near-universal (80.5 percent), and then declined to slightly over 60 percent by 1960. Hence, the decline between 1940 and 1960 in the proportion of all young adults aged 18–24 living with parents reflected two trends: the decrease in age at marriage and the decline in living with parents among unmarried young adults.

Things became much more complicated, however, in the post-1960 period. The marriage boom ended abruptly, with the result that the share of young adults aged 18–24 living in new families they had formed through marriage dropped precipitously, and continued to decline through 2000. This decline in new families formed by marriage resulted in a greater proportion of all young adults remaining in (or returning to) their parental home. The child-of-head category increased from 34 percent in 1960 to nearly 45 percent in 1990. However, despite the continued increase in age at marriage between 1990 and 2000, during that decade the proportions of all young adults aged 18–24 living with parents declined.

Does this 1990–2000 dip indicate a reversal in nest-leaving patterns? Not really, because as the dotted line in Figure 1 shows, the proportions of the unmarried living with parents declined throughout the 1940 to 2000 period. By 2000, about half (51 percent) of young unmarried adults aged 18–24 lived with their parents. Thus, while fluctuations in age at marriage affect the process of leaving the parental home, the influence of marriage age on leaving home has decreased. Those who left home in the latter part of the twentieth century were much less likely to do so via marriage.

This illustration demonstrates that even at the level of the living arrangements of the unmarried, the transitions in young adulthood are complex. Adding in trends in educational transitions (including dropping out and stepping out and returning to school), in early job transitions, and, of course, in union formation and dissolution, would require extensive research, little of which has been done in an integrated manner. For exceptions, see Billari et al. (2001) and Corijn and Klijzing (2001) for Europe, and Brien et al. (1999) for the United States. Most other studies rarely link leaving home

consistently with partnership formation, or with transitions in work and study. As a result, the light they cast on "semi-adulthood" is partial, at best. To understand transitions in young adulthood, research is needed that relates changes in young adult living arrangements to changes in patterns of work and school attendance as well as to changes in marriage and cohabitation.

SEE ALSO: Family Demography; Family Structure and Child Outcomes; Intergenerational Relationships and Exchanges; Life Course and Family; Life Course Perspective; Occupational Mobility; Second Demographic Transition; Urban–Rural Population Movements

REFERENCES AND SUGGESTED READINGS

Billari, F. C., Philipov, D., & Baizán, P. (2001) Leaving Home in Europe: The Experience of Cohorts Born Around 1960. *International Journal of Population Geography* 7: 339–56.

Brien, M. J., Lillard, L. A., & Waite, L. J. (1999) Interrelated Family Building Behaviors: Cohabitation, Marriage, and Nonmarital Conception. *Demography* 36: 535–51.

Cherlin, A., Kiernan, K. E., & Chase-Lansdale, P. L. (1995) Parental Divorce in Childhood and Demographic Outcomes in Young Adulthood. *Demography* 32: 299–318.

Corijn, M. & Klijzing, E. (Eds.) (2001) *Transitions to Adulthood in Europe*. Kluwer, Amsterdam.

Duvander, A. (1999) The Transition from Cohabitation to Marriage: A Longitudinal Study of the Propensity to Marry in Sweden in the Early 1990s. *Journal of Family Issues* 20: 698–717.

Furstenberg, F., Kennedy, S., McLloyd, V., Rumbaut, R., & Settersten, R. (2004) Growing Up is Harder to Do. *Contexts* 3(3): 33–41.

Glick, P. & Parke, R. (1965) New Approaches to Studying the Life Cycle of the Family. *Demography* 2: 187–202.

Goldscheider, F. & Goldscheider, C. (1999) *The Changing Transition to Adulthood: Leaving and Returning Home*. Sage, Thousand Oaks, CA.

Goldscheider, F., Thornton, A., & Yang, L. (2001) Helping Out the Kids: Expectations about Parental Support in Young Adulthood. *Journal of Marriage and the Family* 63: 727–40.

Nilsson, K. & Strandh, M. (1999) Nest Leaving in Sweden: The Importance of Early Education and Labor Market Careers. *Journal of Marriage and the Family* 61: 1068–79.

Oppenheimer, V. K. (2003) Cohabitation and Marriage During Young Men's Career-Development Process. *Demography* 40: 127–49.

Oppenheimer, V. K., Kalmjn, M., & Lim, N. (1997) Men's Career Development and Marriage Timing During a Period of Rising Inequality. *Demography* 34: 311–30.

Schnaiberg, A. & Goldenberg, S. (1989) From Empty Nest to Crowded Nest: The Dynamics of Incompletely Launched Young Adults. *Social Problems* 36: 251–69.

Smock, P. J. & Manning, W. D. (1997) Cohabiting Partner's Economic Circumstances and Marriage. *Demography* 34: 331–41.

White, L. & Lacy, N. (1997) Pathways from Home and Educational Attainment. *Journal of Marriage and the Family* 59: 982–5.

Whittington, L. & Peters, H. E. (1996) Economic Incentives for Financial and Residential Independence. *Demography* 33: 82–97.

Young, C. (1987) *Young People Leaving Home in Australia: The Trend Toward Independence.* Department of Demography, Australian National University Printing Press, Canberra.

Lechner, Norbert (1939–2004)

Miriam Alfie Cohen

Born in Germany in 1939, Norbert Lechner was granted honorary citizenship by the Senate of the Republic of Chile in 2003. He earned a bachelor's degree in law and obtained a doctorate in political science from the University of Freiberg in 1969. He visited Chile as a doctoral student and came to live there. From 1974 he was a professor and researcher in the Latin American Faculty of Social Sciences in Chile (FLACSO). He was its director from 1988 to 1994.

One of the central concerns throughout Norbert Lechner's theoretical analytical work was the creation of a theory of the state in Latin America. Texts such as *La crisis del Estado en América Latina* (1977), *La conflictiva y nunca acabada construcción del orden deseado* (1986), *State and Politics in Latin America* (1981), and *Los patios interiores de la democracia* (1990) speak of the urgent need in Latin American countries

for political reflection as a guide to theoretical analysis, as well as a project to be constructed. Lechner takes on the analysis of the state as an object of research in order to account for the problems posed by social reality.

From this perspective, the existing order is analyzed in order to carry out a critique, a negation of the prevailing situation with the goal of unraveling the logic of the system, transcending it, and creating a theoretical and practical reflection upon social change and the construction of the new order. Thus, politics, order, and utopia are the linked categories that become the core of the exposition in the author's works.

His first writings show a concern for the Chilean social reality of the so-called "legal road to socialism" that brought Salvador Allende to power. This peculiar political situation led Norbert Lechner to question the limited experience of Popular Unity in the study of the state. Although Allende and his team established an economic program for the period of transition to socialism, the lack of a political theory to explain the change was evident. From Lechner's point of view, in Popular Unity's lack of a concrete analysis of politics a determination of the economic order was provoked which considered the state realm to be a mere corollary of the economic realm, the state appearing as an entity at the disposal of one class or another.

With the military coup and the rise of Augusto Pinochet's regime (1977), Lechner came to study the state intensely, emphasizing that the state is neither on the margin of the social process nor an actor above the social process. Chilean authoritarianism pushed Lechner to find common traits in the Latin American region. Guided by Marxist thinking, particularly the currents represented by Antonio Gramsci, Rosa Luxemburg, Ernest Bloch, and the Frankfurt School, he sought out the leitmotif of the Latin American political situation. From his point of view, the distinction between state and state apparatus is fundamental. The central question for Lechner is the nature of the state, the state as a form. The idea is to discover the specific nature of the bourgeois state, in a way analogous to the type of commodities that appear as goods through the lens of Marxist theory. Thus, the state would seem to be the type of generality that atomized social relations assume in the process of production.

The state is necessary because it organizes and guarantees relationships of domination and inequality. Economic coercion (exploitation of the added value) breaks down into objectified political coercion in the state apparatus. The state is an autonomous power that intervenes in the economic sphere and fails to appear as a co-constitutive moment in capitalist production relations. Here it is worth highlighting the Gramscian vision of politics as an autonomous entity that is not determined by the economic realm.

However, for Lechner the serious problem in Latin America is understanding how the state is converted into a social relationship that becomes independent of its producers, becomes distanced from the social praxis that created it, and appears as a real abstraction endowed with a life unto itself. Unraveling the nature of the state in Latin America became a fundamental concern of the author's political analysis. His analytical objective is divided in two facets: first, to carry out a theoretical-conceptual reflection regarding the capitalist state per se based on critique of political economy; secondly, to carry out a historical-concrete study regarding the development of a particular state (Chile, Peru, Mexico, amongst others). The common thread is authoritarianism in different Latin American societies.

Lechner returns to the theoretical assumptions of dependency theory, led by the writings of Fernando Henrique Cardozo and Enzo Faletto (1969), and emphasizes how capitalist dependency is the result of structural heterogeneity, the juxtaposition or overlapping of different relations of production that give rise to the fragmentation of society. In the majority of Latin American countries, the nation does not exist as a mechanism of collective identity, forcing a certain level of social cohesion to be built through authoritarian means. To Lechner, the nonexistence of the "national state" in Latin America is substituted by the state apparatus. Thus, domination becomes more visible when there is little collective identity and the active presence of physical coercion substitutes the lack of social internalization of power in a "consensus of order."

Living under authoritarian conditions tends to lead to overvaluation of the coercive momentum; the state becomes a synonym for physical coercion. Through various subtle forms of social control it expands and intensifies a new rationality, a new culture, and that "one-dimensional man" (Herbert Marcuse) that incarnates in actu authoritarianism begins to appear.

The authoritarian state is a new Leviathan, a representation of the rationalization of domination: reason that becomes domination. The Latin American state is established as a relationship of internal domination and external hegemony. Therefore there is no capitalization of Latin American society to generate the material basis for a general interest. Because of this, it is difficult to construct a "popular-national will." Thus there is a hegemonic crisis, as no social group is able to consider, based on its own individual interests, the whole of society. The task is then the construction of a real and effective solidarity around common interests. Politics is conflict regarding people's sense of order.

For Lechner the construction of utopia is proposed as the abolition of domination within human order, an essential possibility for reality, the good order. Utopia is linked to an anti-authoritarian interest, whose motto consists of never falling for any type of servitude. Lechner emphasizes the struggle for democracy as the battle for popular sovereignty, a struggle against all forms of domination. The anti-authoritarian interest refers to an order of freedom. Freedom is not an idea without a cause, it is the content of a kingdom to be built and its construction anticipates the new society.

Politics is a struggle for the determination of the sense of order and the order that should be, while utopia is a moment of politics. Rationality leads to a good order; it is the critique of the capitalist order in light of an alternative order. Thus, the possibility of a rational order makes the present order irrational. Utopia, then, will be the cleverness of reason that allows society to reflect upon itself.

A third moment in Lechner's work is marked by the fall of the dictatorship and the transition to democracy. The majority of the ideas promoted during this period had transcendence for the rest of Latin America as, along with authors such as O'Donnell and Schmitter, a period of theoretical-political reflection regarding societies in transition begins.

If the concern for order was briefly seen in Lechner's early writings, these gain relevance for him as a central analysis of politics and the transition to democracy. The order tends to be sought out and imposed by either the state or the market. From Lechner's point of view, the debate regarding state and market tends to be polemical because it puts at stake the idea that we are created by the social order. In order to avoid the fetishization of one or another element, the convenience of situating the relationship within their respective historical contexts is proposed.

According to Lechner, the market is a special category; the operation of the market is found to be determined by its insertion into political institutions, social structures, and cultural processes. It is worth mentioning that the market by itself neither generates nor sustains a social order; on the contrary, it presupposes a "politics of order." This implies two integration processes – integration into the global system and social integration – that require the market dynamic as well as, above all, a redefinition of the state. In Latin America, a dual transition process takes place: transition toward democracy and the transition toward a market economy. Thus, the classic question emerges regarding the relationship between democracy and economic development.

Lechner establishes that modern society, along with deploying the differentiation between economics and politics, always proposed (in an affirmative or critical manner) a certain harmony between both spheres. When the countries of Latin America proposed harmonizing political democracy with economic growth and social equality, a novel challenge was posed. On one hand, economic development and, concretely, the market could not be considered a "prerequisite" for democracy. On the other hand, democratic politics did not guarantee economic development either. Thus, the profound question for all of Latin America continues to be how to make democracy and development compatible.

From this perspective, it becomes clear that the determination of the social order is definitively at stake. For Lechner, the debate regarding state and market has traditionally been a point of polarization in Latin America. Ideological discussion led to choosing a priori one or another principle as the exclusive and excluding rationality of social organization. In order to

avoid the fetishization of the state or the market under a form of higher rationality, it became convenient to carry out a historical analysis that allows one to visualize not only the continued existence of the two logics, but also the changing combination of the two. The priority given to one or the other would mark policy.

For Lechner, the field of politics opens a field of conflict, of power and the opportunity to establish a new conception that develops into a critique of the established conceptual models. This critical theory of politics cannot be reduced into any particular political strategy. They are distinct levels, where strategy is the result of deliberation and collective decision, while theory contributes the arguments for convincing others, without supplanting collective creation. There is a perception, in this stage of Lechner's work, of a distancing from Marxist thinking and from a particular conception of the so-called "desired order."

It could be said that as Lechner's interest moves from the study of the state to the analysis of politics, he arrives at the conclusion that social interest does not have to overcome social differences, but rather develops them. To him, it is not about proposing unity regarding the resolution of the plurality of man, but rather examining that plurality as the construction of a collective order. It is a conflictive and never-ending order in which the content varies from one period to another.

Because of this, one cannot think about politics and order without referring to utopia, construction projects that allude to the transformation of the world. Utopia thus functions as a horizon concept that allows us to conceive of society projected into plenitude. It is an ideal through which to understand historical projects. Just by considering what is desirable, the possible is constructed. Utopia forms a part of the social imaginary that all societies externalize as a horizon for judgments. From there, it is necessary to preserve and develop the utopias of good order, because only as related to this image of the perfect, but impossible, society are we able to discover the possible society.

Lechner rejects social revolutions as mechanisms for the construction of a social order and establishes the possibility of consensus as being necessary to the new forms of political processes. Negotiated ruptures are social reforms based on agreements that give rise to political self-determination. The greatest challenge in Latin American transitions is the construction of an order that can combine the possibility to establish consensuses regarding central themes that lead to democracy. From this perspective there are no longer predetermined subjects, nor armed revolutions. Qualitative changes are proclaimed based on political ruptures and conception between what is possible and what is desirable. Facing war and consensus as two limiting ideas, negotiated rupture points toward the construction of collective will, toward politics as the deliberate creation of the future.

Lechner's main contribution is in highlighting the construction of order as a political task. The search for society's diversity is a transformation undertaken as the construction of order, where negotiated ruptures are the constructive elements of a new order shaped according to the idea of what is desirable. Feasible democracy is constituted by a plurality of subjects that arises through reciprocal recognition; even though one has to confront the "Other," it is no longer to annihilate him but rather to confront the differences. Democratization therefore demands the development of plurality and collective responsibility. The construction of order becomes a collective task. Politics is everyone's activity, a citizen activity. There are reciprocity agreements, where trust, loyalty, or respect are real norms through which reciprocal expectations are structured. Thus, it is the linking of economic transformation and political self-determination as emancipatory practices that leads to democracy.

The last part of Norbert Lechner's work is dedicated to the difficult task of constructing Latin American democracy. Democracy needs to be placed in the public light in order to develop, but at the same time it hides skeletons in the closet, some sordid and others simply forgotten. Lechner will delve into the recognition of these nooks and crannies – the cognitive-affective substratum of democracy – in order to obtain a different substratum of politics.

Thus, in the debate regarding democratic alternatives, Lechner says that two moments stand out that pave the way for a transformation of Latin American political thinking. On one hand, there is a reassessment of politics, which rejects the logic of war and substitutes for the political logic; this points not to the annihilation of the adversary but rather to the reciprocal recognition of subjects amongst themselves. The need for difference and plurality is emphasized as a condition for political life itself, and a reconceptualization of utopia is proposed that defines it as an image of impossible plenitude that is nonetheless indispensable in order to discover the possible. On the other hand, there emerges a reassessment of civil society that highlights the interest of intellectuals in establishing democratization in the concrete problems of ordinary people, along with concern for the reconstruction of the social fabric that has been devastated by military dictatorships as well as neoliberal regimes.

For Norbert Lechner, the actual reevaluation of the formal procedures and institutions of democracy in Latin America cannot rest on old habits and norms that are recognized by everyone. It is not about restoring regulative norms, but rather the creation of those norms that are essential to political activity; the beginning of the democratic game and agreement regarding the rules of the game are two simultaneous facets of the same process. Today, the central task in the democratization of Latin America is a change in political culture. The possibilities and tendencies for democratization are conditioned by criteria of normalcy and naturalness, developed by normal people in their daily lives. It is in this sphere that projects of solidarity and social change can be built. Delving into political culture opens a wide expanse of possibilities that range from the mundane to the political.

The lack of a democratic political culture in Latin America is due, according to Lechner, to the growing distance between political institutions and citizens. As more social activities are submitted to political-legal regulation, the man on the street loses more control over his social context, producing a deterioration of political practice upon failing to be able to produce and reproduce the sense of order to which men and women refer in order to contextualize the different aspects of their lives. To the extent that political organizations, which are increasingly specialized and separated from the daily tasks of "people like us," no longer create or guarantee collective identities, these identities tend to recreate themselves on the margins or even in opposition to the institutions.

Because of this, the study of everyday life becomes a fundamental concern for Lechner. He returns to important authors such as Gouldner, Habermas, Touraine, and Heller and proposes that everyday life is a crystallization of the social conditions that allow us to explore the relationship between macro- and microsocial processes. It is the field for the analysis of the contexts in which different individual experiences come to be recognized as collective identities. Democratic construction goes side by side with political culture, with that privileged space in daily life that implies a change of values, perceptions, and images and comes to establish itself. It begins with common visions, the possibility to create collective identities, and democratic consolidation.

However, the construction of a democratic order confronts two great problems: the lack of time and unpredictability. In terms of time, Lechner points out how events suddenly happen and multiply and, on occasions, nothing happens and time languishes, stagnates. In both cases, one bets on the realist's conjecture, to take one's time in order not to be overwhelmed by the urgency of events nor limit the time in order to be able to crystallize emotional energies within a symbolically significant time frame. In terms of unpredictability, he returns to Luhmann and proposes reducing the uncertainty and insecurity of politics. It is not a forecast, it is a bet: it is the commitment to a particular result, which is not foreseeable.

One of the fundamental elements for resolving the distance between the present and the future and increasing the level of acceptable uncertainty is trust. The term implies a commitment to certain future conduct without knowing whether the other will respond to the commitment. It is a voluntary offer, but once the other responds to the trust given, he or she is committed. To trust is to reflect upon uncertainty. Trust in the order is a central element of the stability of a democratic system. Trust involves the citizenry's identification with the political system as well as the system's credibility before public opinion.

As can be seen, Lechner's work shows a substantial change from his proposals of the 1970s. In this final period, concern for political culture, trust, and the construction of a democratic order are the most important points of reference in his work. The transformation of Norbert Lechner's theoretical as well as critical apparatus is a clear sign of political-ideological developments in Latin America, a region of the world that continues to face the consolidation of democratic societies.

SEE ALSO: Authoritarianism; Democracy; Democracy and Organizations; Gramsci, Antonio; Marx, Karl; Marxism and Sociology; State; Utopia

REFERENCES AND SUGGESTED READINGS

Agnew, J. (1987) *Place and Politics: The Geographical Mediation of State and Society*. Allen & Unwin, London.

Bauman, Z. (1999) *En Busca de la Política*. FCE, Buenos Aires.

Cardoso, F. (1979) Sobre la caracterización de los regimenes autoritarios en América Latina. In: Collier, D. (Comp.), *The New Authoritarianism in Latin America*. Princeton University Press, Princeton.

Gramsci, A. (1975) *Notas sobre Maquiavelo: La política y el Estado moderno*. Juan Pablos, Mexico City.

Henrique Cardozo, F. & Faletto, E. (1969) *Dependency and Development in Latin America*. Fondo de Cultura Económica, Mexico City.

Lechner, N. (1977) *La crisis del Estado en América Latina*. Siglo XXI, Madrid.

Lechner, N. (1986) *La conflictiva y nunca acabada construcción del orden deseado*. Siglo XXI, Madrid.

Lechner, N. (1990) *Los patios interiores de la democracia*. Siglo XXI, Madrid.

Lechner, N. (1992) El debate sobre el Estado y el mercado. *Revista Nueva Sociedad* 121, Caracas.

Lechner, N. (1995) La problemática invocación de la sociedad civil. *Espacios* 4 (April/May), Bogota.

Lechner, N. (1998) *Los condicionantes de la gobernabilidad democrática en América Latina de fin de Siglo*. FLACSO, Buenos Aires.

Lechner, N. (2002a) Los desafíos políticos del campo cultural. *Revista Nueva Sociedad* 184, Caracas.

Lechner, N. (2002b) *Las sombras del mañana: La dimensión subjetiva de la política*. LOM Ediciones, Santiago de Chile.

Luhmann, N. (1992) *Sociología del riesgo*. Universidad Iberoamericana, Universidad de Guadalajara, Mexico City.

Marcuse, H. (1989) *Eros y civilización*. Joaquín Mortiz, Mexico City.

O'Donnell, G. (1997) Las fuerzas armadas y el estado autoritario del Cono Sur de América Latina. In: *Contrapuntos*. Paidós, Argentina, pp. 97–127.

O'Donnell, G. & Schmitter, P. (1989) *Transitions from Authoritarian Rule*. Johns Hopkins University Press, Baltimore.

Putnam, R. (1993) *Making Democracy Work: Civil Tradition in Modern Italy*. Princeton University Press, Princeton.

Touraine, A. (1989) *América Latina: Política y sociedad*. Espasa Calpe, Madrid.

Lefebvre, Henri (1901–91)

Michael T. Ryan

Henri Lefebvre had the good fortune to live a long, intellectually productive life in a century of political disasters that drove most intellectuals on the left to despair or worse. Lefebvre was one of the most original Marxist theorists to think with Marx beyond Marx about the changes taking place in capitalism since Marx's death in 1882. He appropriated in a critical manner the concepts of some of the most important social theorists. Lefebvre also developed concepts of his own: everyday life, the production of social space, difference, modernity, and reproduction of the relations of production. He completed his Diplôme d'Études Supérieures at the Sorbonne in 1924 and his dissertation in 1954. Lefebvre considered himself a philosopher/sociologist, and this led him to emphasize conceptual analysis on sociological issues. He became a member of the French Communist Party (PCF) in 1928 and was excluded from it in 1958 for participating in too many oppositional groups to the PCF. He was appointed to a research position in 1948 in the Center of Sociological Studies (CES) at the Centre National de la Recherche Scientifique (CNRS). In 1960 he established the Research Group on Everyday Life at the CES. In 1965 he was appointed to the sociology chair as well as to the directorship of the Institute of Urban Sociology at the University of Paris at Nanterre. Henri Lefebvre was one of the most important influences, along with Guy Debord and the Situationist International, on the student movements and May events in France in 1968 that

raised questions about the bureaucratization of private life in the "bureaucratic society of controlled consumption." His most important publications are: *Critique of Everyday Life*, Vols. 1–4 (1947, 1961, 1981, 1992); *The Production of Space* (1974); *The Urban Revolution* (1970); and *The Survival of Capitalism* (1976).

Henri Lefebvre came of age during the events and aftermath of the Russian Revolution which occurred in the conjuncture of the capitalist crisis and World War I. Lefebvre discovered Marx's concept of alienated labor and extended it to the analysis of private life. It is at this moment that the consumer society emerges in response to the failed proletarian revolution, with the "technocracy" bringing its bureaucratic forms of organization to the reproduction of the capitalist relations of production. The Great Depression and World War II provided a second crisis and moment for Lefebvre's development. He brought Nietzsche's thought together with Marx's in the first volume of his *Critique of Everyday Life*. The process of self-development and public life were as alienated as the working day in Marx's analysis. Lefebvre also confronted a number of other important intellectual currents: institutional Marxism, existentialism, information theory, structuralism, and American sociology. The crisis of the late 1960s provided a third moment in Lefebvre's development when anticolonial wars were proving to be much more risky to the metropolitan centers than the "colonization of everyday life," as Debord put it. Differential groups – racial and ethnic groups, students, youth, women, homosexuals – were contesting bureaucratic authorities across the globe in their struggles to realize the *right to be different*, one of Lefebvre's rights to the city. Lefebvre also had critical encounters with structural Marxists, Heidegger, and postmodern theorists.

Lefebvre first discussed dialectical method in an article on rural sociology written in 1953. He further elaborated on his method in volume 2 of the *Critique of Everyday Life*. Lefebvre's method of analysis takes sociology beyond mere description of society as it exists to an analysis of society in terms of its possibilities for change. His method of conceptual analysis starts by going back to the emergence of a concept, e.g., everyday life emerges in the writings of novelists such as James Joyce in *Ulysses*. Everyday life is a residuum, a moment of history, what is left over after working activities are extracted, humble actions that are repeated daily and taken for granted, the positive moment and power of daily life. This is the "regressive" moment in his dialectical method. Then he links the concept to its place in the current social totality. Everyday life is also the product of modernity, of bureaucratic organization and the programming of private life, "everydayness" as an alienated moment. Everyday life is a contradictory amalgam of these positive and negative moments. In the "progressive" moment he begins in the present to analyze the possible movements of the concept and the totality, from the programmed everyday to lived experience, self-development and generalized self-management, i.e., the revolution in everyday life. For Lefebvre everyday life is *the* social structure of modernity, a mediator between particulars and the social totality, a *level* of the social totality. Everyday life is another instance of uneven development, an impoverished sector that has yet to be developed with the available wealth and technologies to the same extent as other sectors such as capital goods and the military. As long as people can live their everyday lives, modernity will continue to be reproduced in its present forms and structure. When people can no longer live their everyday lives, the possibilities for change in social relations become open.

In *The Production of Space*, Lefebvre distinguishes social space as it is *conceived* in abstract geometric terms, as it is *perceived* concretely in the works of artists like Cézanne, and as it is *lived* in everyday life by different social strata and actors. Social space is organized in ways to facilitate the movement of products and people, reflecting the logic of the technical division of labor; it has also been commoditized and colonized and creates another sector for investment and capital formation. It is an abstract space that develops without regard to the needs and desires of human beings; it enhances the domination of the technocrats and contributes to the reproduction of the capitalist relations of production. It sets in motion a conflict between the producers of this abstract space and the users who want to appropriate space as "lived space."

Difference is another critical concept that Lefebvre linked to the processes of urbanization and urban revolution. Industrialization has a homogenizing logic, reducing everything to commodities. Urbanization has a differential logic. Like Robert E. Park, Lefebvre argues that differences are one of the most unique qualities of cities. While most sociologists analyzed these differences in terms of subcultures, Lefebvre used this concept to emphasize relations of domination and subordination. The differences originate in nature as particularities – race, ethnicity, gender, and age – but they become social differences when the members of these groups struggle for the right to be different. Their struggles take place in an urban context in which they: affirm their difference against the process of homogenization; assert their right to the center against fragmentation and marginalization; and claim their right to equality in difference against the process of hierarchization. Lefebvre uses this concept to explain the new social movements that have developed since World War II. They are at the heart of the urban revolution, although the working class, because of its position in the process of production, still has a role to play.

According to Lefebvre, capitalism has undergone a mutation from its classical nineteenth-century form. When the working class failed to become a revolutionary agent of change, the technocrats brought stability and cohesion to a society that lacked both through their deployment of bureaucratic forms of organization and the ideology of technological modernism, the introduction of trivial technological changes on the surface of this society while the capitalist relations of production remained fundamentally unchanged beneath the surface. Social relations do not have a life of their own; they do not persist due to inertia; they need to be reproduced in everyday life. Marx had demonstrated the social quality of the production, distribution, and exchange moments in the process of production. He did not take his analysis into the moment of consumption, nor did he link this process to social space. In their consumption the members of each social class reproduce themselves as capitalists, workers, and landowners. When workers pay for their material and immaterial needs in everyday life, they recreate their dependence on capital and land and are constrained to return to the labor market. The capitalists take their profits, pay for their own consumption, and reinvest their wealth in whatever economic sector that promises to expand their wealth. This reproduces their dependence on workers whose living labor creates the wealth. Further, capitalists invest their wealth increasingly in space: industrial, commercial, agricultural, and residential and leisure spaces. This allows capital to accumulate beyond the crisis tendency in the industrial sector, although this sector is also subject to crises of falling profits, overproduction, and depreciation. We move from the production of *things* in space in the nineteenth century to the production of *space* and things in space in the twentieth century.

With the creation of modernity, many of the historical tasks of the working-class revolution have been accomplished. Yet, Lefebvre did not see it as a closed system in the way that Baudrillard saw it, and that is why he does not see our society as a postmodern one. He argues that while modernity is efficient at taking care of individual needs, there are social and individual needs that are poorly recognized and met: health care, education, care for the elderly, public spaces, community, love and self-actualization. Social goods are different from individual goods; they are not used up in the same way as a commodity is used up in an act of consumption. Millions of citizens have made use of Central Park in New York City, but they have yet to use it up. There is also a fundamental struggle between consumers and producers over the intended uses and meanings that are attached by the advertising form to goods and acts of consumption. Consumers often use goods in their own ways, attaching their own meanings to commodities. Further, programmed consumption entails incredible destruction of natural resources and the environment, especially when planned obsolescence accelerates the depreciation of commodities through the fashion cycle and the low quality of materials used. The destruction of the earth is a real possibility. Lefebvre proposes a different path for social revolution: revolution in everyday life and urban revolution will complement and extend the proletarian revolution toward generalized self-management and emancipation from bureaucratic domination and class exploitation at work, in public life, and in private life. This process will lead to the creation of an urban society, although it is likely to be a long process since changes in everyday life are slow. This process will require a reduction in time devoted to work.

Modernity is an incredibly complex social formation, and there is a tendency for sociologists to reduce this complexity to single forms (norms), structures (culture), or functions (socialization). Lefebvre argues that we must situate and mediate all of these social forms, functions, and structures within the political, economic, and cultural processes that produce and reproduce modernity. Further, we must be historically specific in our analysis and give up our quest for universals.

SEE ALSO: Built Environment; Capital, Secondary Circuit of; Debord, Guy; New Urbanism; Space; Uneven Development; Urban Movements; Urban Space; Urbanization

REFERENCES AND SUGGESTED READINGS

I want to thank Verso for making the manuscript of the third volume of *Critique of Everyday Life* accessible to me before publication.

Elden, S. (2004) *Understanding Henri Lefebvre*. Continuum, London.
Gottdiener, M. (1993) Henri Lefebvre and the Production of Space. *Sociological Theory* 11, 1 (March): 129–34.
Gottdiener, M. (2000) Lefebvre and the Bias of Academic Urbanism. *City* 4, 1 (April): 93–101.
Kofman, E. & Lebas, E. (1996) Introduction: Lost in Transposition – Time, Space, and the City. In: Lefebvre, H., *Writings on Cities*. Blackwell, Oxford, pp. 3–60.
Lefebvre, H. (1976) *The Survival of Capitalism*. Allison & Busby, London.
Lefebvre, H. (1991a) *Critique of Everyday Life*, Vol. 1, 2nd edn. Verso, London.
Lefebvre, H. (1991b) *The Production of Space*. Blackwell, Oxford.
Lefebvre, H. (1996) *Writings on Cities*. Blackwell, Oxford.
Lefebvre, H. (2002) *Critique of Everyday Life*, Vols. 2 and 3, 1st edn. Verso, London.
Lefebvre, H. (2003) *The Urban Revolution*. University of Minnesota Press, Minneapolis.
Trebitsch, M. (1991) Preface. In: Lefebvre, H., *Critique of Everyday Life*, Vol. 1, 2nd edn. Verso, London.
Trebitsch, M. (2002) Preface. In: Lefebvre, H., *Critique of Everyday Life*, Vol. 2, 1st edn. Verso, London.